AF412397

THE OFFICIAL POINT OF VIEW

GIULIA BER TACCHINI

PAOLO CALCAGNI

LUCIO LUZO LAZZARA

RICCARDO RINETTI

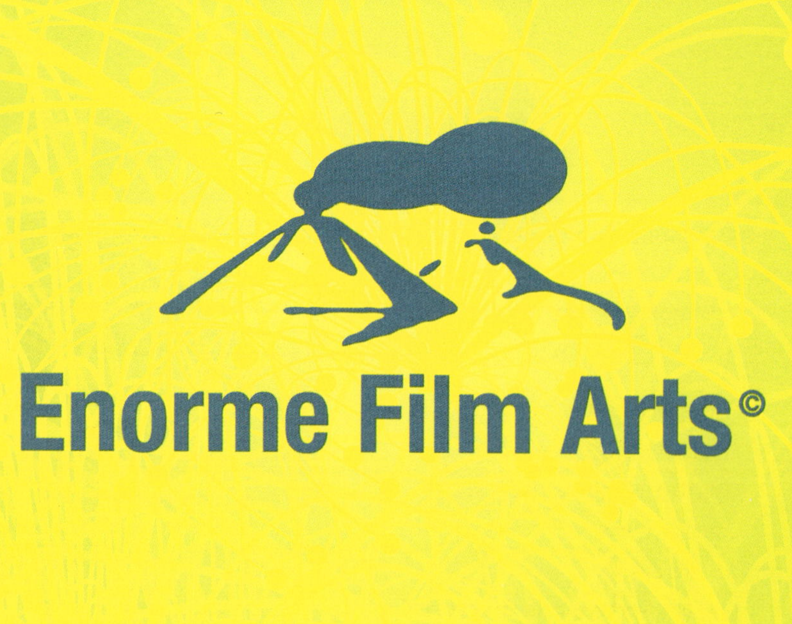

Enorme Film Arts©

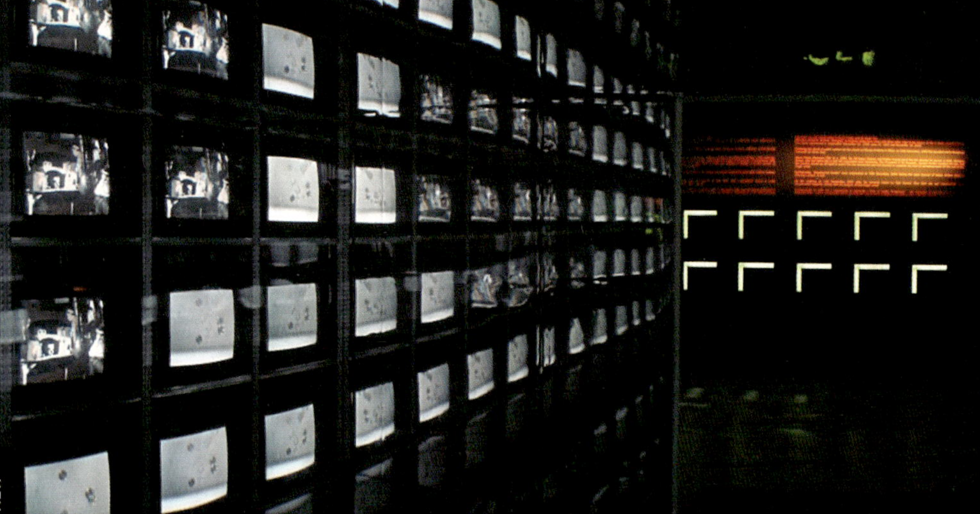

Getting your bearings in the world of design is becoming an increasingly difficult task.

Many of us seem to be waiting for a real and clear-cut trend that can dispel all doubts,

namely something reassuring that can be unquestionably defined as "progress",

whereas others are hunting for minimalism in a harmless effort to get rid of "redundancy".

The boldest ones defy the allure of décor,

of "neo-baroque" and of shape as an art

form standing in its own right.

Also, as it has long occurred in many contemporary art forms, the knock-on effect of

vintage has the power to outshine everything else, besides acting as a fashion revival

whilst bringing about more consumer awareness.

C.G. Jung was once quoted as saying, "A pair of shoes fitting one person will not

necessarily fit another": there is no such thing as a 'life recipe' befitting us all regardless.

The Official Point of View provides us with a few tips on how to approach design,

which is conceived as a journey through life divided into four main categories:

childhood, adolescence, adulthood and old age.

Objects, tools, events, thoughts and people all fall into these categories.

The point of view behind this classification is so personal that it becomes official.

Just like any point of view

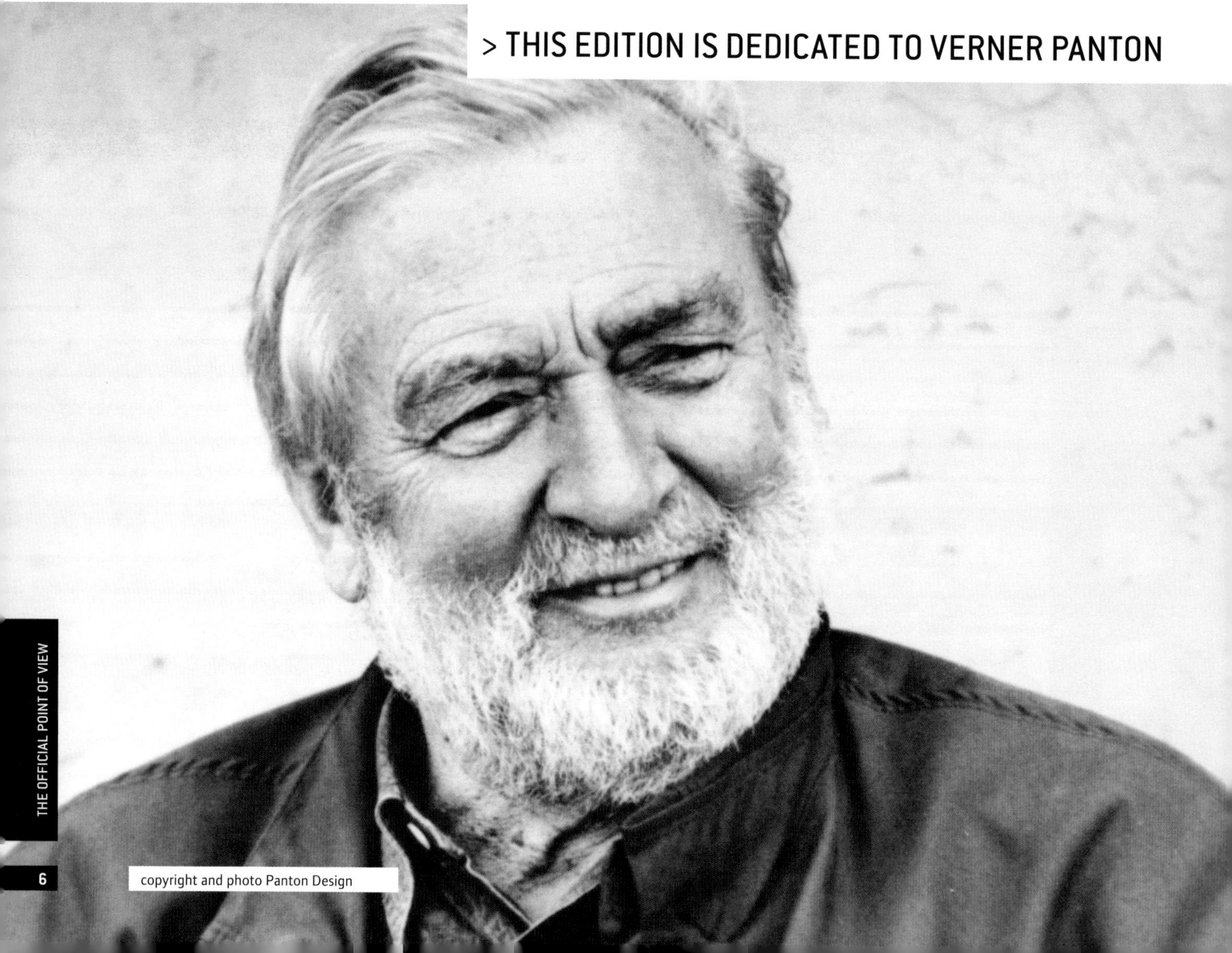

copyright and photo Panton Design

ON COLOURS

[…]" Colour planning is of utmost importance when creating a milieu.
It is not enough to say that red is red and blue blue.I myself normally work with
parallel colours whose tones follow consecutively according to the order of
the spectrum.In this way, I can control the character of the room in terms of
warmth and coolness and thereby create the desired atmosphere.
This does not mean that it is not possible to work with complementary colours
situated opposite each other in the spectrum.In this case, one dominant colour
group is used, with other colours added for emphasis.
One has to take into consideration the fact that light and colours are very
closely related.Colours can acquire a distinctly different character if daylight
alternates with artificial light and when strong lighting is made softer.
Moreover, the appearance of colour is influenced by the structure of
material.Roughly woven material may technically be of exactly the same
colour as a polished enamelled plate, yet their effects are entirely different.
Careful colour planning is therefore of utmost importance, and the complex
composition of colour requires experience.Colour planning is unfortunately
an underdeveloped field in the work of contemporary designers and
architects.Research and development in this area ought to be constantly intensified."[…]

Speech given on 19 of March 1982 @ Bella Center - Copenhagen

Courtesy of Verner Panton private archive, Basel.

> INDEX

Zoo by Kidpele @ Now Underground - binario 21

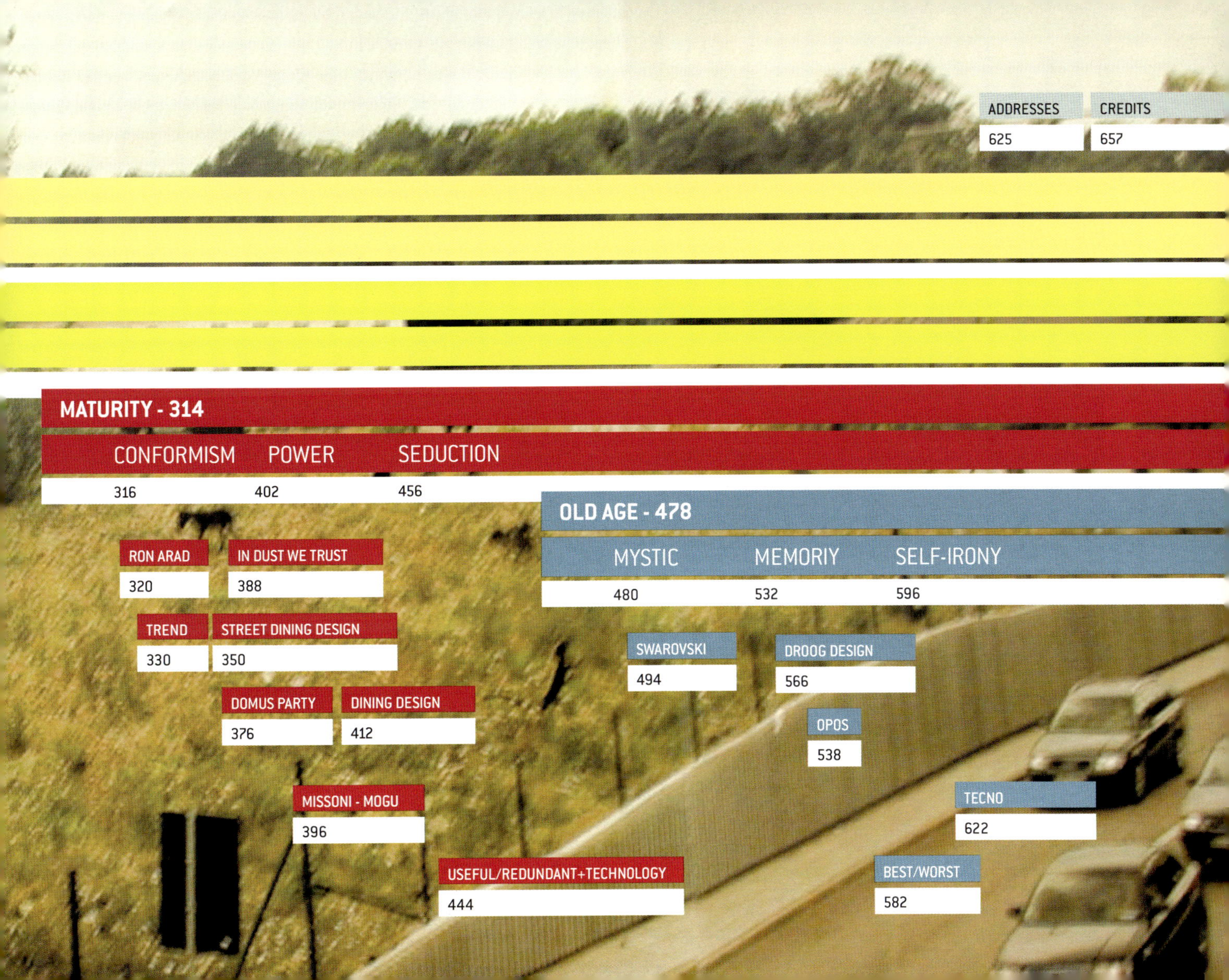

ADDRESSES
625
CREDITS
657
MATURITY - 314
CONFORMISM
316
POWER
402
SEDUCTION
456
OLD AGE - 478
MYSTIC
480
MEMORIY
532
SELF-IRONY
596
RON ARAD
320
IN DUST WE TRUST
388
TREND
330
STREET DINING DESIGN
350
DOMUS PARTY
376
DINING DESIGN
412
SWAROVSKI
494
DROOG DESIGN
566
OPOS
538
MISSONI - MOGU
396
TECNO
622
USEFUL/REDUNDANT+TECHNOLOGY
444
BEST/WORST
582

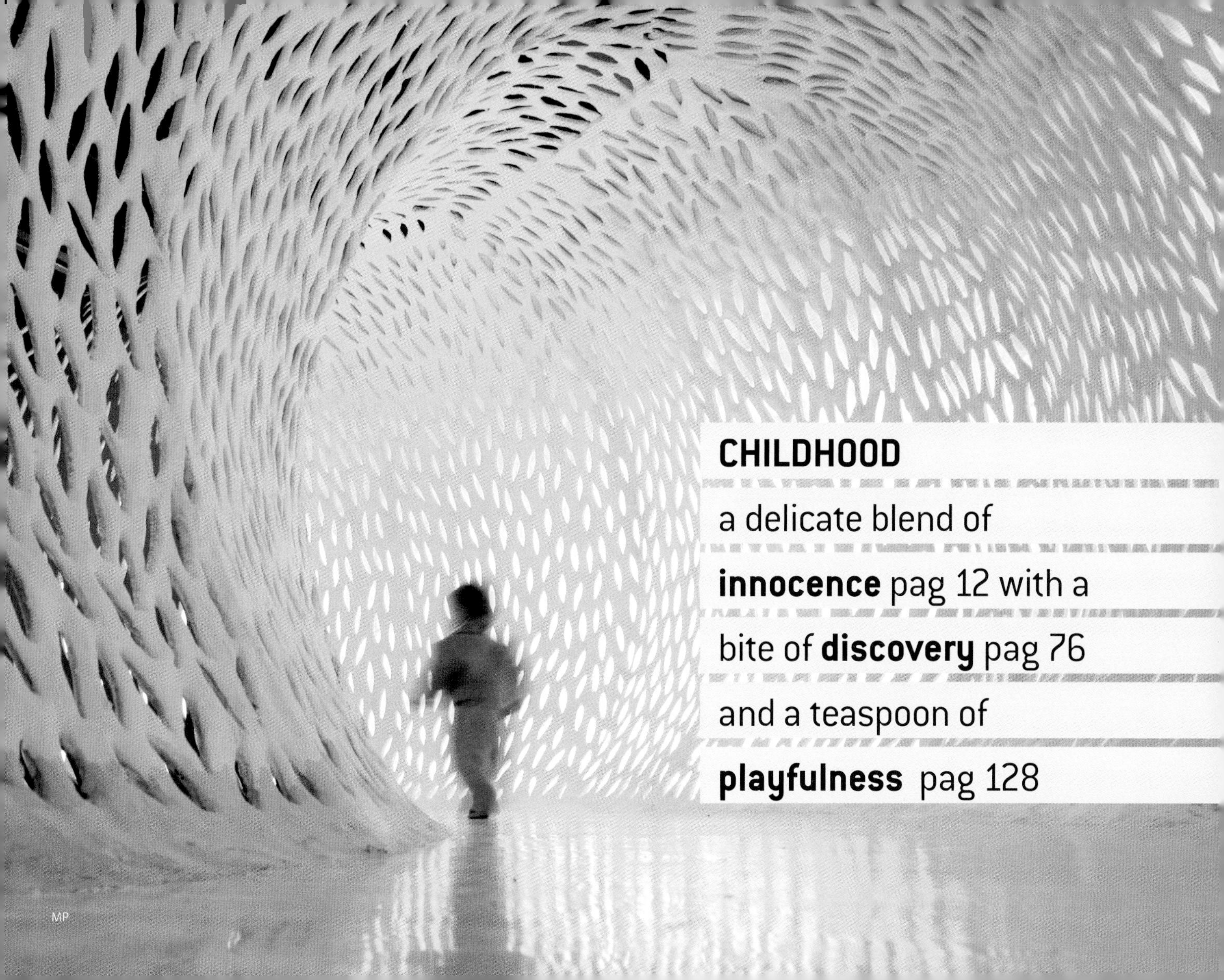

CHILDHOOD
a delicate blend of
innocence pag 12 with a
bite of discovery pag 76
and a teaspoon of
playfulness pag 128
MP

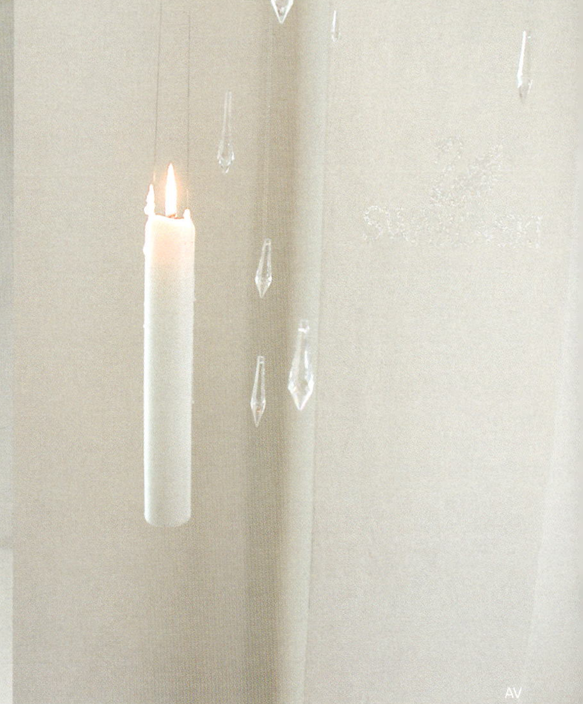

12

Shigeru Uchida Design Institute

"Fly Candle Fly!" by Ingo Maurer

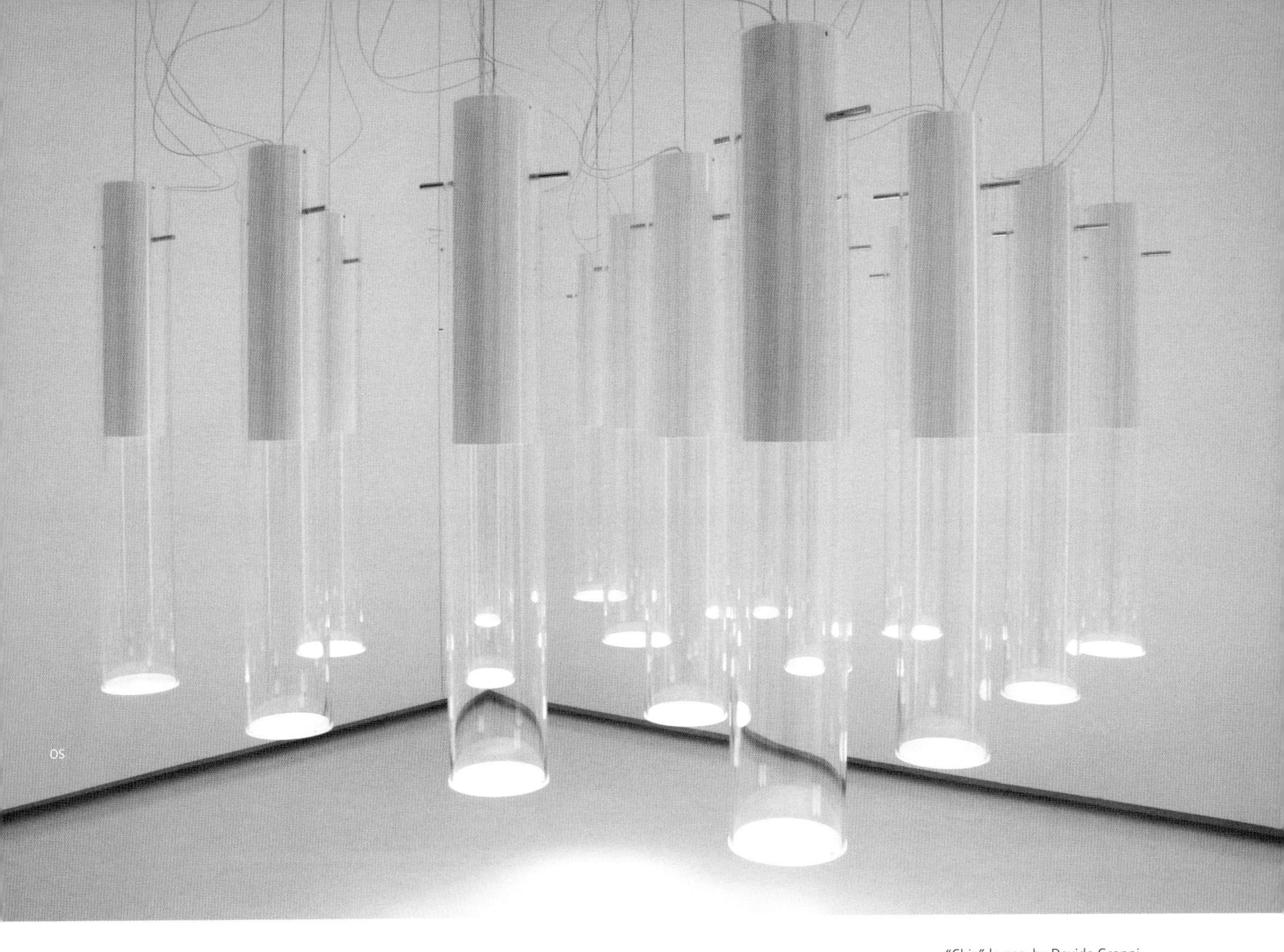

"Chic" lamps by Davide Groppi

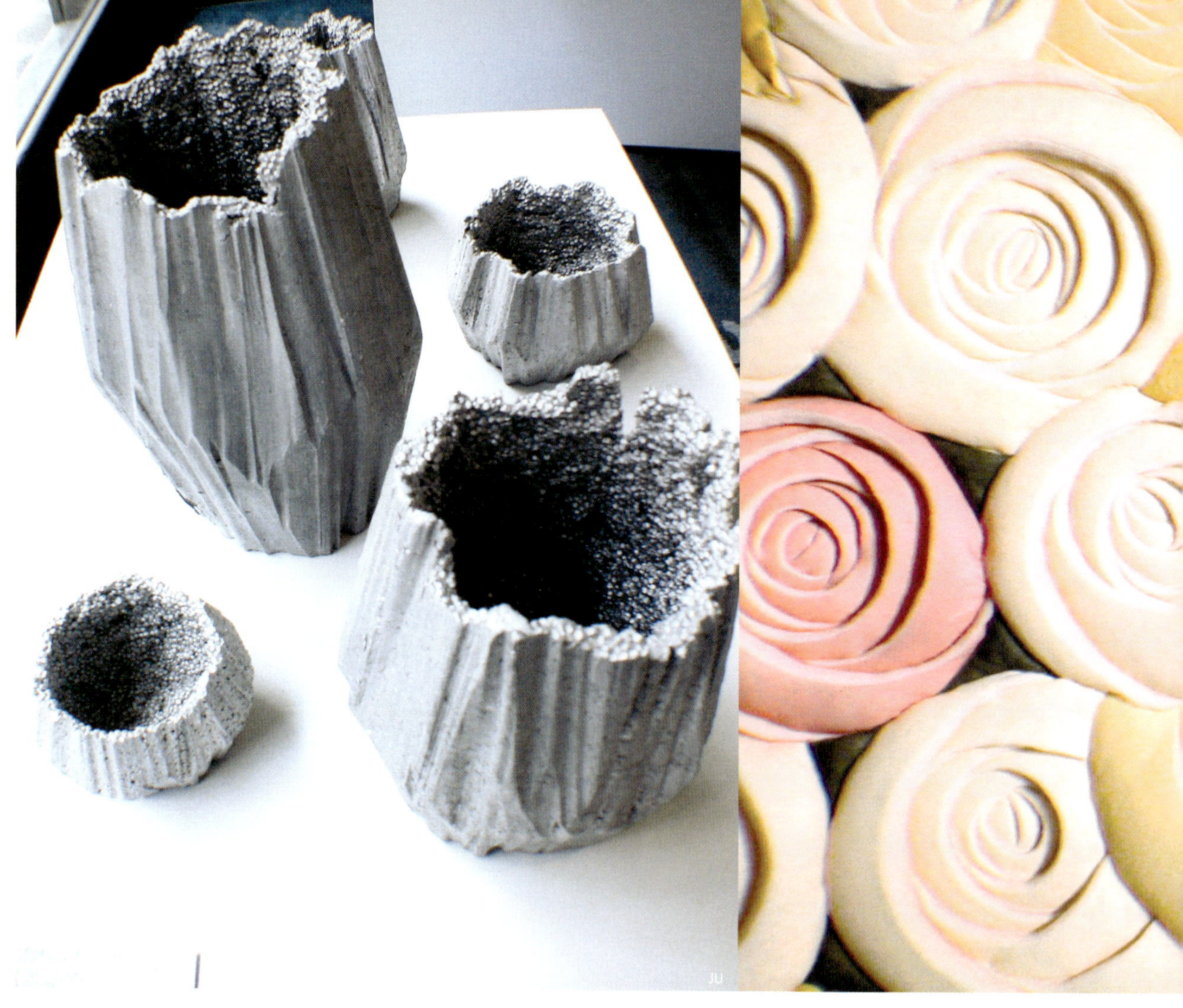

Concrete Poetry by Design Academy Eindhoven

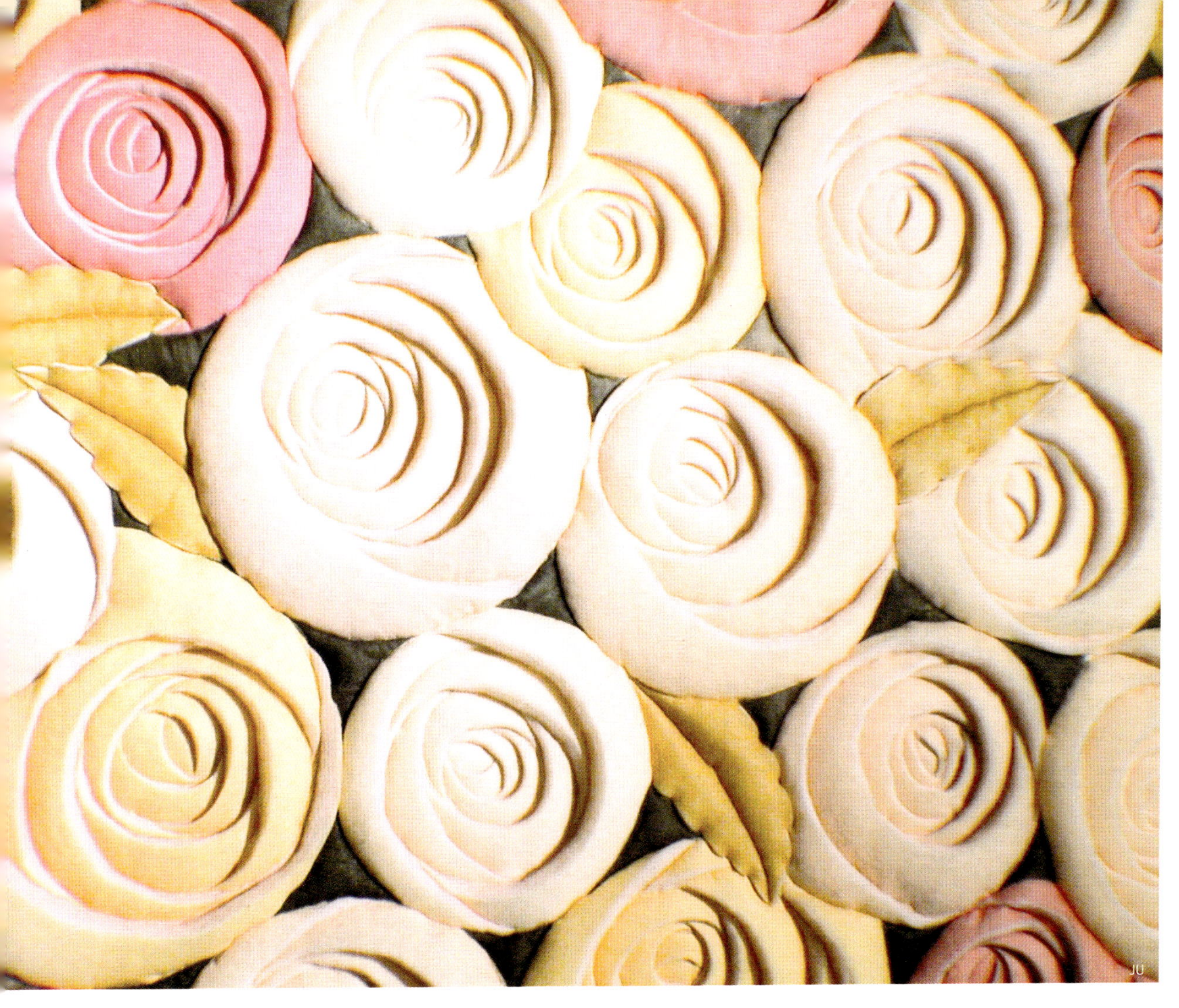

Helen Amy Murray @ Intrecci exhibition

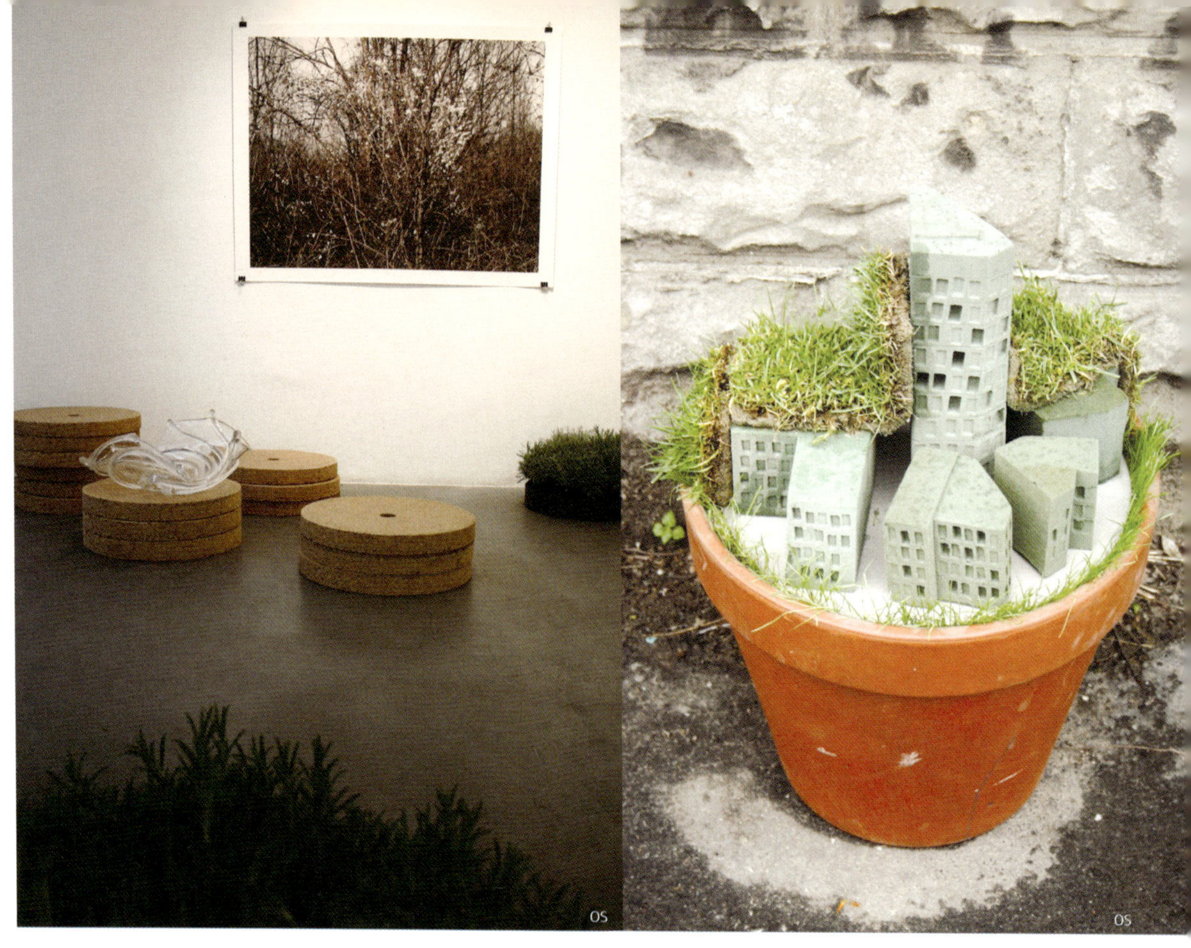

Mishima+Castella @ Blanchaert Gallery

Naba

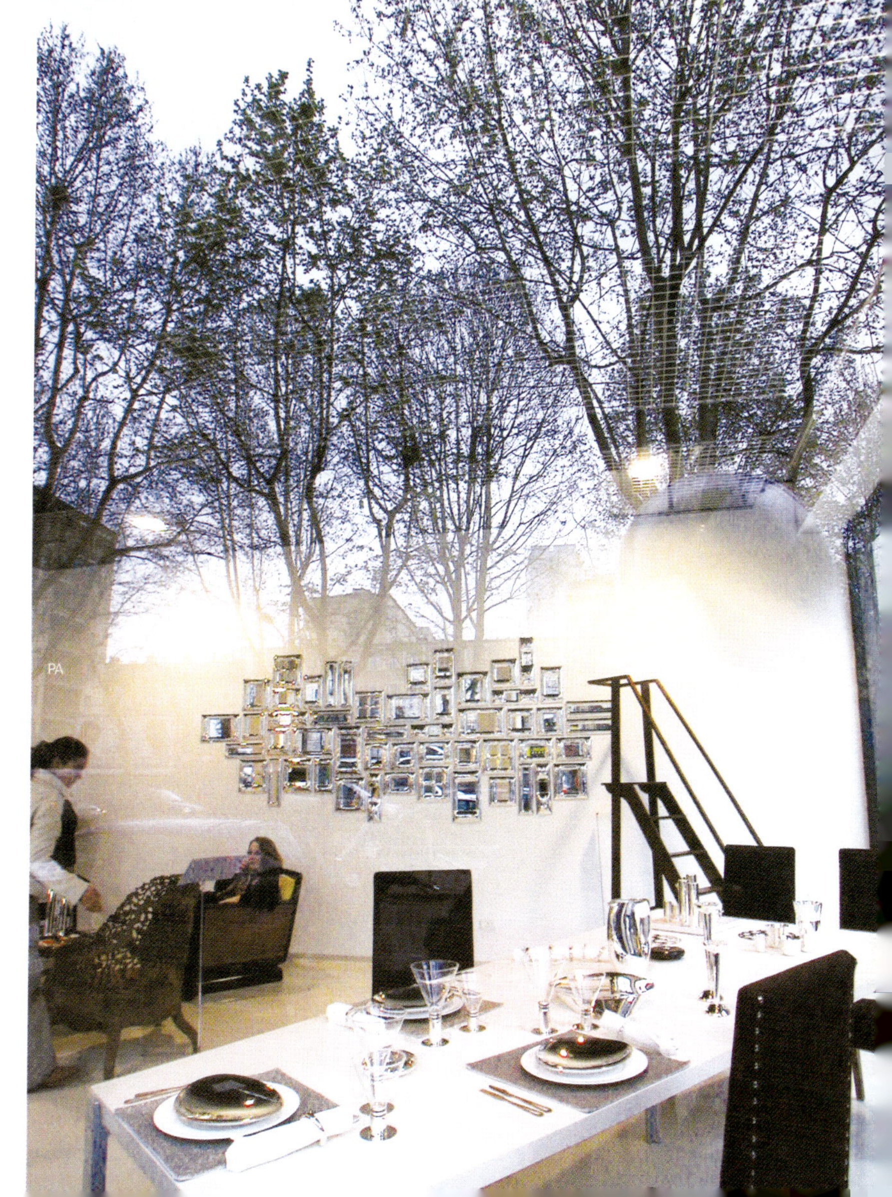

silver tabletop
by Gabriele De Vecchi
@ Understate design store

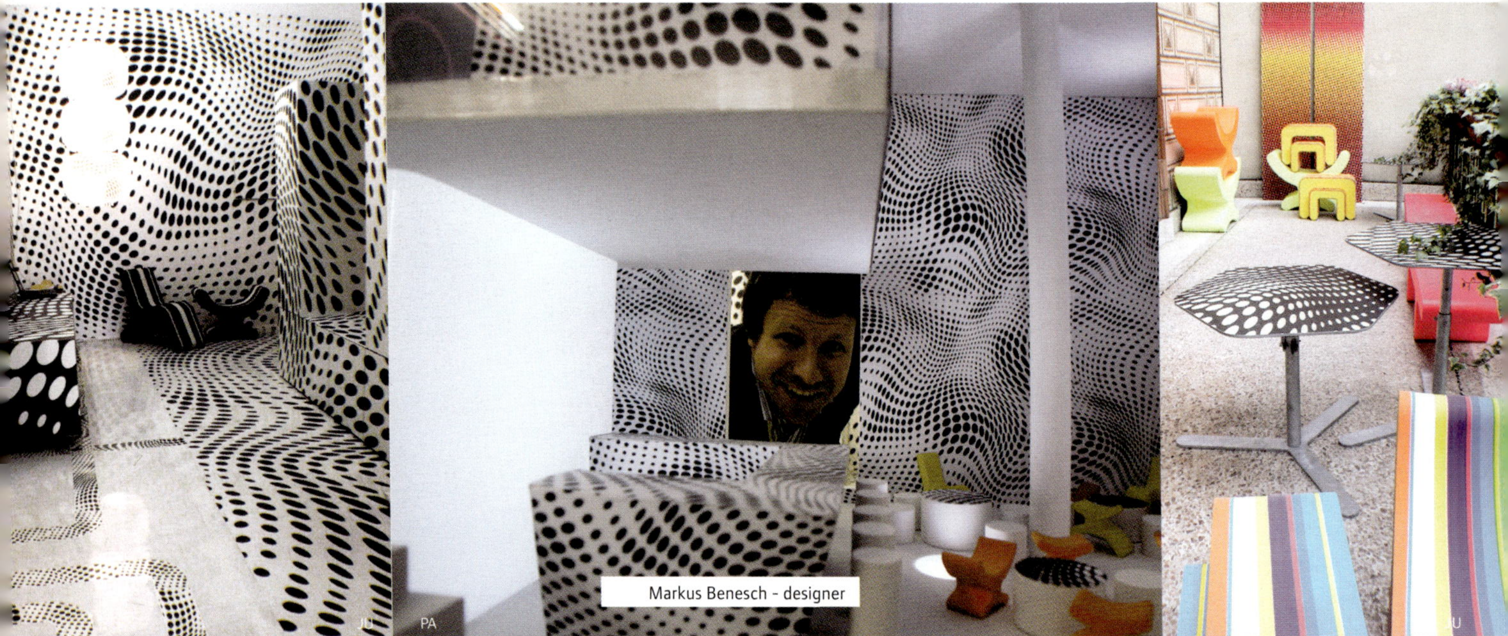

COLORFLAGE IS A FLEXIBLE TOOL THAT DESIGNS SPACES IN A NEW AND CHALLENGING WAY.

It consists of wallpaper, paint, fabric, furniture and lamps.

By weaving a pattern between objects and architecture **we create a fused and uniform space.**

Working with the same colour or pattern for walls and furniture, the furniture blends into the background and appears

less visible. Space is being camouflaged by colors and patterns. **Colorflaged.**

We visually free the rooms from redundant but still necessary objects.

" I always wanted to have a tool- which combines the creative fields of graphic design, product design and architecture.

I believe that in order to create out-standing results these professions should interact and work closer together!"

MARKUS BENESCH

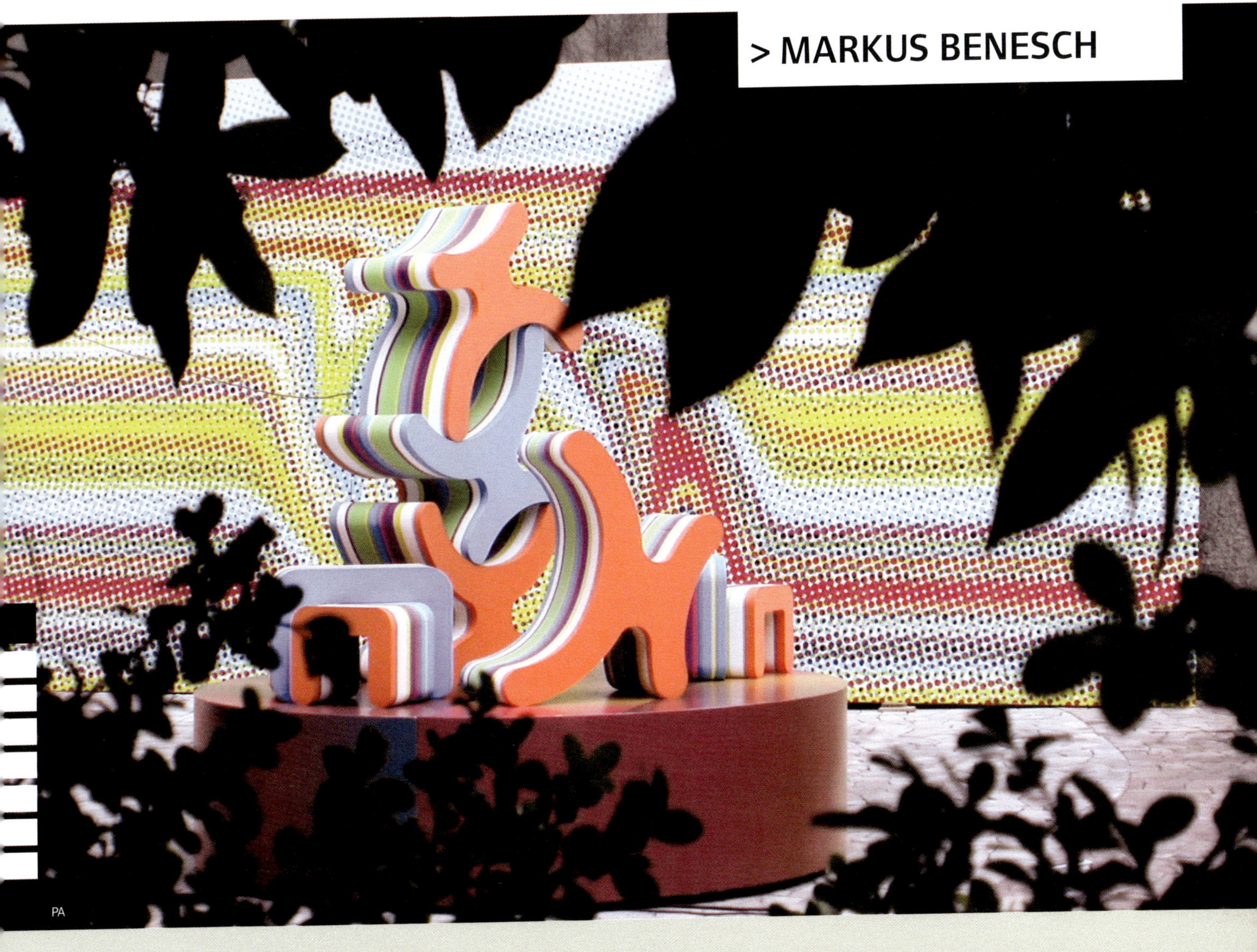

> MARKUS BENESCH
PA

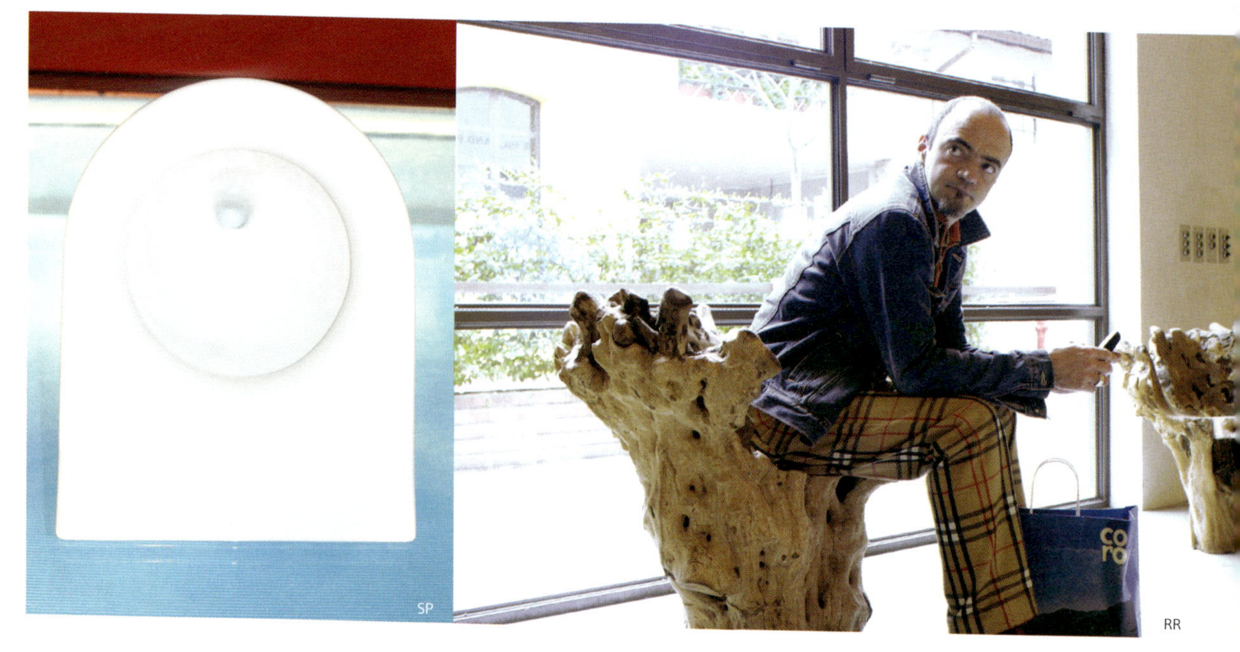

Catalano

@ C.P. Company-Stone Island shop

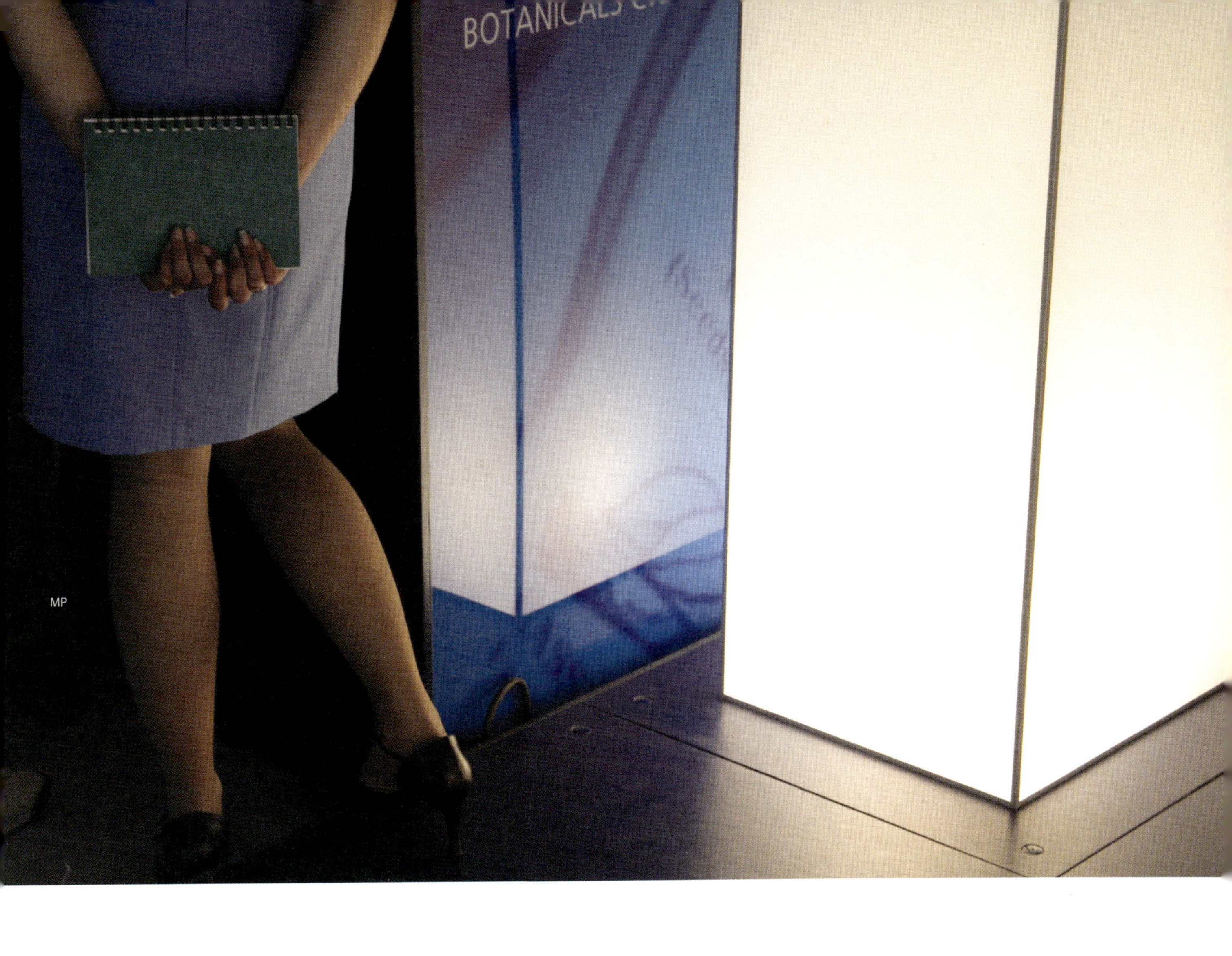

BOTANICALS C
MP

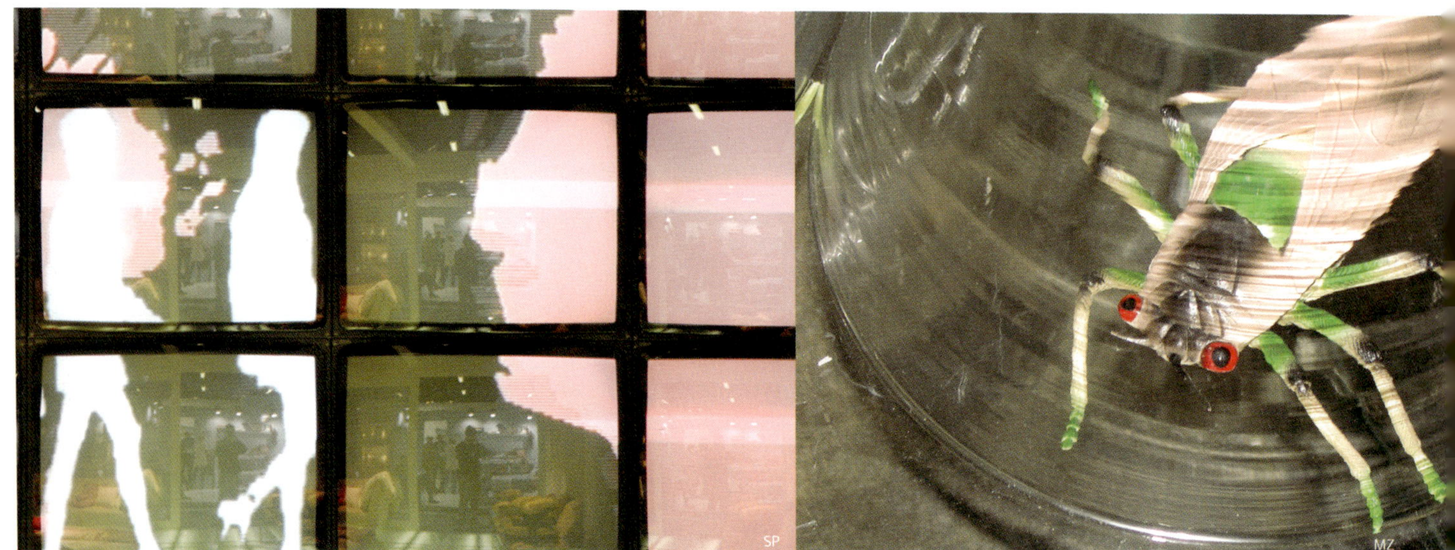

Blumarine

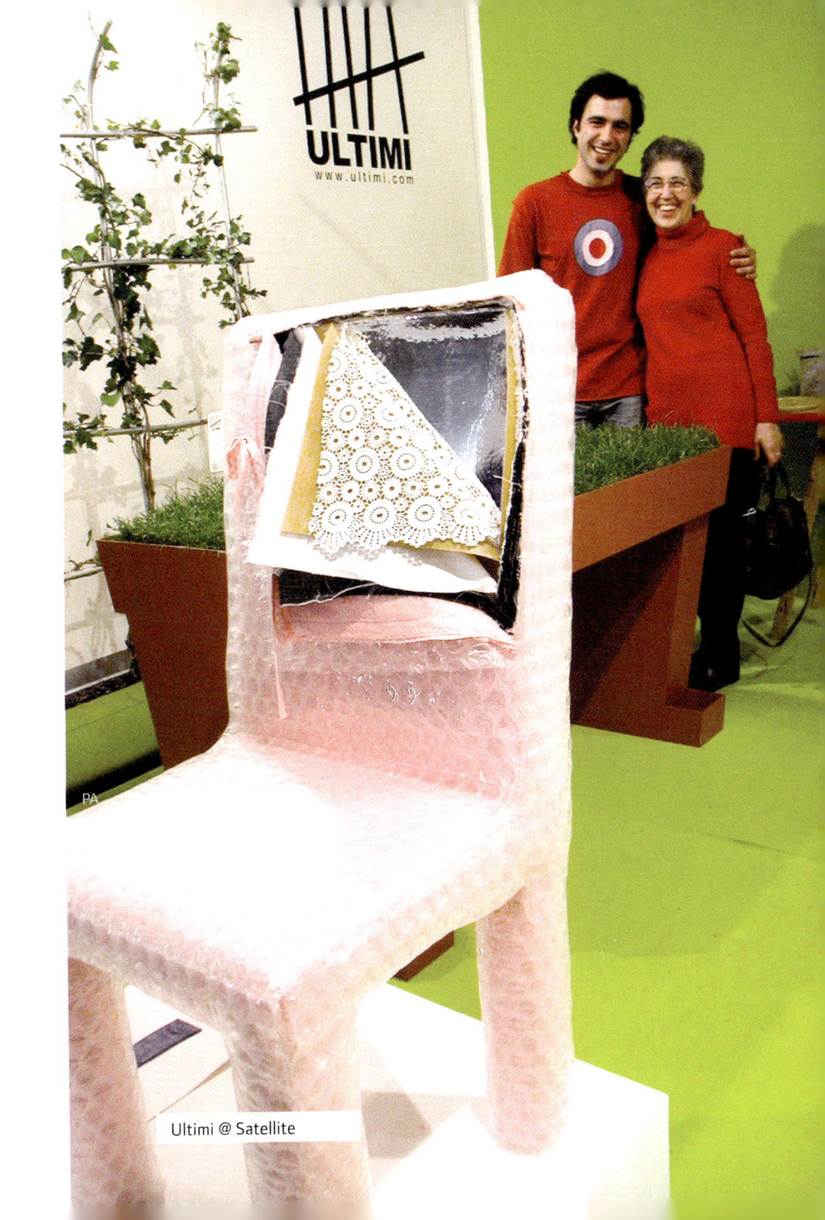

Ultimi @ Satellite

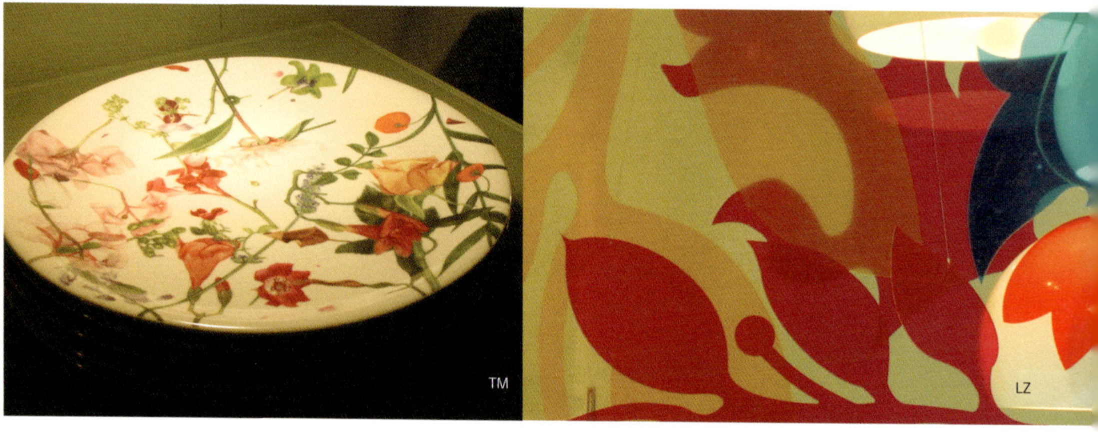

Kartell

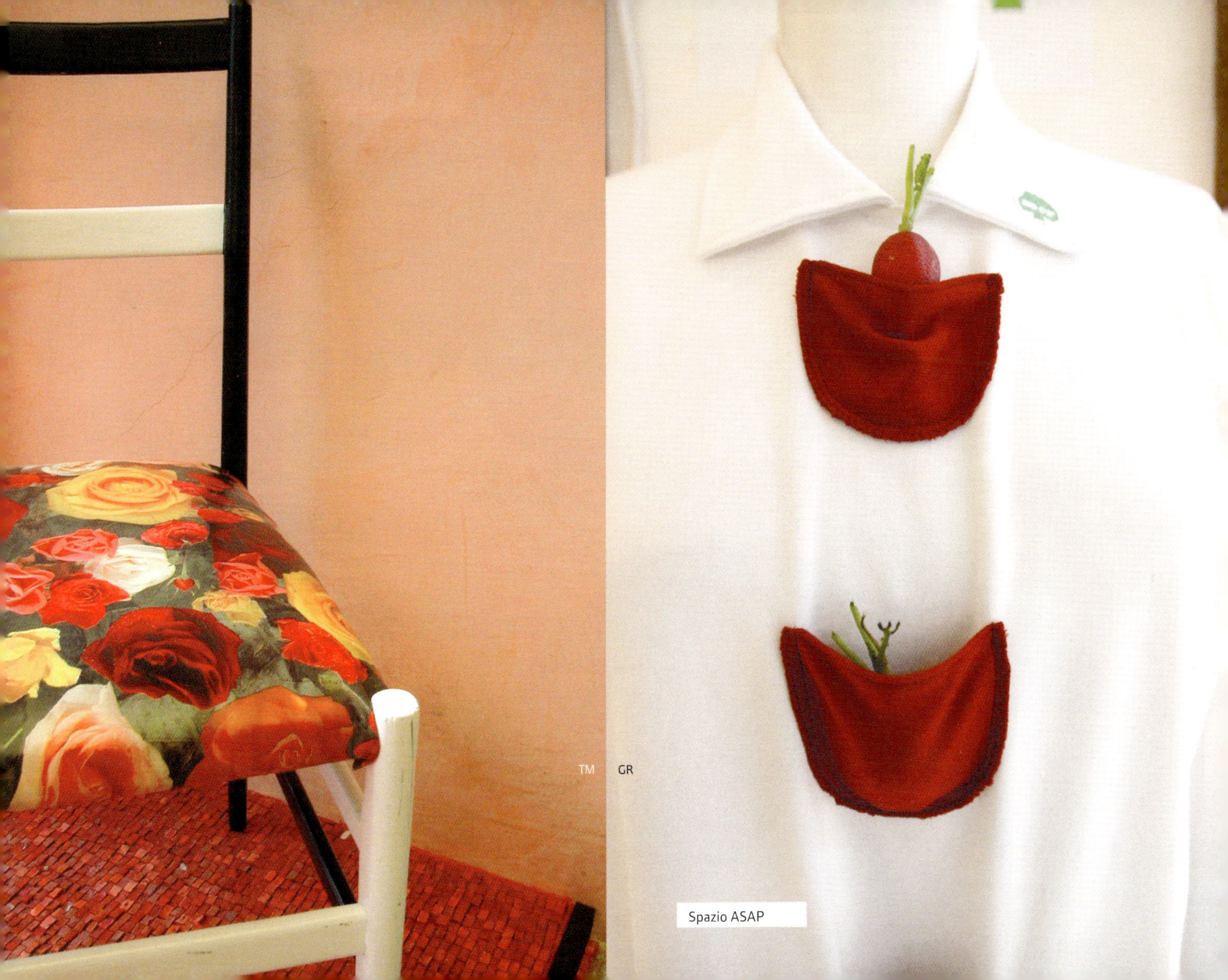

TM   GR
Spazio ASAP

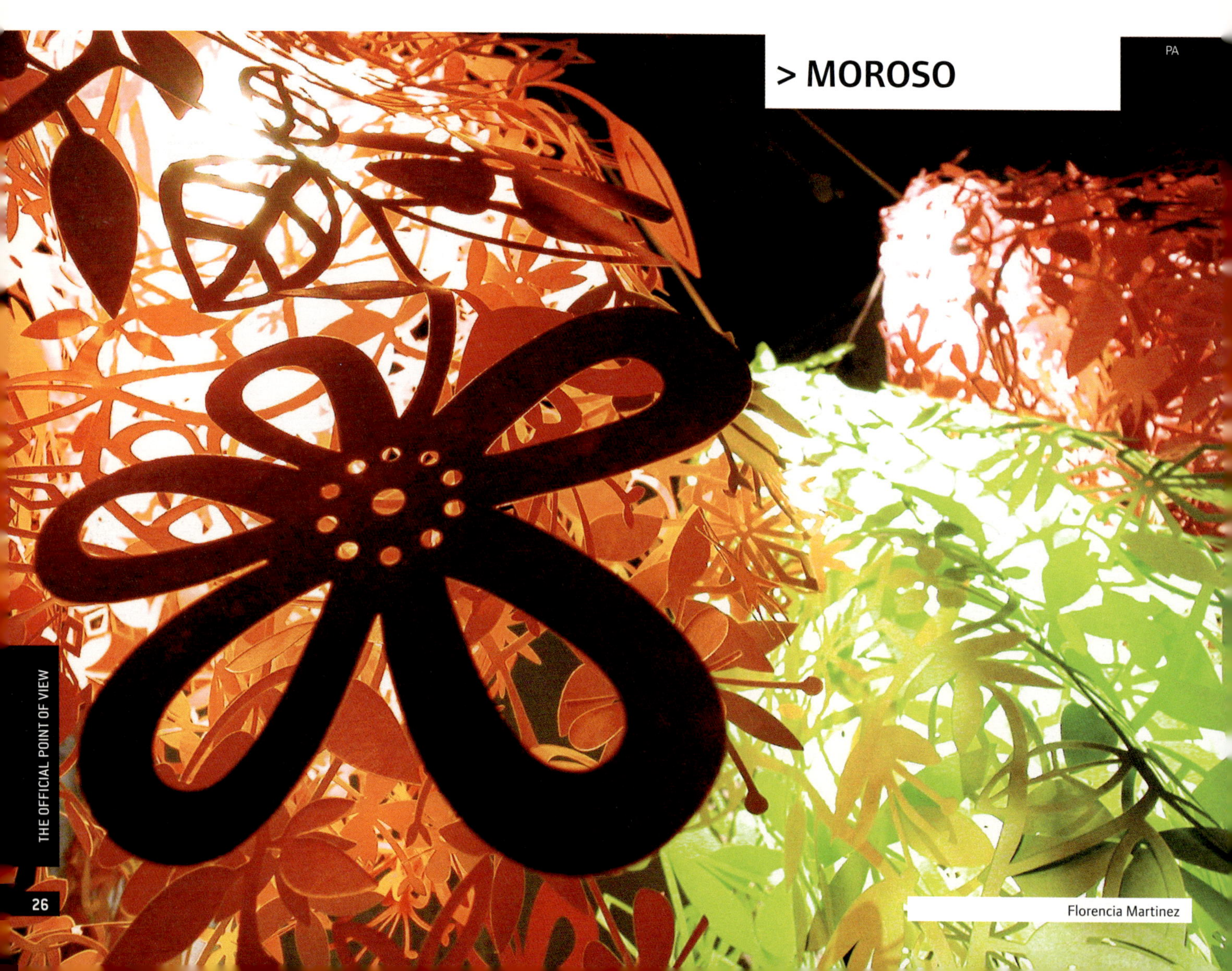PA
> MOROSO
THE OFFICIAL POINT OF VIEW
26
Florencia Martinez

"The installation is **like a fantasy world** that recalls a forest, full of colours,

imaginings and images of animals and flowers.

Experiments with different fabrics are applied to furniture.

The pieces are created by **combining digital production techniques with craft processes.**

We have developed four new articles with laser and water-cut fabric covers: a bench, a swivel chair, a rocking chair and two swings.

There are also various embroidered chairs, which have different personalities:

dreaming, seductive, sinister, playful, innocent, luxuriant and in-your-face".

TORD BOONTJE

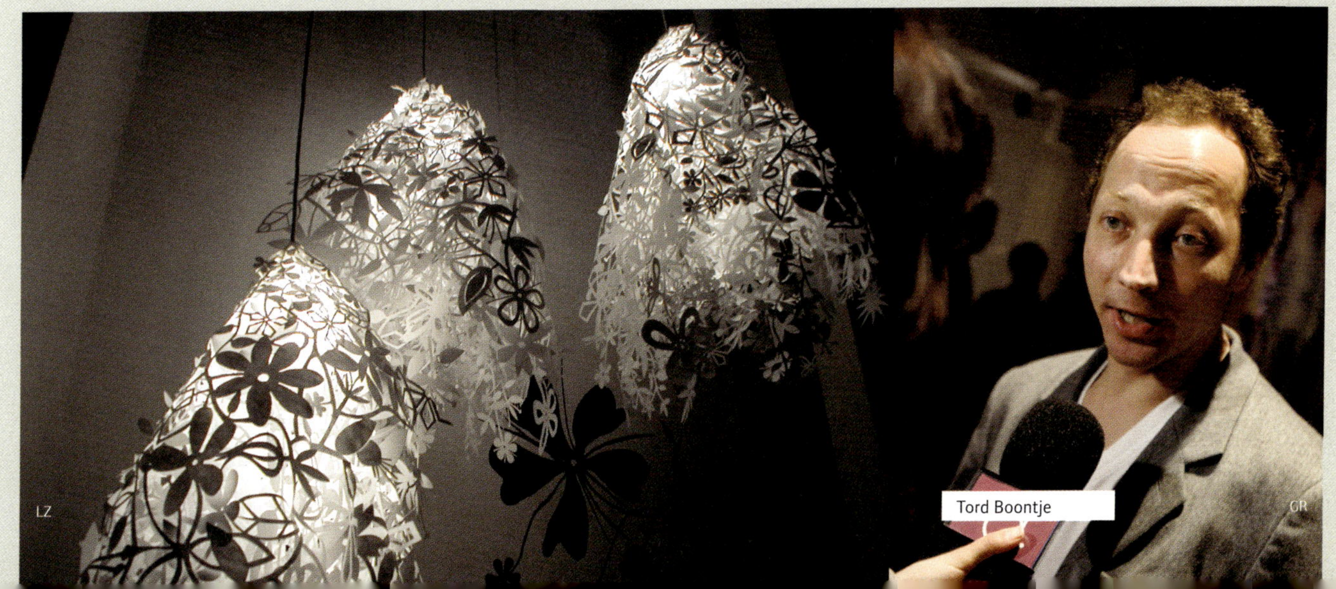

Tord Boontje

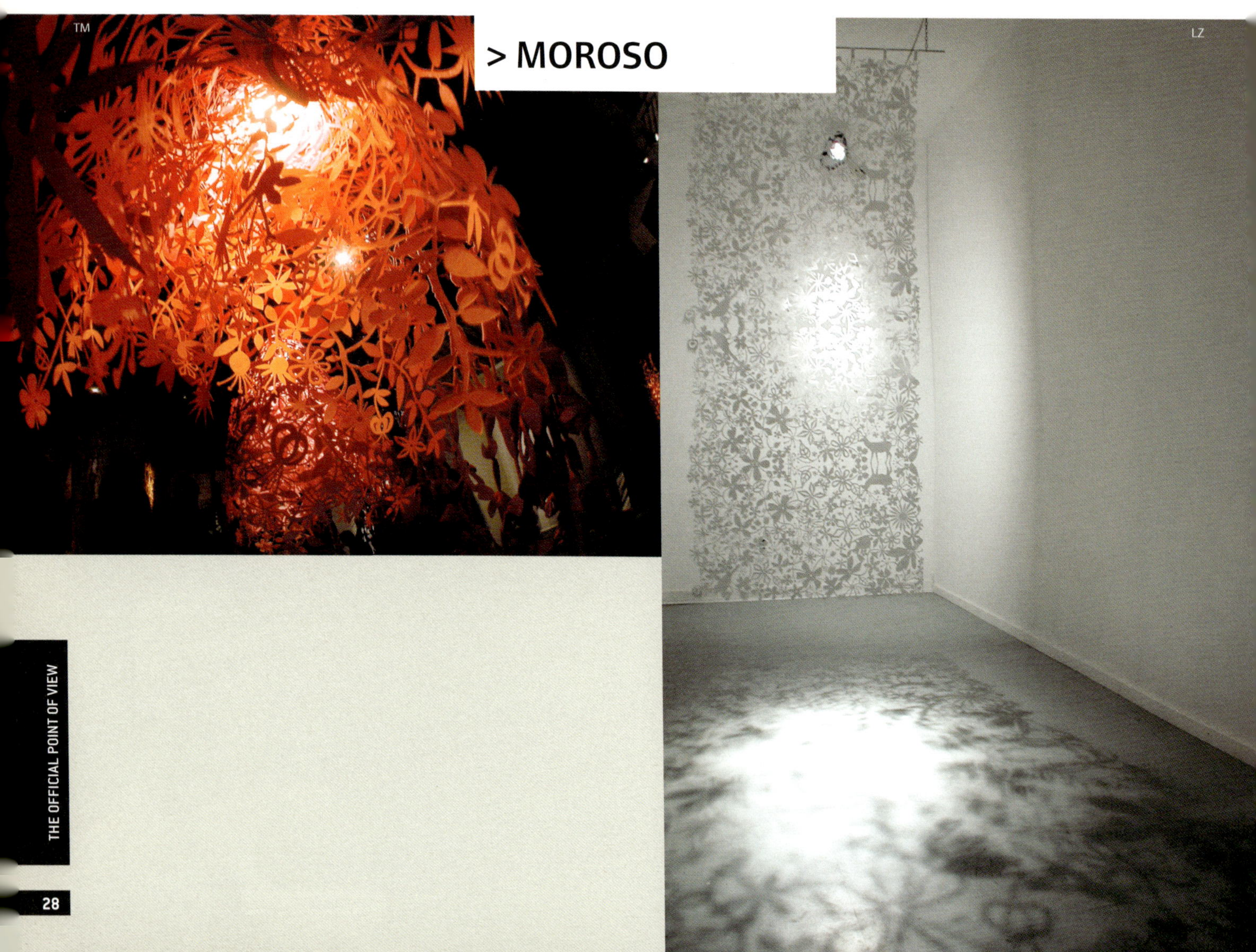

> MOROSO

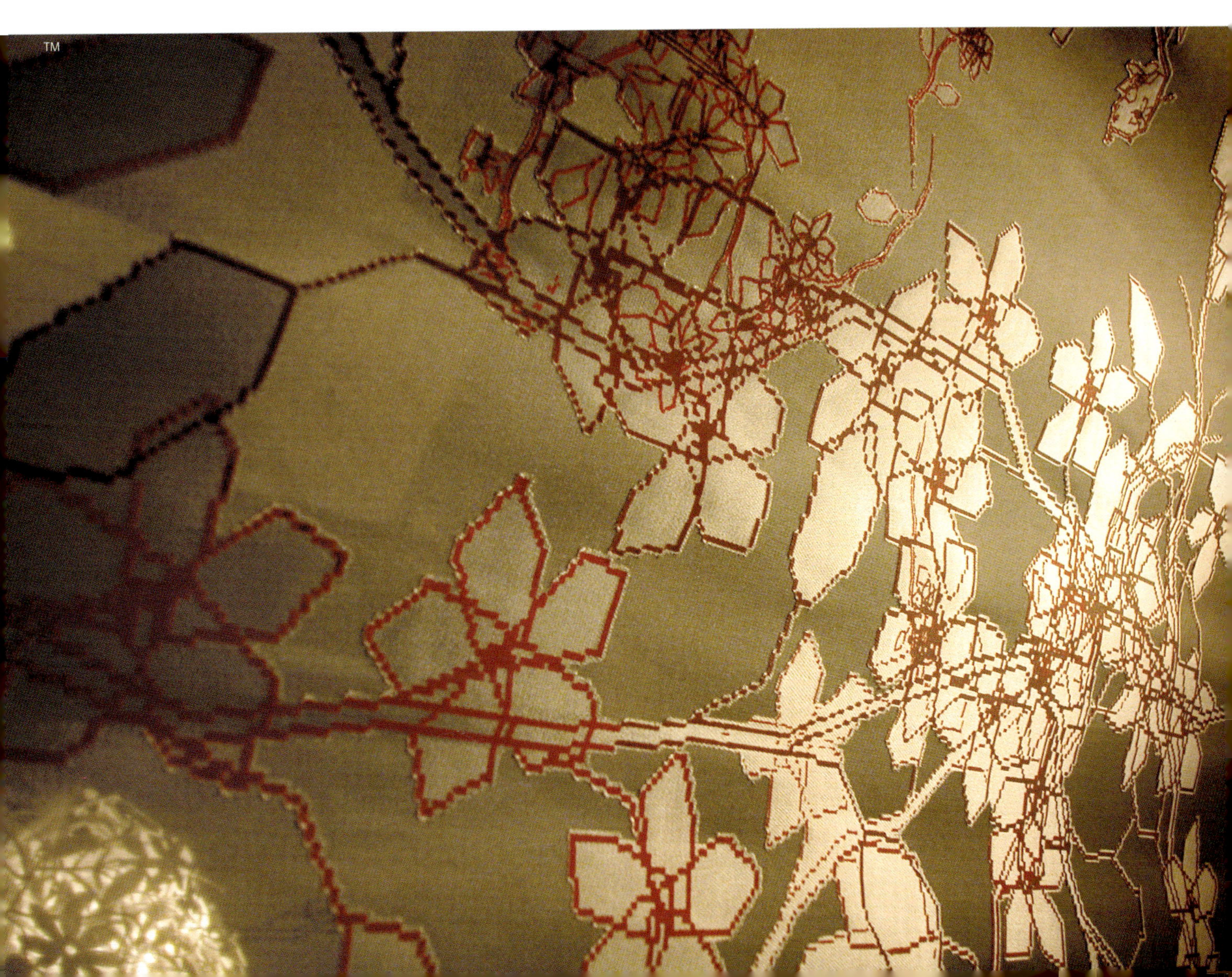
TM

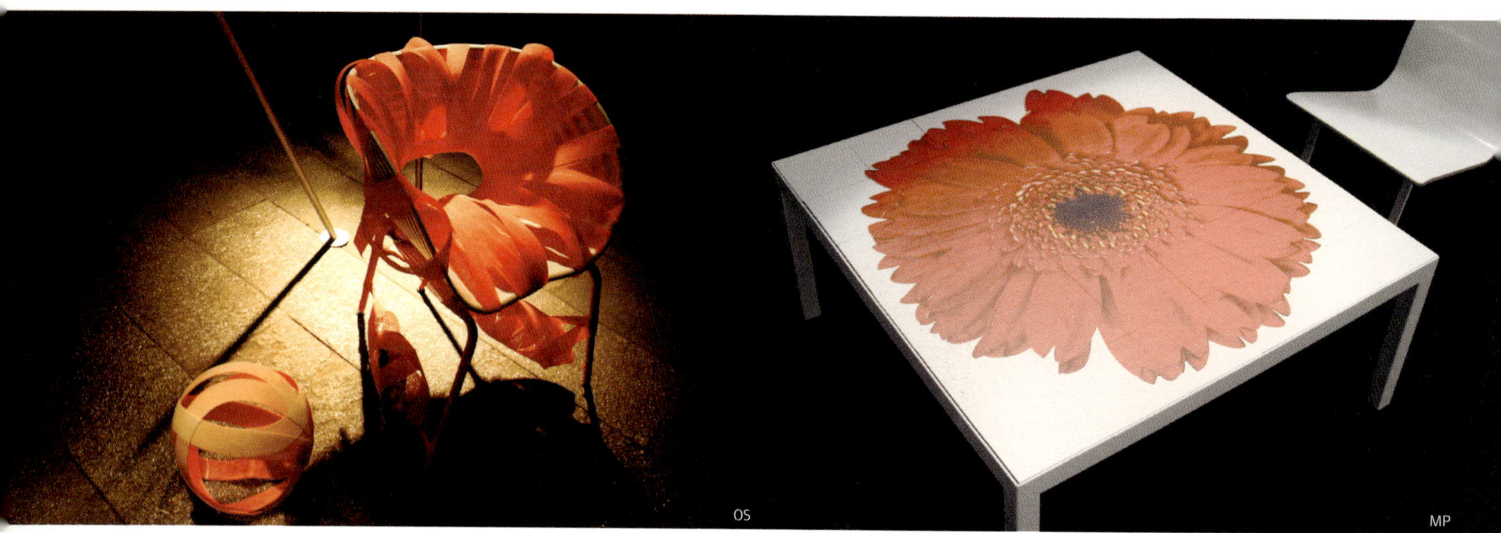

Julie Mathias @ Satellite

Walter Rumsey

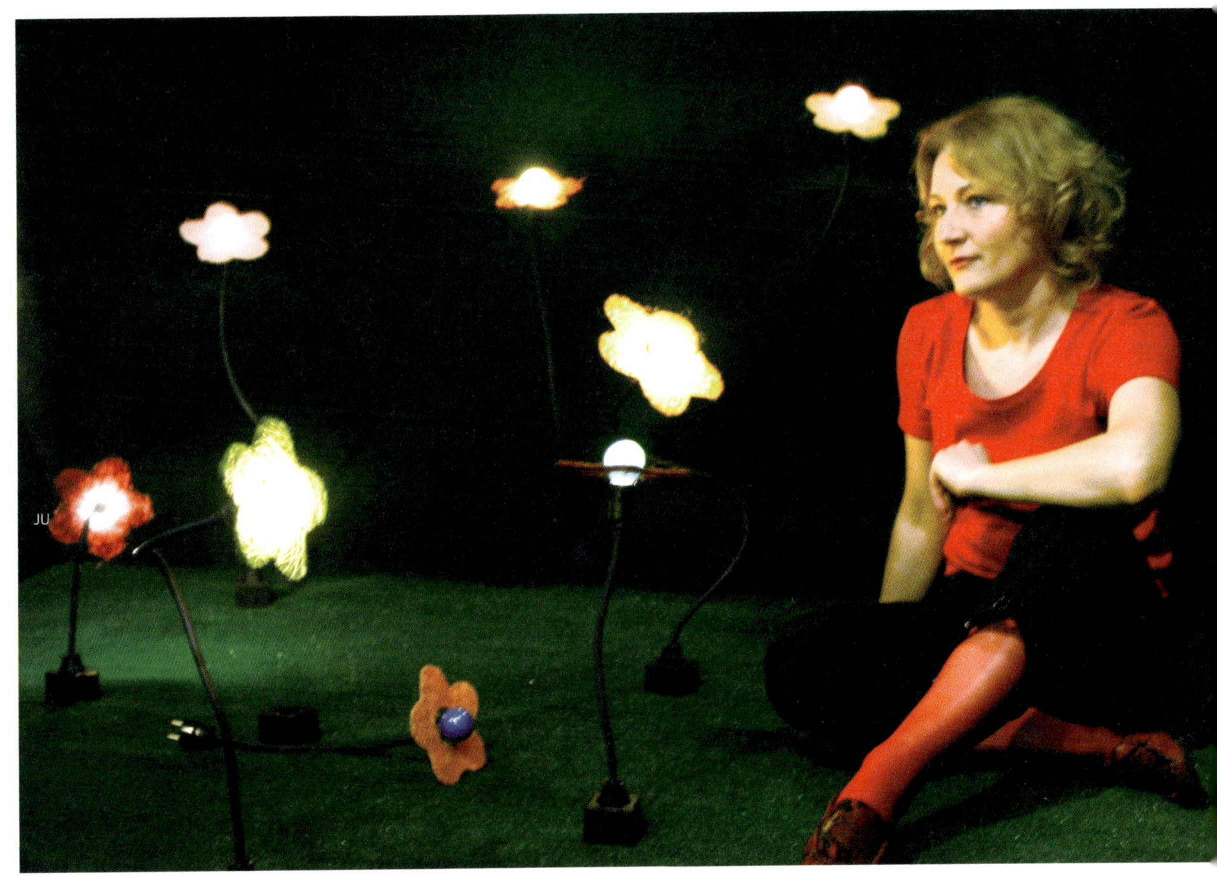

Marton, Maté, Ildiko @ Satellite

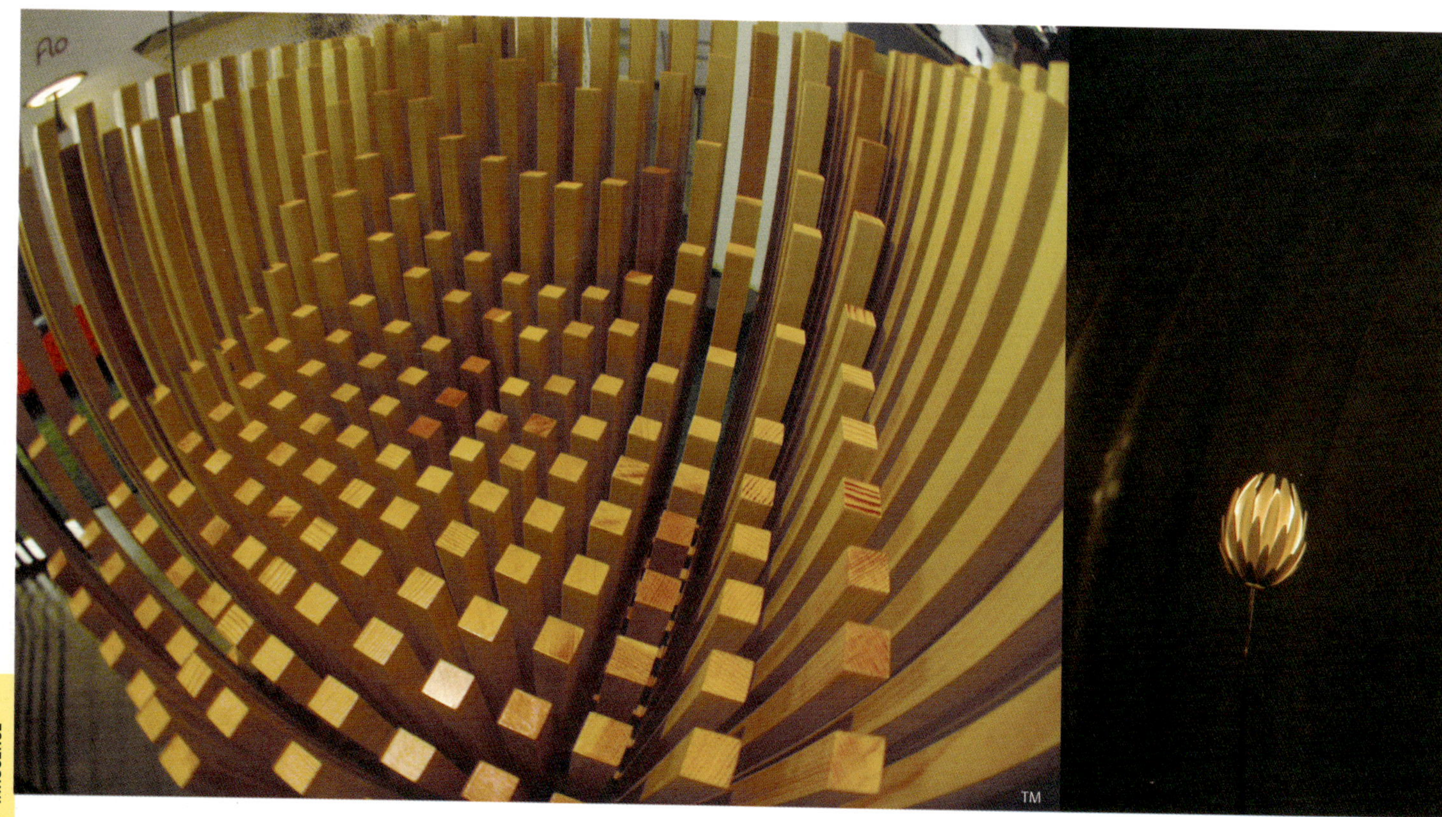

@ Superstudio

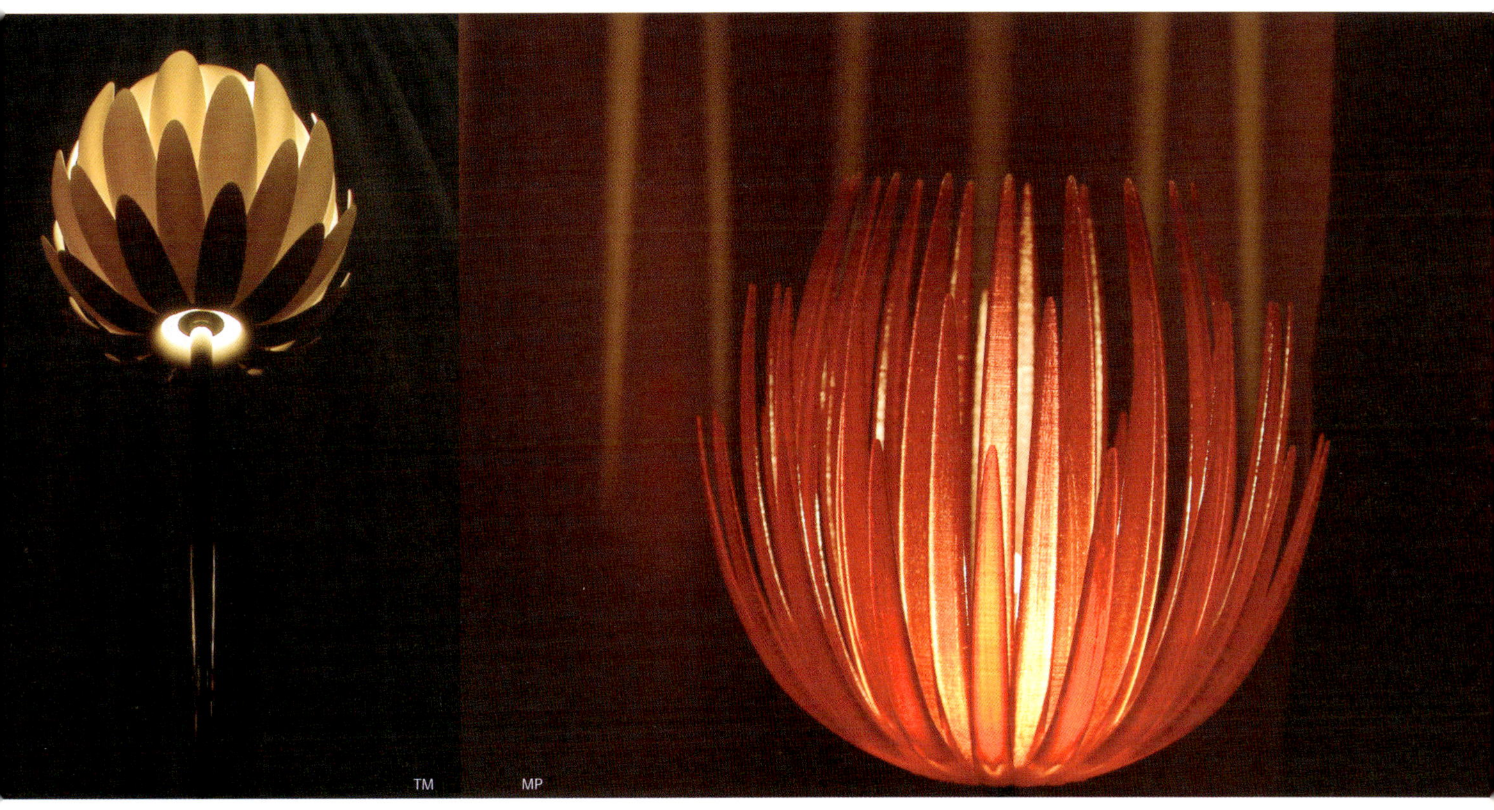

MGX @ Superstudiopiù

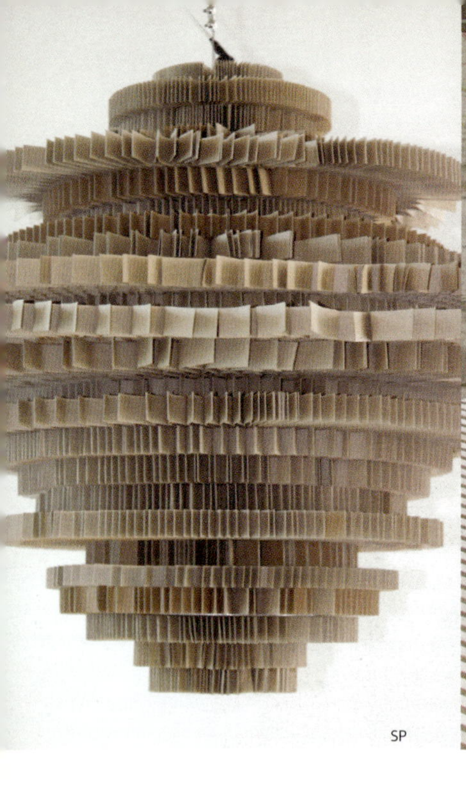

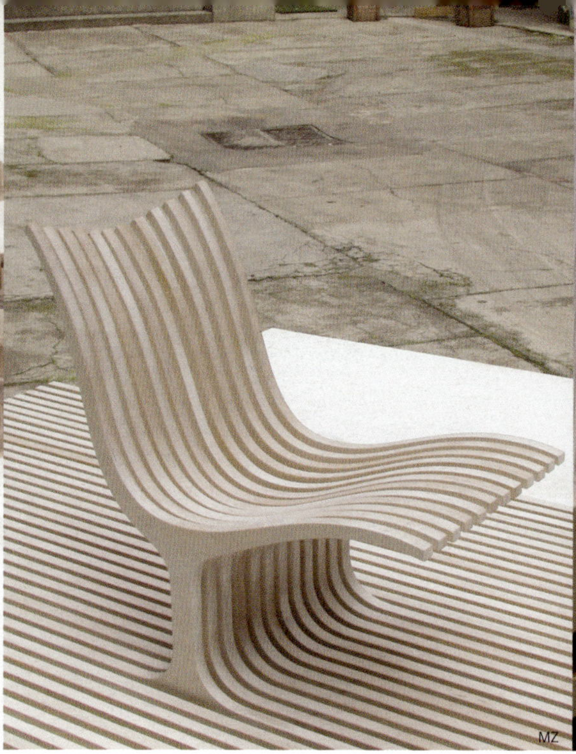

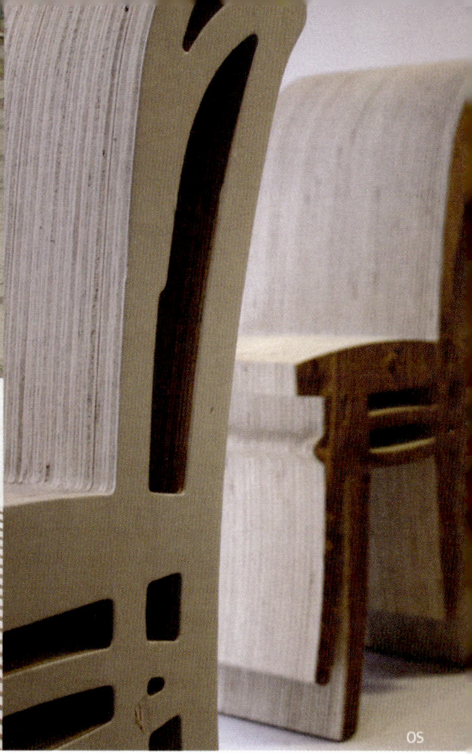

George Baldele
@DesignersBlock

Lente

Laura Cramwinckel @ Design Academy Eindhoven

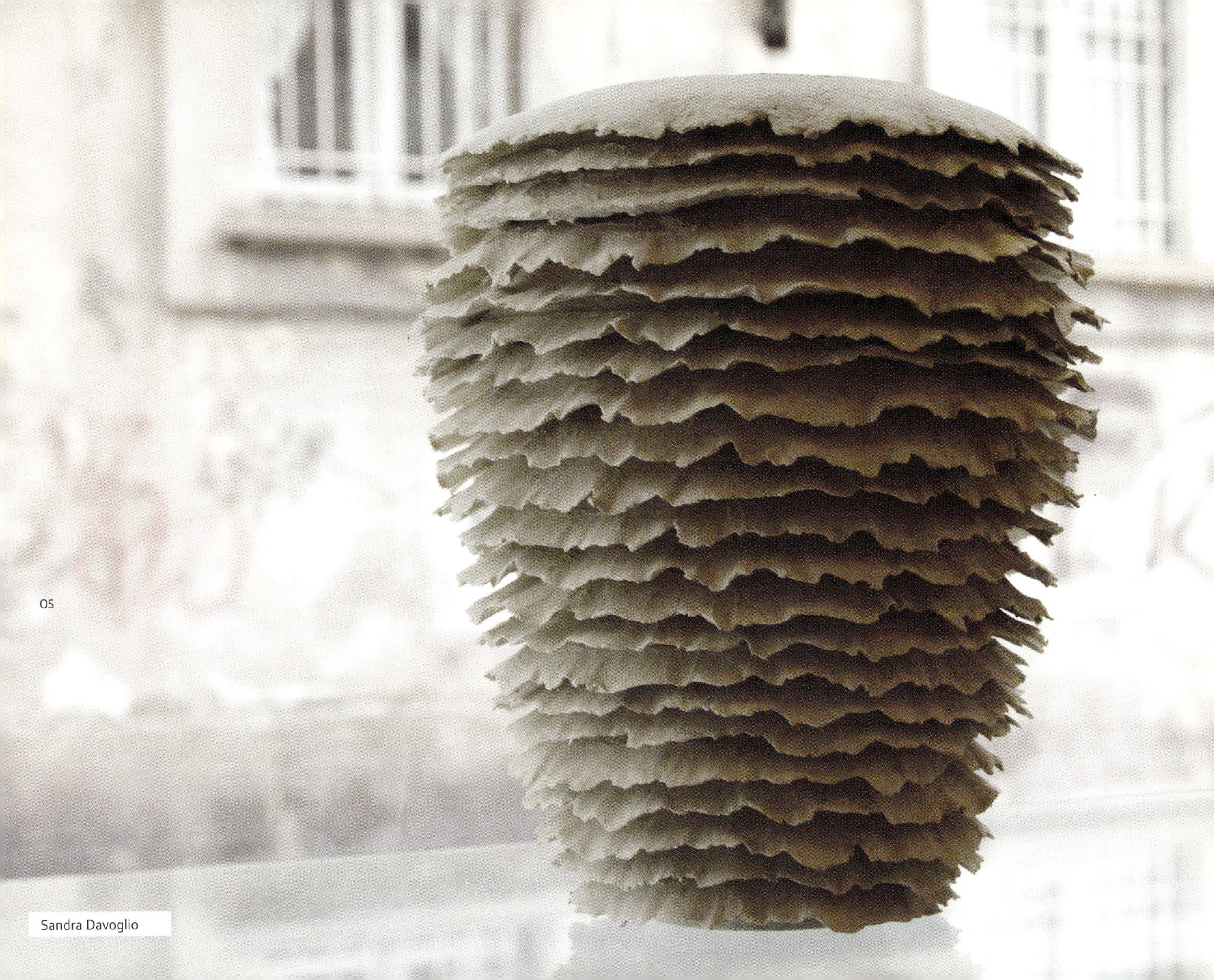

Sandra Davoglio

RR   TM

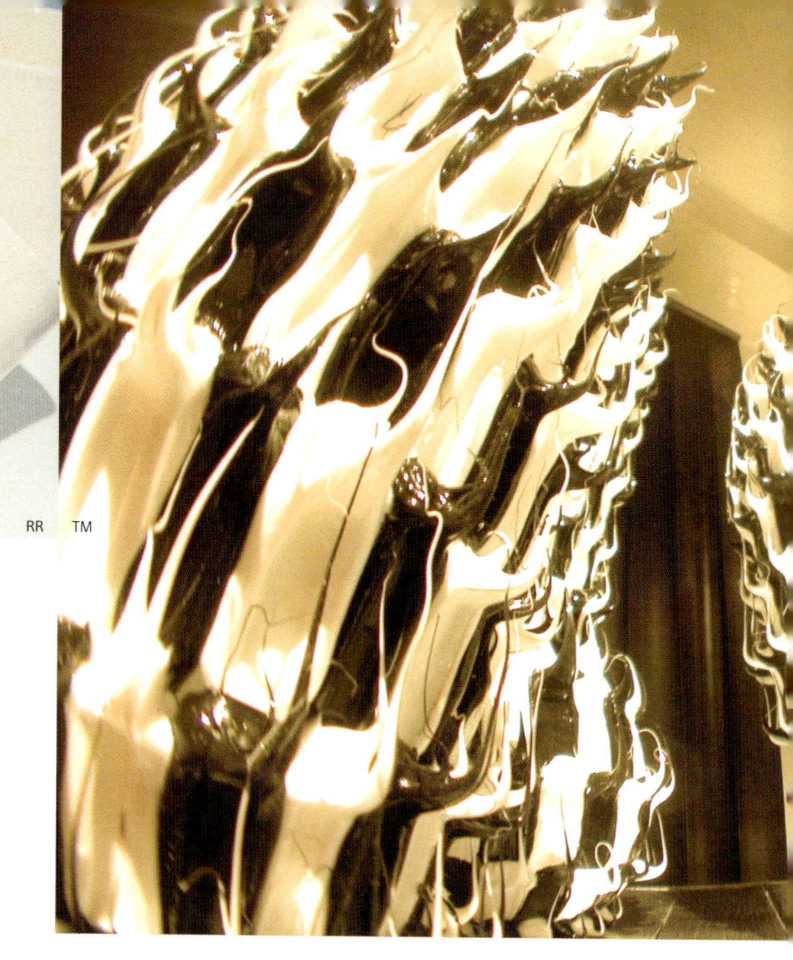

Gariselli Associati @ Satellite

Tipico vases by Alessandro Ciffo @ Dilmos

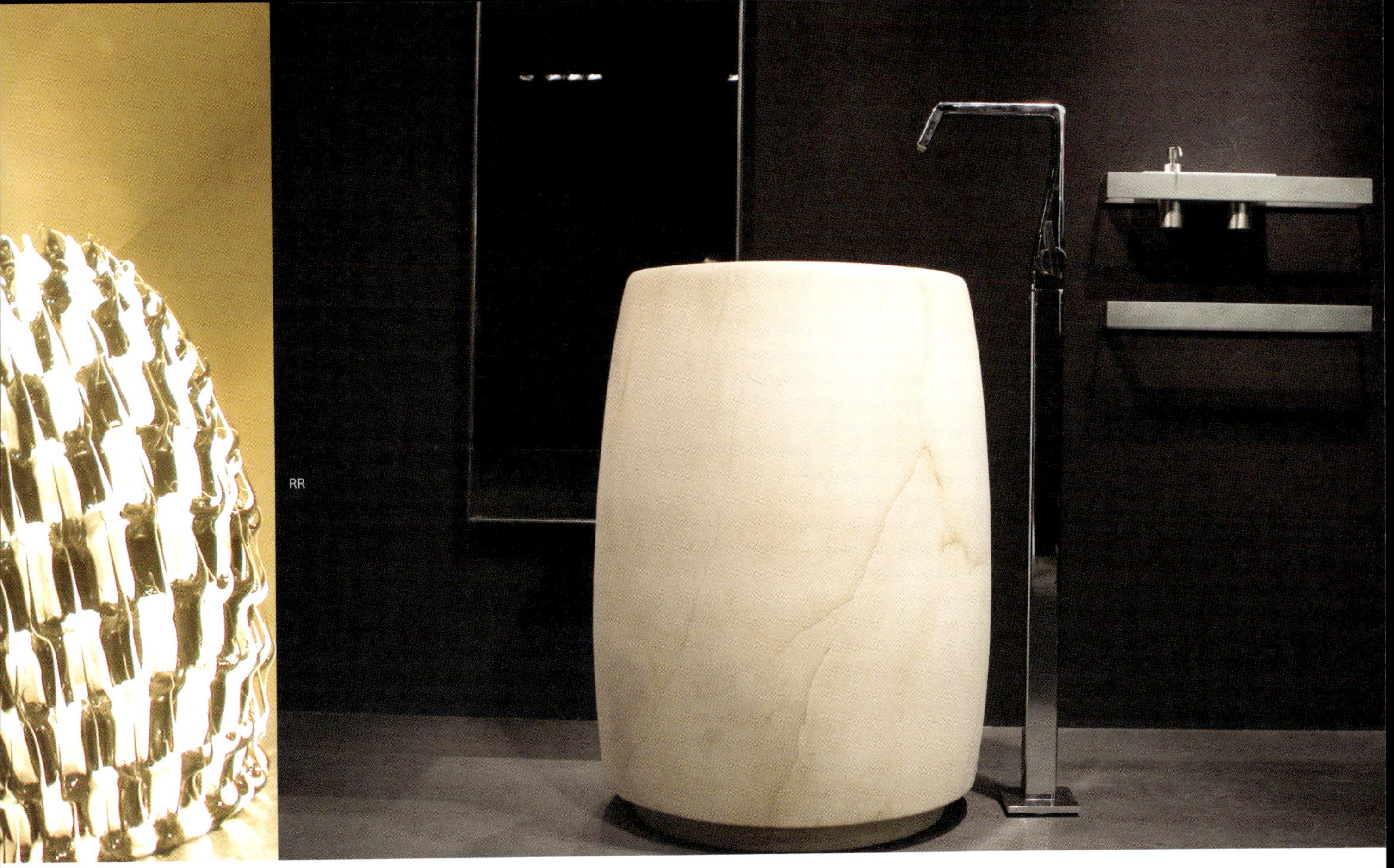

Materia collection by Carlo Colombo

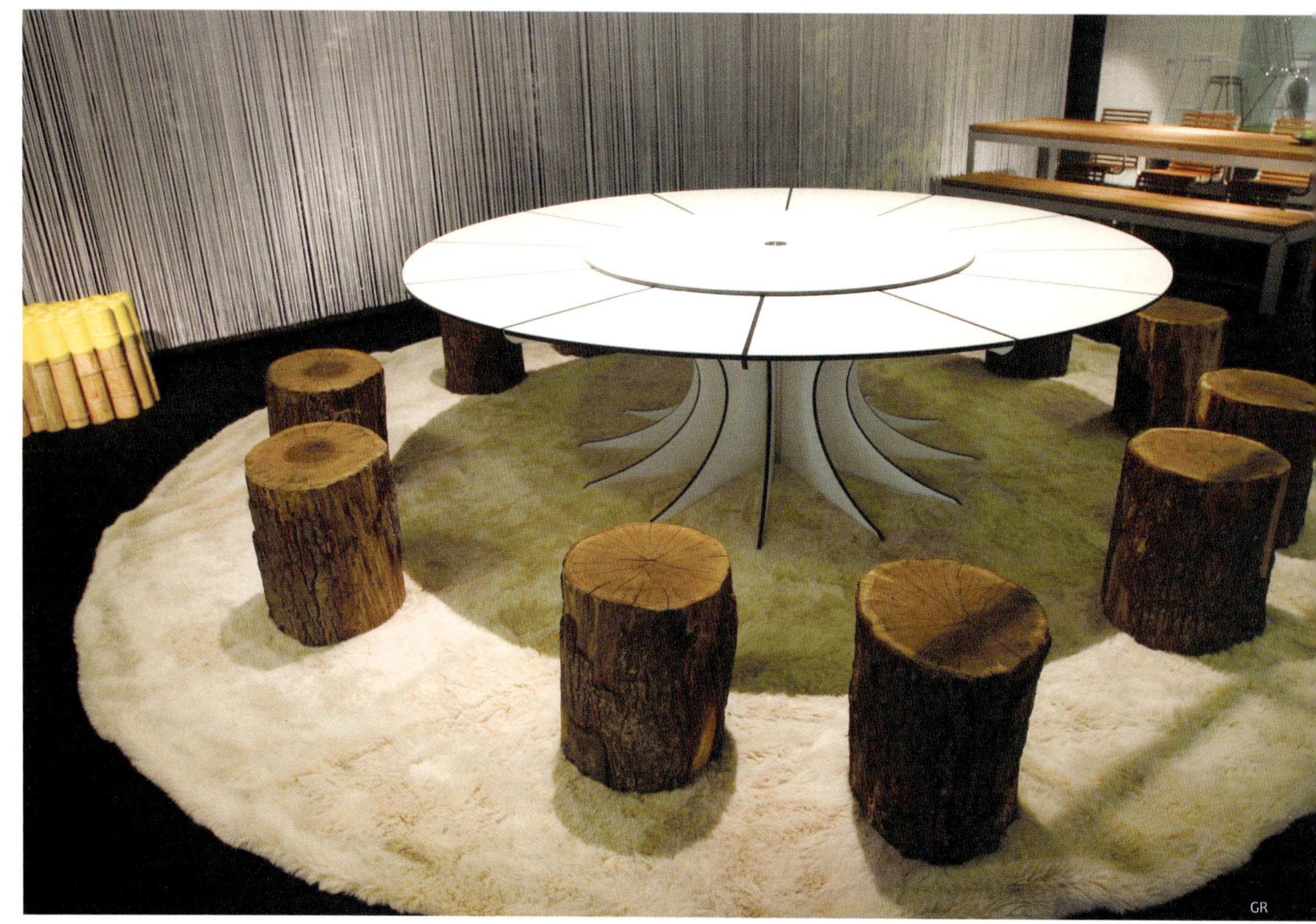

Extremis (outdoor furniture) @ Zona Tortona

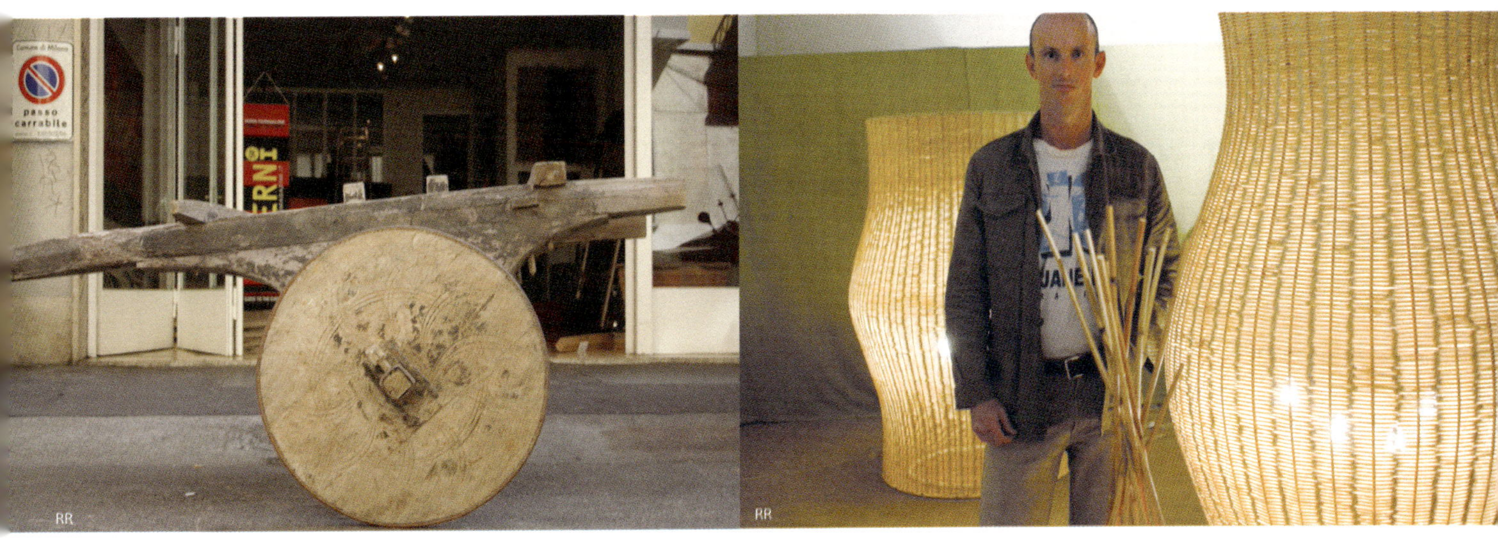

Darcy Clarke for Studiosoft

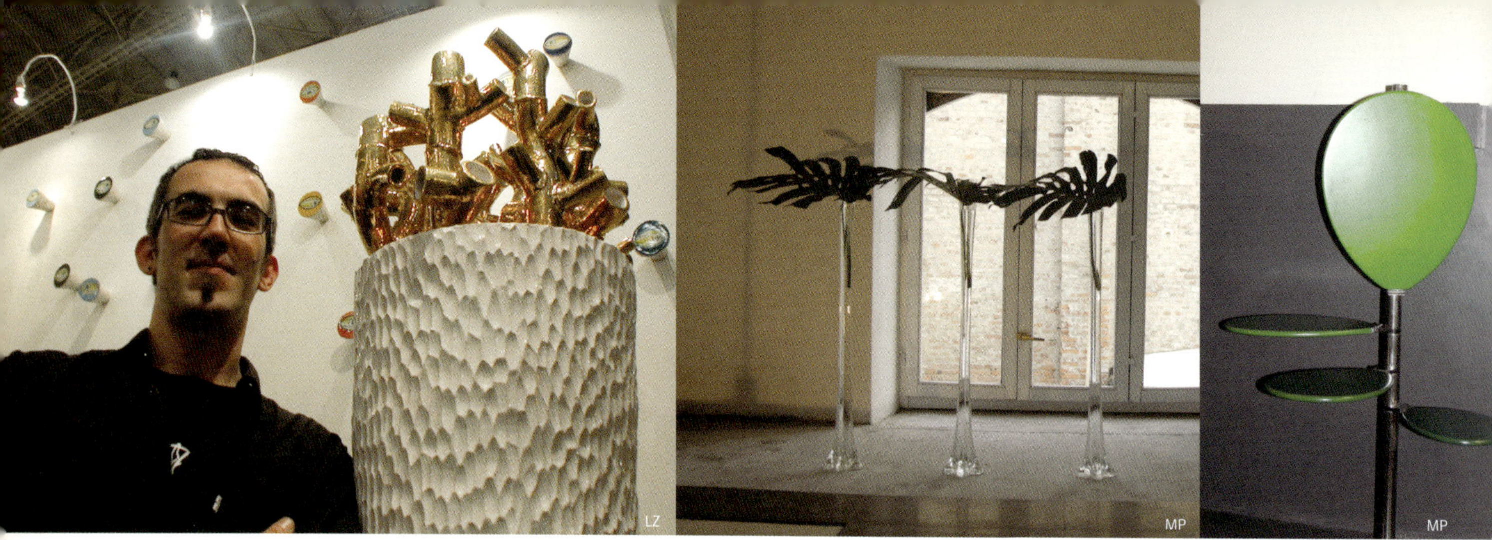

CHILDHOOD - **INNOCENCE**

Fausto Salvi

Segio Mori for Bonomi

@ Cappellini

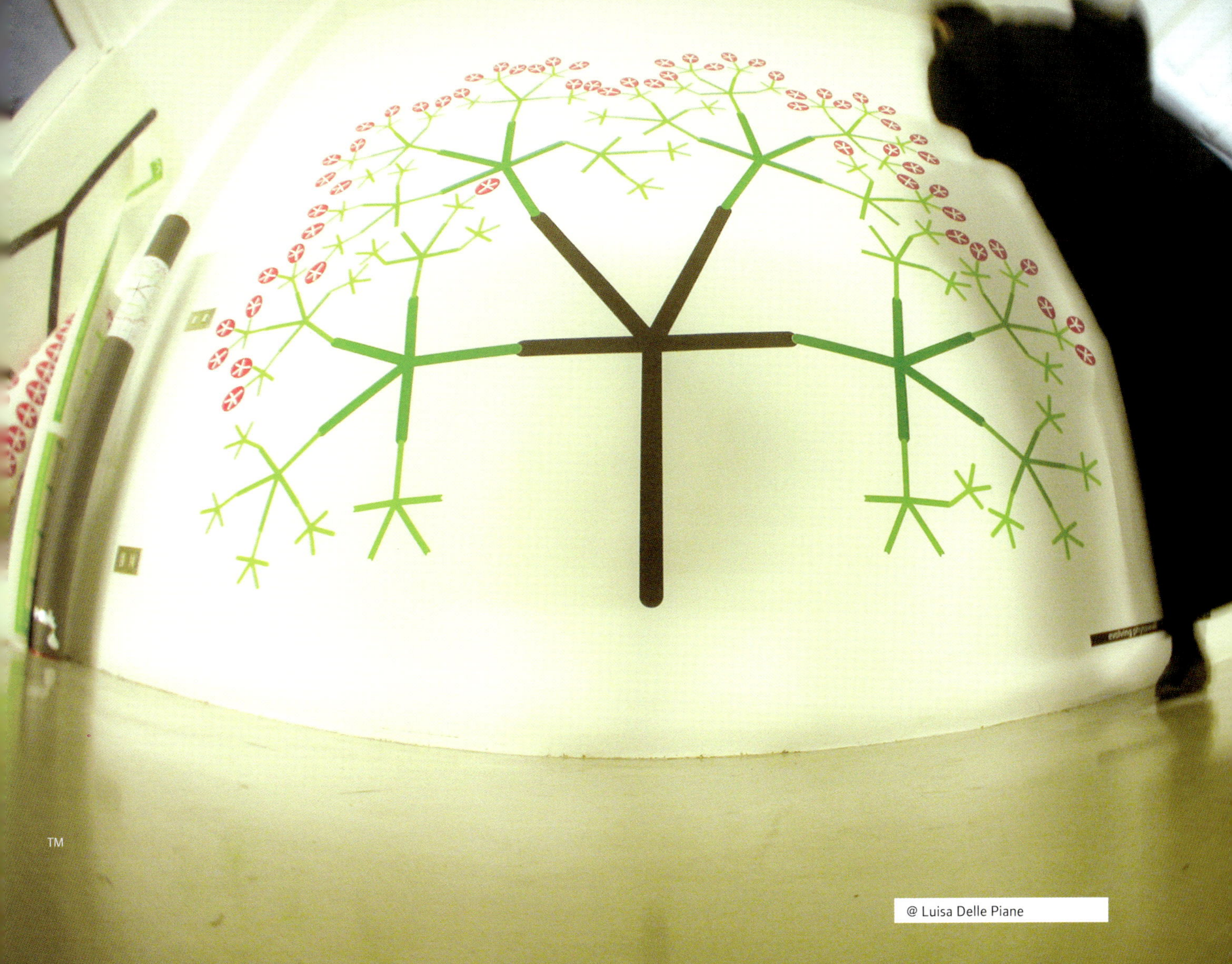

@ Luisa Delle Piane

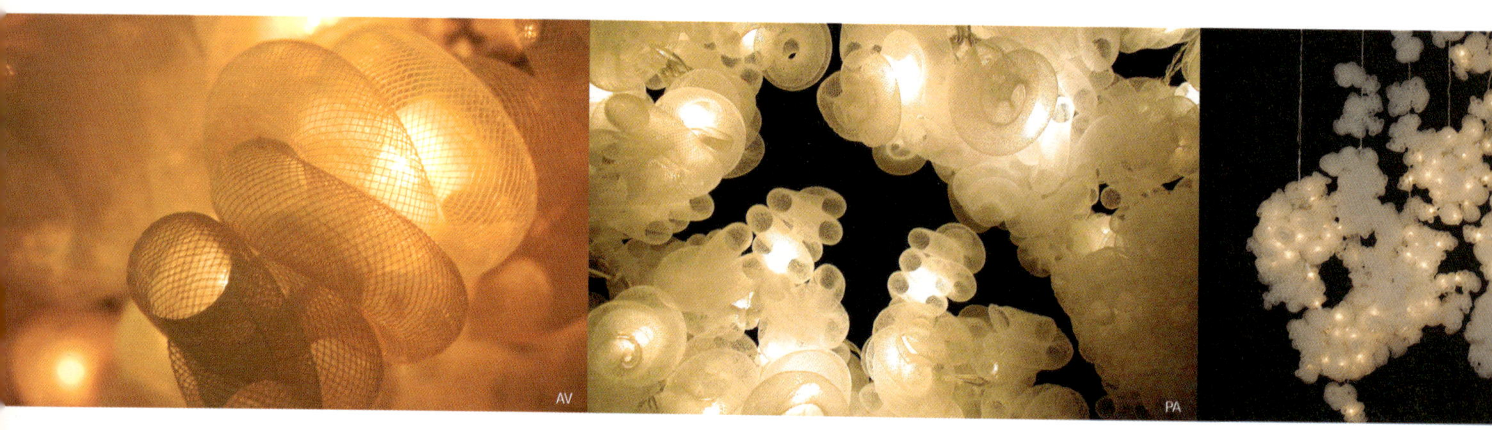

Jess Shaw @ Designersblock

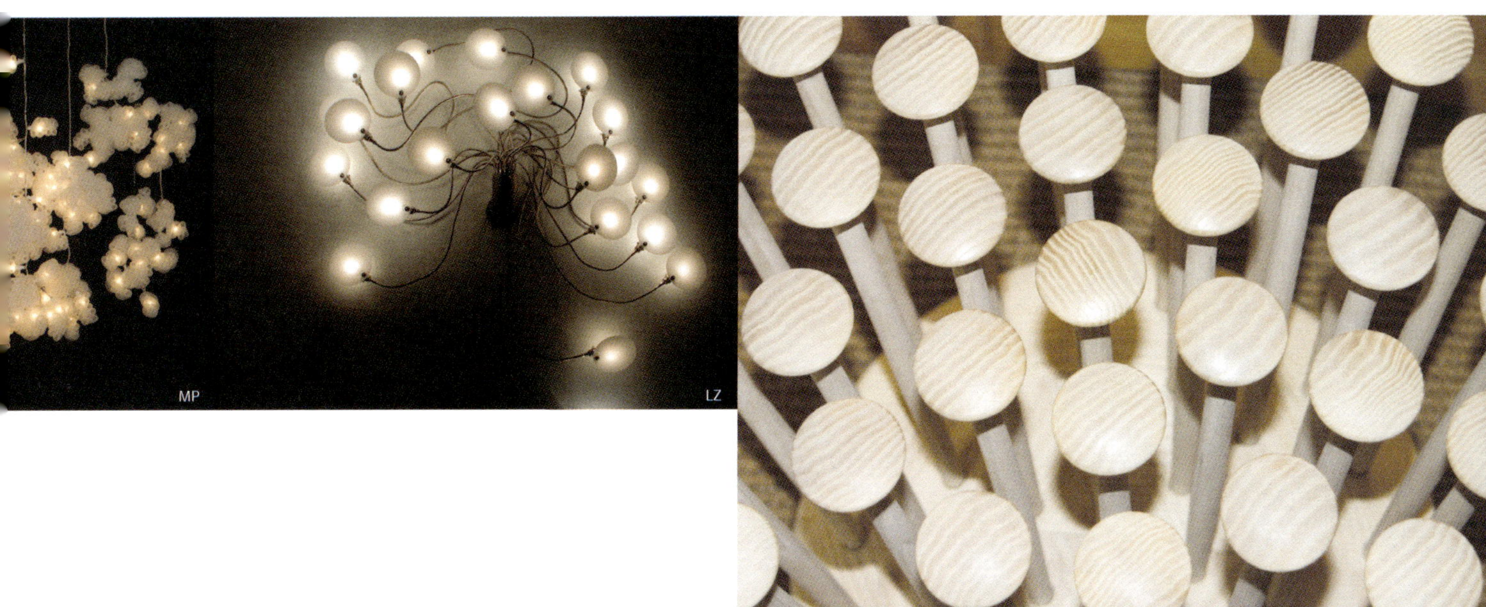

Turciù by Catellani&Smith @ Dilmos

Mc Selvini

Blow up by Alejo Ruocco @ Dovetusai

MP

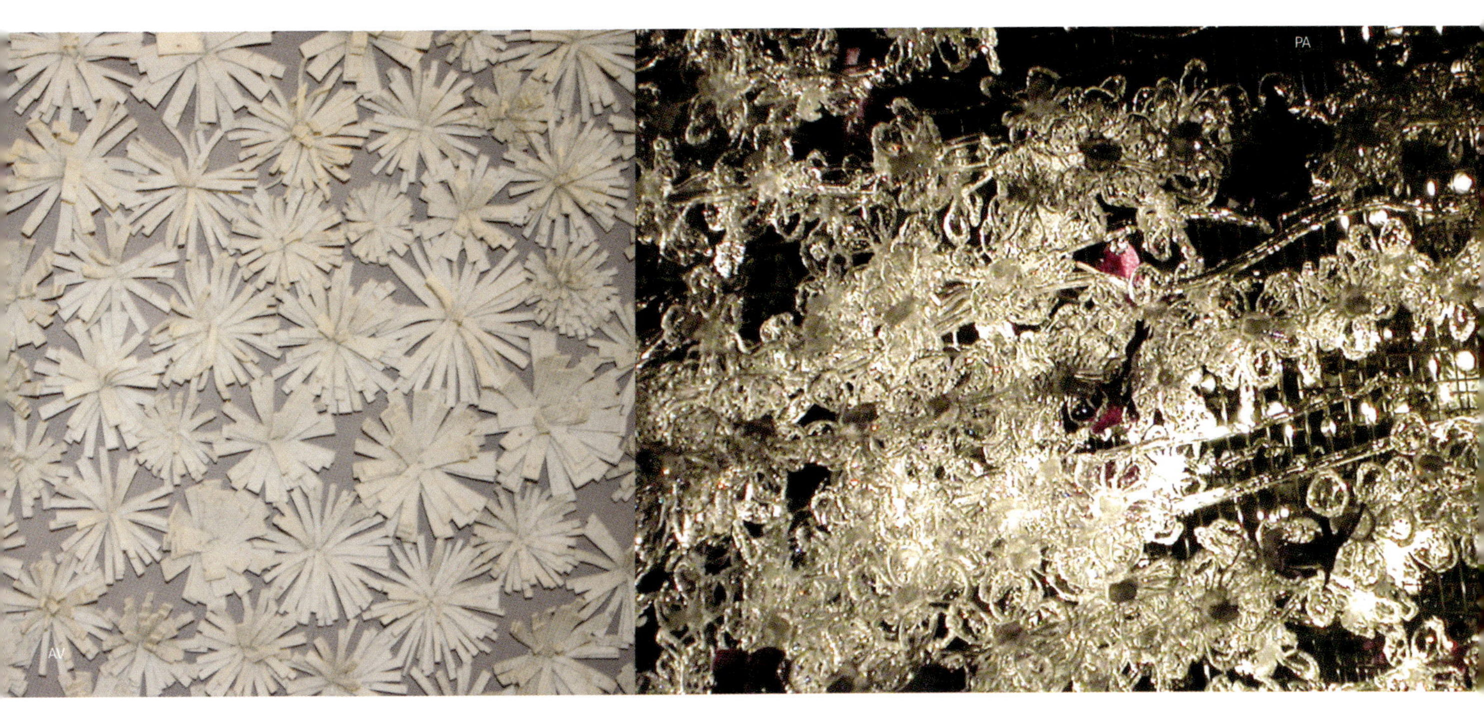

@ Fabbica Del Vapore

Process by Lisa Farmer

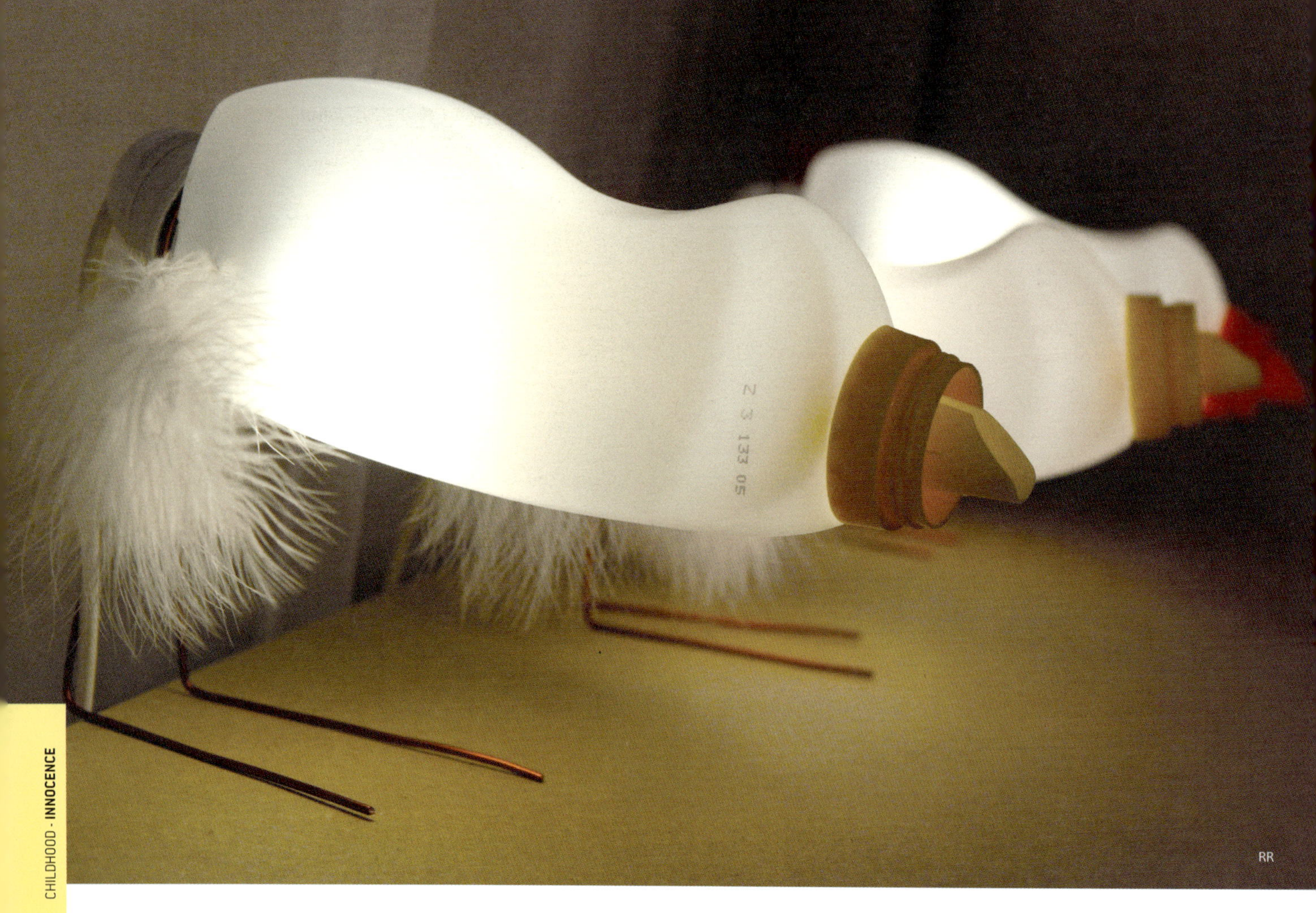

Marc Savary Design

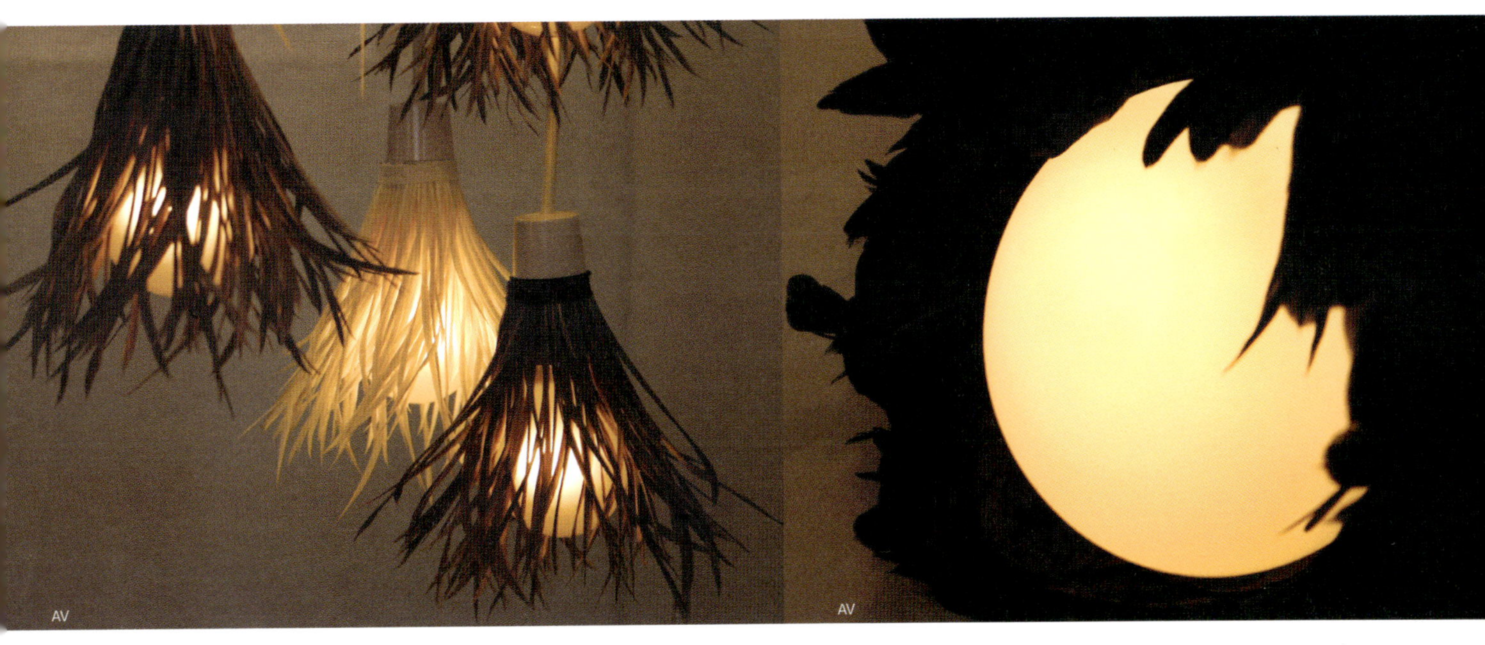

Jess Shaw @ Designersblock

Jess Shaw @ Designersblock

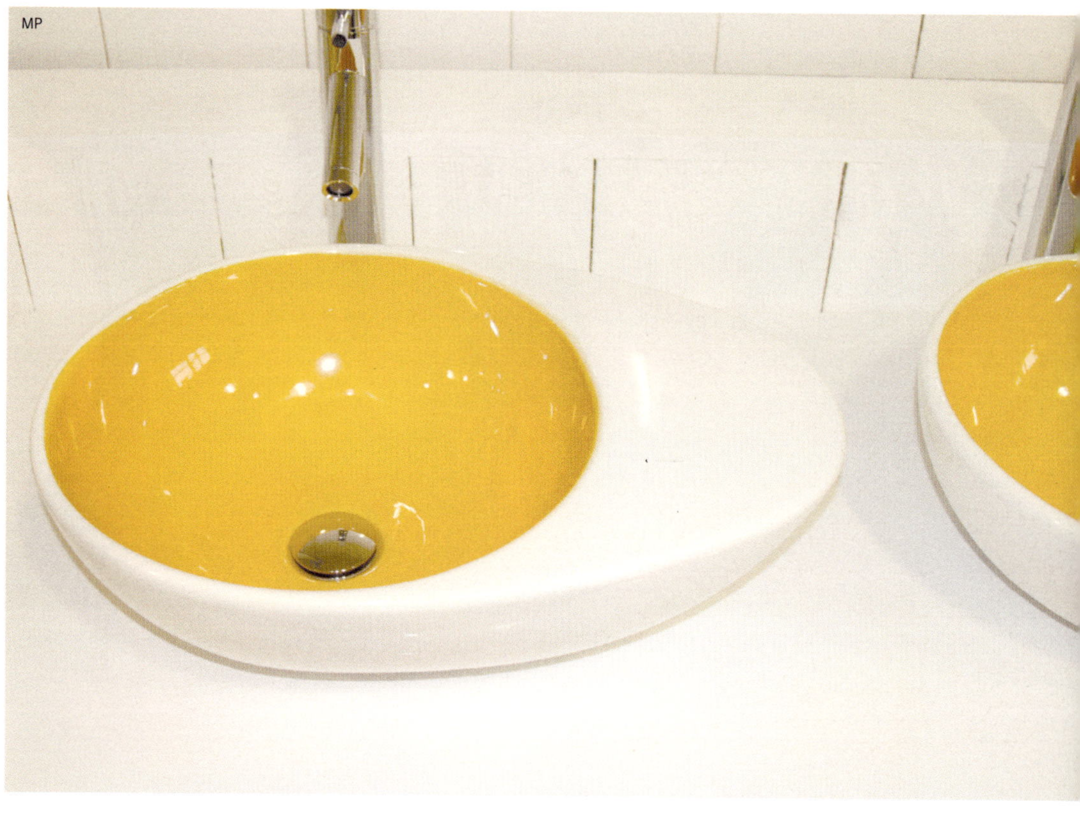

Yolker @ Dinamo

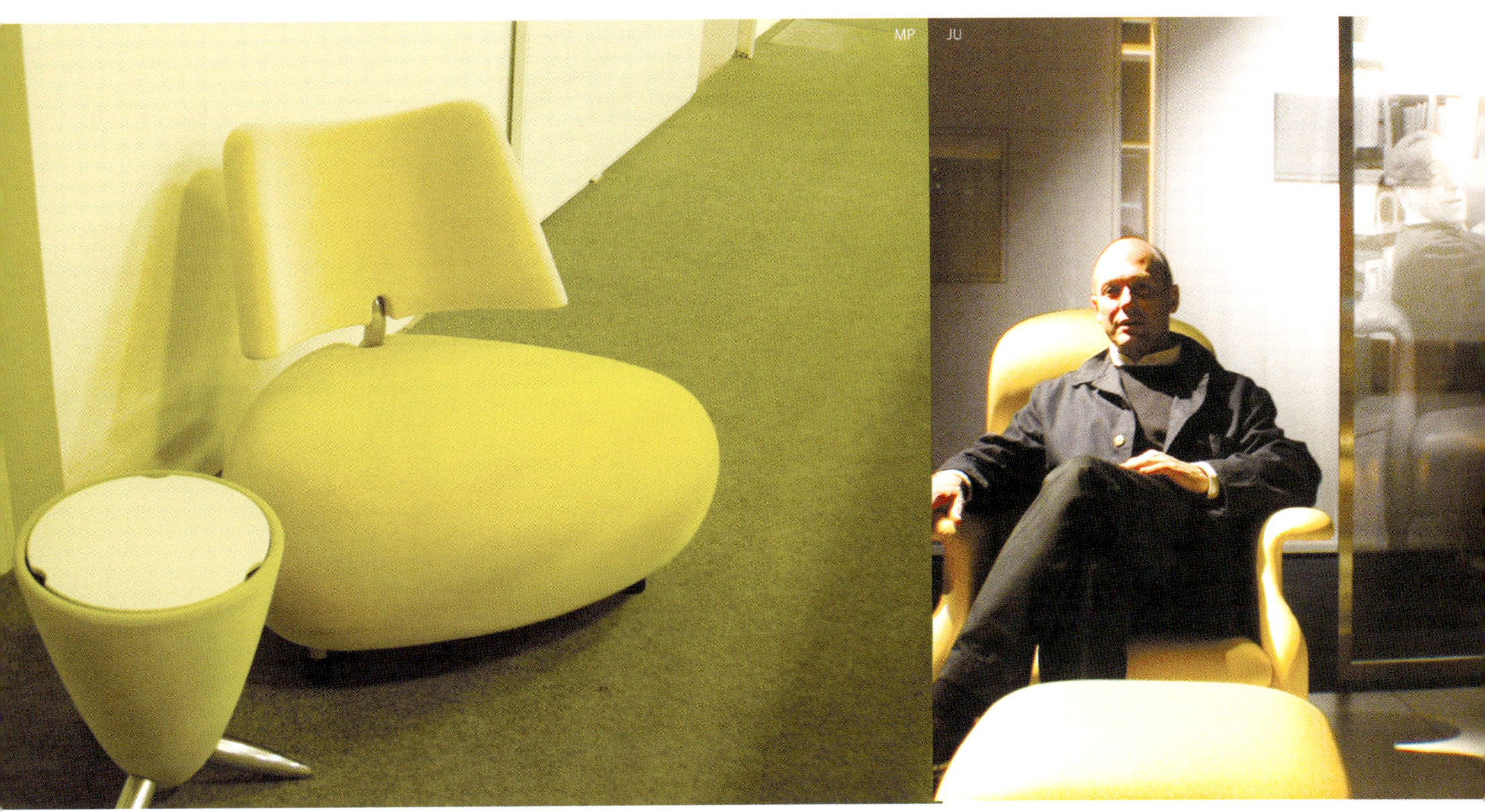

The Silly Side @ Tutto BeNe

Ico Migliore

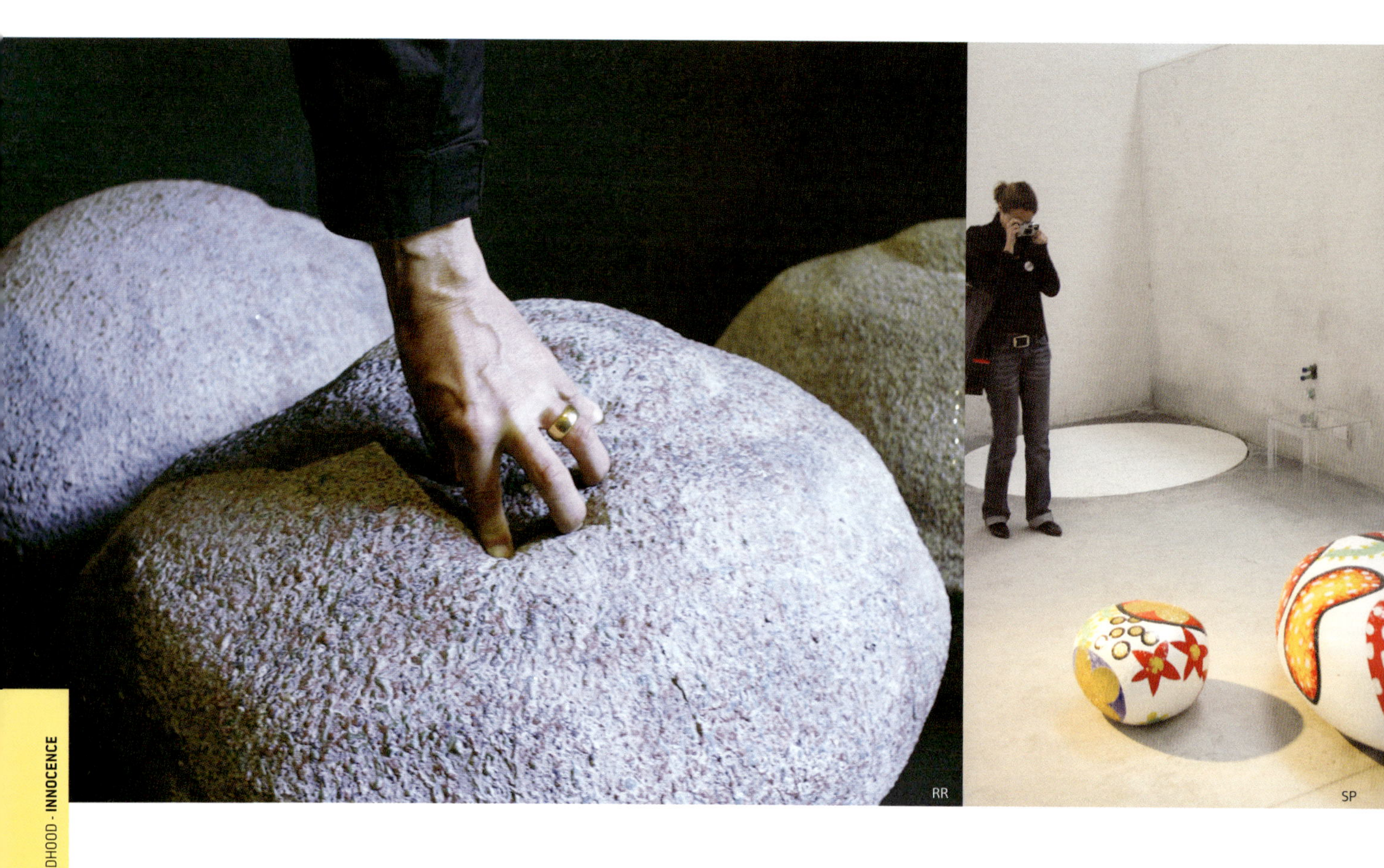

50   Sassi by Pietro Gilardi for Gufram @ Cappellini

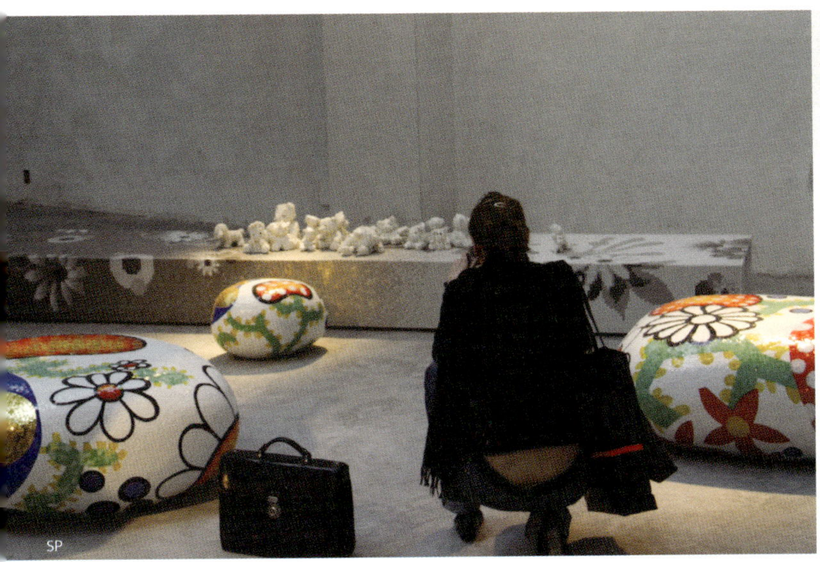

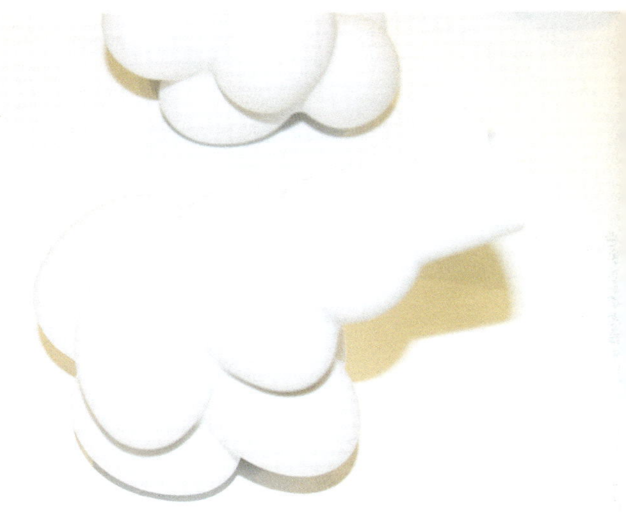

Wip Work In Progress by Bisazza @ Fabio Novembre studio; stools by Marcel Wanders

Moooi

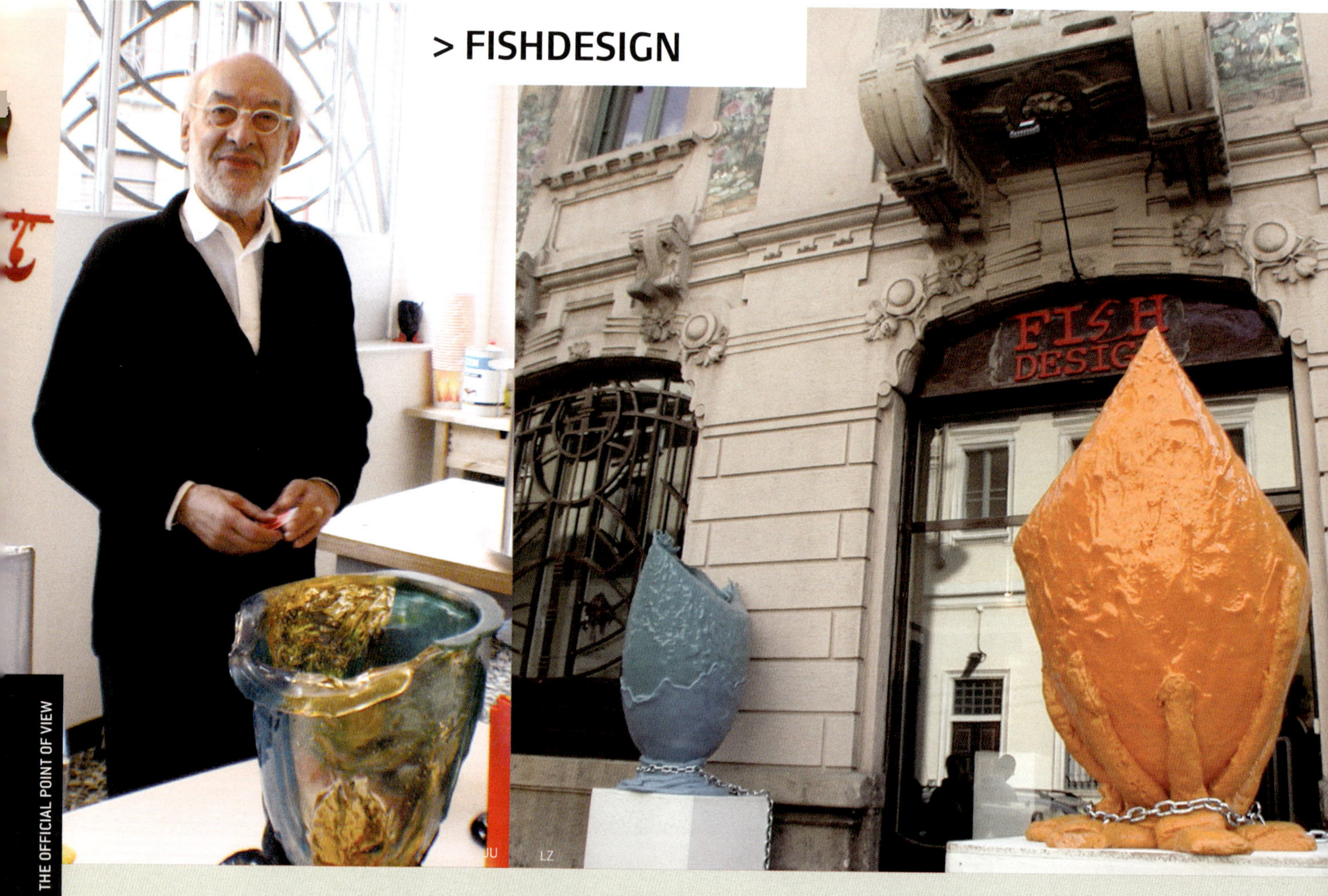

Gaetano Pesce

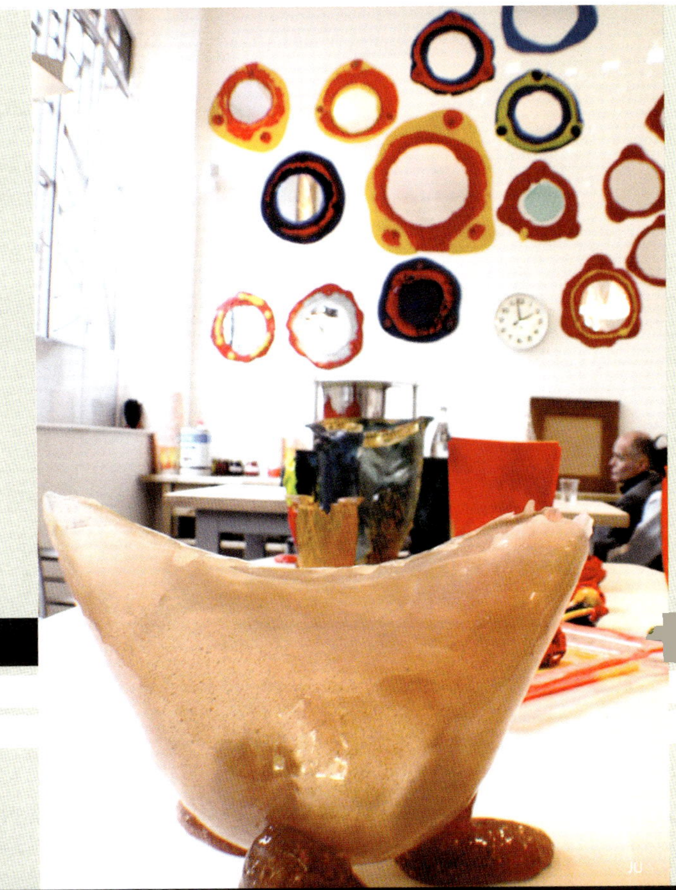

WHAT IS DESIGN ABOUT?

It is about discovering new methods

as opposed to putting shapes together.

IN TODAY'S DESIGN, WHAT IS USEFUL AND WHAT IS REDUNDANT?

The stool made by an African tribe serves the same purpose as a stool manufactured by a leading designer company.

Functionality is definitely its most immediately obvious feature, as it conveys its pragmatic character,

i.e. functionality as opposed to serving a decoration purpose. I therefore believe that art still holds a good functional character.

TO WHAT EXTEND DOES TECHNOLOGY CURRENTLY AFFECT A DESIGNER'S CREATIVITY?

It affects it greatly. Technology is moving incredibly fast and soon we might be in a position to drive our own customized car.

CAN DESIGN AFFECT TECHNOLOGY?

Technology is a crucial learning tool, but it should not level the market out.

One must keep pursuing originality against mass-production. Originality is paramount within this global system,

as it is a synonym of uniqueness aimed at preserving a well-defined identity. It would be nice to be able

to identify the origin of an object from the wood it is made from or from its make. An office in Rome should not look like

one in Tokyo; it's absurd, as different cultures should be kept separate. Technology on its own is not enough.

The Japanese have been able to manufacture great cars thanks to technology but they have a long way to go yet before

they can copy a Ferrari. "Made in Italy" is what makes the difference. Italy has no natural resources, like oil or electric power.

Creativity is our only resource, which is responsible for made in Italy manufacturing, although sadly it is weakening. T

he third industrial revolution will focus on customized objects and creative designers will produce objects no longer manufactured in a factory.

HOW ABOUT THE CURRENT OFFICE PLACE?

Nowadays, an office is not just a workplace, but also a place or rather the place where one

can meet people sharing our own opinions and sensitivity.

The office then becomes a kind of big club, a place where to spend time.

It is the world itself, as through computers we can be anywhere in an instant.

HOW ABOUT THE OFFICE OF THE FUTURE?

The offices I see are rather ordinary. The office of the future has feminine features

and a nice shape, in contrast with what we have been taught, namely a male

oriented mentality, predominantly here in Italy. In spite of what we have been

taught, the driving element is definitely female and certainly far more crucial, as it

is able to create, renew, breath new life into things, whilst appealing to the senses.

WHAT IS CURRENTLY REGARDED AS

THE BEST DESIGN OBJECT OR CONCEPT?

Objects are made and conceived to comfort us, or at least that's how it should be. When we switch the TV on we are bombarded

with bad news, tragedies and wars. Our home is our castle and should be a comforting place, a shelter from a world that is going to the dogs.

NOWADAYS, WHAT CAN BE ASSOCIATED TO THE CONCEPT OF

'ENTERTAINMENT' IN THE WORLD OF DESIGN?

We are slowly leaving abstractionism behind in favour of a more or less unaware

will to draw inspiration from science fiction, from cartoons and from the cinema,

in terms of sensuality, colours and past feelings that help us live the present better.

The abstract elegance of the past no longer lives up to our expectations, as spontaneity,

i.e. the spontaneous creation of an object exemplifies the concept of entertainment.

GAETANO PESCE - DESIGNER

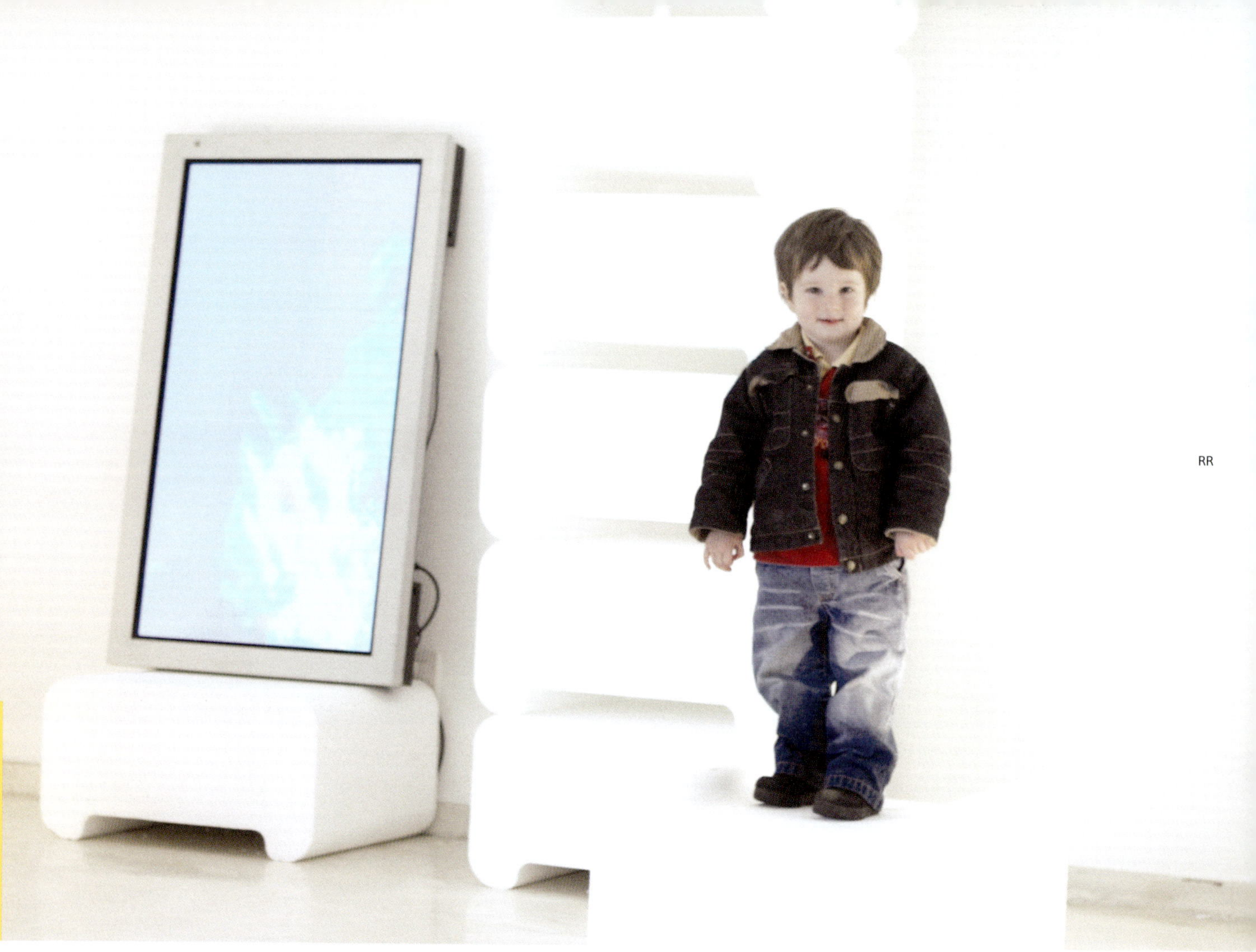

Cibic & Partners

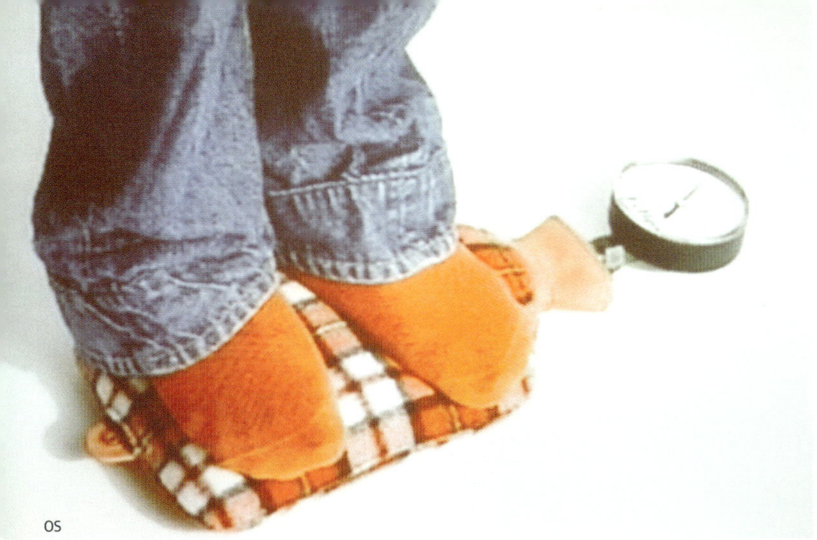

A useful thing is a sustaining thing, something we enjoy using daily

or simply something pleasing to the eye, made with useful materials

and the result of a caring, moderate process that shows consideration

for the environment and devoid of any superfluous add-ons.

Something that is easy to fix, i.e. something worth fixing instead of throwing it out,

something that is bound to improve as time goes by and that can be recycled.

Ernst Gampler

Argudo y Gutierrez for Diseño Español

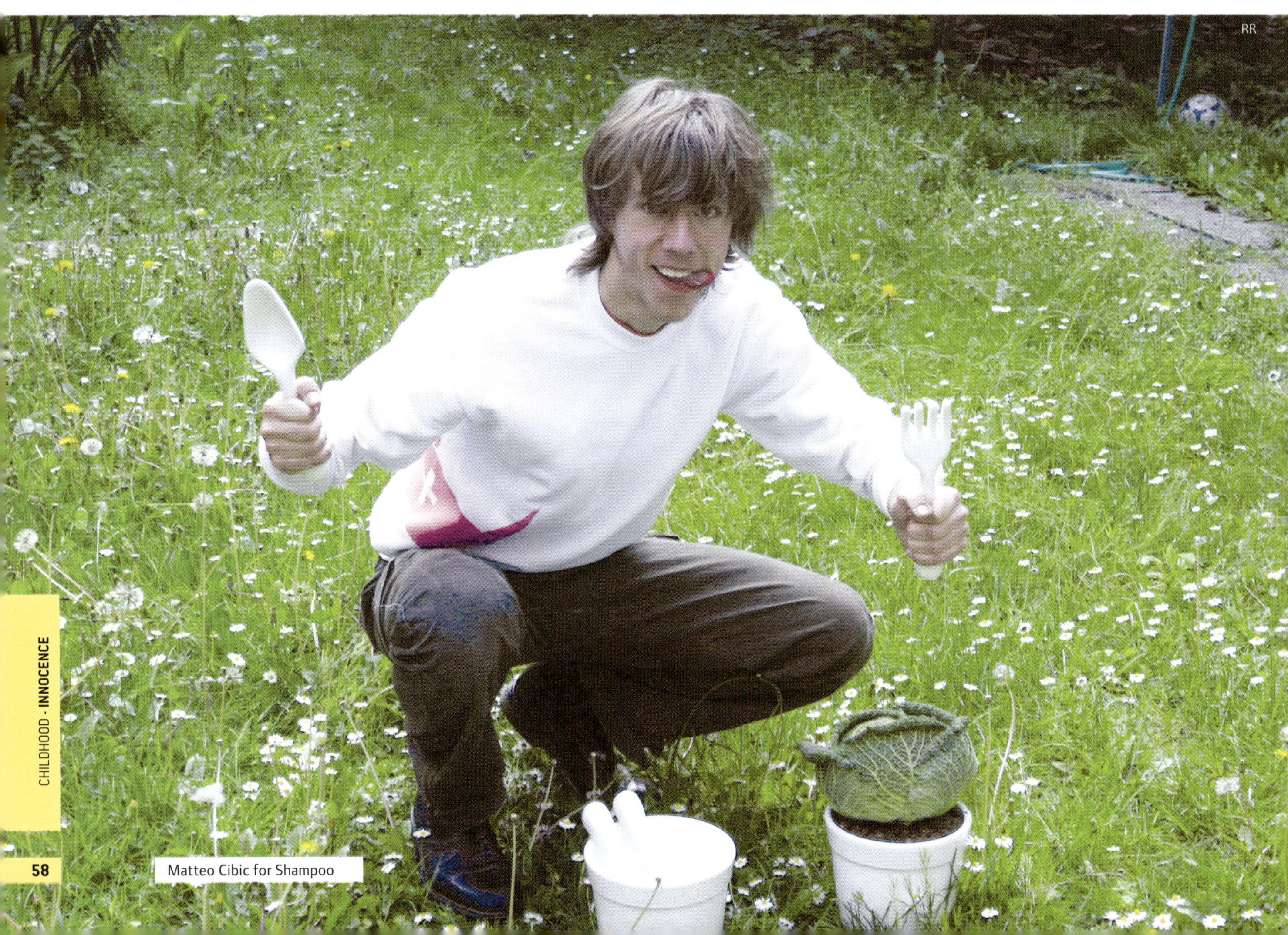

58 Matteo Cibic for Shampoo

SHAMPOO

Six young designers from Italy, Brasile and Argentina present their project.

Their desire to free themselves from behavioral standards,

from premeditated and static thoughts, from prepackaged and steril realities.

The vision of a different world, in which one moves and discovers new sensations,

a world to look at, and not only see, to listen to, and not just hear.

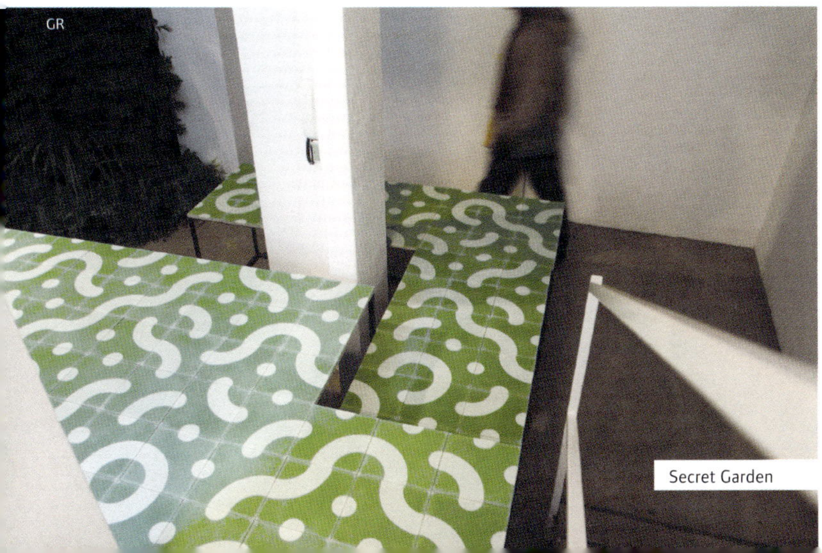

Secret Garden

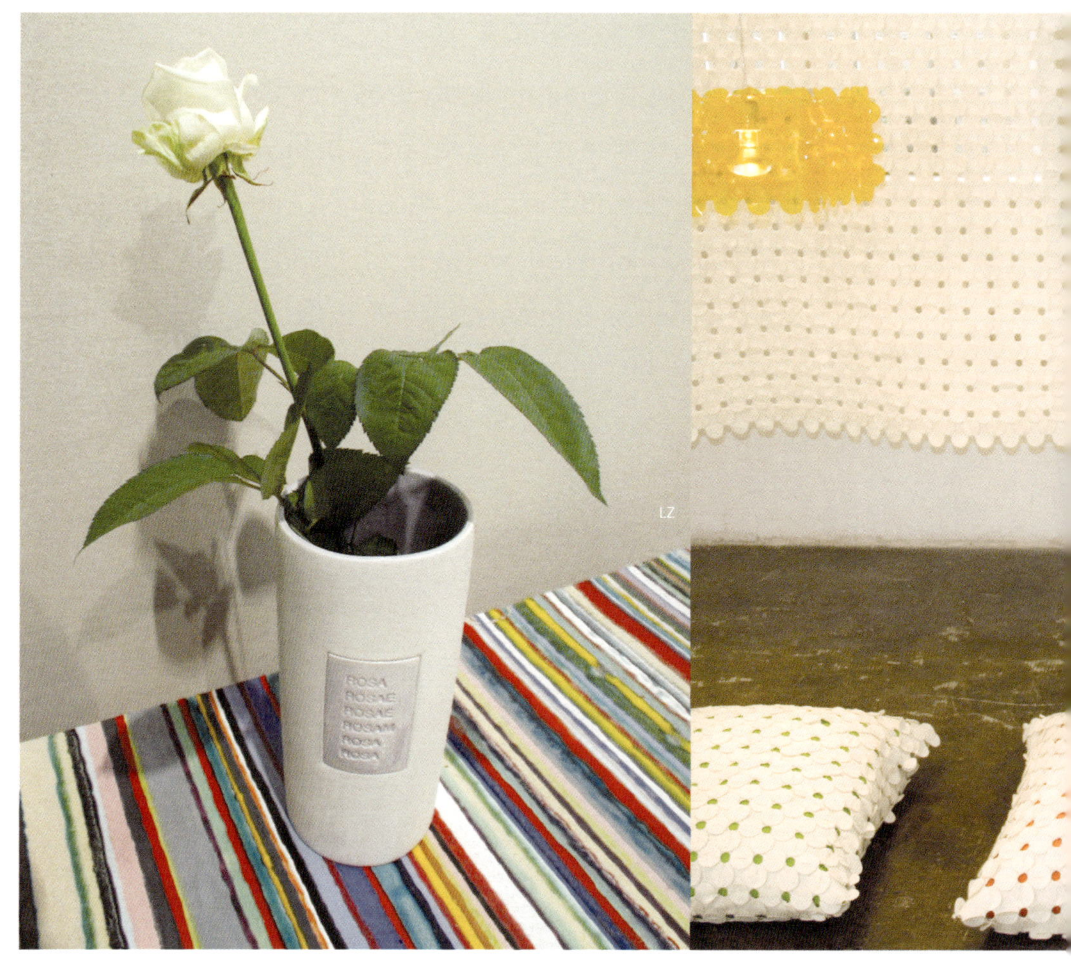

MV%

Mia Cullin @ Designersblock

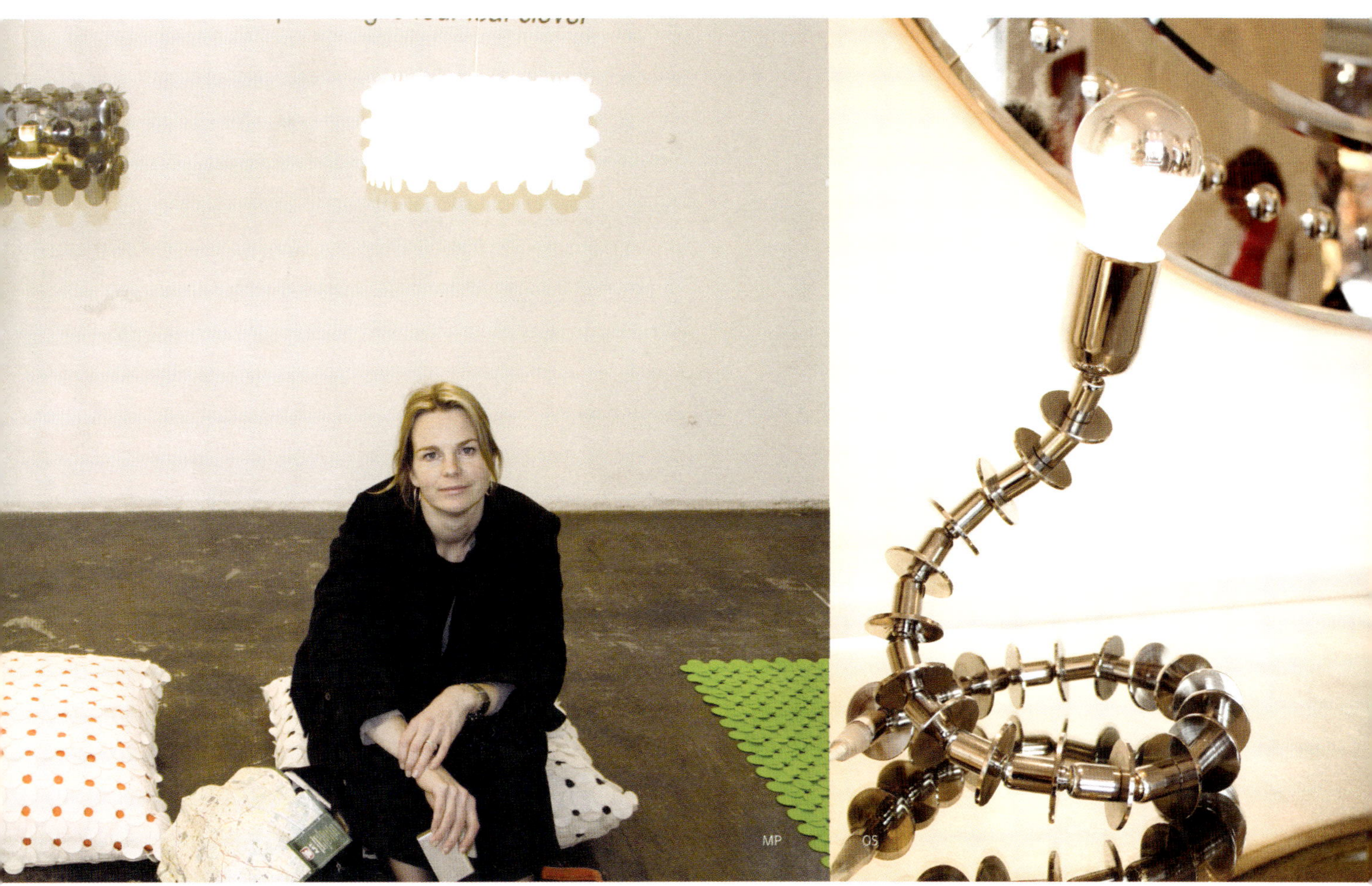

Vertebra lamp and table by Luca Finocchiaro @ Visionnaire

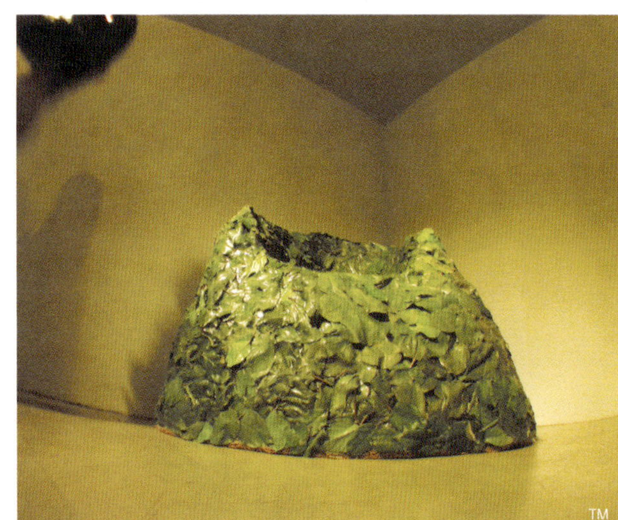

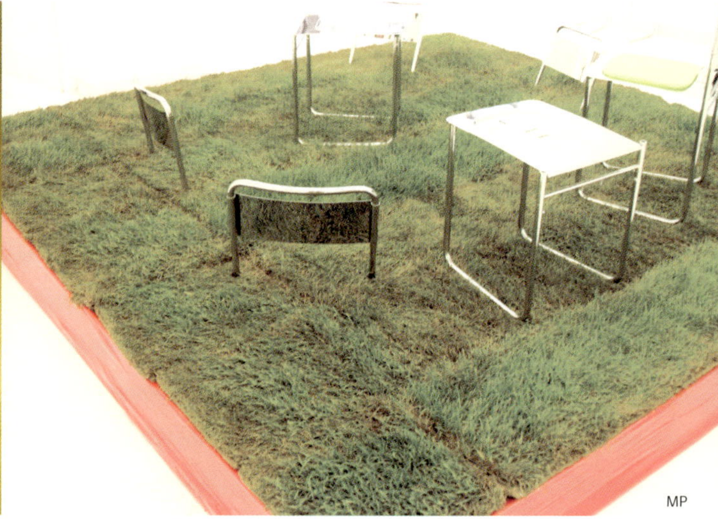

Bosco of Alessandra Baldereschi @ Dilmos

Zani + Zani

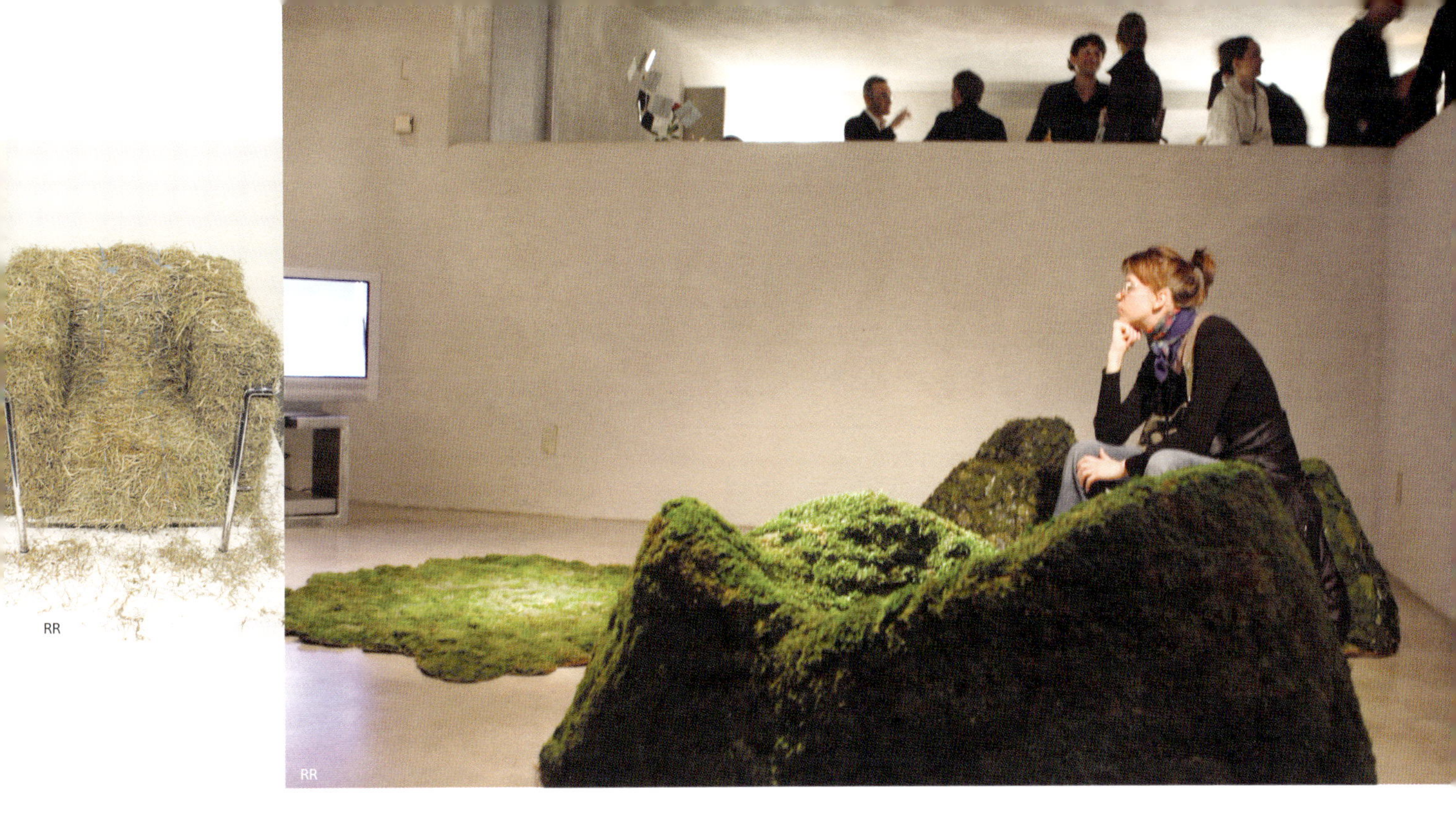

John Angelo Benson   Bosco of Alessandra Baldereschi @ Dilmos

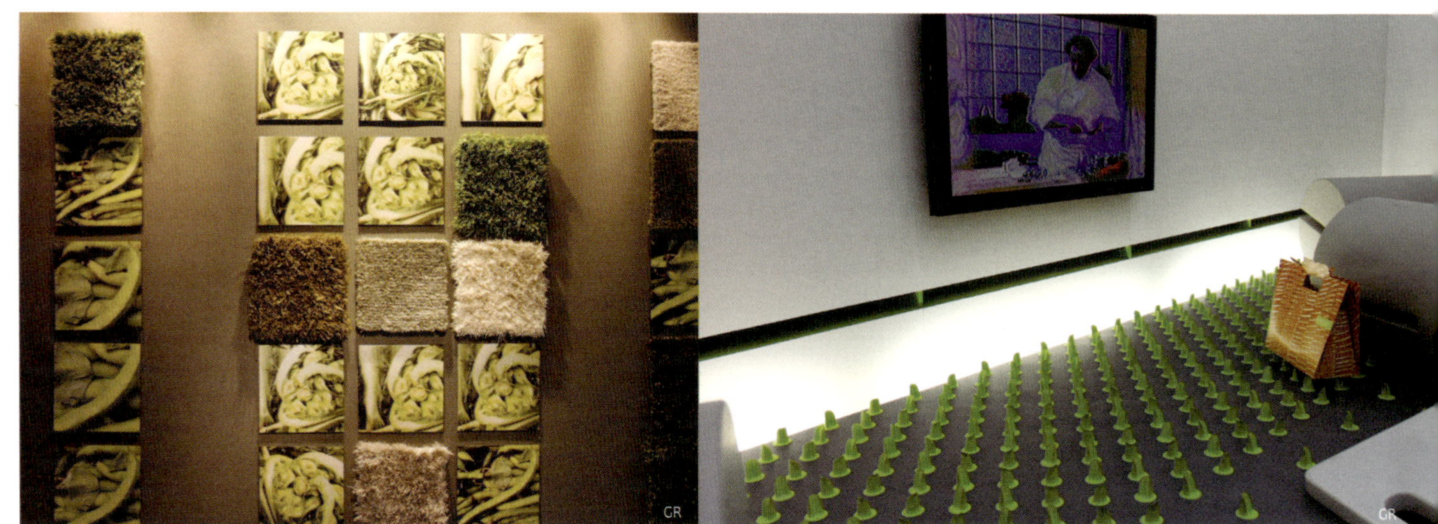

Kasthall

QuickNic @ Dining Design

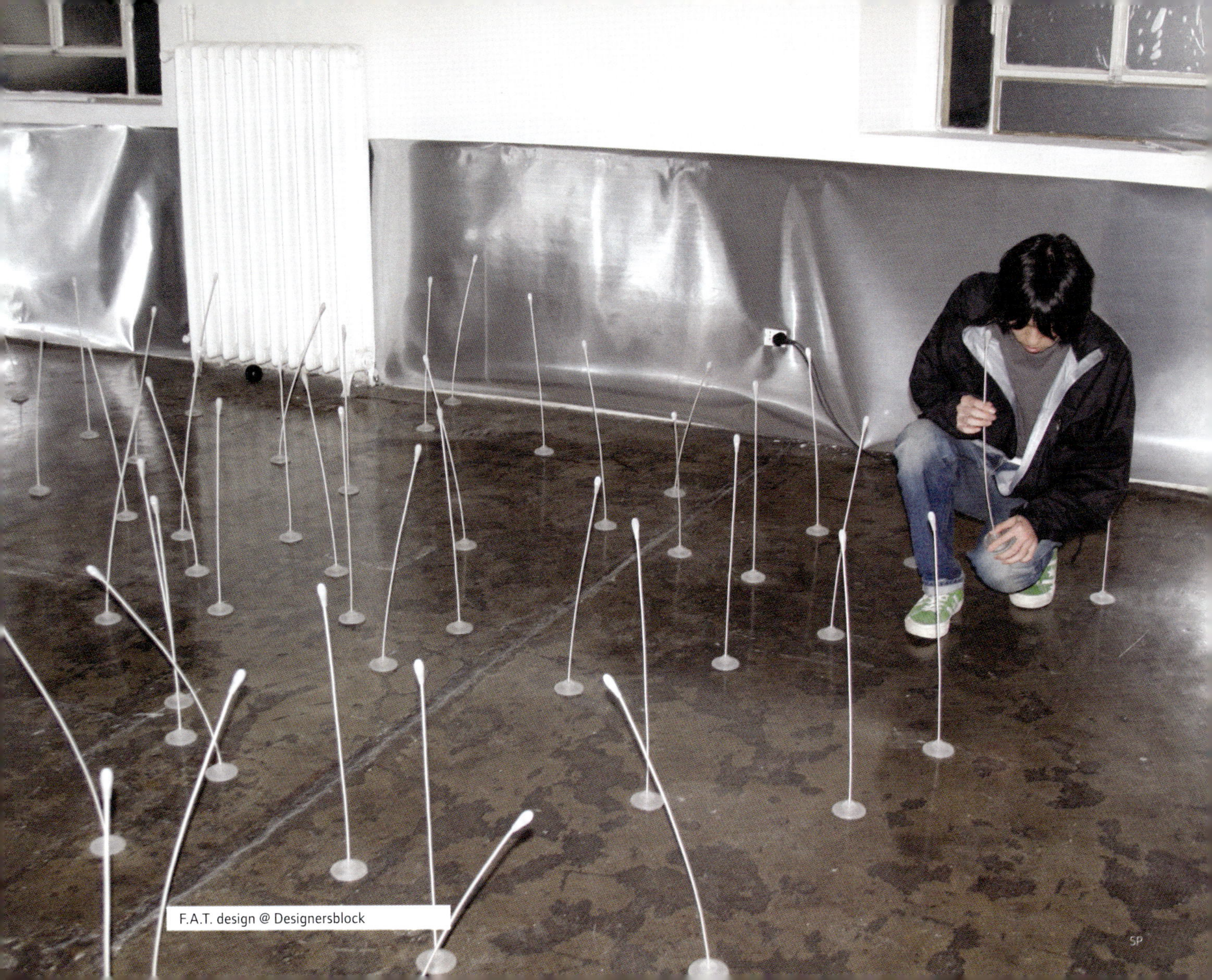
F.A.T. design @ Designersblock

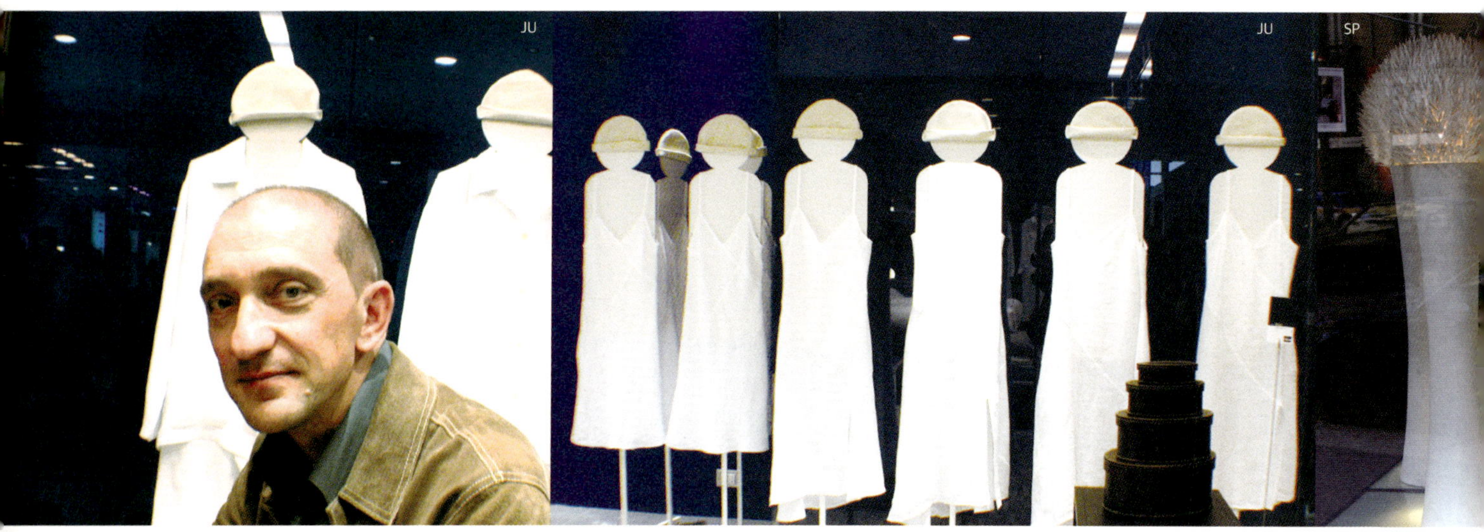

Rodolfo Dordoni @ Flou

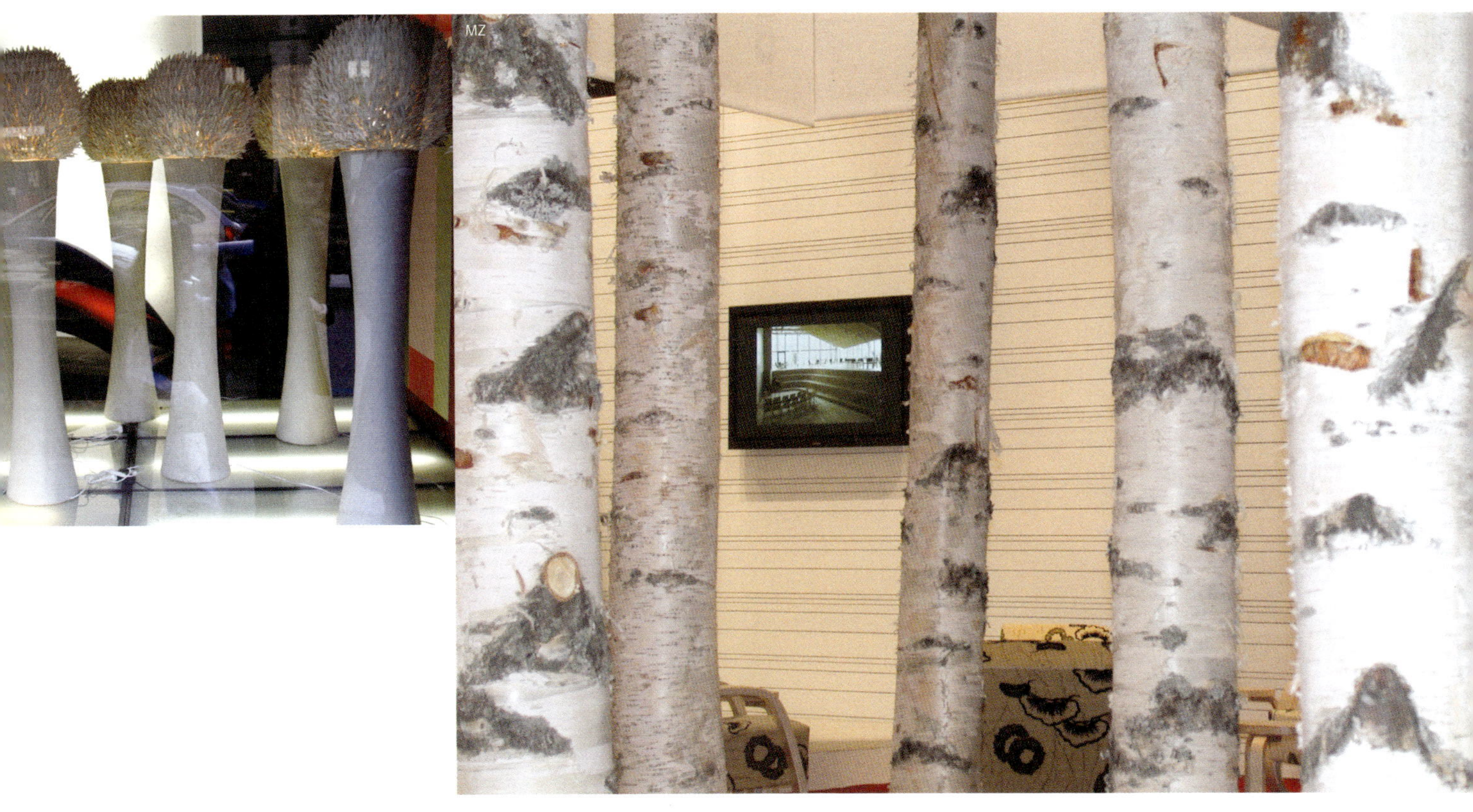

NewTrend

Artek @ Zona Tortona

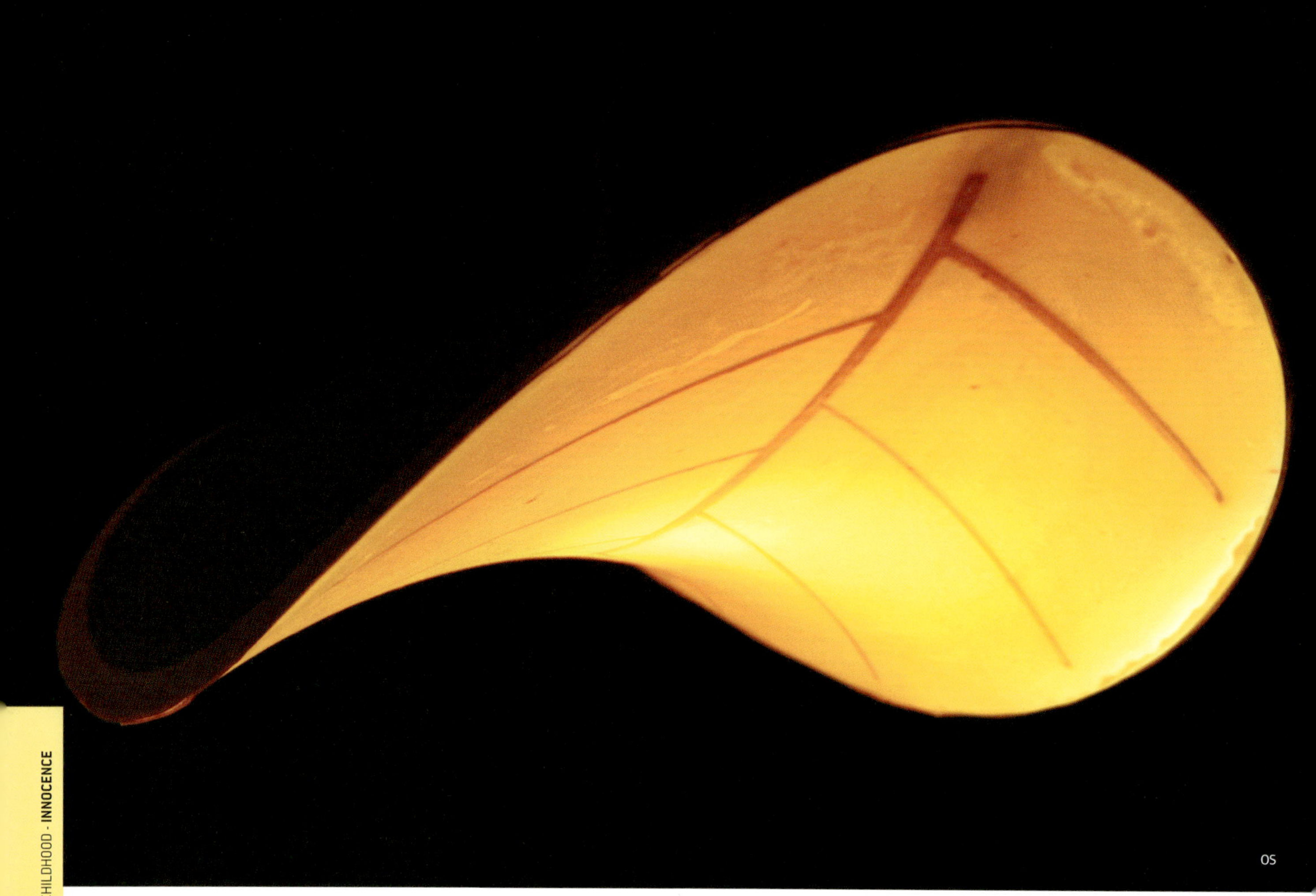

OS

Cul de sac by Cervantes Institut

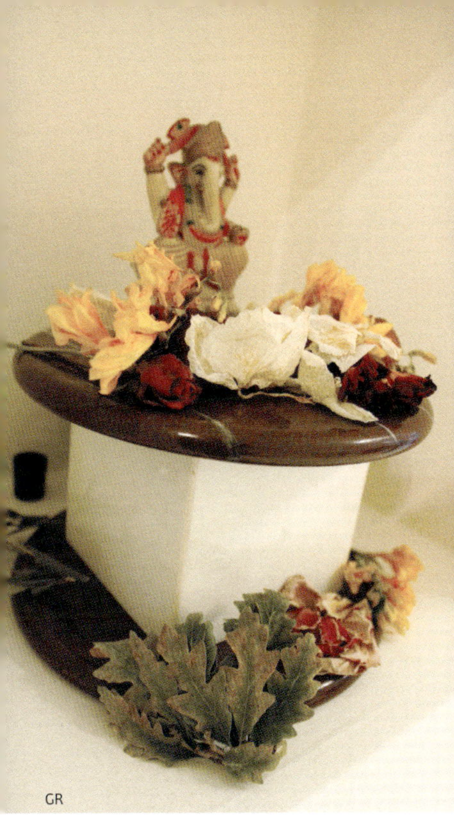

GR

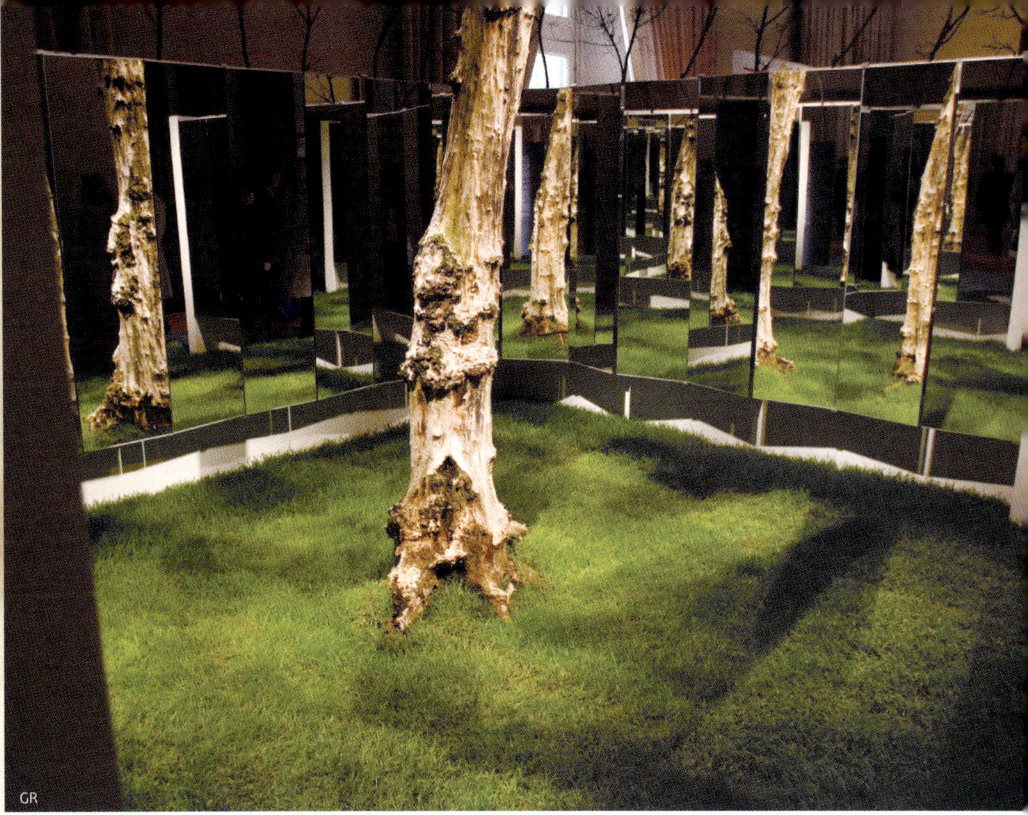

GR

Ganesh @ Galleria Clio Calvi Rudy Volpi

Agape

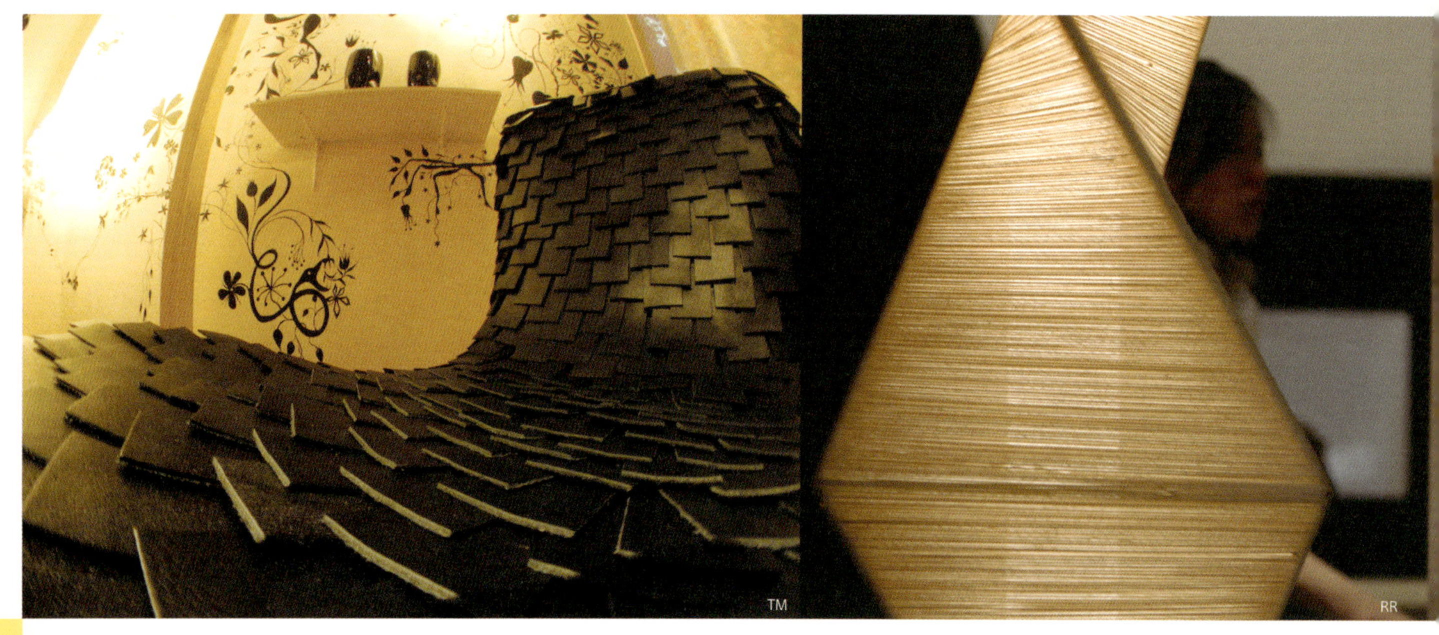

@Moroso

Granese Design Studio

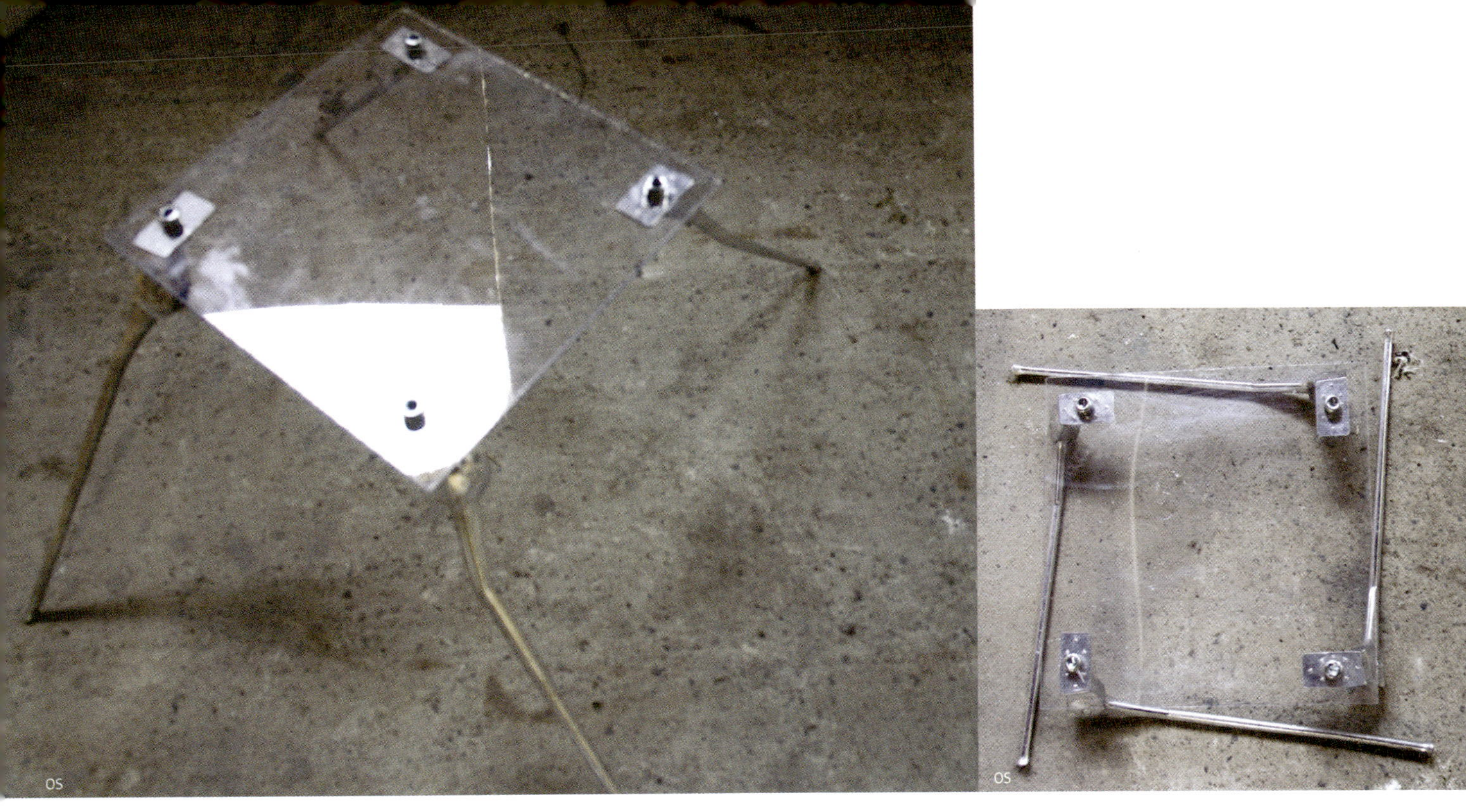

Stefano Reboli

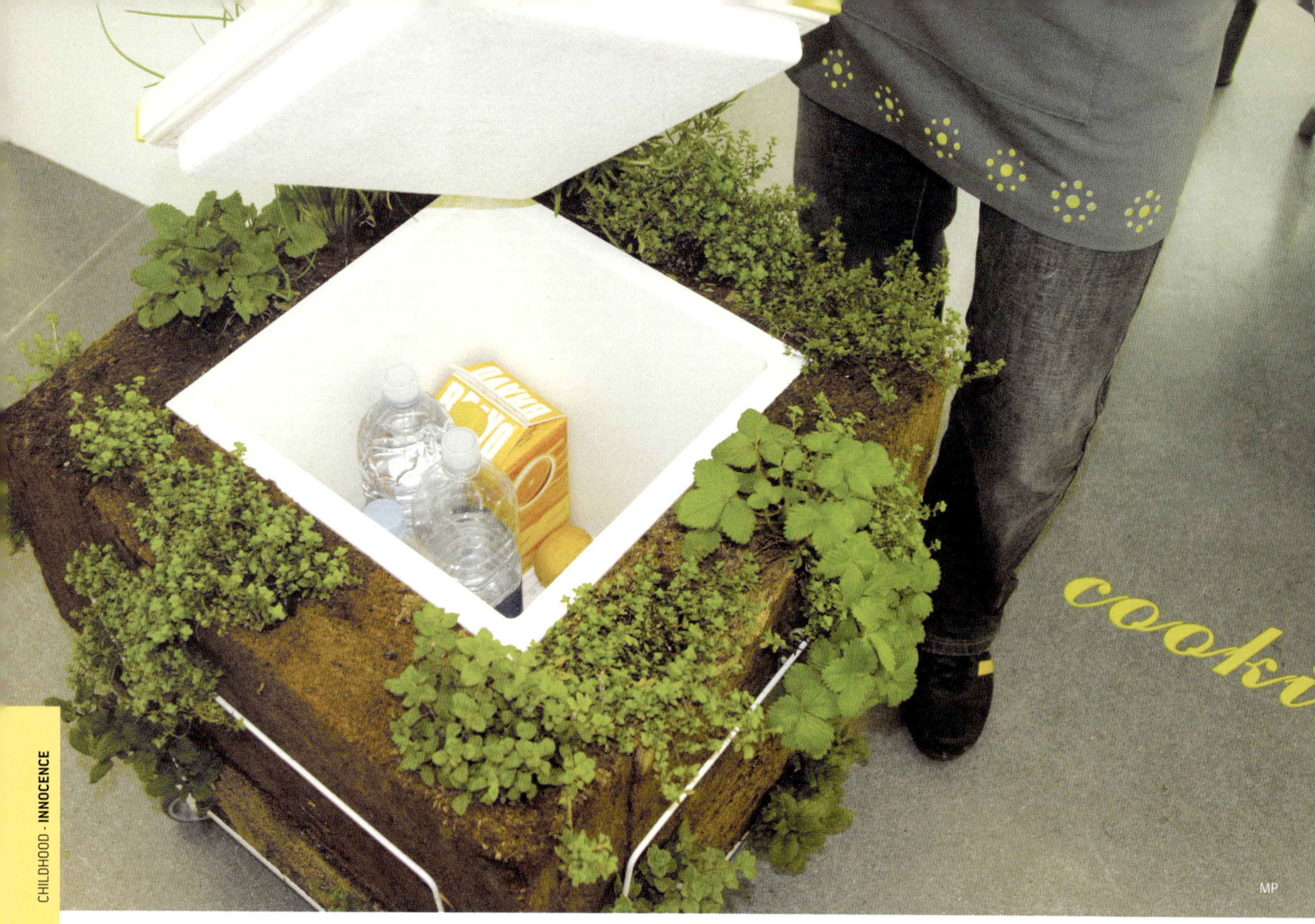

Land University

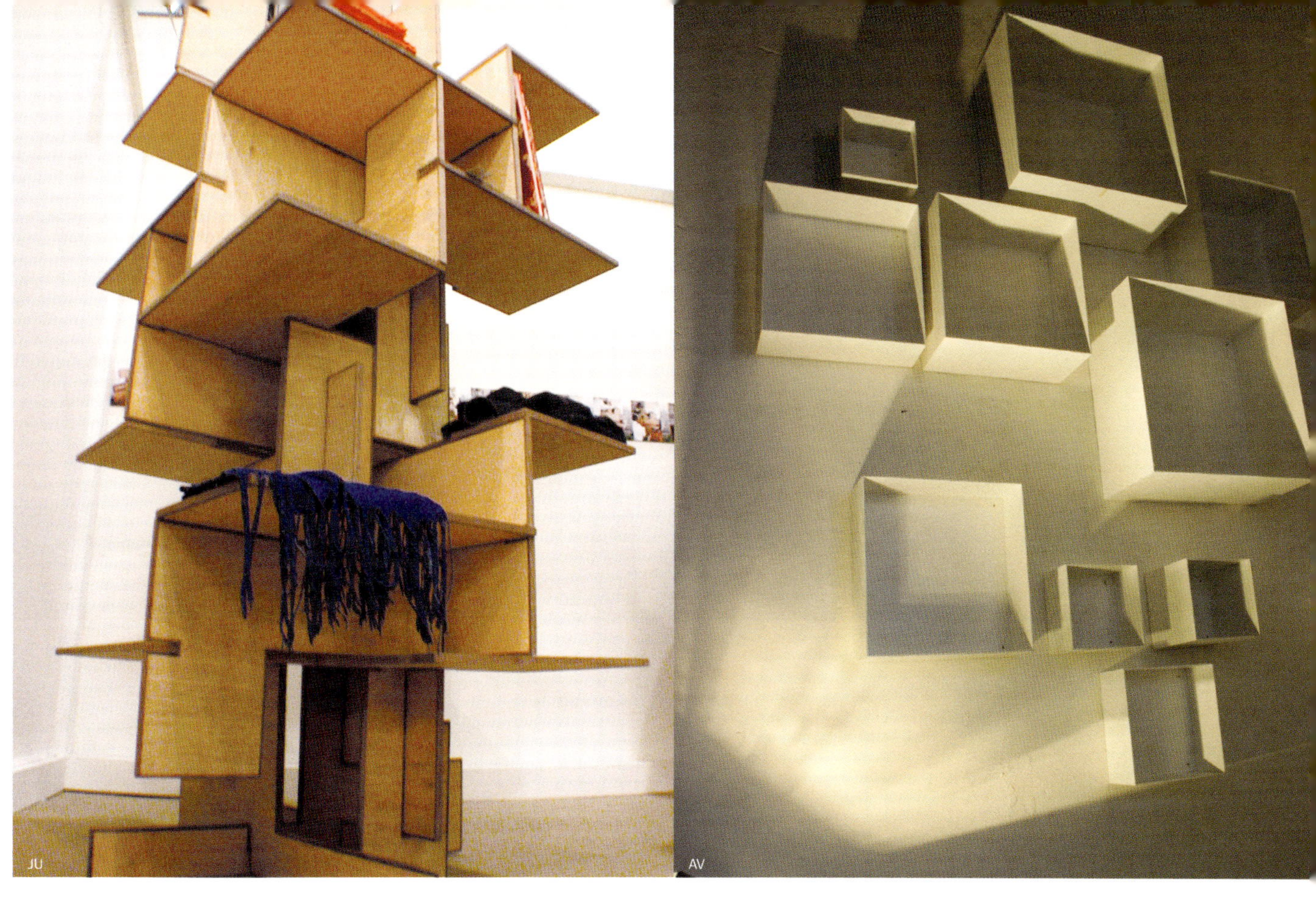

Rui Leao-Leao atelier de arquitectura @ Satellite

Process by Lisa Farmer

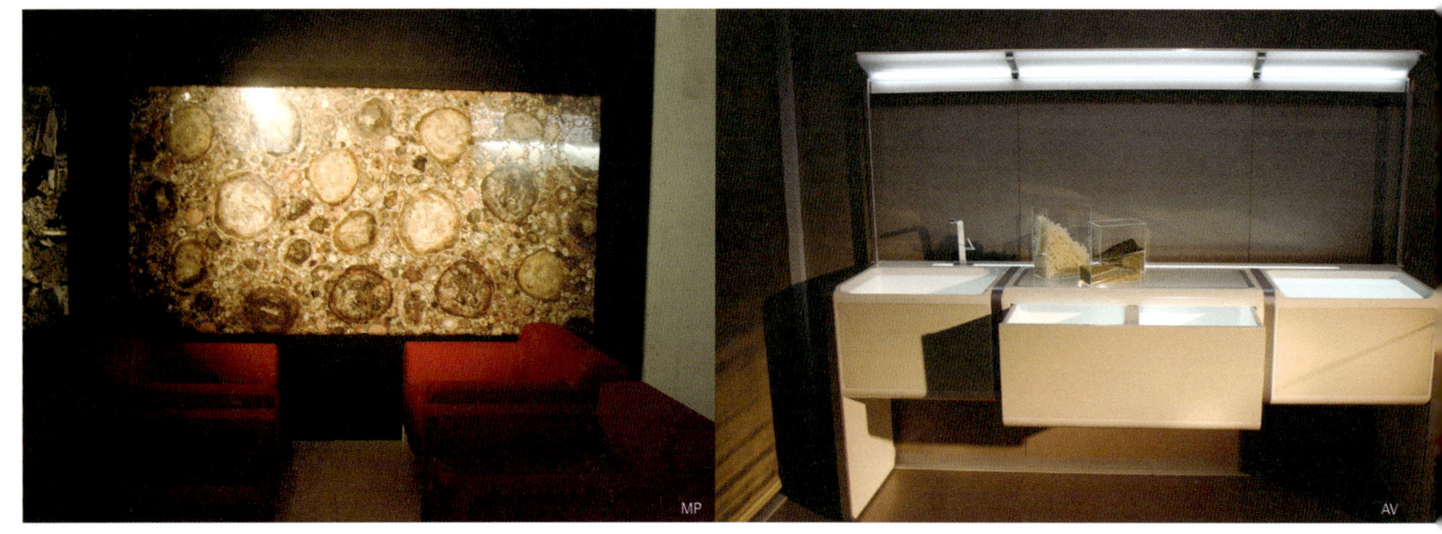

Flaminia

@ Adi

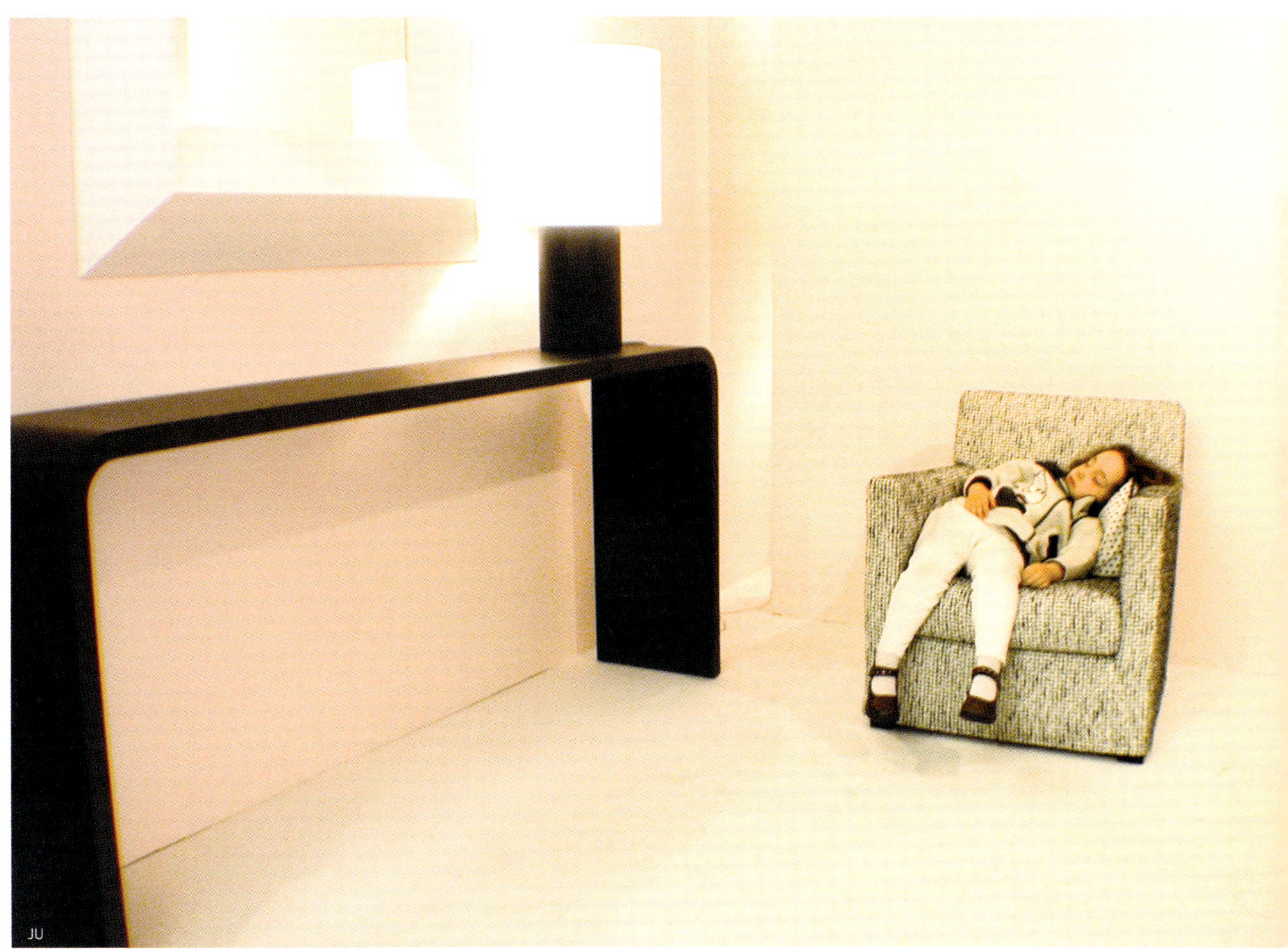

Ceccotti collezioni

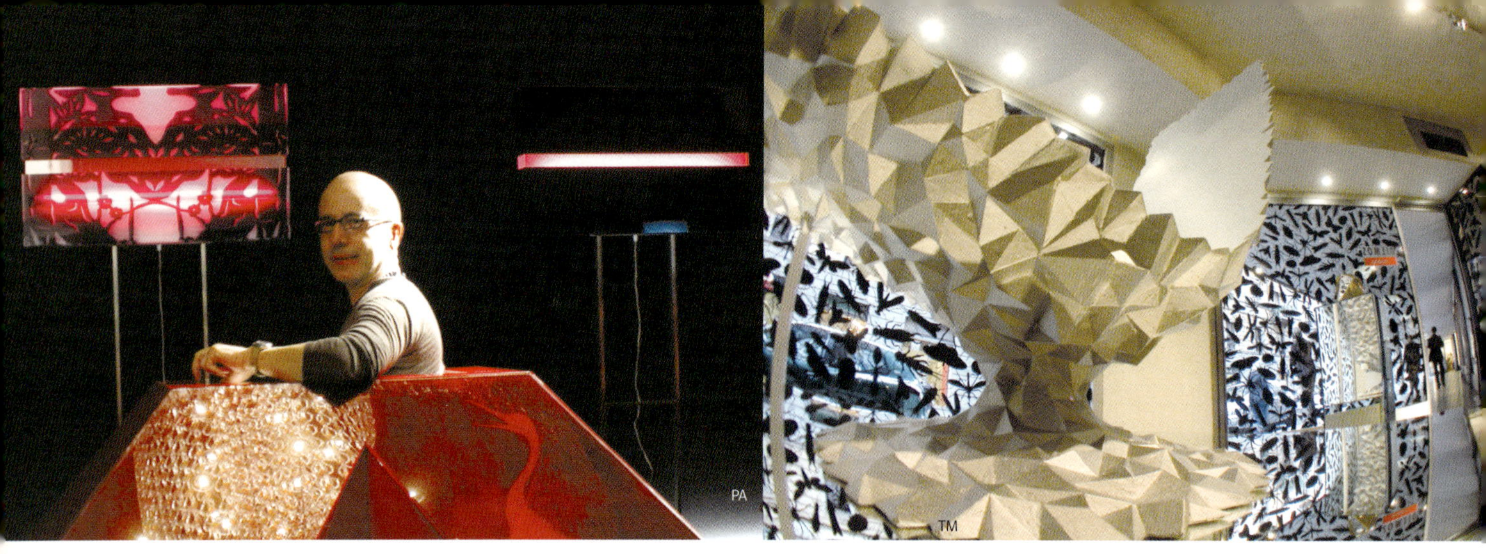

Gianfranco Fenizia of Fenizia Design Studio

Job Zoom @ Dilmos

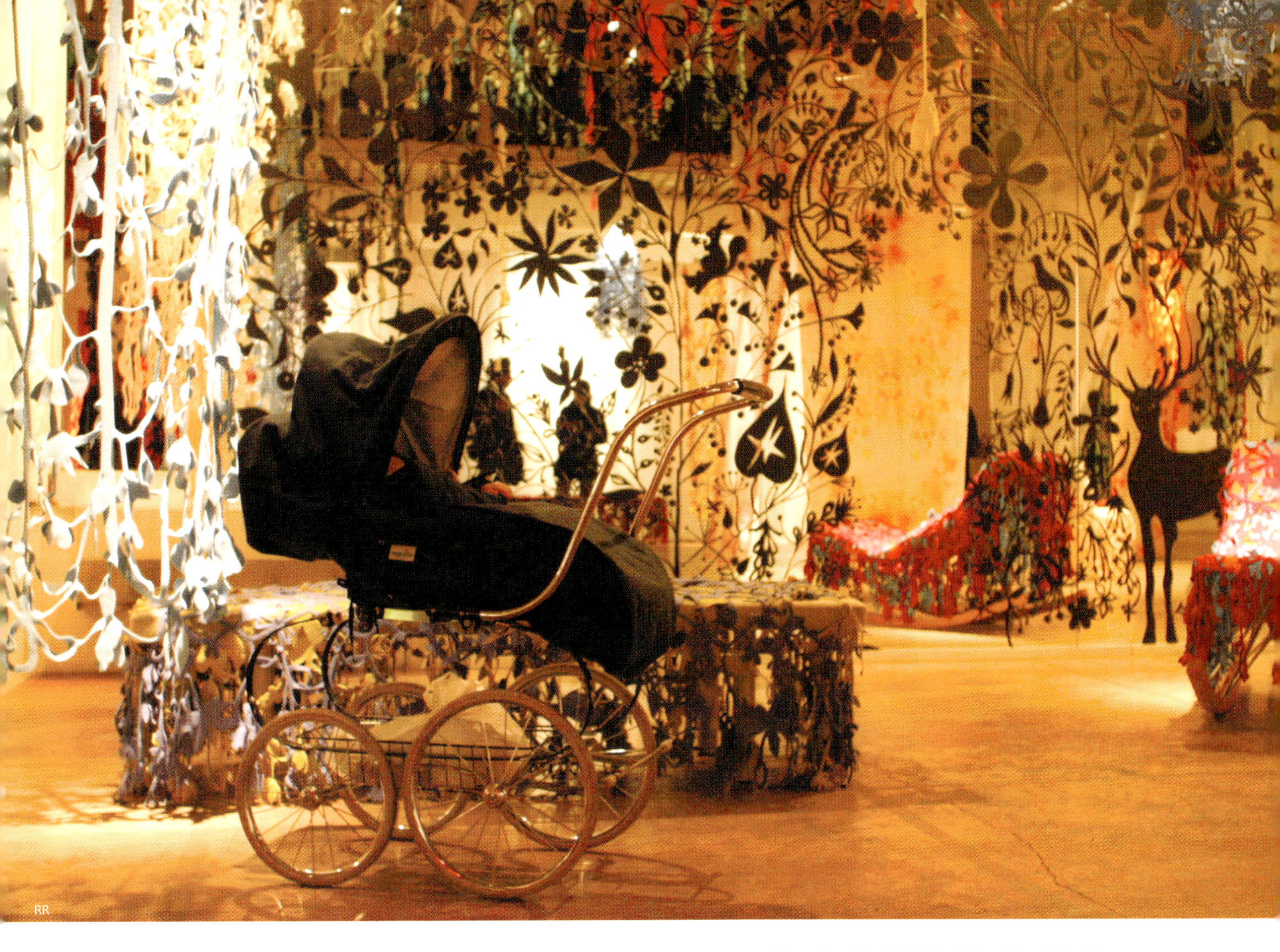

Happy Ever After installation by Tord Boontje for Moroso

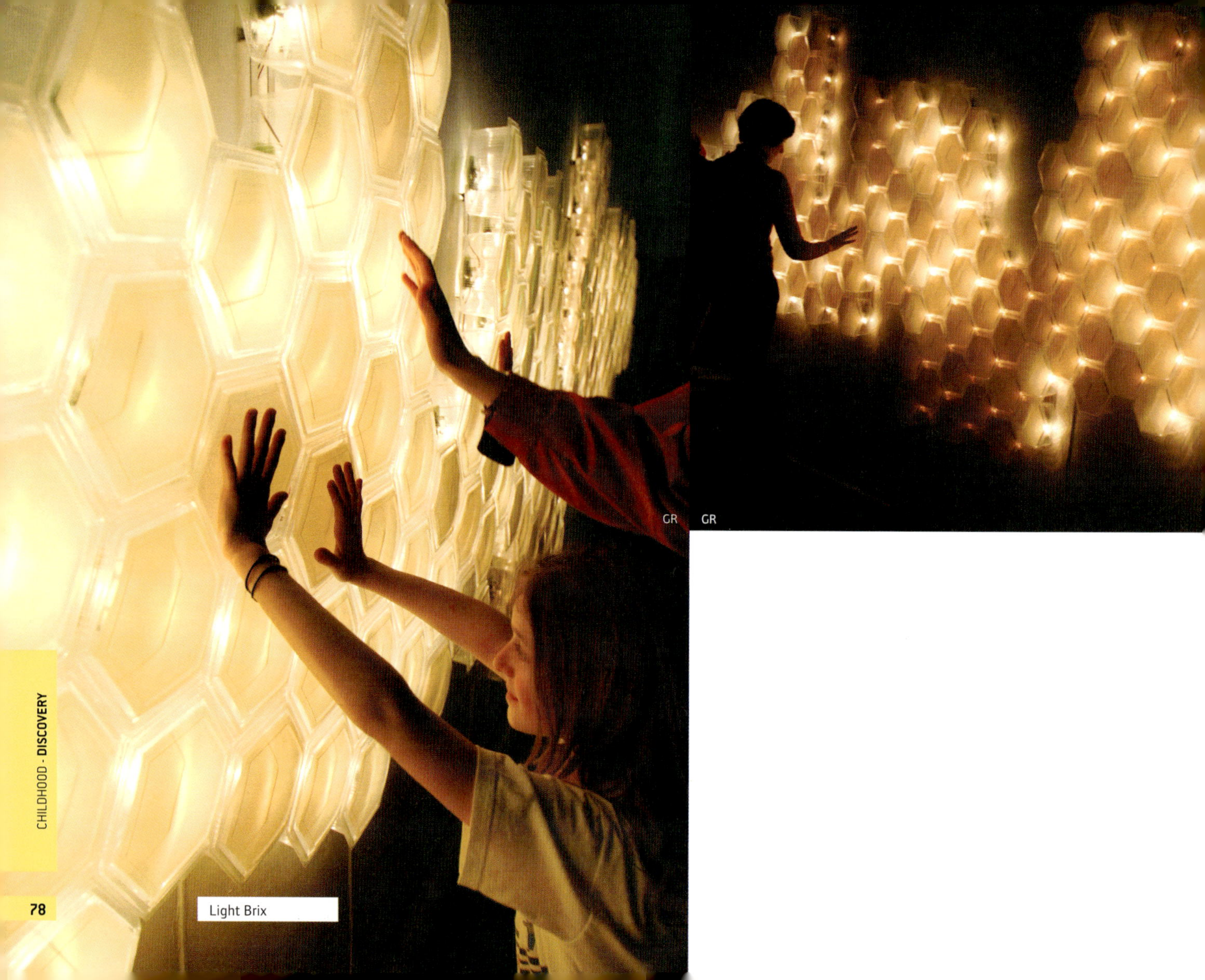

Light Brix

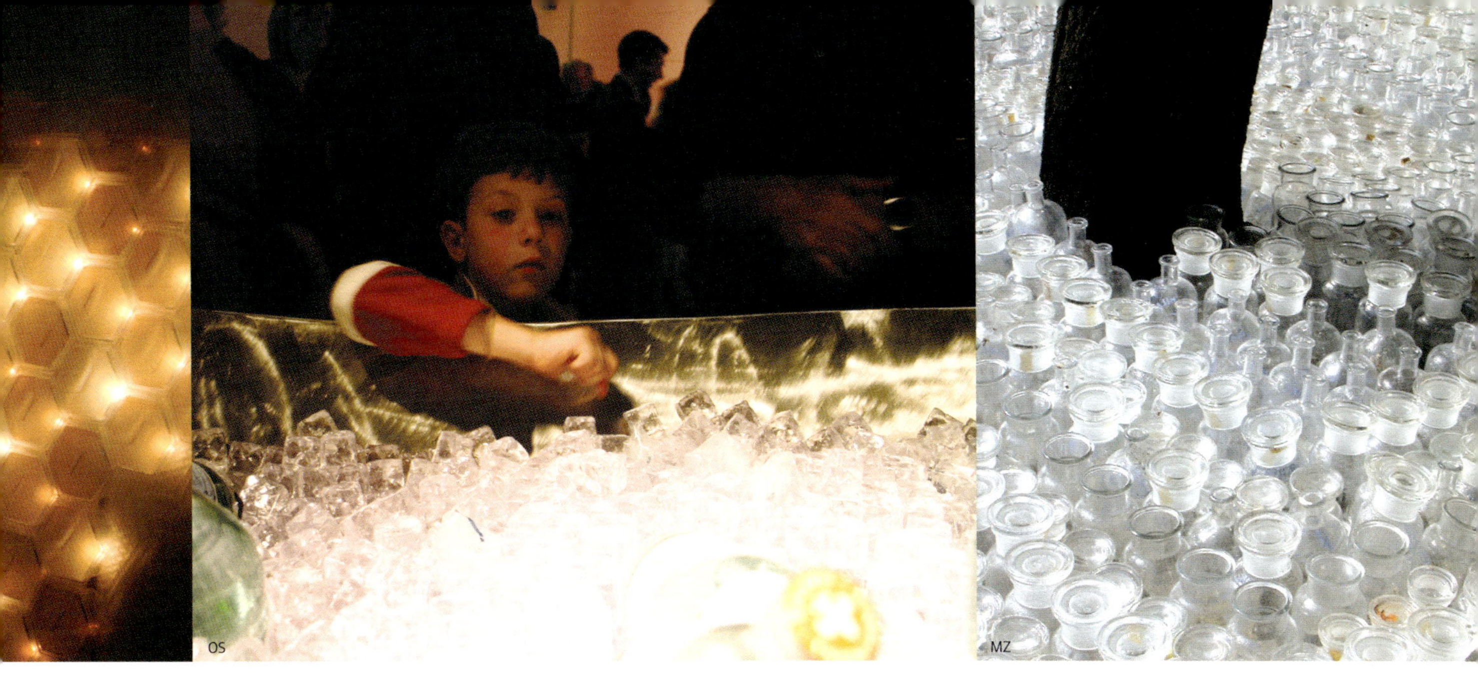

San Pellegrino installation @ Street Dining Design

Process by Lisa Farmer

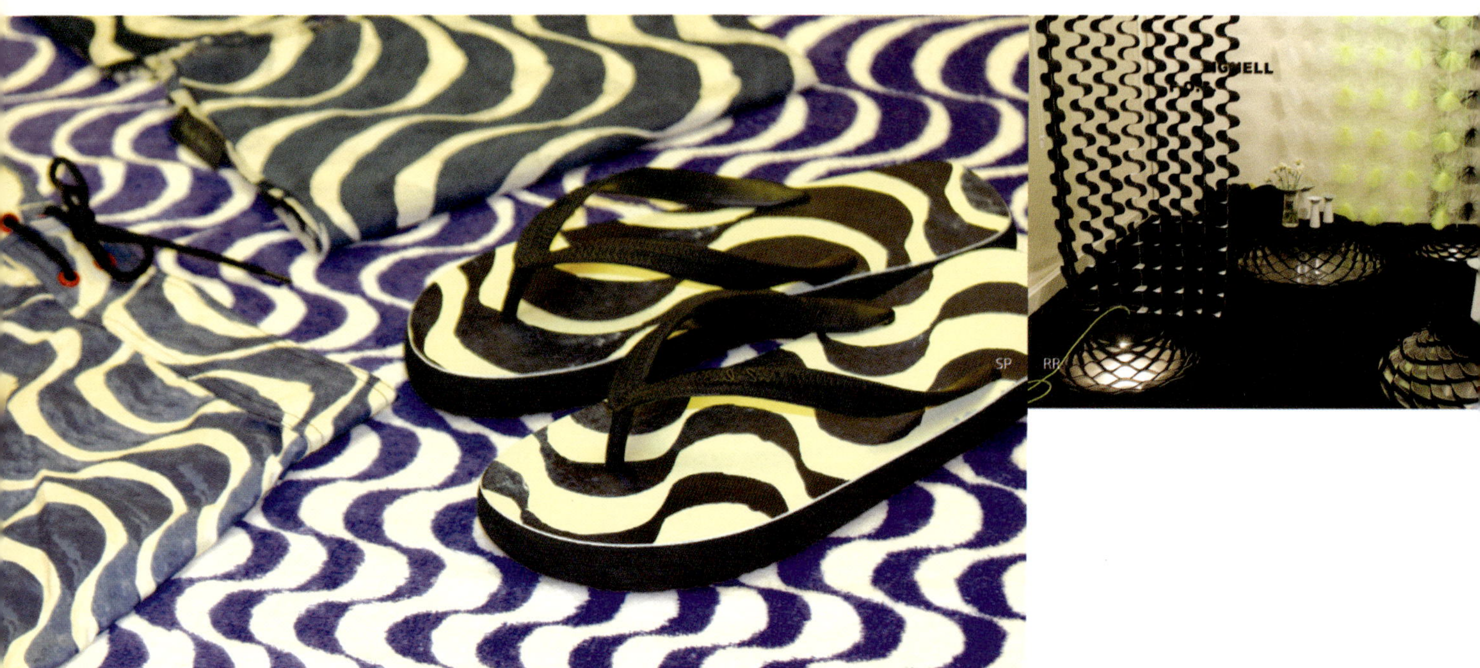

Paul Smith

Hogberg / Signell @ Satellite

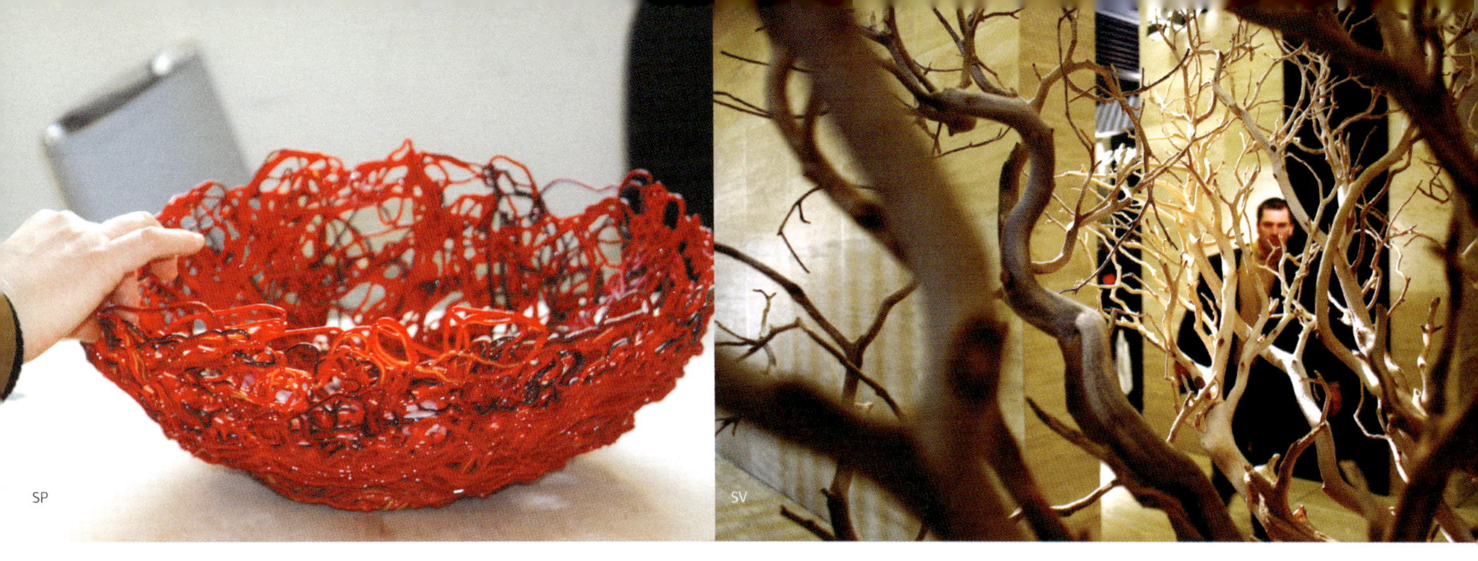

Gaetano Pesce for Fish Design

Rimadesio

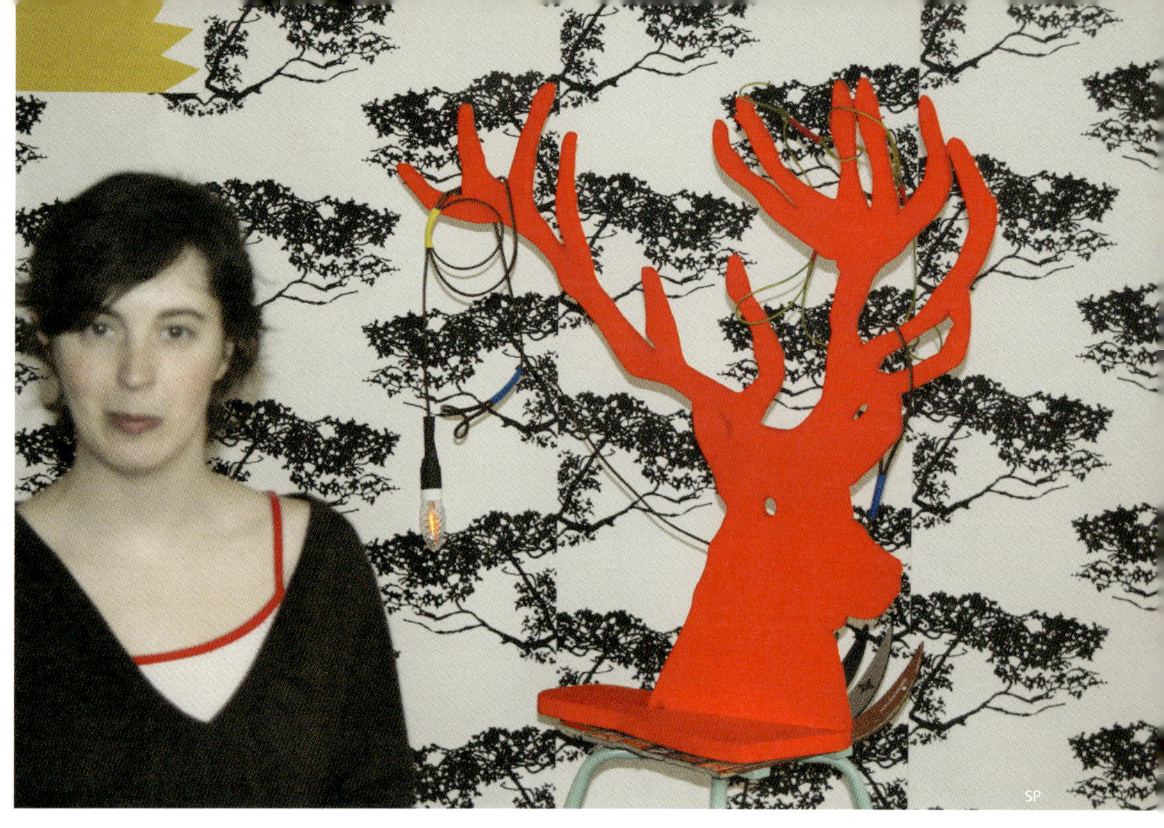

Defyra @ Designersblock

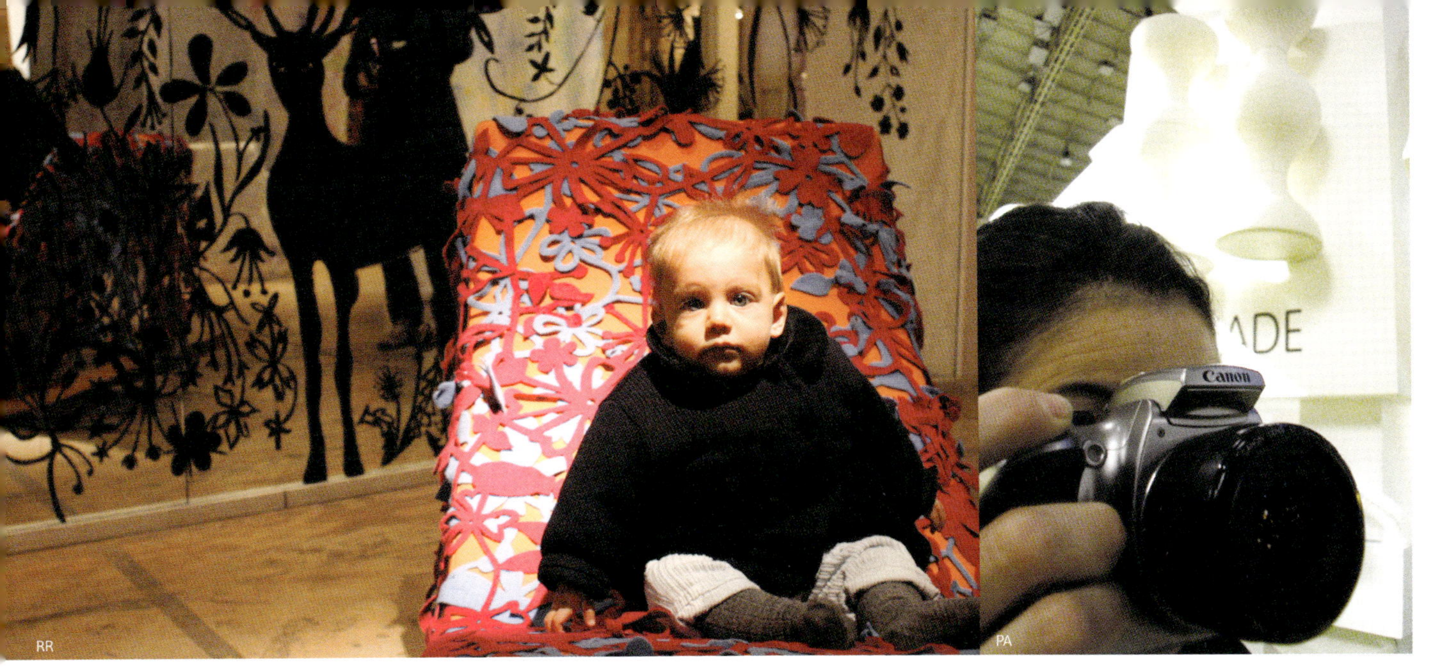

Happy Ever After installation by Tord Boontje for Moroso   Canon EOS 300 Digital

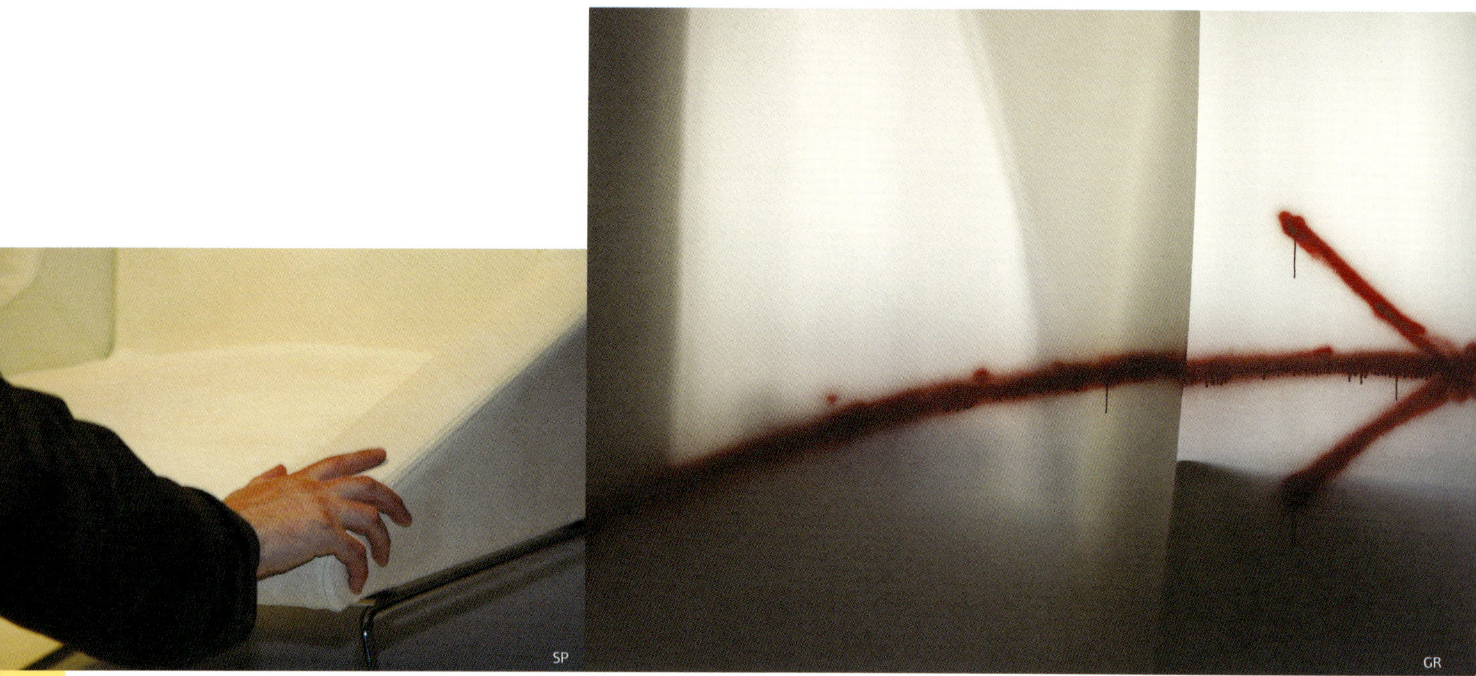

Percorso Divino @ Zona Tortona

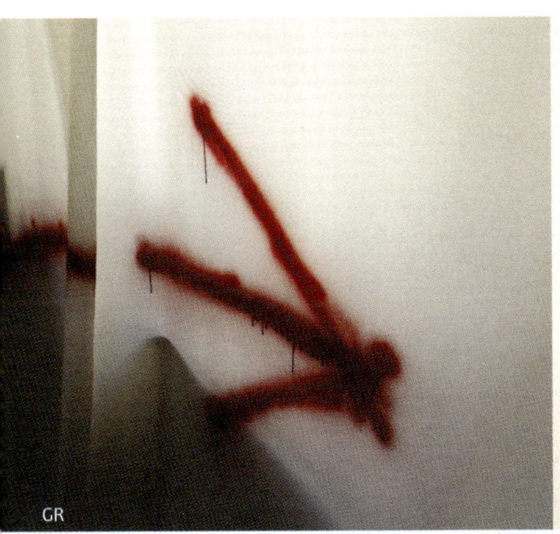

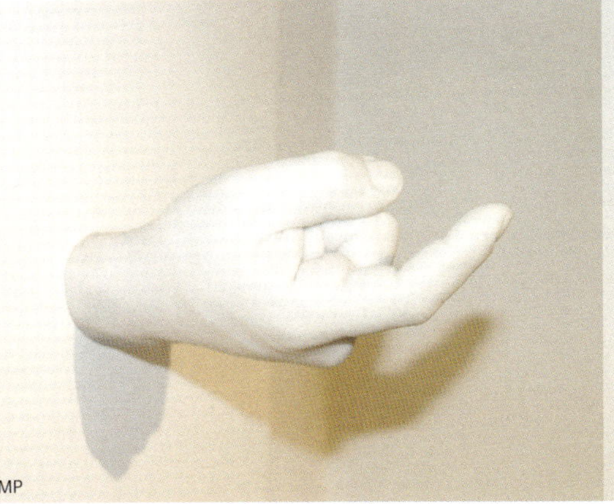

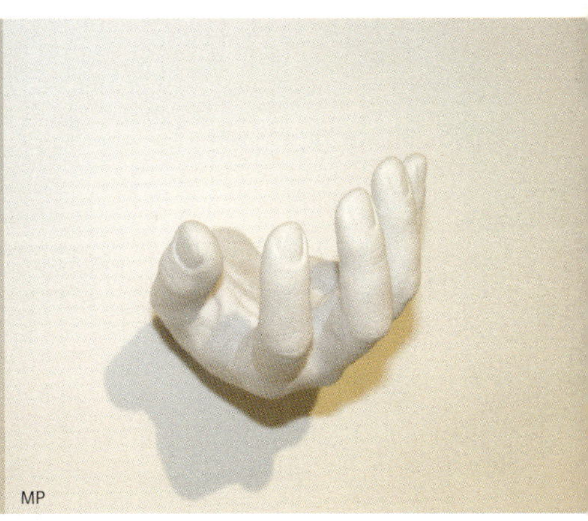

Harry Allen

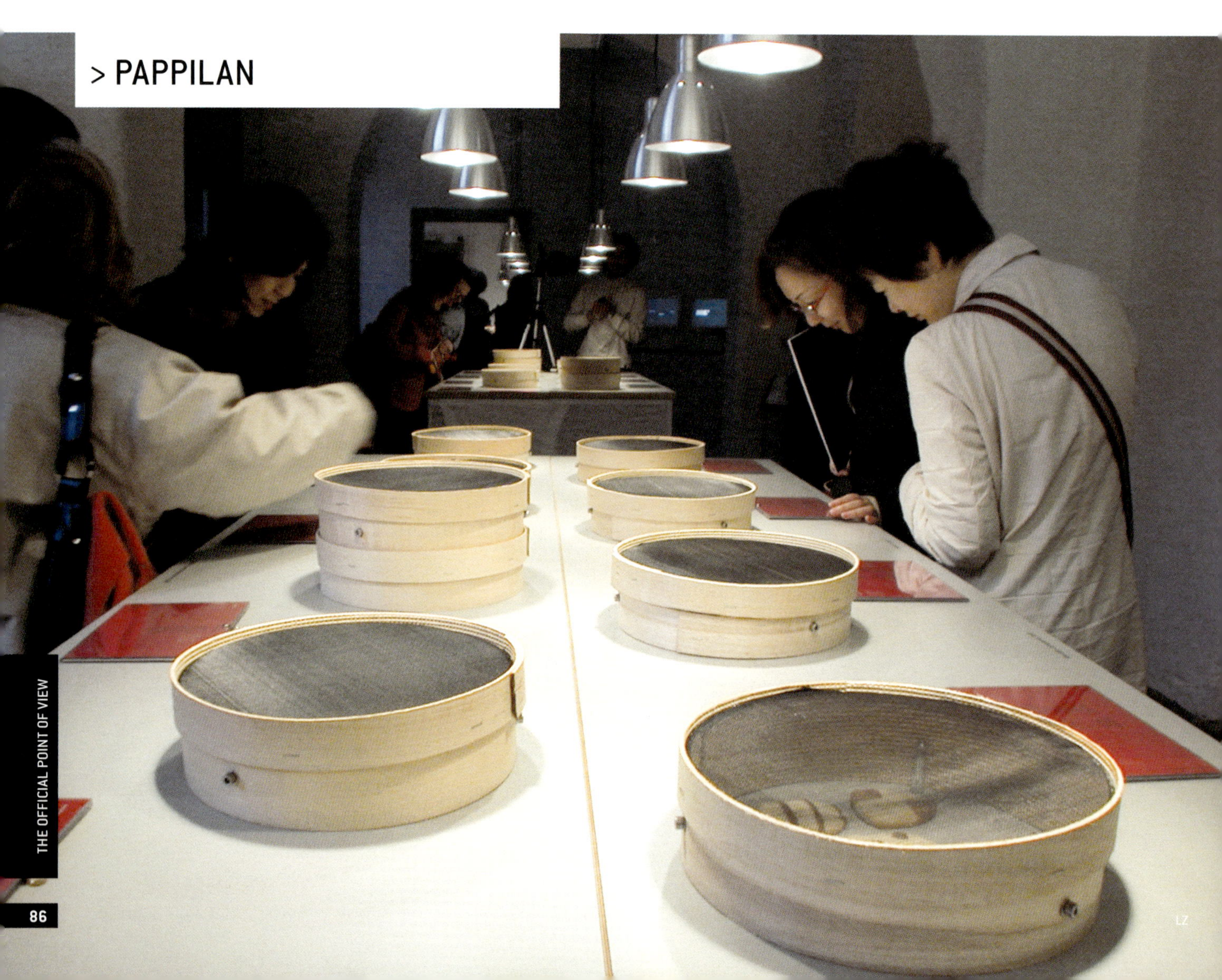
> PAPPILAN

The new Art and Design Faculty moves its first steps in the

world of design by asking 24 known designers to **explore the idea of biscuit:**

invent -and cook- new shapes and new flavours.

The result is a sweet collection and a catalogue-recepy book

that reflect the interdiscipliary and practical/conceptual approach of the University of Bolzano.

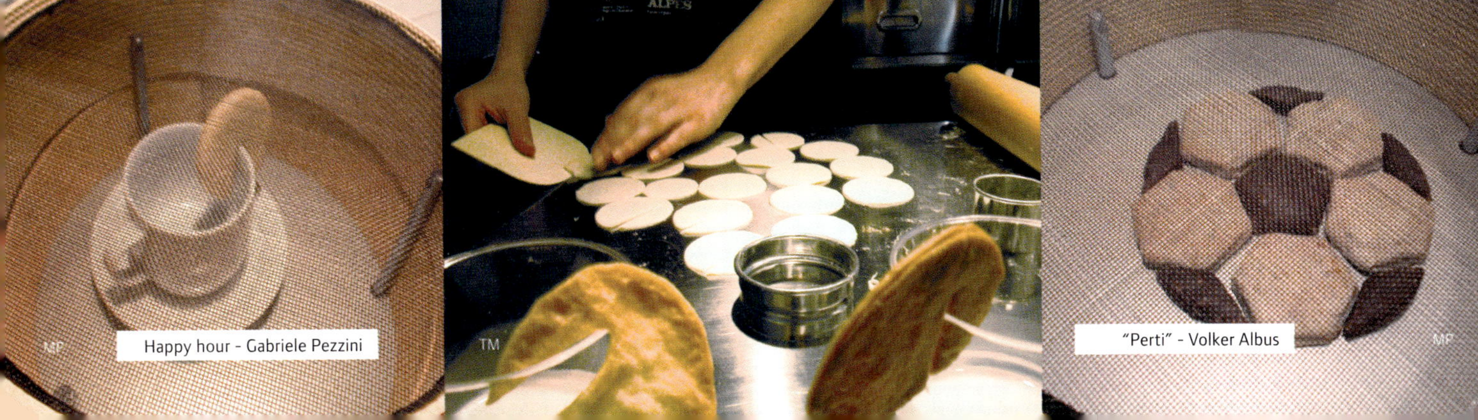
Happy hour - Gabriele Pezzini

"Perti" - Volker Albus

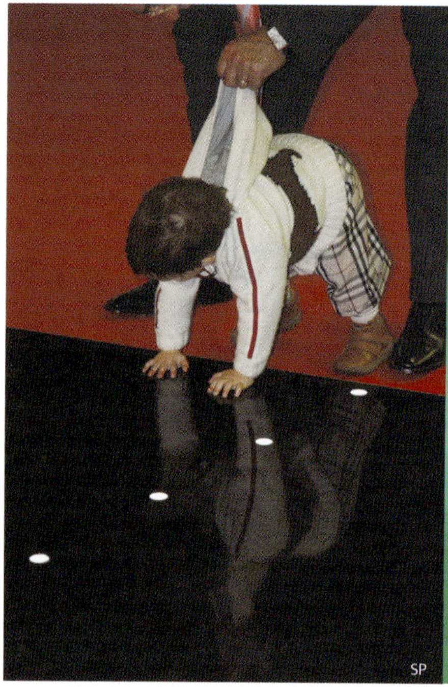

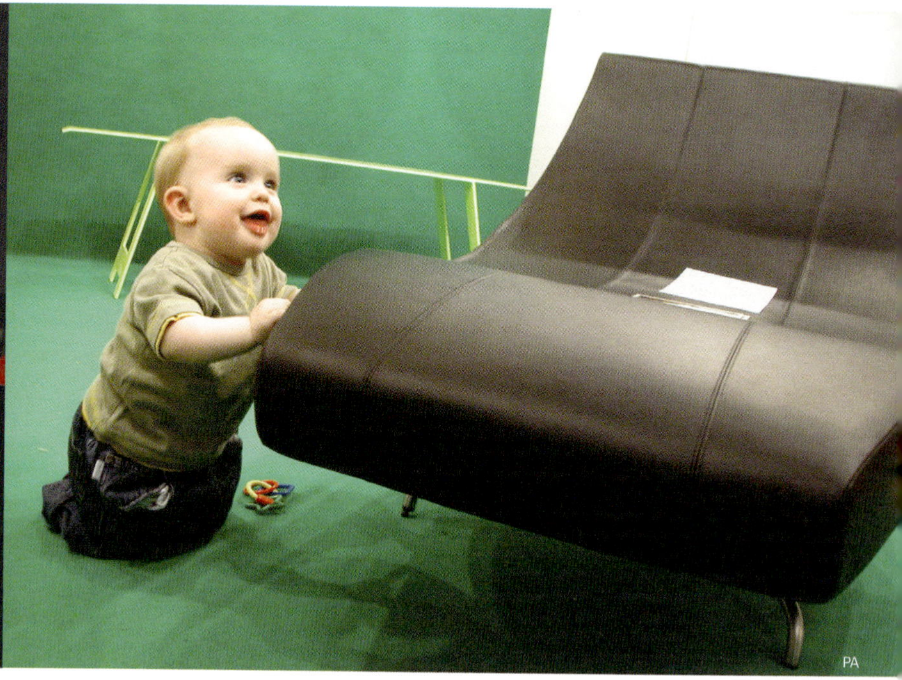

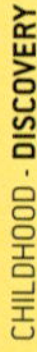

Rossi di Albizzate

Guggenbichlerdesign... @ Satellite

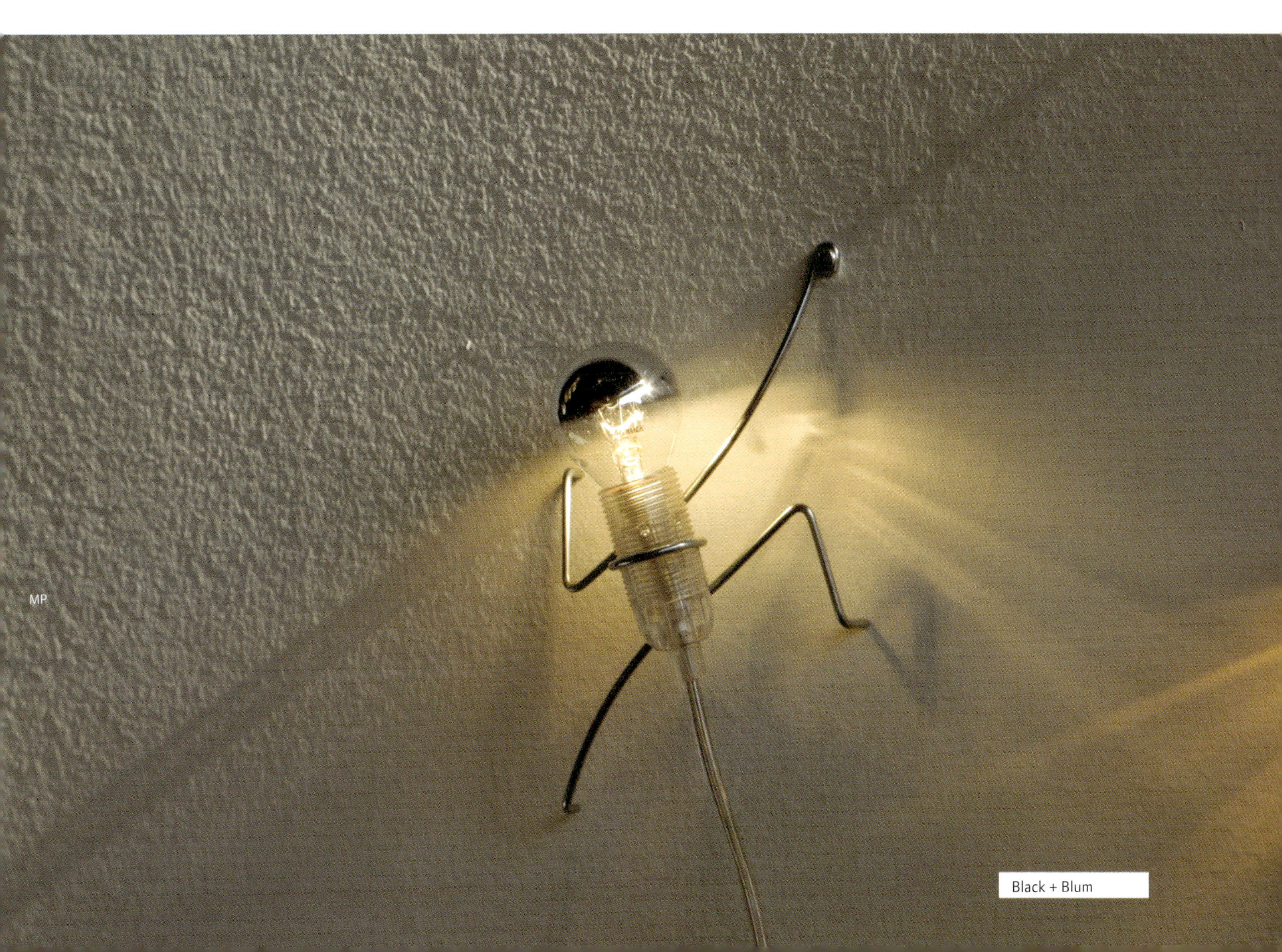
MP
Black + Blum

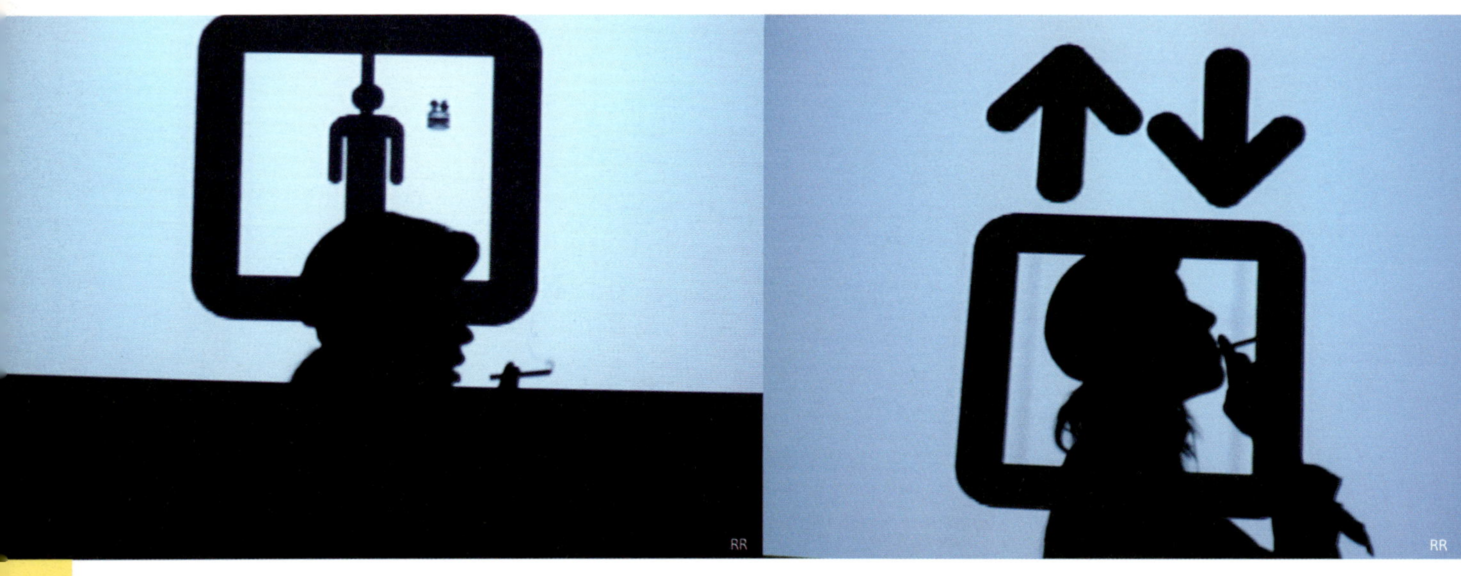

MMM (Metal Machine Muzak)

RR

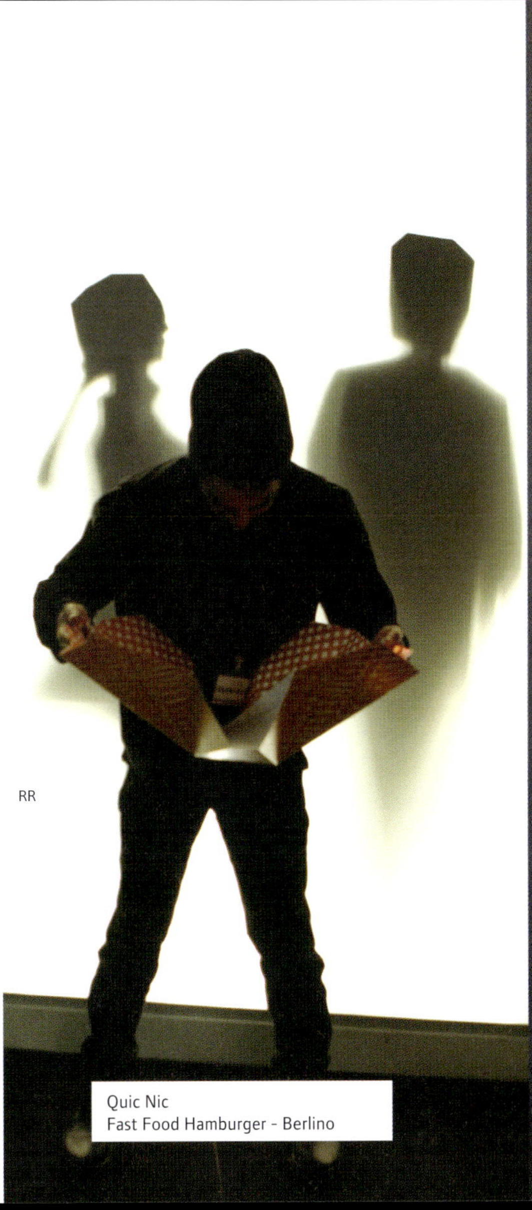

Quic Nic
Fast Food Hamburger - Berlino

SV

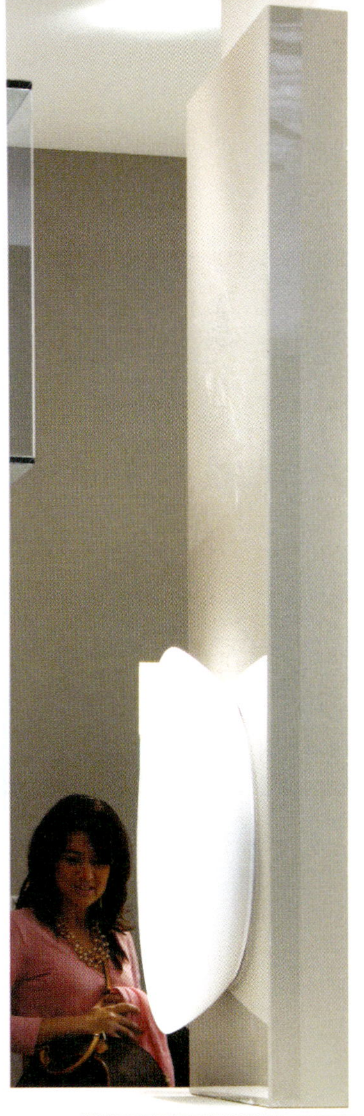

Agape

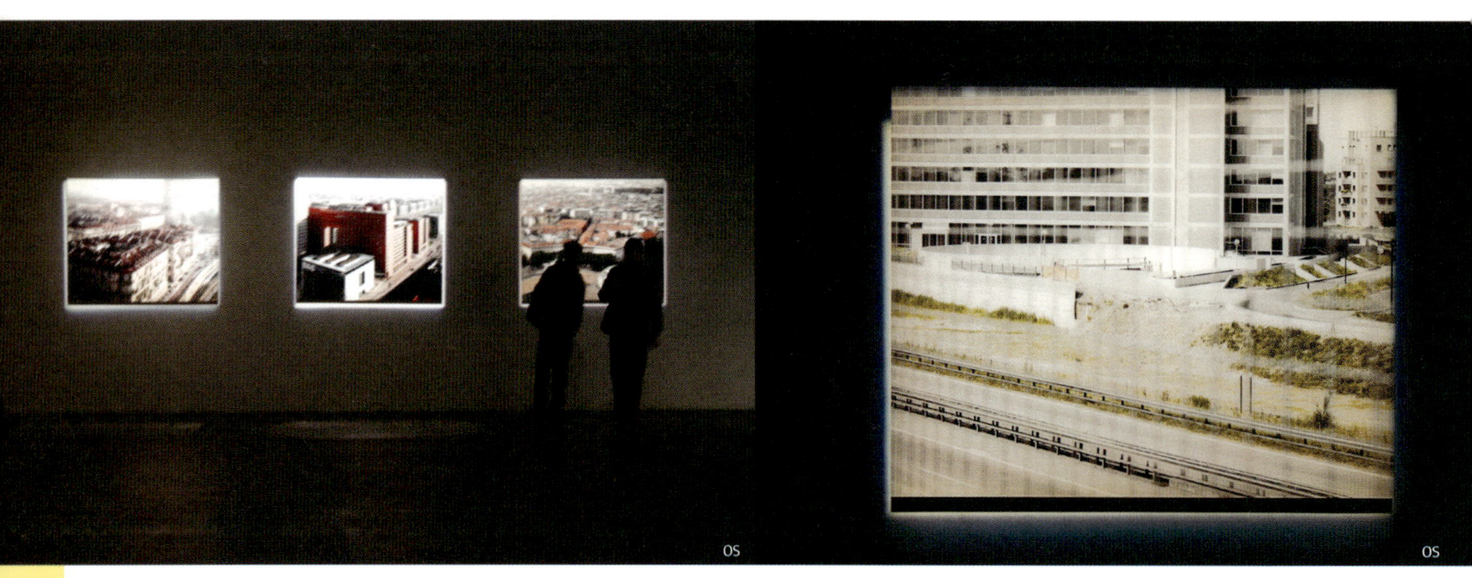

Vincenzo Castella

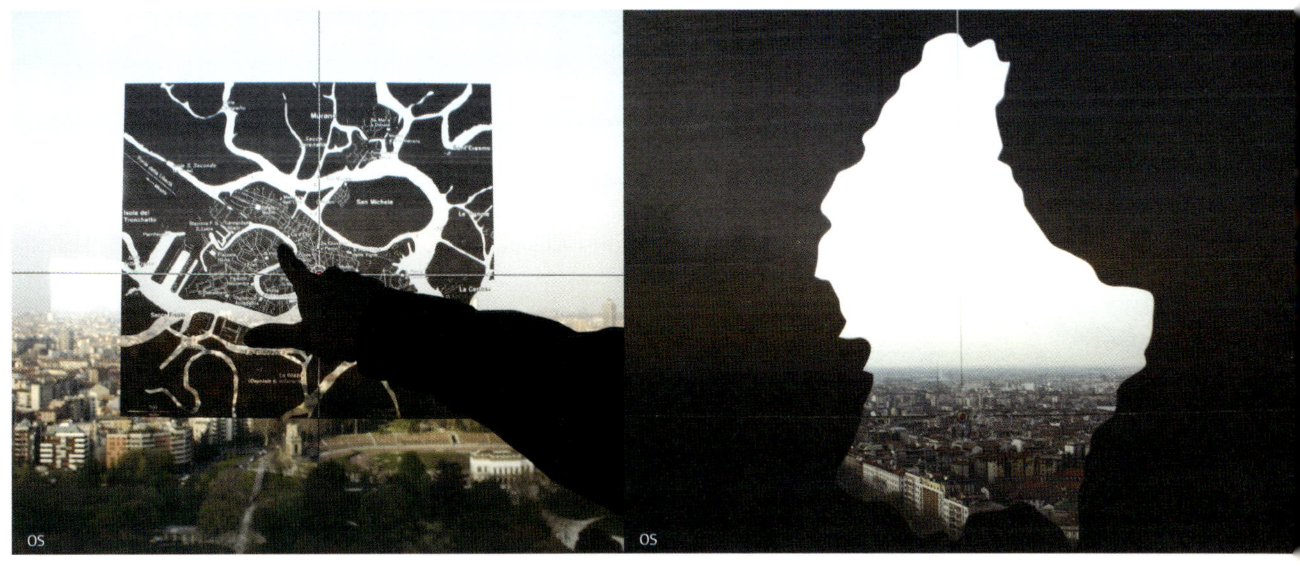

Torre Branca

Fabbrica Del Vapore

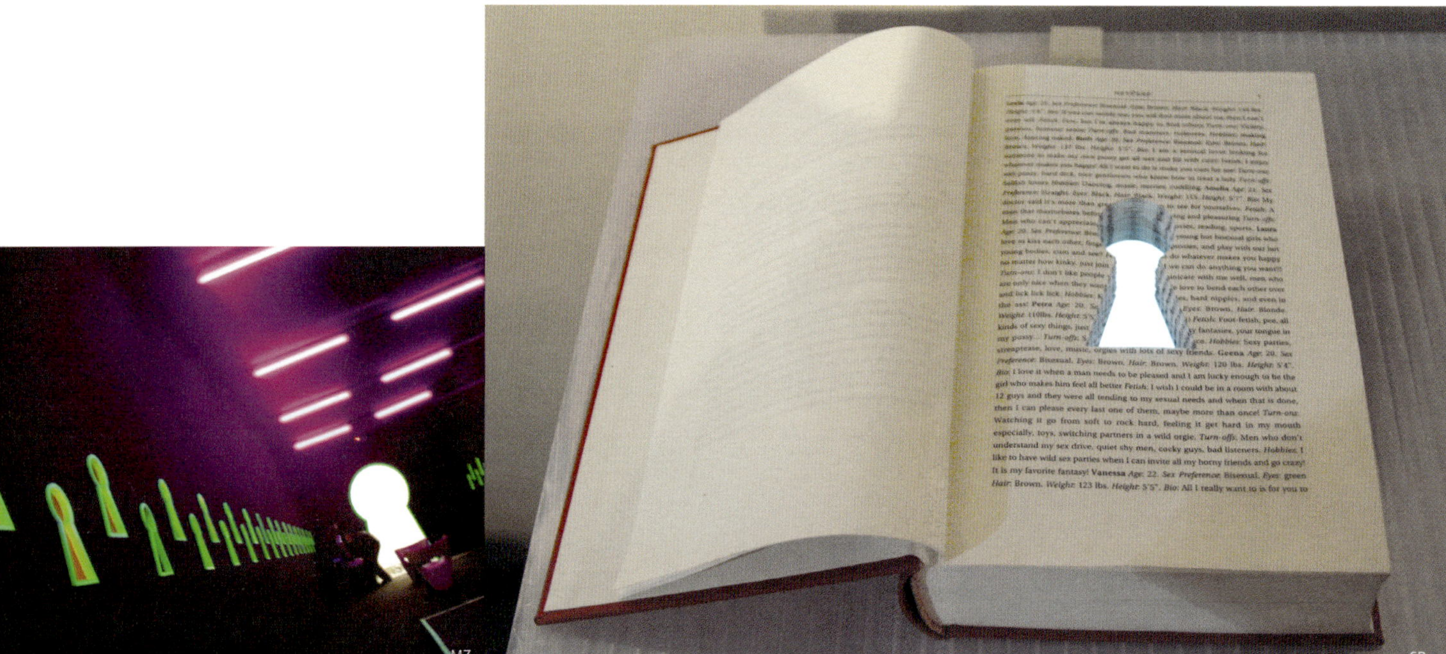

Beck's Prize

@ designersblock

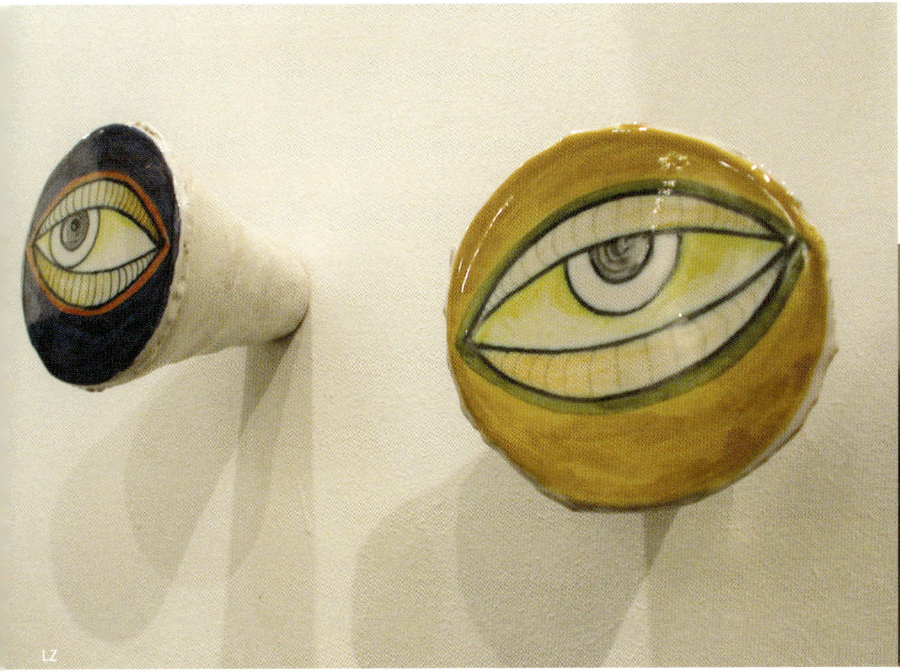

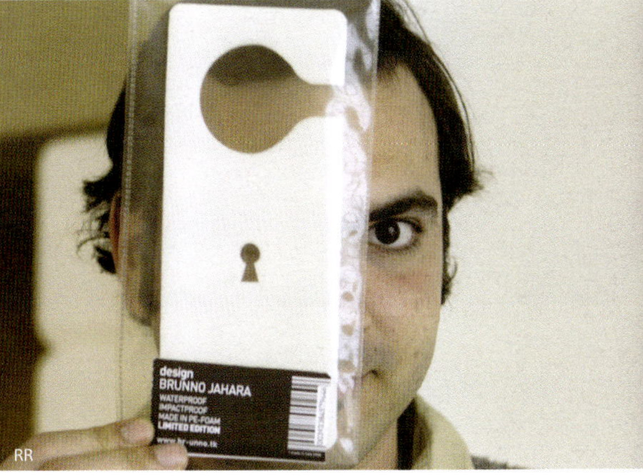

Salvi + Zotta

Bruno Jahara @ Cibic & Partners

96

@ Fiera

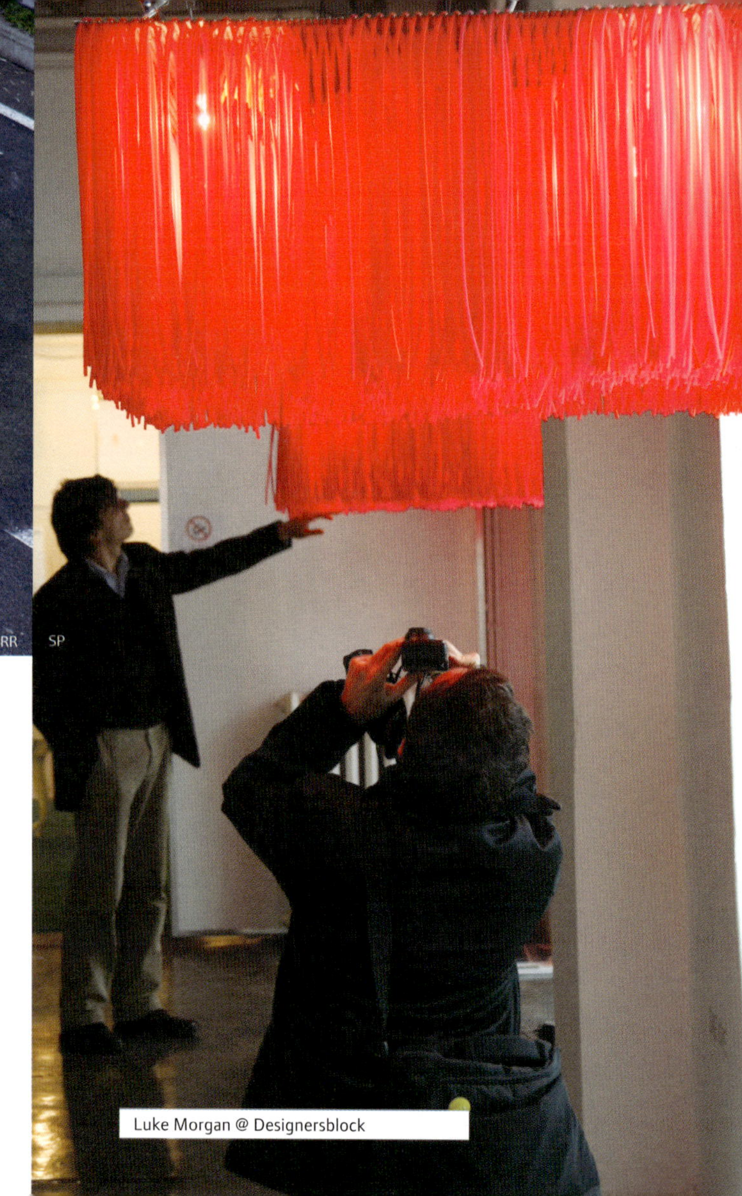

Luke Morgan @ Designersblock

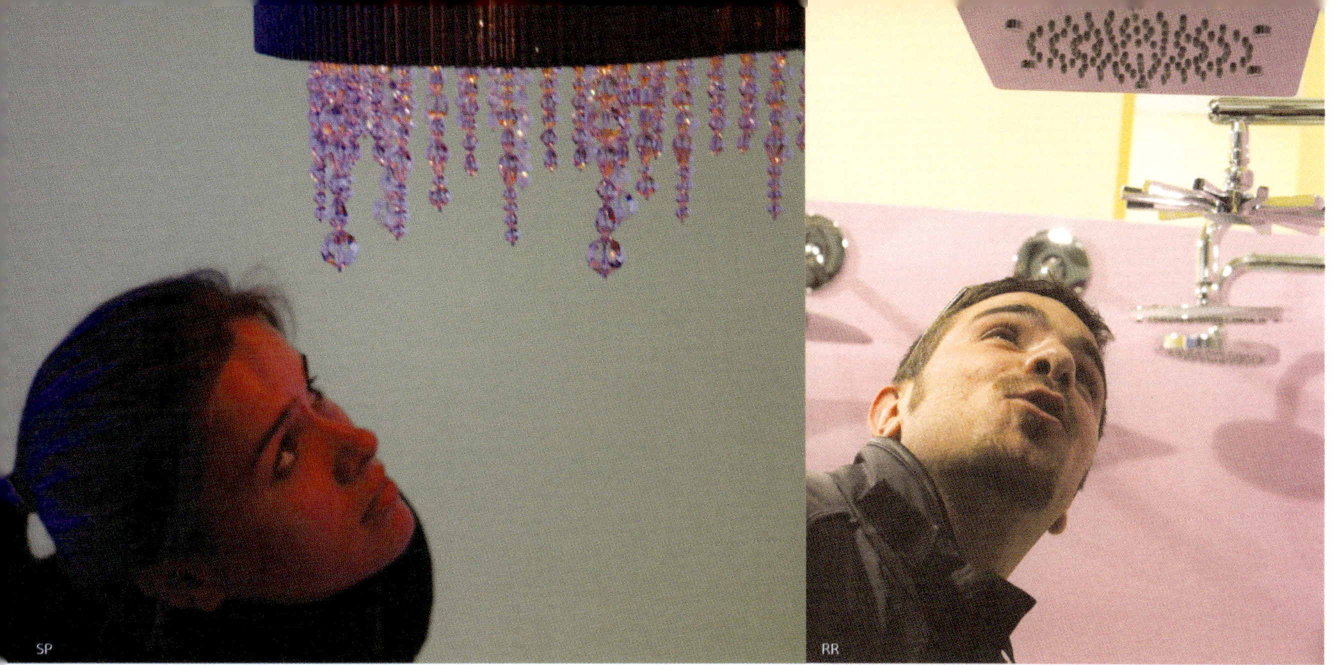

@ Sawaya&Moroni   Flex Doccia

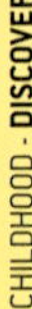

Deltagroove

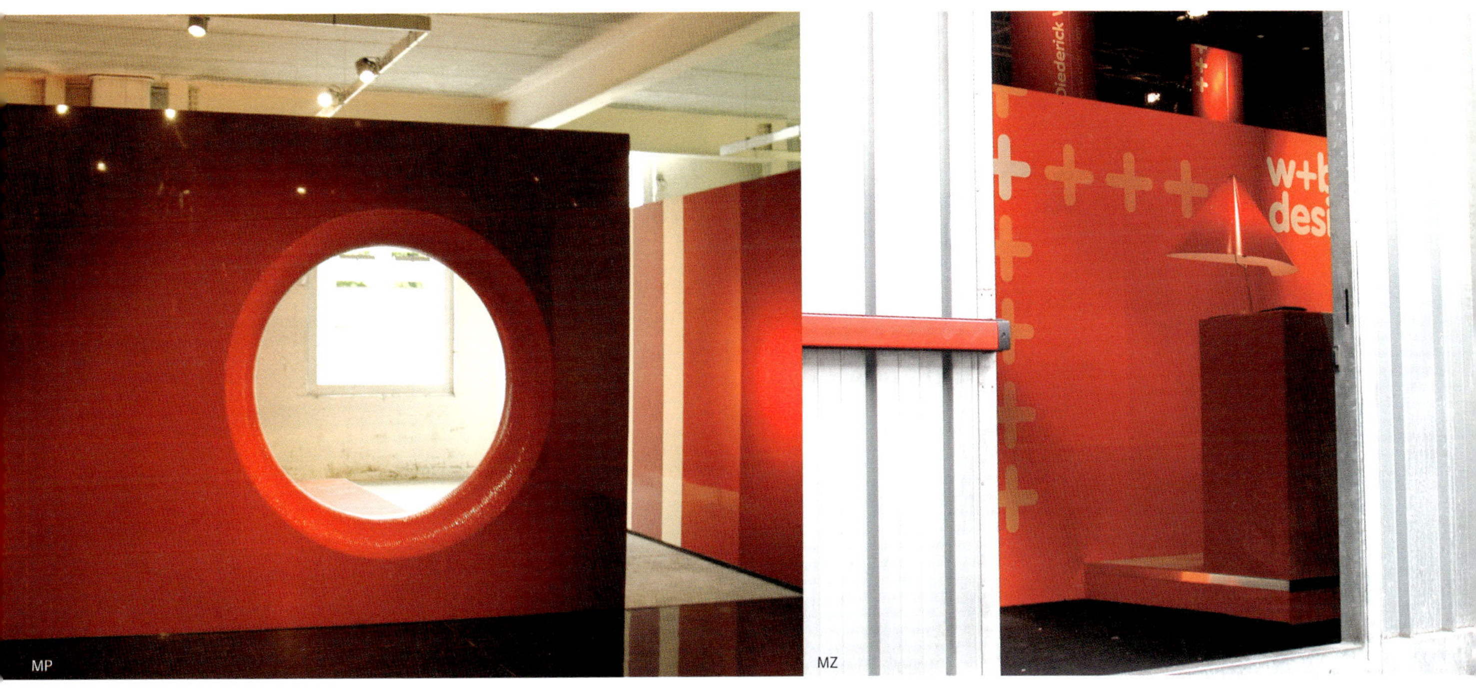

MP

MZ

Bisazza

W+B Design 2004 @ zona Tortona

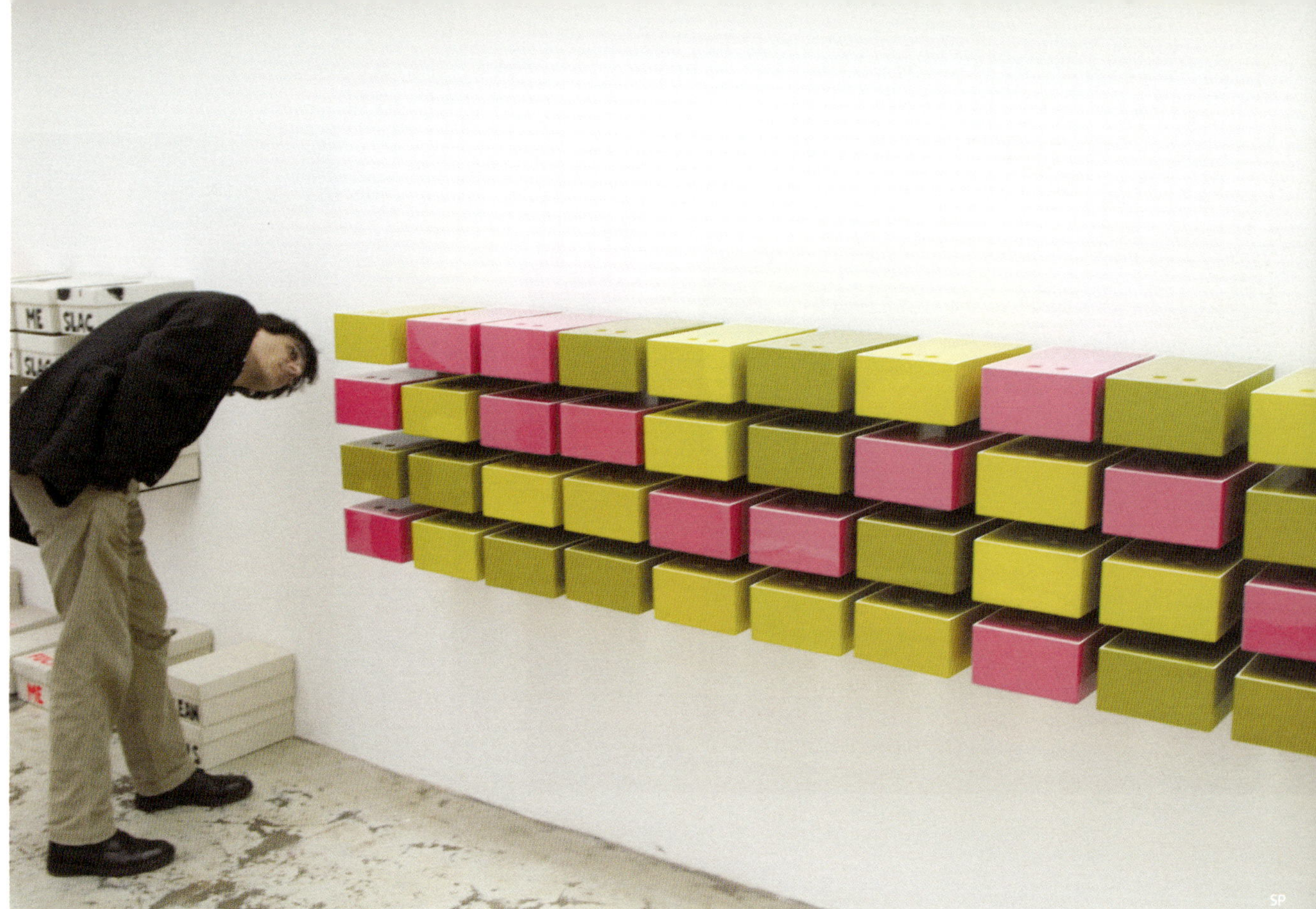

Her House Products by Luke Morgan @ Designersblock

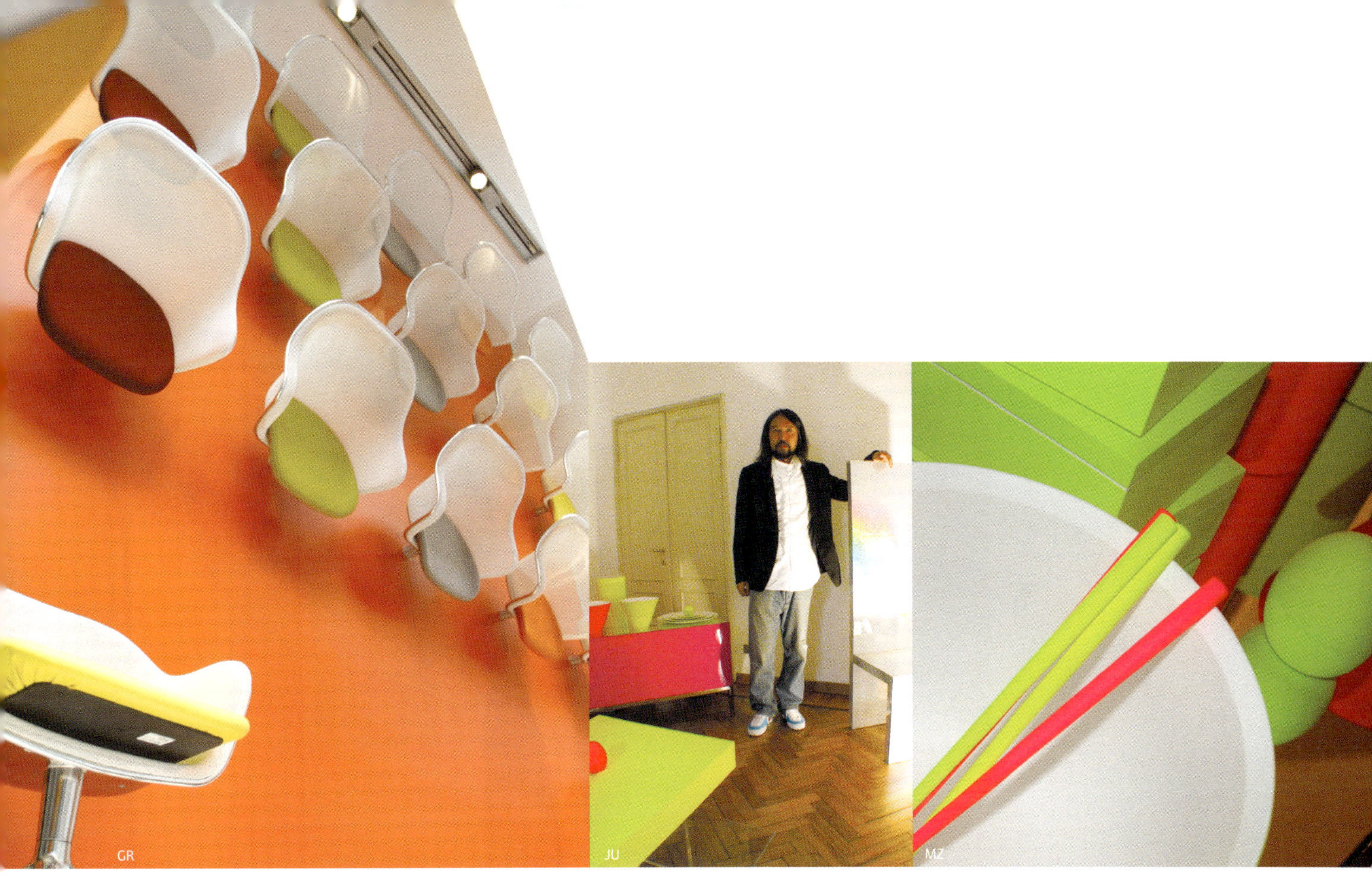

B&B Italia

Koichiro Kimura @ Internos

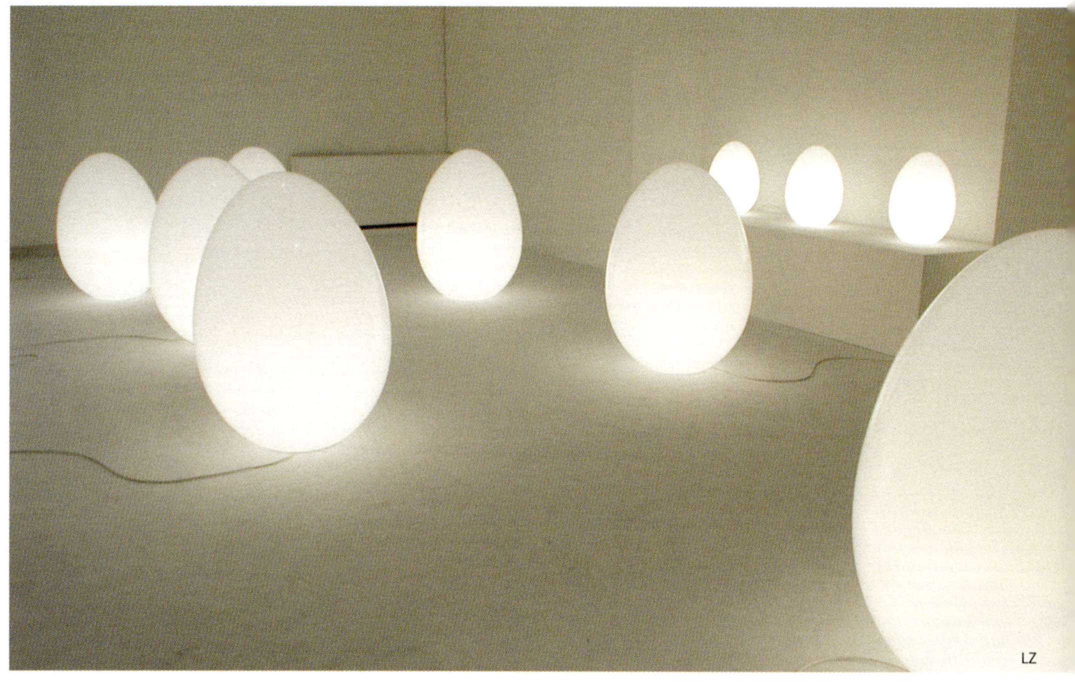

102   Shigeru Uchida Design Institue @ Posteria

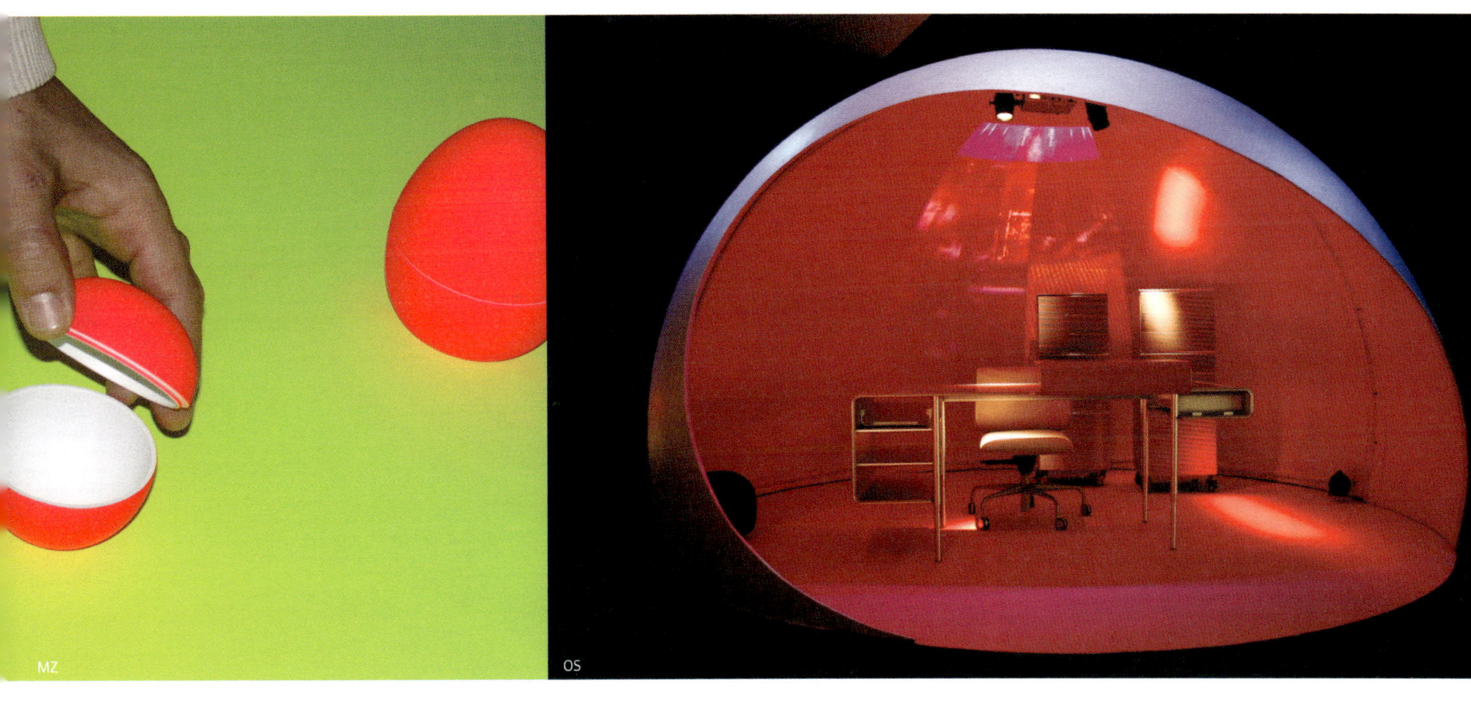

Koichiro Kimura @ Internos

Ycami

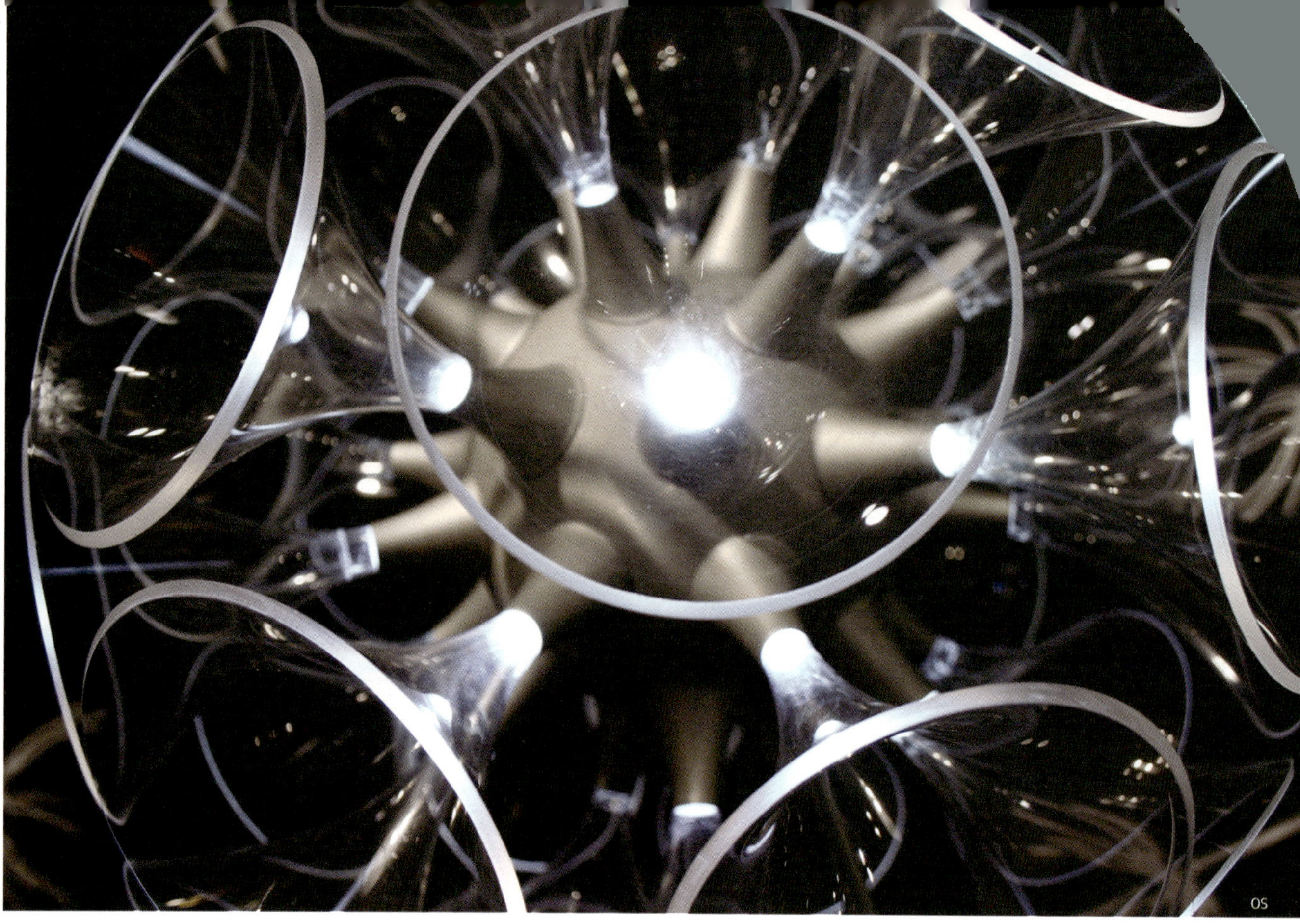

Dandelion by Deep Design @ Satellite

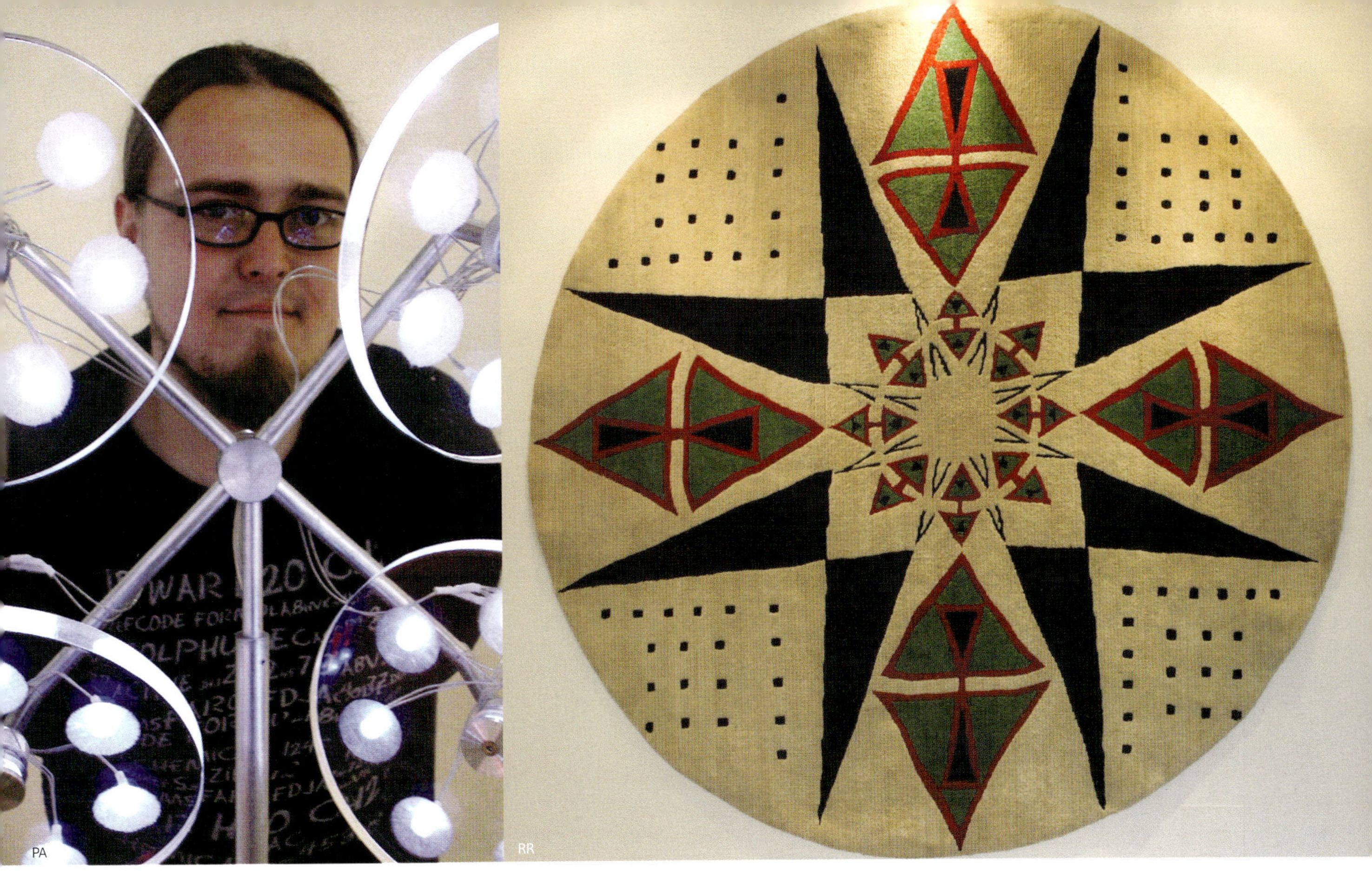

Puff Buff @ Satellite

Nanda Vigo for Life Commodities @ Post Design

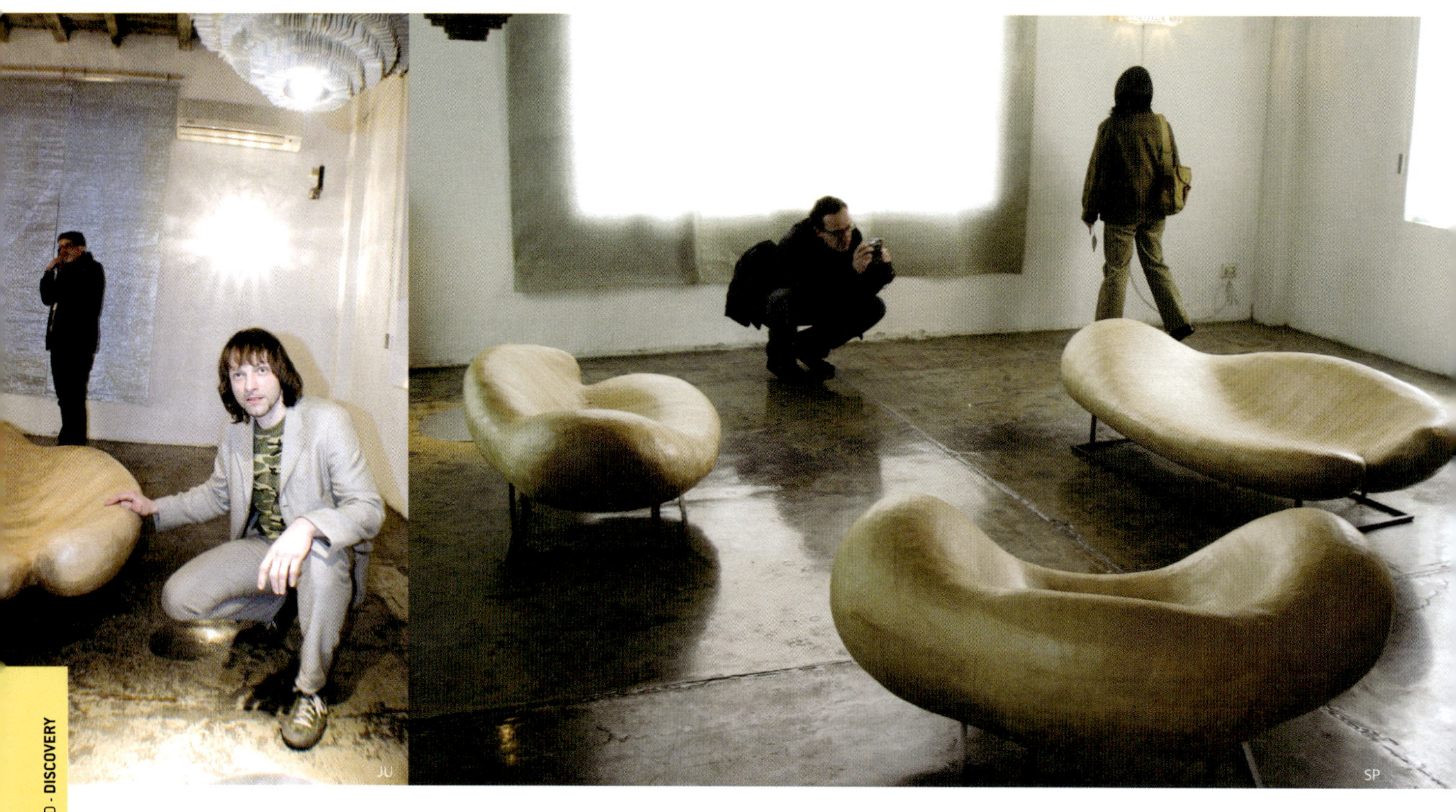

Georg Baldele @ Designersblock

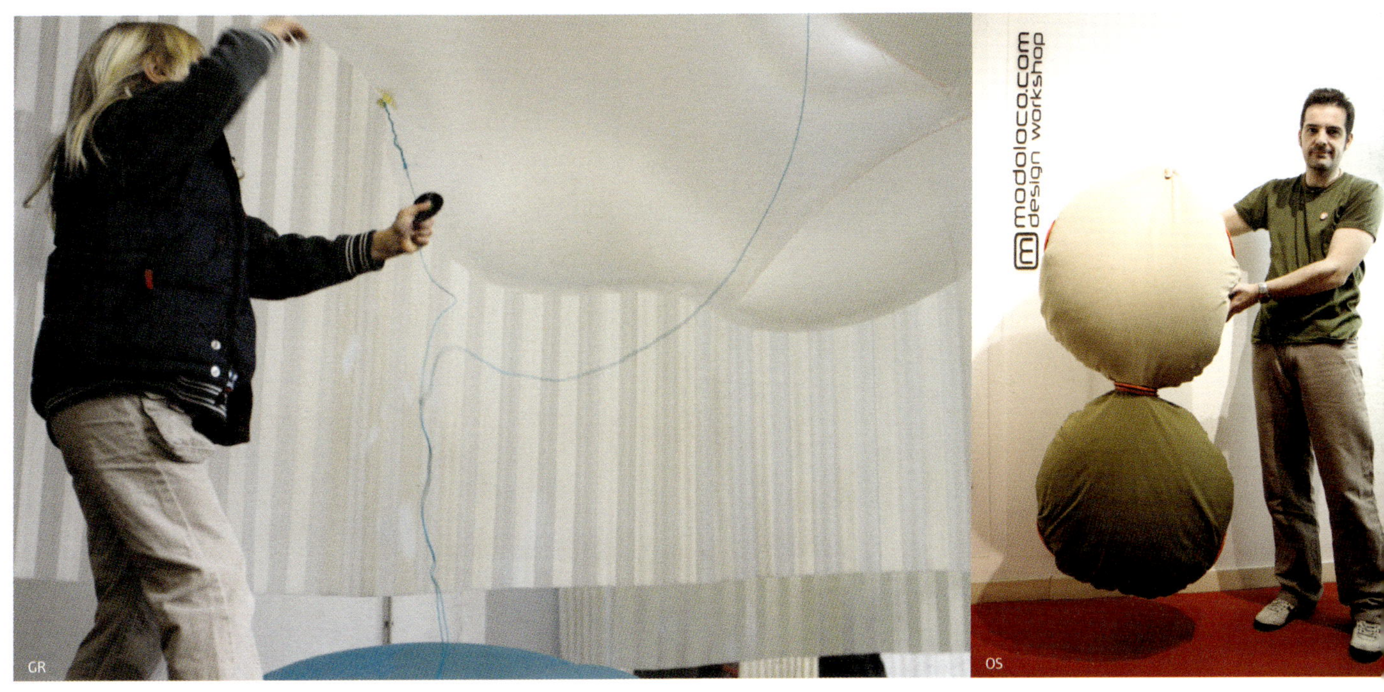

Takeaway   Diseño Español + Modoloco

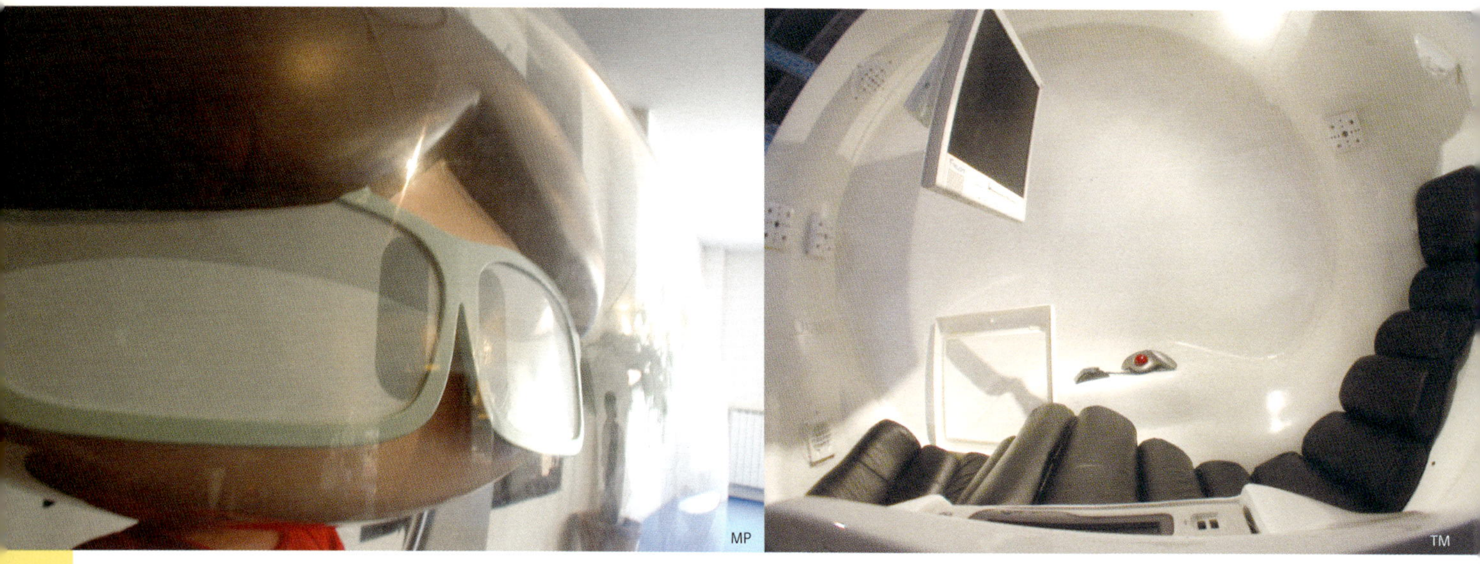

Sooper Double @ Designersblock

Oculas

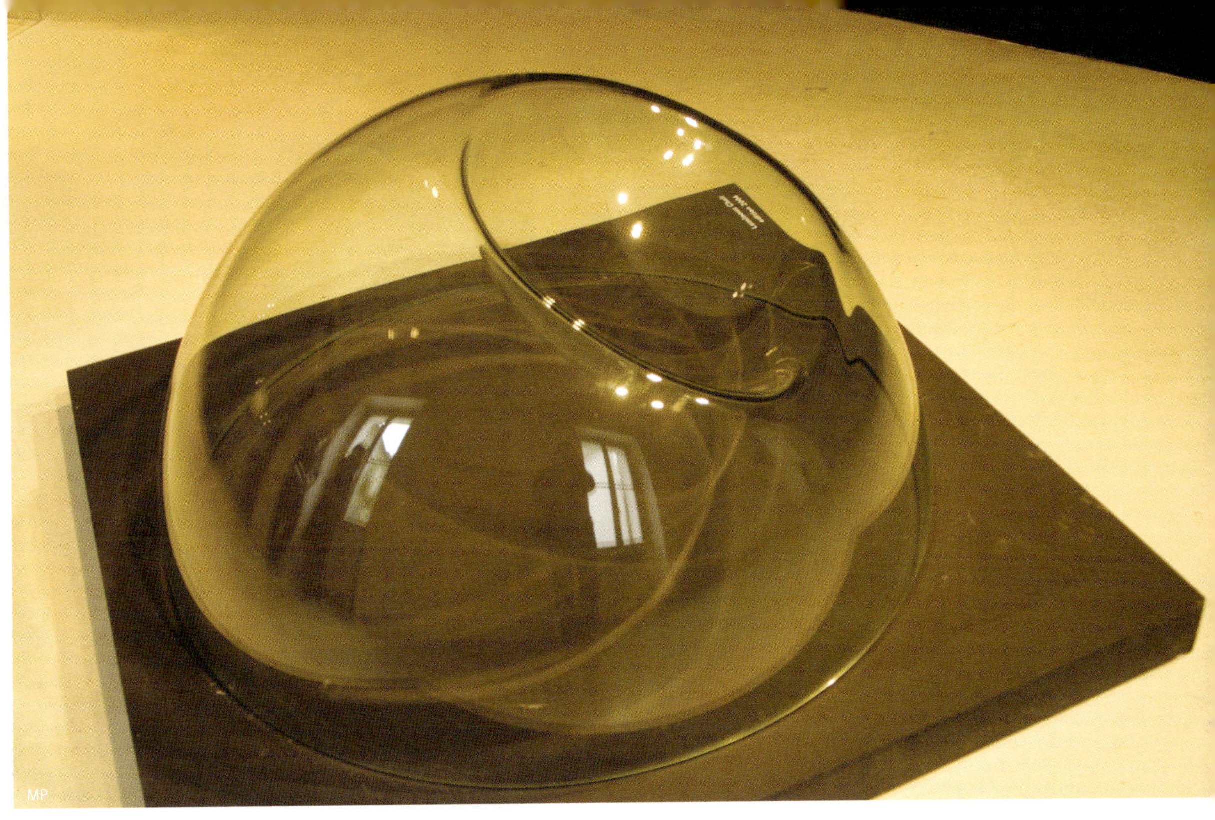

Shiro Kuramata

> DESIGNOSAURUS

An installation by Ross Lovegrove
"This is my first solo installation in Milan
dedicated to **conceptual art rather than
manufactured furniture or product.**
This installation has been conceived therefore
to communicate my facination with stucture,
technology and materials.
I've responded to the volumetric
dimensions of Segheria.

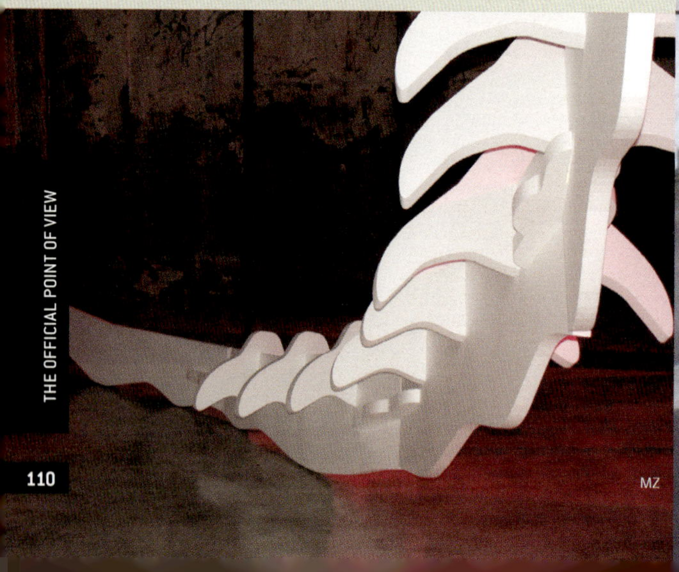

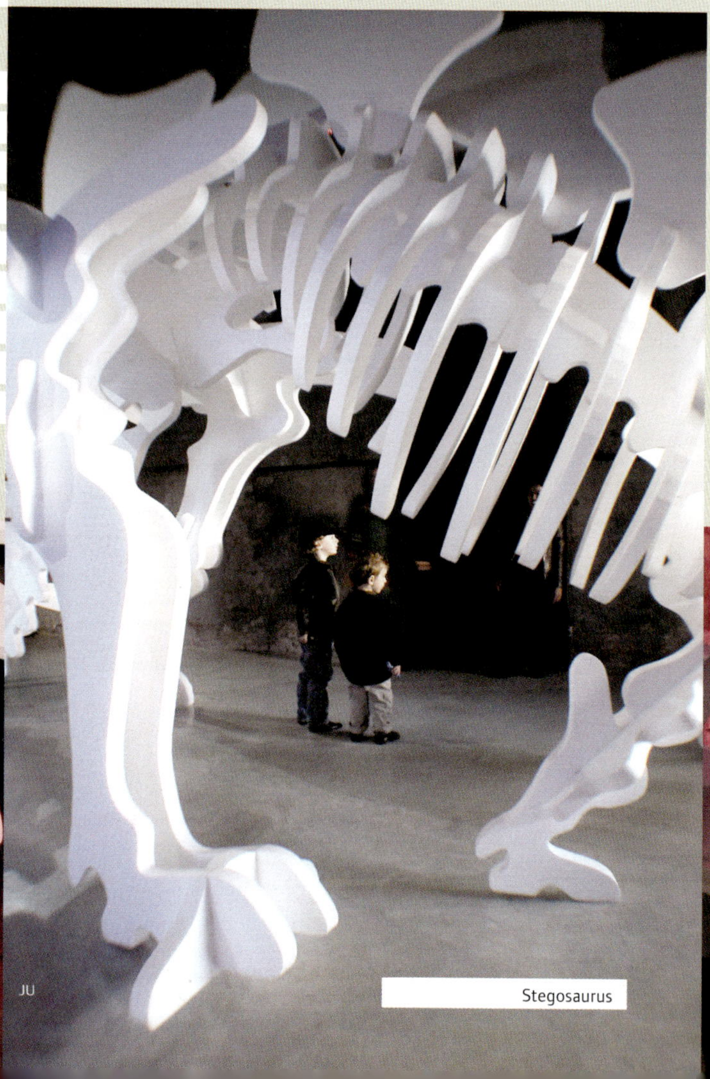

MZ   JU

Stegosaurus

PA

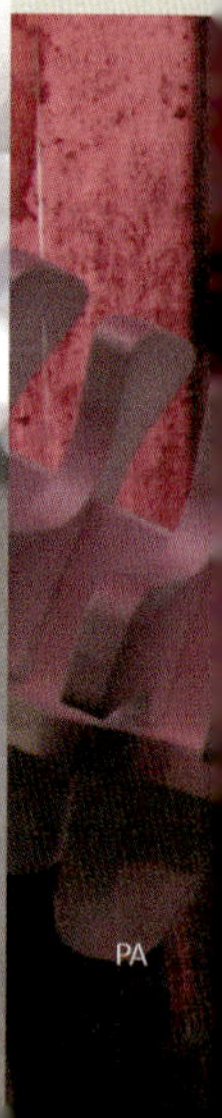

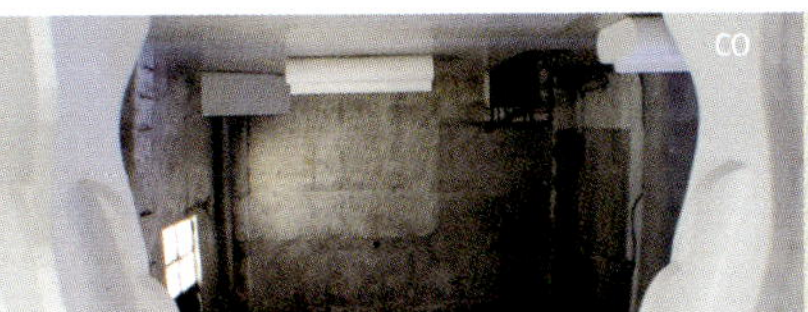

This space can stimulate and highlight perception of design in an even more modern way through the contrast of juxtaposition.

The installation has been made possible by the material's inherent magical lightness and with it, the economic availabity of

polystyrene with its ease of shape creation.

These three pieces consist of a Brachiosaurus, a T Rex and a Stegosaurus constructed that **lie somewhere between Archeology and Architecture**.

They are forms that we all know but created with purpose by evolution in a reductive rather

than additive process that has been going on over millions of years...

Designosaurus is my contribution to the Milan Salone this year."

ROSS LOVEGROVE

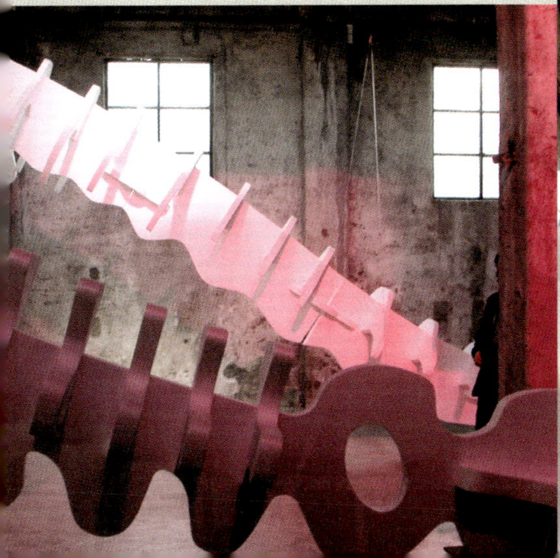

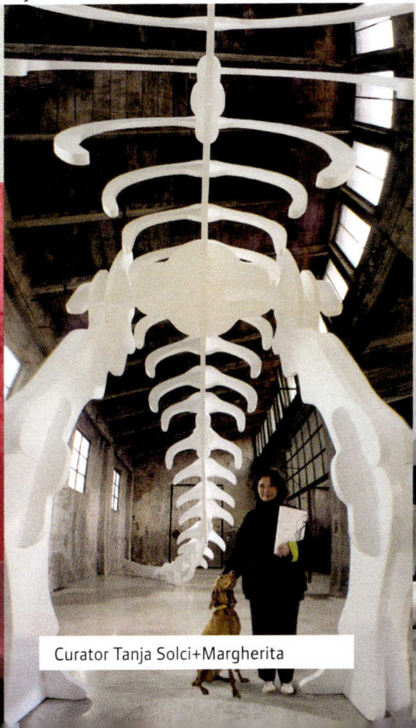

Curator Tanja Solci+Margherita

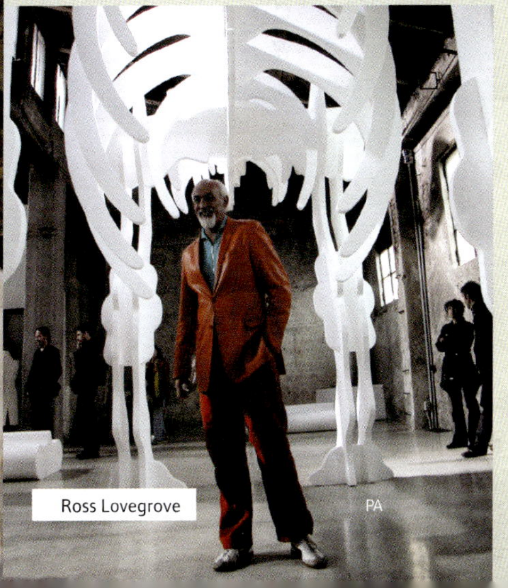

Ross Lovegrove

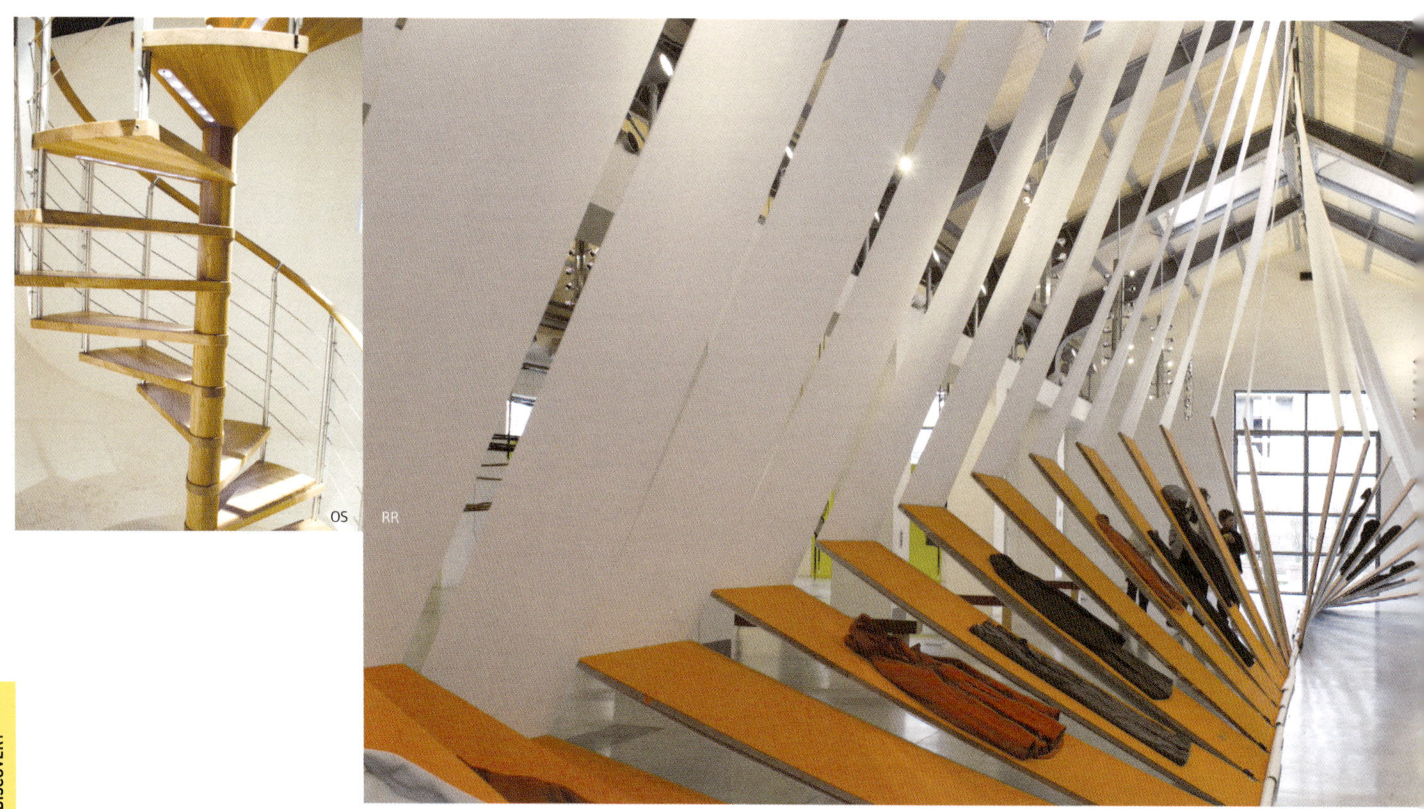

Albini e Fontanot
@ Zona Tortona

CP Company Store

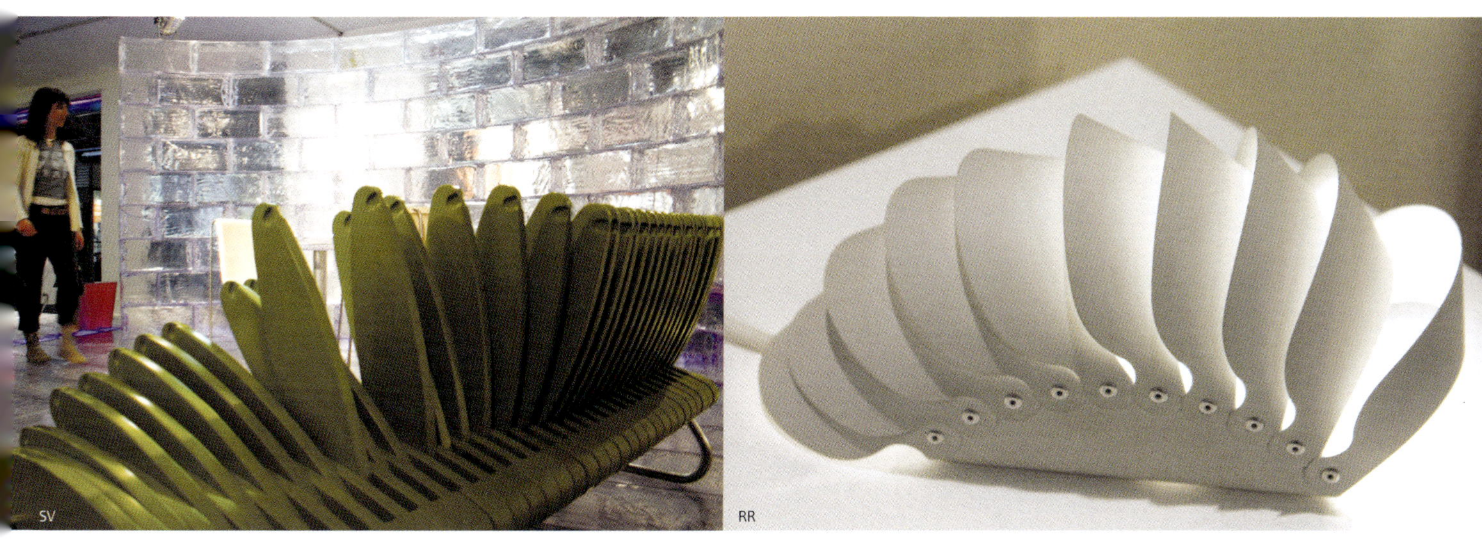

Double Up by Sturmundplastic

Sentinel by Marc Savary Design

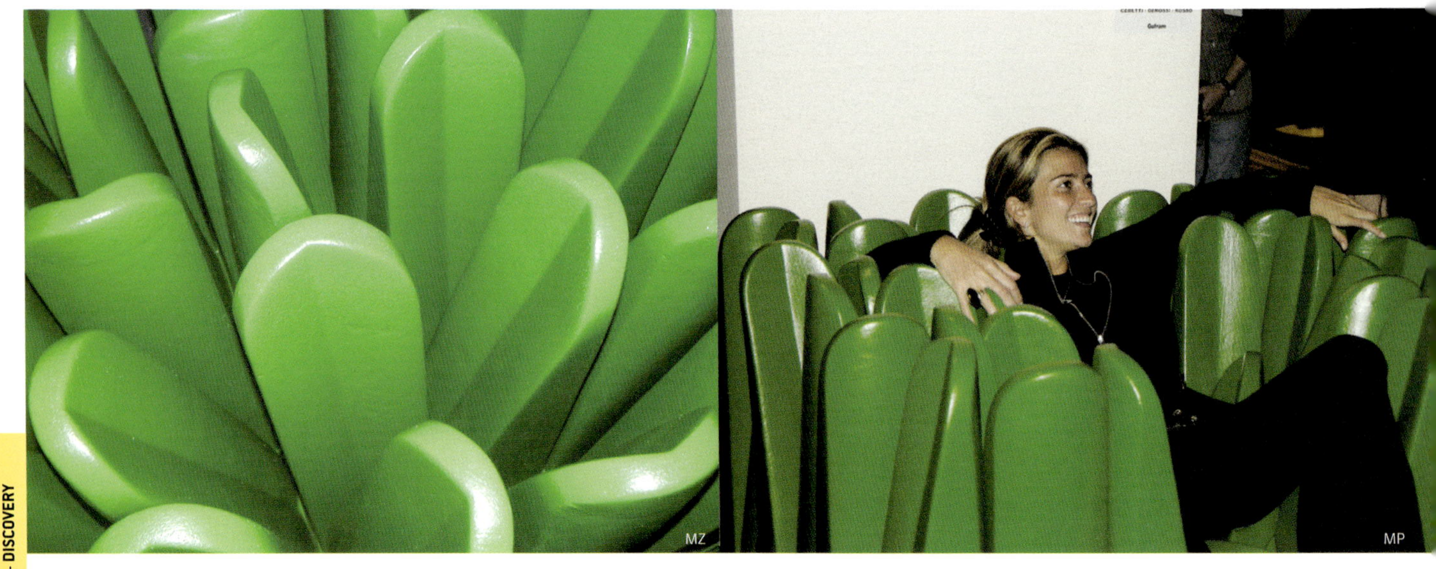

114 Pratone by Gufram @ Cappellini

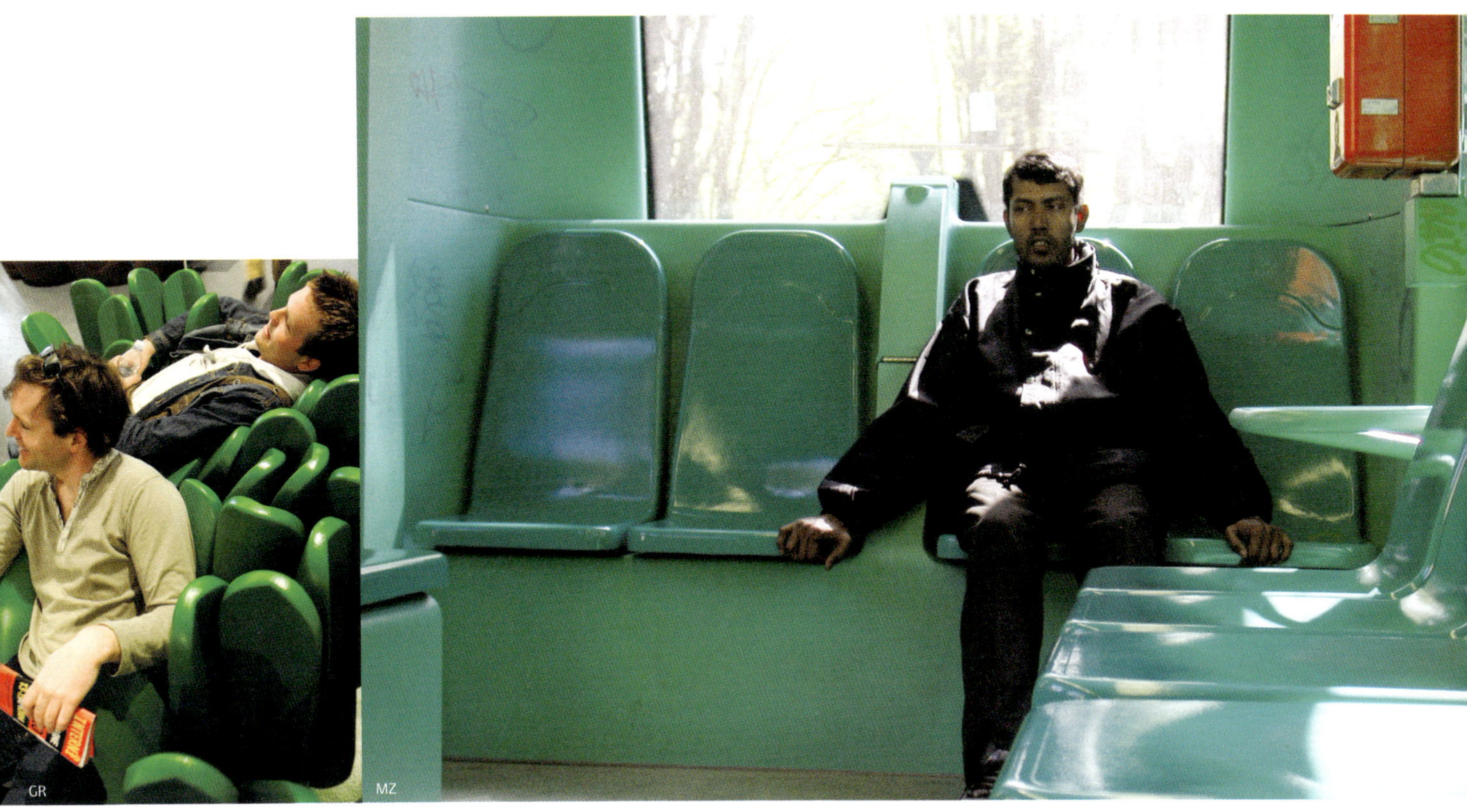

ATM bus Milano

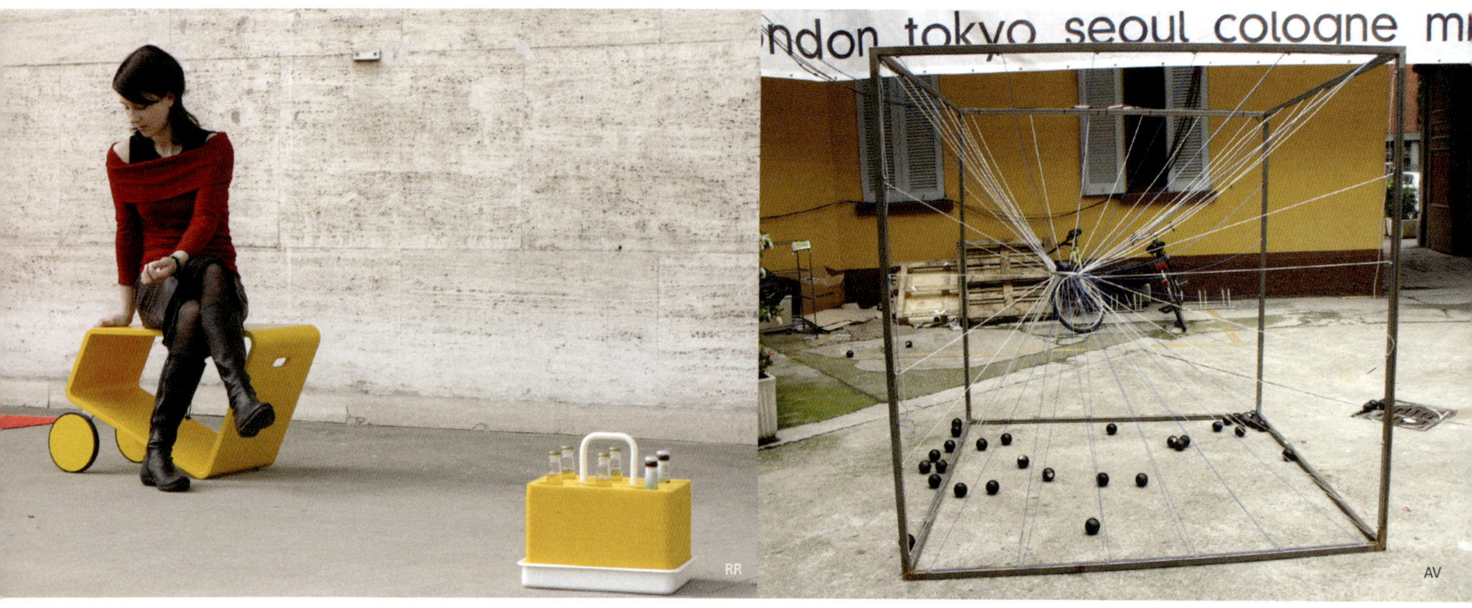

@ Fiera

@ Designersblock

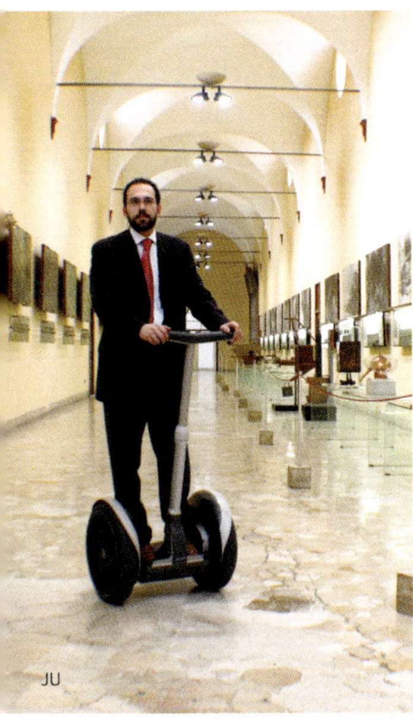

Human Transporter by Segway @ Well Tech

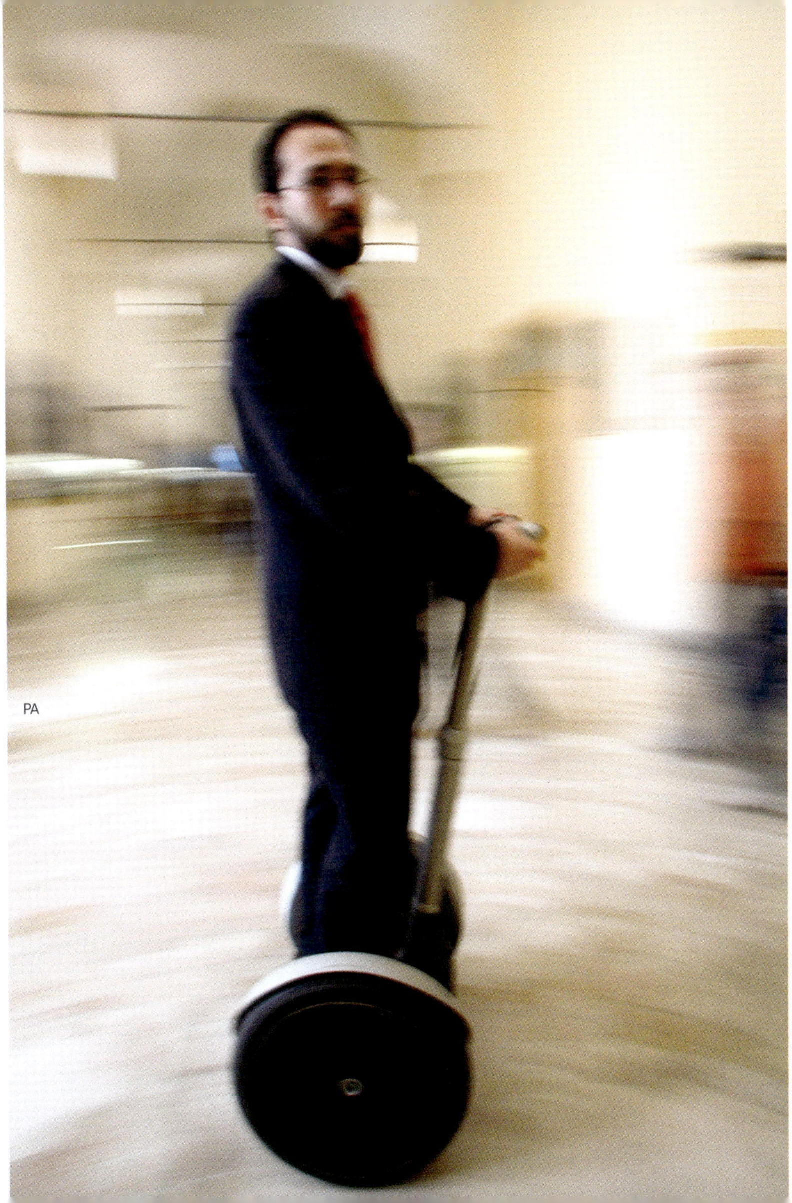

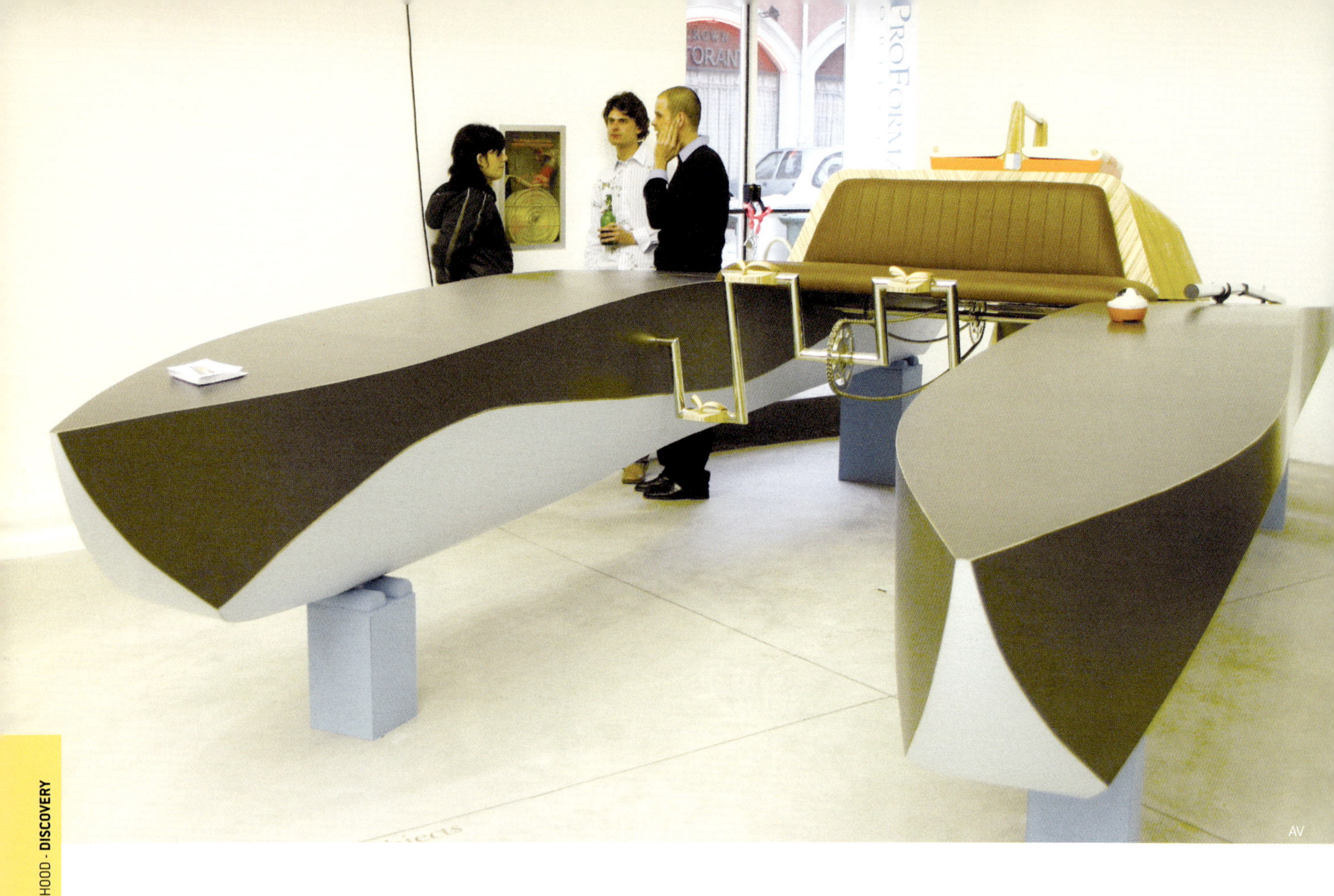

Pro Forma Objects @ Tutto BeNe

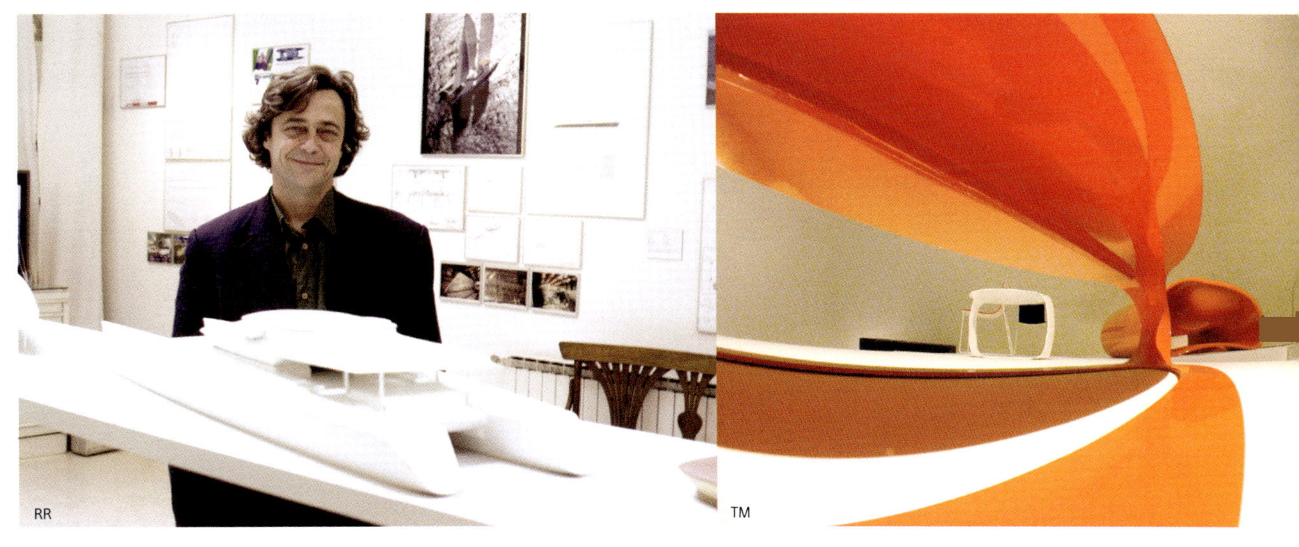

Marc Van Peteghem, Naval Engineer

Shaus @ Zona Tortona

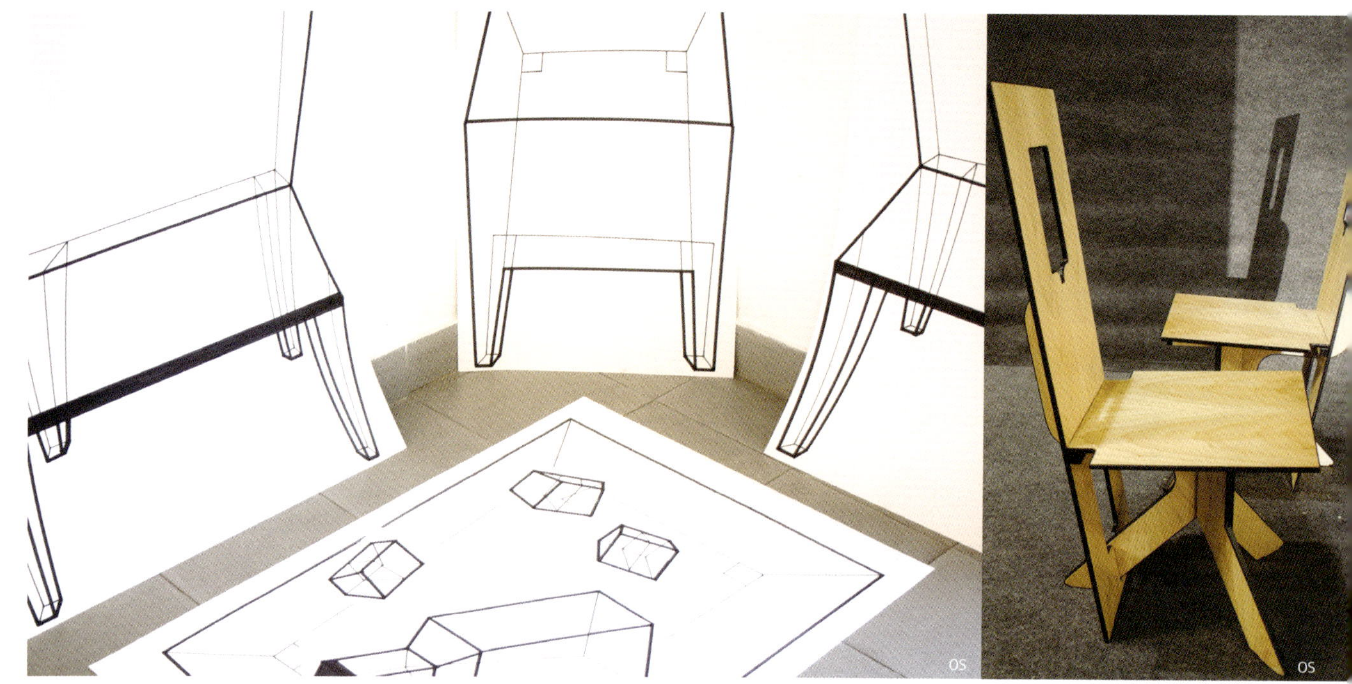

Cadrega

Jacopo Gardella

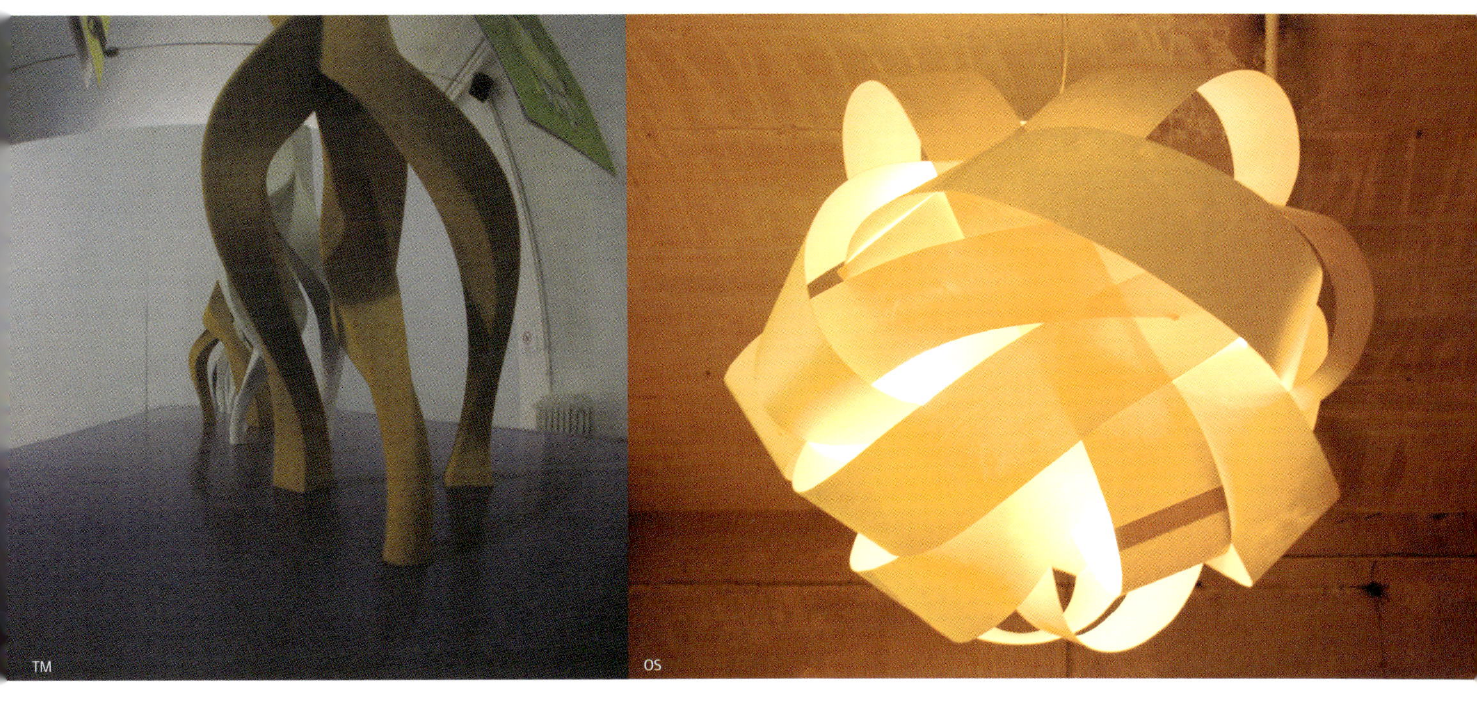

Twist by Future Factories @ Designrsblock

Santa & Cole

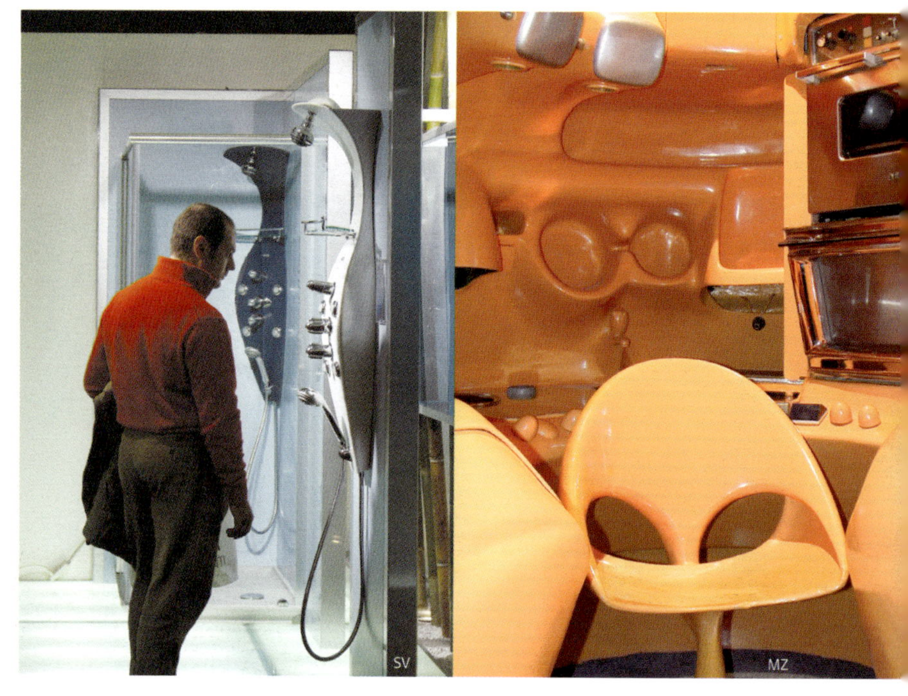

Teuco

Poggenphol

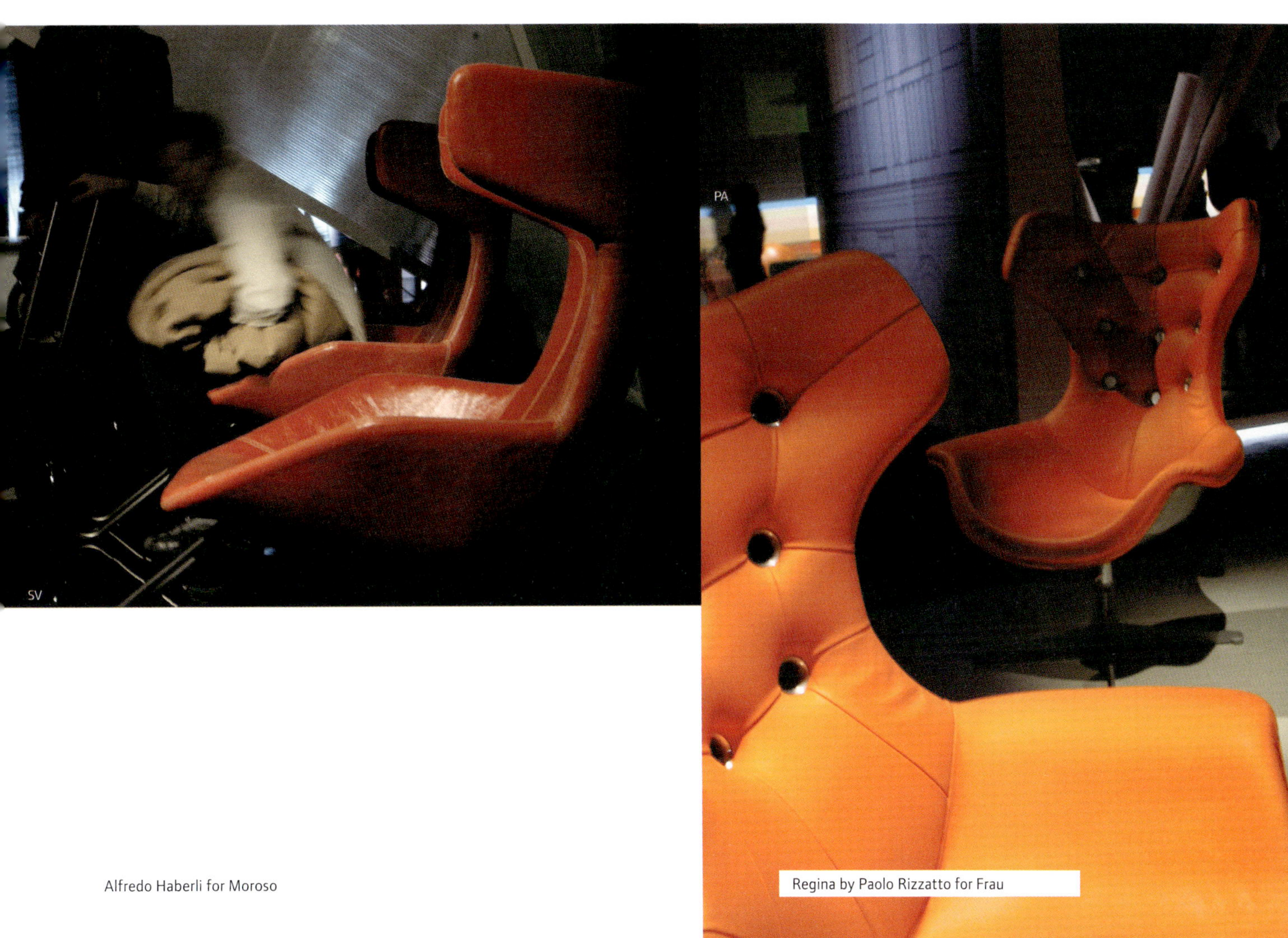

Alfredo Haberli for Moroso

Regina by Paolo Rizzatto for Frau

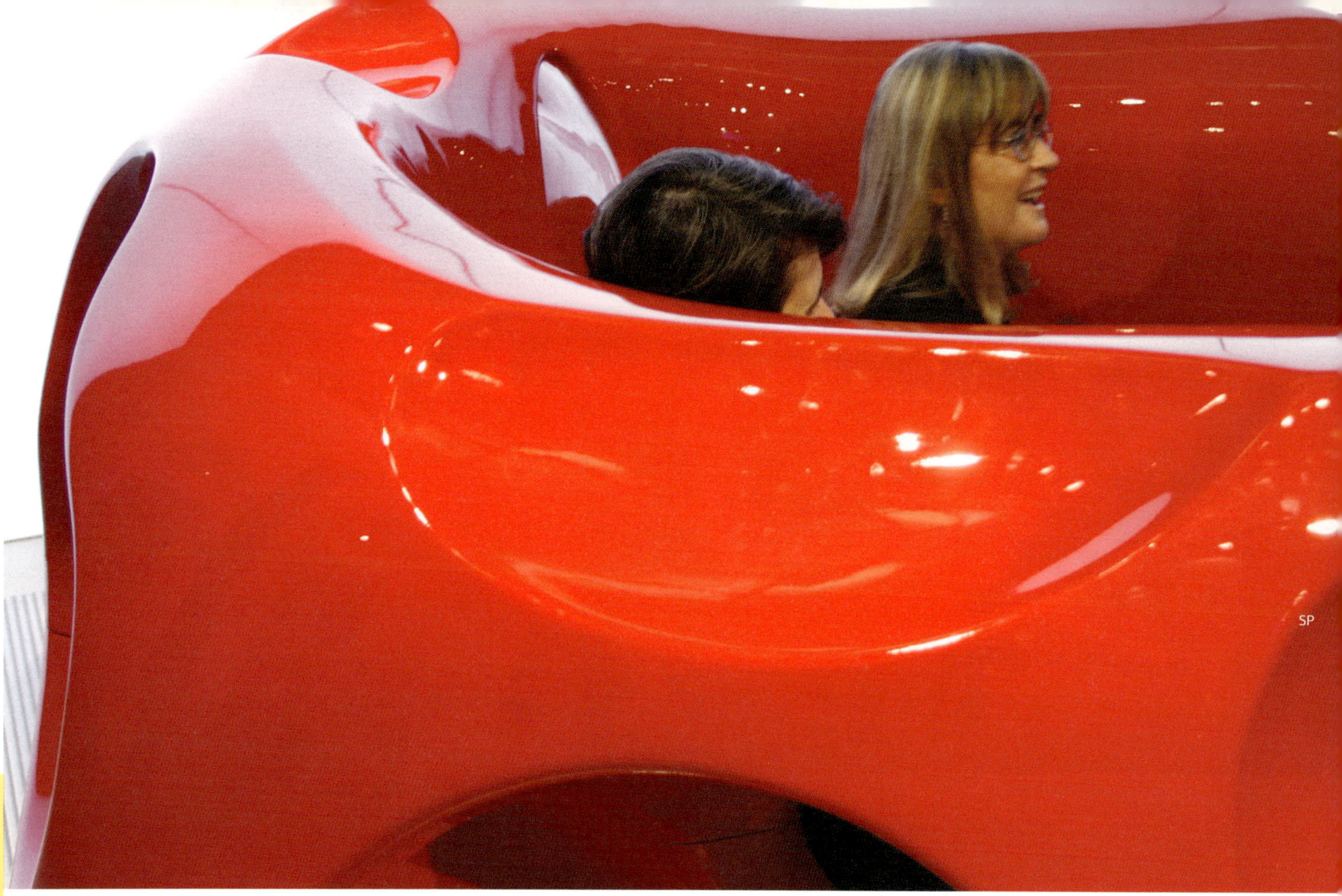

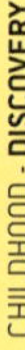

SP

Gilda Bojardi @ Sawaya&Moroni

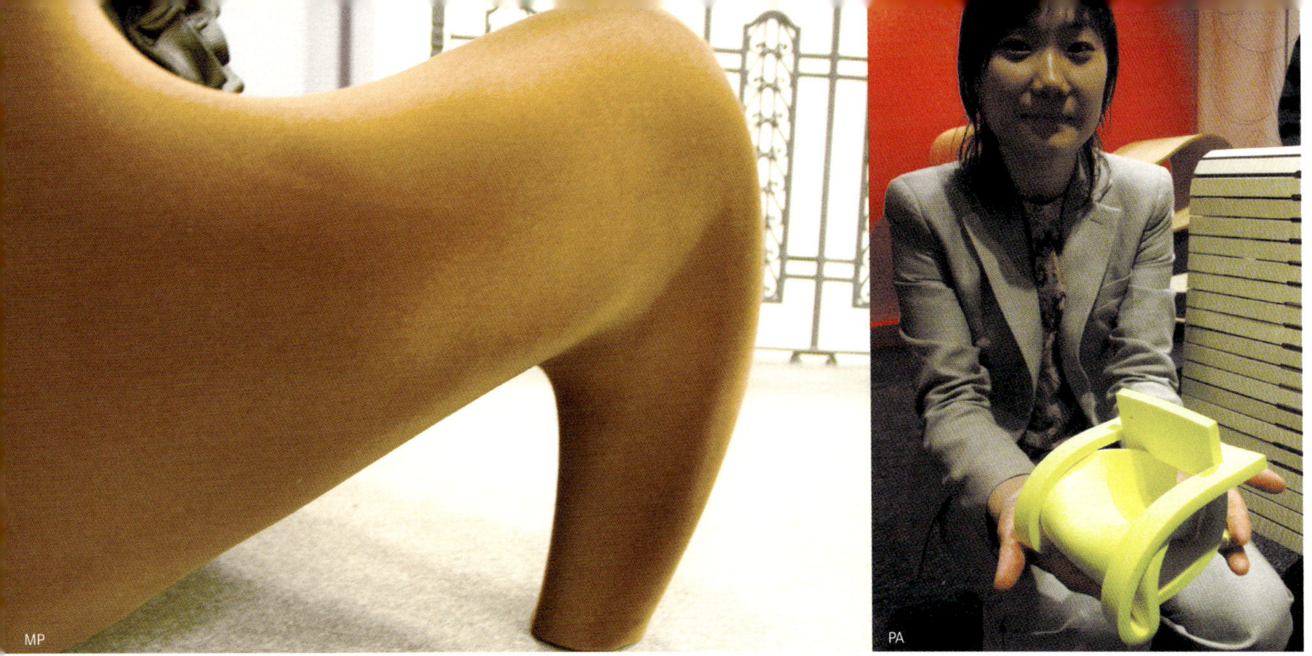

The Silly Side @ Tutto BeNe   Hong-Ik University @ Satellite

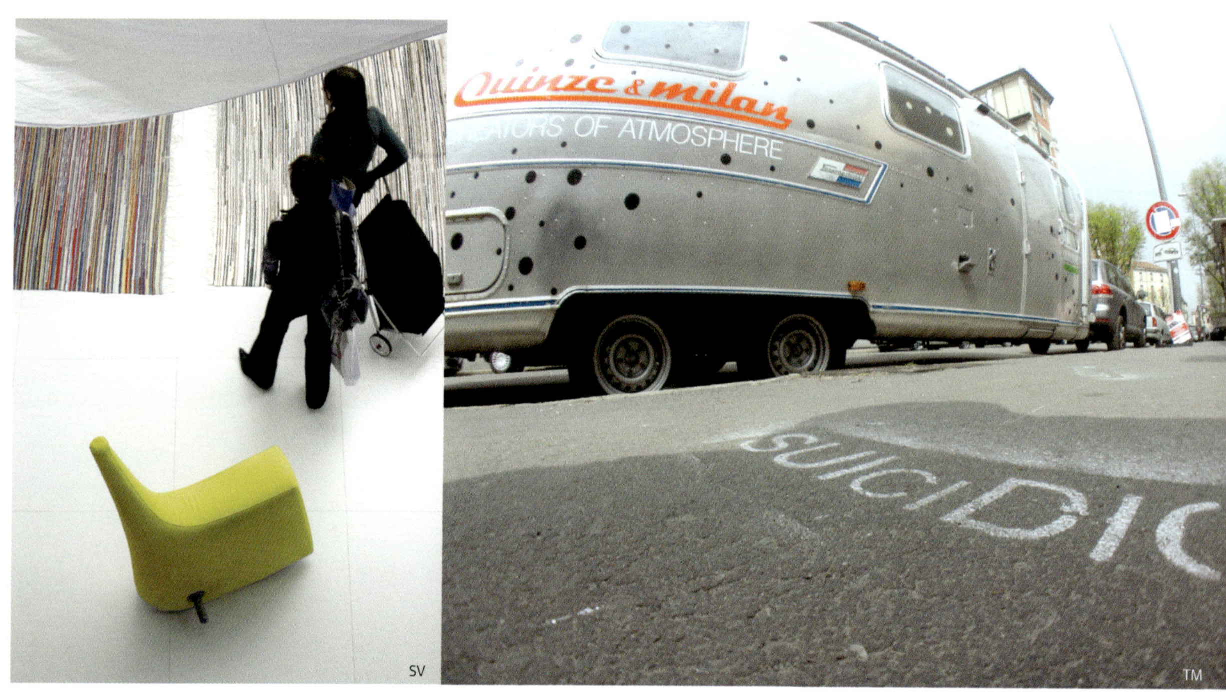

Campeggi

Quinze&Milan

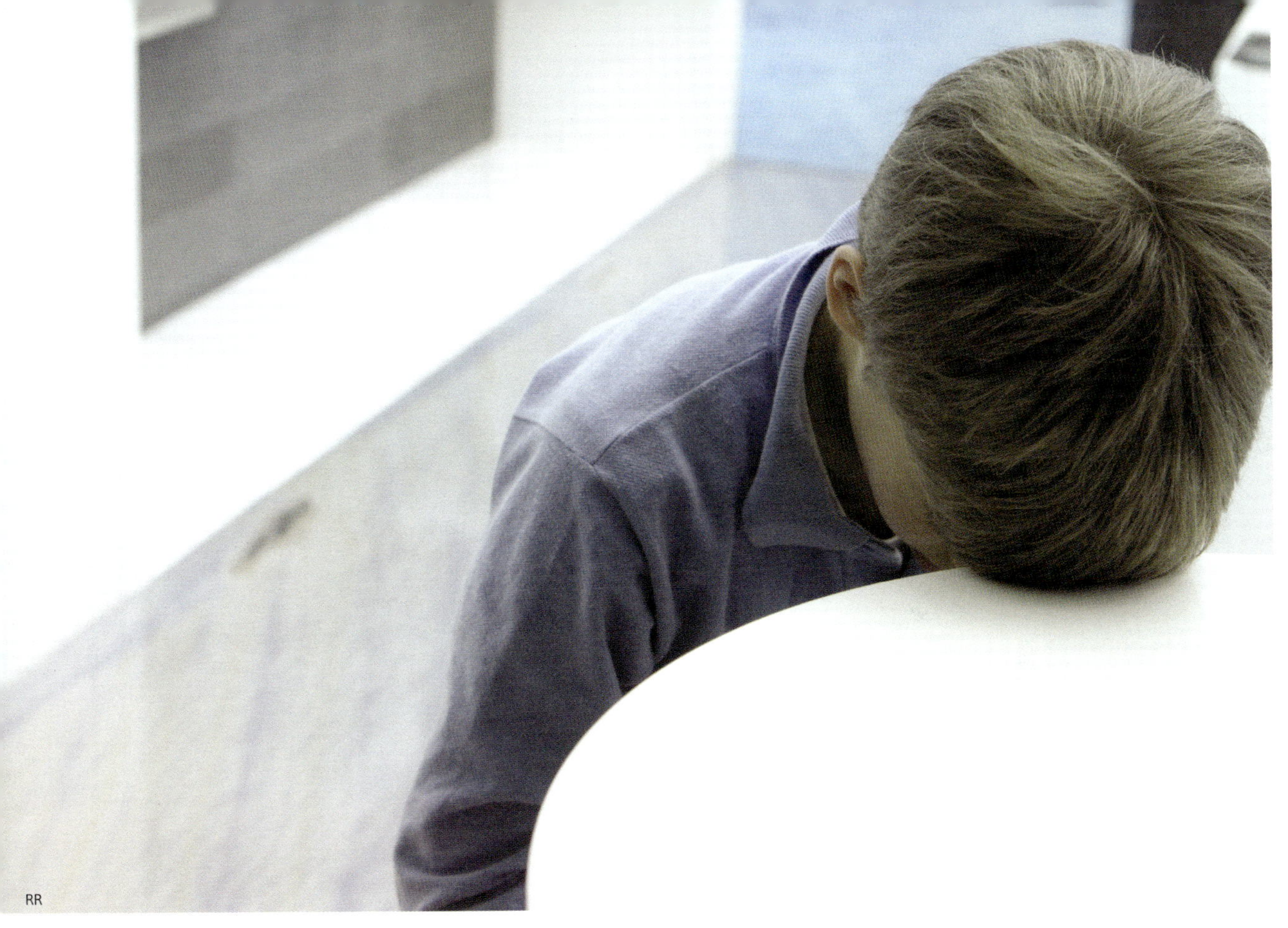

RR

@ Fiera

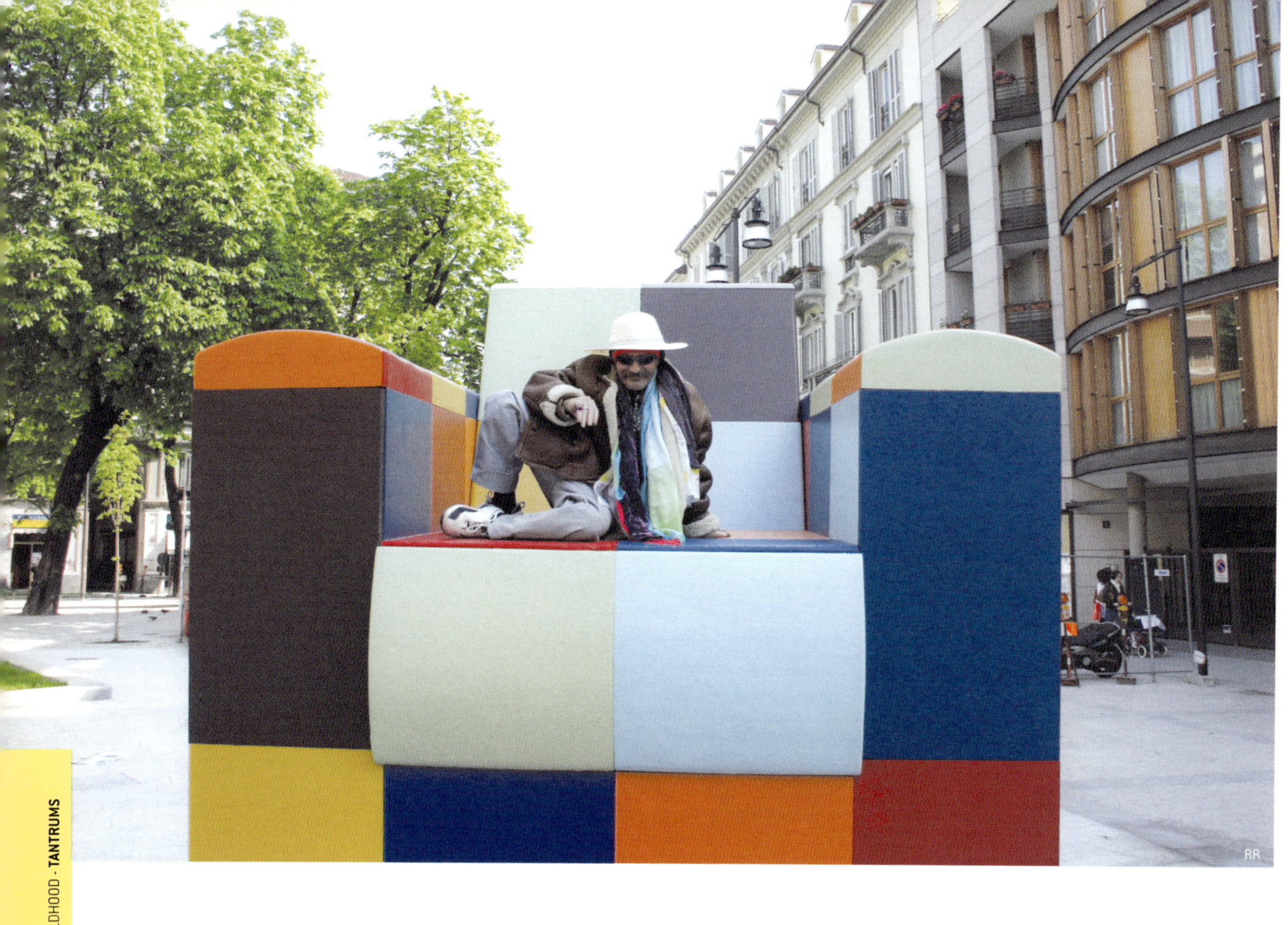

Nicoletti installation

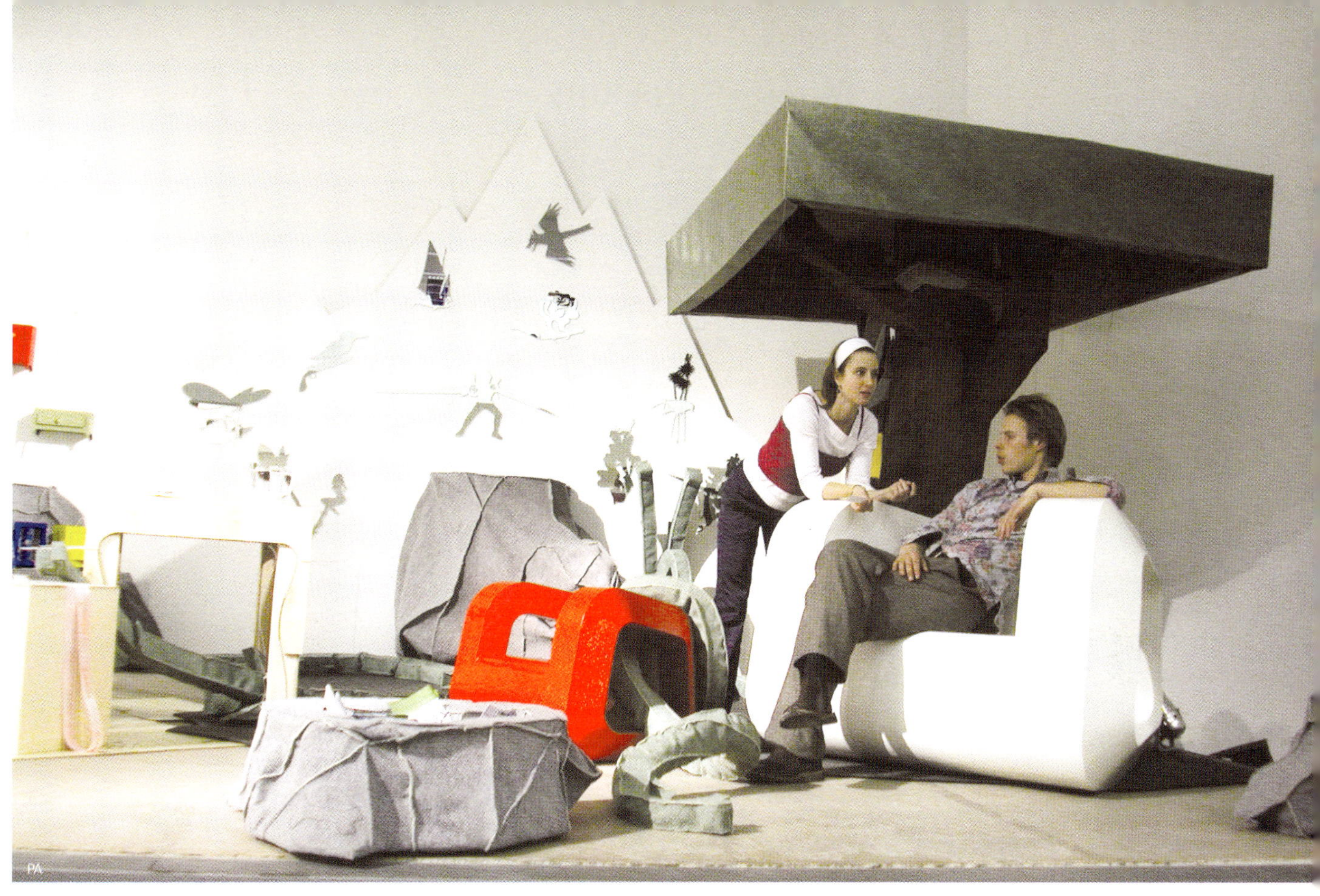

Recreation Enterprises @ Tutto BeNe

> ZONA TORTONA KIDS

THE SENSE OF DESIGN FOR KIDS

A.PR.I. (Projects for childwood) and Recapito Milanese (Public Relations and Press Agency)
promoted the only event, to coincide with Milan's 2004 Furniture Fair, that presented researches,
projects, materials and products, created by **"sensitive to childhood"** companies and designers,
to help children develop their creativity and structural ability.

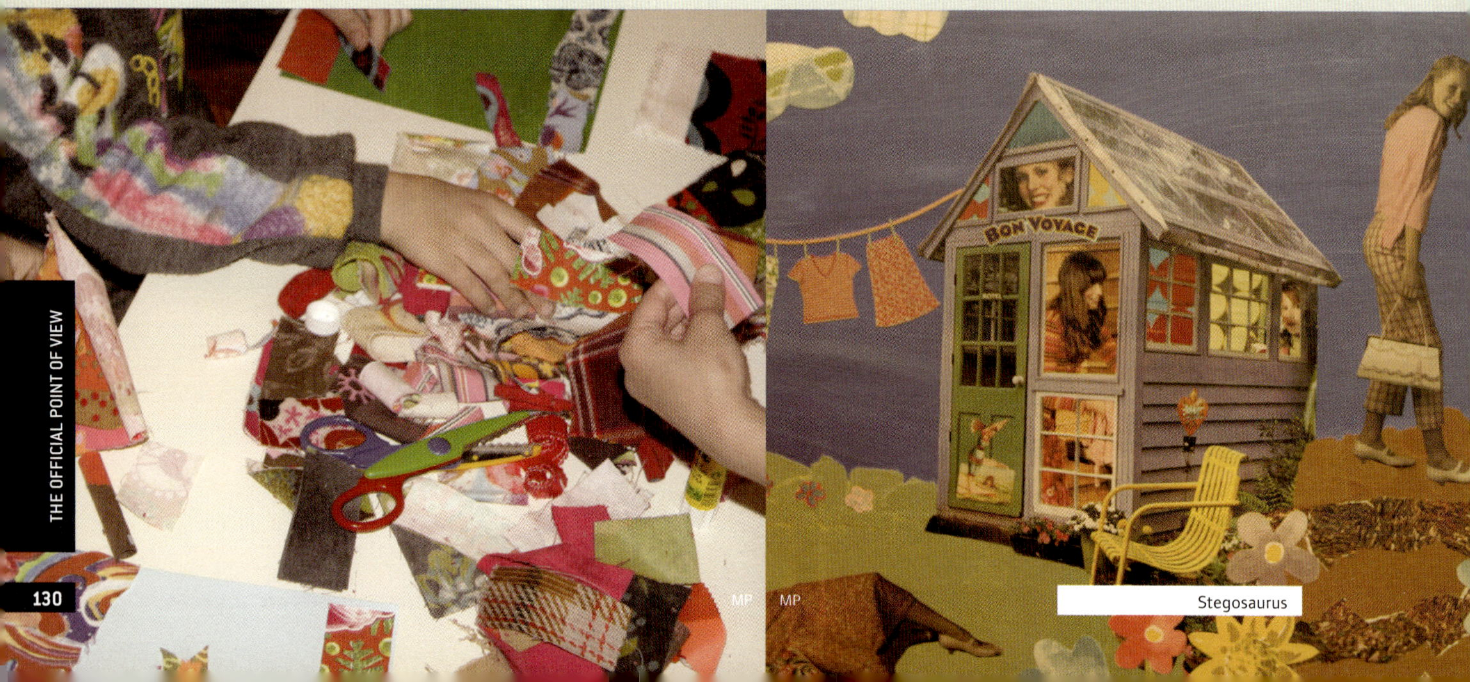

Stegosaurus

The exhibition included a ludic and interactive path, an exposition of objects and a hospitality service for kids, and is part of Zona Tortona's happenings.

The exhibition was divided into three interactive and expositive areas: the "disguising area", the "house of things" and the "nature laboratory".

The event gave the opportunity to start a qualitative research that mainly involved children between 5 and 12 years old: on the basis of a collection of pictures that children could take during the events of the "Fuori Salone", it was possible to identify, and then critically interpret, their point of view about the design world.

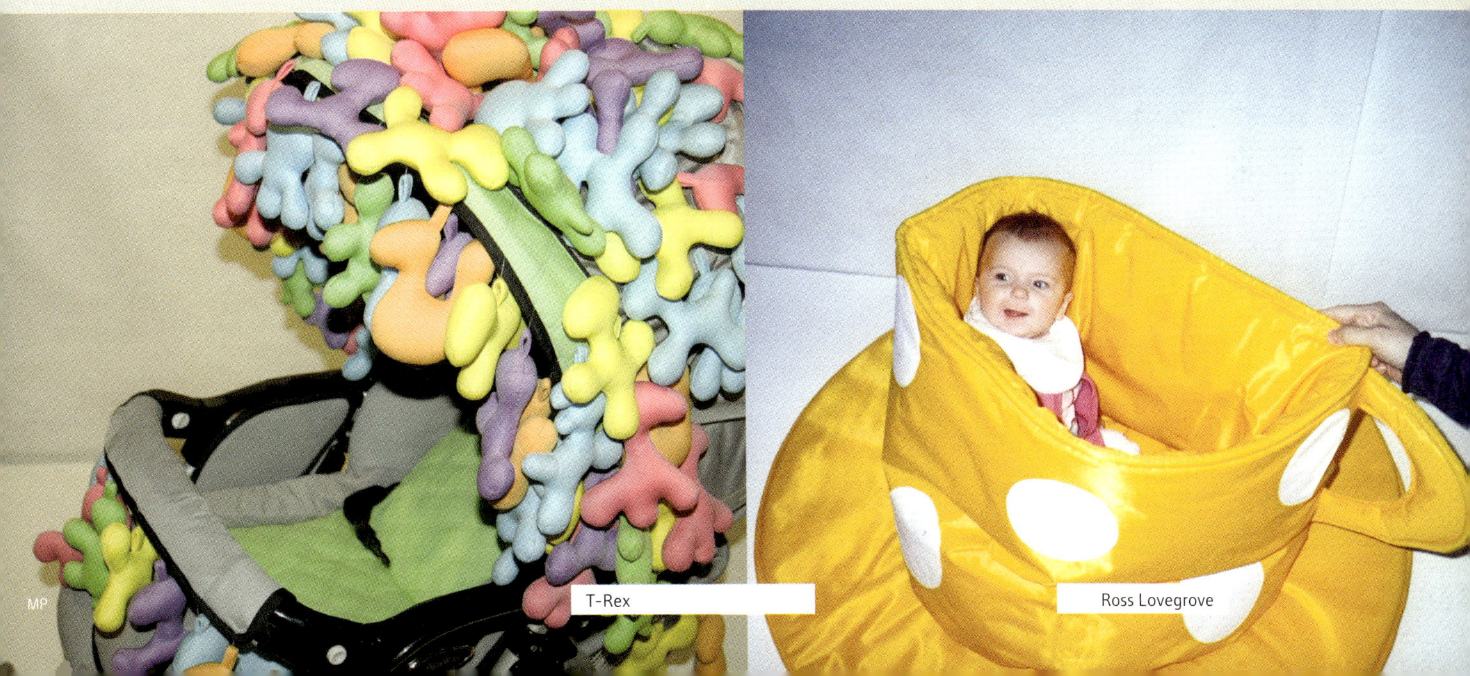

T-Rex

Ross Lovegrove

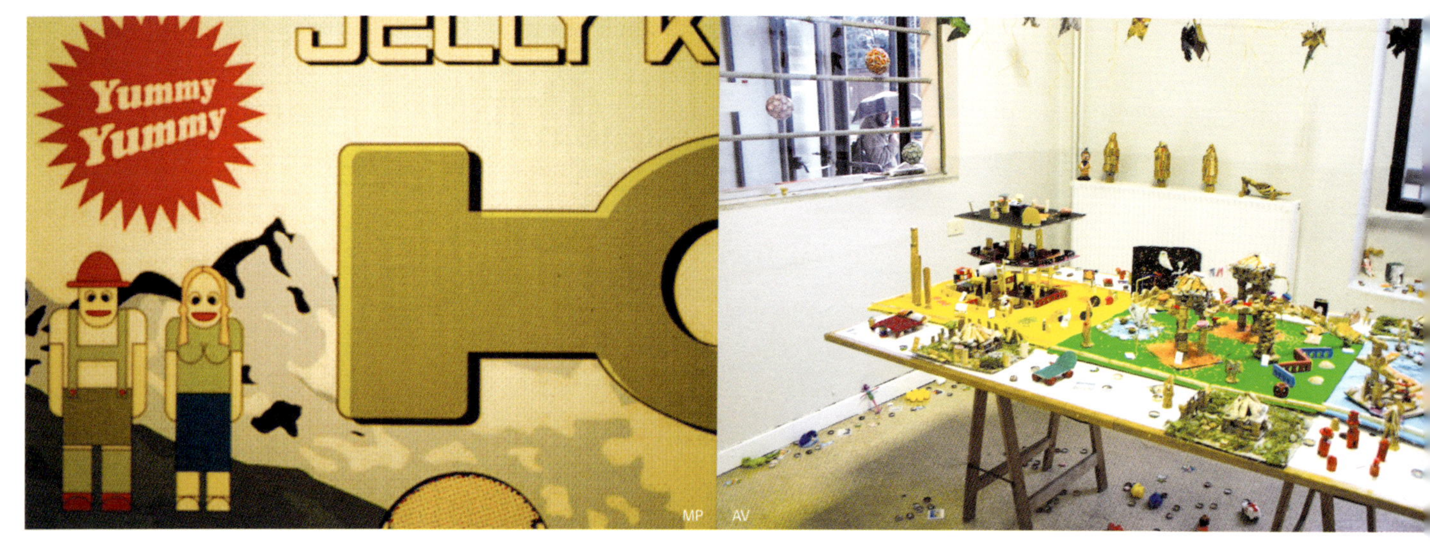

@ Beck's prize

Ludocasa

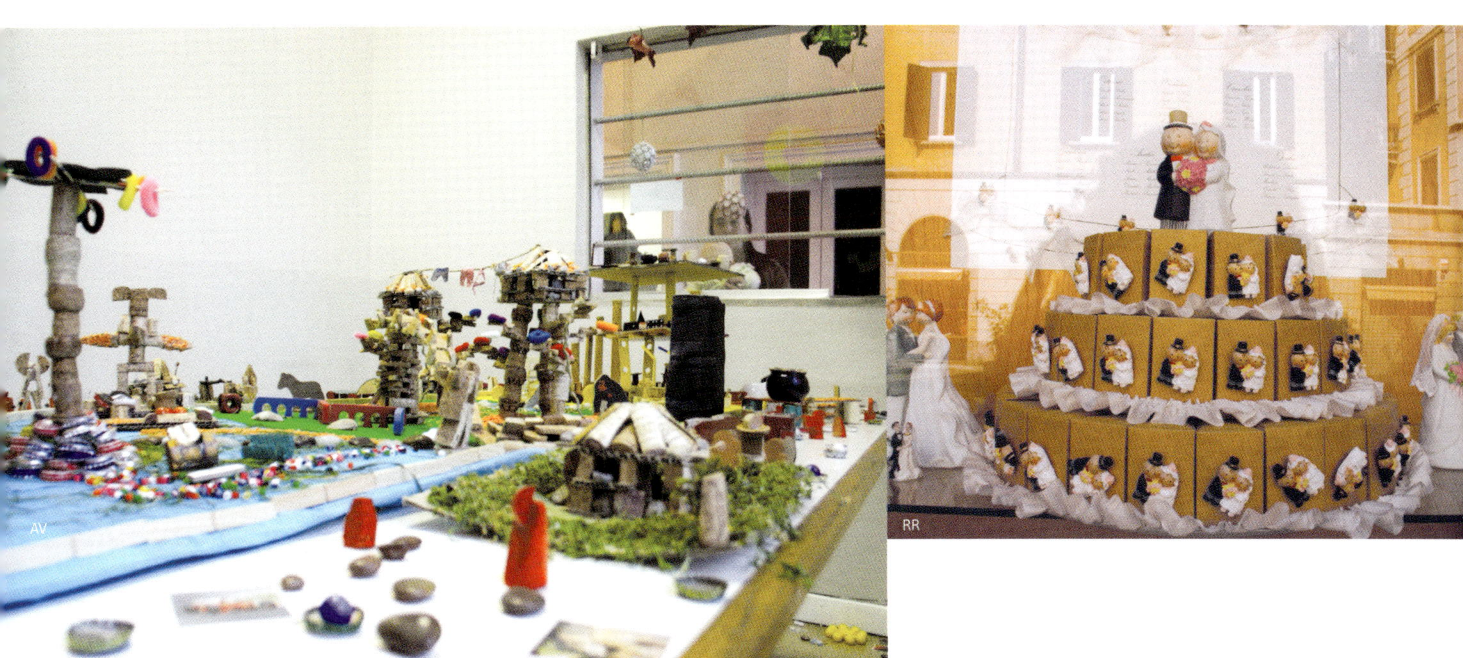

Milano´ shop

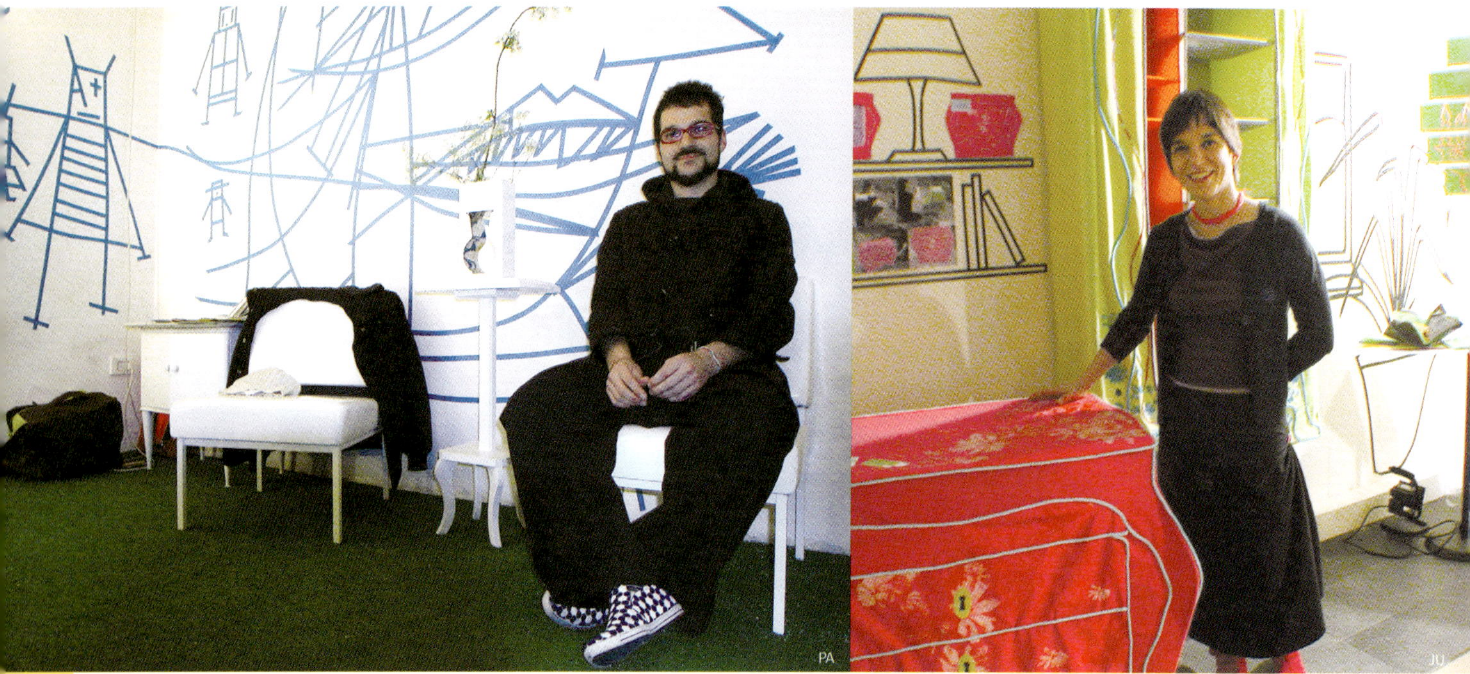

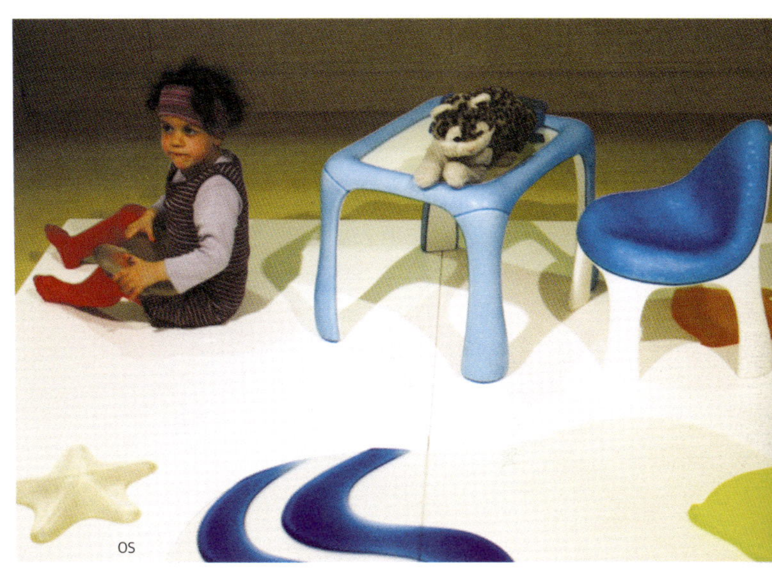

Keiko Oyabu & Technogel

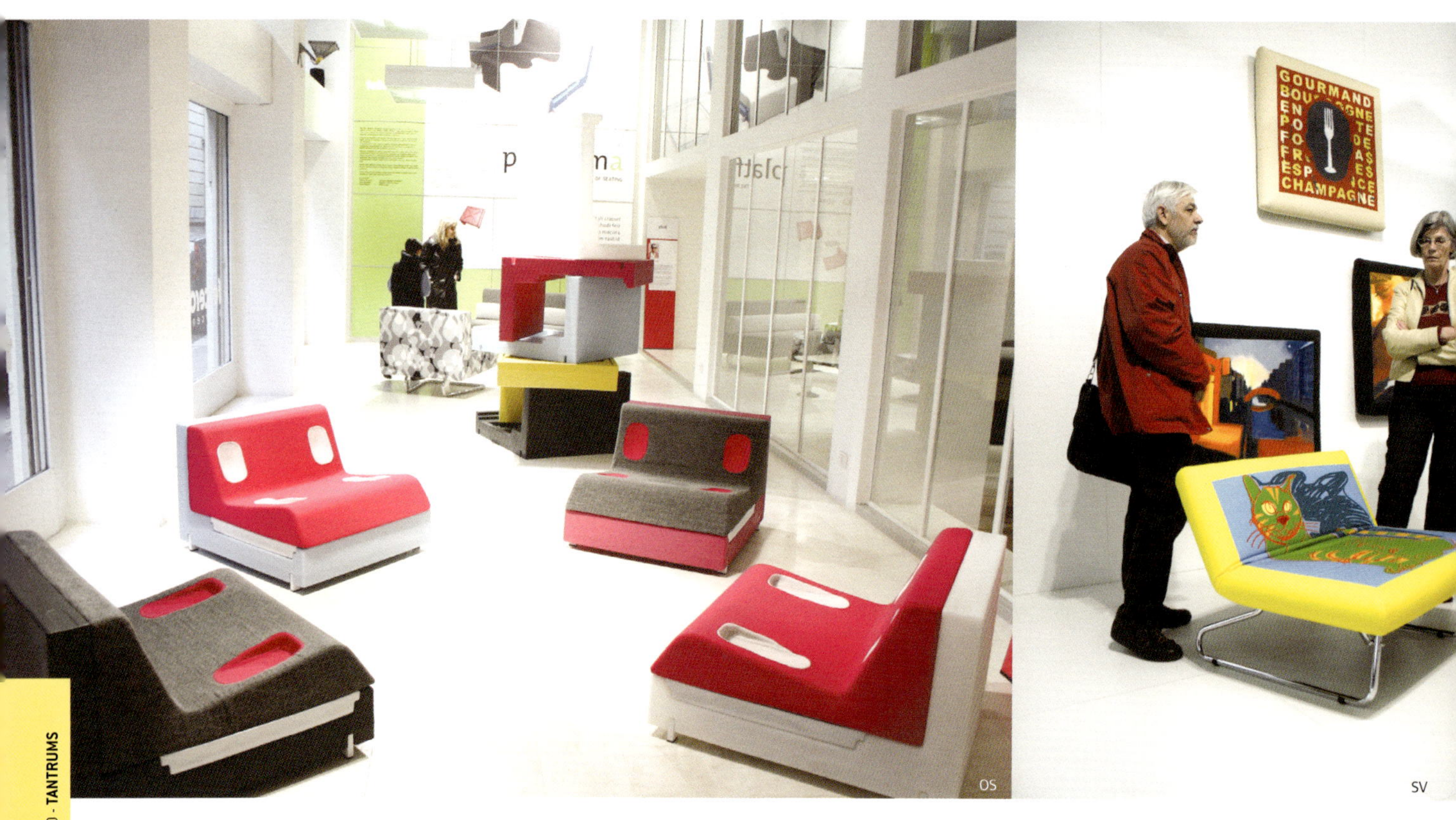

OS

SV

Karim Rashid for Felice Rossi

Campeggi

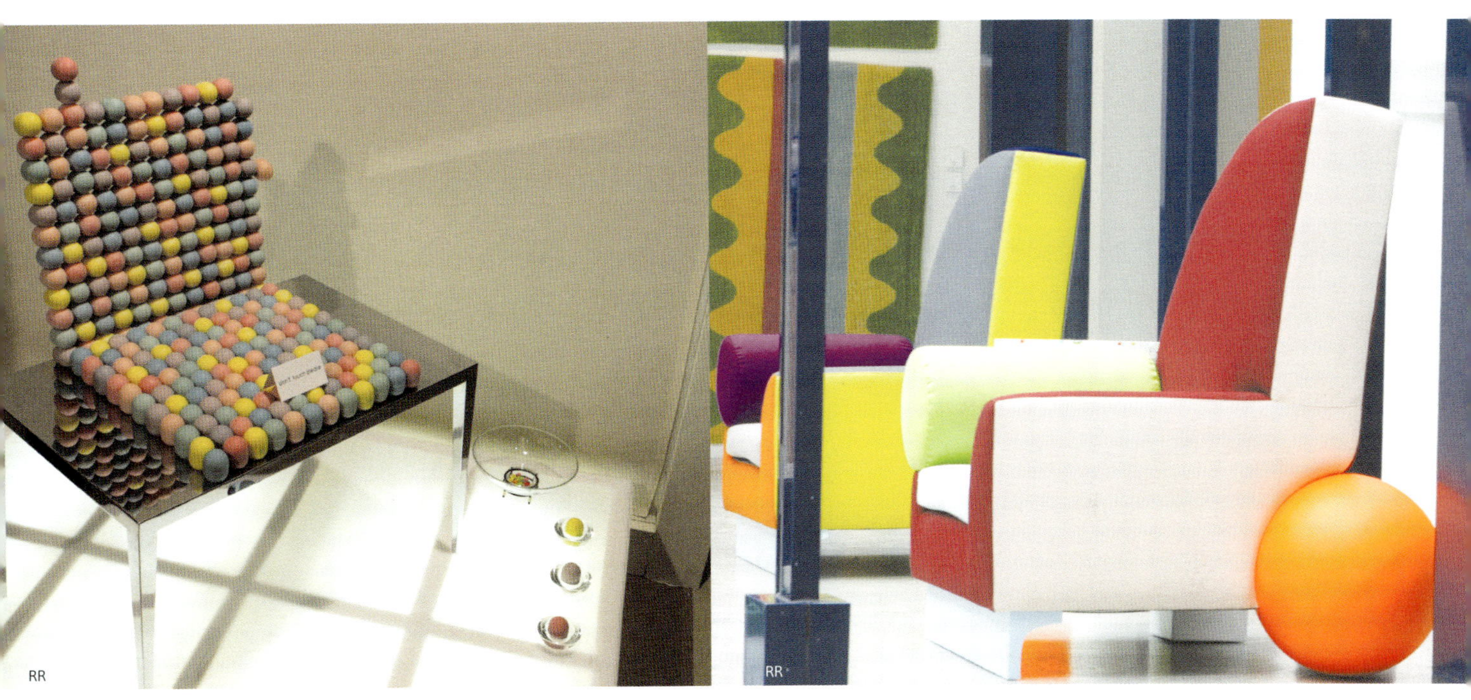

Plustic Minustic   Menphis

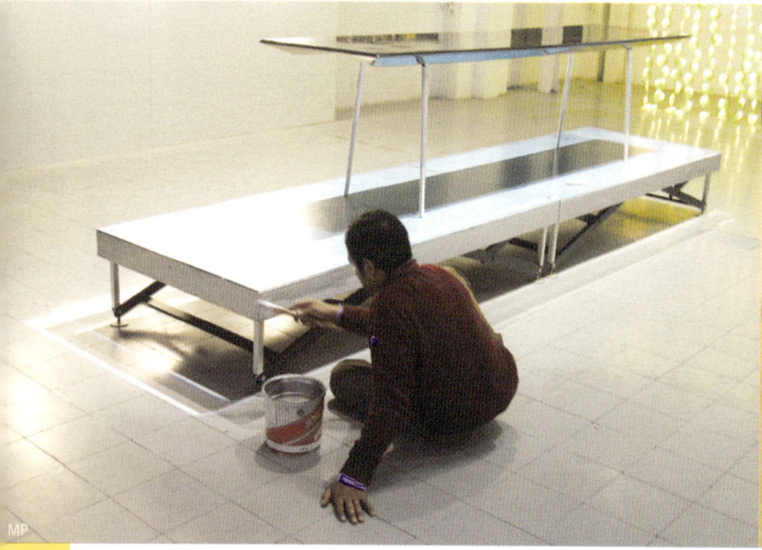

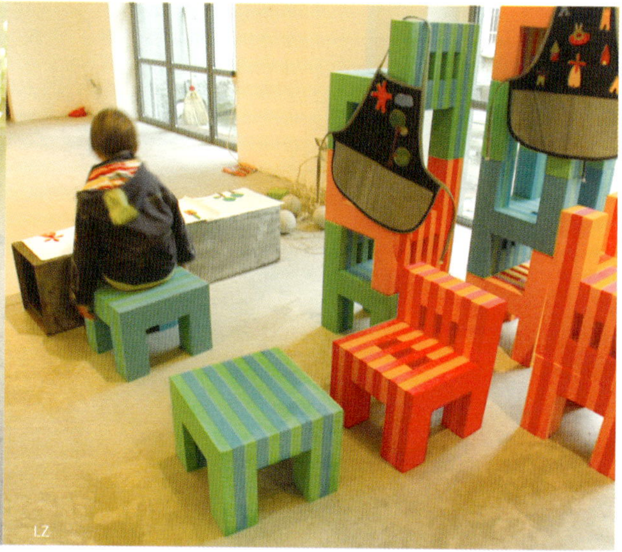

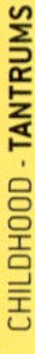

138   TableU_O' by Odile Decq with Domeau&Peres @ VIA

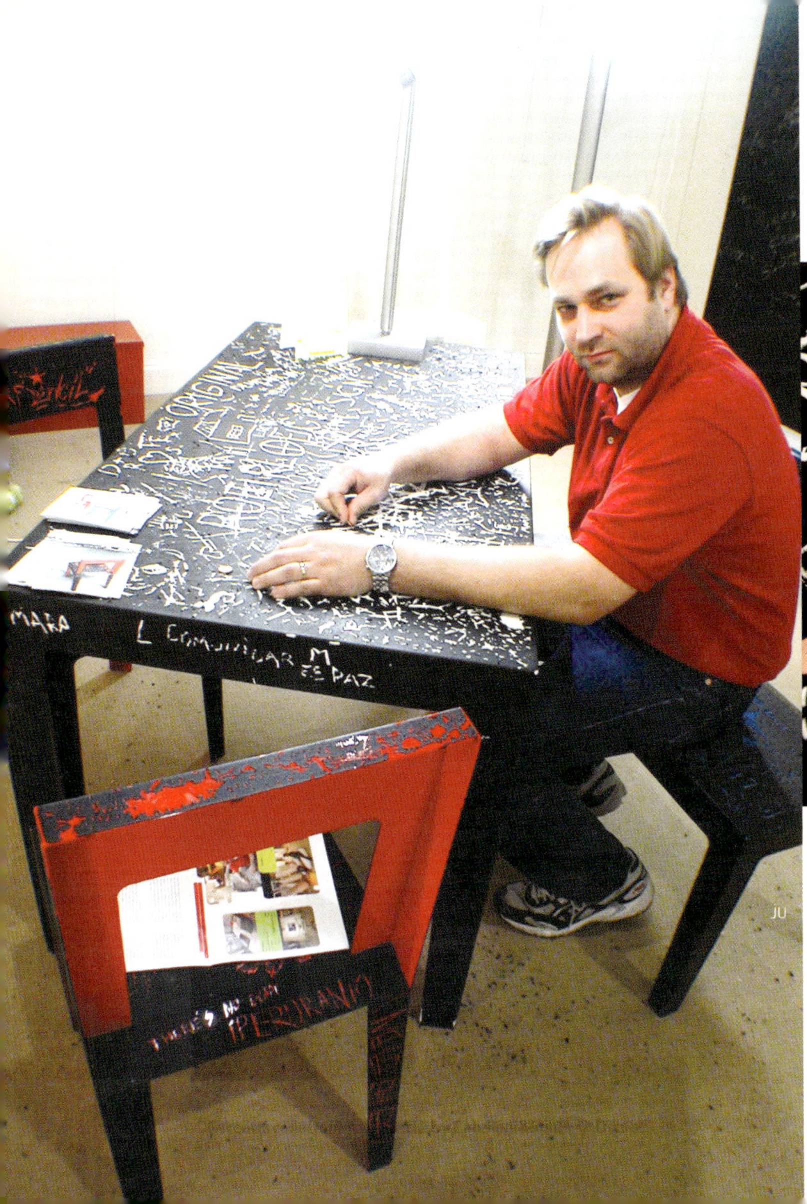

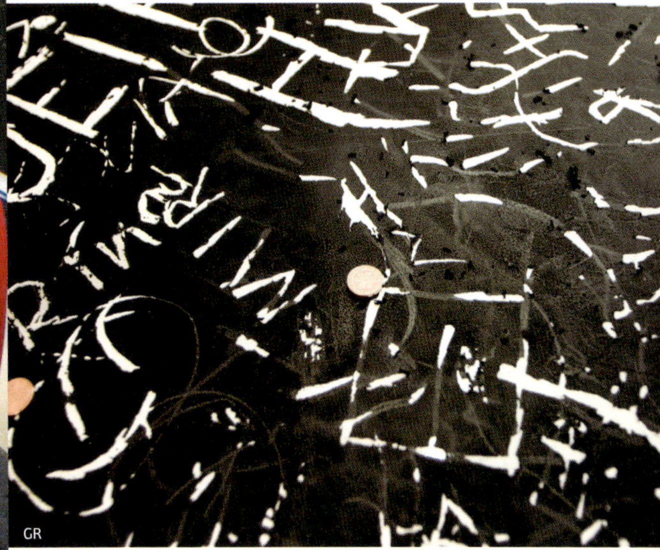

David Caspar Schaefer for MIR-Studio.com

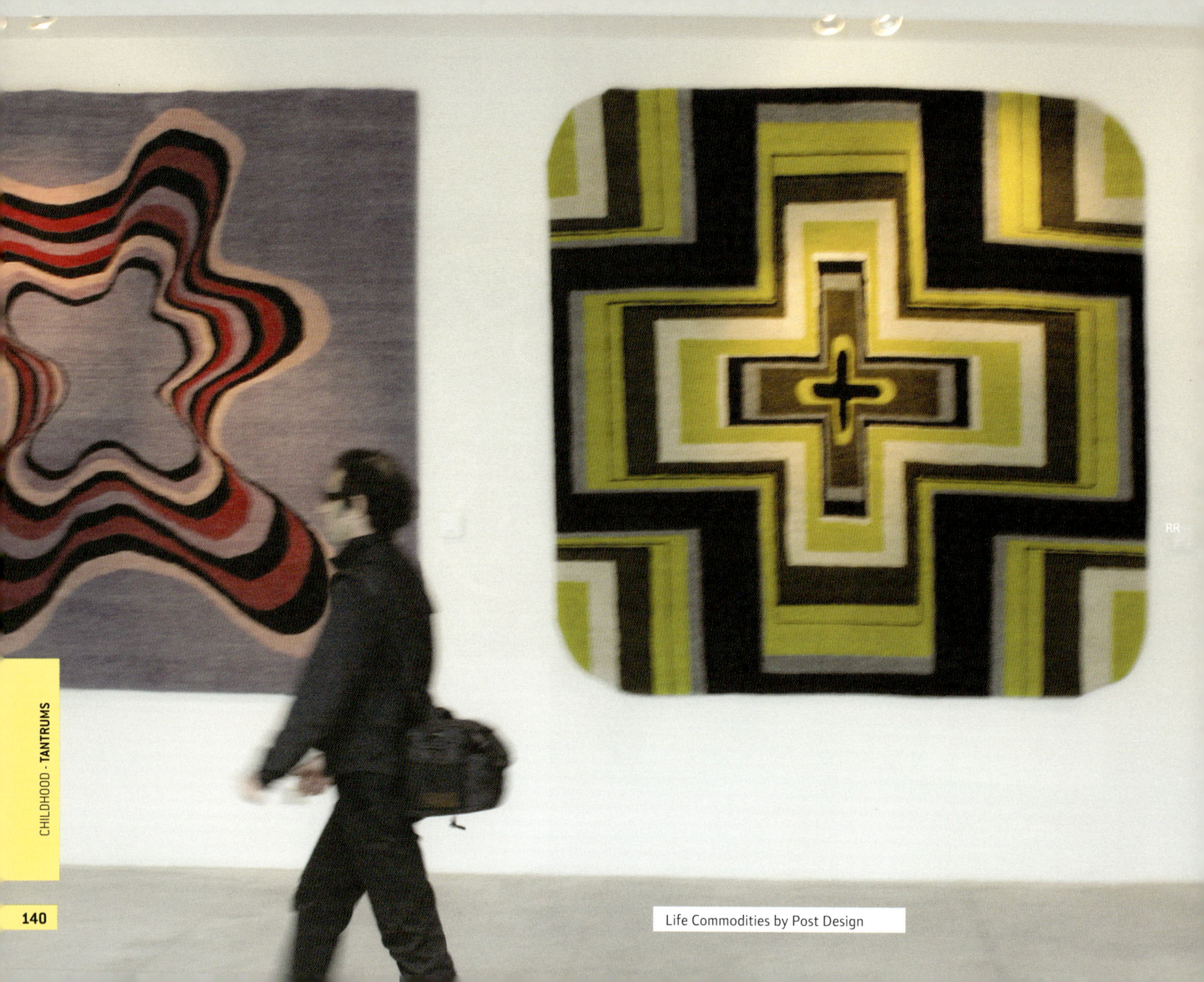

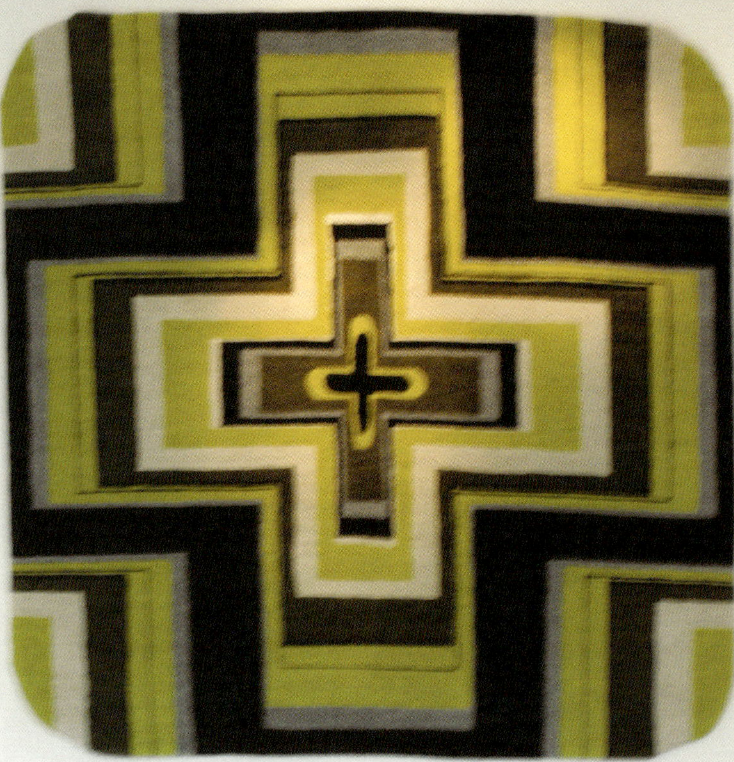

Life Commodities by Post Design

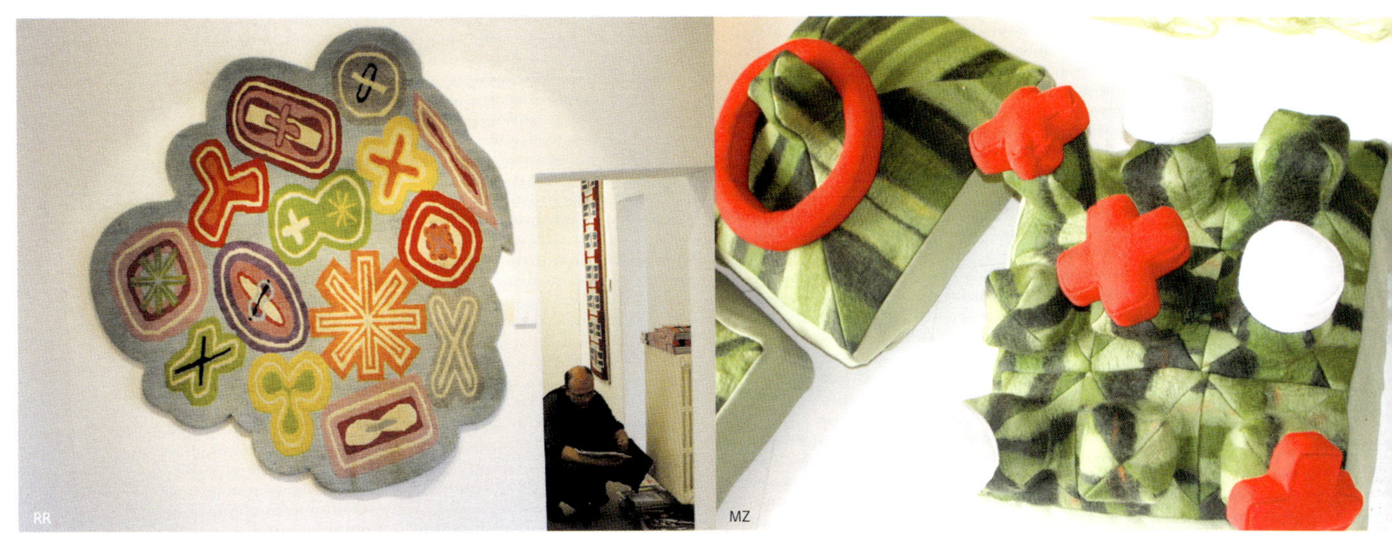

Design London @ Zona Tortona

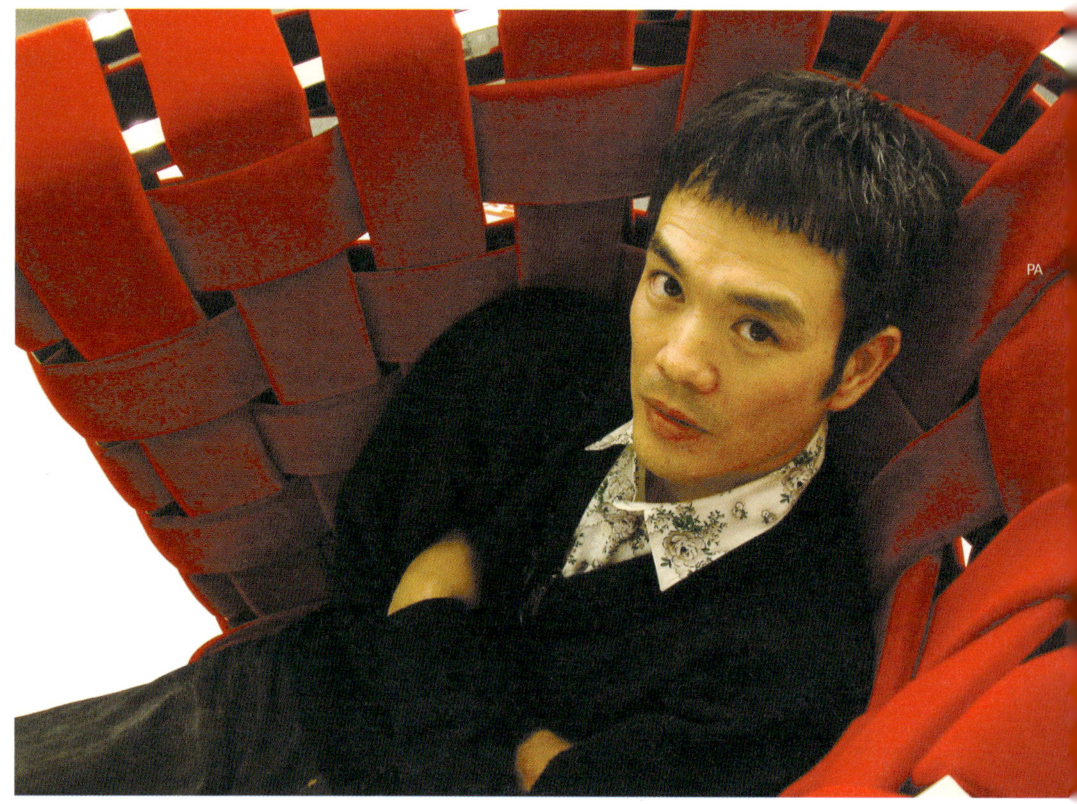

Masashi Sawada @ NU light

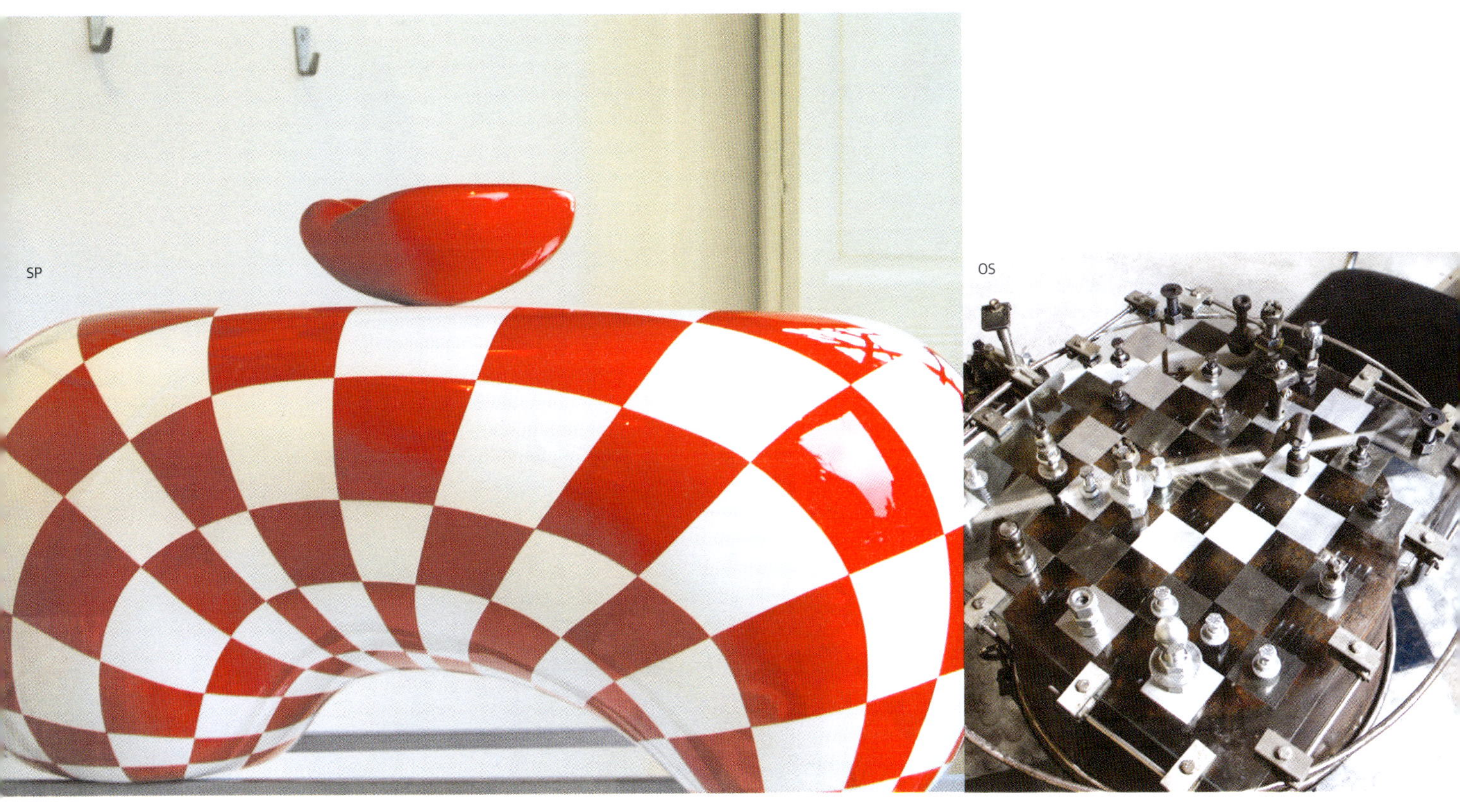

Leblon Delienne

Lucio Forte and Francesca Albanesi

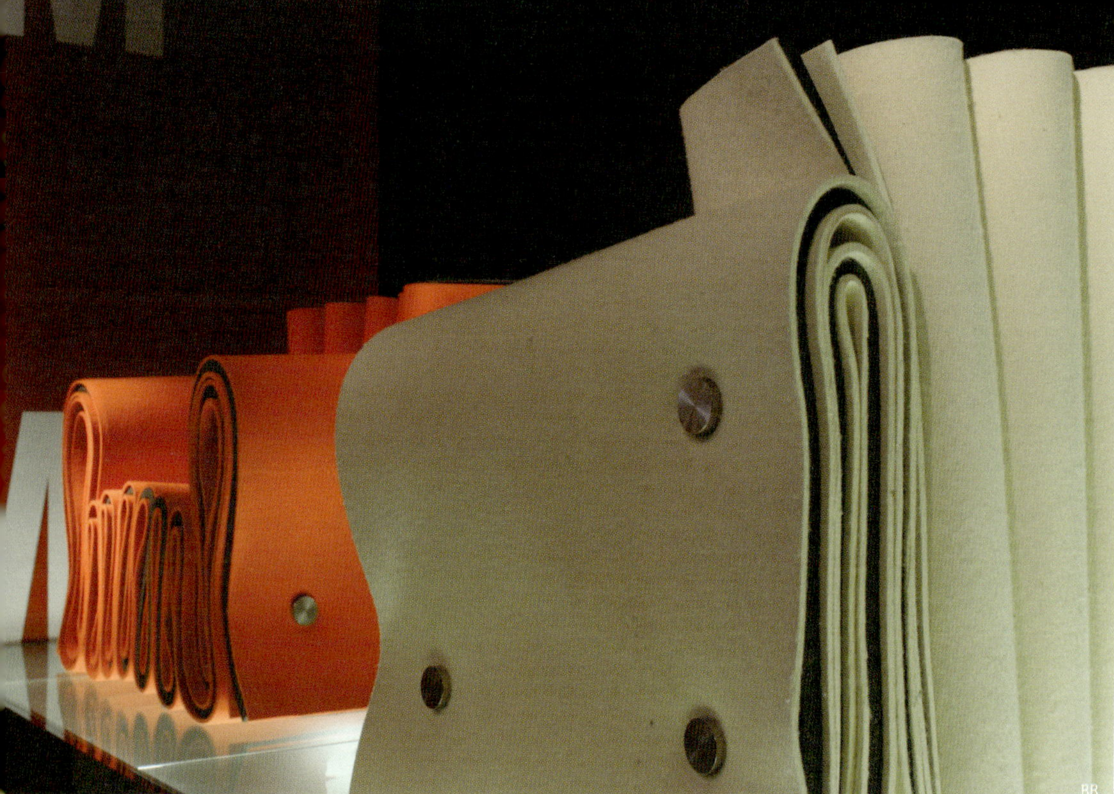

144

"Joseph' chair" by Lothar Windels for Parentesi Quadra

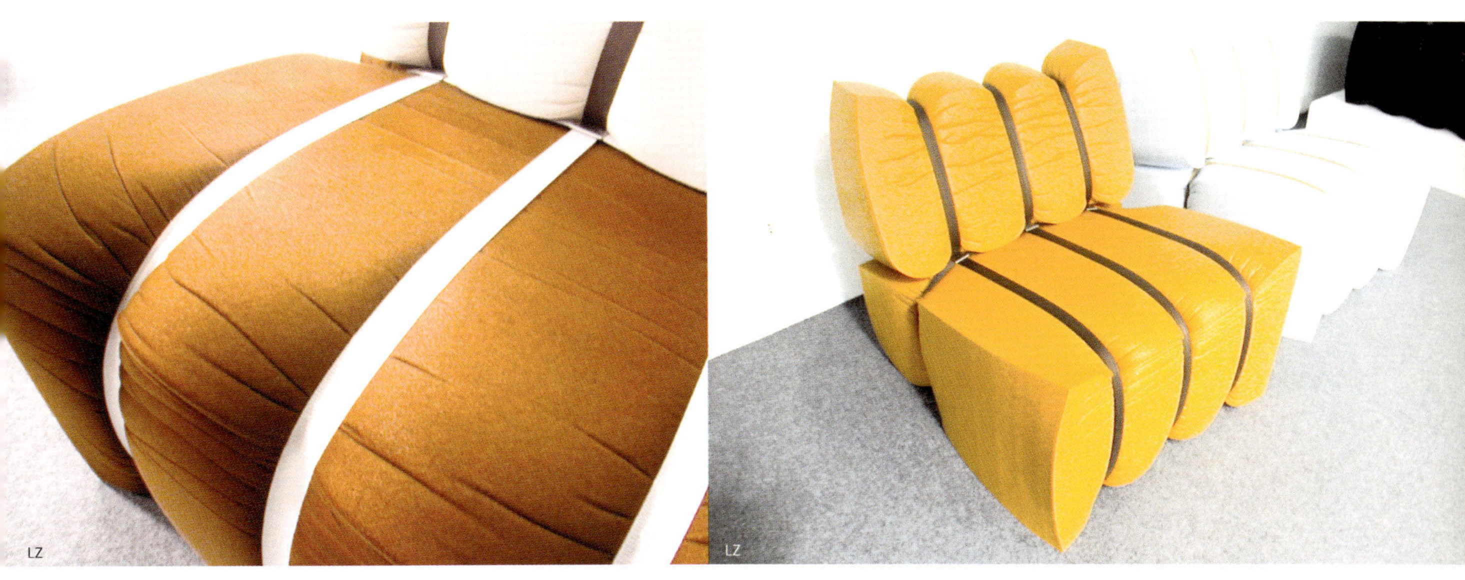

The Silly Side @ Tutto BeNe

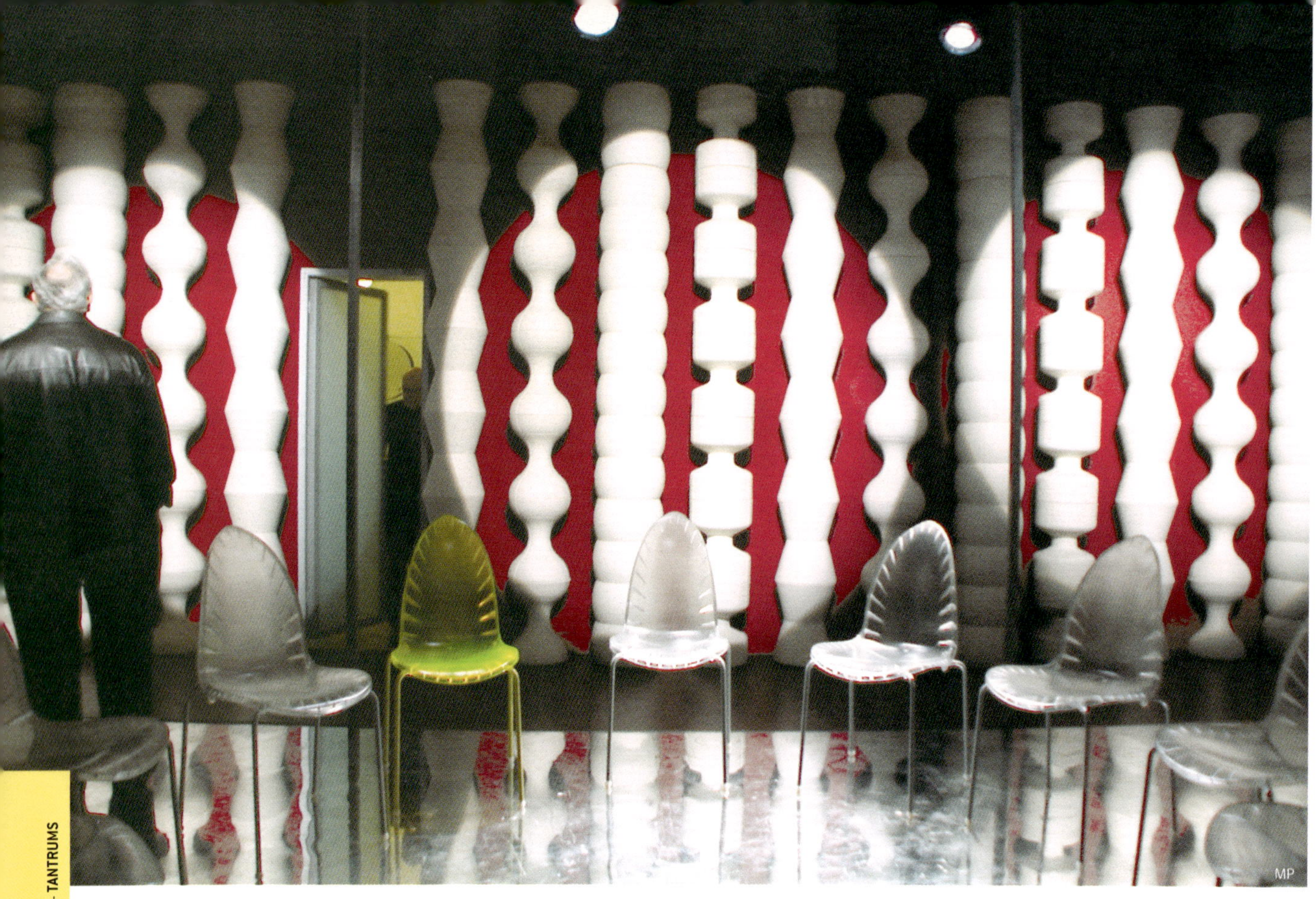

146   Driade Aleph

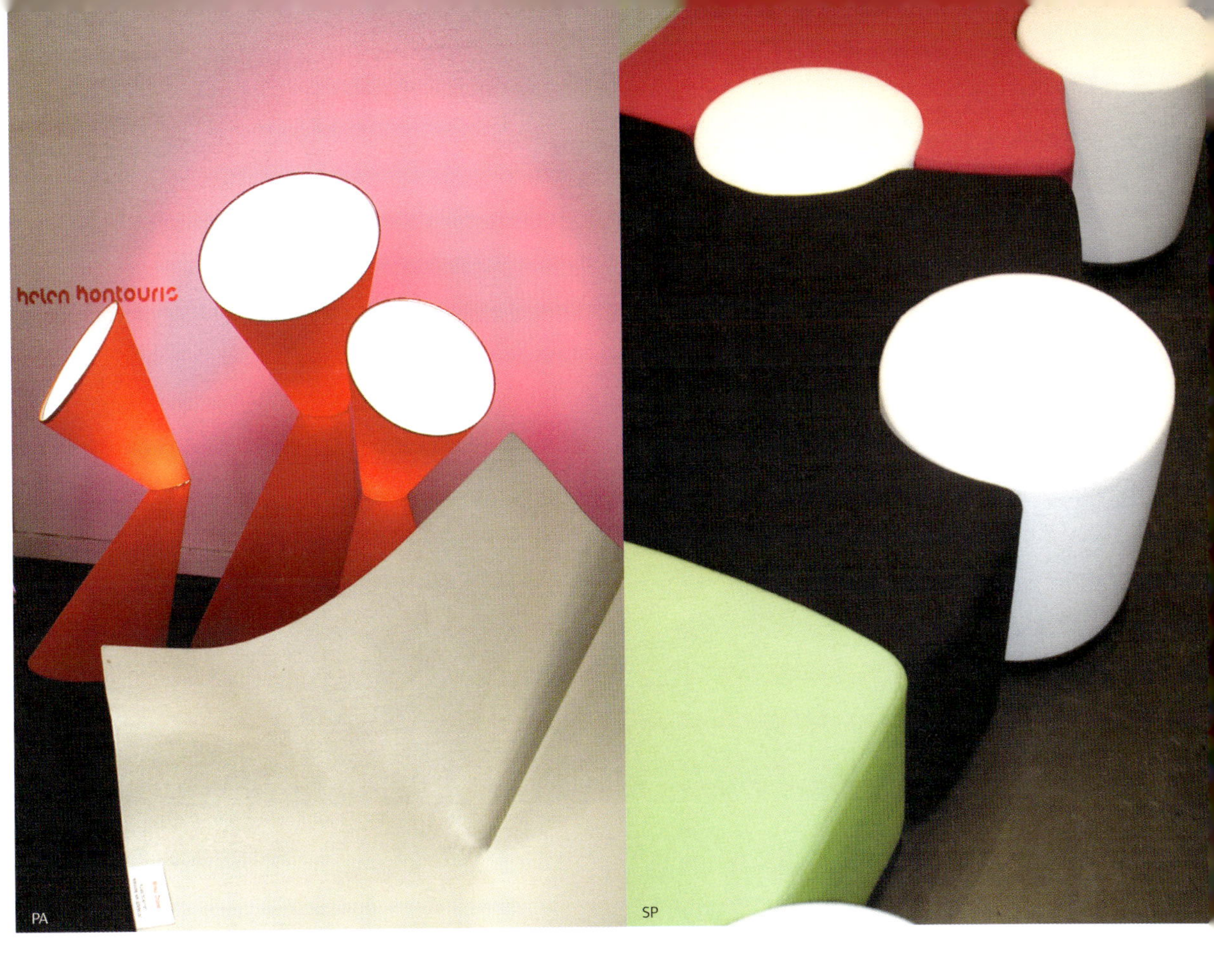

Helen Kontouris design @ Satellite   Toys sofa by Arflex

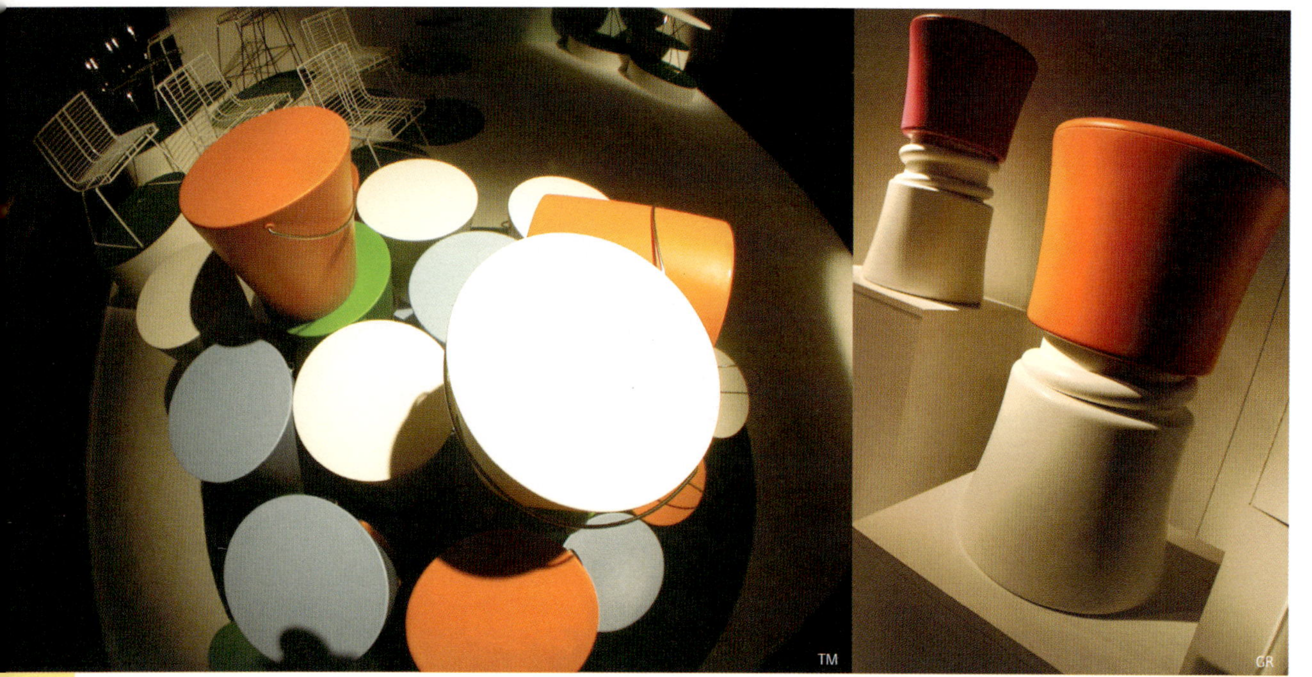

Max Design @ Zona Tortona

Ghaadé

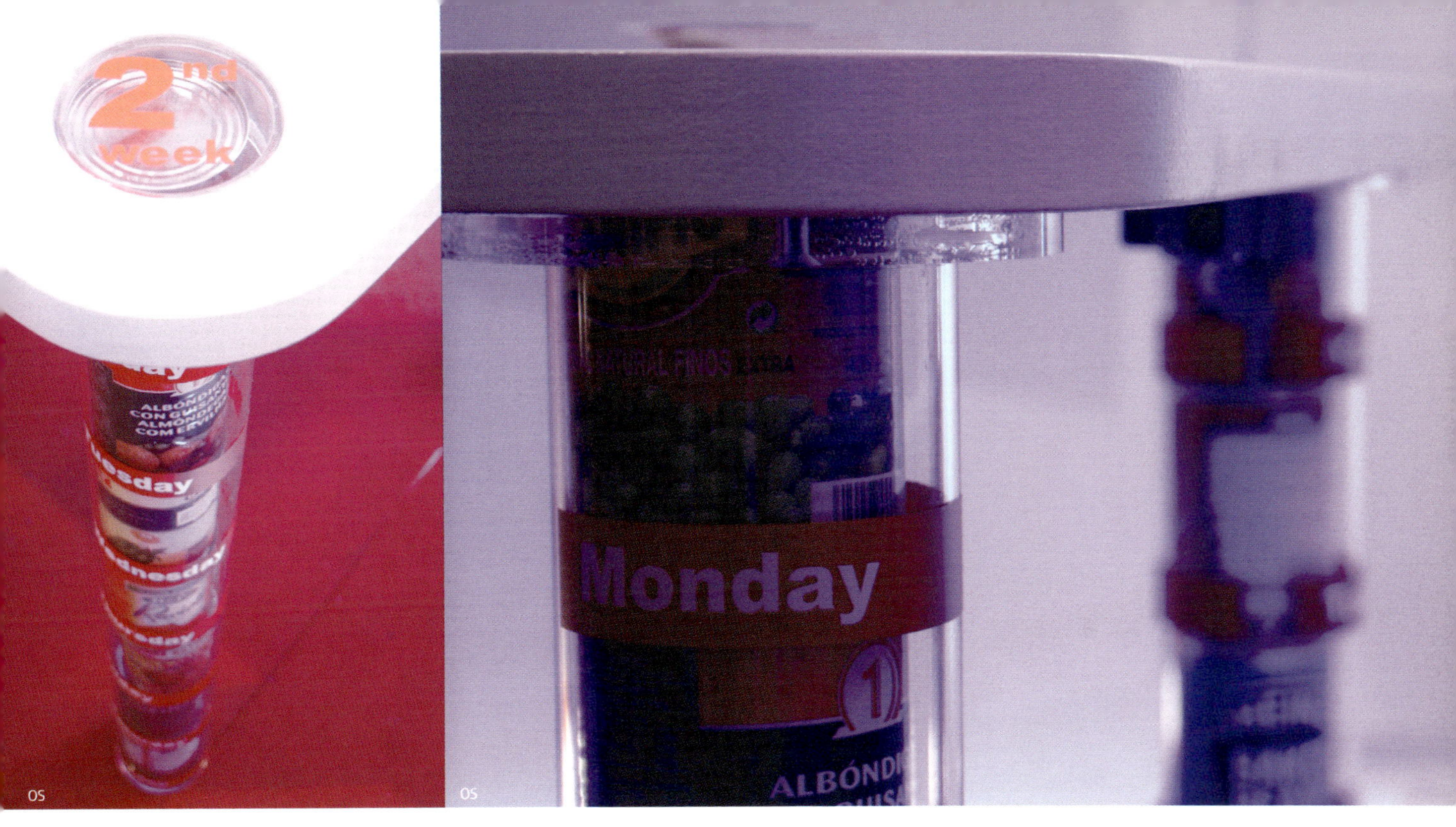

Stone Design

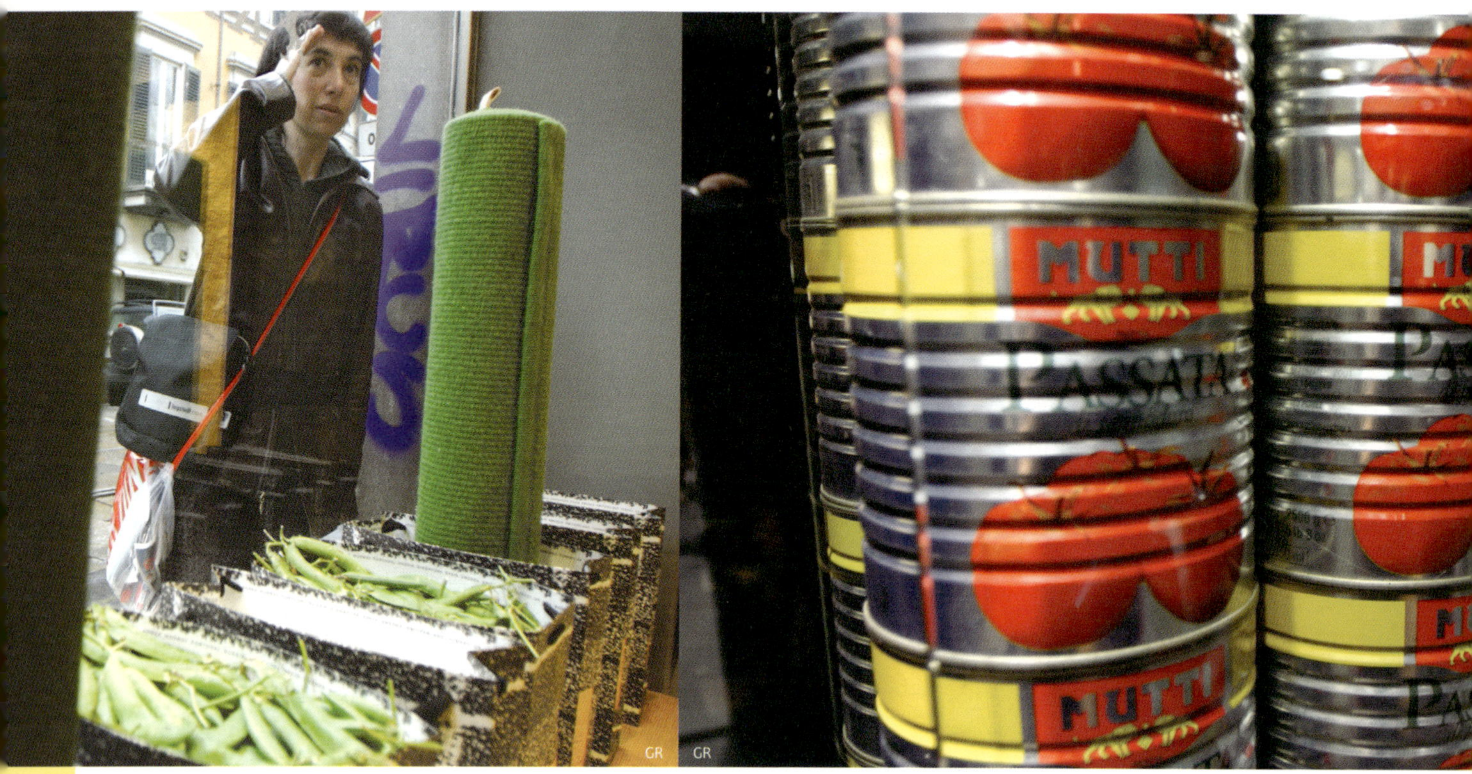

Kasthall showroom

Elma

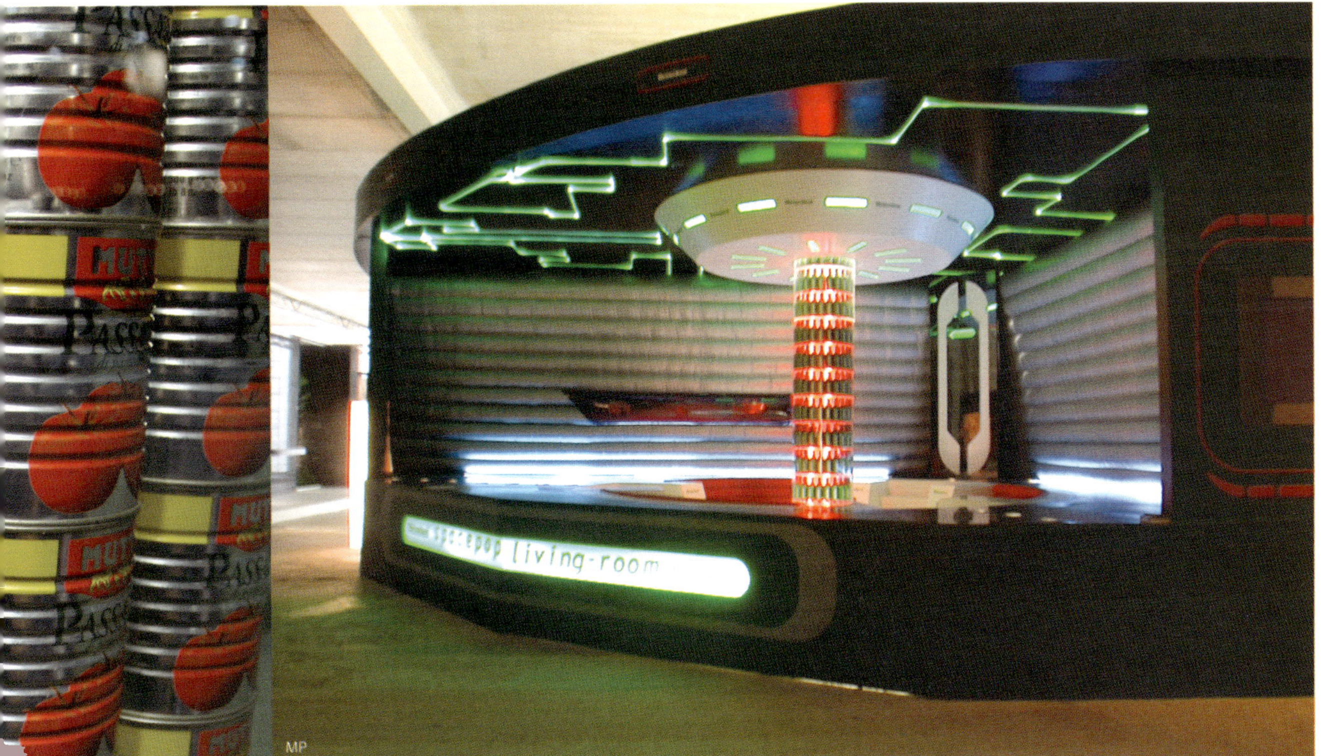

Heineken installation @ Zona Tortona

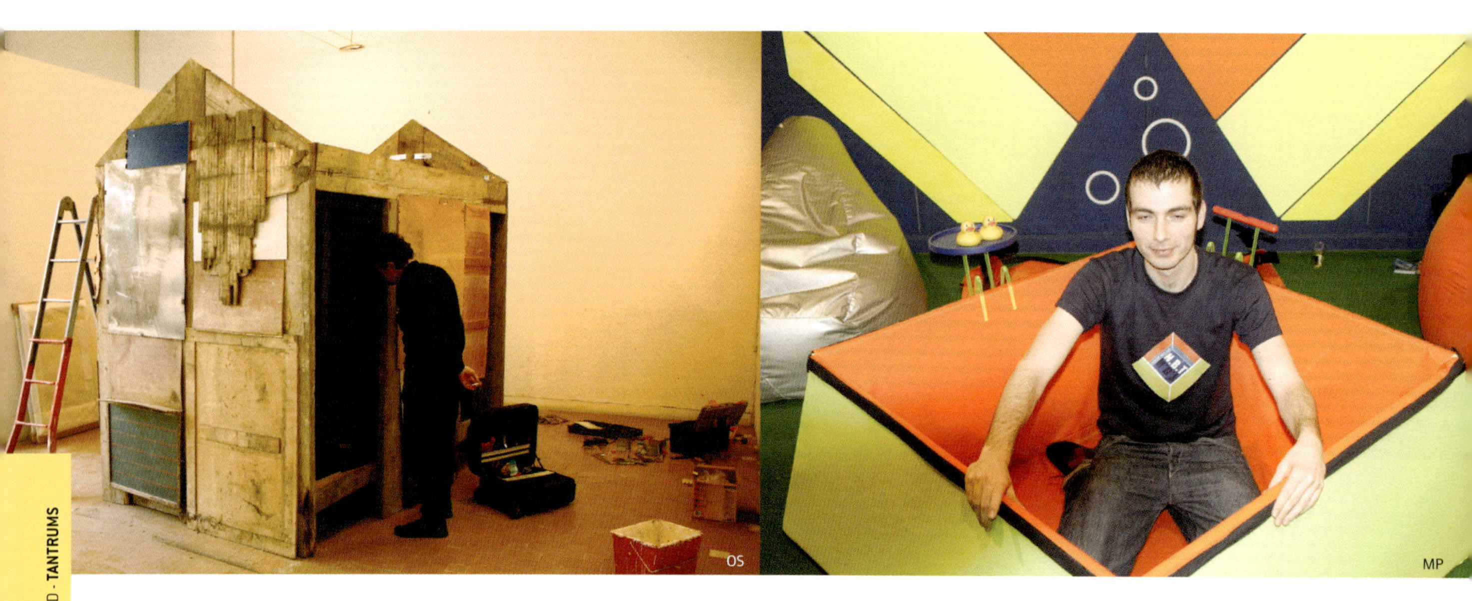

@ Fabbrica Del Vapore

Modan @ Satellite

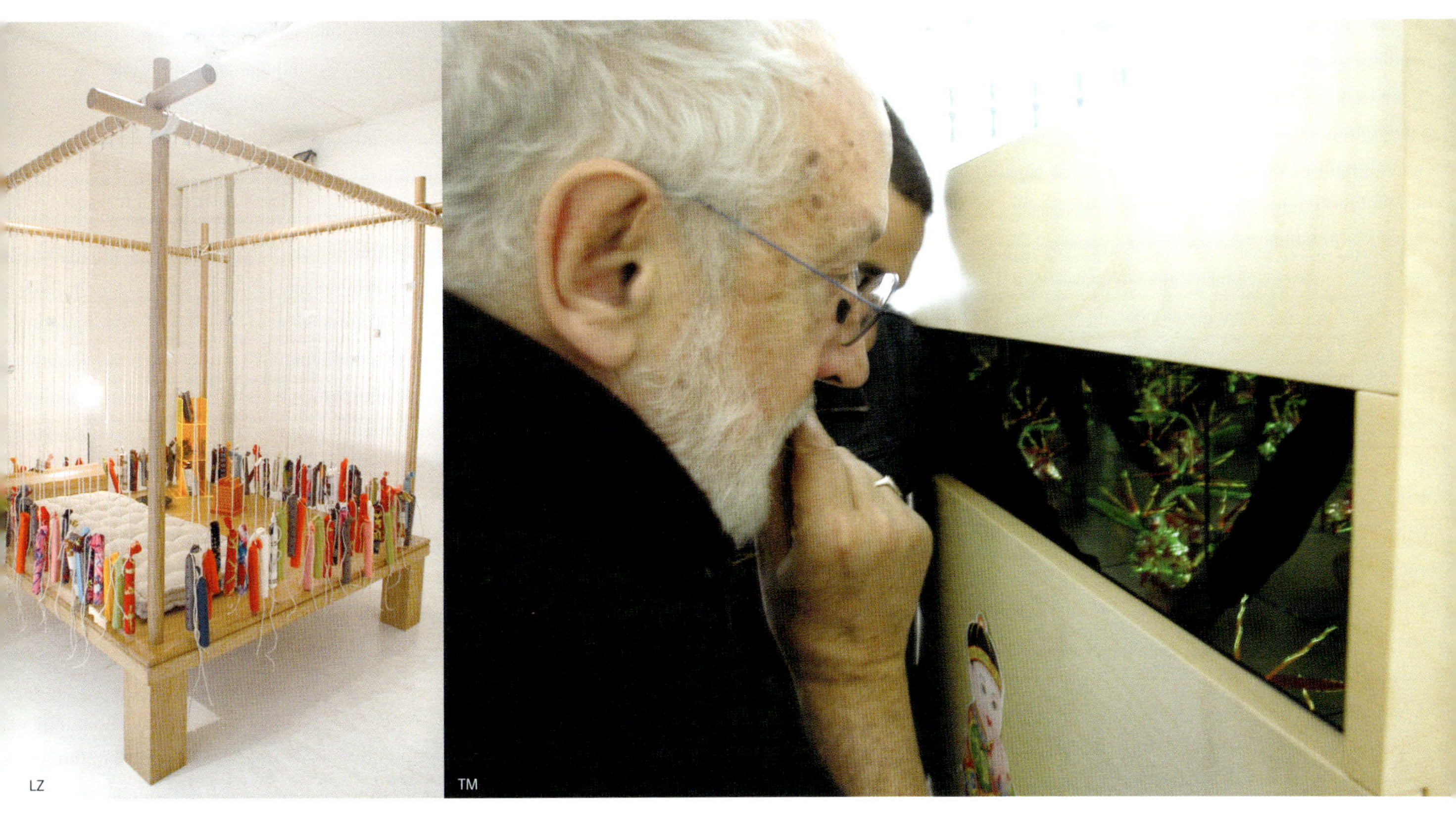

Riposi by Andrea Branzi and Ettore Sottsass

Andrea Branzi

> THE HOUSE OF THE FUTURE

HOW DO YOU ENVISAGE THE HOUSE OF THE FUTURE AND THE FUTURE ITSELF?

I don't know about the house of the future, but I do know that the future is bound to be extraordinary.

The future is made of unique things. The design of the future is the design of the present, which privileges original items as opposed to copies.

I remember a stunning exhibition by Issy Miyake at Vitra Design Museum in Berlin, where people could cut their own personal and unique lothes out of a roll of cloth available to them for that purpose. It is the concept of unique items for each one of us in the same way as art and handcrafted products are something unique.

Our relationship with an object is the same as the relationship between two friends, between two individuals (individual = inseparable).

It is therefore a unique relationship, made of feelings of jealousy and manias, just like a romantic relationship. In the past, a desk merely served a purpose and did not 'interact with us'.

It was used as a tool to write upon, it served a purpose and it would be disposed of when no longer needed.

Nowadays, the objects provide a psychological pleasure and that's the reason why I believe that the present is the most interesting time in the history of mankind.

As to a house, it has to look like the person living in it; it has to be a reflection of its owner's personality.

That is the reason why I always tend to get close to the people I design a house for, in order to understand what they are like. If this does not happen then the exercise will fail. Anyway, I do think that the house of the future will not require an architect's involvement.

GAETANOPESCE

The house of the future will be composed of simple, well lit spaces - made of ultralight, high-strength bio-engineered natural materials - which can be re-configured and re-proportioned with a breath of a gesture to accommodate any changing convivial or solitary scenario in a moment's notice. As a response to the ever-increasing premium on space, a new domestic luxury will be defined through our ability to inhabit a multi-dimensional home which is transformable in time.

JOZEPH FORAKIS

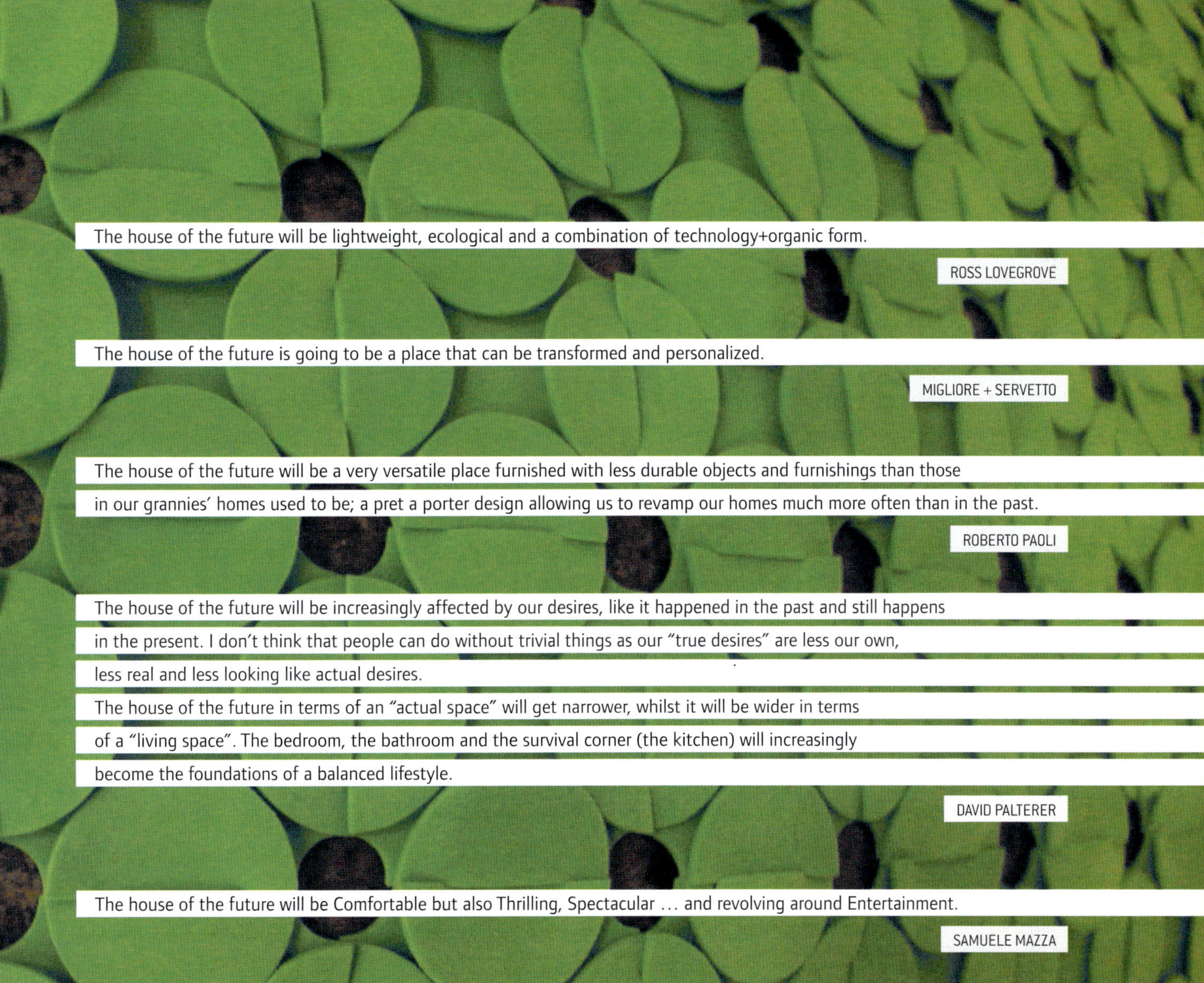The house of the future will be lightweight, ecological and a combination of technology+organic form.

ROSS LOVEGROVE

The house of the future is going to be a place that can be transformed and personalized.

MIGLIORE + SERVETTO

The house of the future will be a very versatile place furnished with less durable objects and furnishings than those
in our grannies' homes used to be; a pret a porter design allowing us to revamp our homes much more often than in the past.

ROBERTO PAOLI

The house of the future will be increasingly affected by our desires, like it happened in the past and still happens
in the present. I don't think that people can do without trivial things as our "true desires" are less our own,
less real and less looking like actual desires.
The house of the future in terms of an "actual space" will get narrower, whilst it will be wider in terms
of a "living space". The bedroom, the bathroom and the survival corner (the kitchen) will increasingly
become the foundations of a balanced lifestyle.

DAVID PALTERER

The house of the future will be Comfortable but also Thrilling, Spectacular … and revolving around Entertainment.

SAMUELE MAZZA

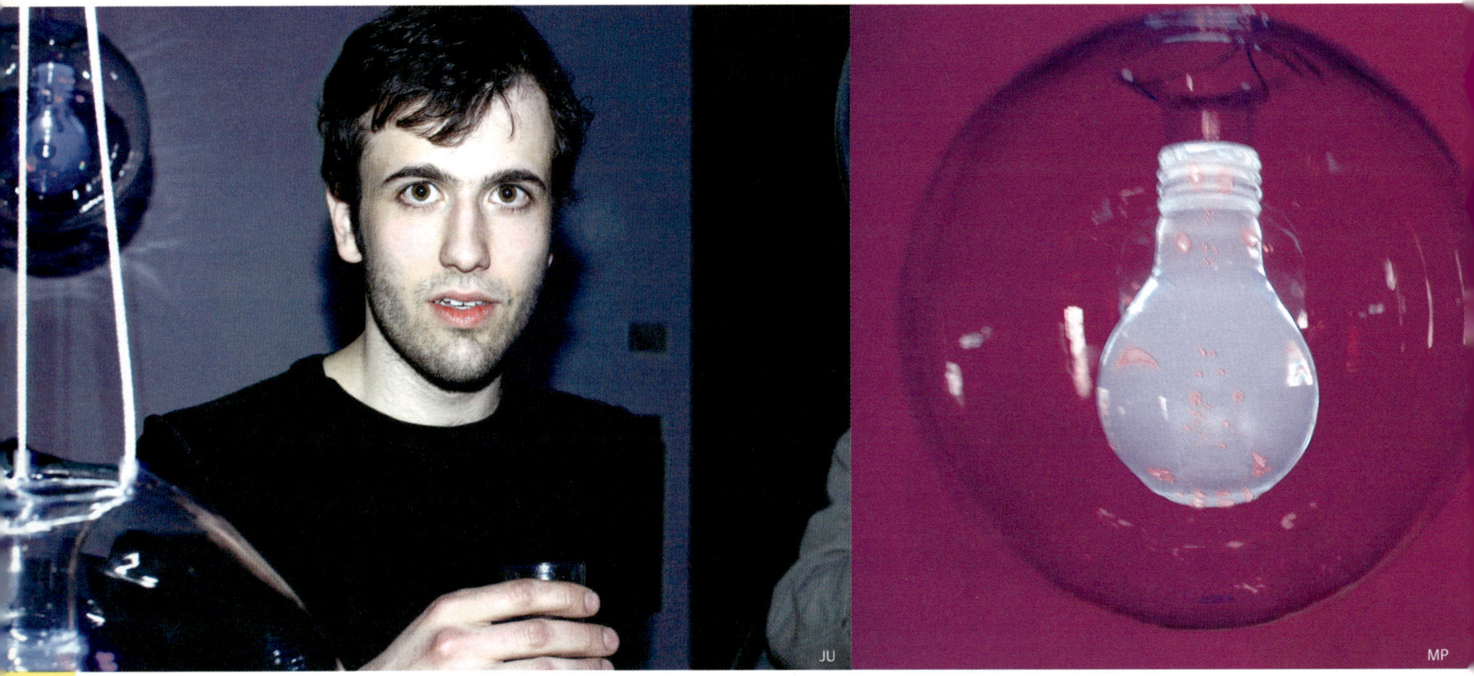

Paul Cocksedge

Sapphire&Tonic by Paul Cocksedge @ Spazio Krizia

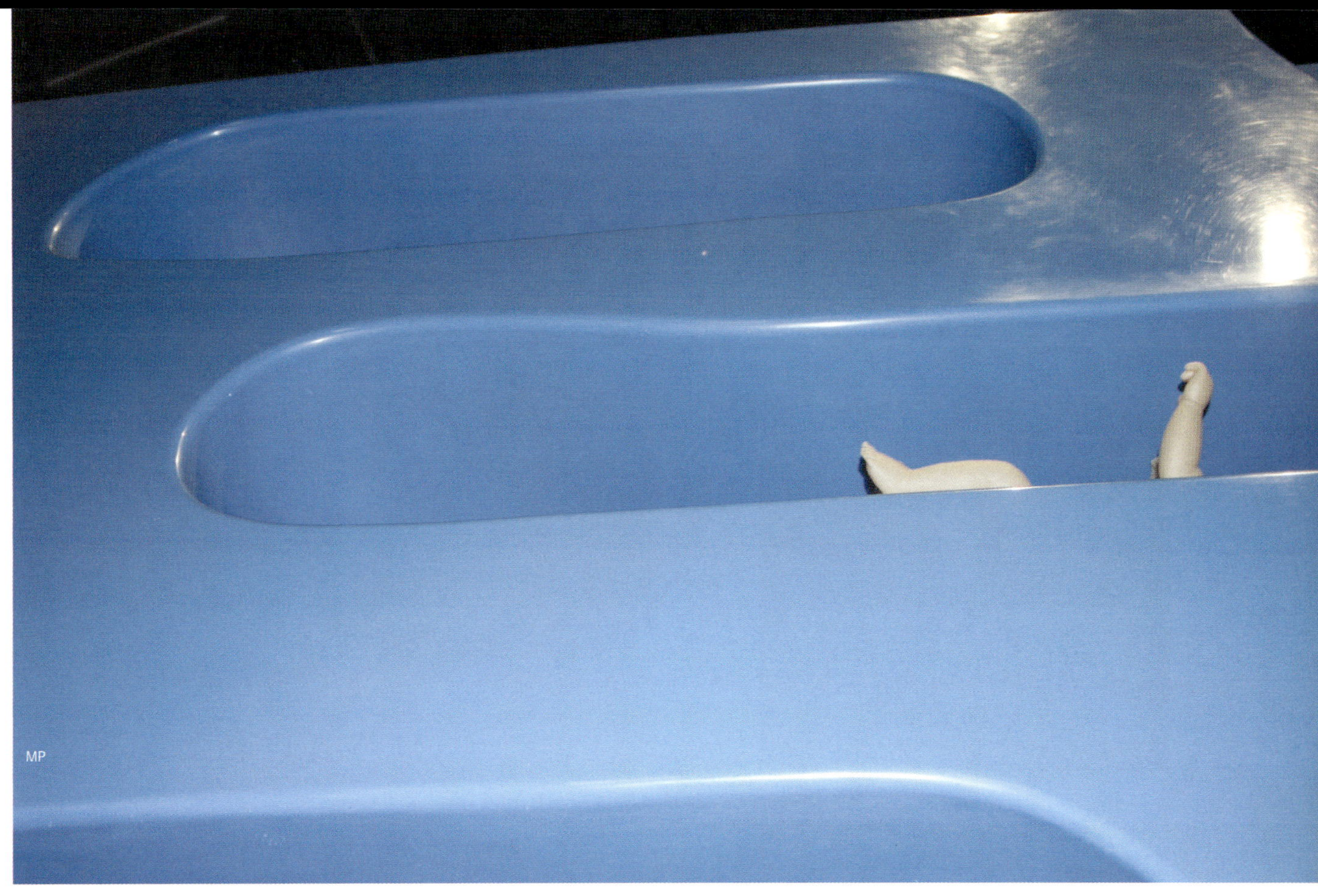

Bookshelves by Ingo Maurer @ Spazio Krizia

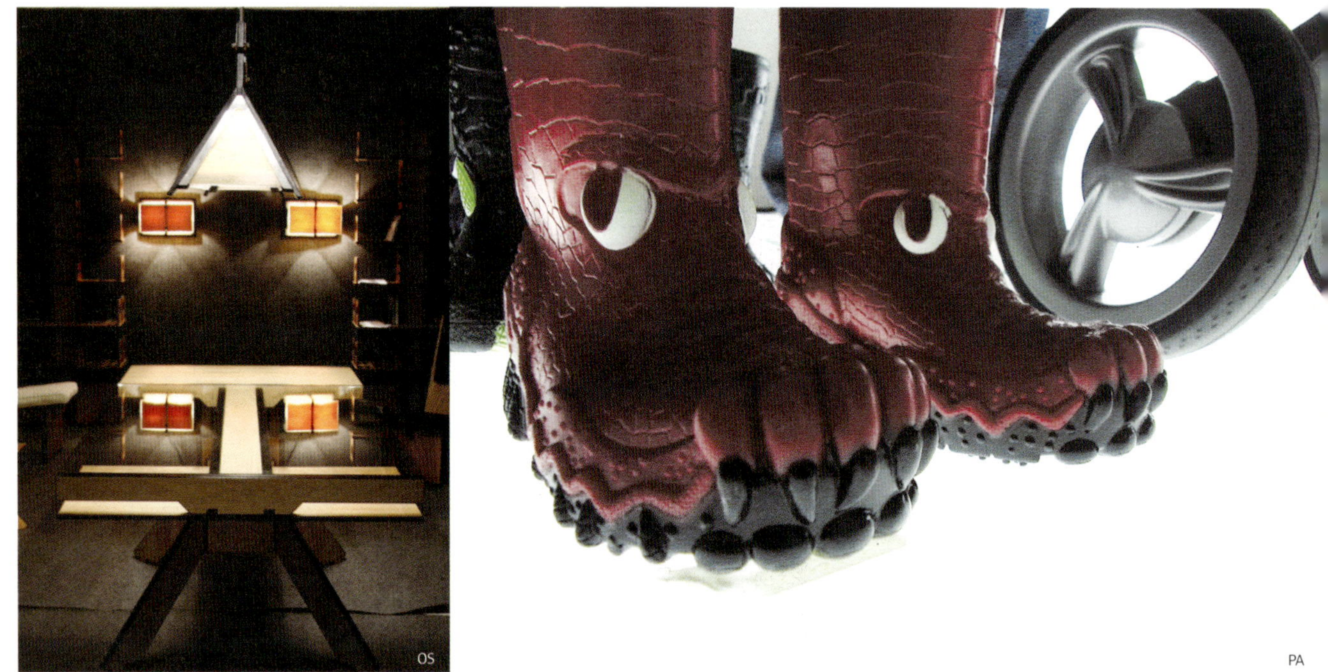

Jacopo Gardella

Urban stroller and boots @ Scandinavian design

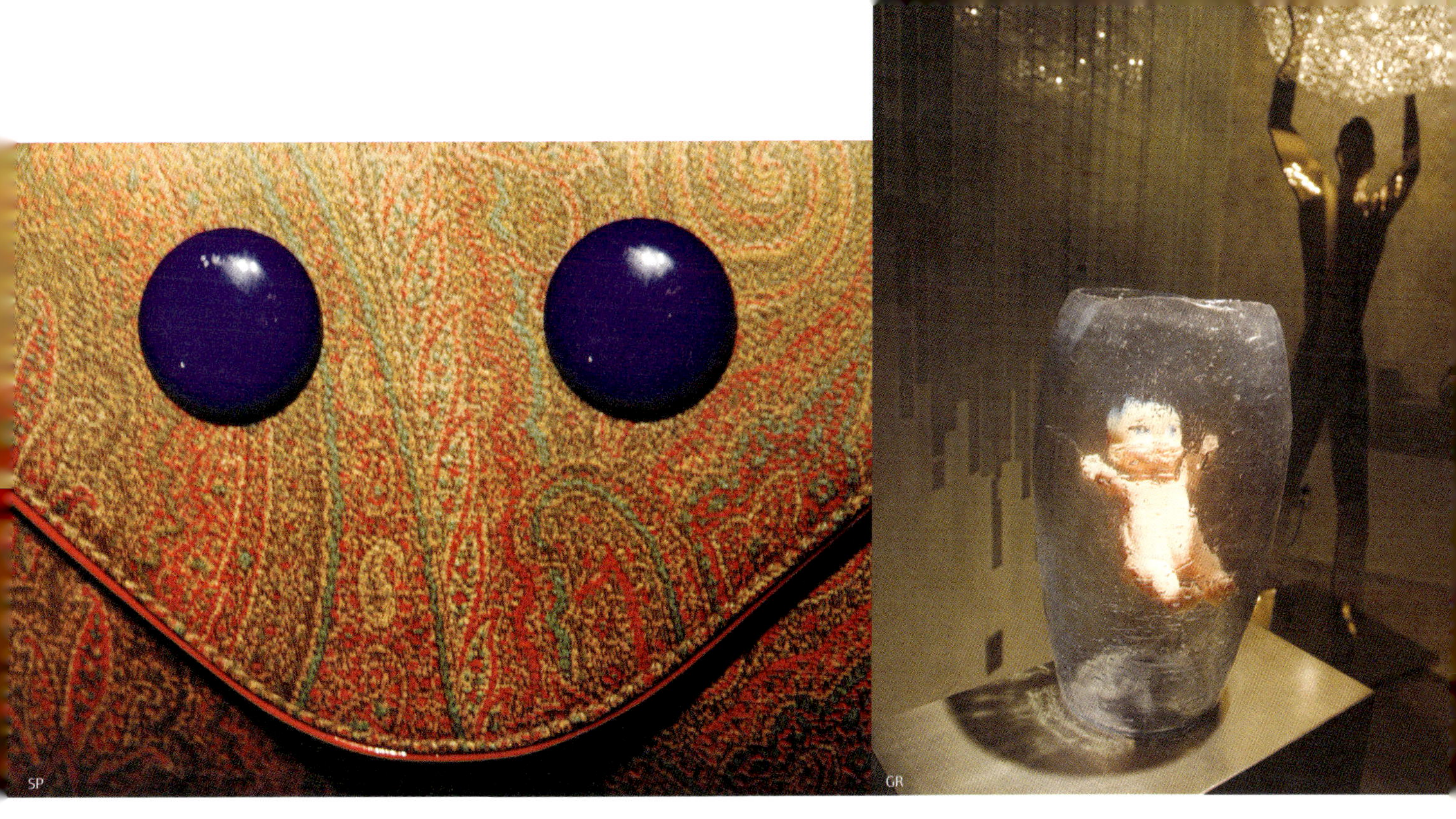

Bag by Alessandro Mendini for Etro

Vase by Alessandro Ciffo,
Lamp by Catellani&Smith
Tent by Gianfranco Coltella @ Dilmos

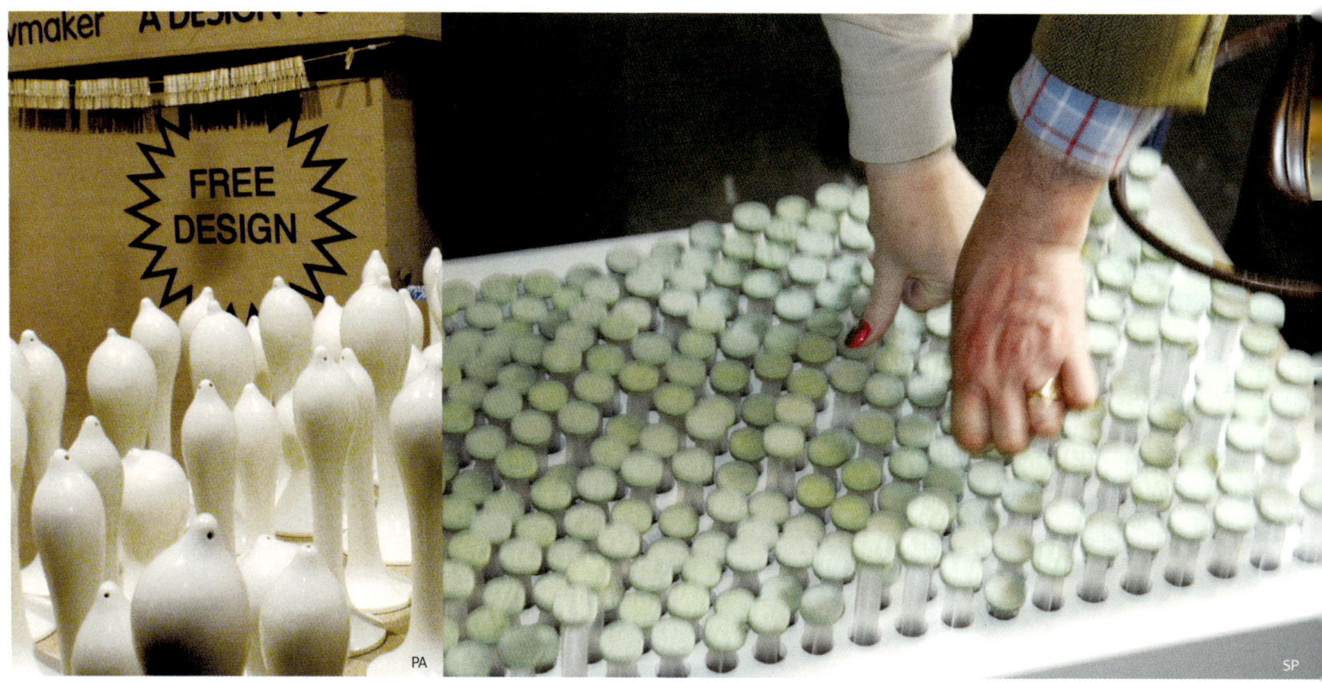

Wemake @ Satellite

Annick Collins @ Designersblock

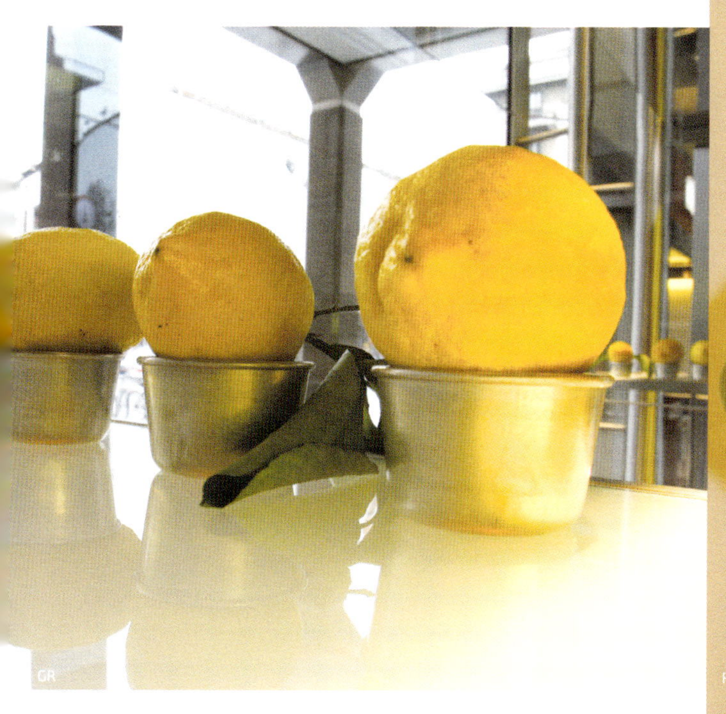

Spazio Miele

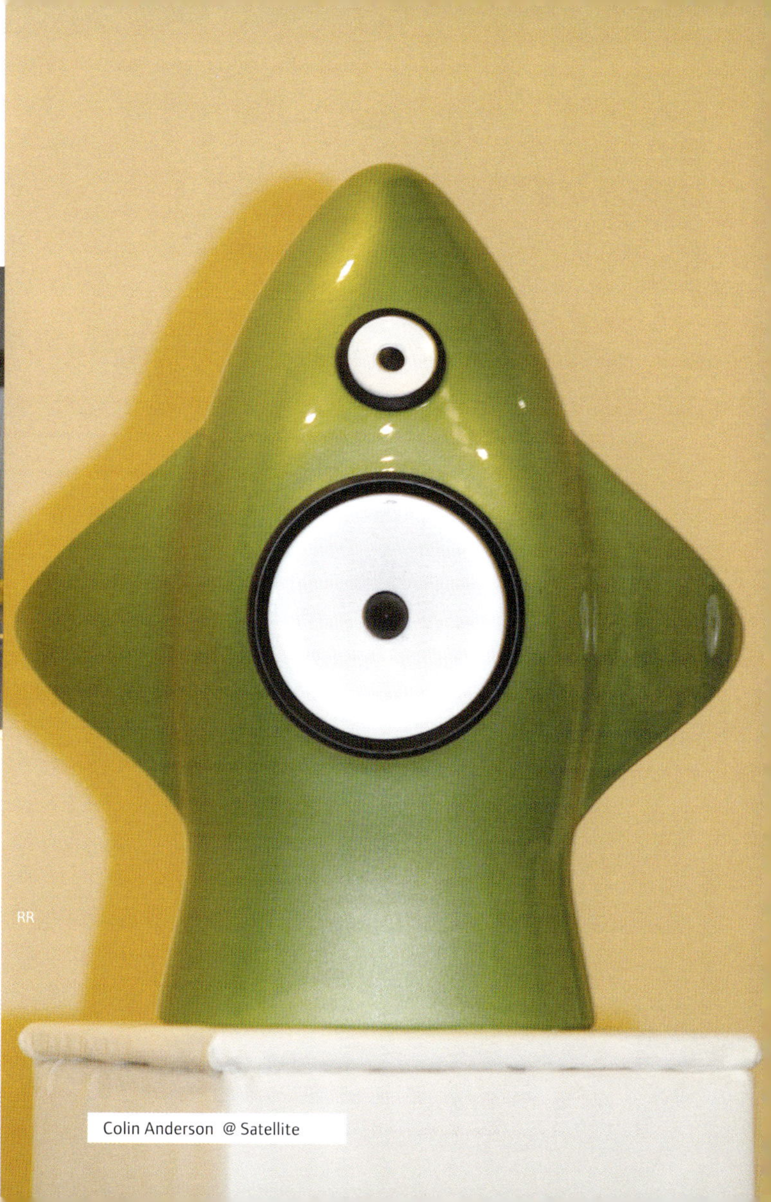

Colin Anderson @ Satellite

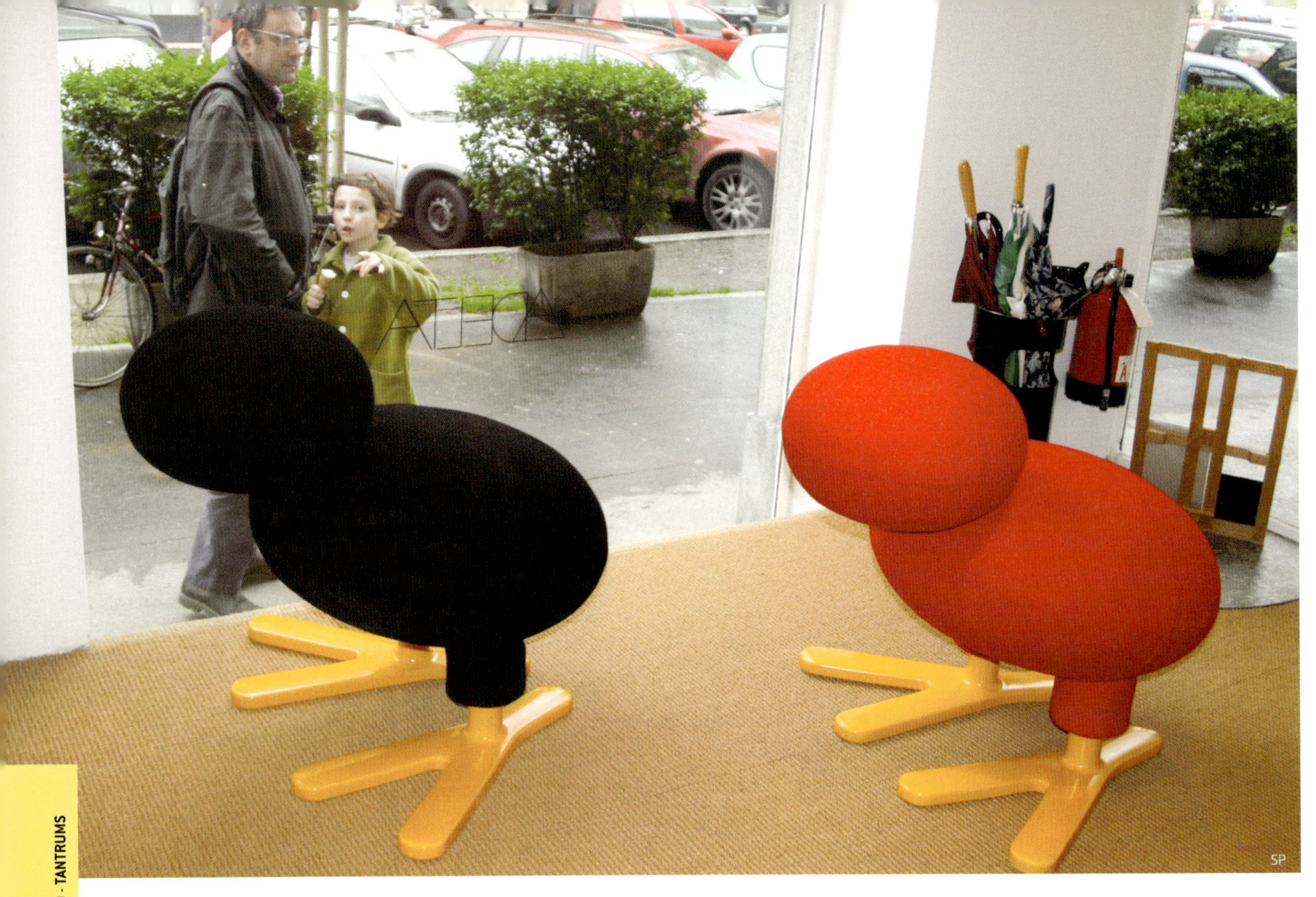

162   Tipi by Eero Aarni

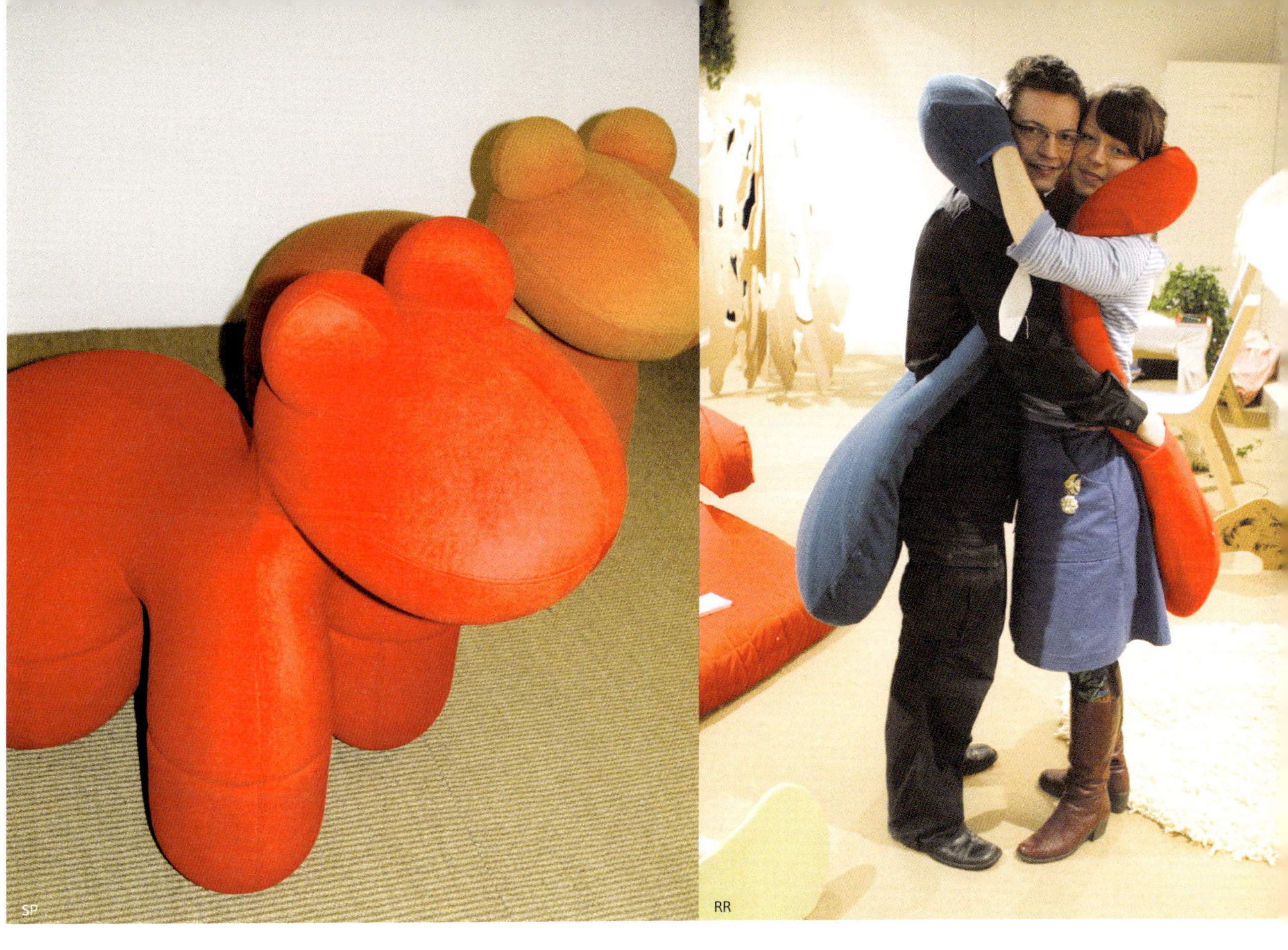

Pony by Eero Aarni

Go Ping pong APS @ Satellite

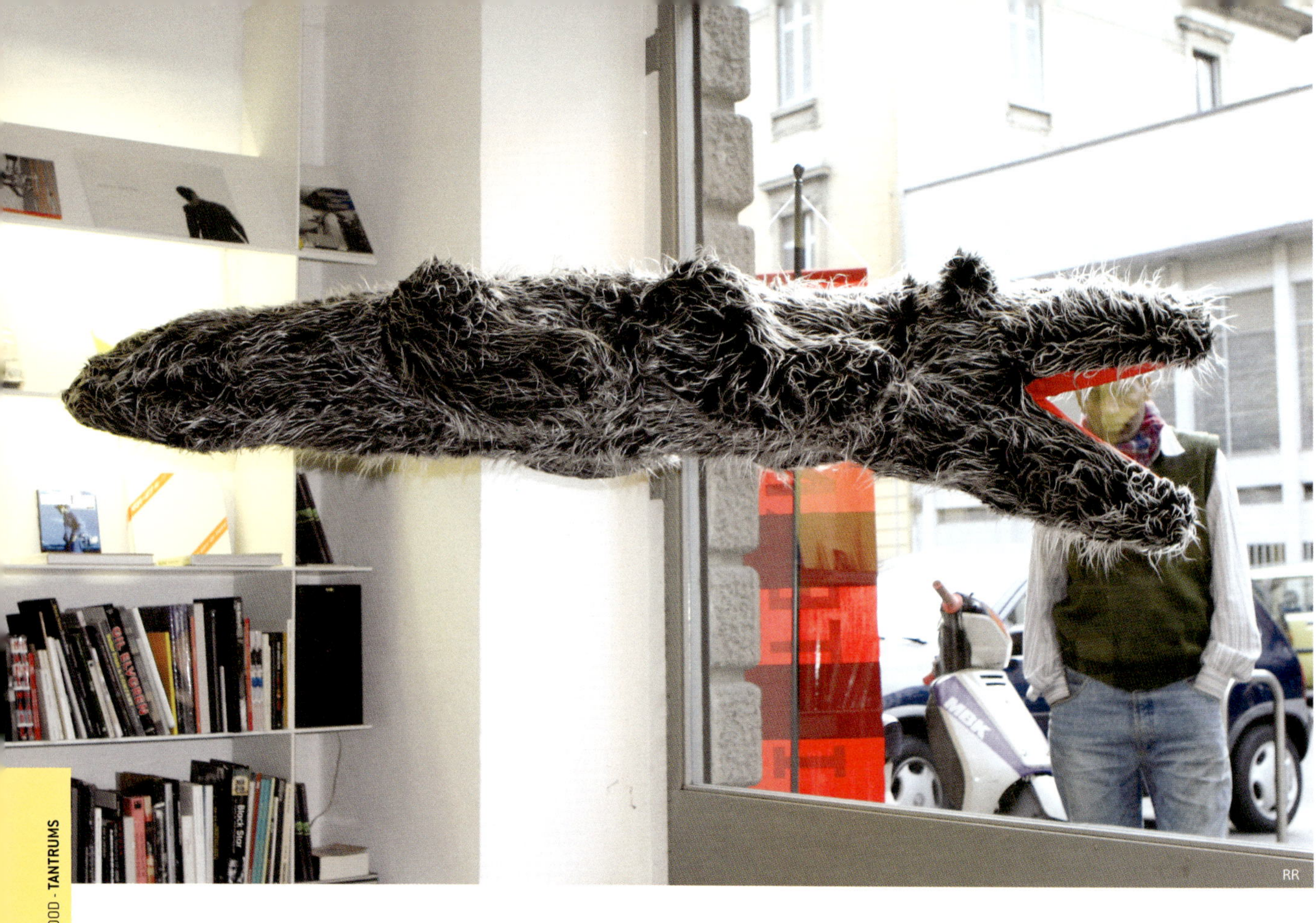

164 Rocco del Crocco, enflatable sofa by Nunzia Carbone, Gaoyi Li, Zhang Jin and Yang Yi Feng

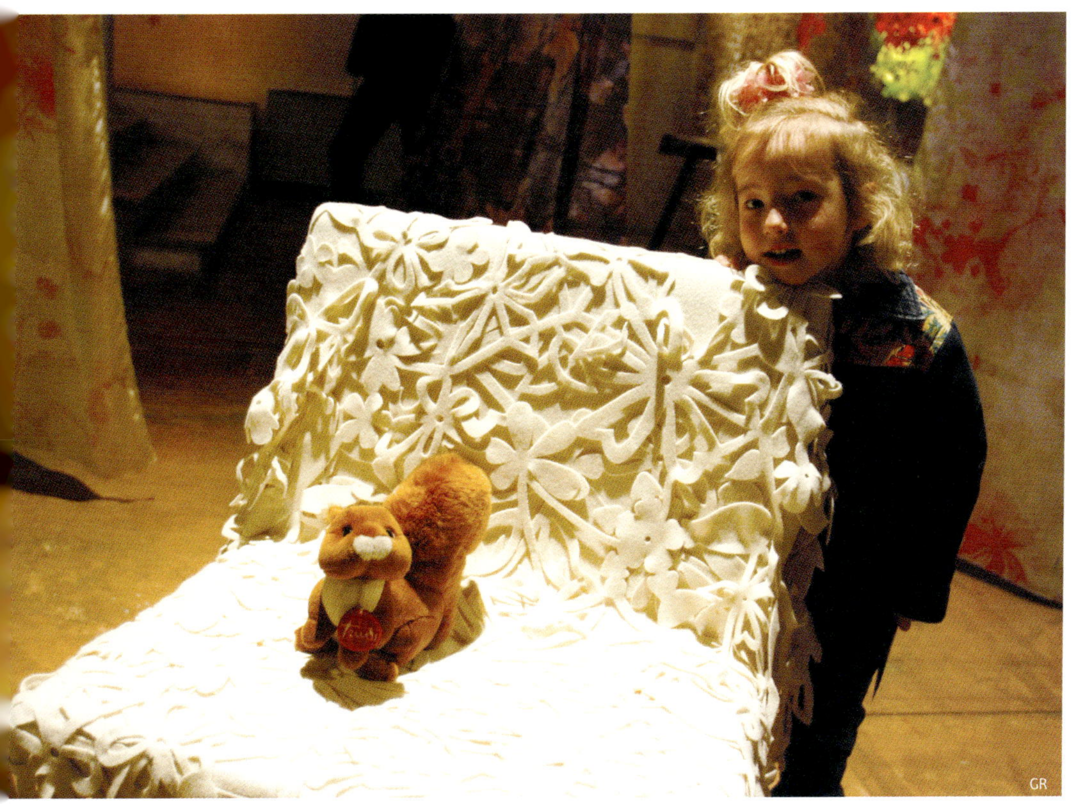

Moroso installation

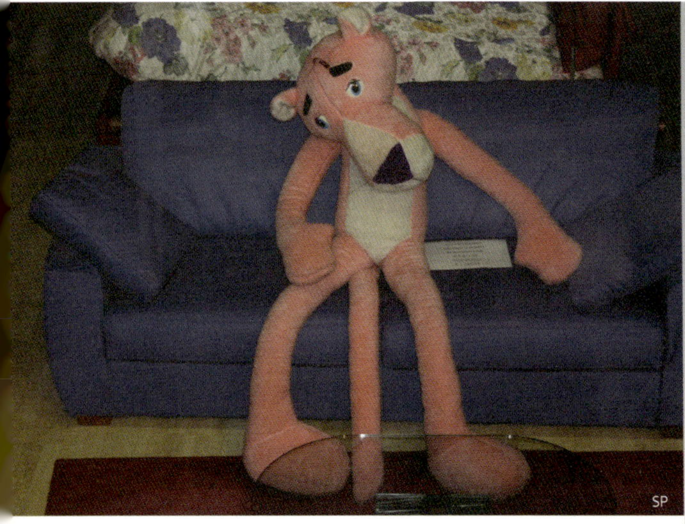

Cibic & Partners

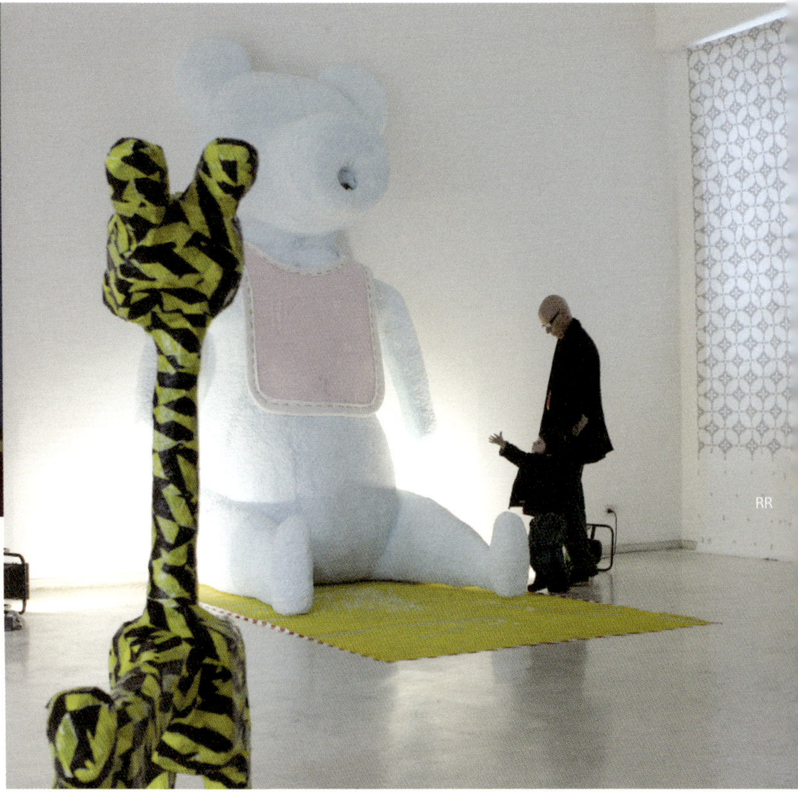

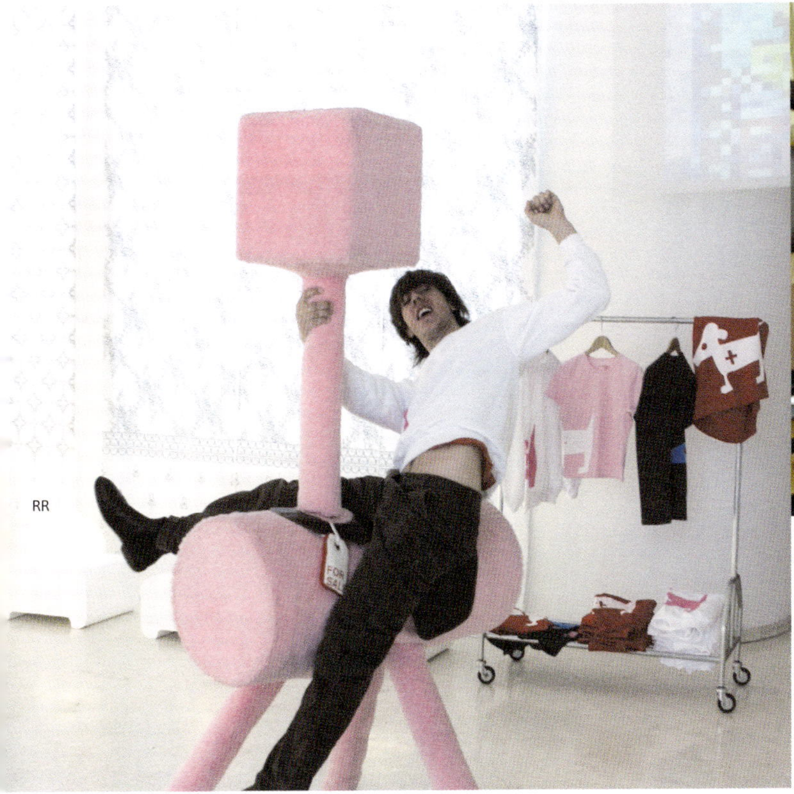

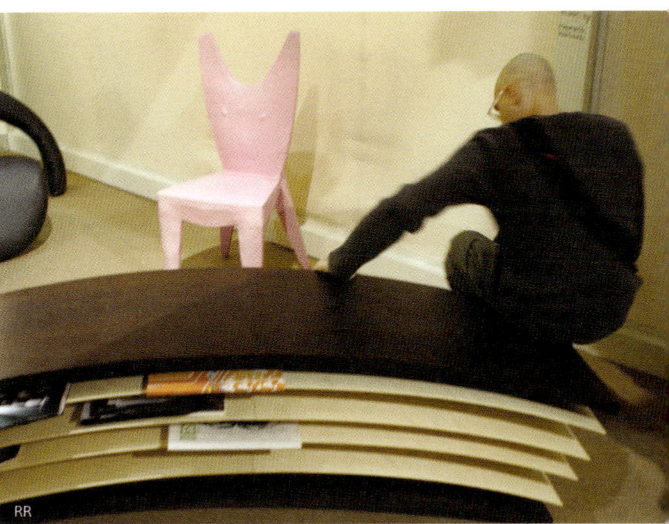

W+B design ASBL @ Satellite

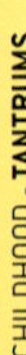

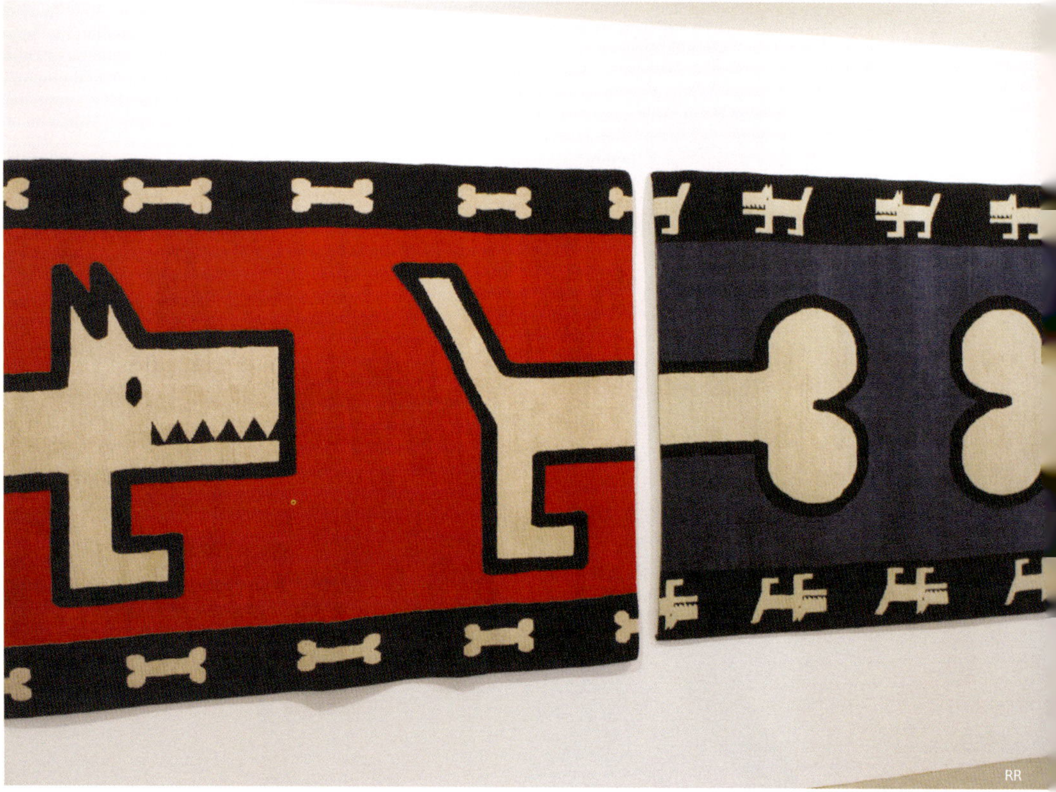

Carpet by Stefano Giovannoni @ Post Design

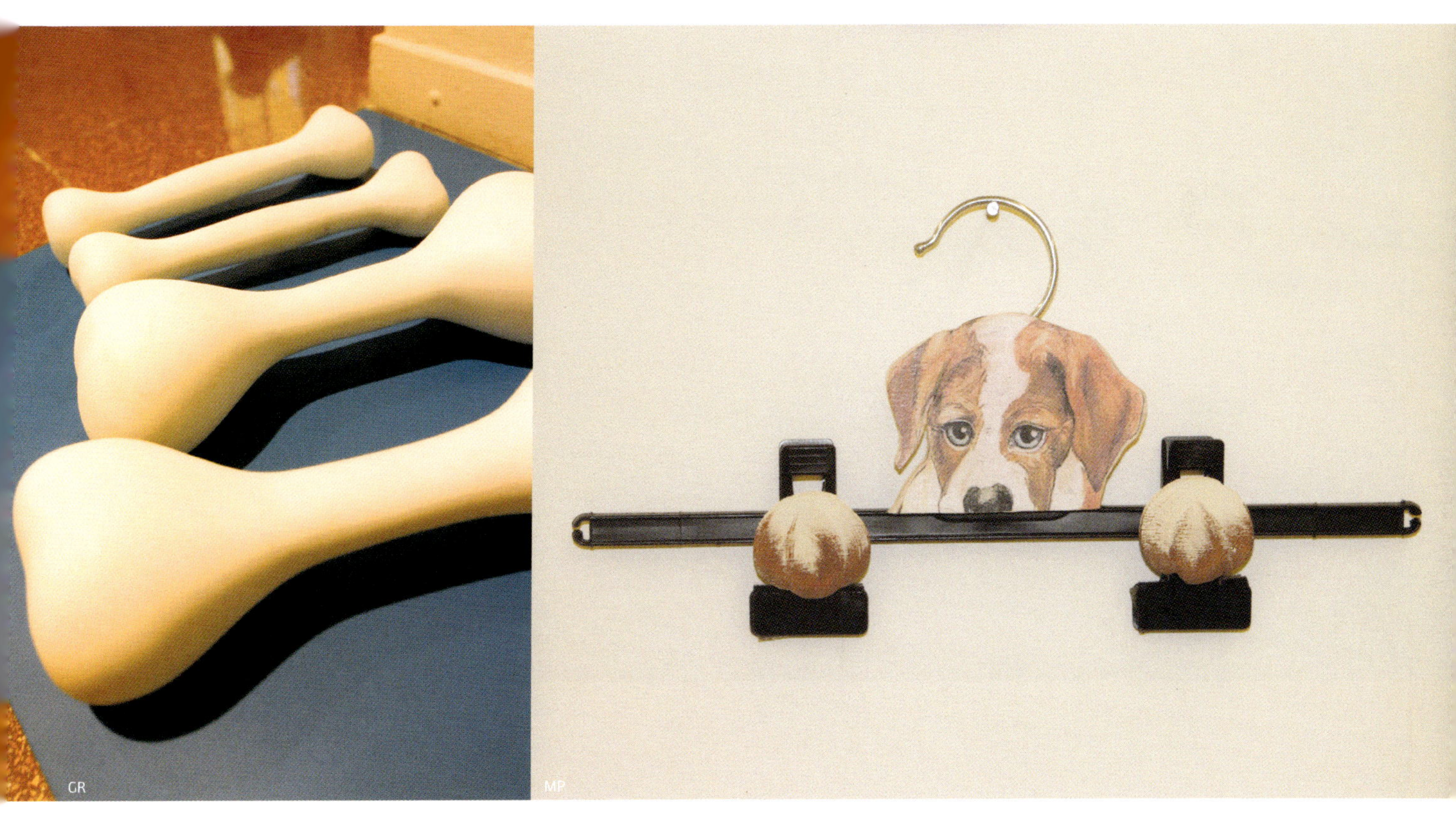

Vanishing Point 1

Appendimi @ Emporio 31

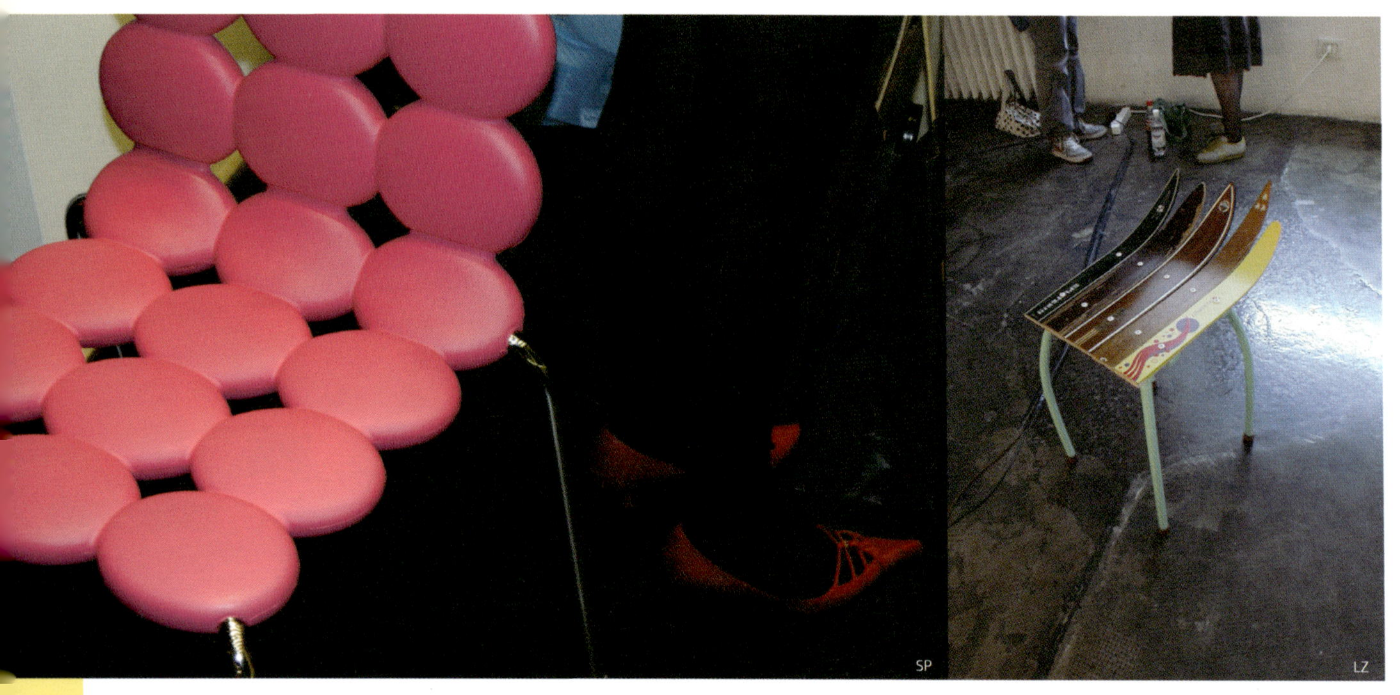

Mints by Arflex

Defyra @ Designersblock

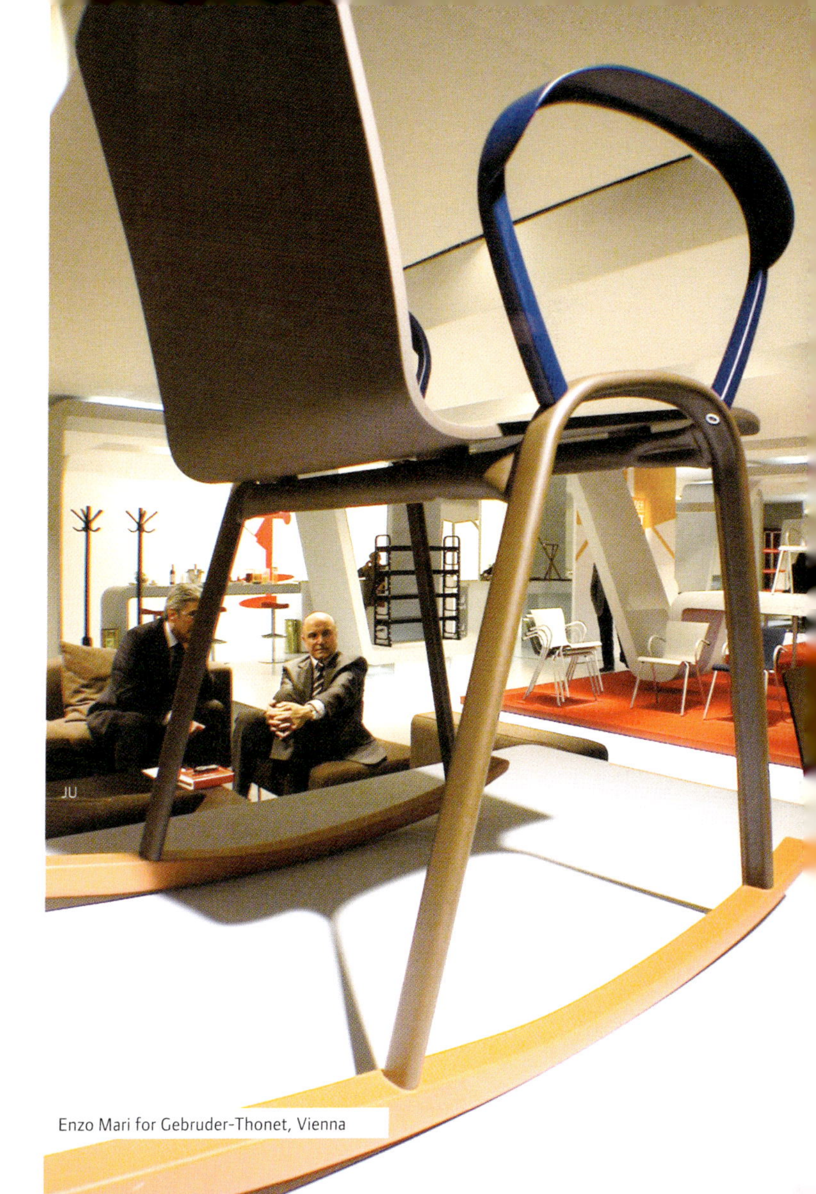

Enzo Mari for Gebruder-Thonet, Vienna

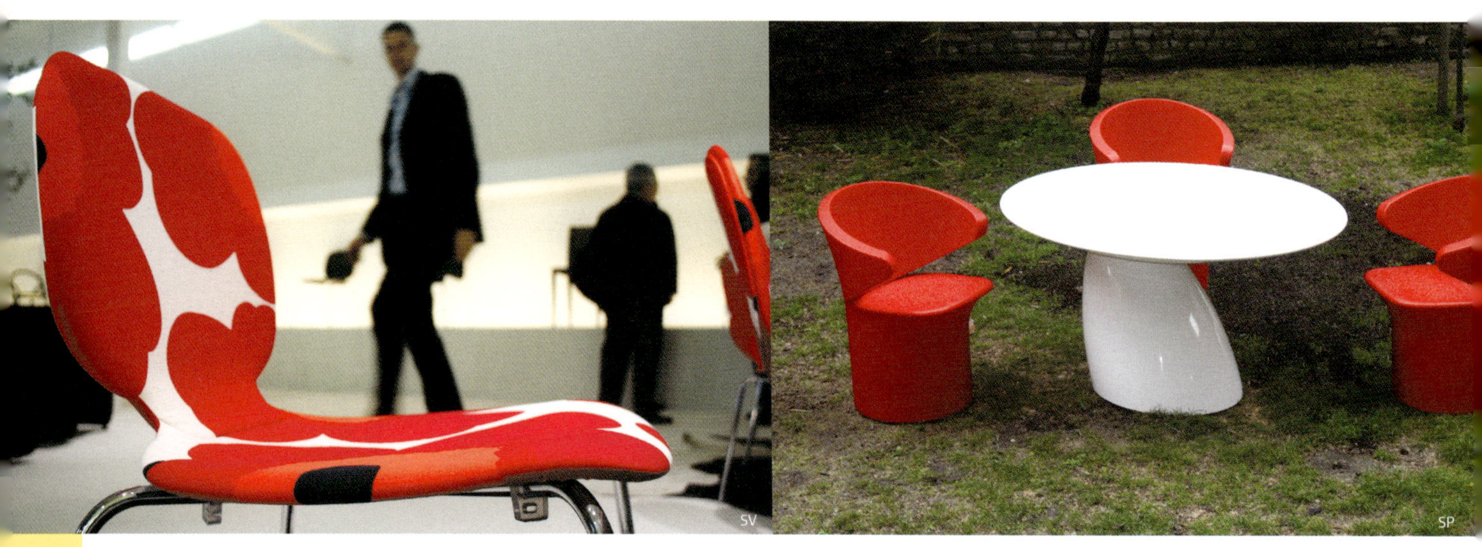

Crassevig

Eero Aarni

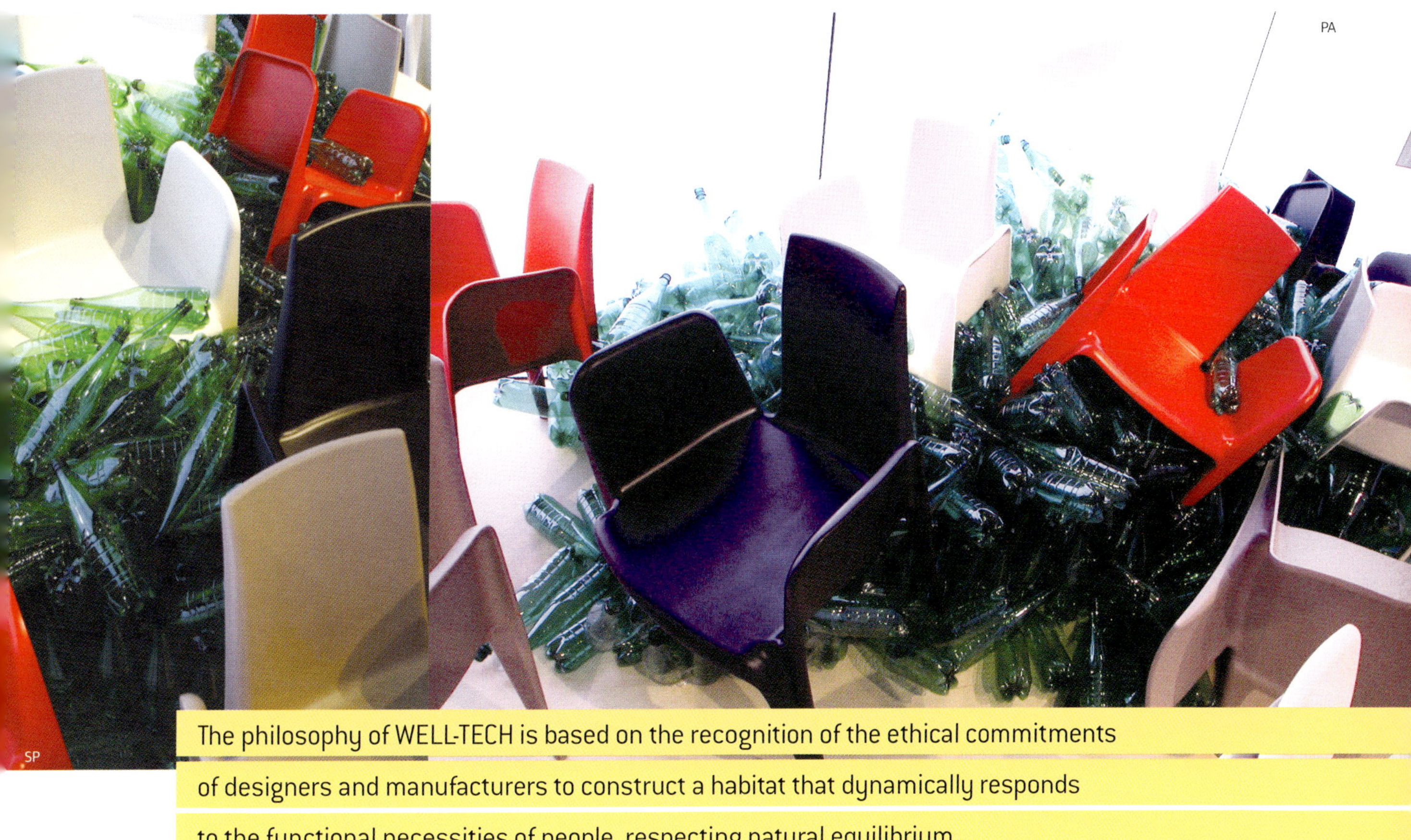

The philosophy of WELL-TECH is based on the recognition of the ethical commitments

of designers and manufacturers to construct a habitat that dynamically responds

to the functional necessities of people, respecting natural equilibrium.

WELL-TECH helps various businesses to renew their products through coherent

and sustainable planning, creating innovative products using technology and materials

that have minimal environmental impact.

Bella Rifatta by Sawaya&Moroni with Corepla (Eco Design with Recycled Plastics) @ Well-Tech

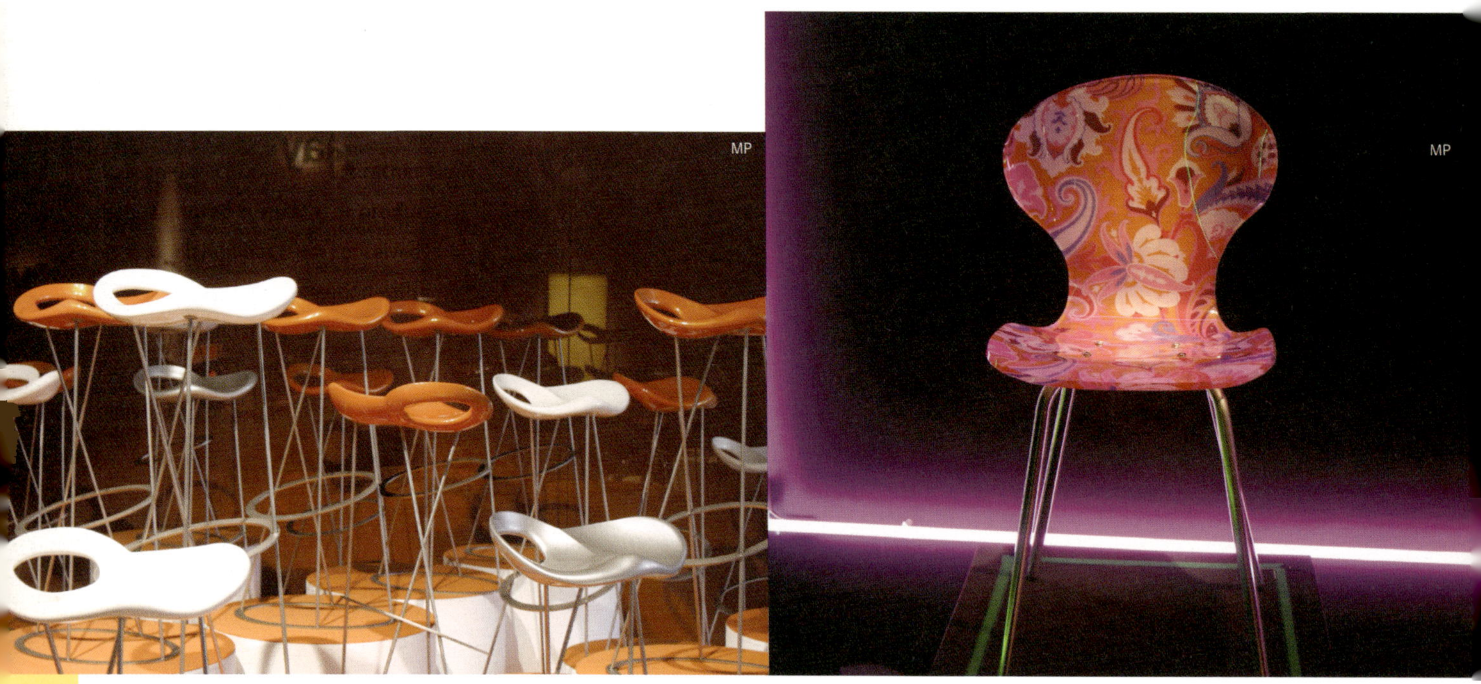

Marco Maran @ Zona Tortona

Etro

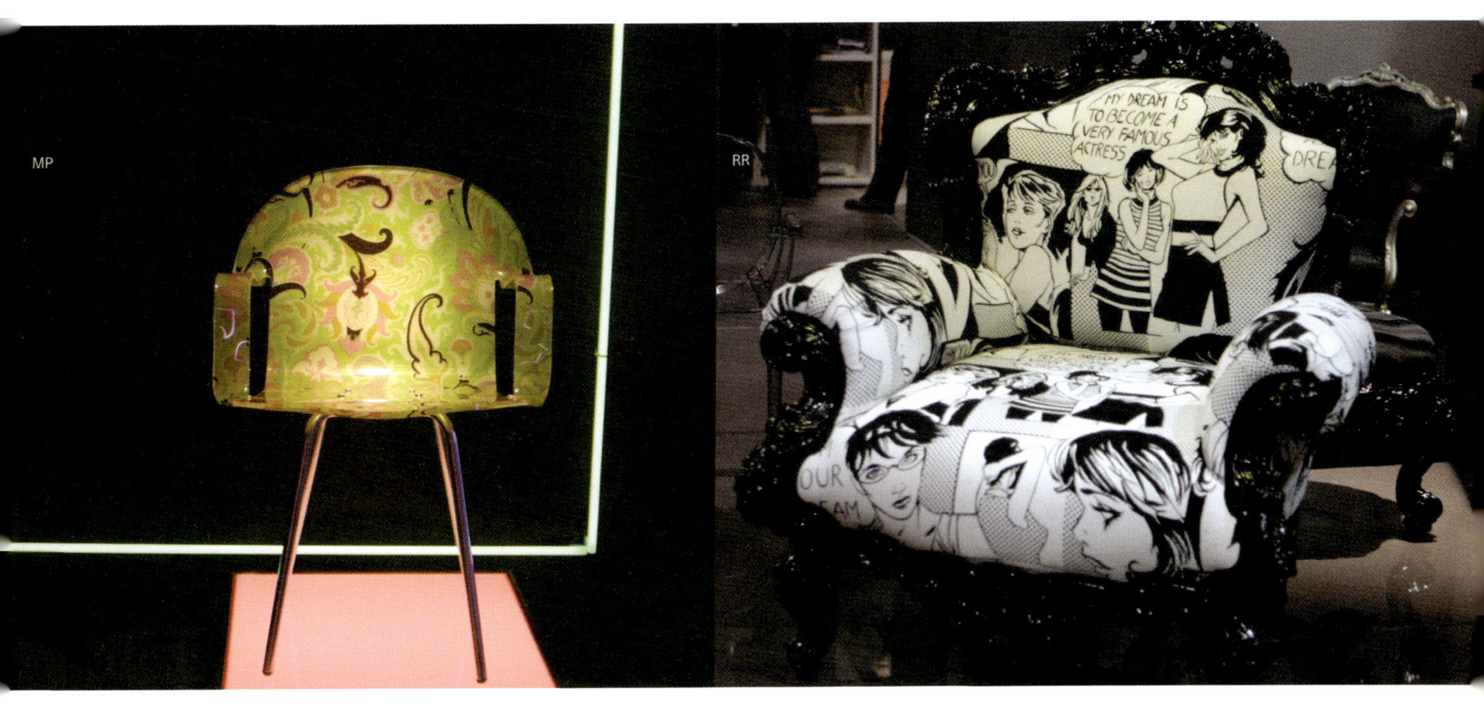

MP

RR

Di Liddo & Perego

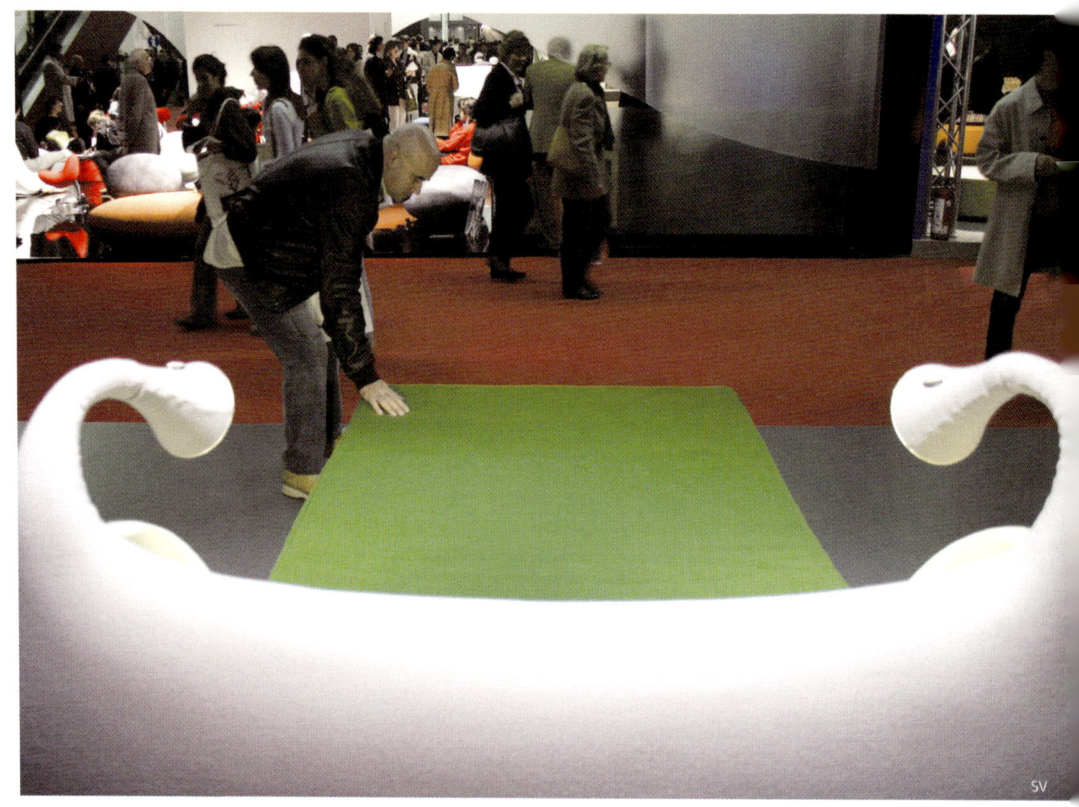

Domodinamica

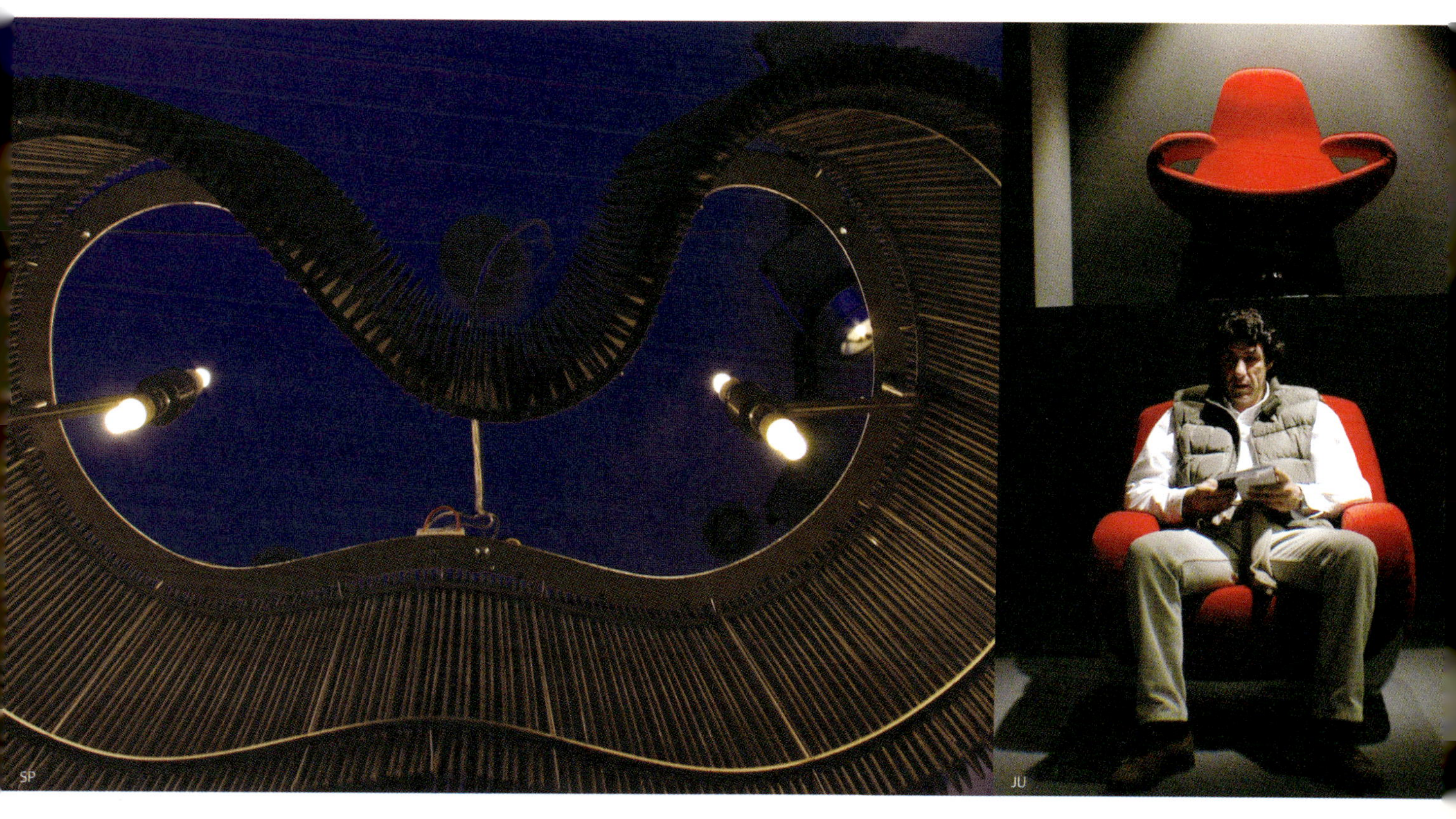

Chandelier by Dominique Perrault for Sawaya&Moroni   Domodinamica

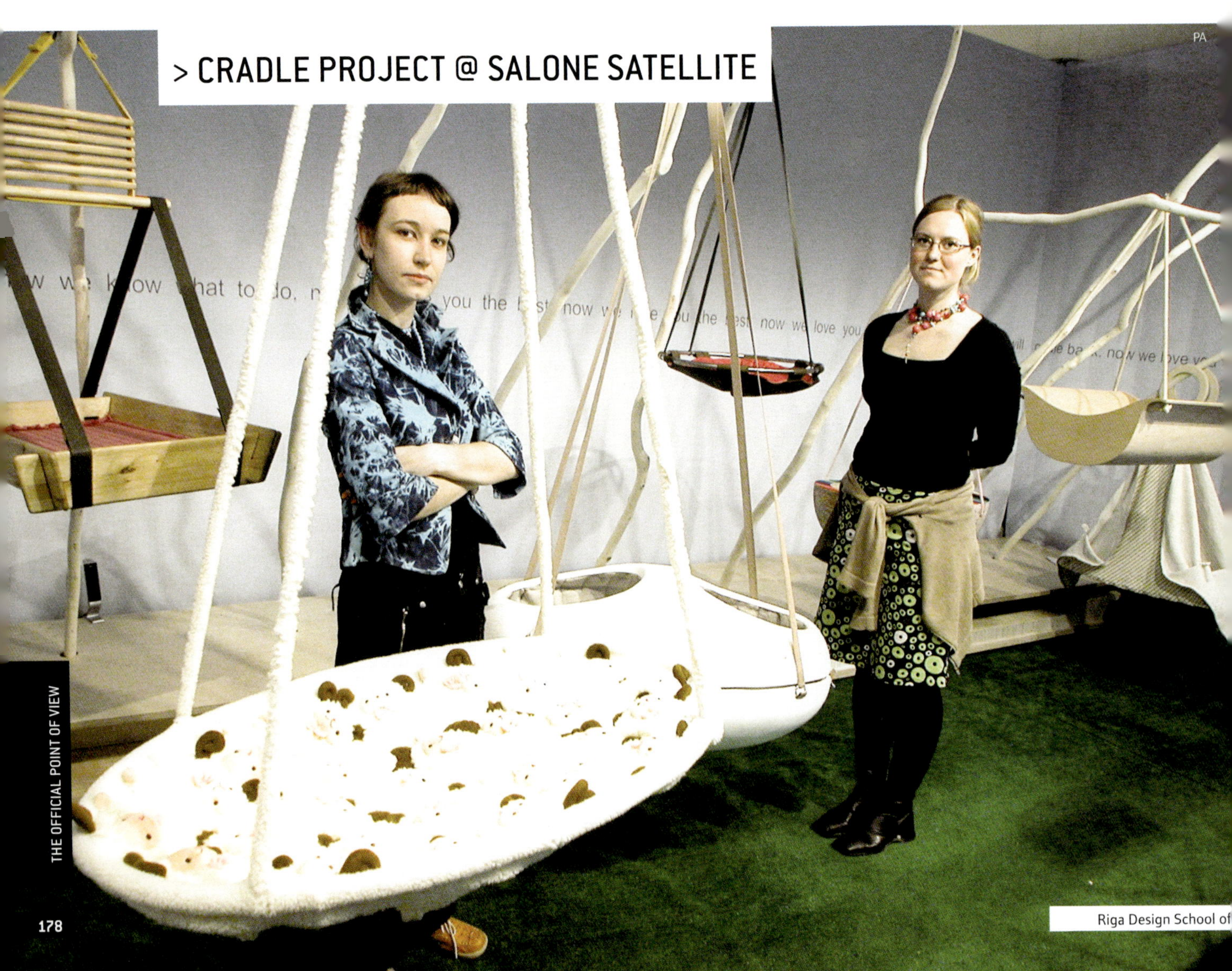

Riga Design School of

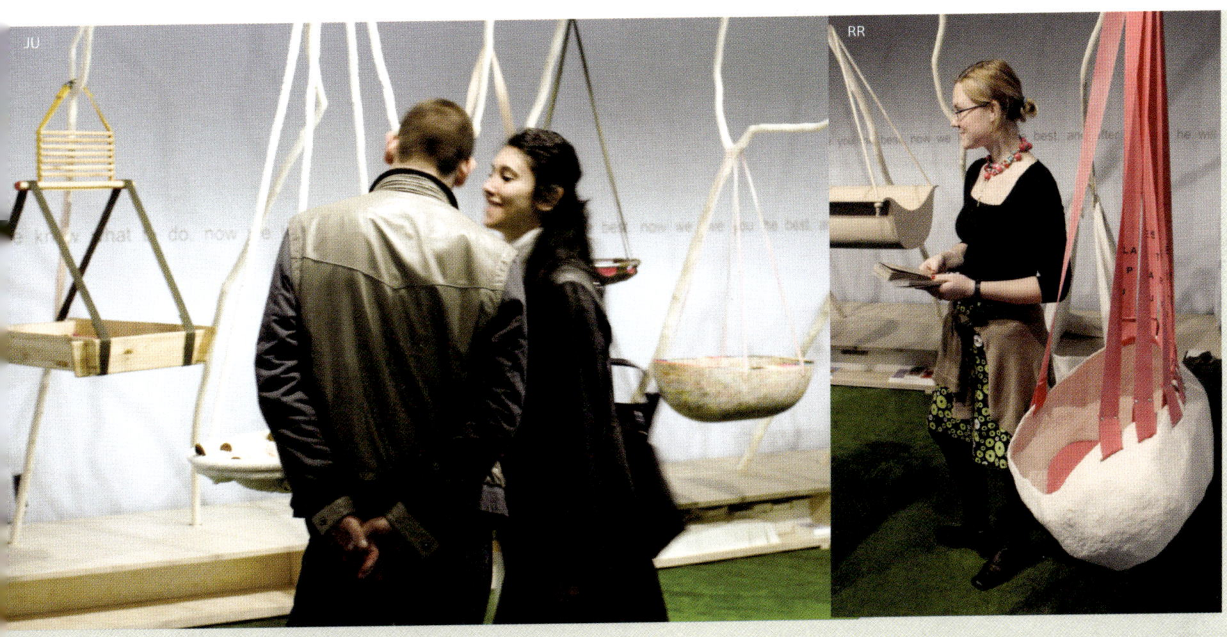

THE FIRST PIECE OF FURNITURE IN HUMAN LIFE

The Project's source of inspiration is a cradle found in the collection of the **Latvian Museum of History.**

This cradle comes from the Liepaja region, dates back to 1860, and was commonly known as the **"Wind's cradle".**

Ilt was made from flaxwaste cloth, trimmed with birch-wood hoop and the cord for hanging up the cradle was had three fixation points.

The cloth was woven in herring-bone pattern.

It was used by mothers who went to work in the fields; she stuck a pole into the ground and hung the cradle with the baby on it.

While she was working **the wind gently rocked the baby** and he slept peacefully, covered with a small cloth, sheltered from the sun and insects.

This cradle has a very ingenious construction, it is very mobile, true to the ideas of functional or applied design, could be well suited to contemporary busy women, who return to work soon after the birth of the baby or set up their office at home.

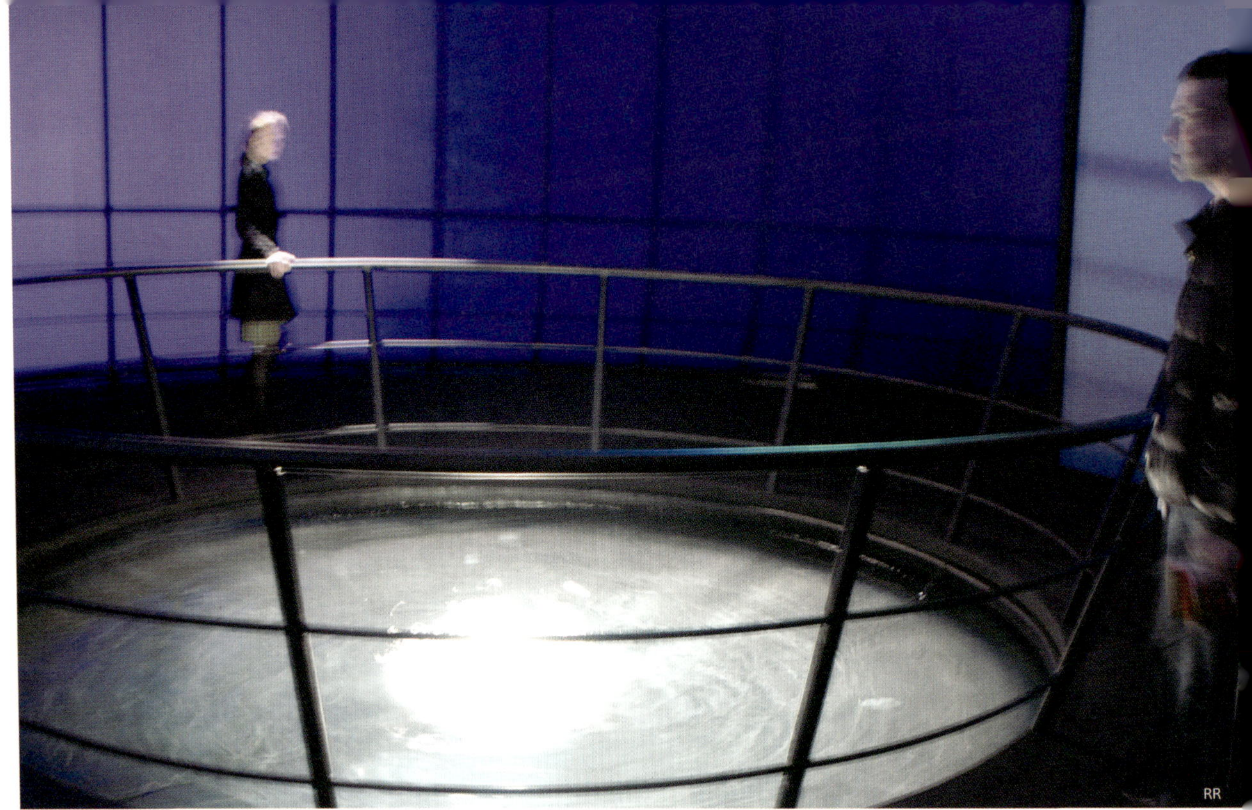

Morphosis @ Pelota

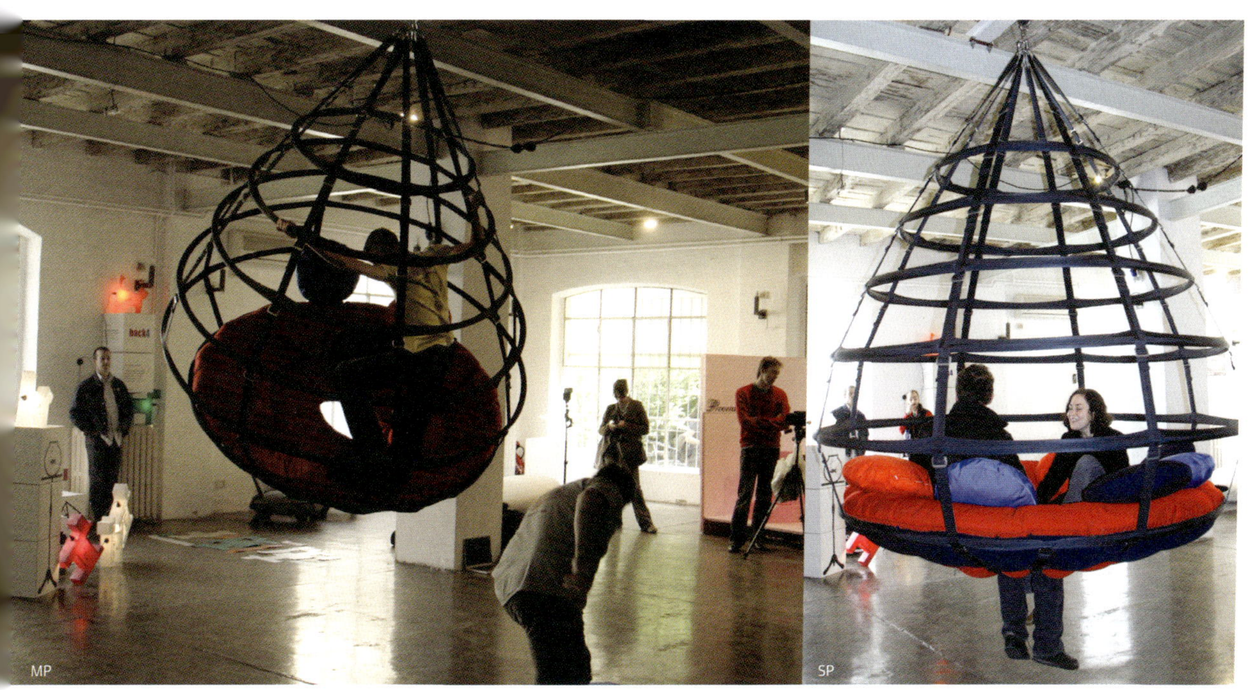

Pod-Life by The Collaborators @ Designersblock

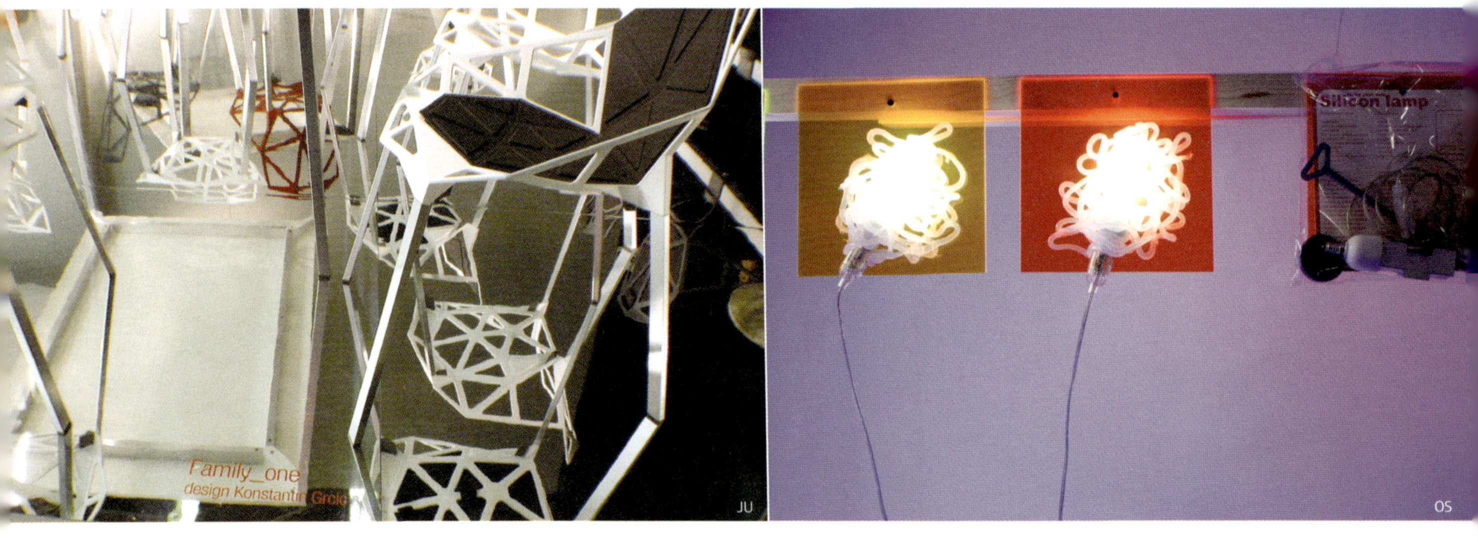

182   Family_one by Constantin Grcic for Magis   Stone Design

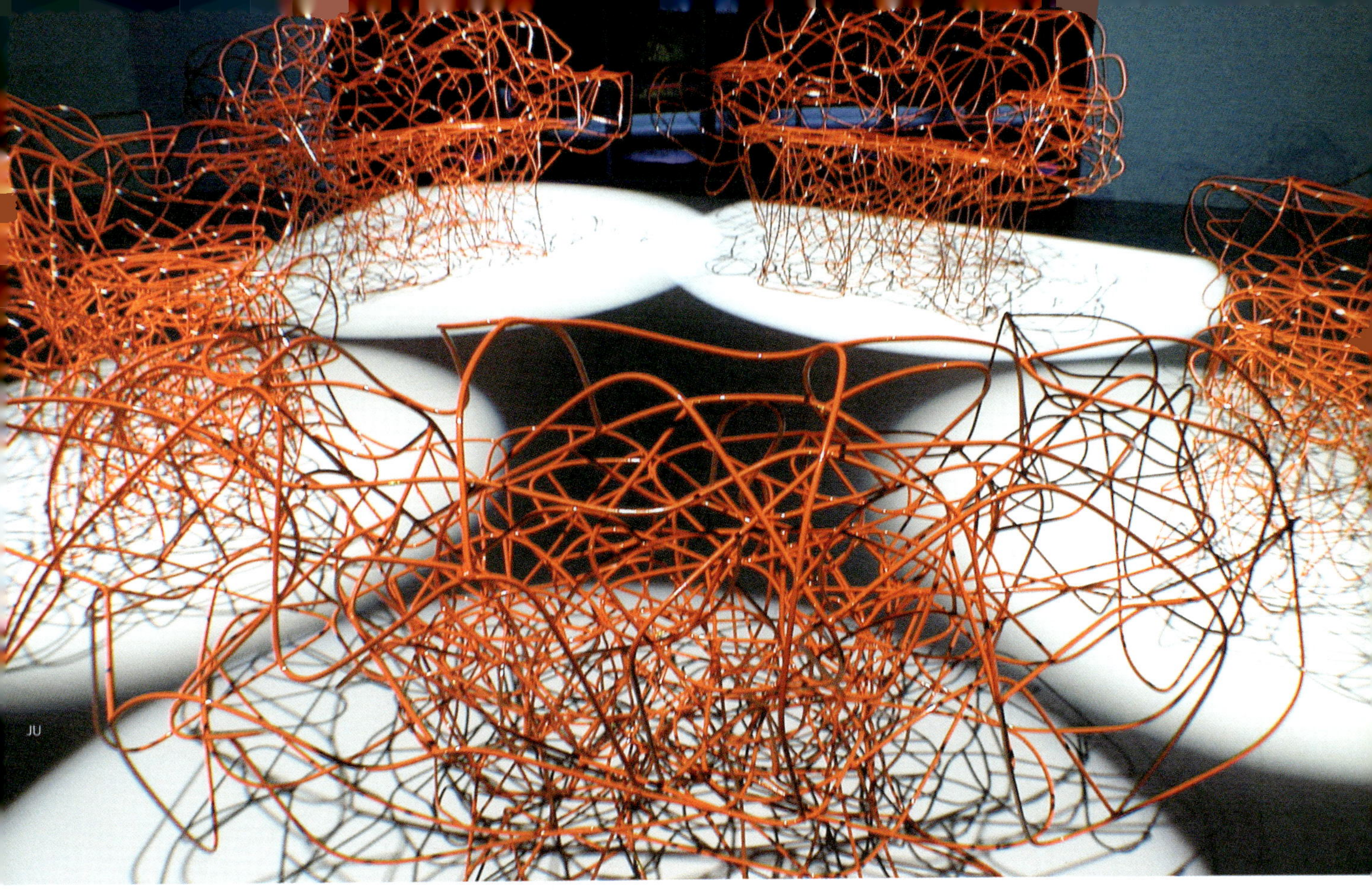

Corallo by Fernando and Humberto Campana for Edra

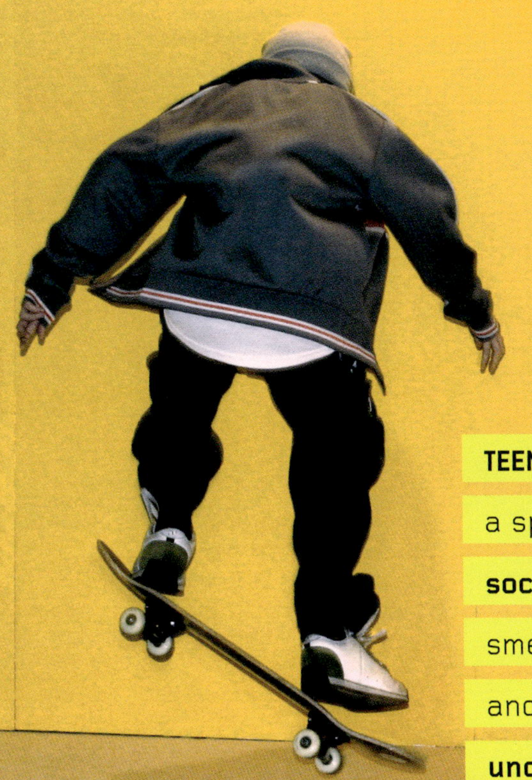

TEENAGER

a spicy mix of

socialization pag 186 with a

smell of **dream** pag 242

and a slice of

unconventionality pag 290

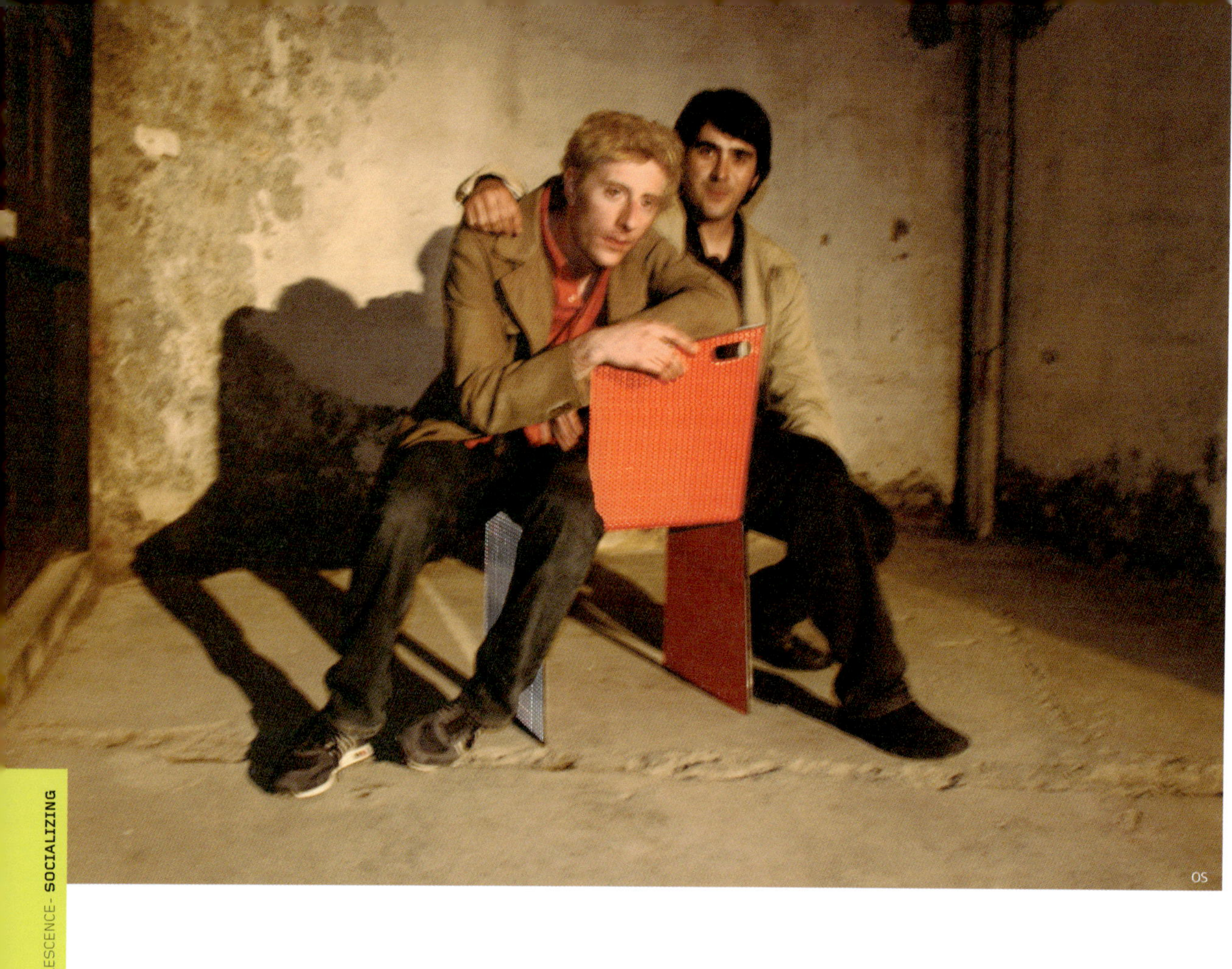

Andrea Borri

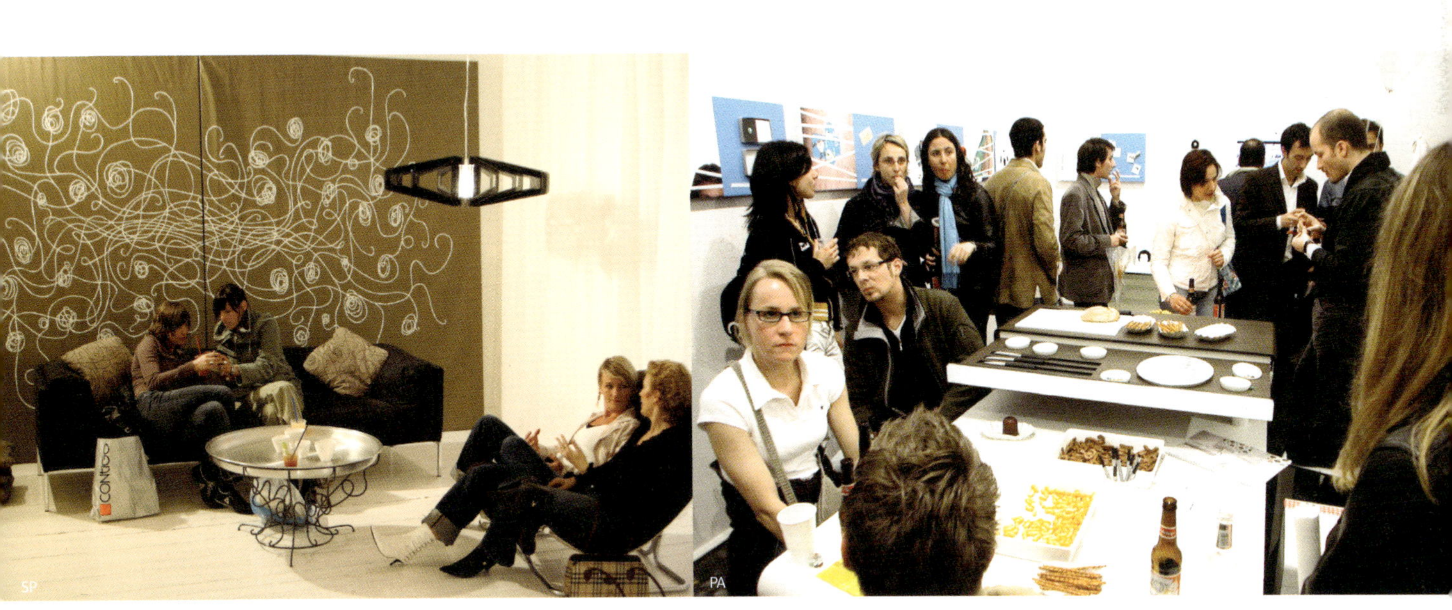

David Design

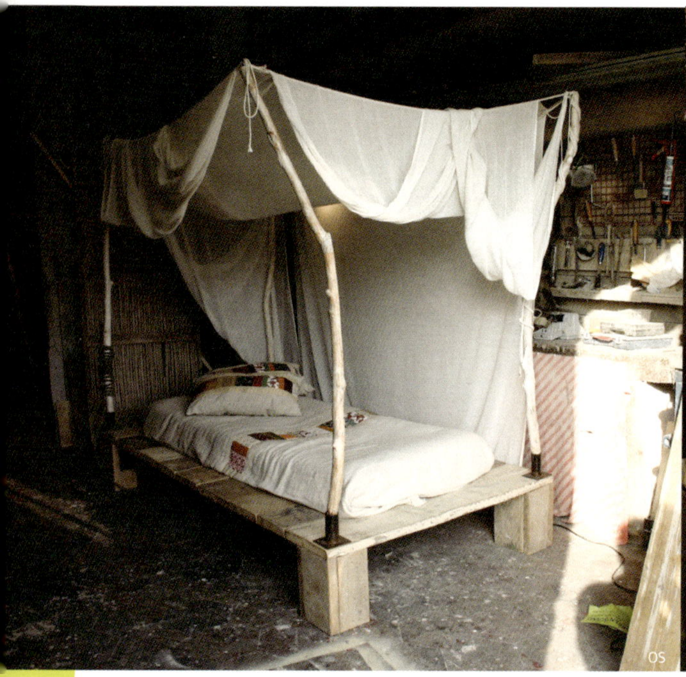

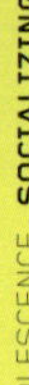

Isola Verde

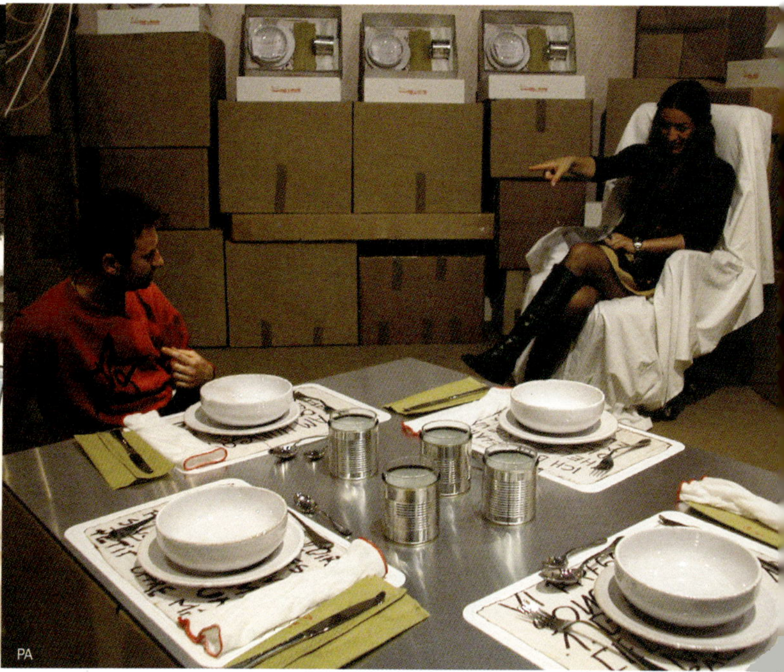

Daniele Pario Perra @ Satellite

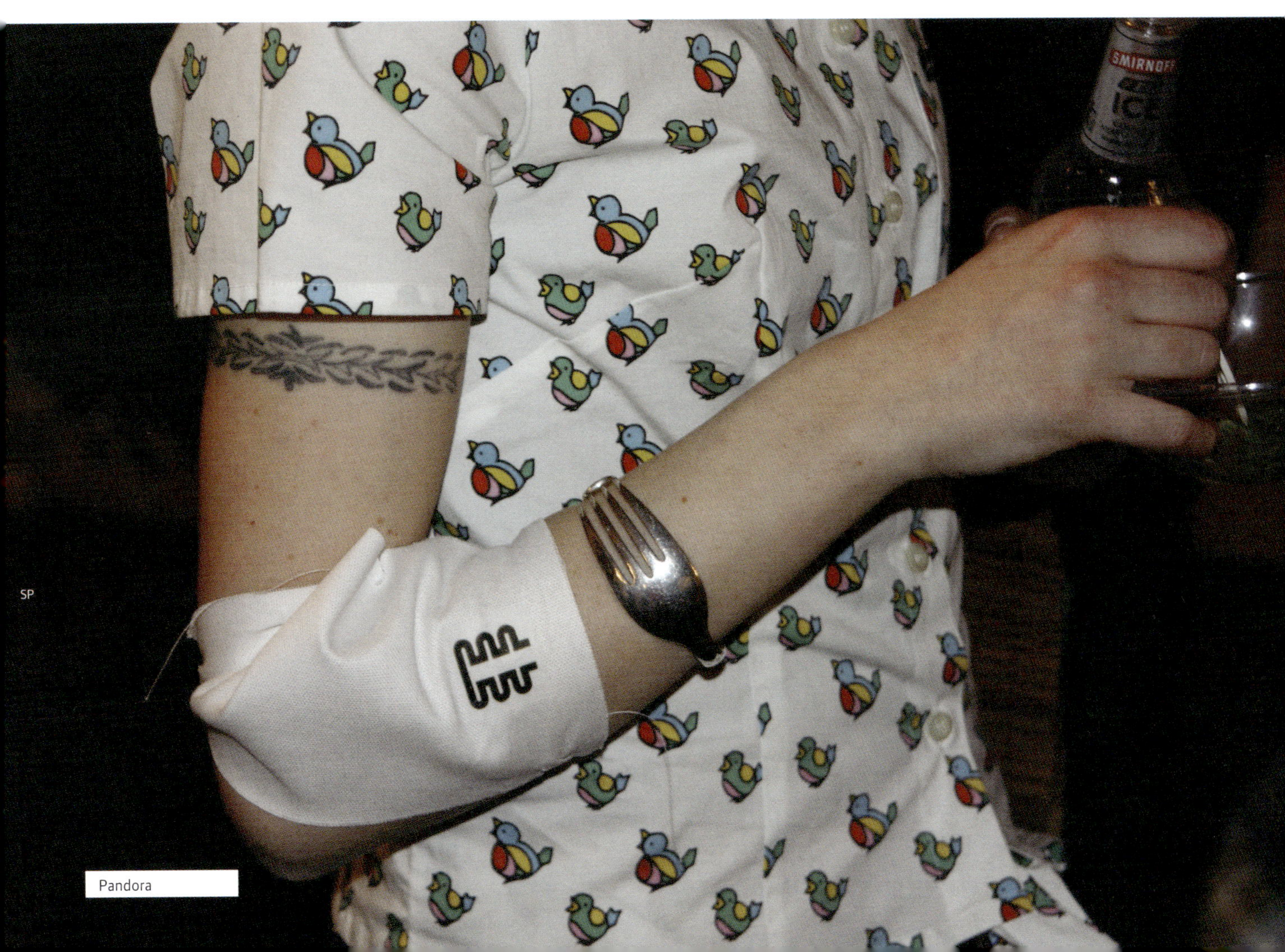

SP

Pandora

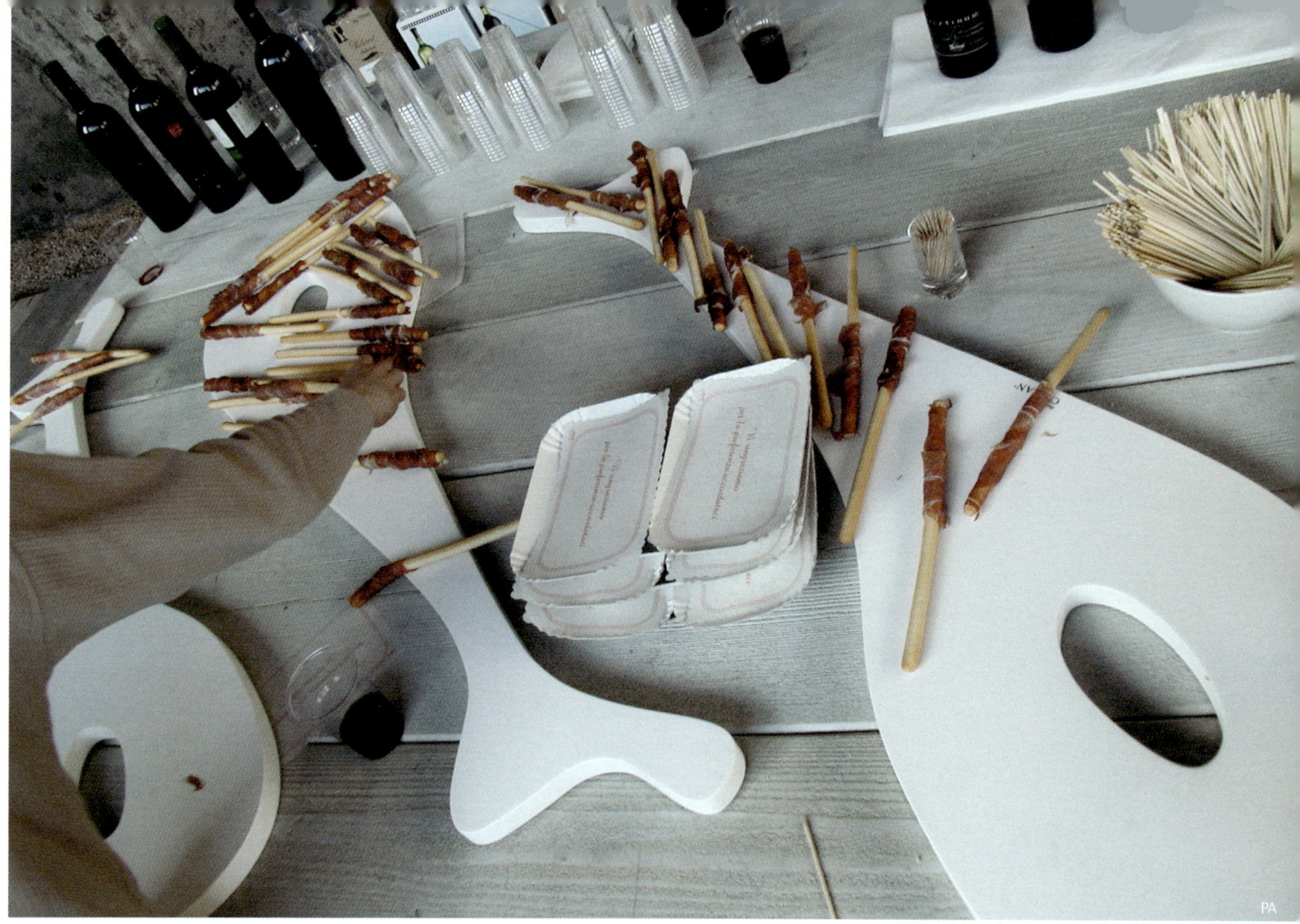

@ Designosaurus

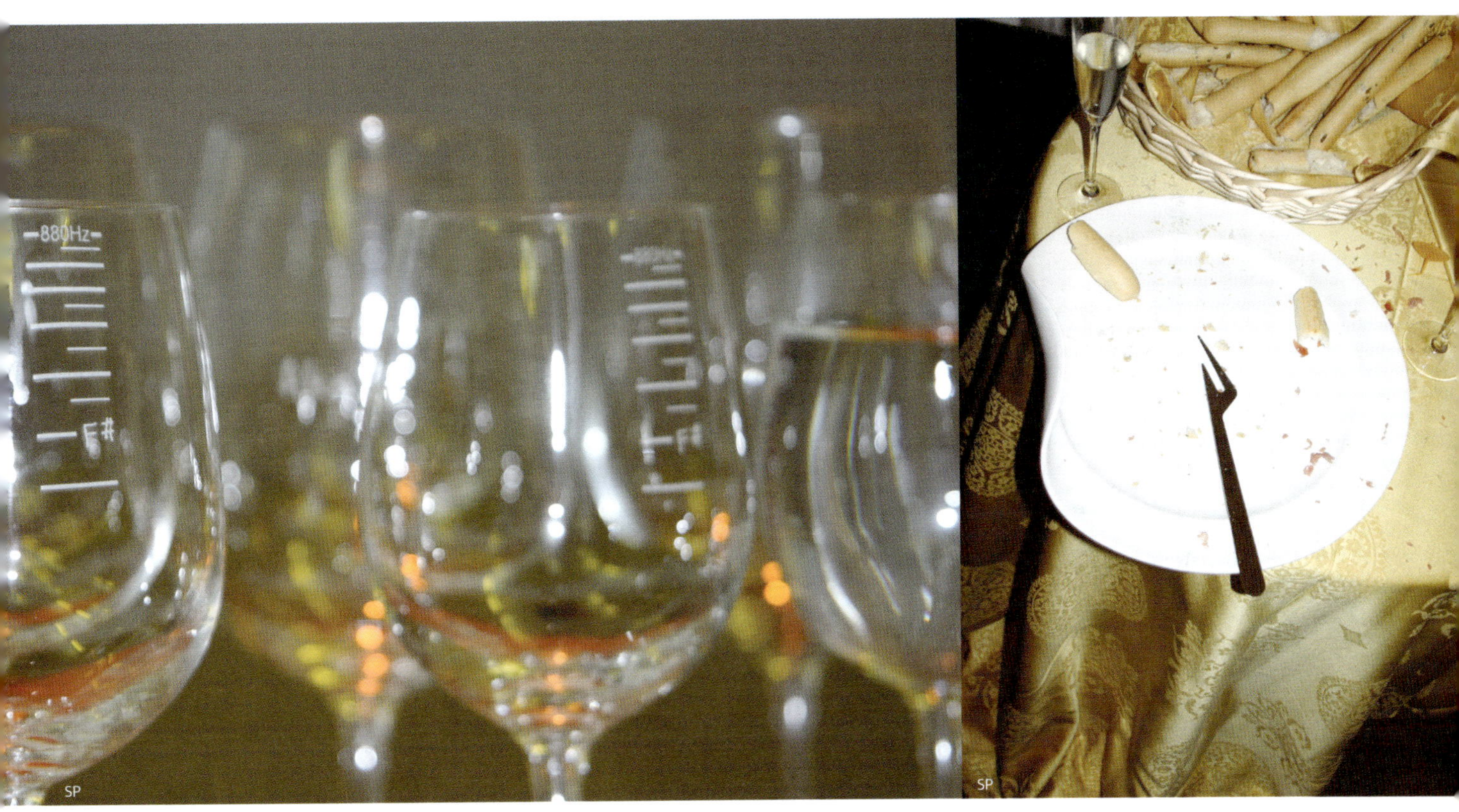

LaLala

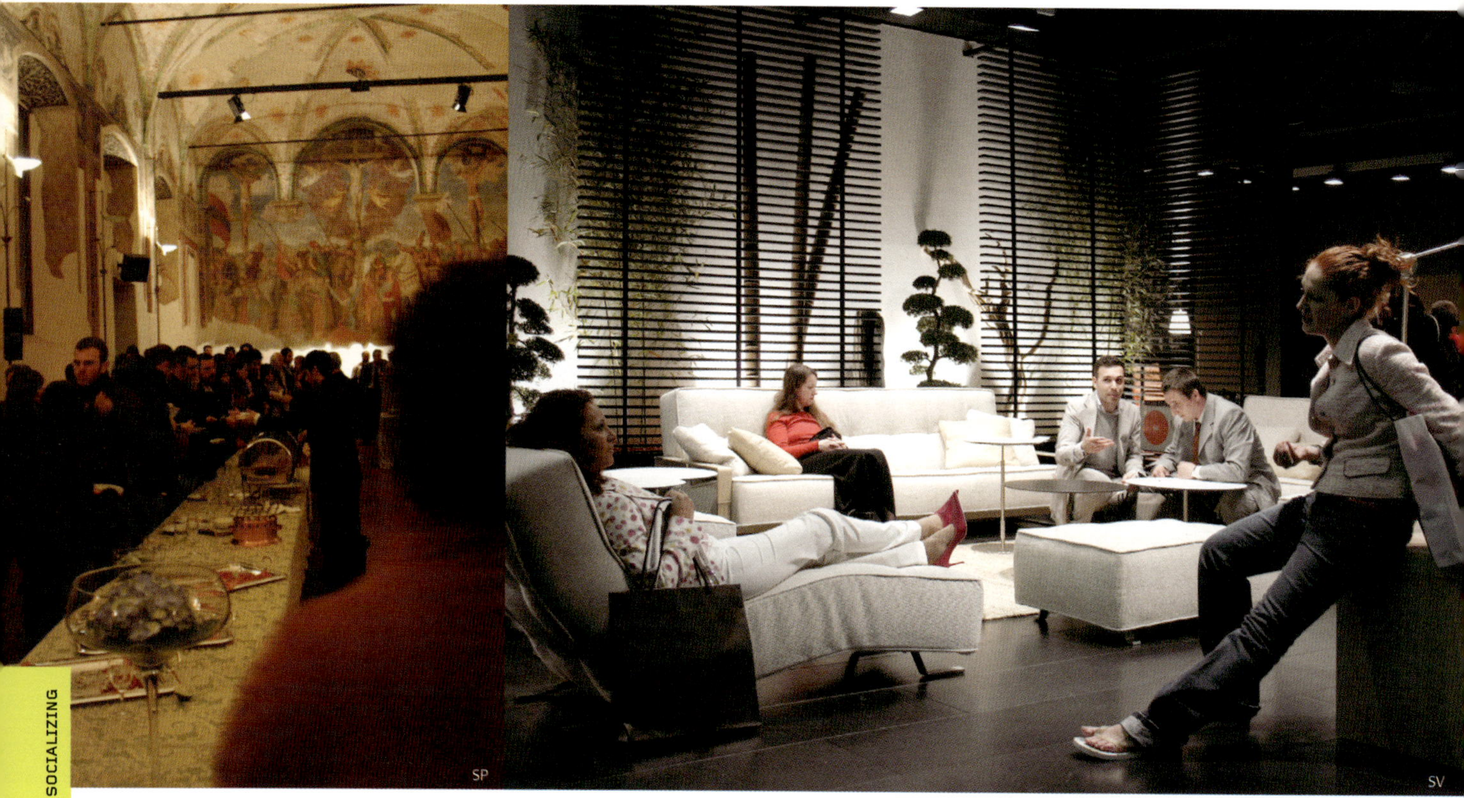

Meritalia

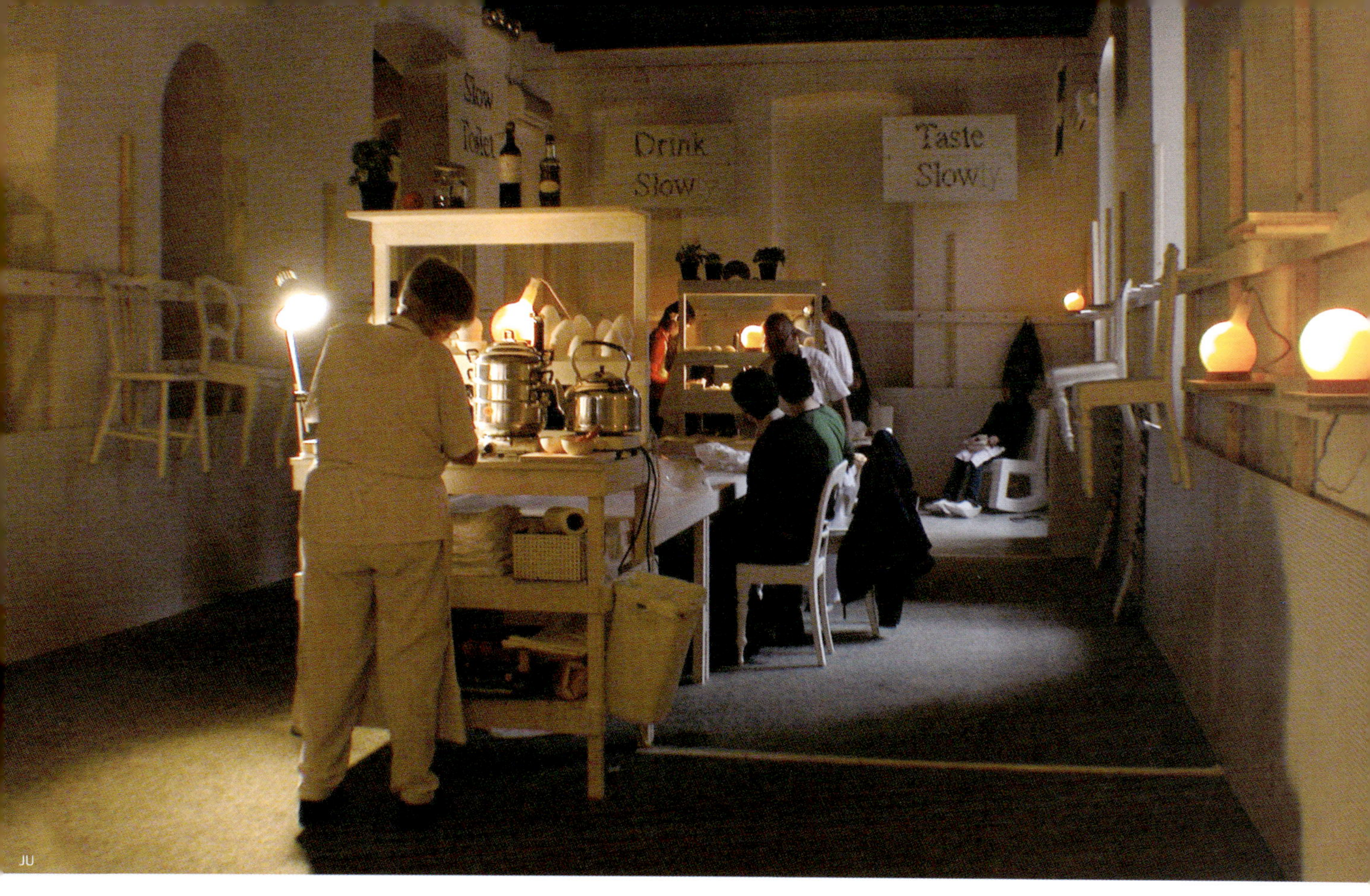

"Go slow" by Droog Design

INAM
Individuality in glass and metal.
FRENER & REI
MP
MP

ADOLESCENCE- SOCIALIZING

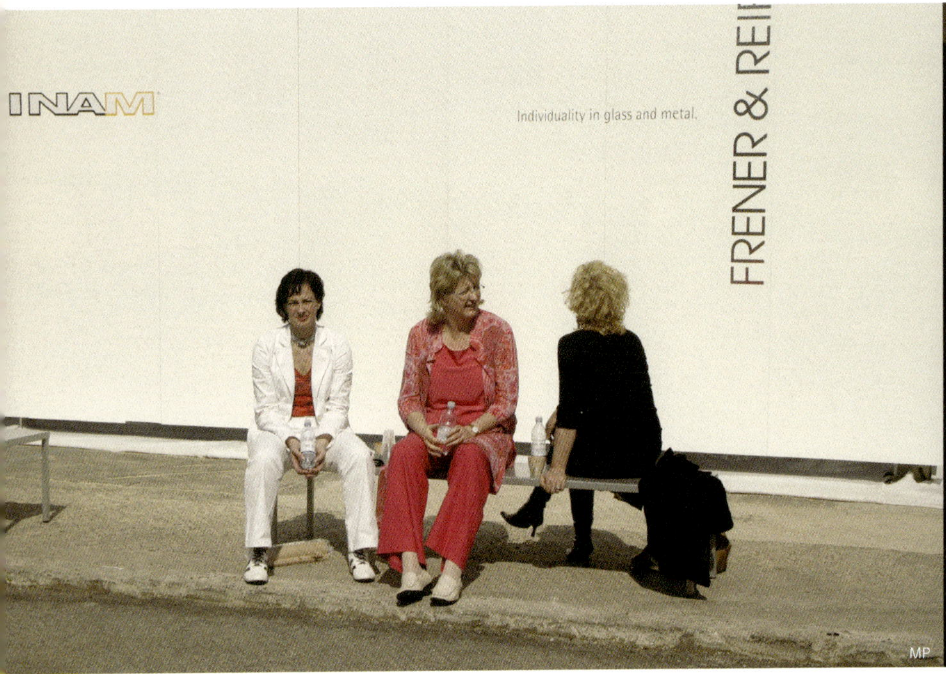

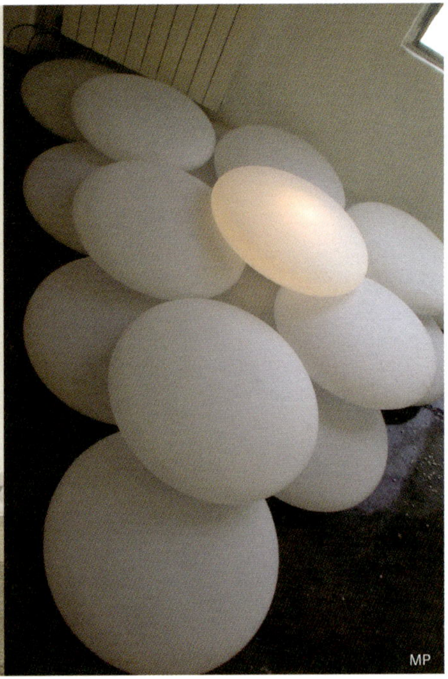

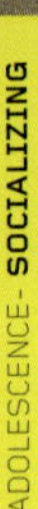

194

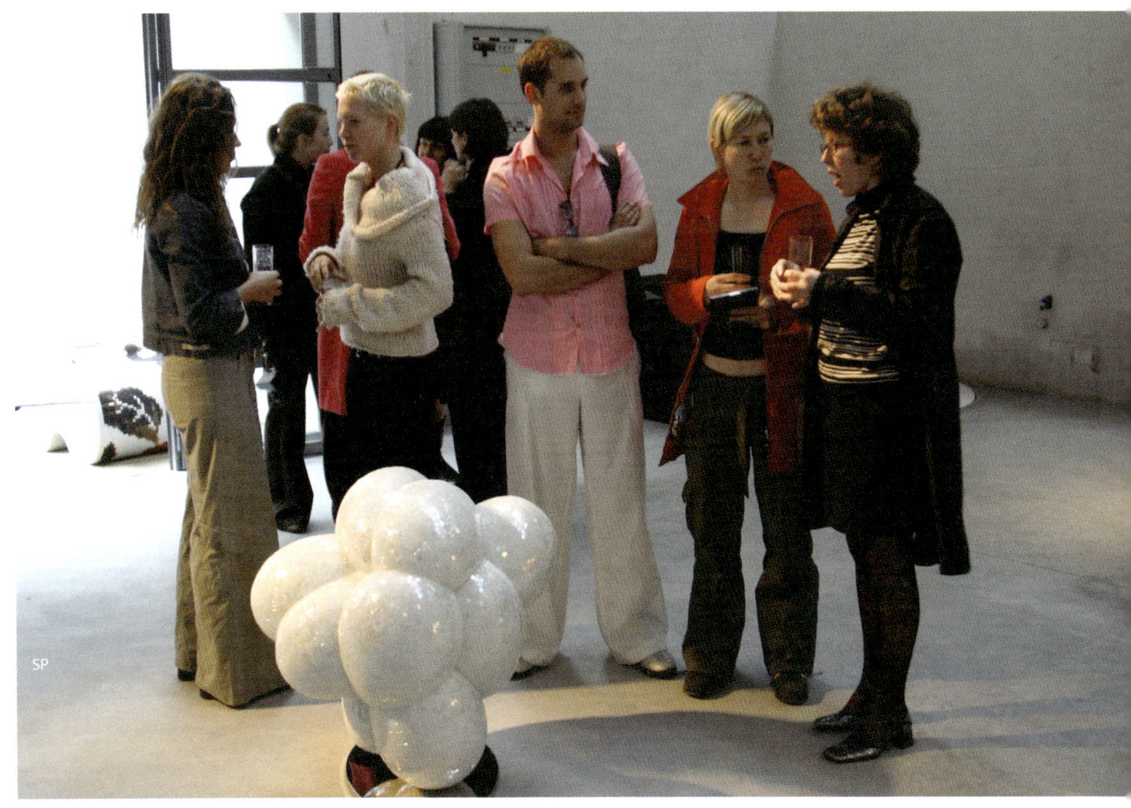

Bisazza

> MATCH THIS "FLAVOURS WITH DESIGN

SPICY	intriguing
CRUNCHY	scrummy
TASTY	when something is missing to turn a "normal" product into something extraordinary
TASTELESS	dull
YUMMY	a product that is a "hit" with the market… who knows why and on whom does it depends
SALTY	something stepping over the mark and resulting in "bad taste"
SWEET	with predictable colour effects
BITTER	a strong object, with distinctive features
ORGANIC	trying to profit from something undeservedly
ACID	an exciting and perhaps fluorescent colour
OUT OF DATE	a cutting edge project
VEGETARIAN	I am ashamed to answer since I am a vegetarian myself!
ALCOHOLIC	the infinite stupidity of glam "bottle design" for grappa
ITALIAN CUISINE	by now an ambitious project we hunger for
SUSHI	a real and raw reality
INDIAN CUISINE	the time and space where spices make all the difference
FUSION CUISINE	something to look at and not destined for consumption
BOILED	seen over and over again and yet successfully recycled

DAVID PALTERER

Enzo Mari	SPICY	A new project!
The objects by Achille Castiglioni	CRUNCHY	A brainstorming session
Made in Italy	TASTY	An original project
Minimalism	TASTELESS	A copy
Alessi	YUMMY	A designer
Scandinavian design	SALTY	A fine achievement
The bean bag chair	SWEET	Another fine achievement
Black and white	BITTER	A client rejecting a project
Multi purpose objects	ORGANIC	Recyclable
Packaging	ACID	An ironical project
Hyper high tech objects	OUT OF DATE	Out of date
Overstated interior decor	VEGETARIAN	An organic project
Computers	ALCOHOLIC	An opening ceremony!
The corkscrew by Anna G.	ITALIAN CUISINE	1960's design
Shigeru Ban	SUSHI	Japanese sophistication
Sottsass	INDIAN CUISINE	Bollywood
French design	FUSION CUISINE	Young designers
Details	BOILED	Old designers

MIGLIORE + SERVETTO

GALA FERNANDEZ

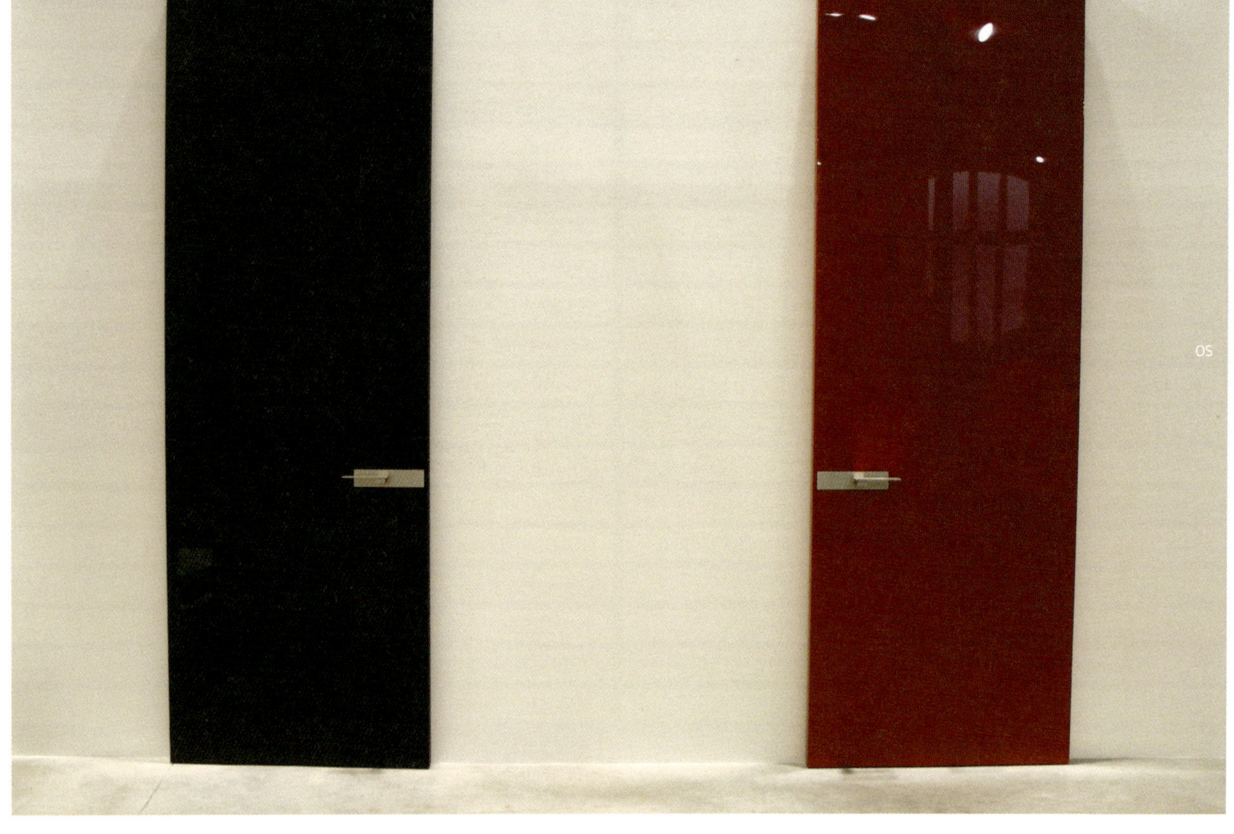

Lualdi Porte

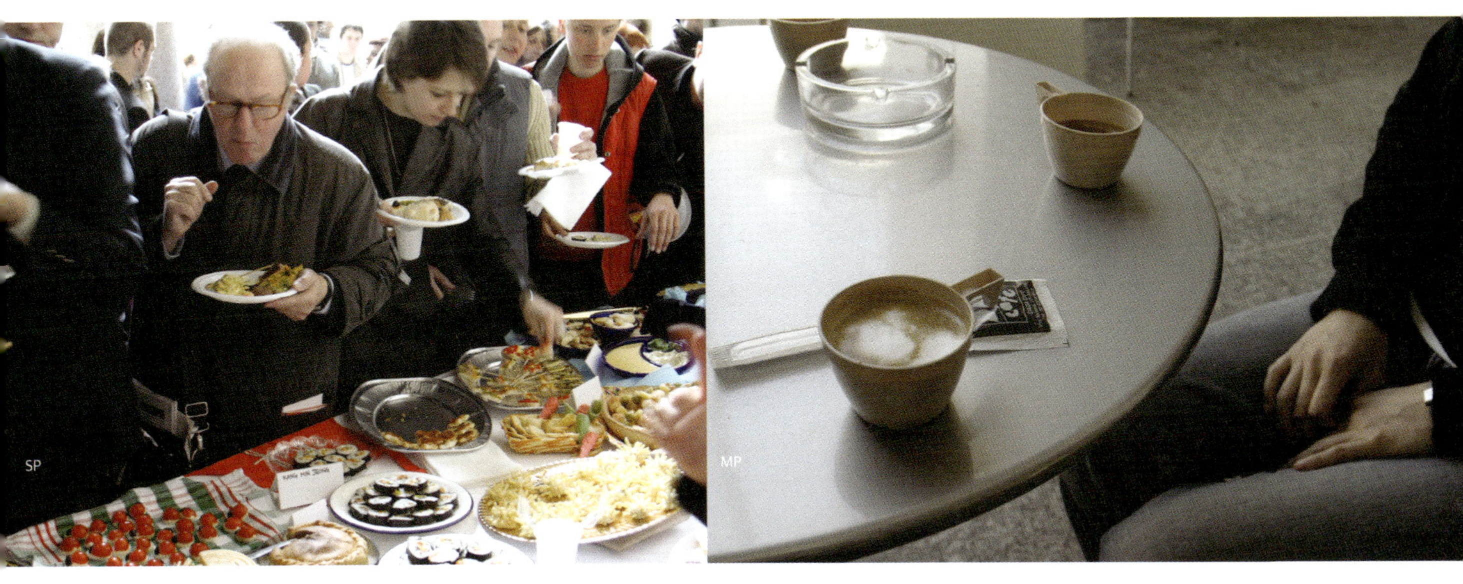

Accademia di Belle Arti

Food takeaway @ Dining Design

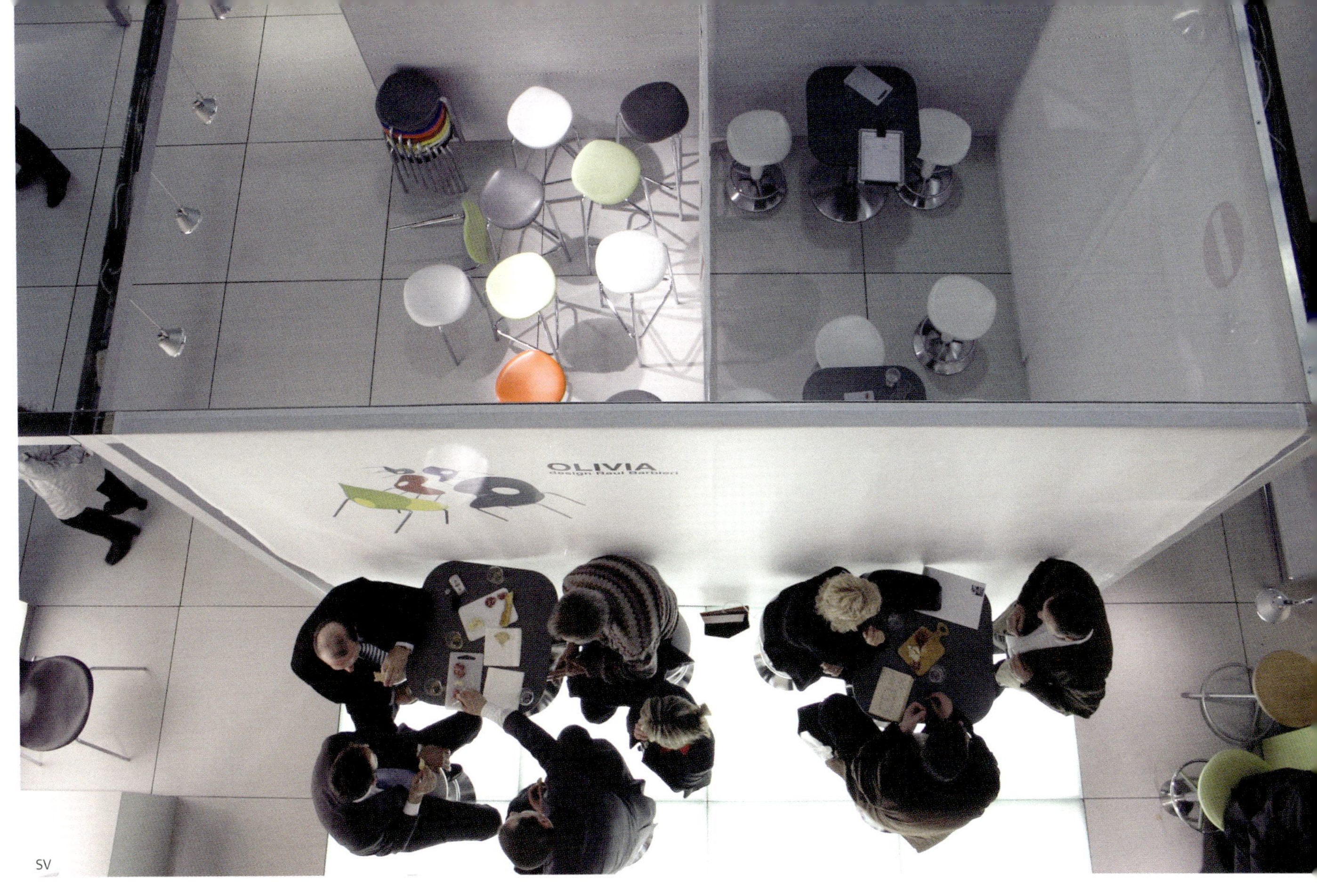

SV

Rexite

Like aliens from another planet, students, designers and teachers from Interaction-Ivrea

landed at the Triennale di Milano with their exhibition that bringed together some of

their more typical works: a classic Olivetti "Lettera 22" typewriter sending email, a table

functioning as a virtual fortune-teller, a vintage Fiat 500 car "downloading mp3 files

while being refueled, etc.

A kaleidoscope of suggestions (24 projects in all) in which the technological core of the

objects, deliberately hidden, is combined with their soft, bright, translucent, inflatable, metallic or transparent exteriors.

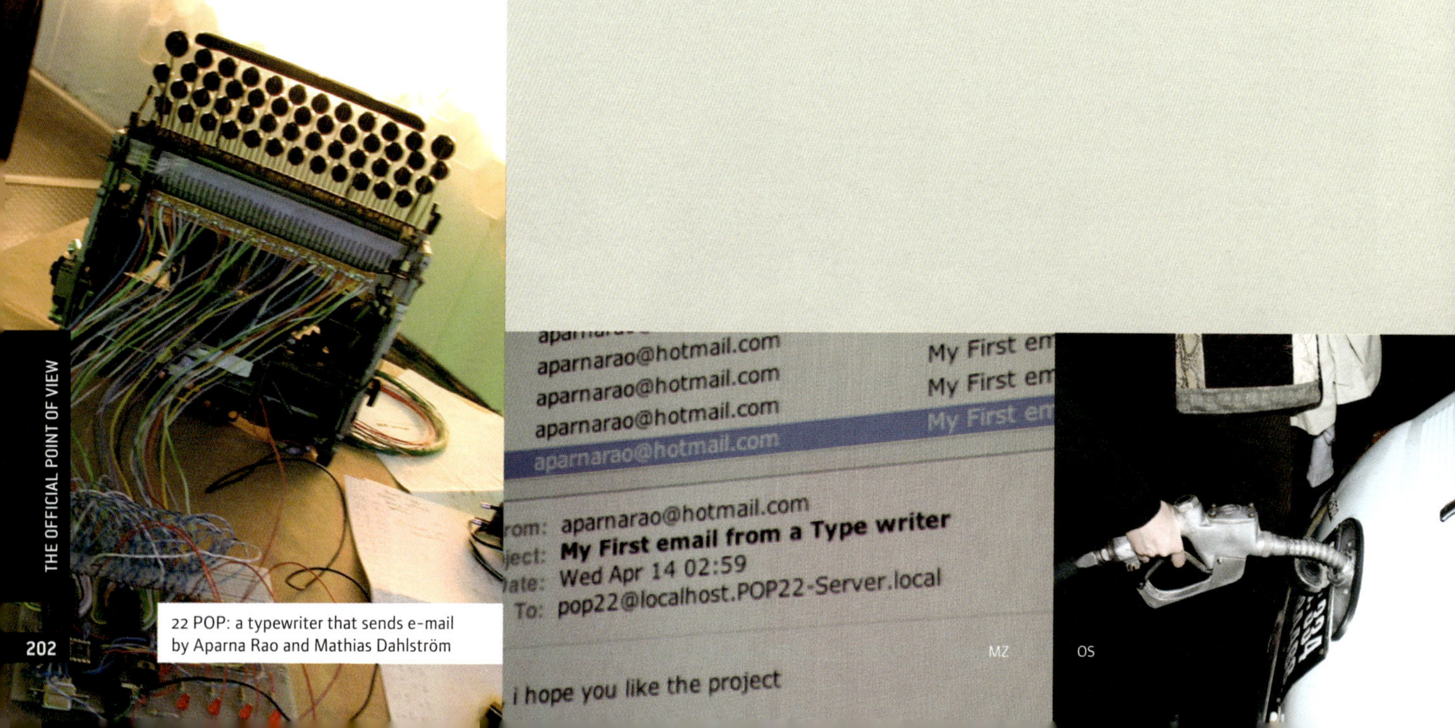

22 POP: a typewriter that sends e-mail
by Aparna Rao and Mathias Dahlström

202

MZ   OS

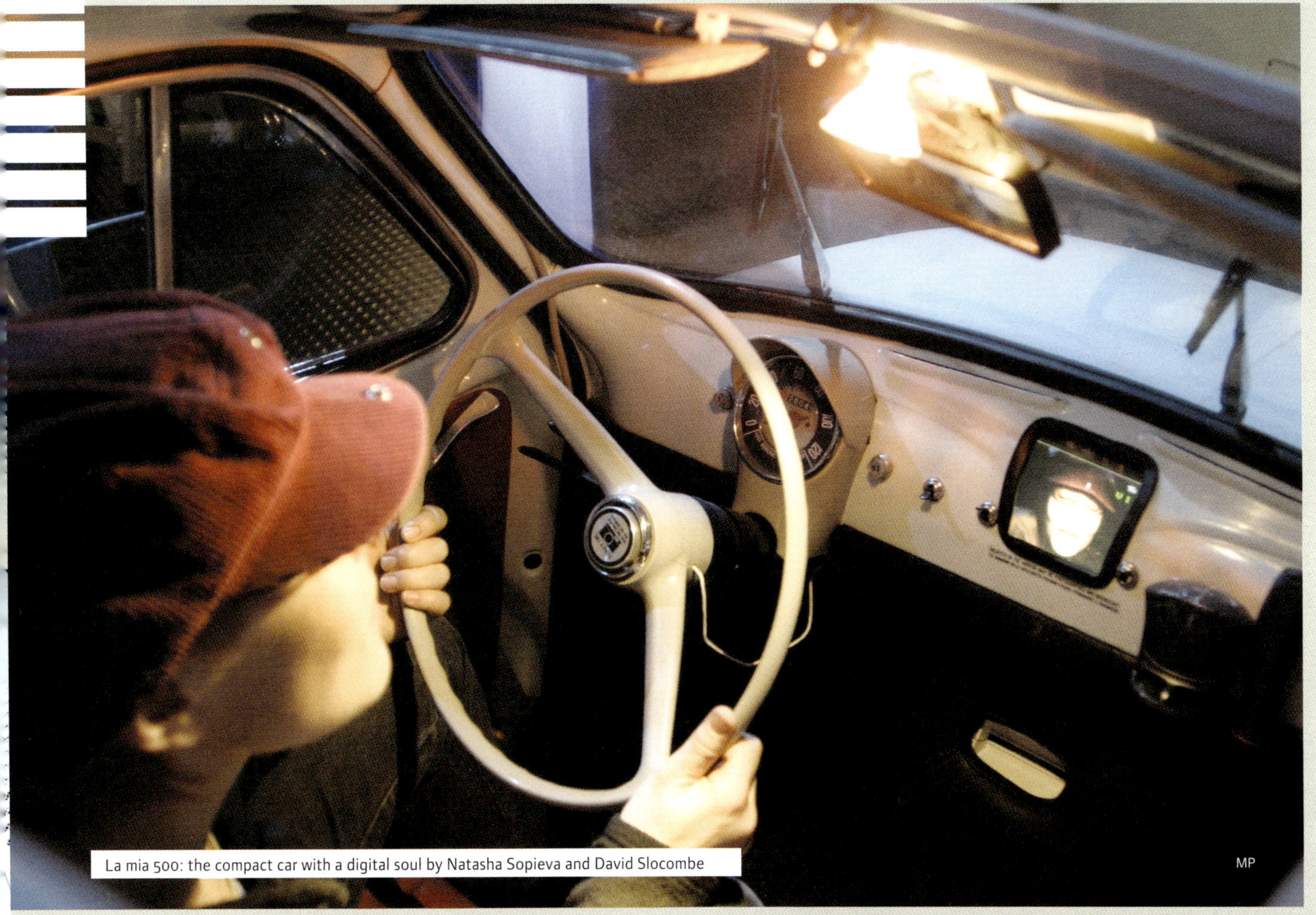

La mia 500: the compact car with a digital soul by Natasha Sopieva and David Slocombe

MP

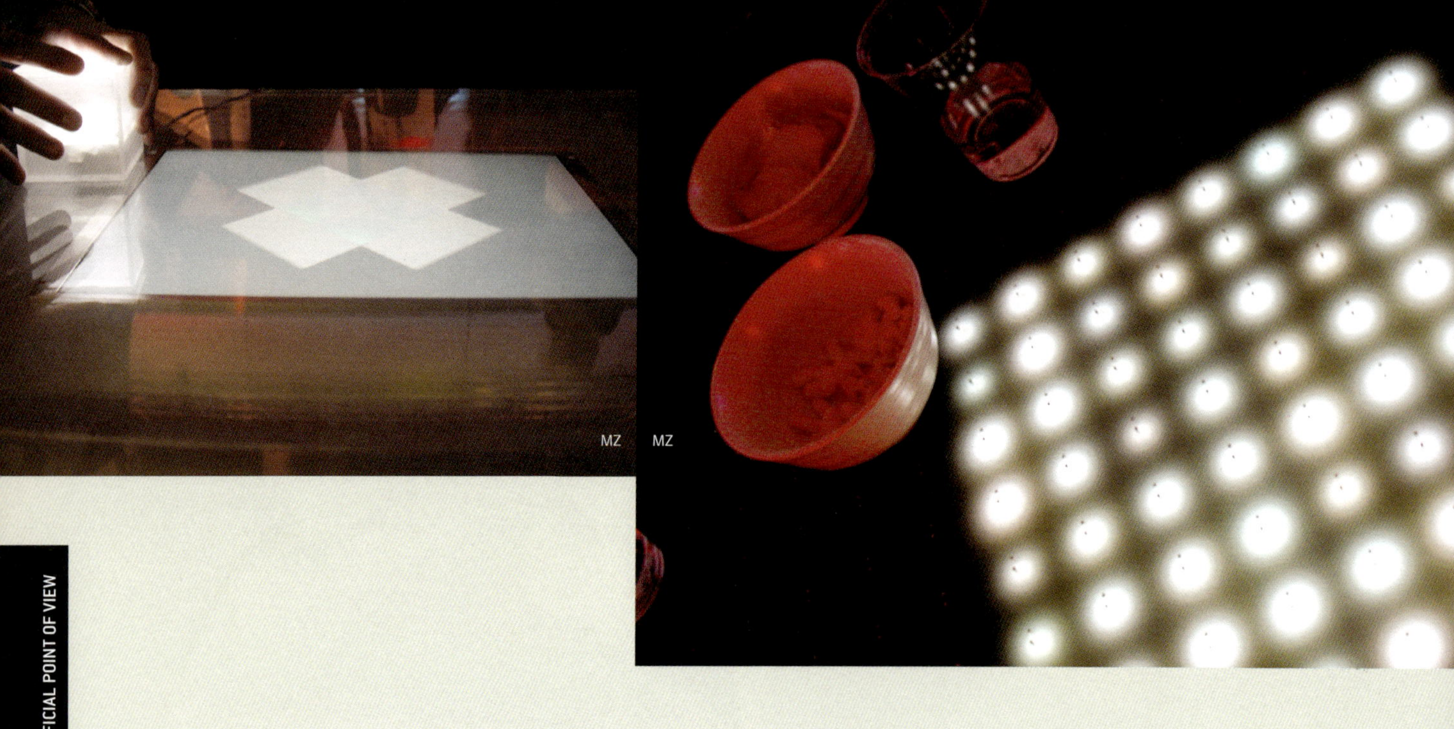

Wirng: Lines of code that brighten up a cube
by Hernando Barragan

Tableportation: café tables for virtual seduction
by Giorgio Olivero and Peggy Thoeny

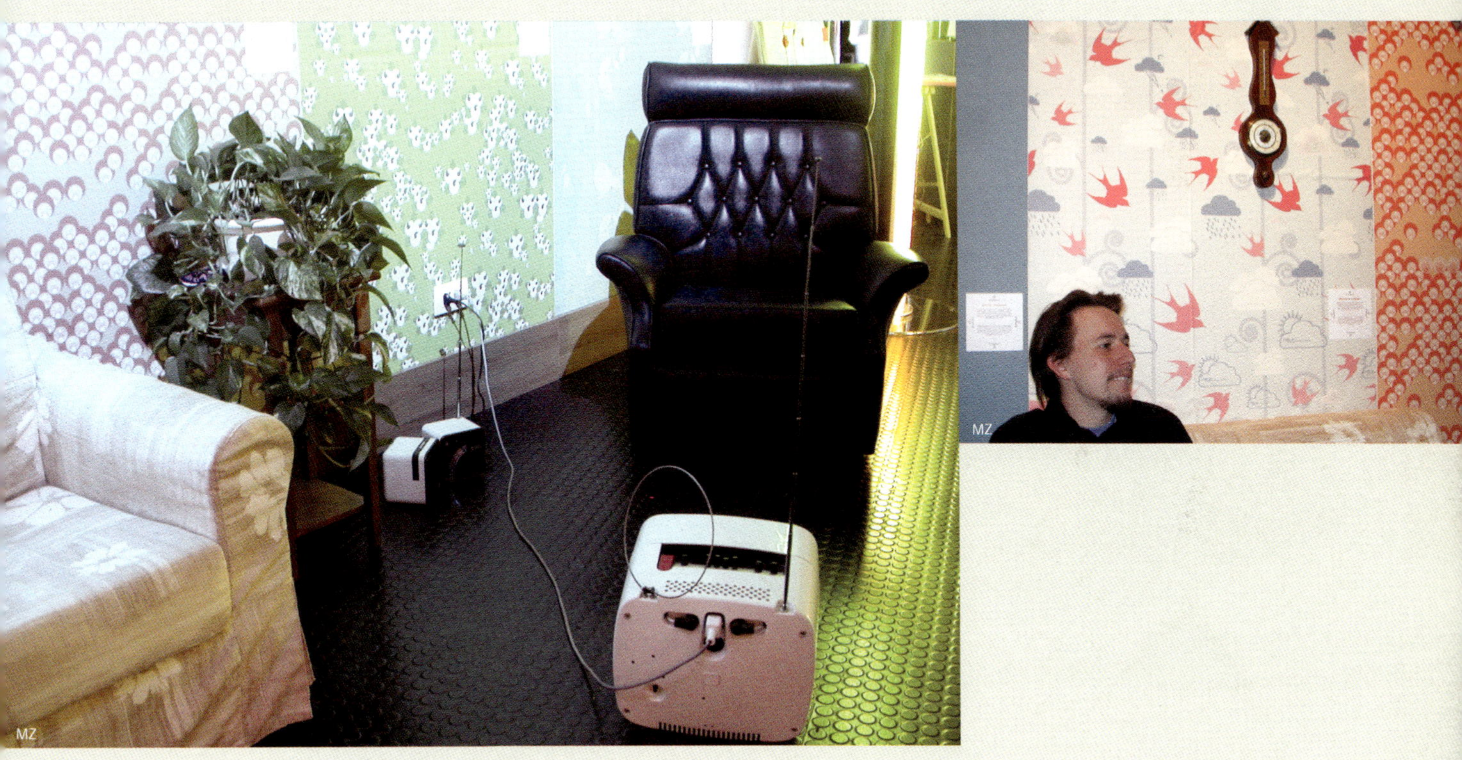

Not-So-White Walls: interactive wallpapers by Dario Buzzini

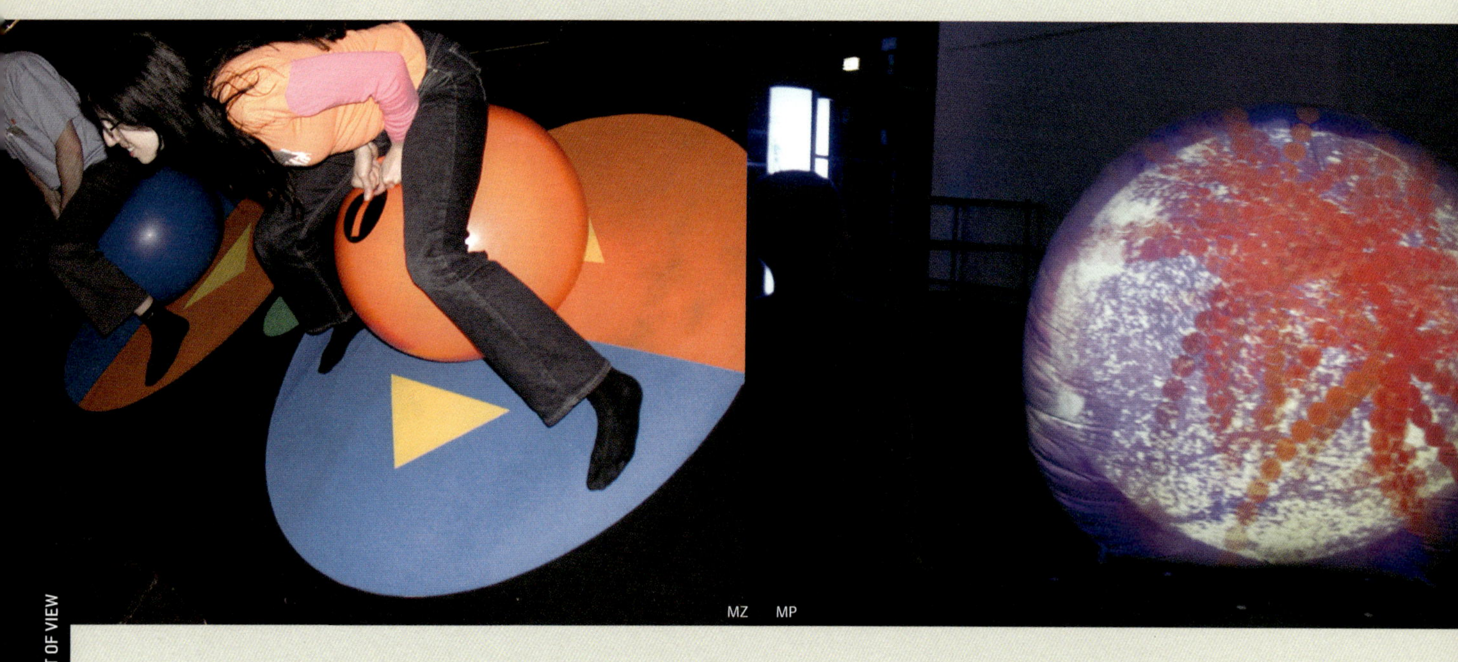

Collabowobble: the videogame you jump around on until you drop
by Jennifer L. Bove, Simone Pia, Nathan Waterhouse

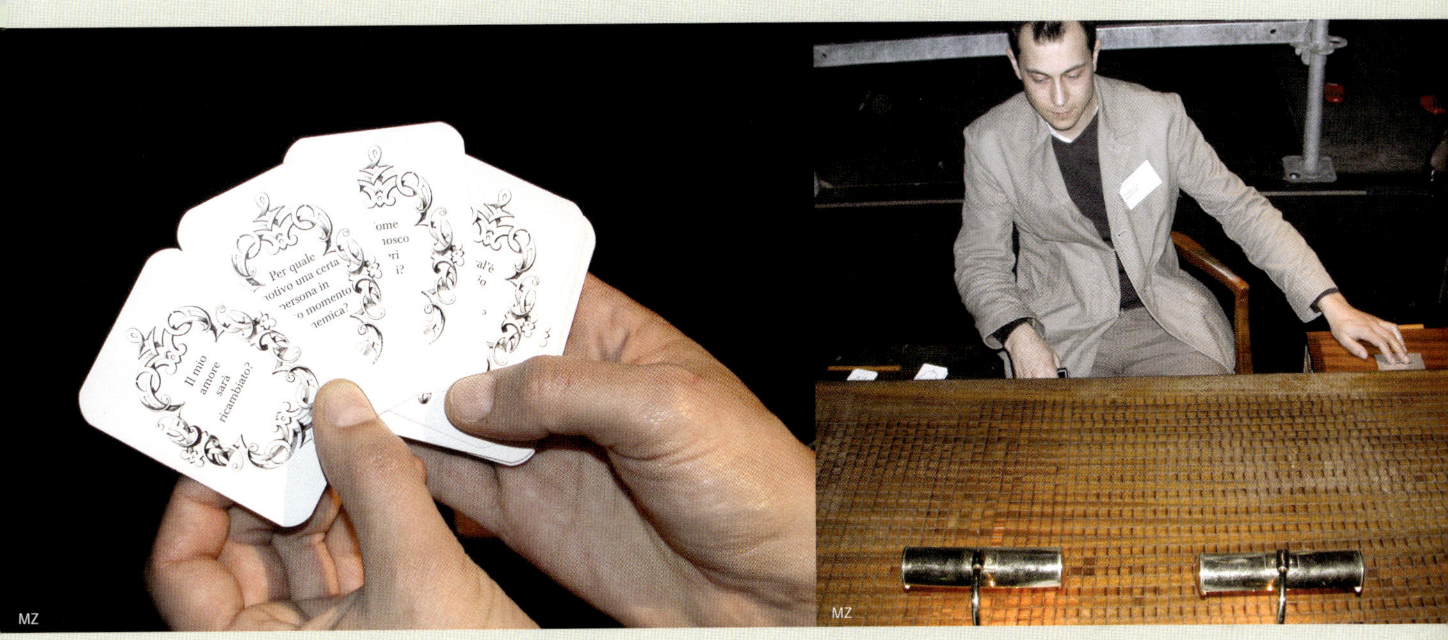

Invisible Force: digital fortune telling with a sdistic touch by Crispin Jones

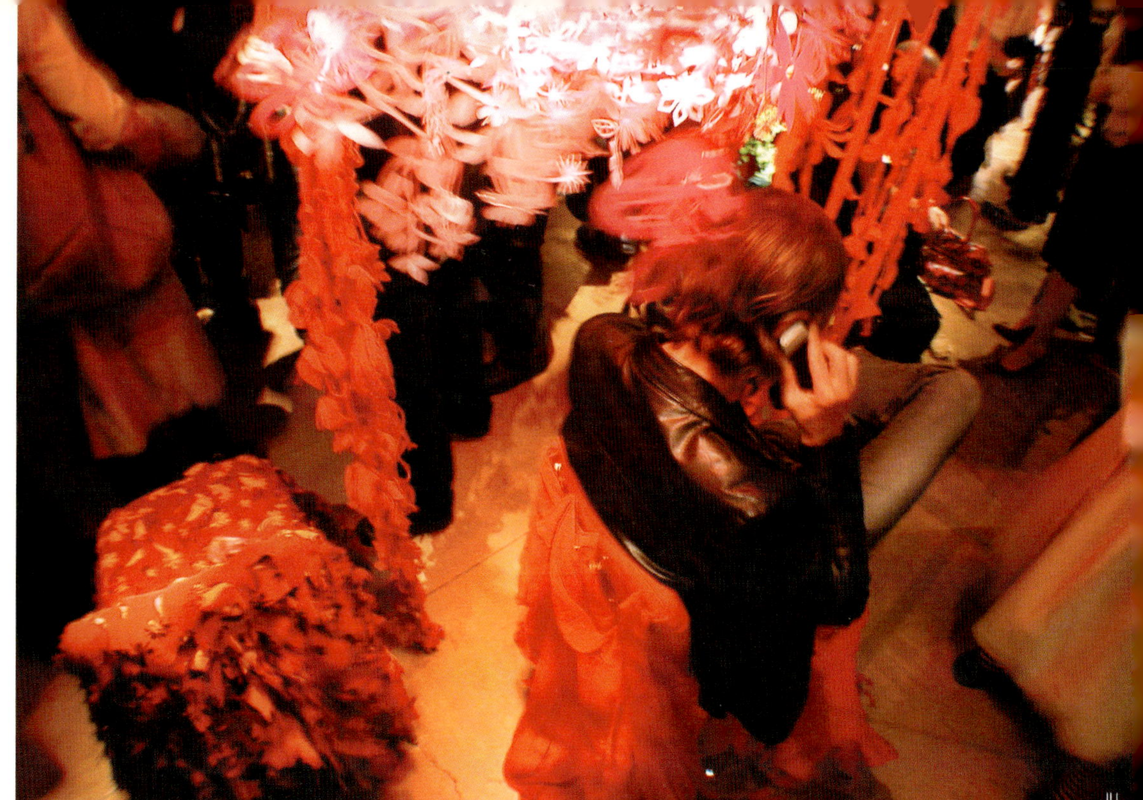

@ Moroso

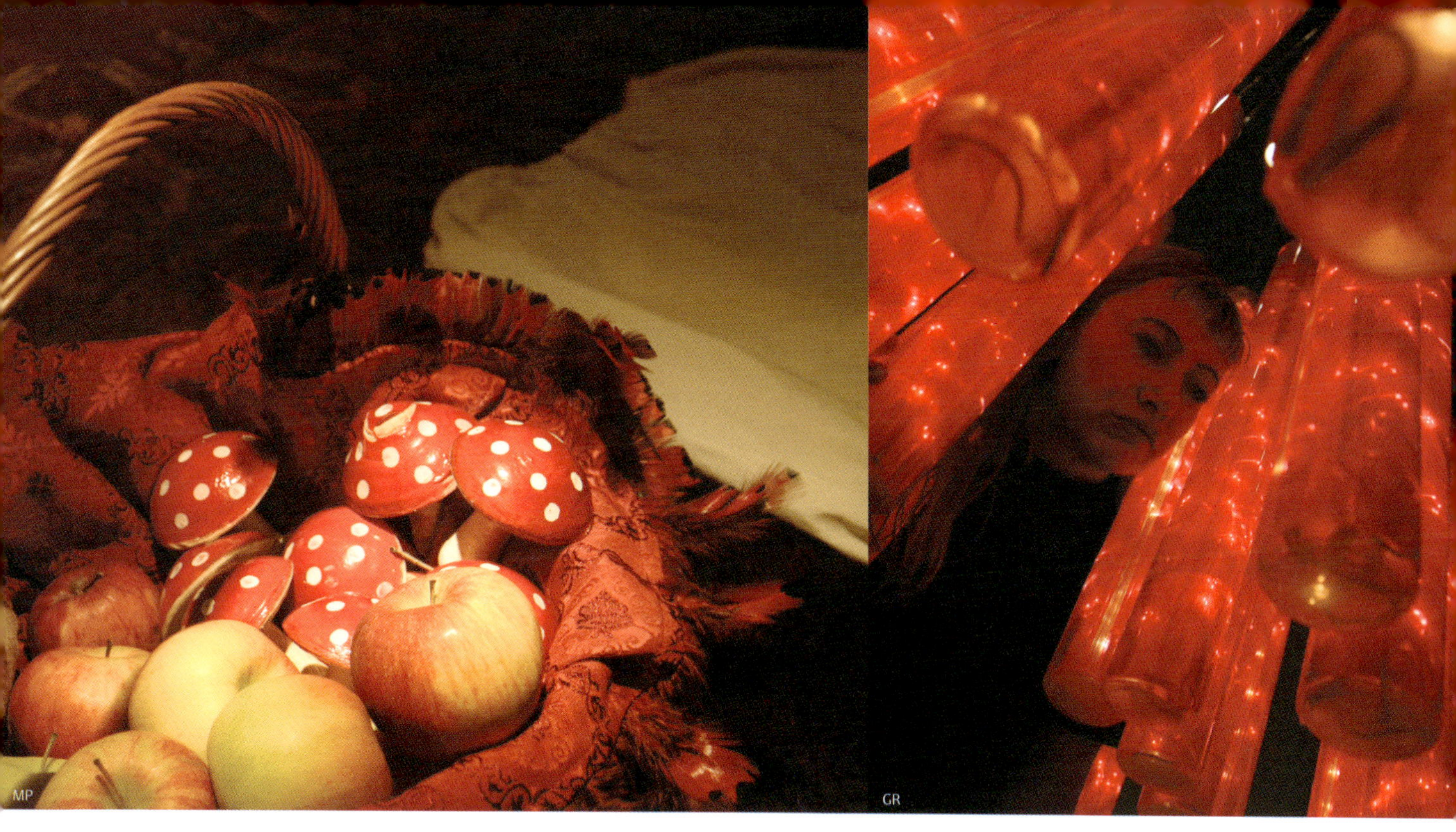

Etro

Florence Jaffrain

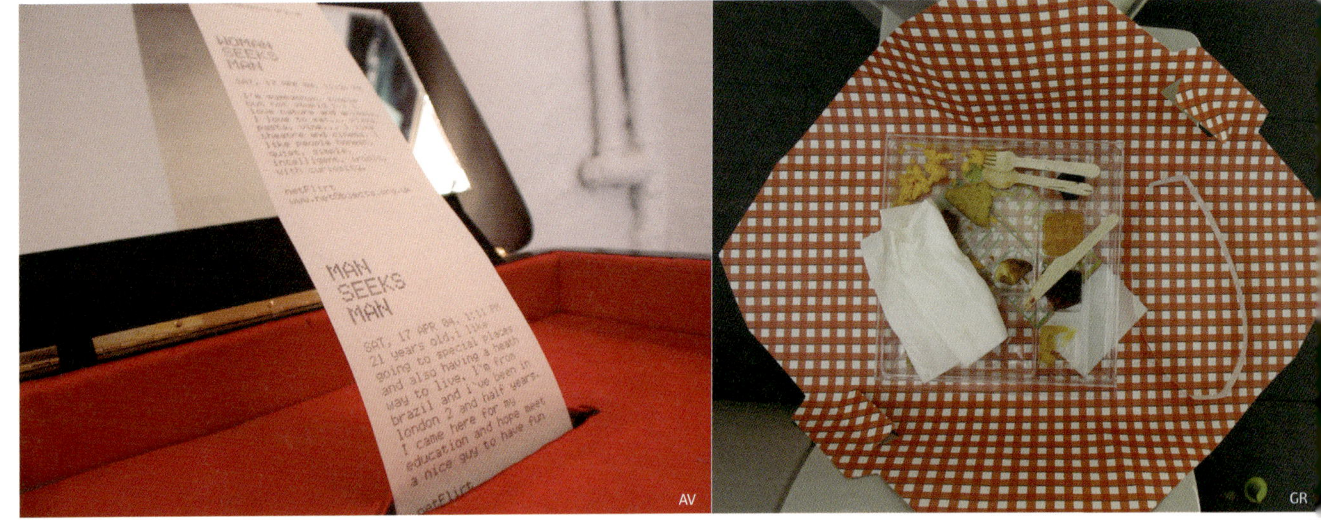

Net Objects @ Tutto BeNe

Quicnic Fast Food Hamburger in Berlin @ Dining Design exhibition

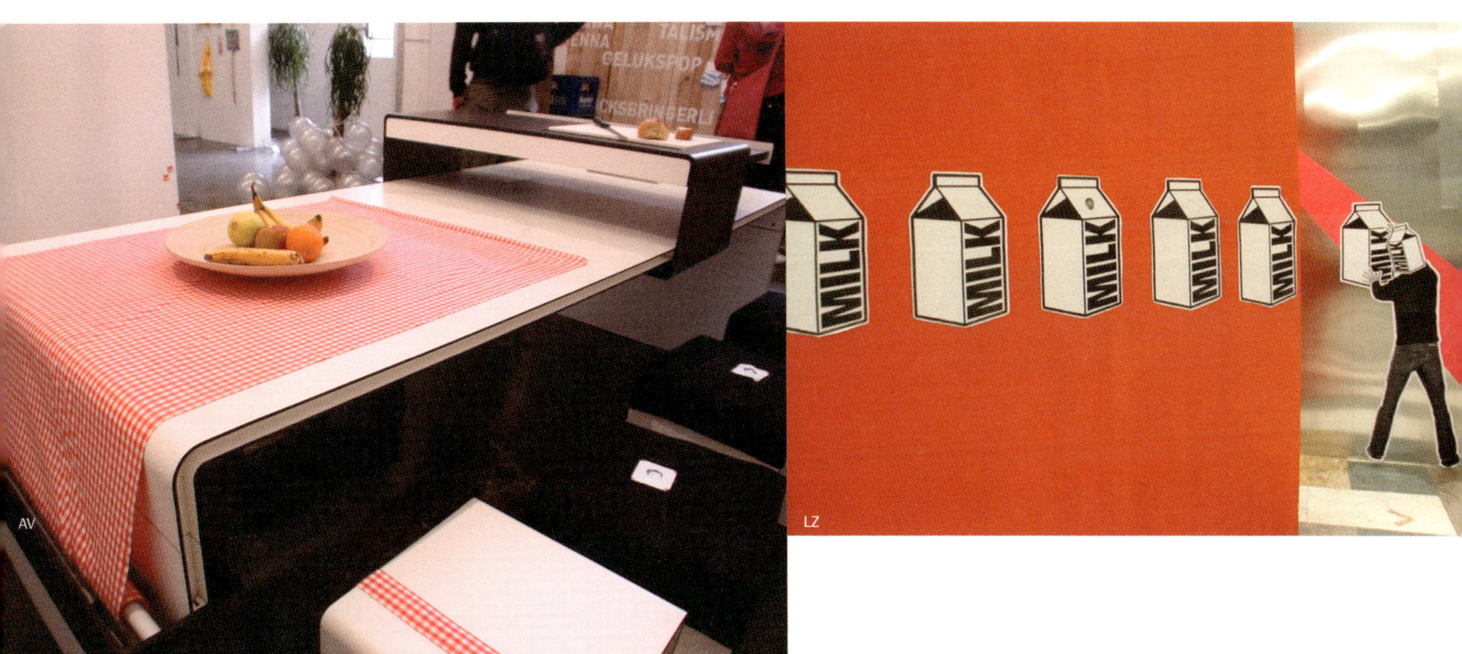

Team 4 @ Designersblock

Daniele De Giorgis

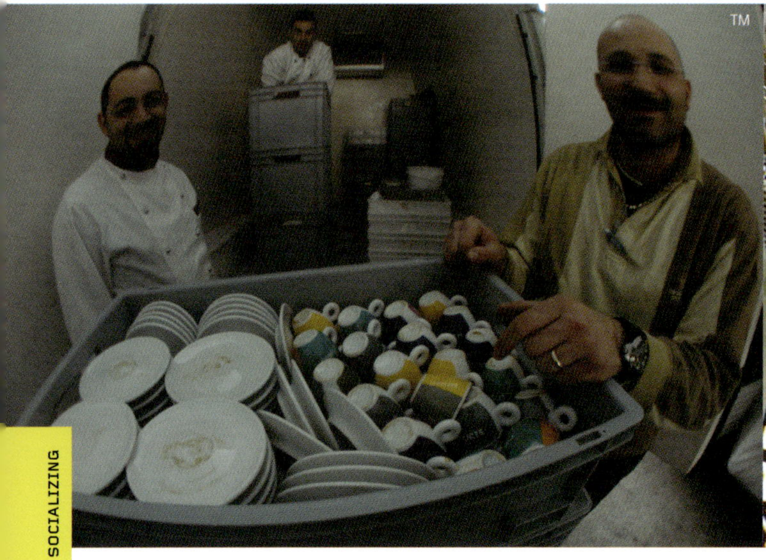

TM

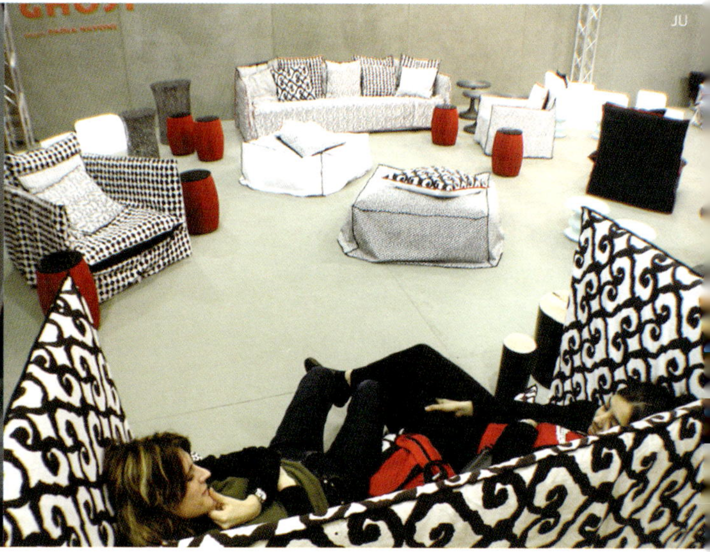

GHOST
JU

Gervasoni

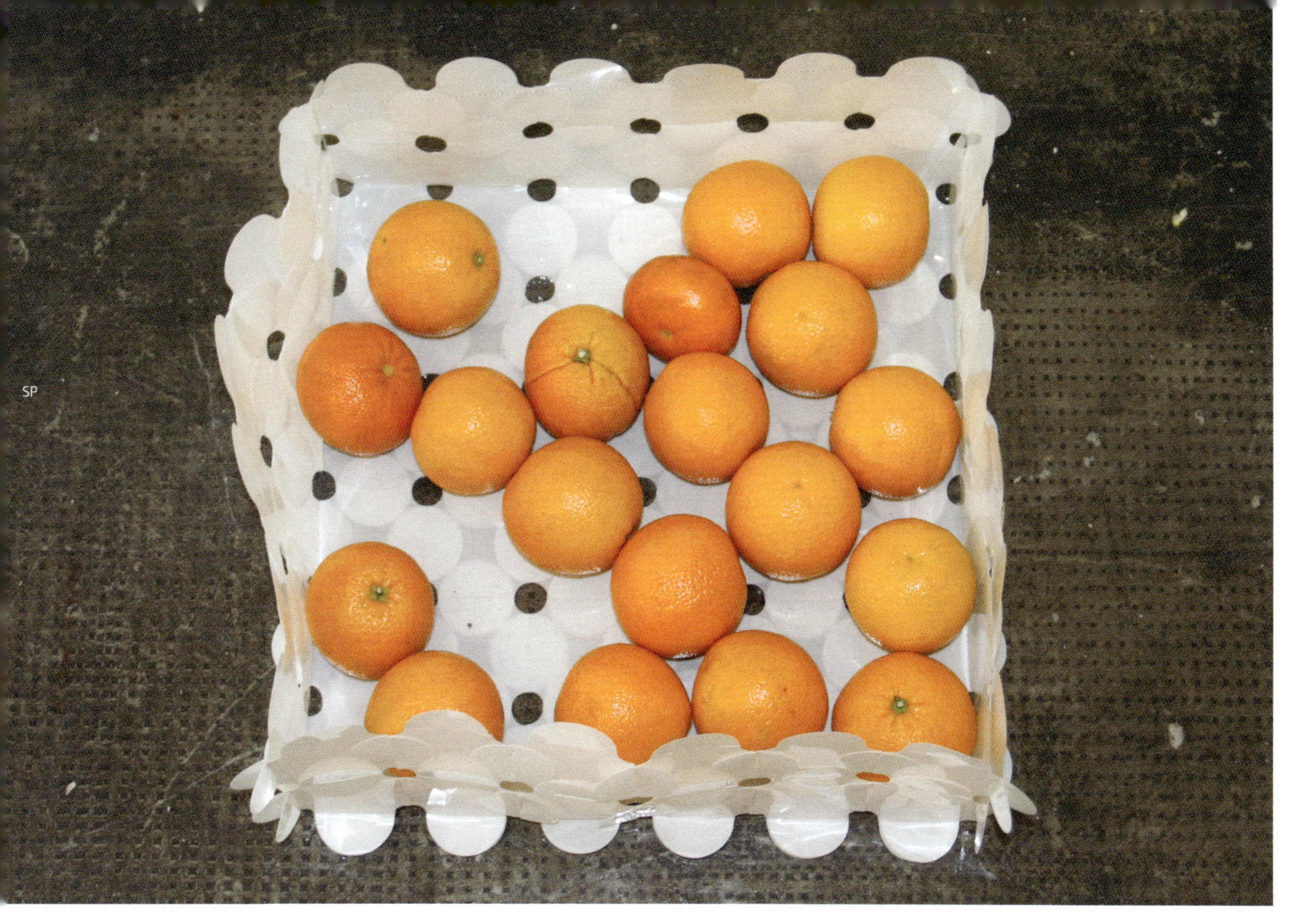

Mia Cullin @ Designersblock..

"The Furniture Fair?
It is like a IKEA on steroids
with nothing for sale!!!"

Darren Almond

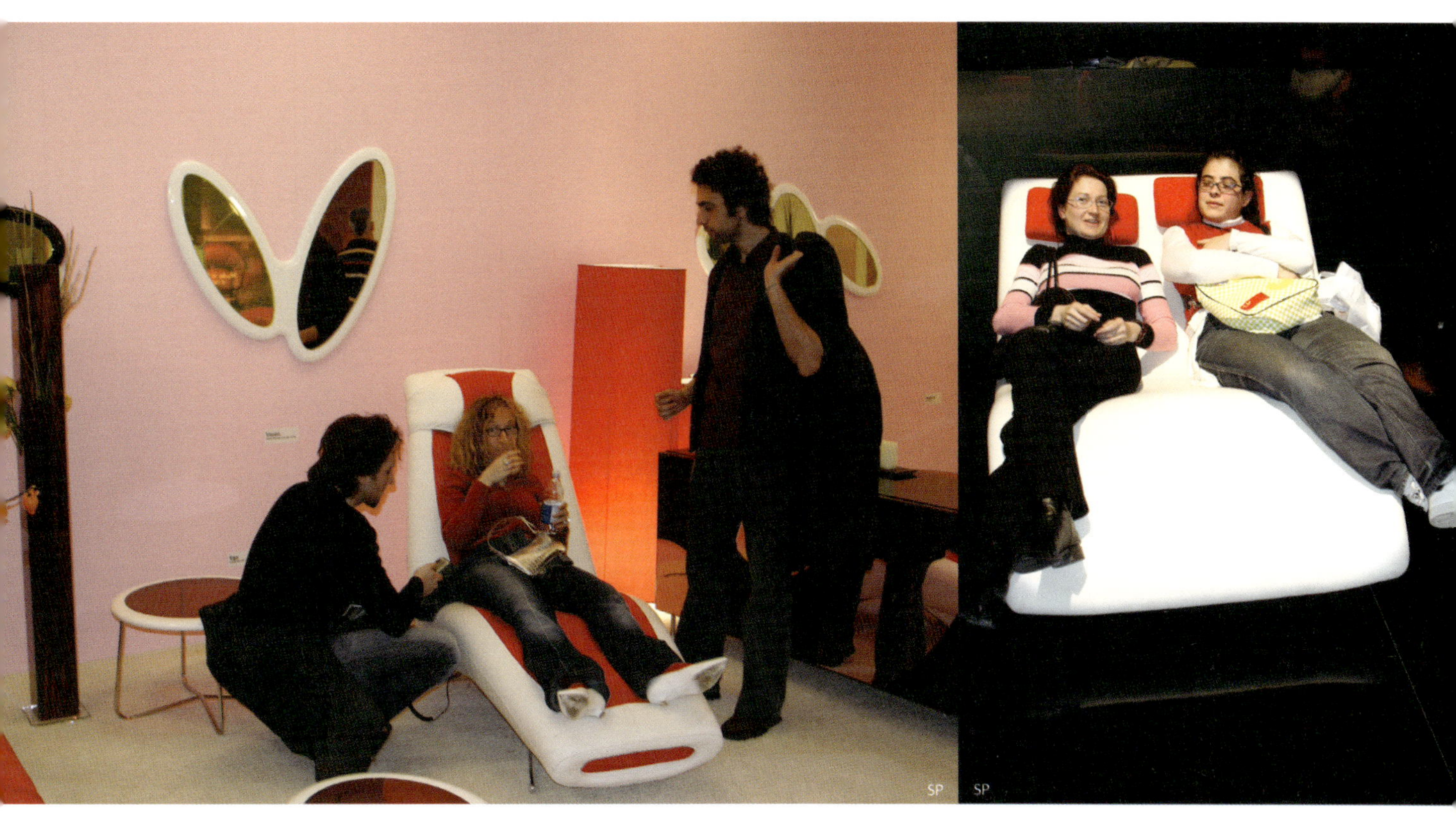

Poltrone Mec

Rossi di Albizzati

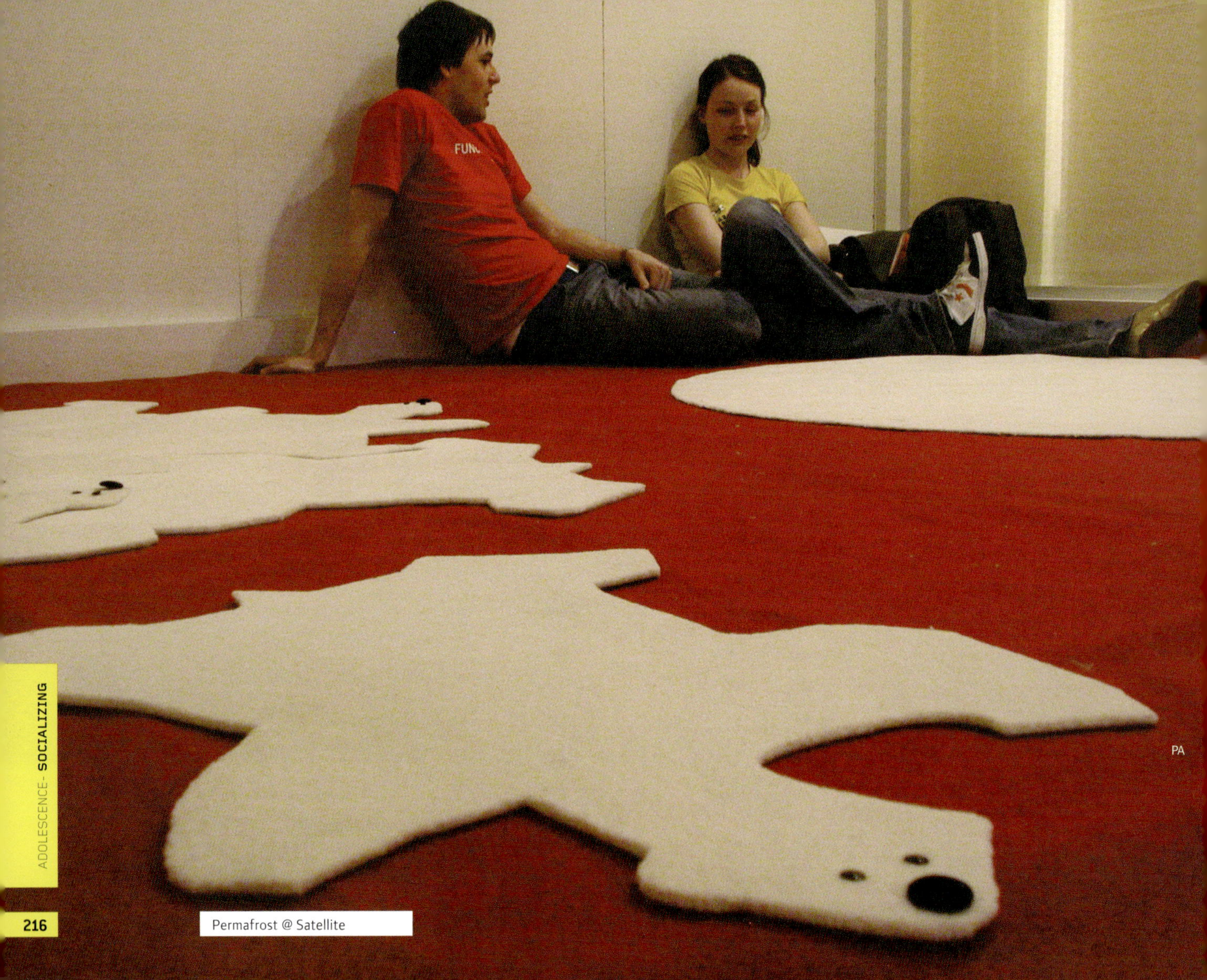

PA

Permafrost @ Satellite

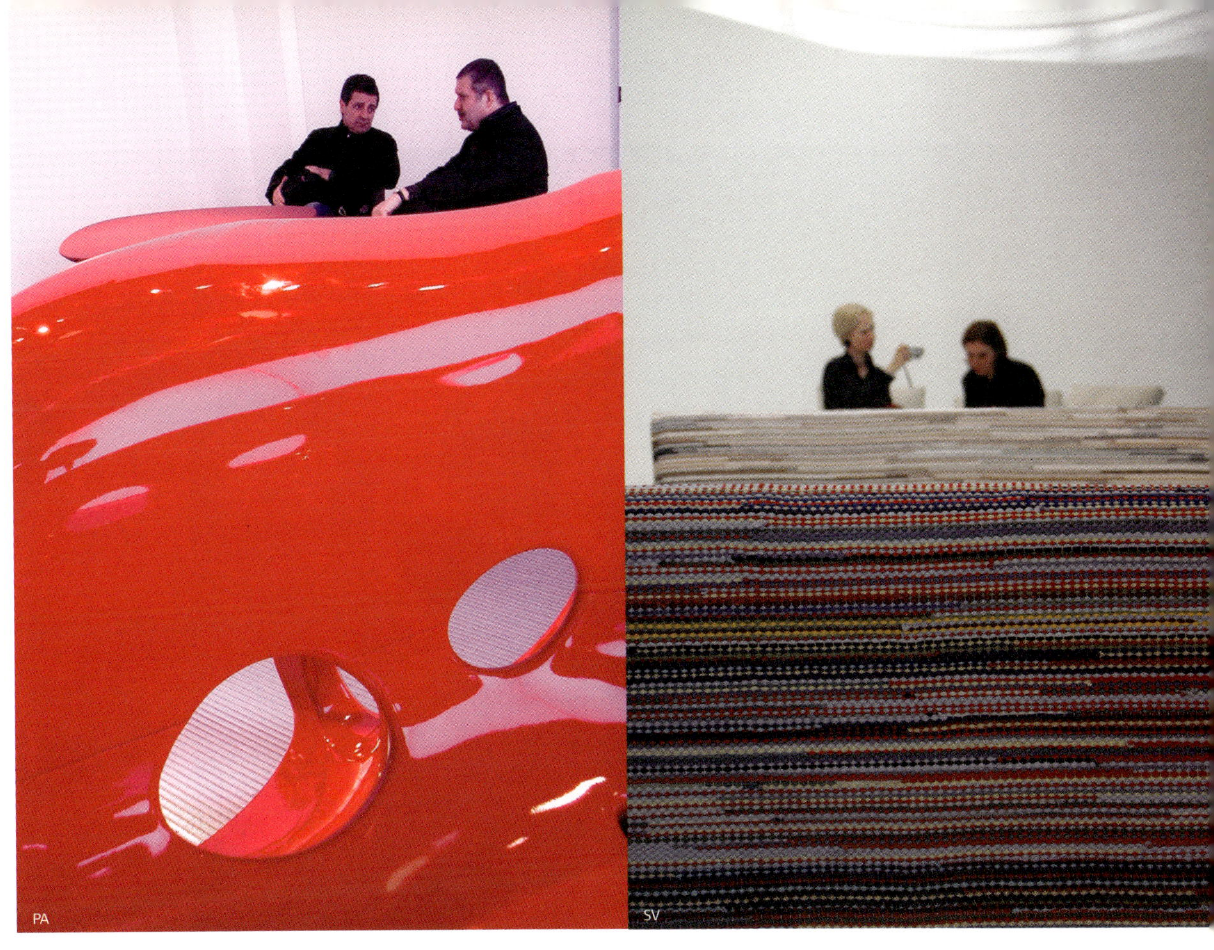

Sawaya&Moroni   Campeggi

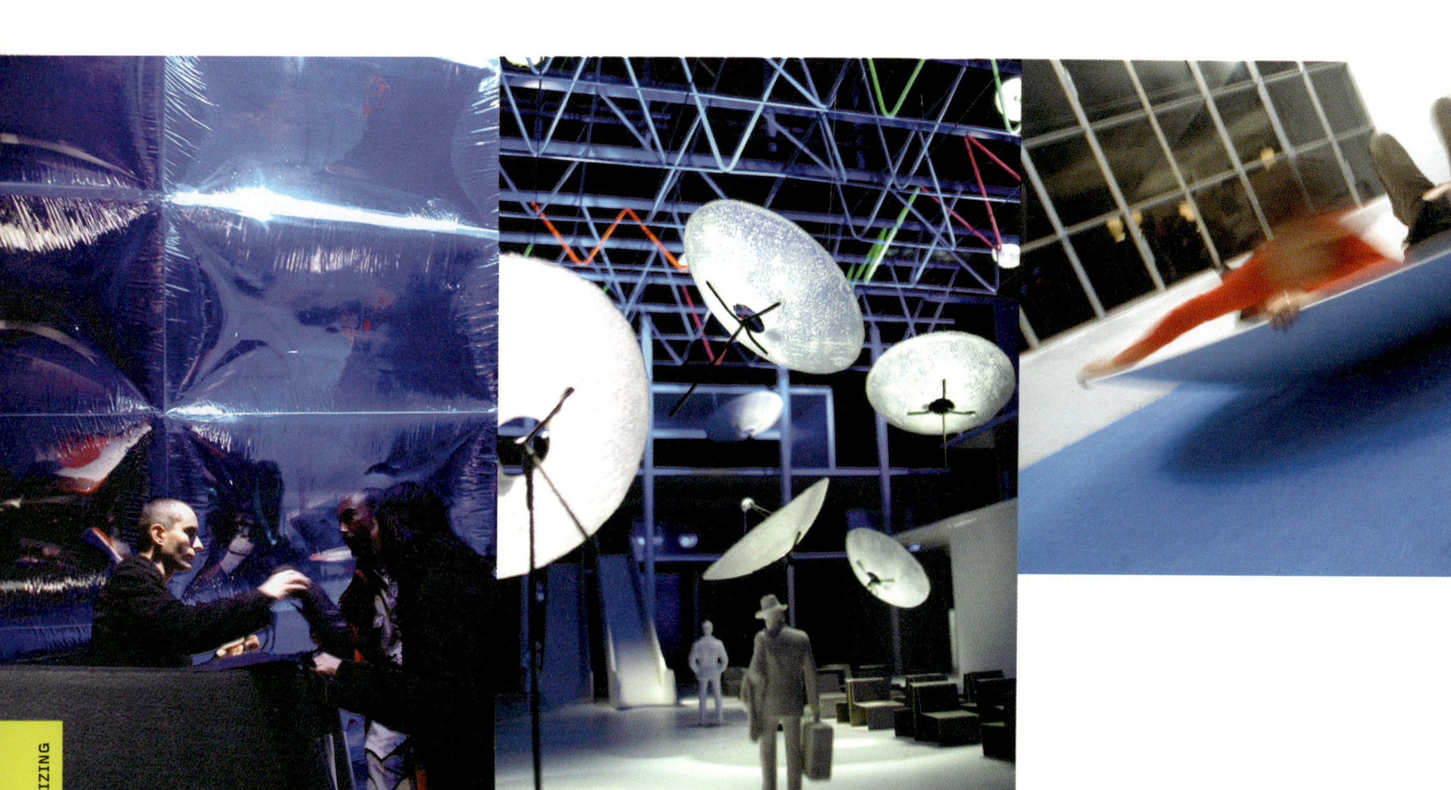

218   Via   Ingo Maurer @ Spazio Krizia

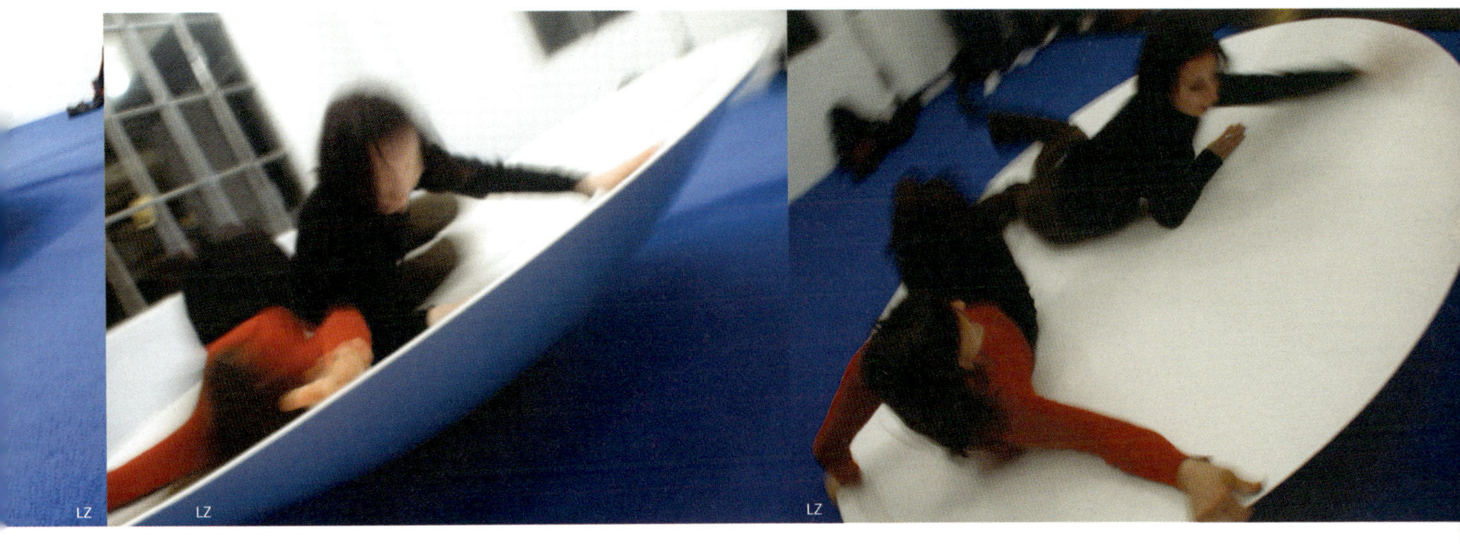

The Temple by Jephson Robb @ Designersblock

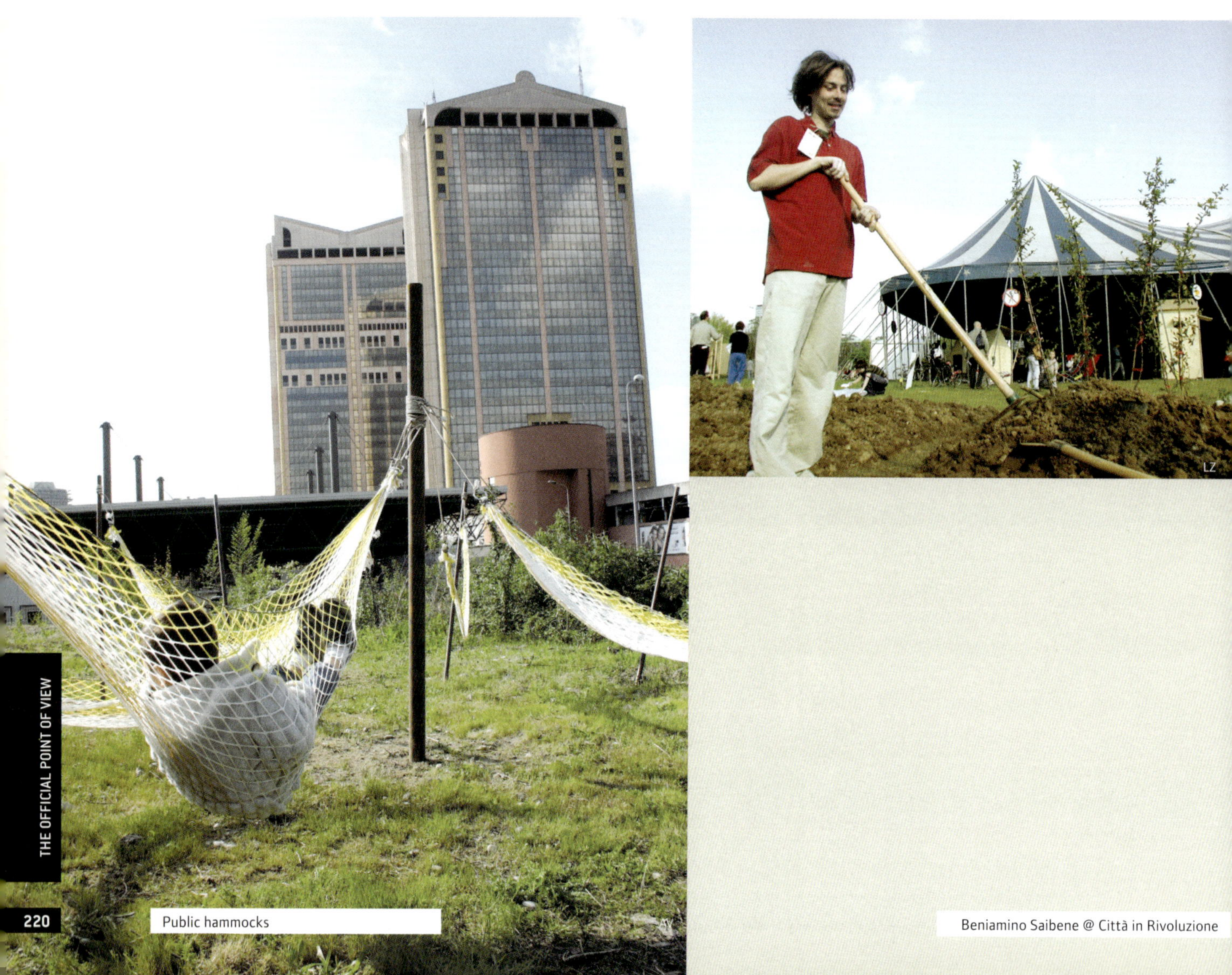

Public hammocks

Beniamino Saibene @ Città in Rivoluzione

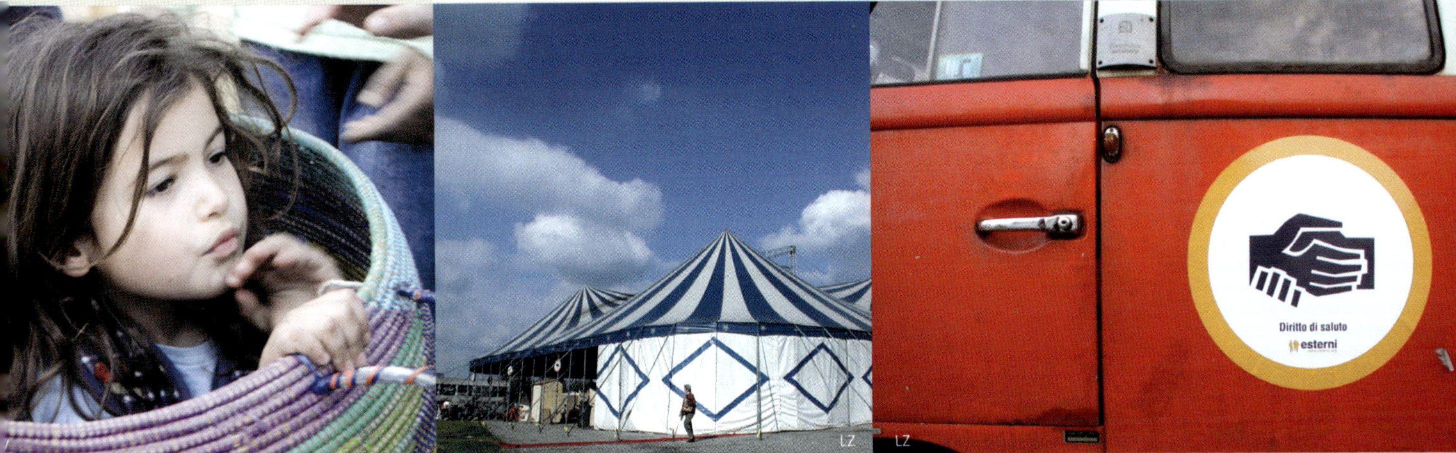

CITTÀ IN RIVOLUZIONE

Nine days workshops, concerts, projects, music and happenings

in one of the many **abandoned public spaces** in the center of Milano.

A **collective experiment** to build a new urban reality, where encounters and socialization are precious **values.**

24.000 visitors and citizens has been involved in the project days and nights, including families, students, children, old people.

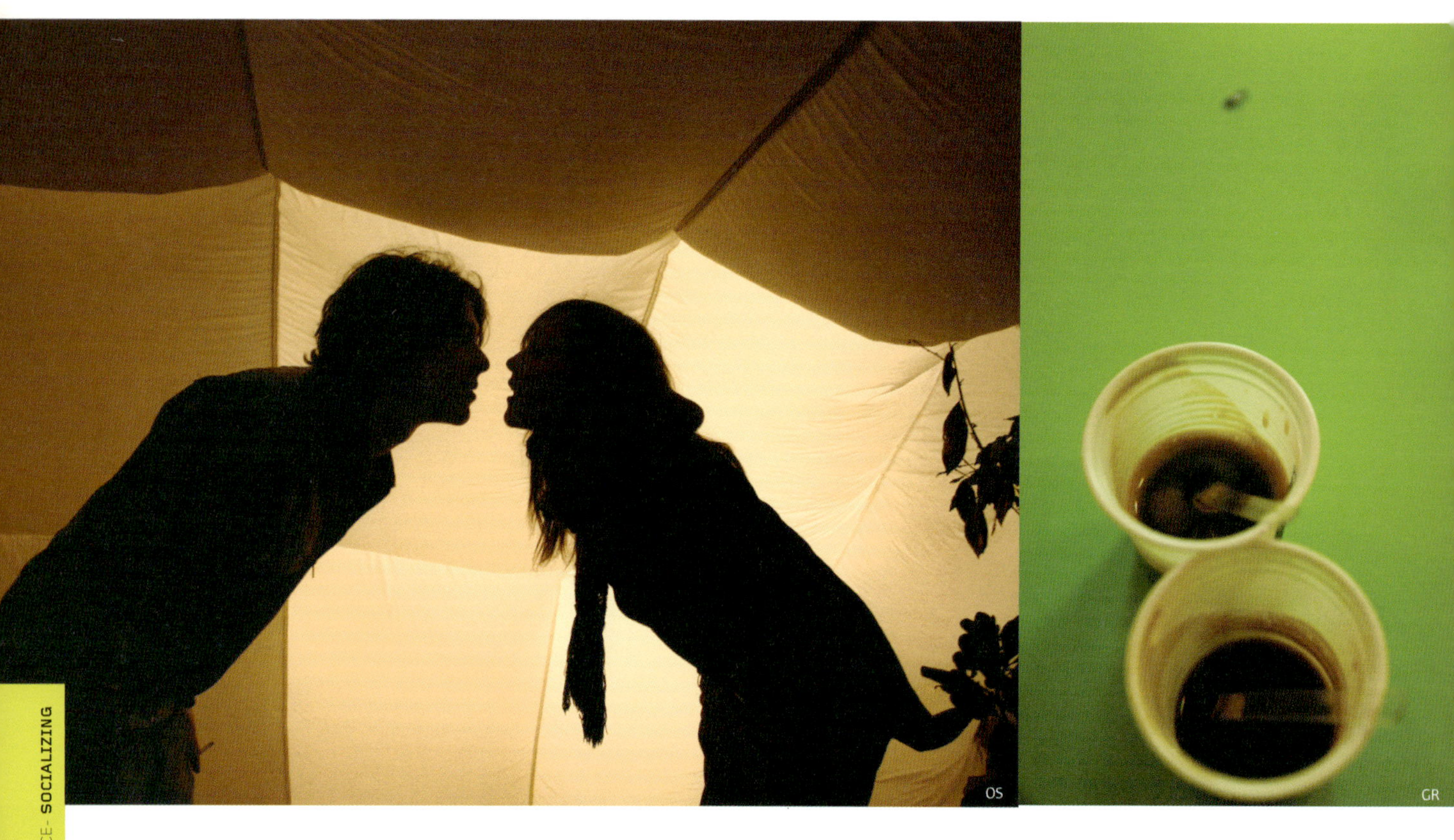

Horge Perez

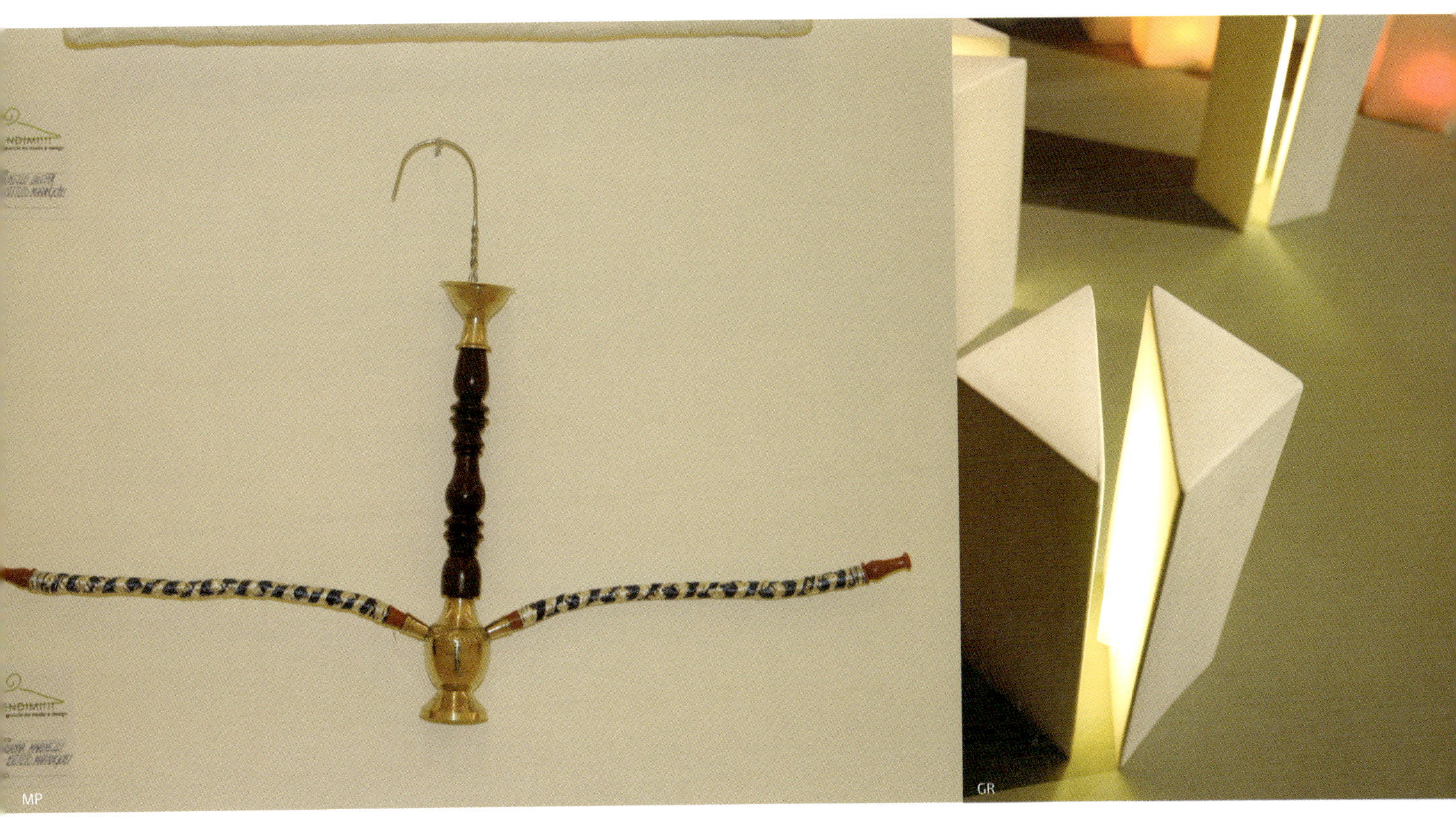

Appendimi @ Emporio 31

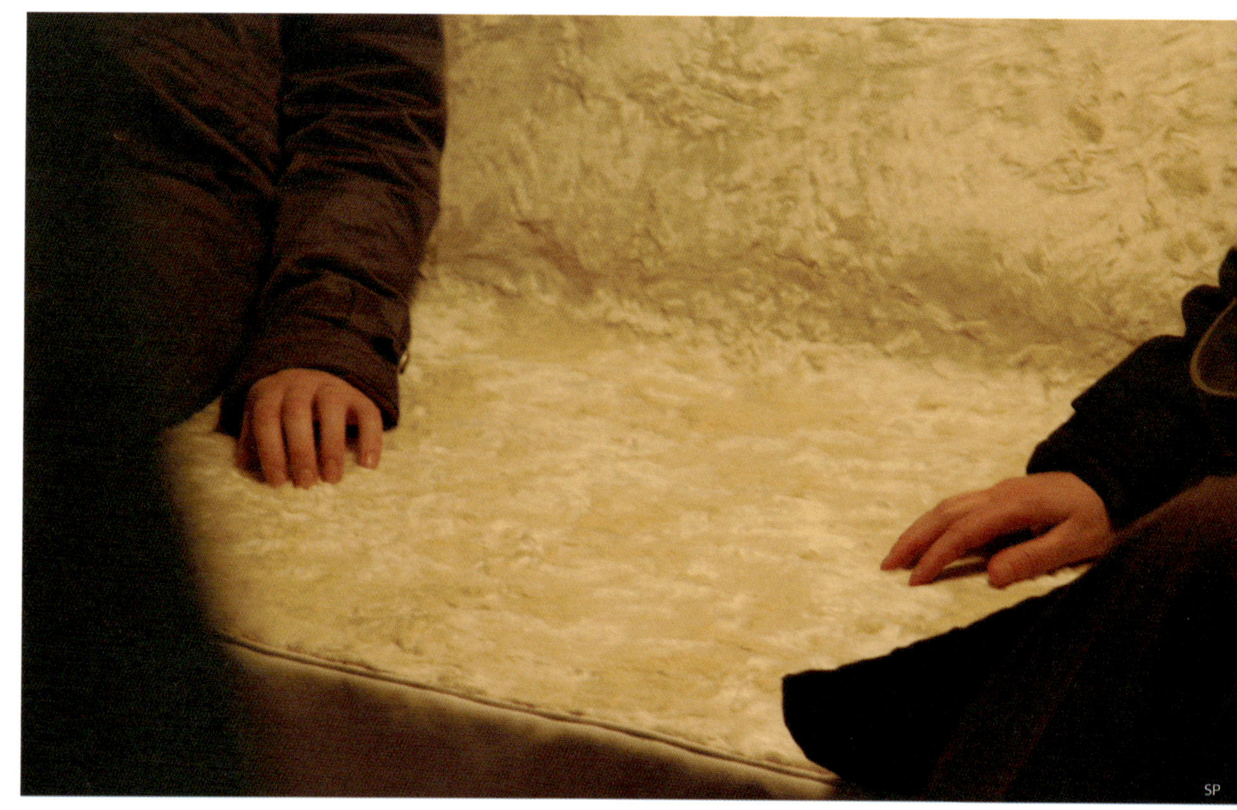

@ Driade

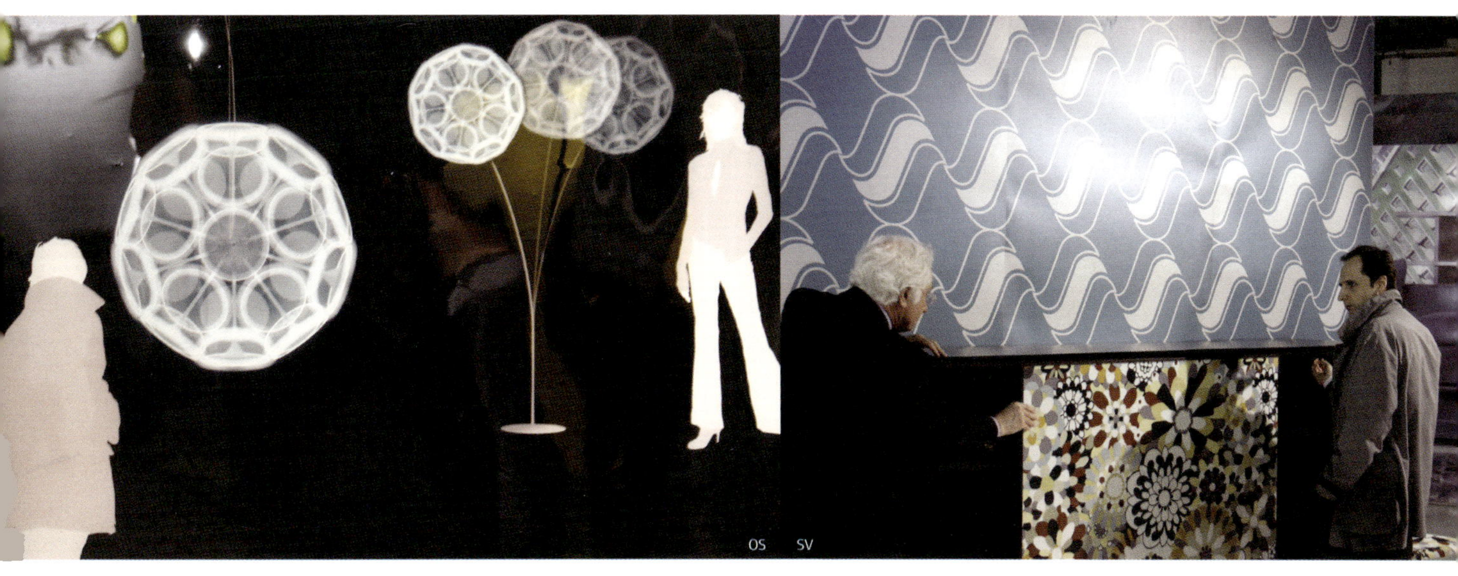

Deep Design

Zanotta

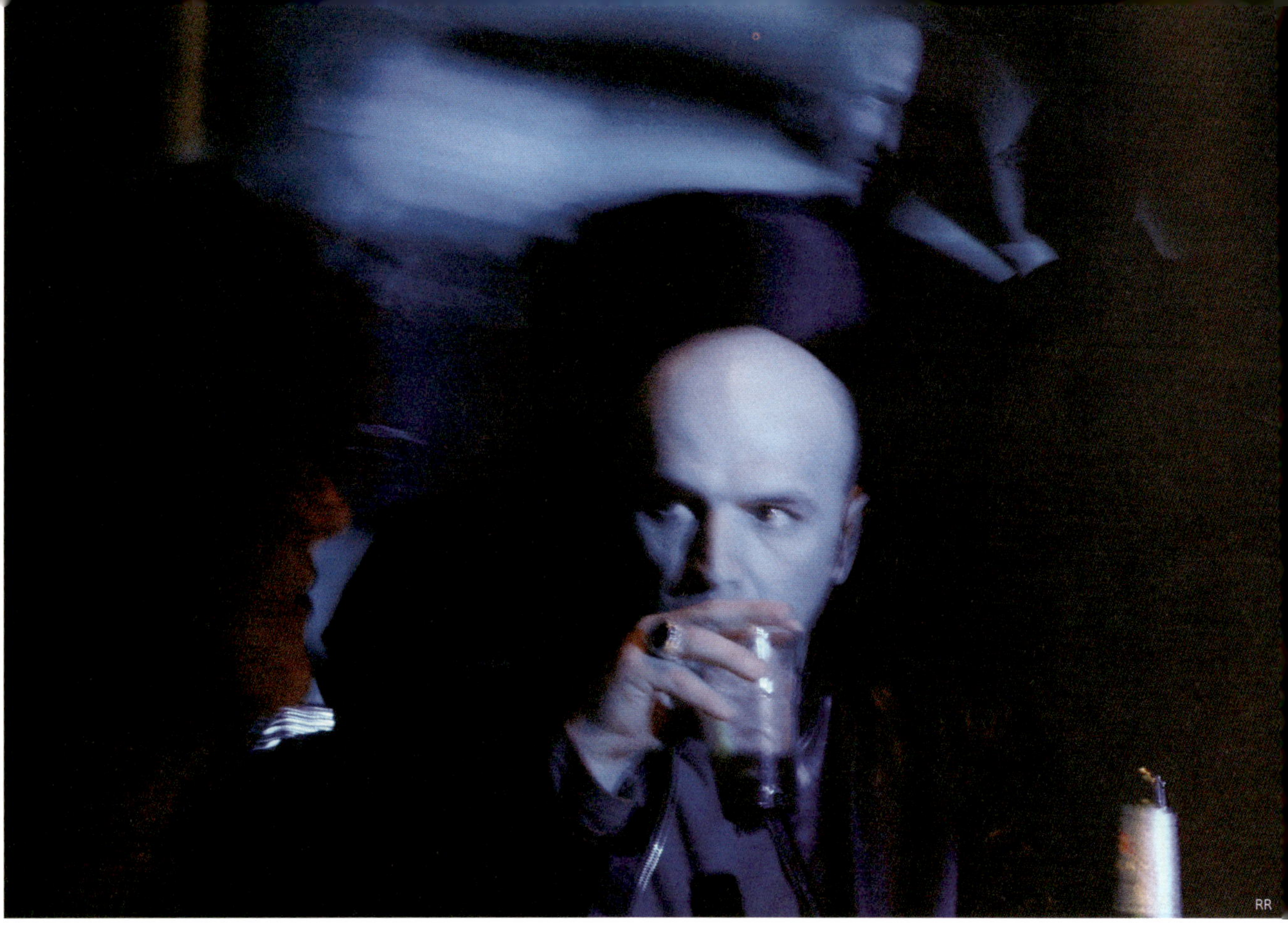

@ Plastic

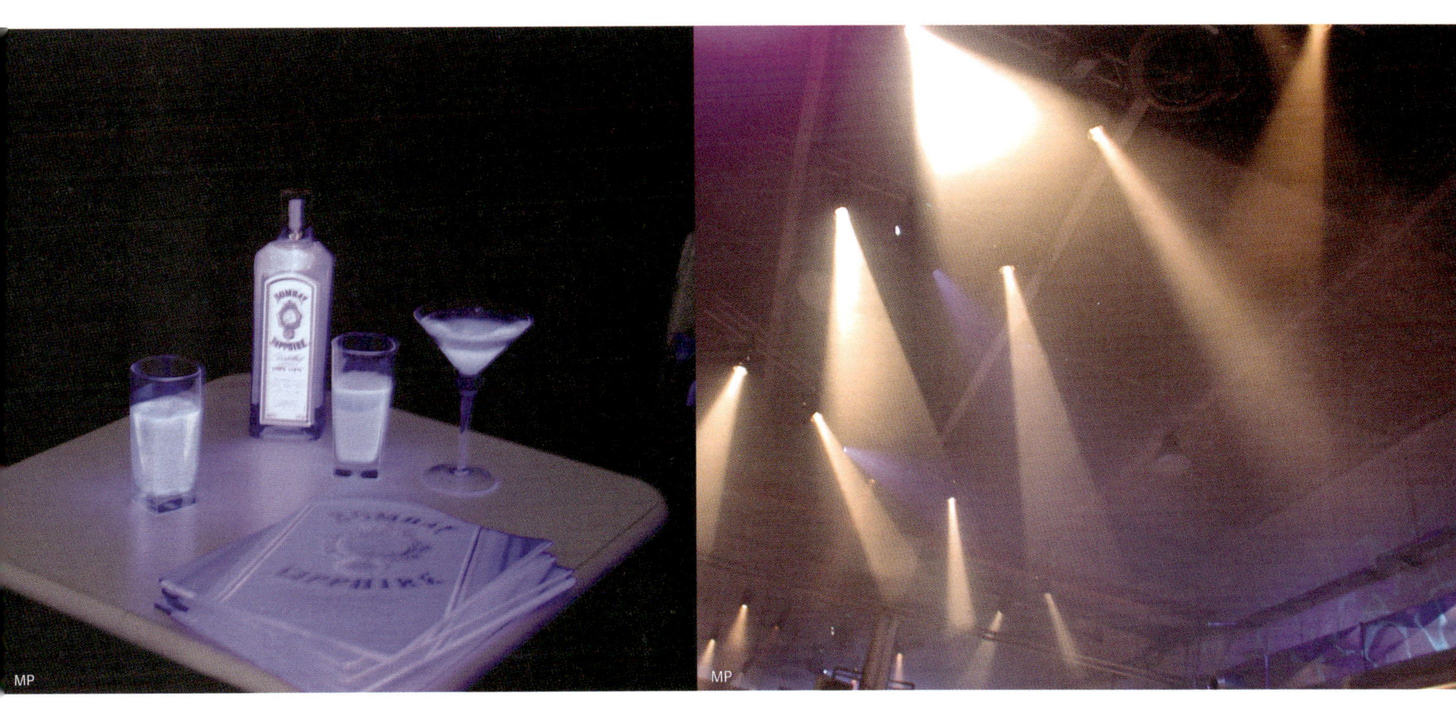

Via

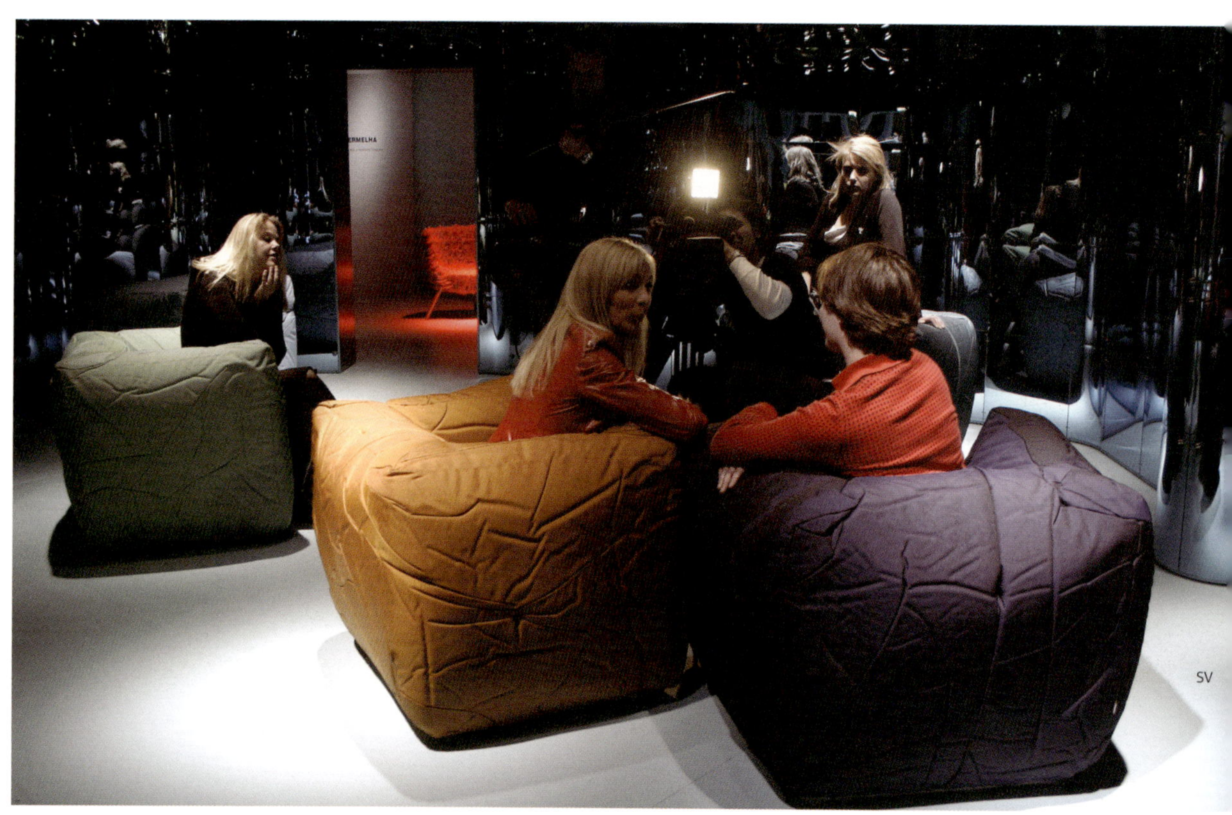

Edra

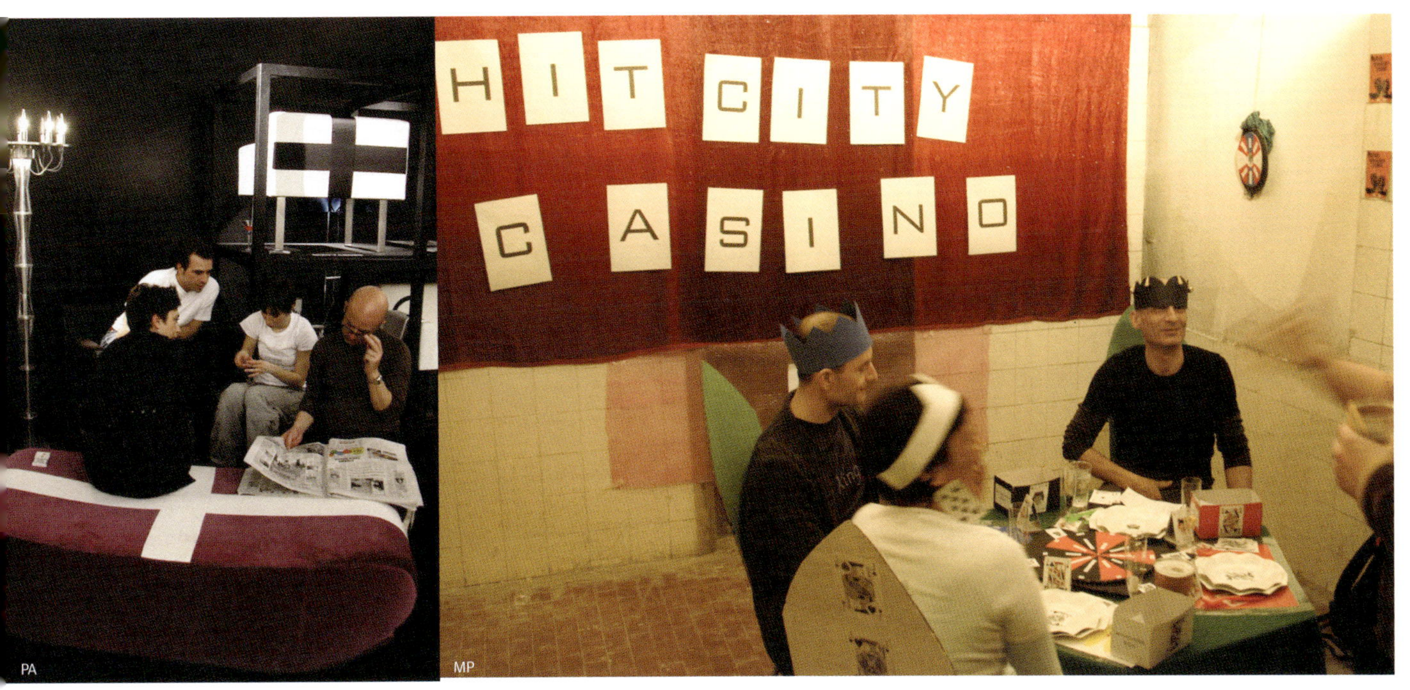

Fenizia Design Studio

Shit Design

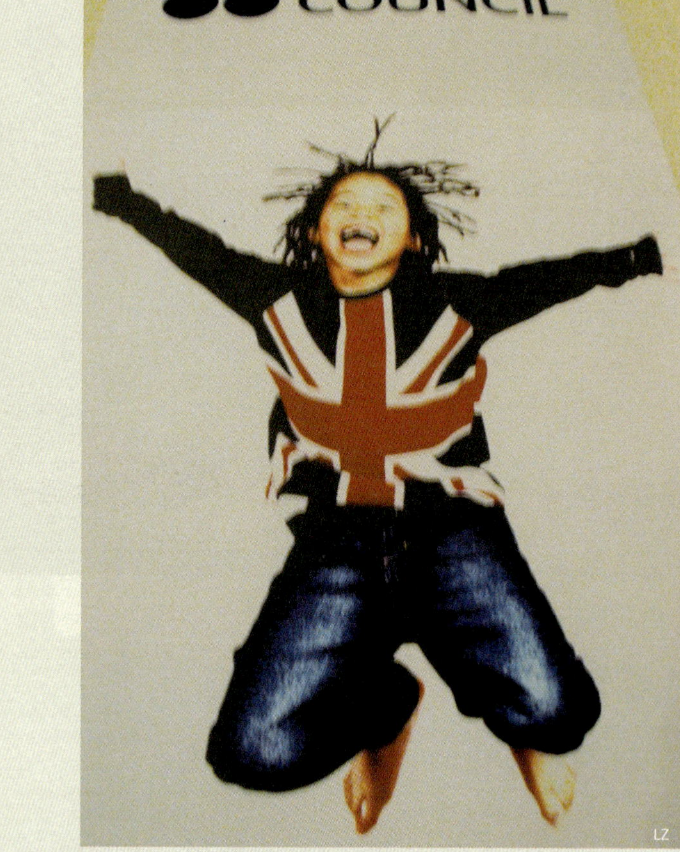

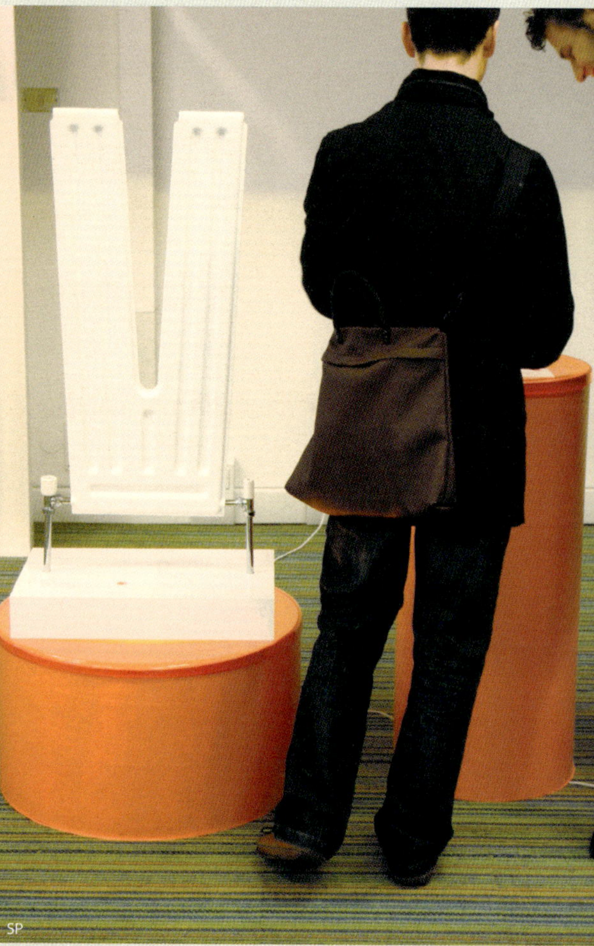

LZ   SP

Gina Reimann

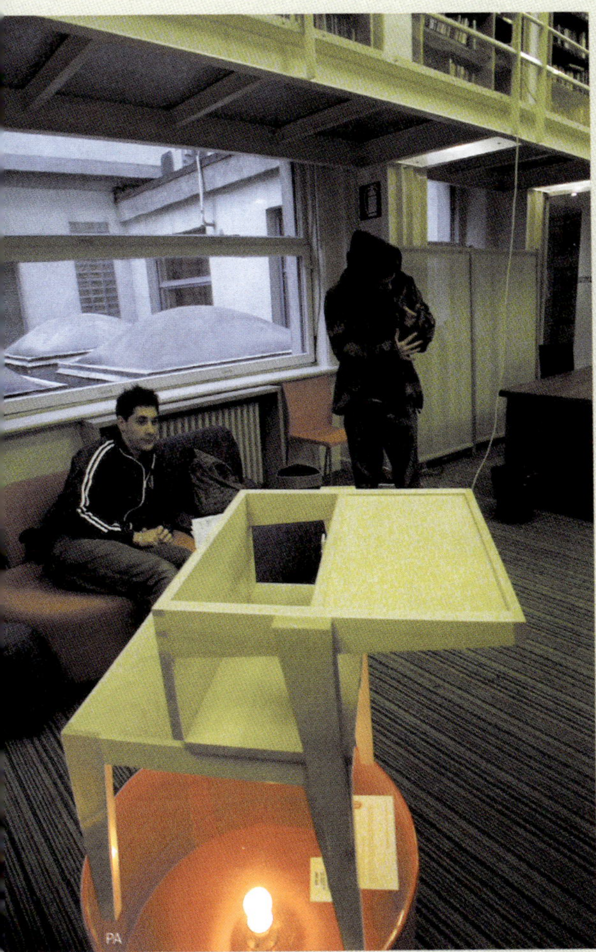

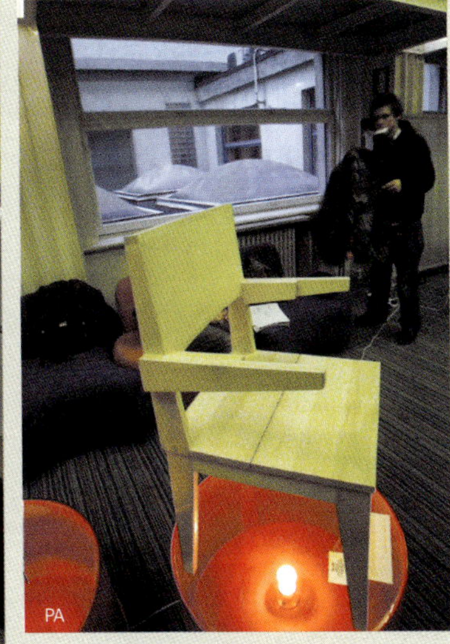

T-Rex

YOUNG AND "DIVERSE"

Seventeen young designers at the British Council in Milan.

An exhibition of prototypes projected by the students of some
of the most famous design schools in the UK. Selected by Tom Dixon,
and by Sheridan Coakley, the designers exhibiting are an important example
of **"diversity", a dominant feature of British design.**

This is a reflection of the heterogeneity of the British society,
which is pushing young designers to develop highly original and individual styles.

Many of the young designers are foreign born, but British-trained and UK based.

Also significant is the sheer volume of the **healthy cross-fertilisation
between different disciplines.**

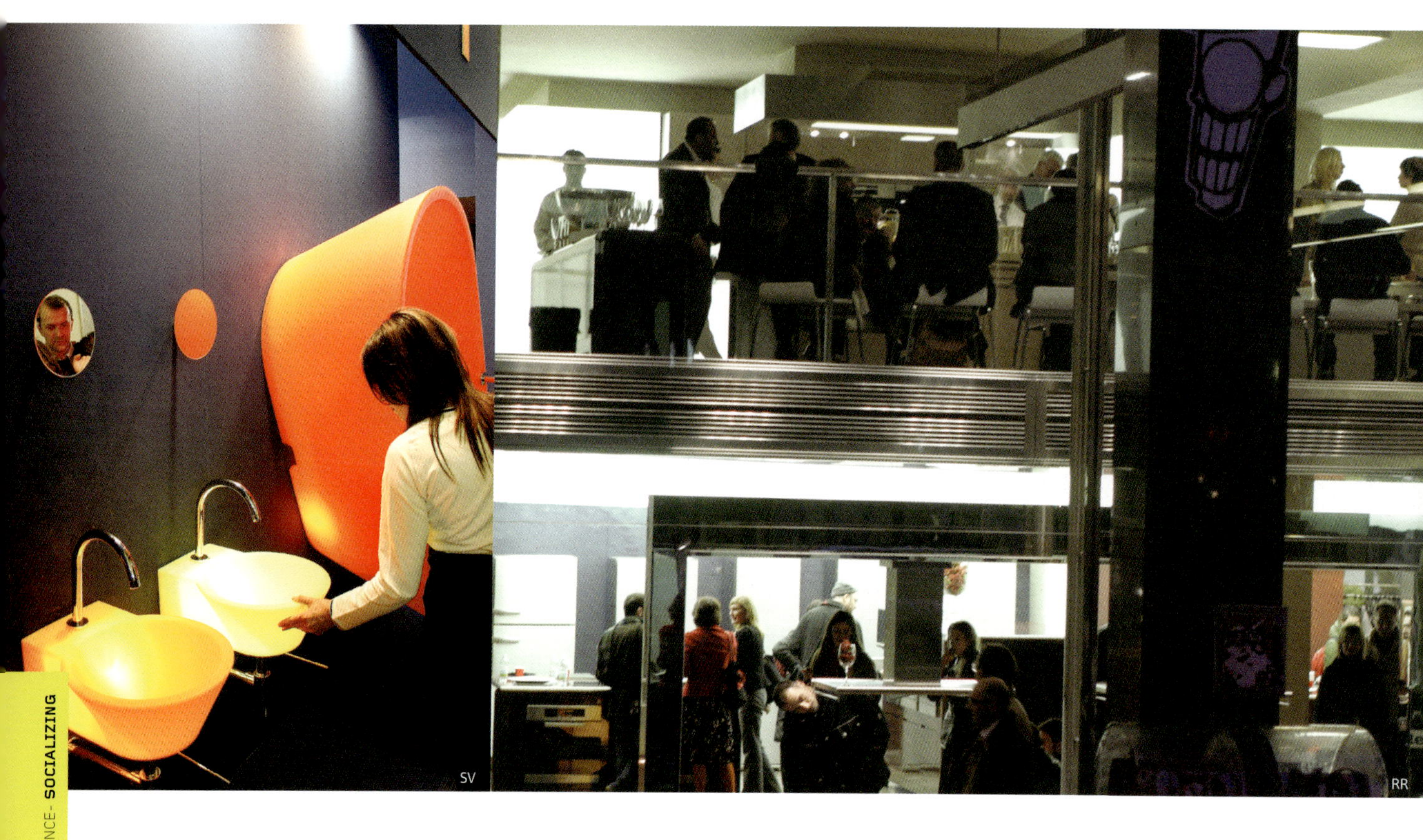

Wet

Miele

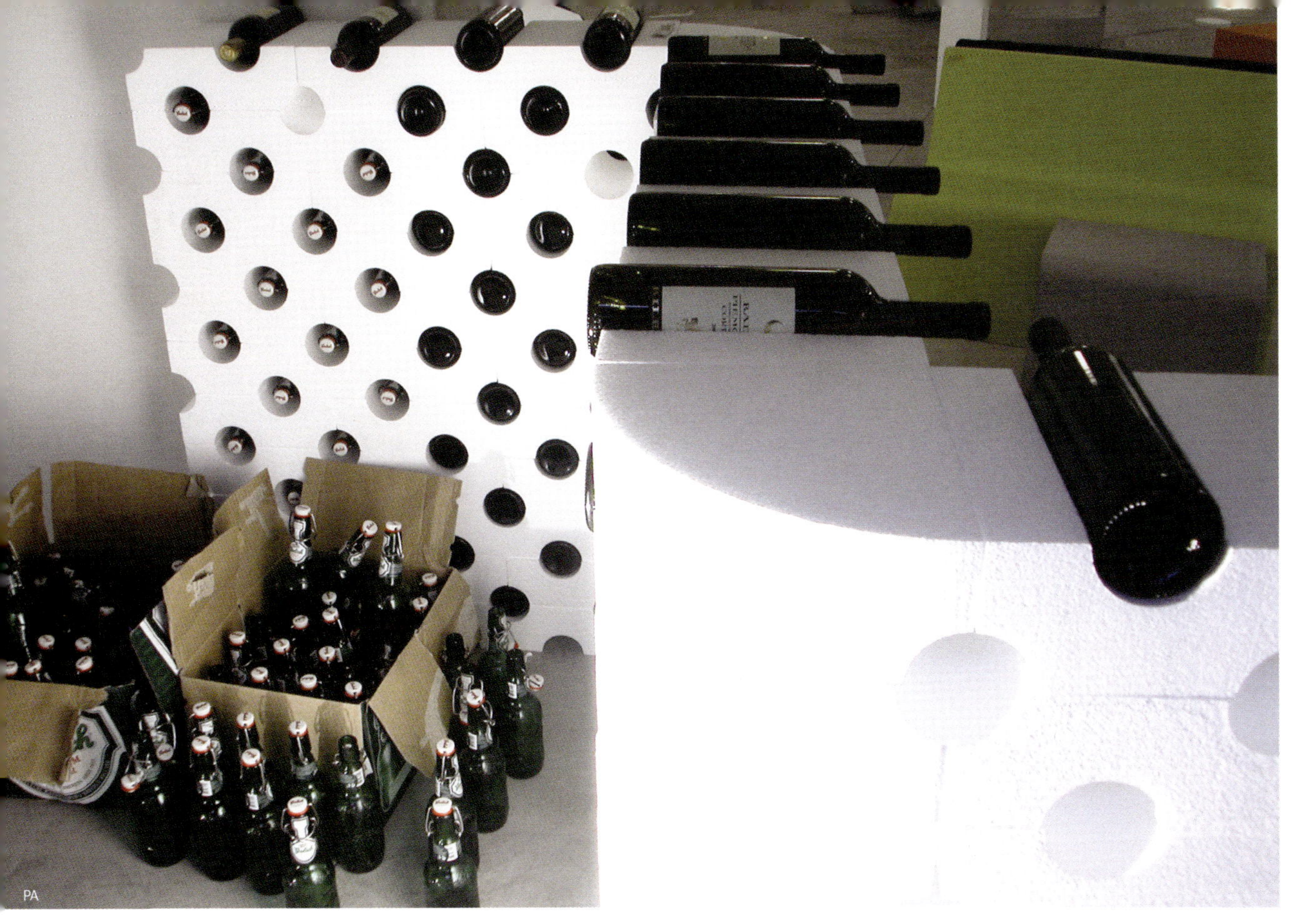

@ Tutto BeNe

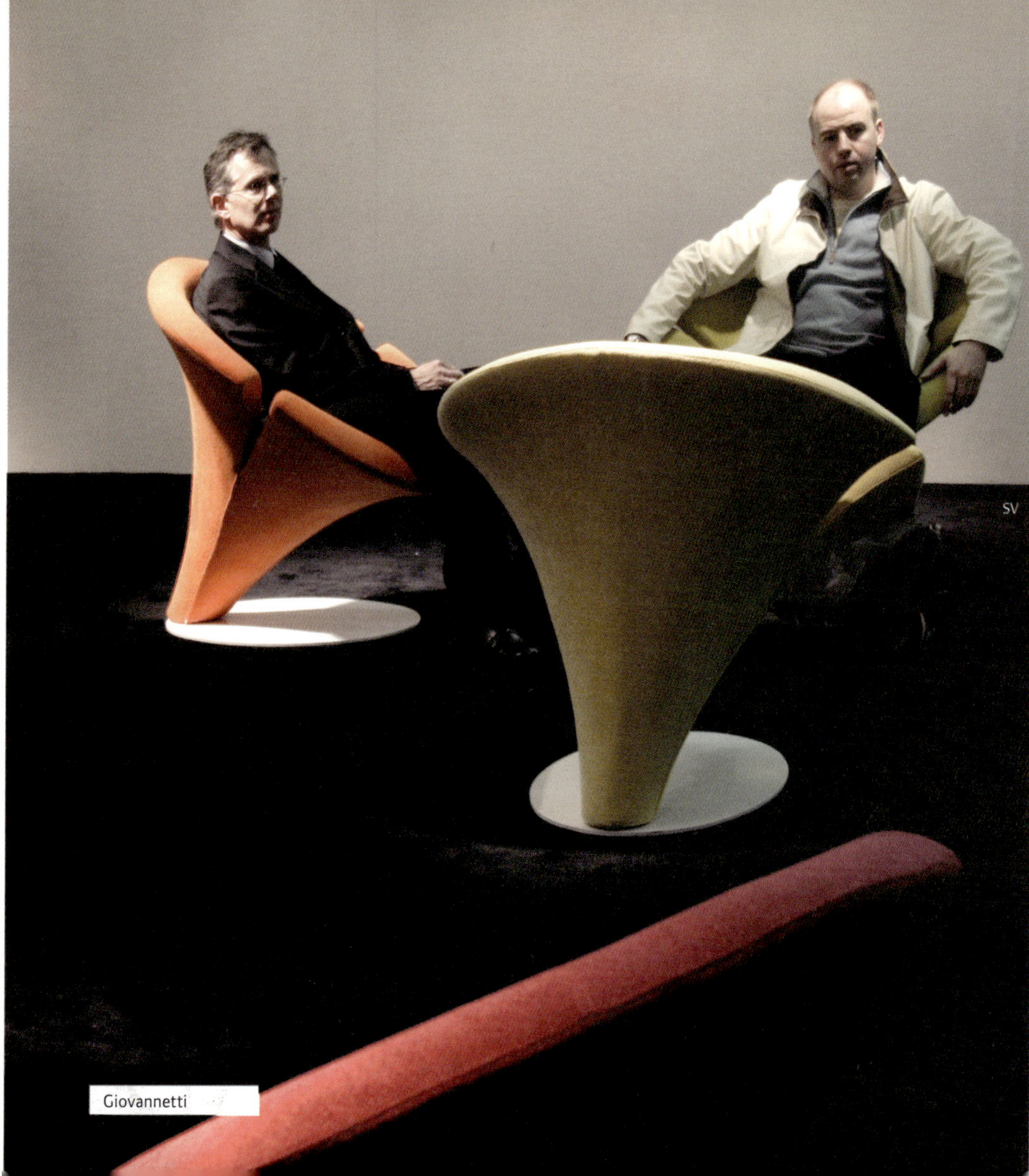
SV
Giovannetti

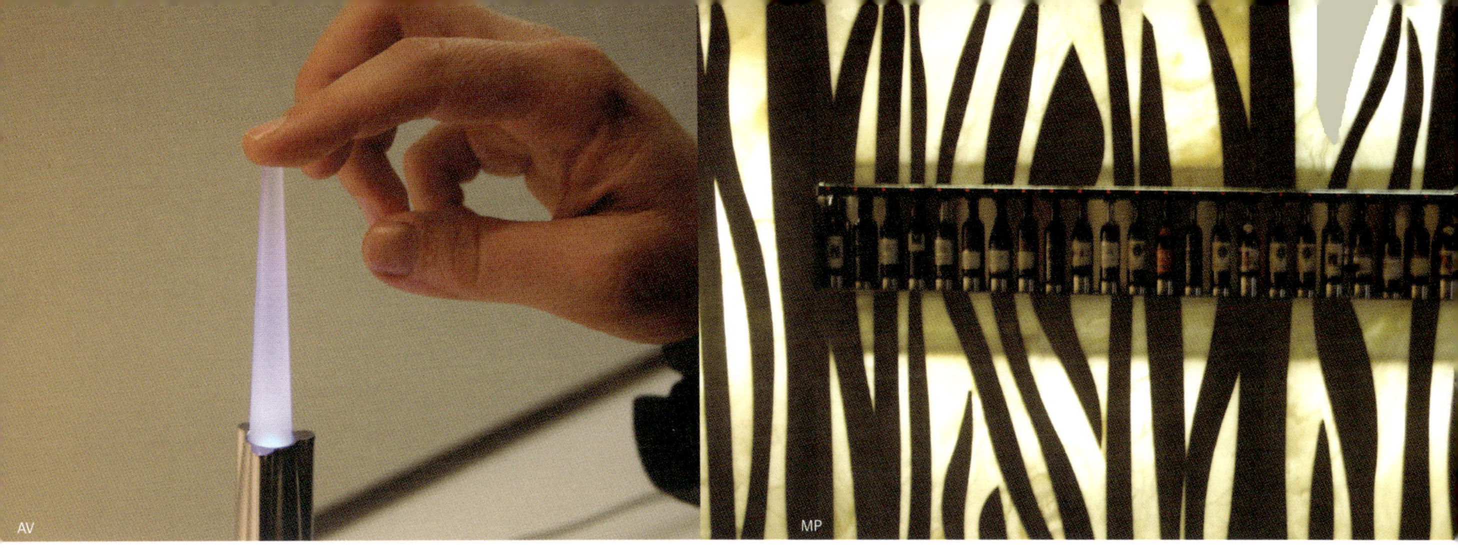

Lumen Center   Daniele De Giorgis

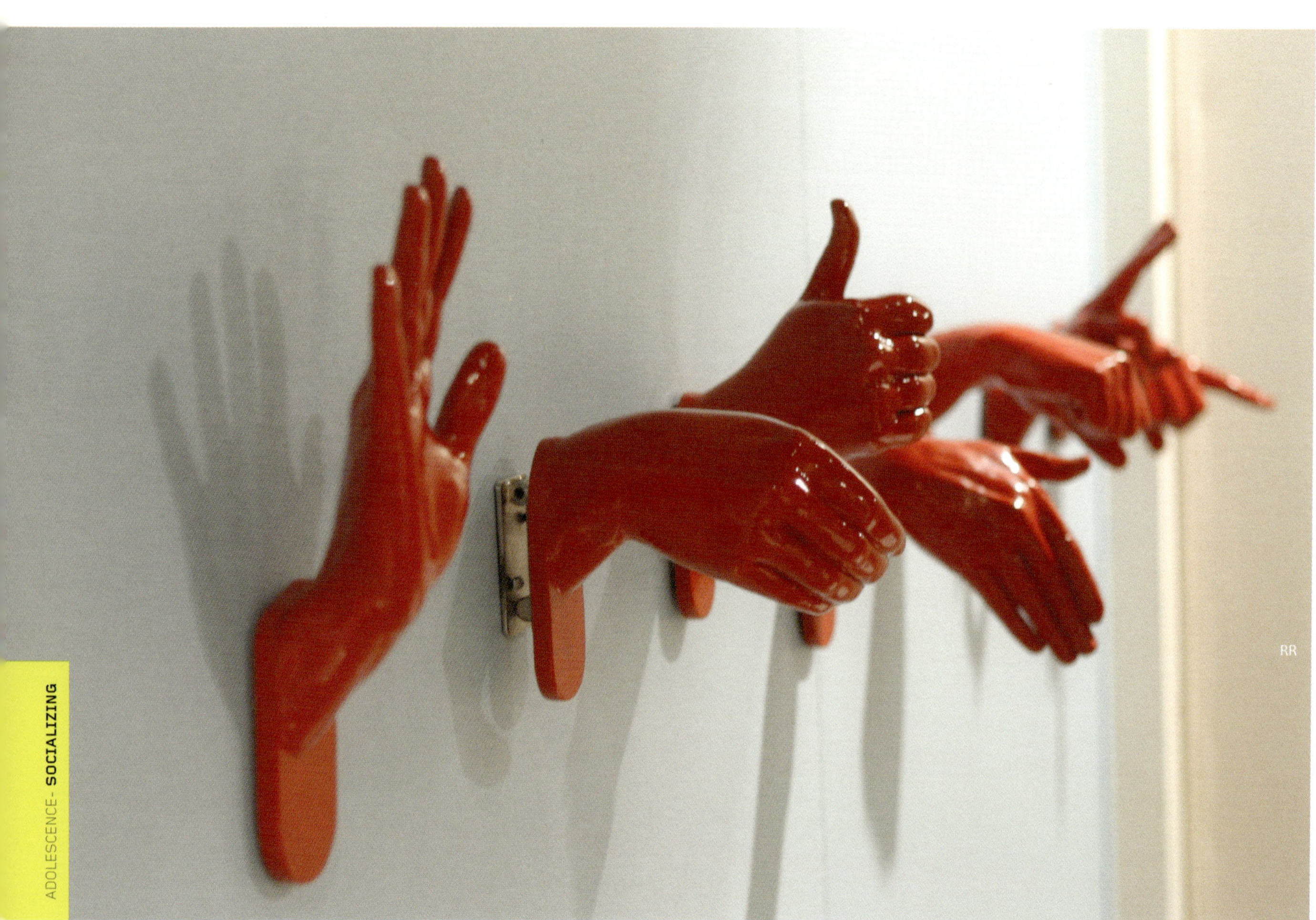

236 Gariselli Associati @ Satellite

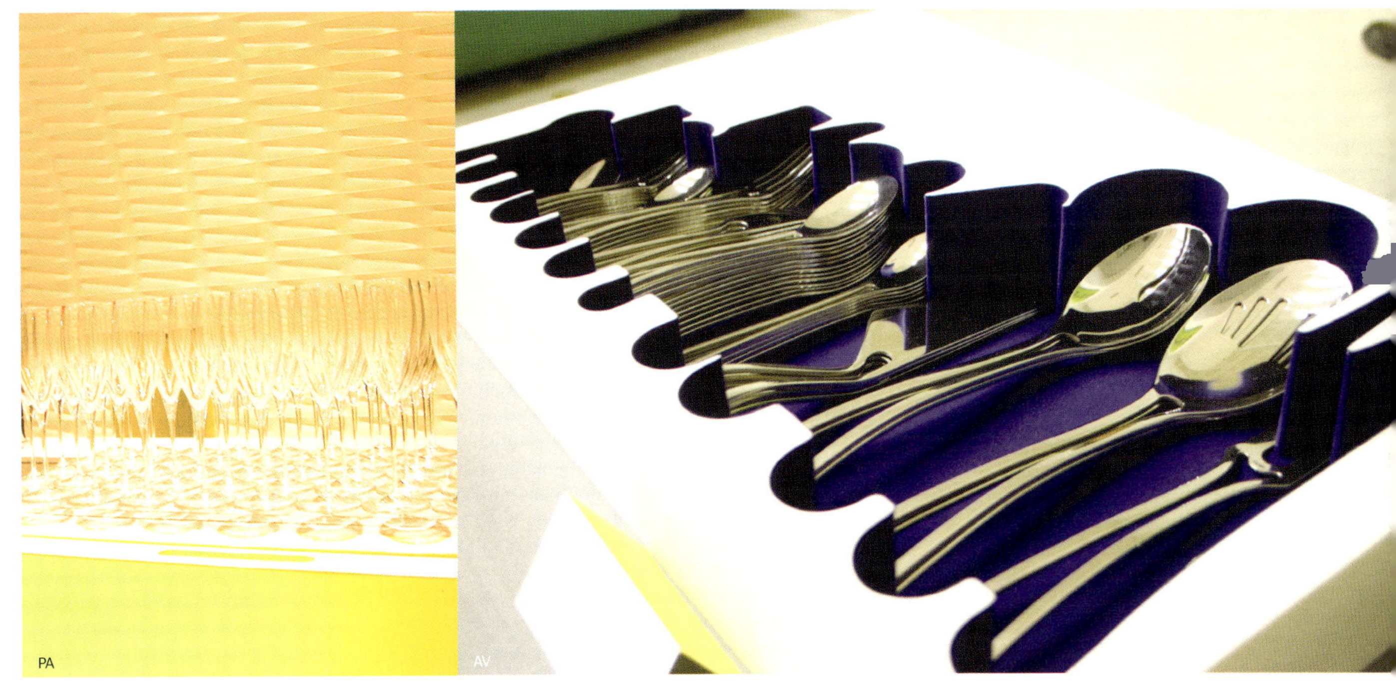

Maarten Baptist for Wat design

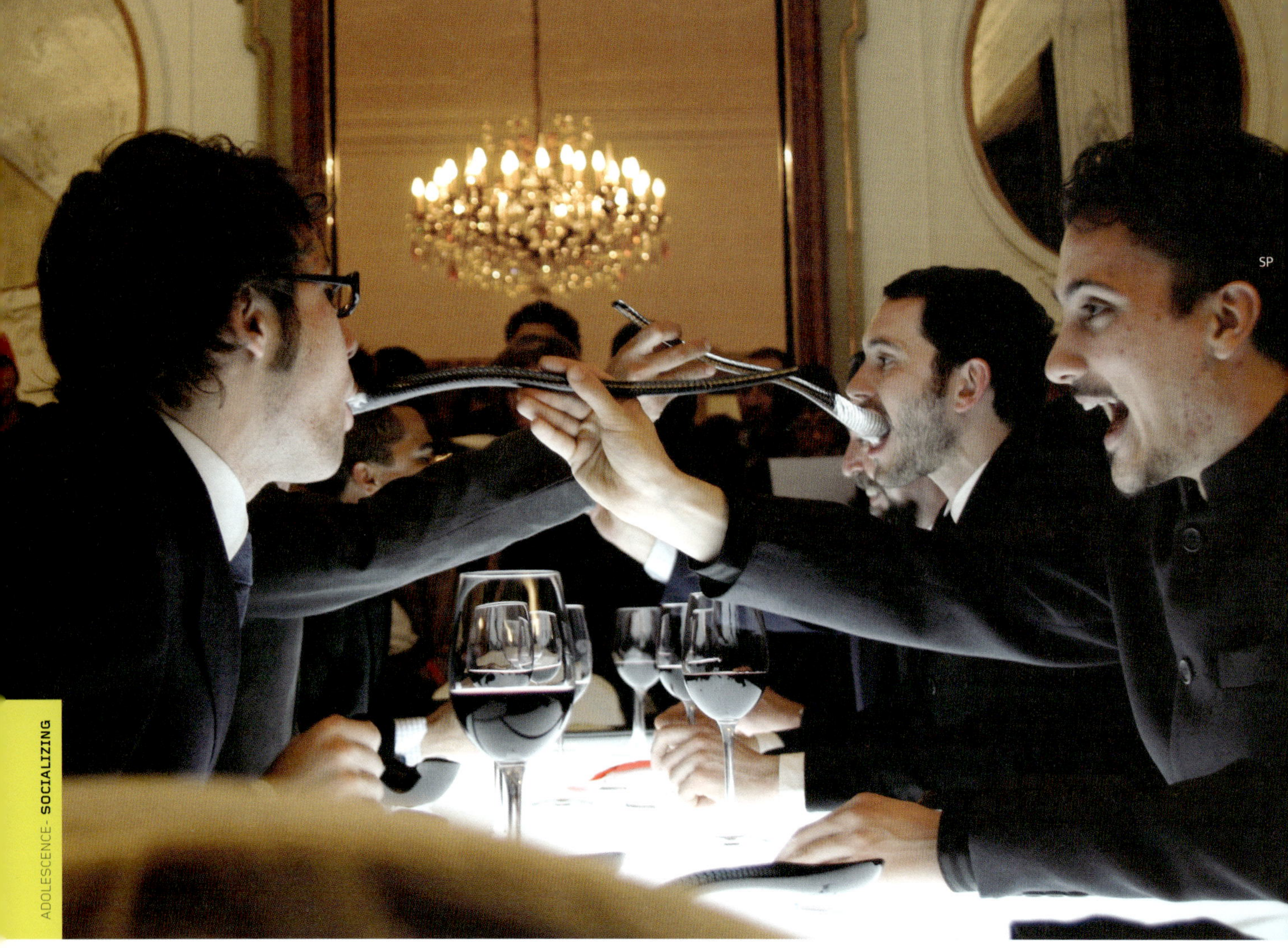

Alessandra Cassinelli performance @ Pandora

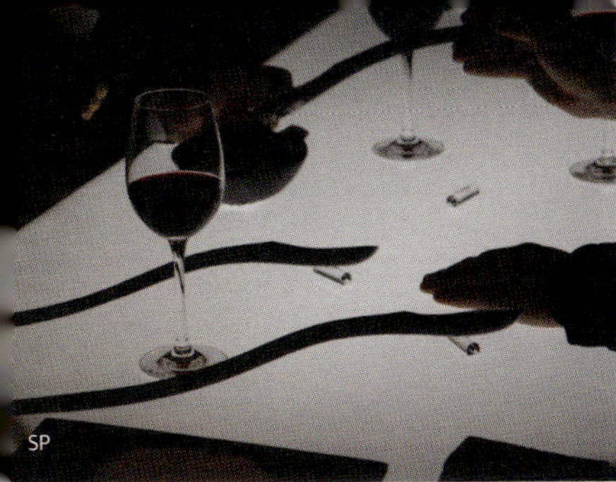

In the setting of The Residenza alla Scala,

Alessandra Cassinelli has presented her performance Oris Hiatus:

eight elegant and detached men had a dinner feeding each other

across the table with long glass spoons – created by the artist –

talking about different subjects, often in different languages,

drowning out each others words.

The idea of the long spoons PRO–TESE, was born thinking about the necessity

to keep the distance between the interpersonal relationships

while the overlapping of the different languages and words

represent the difficulty in the communication, hidden by a formal indifference.

Denise Bonenti

Spoons by Alessandra Cassinelli for Pandora

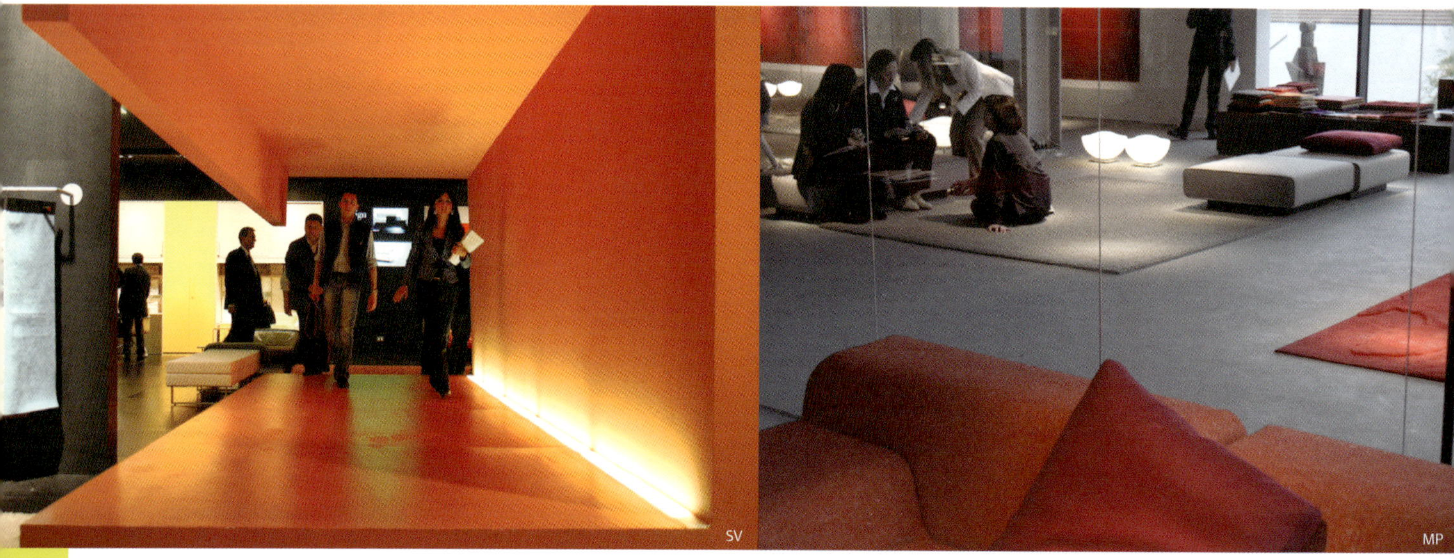

Zalf

Paola Lenti

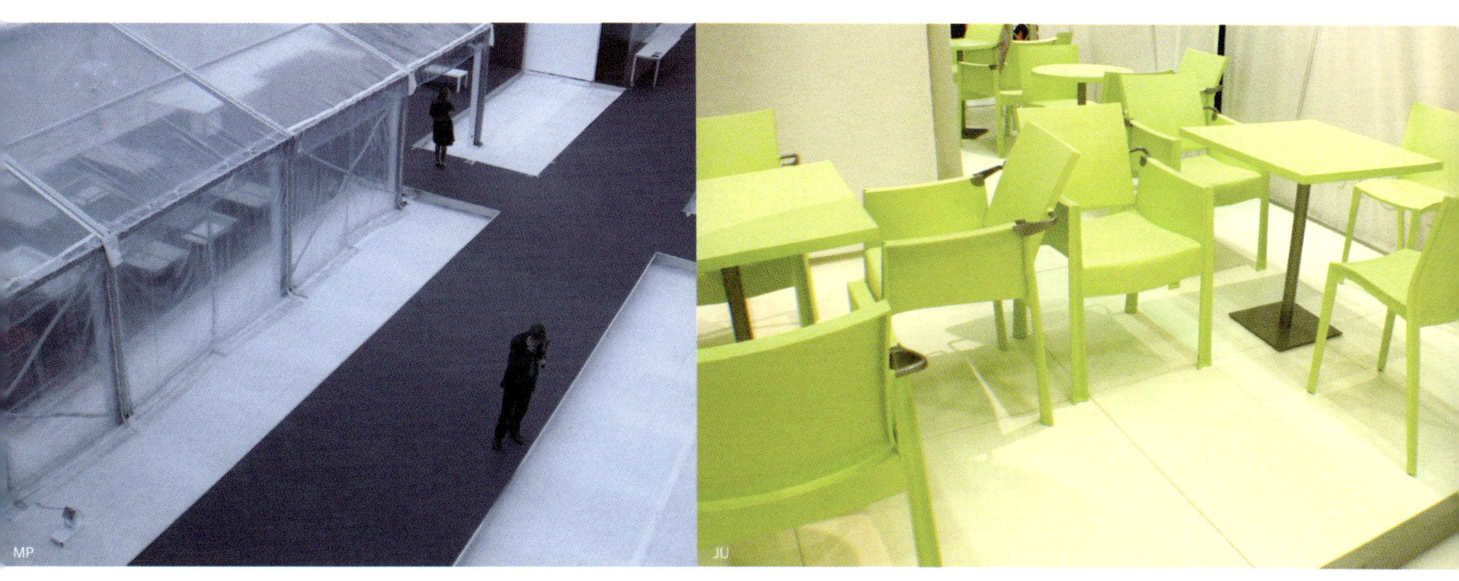

Monica Armani   XO by Starck

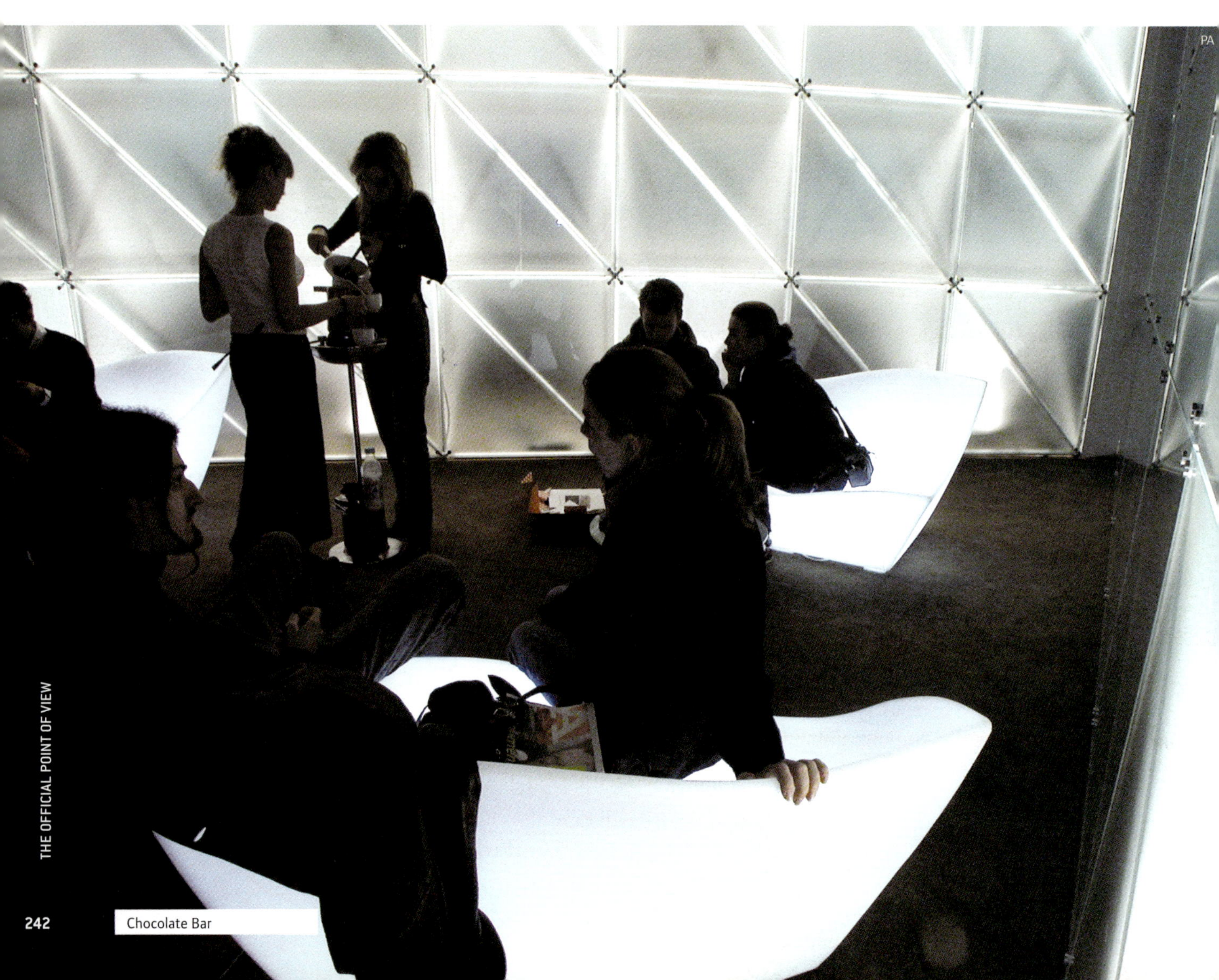

Chocolate Bar

> DINING DESIGN

AN EXCITING JOURNEY THROUGH THE GALAXY OF INTERNATIONAL RESTAURANT DESIGN.

A DYNAMIC, INTERACTIVEEVENT DESIGNED TO ENTICE, EDUCATE, AND ENTERTAIN THAT

HIGHLIGHTS THE VISUAL, FUNCTIONAL, AND ATMOSPHERIC ELEMENTSOF THE DINING EXPERIENCE.

STREET OF RESTAURANTS

10 restaurants x 10 schools x 10 companies = Future Restaurants by Future Architects

Every sample corner of the restaurant features models, sketches, and prototypes

and their partial realizations by the participating companies.

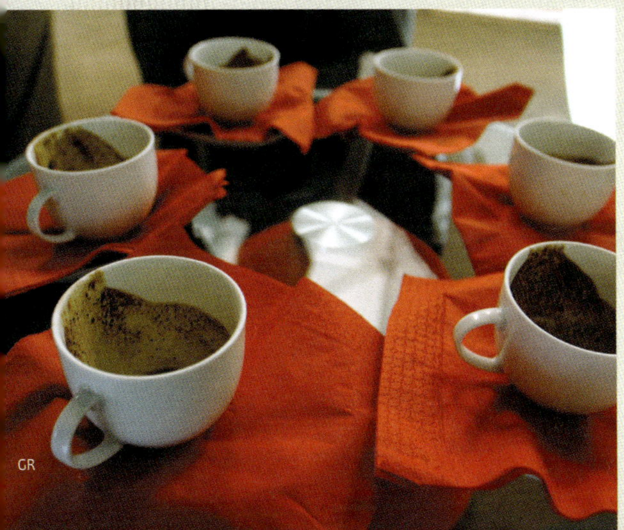

CHOCOLATE BAR

The place for a steaming hot chocolate

in a comfortable, relaxing atmosphere.

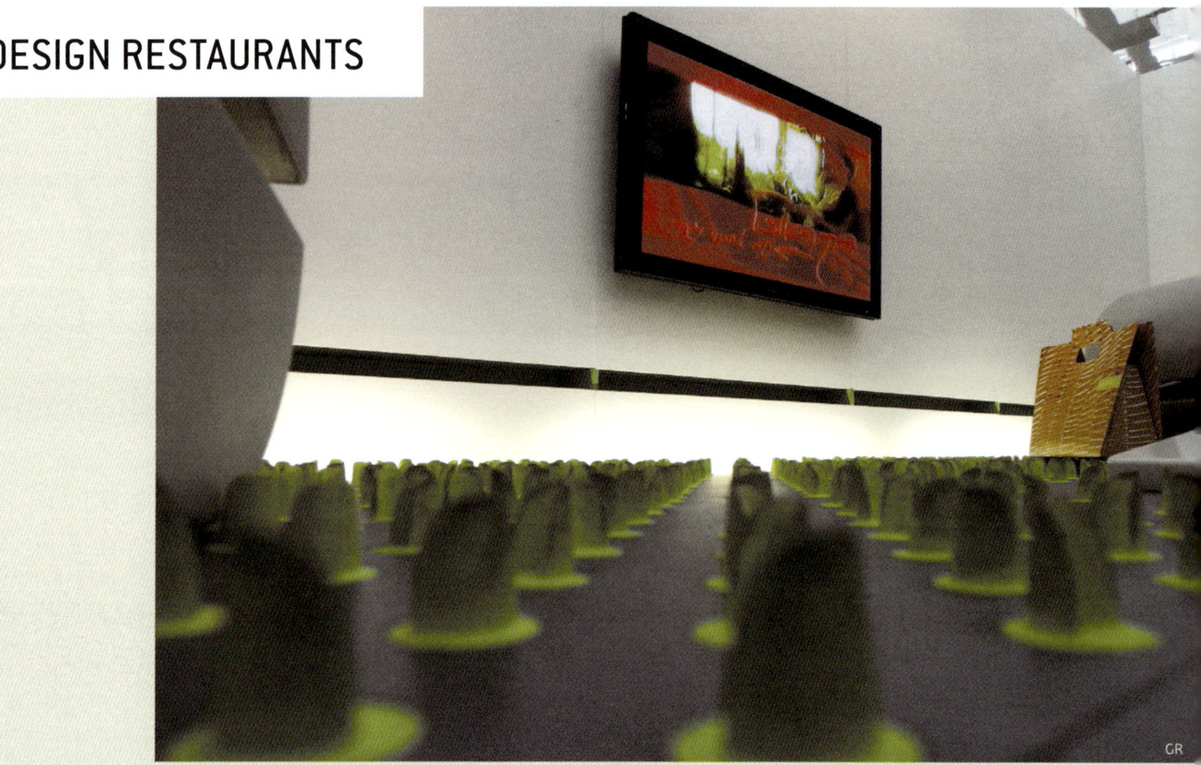

"QUICNIC" FAST FOOD HAMBURGER IN BERLIN - STAATLICHE HOCHSCHULE FÜR GESTALTUNG KARLSRUHE (GERMANY)

The design works with a futuristic and succinct reinterpretation of the "picnic" for an urban culture:

Quicnic = quick + picnic. The concept behind Quicnic is a "quick urban interlude."

Quicnic offers a new natural/artificial space and a new, stage-managed version of a pleasant picnic outing

by creating an open area inside a closed building.

Diners don't come to eat but to celebrate their picnic within the restaurant space.

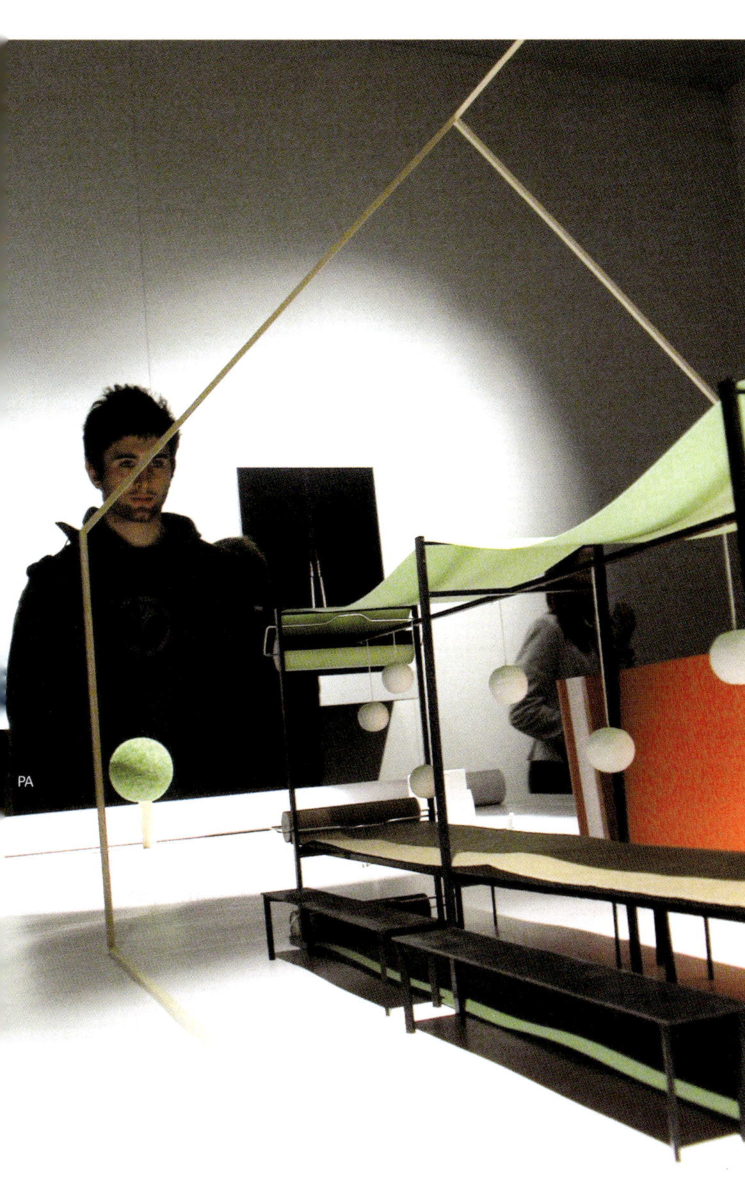

"ROLL-AWAY" KARAOKE SUSHI BAR IN LAUSANNE.

ECAL ECOLE CANTONALE D'ART DE LAUSANNE (SWITZERLAND)

The aim of this project is to create a restaurant that can be moved from one place to another while still encompassing all those decorative elements that give a restaurant its identity. The project consists of numerous rolls of fabric, paper, and carpet, as well as a table system. The basic structure makes it possible to set up in different spaces.

The restaurant can be dismantled, reassembled, lengthened, and increased in size as needed.

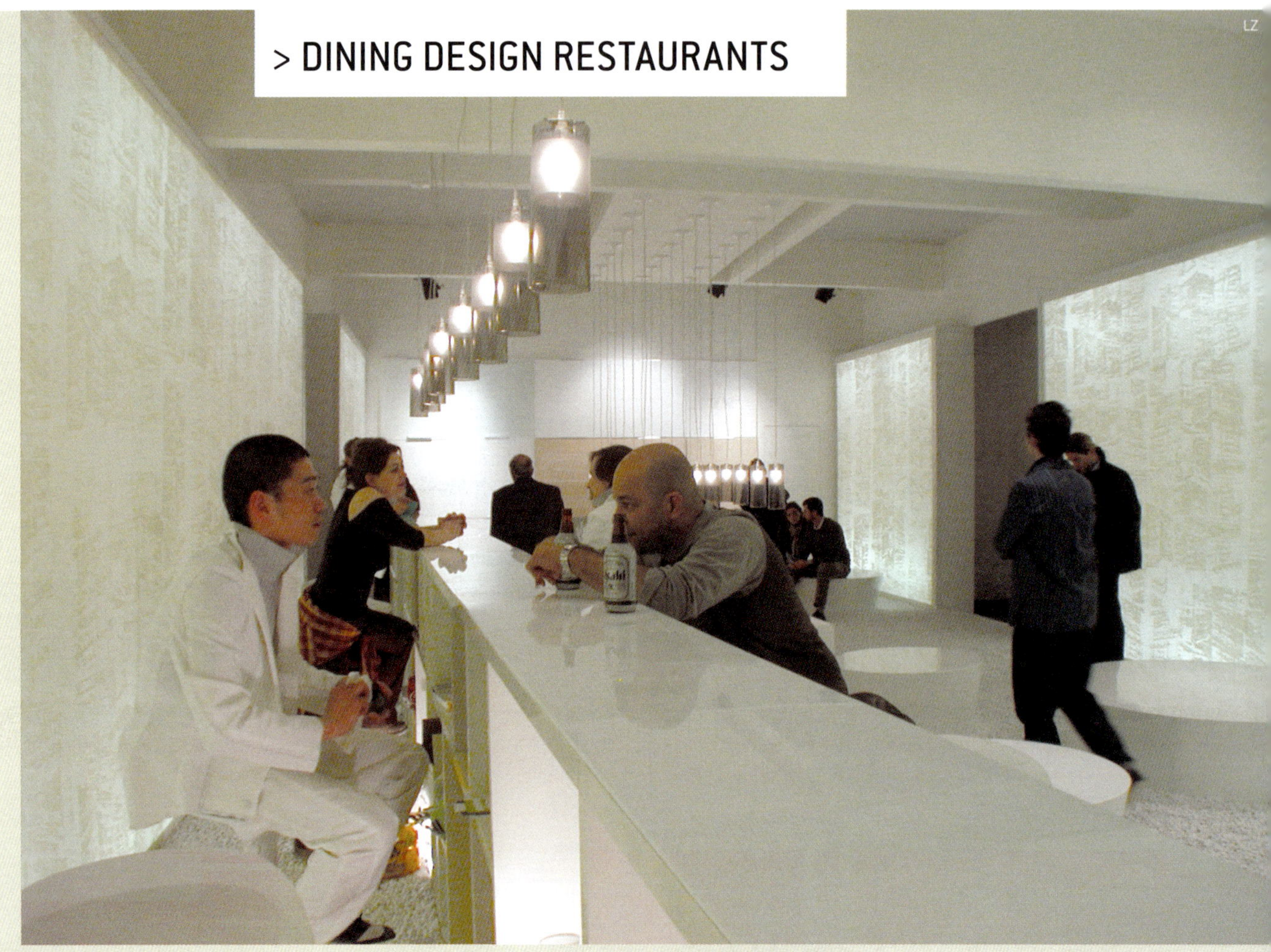

> DINING DESIGN RESTAURANTS
LZ

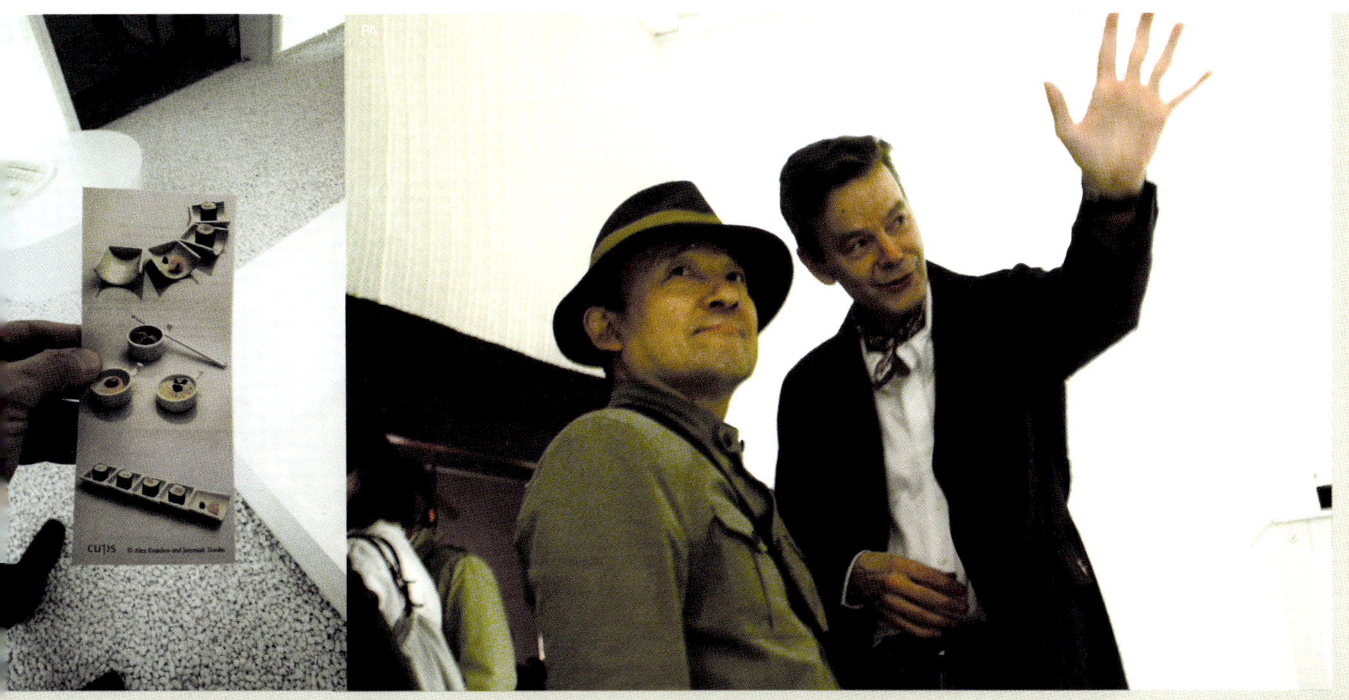

"WHITE2" JAPANESE RESTAURANT IN HELSINKI - UNIVERSITY OF ART AND DESIGN HELSINKI (FINLAND)

The design concept consists of bringing together the hot, colorful, and contemporary clamor of Tokyo and the cool, black and white melancholy of Helsinki by uniting different cultures, culinary traditions, and customs in a new and creative way. The restaurant is an open space containing a lounge, a sushi and sake bar, a main dining area, and a tatami area. The space is pure white, with floors, walls, and ceilings all made of different white materials. The food and diners occupy the center.

A friend with Martin Relander

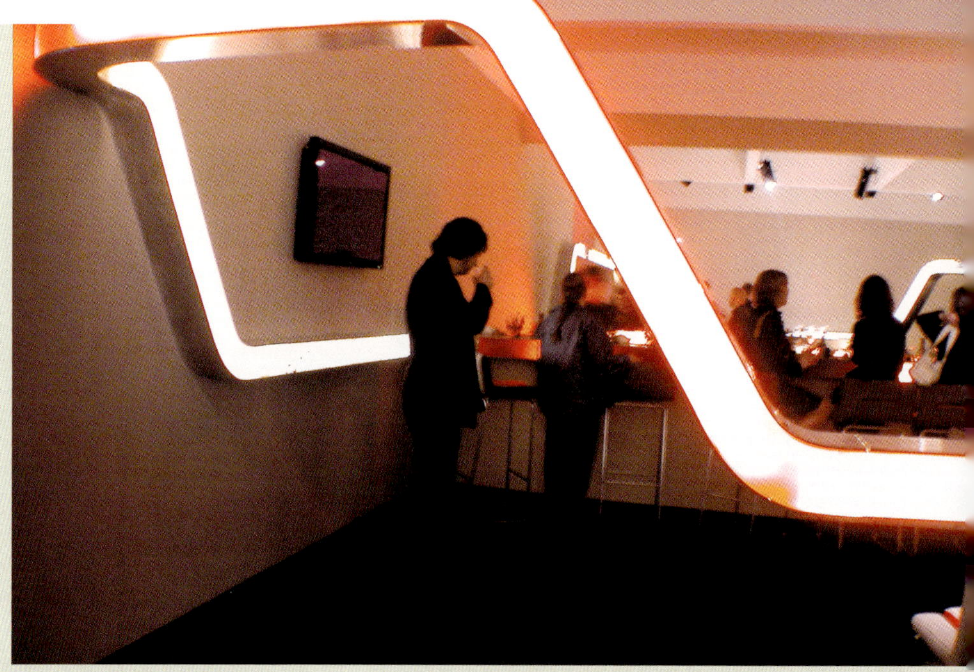

"PATRINGLINE" FRENCH HAUTE CUISINE RESTAURANT IN TEL AVIV - BEZALEL ACADEMY OF ART & DESIGN (ISRAEL)

By sitting on the barstools, people animate the surrounding space as, little by little, the light surrounding

the seated patrons is increased. The dining table changes throughout the meal: composed of two parts,

one part changes for each course, creating a unique atmosphere that complements each dish.

Split into two moving surfaces,the chairs only work as chairs when someone is actually seated.

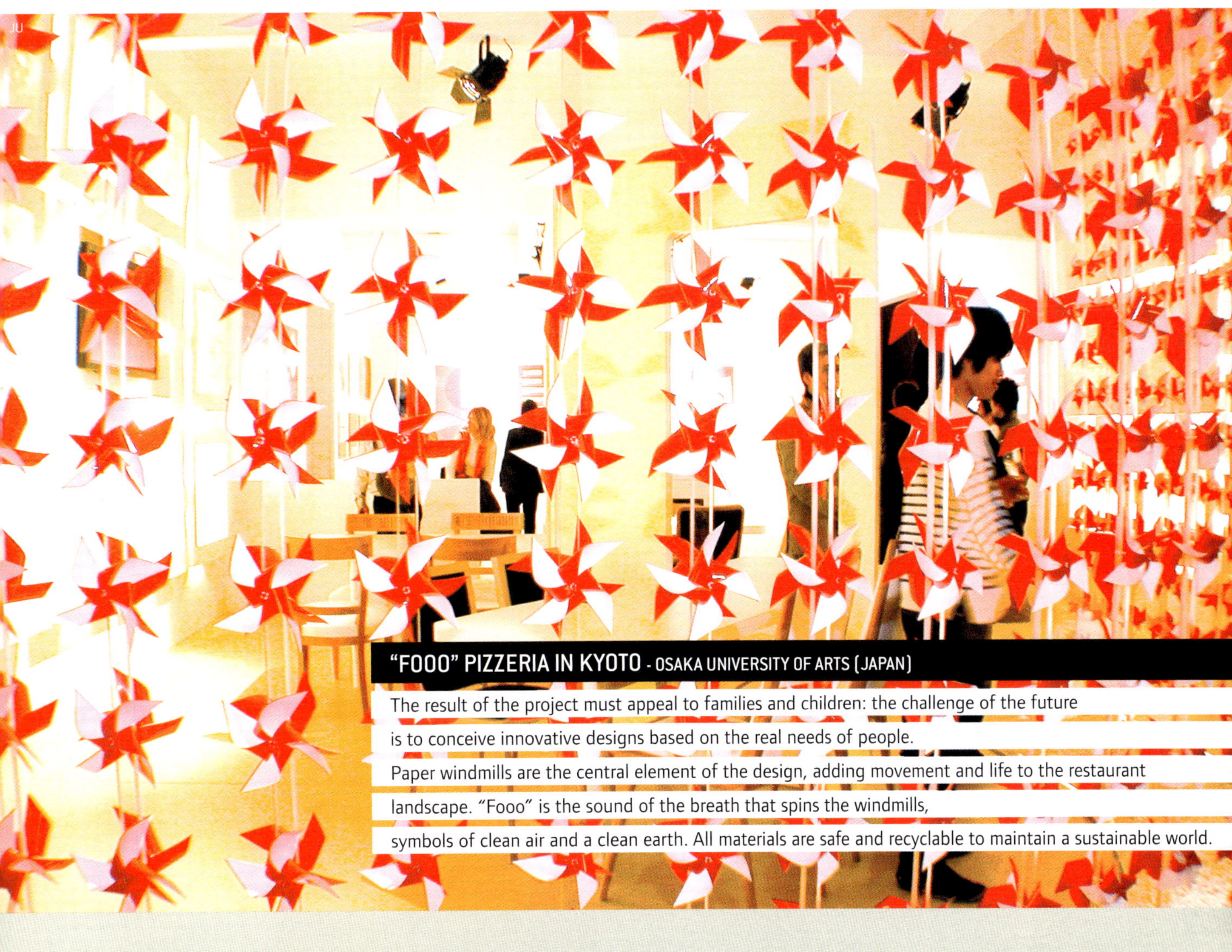

"FOOO" PIZZERIA IN KYOTO - OSAKA UNIVERSITY OF ARTS (JAPAN)

The result of the project must appeal to families and children: the challenge of the future is to conceive innovative designs based on the real needs of people.
Paper windmills are the central element of the design, adding movement and life to the restaurant landscape. "Fooo" is the sound of the breath that spins the windmills, symbols of clean air and a clean earth. All materials are safe and recyclable to maintain a sustainable world.

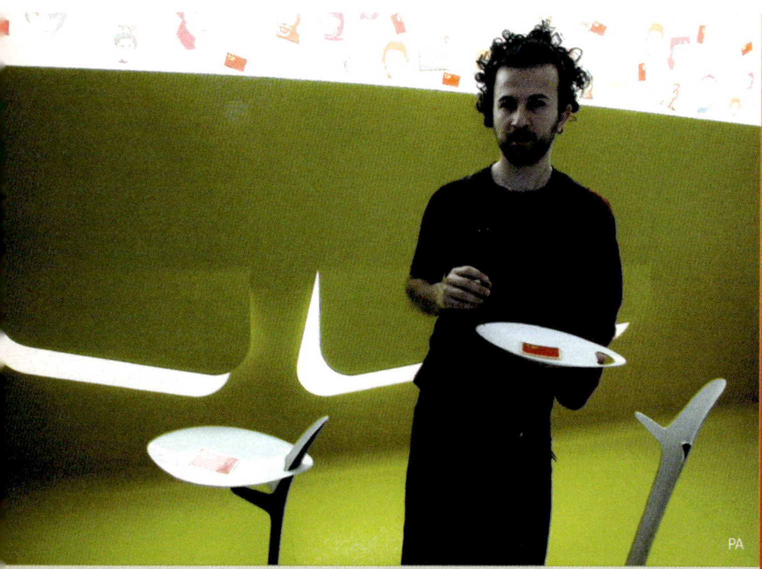

"PIÙ-YIÙ" CHINESE RESTAURANT IN ROME

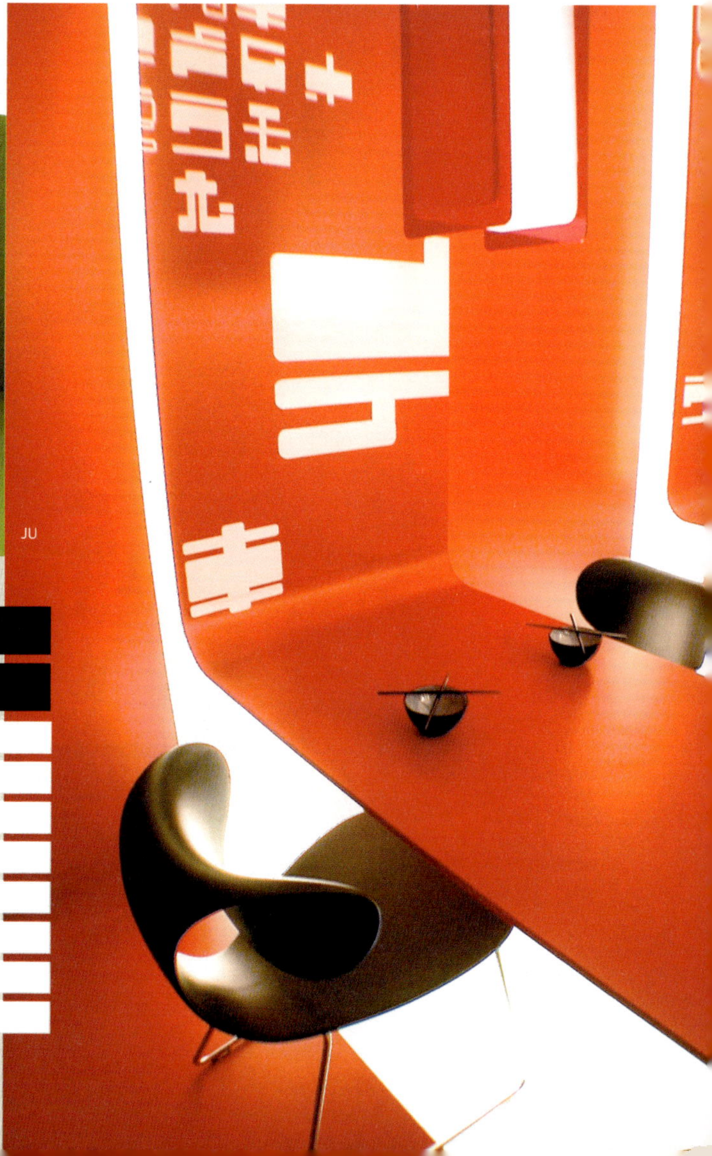

POLITECNICO DI MILANO (ITALY)

The restaurant is clearly divided into two zones that are different in their function (standing/seated service), rhythm (slow/fast), and density (rarefied/intense).

The red zone on the right has been conceived as a traditional restaurant, with tables and chairs. In the yellow zone on the left, diners experience the chic lifestyle of Roman nights over aperitifs and appetizers. Beams of white light lead the eye to the restaurant's key element: the bar, an extension of the kitchen space.

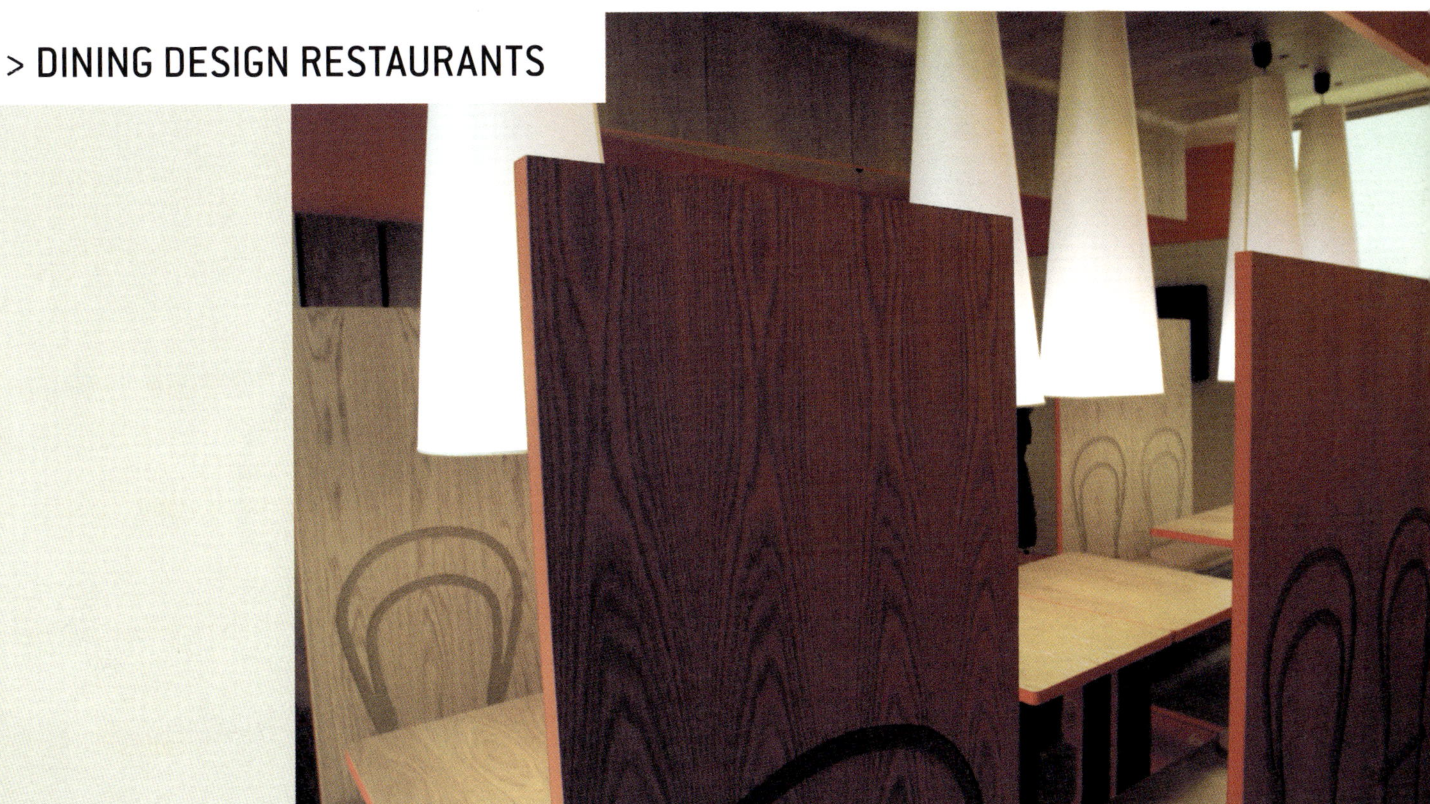

"BISTO'" FRENCH BISTRO IN TURIN - ISTITUTO EUROPEO DI DESIGN (ITALY)

The functional core of the layot is the kitchen –a translucent, hi-tech space that

commands the attention of passers-by and dictates the layout of the surrounding areas and passages.

Like a theatre backdrop, a series of decorative wall-panels, designed around the theme of the wine bottle,

welcomes diners at the entrance and guides them to the intimate interiors of the bistro and the modular bar.

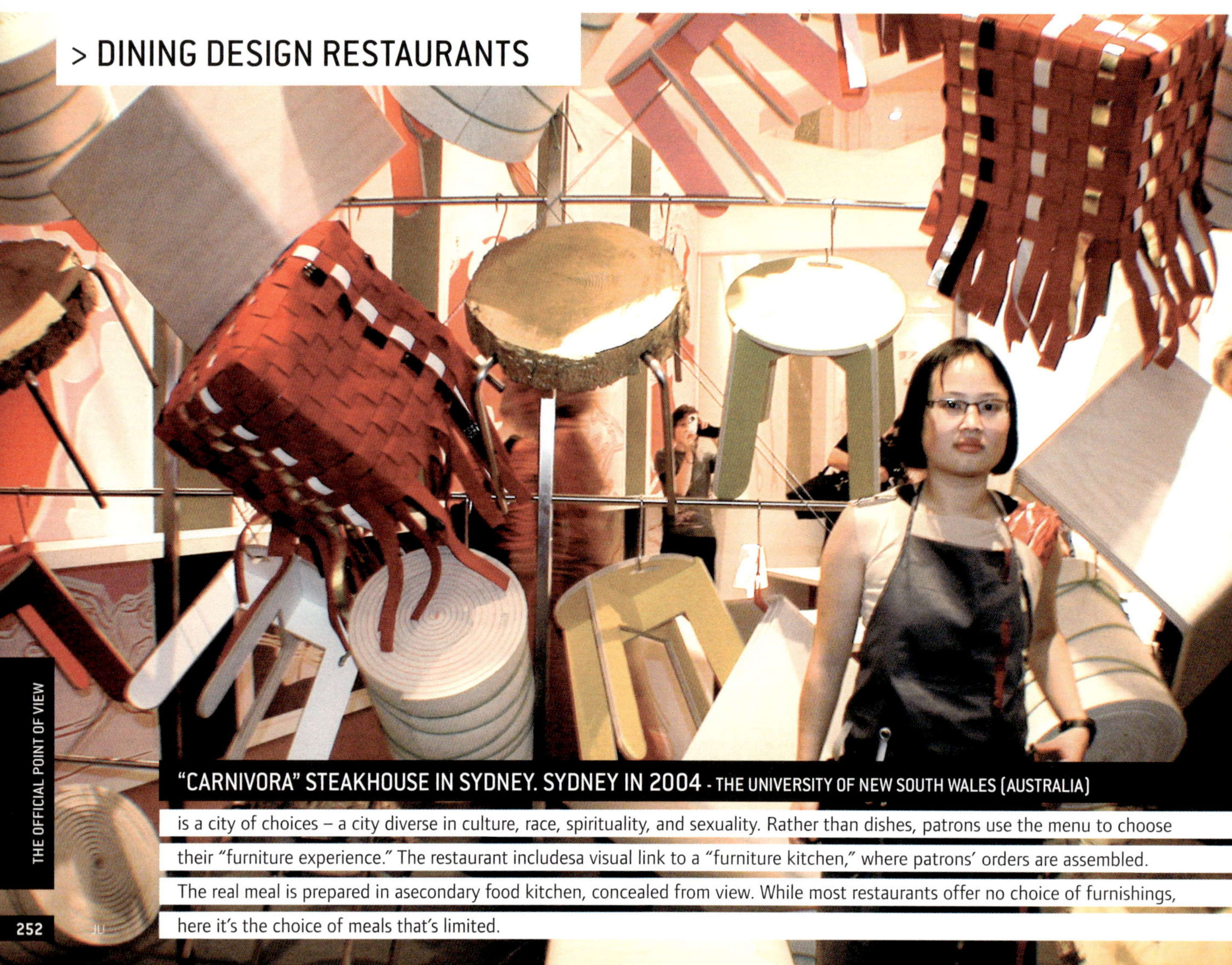

"CARNIVORA" STEAKHOUSE IN SYDNEY. SYDNEY IN 2004 - THE UNIVERSITY OF NEW SOUTH WALES (AUSTRALIA)

is a city of choices – a city diverse in culture, race, spirituality, and sexuality. Rather than dishes, patrons use the menu to choose their "furniture experience." The restaurant includesa visual link to a "furniture kitchen," where patrons' orders are assembled. The real meal is prepared in asecondary food kitchen, concealed from view. While most restaurants offer no choice of furnishings, here it's the choice of meals that's limited.

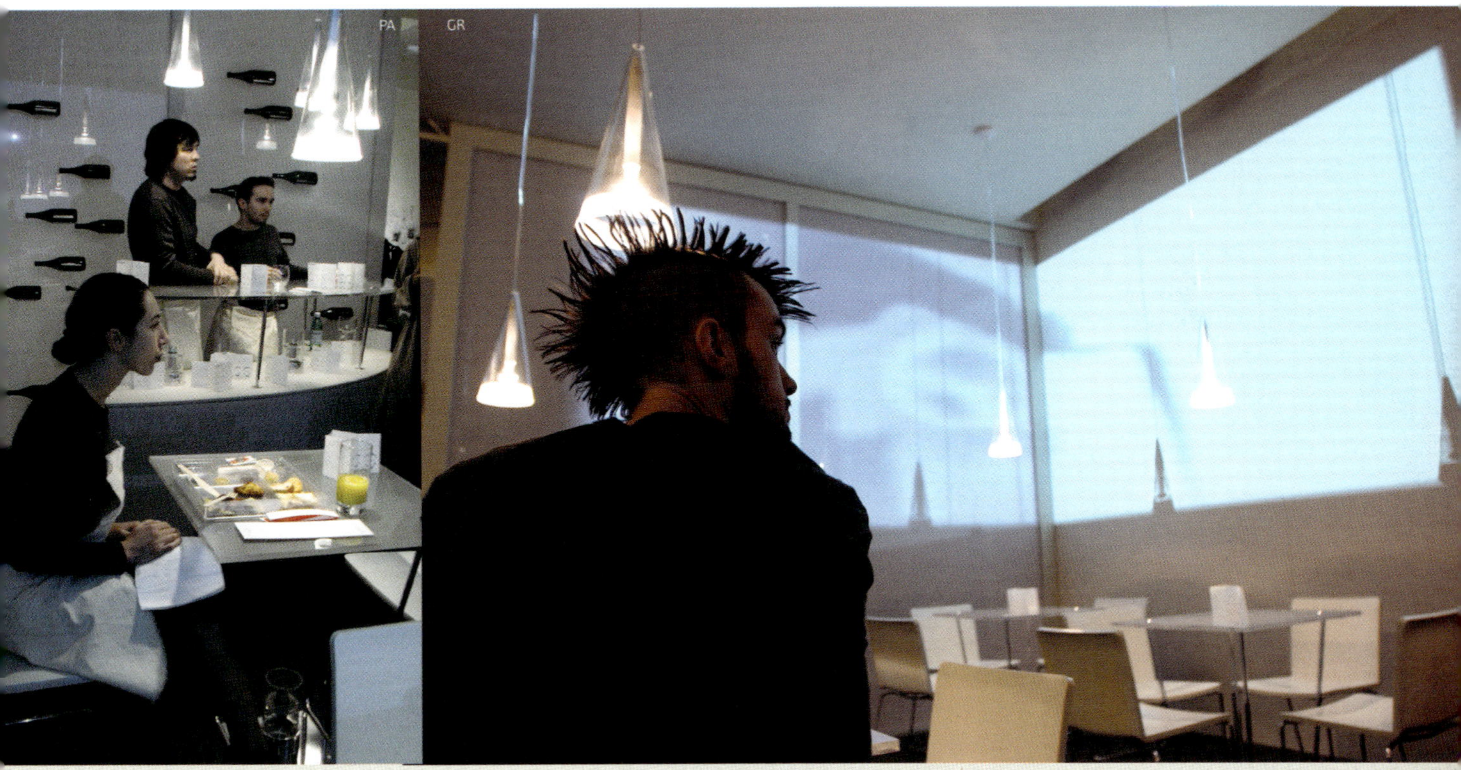

"TRACE" WINE-BAR IN TRIBECA, NEW YORK CITY - RHODE ISLAND SCHOOL OF DESIGN (USA)

The project is based on a visual experience that blends people together: the gestures and movements of patrons

in the bar are superimposed and projected larger than life onto the entrance wall, forming an ever-changing tapestry.

The environment reflects the social interactions of the people within: using new digital technology, the crowd makes

the space and the space reflects the crowd. The surfaces of the tables and the bar are translucent, allowing

the shapes and shadows of anything on them to show through.

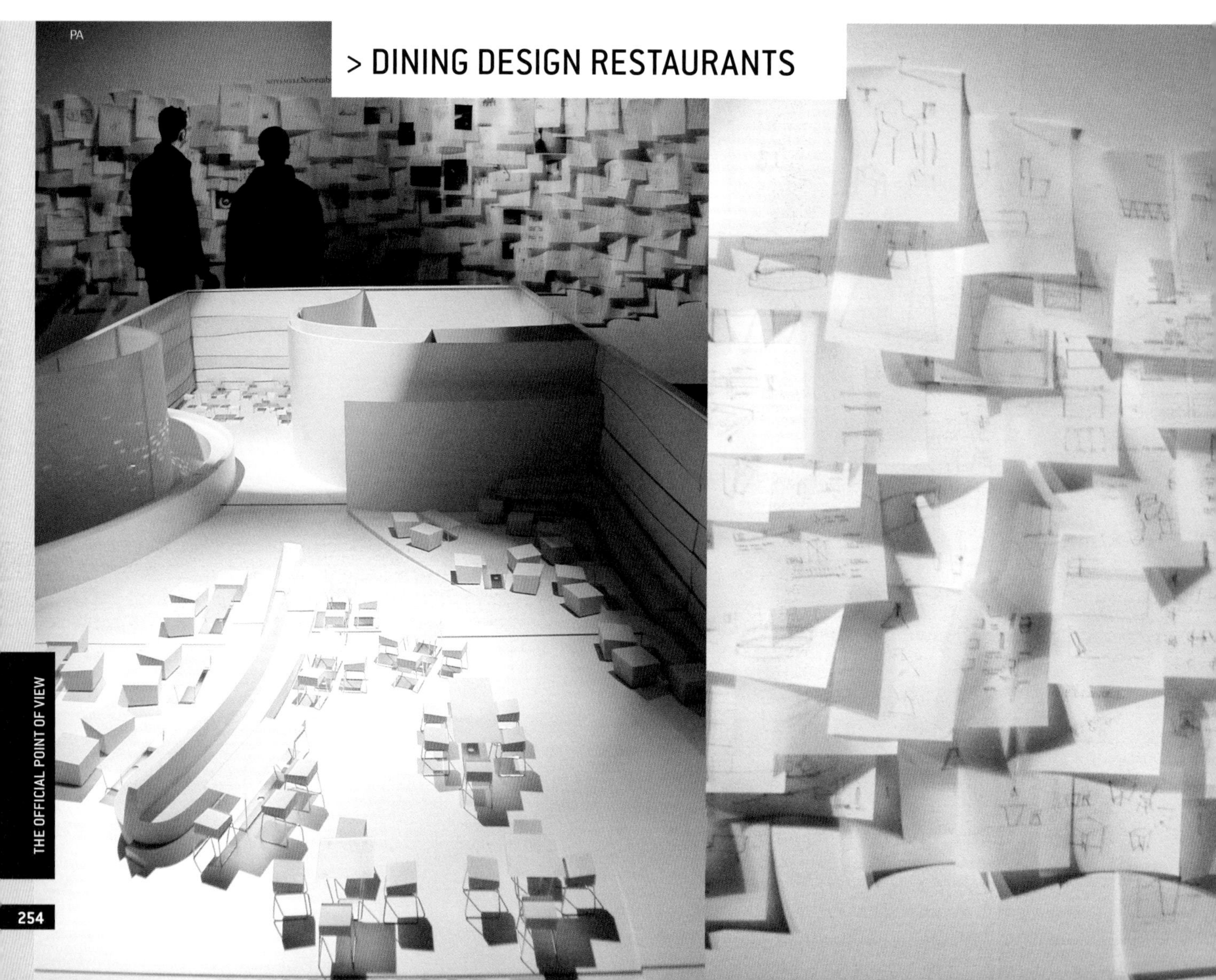

PA

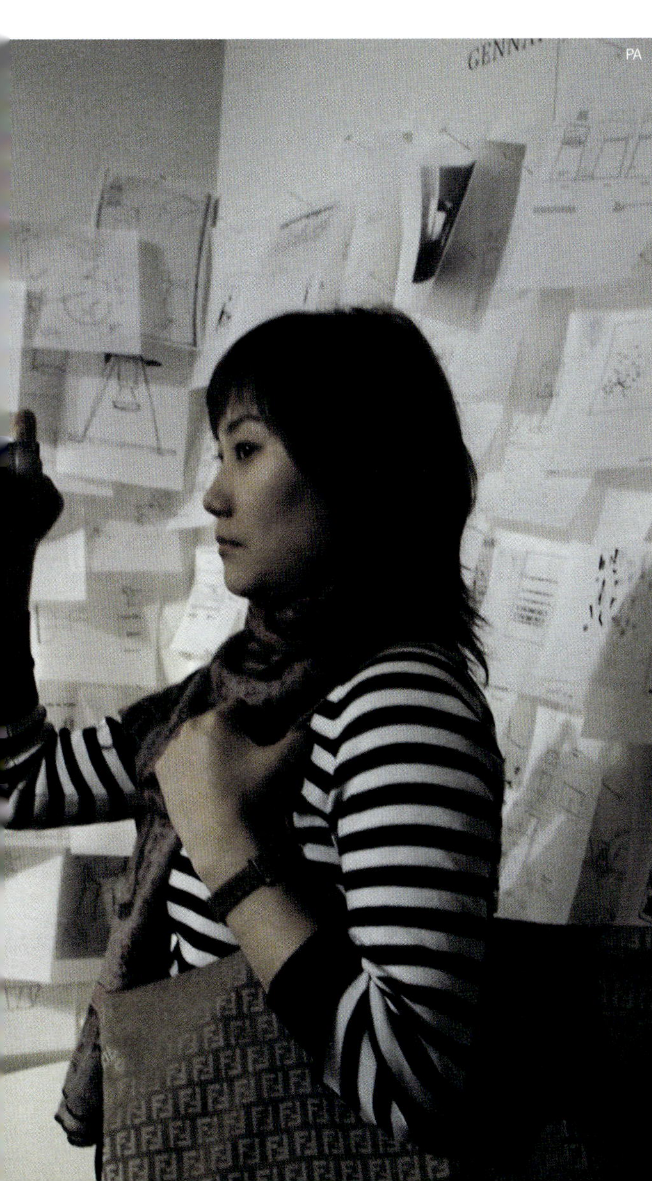

"B:ROQUE" VIENNA COFFEE HOUSE IN BRIGHTON

- BUCKINGHAMSHIRE CHILTERNS UNIVERSITY COLLEGE (UK)

The key element of the restaurant is a "spine wall" unfolding and uncoiling in space to generate create the diverse areas – from bar to bar lounge, main dining area and through to the private dining room at the back of the restaurant.

The space is composed of elements that fold out from the walls, ceiling, and floor.

Upholstery and carpets lend their personalities to the surfaces of tables and chairs, weaving, twisting, and turning to reveal hidden qualities and surprises.

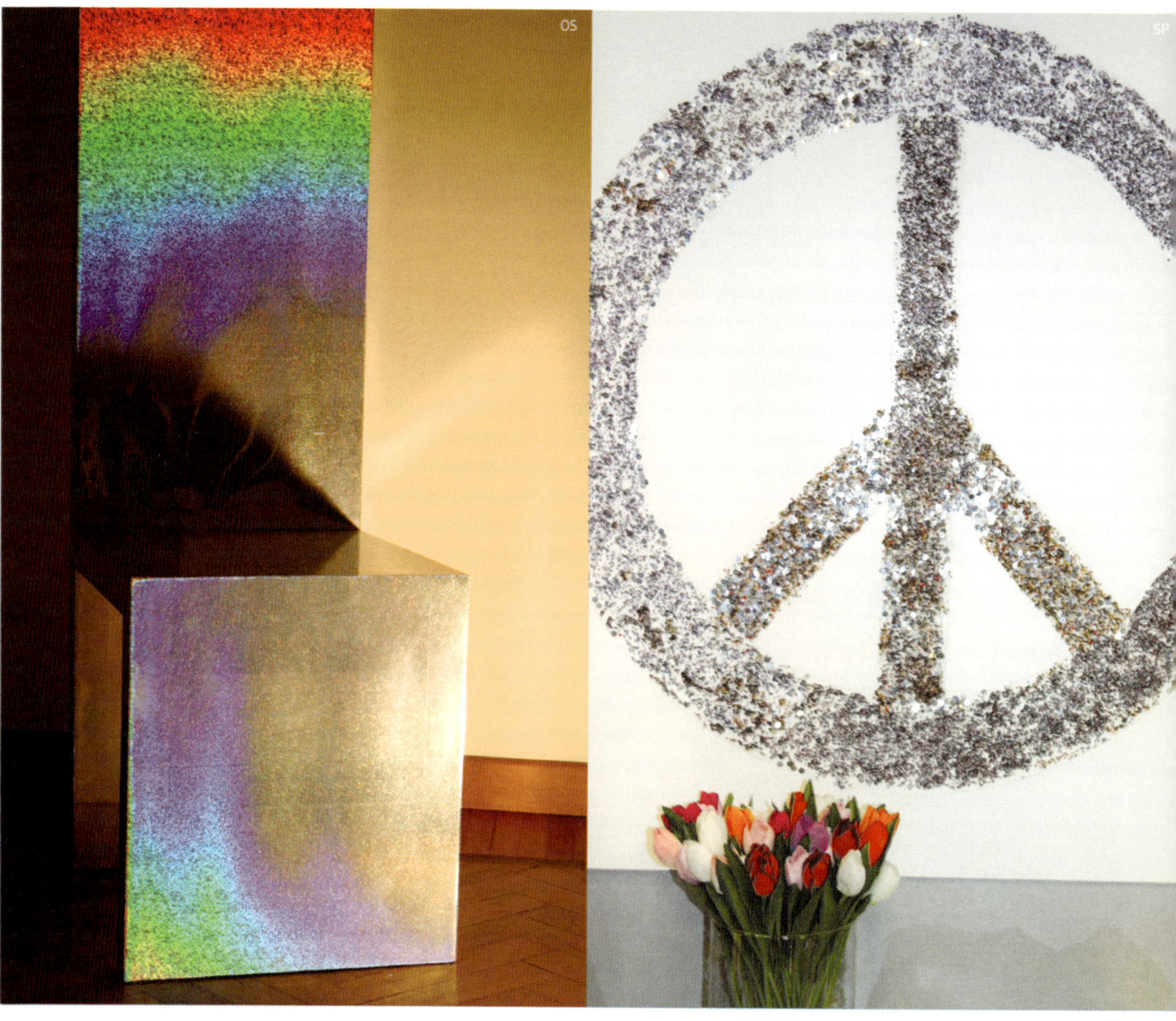

256

Koichiro Kimura

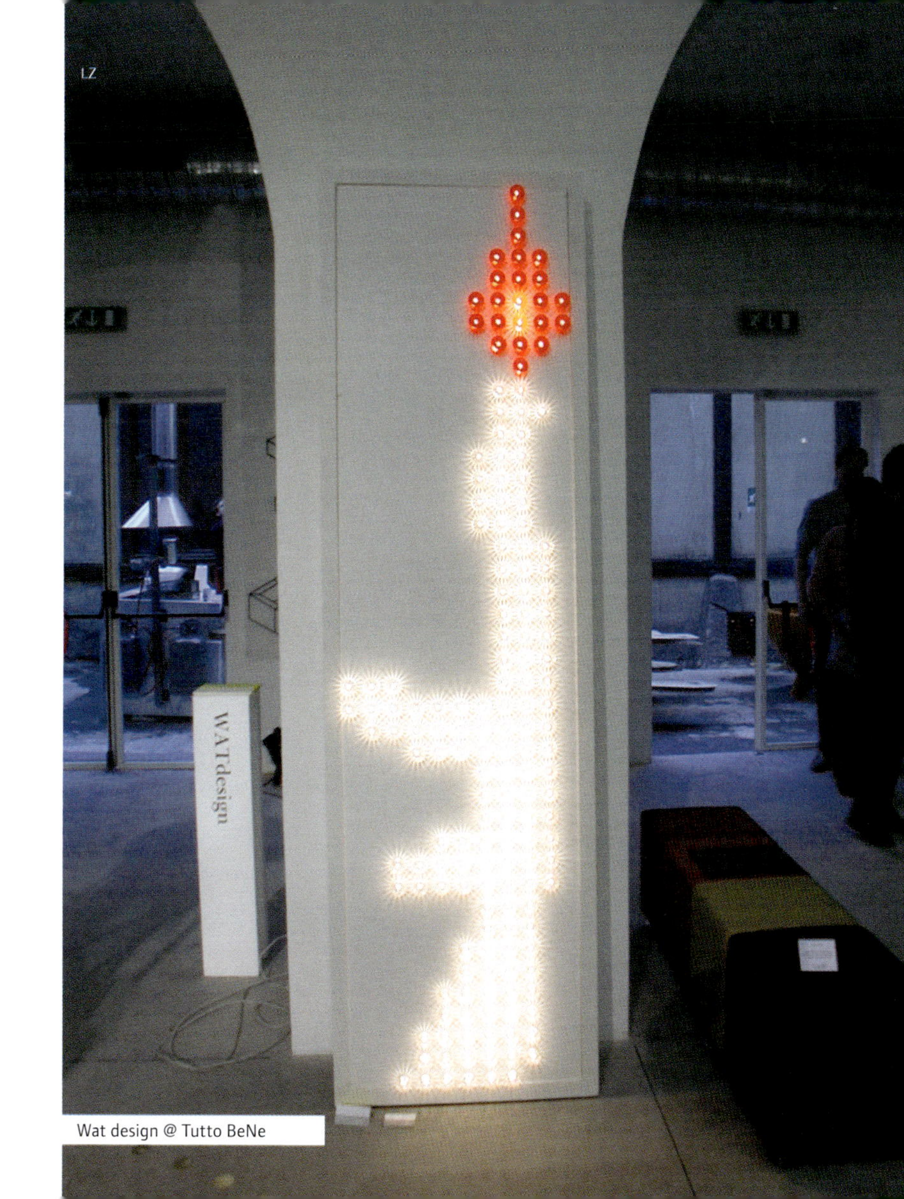

Wat design @ Tutto BeNe

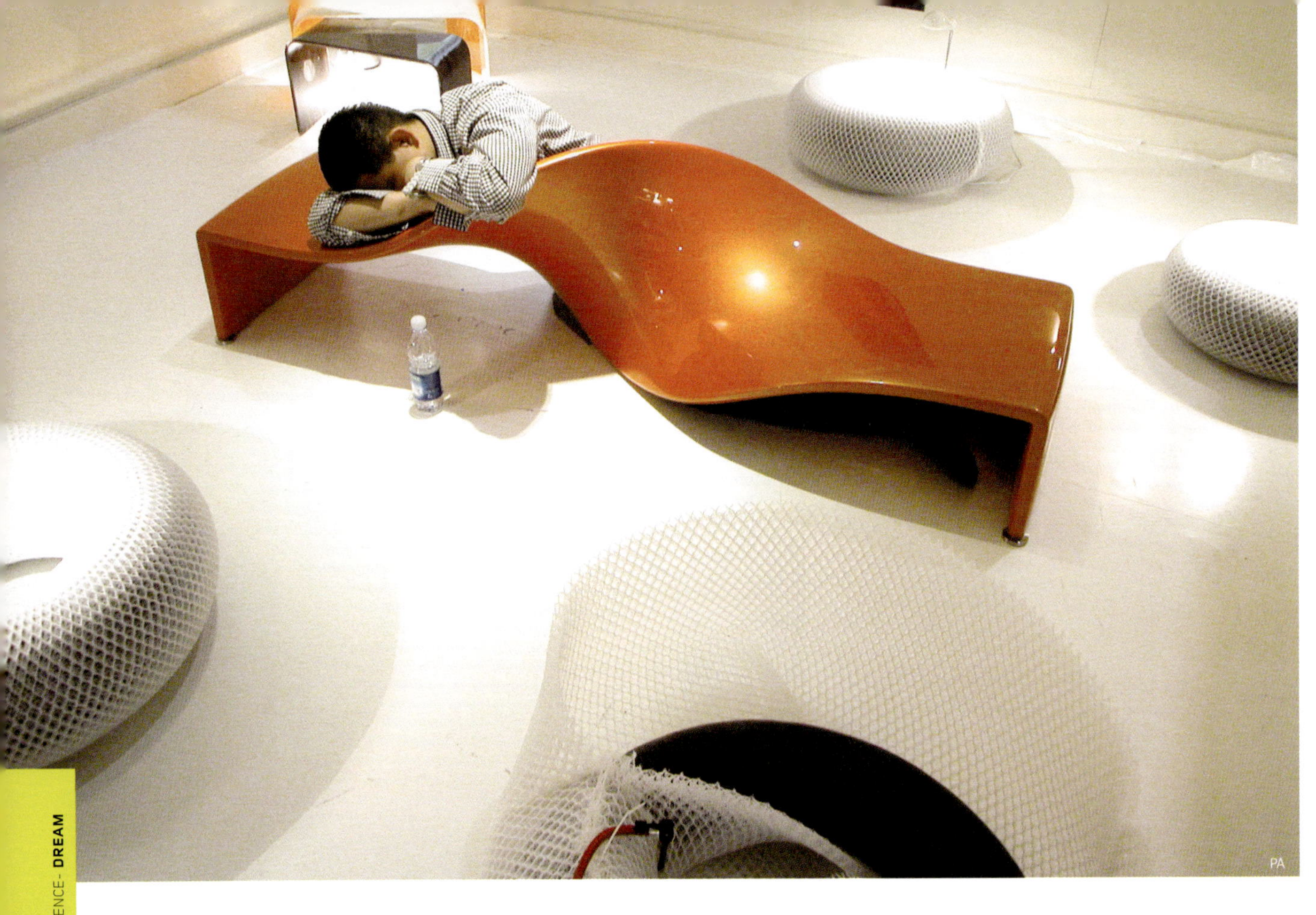

Sachio Hihara @ Satellite

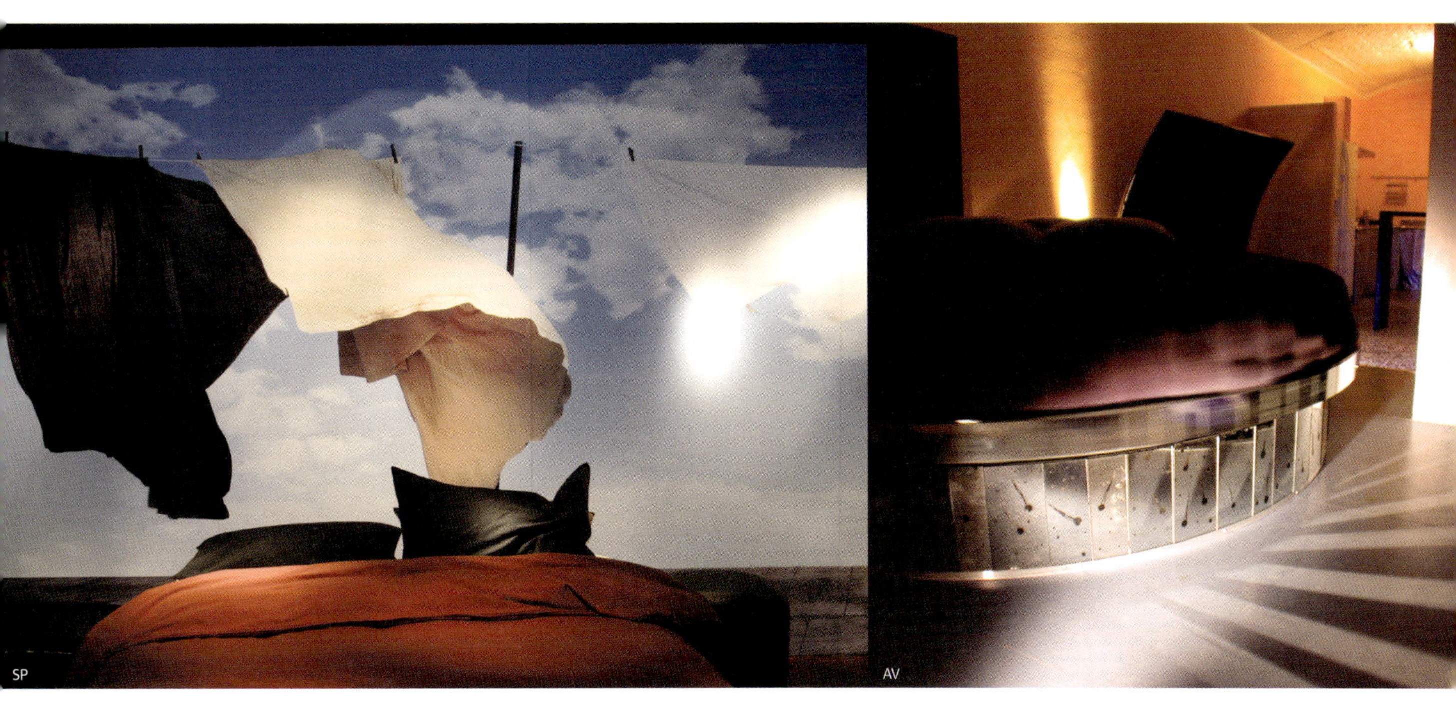

Claudy Jongstra

Drreams

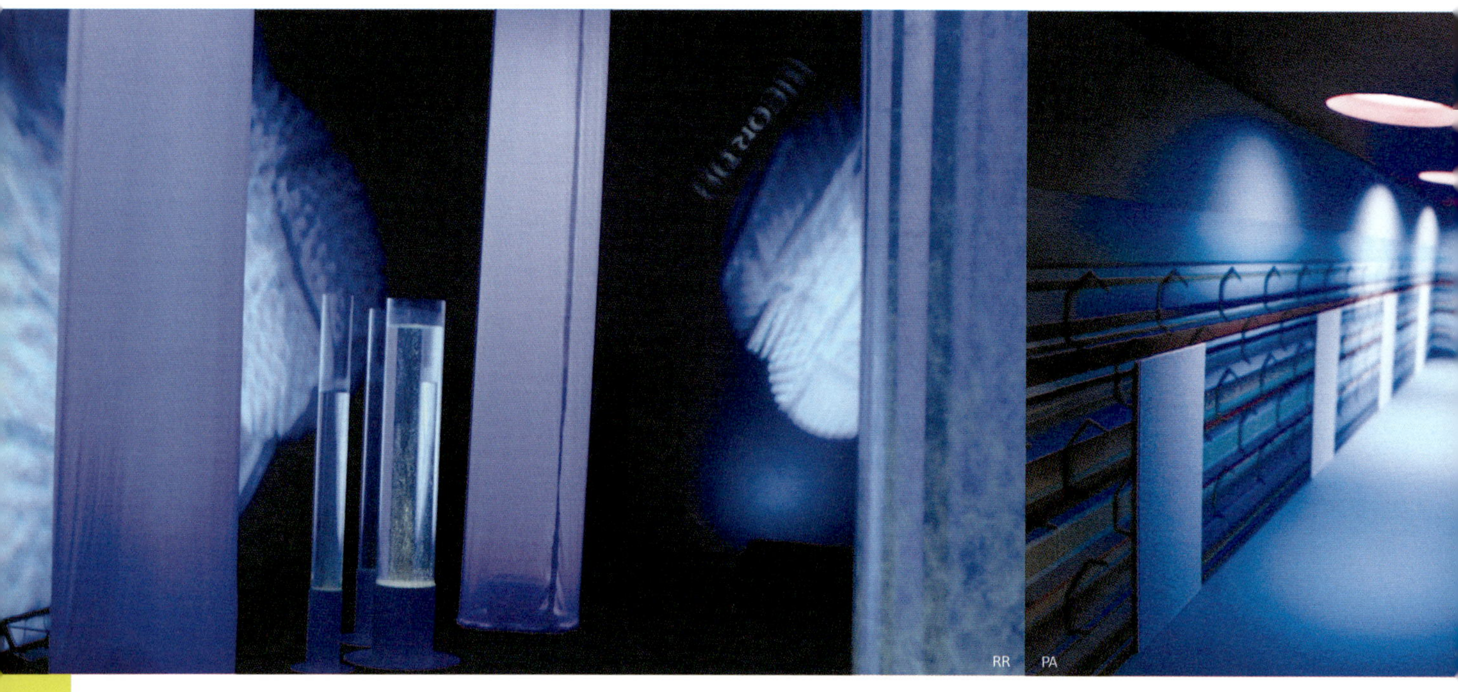

Morphosis by Jacuzzi @ Pelota

Colorflage" by Markus Benesch

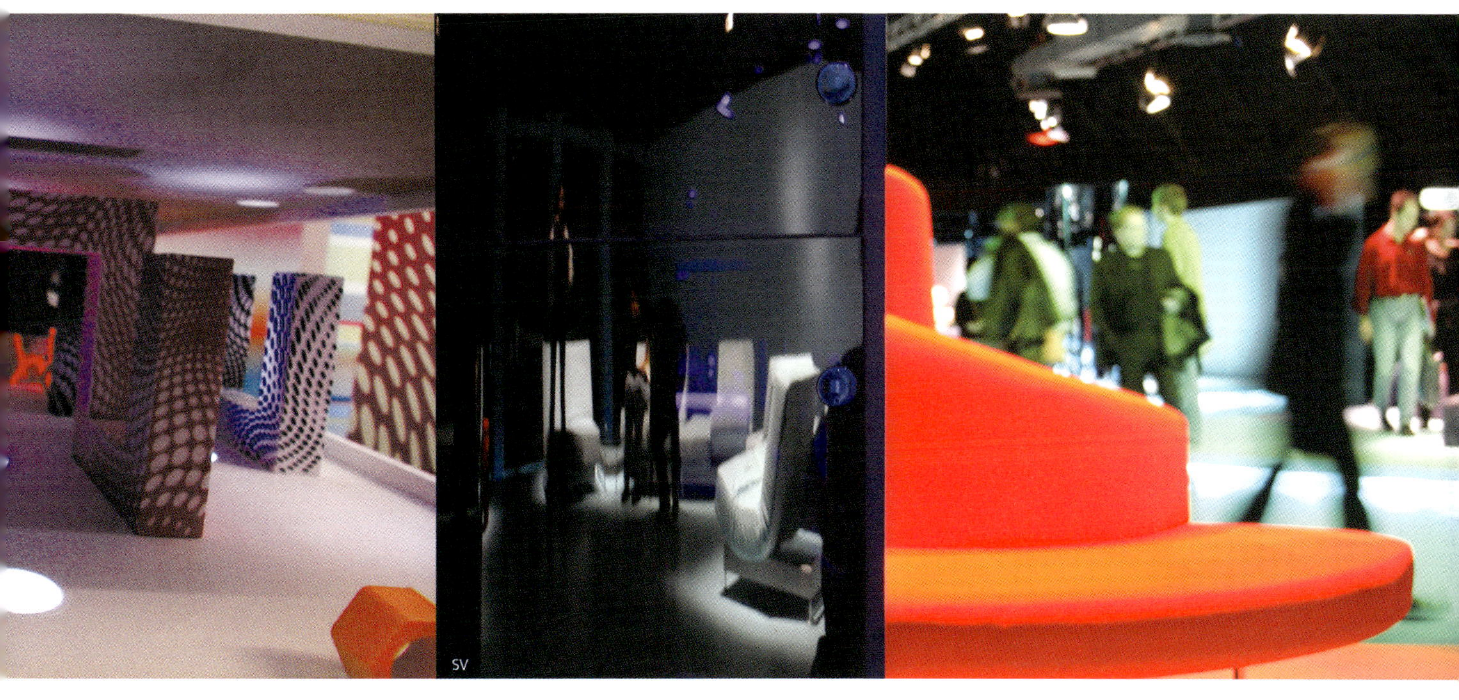

Edra

> SCANDINAVIAN DESIGN

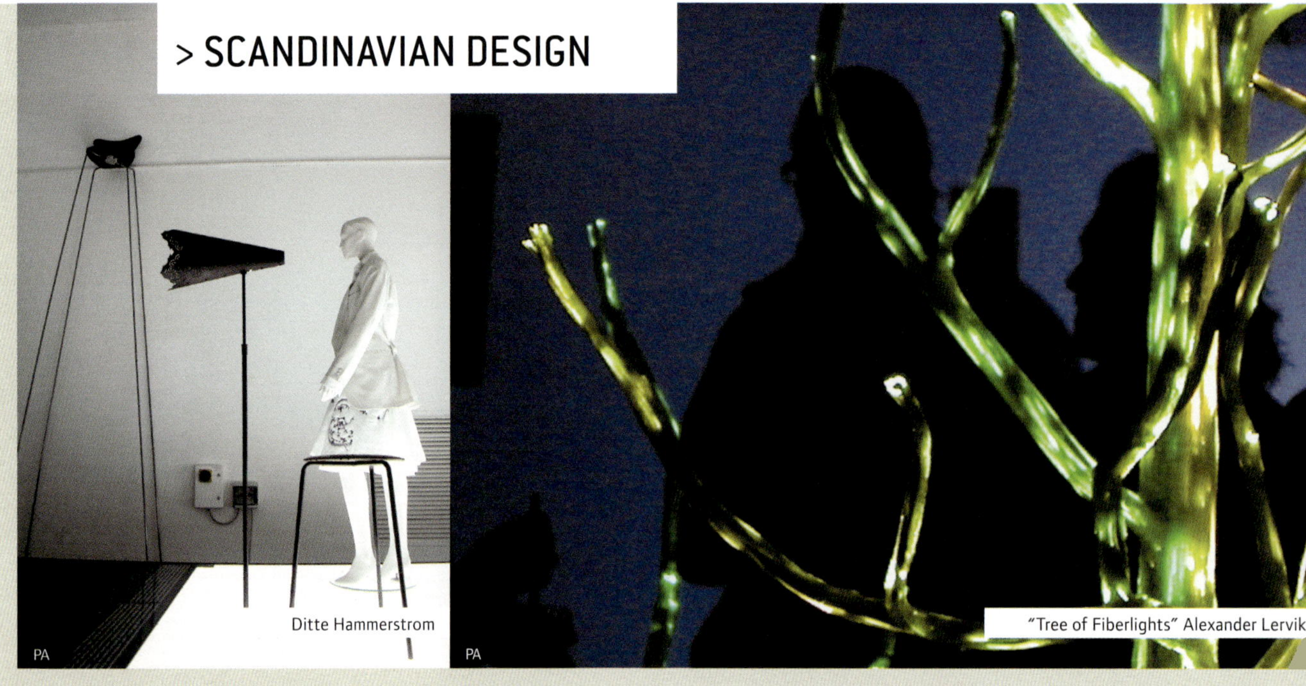

Ditte Hammerstrom

PA

PA

"Tree of Fiberlights" Alexander Lervik

BEYOND THE MYTH

This exhibition will confirm the Scandinavian design movement as a **crucial element in design history**,

but will also debate the myths and **stereotypes** that have flourished around this topic.In order to obtain a

fresh view the exhibition has been structured on Italo Calvino's **Six Memos for the Next Millenium** as a point of departure.

Calvino emphasizes some values that will be important for creative people in the

new millenium:Lightness, Quickness, Exactitude, Visibility, Multiplicity and Consistency.

Such vital qualities are easily associated with many aspects of Scandinavian design.

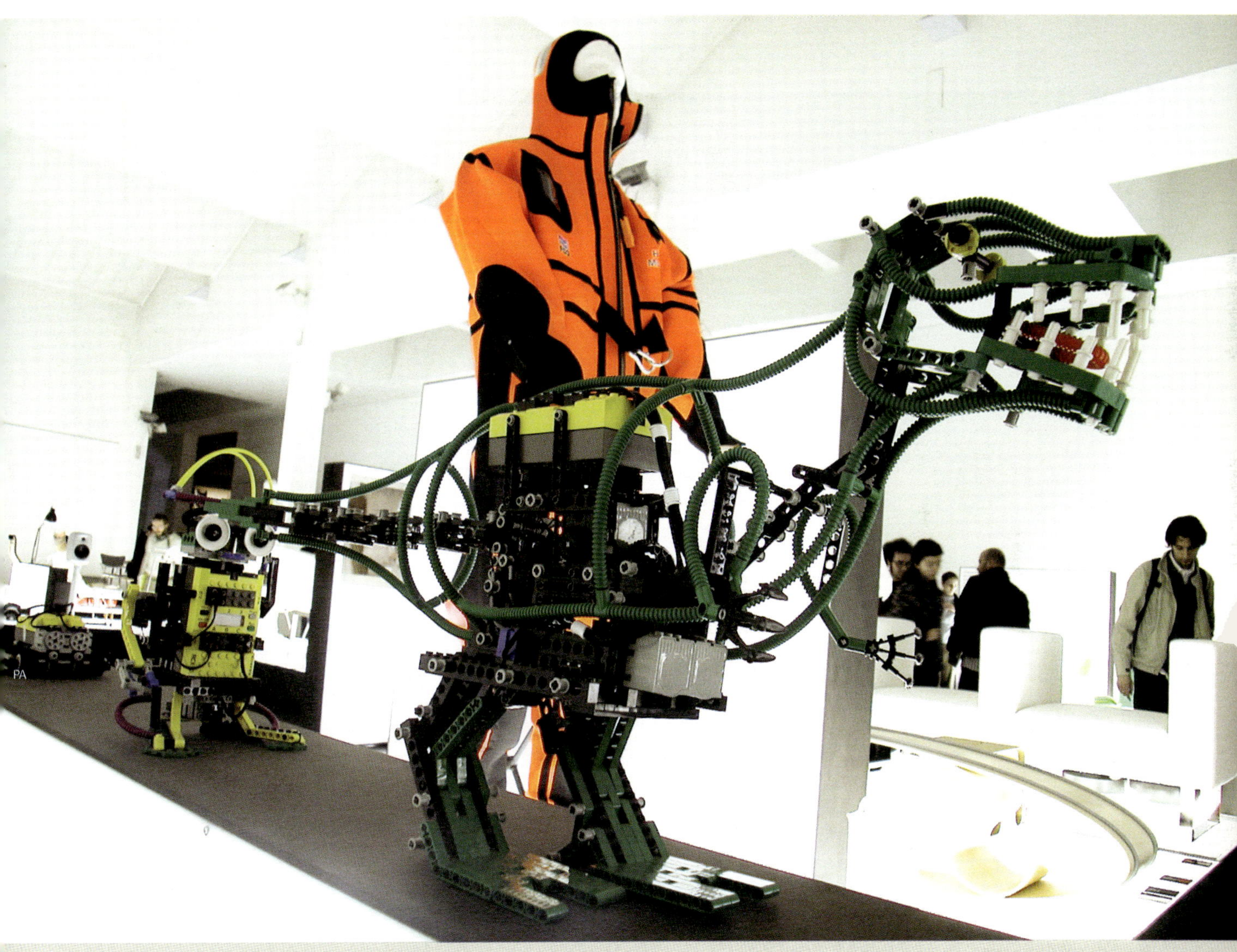
PA

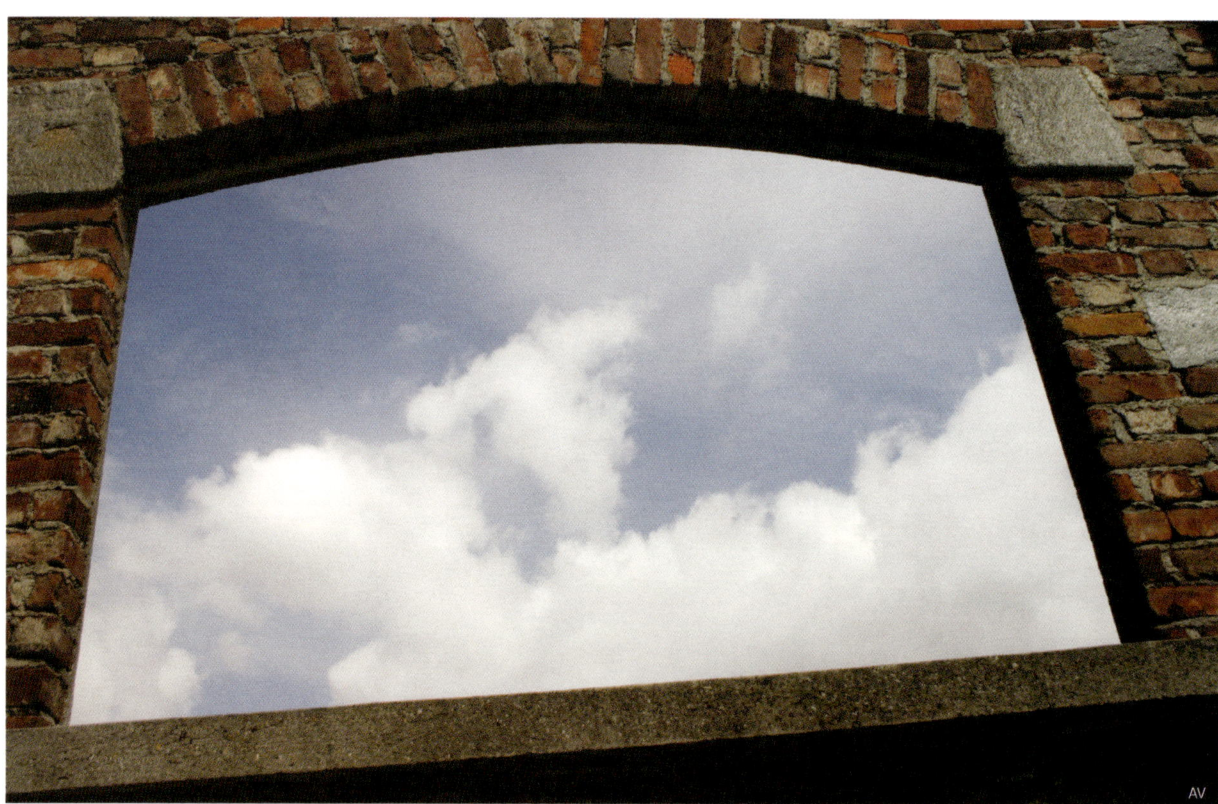

AV

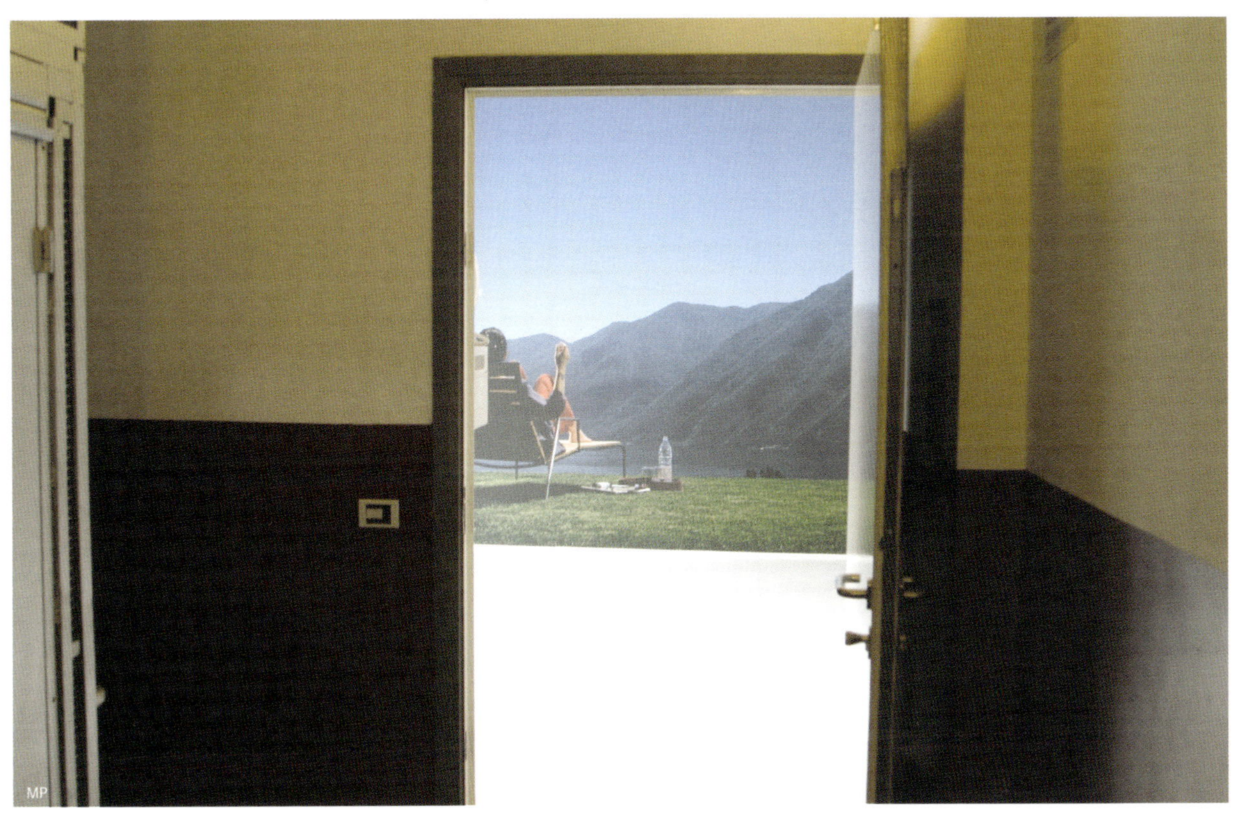

Co Ro

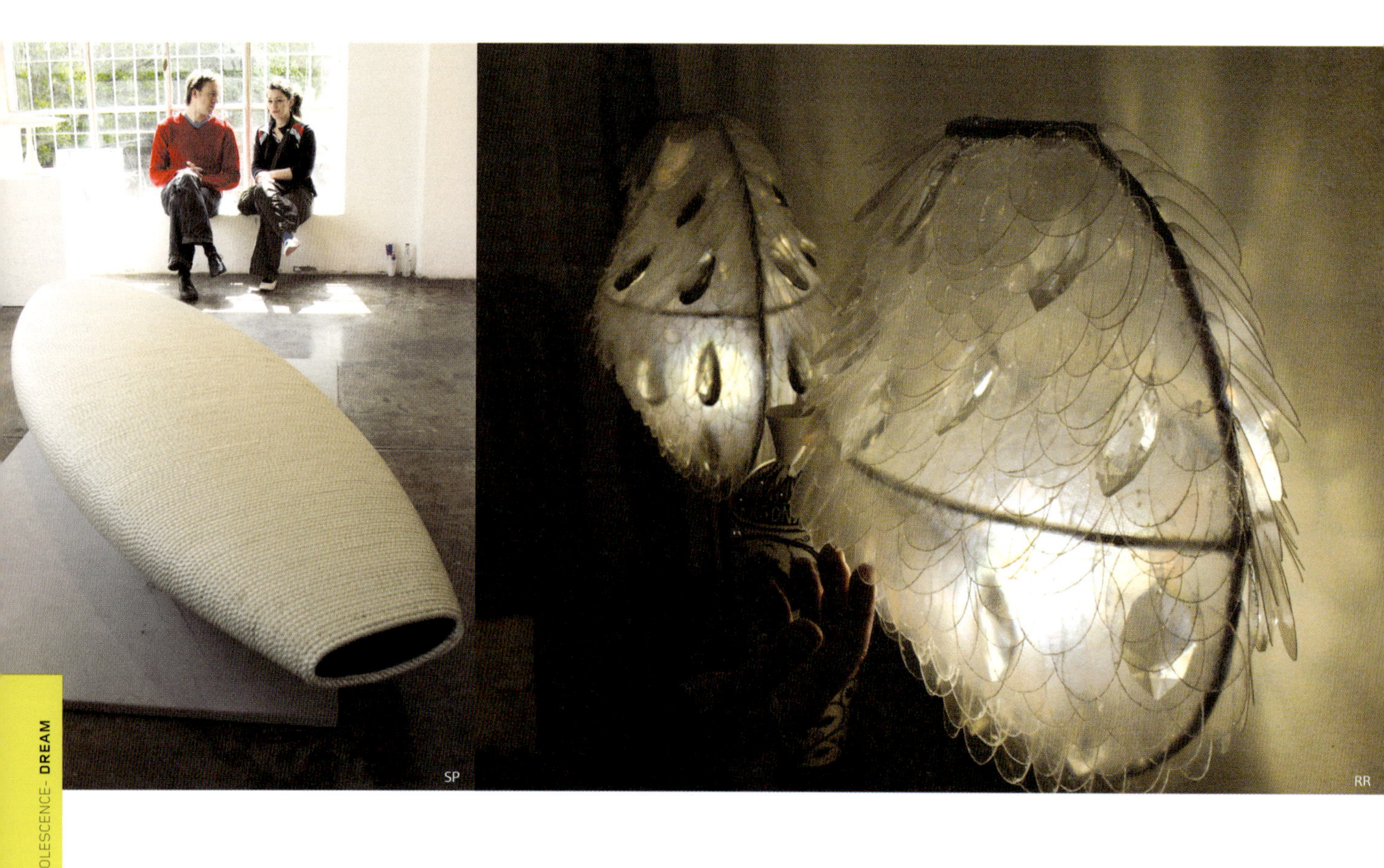

Charlie Davidson @ Designersblock   Amalgama

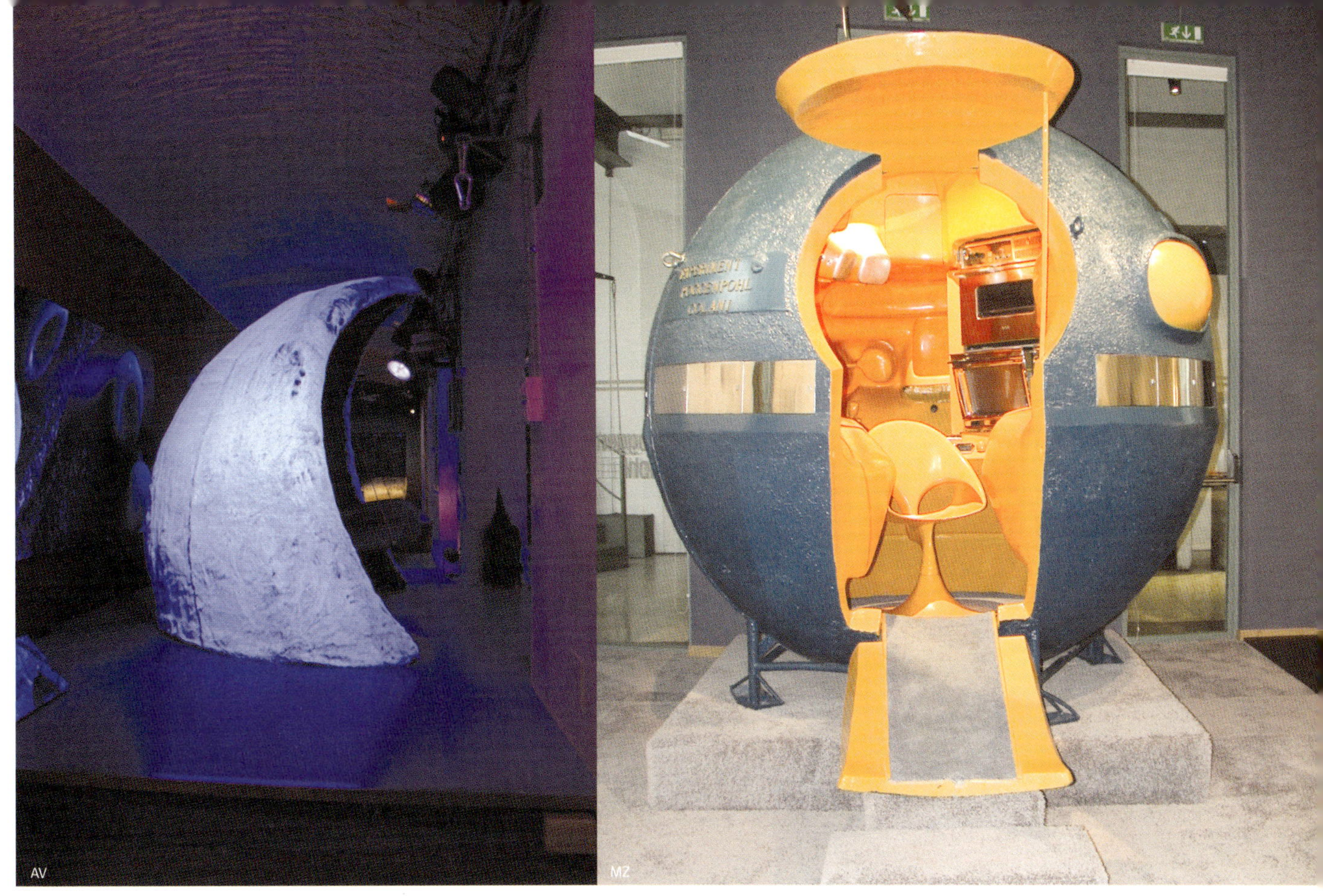

Dreams   Poggenpohl

> SCIENCE FICTION

WHICH DESIGN OBJECT/S OR CONCEPTS EXEMPLIFY A NEW KIND OF SCIENCE FICTION?

I think most – though certainly not all - of the blow-molded plastic furniture is a kind of failed science-fiction: primarily focused on image rather than any new, liveable reality. Especially when it's illuminated from within like some Hollywood B-movie for cheap special effects. We have real challenges to produce democratic design, but how many oversized, hard plastic balloons do we need in our spaces?

JOZEPH FORAKIS

IPOD is a design object that currently exemplifies a "new" kind of science fiction.

MIGLIORE + SERVETTO

"Science fiction" does not involve design but marketing instead.

DAVID PALTERER

Design is made to activate fantasy in people, otherwise it is not made any experience

DROOG DESIGN

Fake spacey design which looks modern but is not modern.

ROSS LOVEGROVE

Some wishes are of a science fiction nature and there are designers trying to fulfil them. Everything originates from a request. Castiglioni would analyse his people in order to produce something to share.
Contemporary design looks for striking solutions whilst failing to focus on people's wishes.

TANJA SOLCI

> ENTERTAINMENT

NOWADAYS, WHAT CAN BE ASSOCIATED TO THE CONCEPT OF "ENTERTAINMENT"

IN THE WORLD OF DESIGN?

The sicker and louder the cry is, the more it's entertainment.

INGO MAURER

Entertainment is currently connected with the concepts of 'immediate familiarity' and 'fast consumption'. Boredom is always lingering!

DAVID PALTERER

Nowadays, the majority of communication tools and objects can be associated to the concept of "entertainment" in the world of design.

MIGLIORE + SERVETTO

The concept of "entertainment" in the world of design is a showy, simplistic design thats full of pretension.

ROSS LOVEGROVE

In the world of design the concept of "entertainment" is giving a house a new make over like you would change your clothes. Having fun is "wearing" an ever-changing context, i.e. a Mood house.

SAMUELE MAZZA

We make some amusing objects, for example tha porcellane cat house, the moon carpet; I produce them to make on people a little smile.

DROOG DESIGN

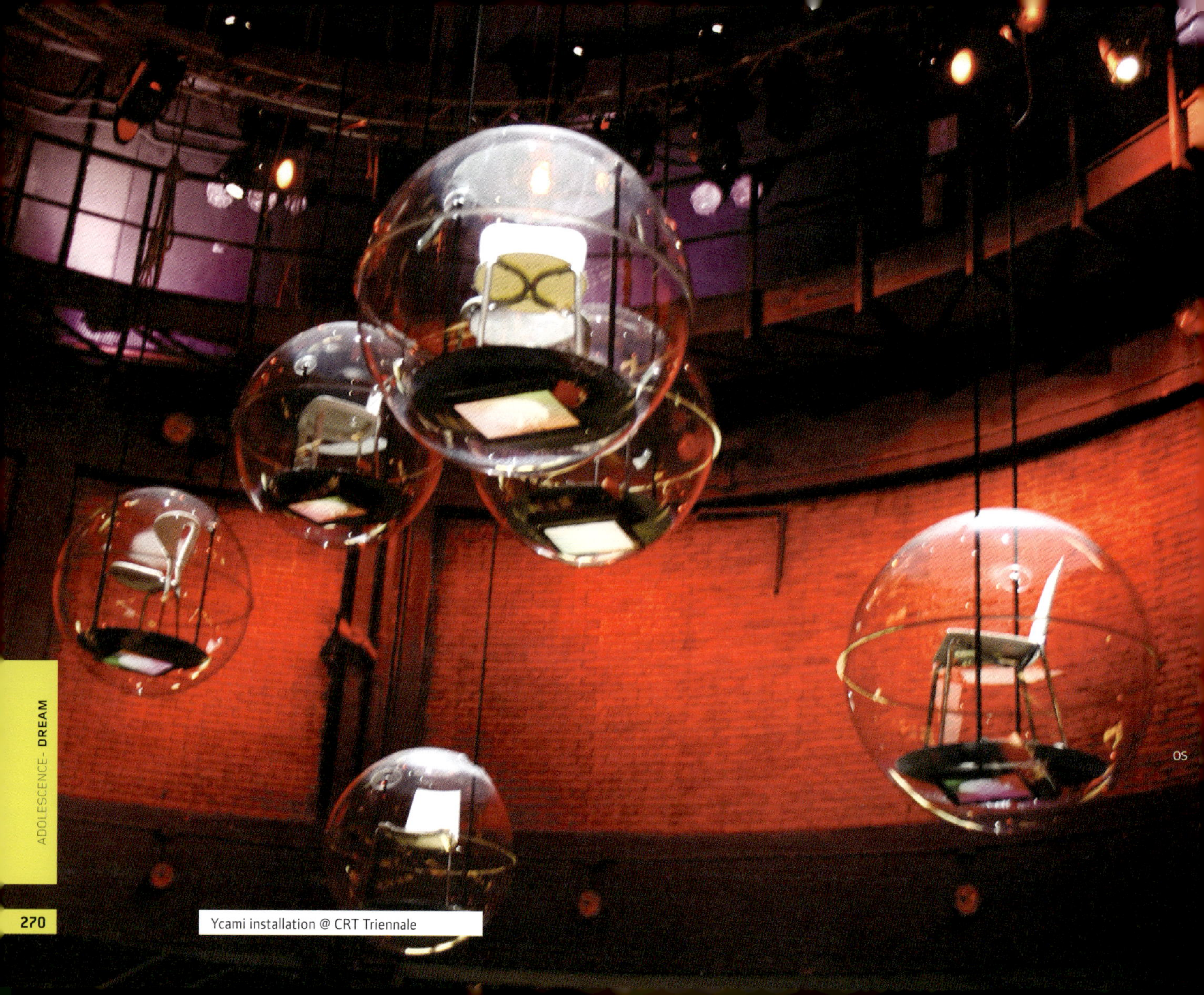

Ycami installation @ CRT Triennale

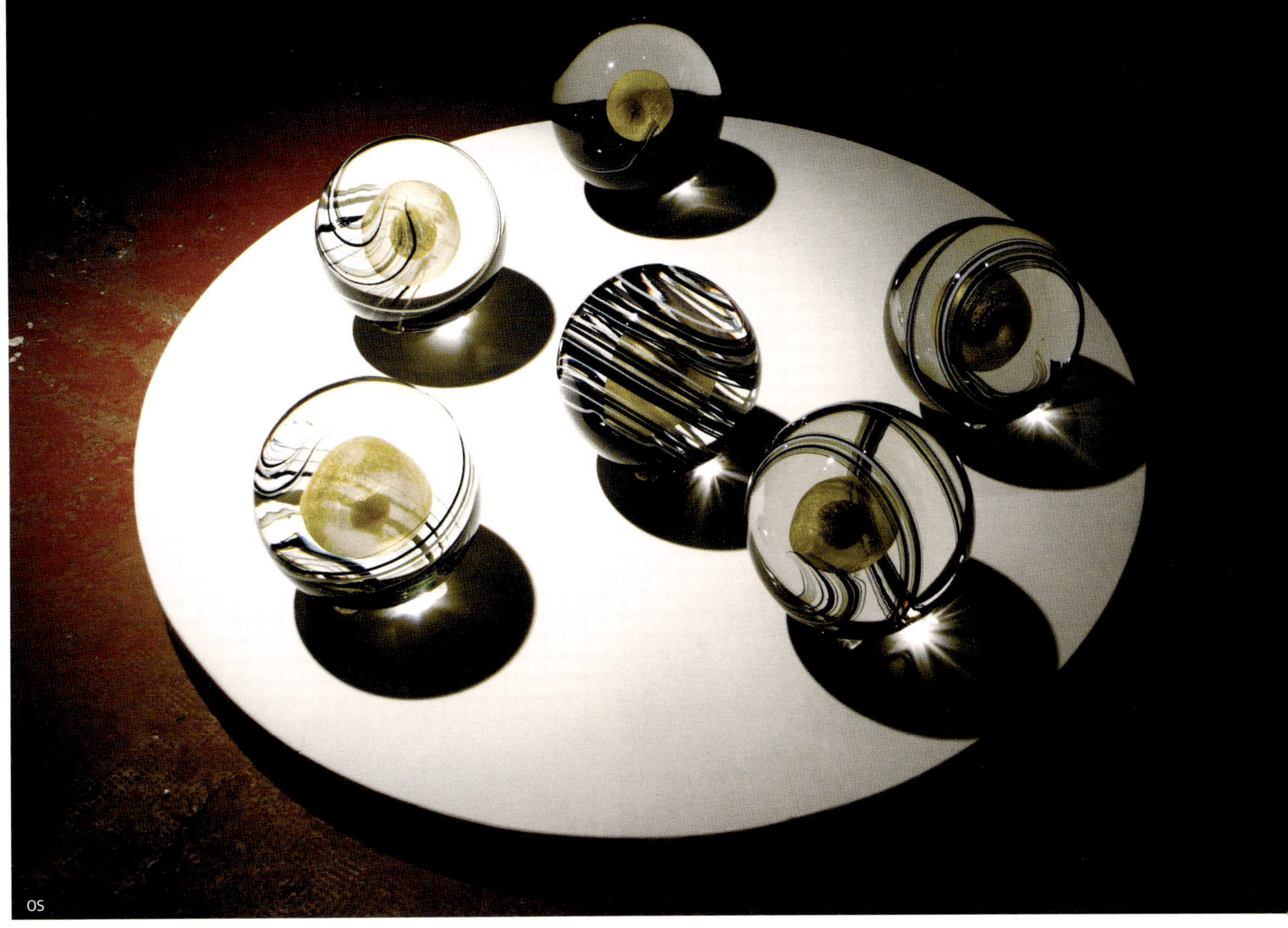

Vettor Frattini

Ritsue Mishima @ Galleria Blanchaert

Jess Shaw @ Designersblock

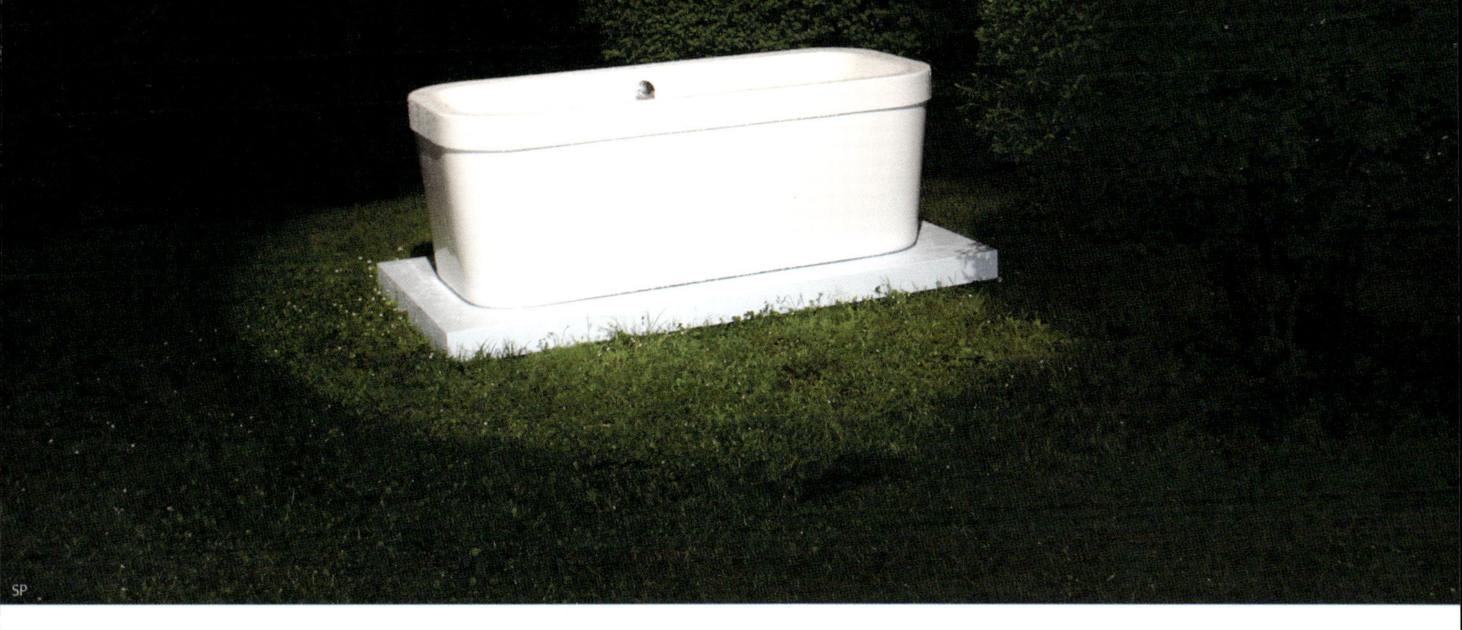

Duravit

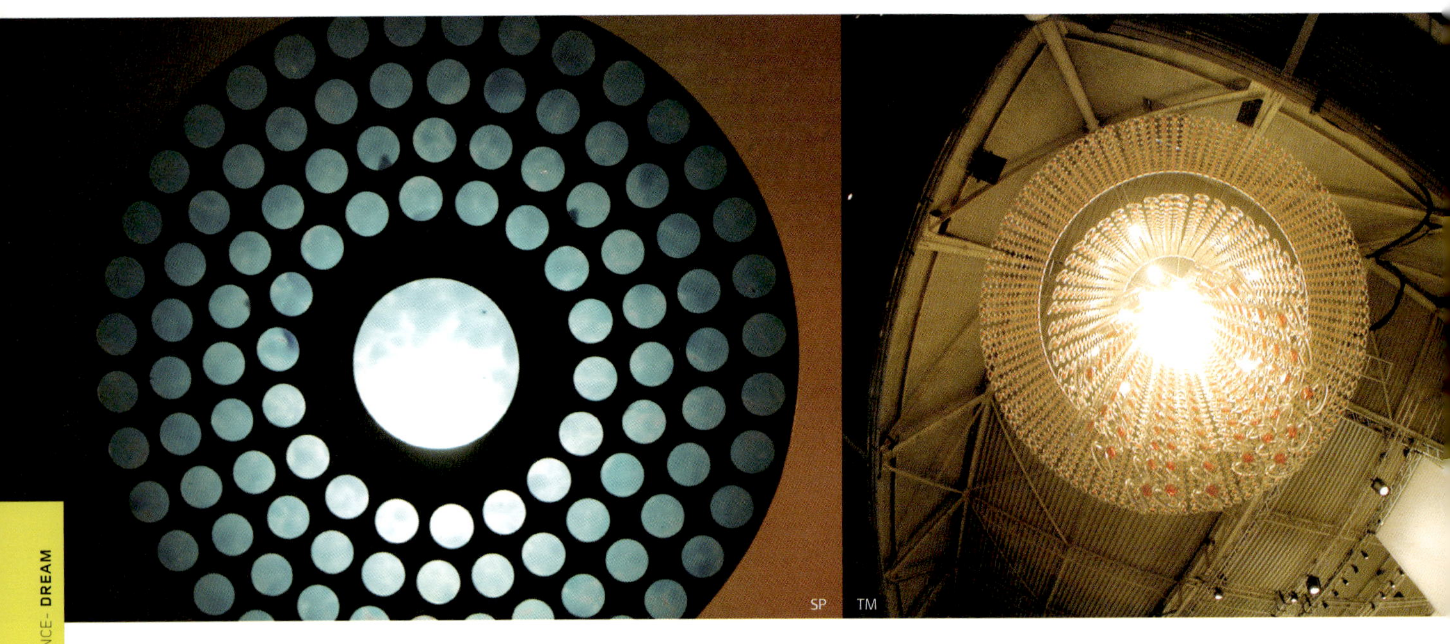

Studio Marcelio

Jacopo Foggini

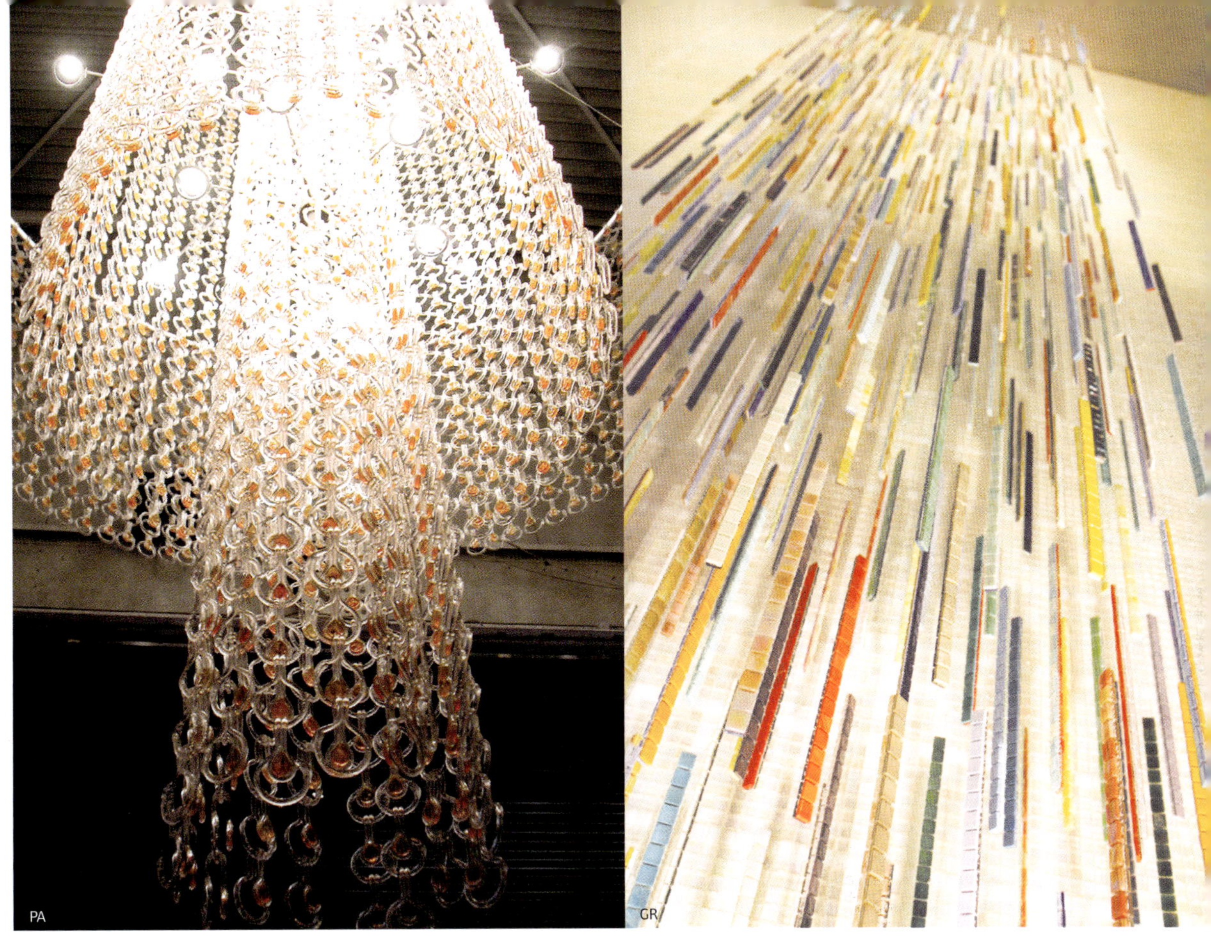

Jacopo Foggini   Drreams

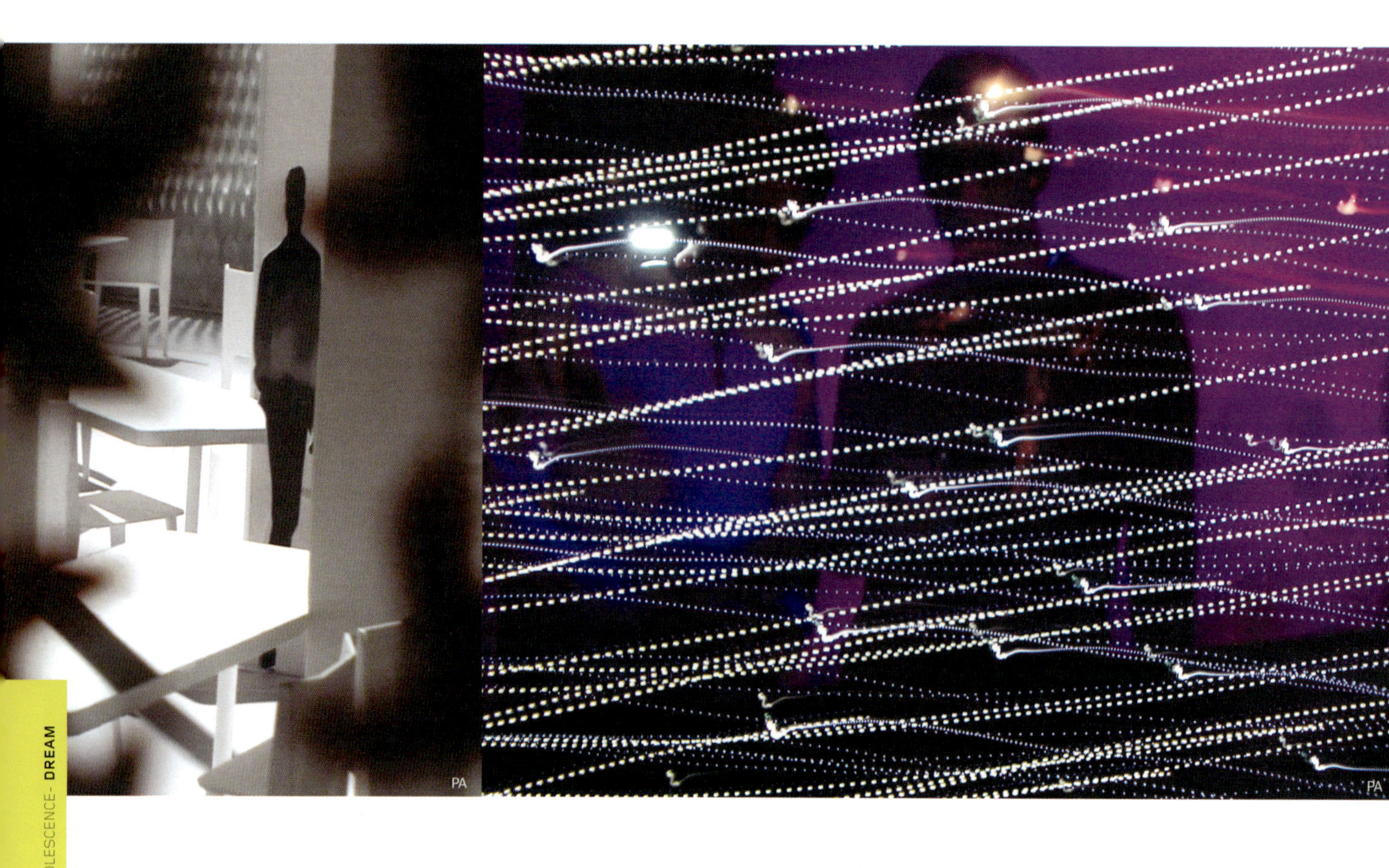

Pizzeria Fooo
by Osaka University of Arts
@ Dining Design exhibition

Injom

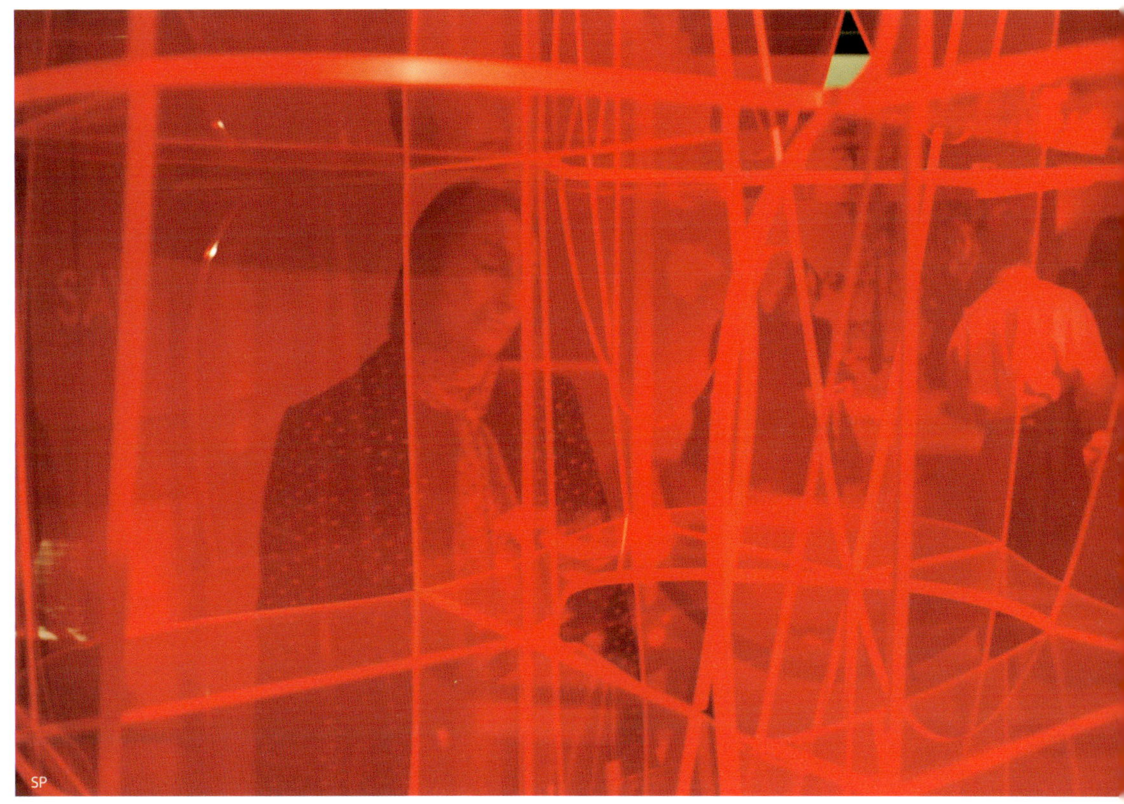

Sawaya&Moroni

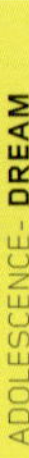

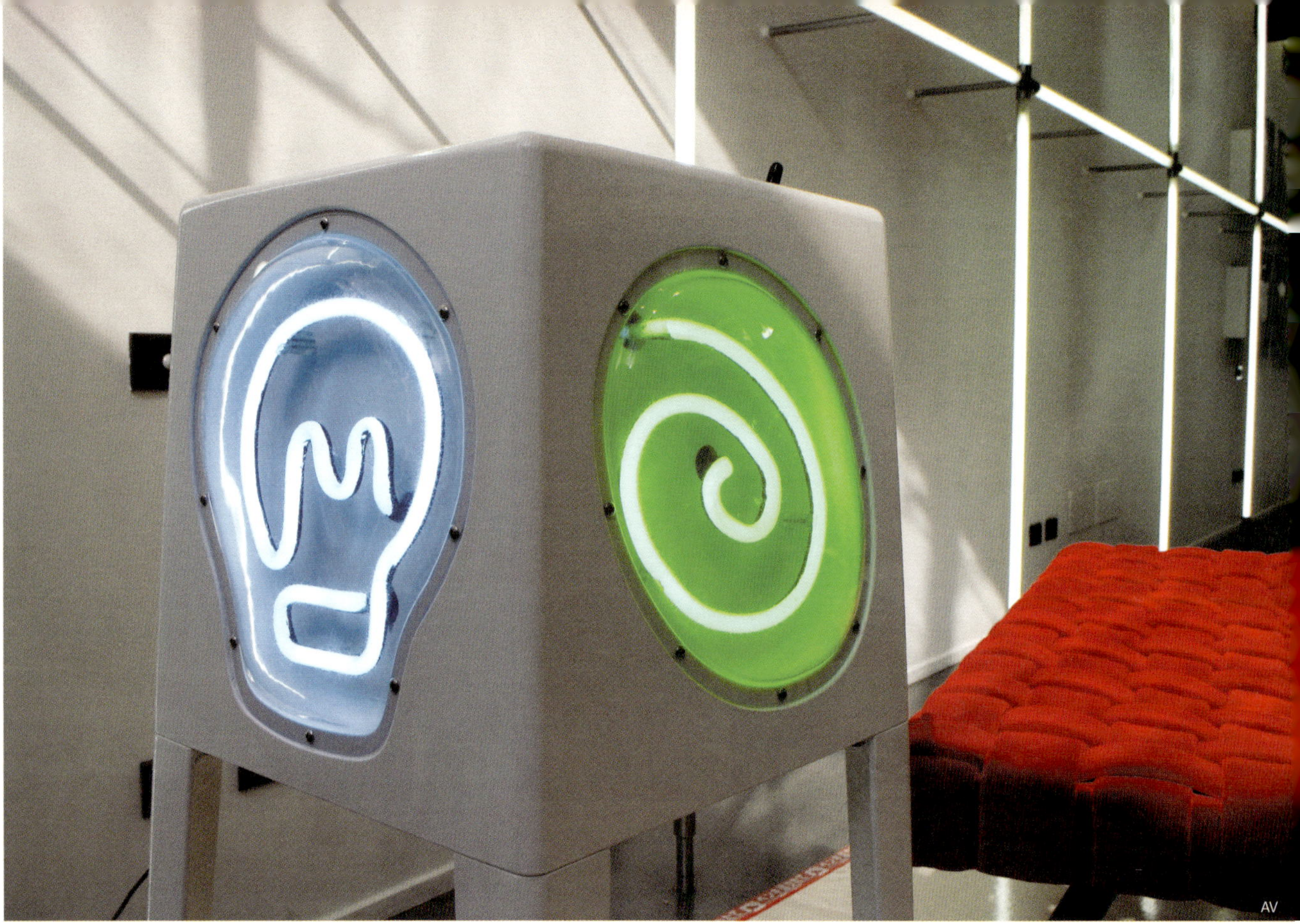

Masashi Sawada @ Nu light

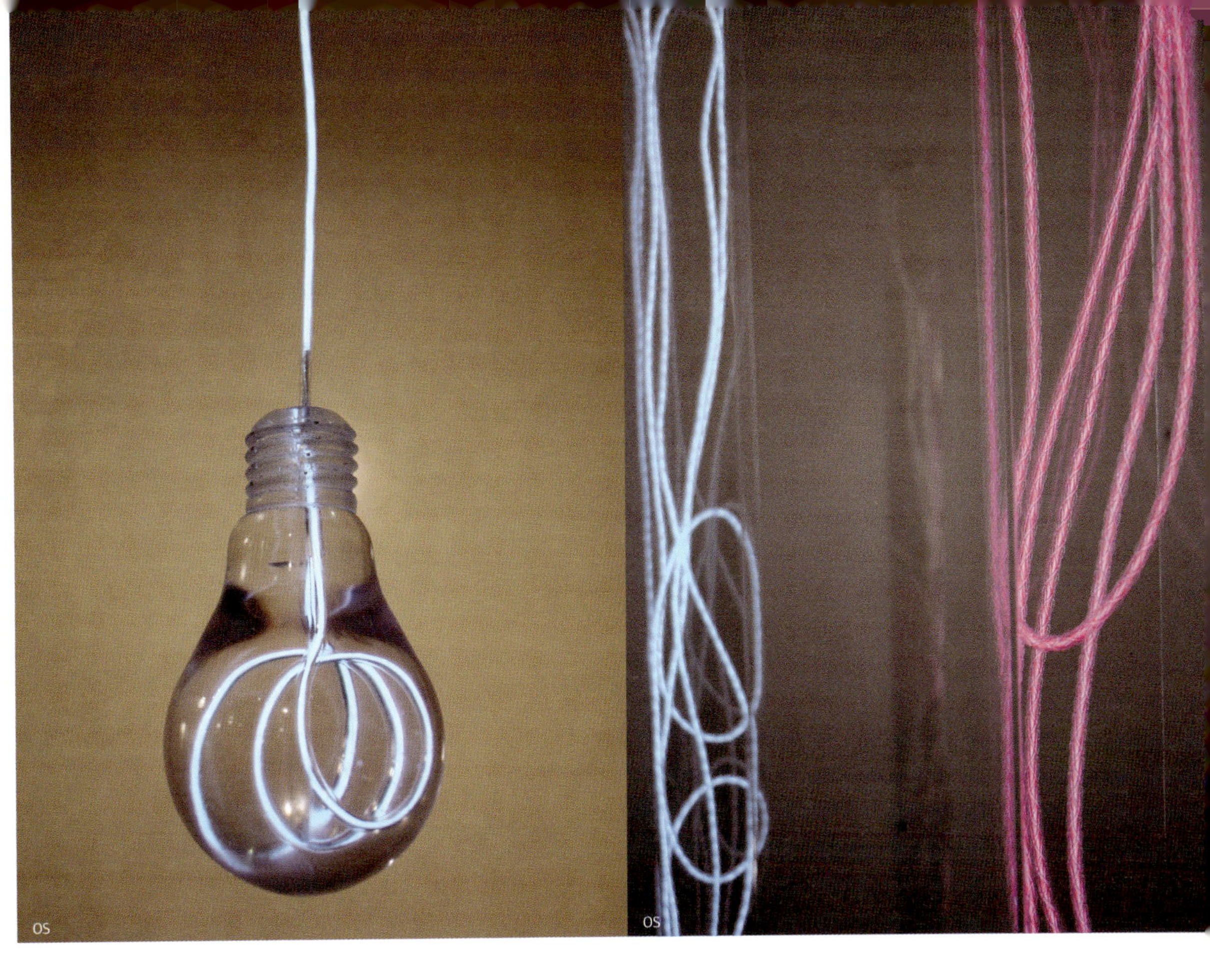

Johee Lee

Koichiro Kimura @ Internos

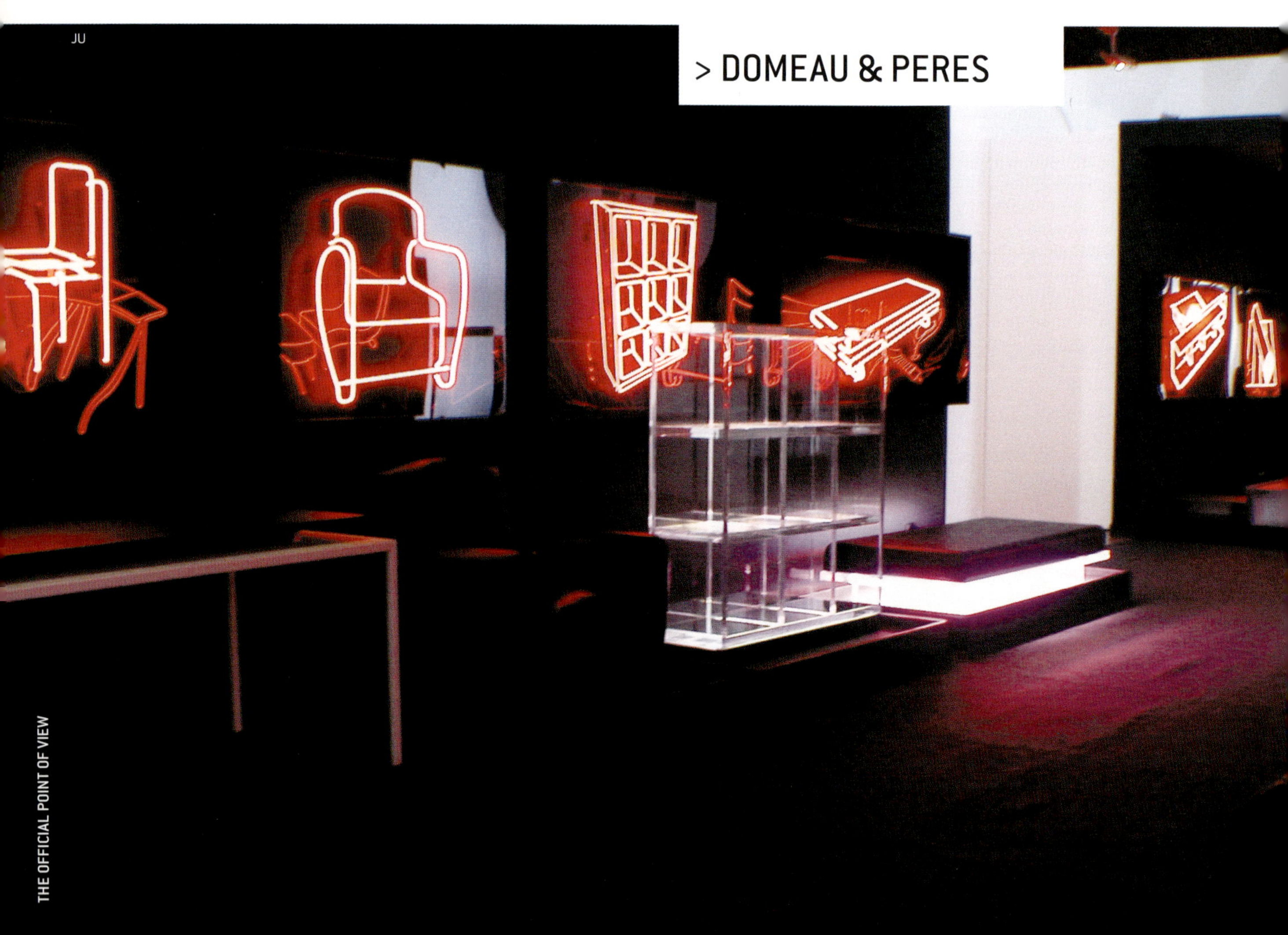

Florencia Martinez

For the first time Domeau&Peres was shown in Milan at the Centre Culturel francais de Milan.

Fourteen pieces of furniture, coming across the icons of the brand such as Ronan and Erwan Bouroullec, Matali Crasset,

Agence Odile Decq et Benoit Cornette, Elodie Descoubes and Laurent Nicolas, Christophe Pillet, Andree Putman

as well as newcomers such as Francois Azambourg, Alexandre de Betak, Vincent Dupont-Rougier,

Jerome Olivet and Milan Vukmirovic. Alexandre de Betak has taken charge of designing the setting.

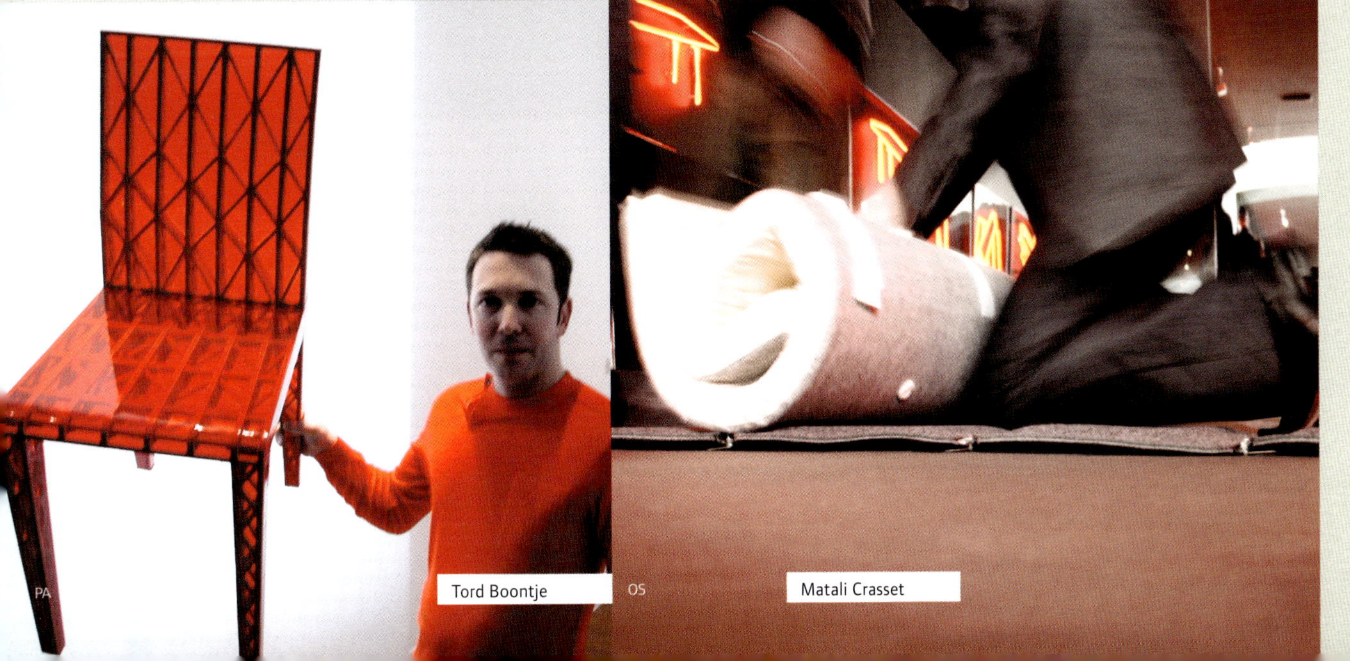

PA
Tord Boontje
OS
Matali Crasset

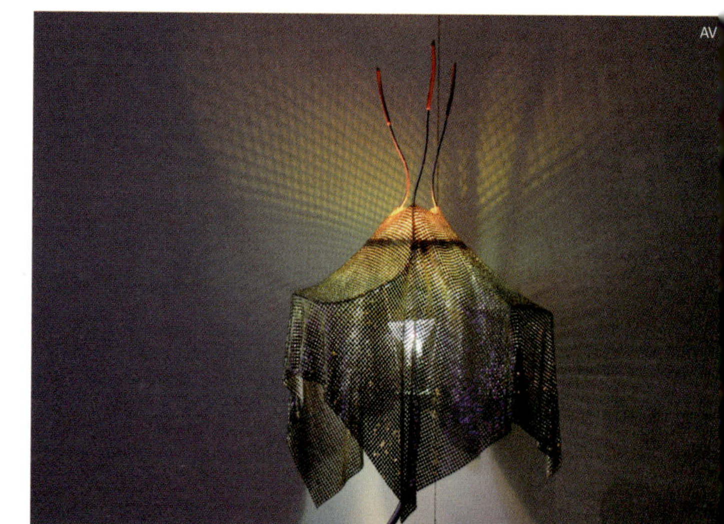

Lucifero Illuminazione @ Nu light

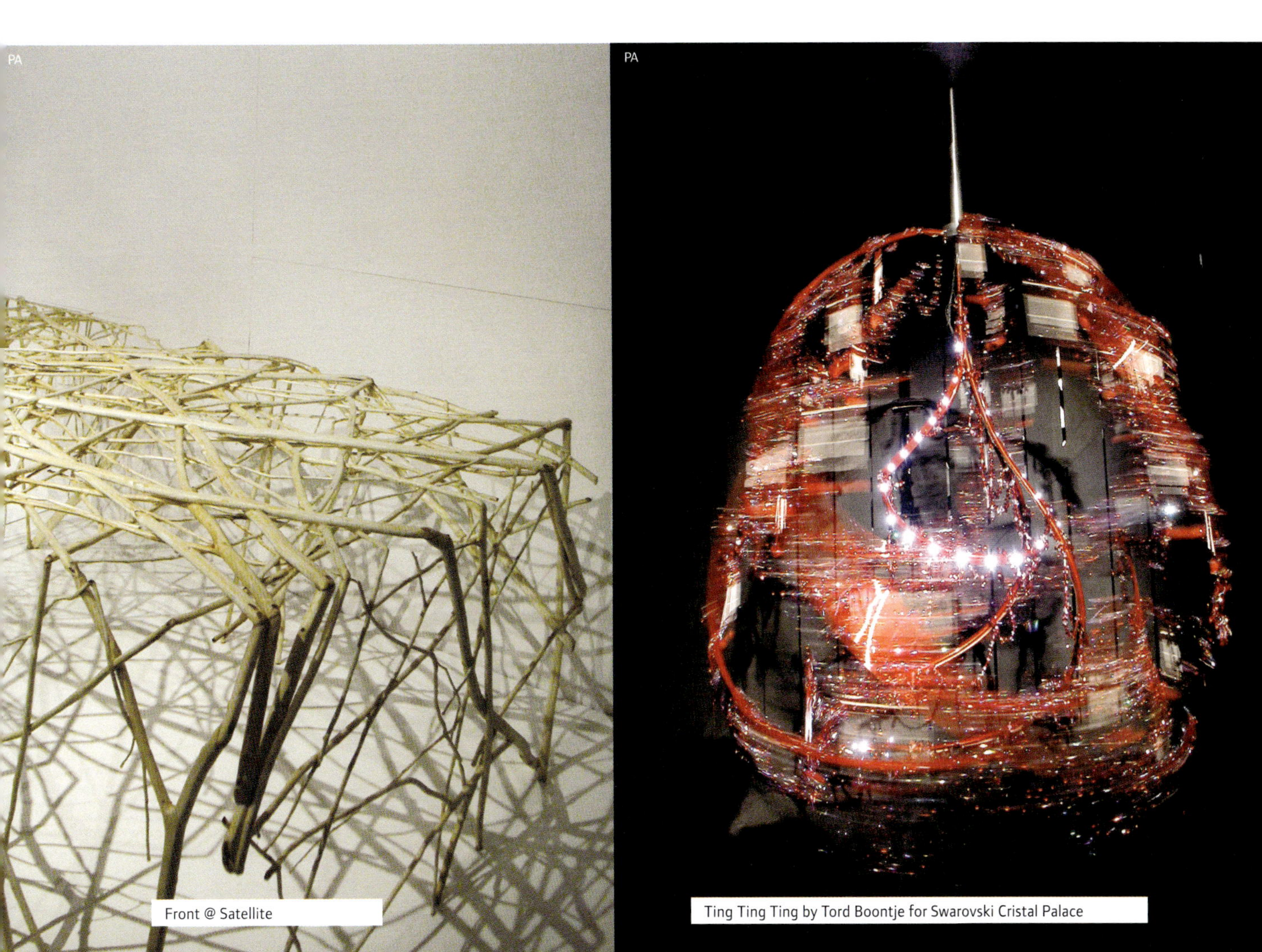

Front @ Satellite

Ting Ting Ting by Tord Boontje for Swarovski Cristal Palace

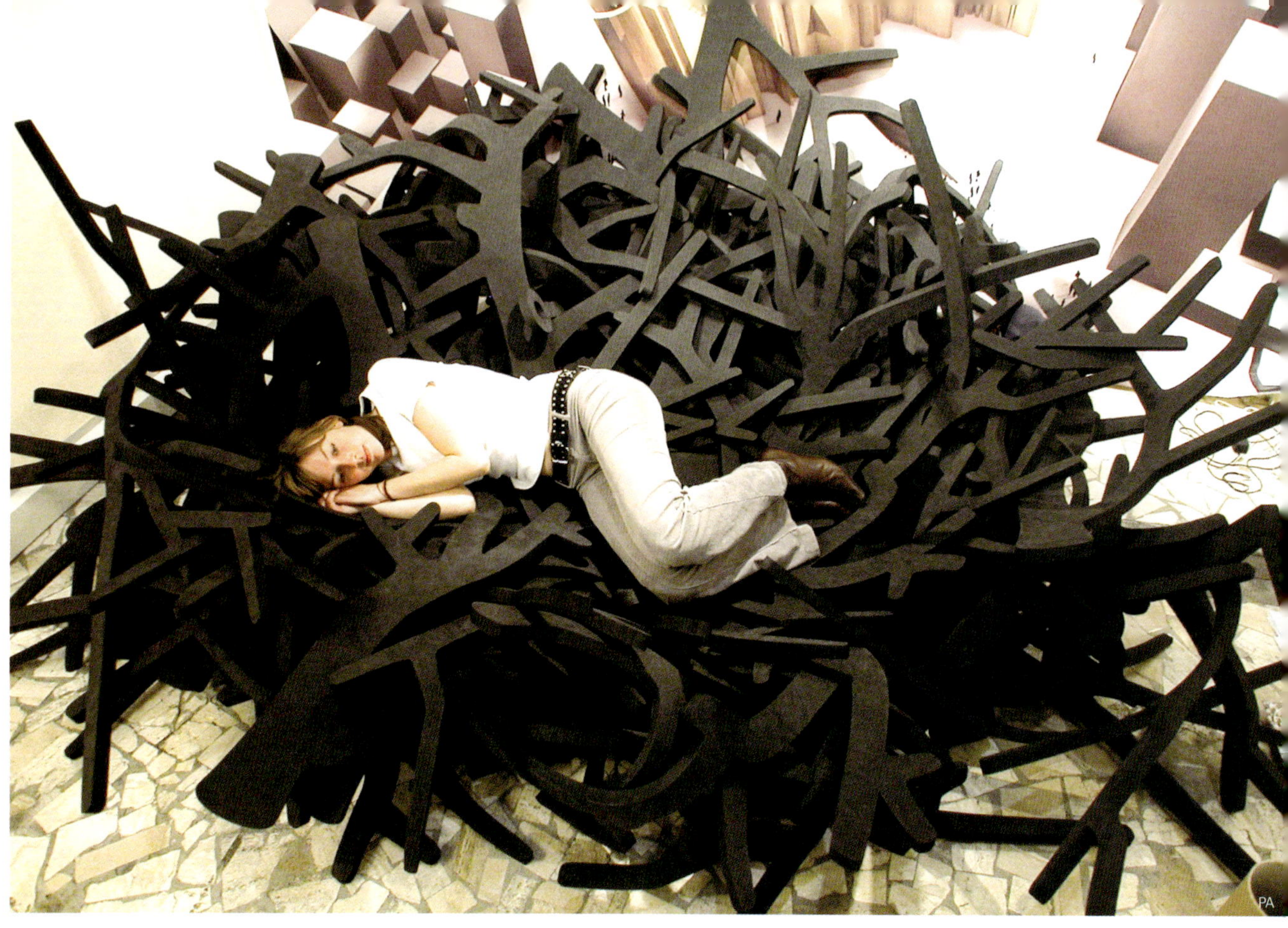

Frank Tjepkema @ Satellite

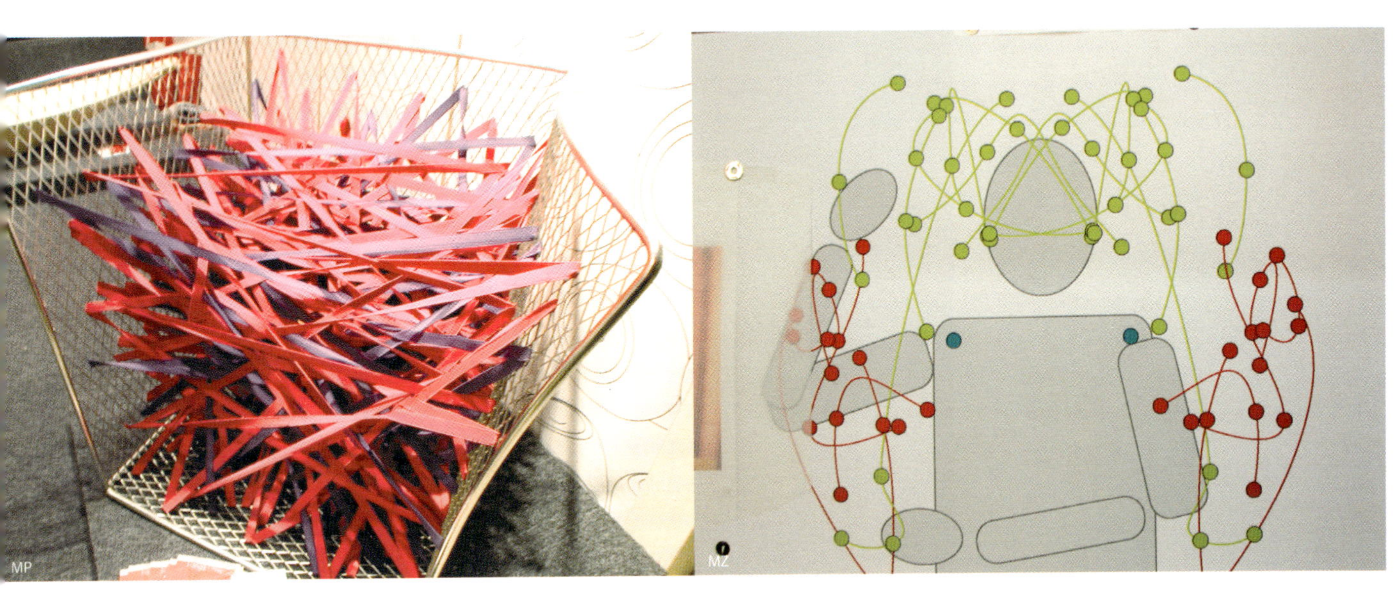

University   Dornbracht

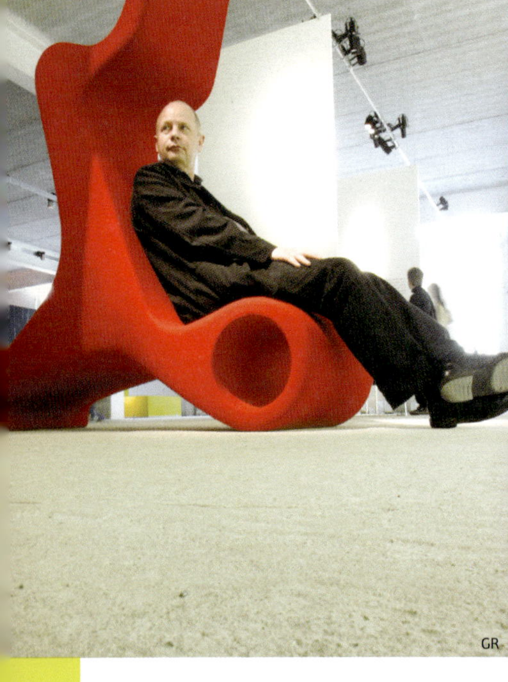

Amisa Satyendra Pakhalé   Tuber by Future Factories @ Designersblock

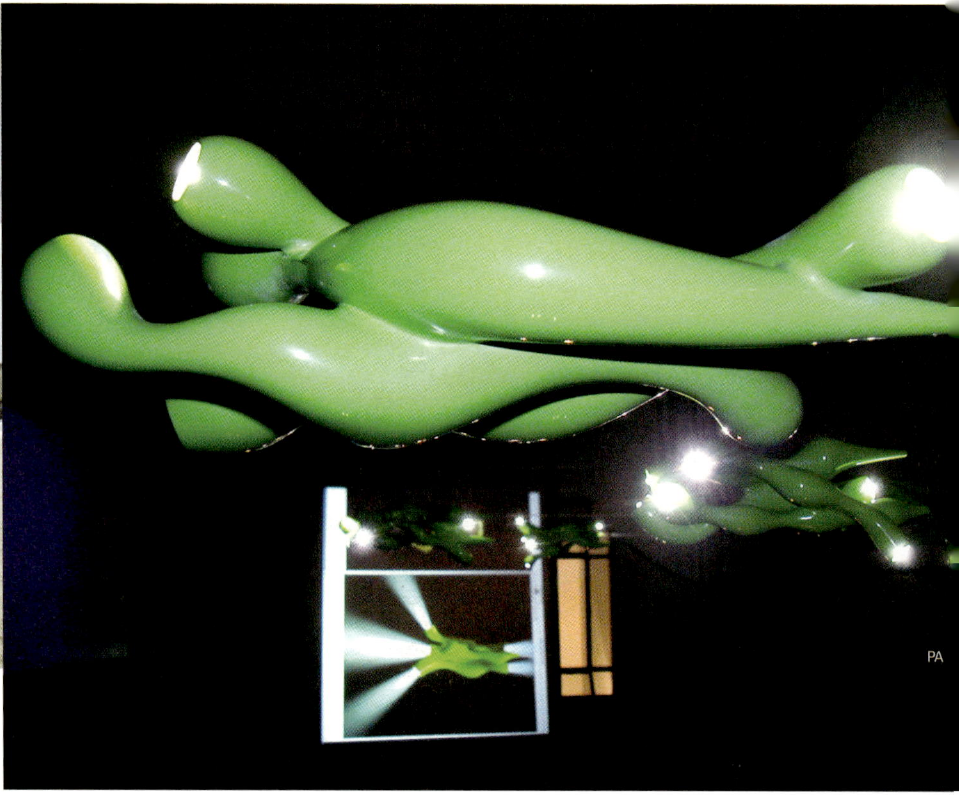

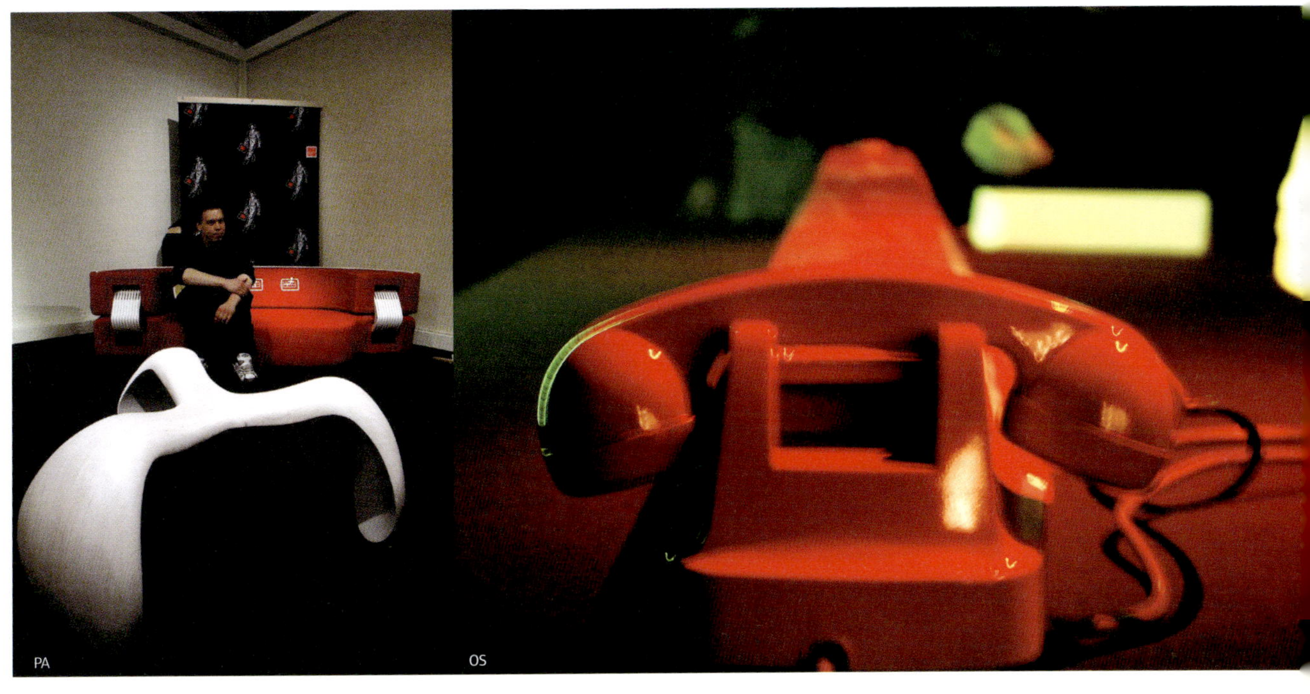

Seinajoki Polytechnic @ Satellite

Uncle Phone by Interaction Design Institute Ivrea @ Triennale

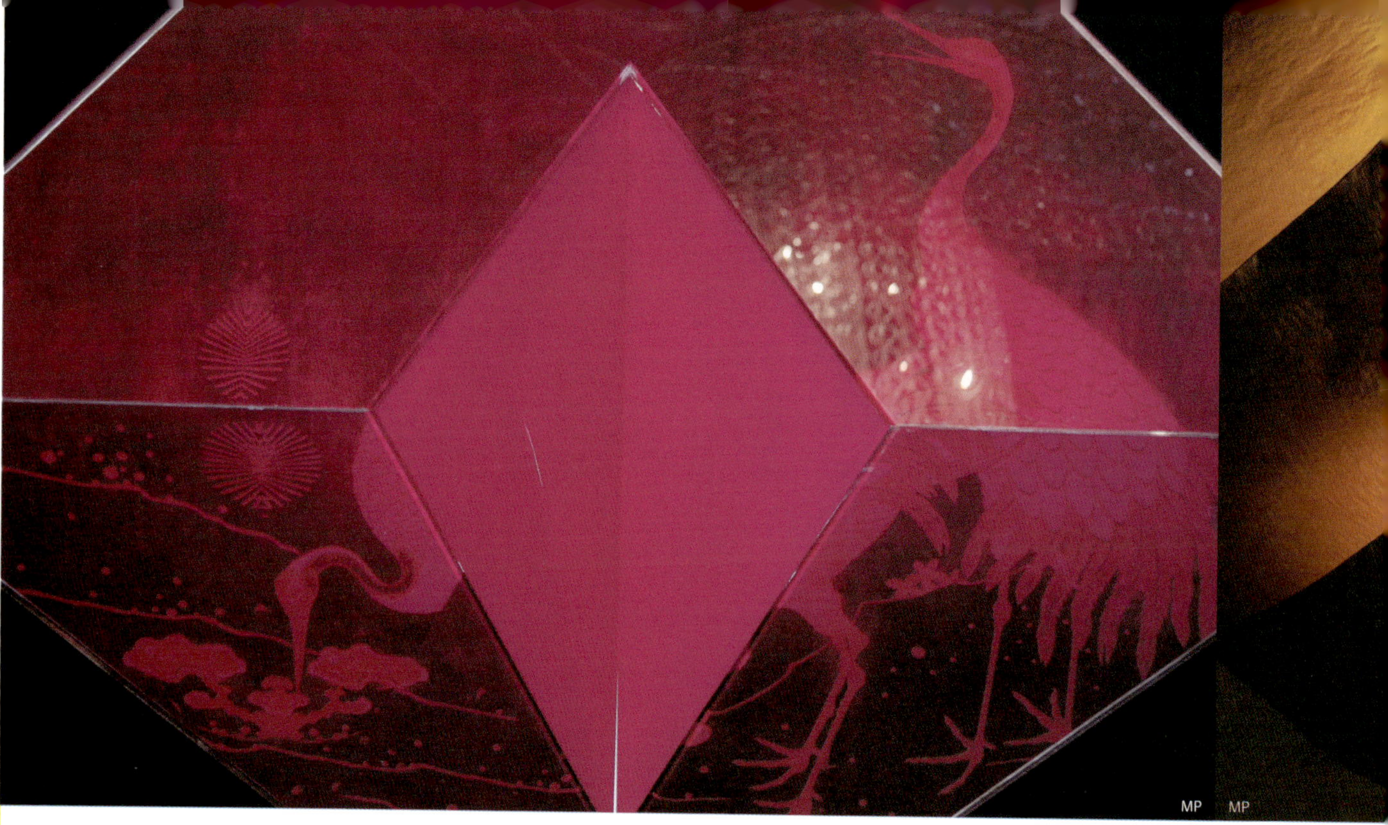

288   Fenizia Design studio

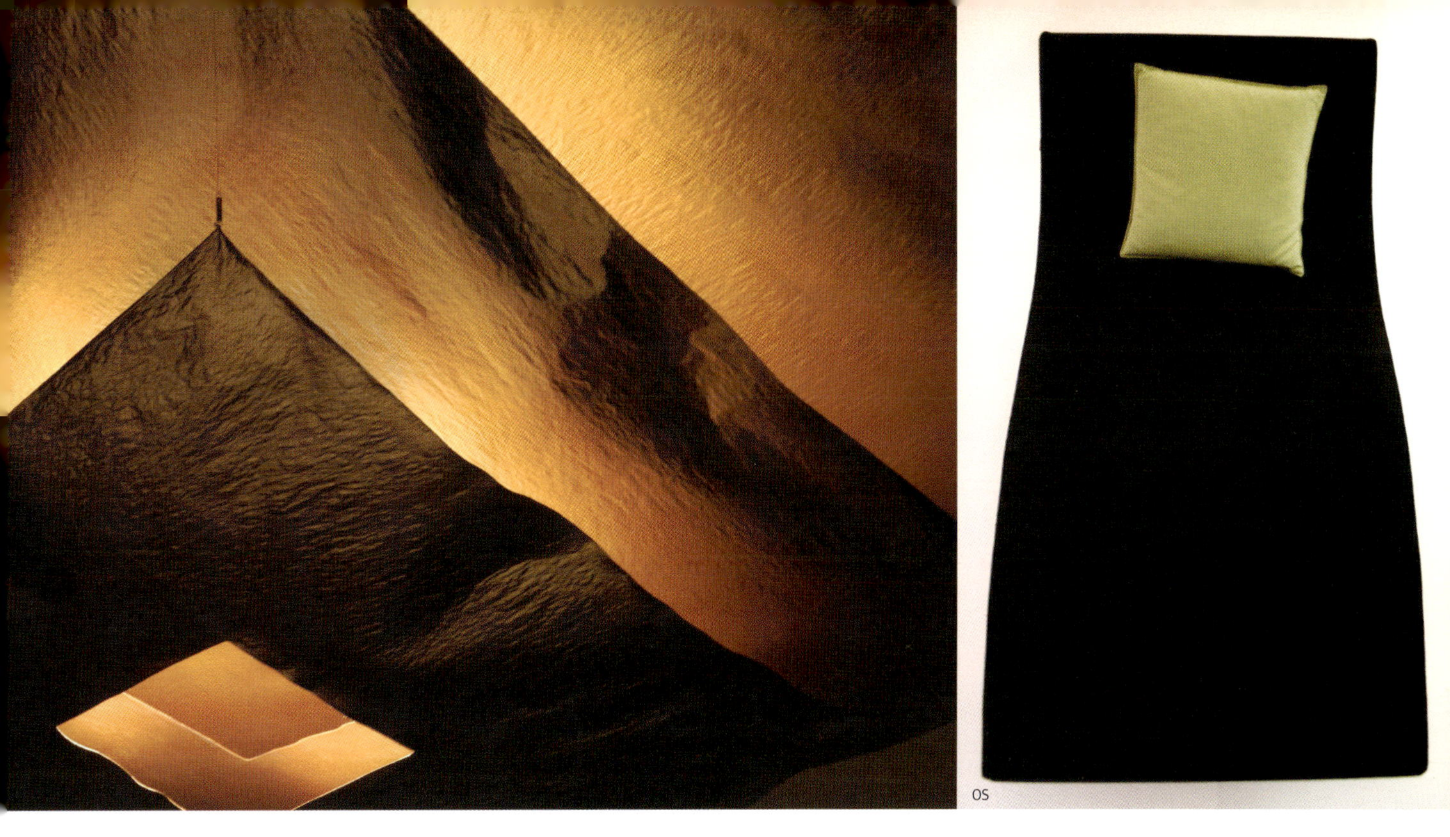

Ingo Maurer

MDF

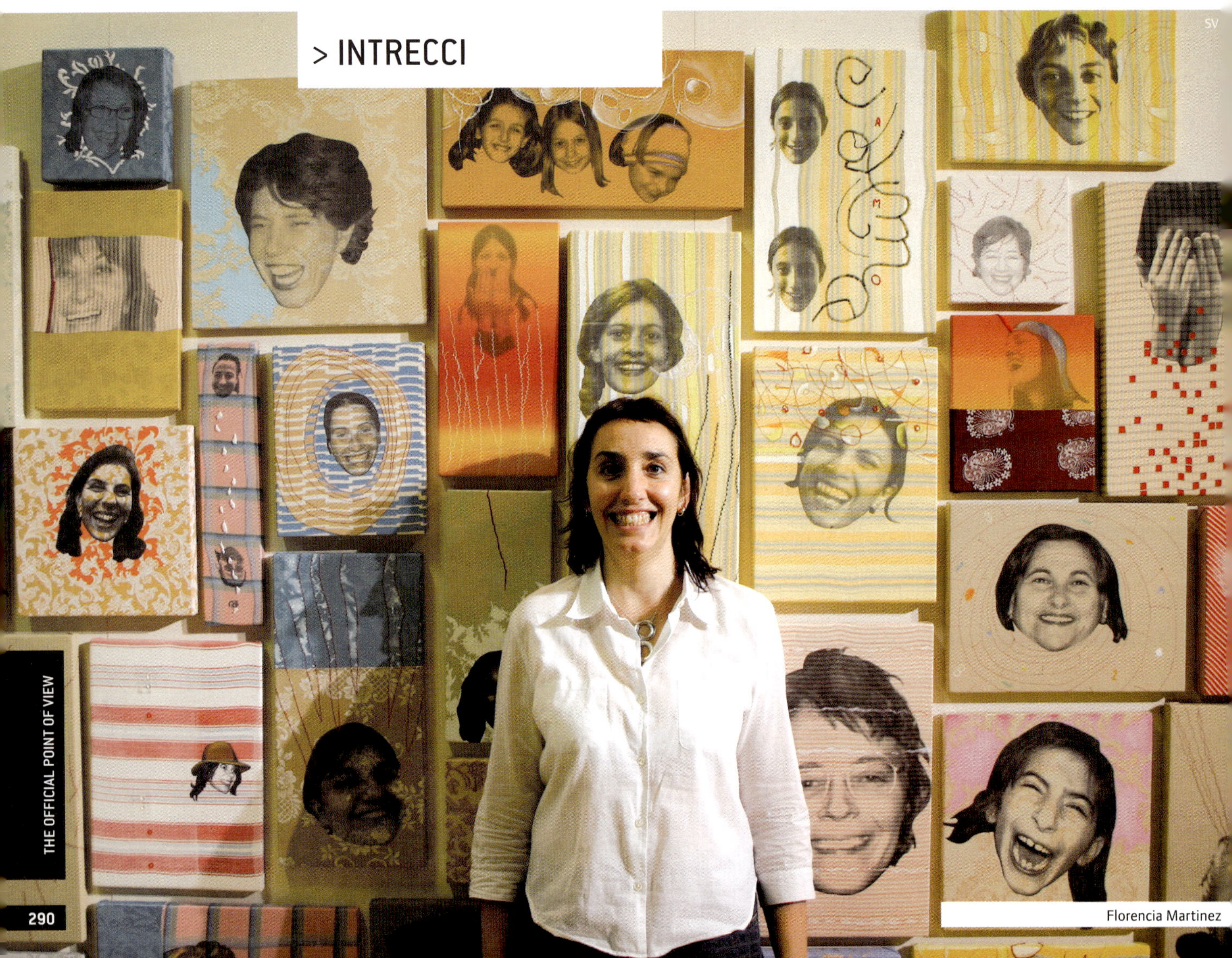

Florencia Martinez

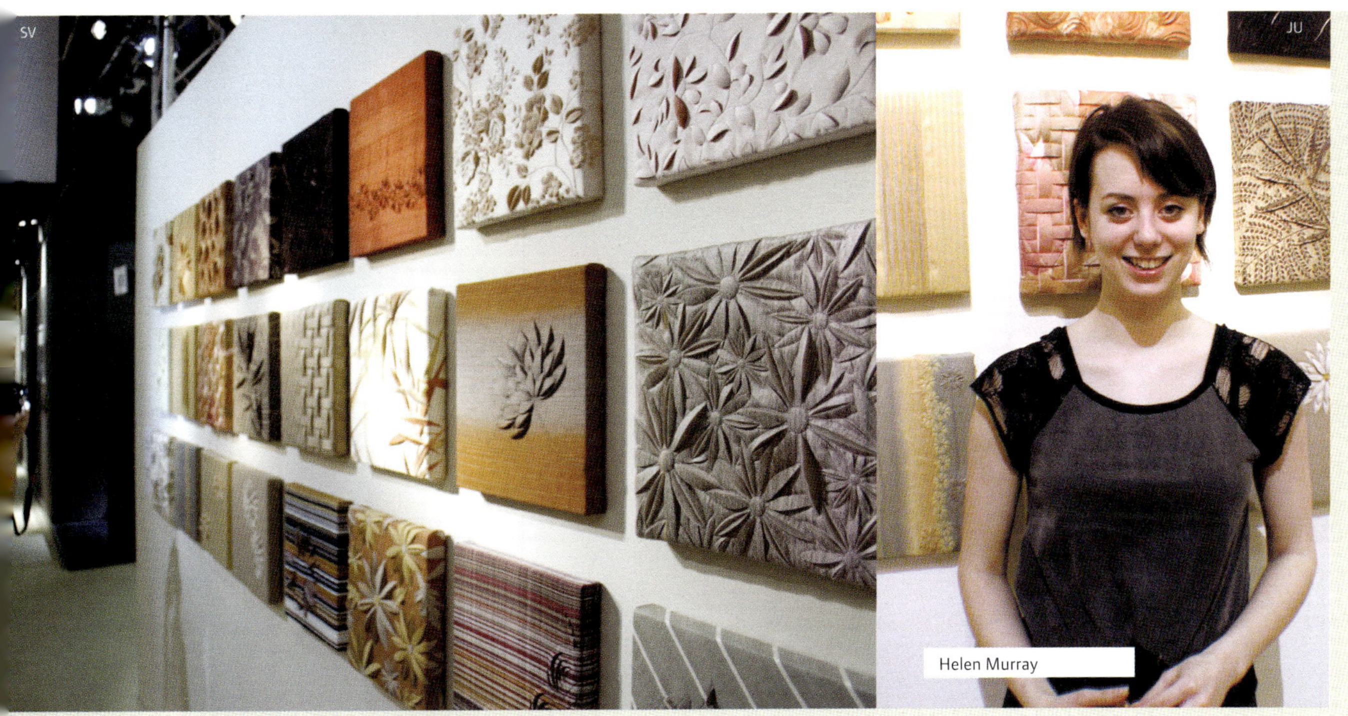

A parallel event stretches the horizons of lifestyles and interior to include the world of art.

During the Salone, "Intrecci" hosts two **internationally acclaimed artists** as they weave their skills,

experiences and inspirations into art works using materials supplied by the exhibitors, to emphasize the untold potential of textiles.

Florencia Martinez's work employs fabrics to create an intimate memoir supporting her photographic images: a gallery of women smiling at the fairgrounds.

The images are completed with brushstrokes and embroidery to preserve the manual element which is the very essence of art, and to permit the

past and the future to communicate through the multimedia of the present.

Helen Amy Murray creates, behind the scenes, a three-dimensional story of colors and decorative themes using a highly personal technique

that is in the processof being patented. Using a variety of textiles, the artist forms a picture gallery of sculpted shapes invented especially

for the occasion, either highlighting or deliberately contrasting the fabric's pattern.

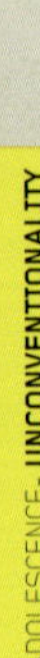

Appendimi @ Emporio 31

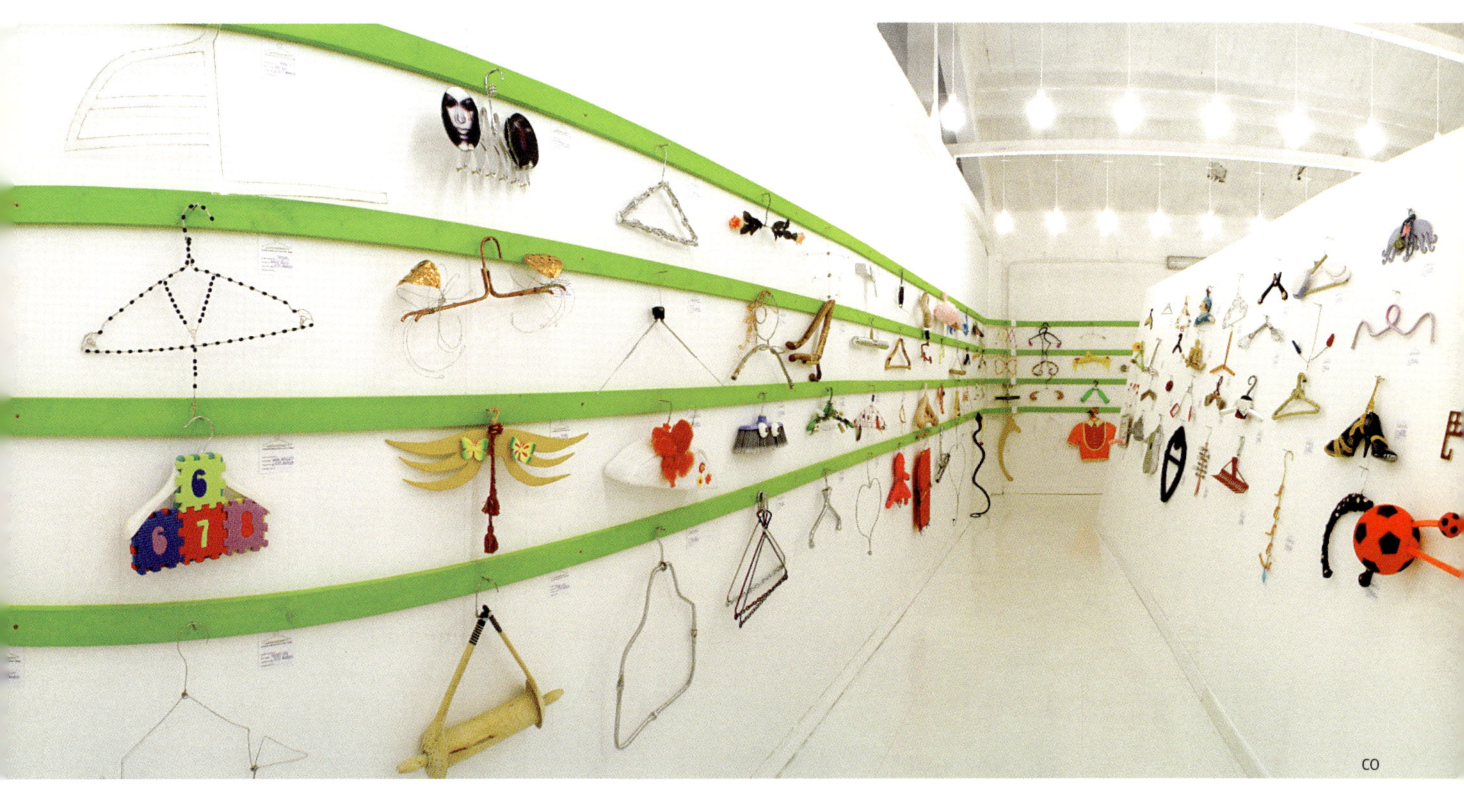

CO

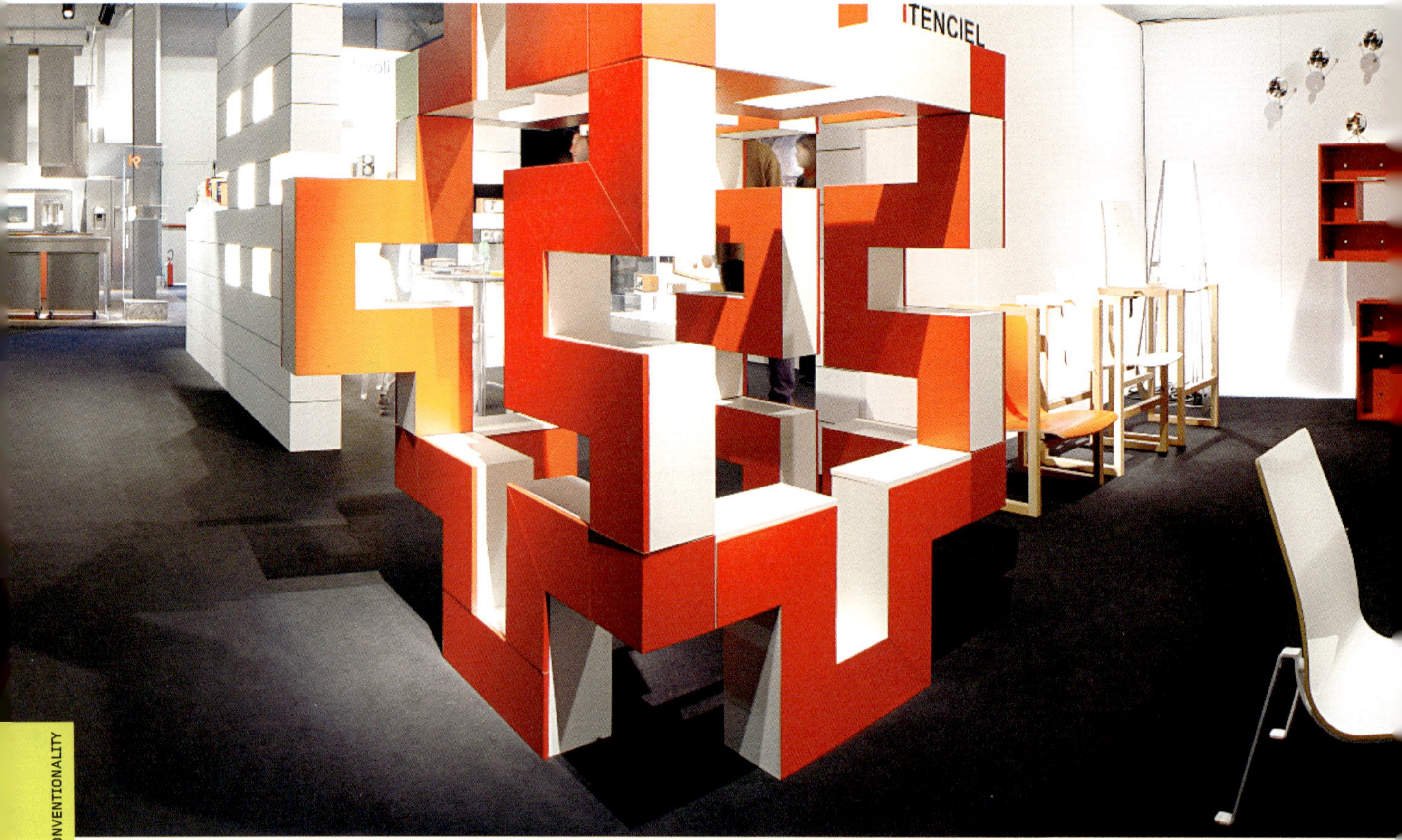

Artenciel

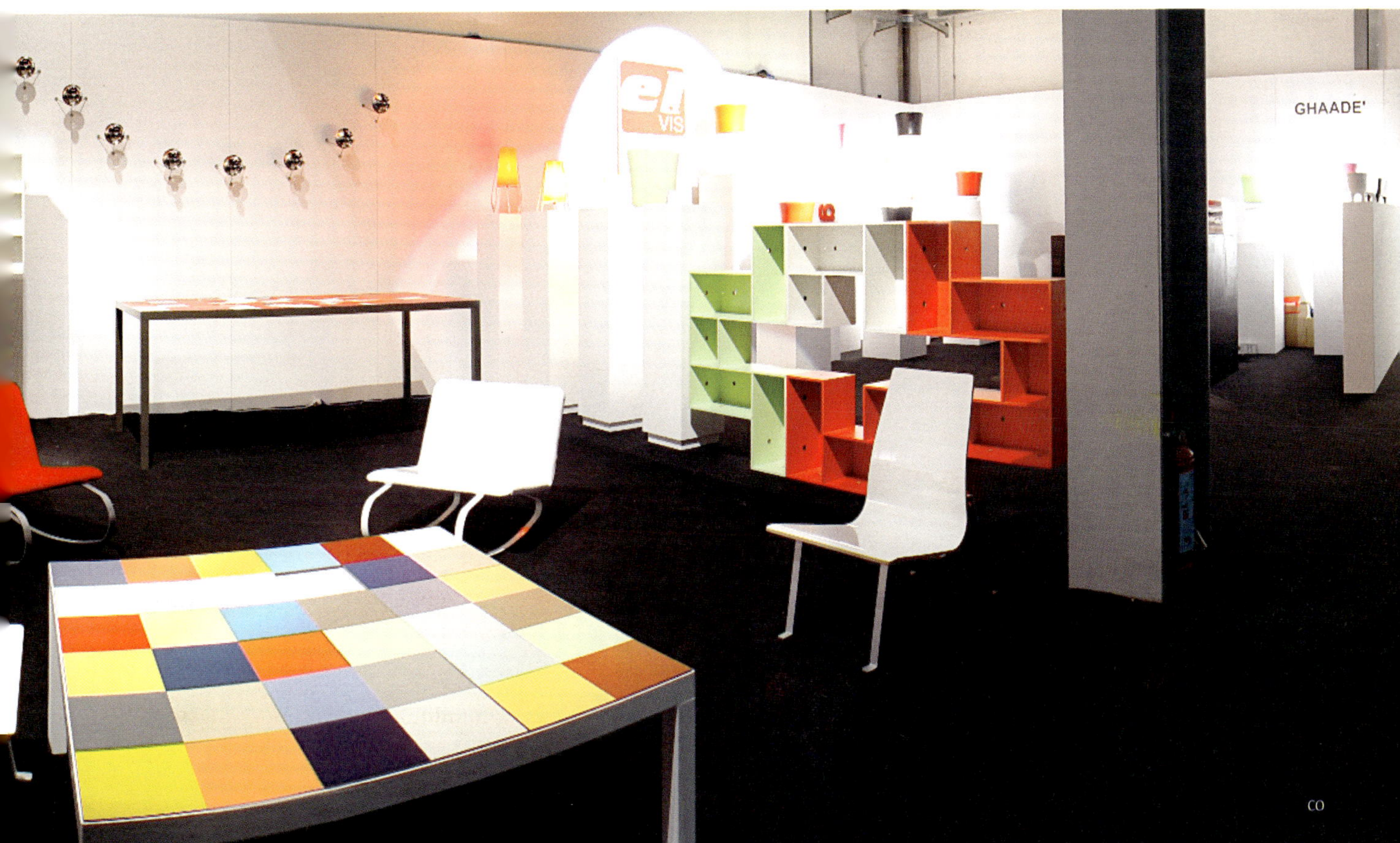

el
vis
GHAADE'
CO

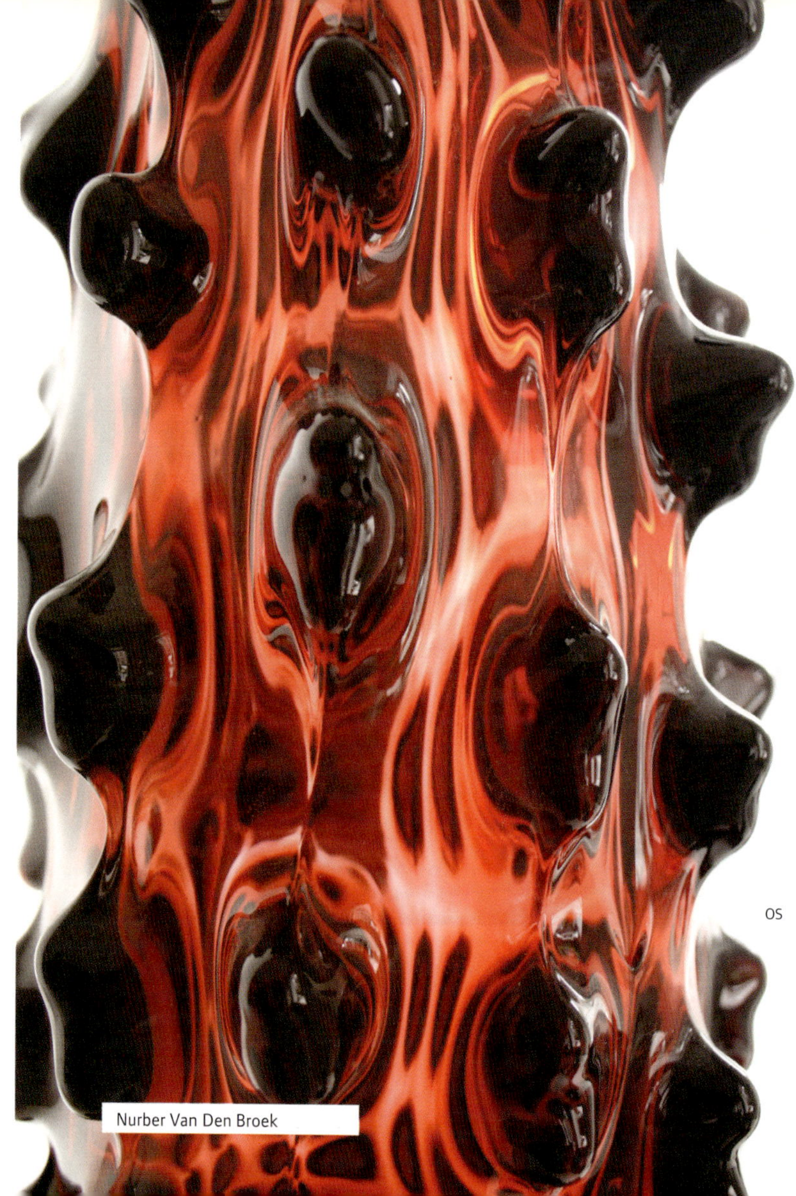

Nurber Van Den Broek

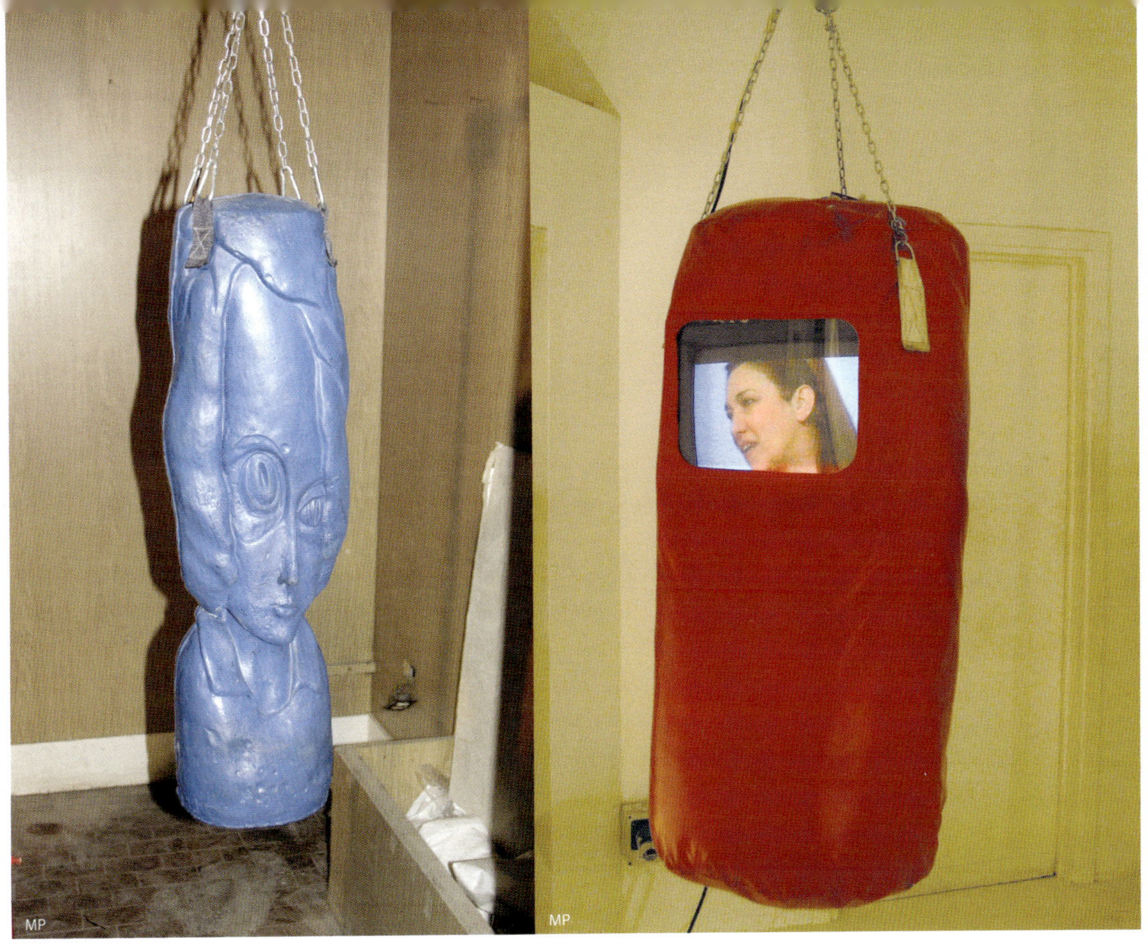

Shit Design   Eugenia Chiara

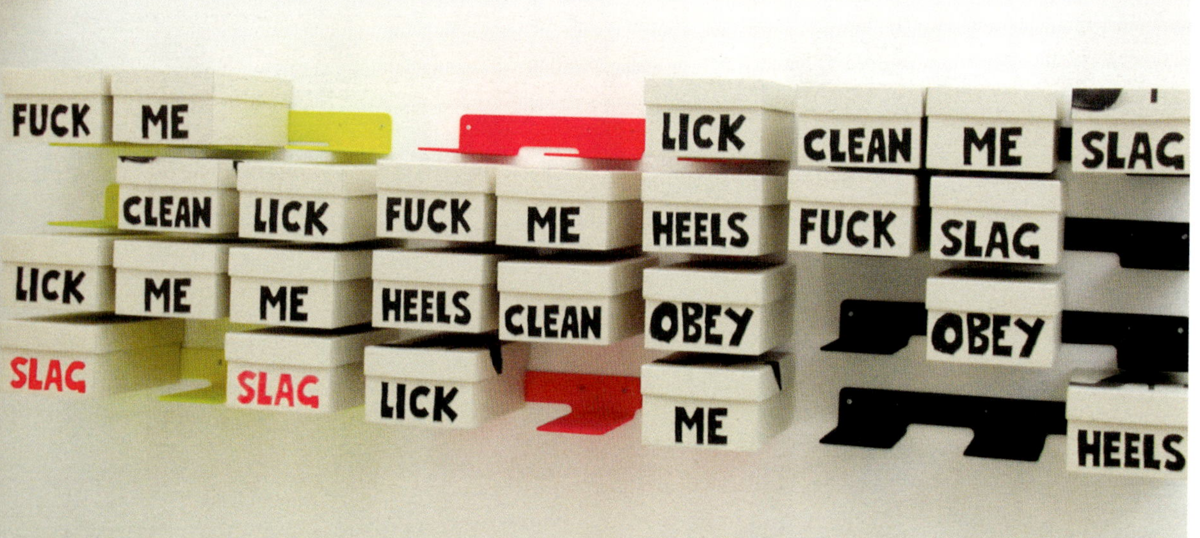

298   Her House Products by Morag Myerscough and Luke Morgan @ Designersblock

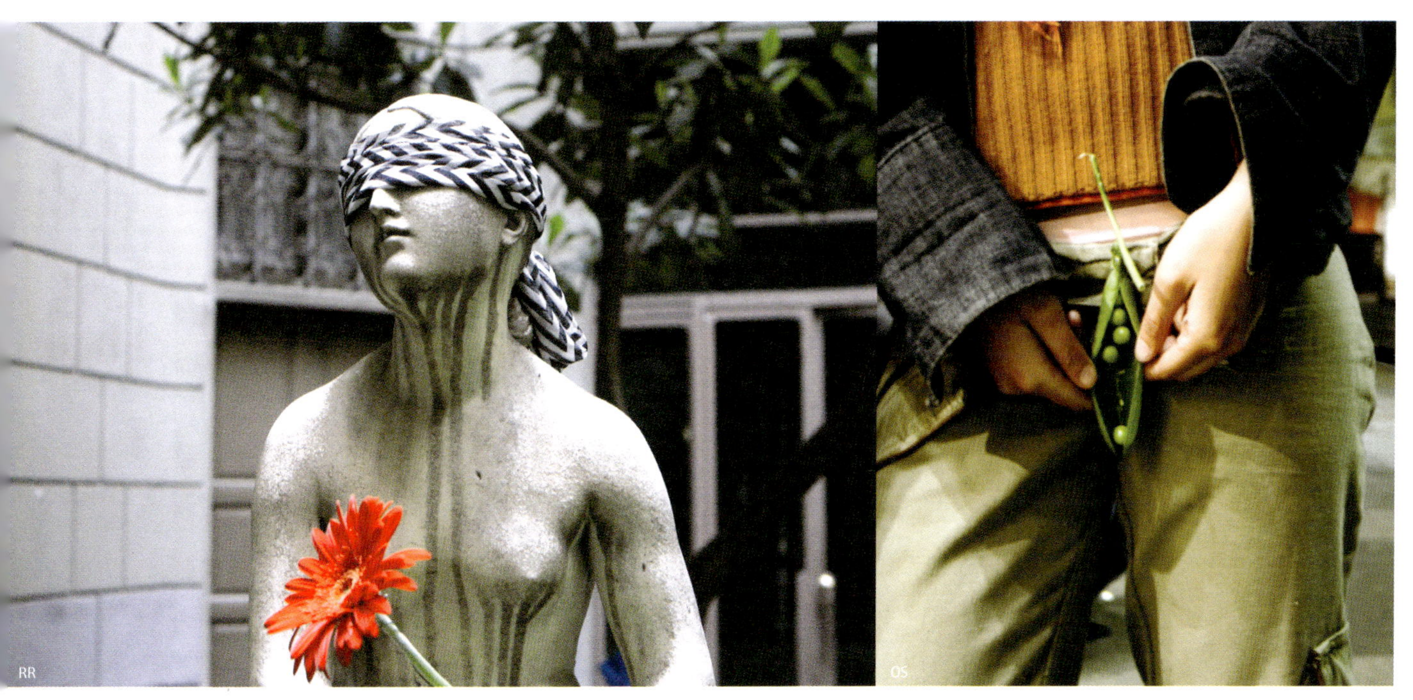

Amalgama

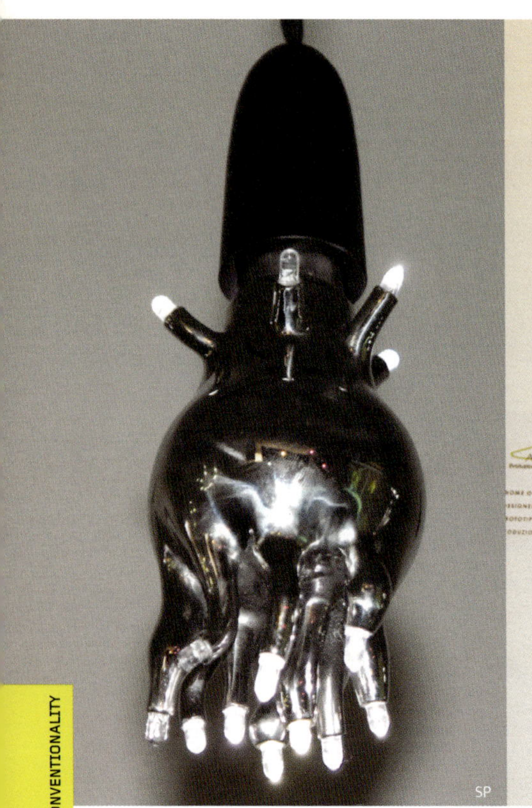

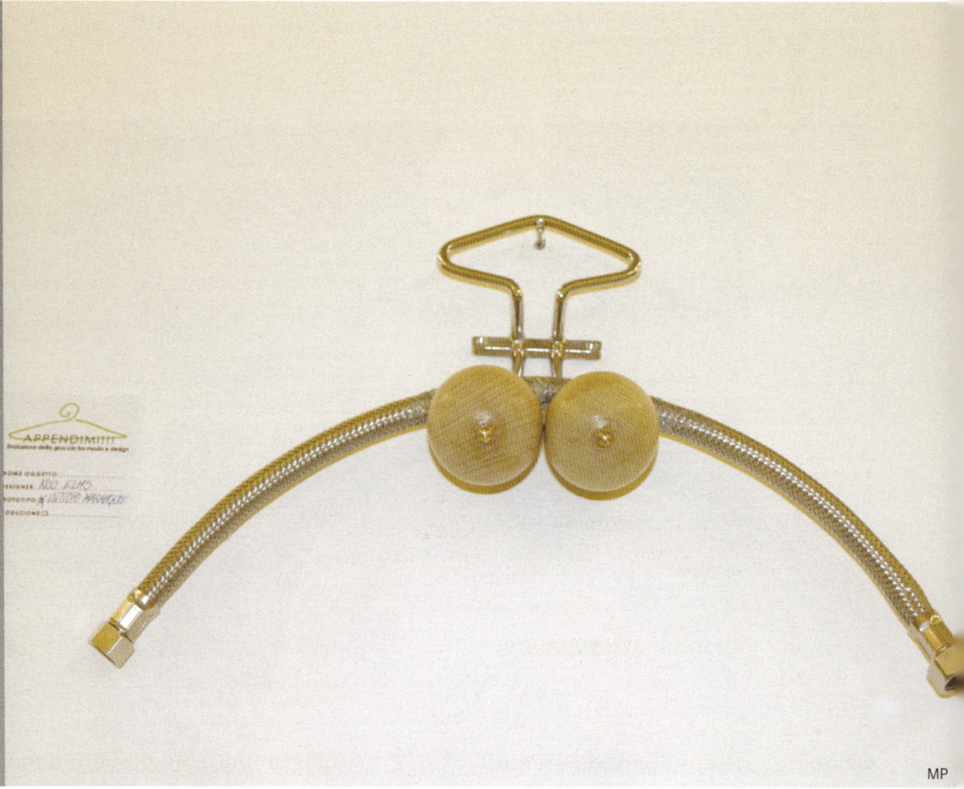

Lampadina Mutanta
by Future Factories
@ Designersblock

Appendimi @ Emporio 31

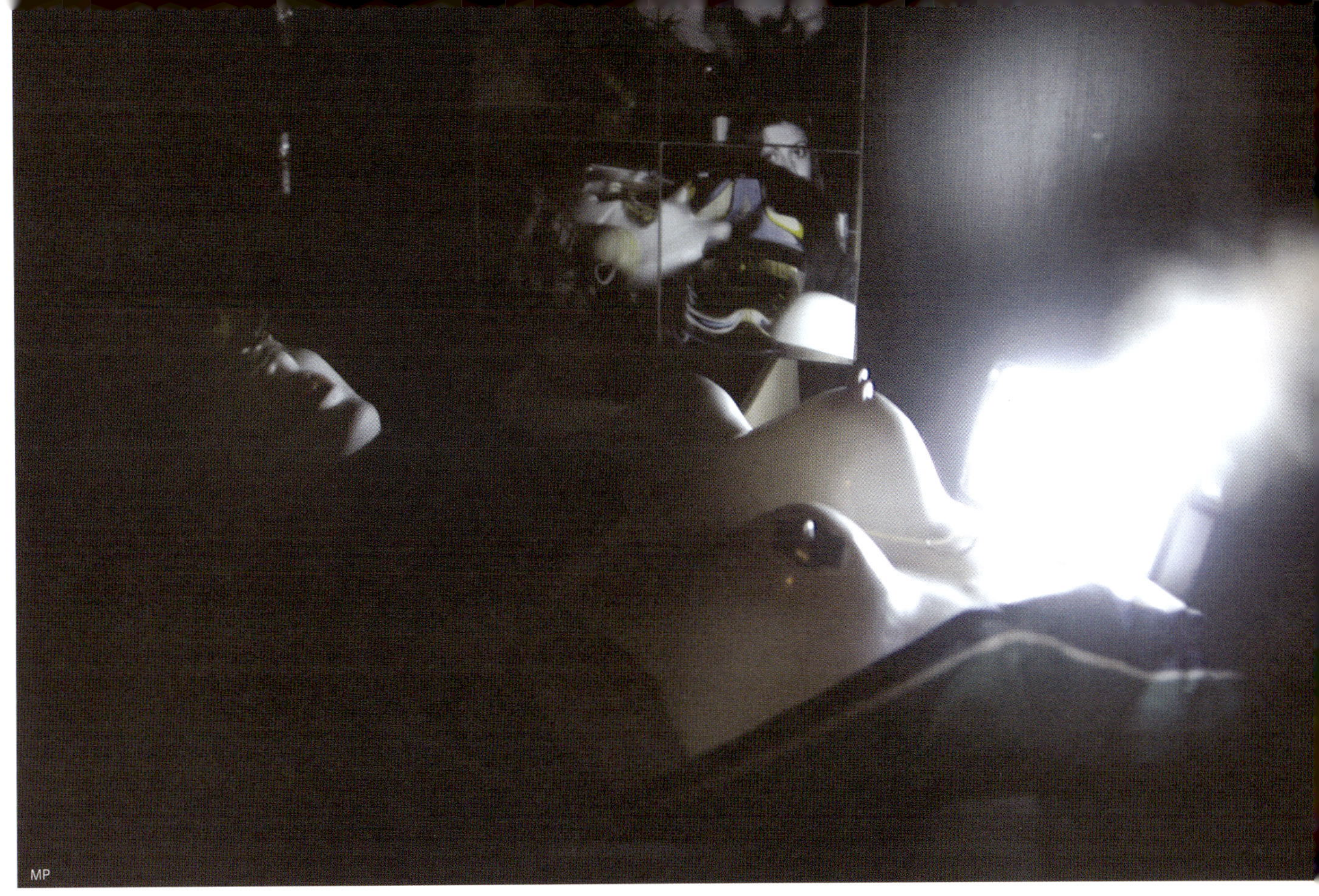

Andrea De Andrea and Laura Castelli

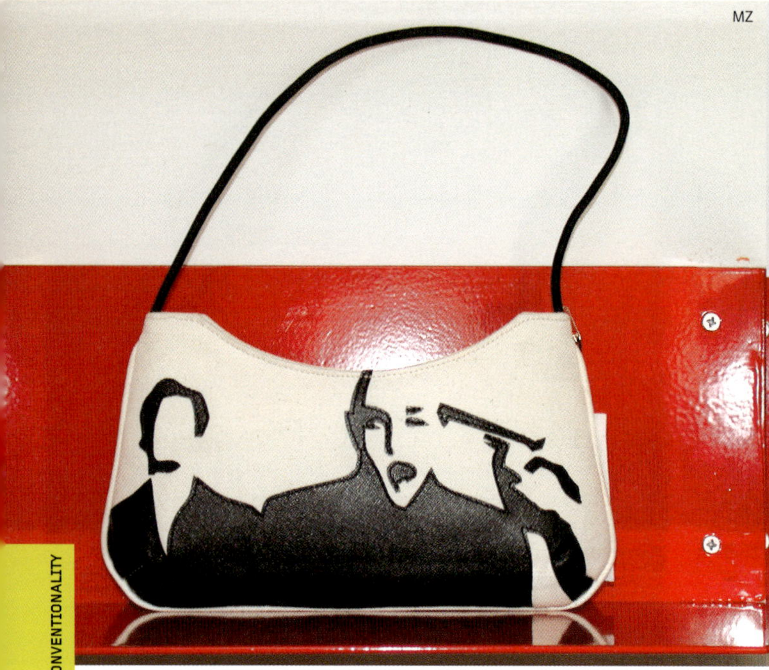

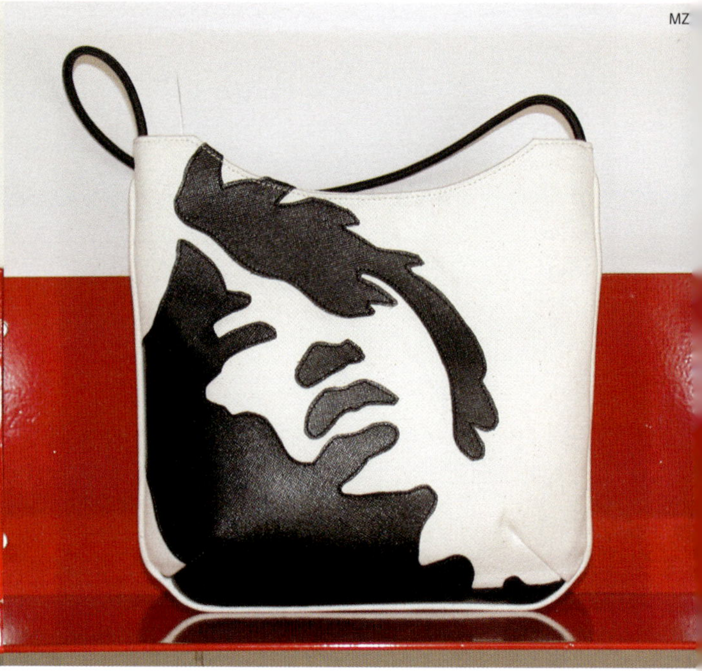

@ Fabbrica Del Vapore

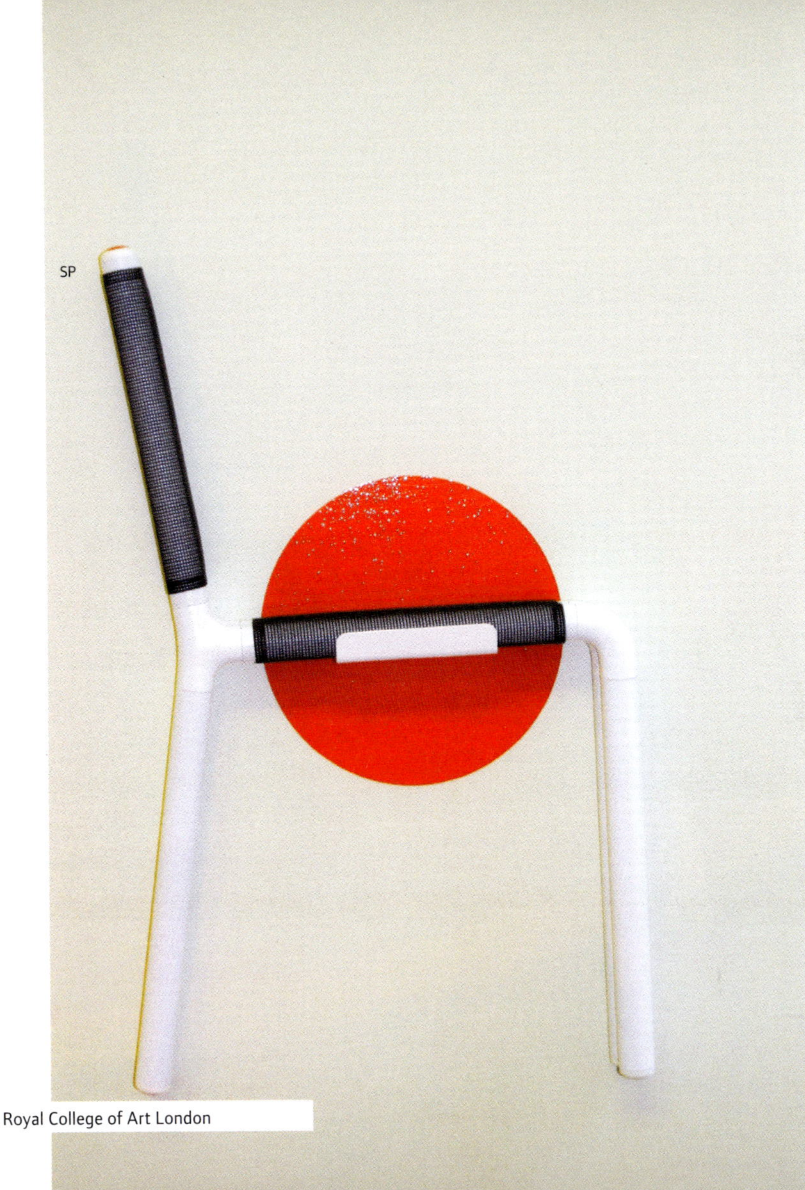

Nicol Boyd and Thomas Rosen of Royal College of Art London

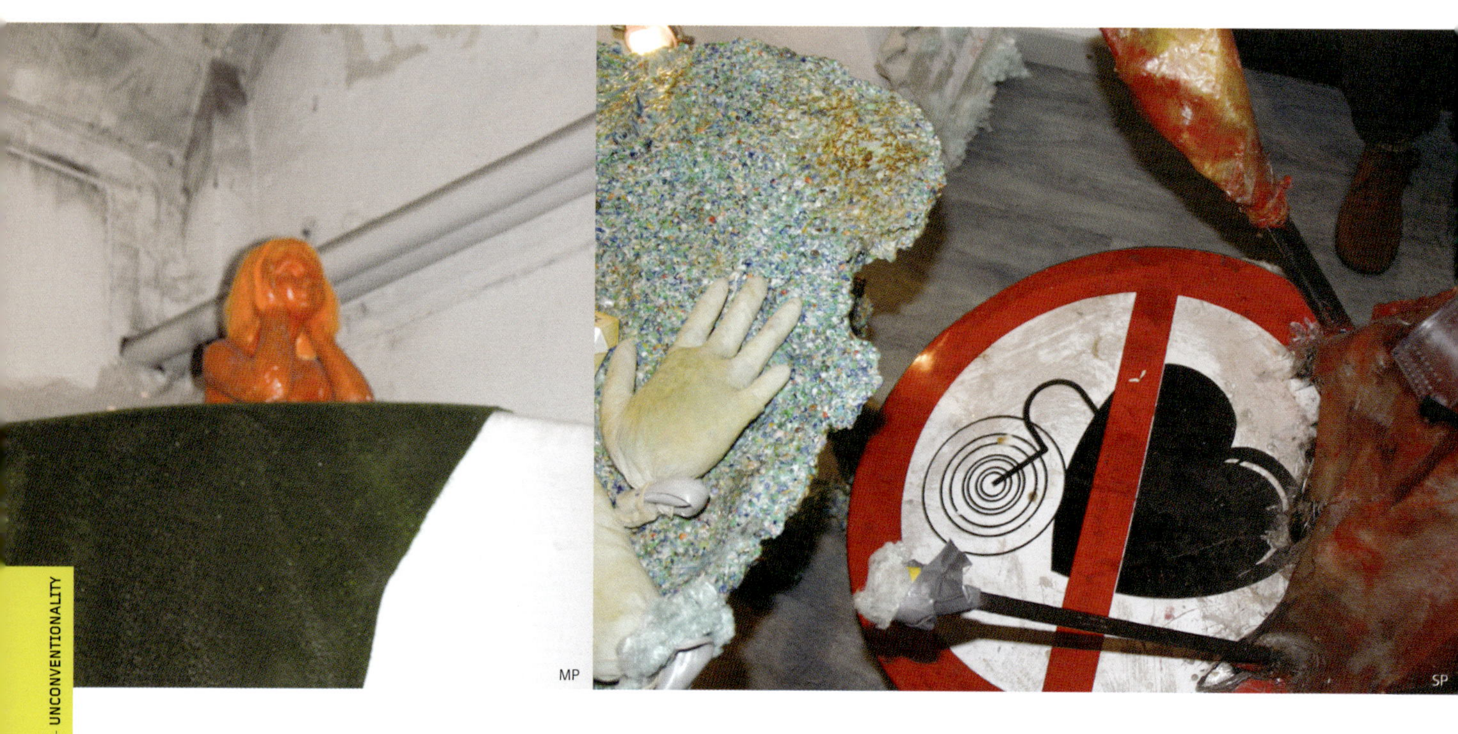

Grace' seat

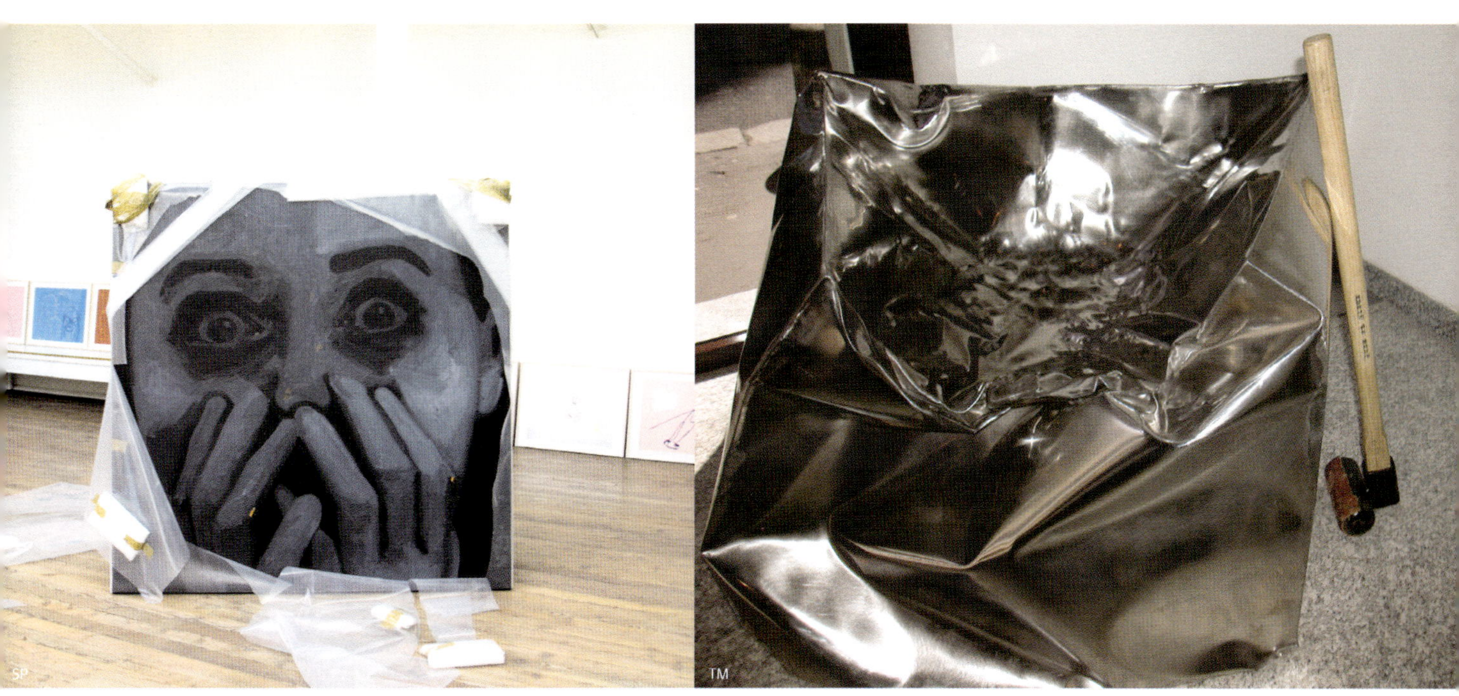

Ryan Mendo

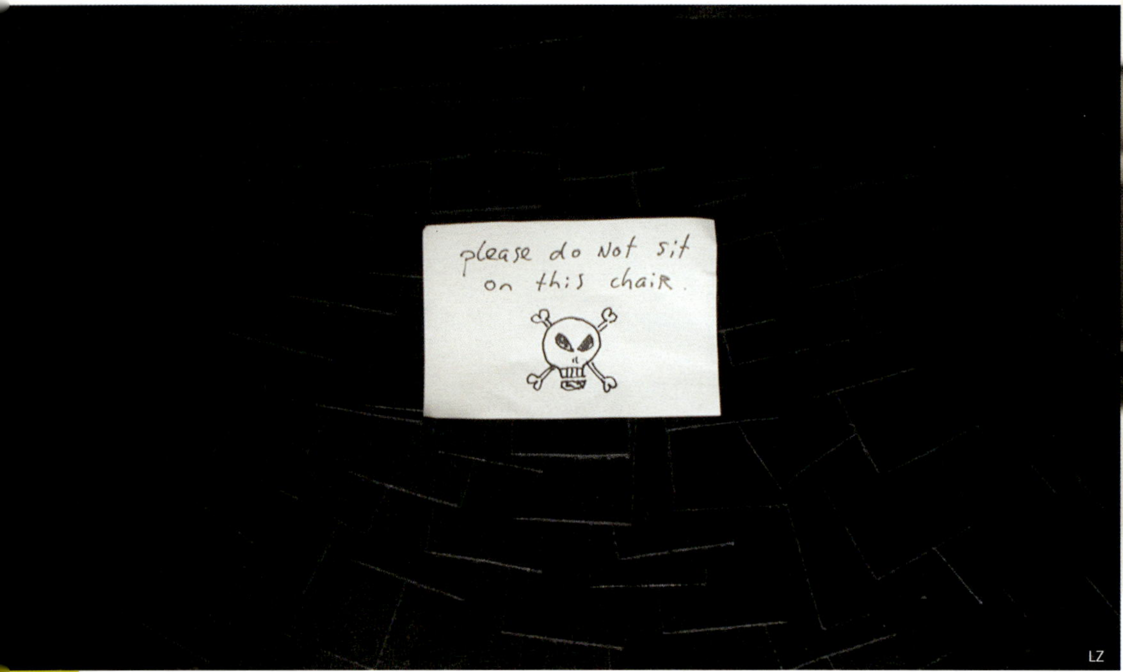

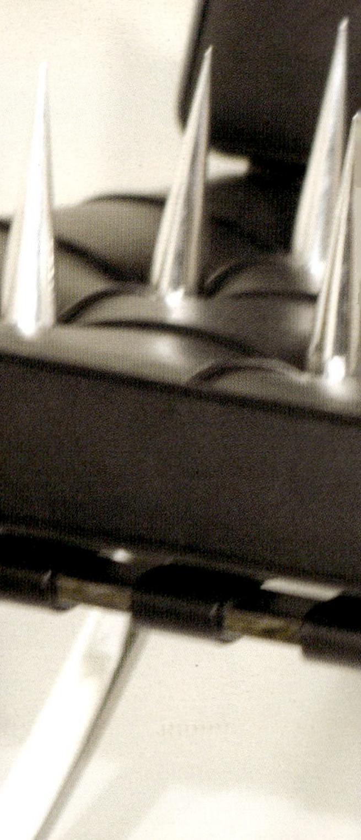

@ Moroso

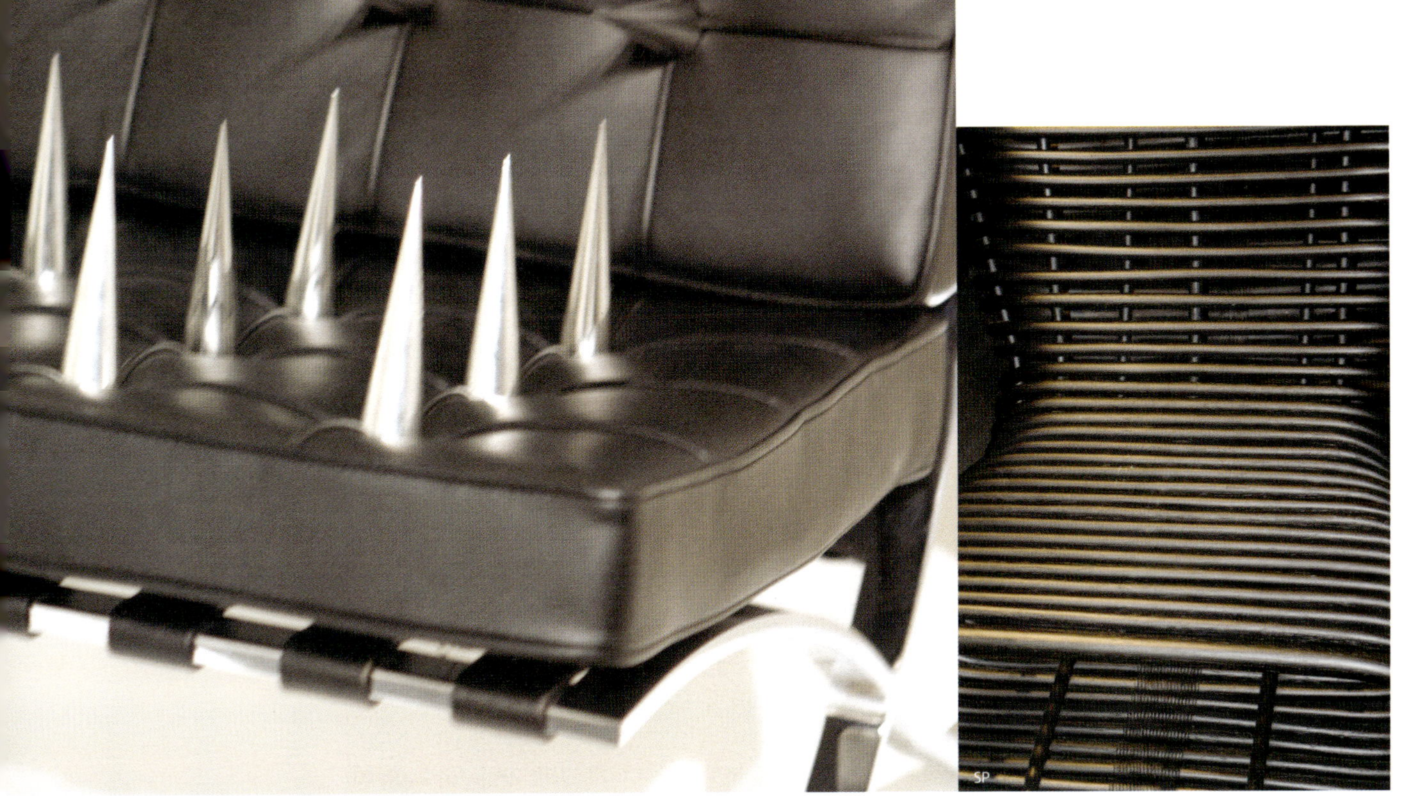

John Angelo Benson @ Satellite

Kora by Enzo Berti

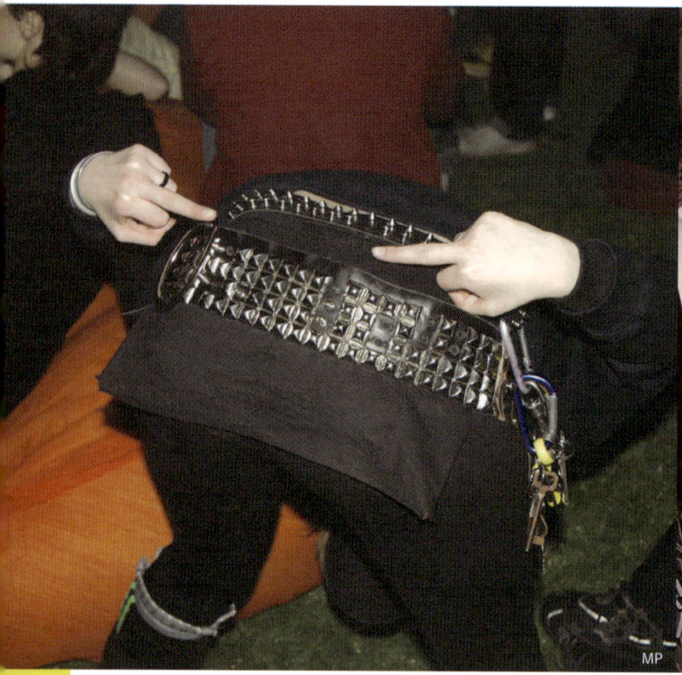

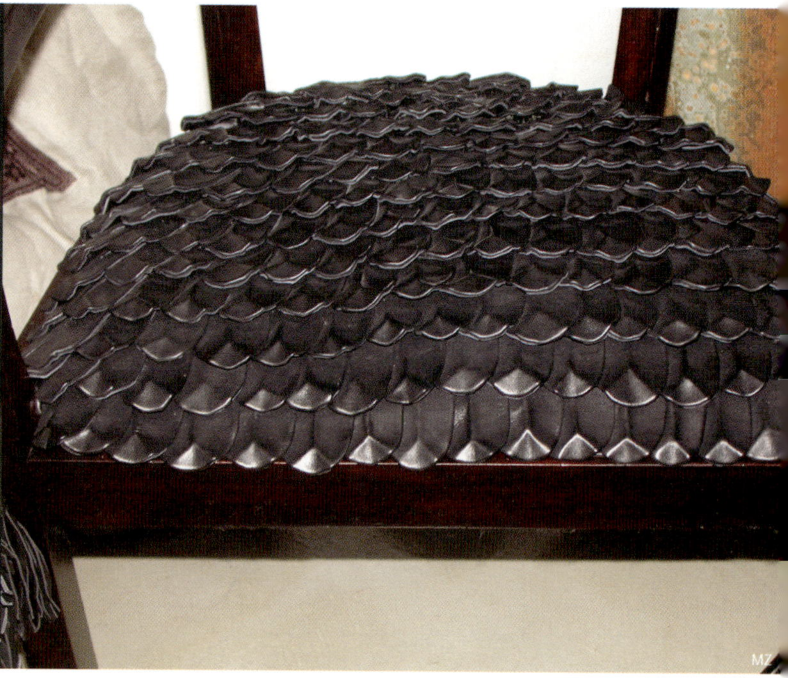

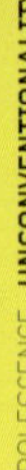

Shit Design

Designer Minero

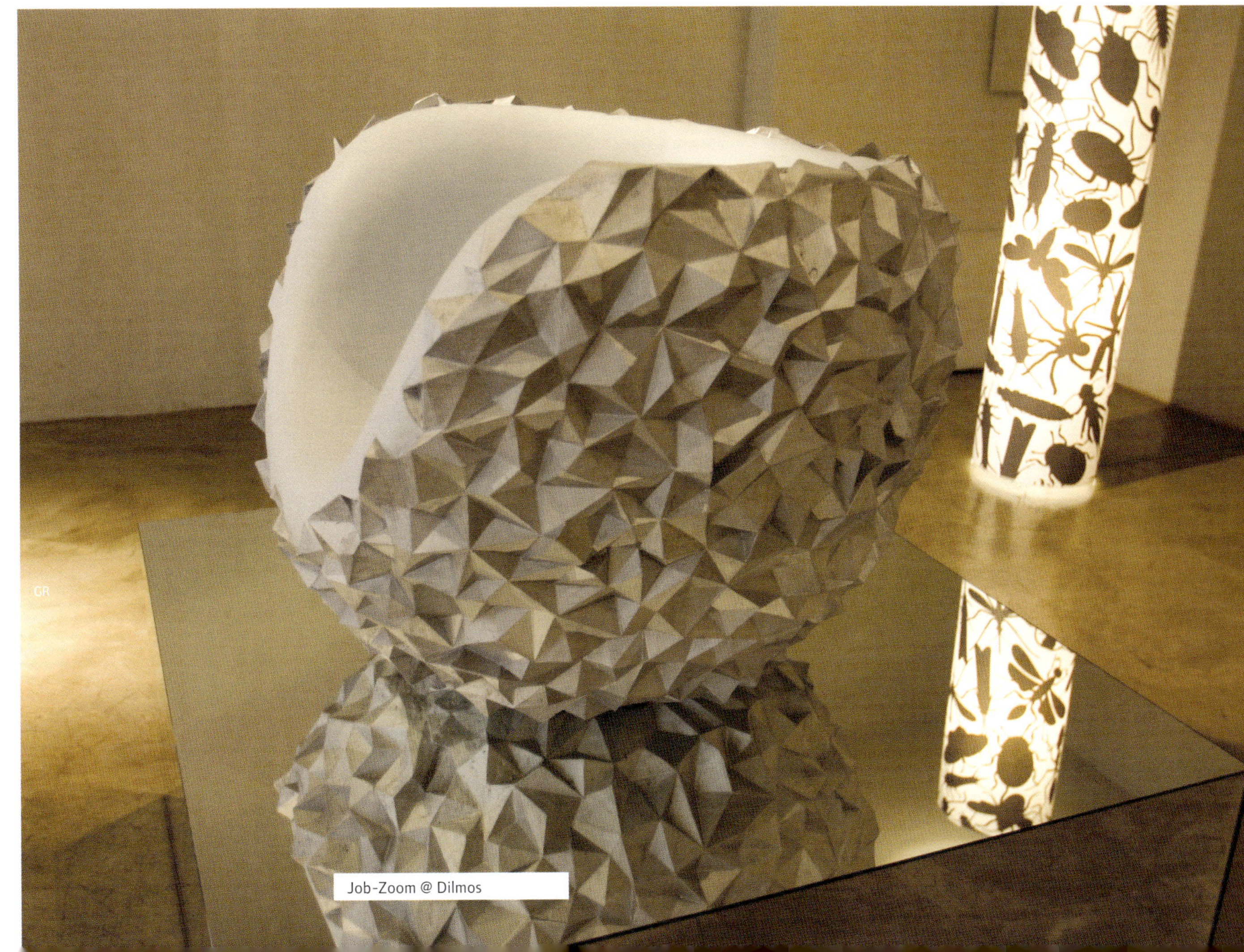

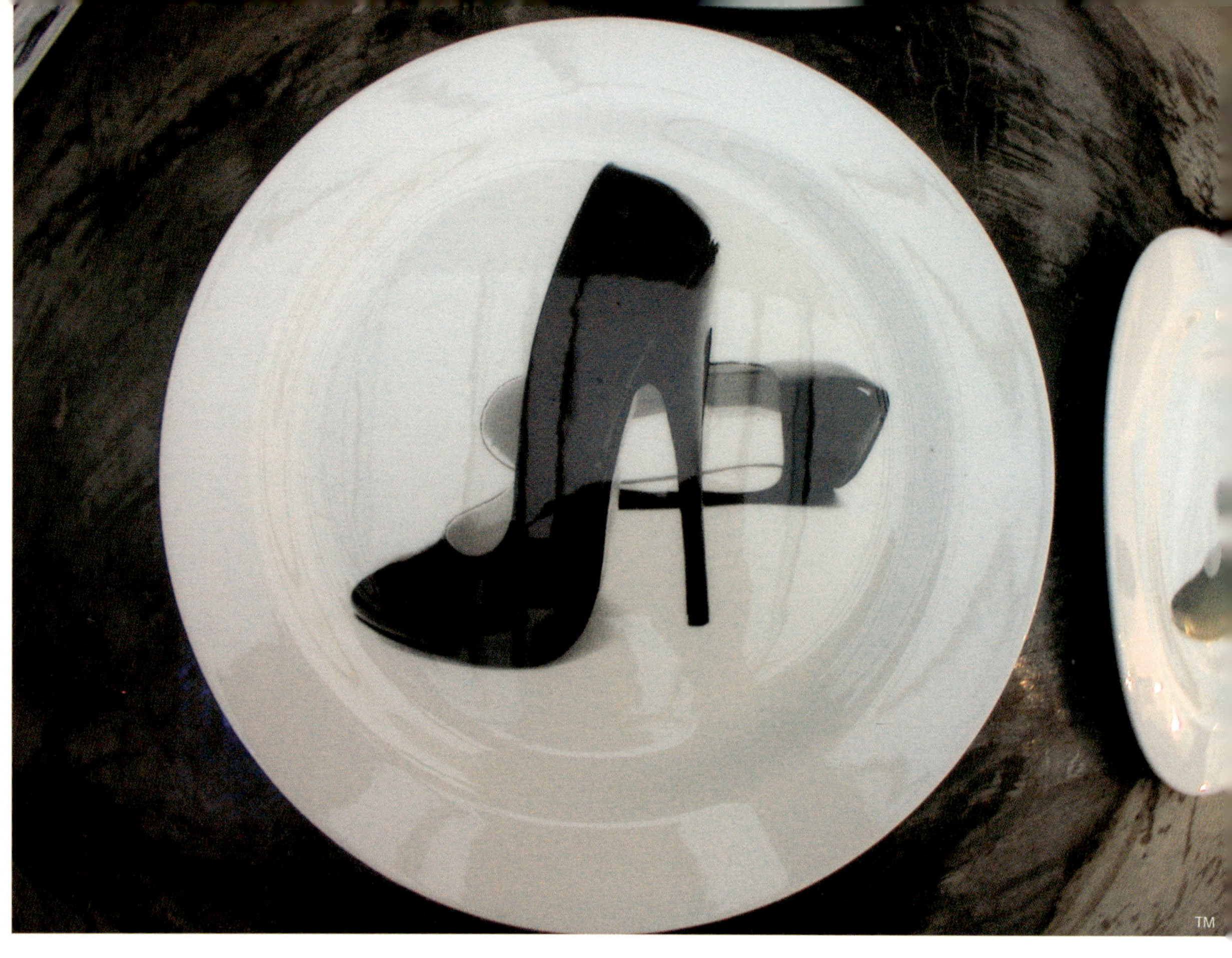

Her House Product by Luke Morgan @ Designersblock

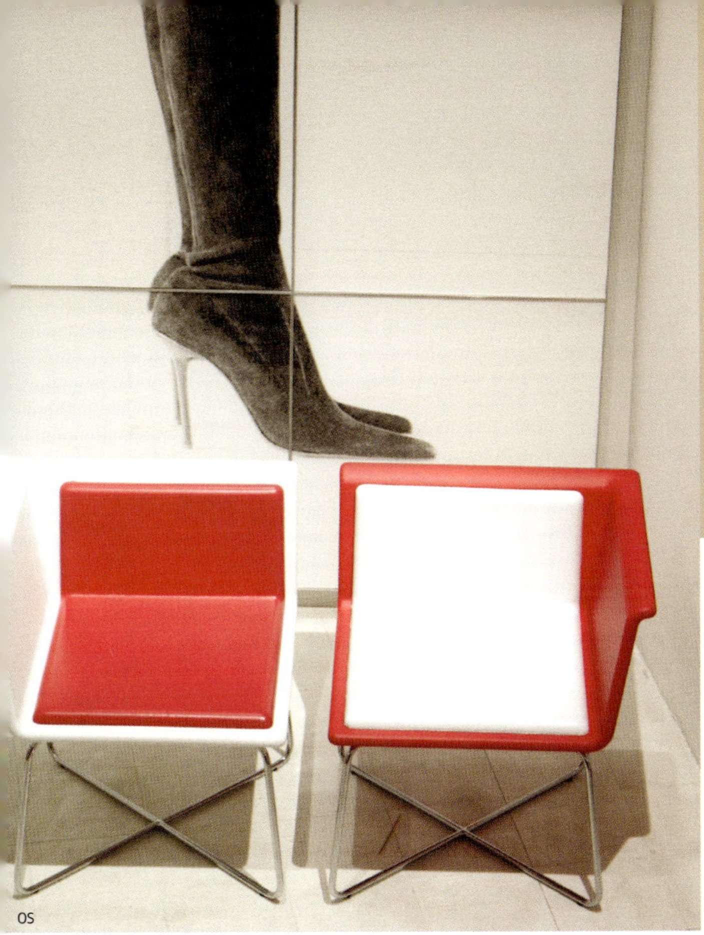

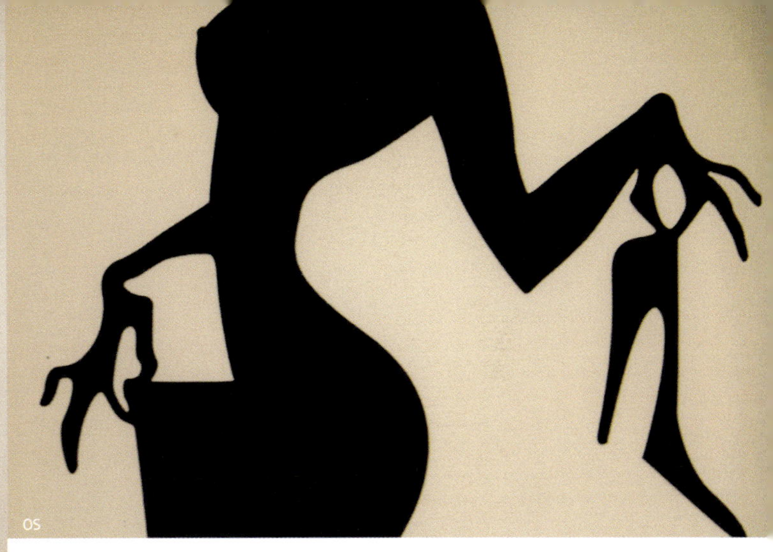

karim Rashid for Felicerossi

Diseño Español

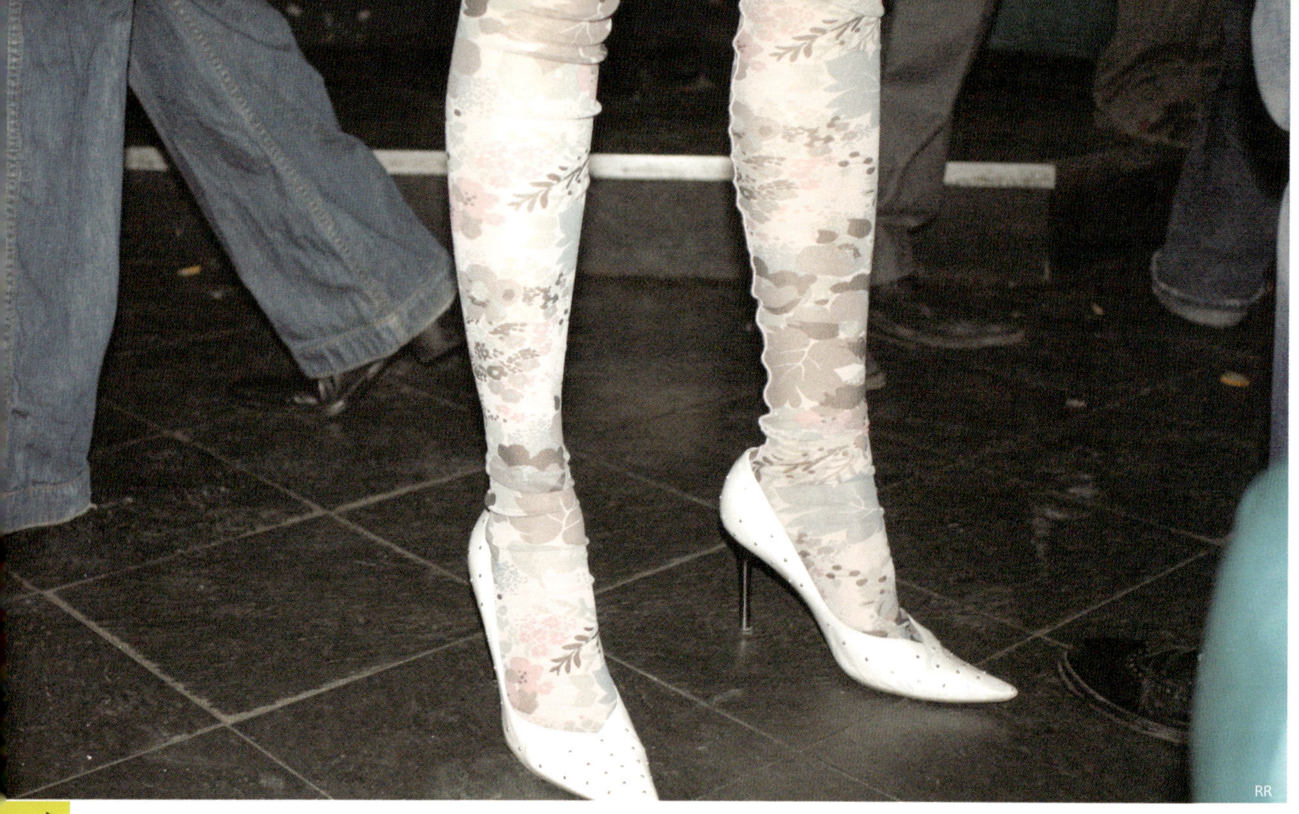

@ Plastic

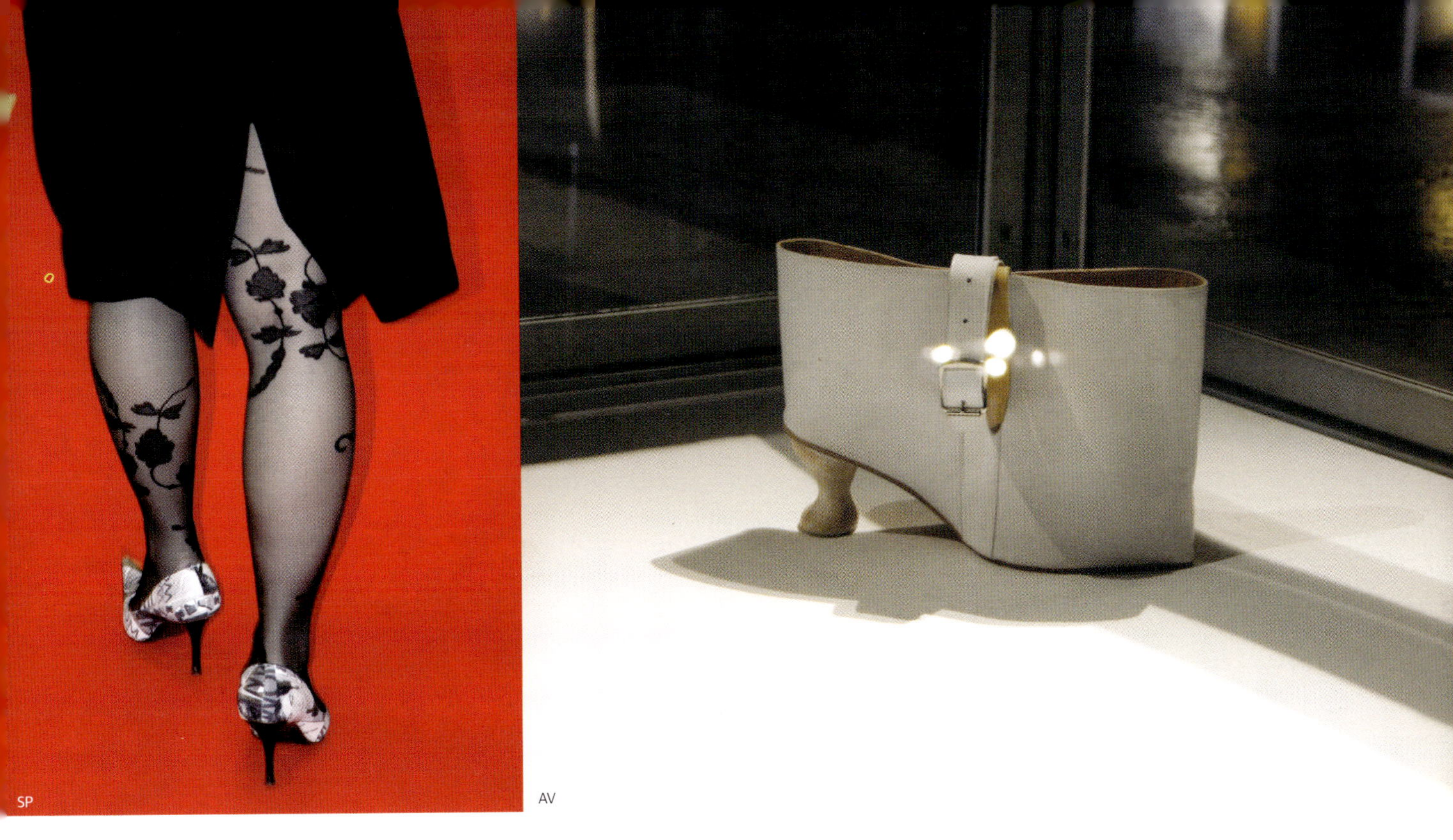

Adi

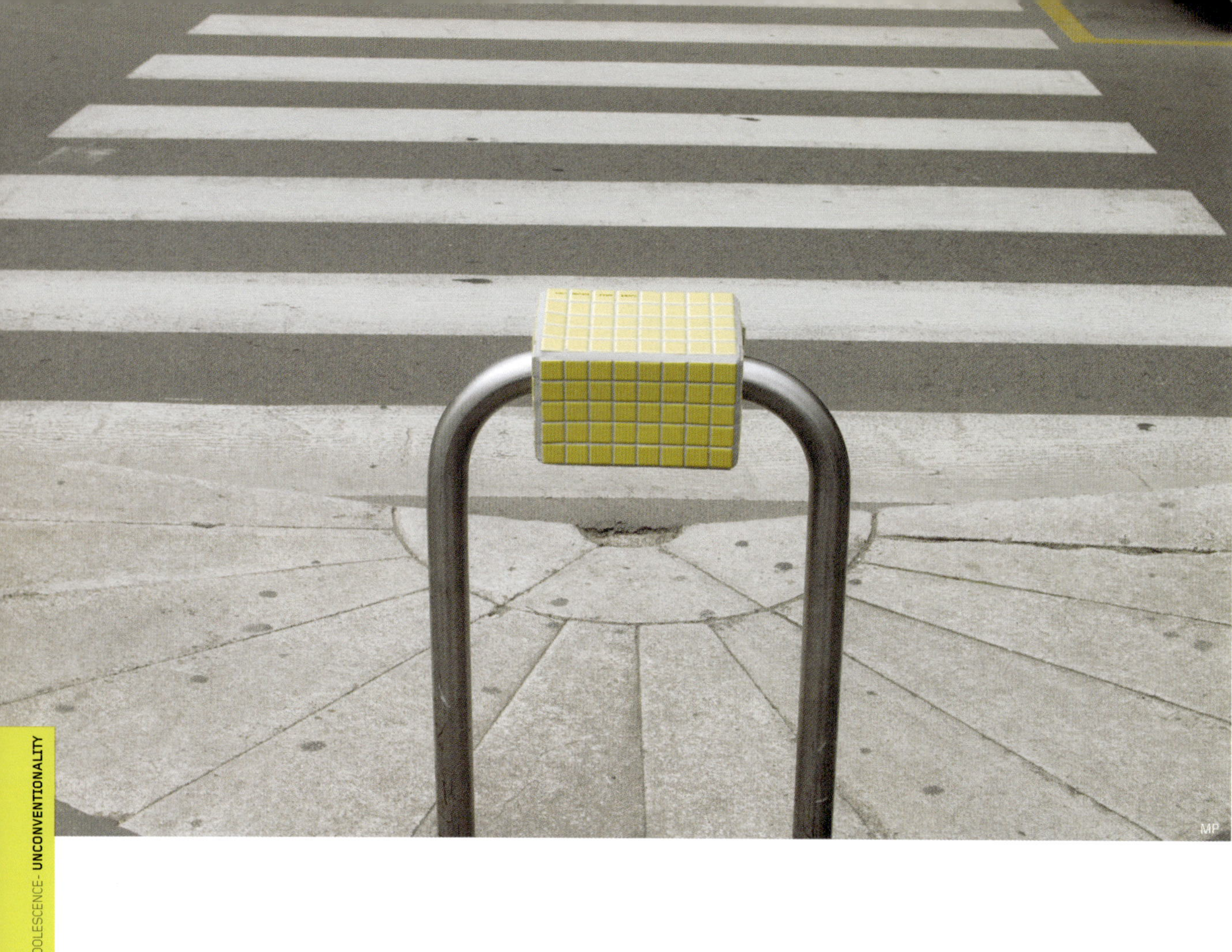

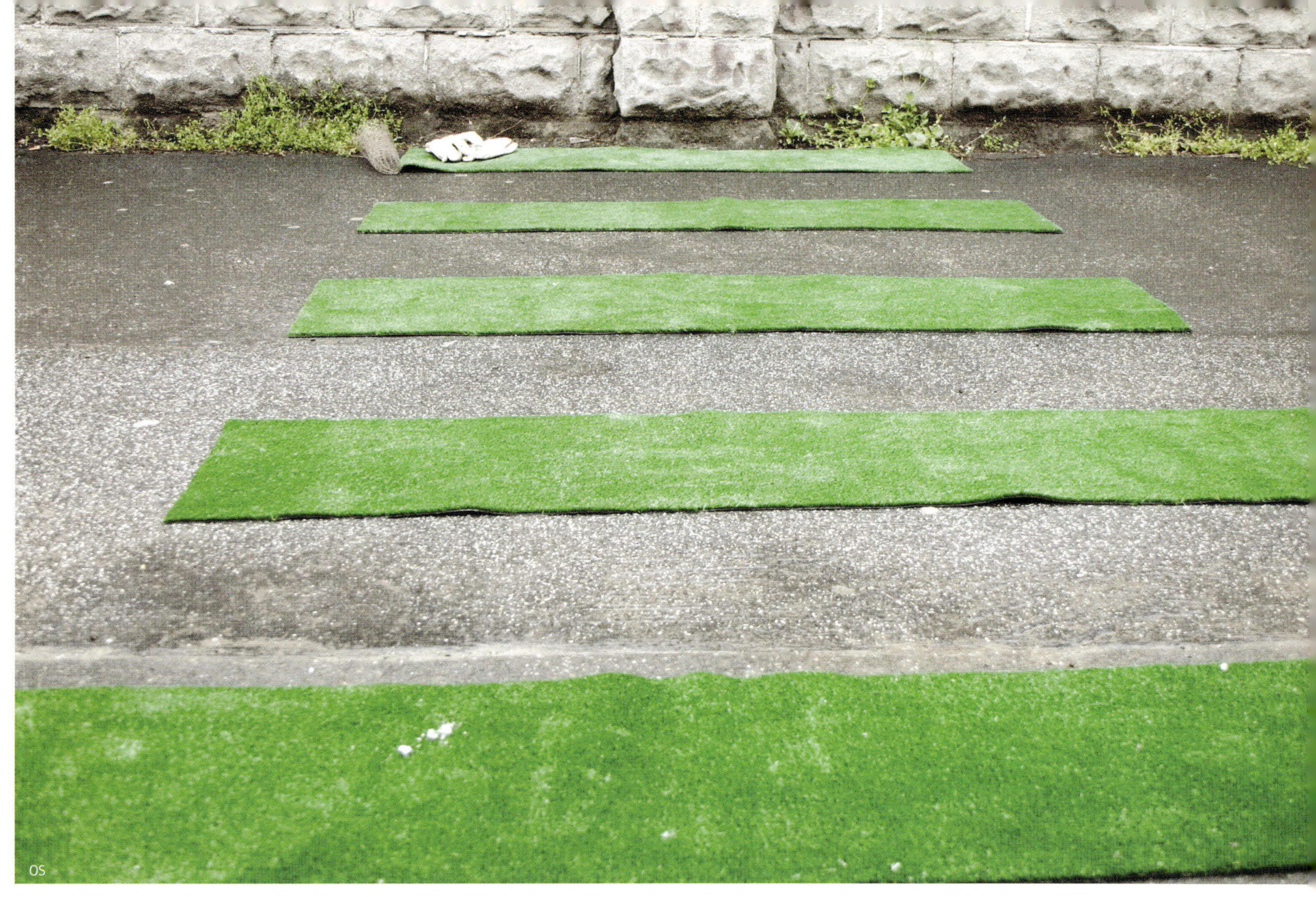

NABA for Nuova Accademia di Belle Arti

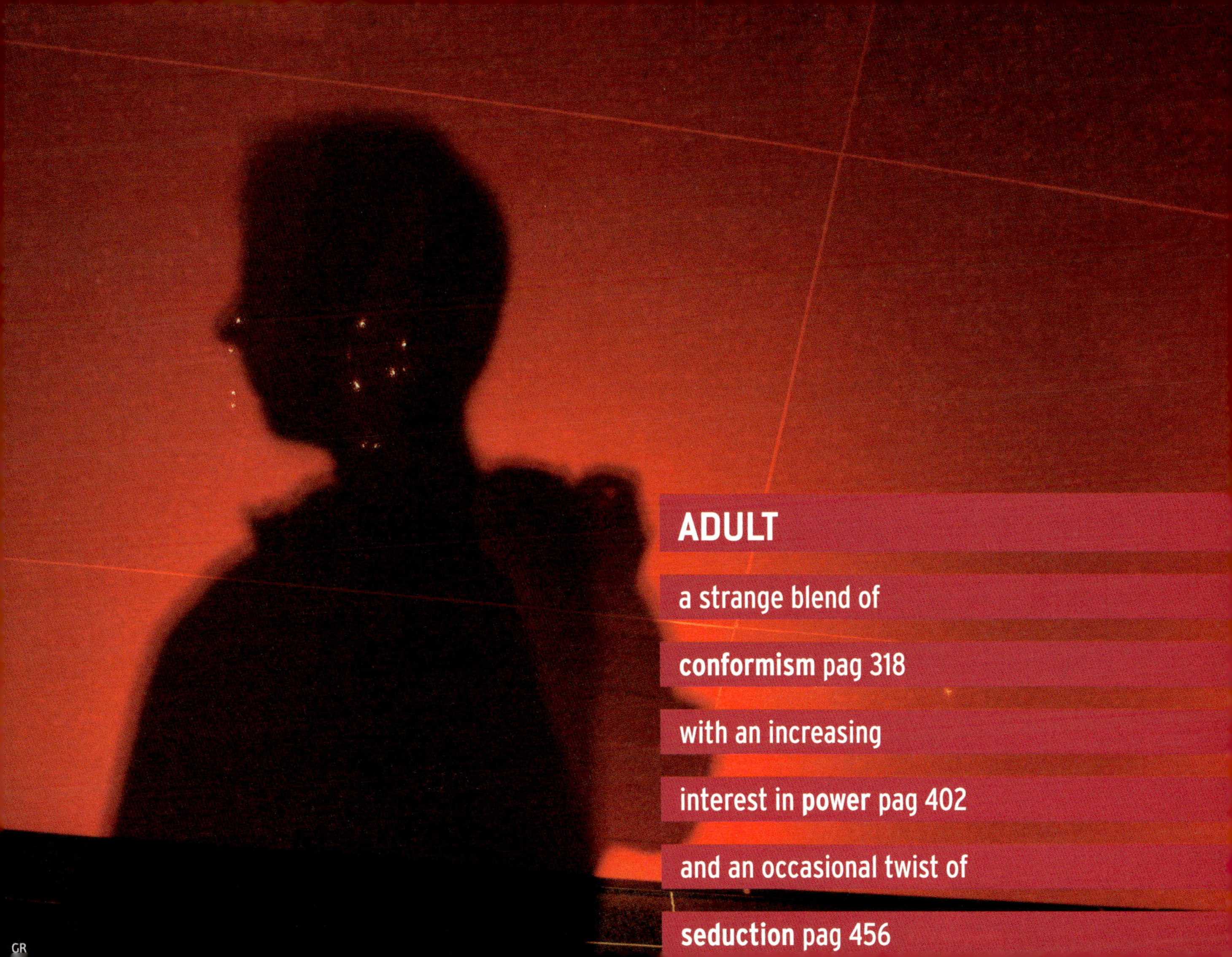

ADULT
a strange blend of
conformism pag 318
with an increasing
interest in power pag 402
and an occasional twist of
seduction pag 456
GR

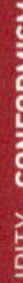

MisuraEmme

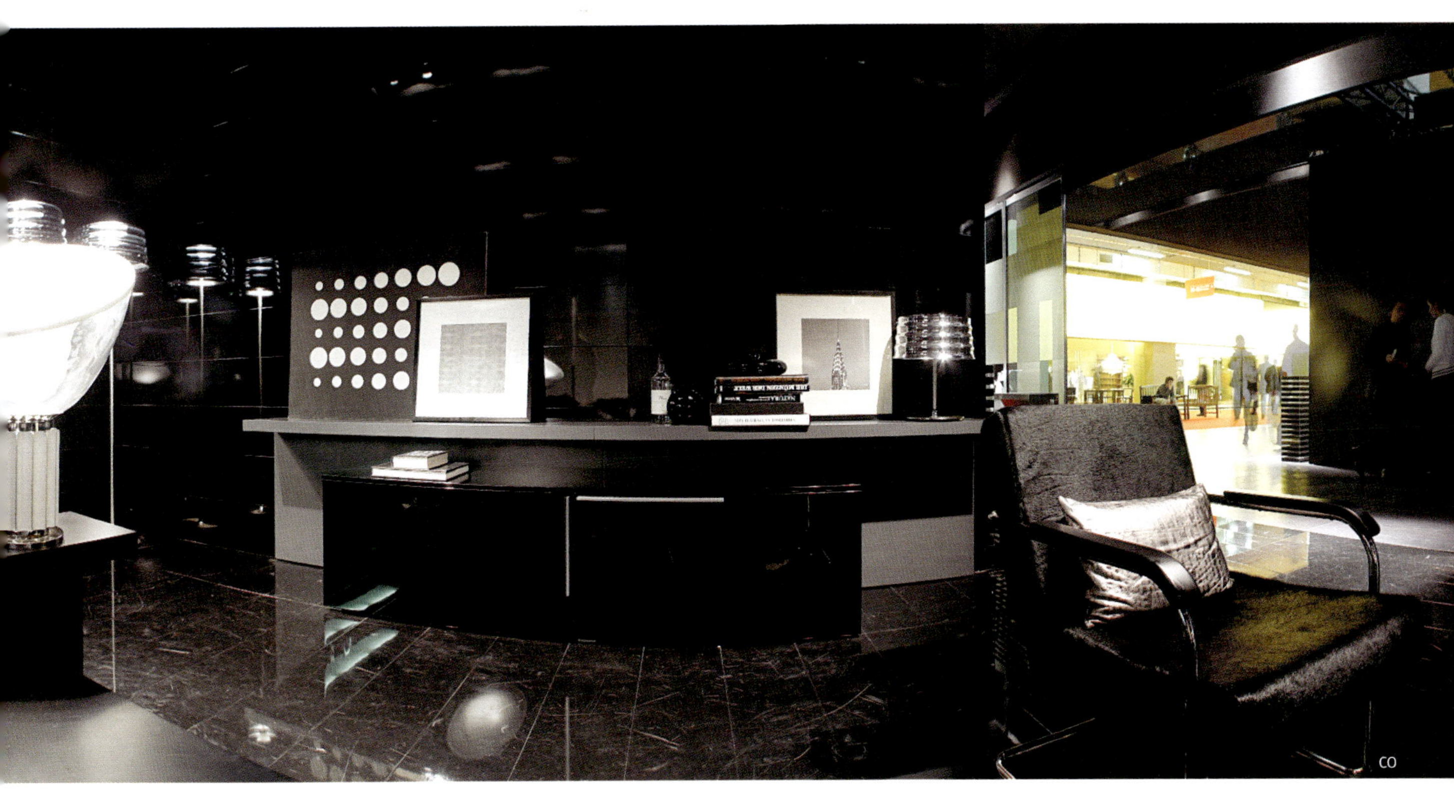

CO

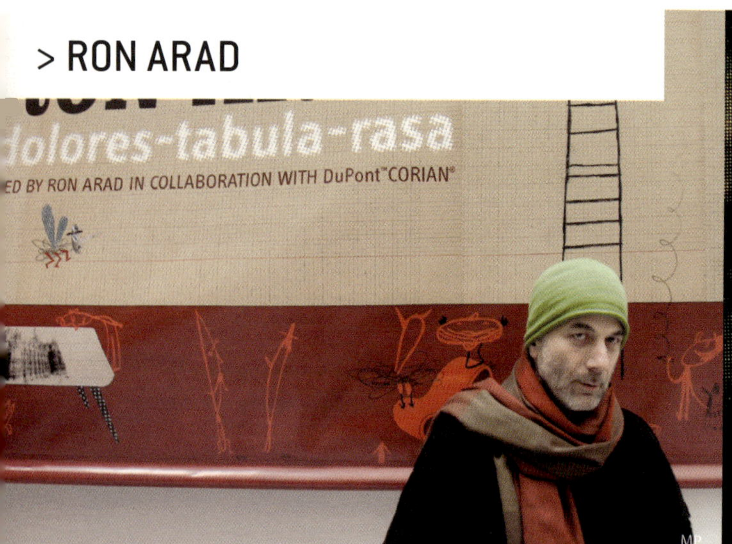

LO-REZ-DOLORES-TABULA-RASA

" **Imagine** an empty space with tactile satin smooth white walls – DuPont™ Corian® shows "stucco lustro" how perfect walls can be.

Imagine a huge cylindrical column in the centre of the space, possibly a large table somewhere in the room … just when you're not looking…

moving images emerge in the depth of the wall, you think you see runningmessages, or are there people inside the column?

The wall may play Vittorio de Sica's Miracolo a Milano, the column may become a "brand new leopard

skin pill-box hat" while the table is busy running "Pulp Fiction". Then … all is white again, no trace, no memory…tabula rasa.

This is **a marriage between the material world and the ephemeral images** conjured up by arteries of light.

Writing this may feel like writing science fiction and it is indeed still fiction but a lot of hard work is frantically taking place in

London, Belgium, France and Italy for this fiction realized at Gallery Gio' Marconi (Milano) during April 2004.

Oh yes, there are also some heavy furniture landscaped in coloured Corian® and contoured

by contrasting coloured glue, of course. "

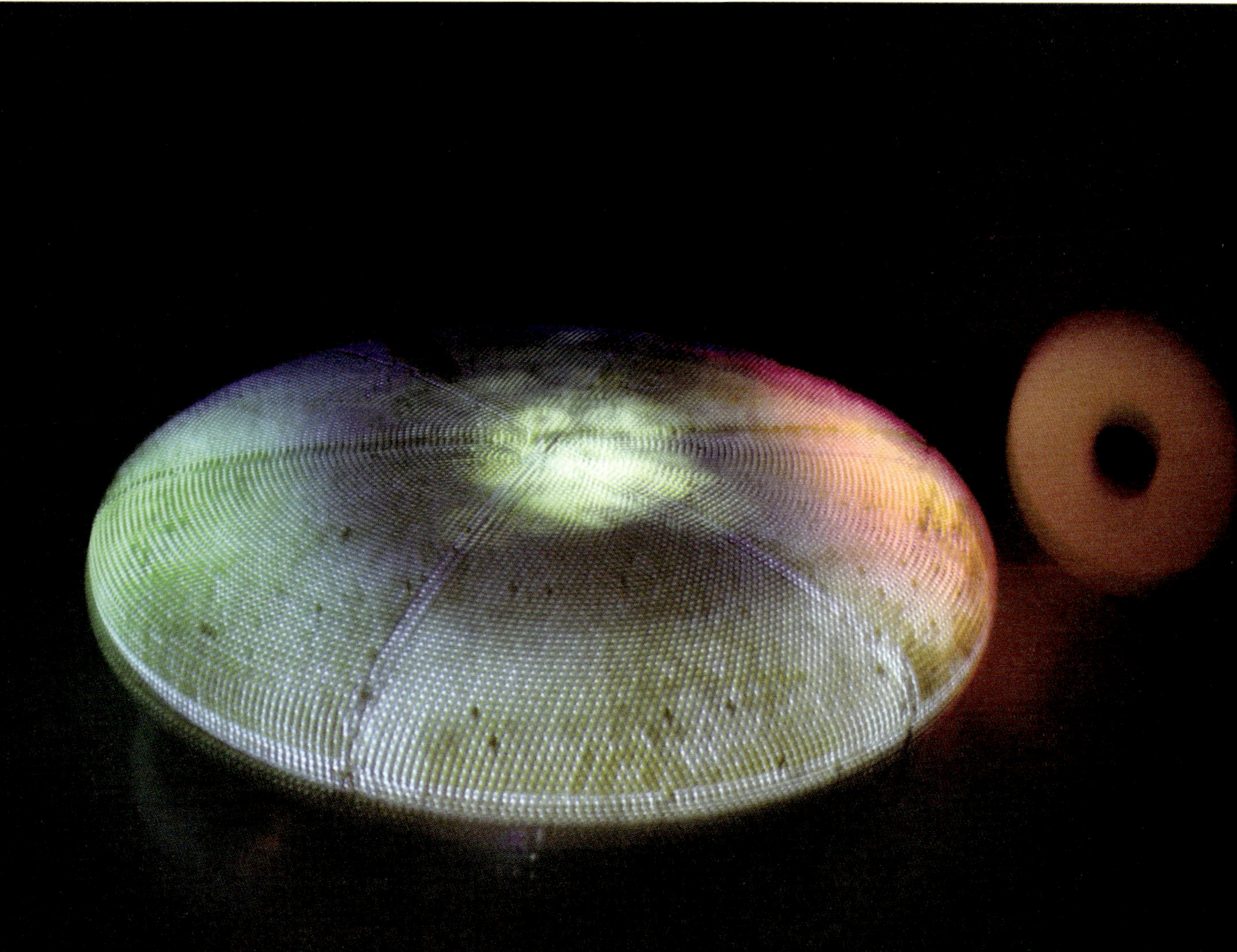

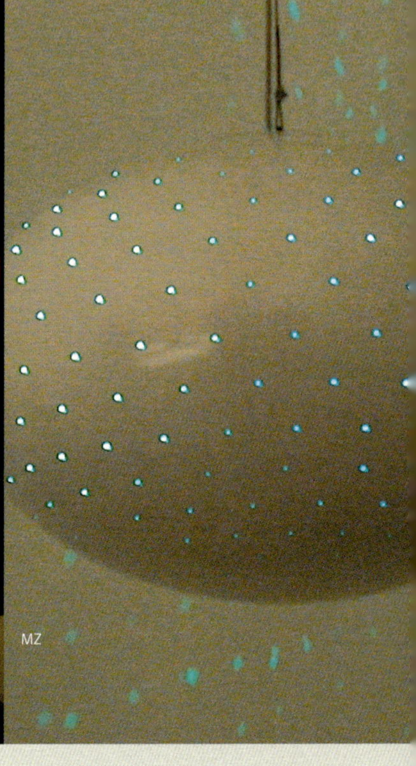

MP   MZ

Ron Arad -designer

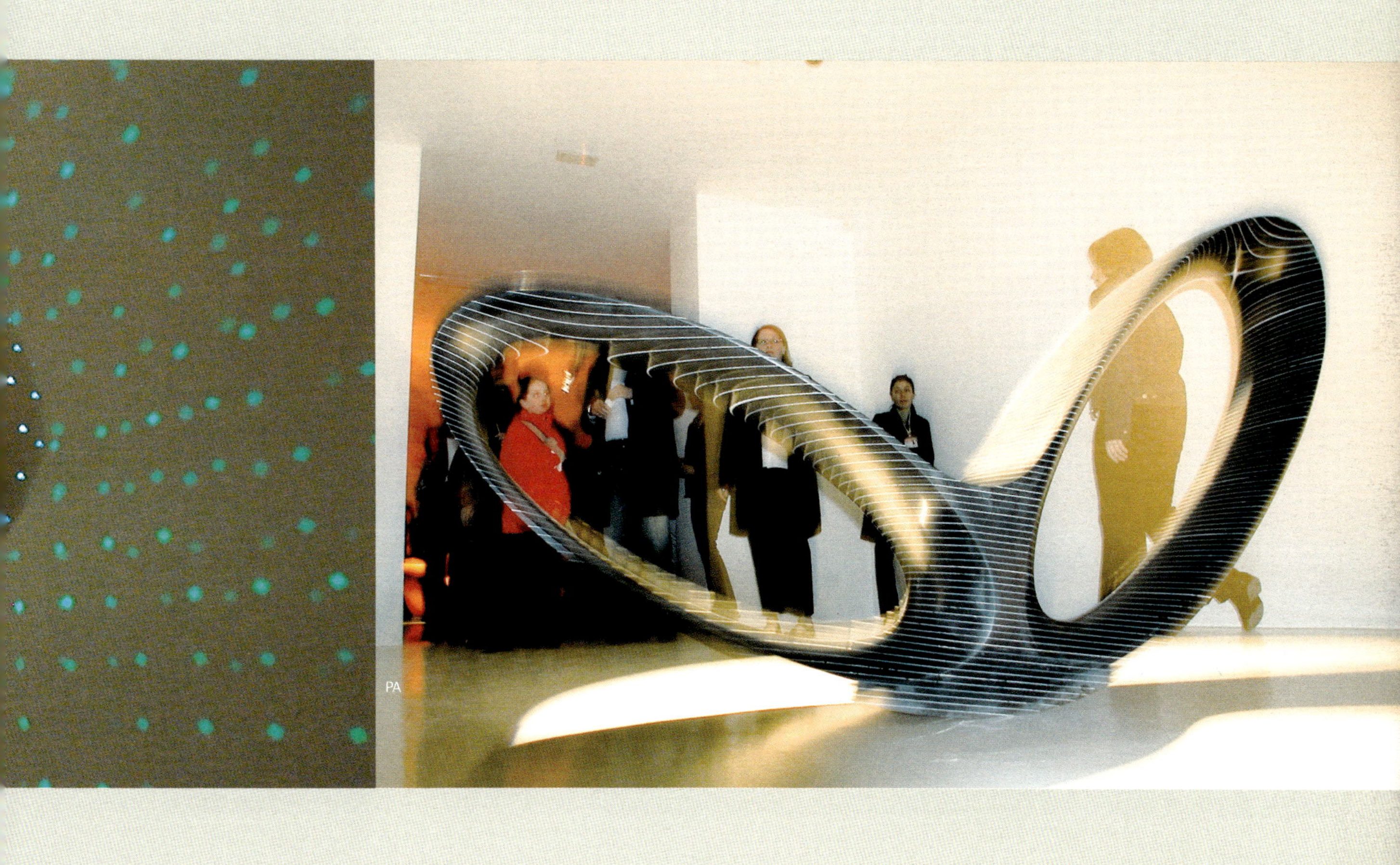
PA

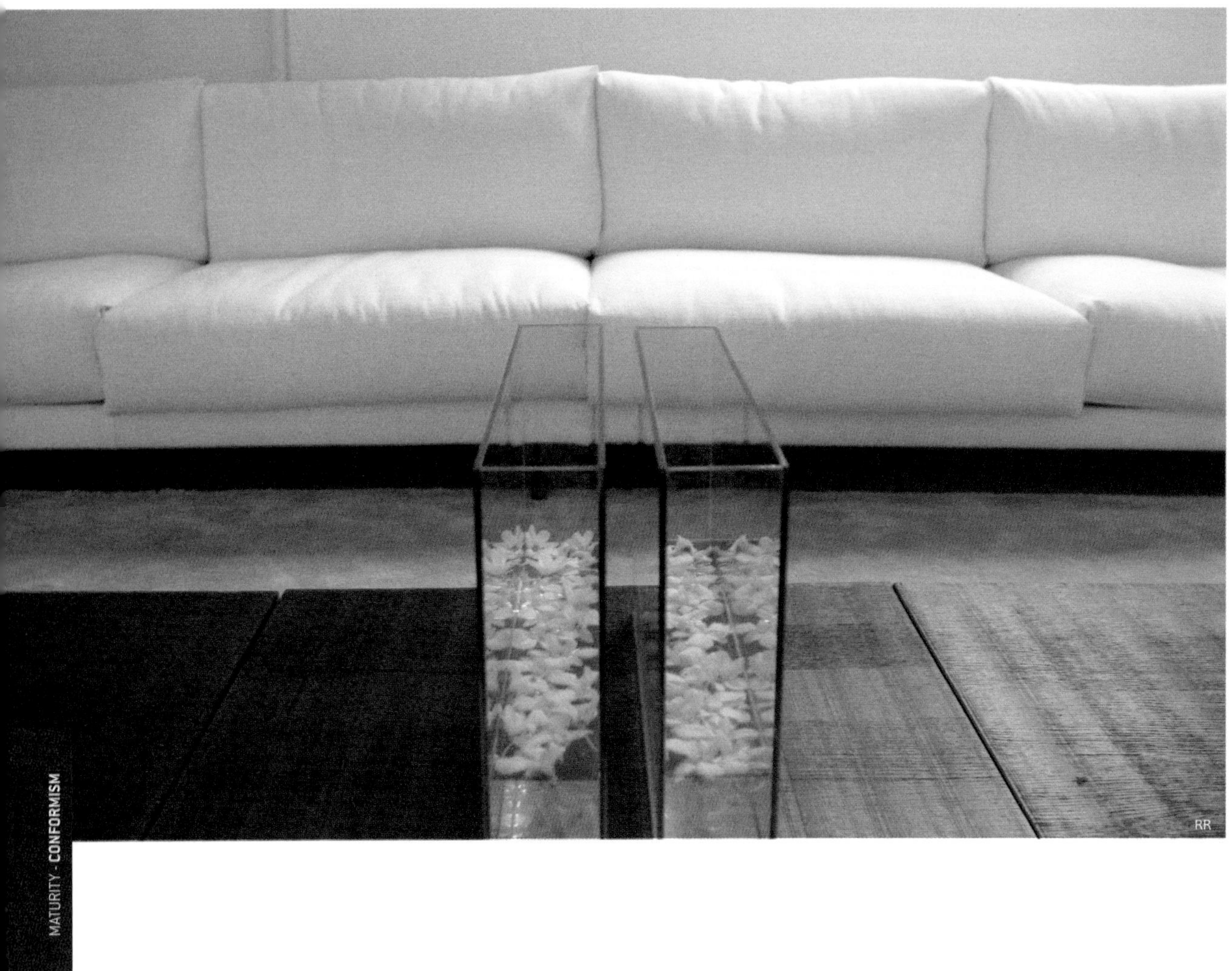

Living divani

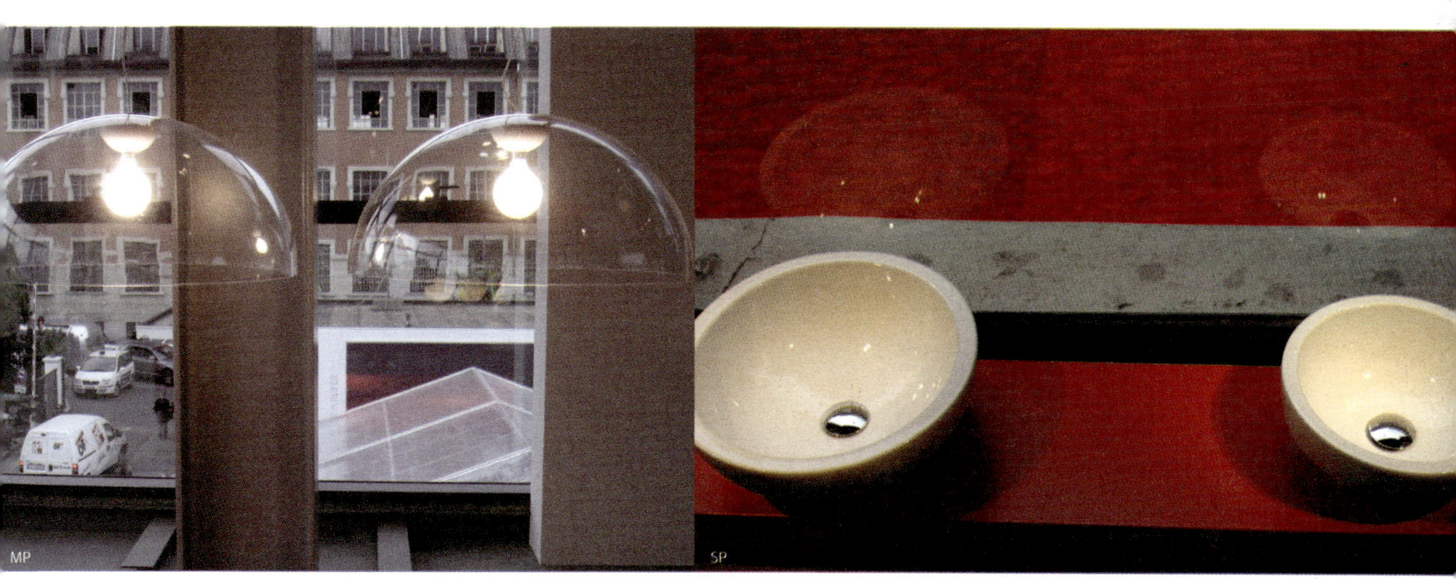

Paola Lenti   Catalano

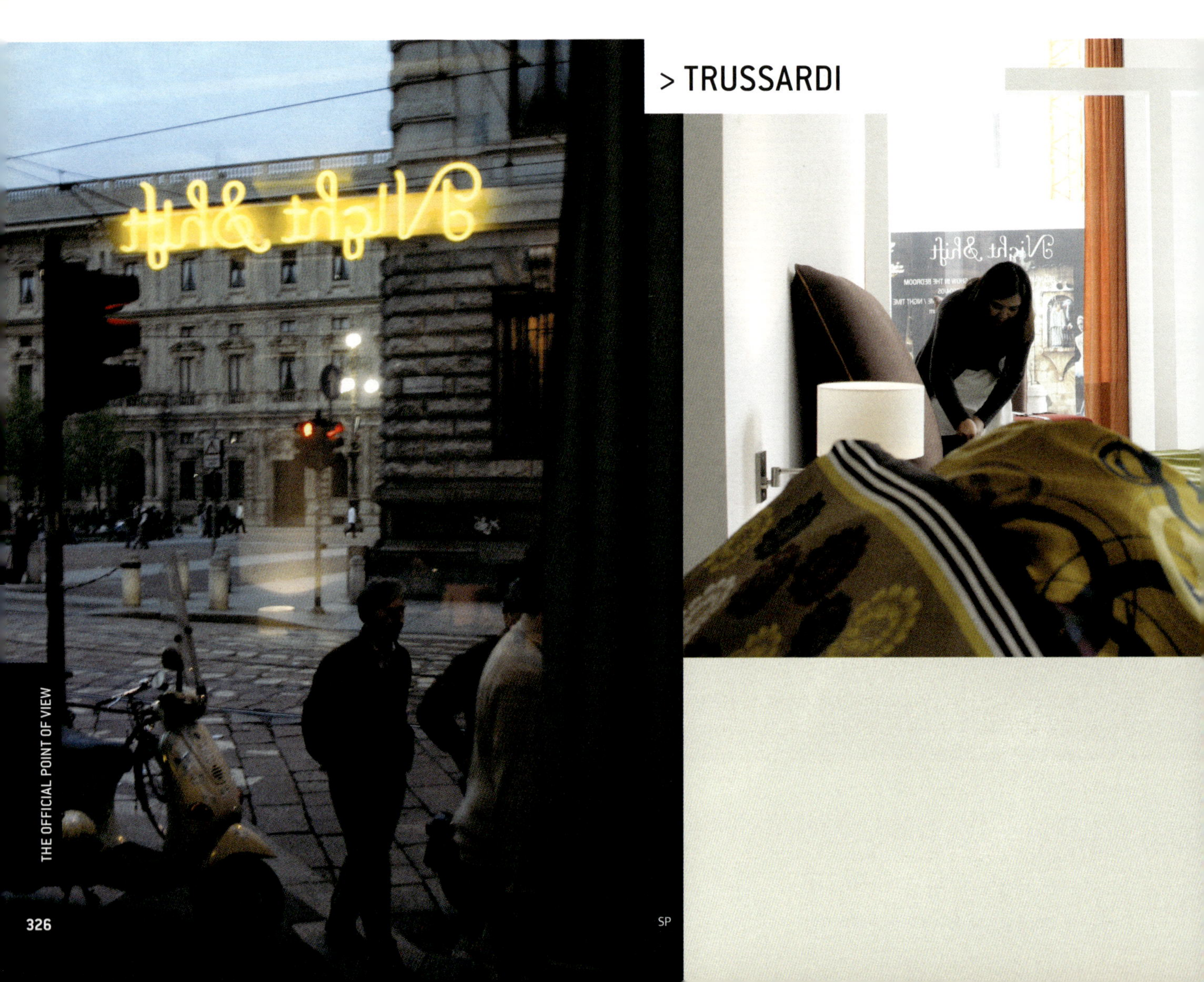

> TRUSSARDI

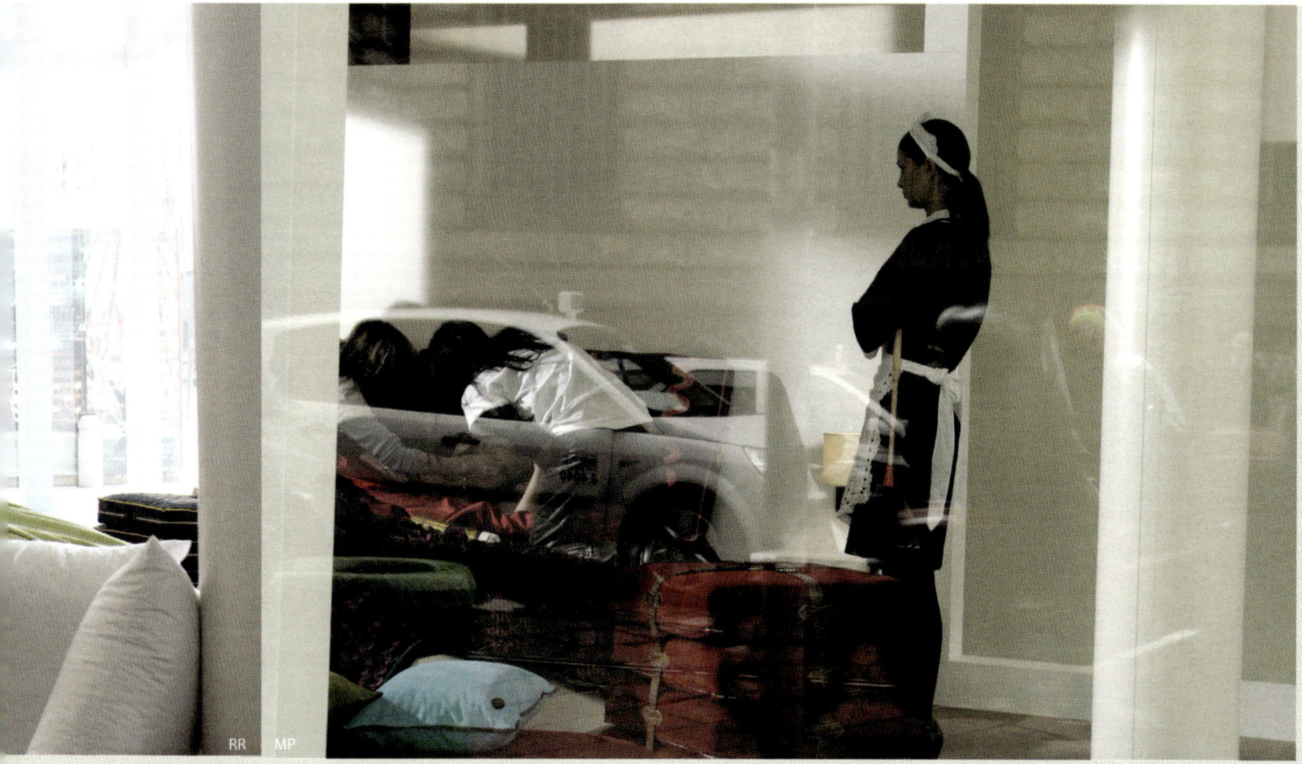

A COLLECTION OF EXPERIENCES MIXING THE PUBLIC AND PRIVATE SPHERES

Trussardi presented Night Shift: the windows of Trussardi Marino Alla Scala, a reality show involving the public with a series of meetings, performances, discussions, presentations, live sets, music, design, cooking, cinema and fashion.

Continuous scenery changed and alternating personalities and situations transformed the Trussardi areas into the ideal setting for the visions and dreams of a changing city: a private place and at the same time in the public eye,

Night Shift is a platform to look at Milan from an unusual point of view with as protagonists personalities from design, music, fashion and society who, with their original contribution.

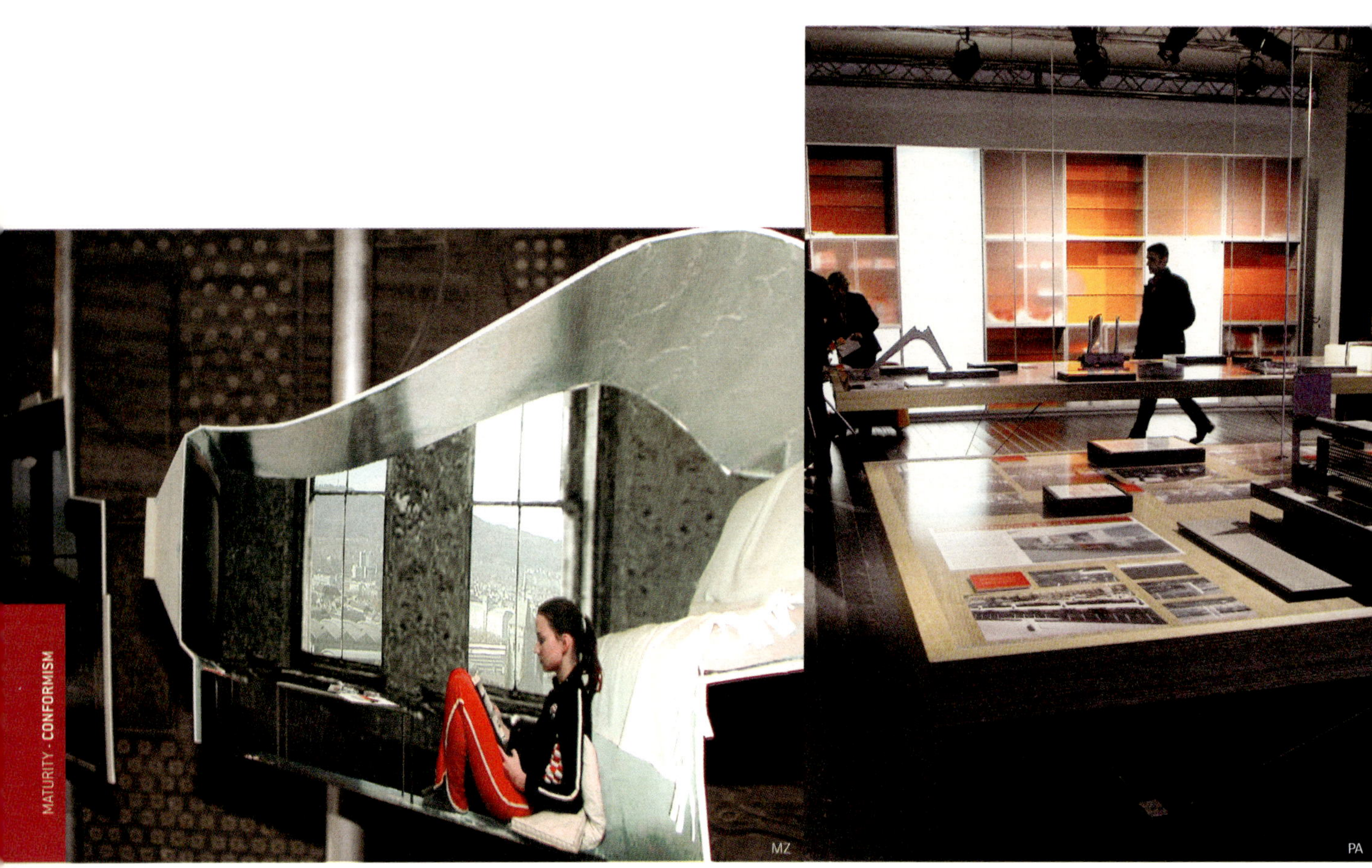

Dormbracht

Tecno

328

Barcelona Mies van der Rohe
Kazuhide Takahama Suzanne
Knoll

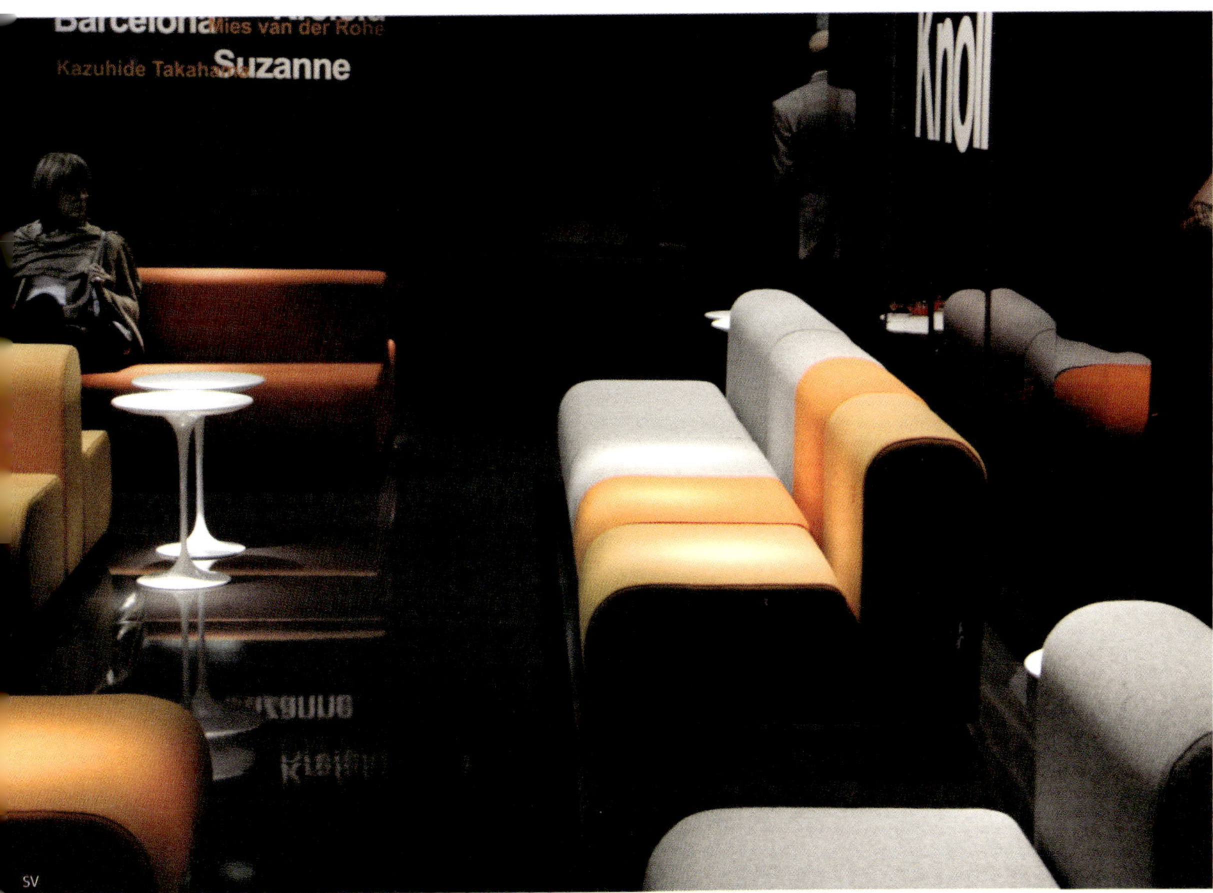

SV

Knoll

IS THERE A TREND AS SUCH IN THE WORLD OF DESIGN?

There has always been one and it will continue to exist.

Quality is admired and then copied: being able to separate an original from an imitation is what matters.

GALA FERNANDEZ

There is no trend as such, as design is made of all sorts of stuff.

Objects taking into account the environment, sustaining objects,

nachhaltige, ressourchenschonende Produkte are what I am interested in.

I think that sooner or later nature is bound to impose sustainable and respectful methods.

ERNST GAMPLER

Trends? There are loads of them and they are all different from one another.

Some people think (a way of thinkign perhaps

actually pertaining to the phenomenon) they've got one,

i.e. the "real thing", "Cultivated" design is probably the most

exposed trend, although all trends tend to follow "opinion leaders",

worshipping "holy cows" – many cows but not that holy!

DAVID PALTERER

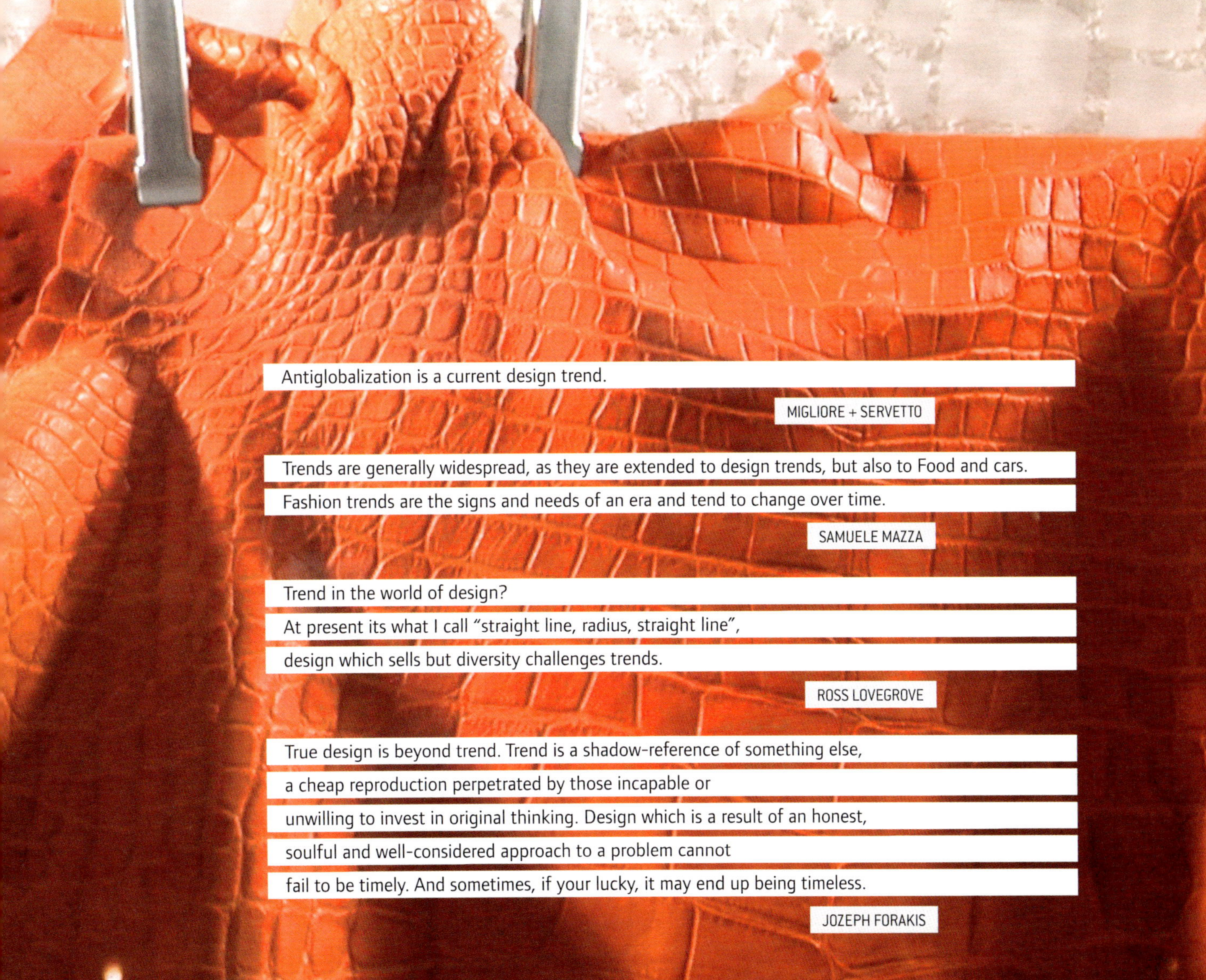

Antiglobalization is a current design trend.

MIGLIORE + SERVETTO

Trends are generally widespread, as they are extended to design trends, but also to Food and cars.
Fashion trends are the signs and needs of an era and tend to change over time.

SAMUELE MAZZA

Trend in the world of design?
At present its what I call "straight line, radius, straight line",
design which sells but diversity challenges trends.

ROSS LOVEGROVE

True design is beyond trend. Trend is a shadow-reference of something else,
a cheap reproduction perpetrated by those incapable or
unwilling to invest in original thinking. Design which is a result of an honest,
soulful and well-considered approach to a problem cannot
fail to be timely. And sometimes, if your lucky, it may end up being timeless.

JOZEPH FORAKIS

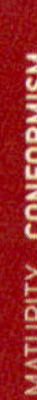

332

Frau

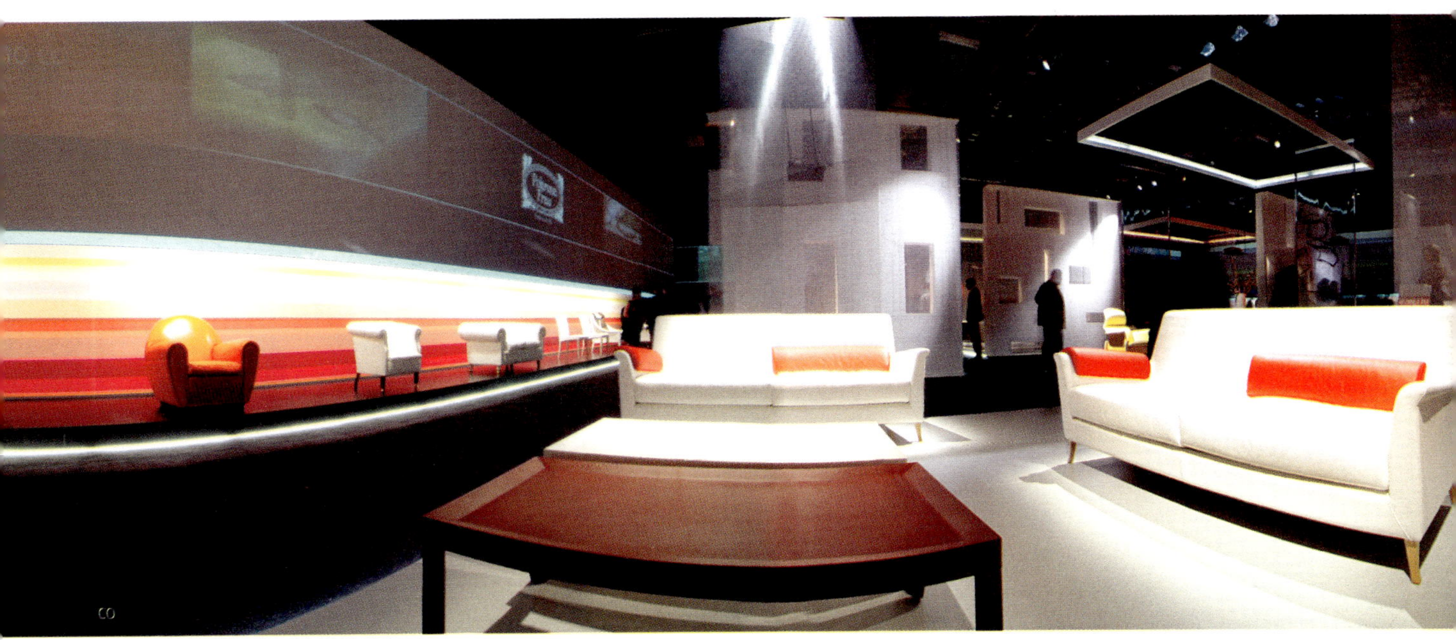

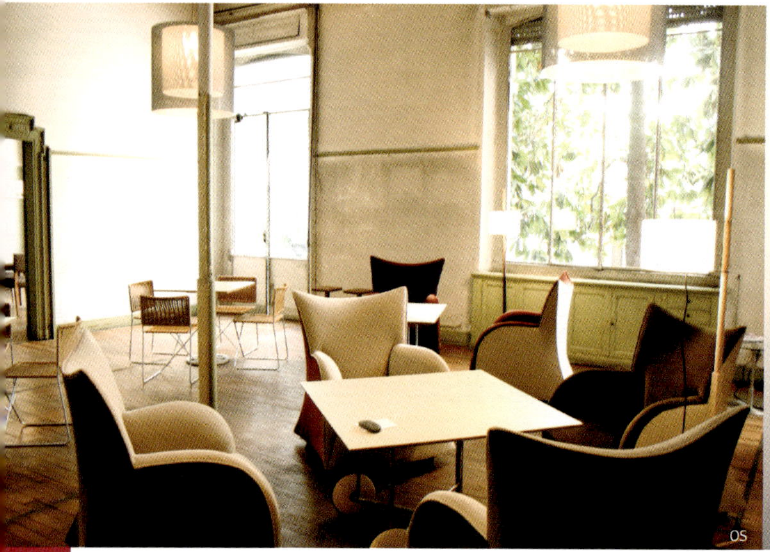

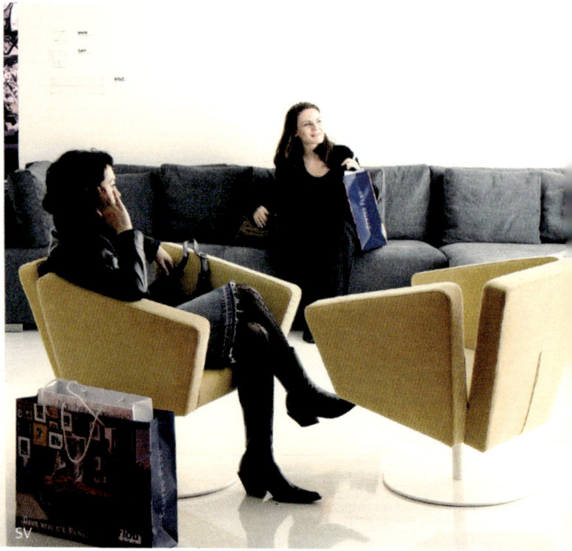

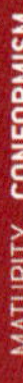

Santa & Cole

Ferlea

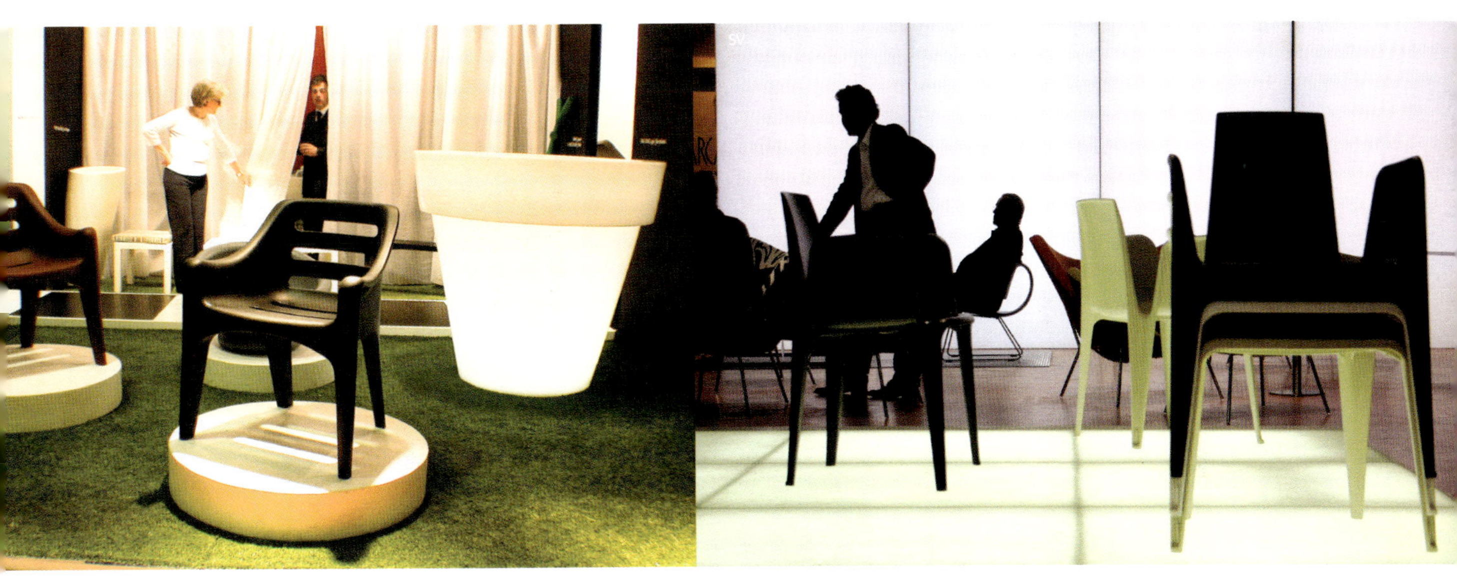

Serralunga

Sawaya e Moroni

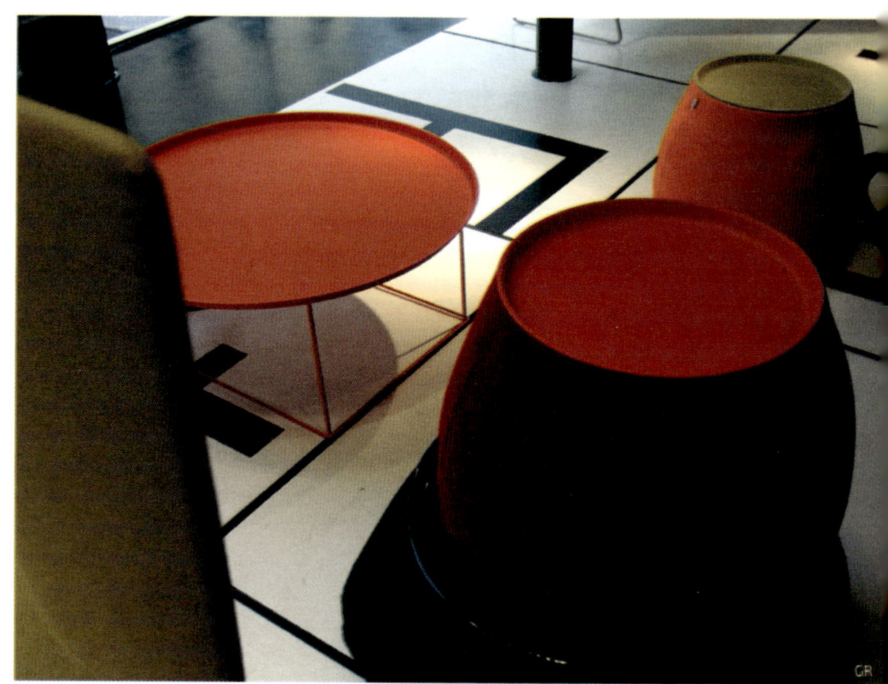

B&B italia

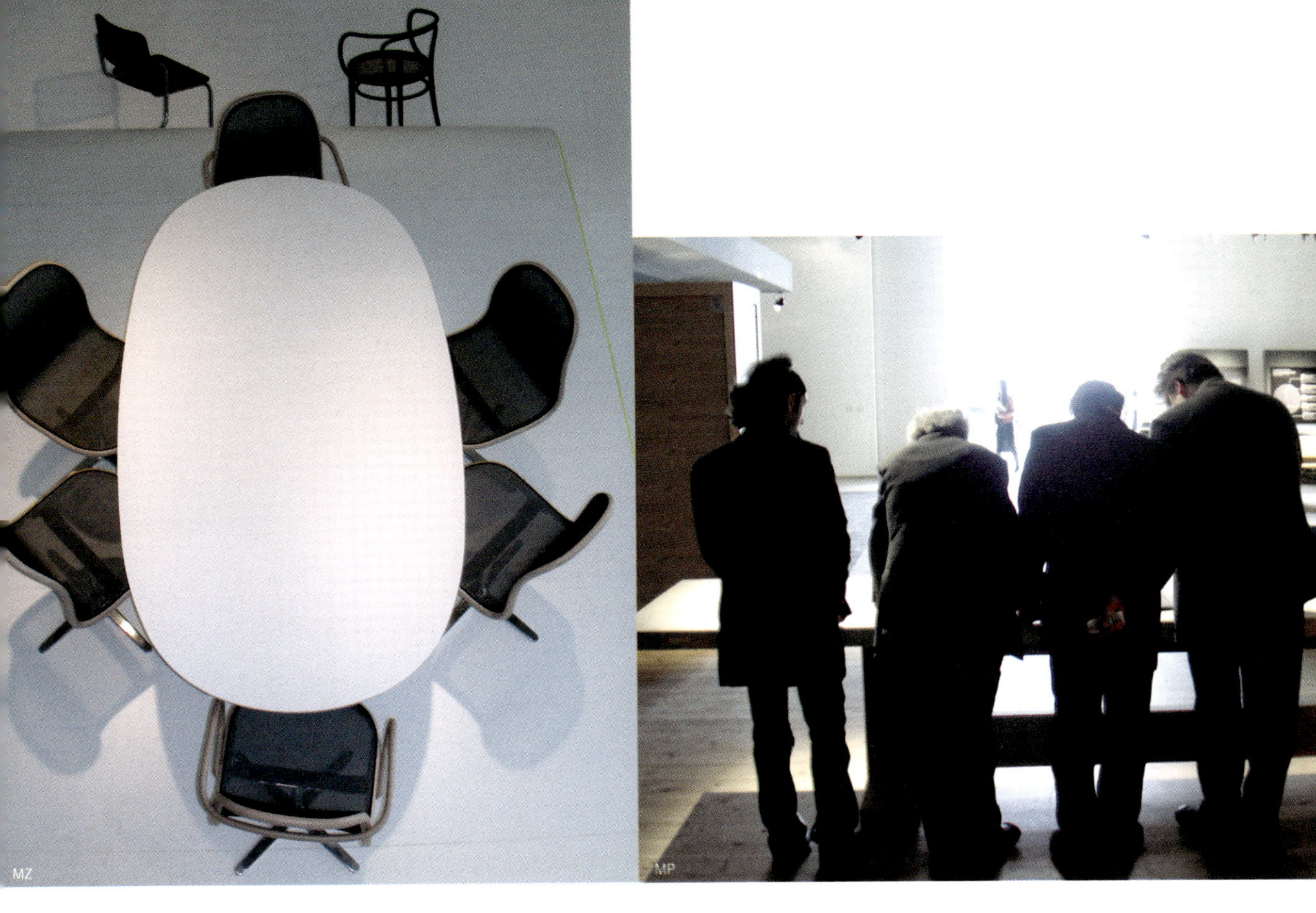

Thonet @ Superstudiopiù, Zona Tortona

EffeTi Cucine @ Zona Tortona

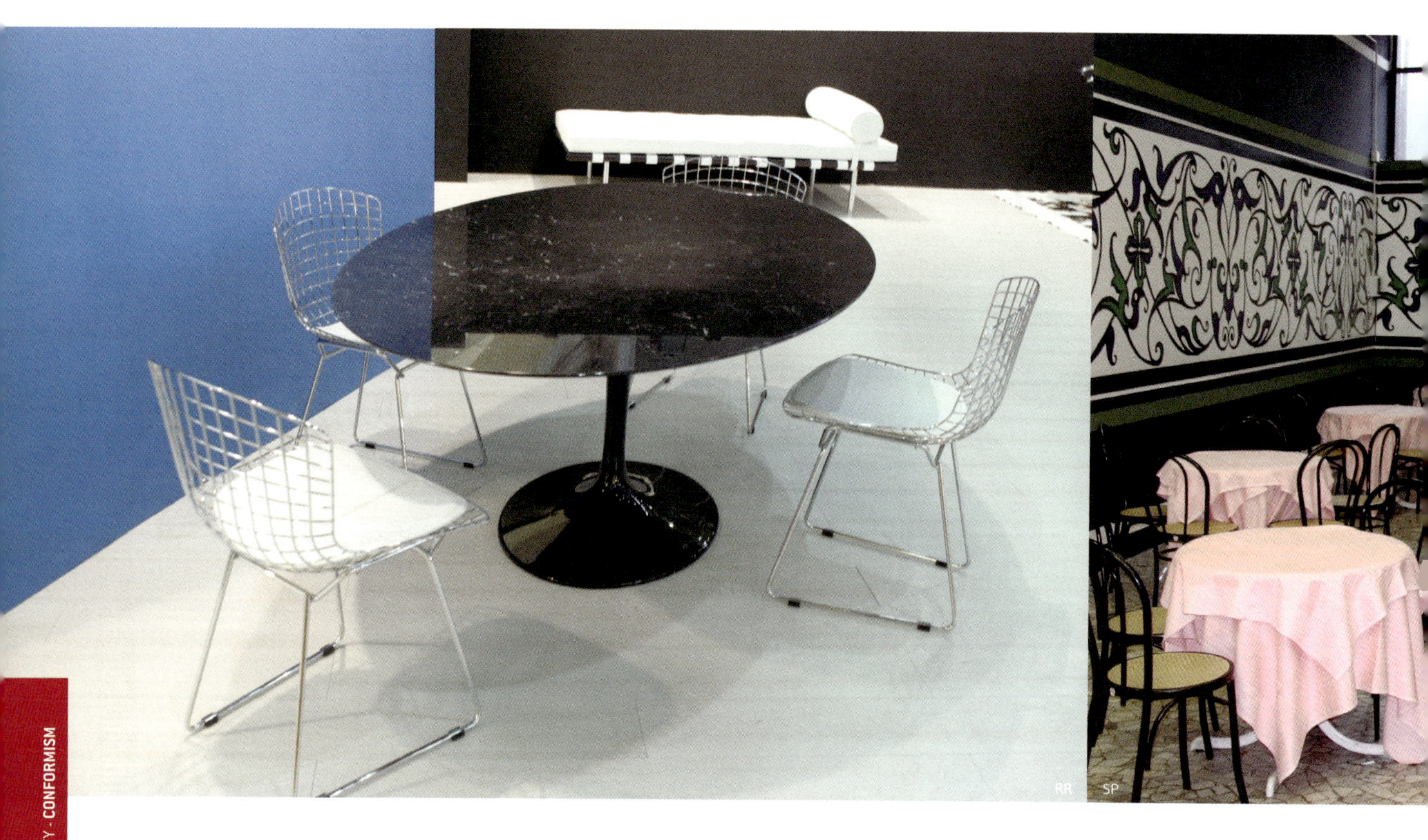

Tekno

Bar

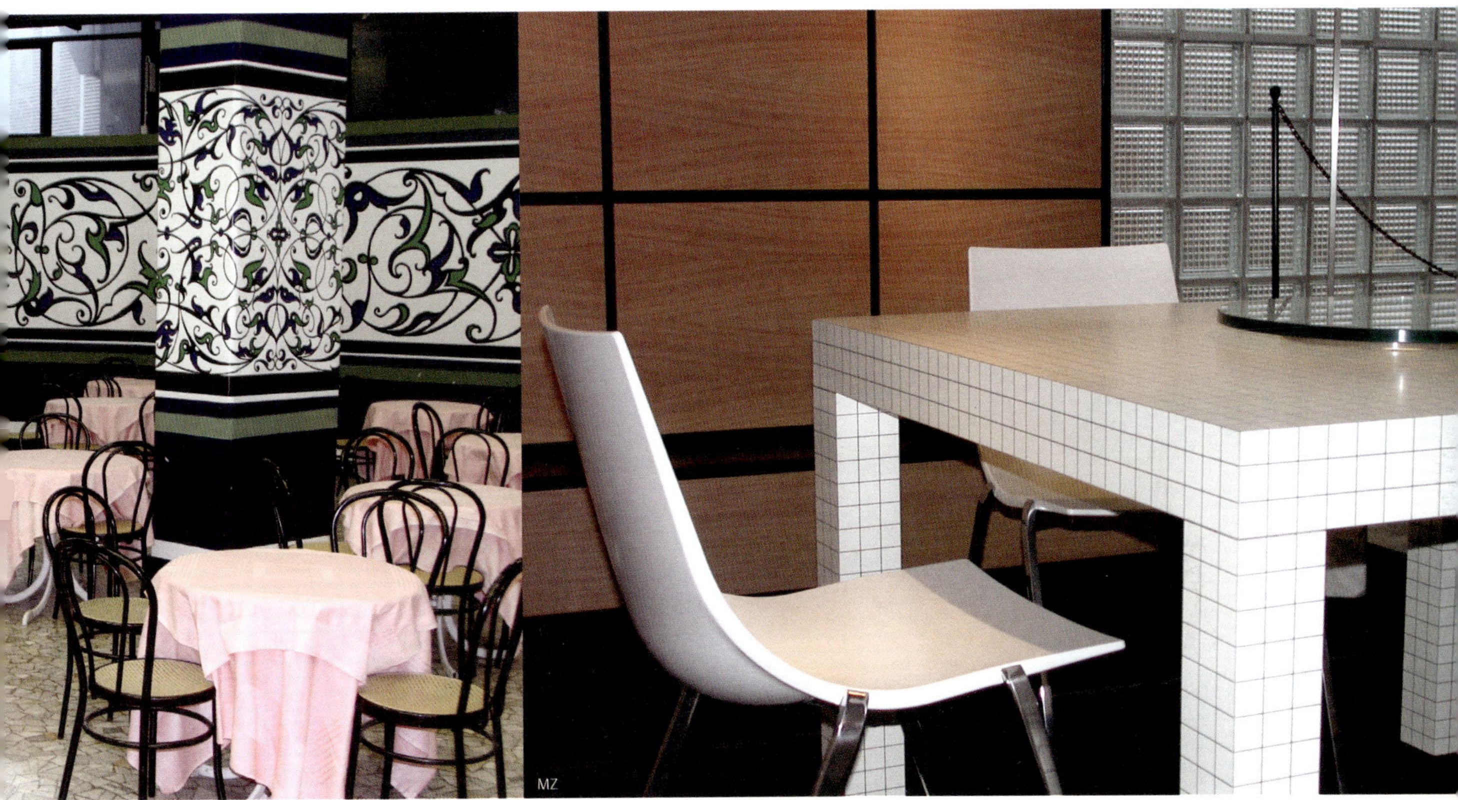

Zanotta

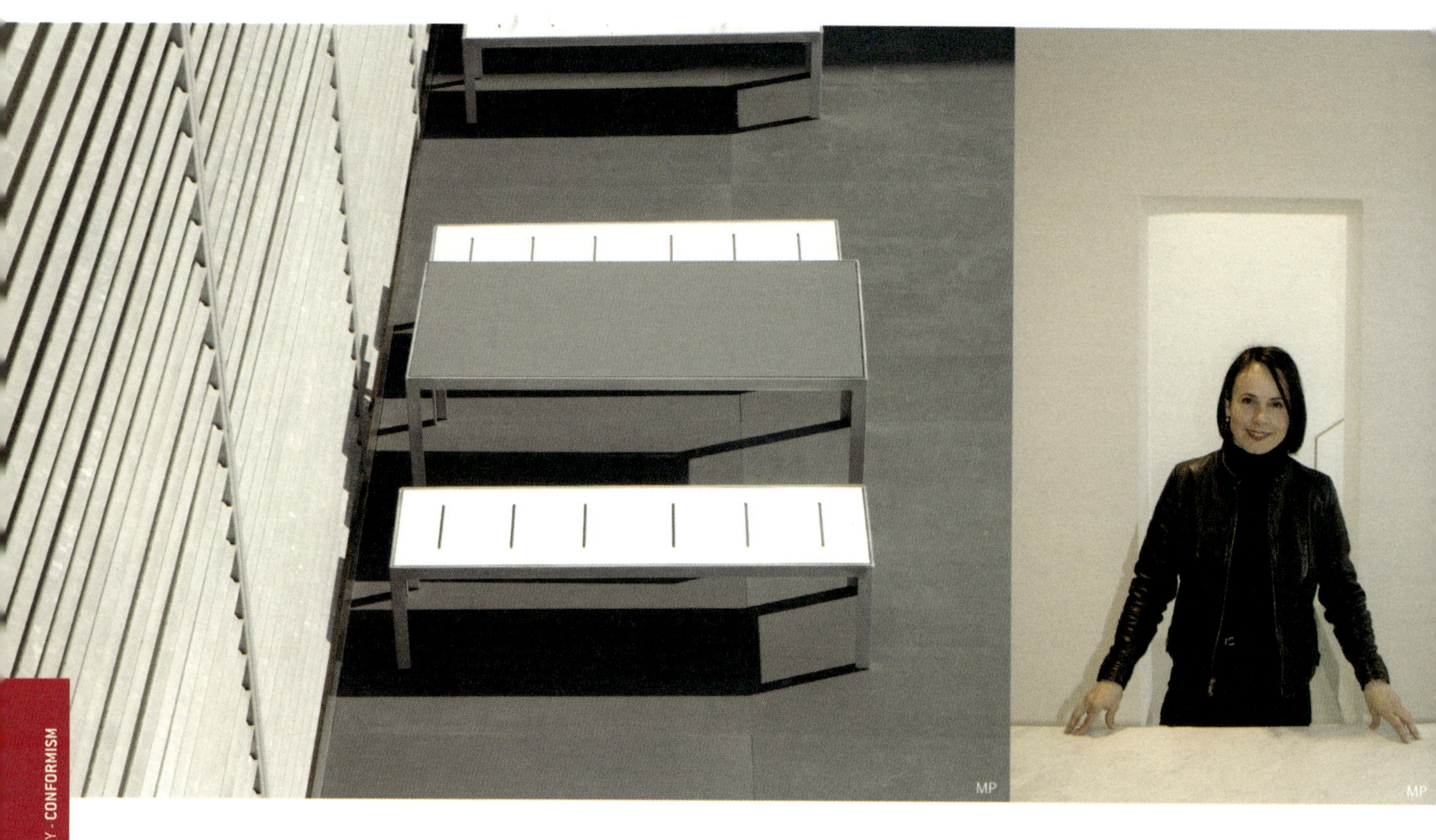

Monica Armani

Monica Armani

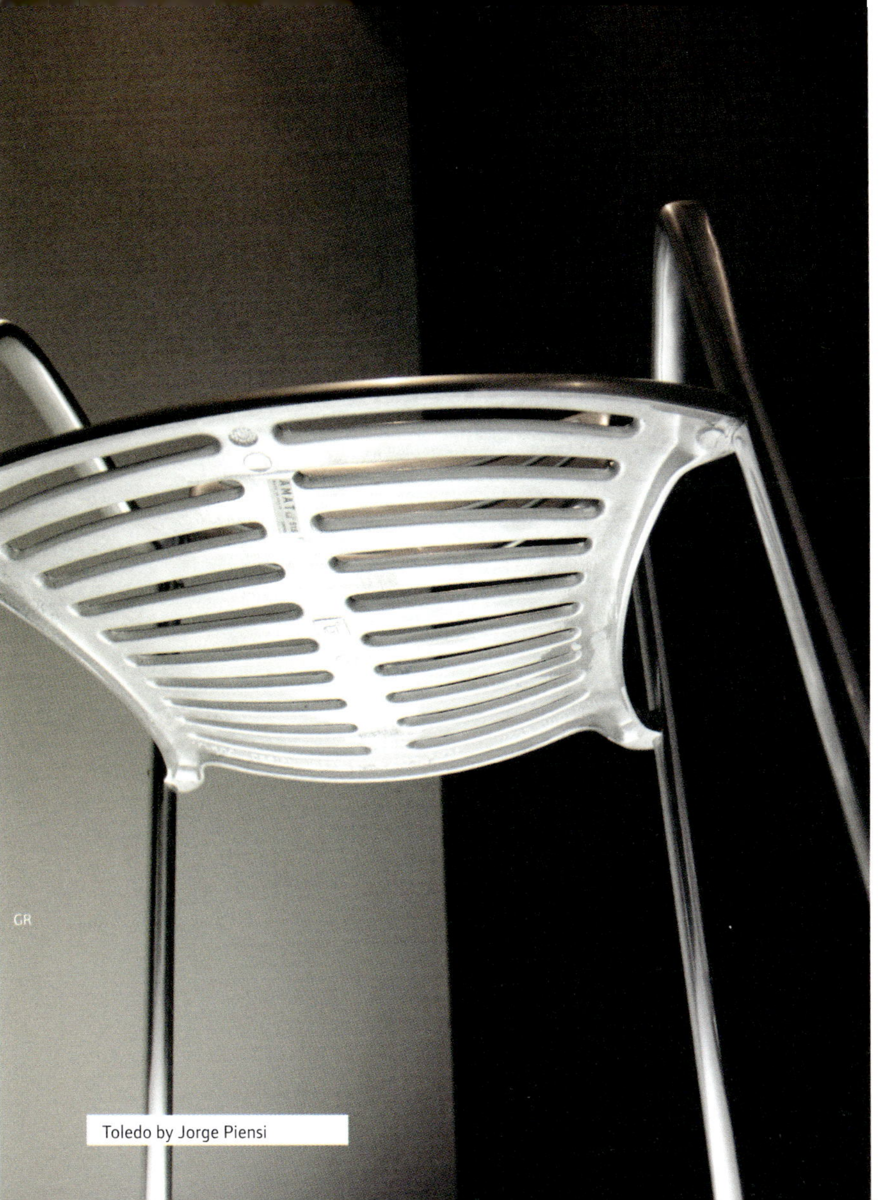

Toledo by Jorge Piensi

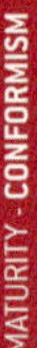

Molteni

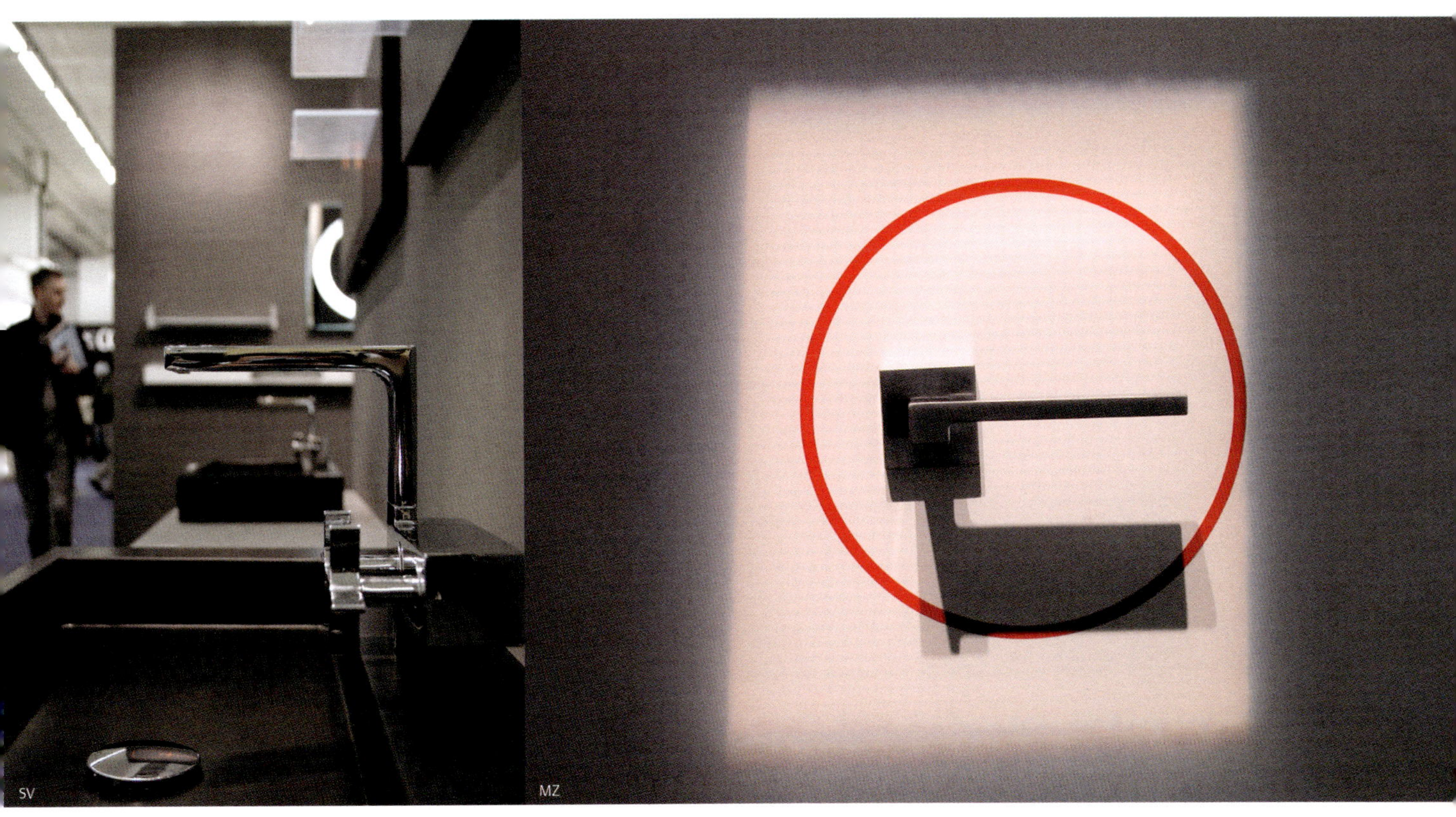

Merati

Bisazza

IMS Italia

Matteo Grassi

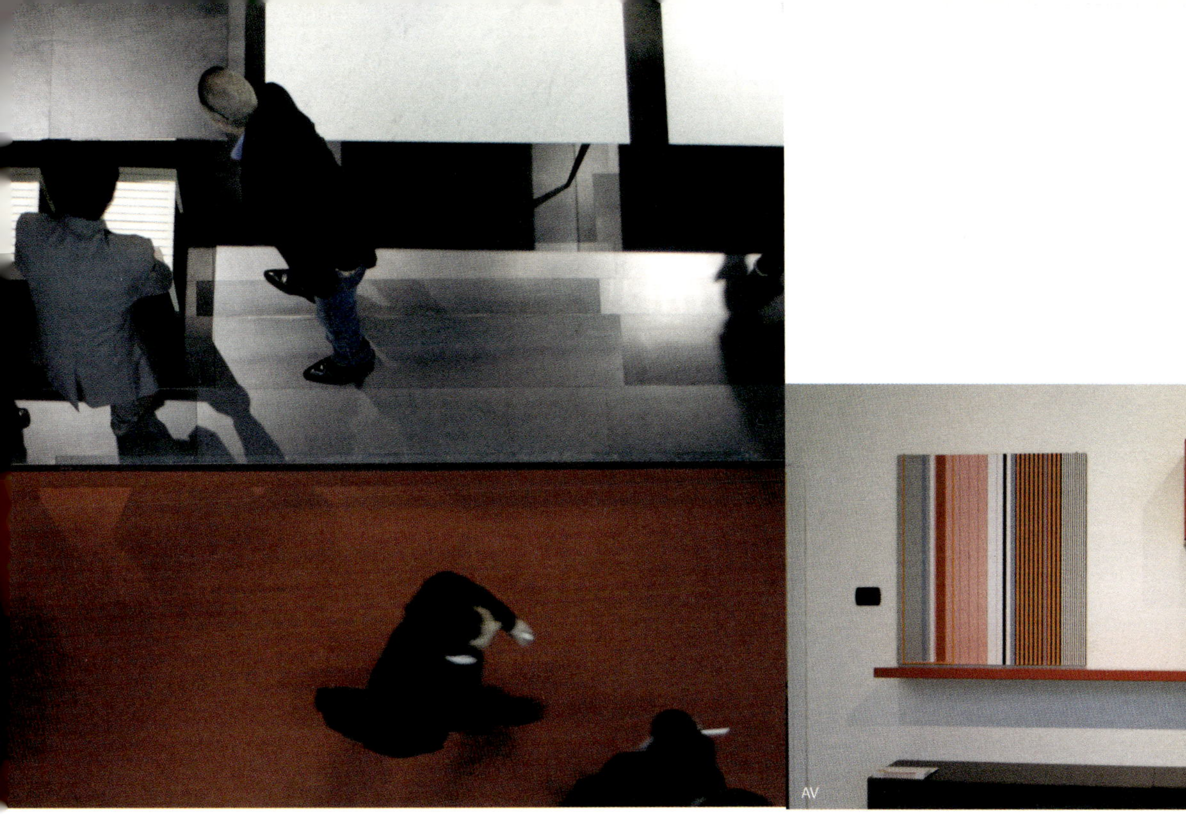

Targa Italia

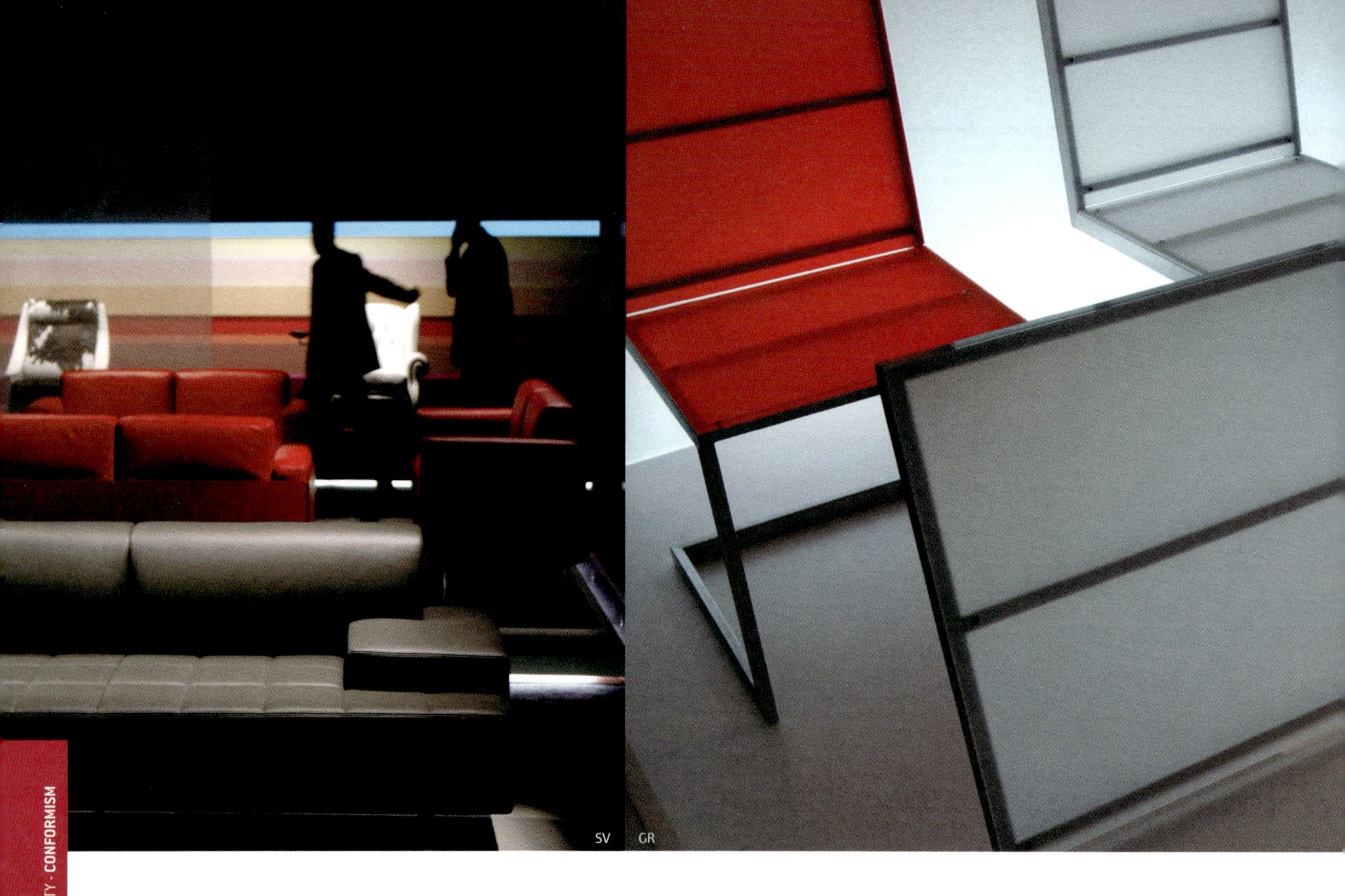

346   Poltrona Frau   Luna" by Ramon Esteve

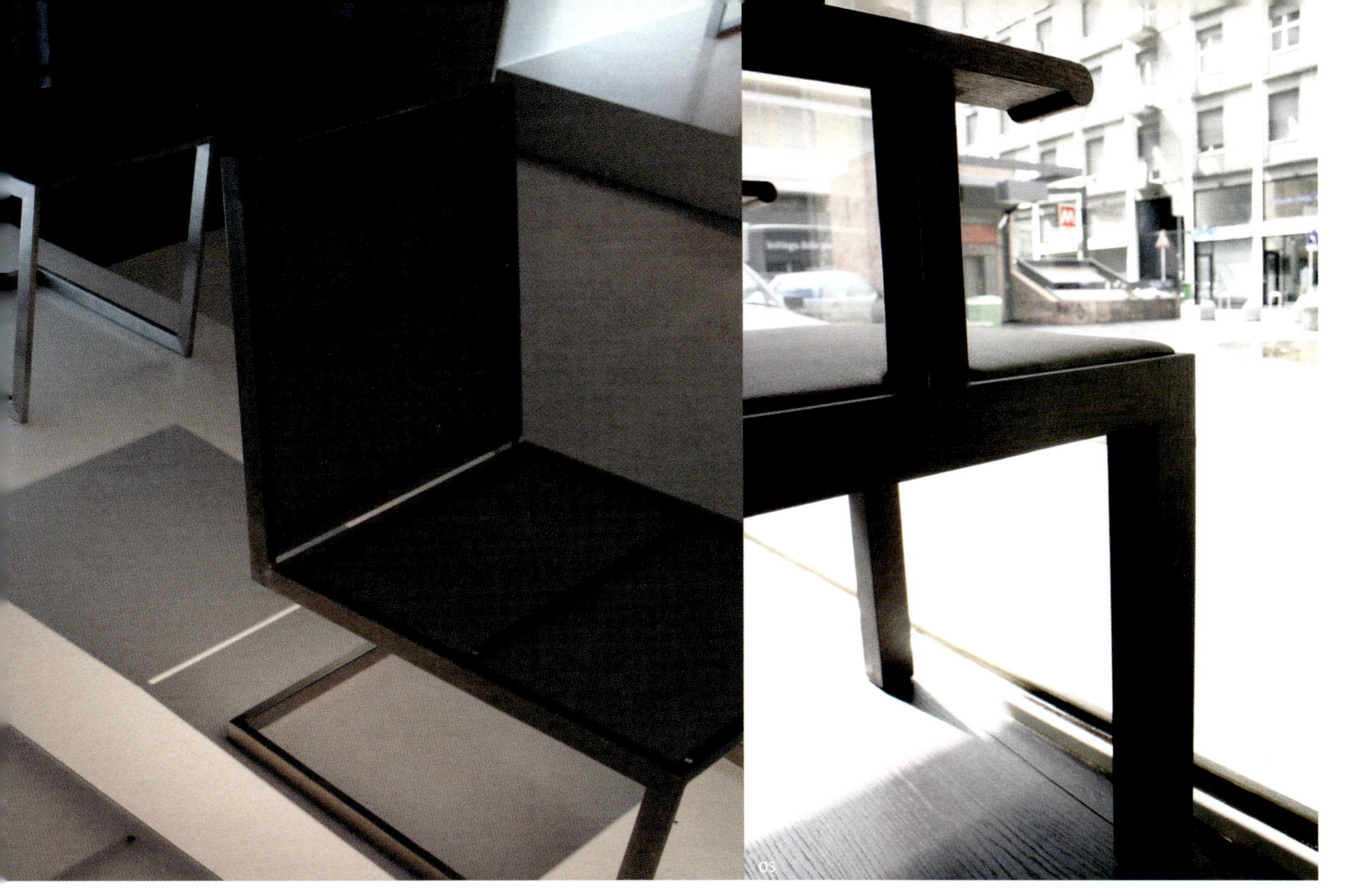

Molteni

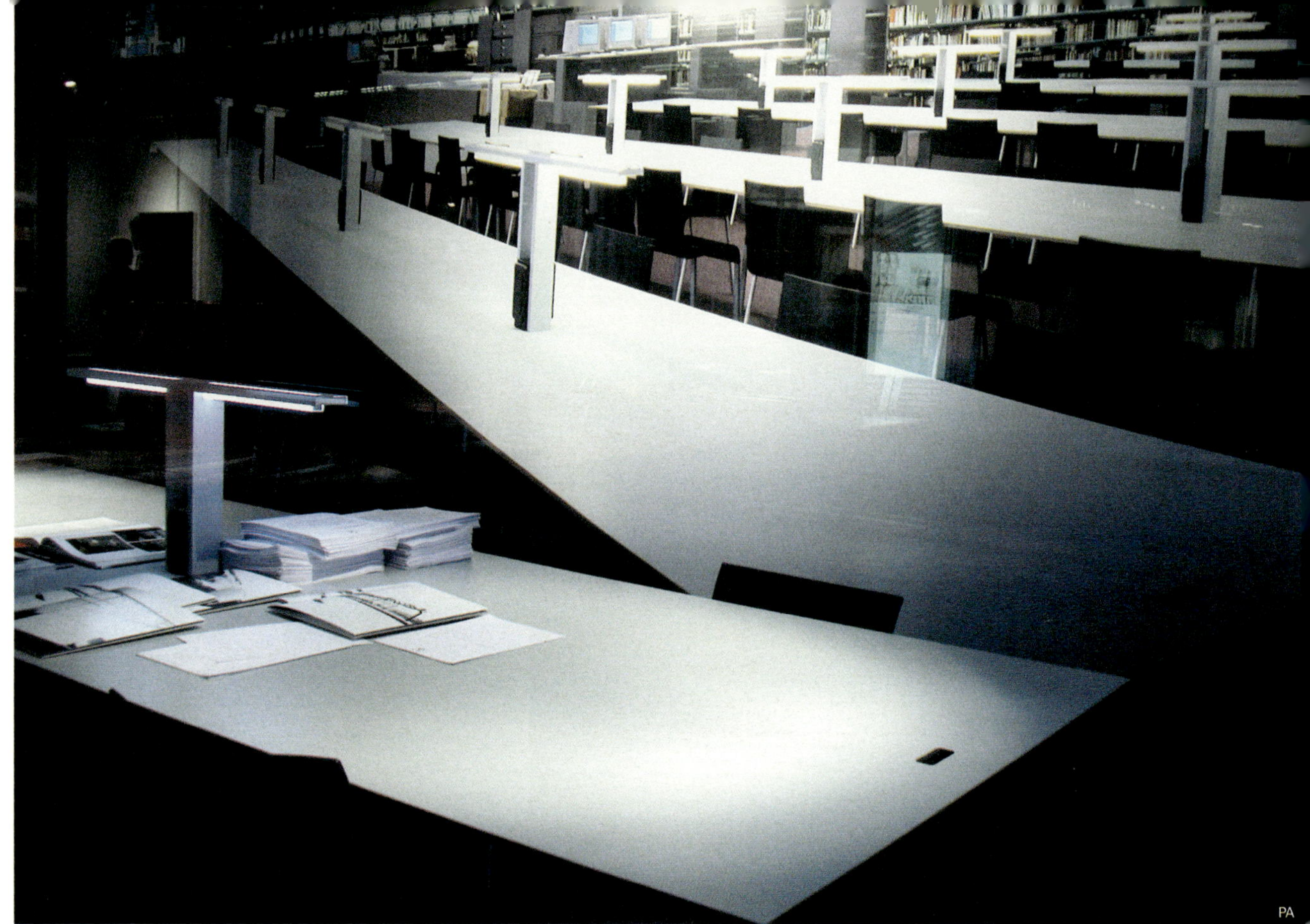

 Tecno

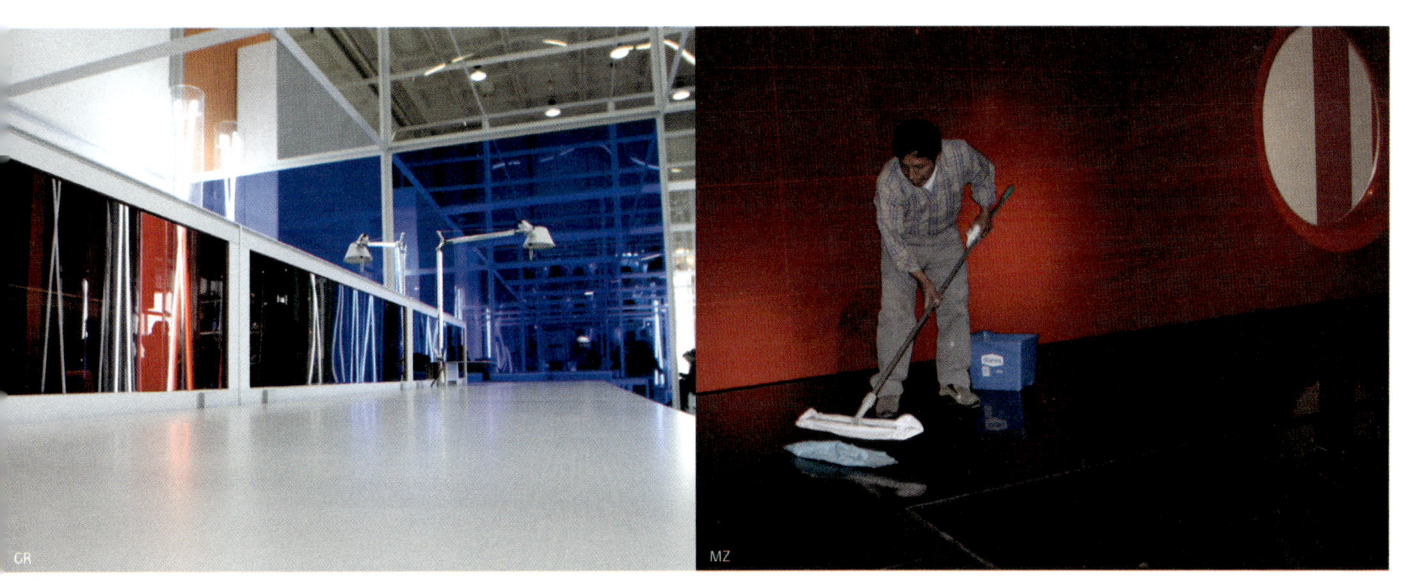

Bisazza @ Zona Tortona

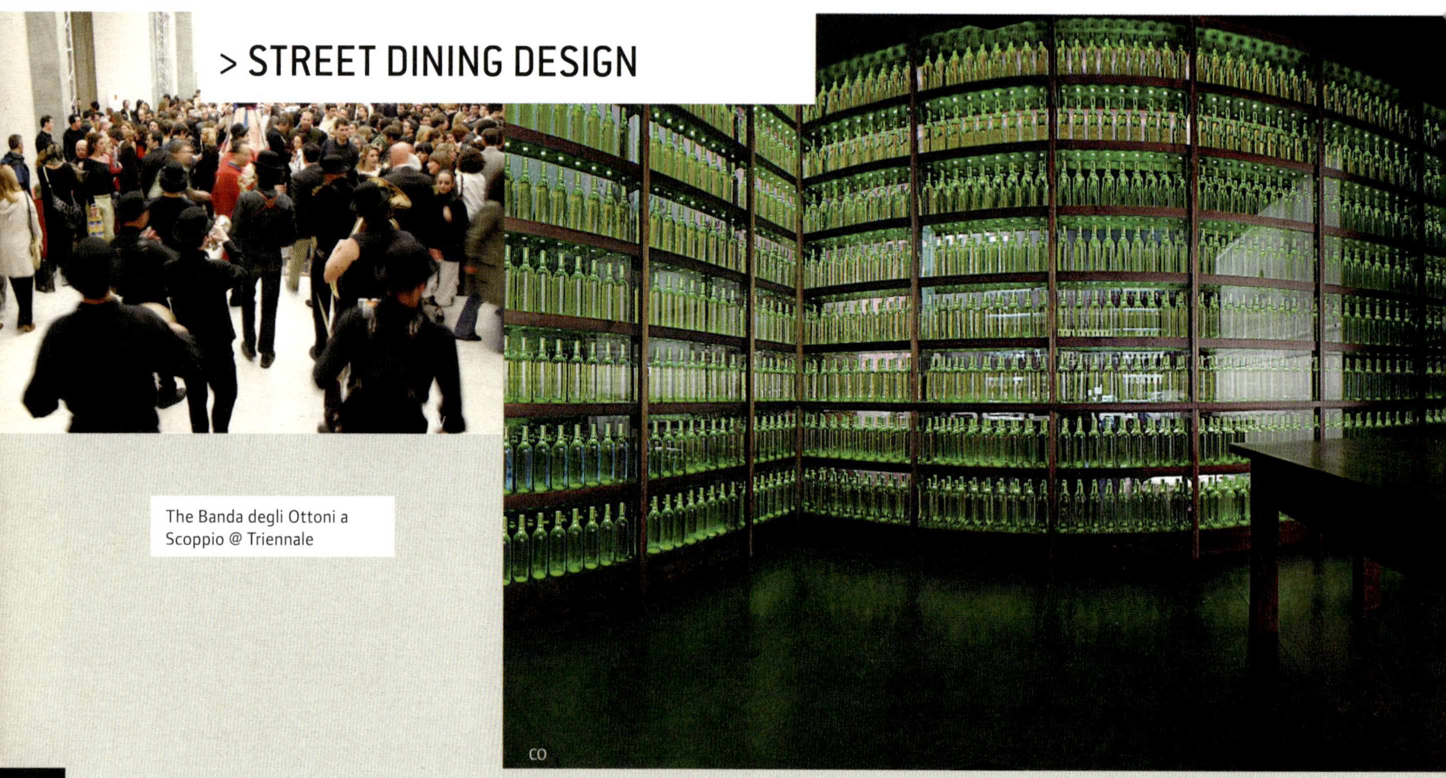

The Banda degli Ottoni a
Scoppio @ Triennale

STREET DINING DESIGN

INTERNI presented at the Triennale di Milano, **Street Dining Design**, an exhibition of food consumption projects through

the expression of different contemporary Interior Architectures with the participation of new designers.

The exhibition showed **10 Kiosk**s, designed by architects/designers and characterised by strong experimentation

in terms of design, which created an architectural itinerary connected to theconception of spaces for people

in the streets, and a gastronomic itinerary with different types of food to eat while standing, at different moments during the day.

Ten famous designers have been invited to interpret this theme: they belong to the last generation of designers and their

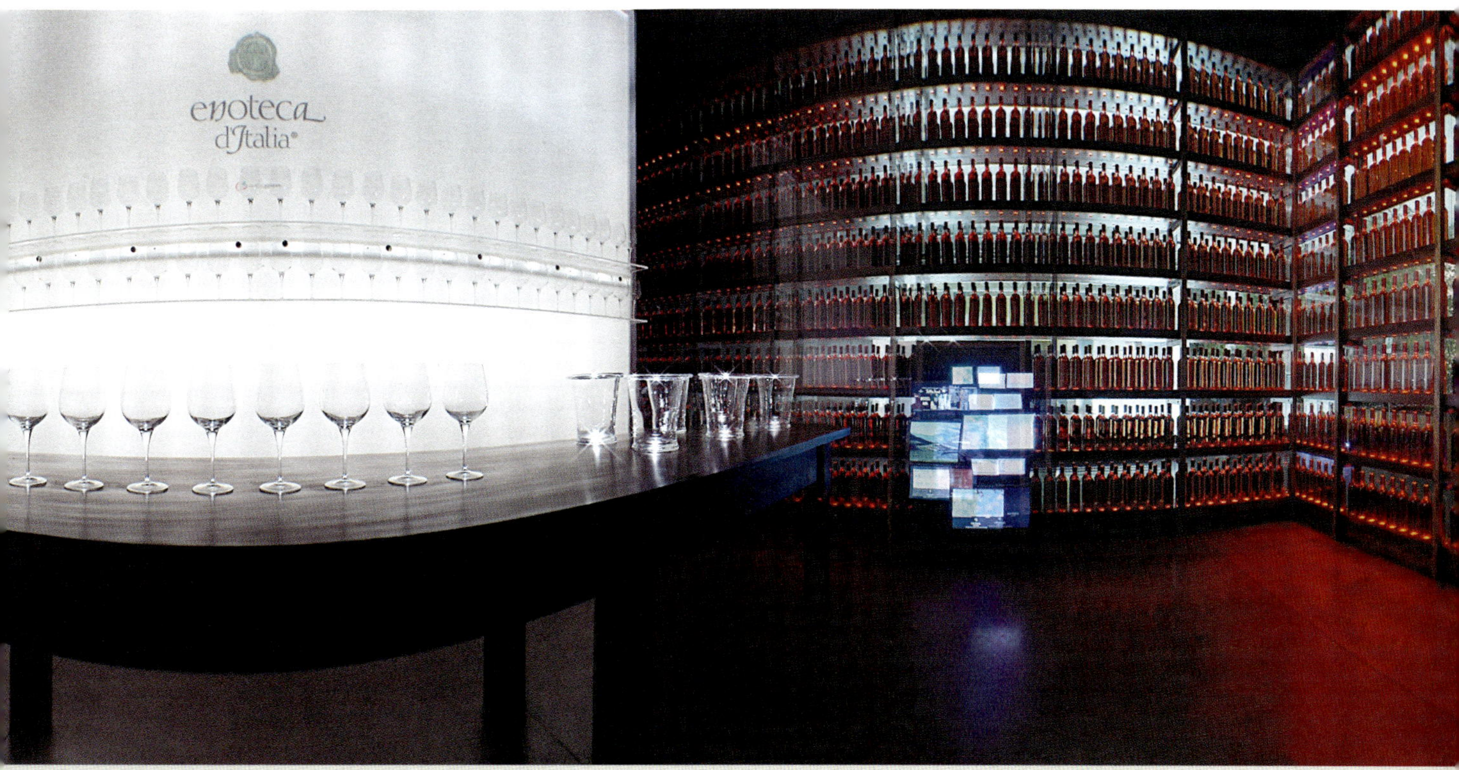

Kiosks were made with the technical contribution of sponsoring companies for their construction and food distribution.

Great importance was devoted to the packaging and graphics of: cups, napkins, coasters.

Each space was operating and was furnished to host guests and visitors who would

try creative menus from breakfast to the cocktail hour, from lunch to the happy hour.

"Enoteca" by Claudio Monti & Francesco Muti with Cenacchi and Enoteca d'Italia

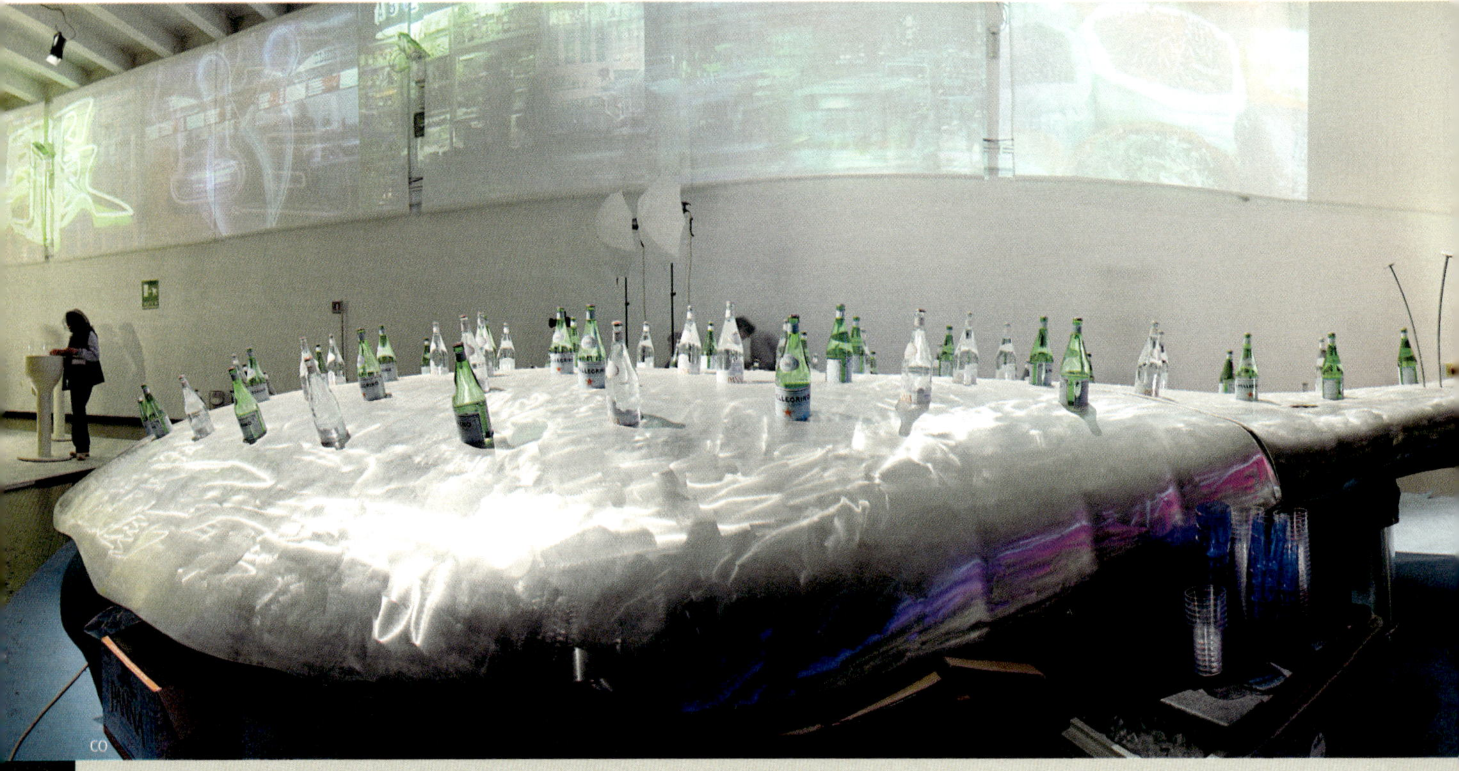

"Acquae" by Future Systems with Marzorati Ronchetti and S.Pellegrino, Acqua Panna

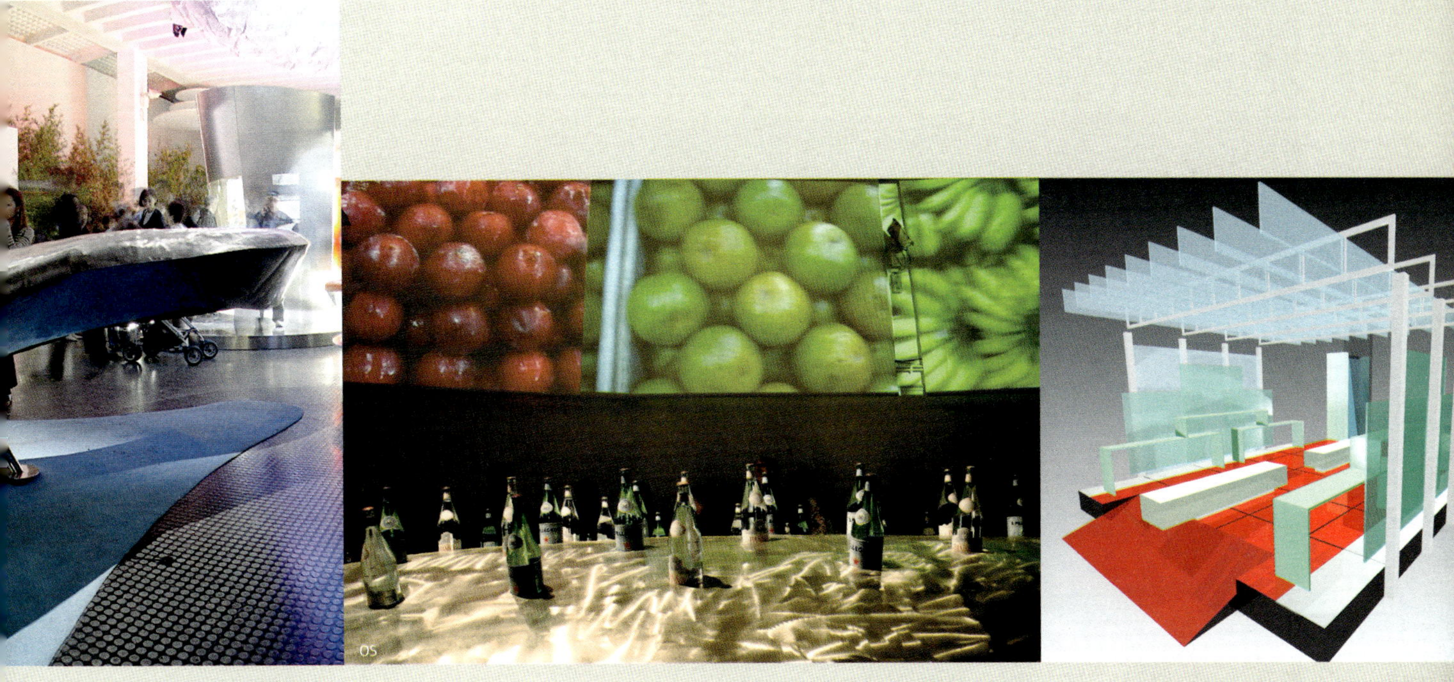

"Fine Chocolate Glass Garden" by Studio Sigla

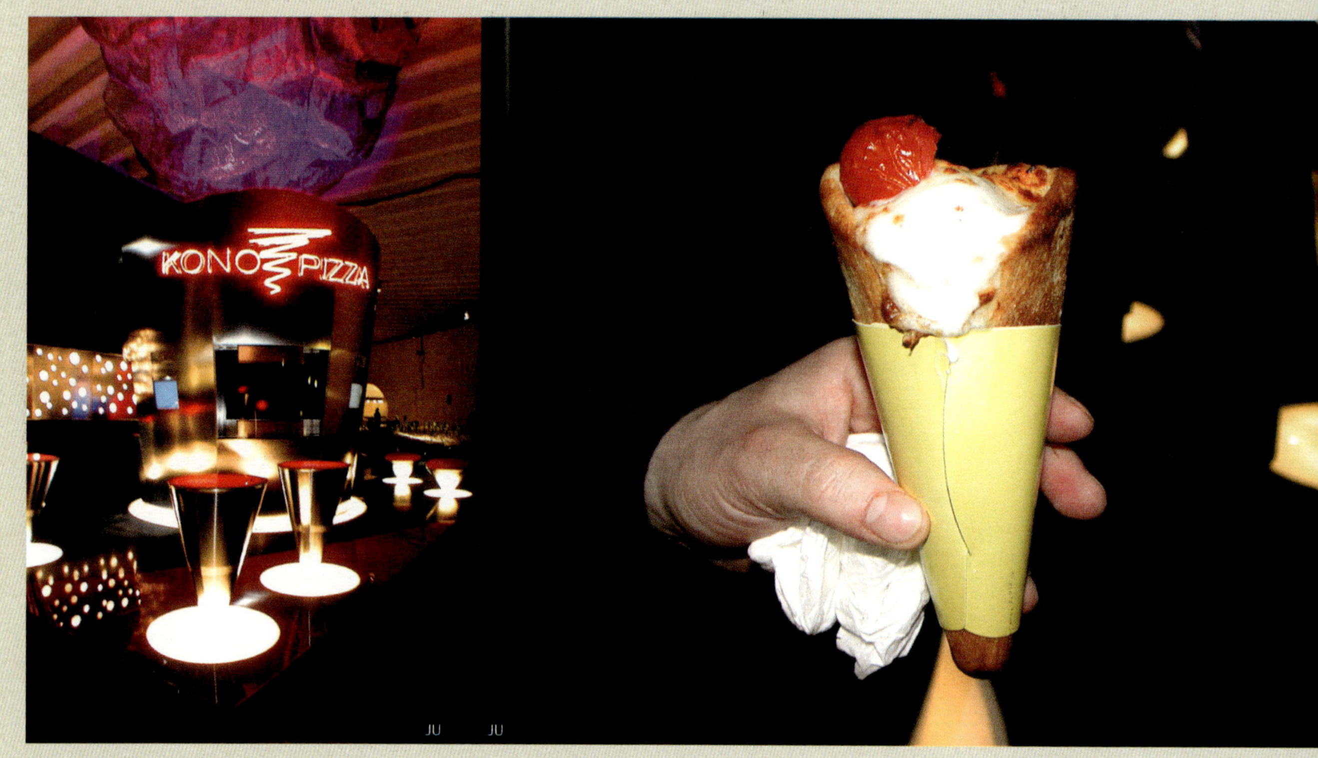

"Kono Pizza" by Marco Piva with GMC Contract&Mobili and Boscolo Etoile

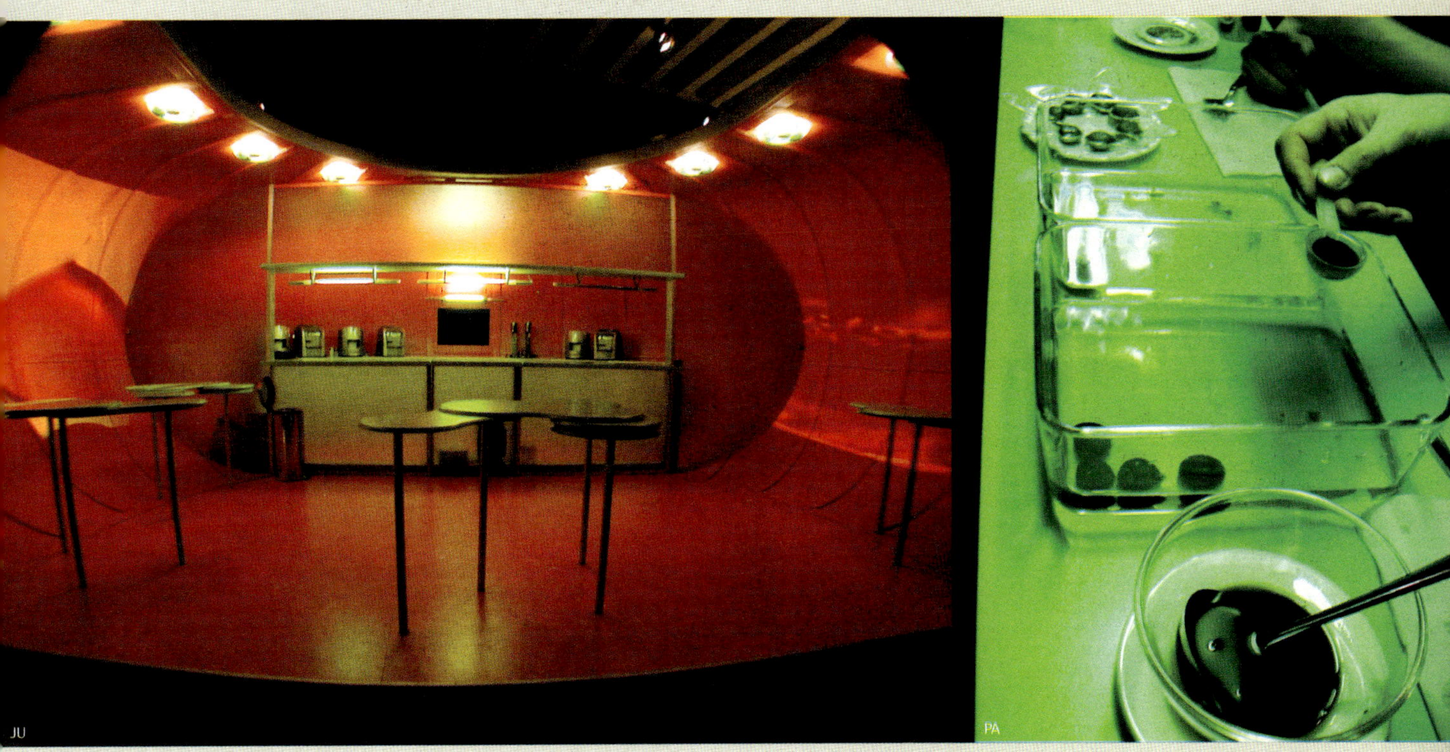

"Biomorphic Cafe" by Karim Azzabi with Lavazza, Mostre e Fiere and Ferran Adria'

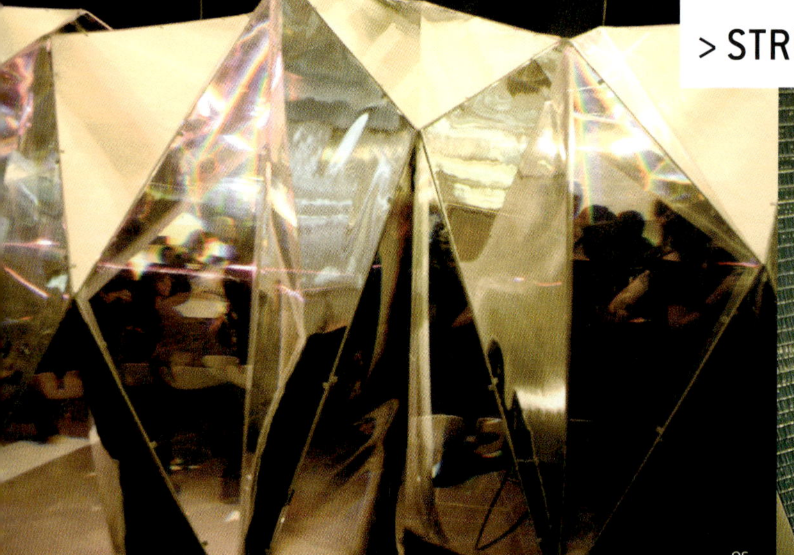

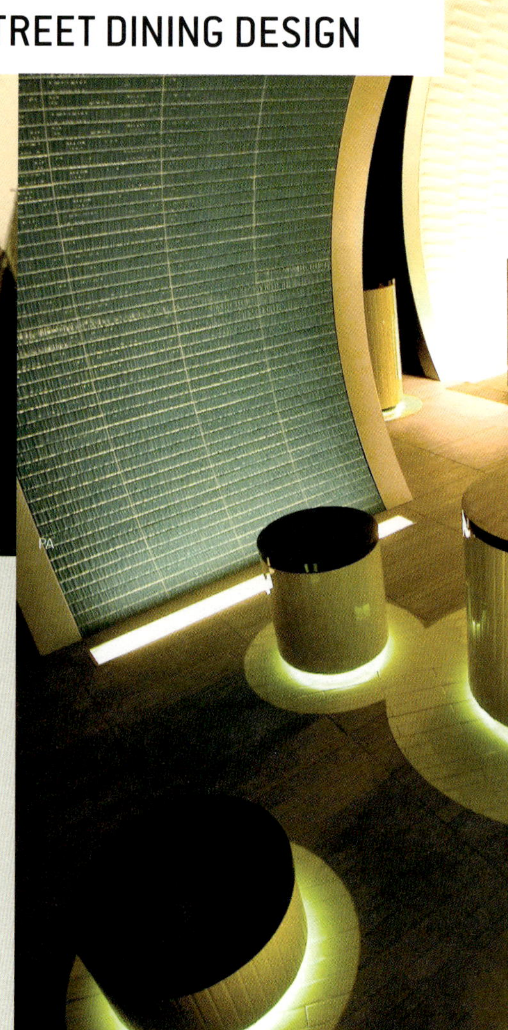

356

"Risotteria" by Patricia Urquiola & Martino Berghinz with Scholtes

"Bubble Blog" by Diego Grandi with Laurent Perrier and Carpene Malvolti/D&C

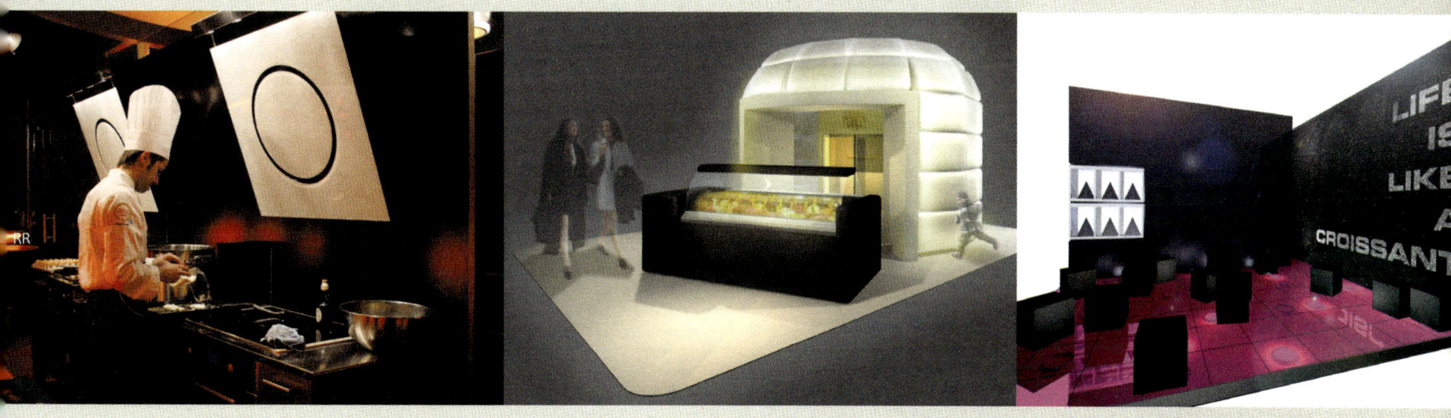

"Om FoodLoose" by Riccardo Diotallevi with Elica   "Gelateria" by Aldo Cibic & Partners   "Ice Croissanterie" by Simone Micheli

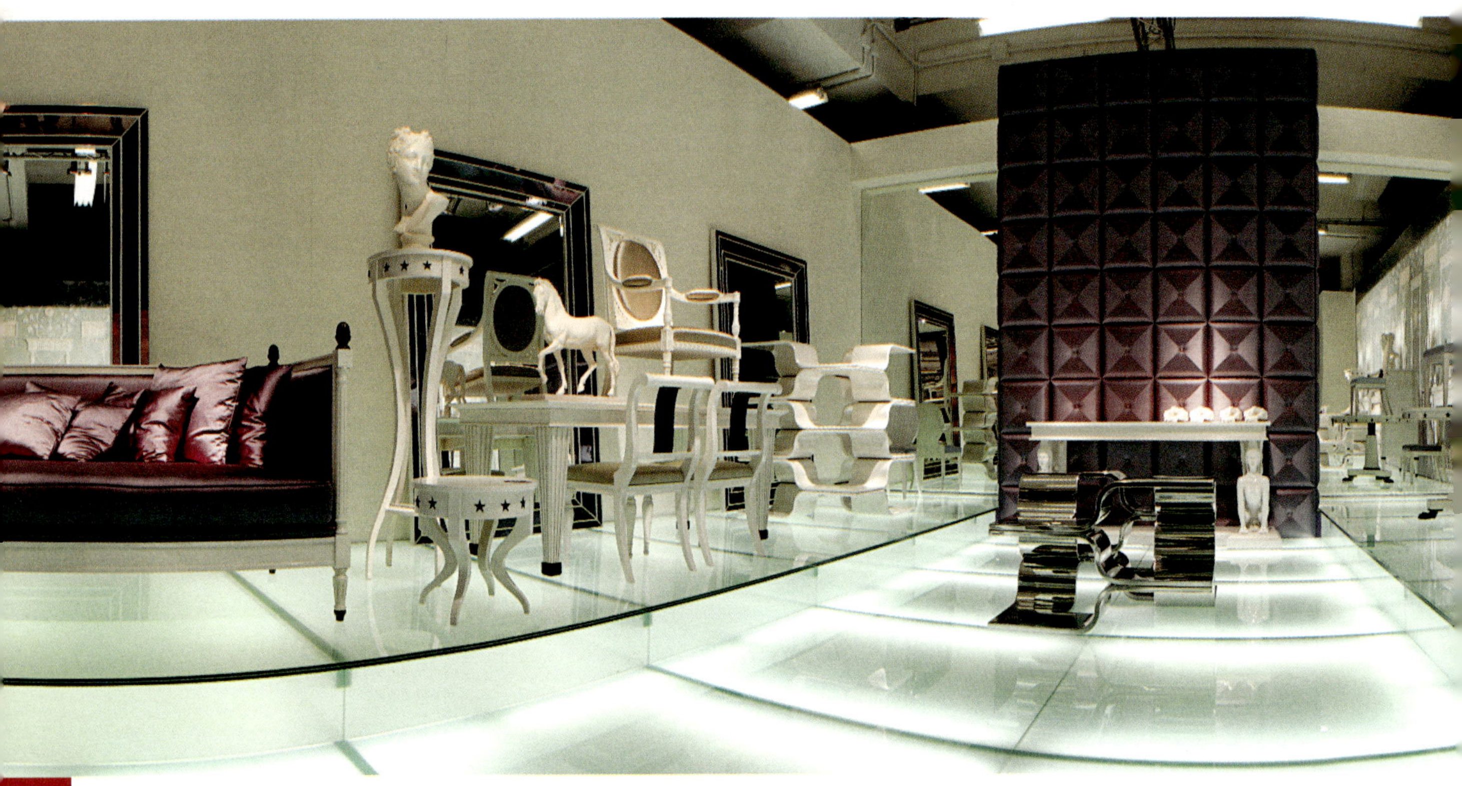

F.lli Boffi

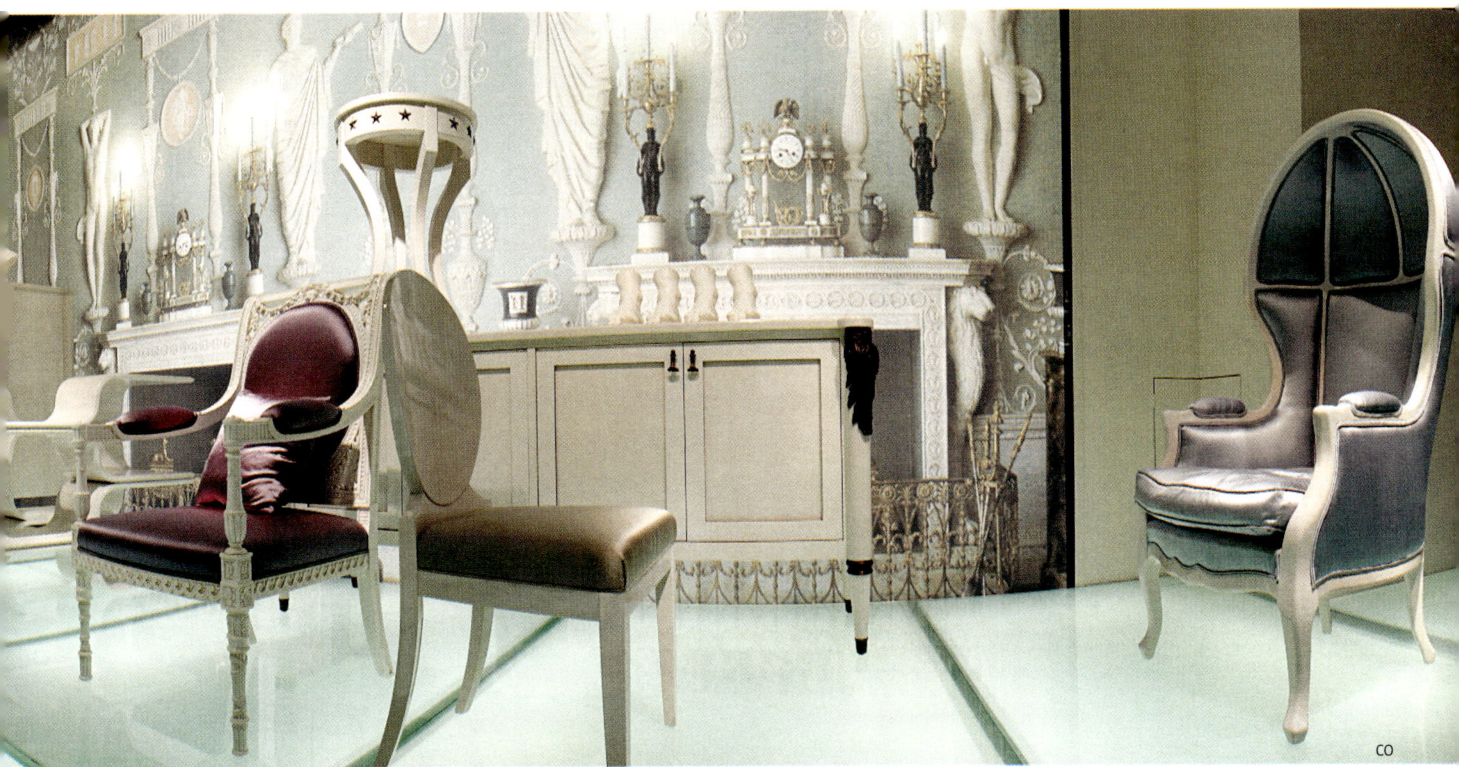

CO

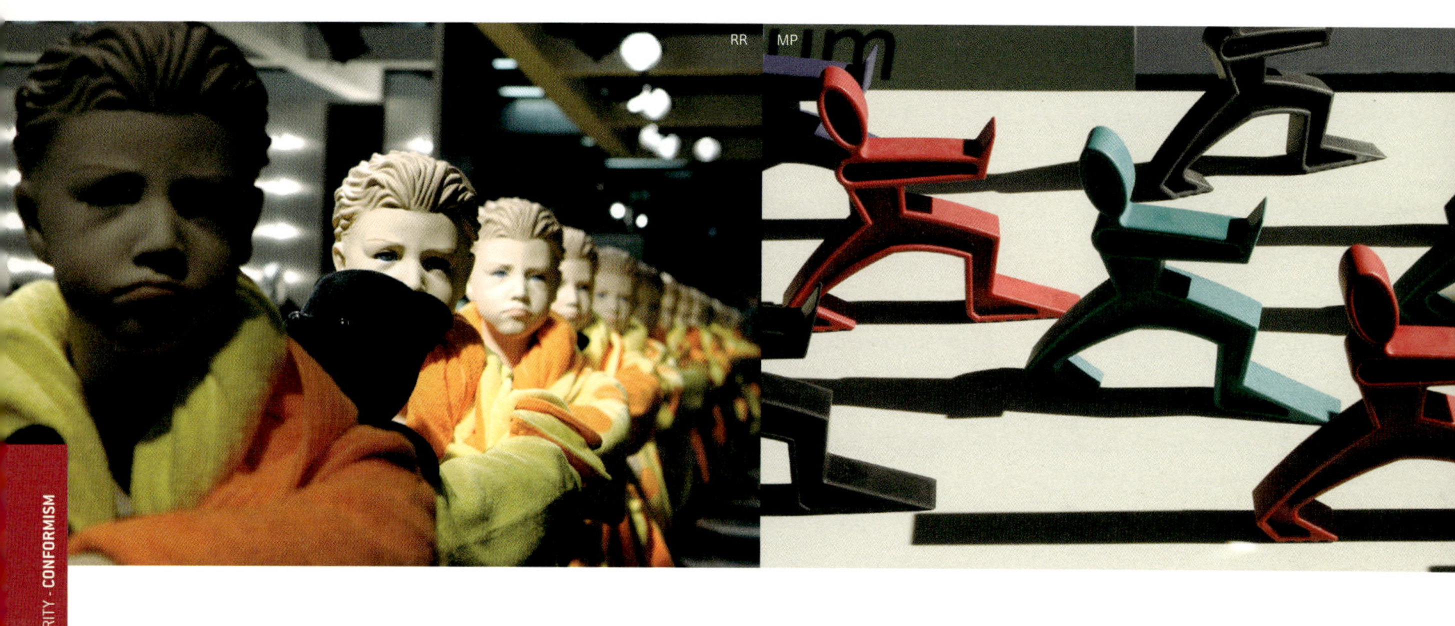

Carrara

Black & Blum

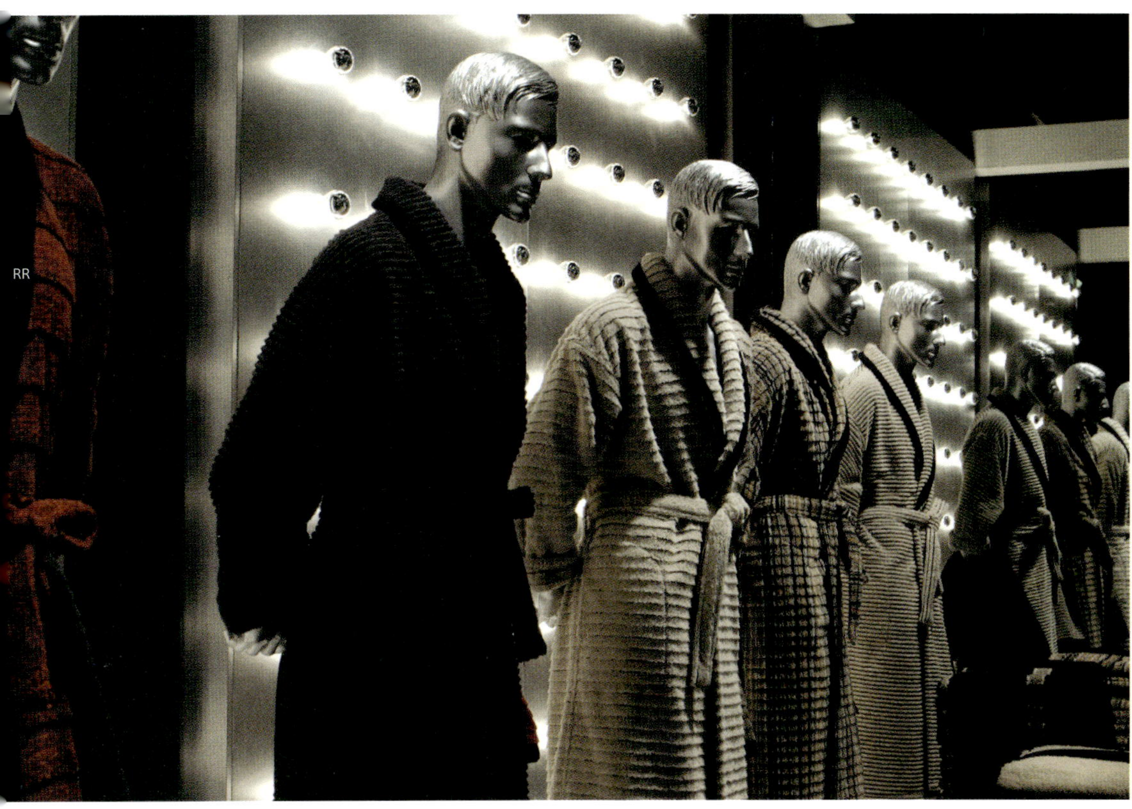

Carrara

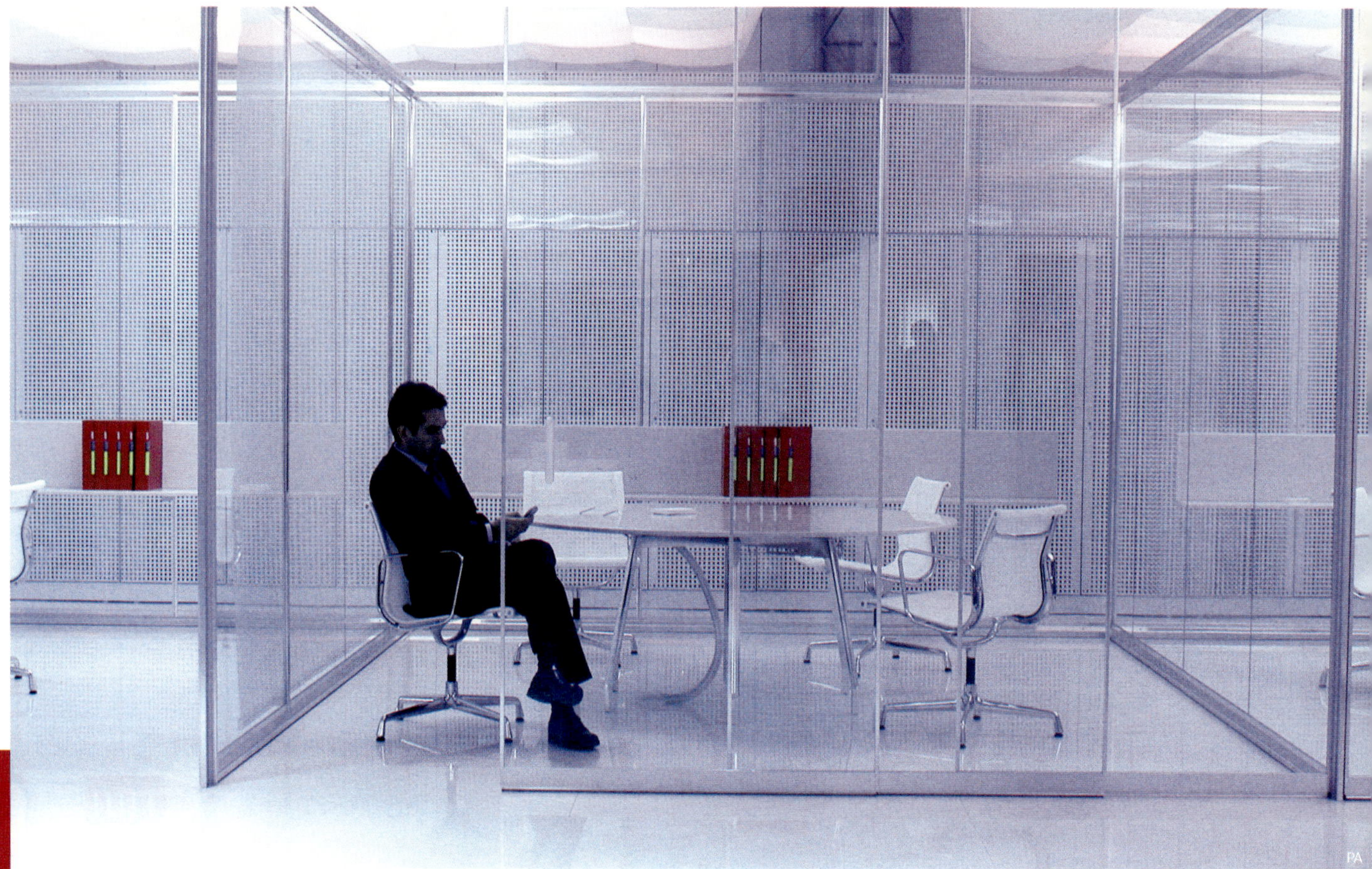

Unifor

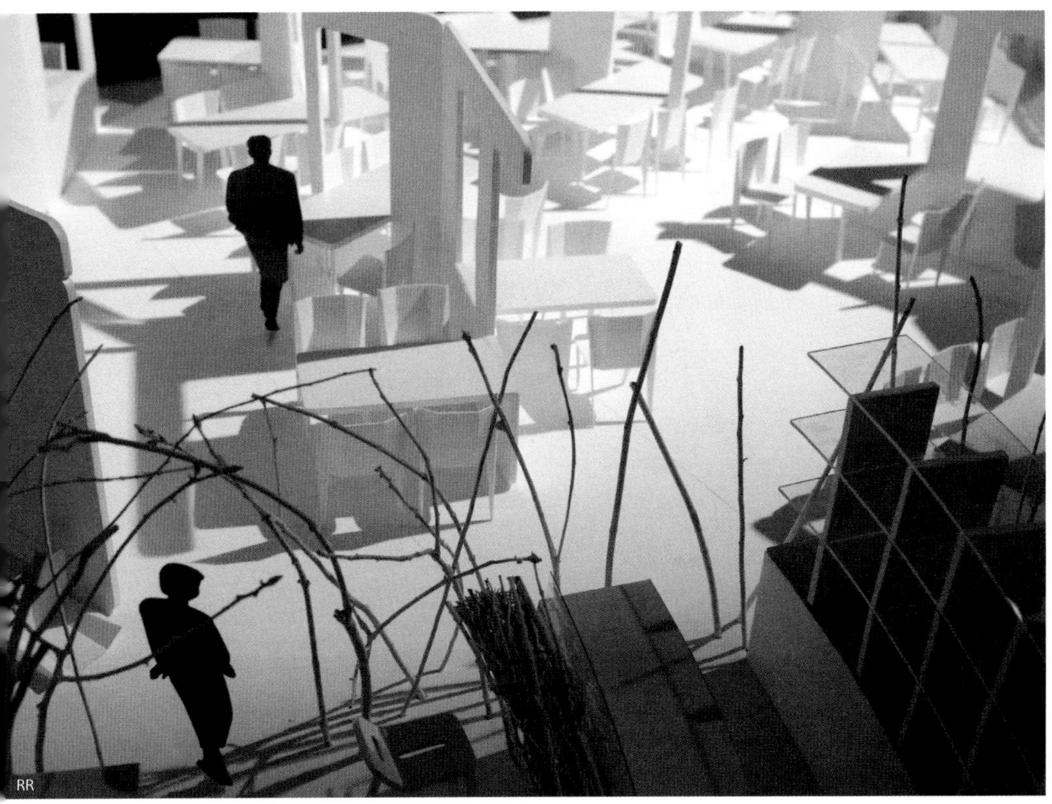

Pizzeria Fooo by Osaka University of Arts @ Dining Design exhibition..

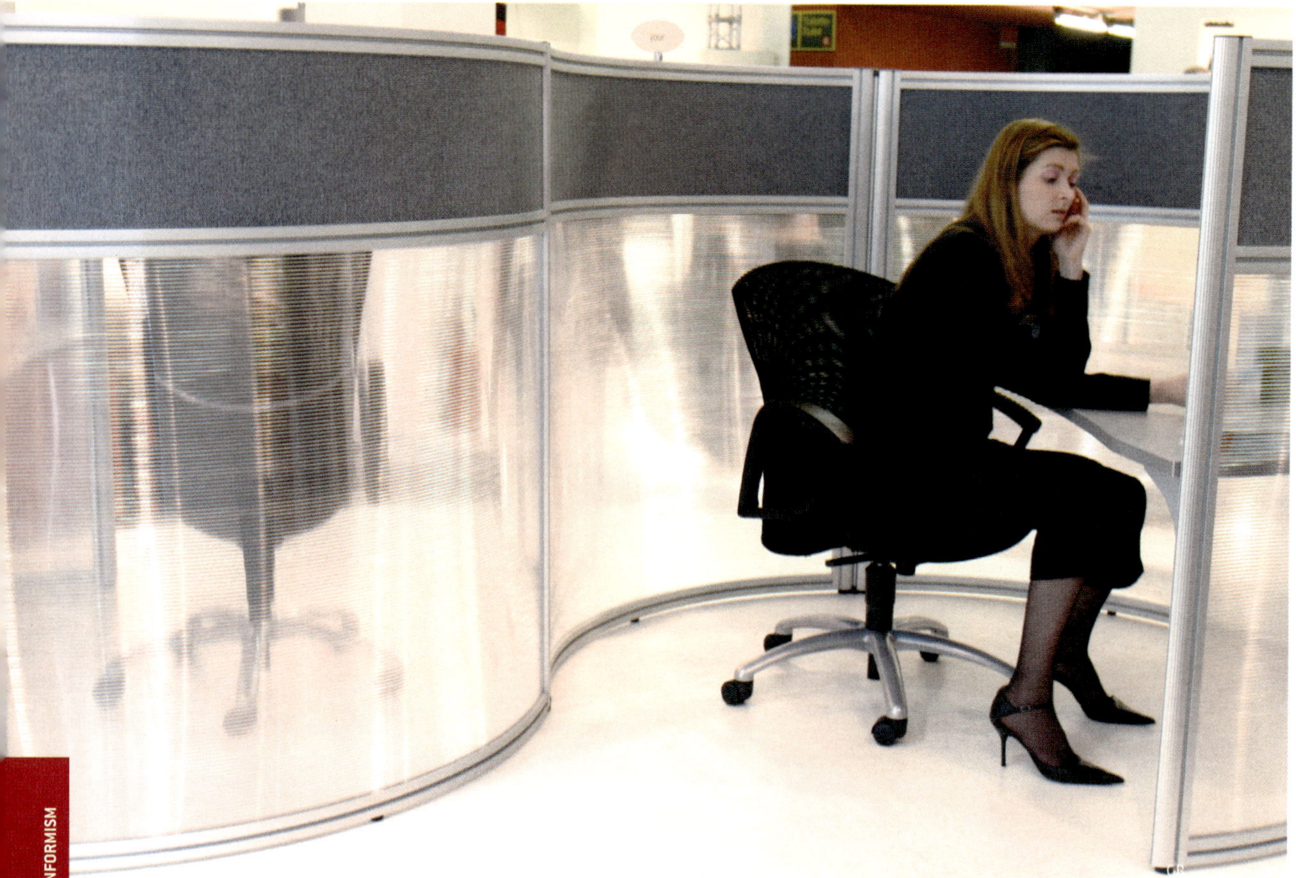

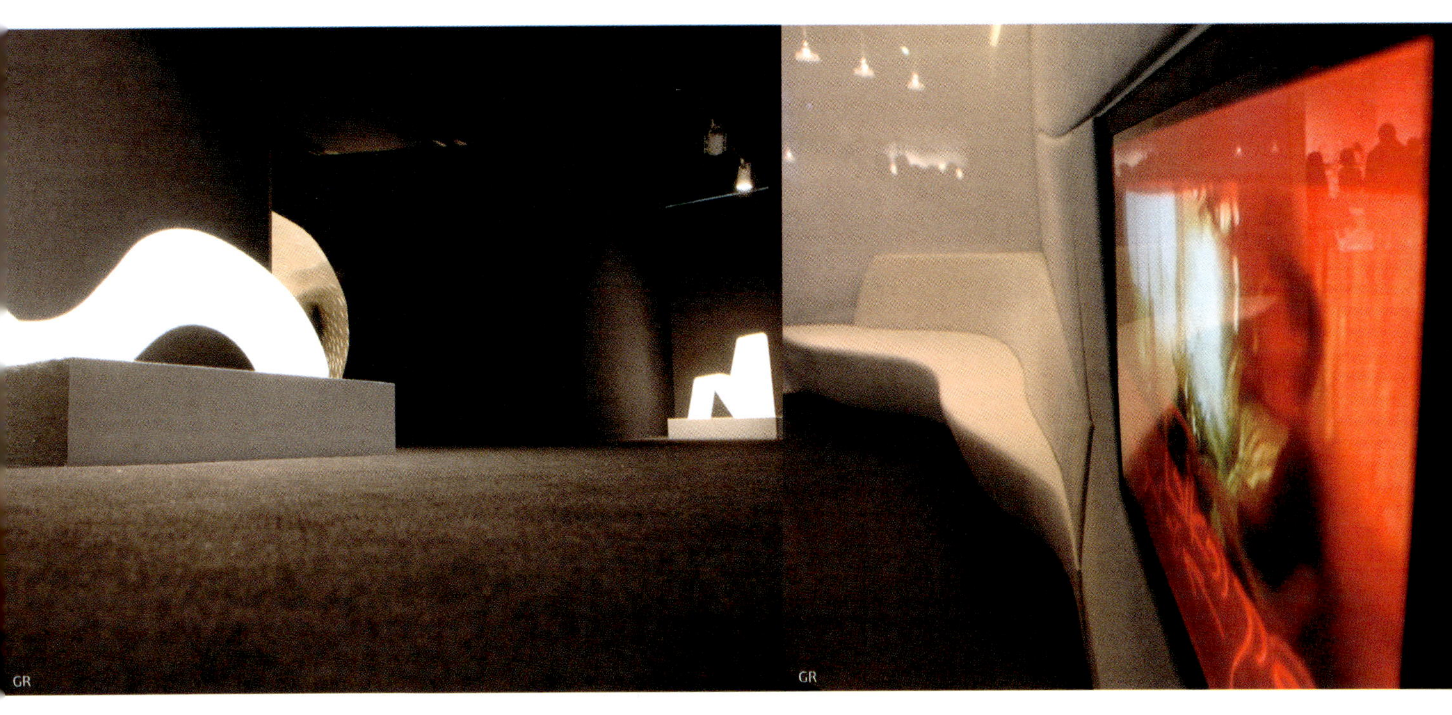

Kris Ruhs @ Galleria Carla Sozzani

Trace by Rhode Island School of Design

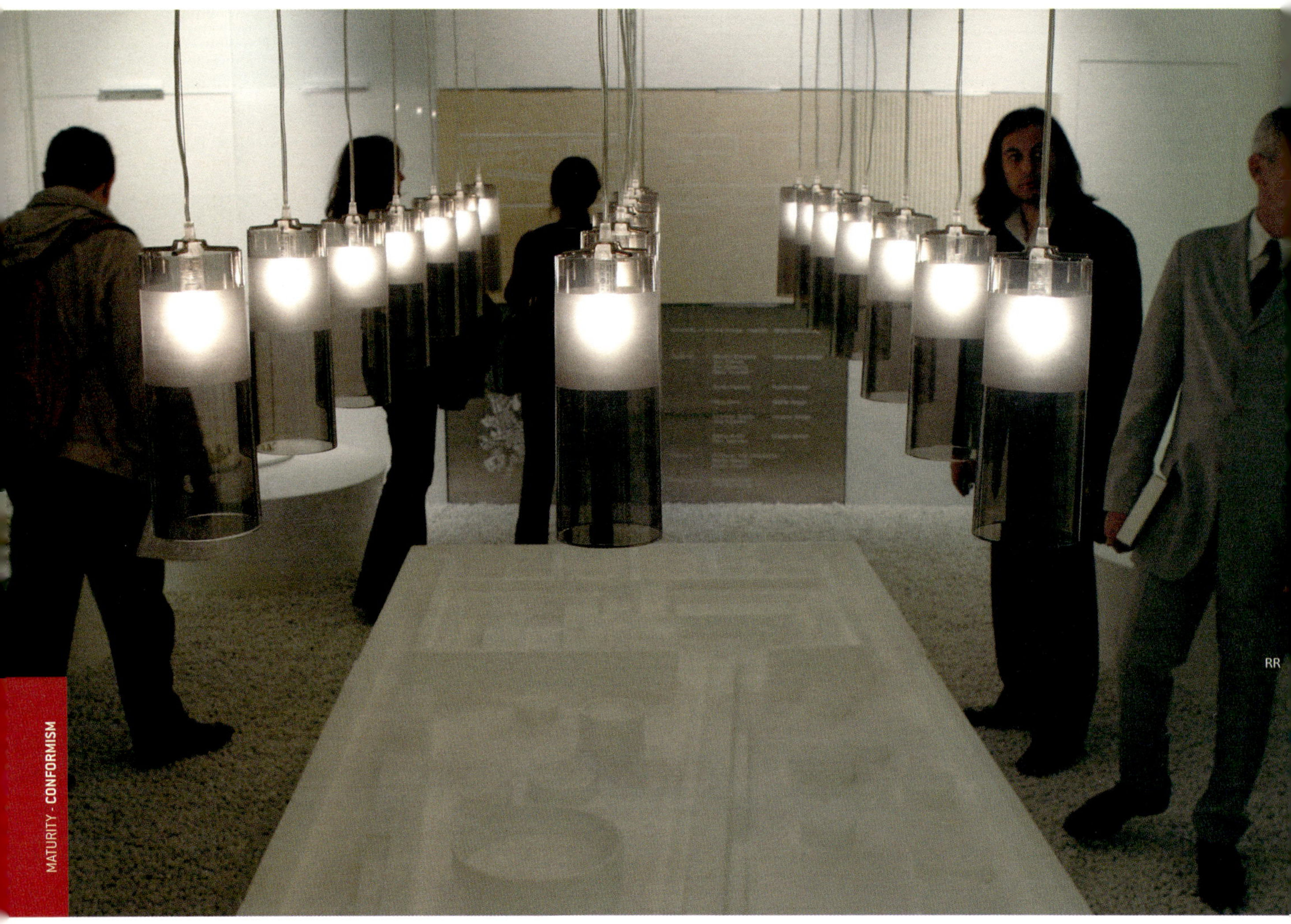

White by University of Art and Design Helsinki @ Dining Design exhibition

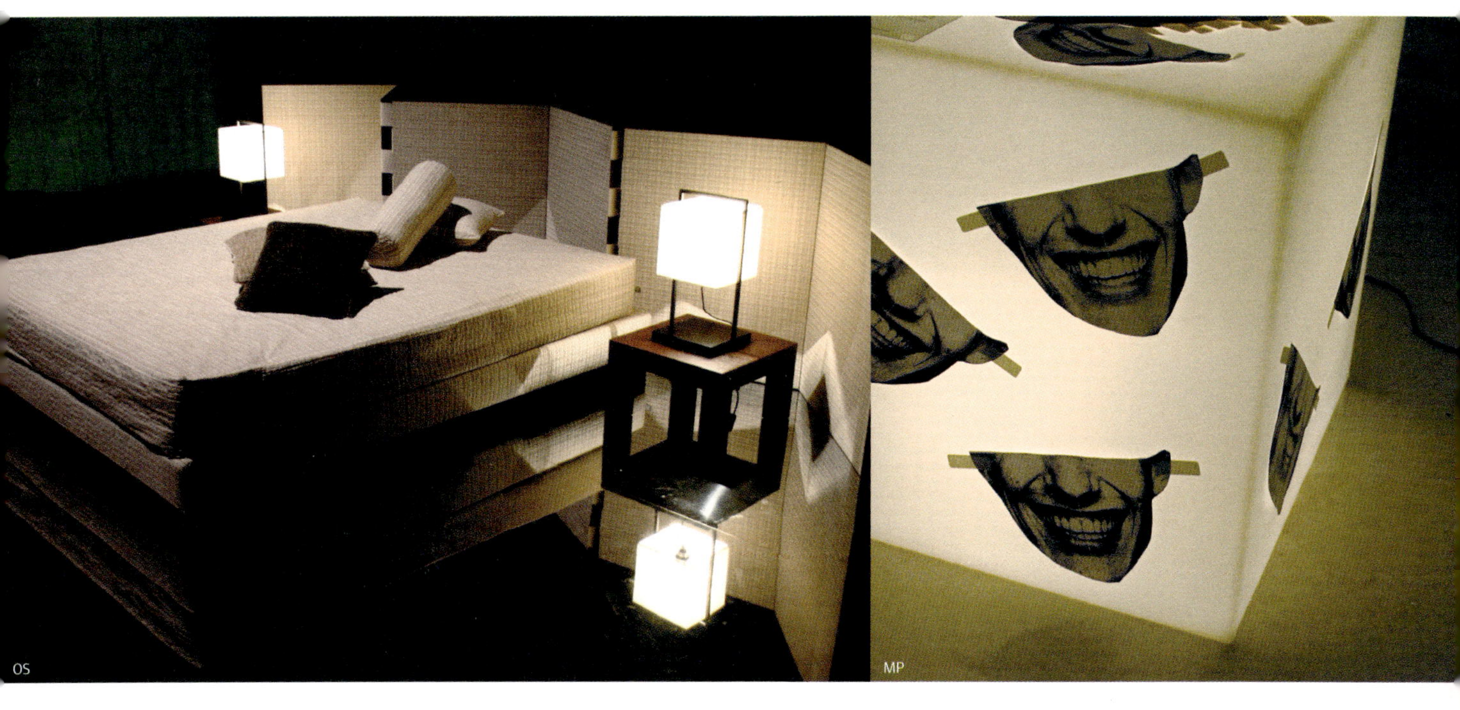

Armani   Daniela Caputo and Antonio Giuliodori

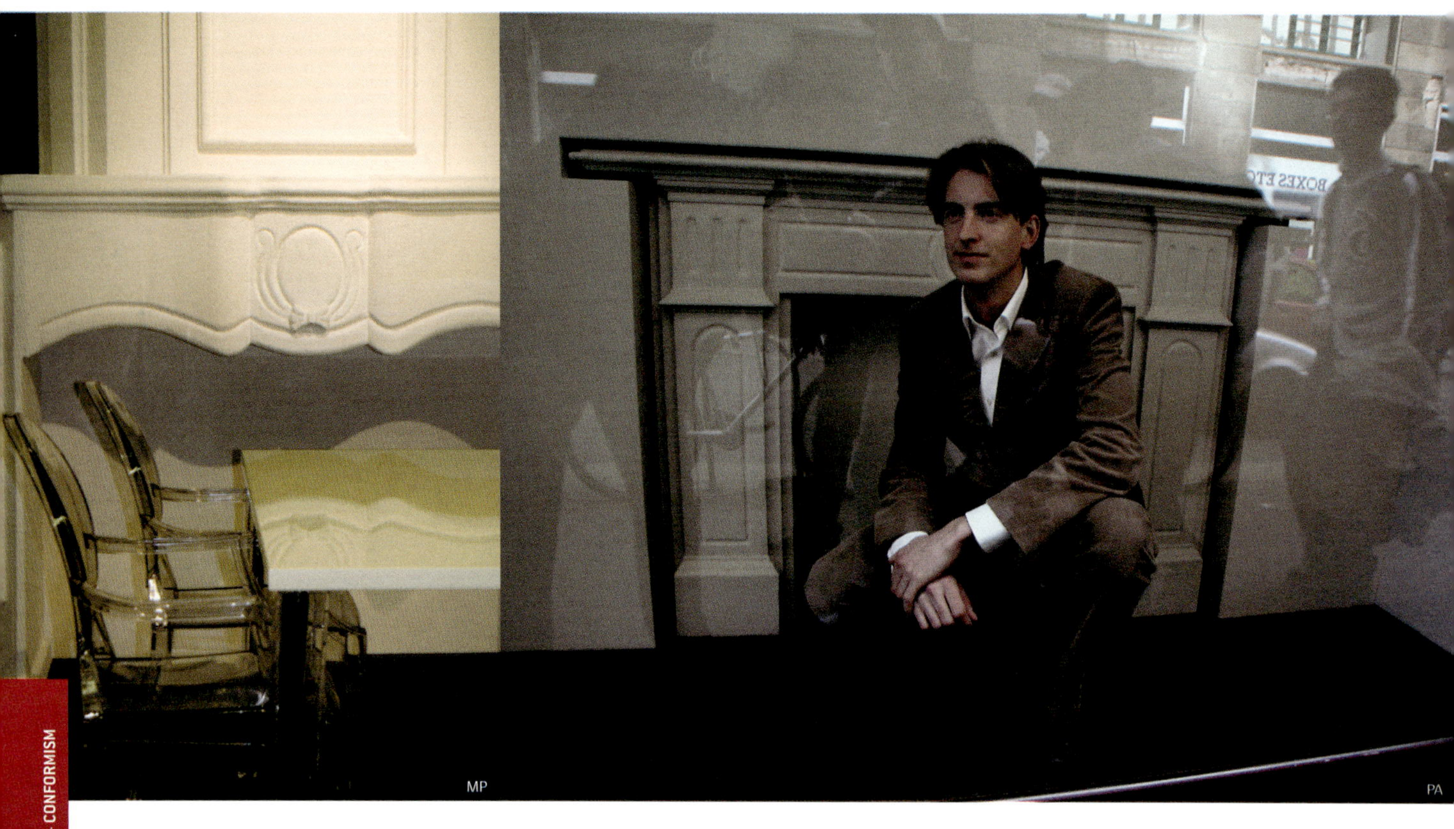

370   Kartell   Luc Schouten @ Design Academy Eindhoven

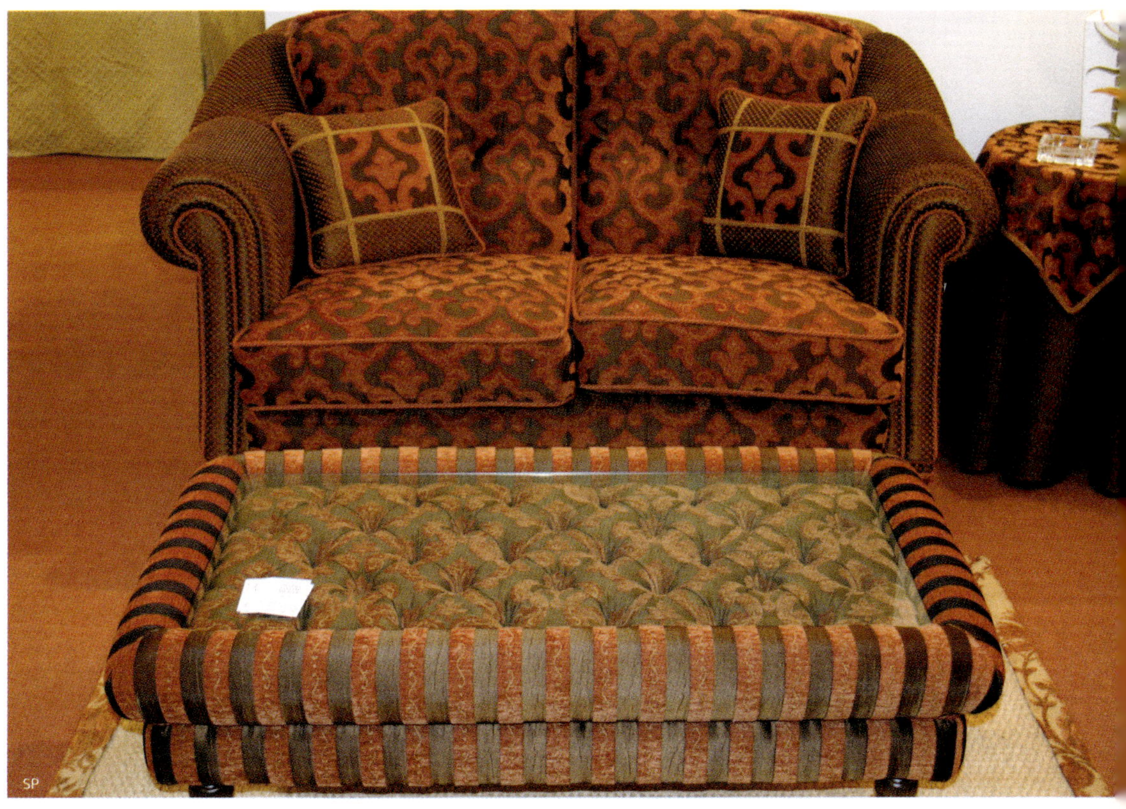

Galimberti Mario

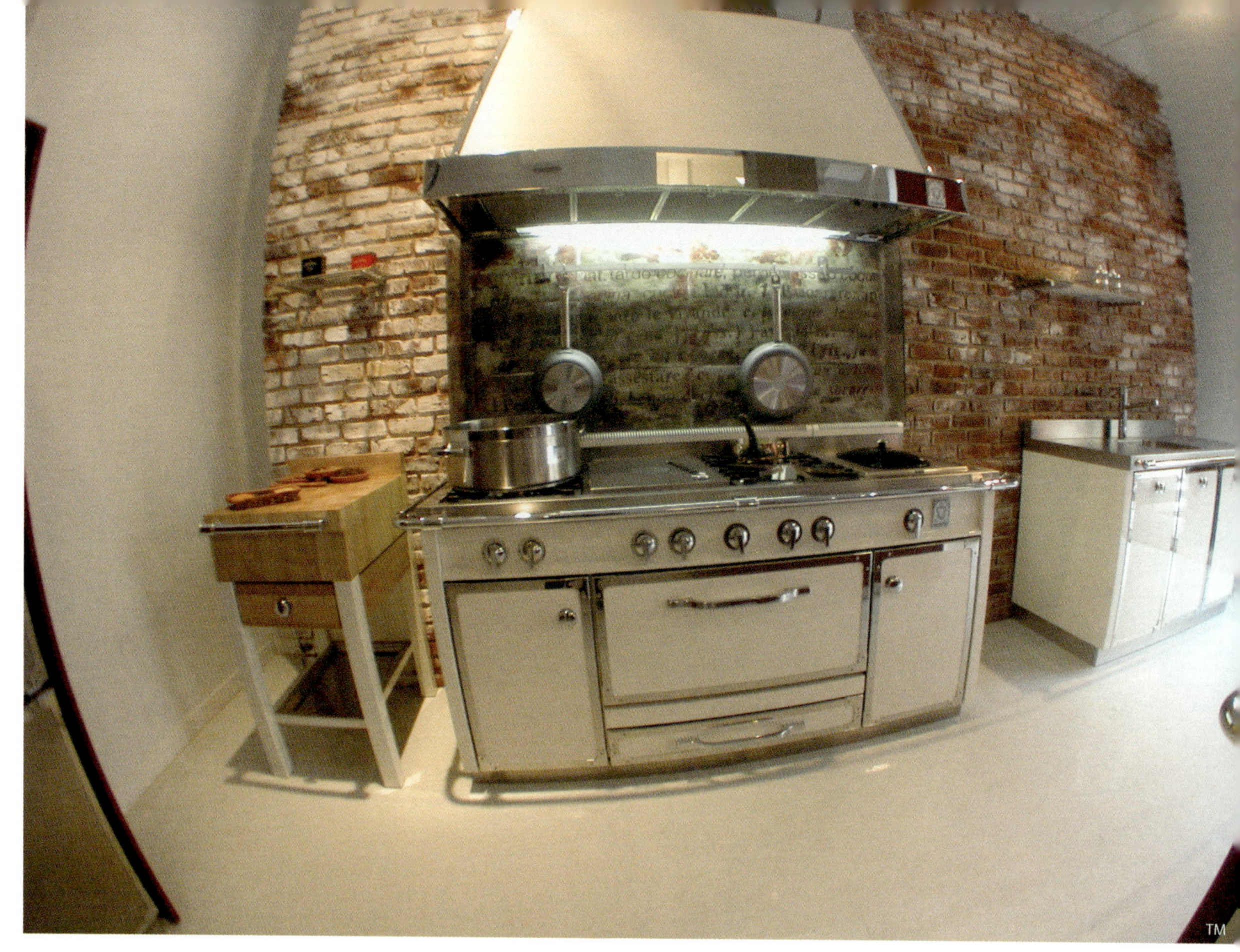

TM

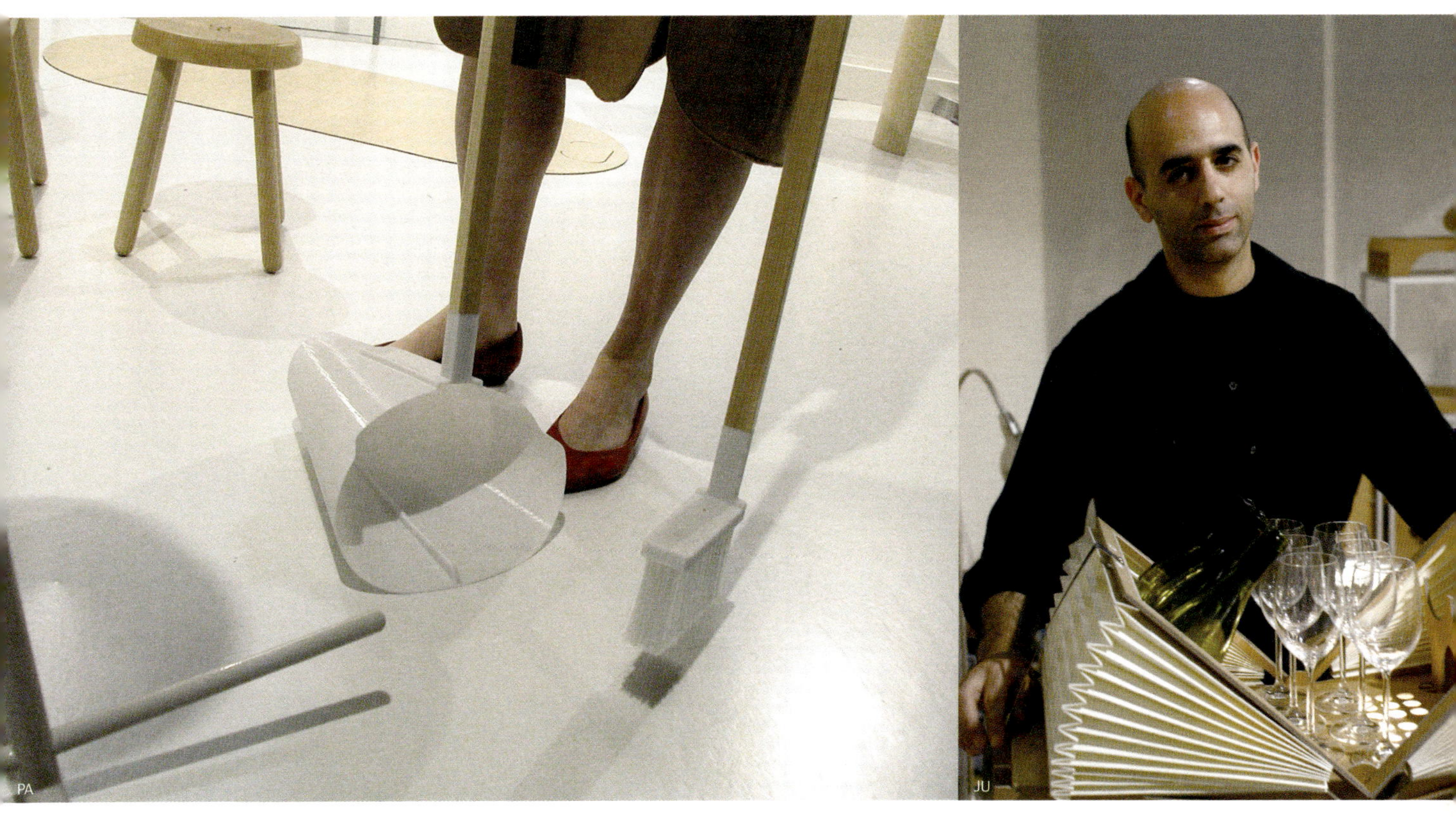

Leon Ransmeier @ Satellite

Store @ Satellite

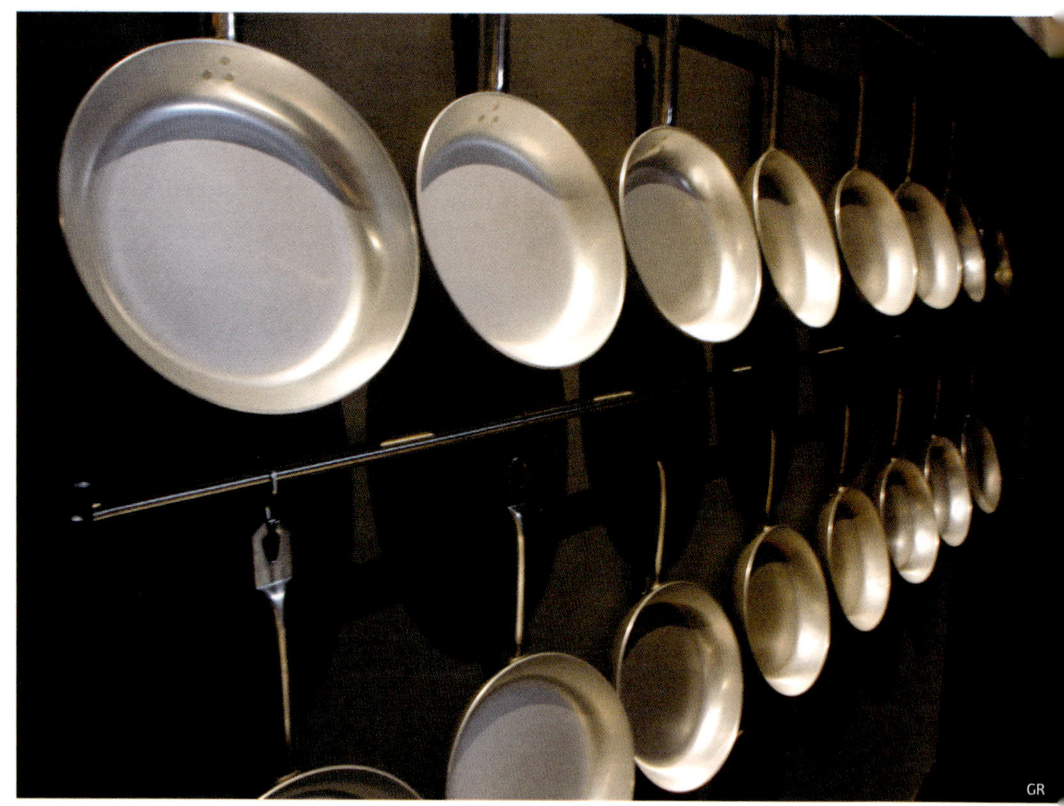
GR

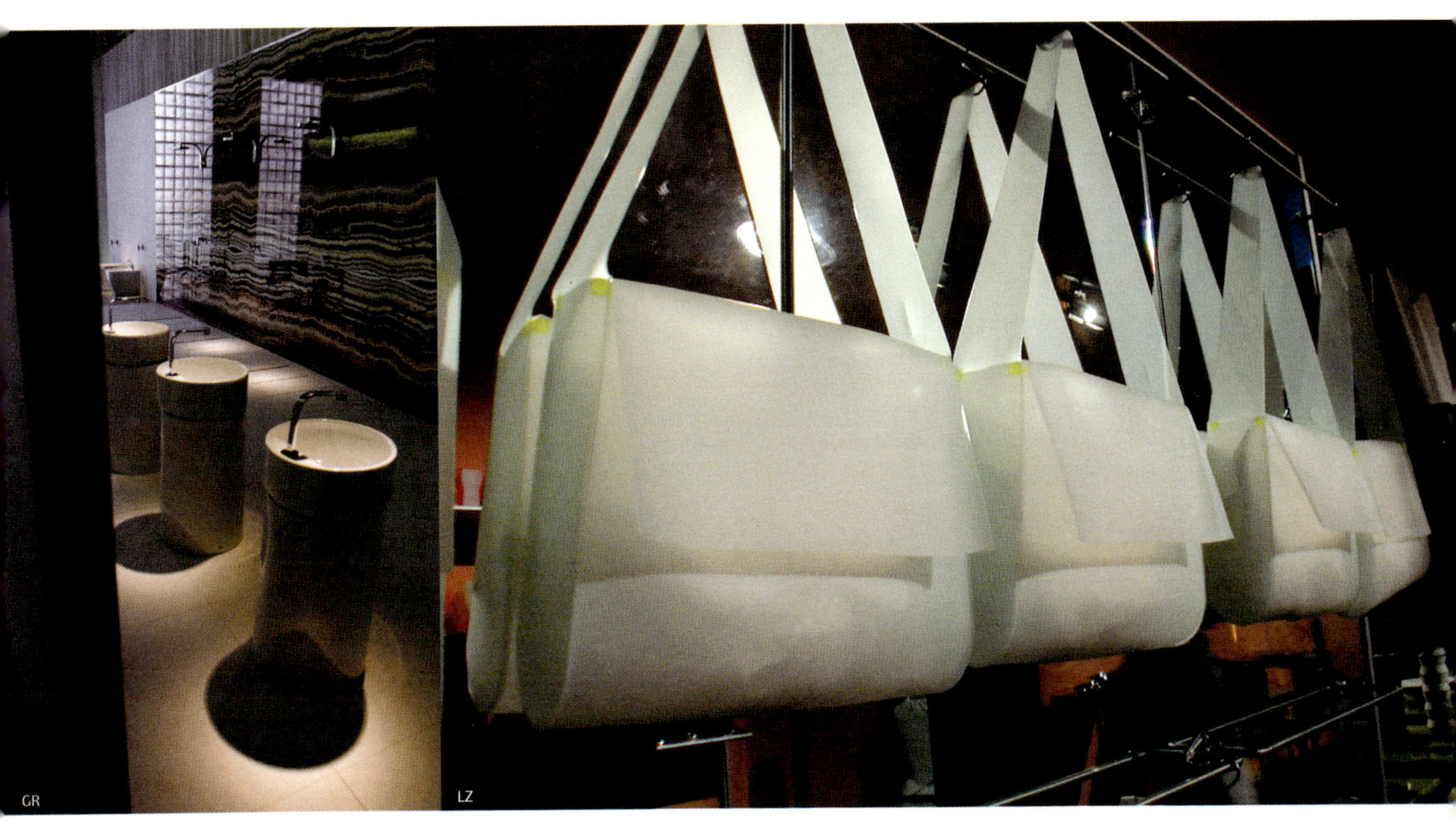

Bisazza @ Zona Tortona

Driade

> IN DUST WE TRUST

When technology reduces to a minimum the steps of the production process.

When the distance between thought and object is whittled down.

When creative inspiration need no longer be dependant on the laws of mass production.

This will be a great day for creativity and design.

23 designers show 40 products, all made with **3d rapid prototyping tecnology.**

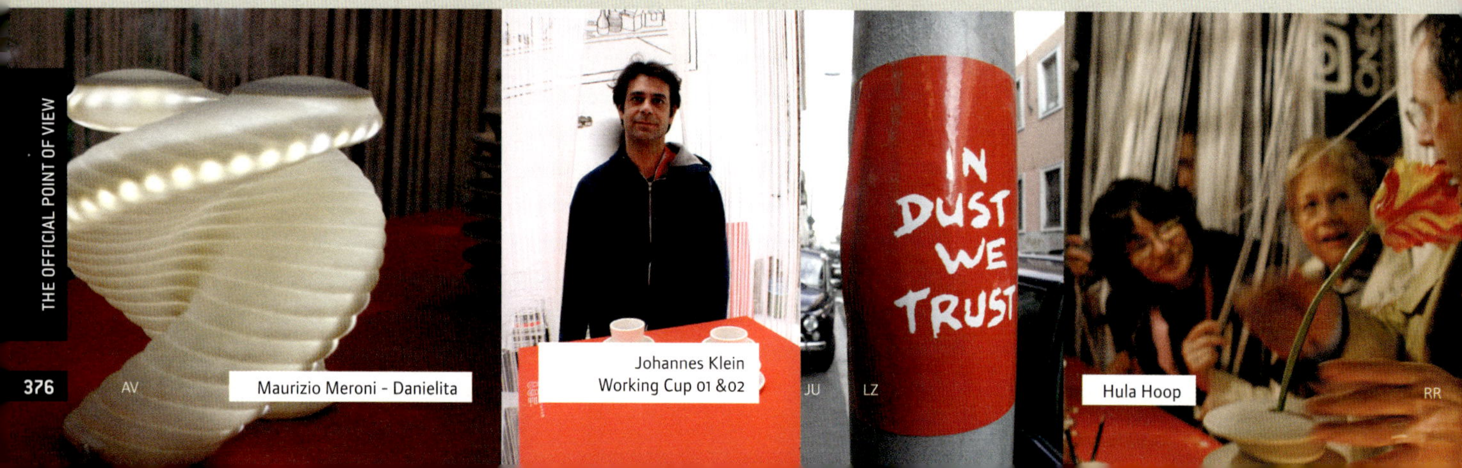

AV

Maurizio Meroni - Danielita

Johannes Klein
Working Cup 01 &02

JU   LZ

Hula Hoop

RR

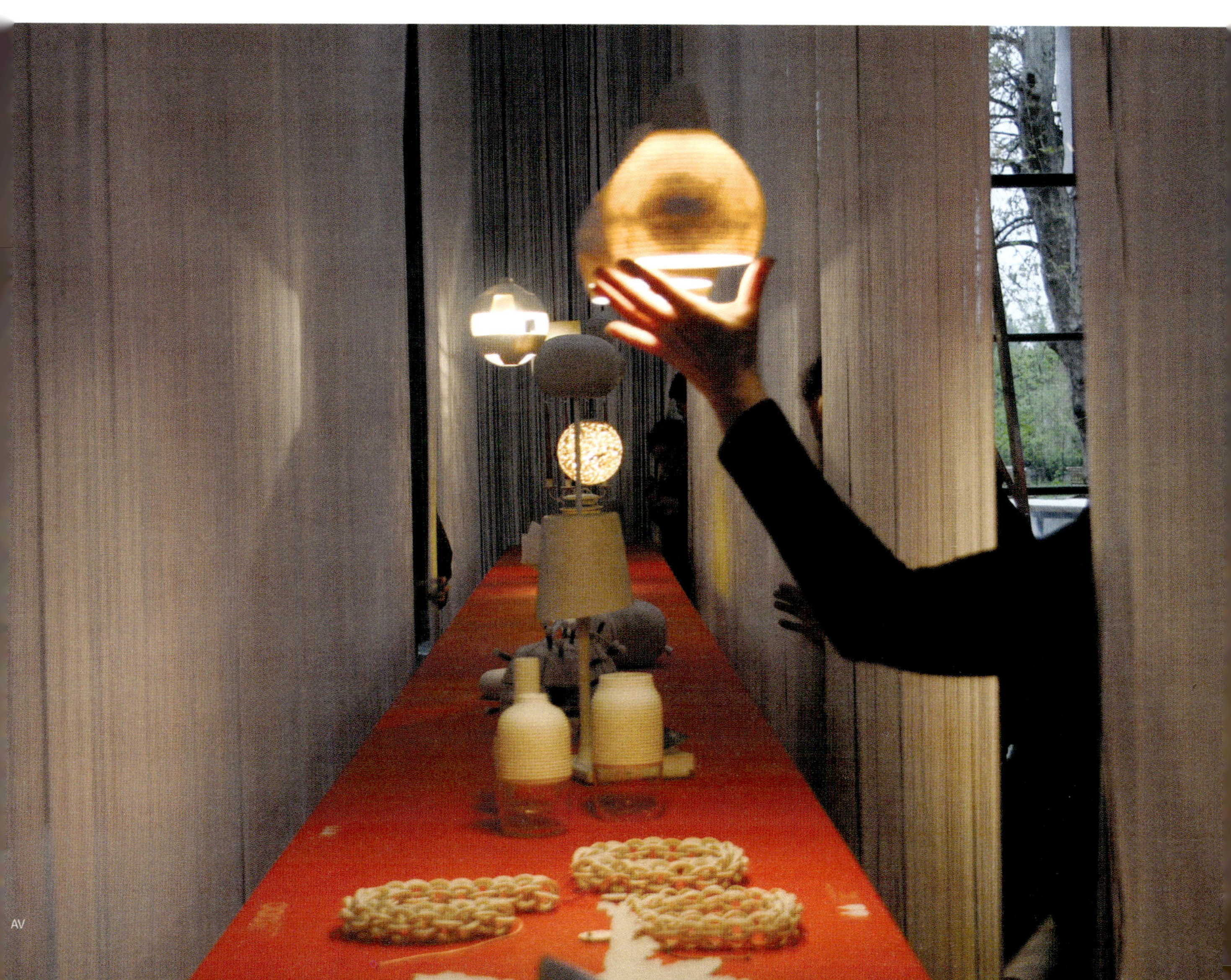
AV

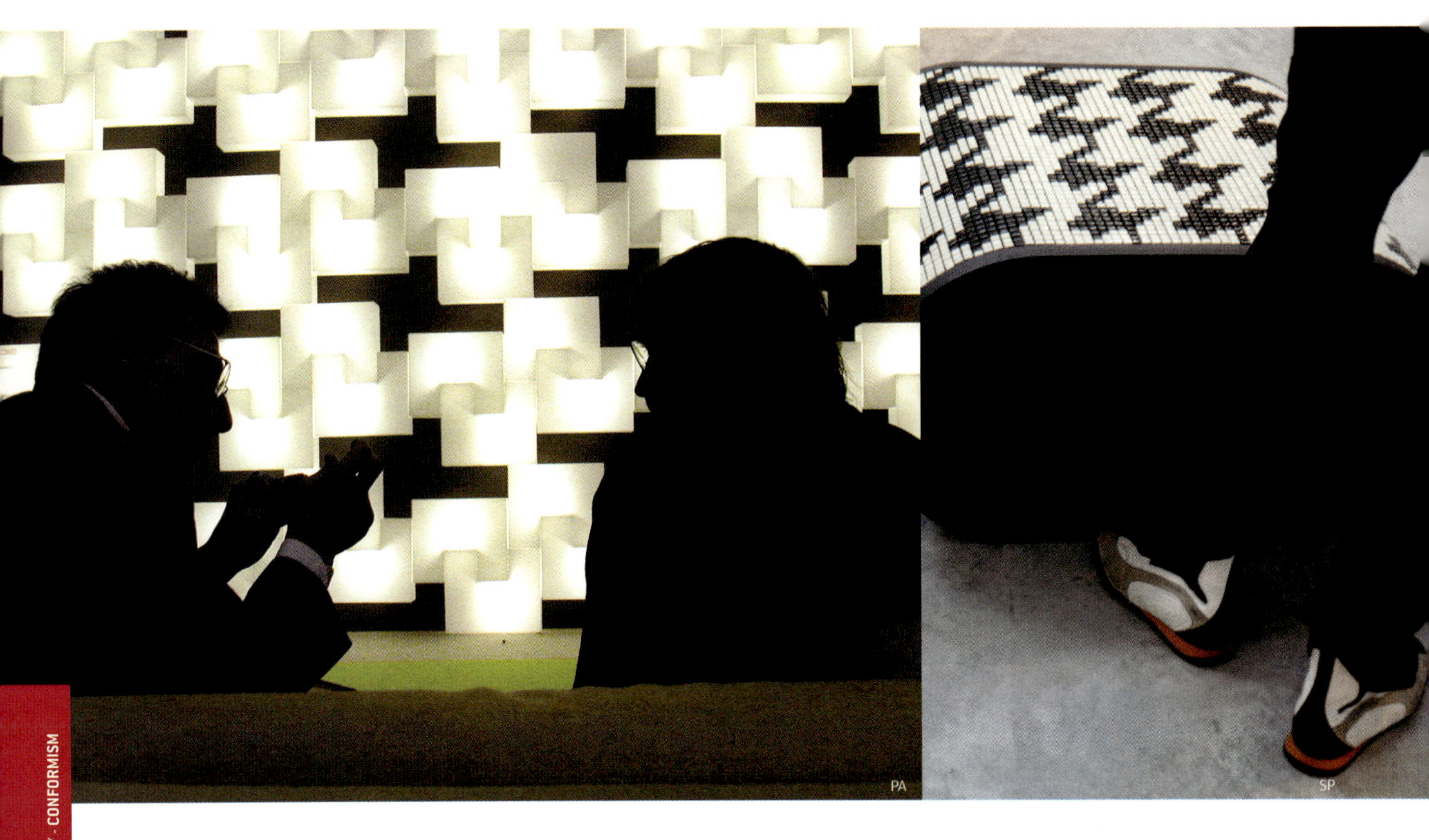

Sloe @ Satellite

WIP work in progress by Bisazza

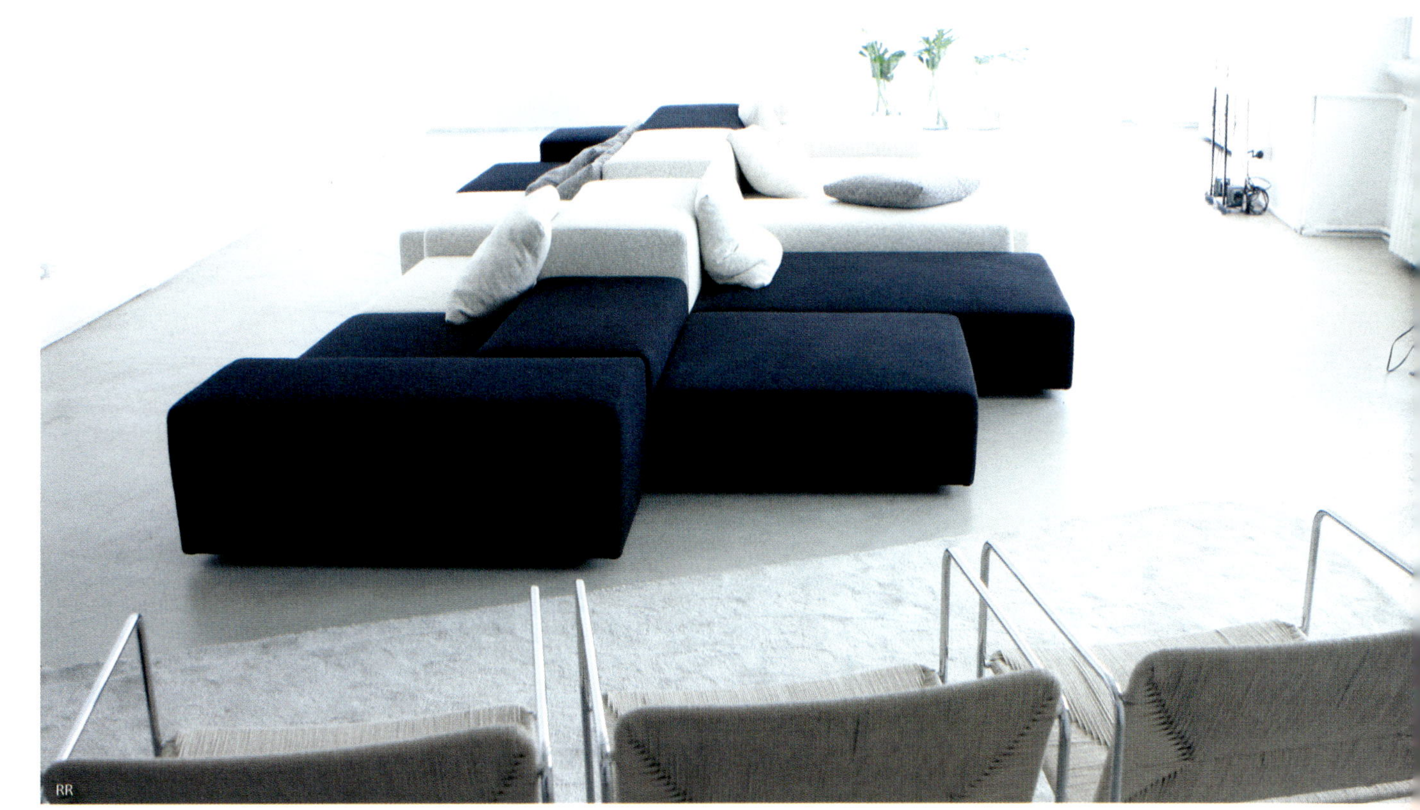

Living Divani

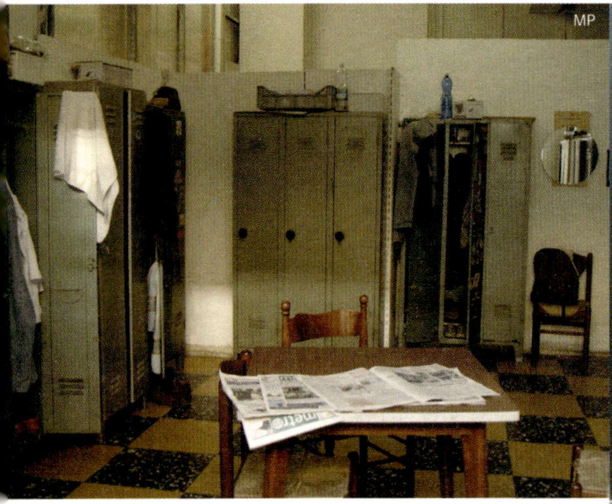

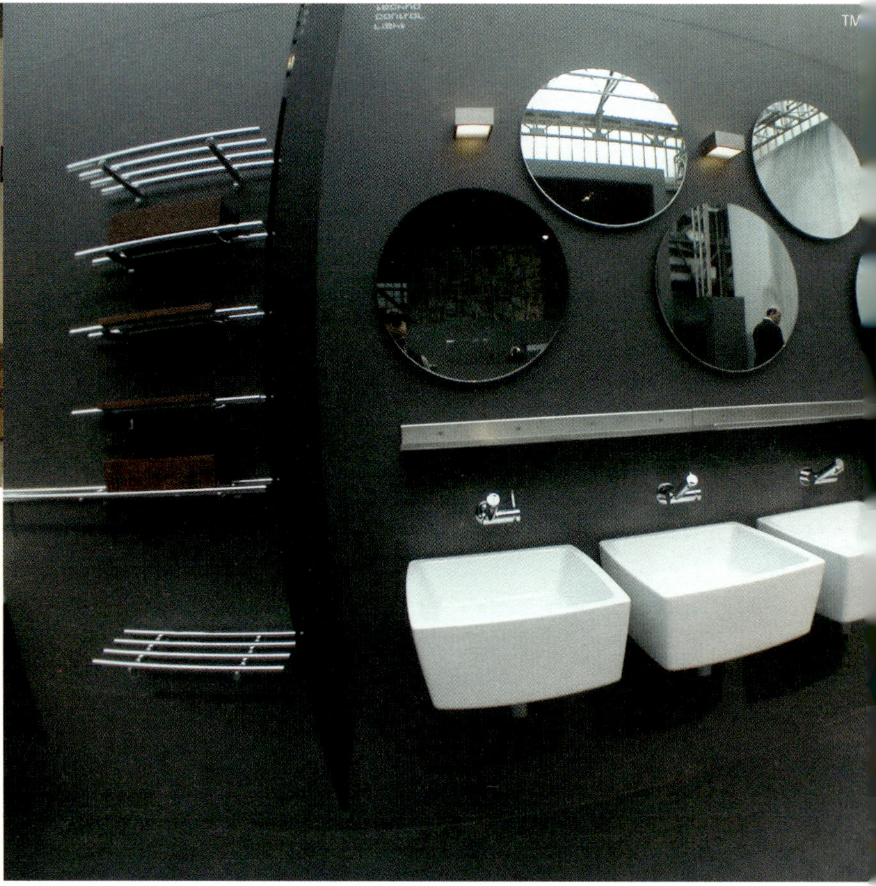

Cosmic @ Superstudio, Zona Tortona

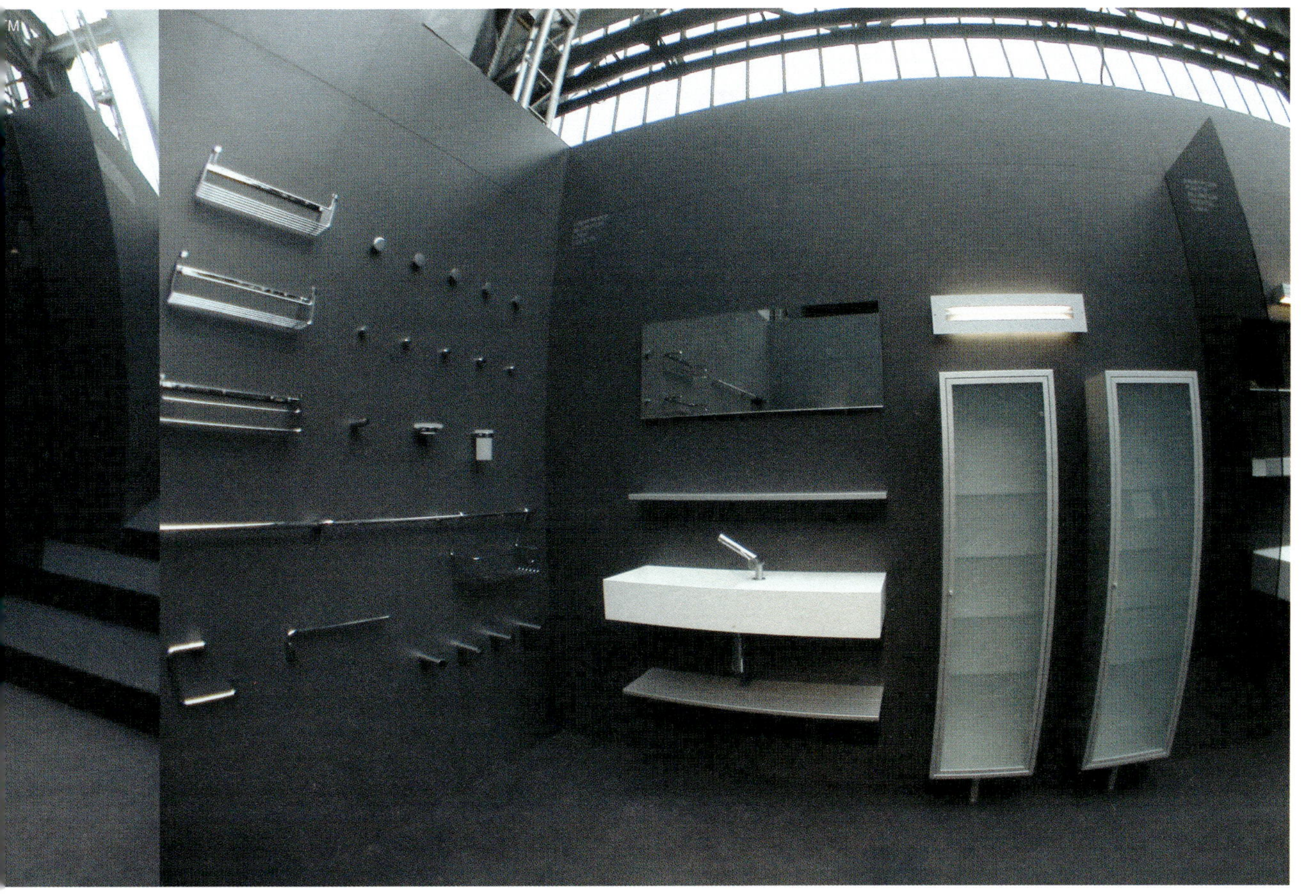

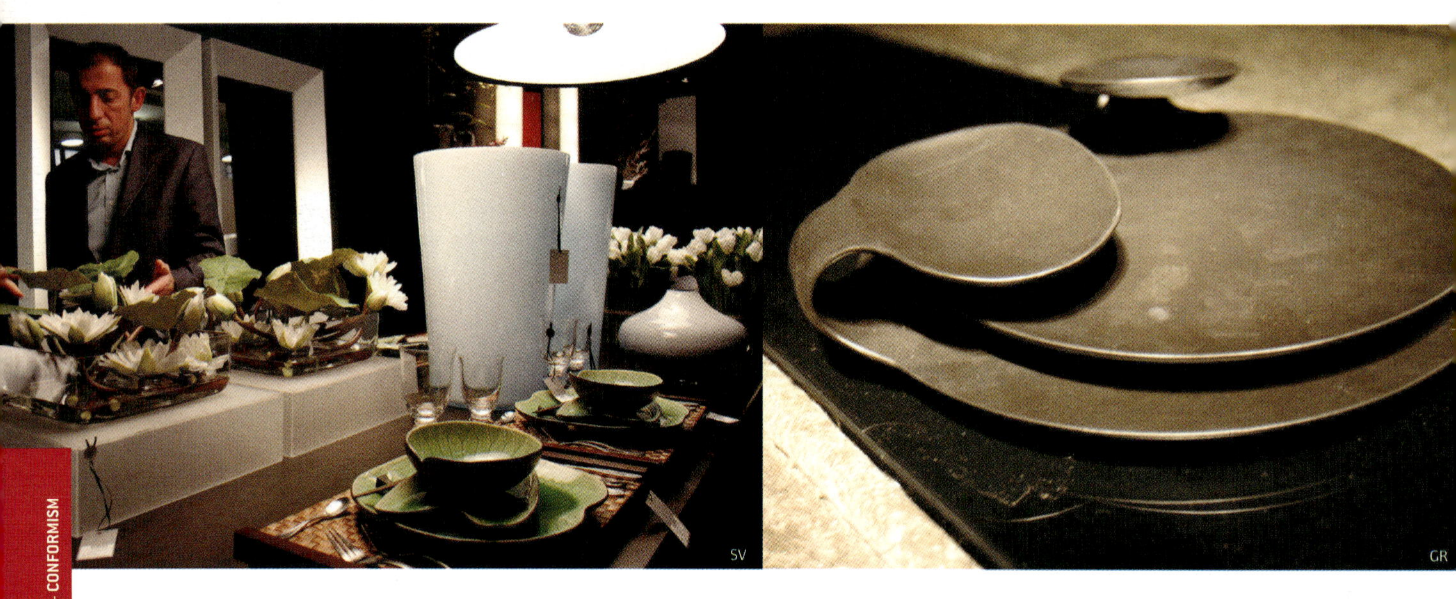

VG Newtrend

Vincenso De Cotiis

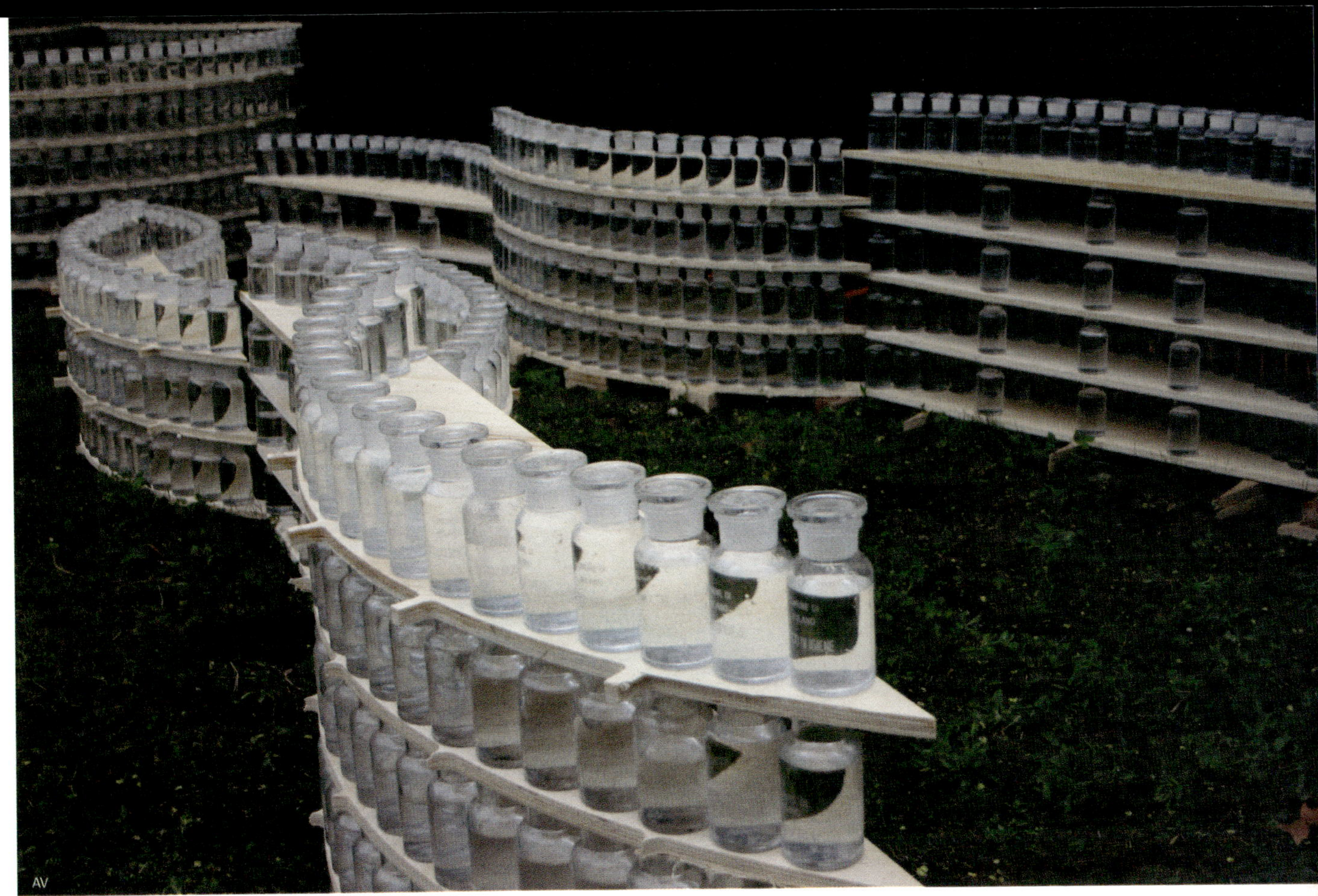

Process by Lisa Farmer

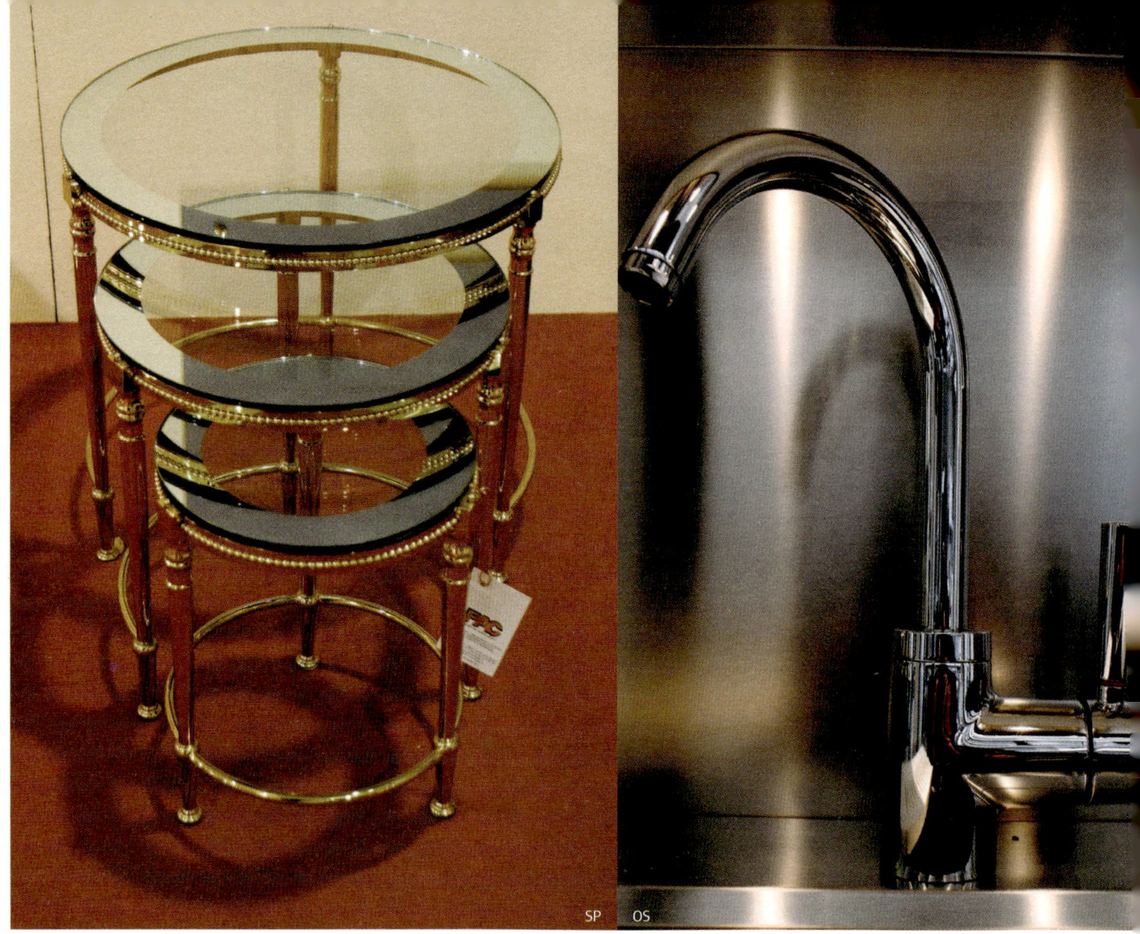

PAC   Dada

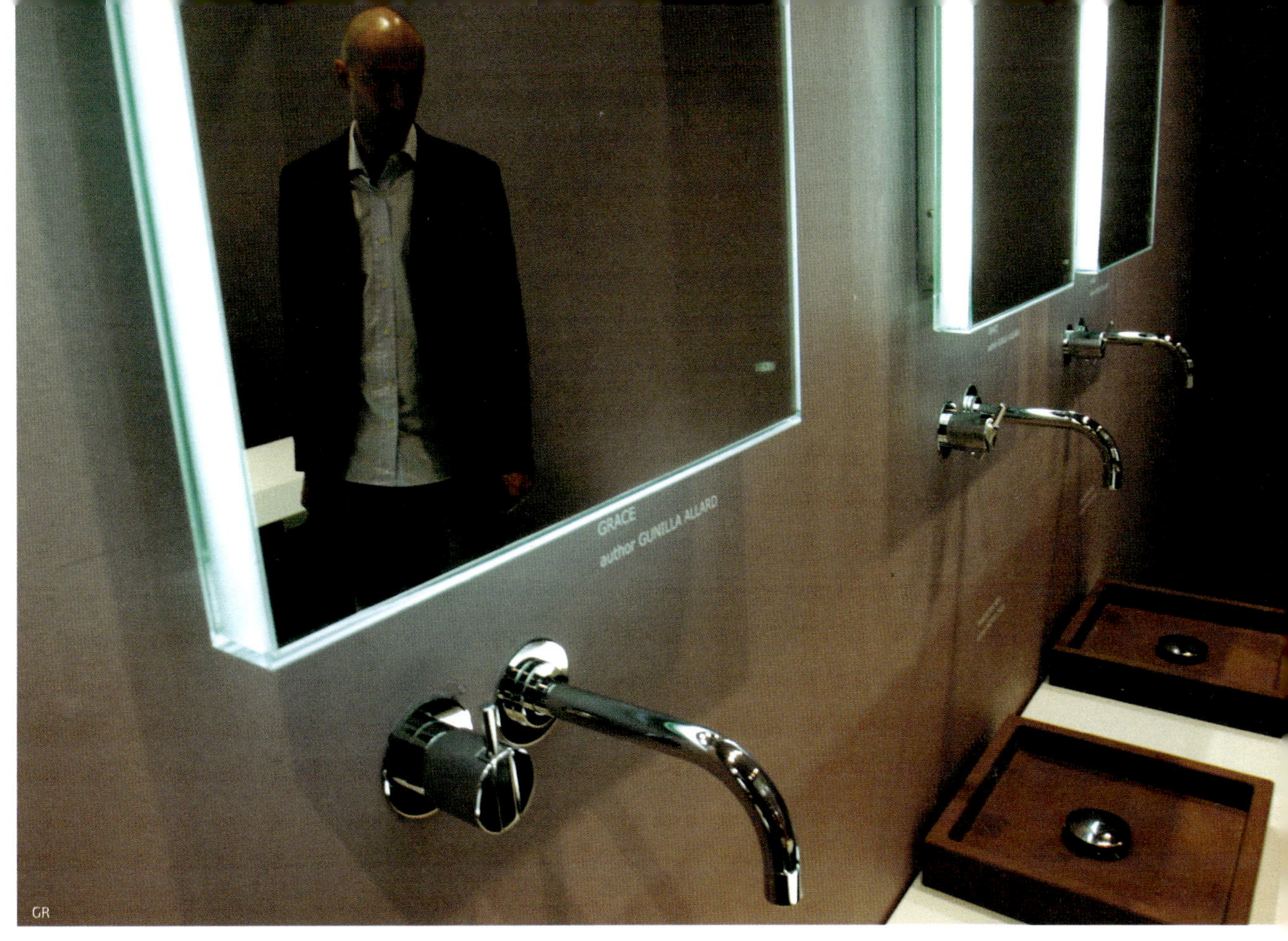

Grace" by Gunilla Allard for Rapsel

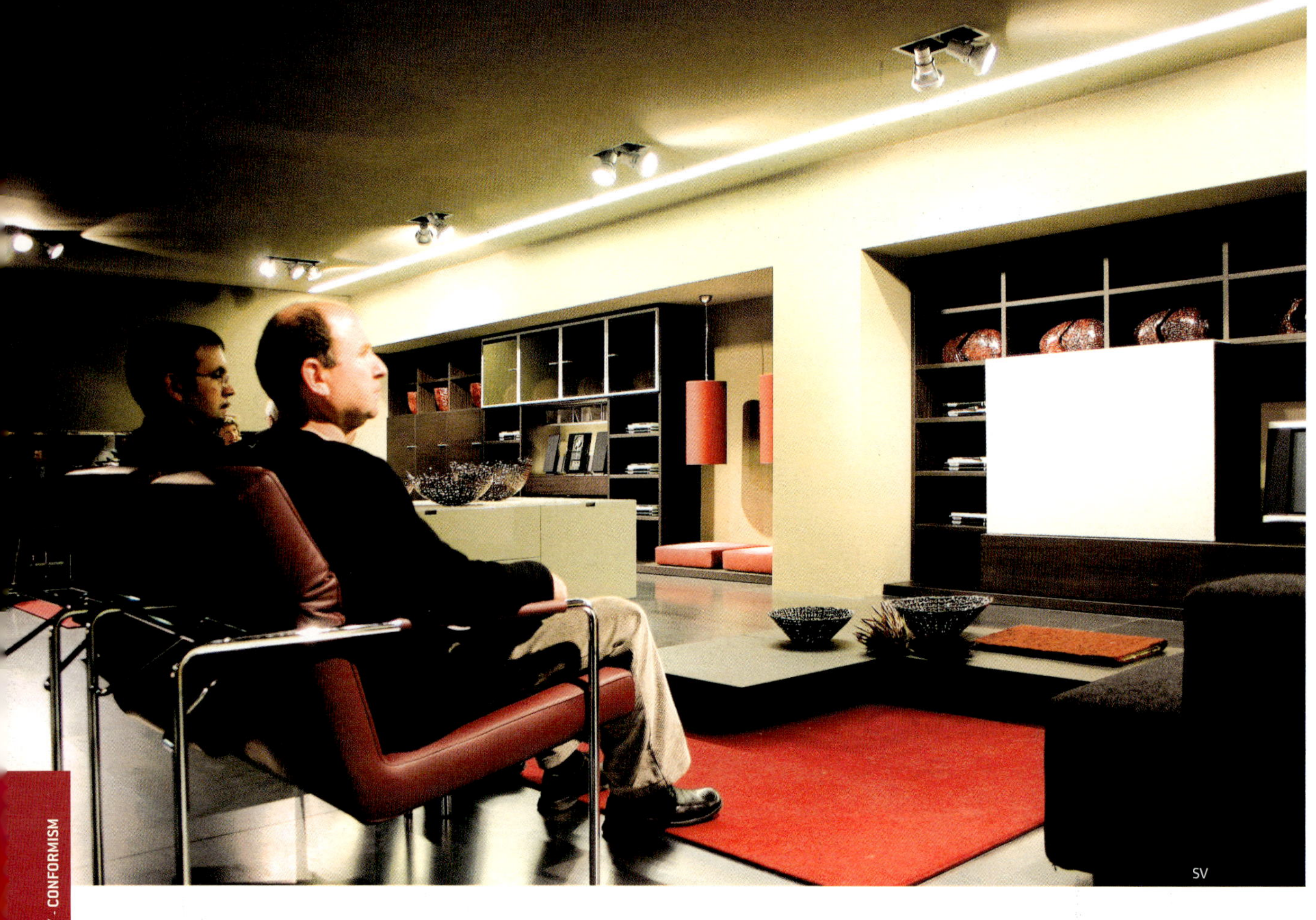

Feg

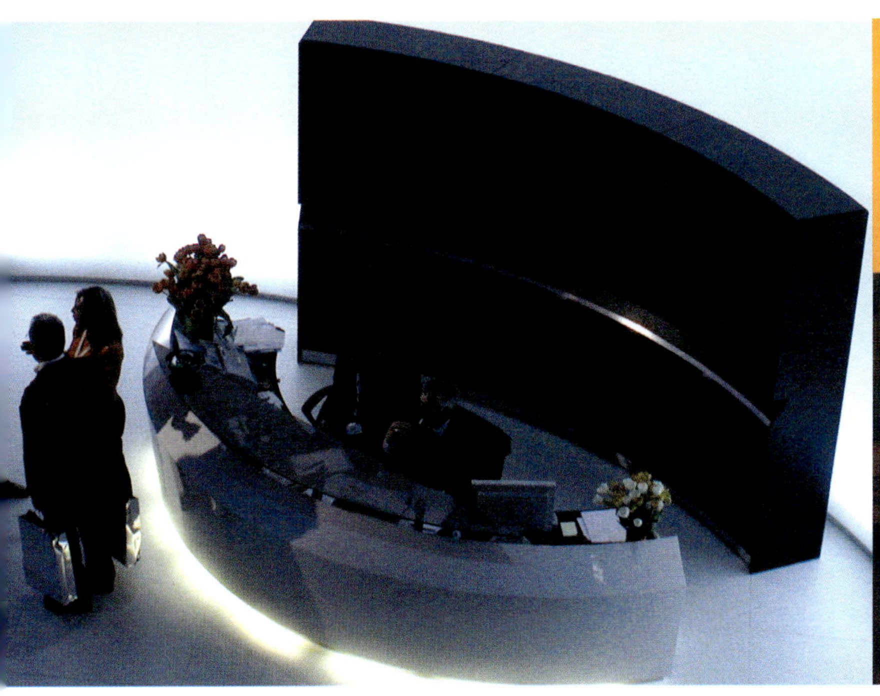

Estel Atelier

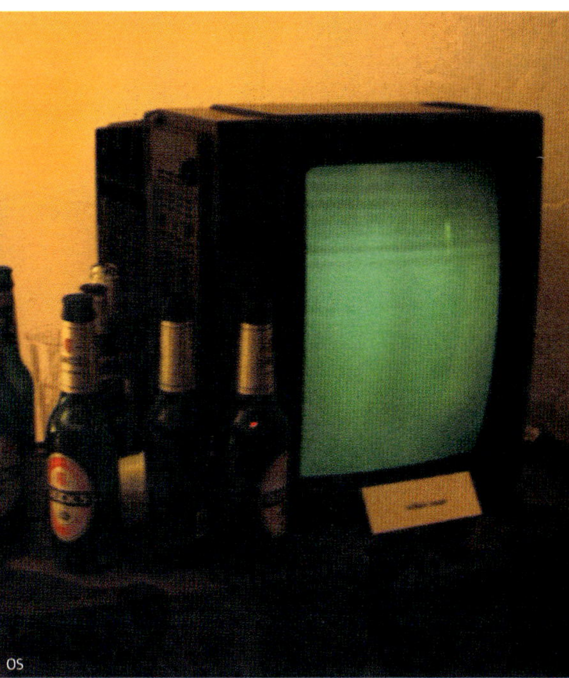

Andrea Burri

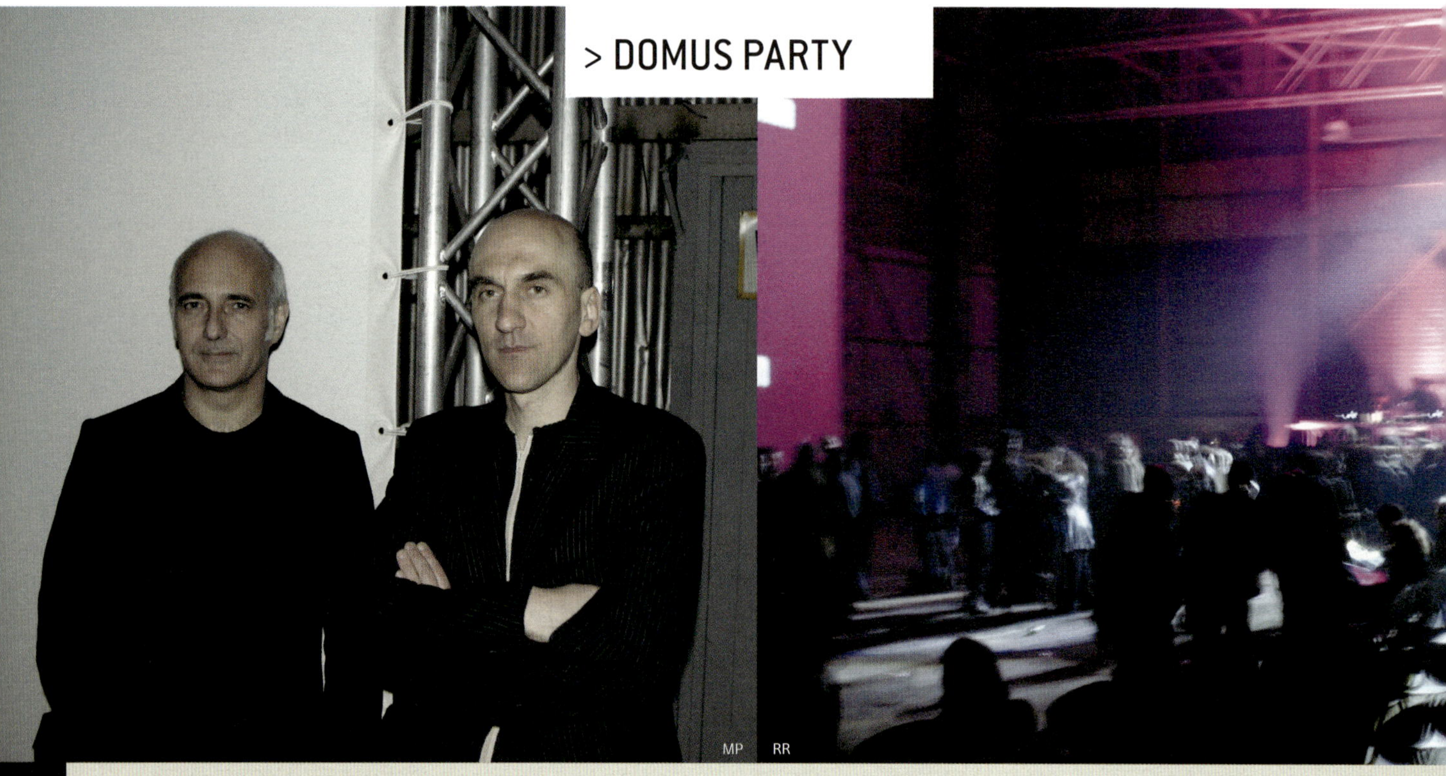

"In Milan design outshines fashion, first and foremost because it is accessible to everybody.

As opposed to fashion, there is no need for a pass or a special invitation.

During the Salone event, the city turns into a creative workshop with exhibitions, performances and parties galore.

Lofts, workshops, big sheds and old factories display and future décor and furnishing trends, thus becoming 'accessible' to all".

A jolly good example of artistic democracy.

LUISA TALIENTO

Ludovico Einaudi

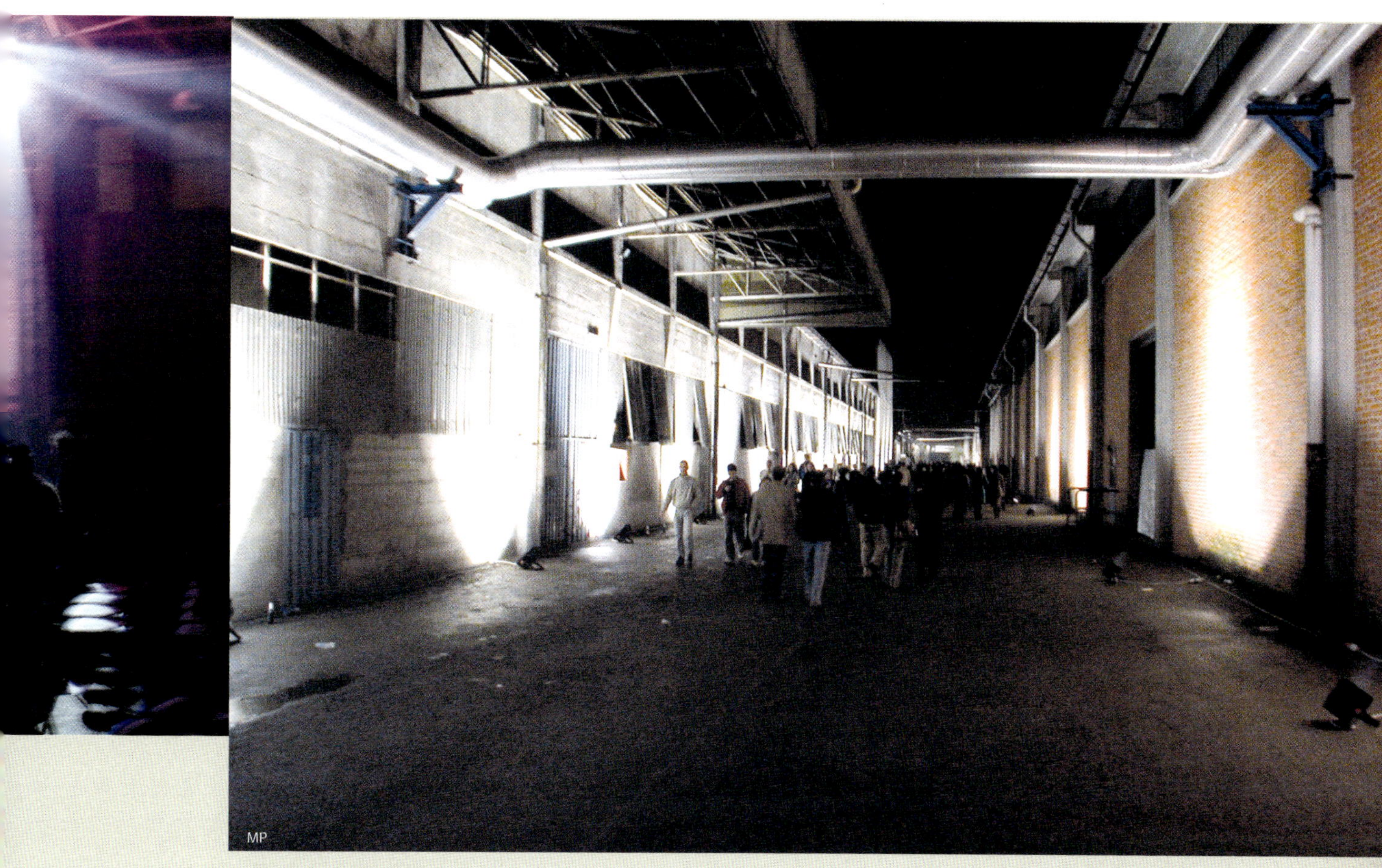

ex Cartiere Binda

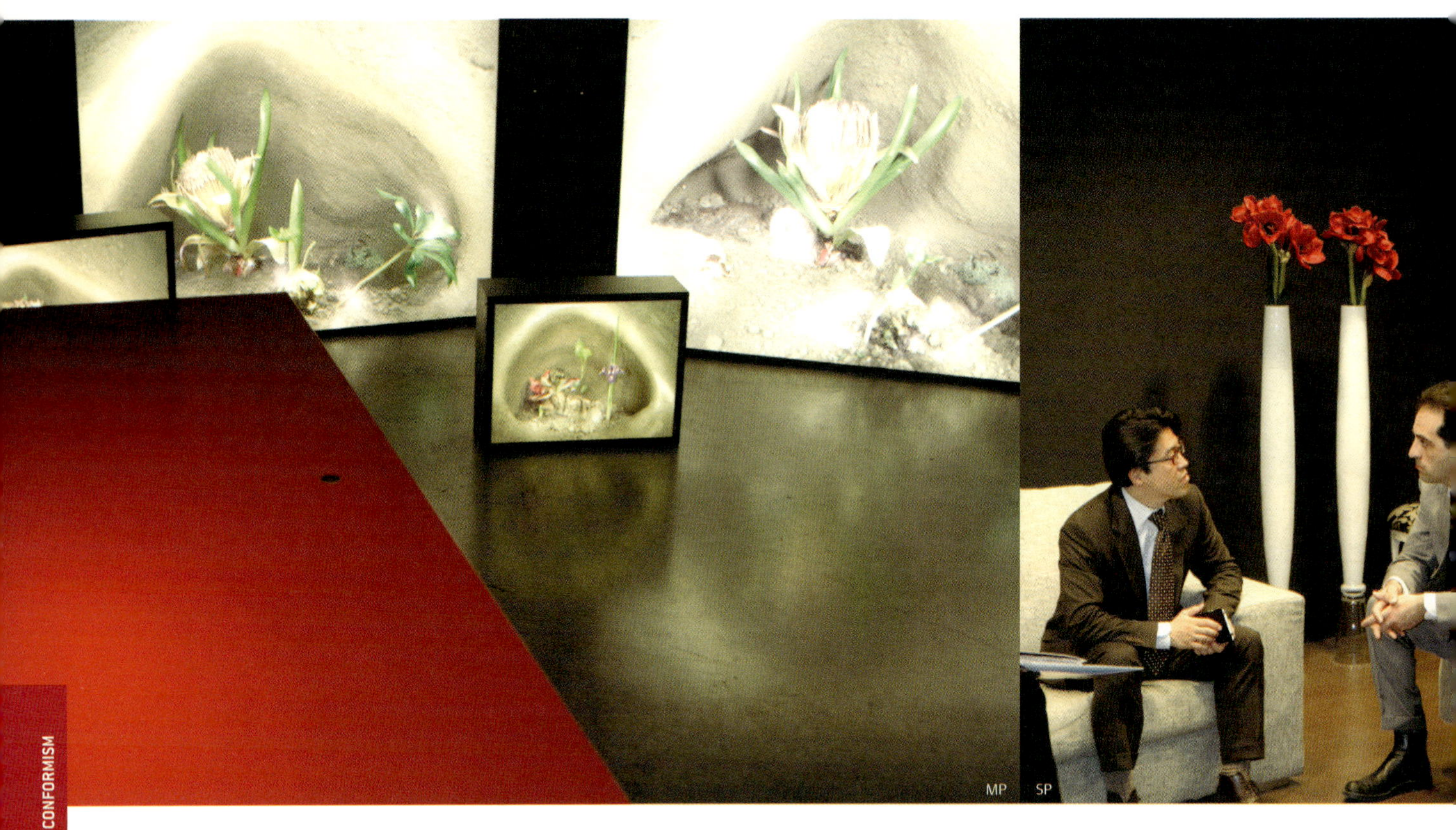

Sphaus @ Zona Tortona

Mobilinea 80

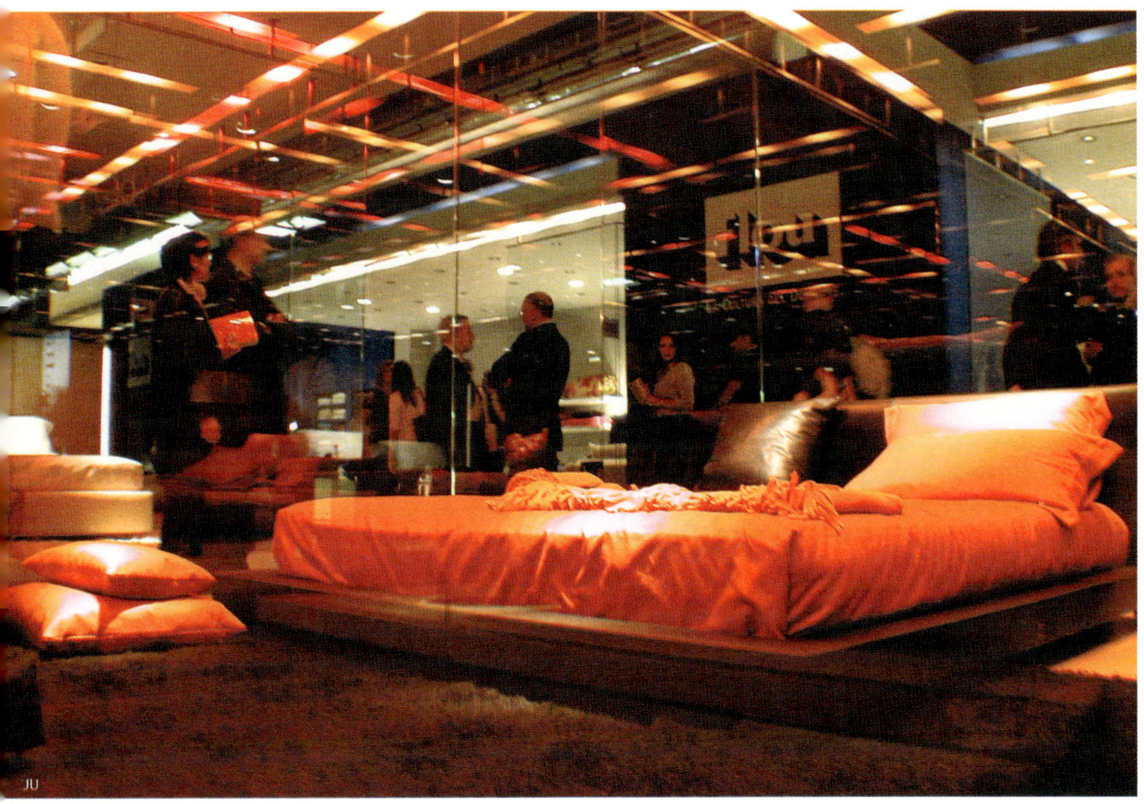

Rodolfo Dordoni for Flou

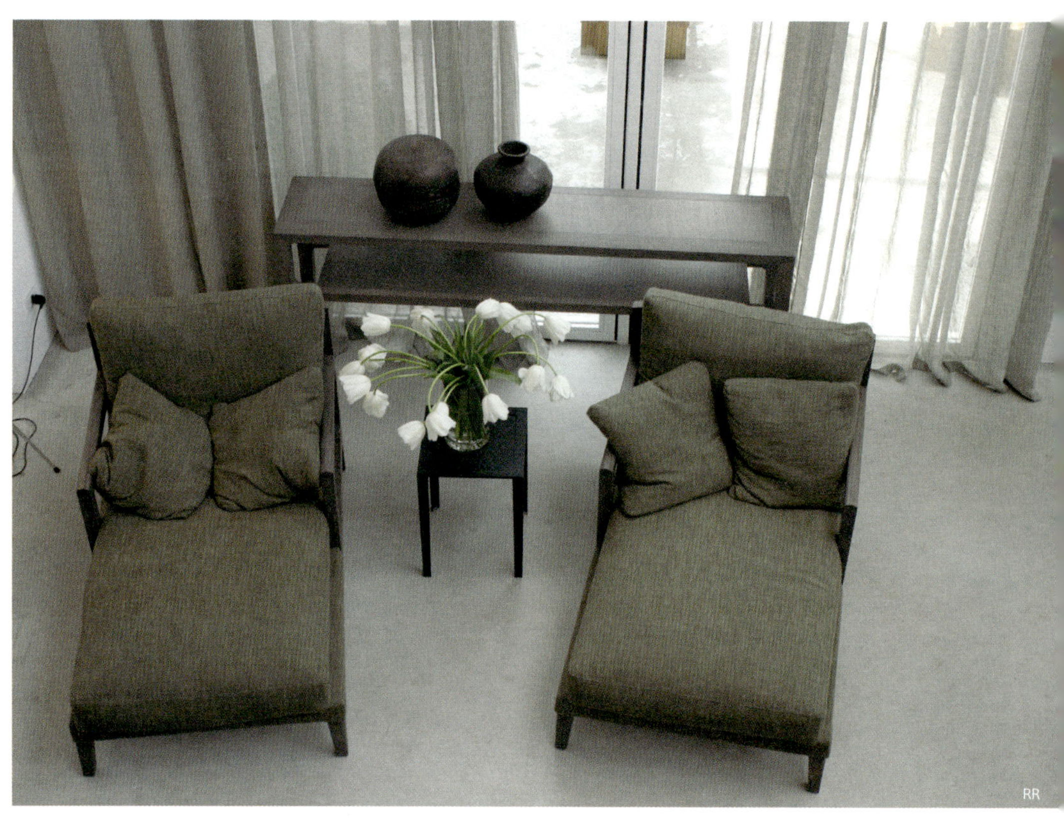

Malofancon

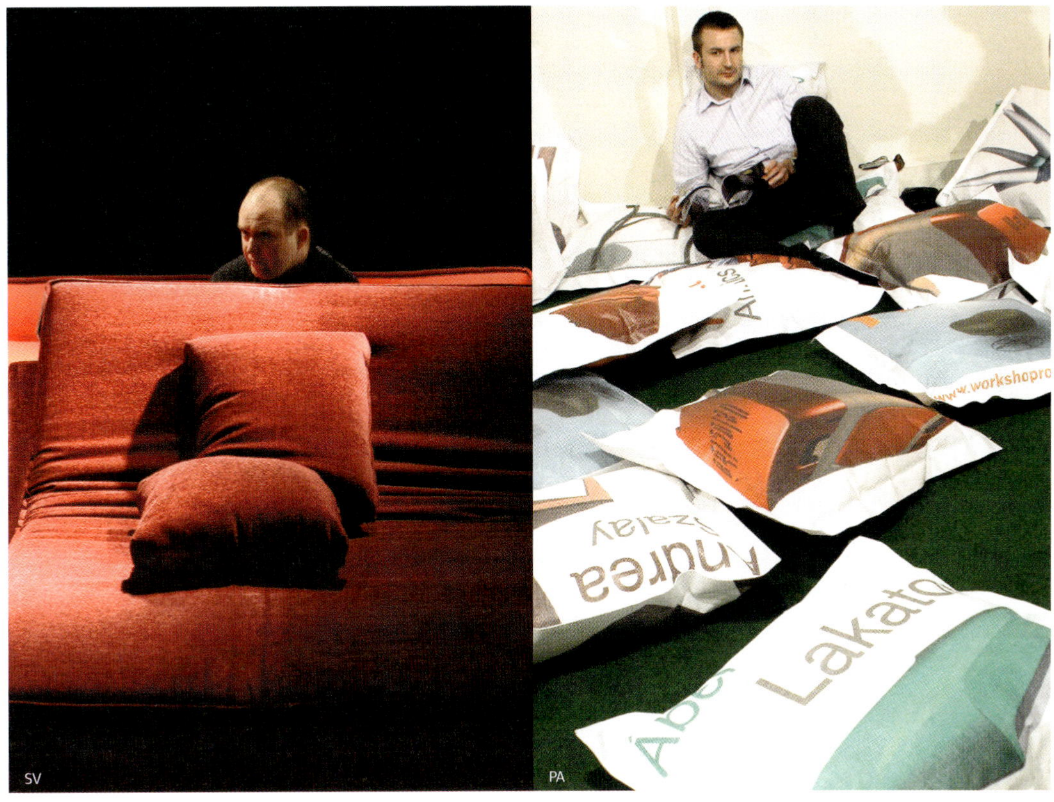
SV
PA
Andrea Szalay
Ábel Lakato
www.workshopro

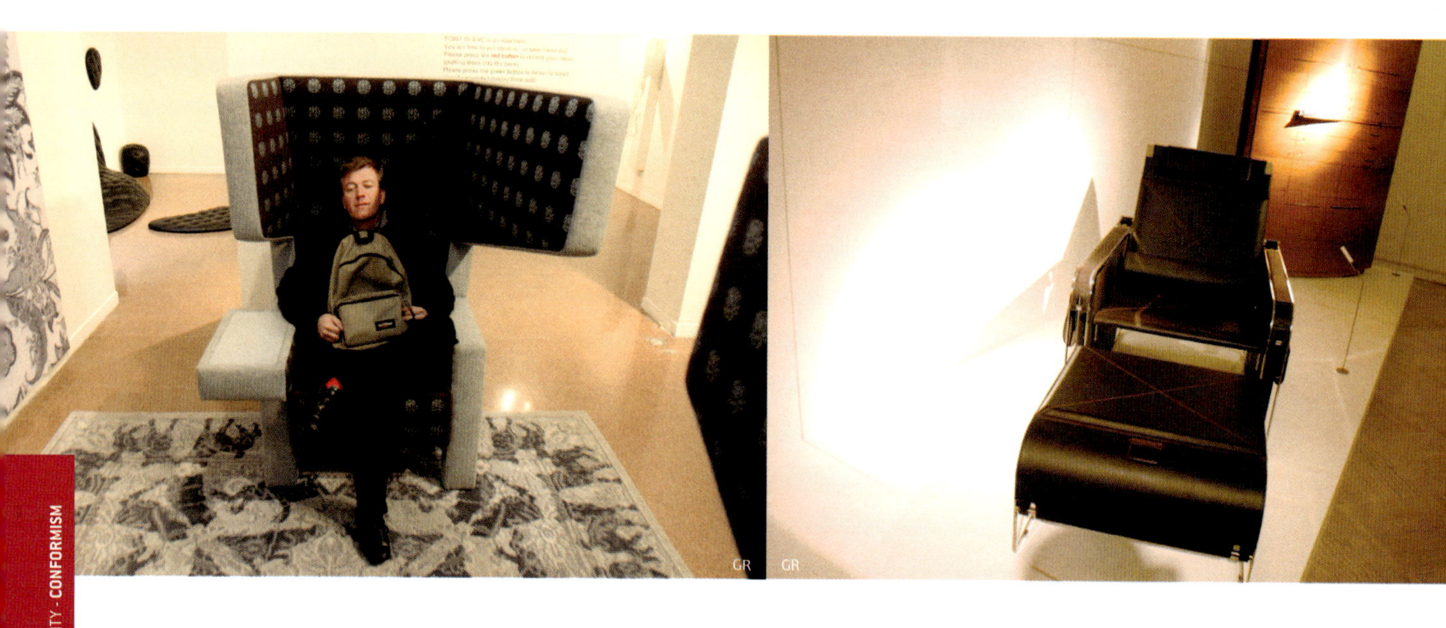

Vanishing Point

Tressera

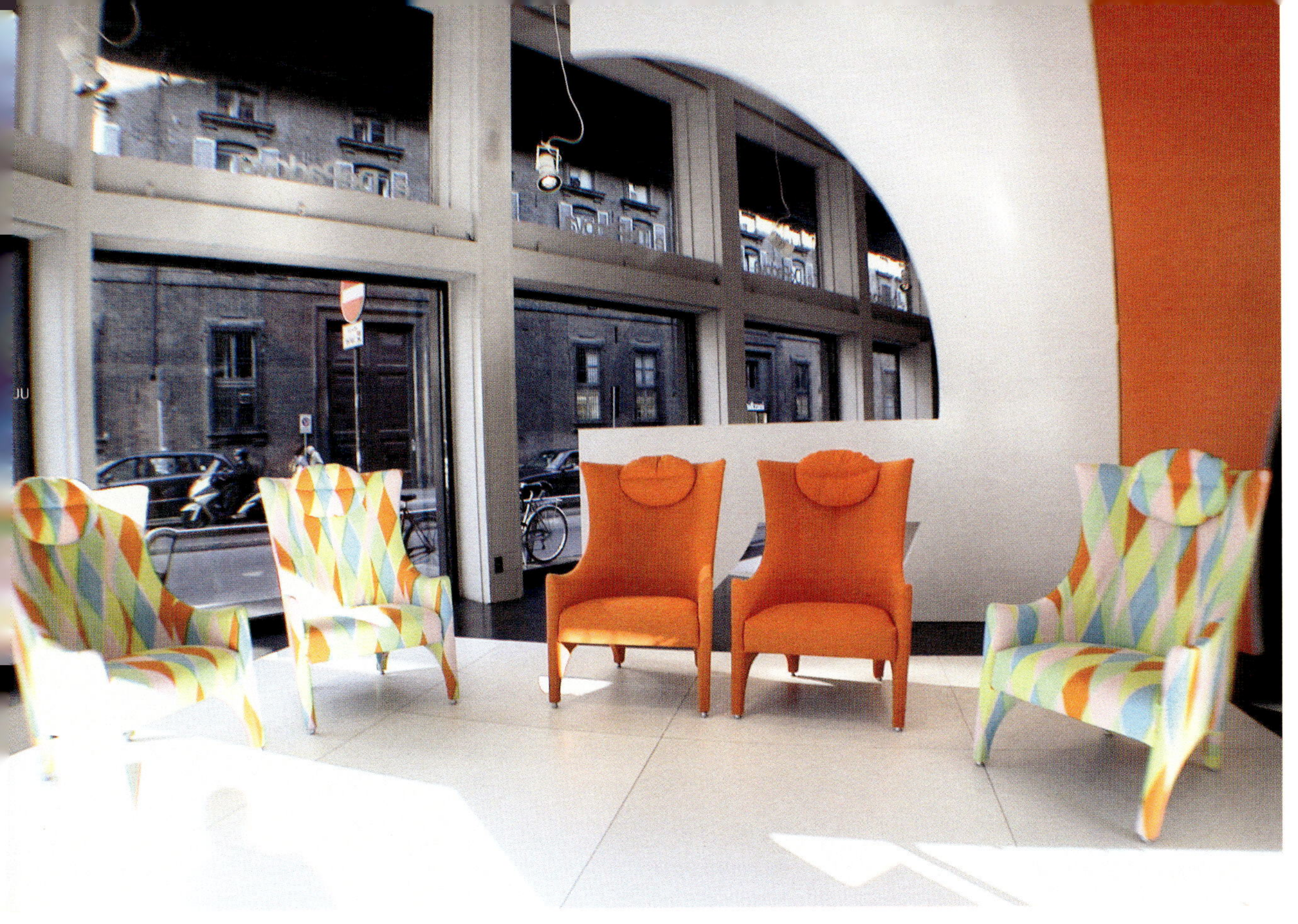

Girotondo by Vico Magistretti, redesigned by Alessandro Mendini for De Padova

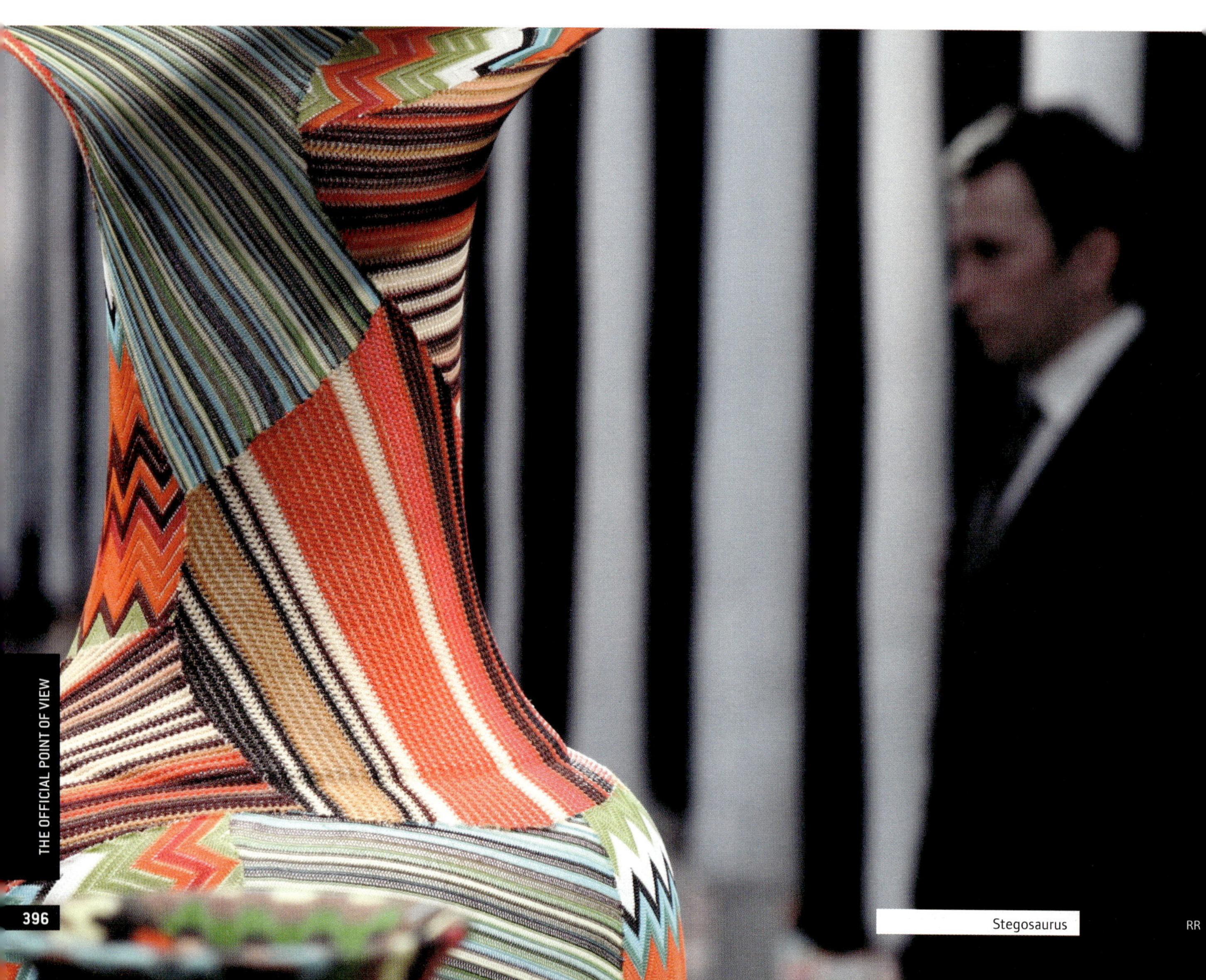

Stegosaurus

RR

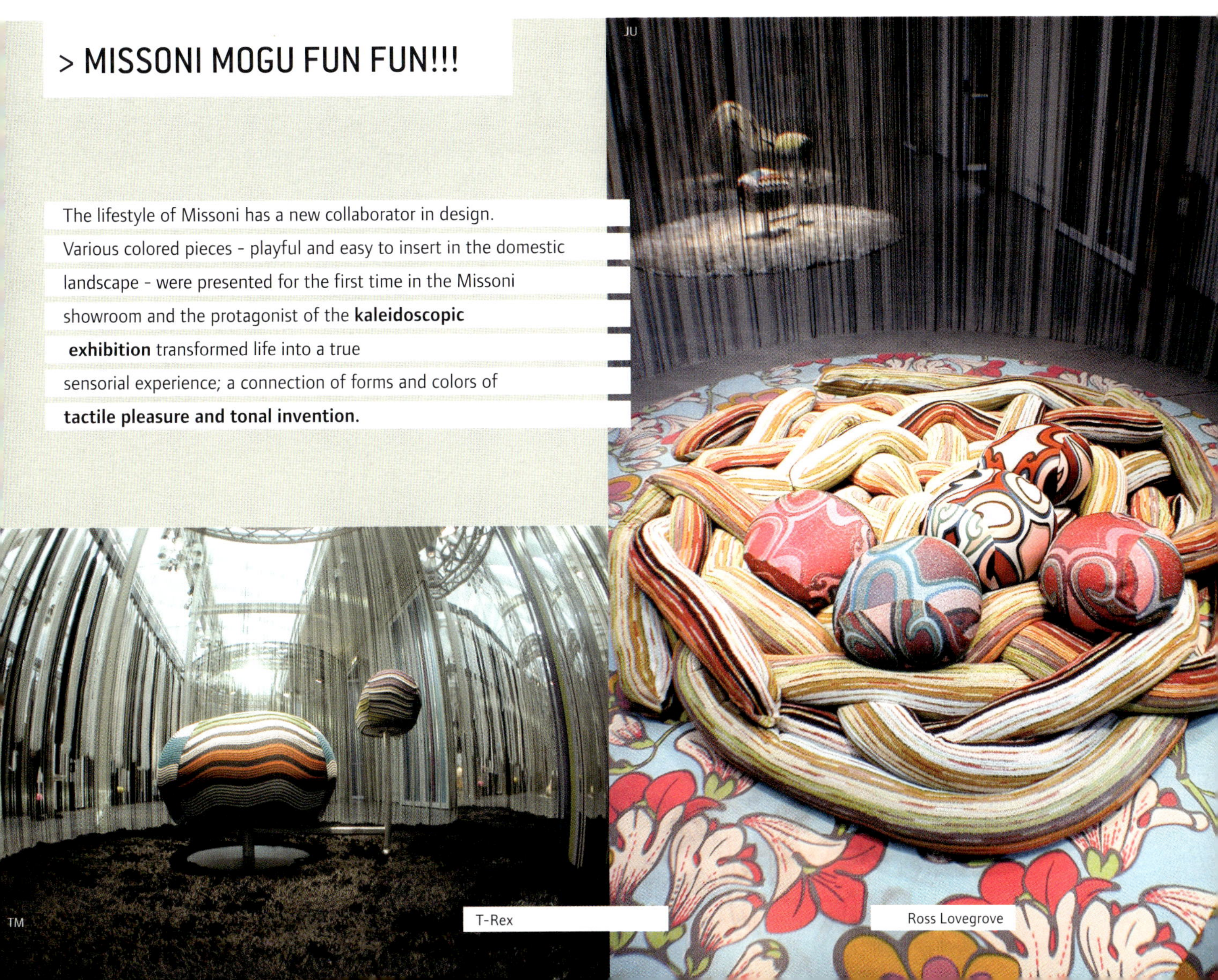

> MISSONI MOGU FUN FUN!!!

The lifestyle of Missoni has a new collaborator in design.

Various colored pieces - playful and easy to insert in the domestic

landscape - were presented for the first time in the Missoni

showroom and the protagonist of the **kaleidoscopic**

 exhibition transformed life into a true

sensorial experience; a connection of forms and colors of

tactile pleasure and tonal invention.

T-Rex

Ross Lovegrove

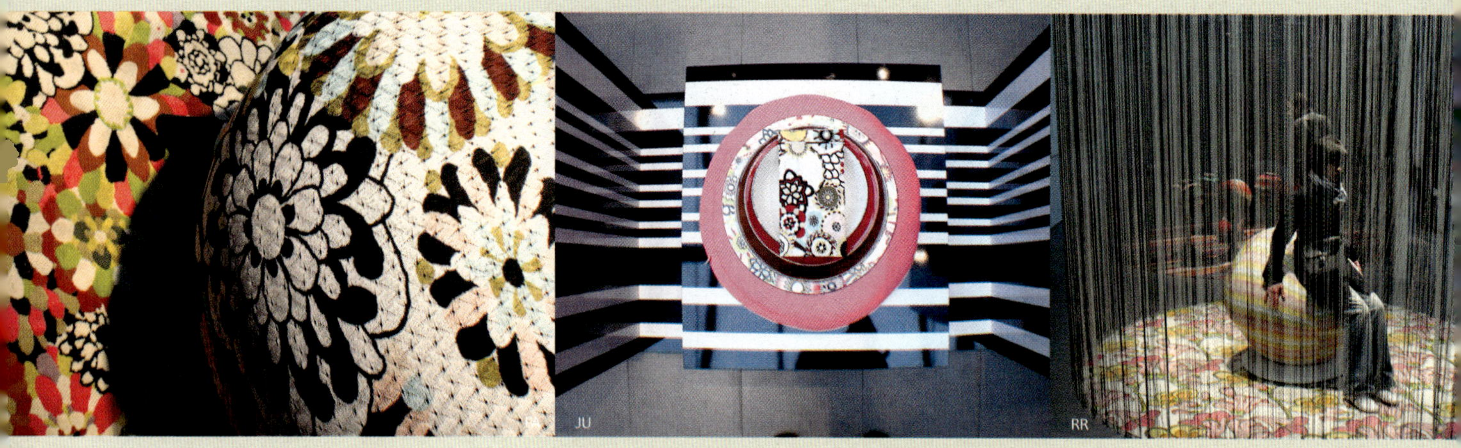

It's impossible to misunderstand this landscape of floral and graphic patterns of black and white modules and colored fringe.

We are talking about new components of furniture born from the collaboration of Missoni and the Japanese brand Mogu.

Internationally known for its upholstered collection of objects filled with powder-beads of polystyrene

and covered in colored lycra, Mogu presented **a new family of comfortable domestic companions.**

The Missoni Mogu Funfun environment designed by Stephen Burks (international art director of Mogu)

in collaboration with Eva Gundersen (Missoni Home stylist).

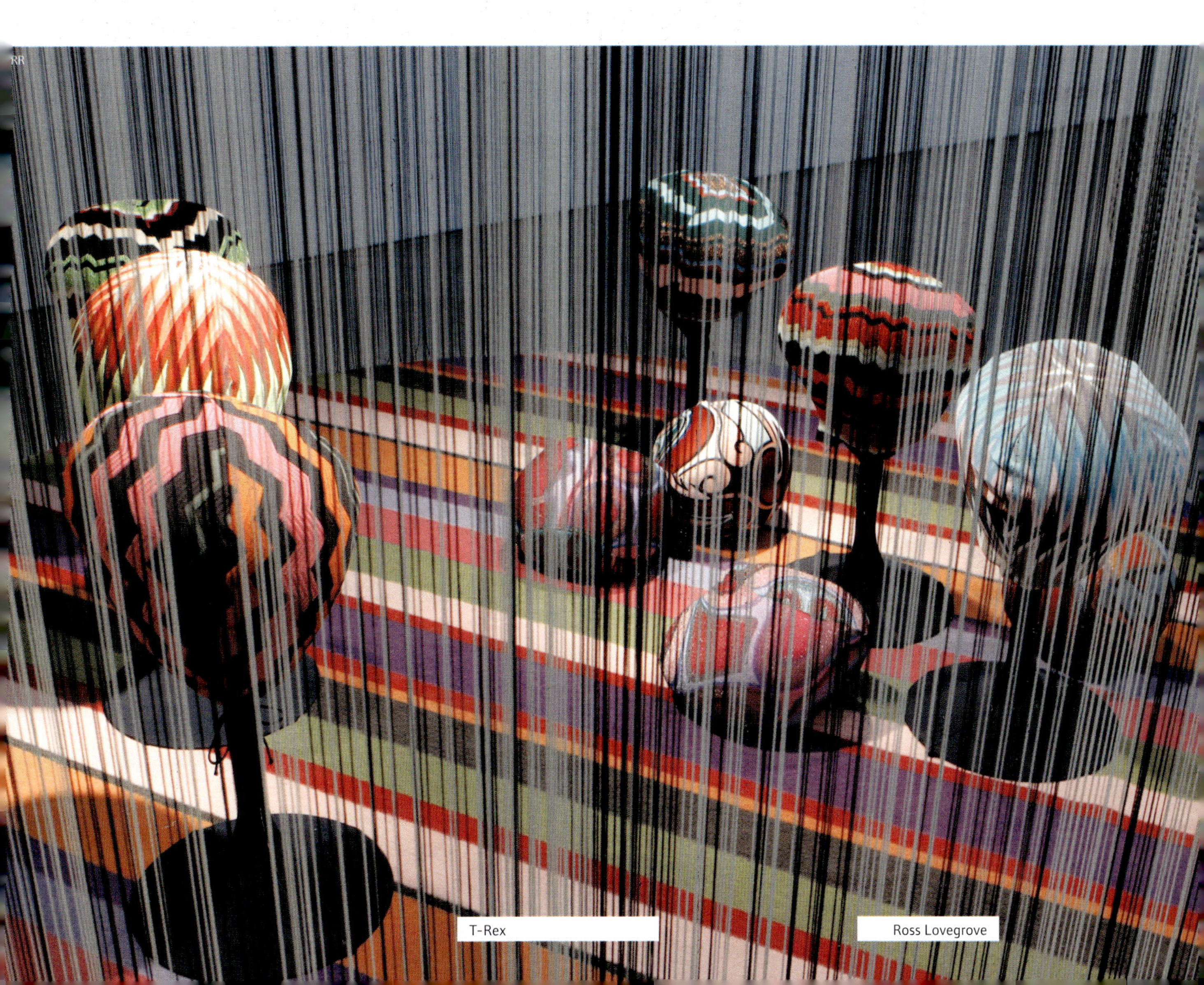

RR
T-Rex
Ross Lovegrove

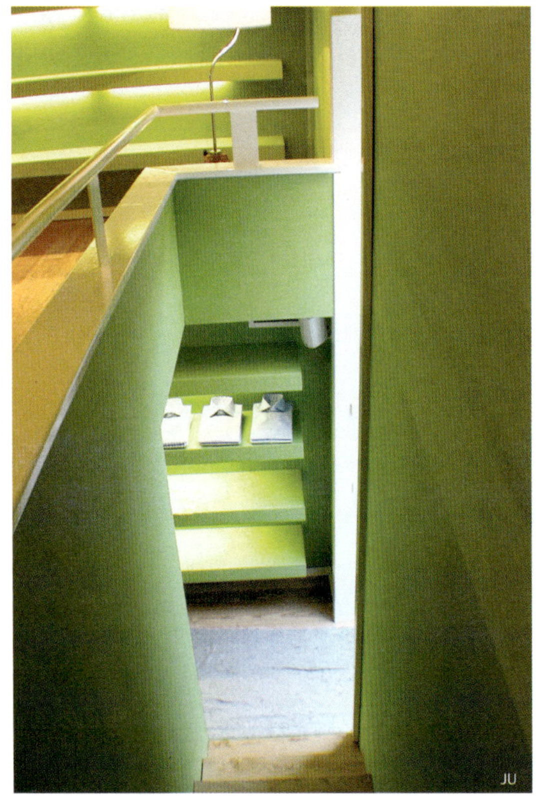

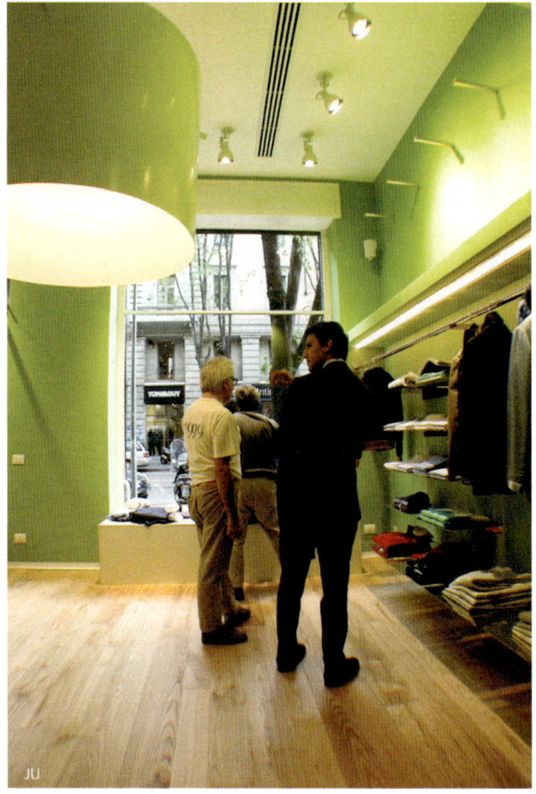

Nicola Quadri for Curatolo

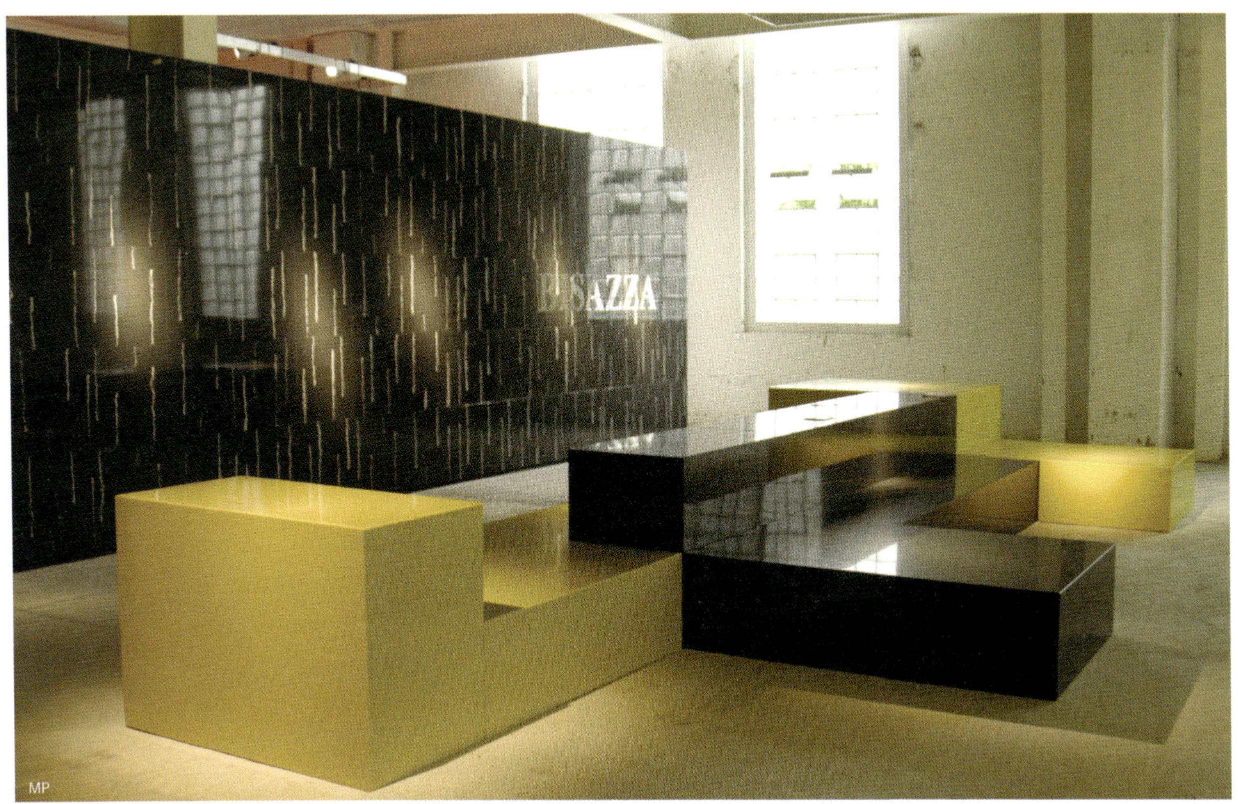

Bisazza

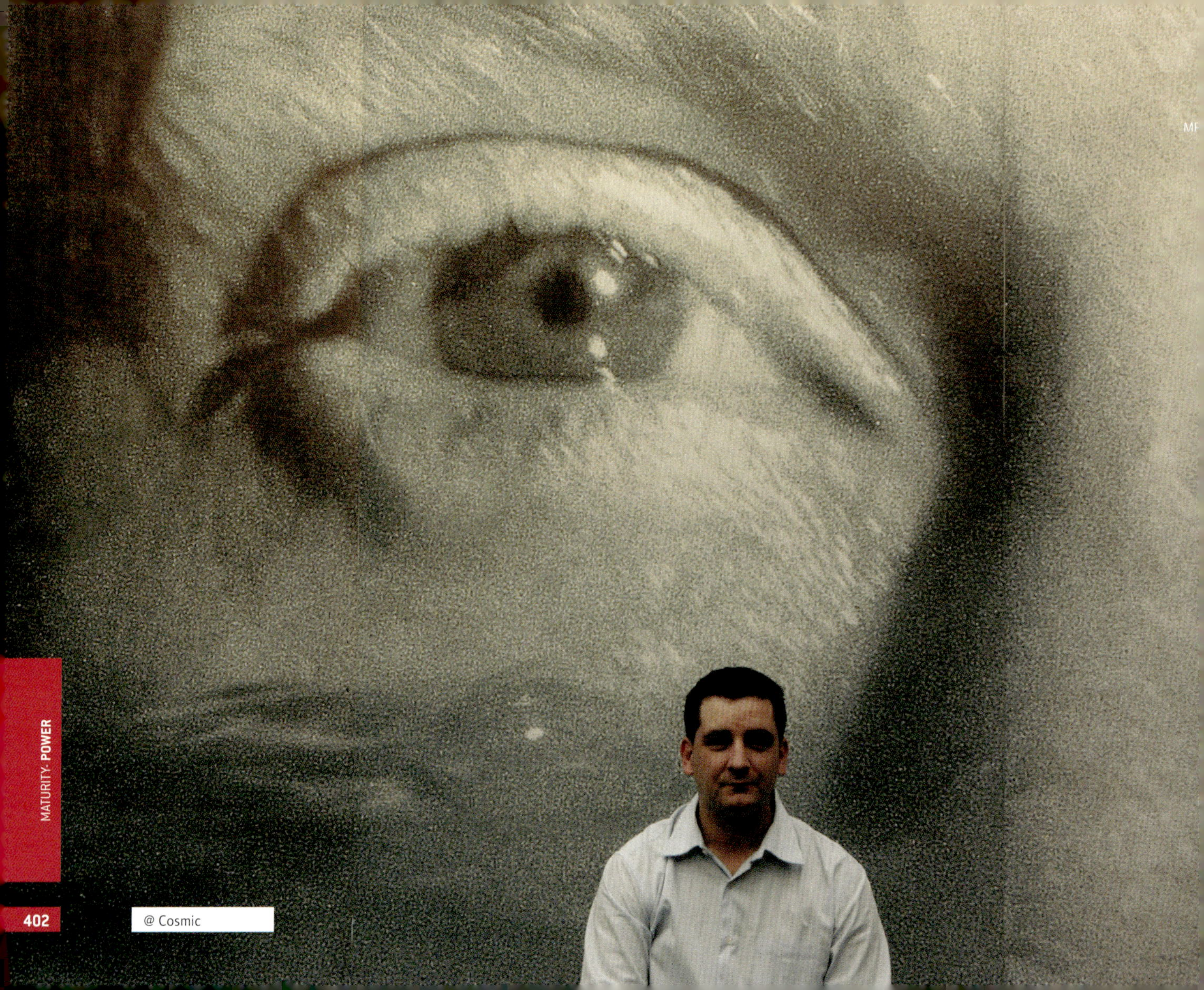

MATURITY- POWER
402
@ Cosmic

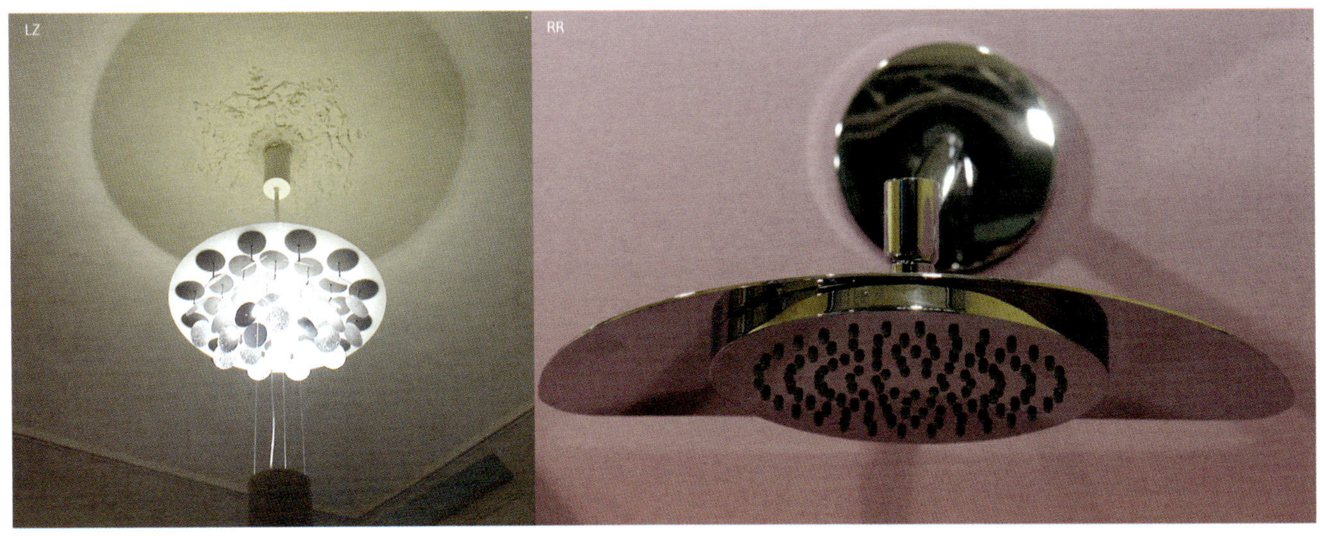

Odegard

Flex doccia

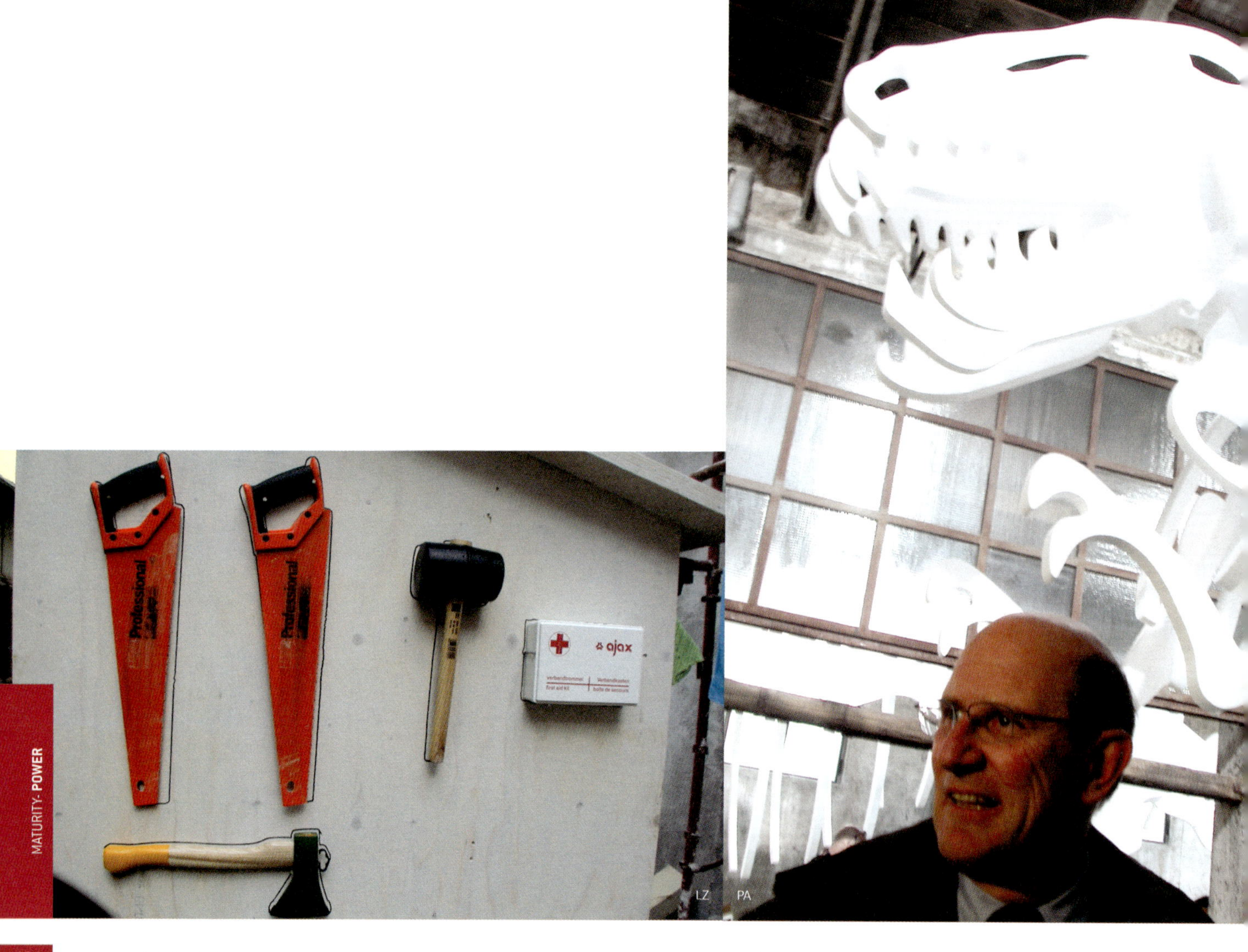

MATURITY - POWER

LZ   PA

@ Tutto BeNe

@ Designosaurus

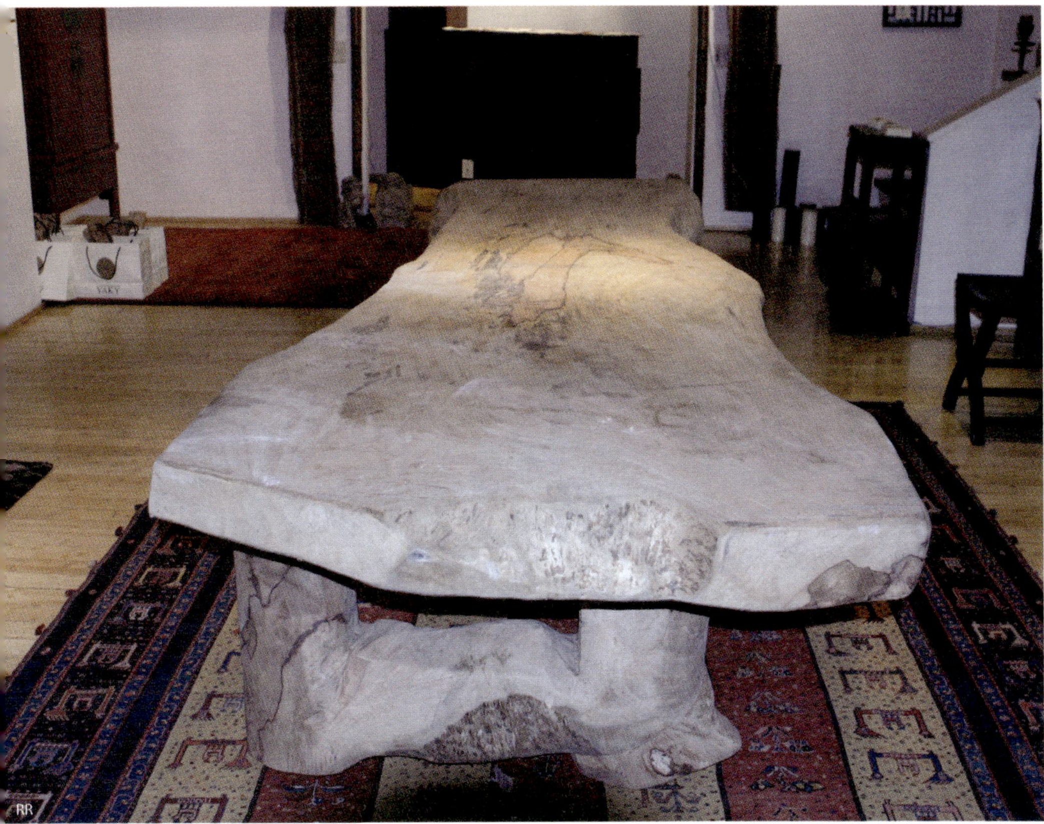

Yaki, table

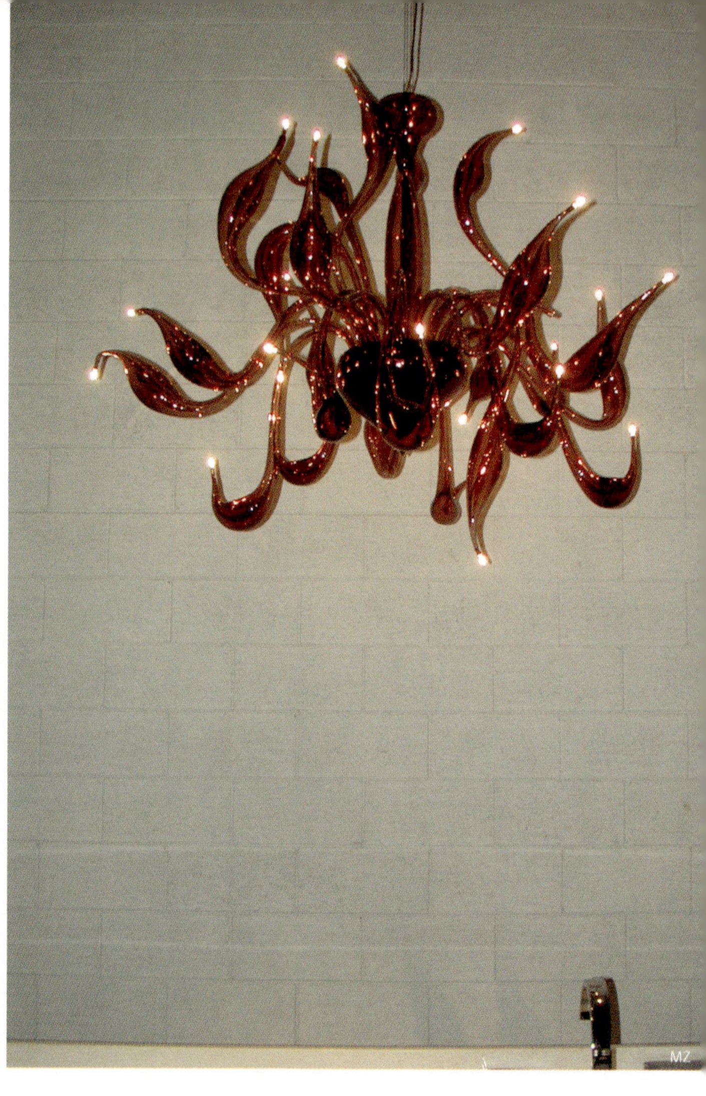

Bisazza

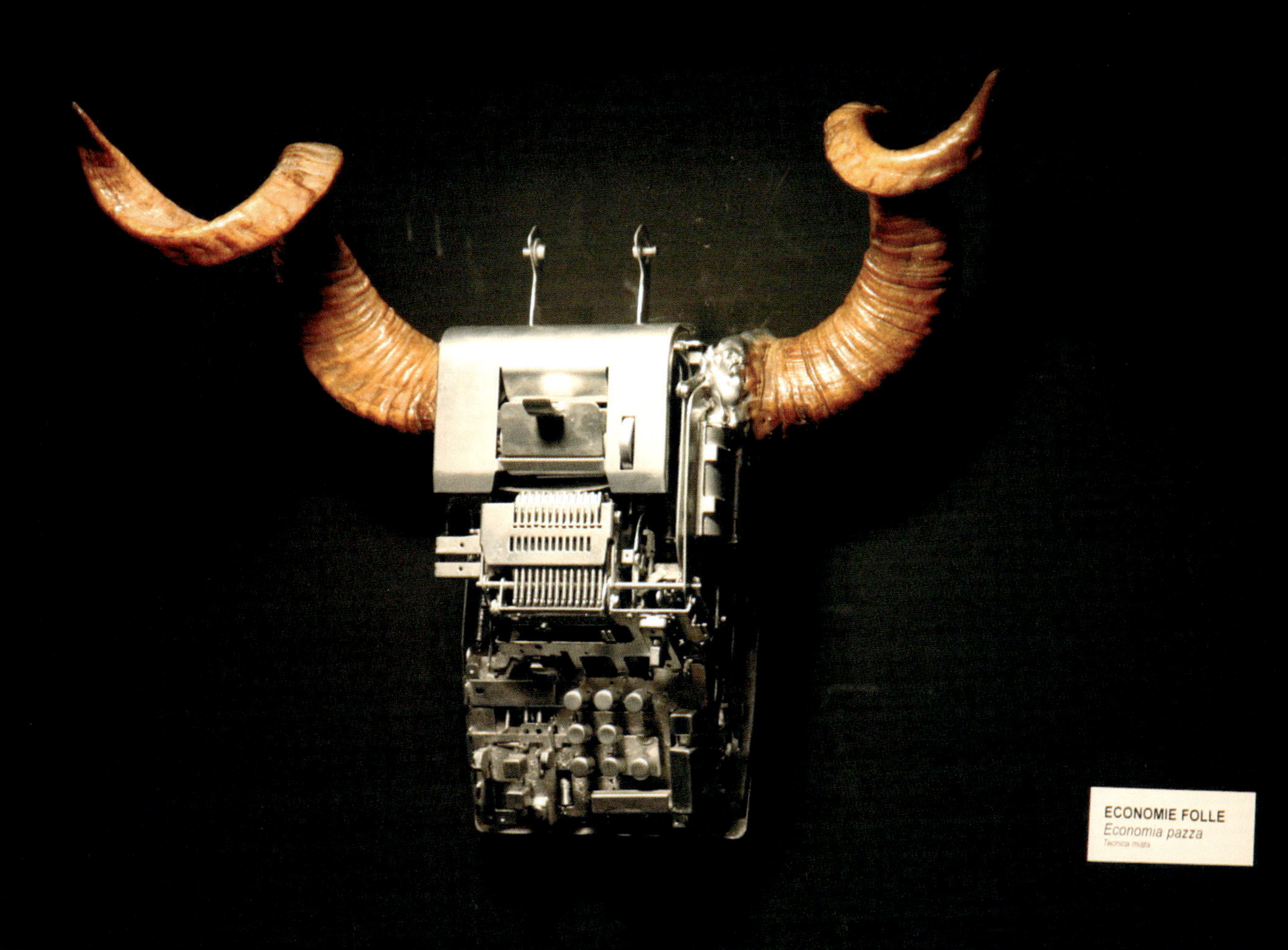

Designplaza

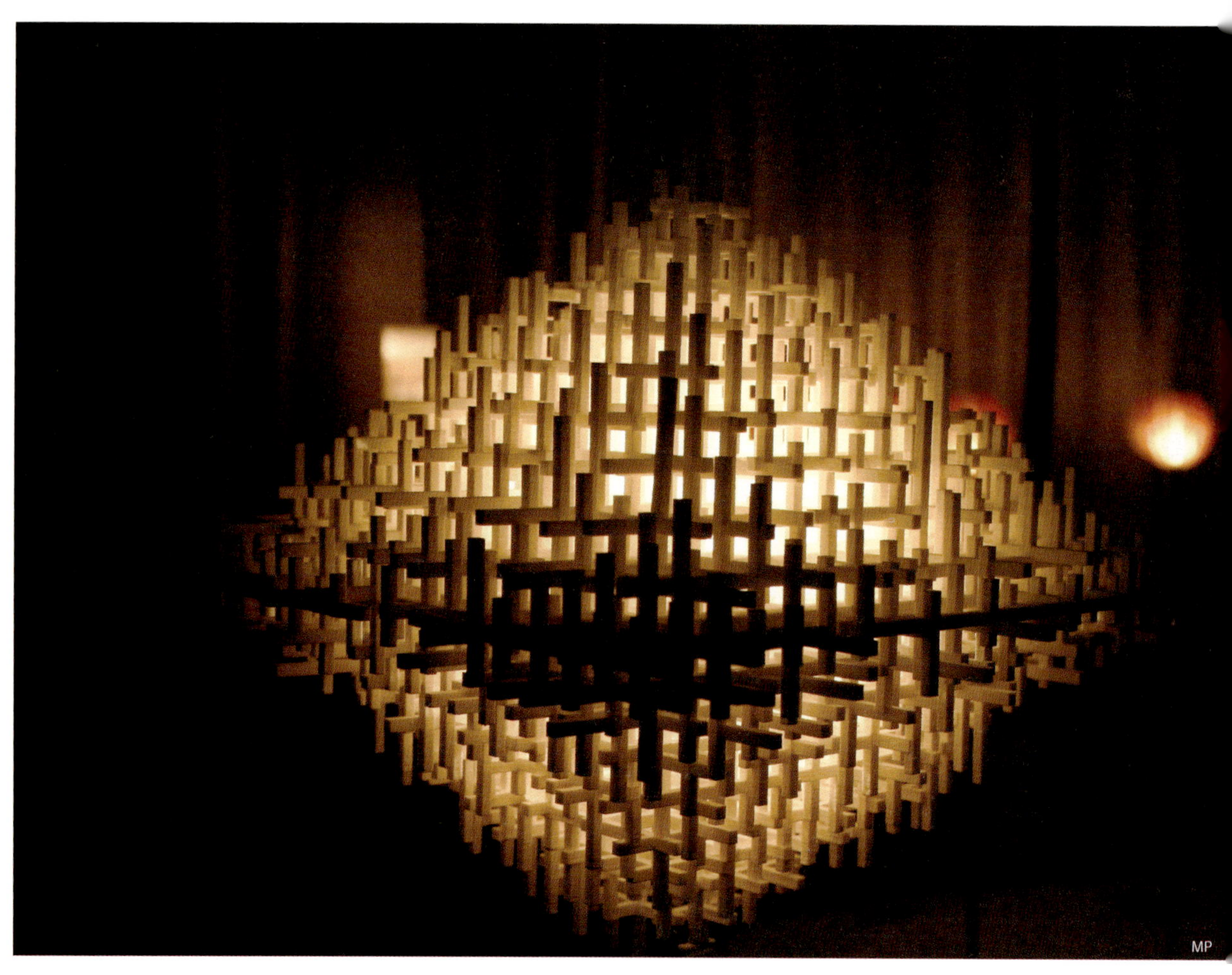

MGX @ Zona Tortona

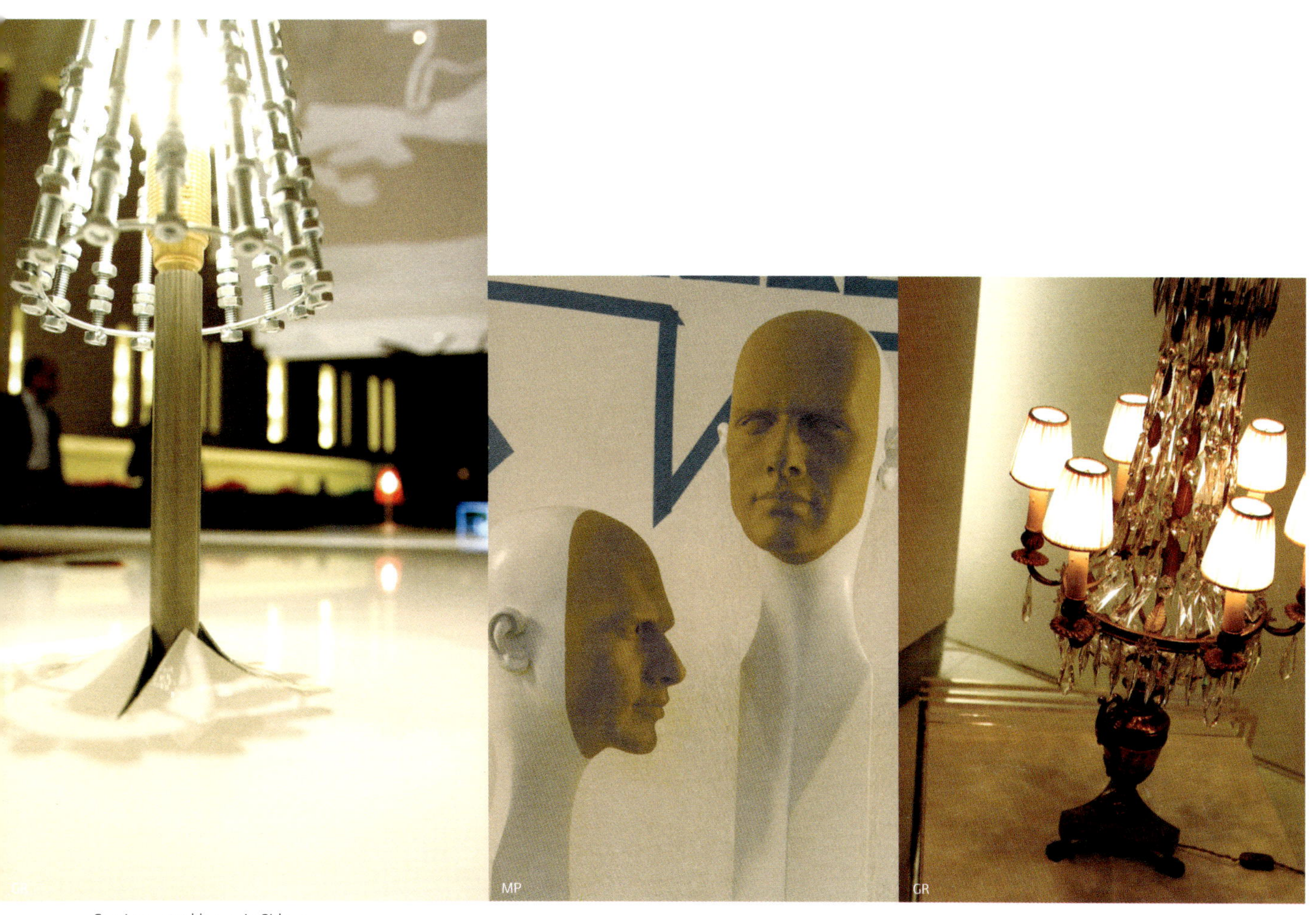

Carnivora steakhouse in Sidney
by The University of New South Wales

Fabrica Features by Fabrica @ Designersblock

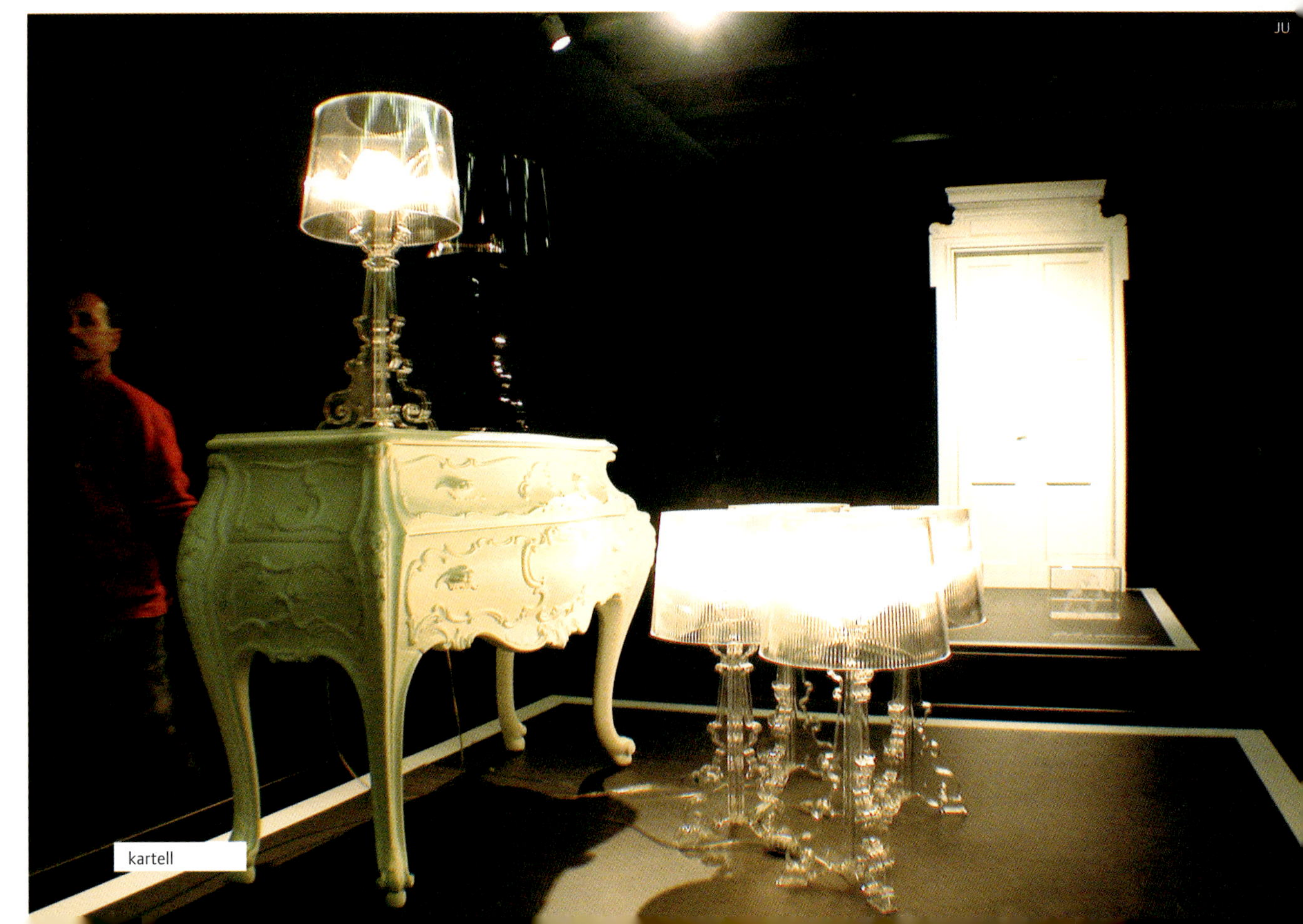
kartell

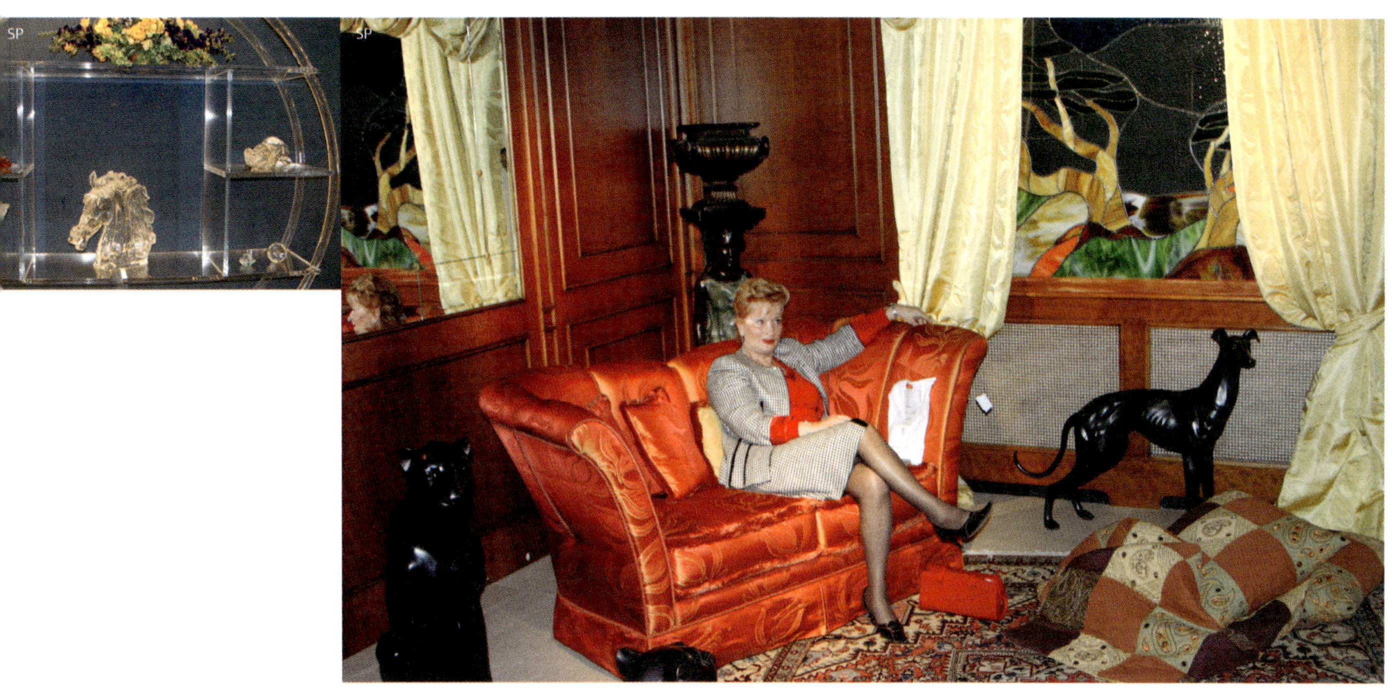

Crisaform

Gigi Santamaria

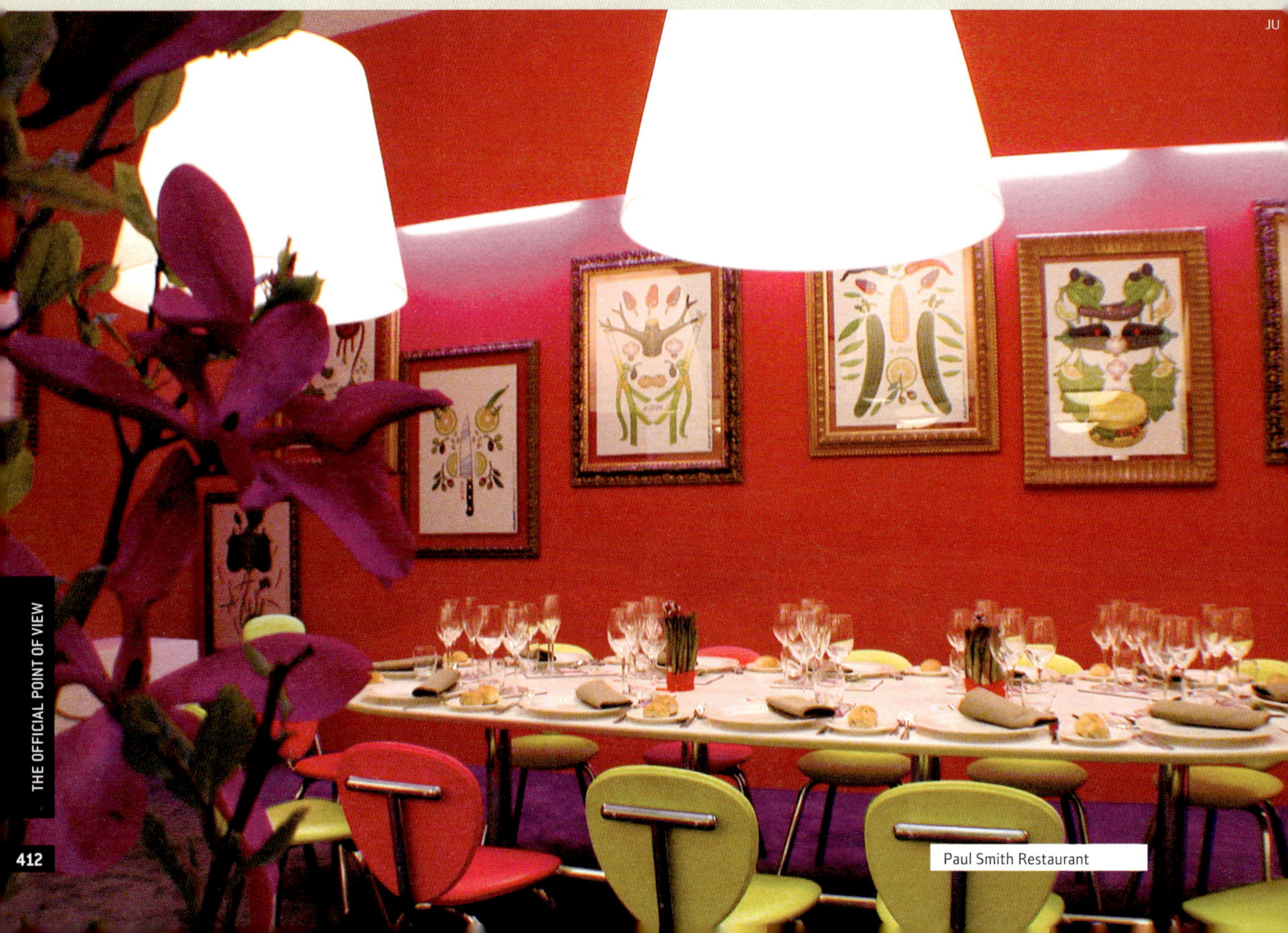

Paul Smith Restaurant

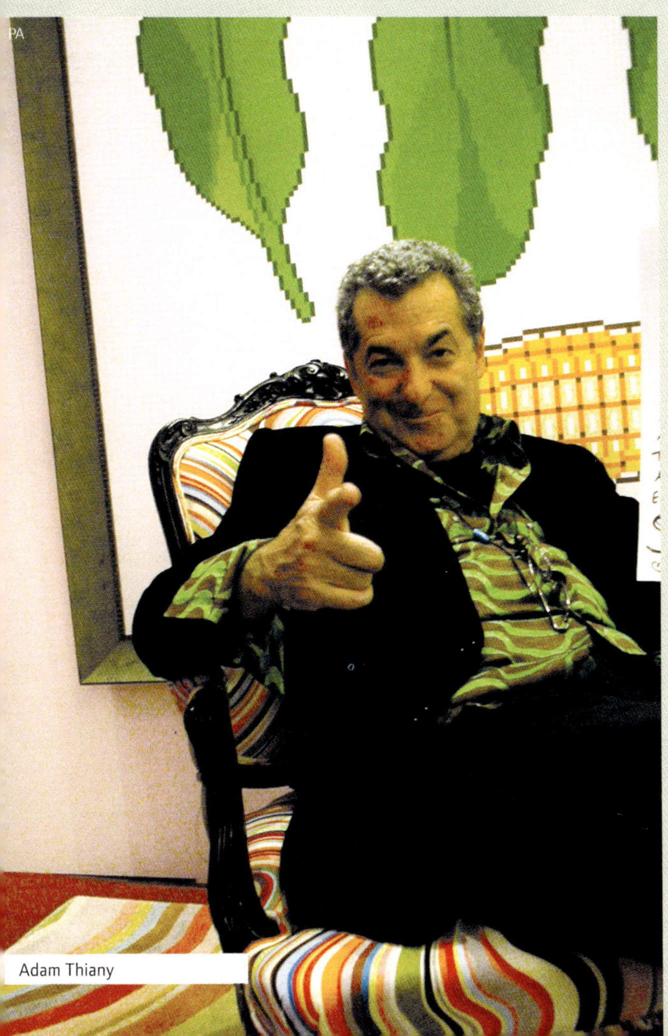

DINING DESIGN RESTAURANT

An invitation-only restaurant,

by Rosita Missoni and Paul Smith.

Rosita Missoni manipulates flowers, lines, and

three-dimensional, kaleidoscopic decor elements in black, white.

At the entrance, a large multi-coloured carpet.

Paul Smith works on the surface of things,

playing with the idea of "dressing" floors with pink

carpeting; tables, with khaki tablecloths; chairs,

with shirts; and walls, with huge images inspired

by food specially created by **Eboy,** a group of young

Berlin-based designers.

FOOD ART

For Dining Design, respected food stylist **Nir Adar** has

created a video installation entitled "Heat as Directed,"

consisting of projections of magical multimedia still lifes.

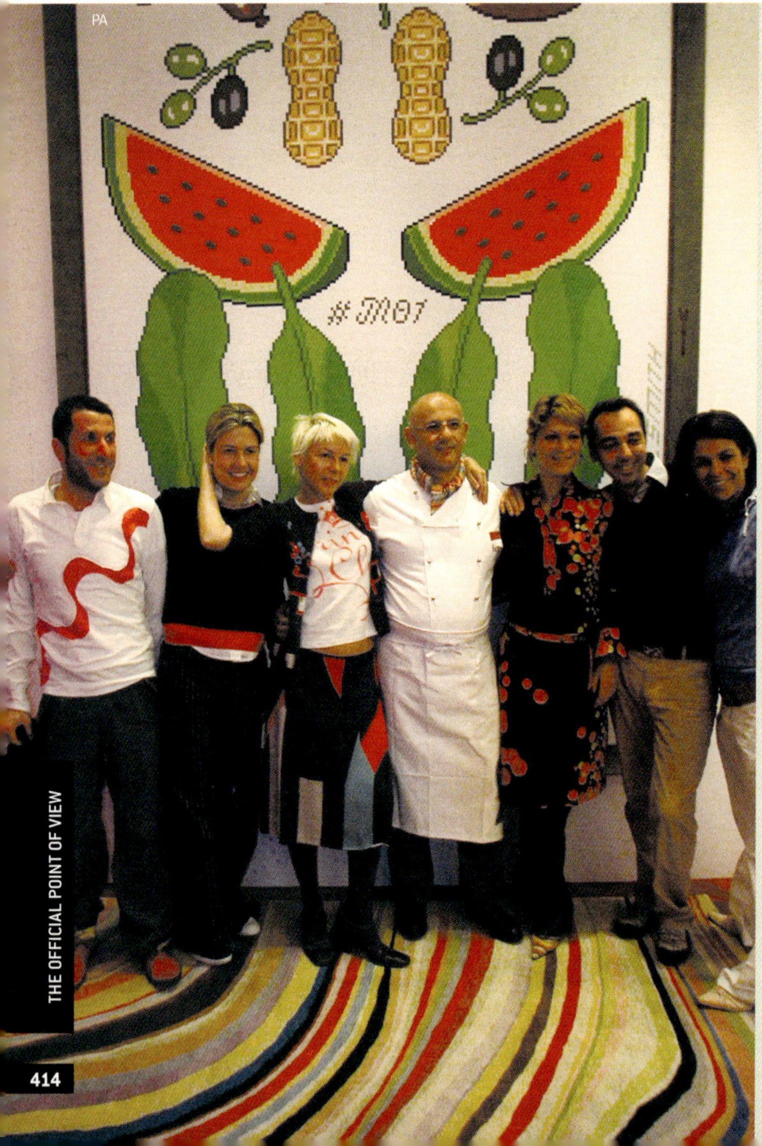

CLAUDIO SADLER

IS FOOD SUBJECT TO PLANNING

JUST LIKE DESIGN IS?

I consider myself as a food designer and as an architect
I use the tools befitting the planning process and
implementation. My ultimate goal is creating new flavours
and to that end I employ my own style and tools.
I start from the materials, the various combinations and
contrasts when thinking of a new dish.

YOUR IDEAL DINNER/SUPPER?

It must be light, exciting and reassuring.

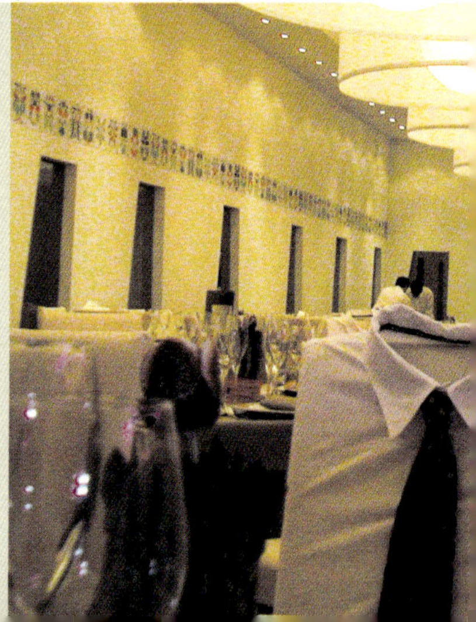

> DINING DESIGN

AN EXCITING DISH?

Prawns covered with almonds and ginger sauce.

A REASSURING DISH

Milanese style veal sirloin.

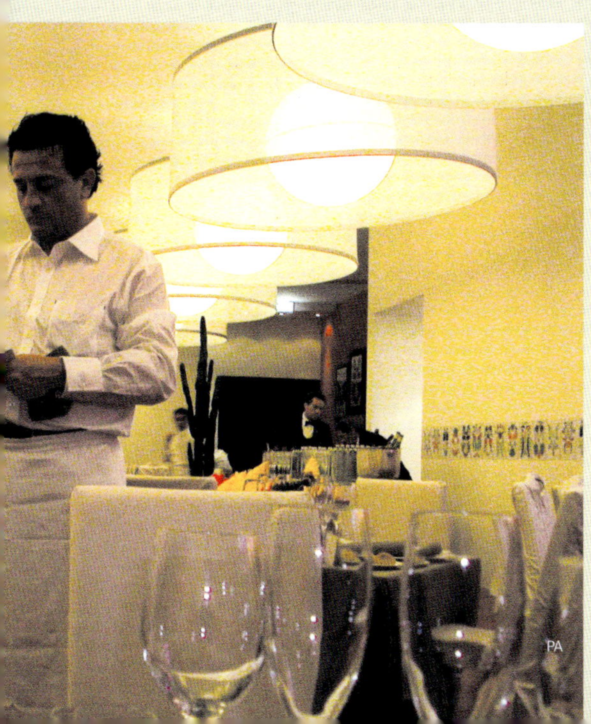

WHAT CAN BE CURRENTLY ASSOCIATED TO THE CONCEPT OF "ENTERTAINMENT" IN THE CULINARY SECTOR?

Pasta, I think, as cooking it is sheer pleasure – at home, of course! You can cook it in the company of friends, who can all give their own contribution. The guests can be actively involved so that cooking becomes a social event bringing people together.

HOW DO YOU ENVISAGE FUTURISTIC FOOD?

Virtual food as a source of fun and performing art, a real and fanciful combination at the same time. Food presentation is crucial as it stimulates the brain, thus making food look more appetizing. Also, cooking for a restaurant, i.e. for many people is a tough task as personal heritage bears considerable weight, like our childhood memories as well as our mother's cooking. Hence innovating and changing is not so simple a task as it must be a gradual process aimed at winning increasing appreciation. The best possible solution for a chef is to be able to transform food and his/her heritage gradually by relying on personal skills. I think this is fairly close to design. In the future people will be eating less and lighter food as quantity is no longer bound to be crucial.

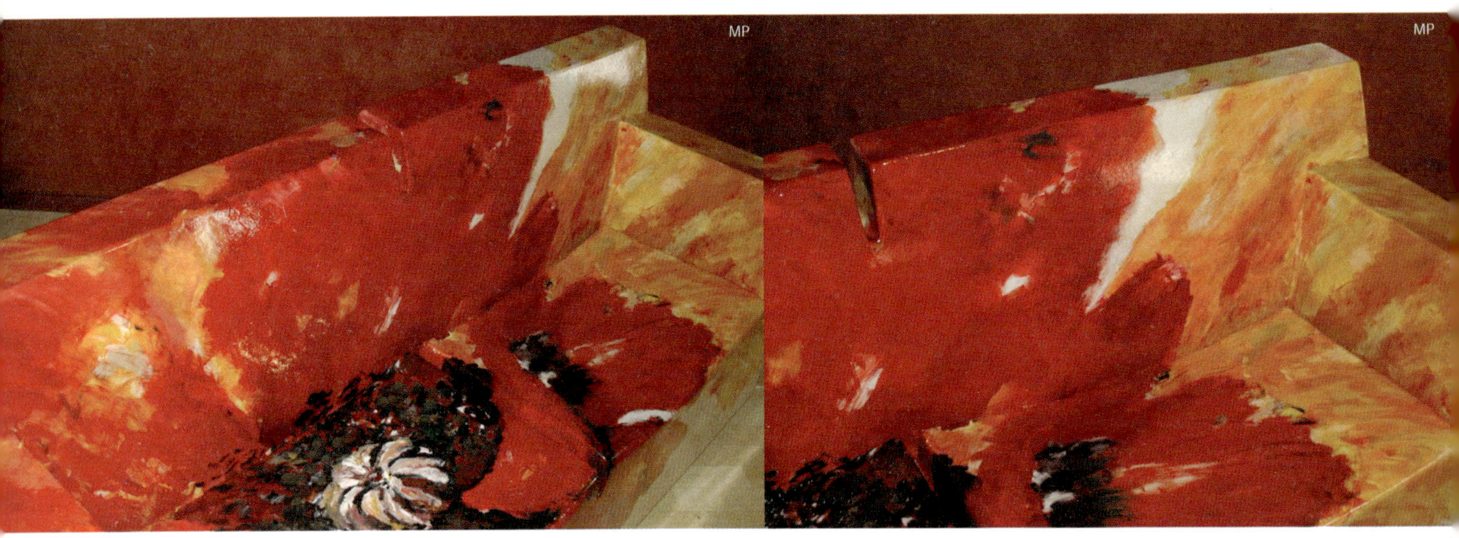

Christiane Guth

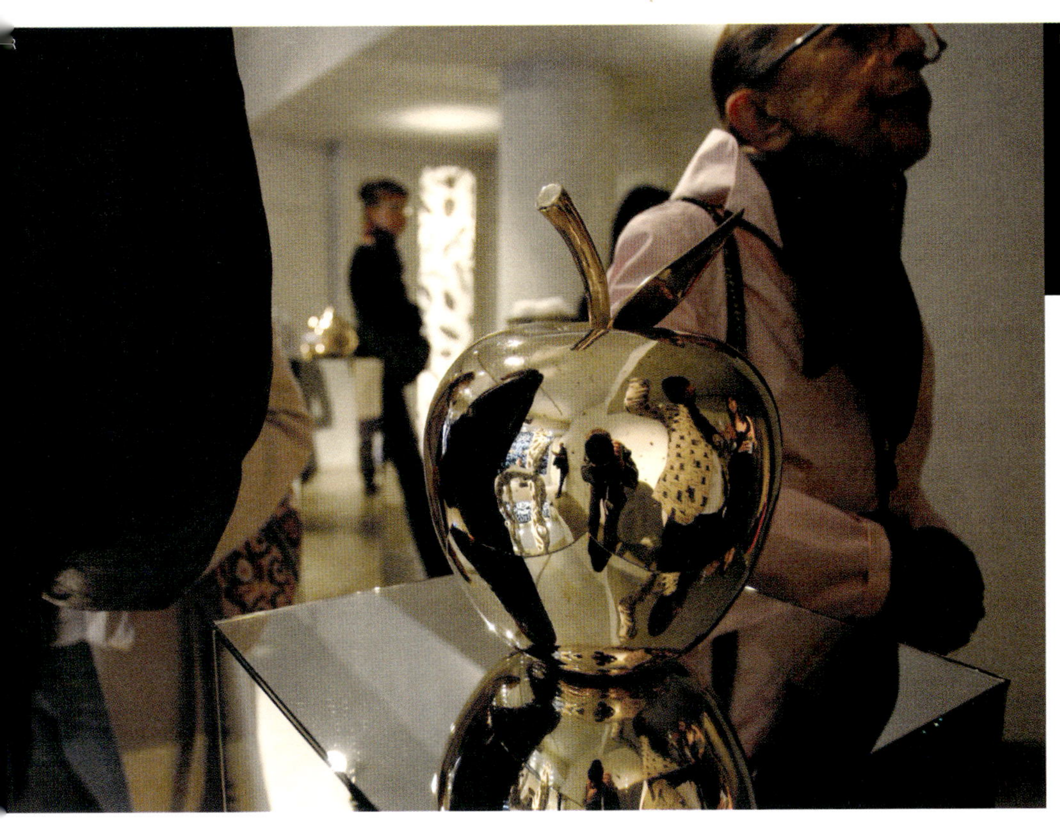

Studio Job @ Dilmos

Krizia's hand

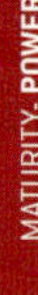

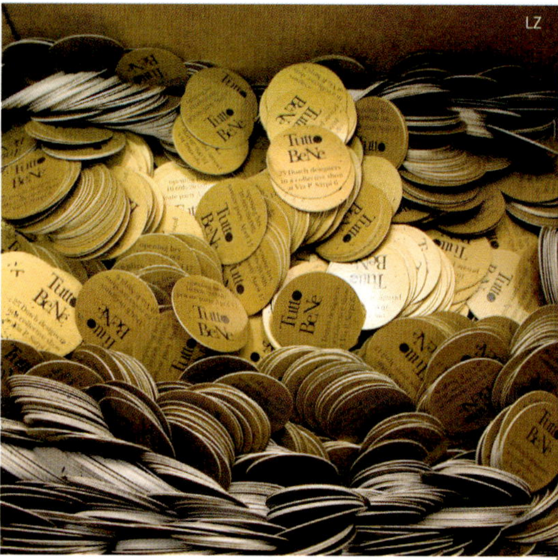

Business cards of Tutto BeNe

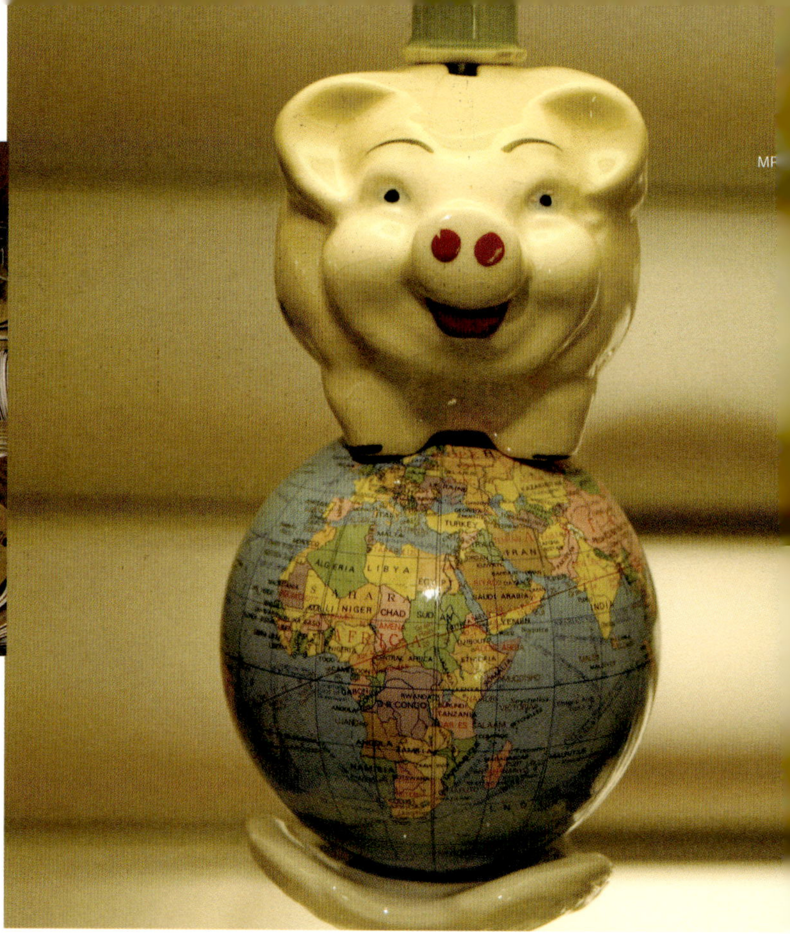

Harry Richardson Design London Committee

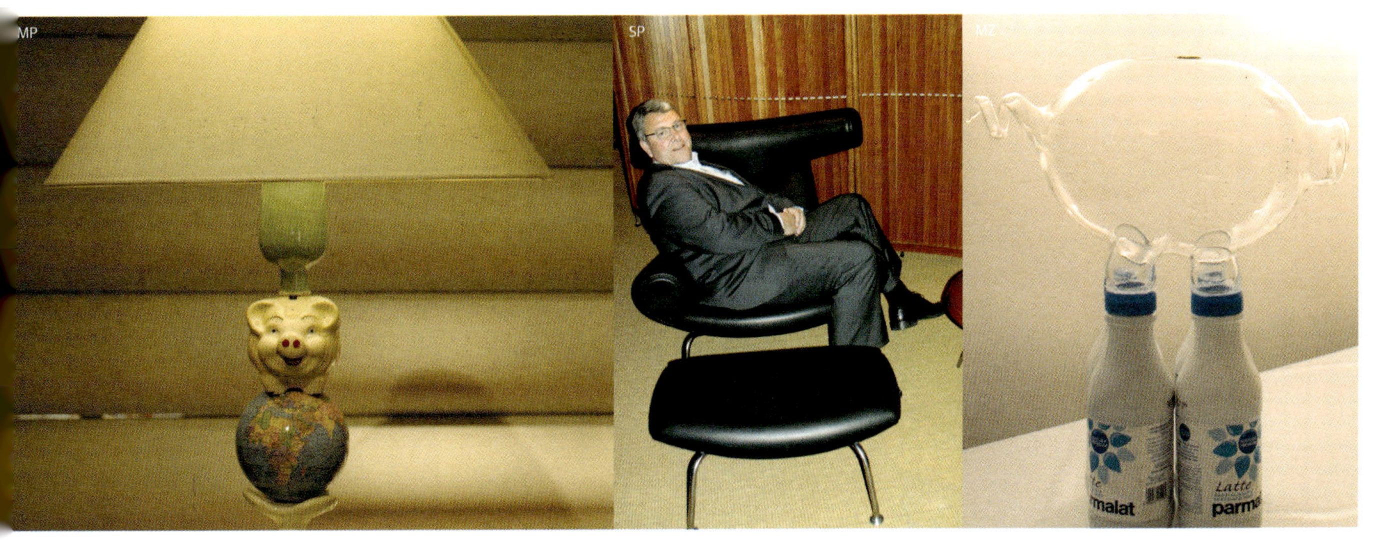

Handustrial @ Internos

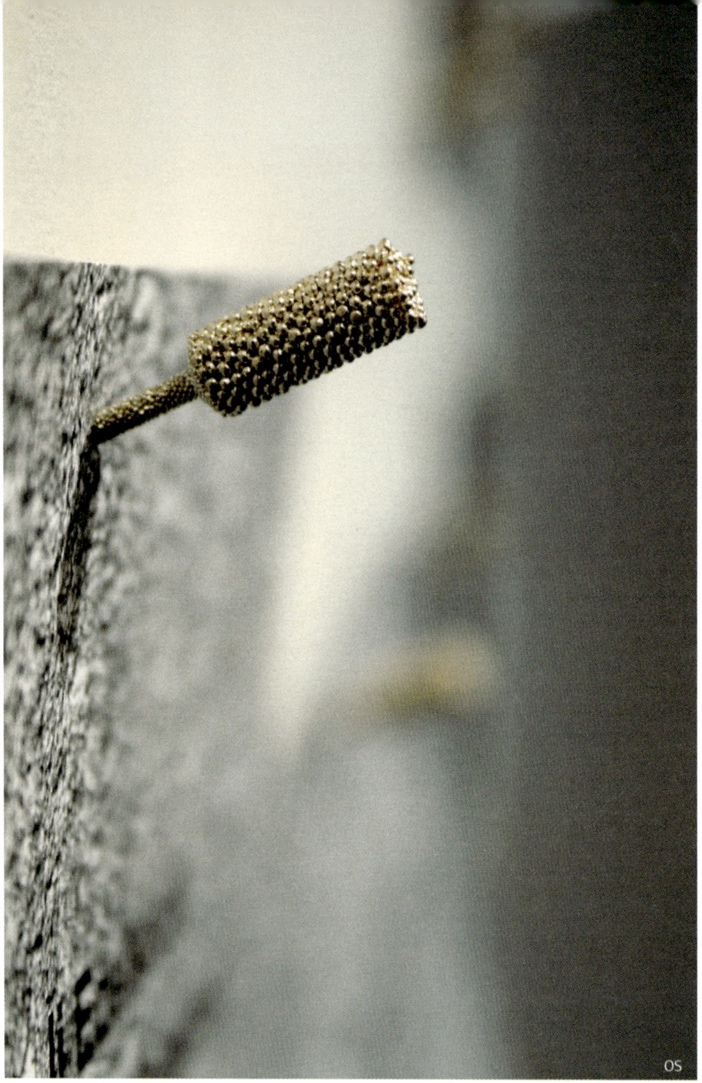

"Concrete poetry" by Design Academy Eindhoven

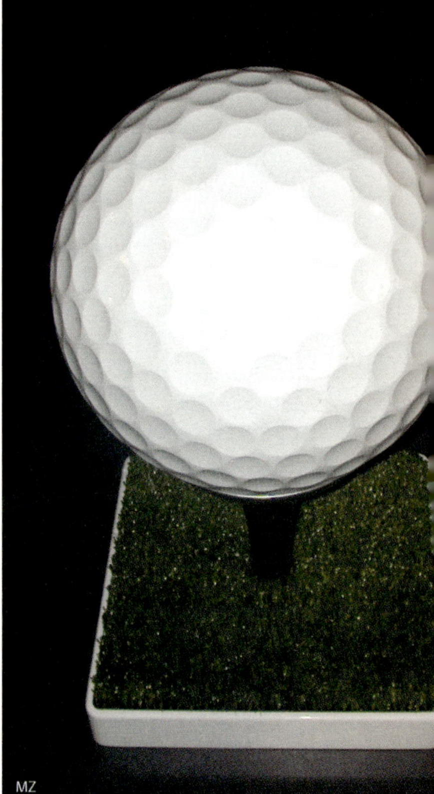

@ Cappellini

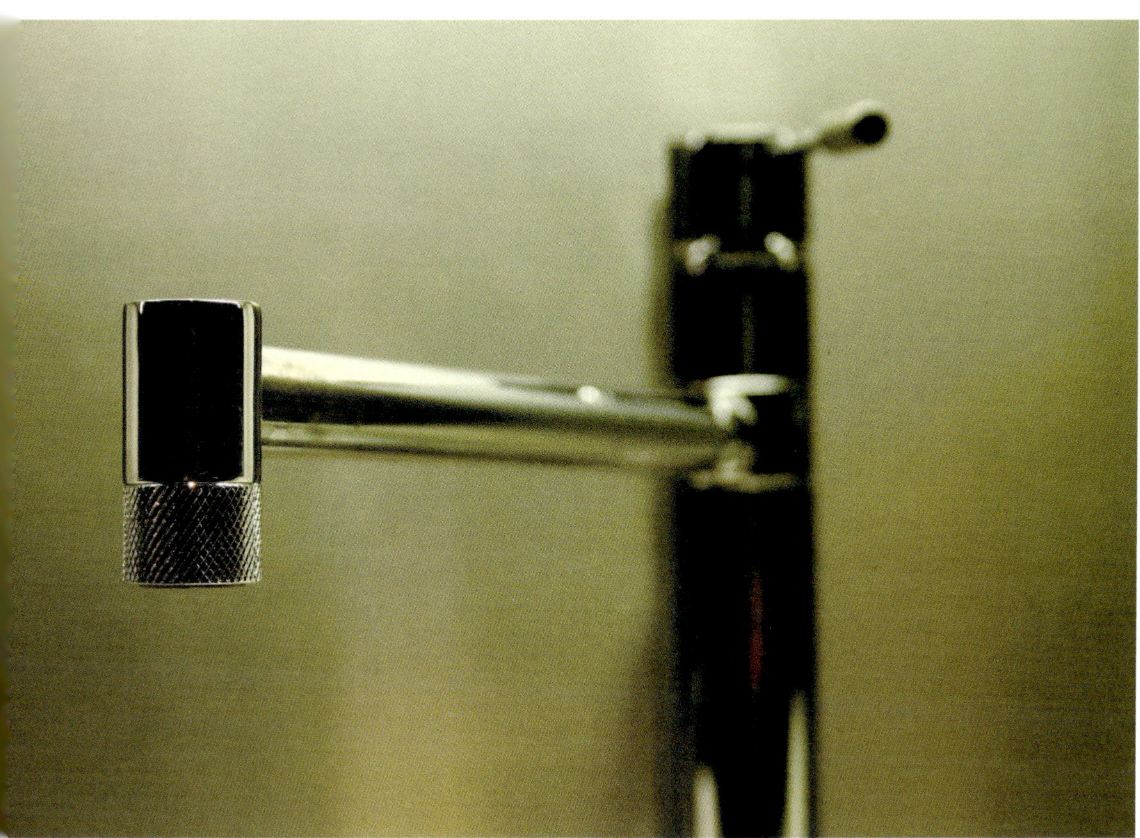

Ycami installation @ CRT Triennale

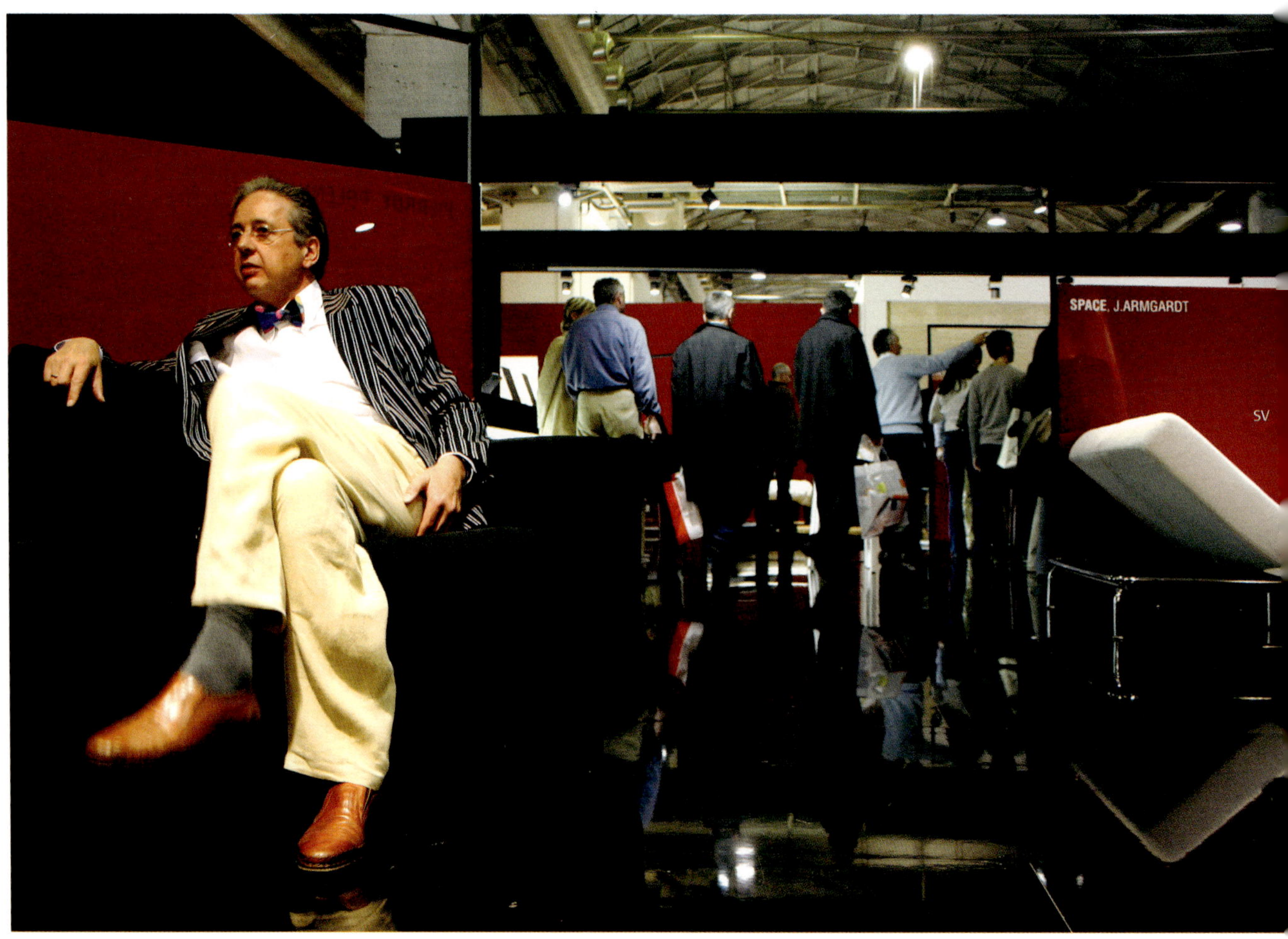

Bonaldo

RR
SP
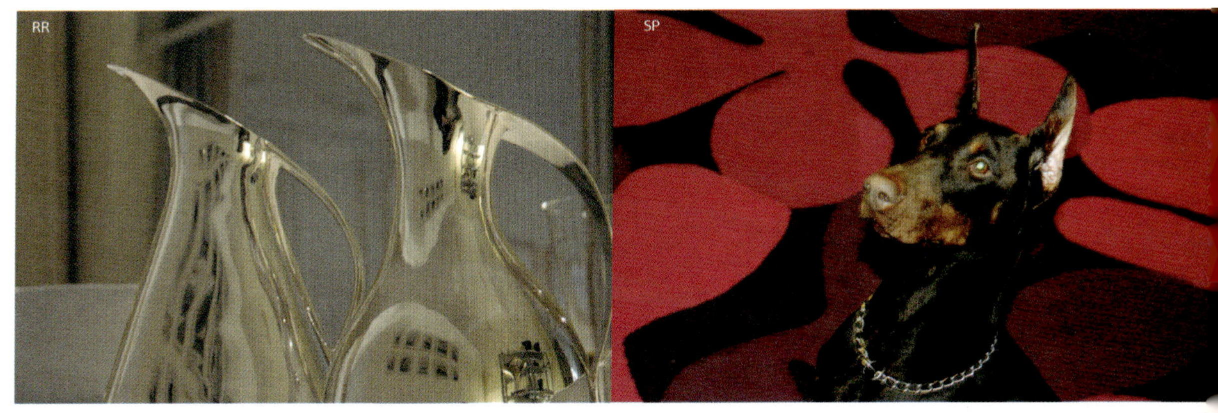

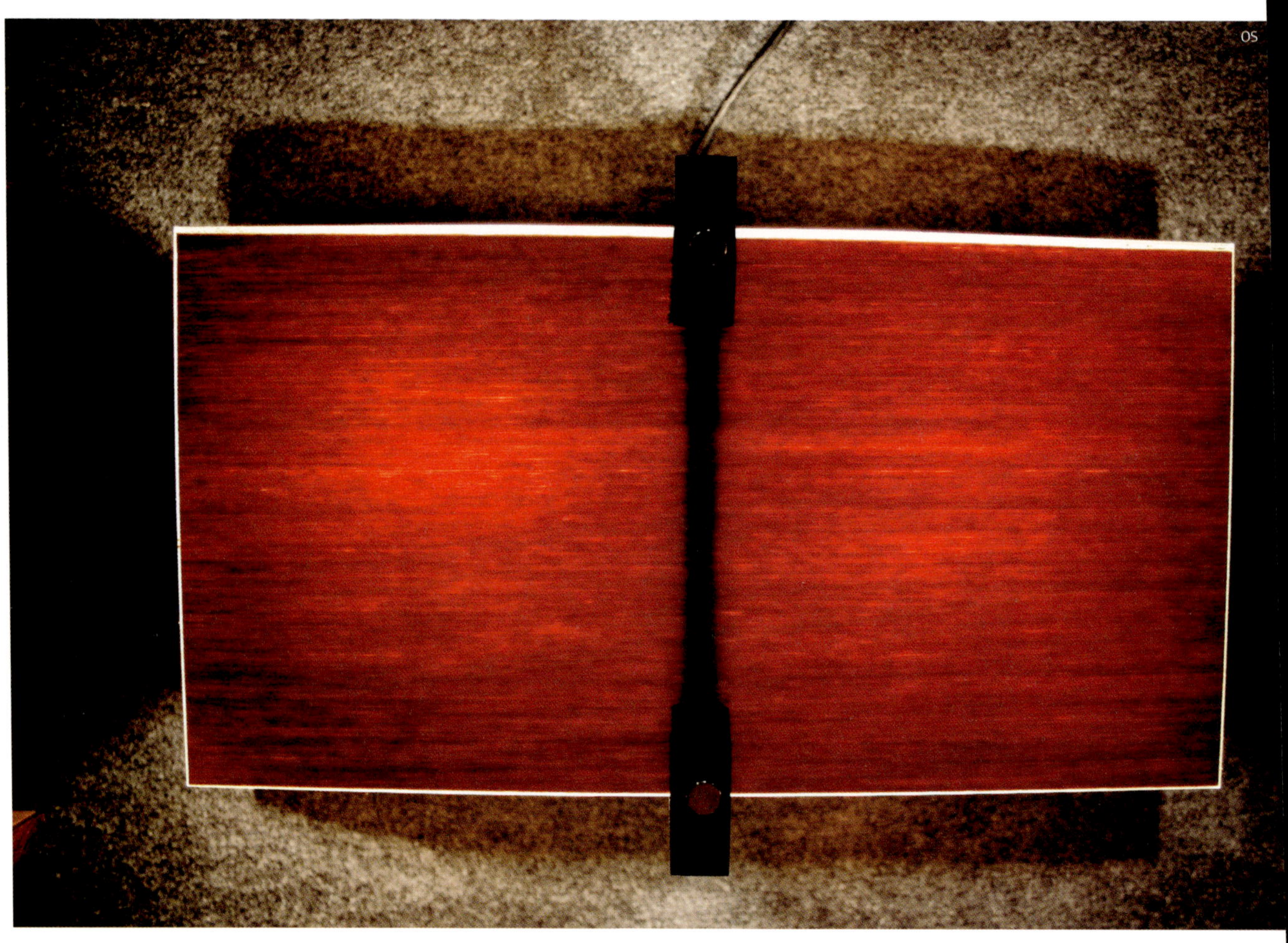

Jacopo Gardella

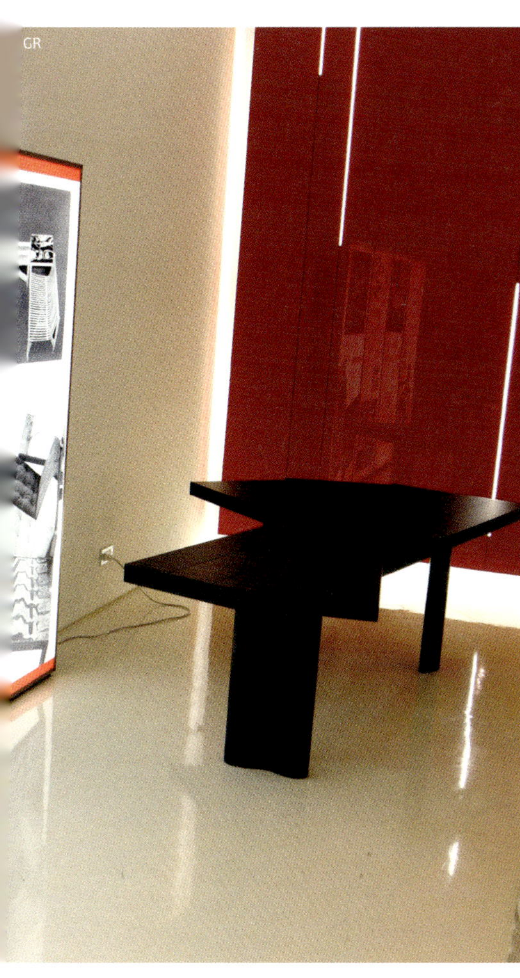

Cassina

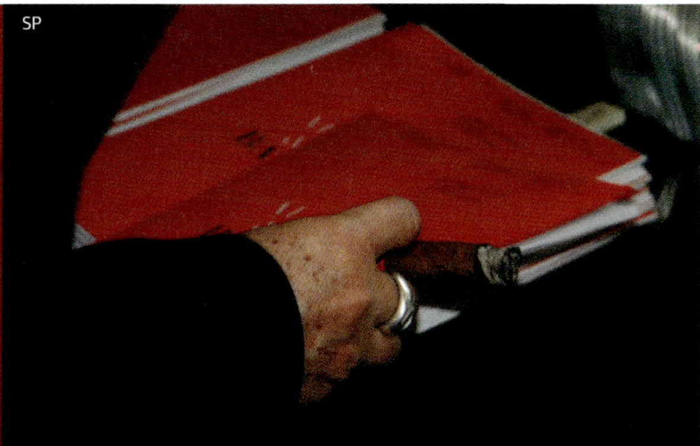

Au Doight

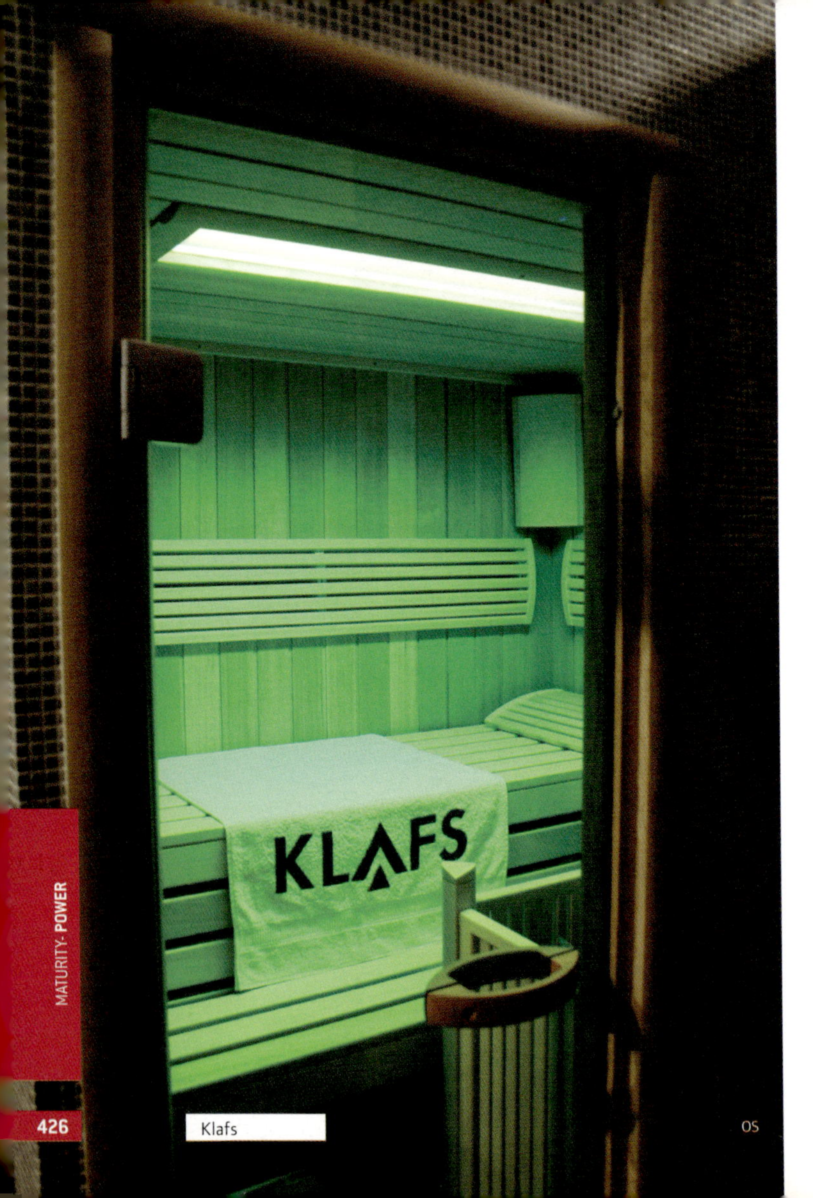

Klafs

OS

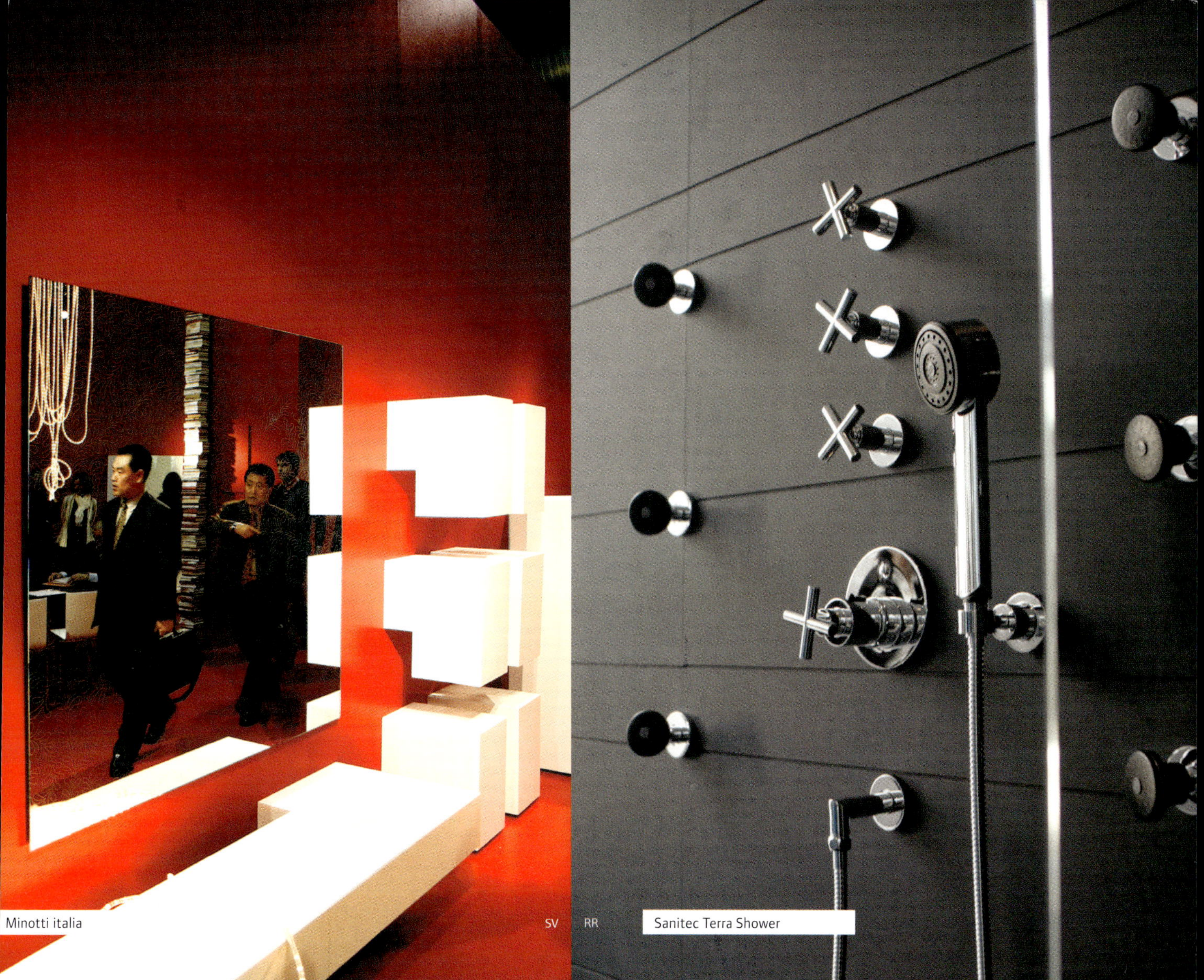

Minotti italia

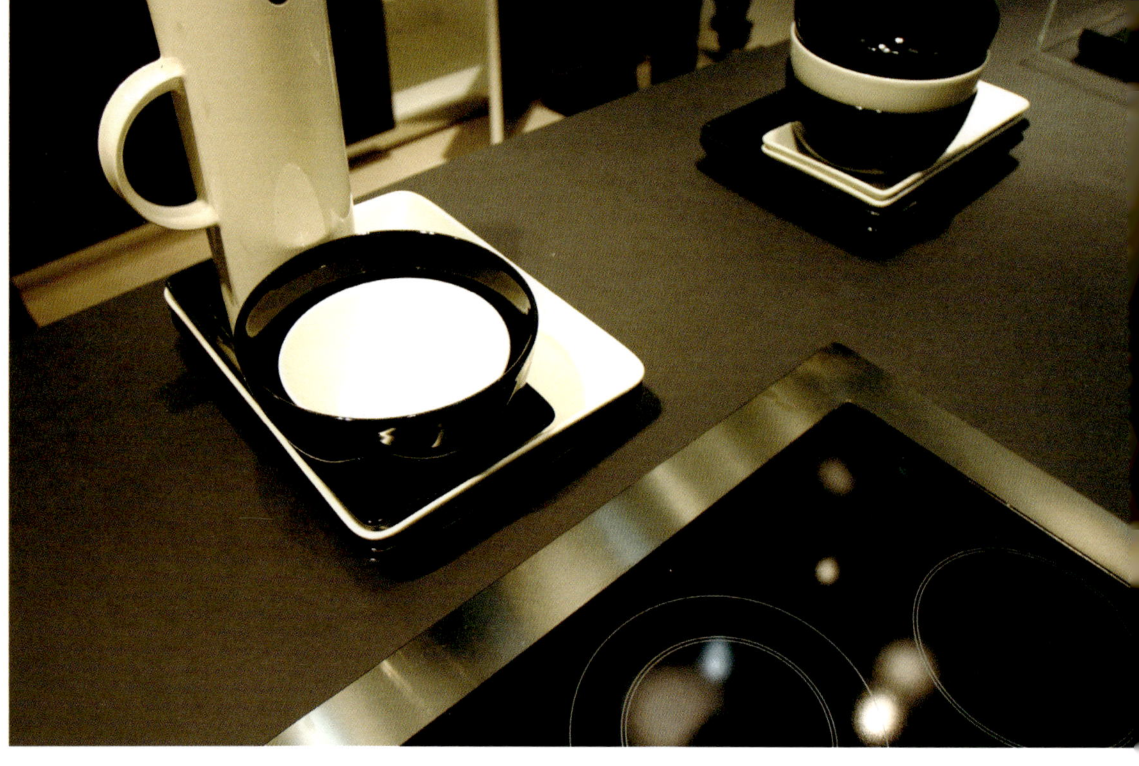

Spazio Dada

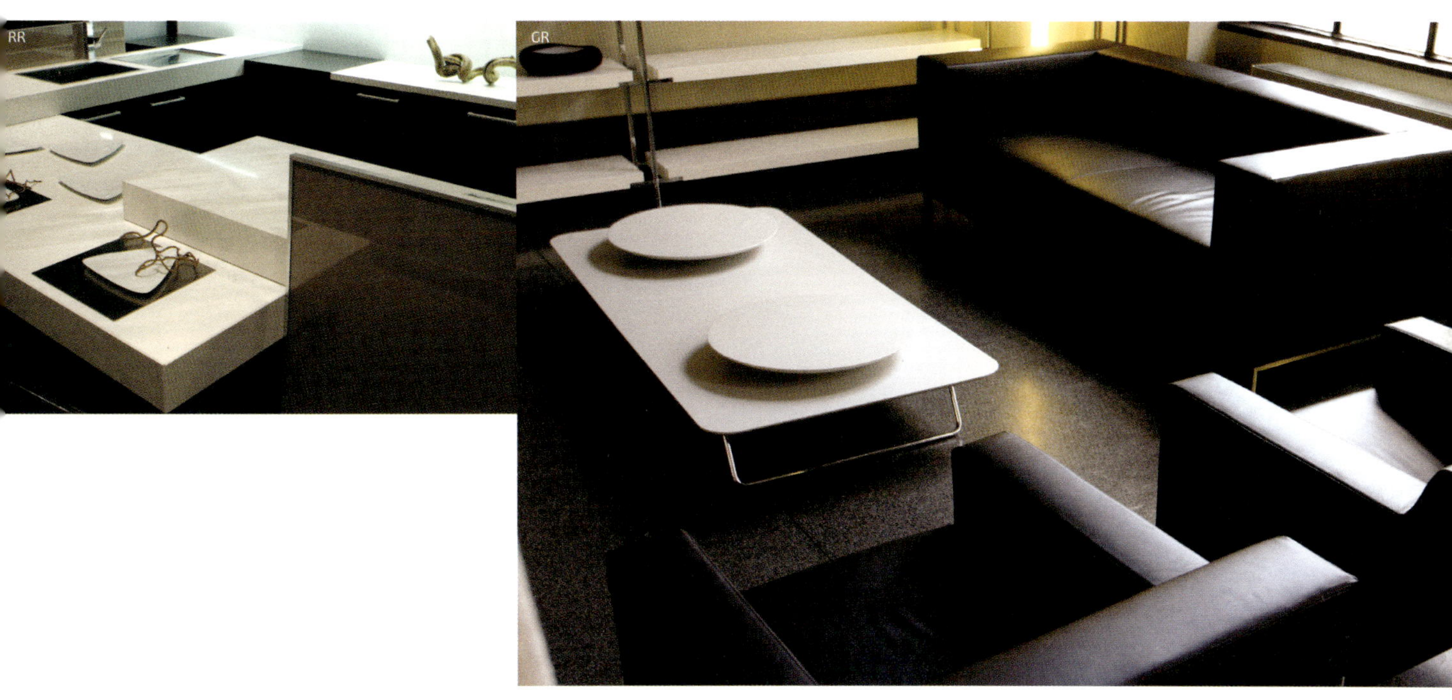

Arrital Cucinev

Maxid

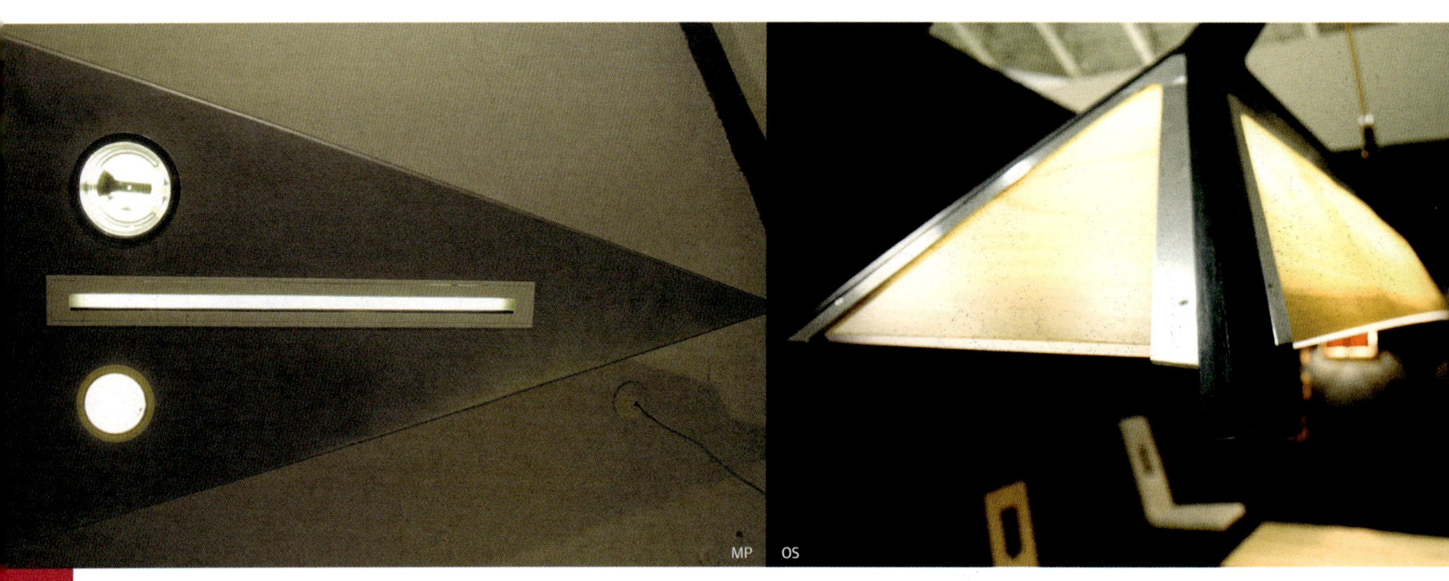

Regiolux

Jacopo Gardella

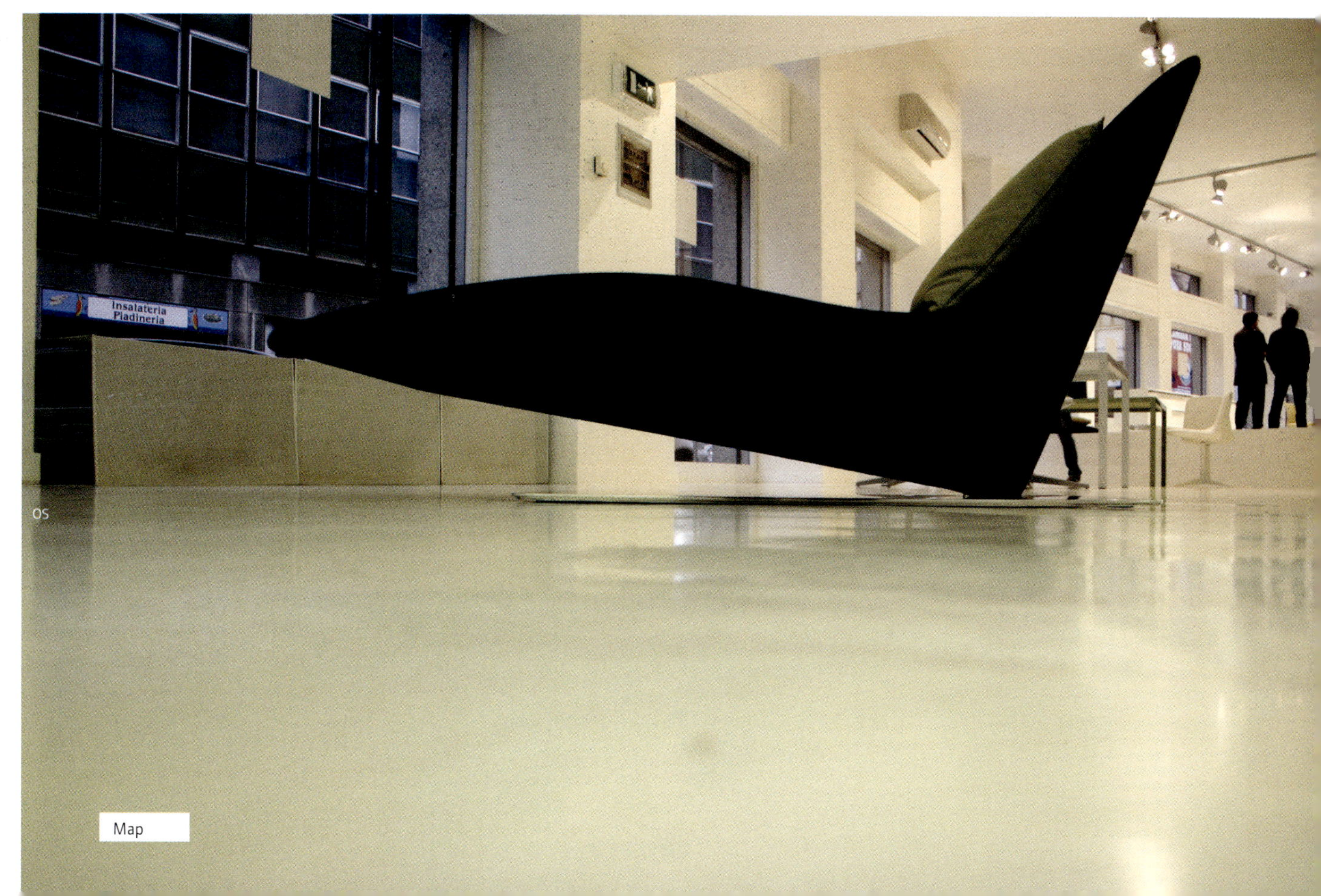
Insalateria
Piadineria
OS
Map

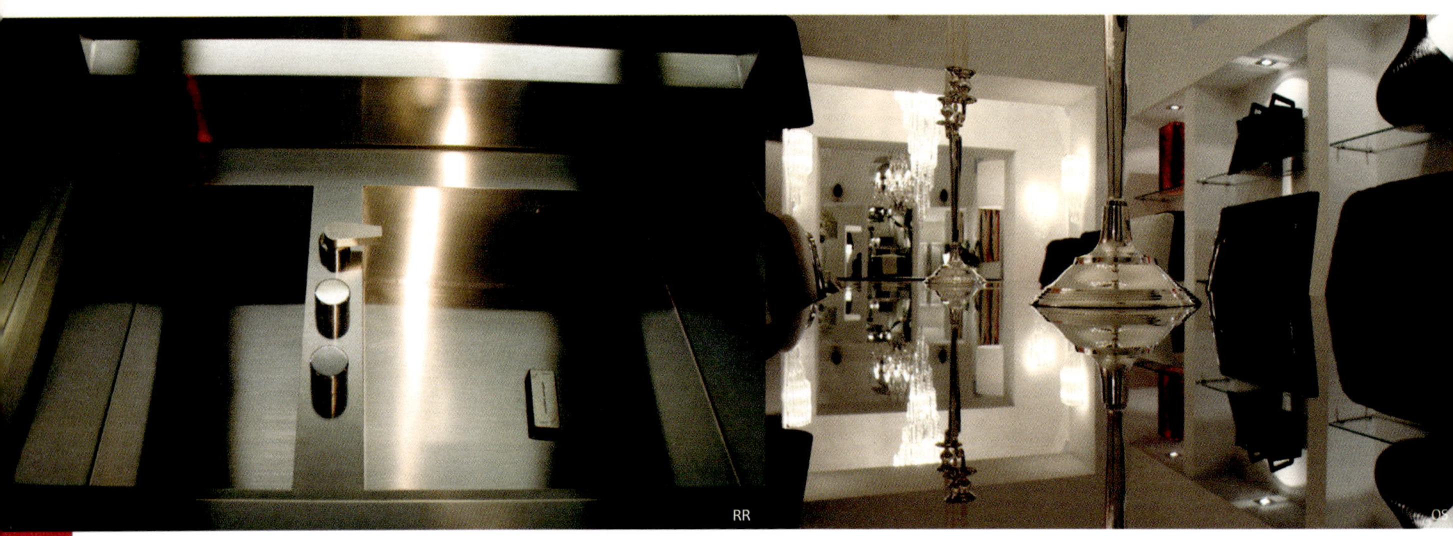

Boffi

Visionnaire

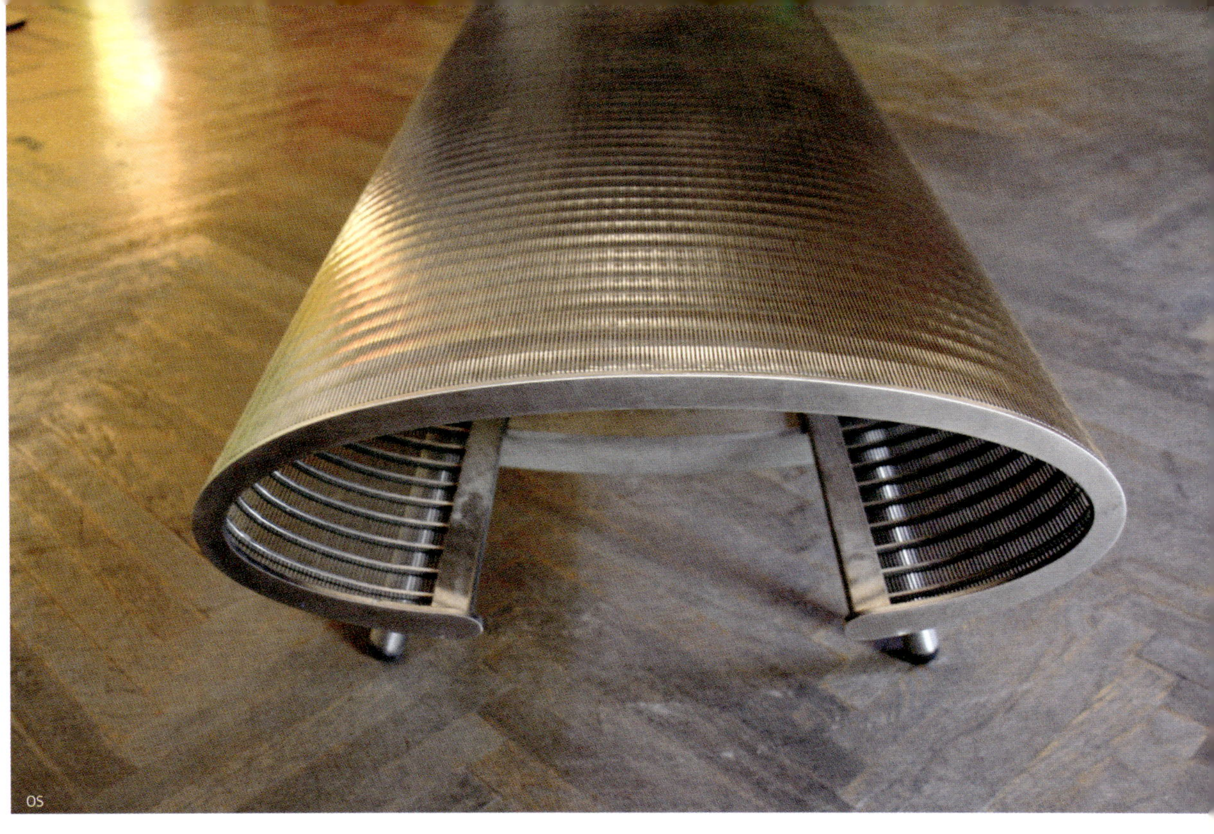

Santa&Cole

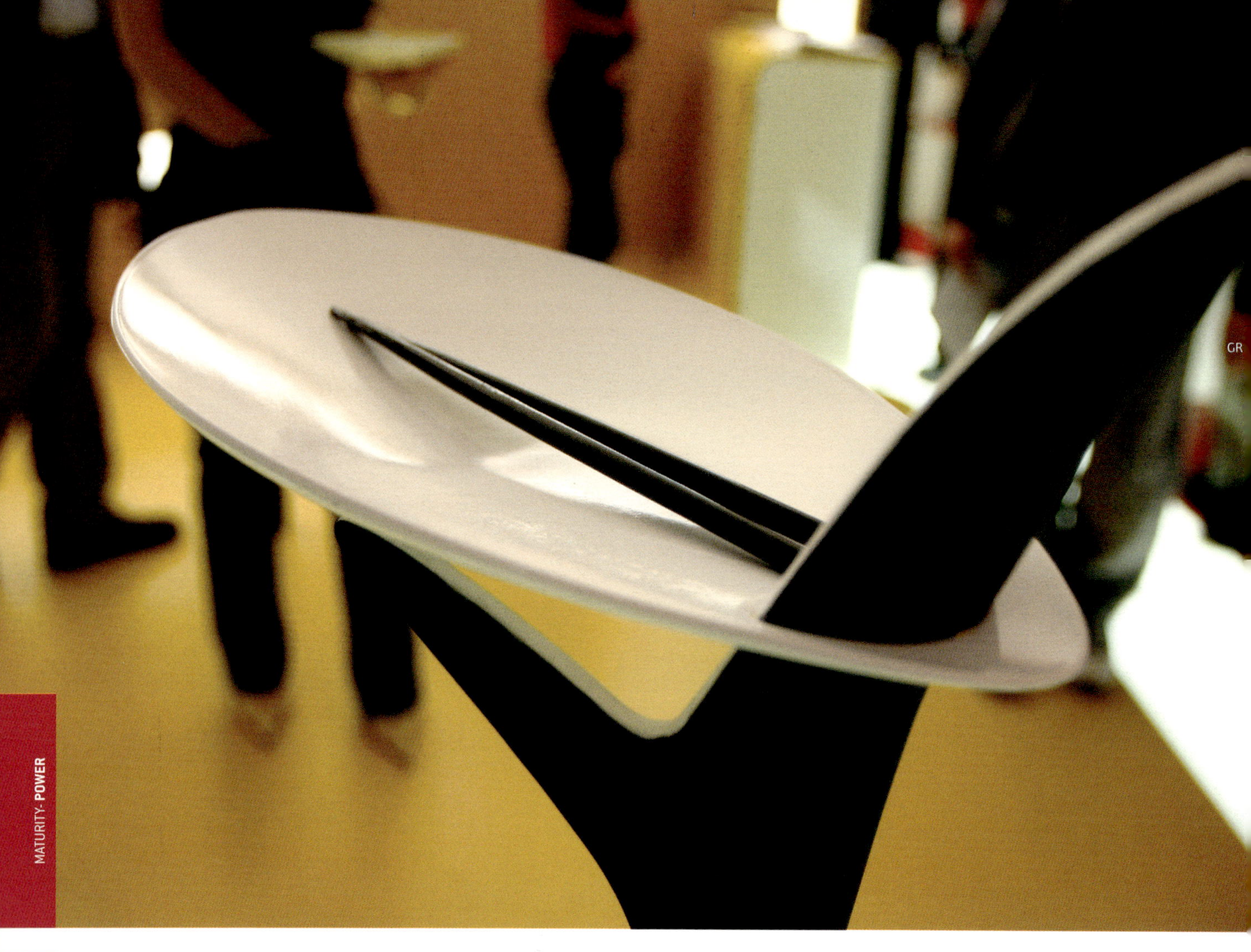

Più-Yiù chinese restaurant in Rome by Politecnico di Milano @ Dining Design

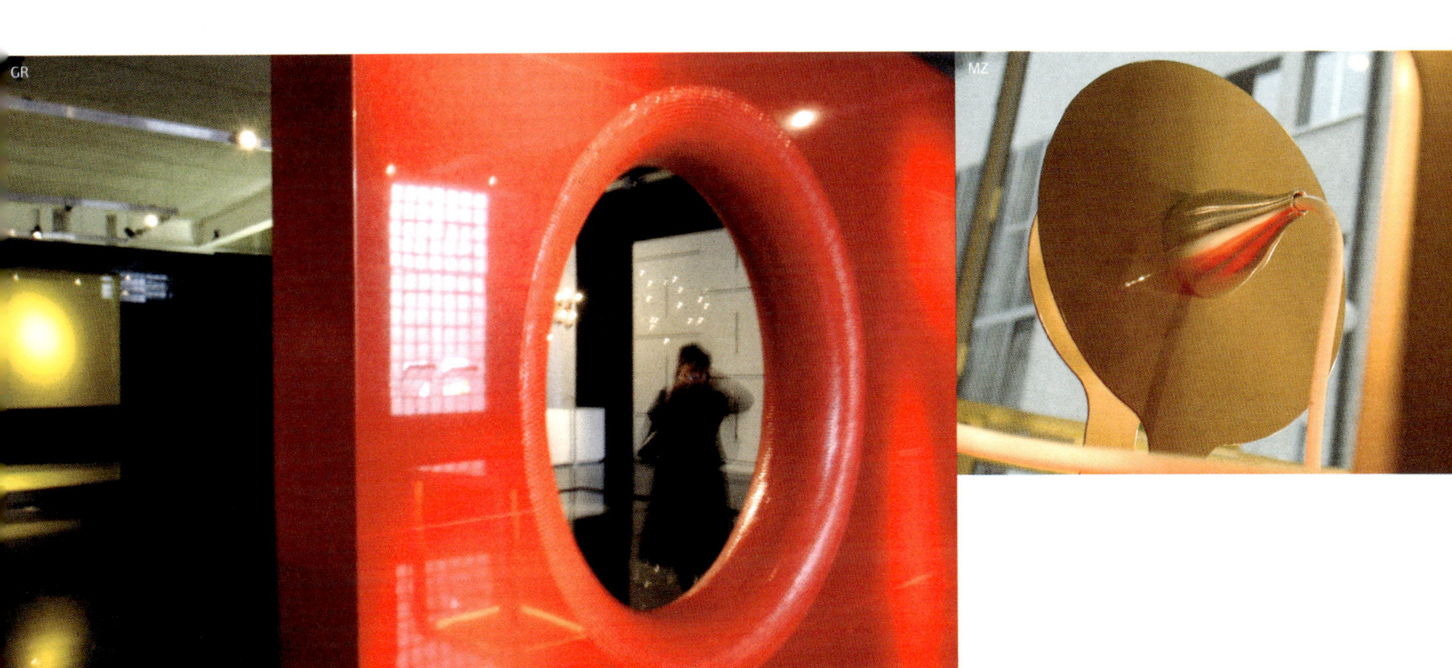

Bisazza @ Zona Tortona

Swiss design

> MMM - Metal Machine Muzak

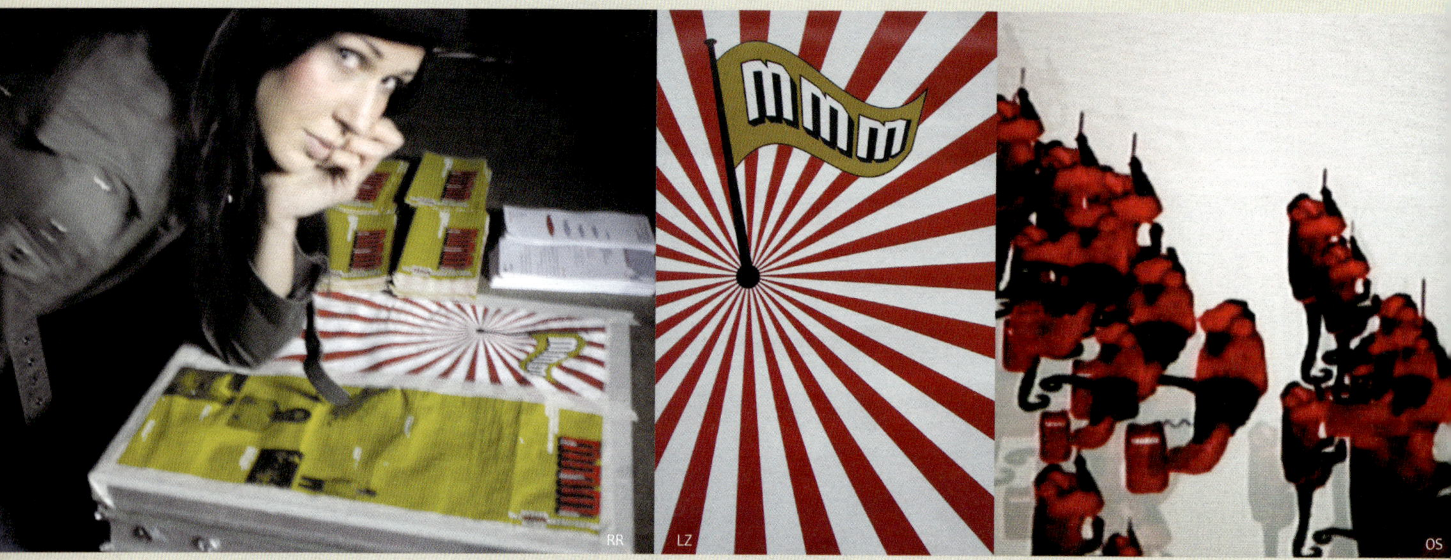

MMM was the first edition of an original experimentation of **public art**:

a summary of new artistic contents, an original requalification of public space.

It was a place where free creativity and the **spirit for research** dominated.

It was an experimental laboratory based on the concept of design applied to open spaces that **hosted the performance**

of visual artists and sound designers, dj sets and concerts in which the technological element

mixed with the human one giving a different interpretation of the contemporary electronic landscape.

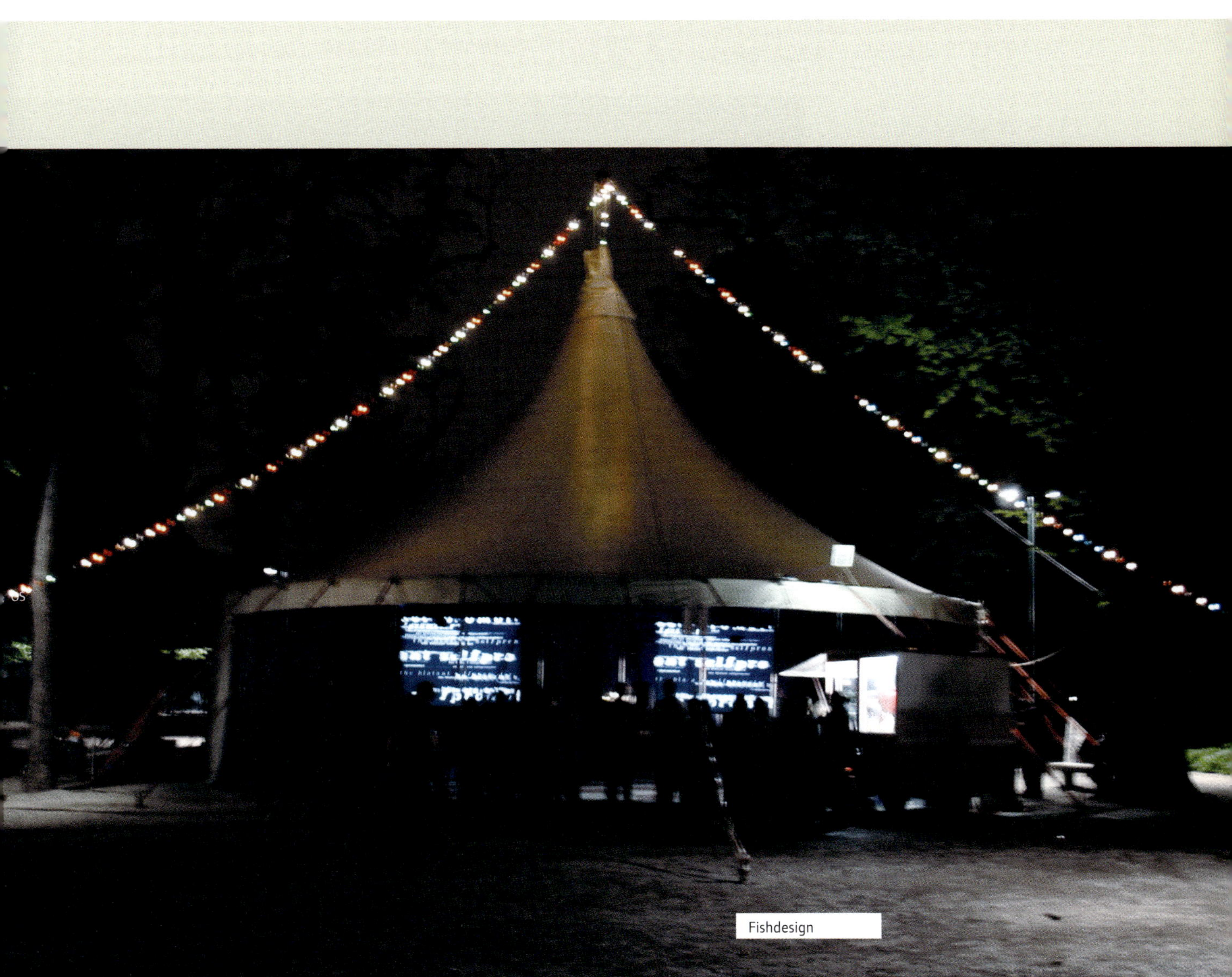

Fishdesign

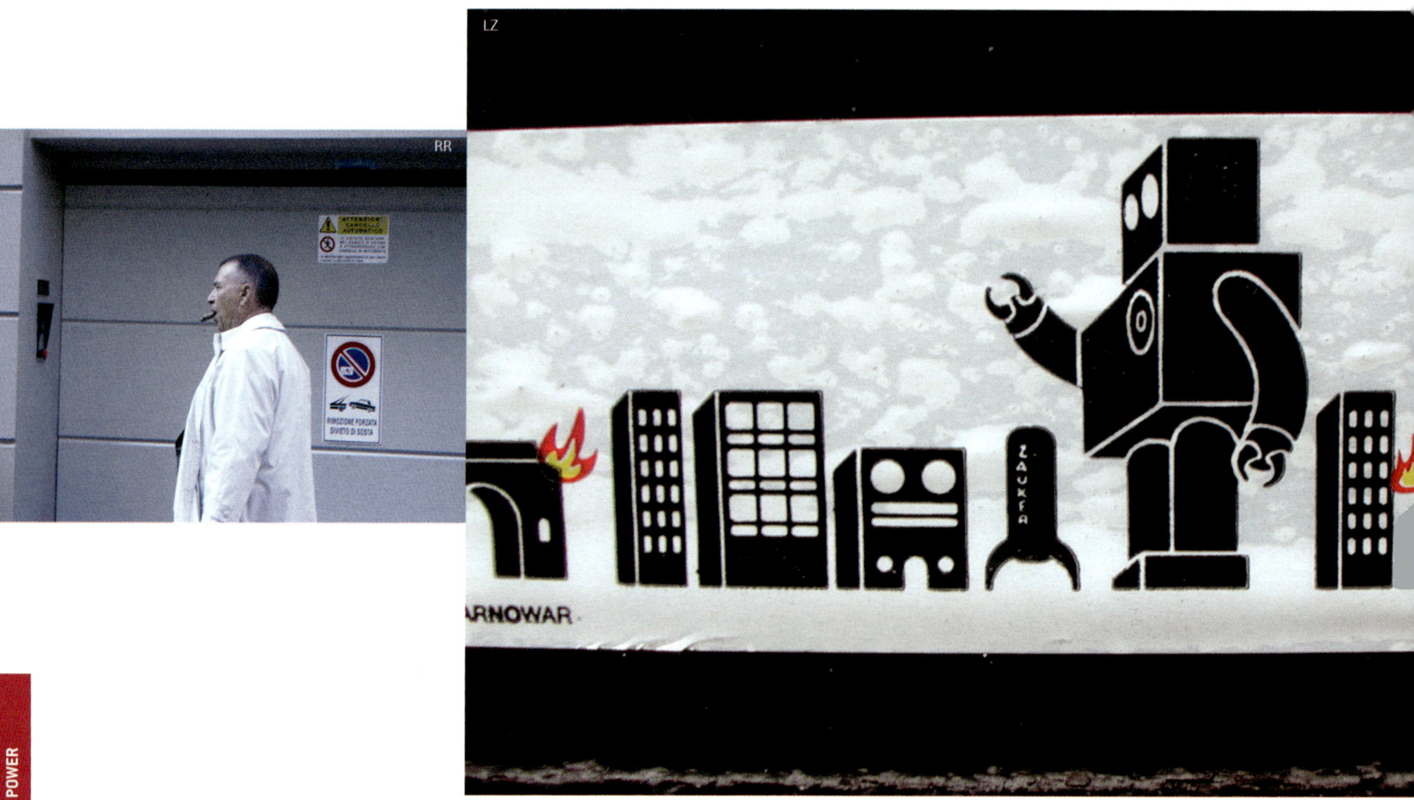

Sticker

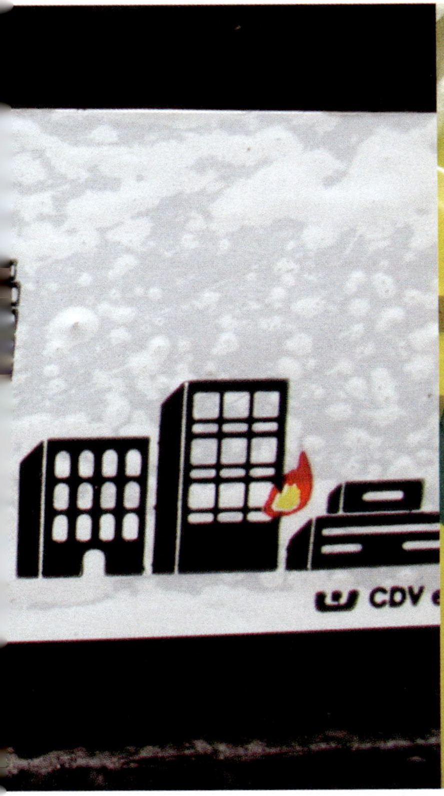

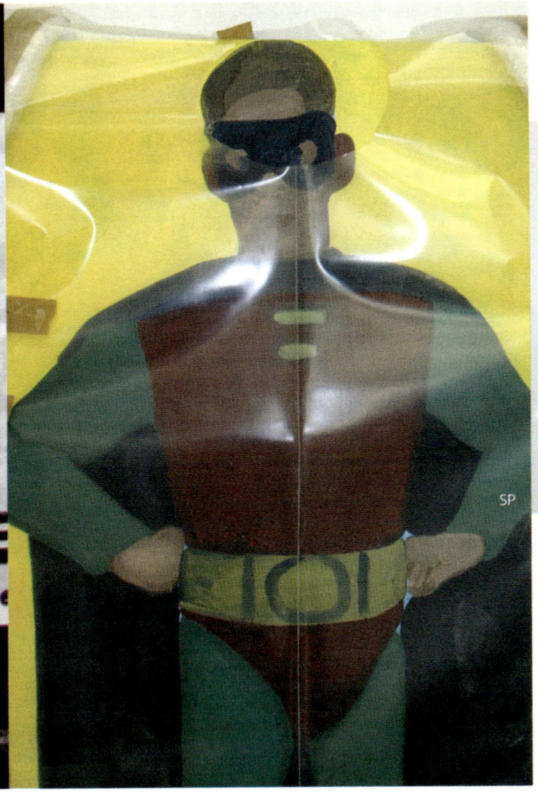

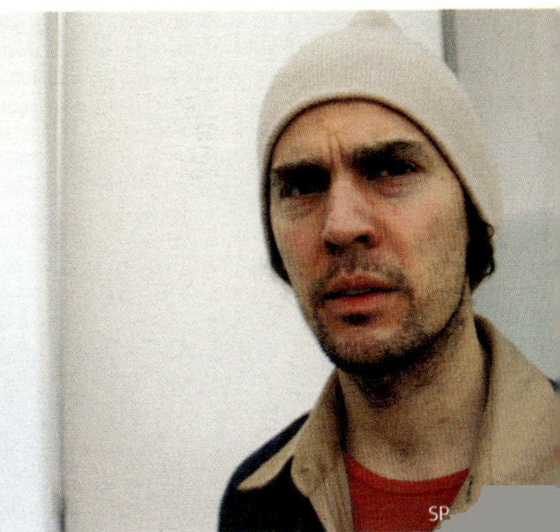

Ryan Mendo

Ryan Mendo

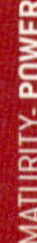

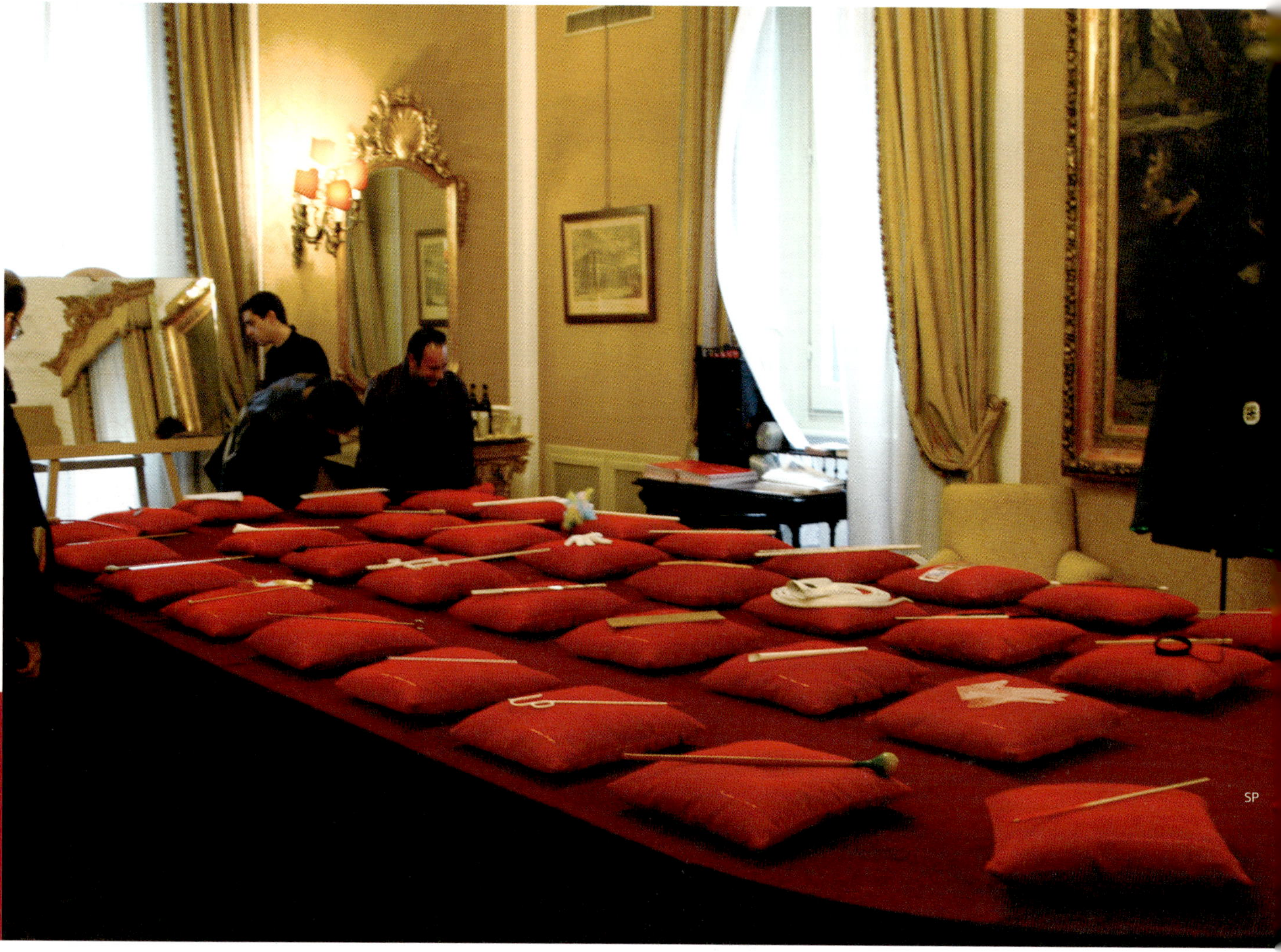

AuDoigt

Italian design is about to begin a new chapter through the acquisition
of some of the most important brands by some large investment companies,
which are bound to change production and distribution policies throughout.
Italian design was a phenomenon originating from the enthusiasm of some of its promoters.
The era of managers in business suits is a-coming. God help us.

FABIO NOVEMBRE

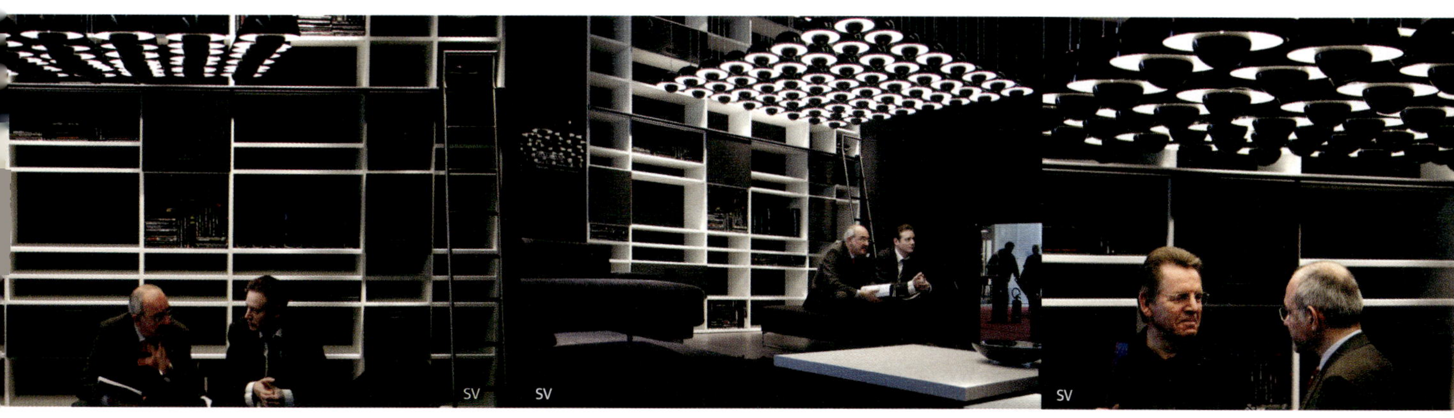
SV
SV
SV

Tisettanta

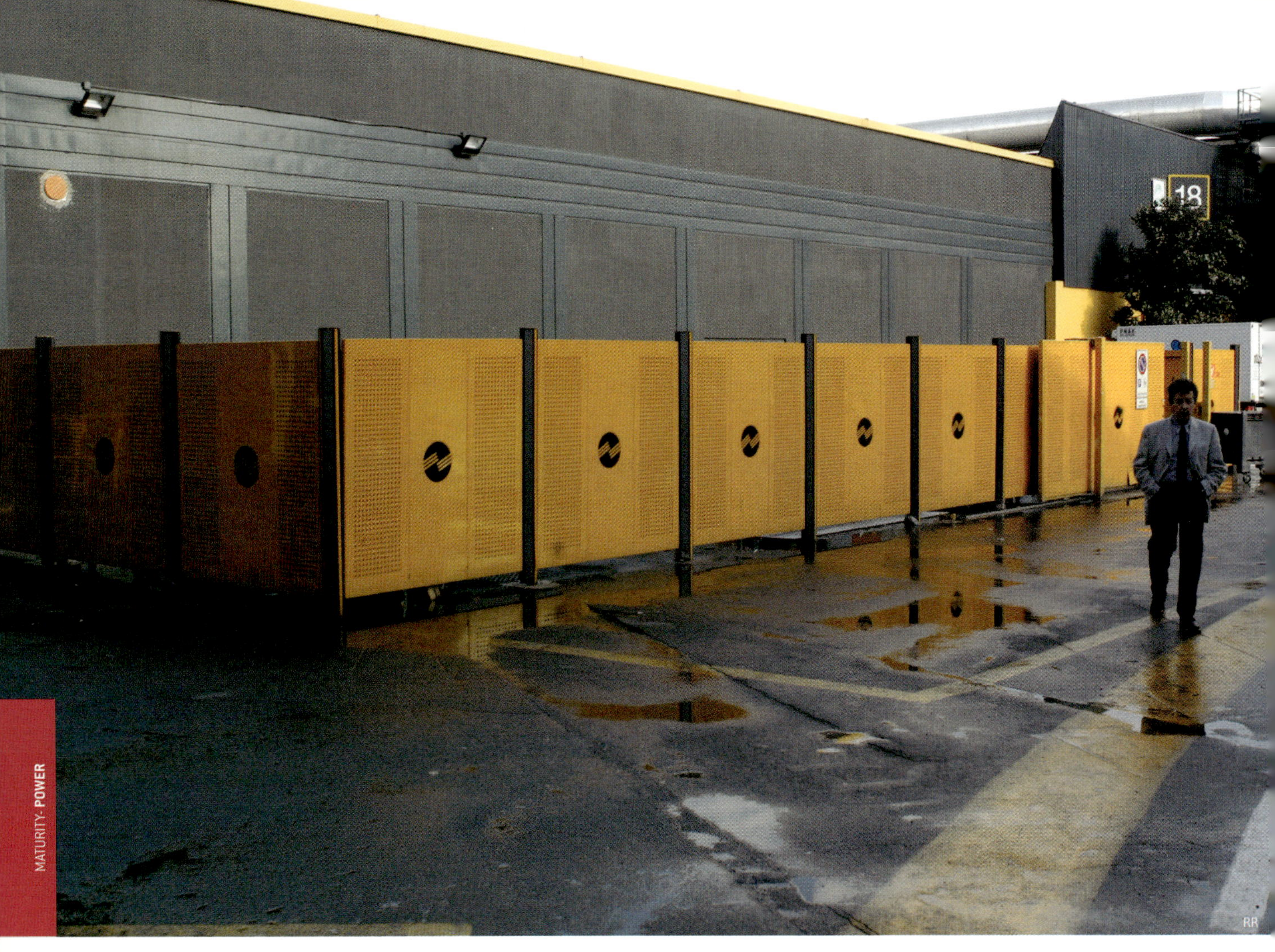

@ Fiera

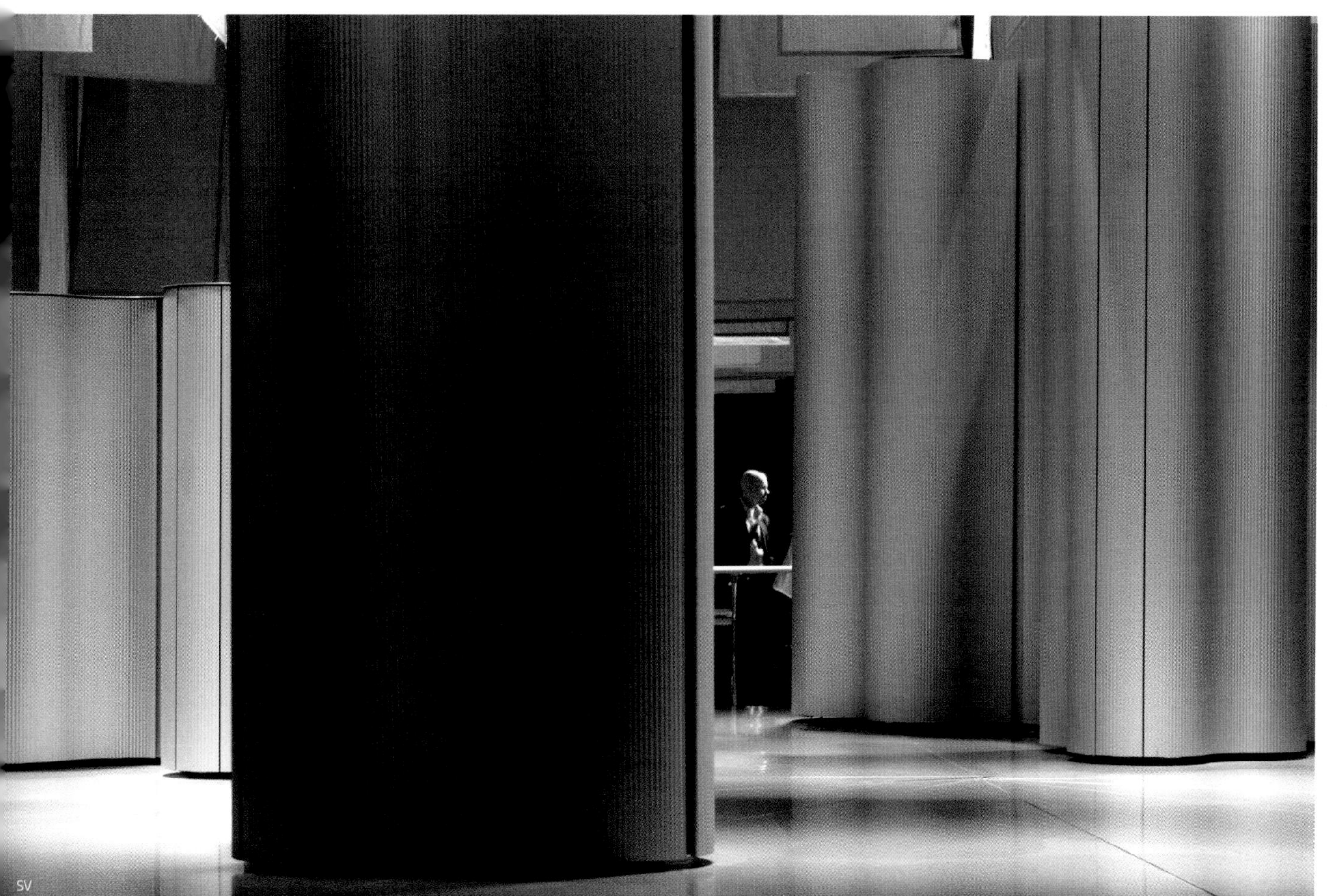

Alias

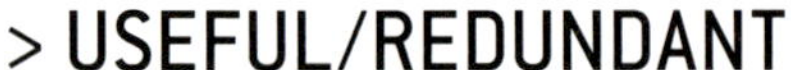

> USEFUL/REDUNDANT

IN TODAY'S DESIGN, WHAT IS USEFUL AND WHAT IS REDUNDANT?

Redundant is the noise, which is made about design.

INGO MAURER

In today's design beauty and logic are useful. Too much design without thought is redundant.

ROSS LOVEGROVE

Thought provoking design is useful, whereas copying is useless.

MIGLIORE + SERVETTO

Emotion is useful whereas designer names are useless.

SAMUELE MAZZA

Design has to have a function otherwise it is not design; il is very hard to get an object useless;

now we could seat on a nice and decorated chair but we could also seat on a wooden box.

DROOG DESIGN

> TECHNOLOGY

Somehow technology can affect design in the sense it can increase the price of production of a piece; then we need to experiment in order to get, in the future, the same refined object with law cost of production even if I believe that some special pieces they will never be mass produced even in the future.

DROOG DESIGN

Technology is engineering, mechanics and not "aesthetics".
A designer must be an aesthete through and through.

SAMUELE MAZZA

When design affects technology it usually doesn't work.

ERNST GAMPLER

TO WHAT EXTENT DOES TECHNOLOGY CURRENTLY AFFECT A DESIGNER'S CREATIVITY?

Right from the beginning, and the whole process through.

INGO MAURER

A designer works "beyond technology". Real technology is devoid of the (sometimes extreme) "desire to be in the limelight". Nowadays, technology often takes on a "redundant decorative" quality – thus becoming an excuse to do something else.

DAVID PALTERER

Technology drives new horizons.The digital age is changing everything: structures, form, precision, function, intelligence, economy.

ROSS LOVEGROVE

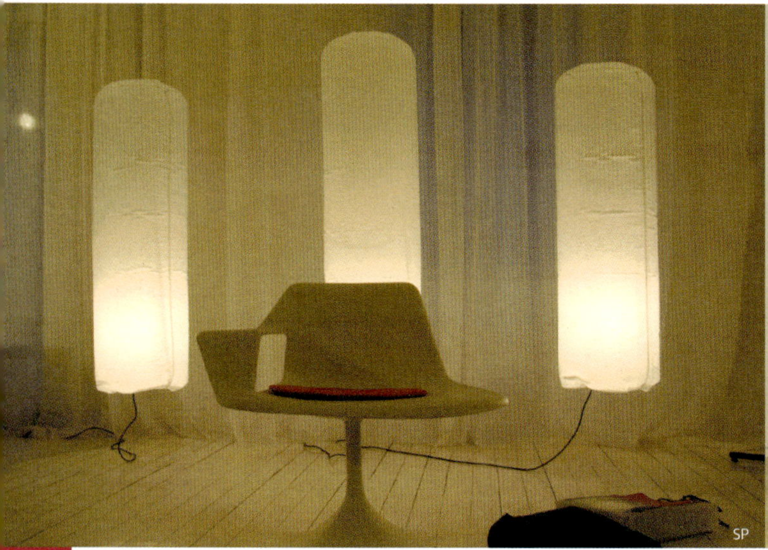

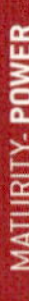

David Design

Monica Armani

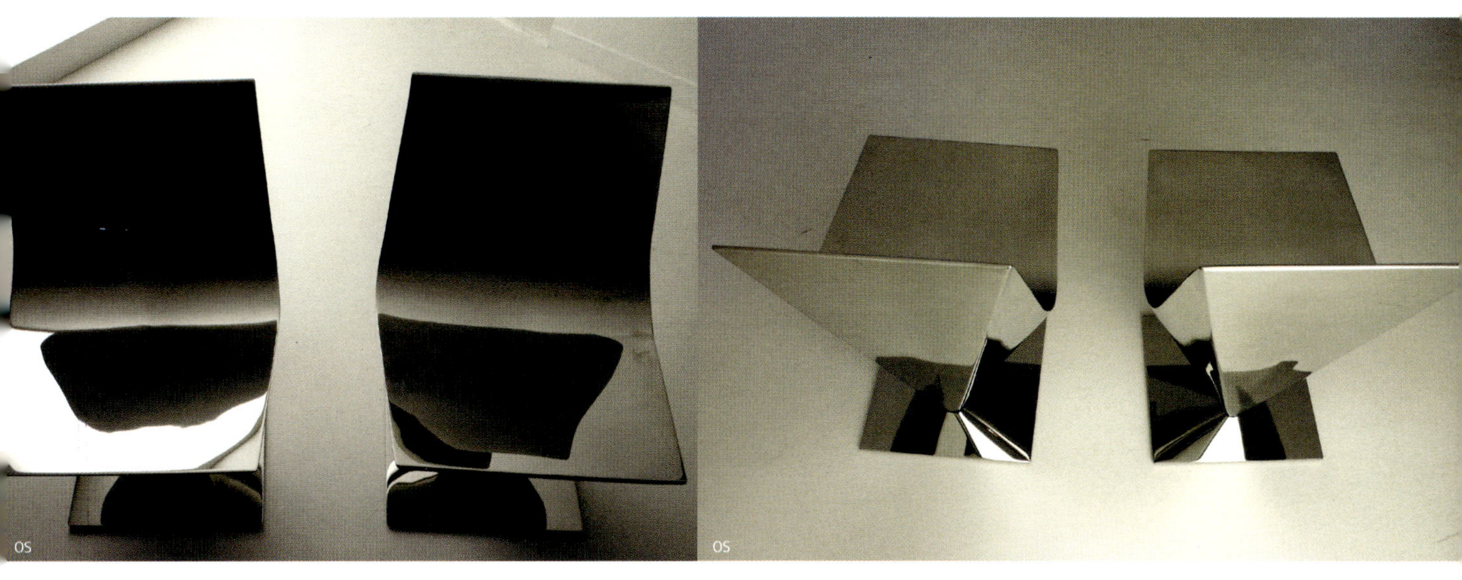

Mdf

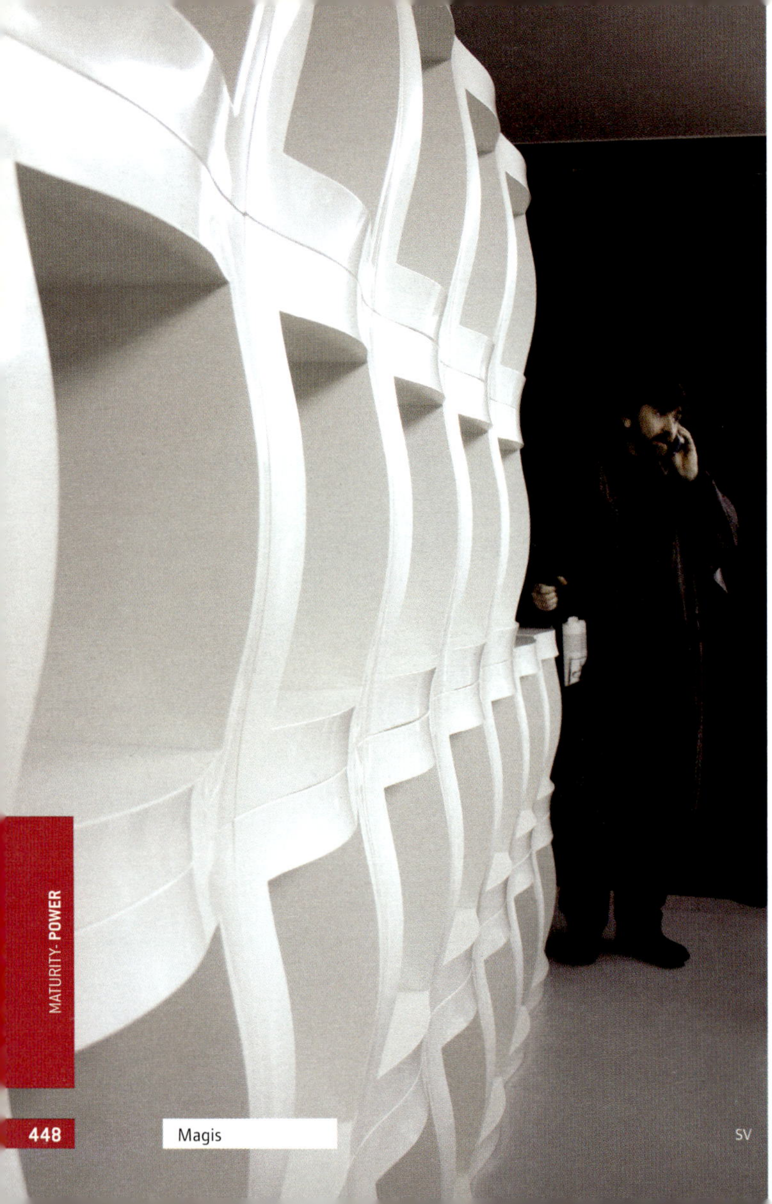

Magis

SV

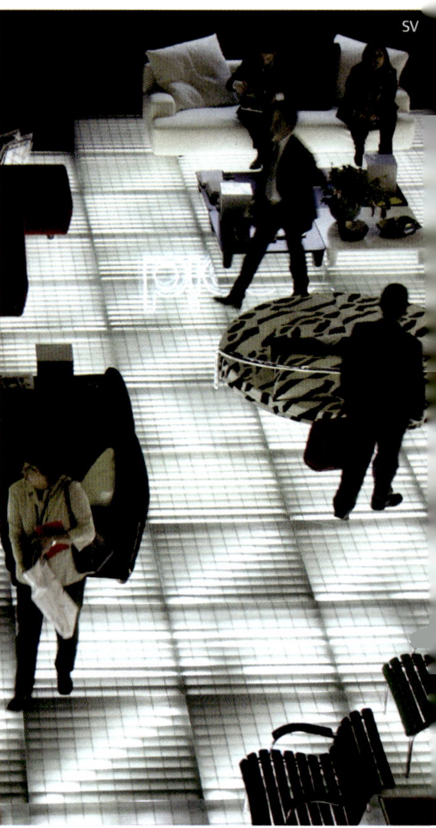

SV

Biesse

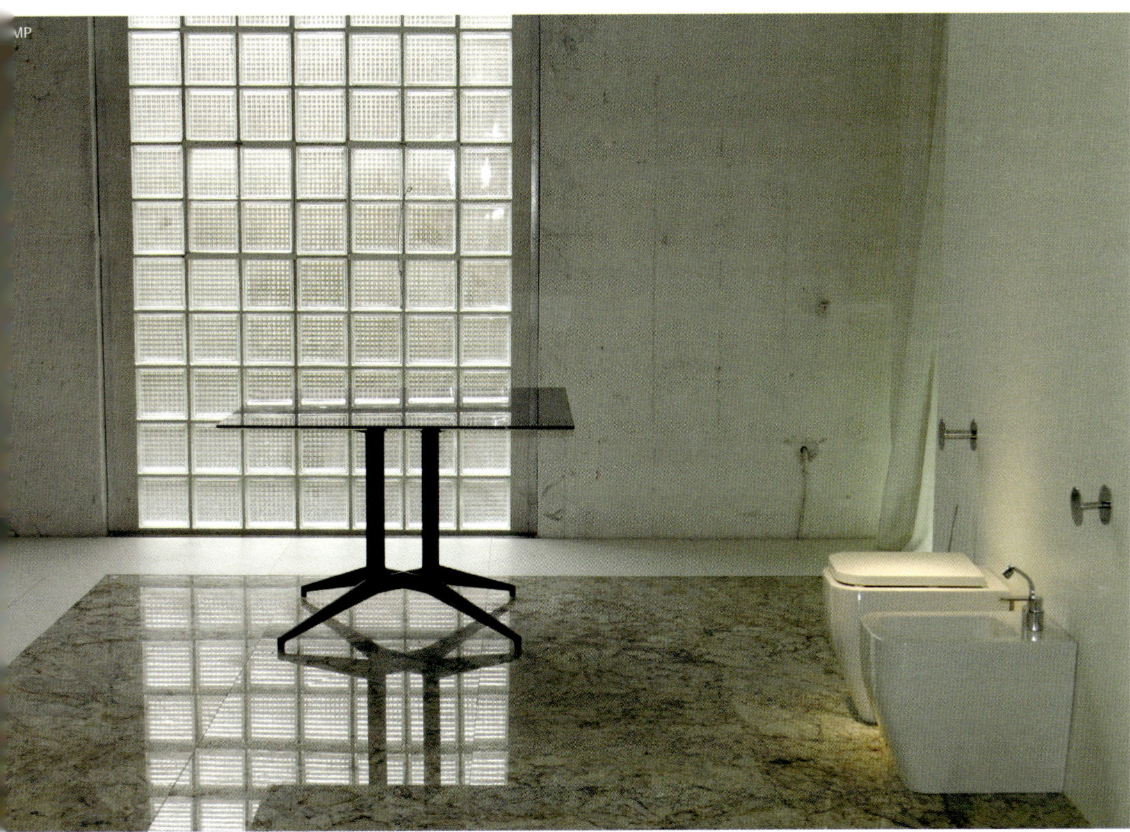

Flamina

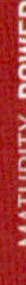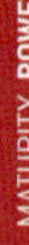

Musa Italia

Colombo Stile

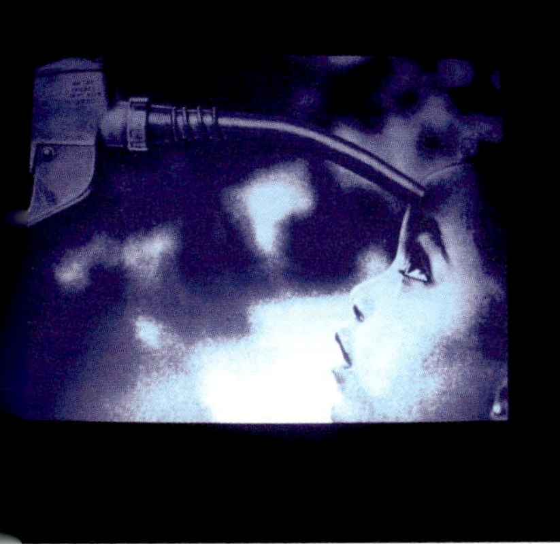

Andrea Borri

Contemporary design tends to use less durable materials

as part of the already mentioned new trend

based on replacingour objects more often.

As one can easily guess, these materials are cheaper

and will hopefully attract more design fans.

ROBERTO PAOLI

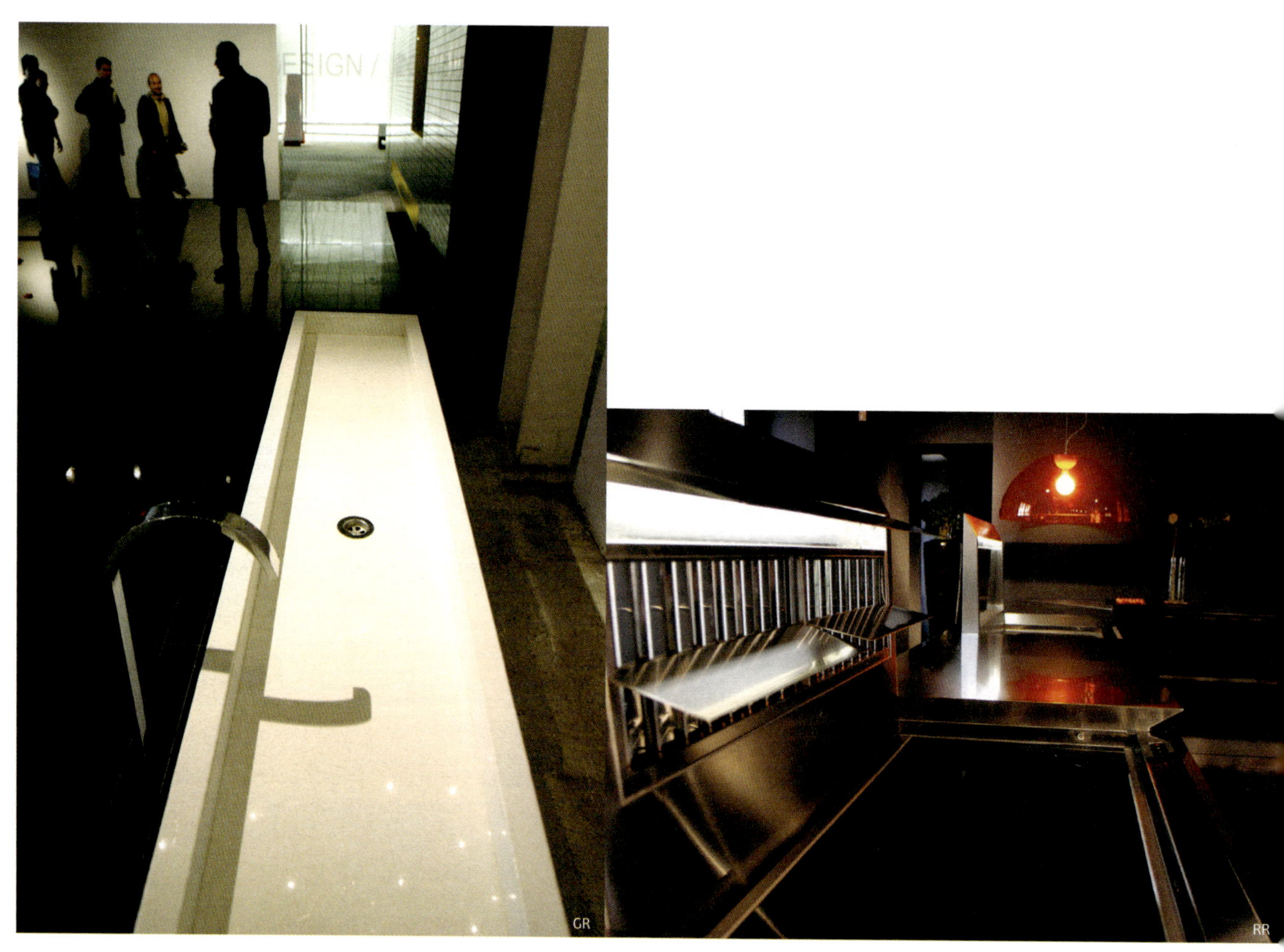

Bisazza @ Zona Tortona

Buffi

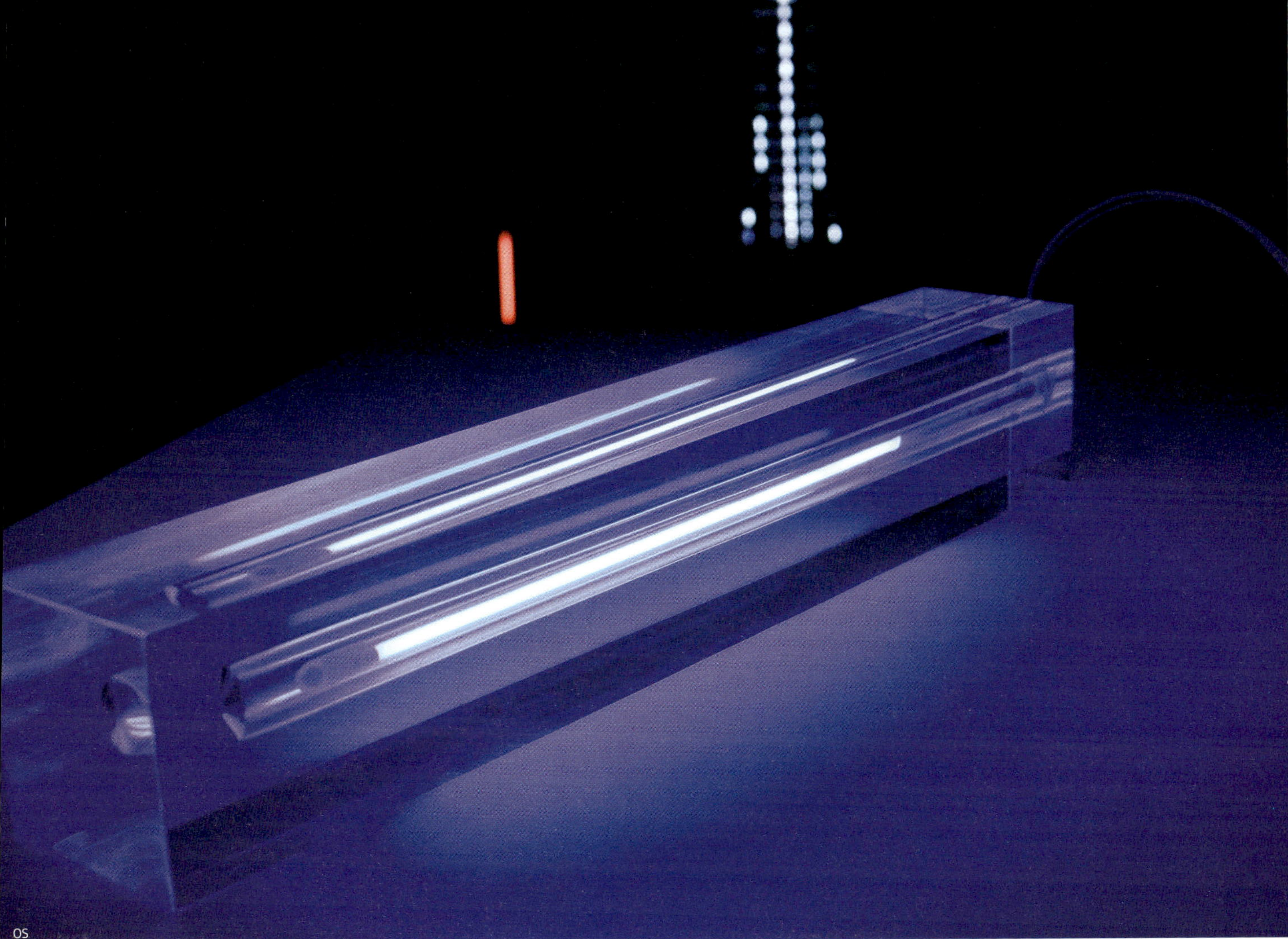

M+K design

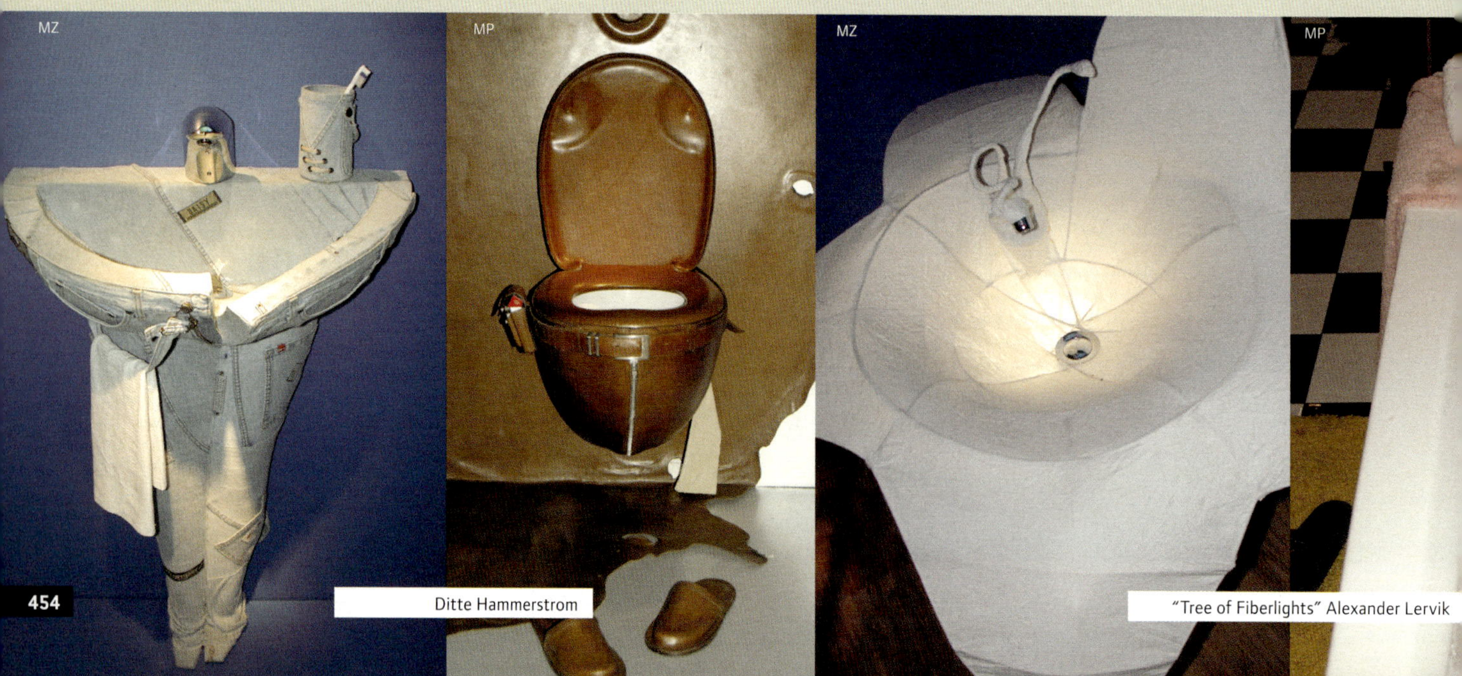

Ditte Hammerstrom

"Tree of Fiberlights" Alexander Lervik

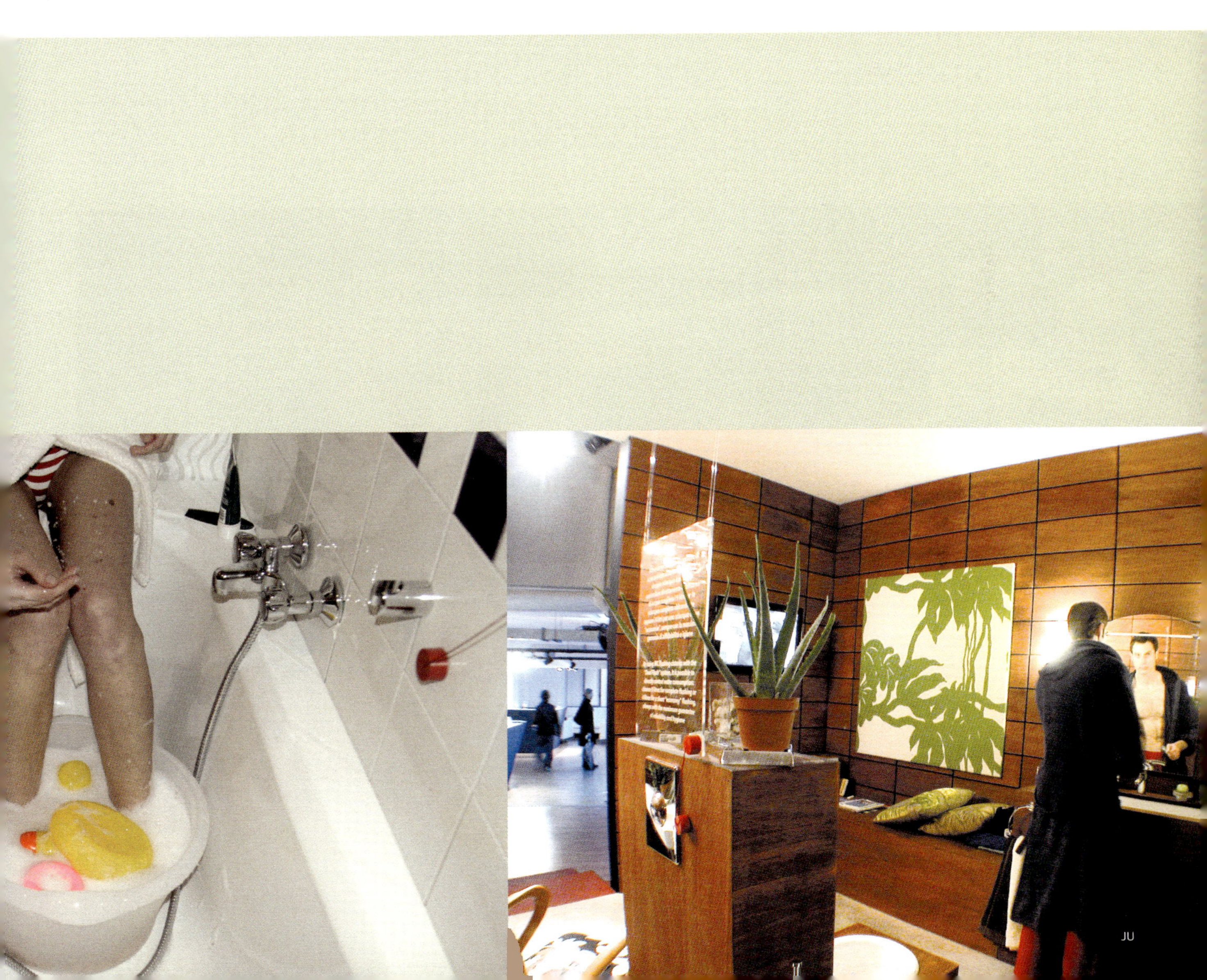

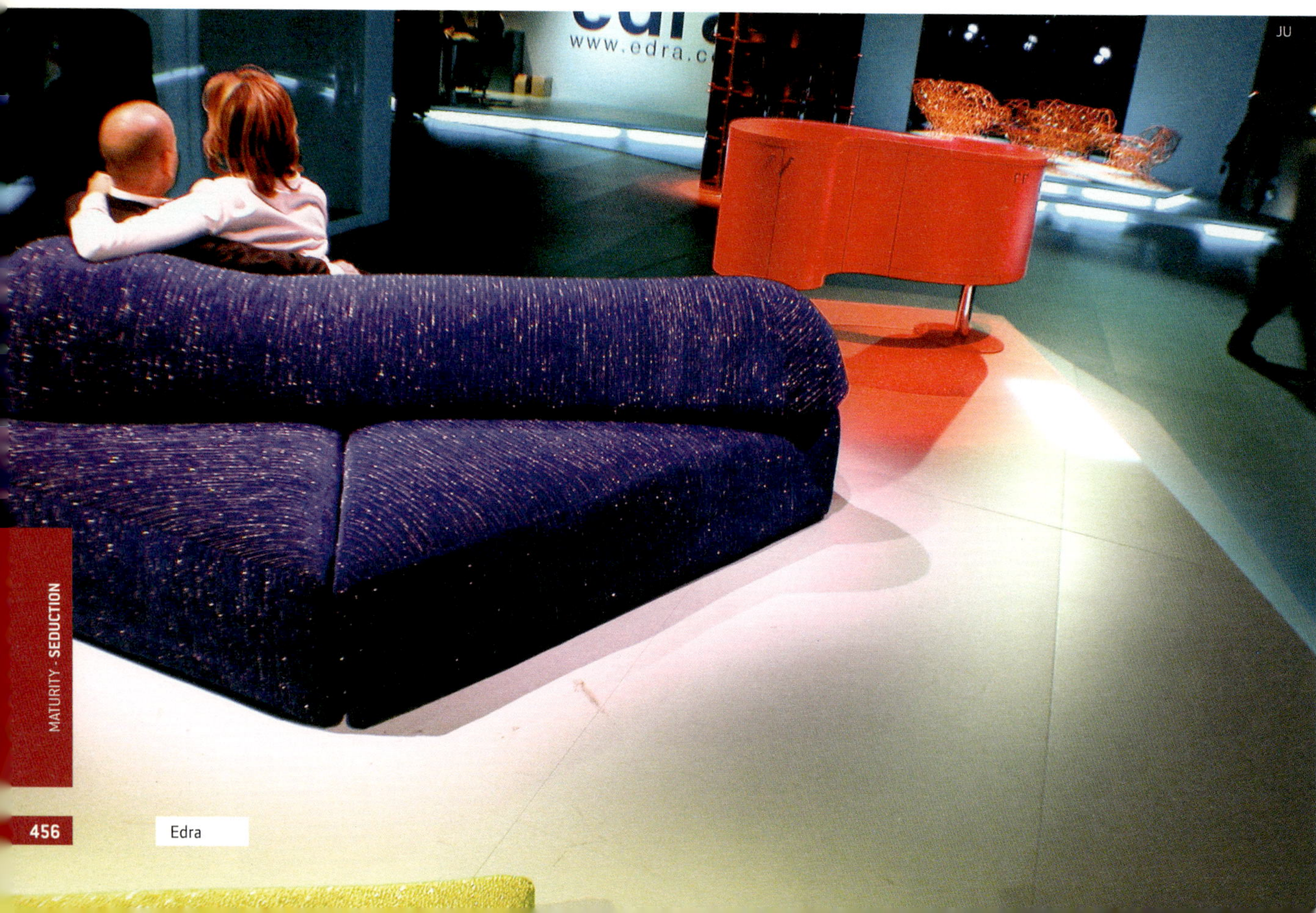

Edra

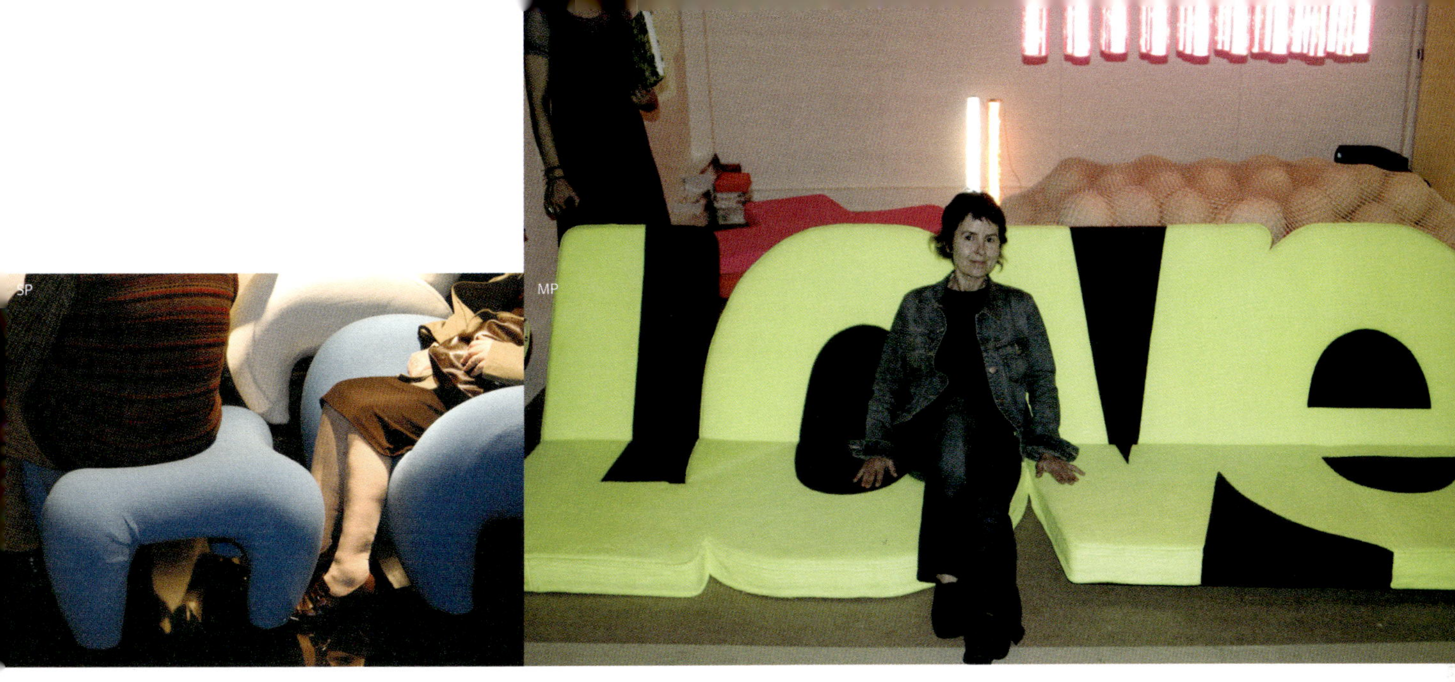

Rossi di Albizzate

Florence Jaffrain

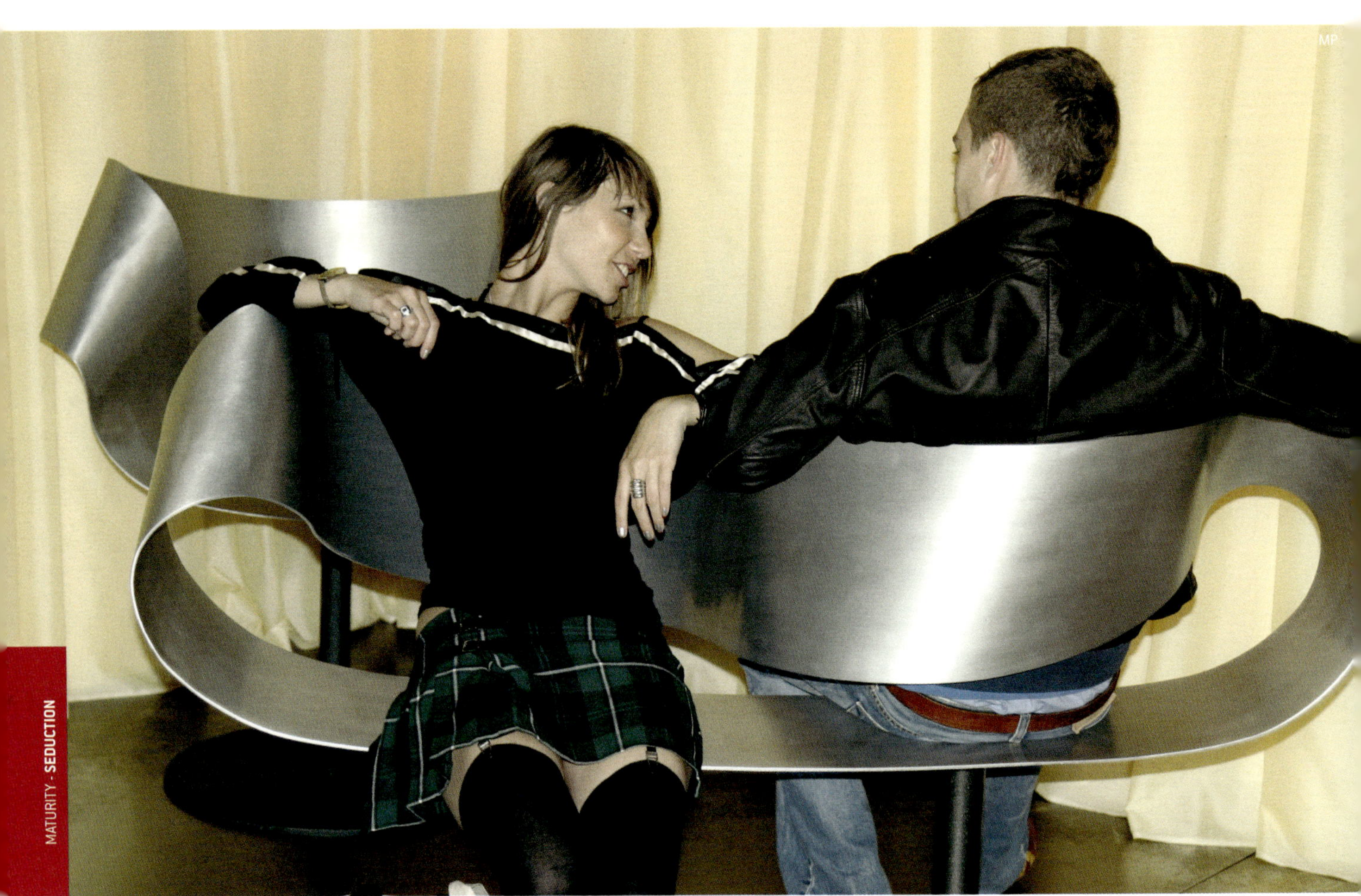

Albera, Arrigoni, Induni, Monti @ Satellite

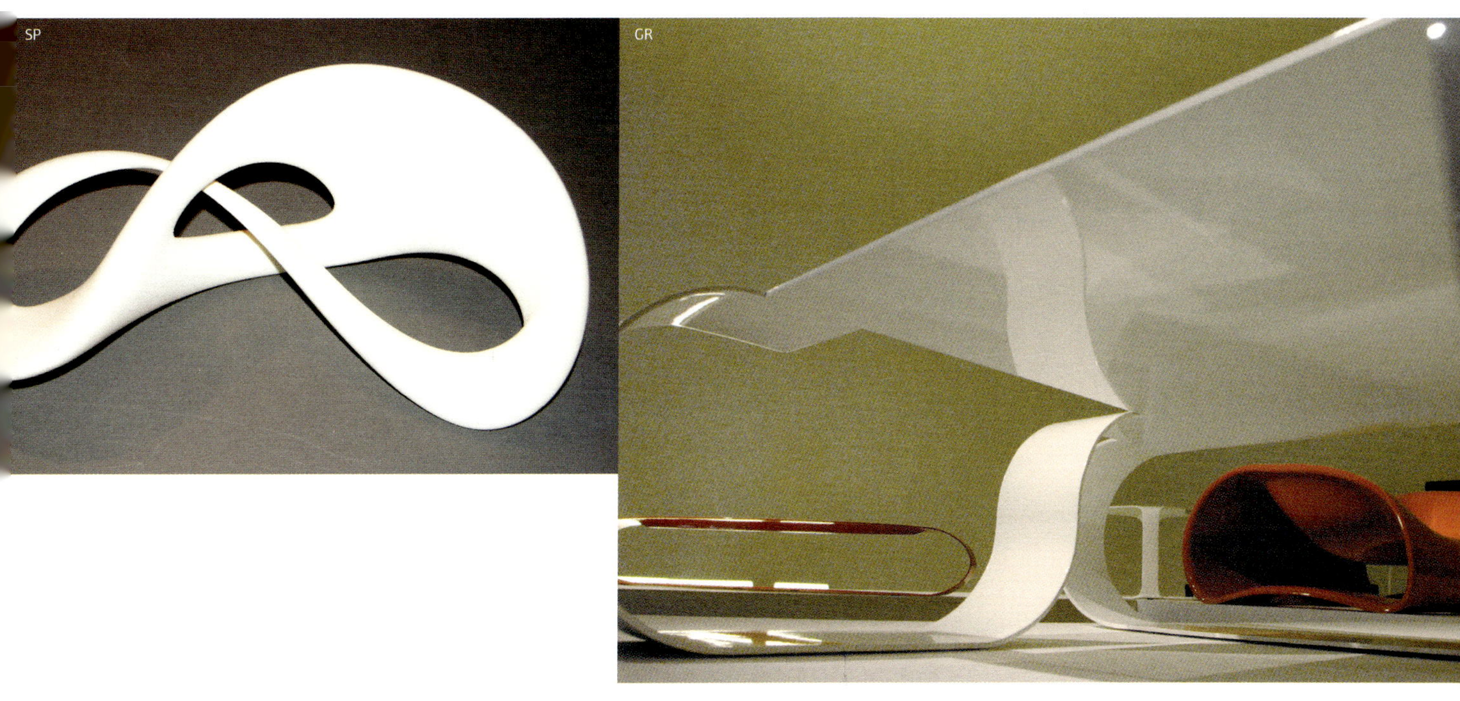

Sphaus @ Zona Tortona

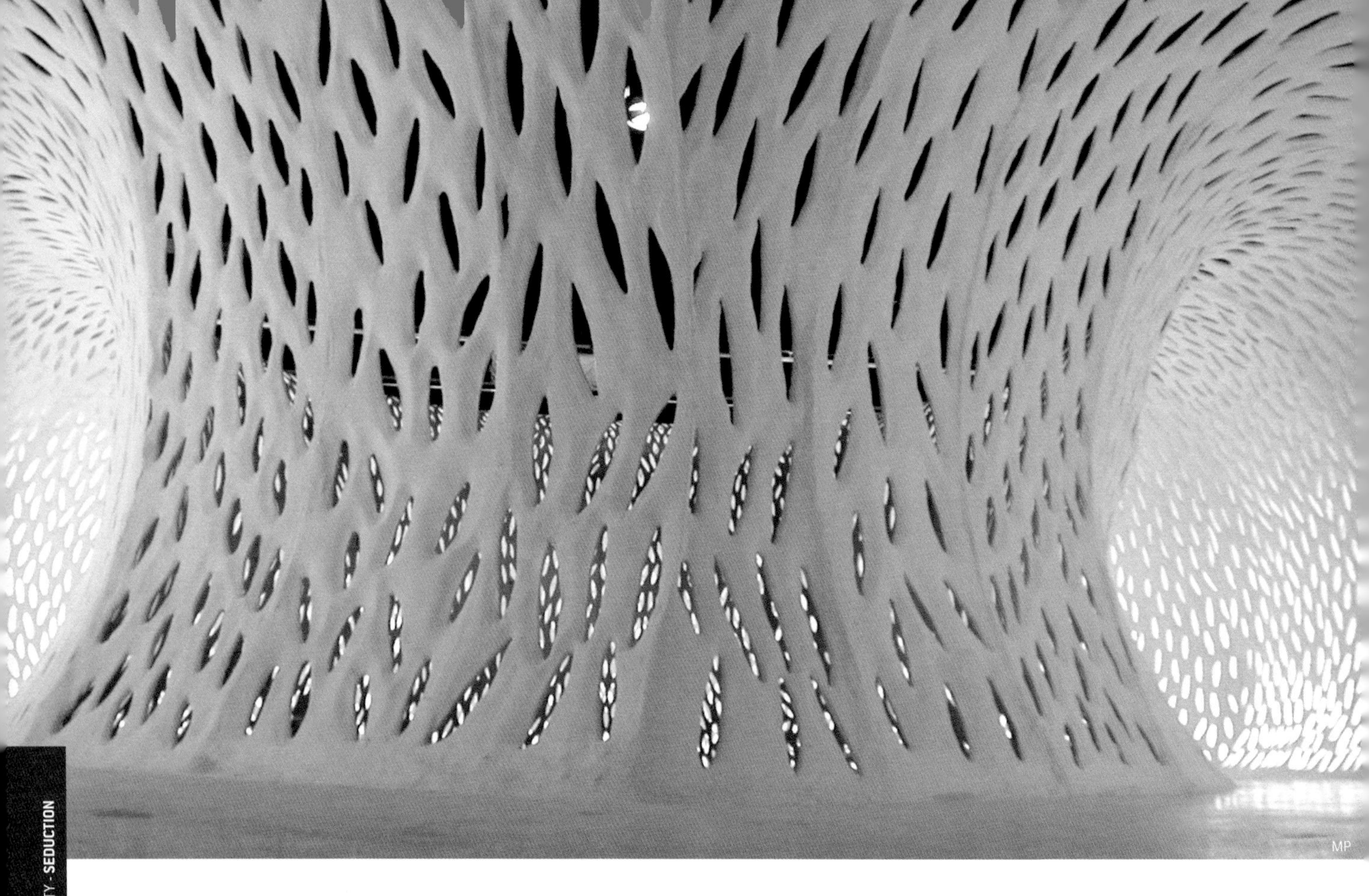

Kris Ruhs

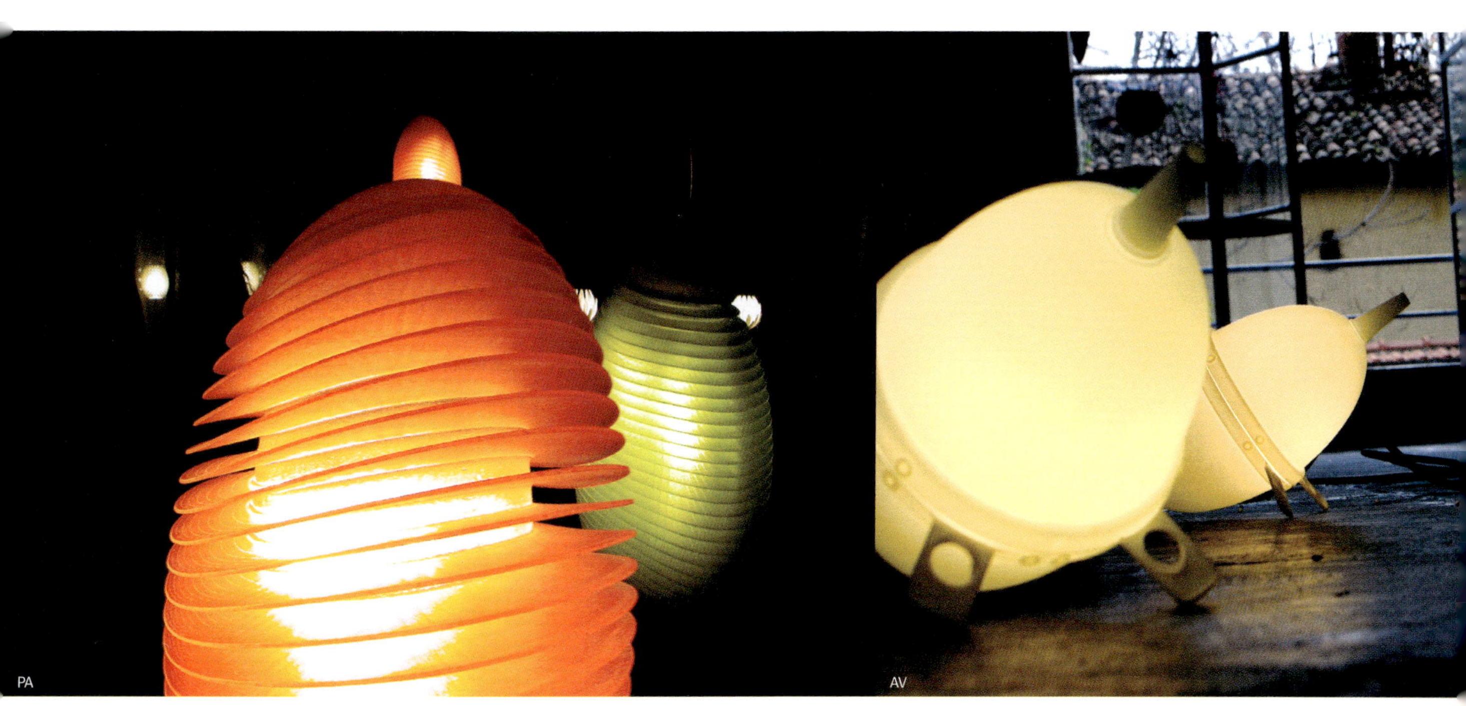

MGX

Glasvegas @ Designersblock

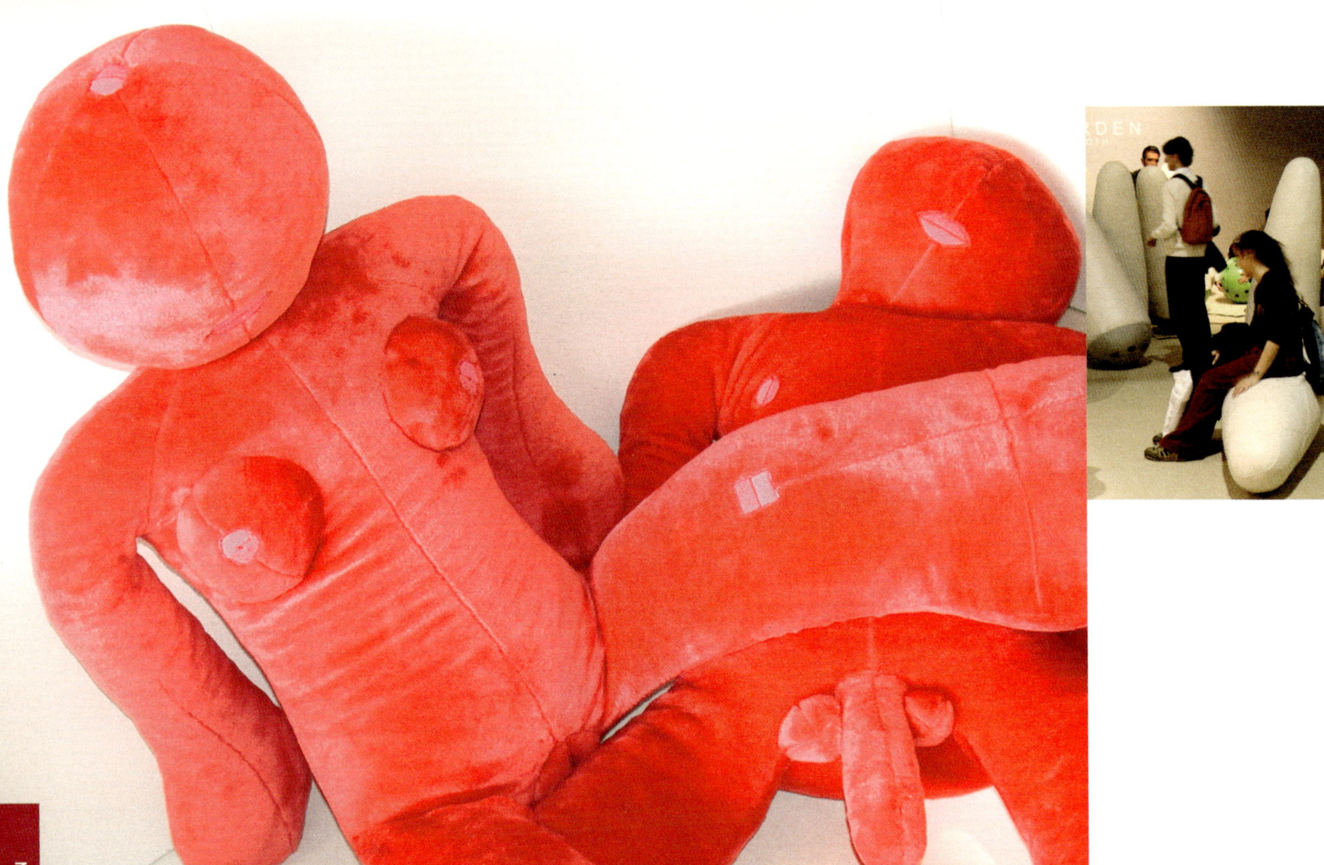

Design London

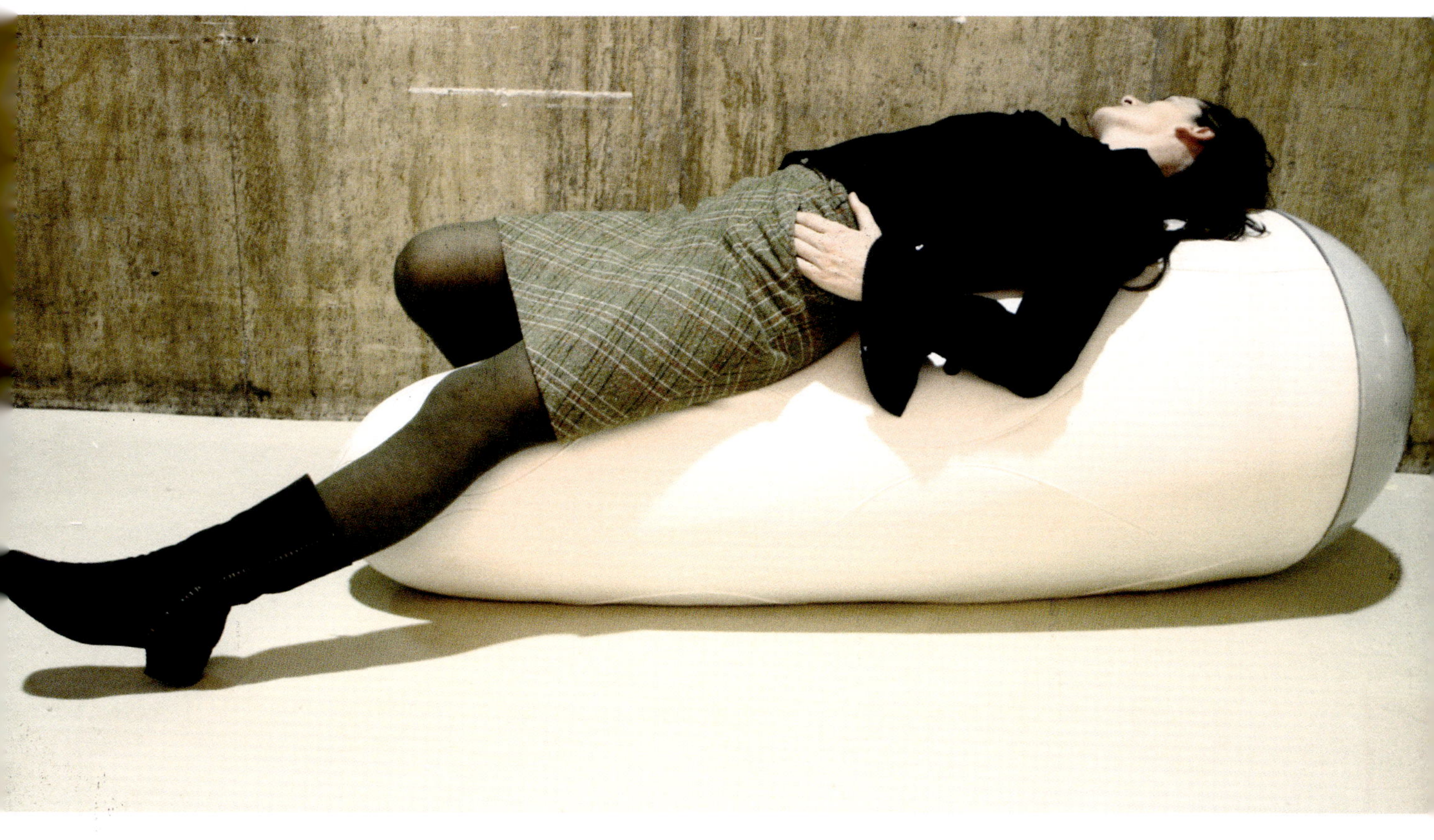

Sonicgarden by Gil Inbal, Roy Roth @ Satellite

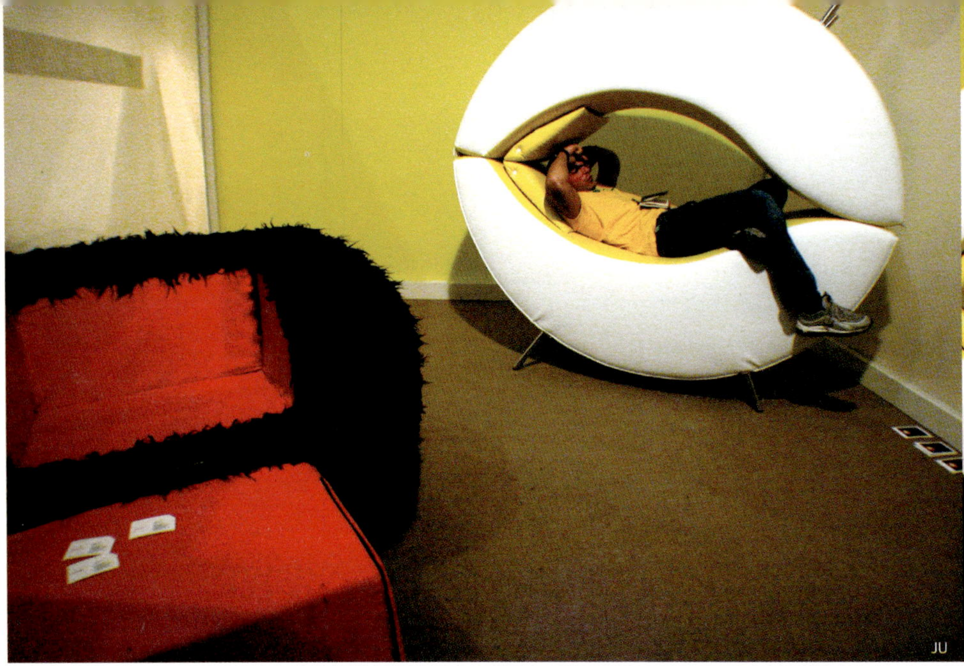

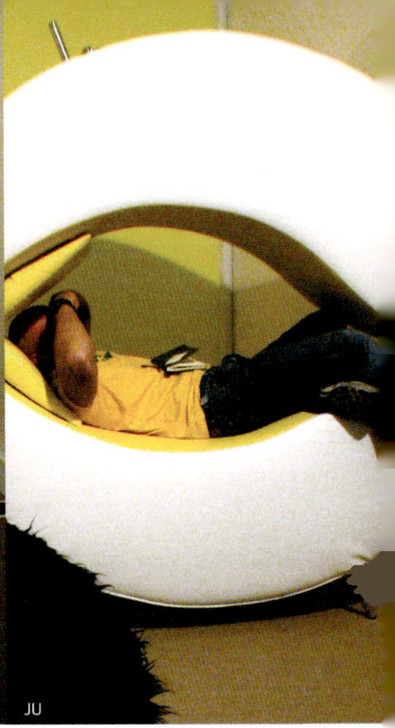

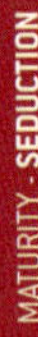

Ivano Verde @ Satellite

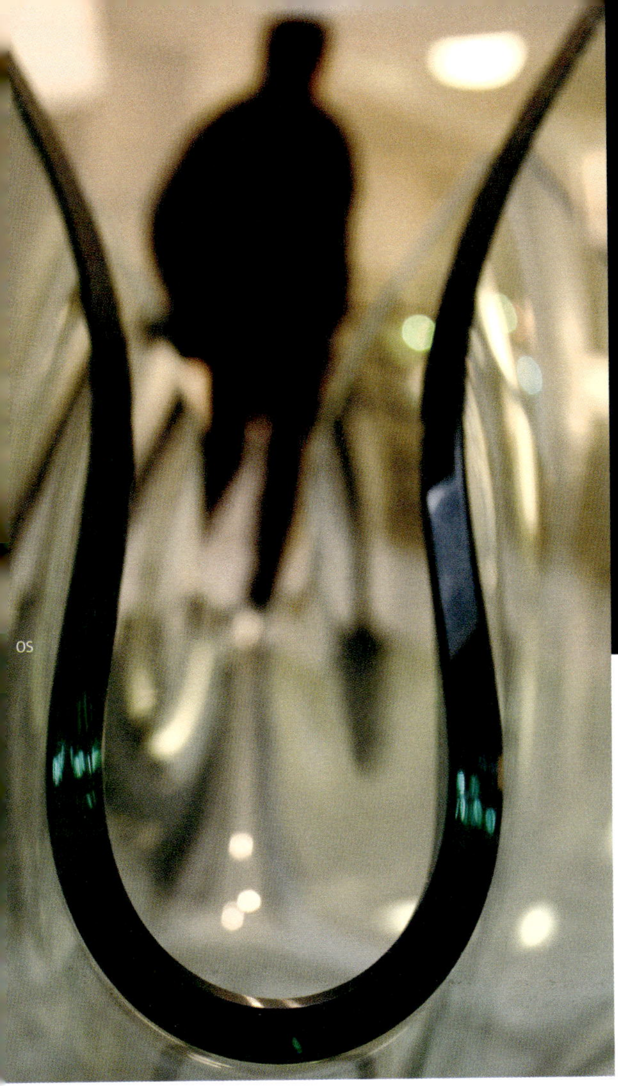

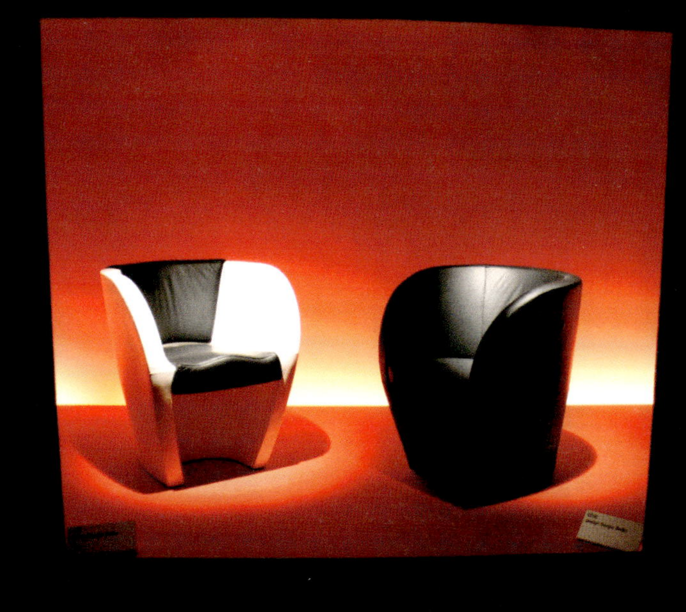

Fontana arte

"Chic" and "Cup" by Sergio Bellin @ Zona Tortona

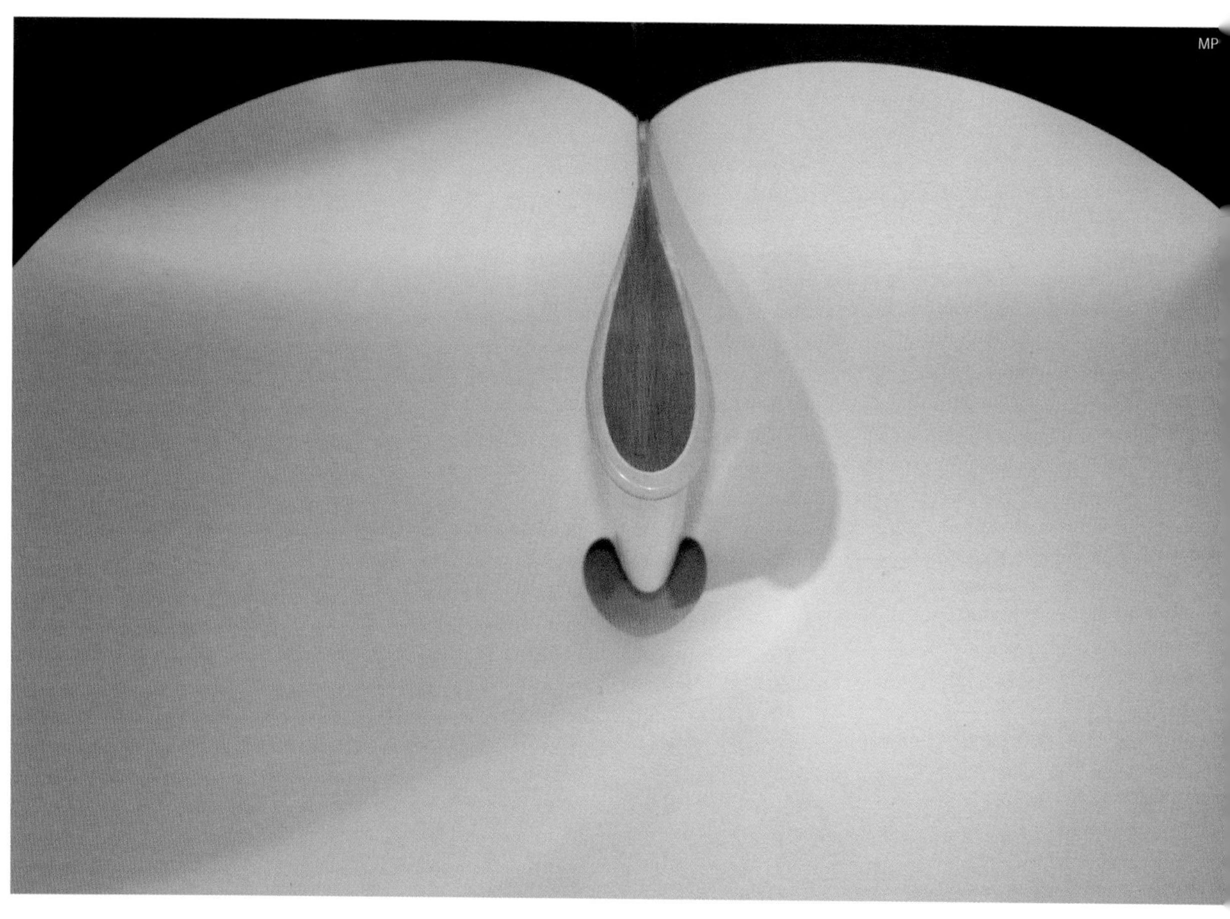

Annalisa Galushko @ Grohe

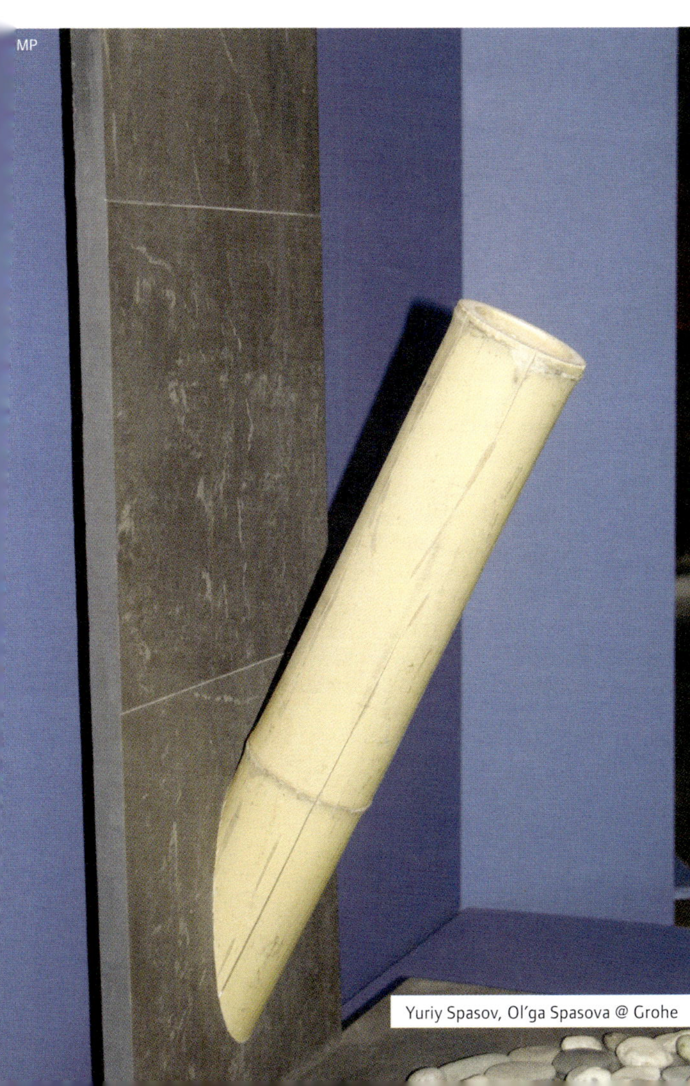

Yuriy Spasov, Ol'ga Spasova @ Grohe

In Greek philosophy the difference between hedonism and eudaimonism

was at the centre of ethical speculation. Hedonism gave individual pleasure a central role

while eudaimonism put happiness at the centre of ethical concern as a virtue belonging to all.

Our modern perception of entertainment is utterly hedonistic

but it would be nice to have eudemonistic forms of entertainment in the future.

Fabio Novembre

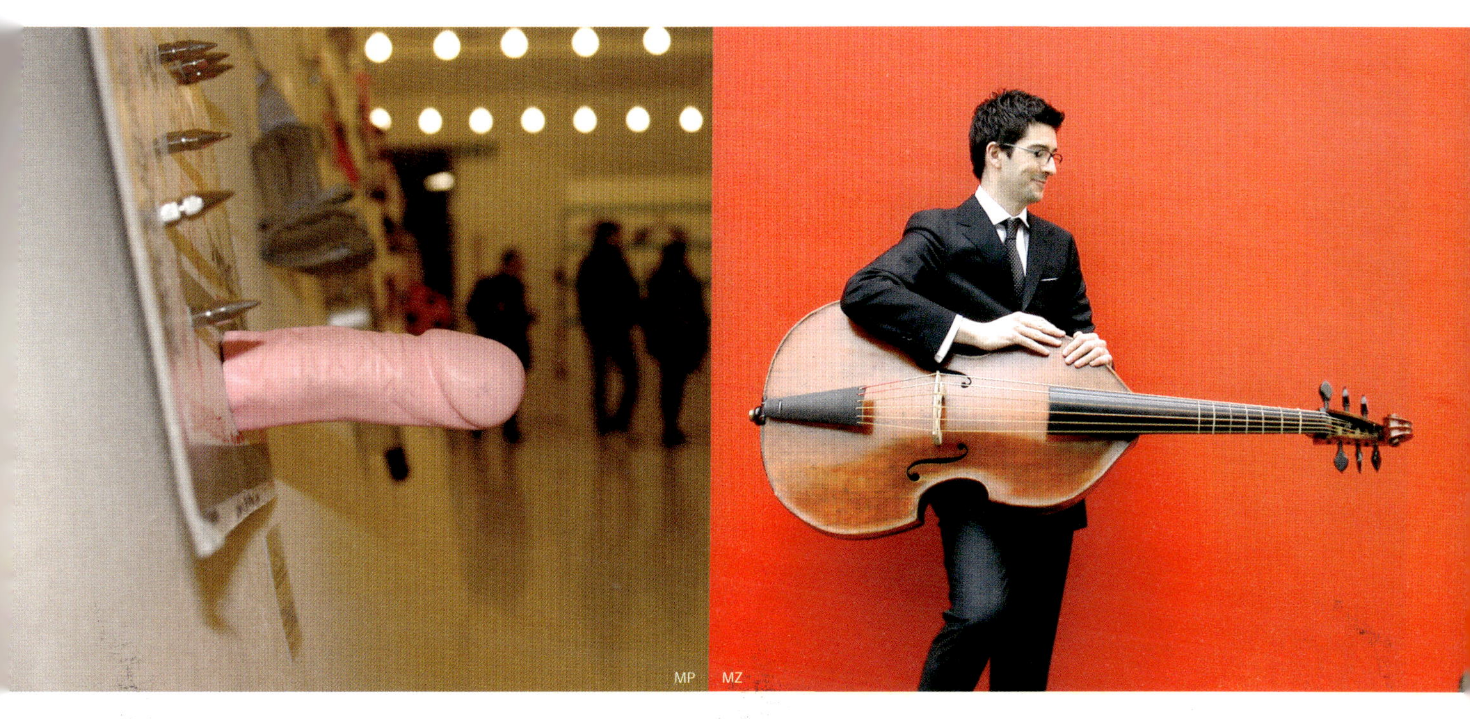

Appendimi @ Emporio 31

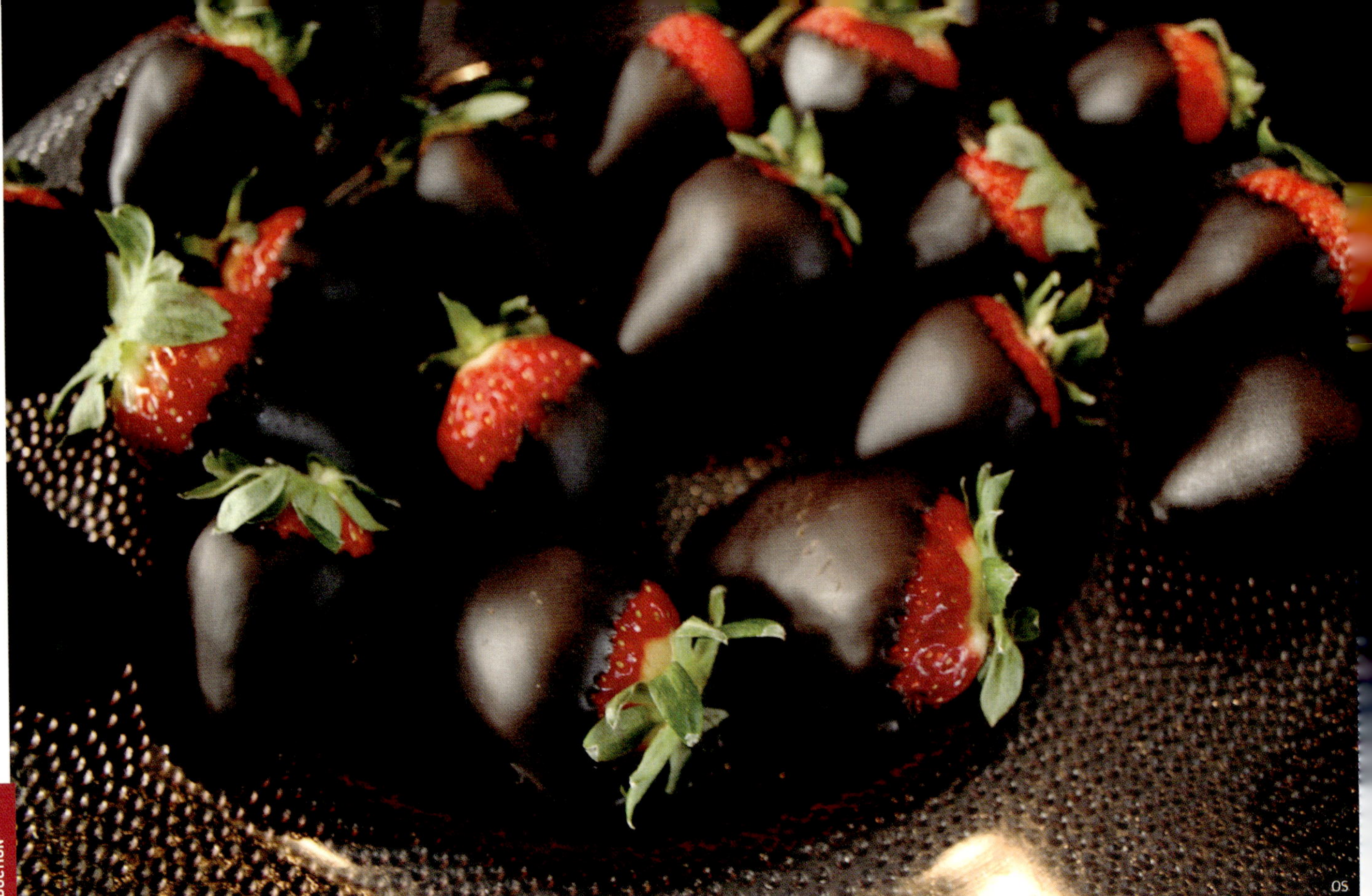

Torre Branca

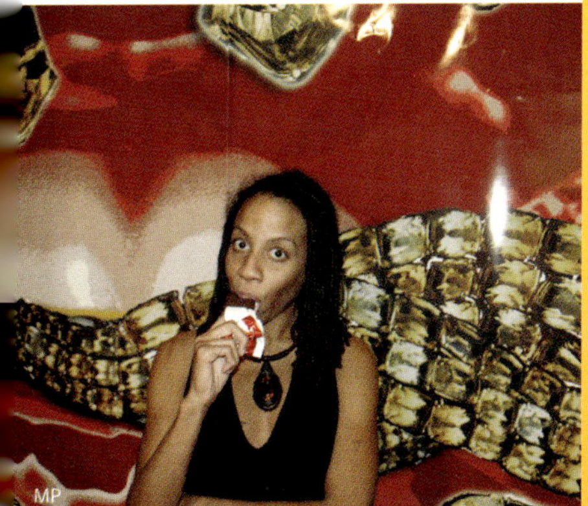

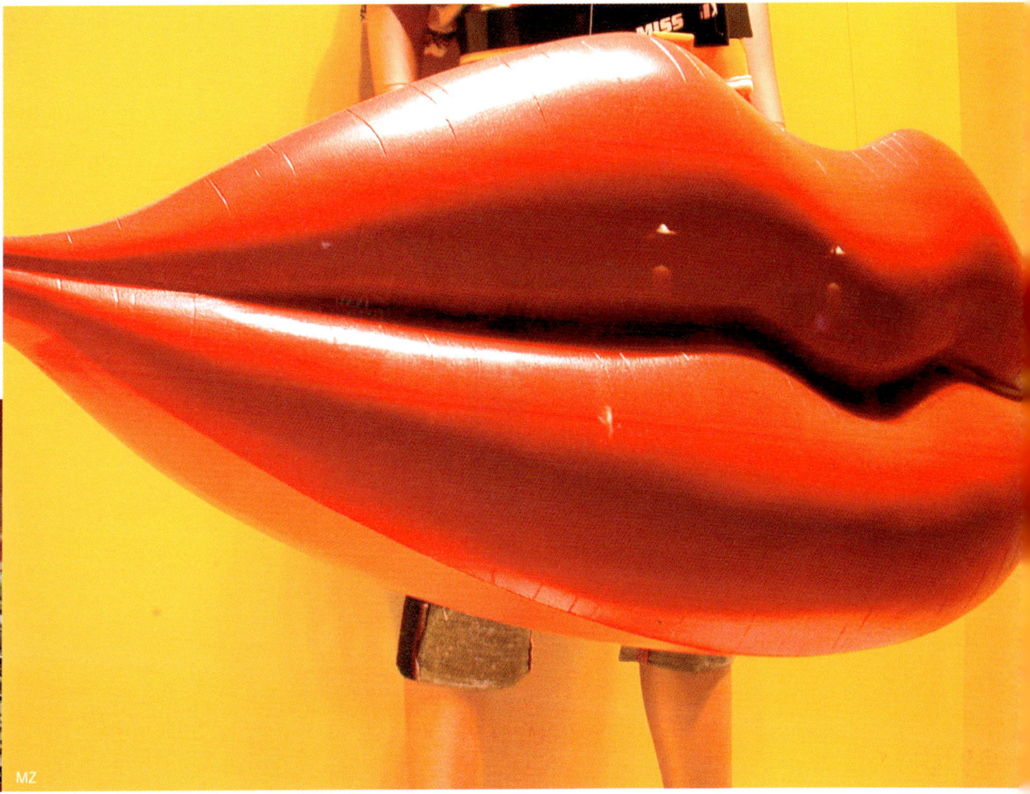

Pun/Antoinette Prattis @ Satellite

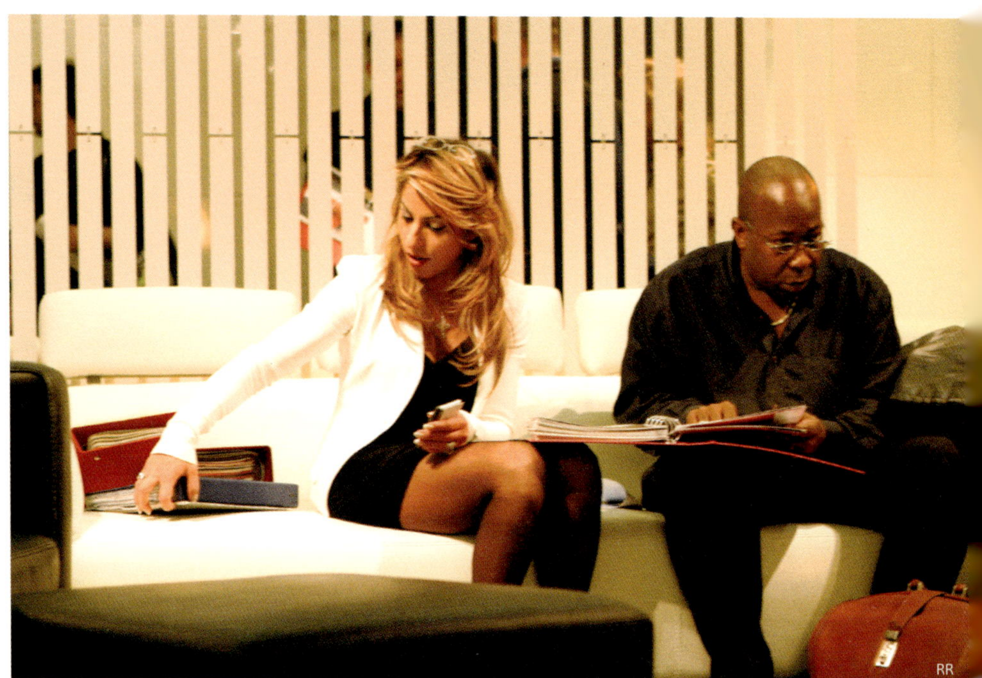

Divani Lux form

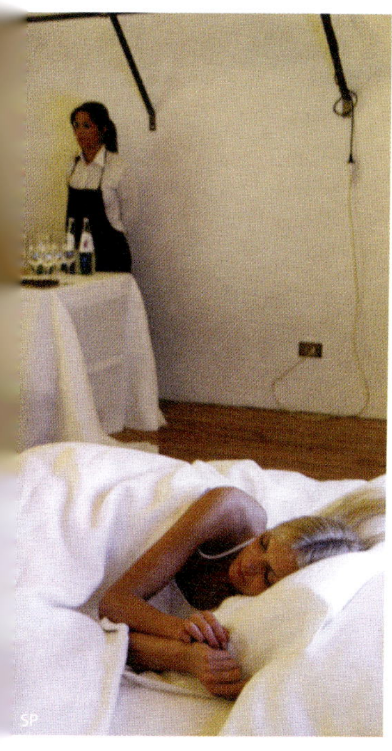

Domo Adami

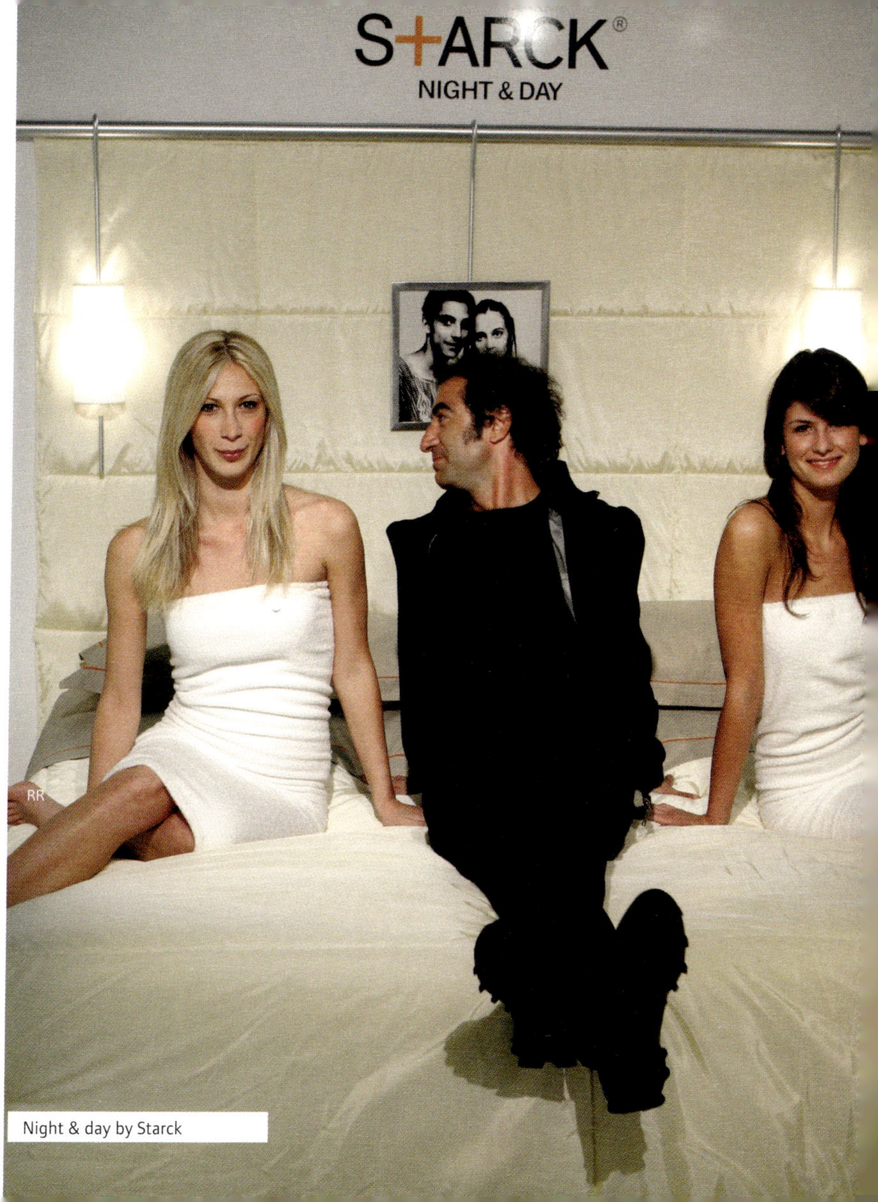

Night & day by Starck

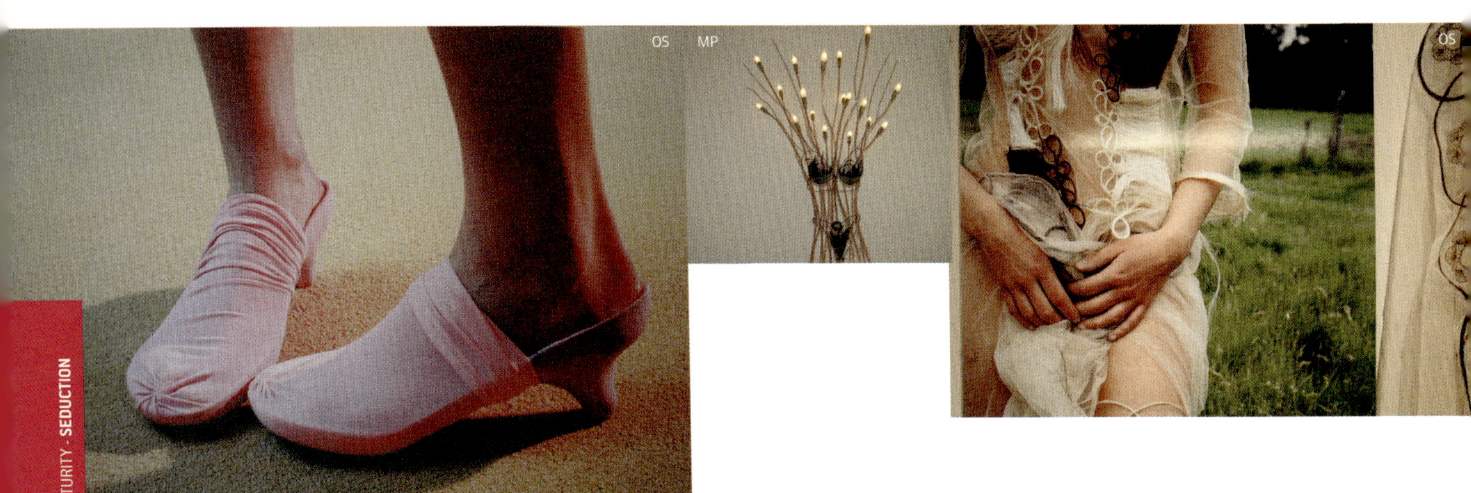

Egill Karlsson @ Design Academy Eindhoven

Lucifero

Kim Van Leuken @ Design Academy Eindhoven

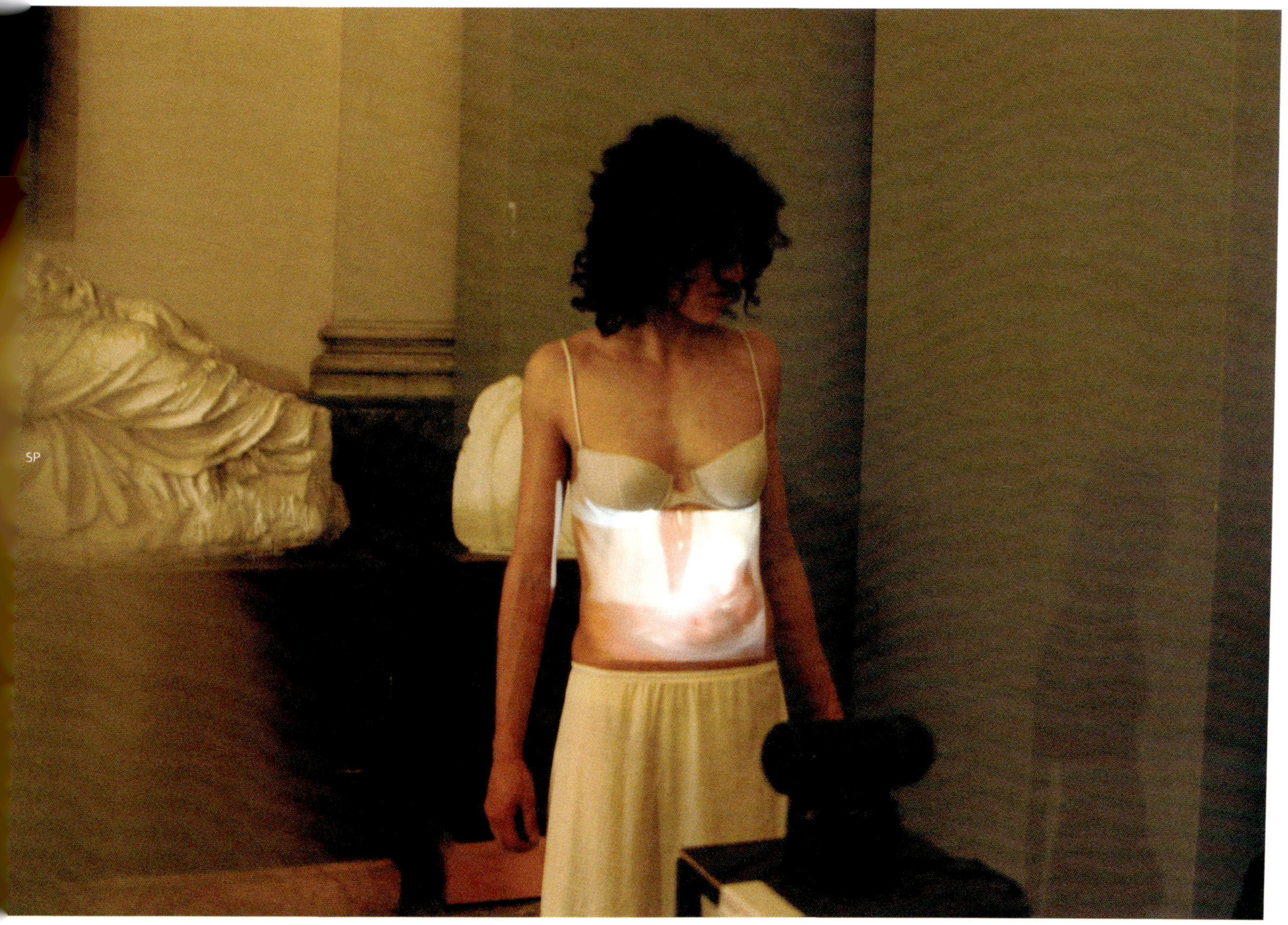

Antonella Gricco @ Accademia Belle Arti

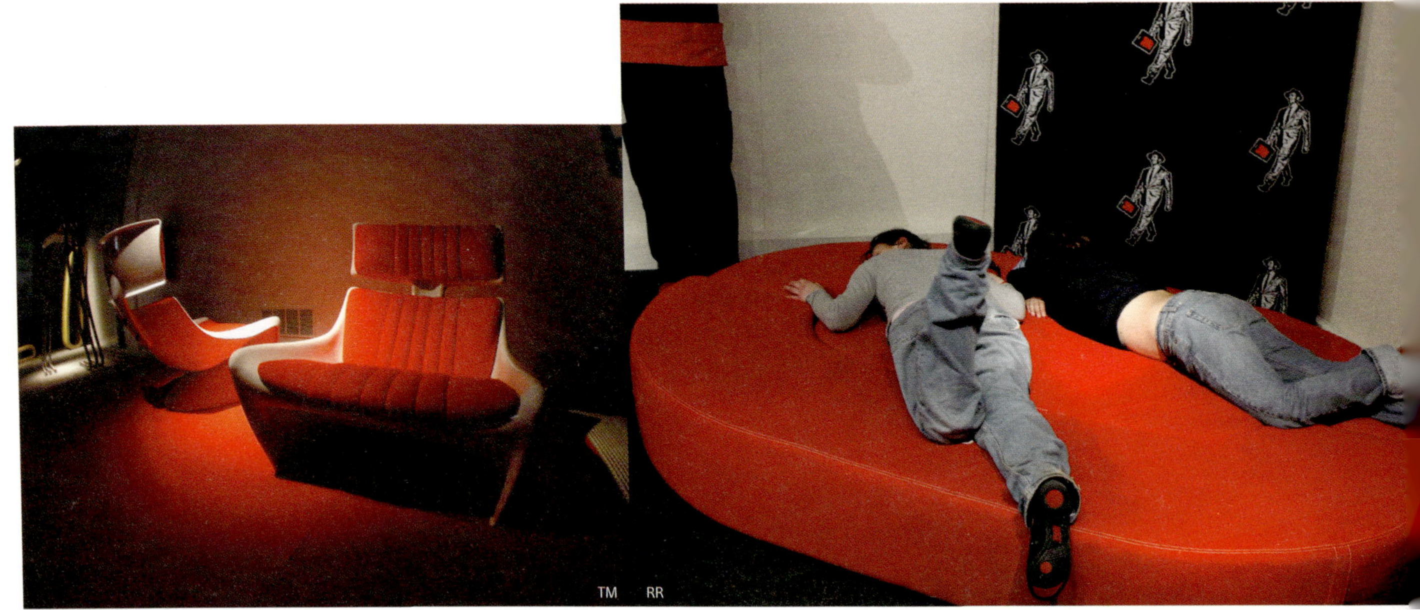

Hay

Seinajoki Polytechnic @ Satellite

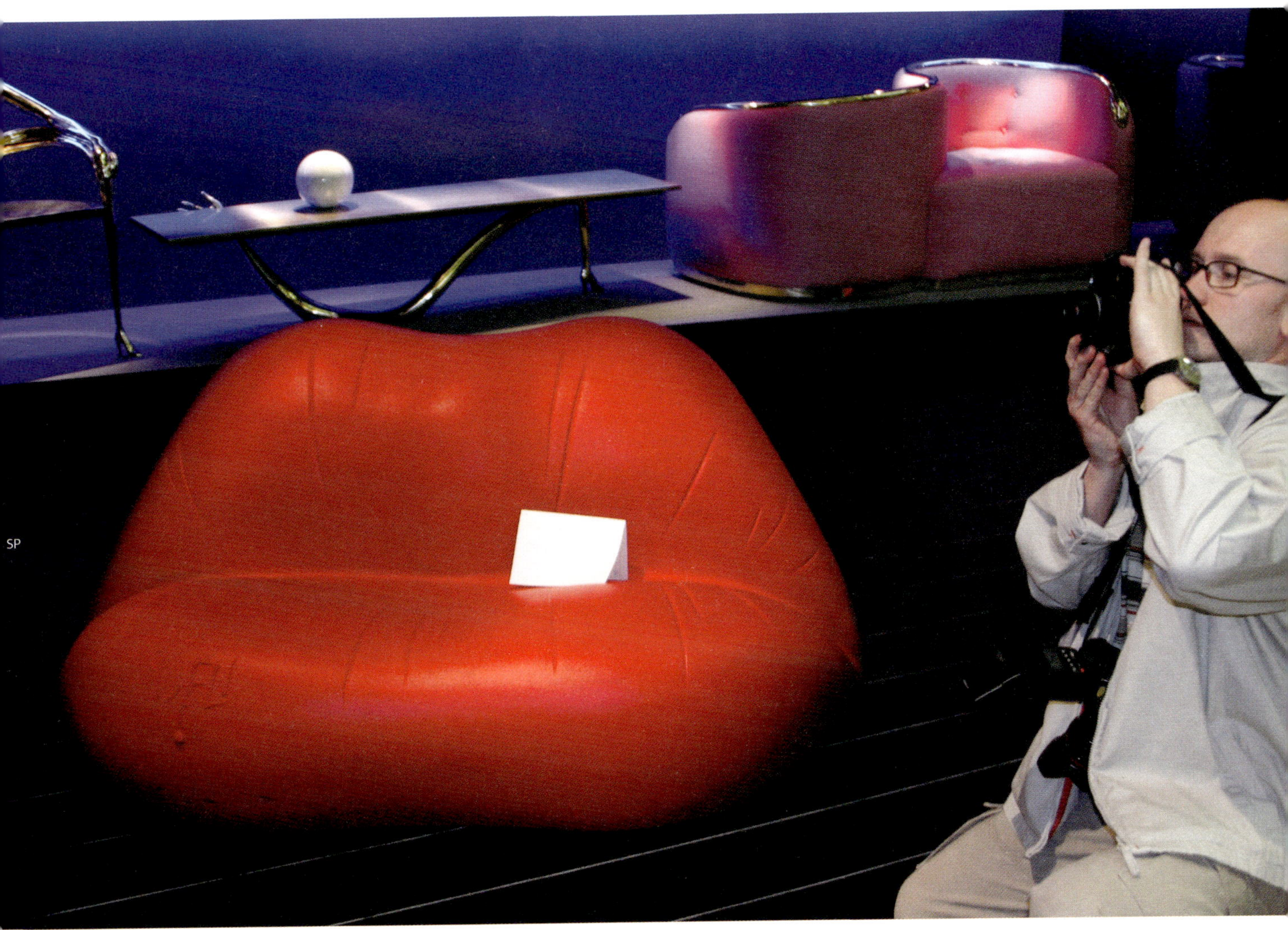

Dalì chair

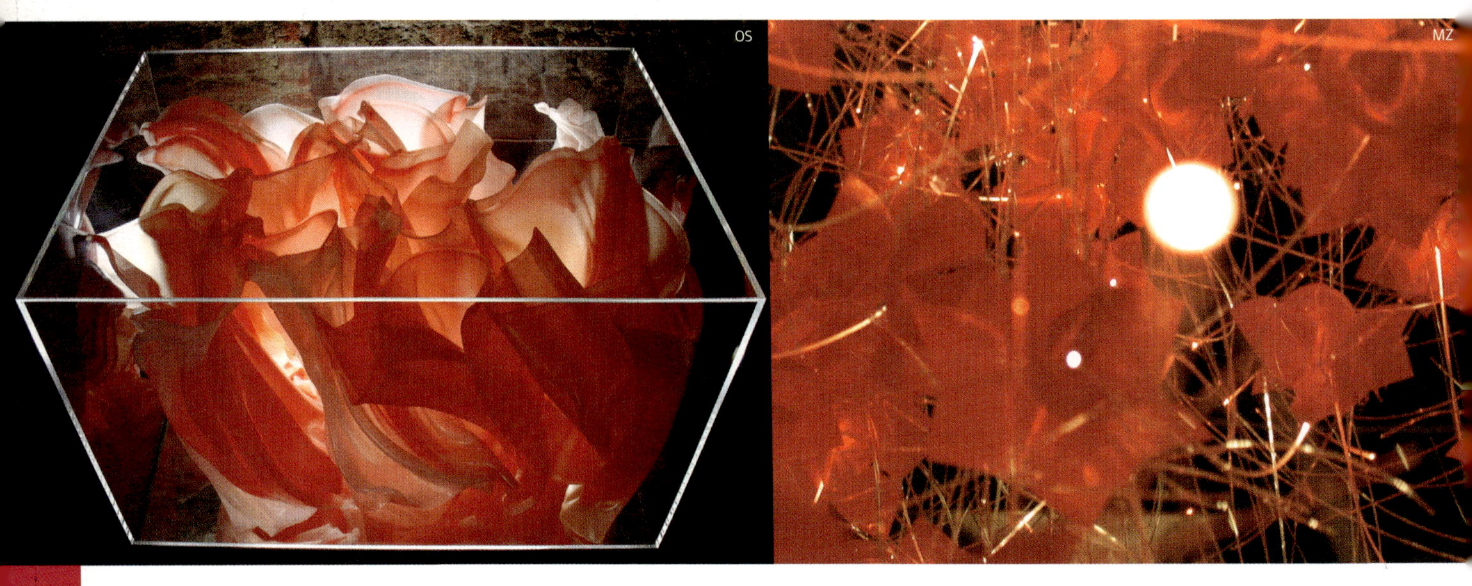

Marles Von Suden   Design London

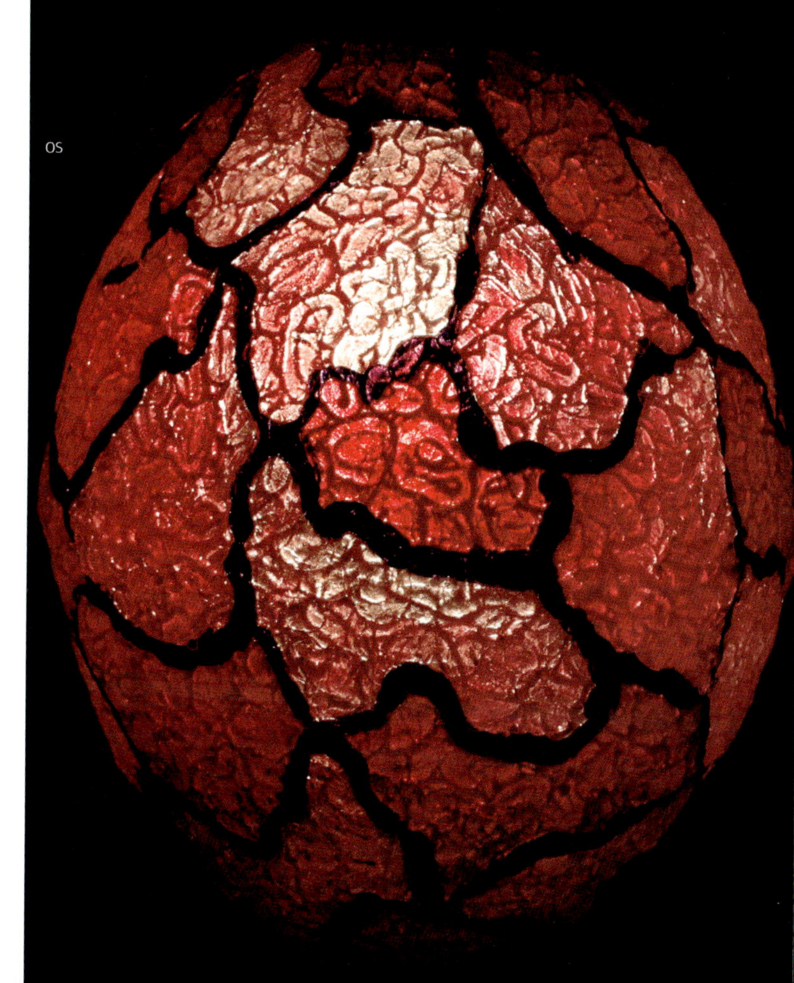

Jacopo Fogoni

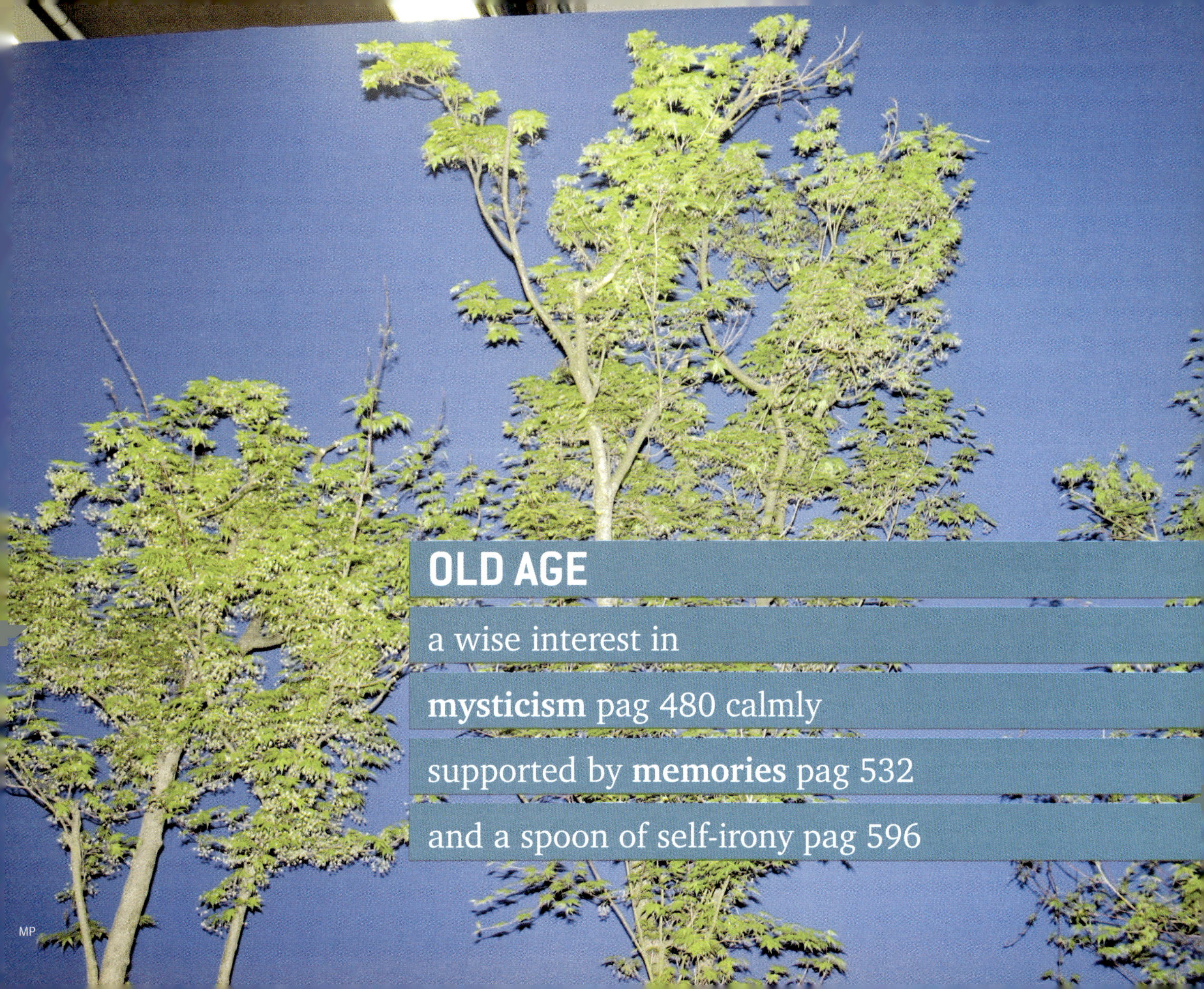

OLD AGE

a wise interest in

mysticism pag 480 calmly

supported by **memories** pag 532

and a spoon of self-irony pag 596

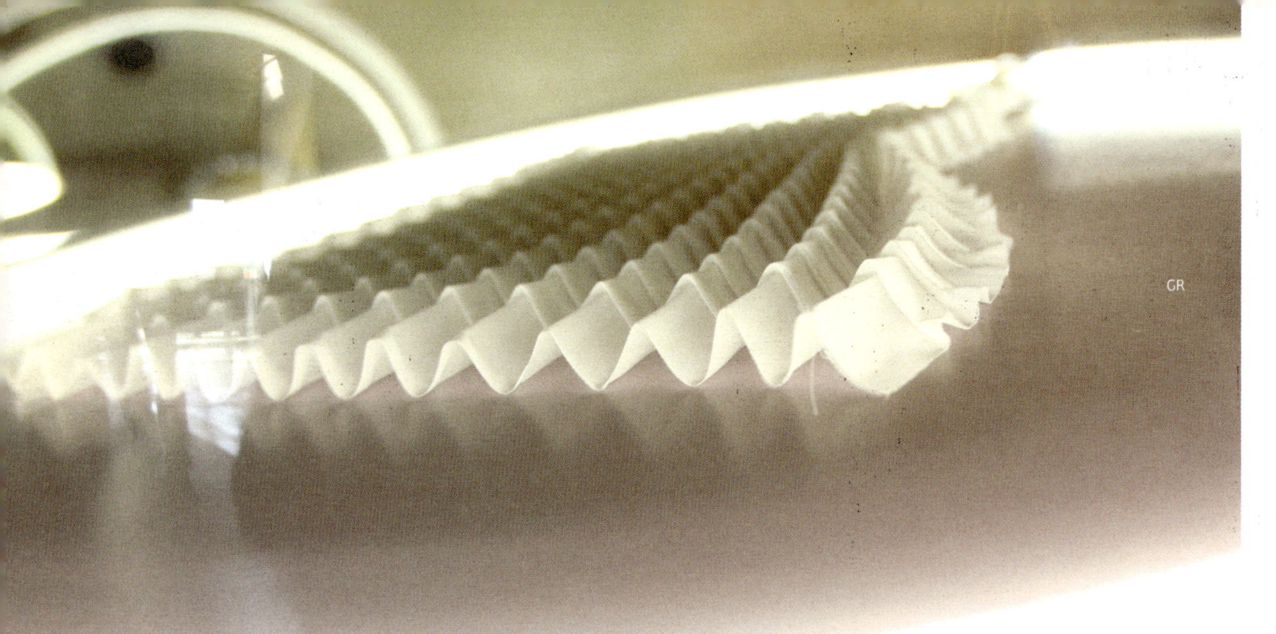

Material ConneXion Milano, the first research center of innovative materials in Milan,

has selected a range of the latest materials, to inspire designers with new ideas

and creative spurs. Each object communicates with who is watching, touching and using it;

while the material it is made of performs a definite differentiation task,

by giving the objects diverse values and tangible performances.

The surfaces of objects become complex, endowed with their own identity

and independent behaviours, while design is committed in the research of new materials

and in the realization of objects, which are able to give intelligent answers.

Material Connexion

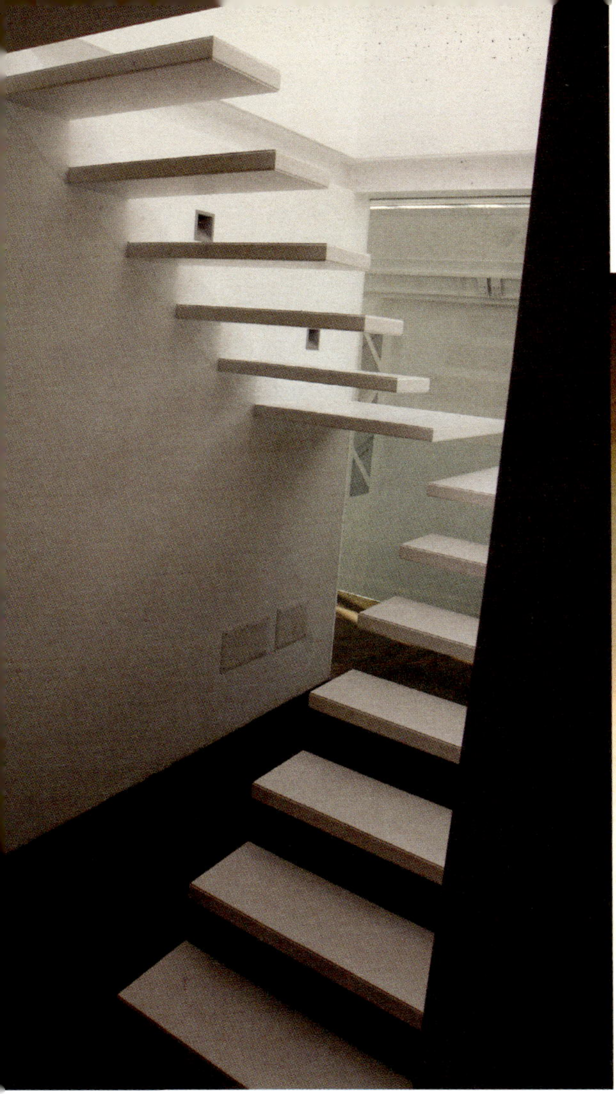

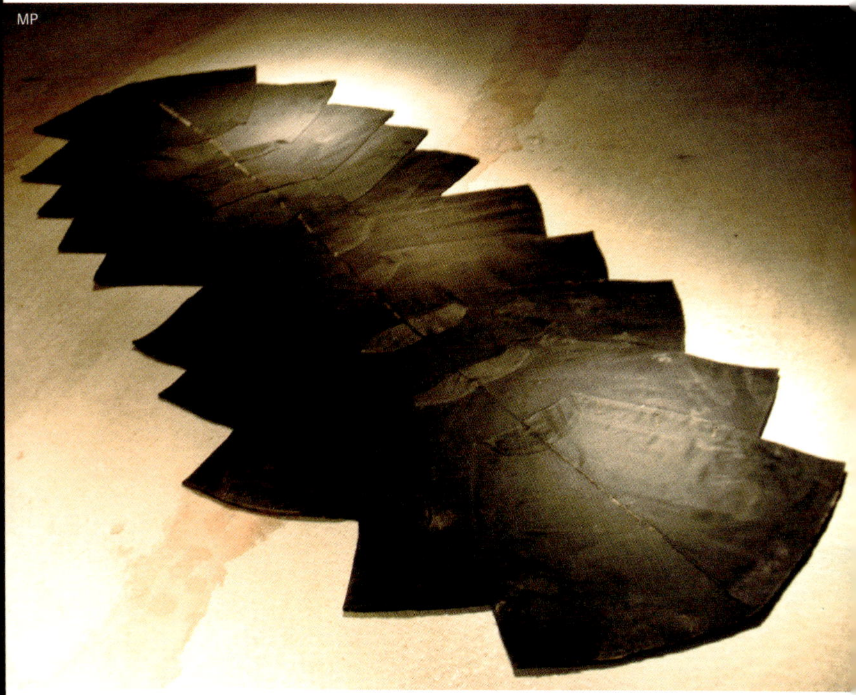

Vicenzo de Cotiis - Massimo del Monte

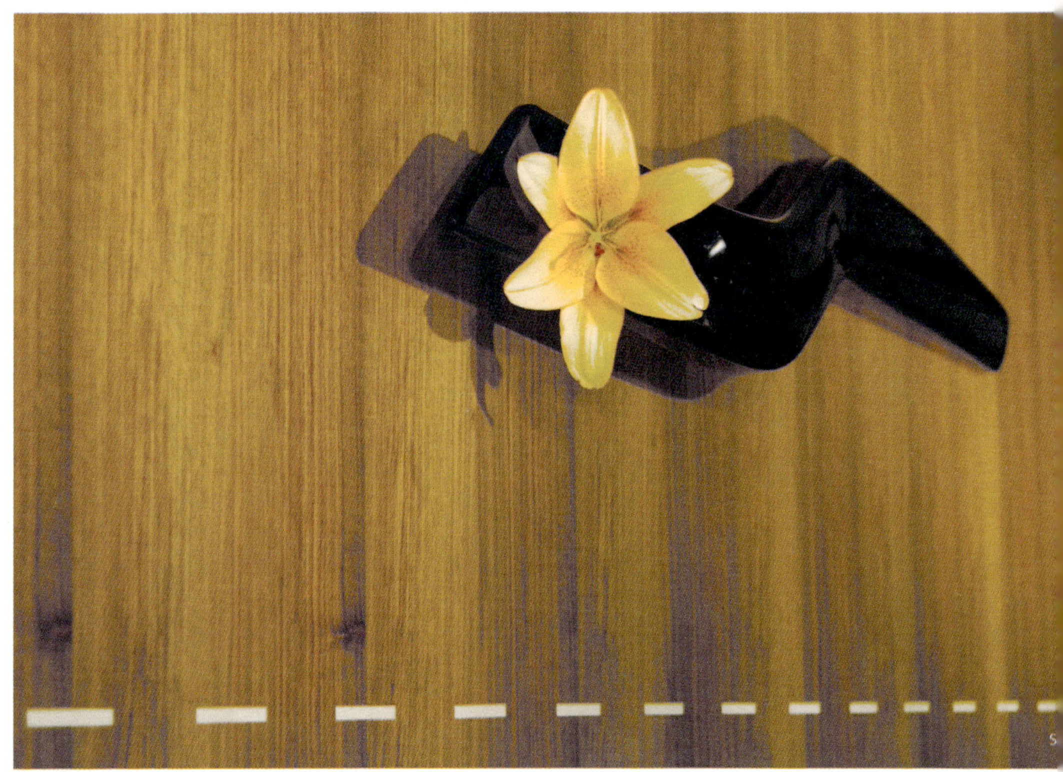

Sawaya&Moroni

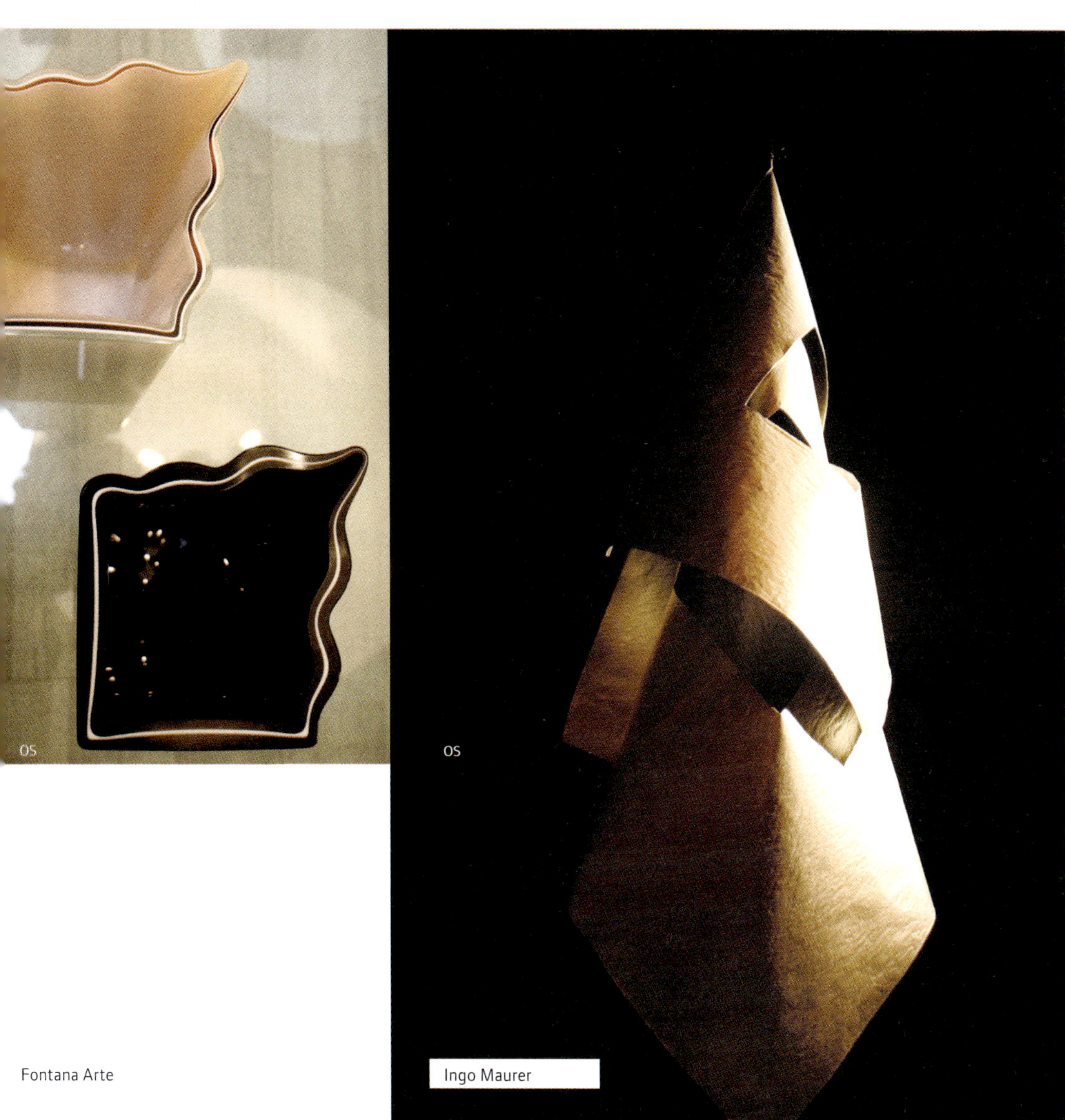

05
OS
Fontana Arte
Ingo Maurer

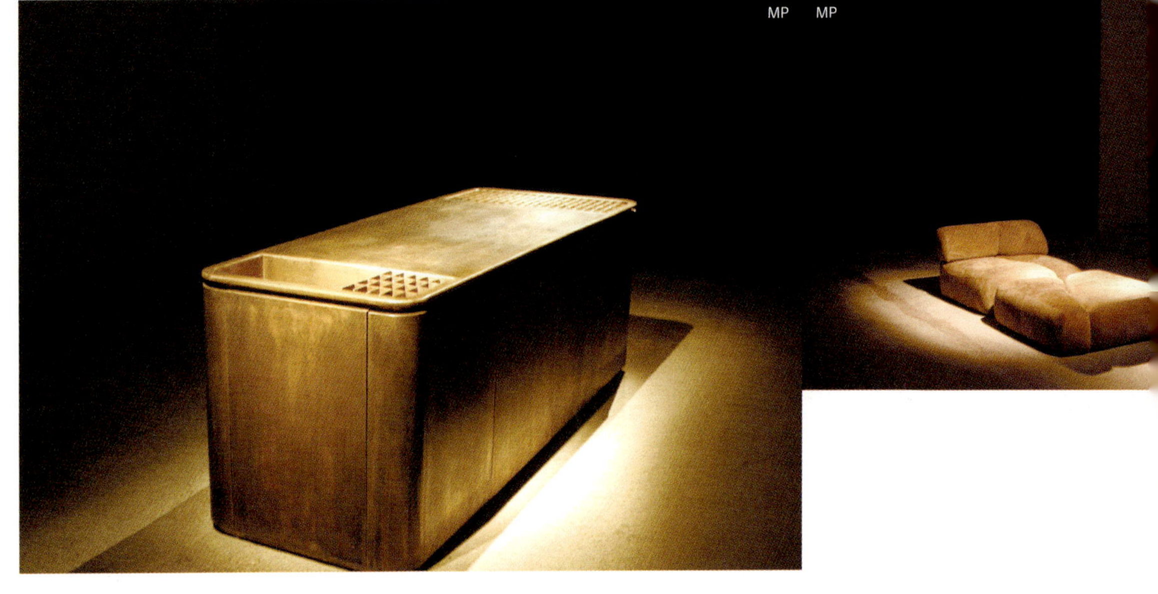

Vicenzo De Cotiis - Massimo del Monte

Vicenzo De Cotiis - Massimo del Monte

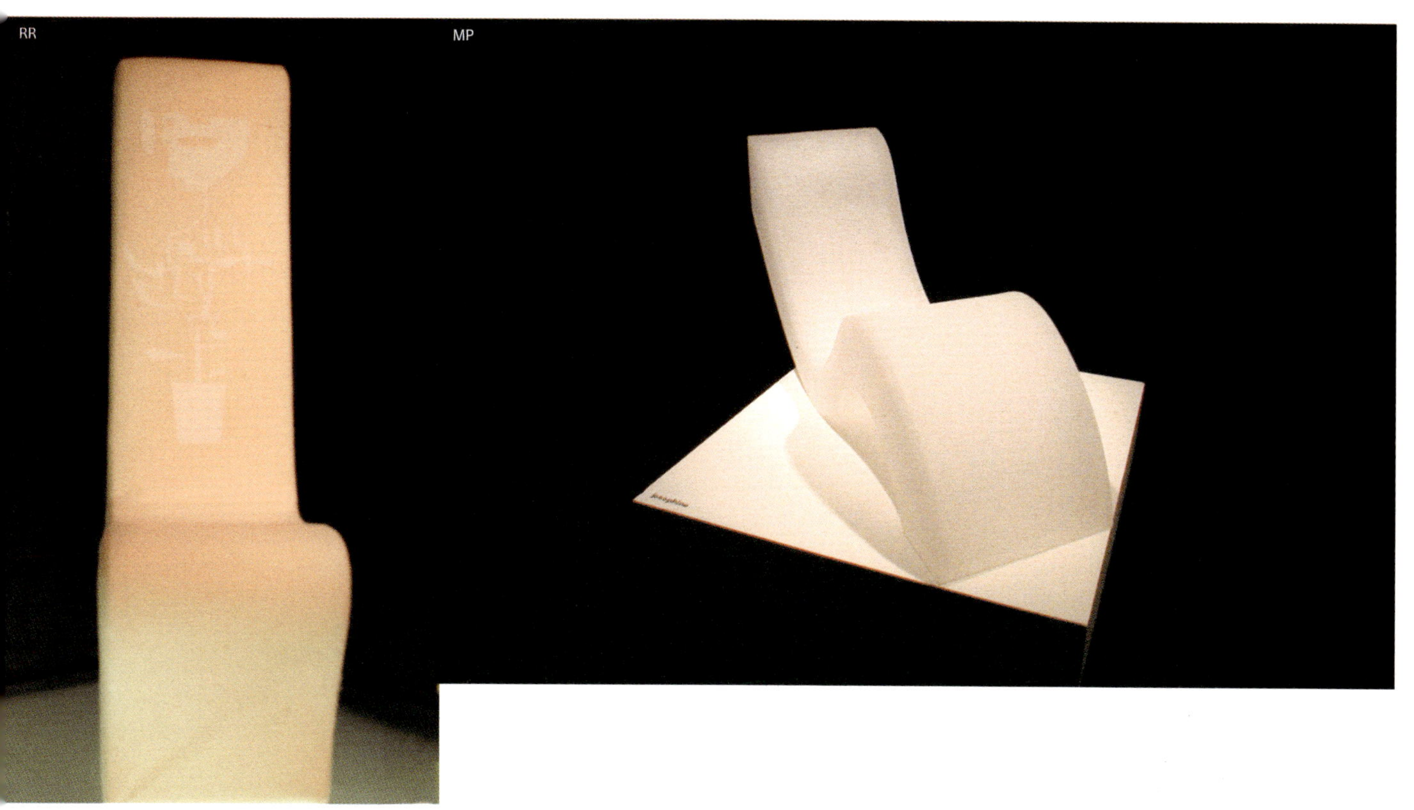

Ginevra seat by Parentesi Quadra   Kris Ruhs

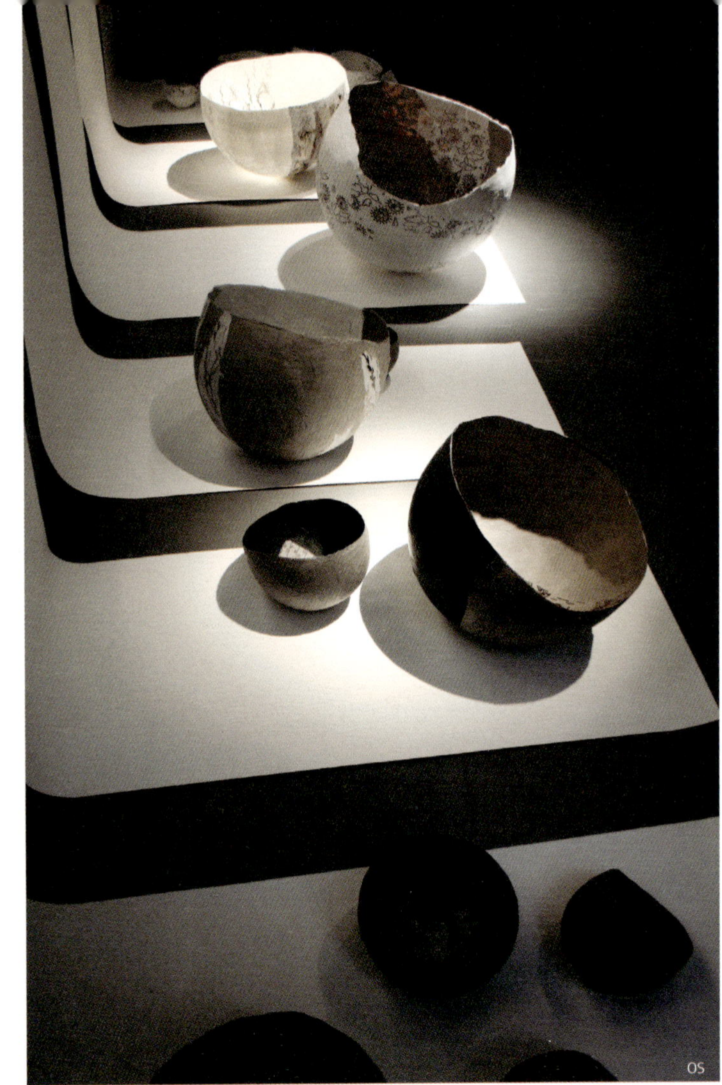

Francesca Davoli

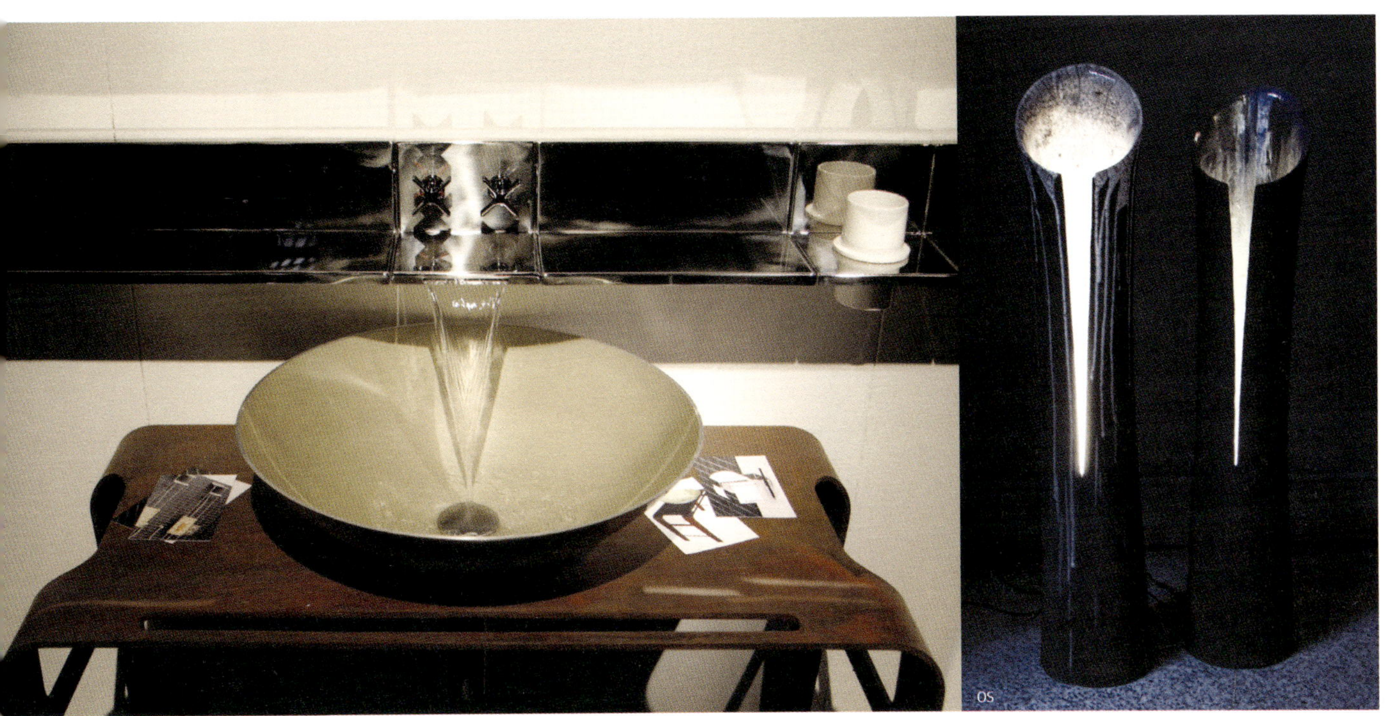

Ritmonio

David Sorgato

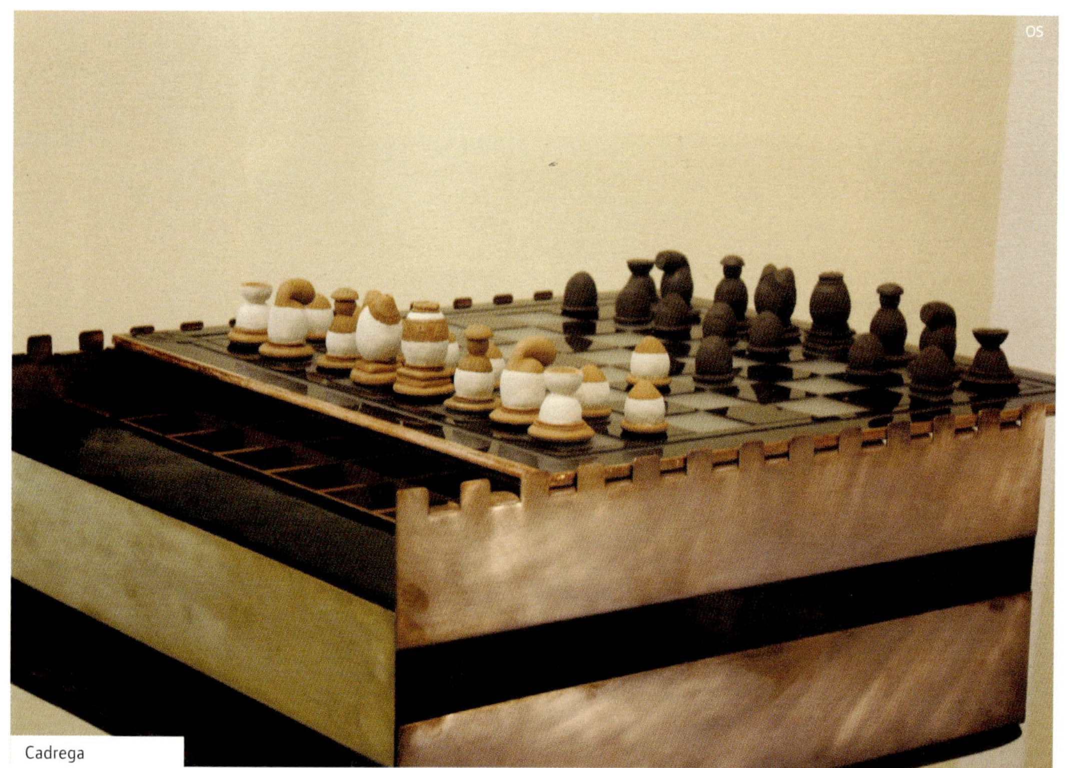

Cadrega

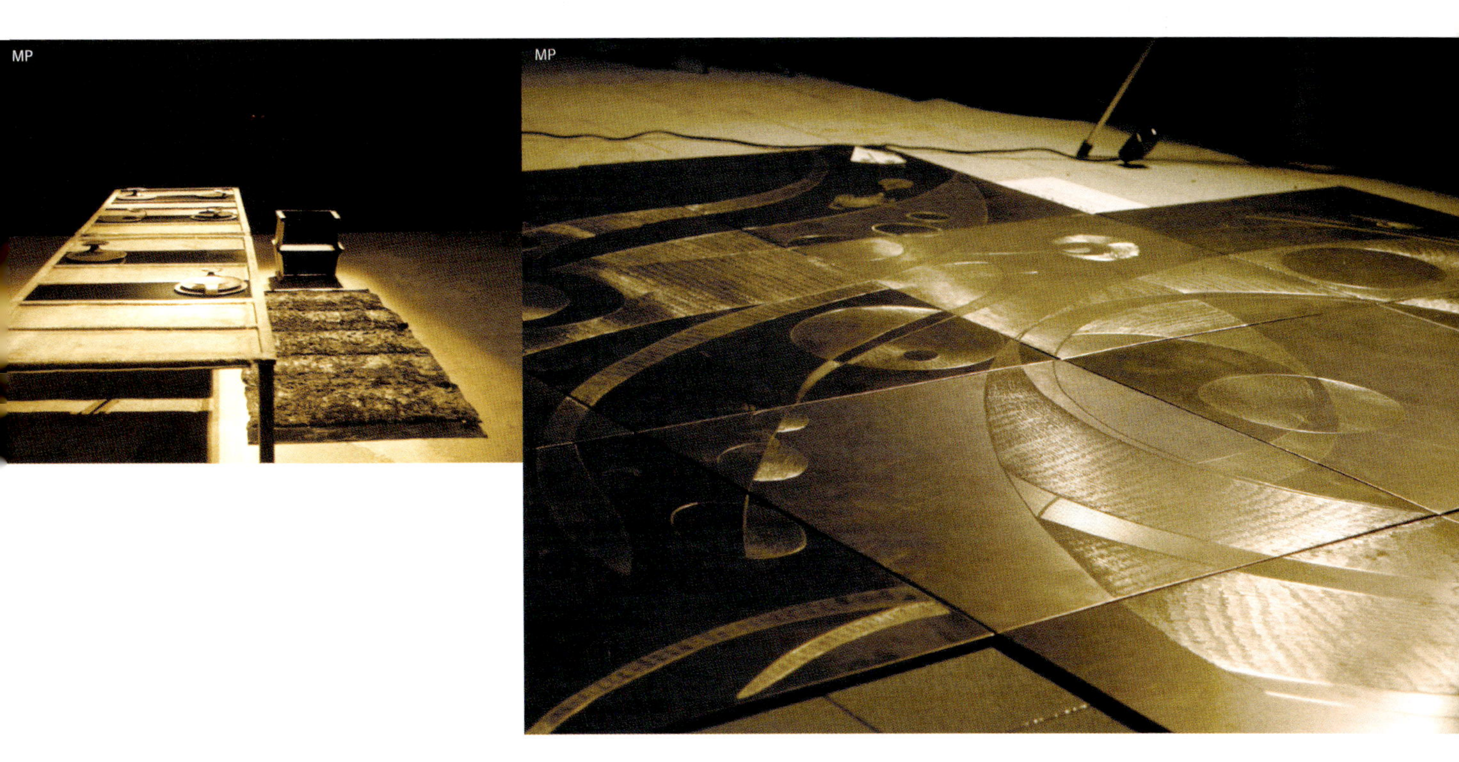

Vicenzo de Cotiis - Massimo del Monte

Shit Design

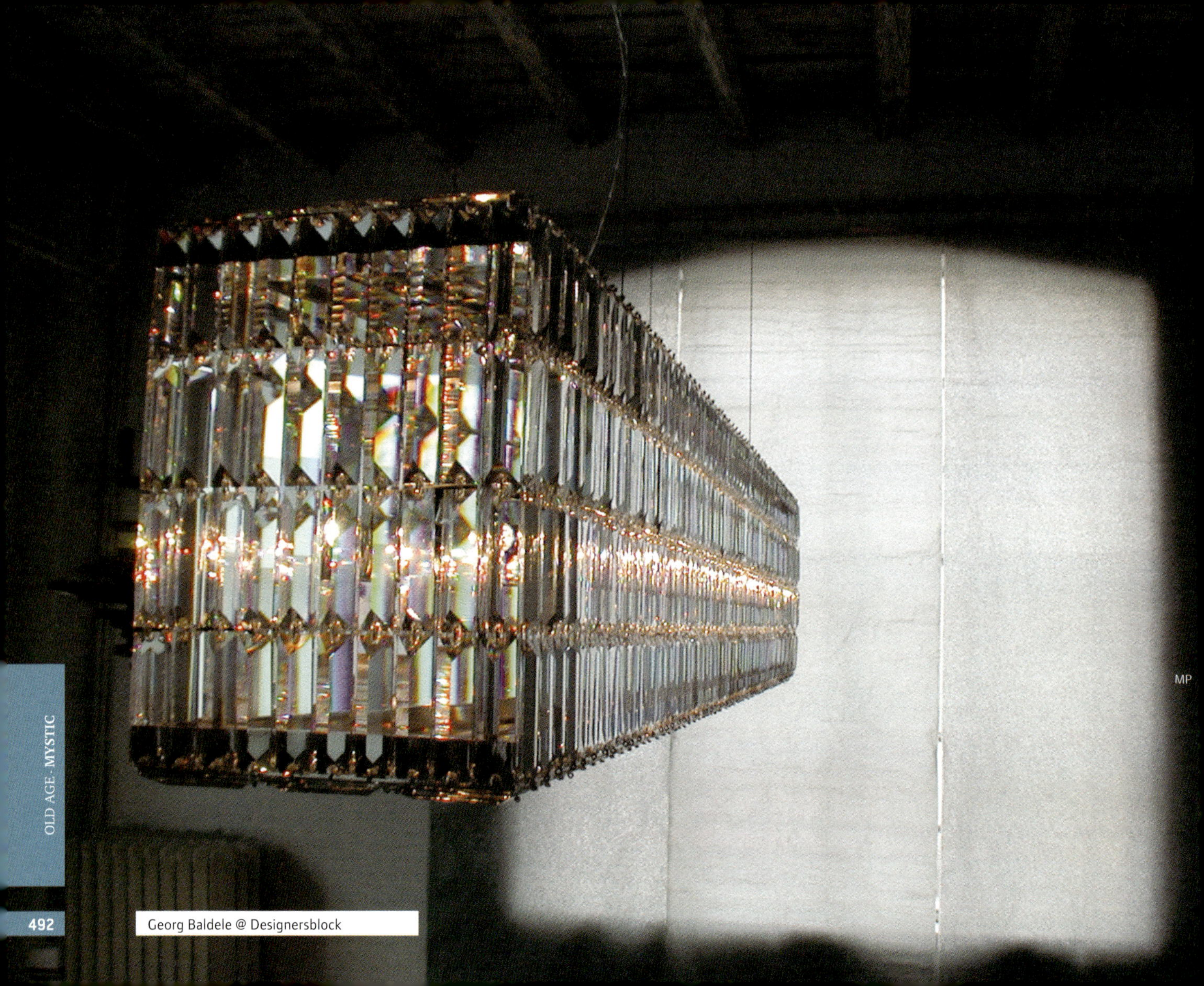

Georg Baldele @ Designersblock

MP

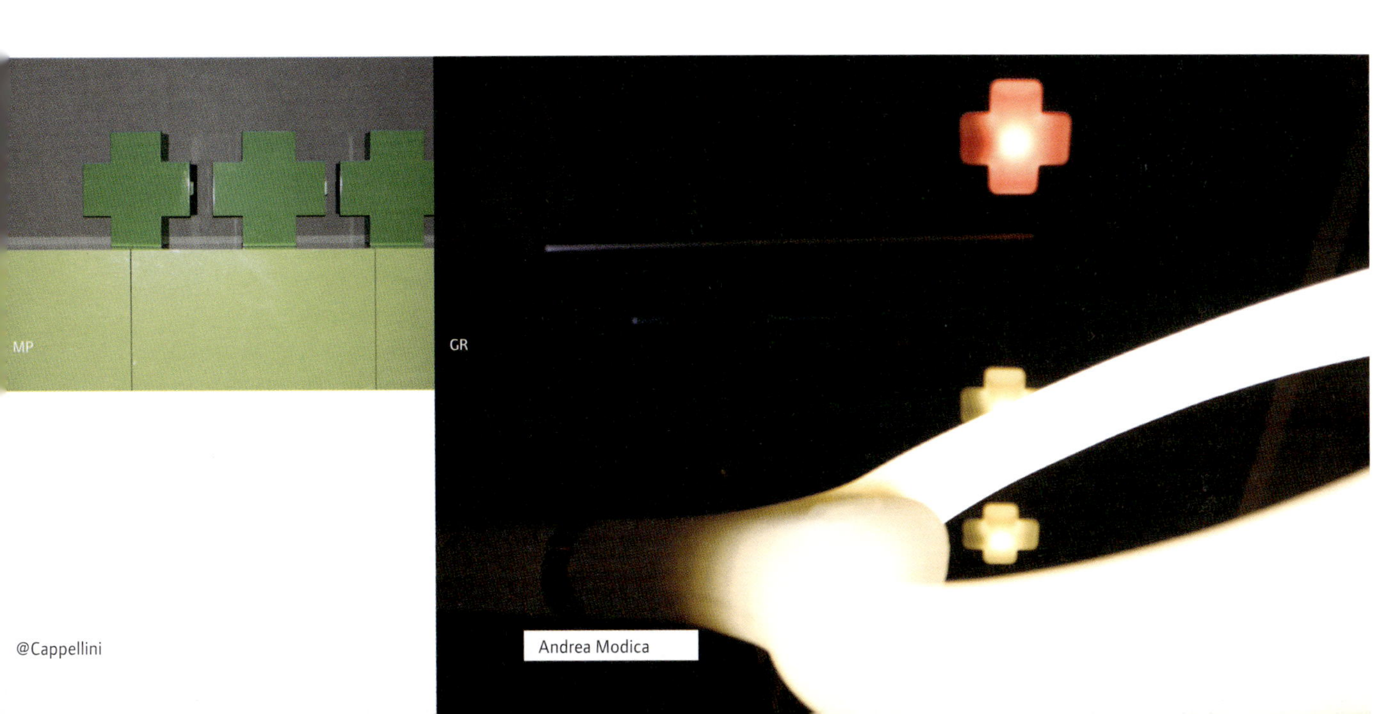

MP
GR
@Cappellini
Andrea Modica

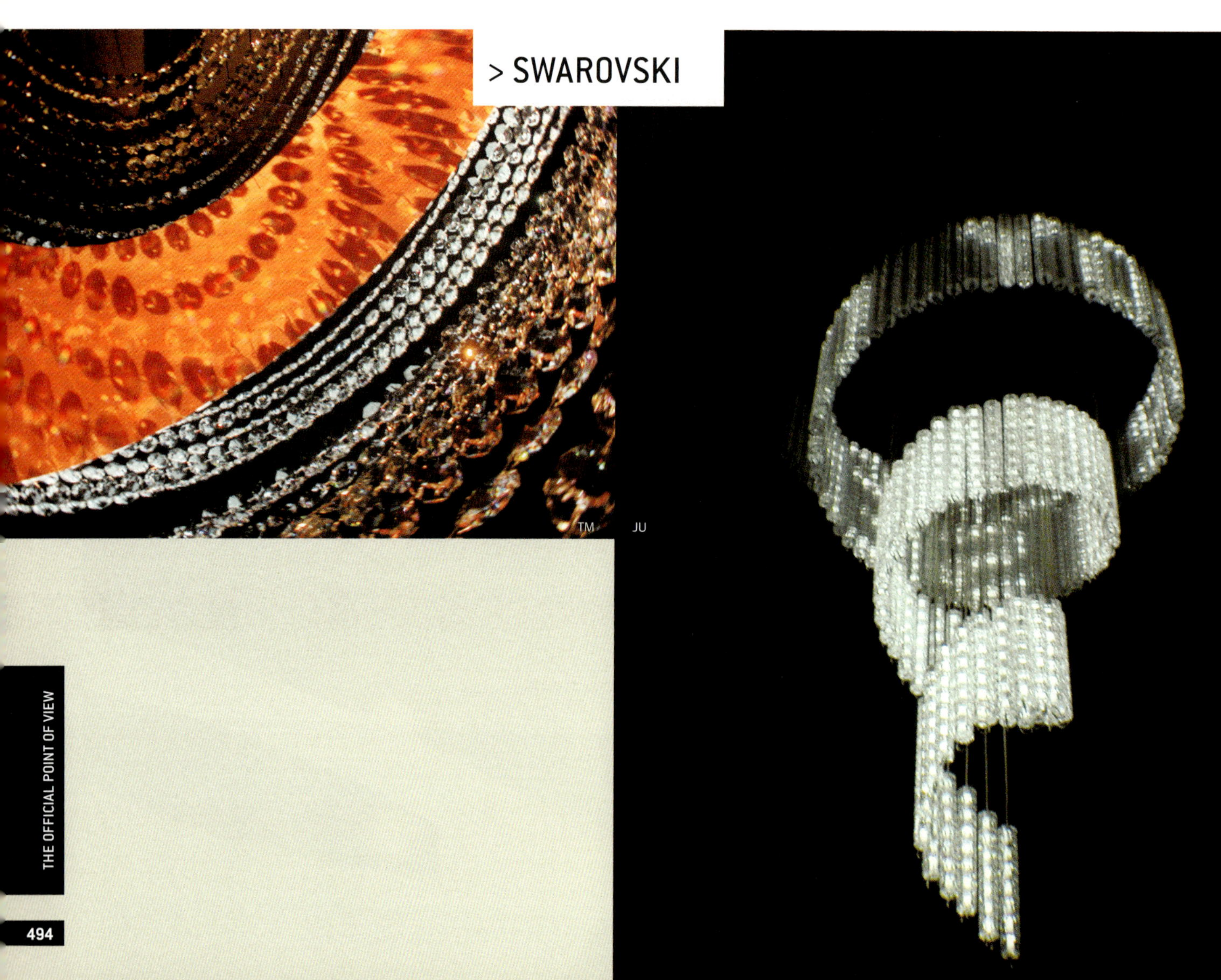

> SWAROVSKI

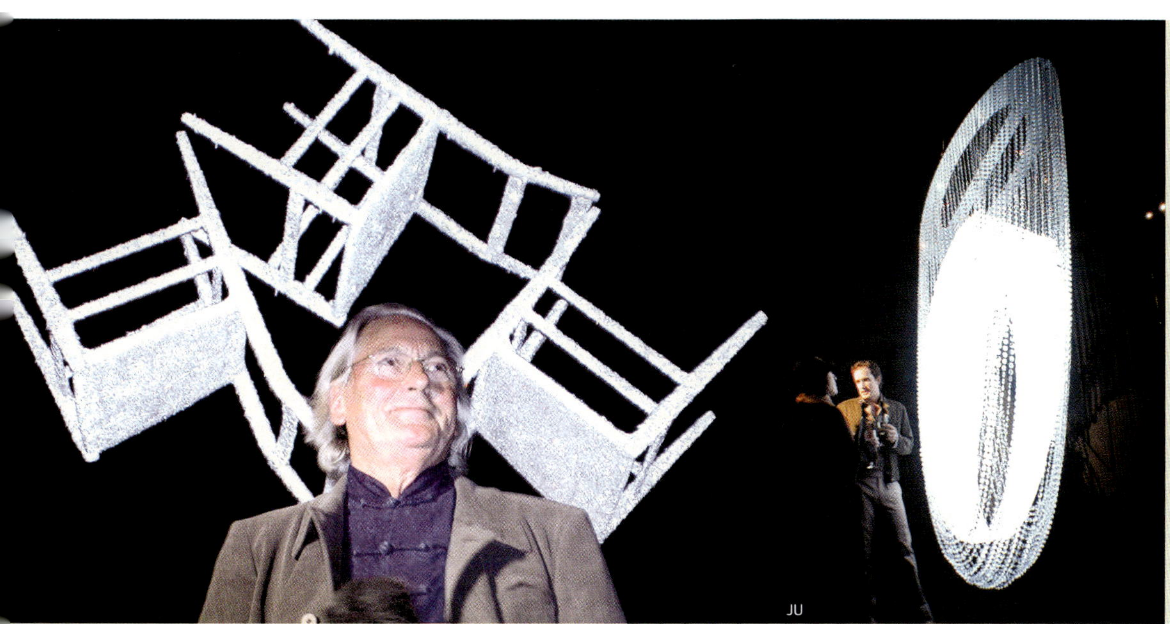

SWAROVSKI CRYSTAL PALACE COLLECTION 2004

For the third consecutive year, a selection of designers and artists from all over the world have been invited **to exploit**

not only the beauty, but also the technical possibilities of Swarovski crystal.

Their mandate, once again, was that of **reinventing the chandelier.**

Their means Swarovski's entire components collection,

inexhaustible material knowledge and technical expertise.

Ingo Maurer

"Tree of Fiberlights" Alexander Lervik

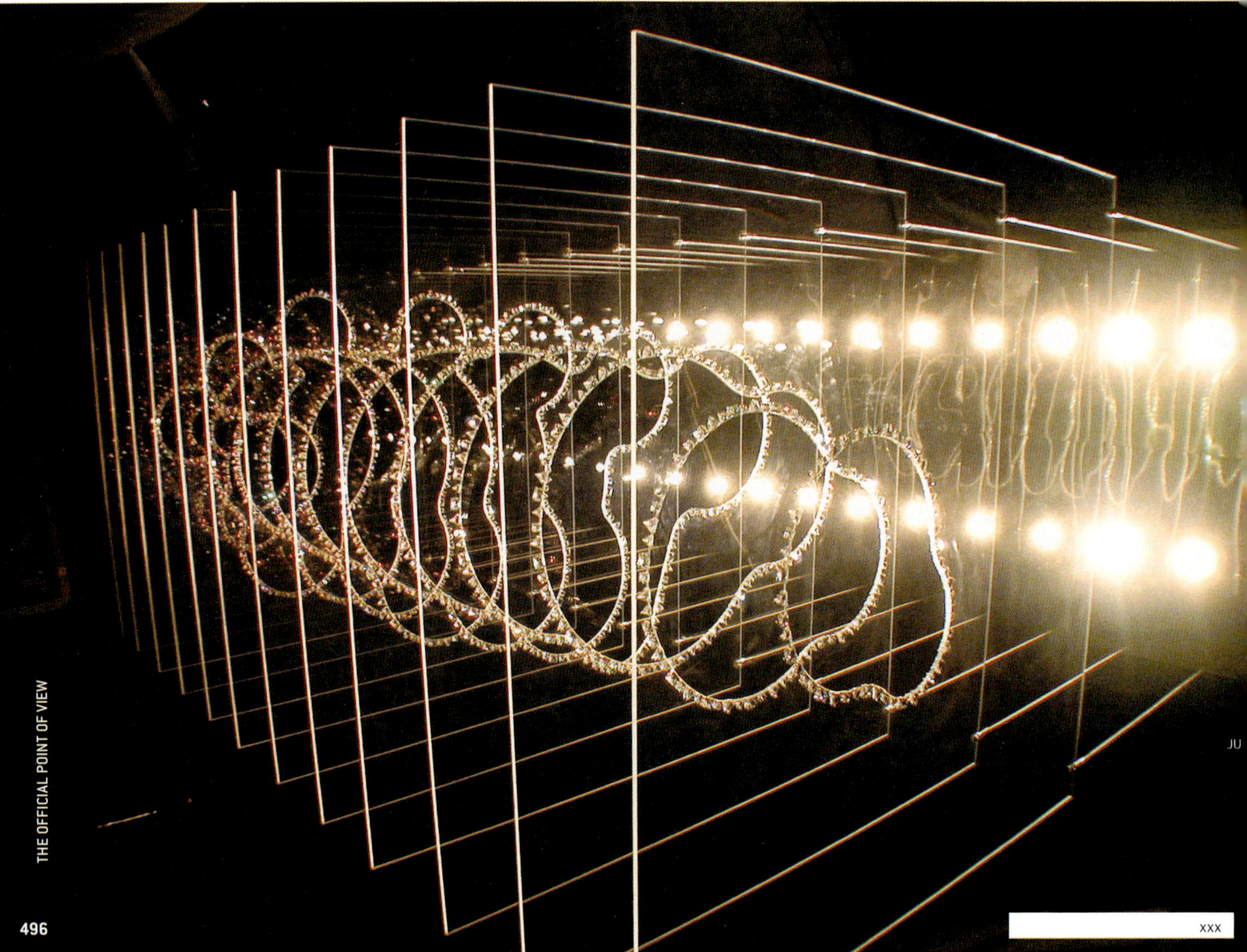

XXX

Fourteen designers presented ten brilliant solutions, each one a personal and innovative interpretation of the theme.

Ron Arad – 'Lolita', Barber Osgerby – 'Supernova', Yves Bèhar – 'Nest', Tord Boontje – 'Ting Ting Ting', Constantin and Laurene Boym – 'Crystal Rugs', David Collins and Chris Levine – 'Satellite', Matali Crasset – 'Sky', Ben Jakober – 'Bucky Life', Jeff Leatham – 'Orchidée', Ingo Maurer "Giò ponti in the sky with diamonds",

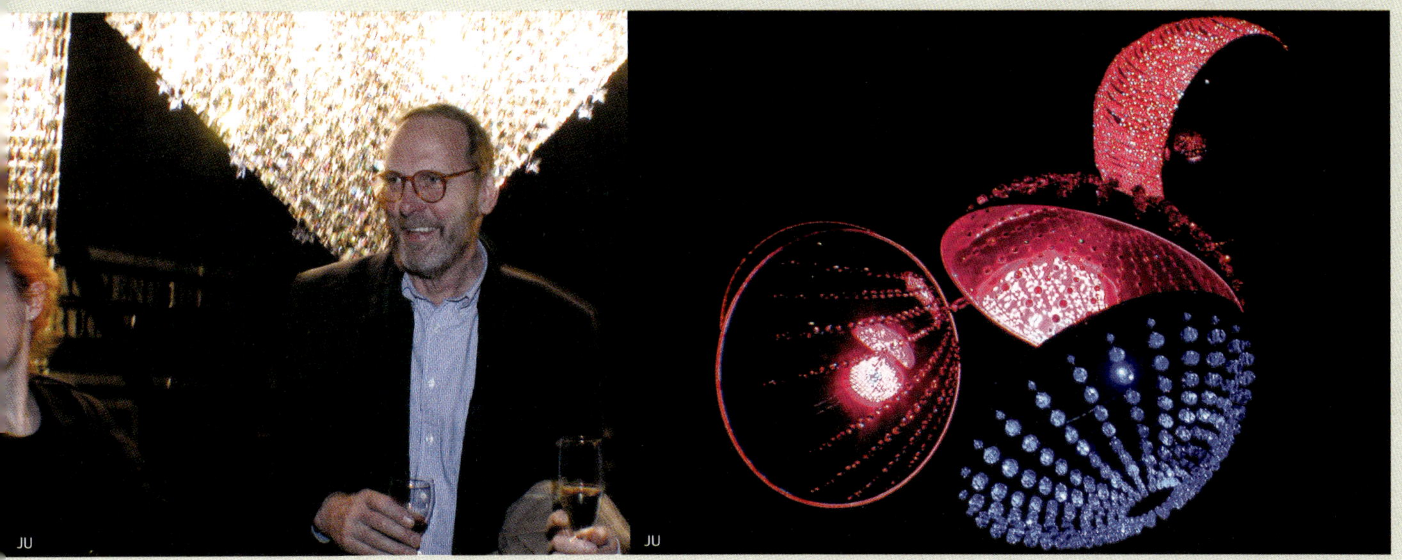

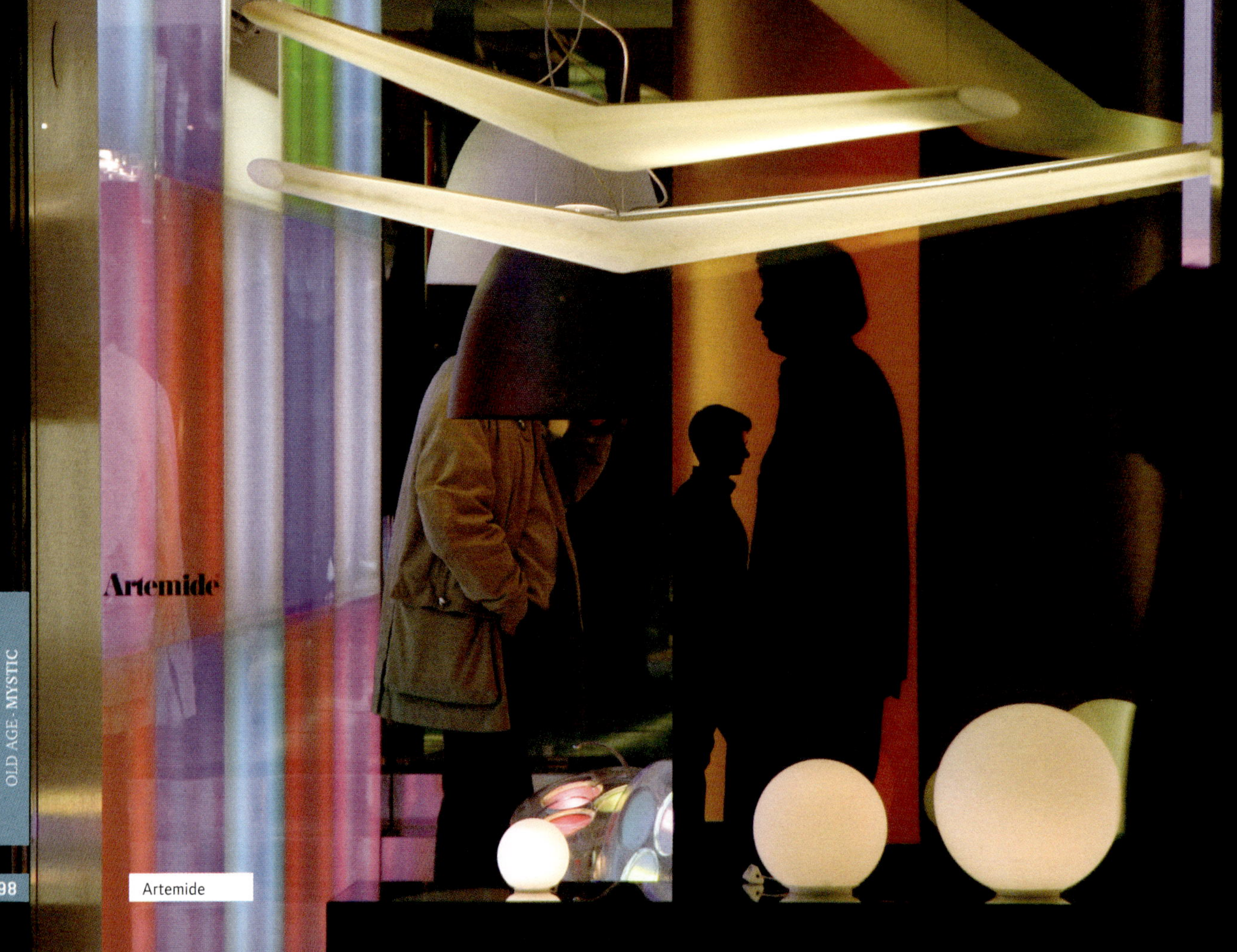

Artemide

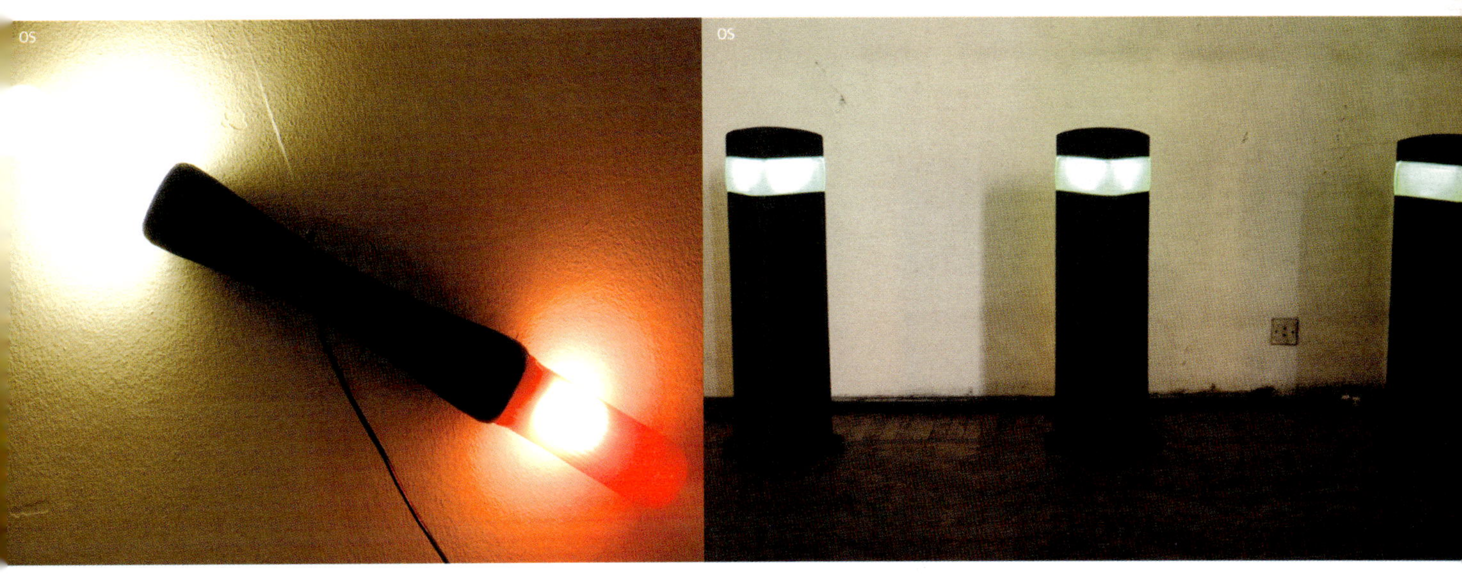

Disegno Espanol   Santa & Cole

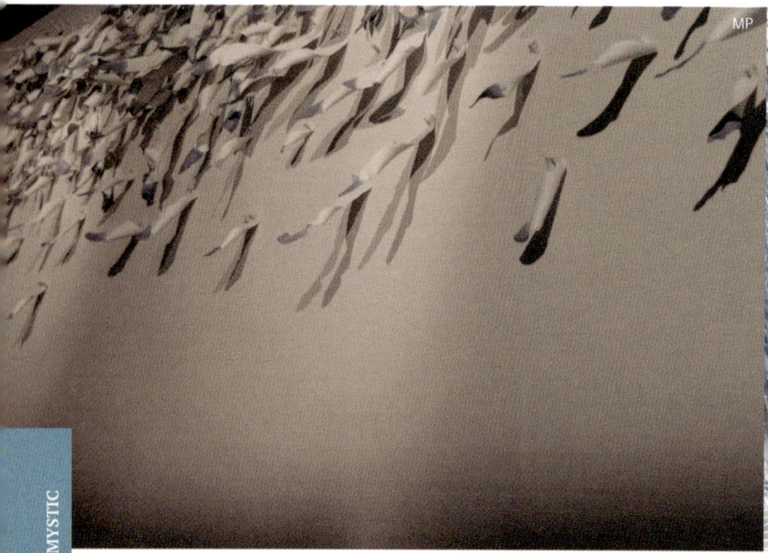

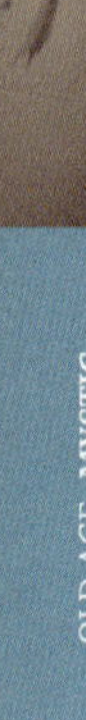

Paola Lenti

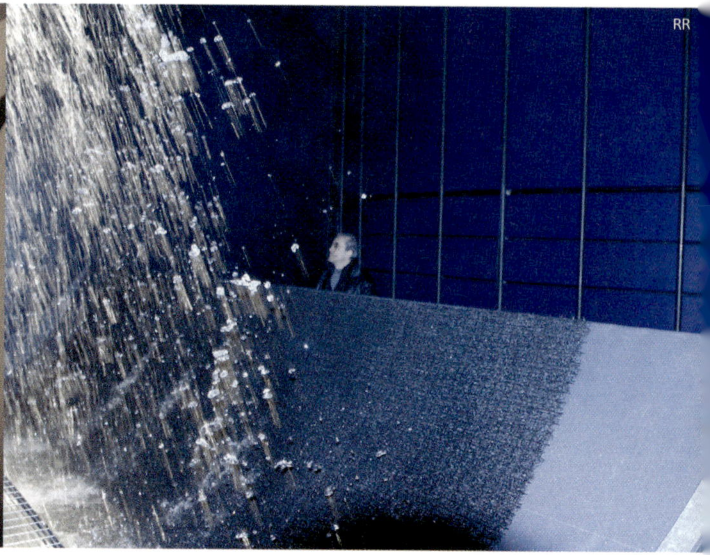

Jacuzzi-Morphosis-pelota

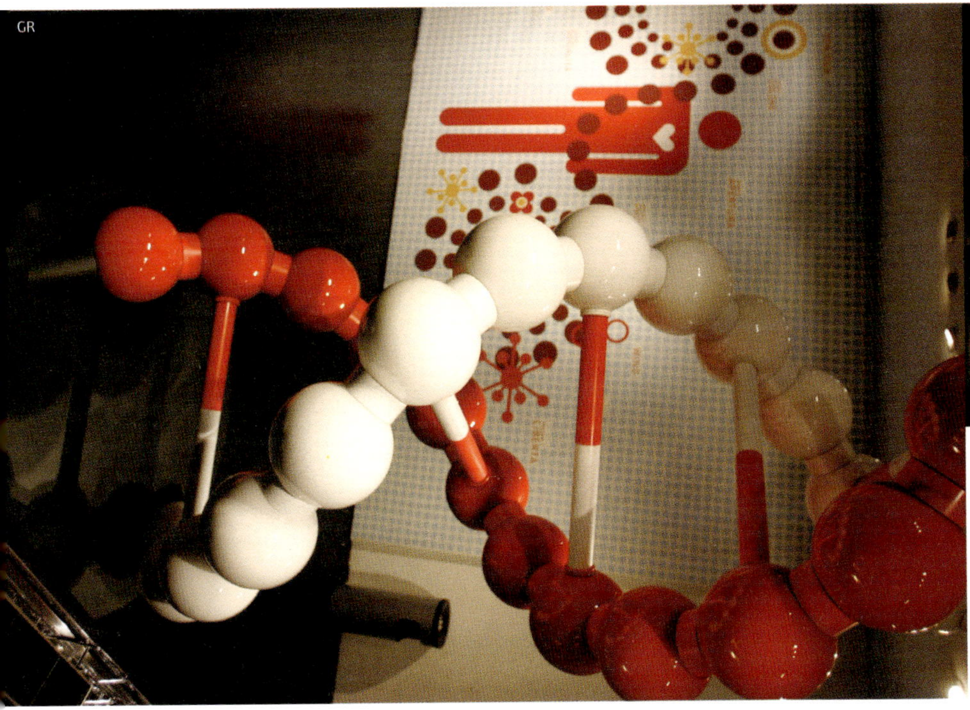

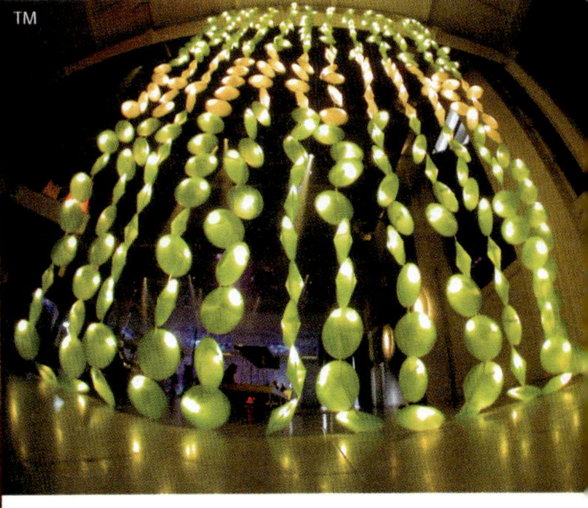

DNA

VIA

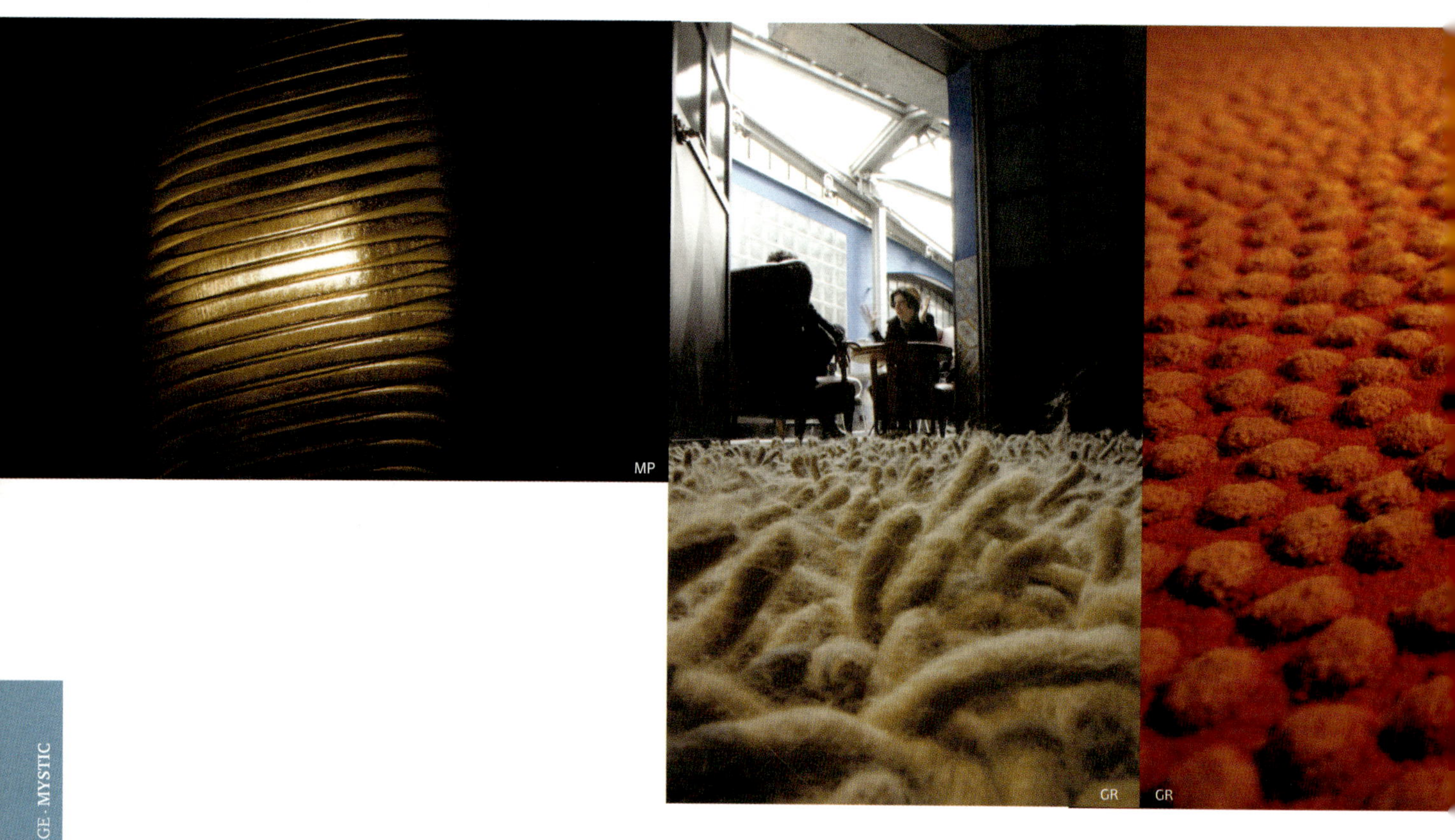

MGX

Nani Marquina - S.S. industria

Nani Marquina @ Superstudio

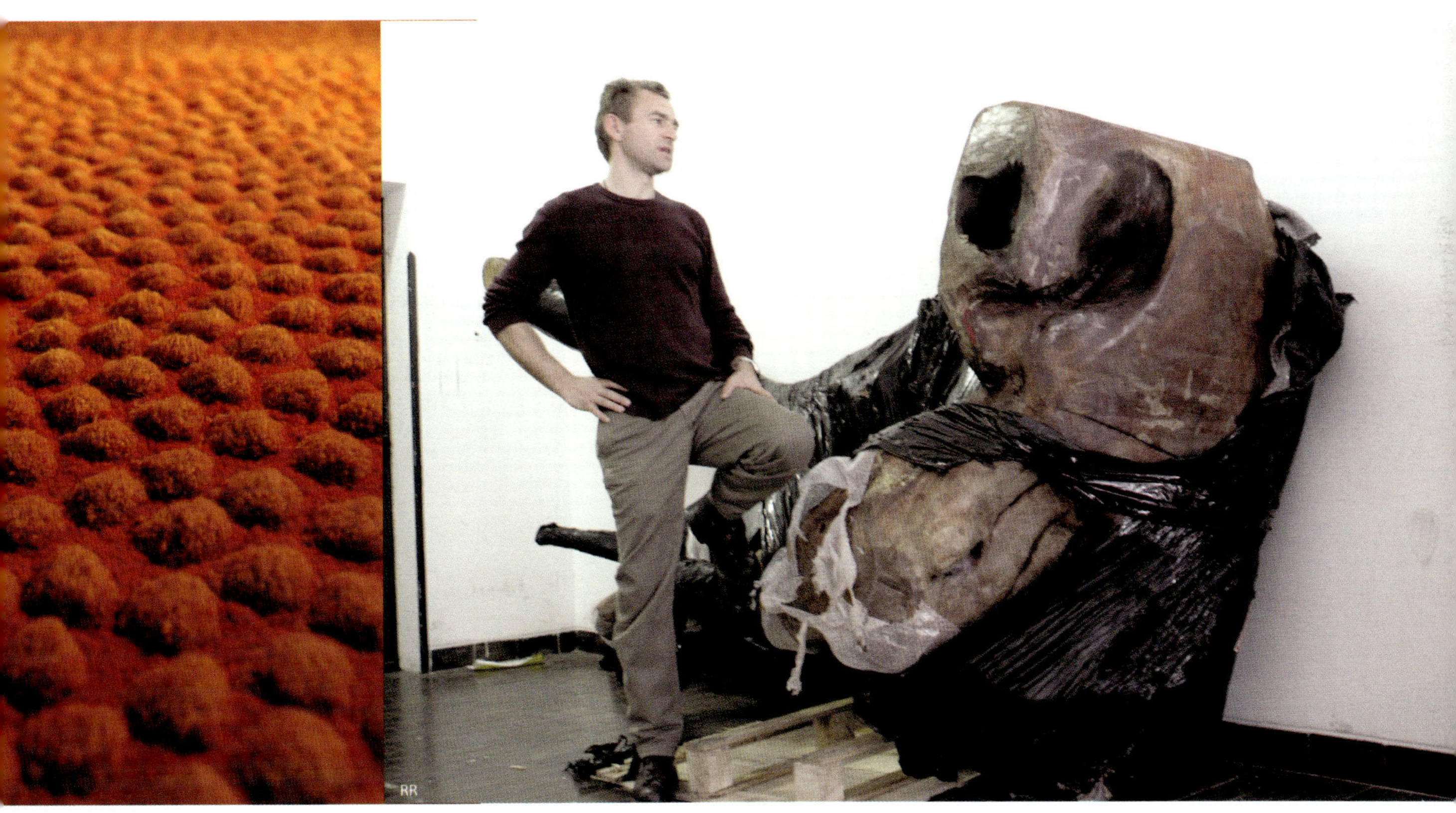

Yaki

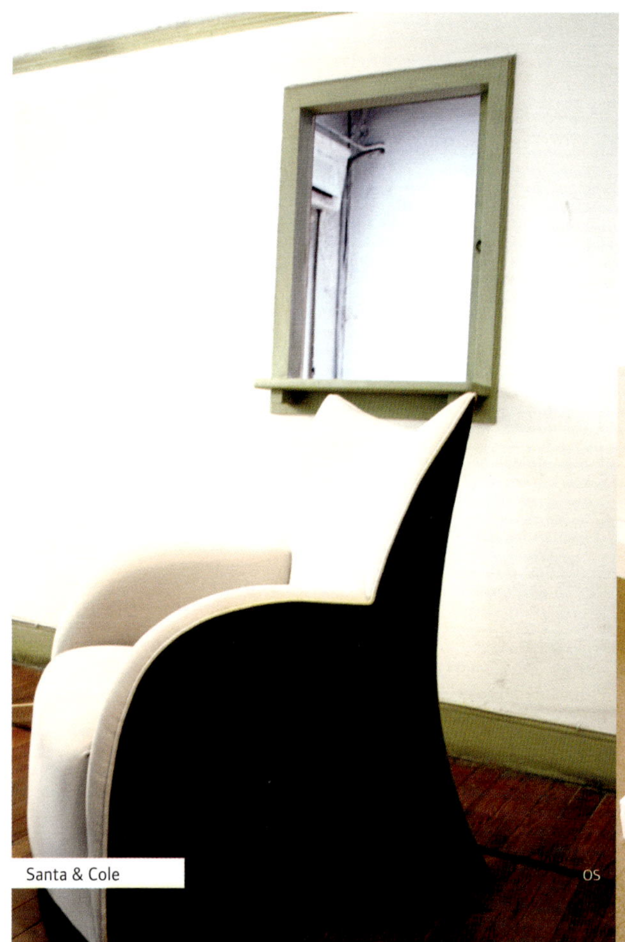

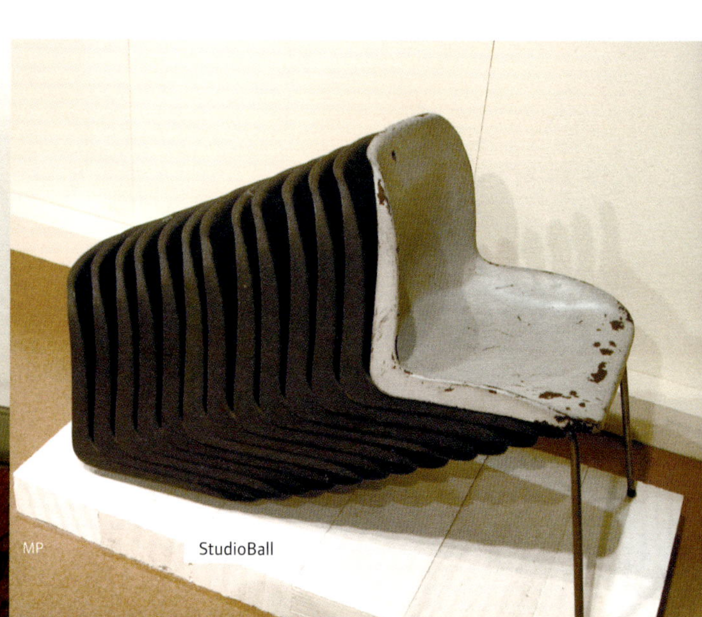

Santa & Cole

OS   MP   StudioBall

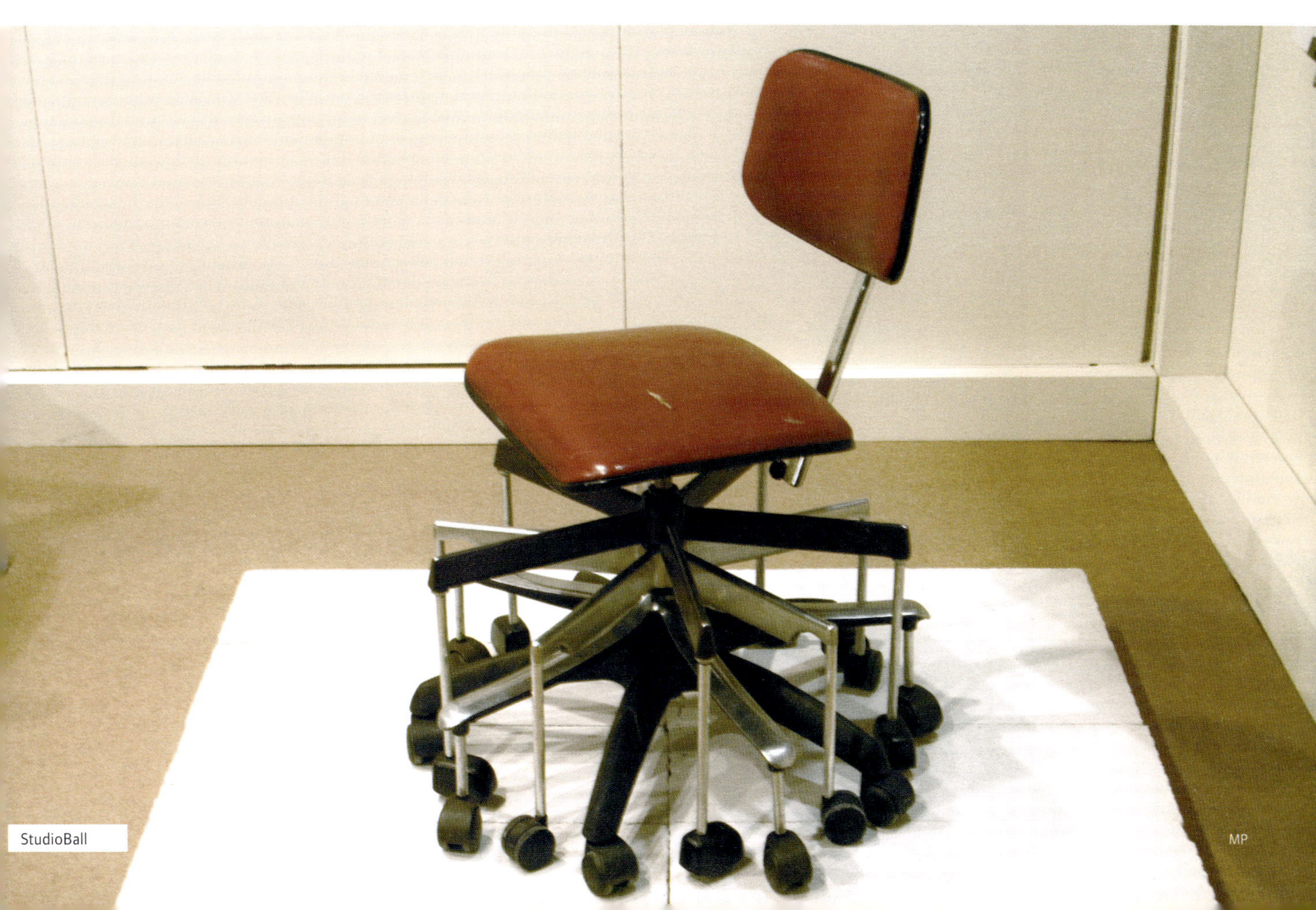
StudioBall
MP

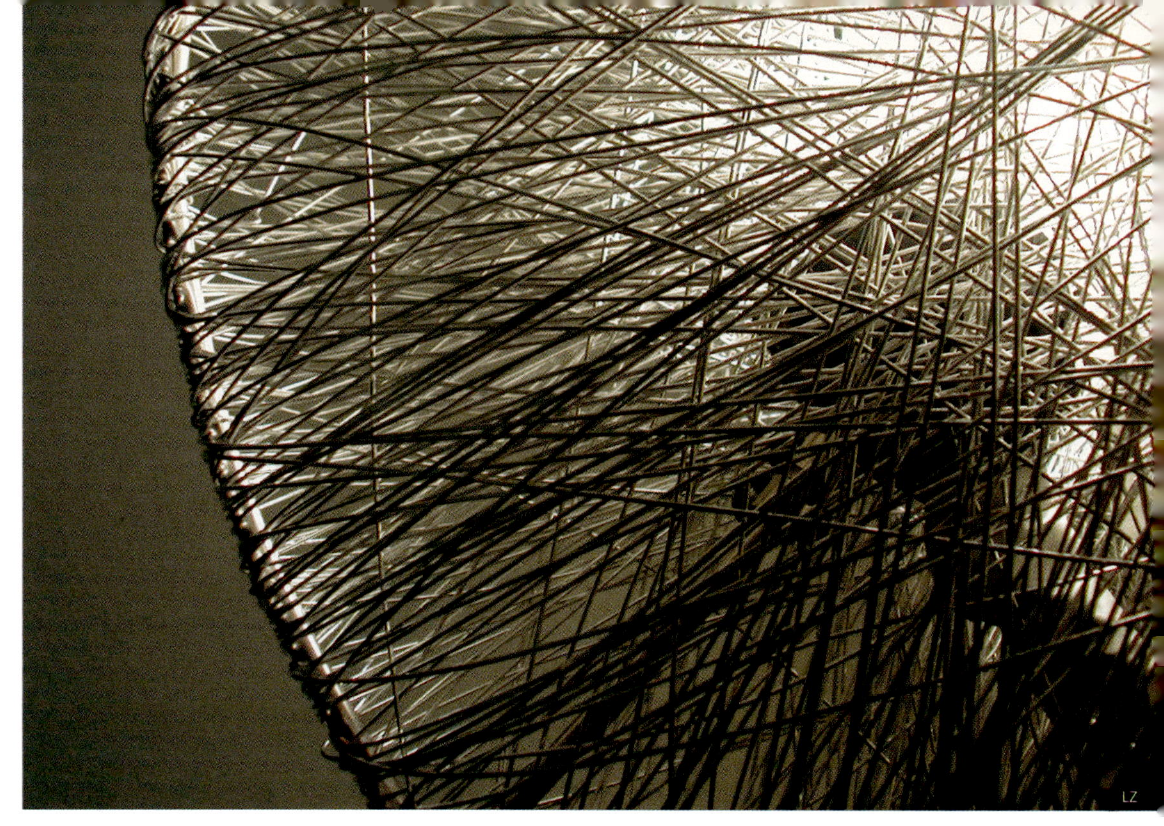

"Coco" by Matthias Bader

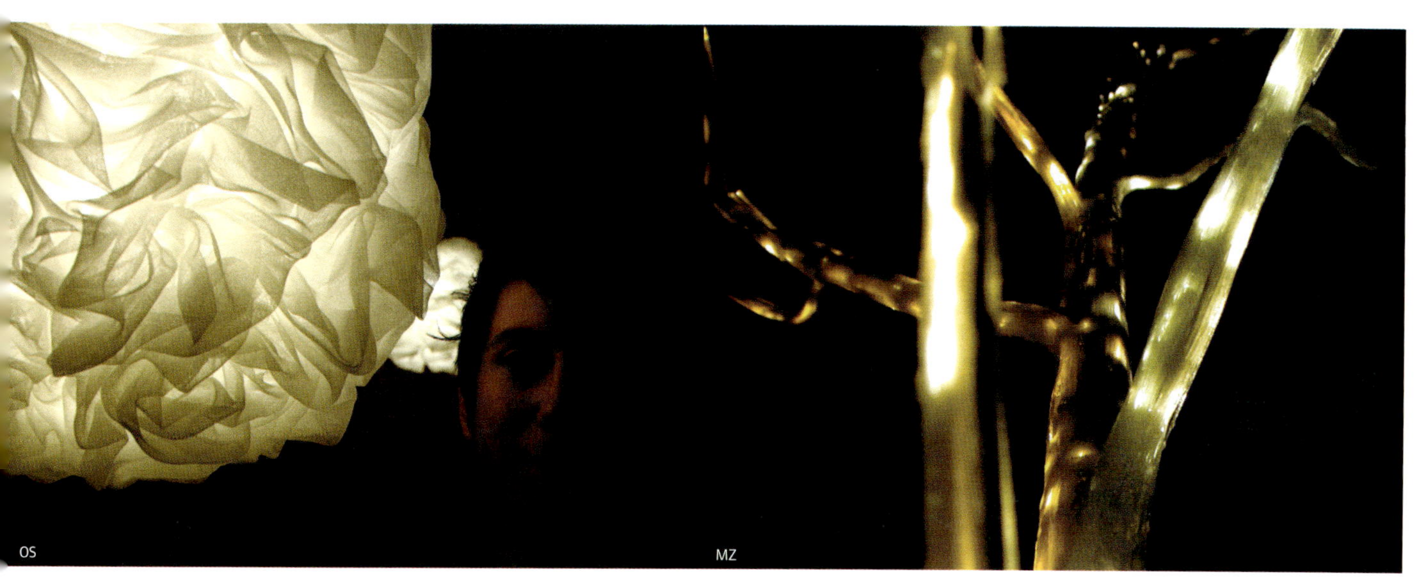

Aaodesign

Scandinavian design @ Triennale

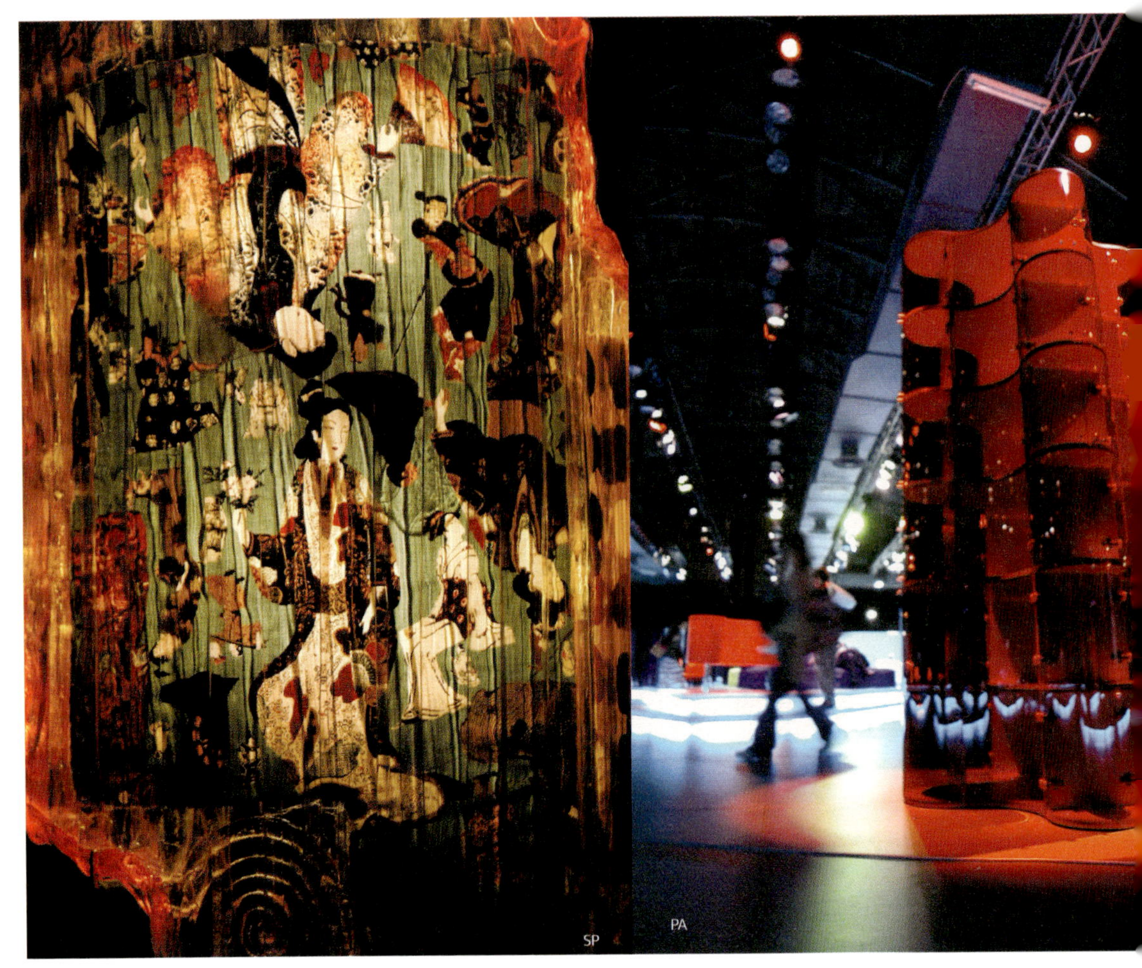

Lamp by Jacopo Foggini and Jacopo Etro

Edra

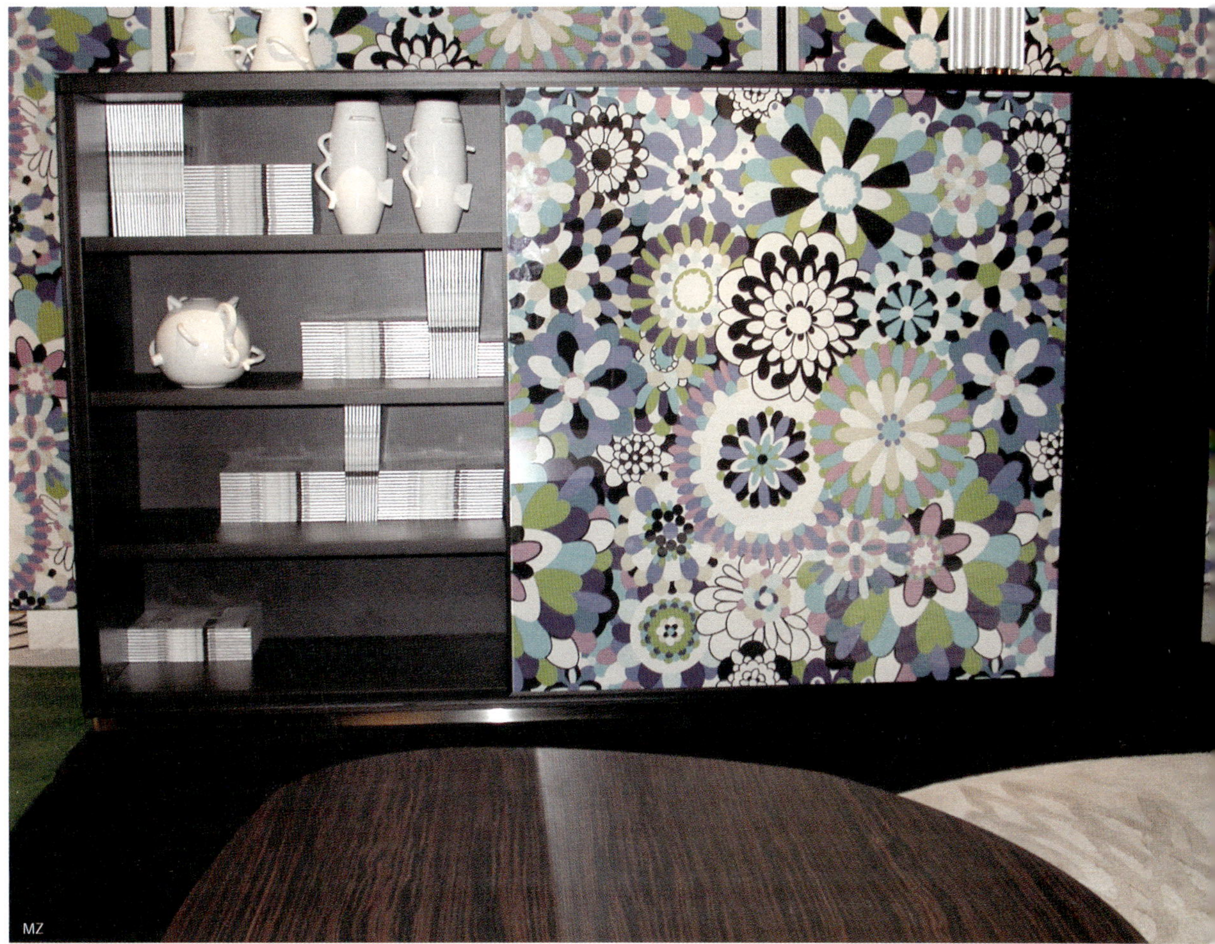

Missoni

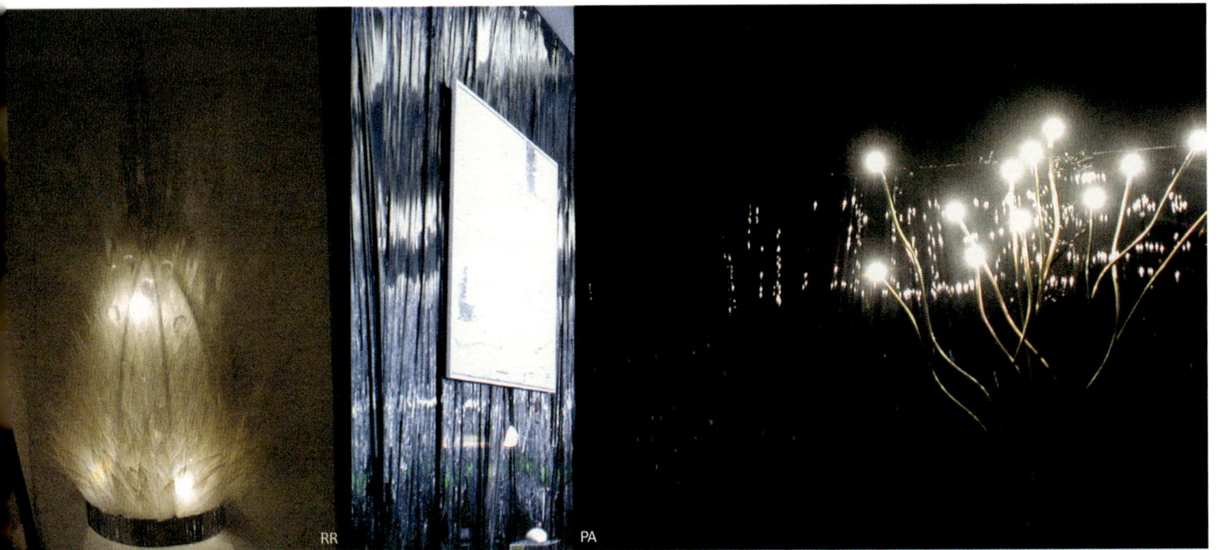

Amalgama - Valentina Giovando

Lucifero Illuminazione @ Nu light

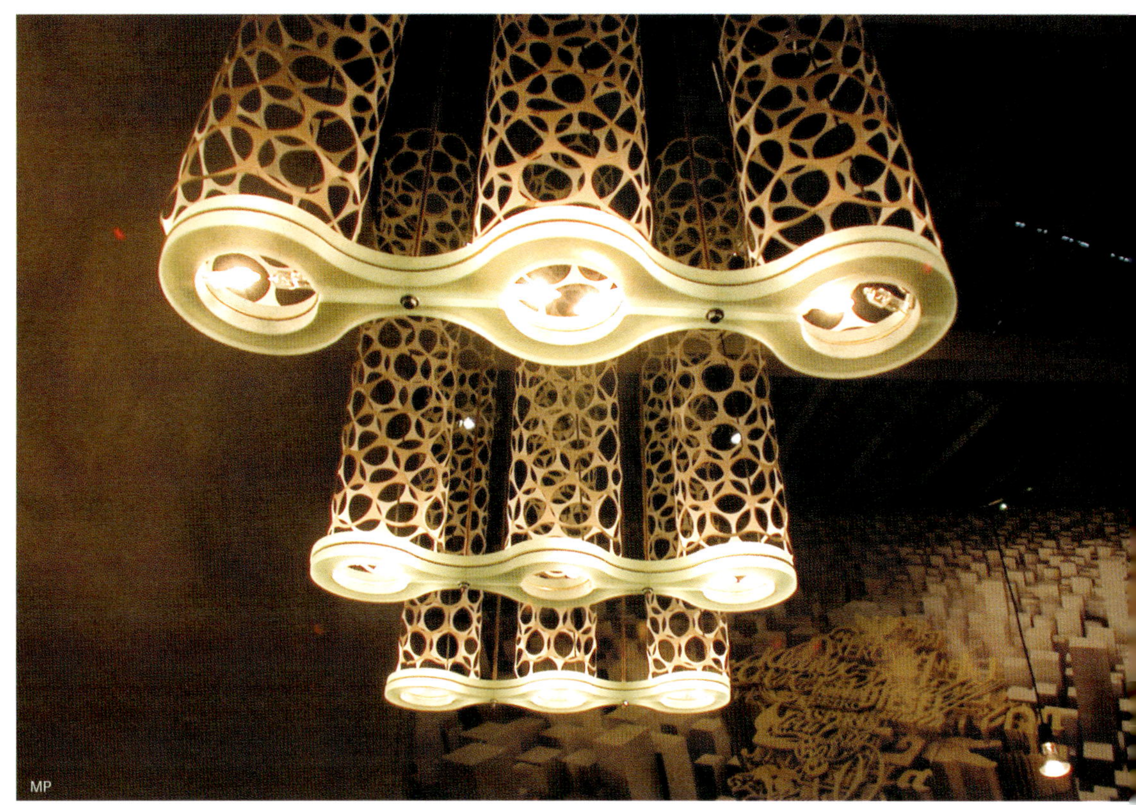

Frank Tjepkema @ Satellite

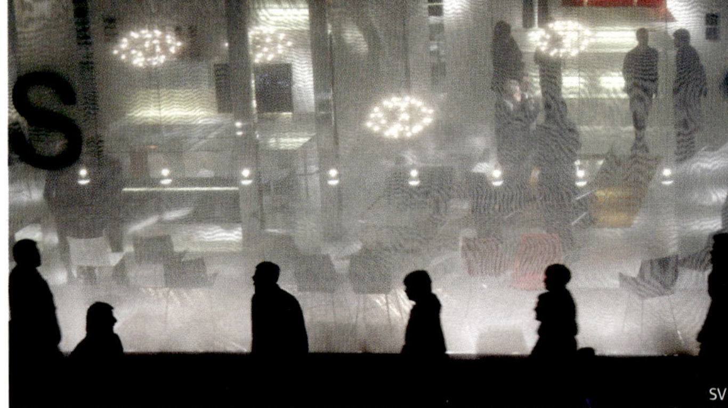

Acerbis

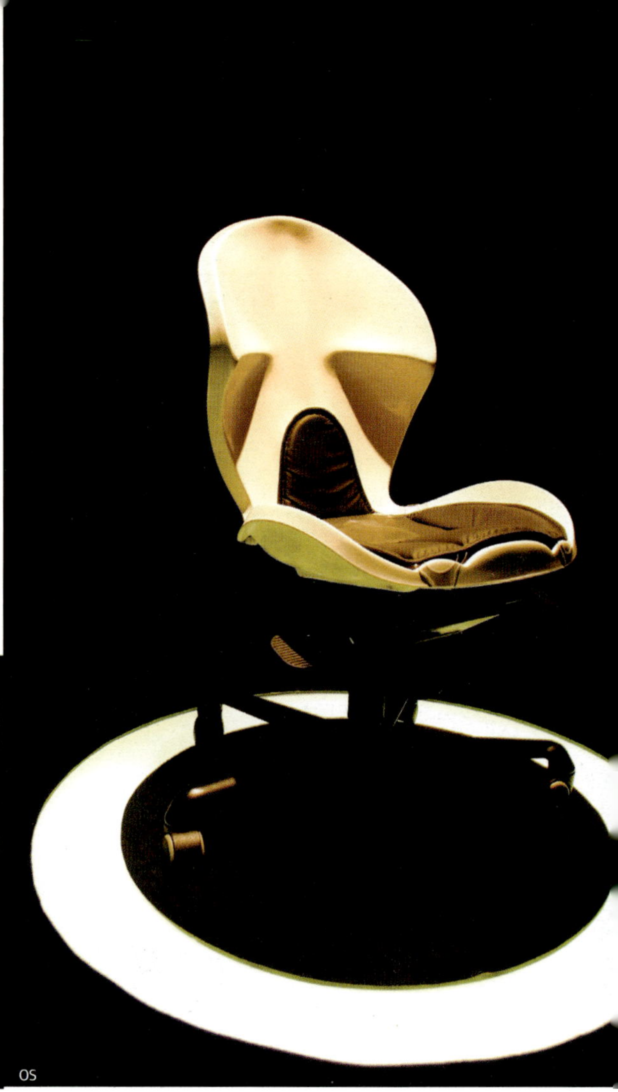

Ycami @ CRT, Triennale

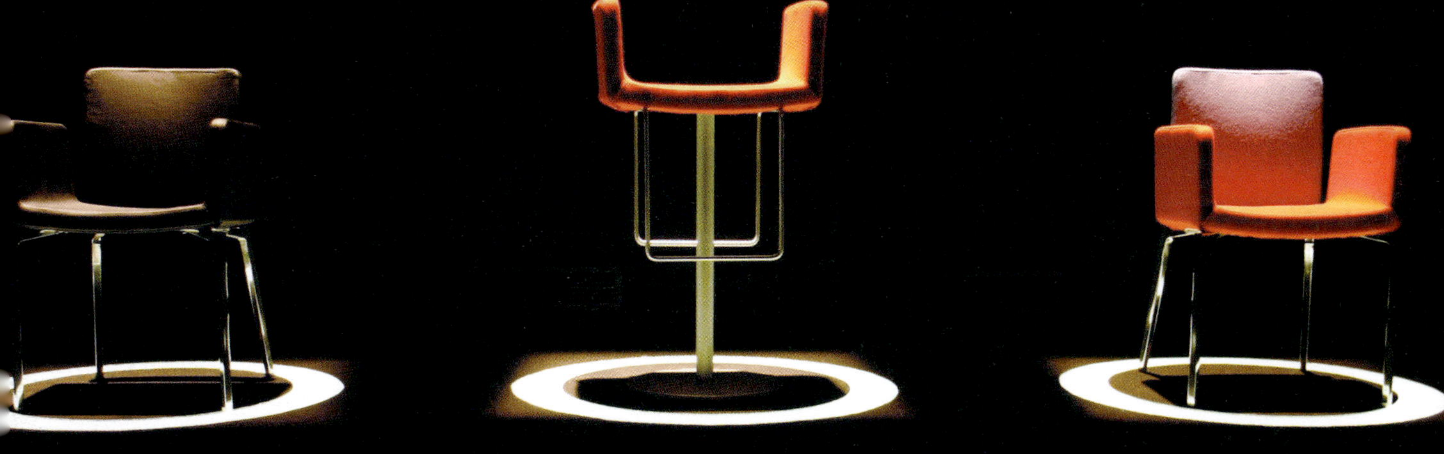

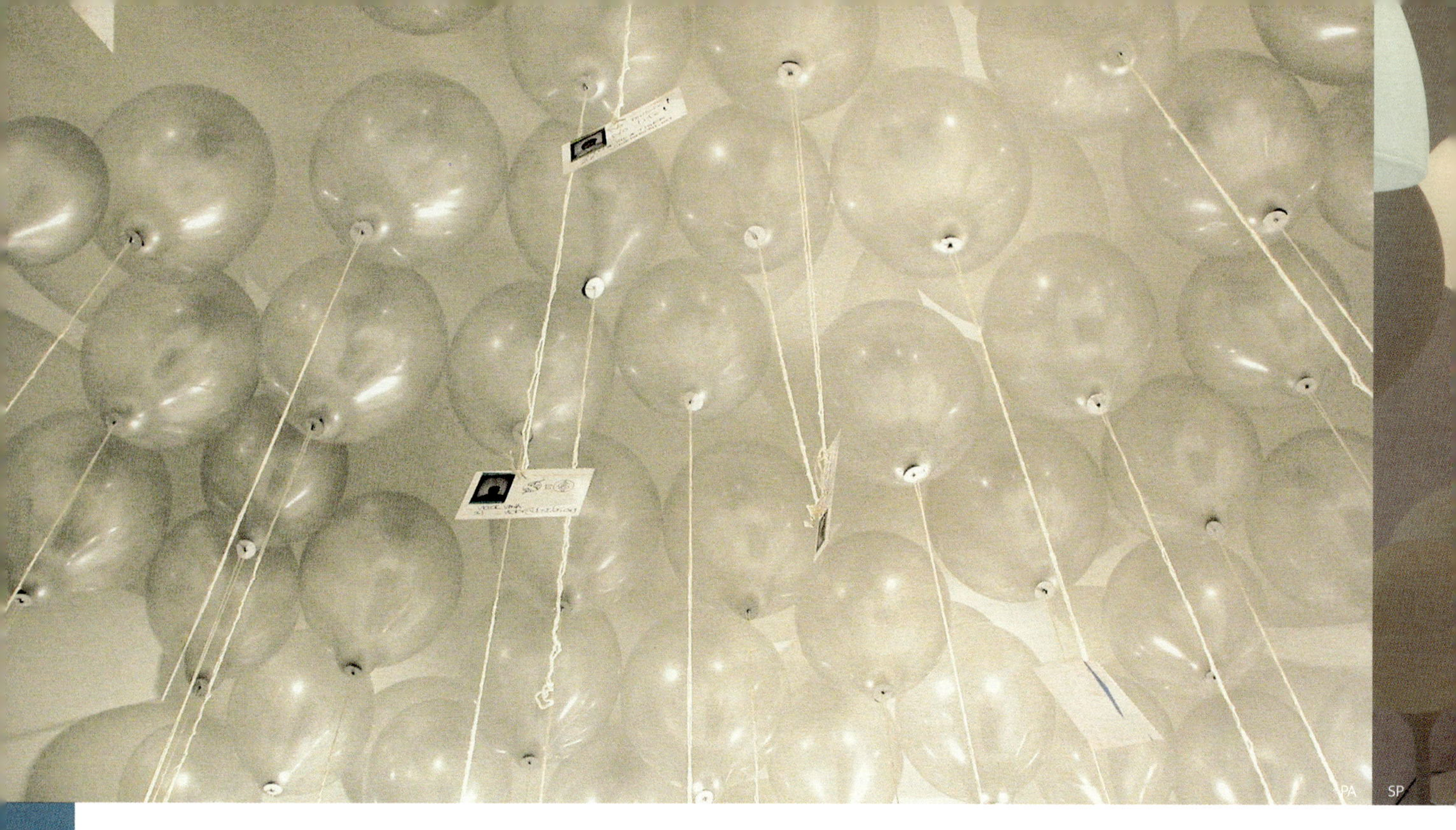

It is no use producing for the umpteenth time

an object resembling the umpteenth product

imitating the umpteenth object already produced.

Fabio Rotella

Team4 @ Designersblock

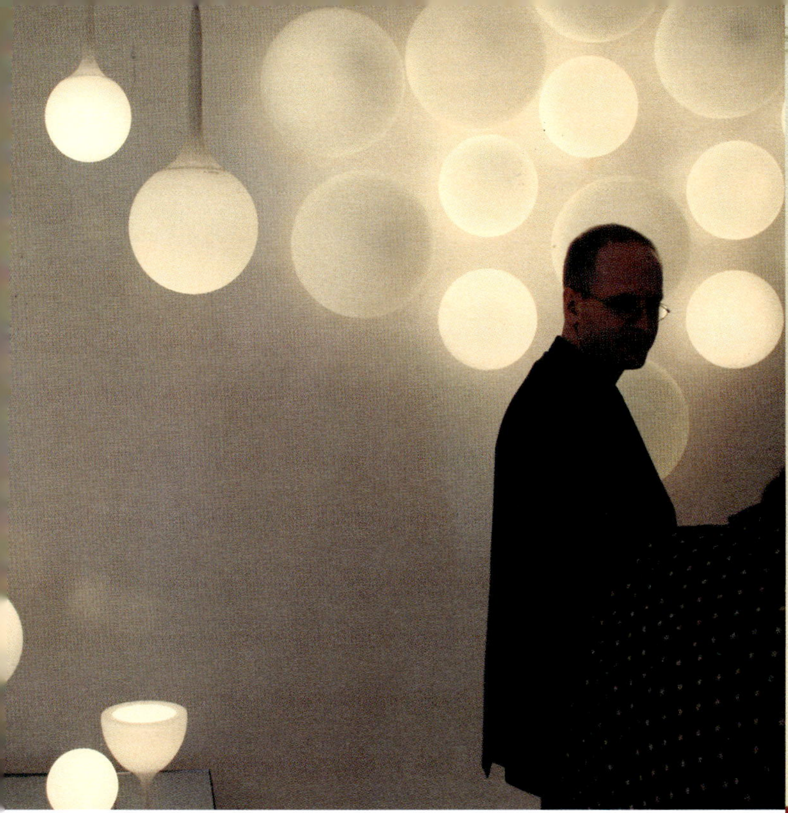

Artemide

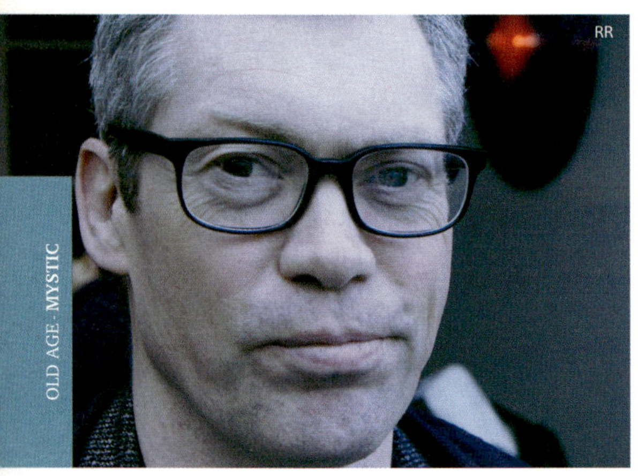

Jasper Morrison

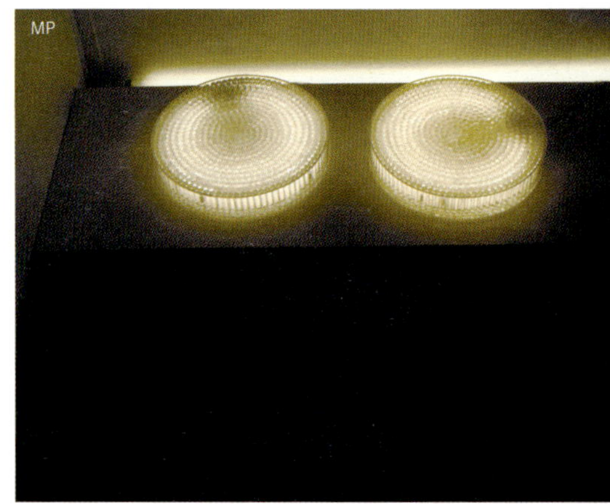

806 D

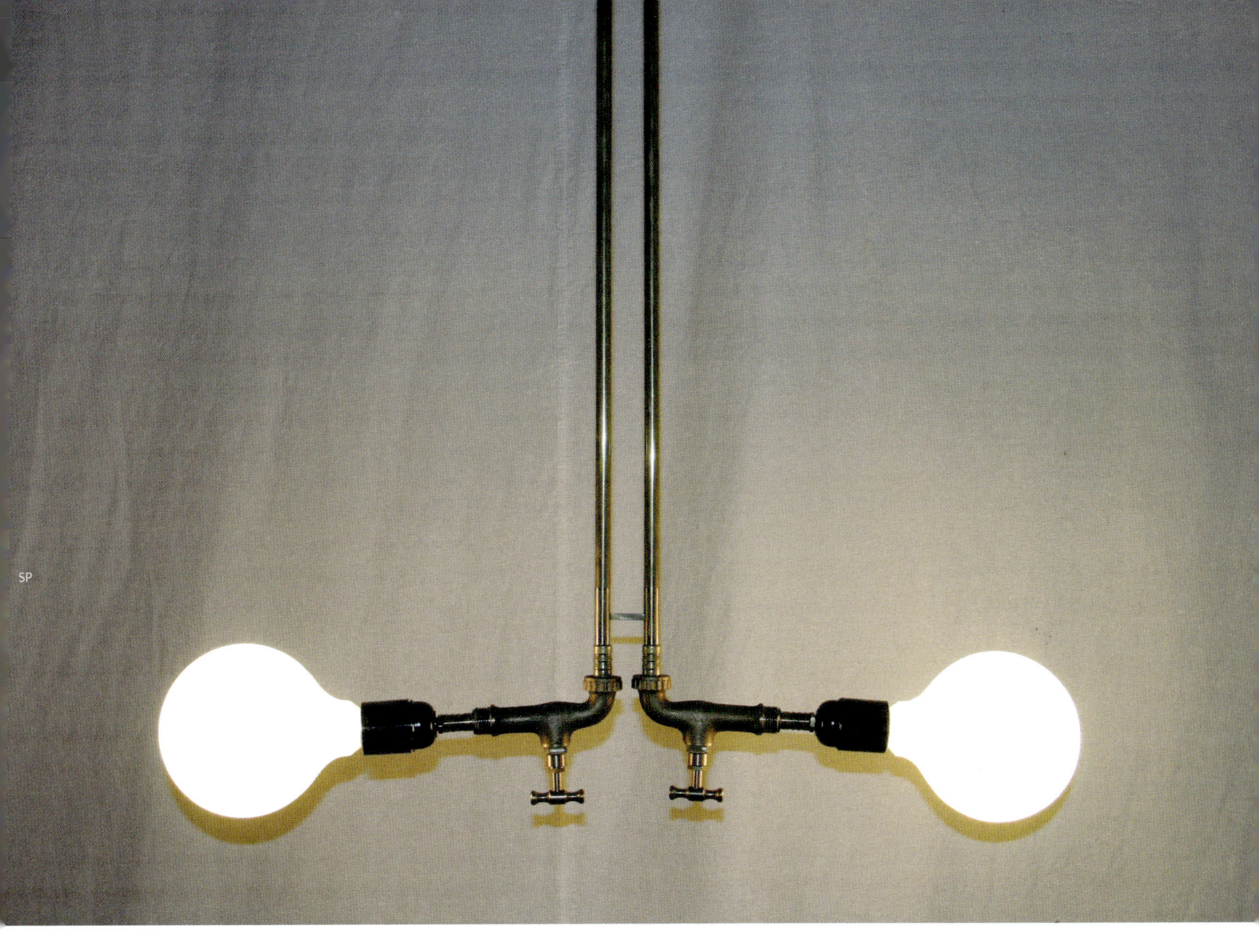

Studio Marcelio

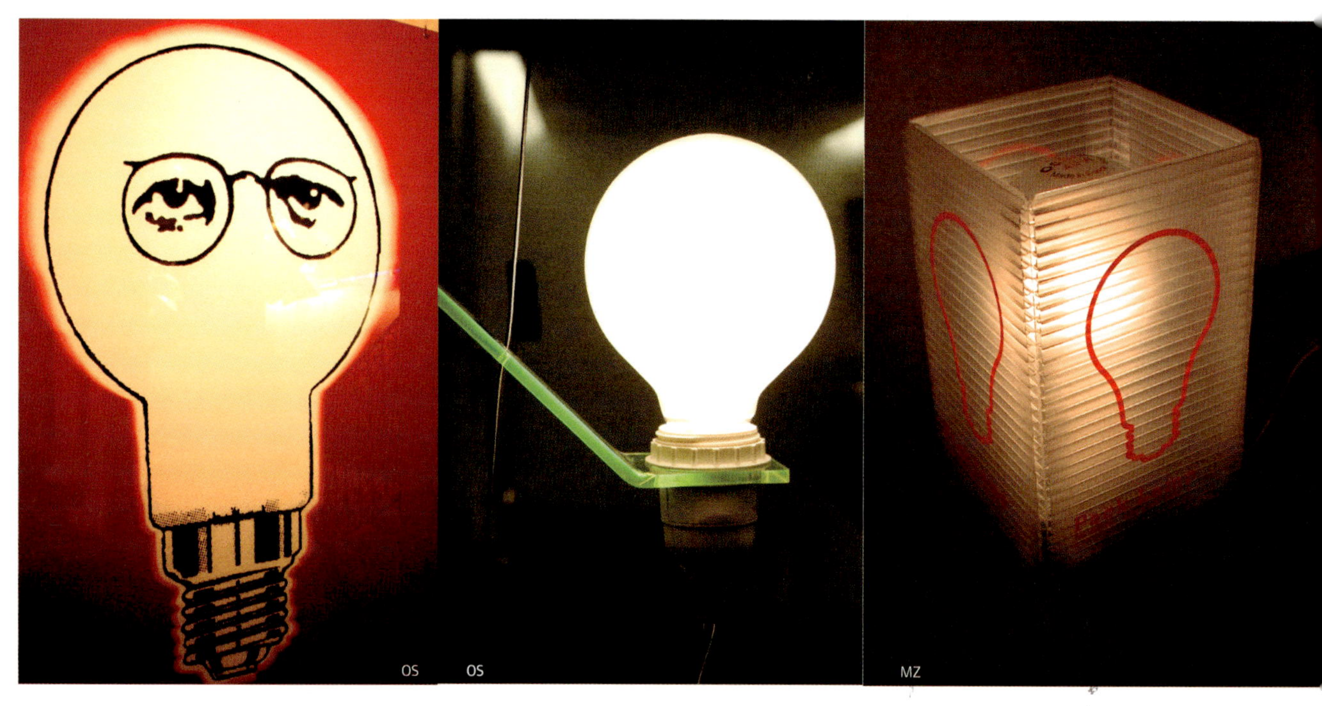

Santa & Cole

Fontana Arte

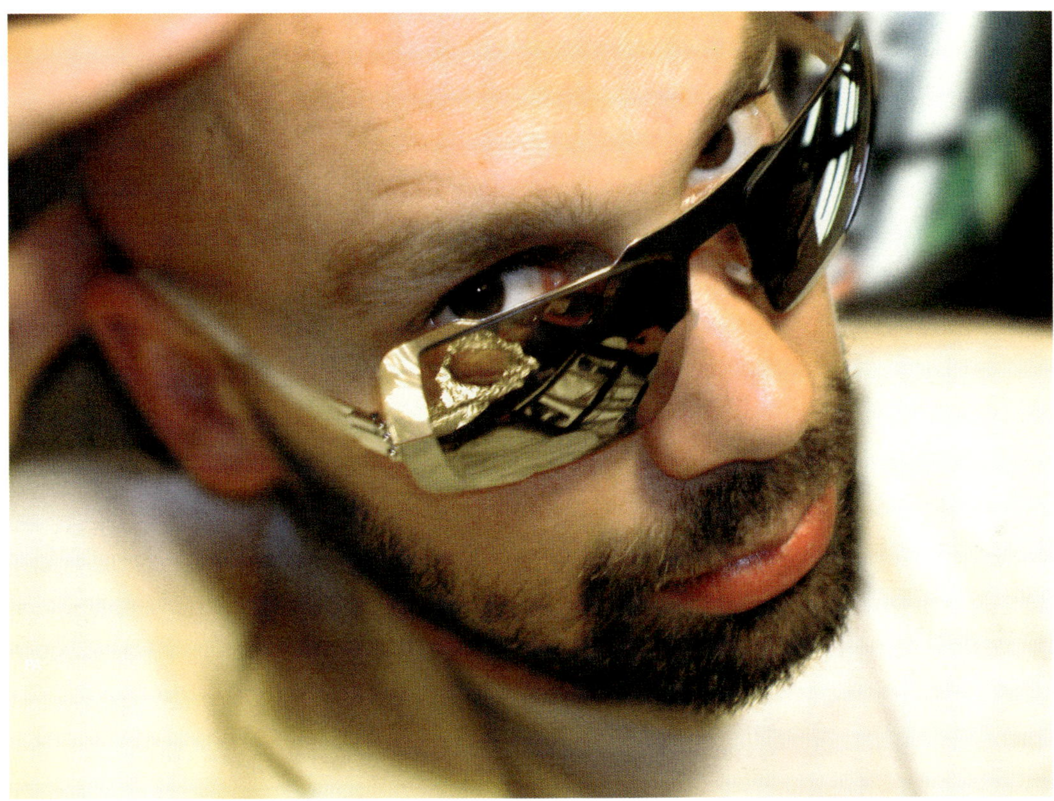
Ralph Anderl of IC-Berlin

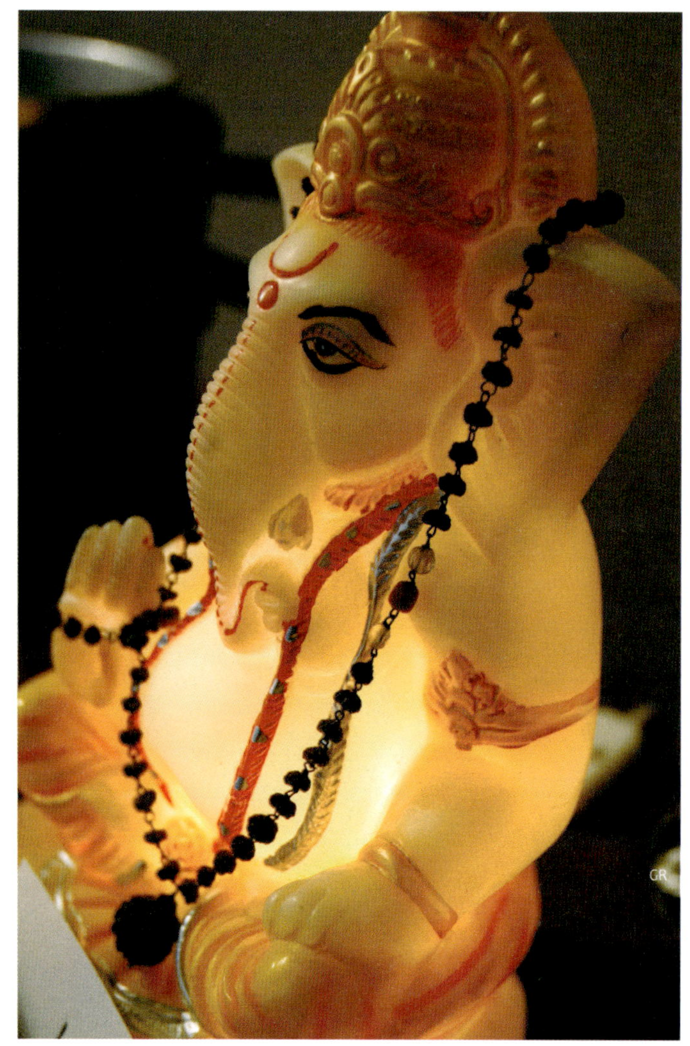

Ganesh

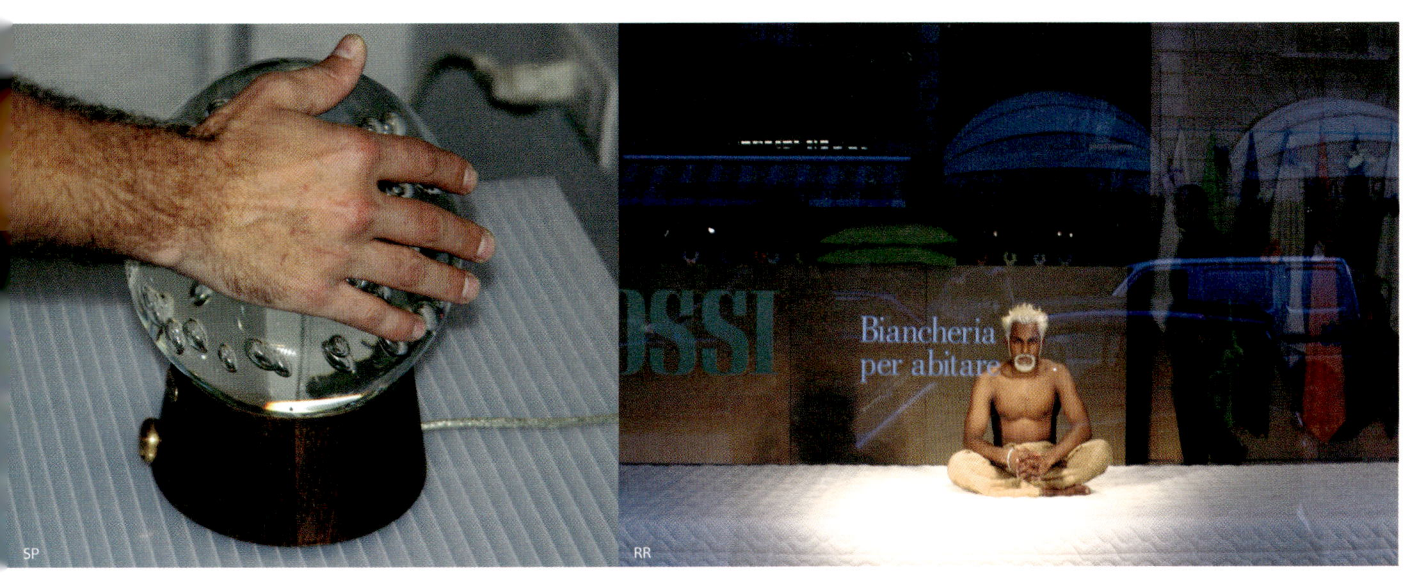
OSSI
Biancheria
per abitare
SP
RR

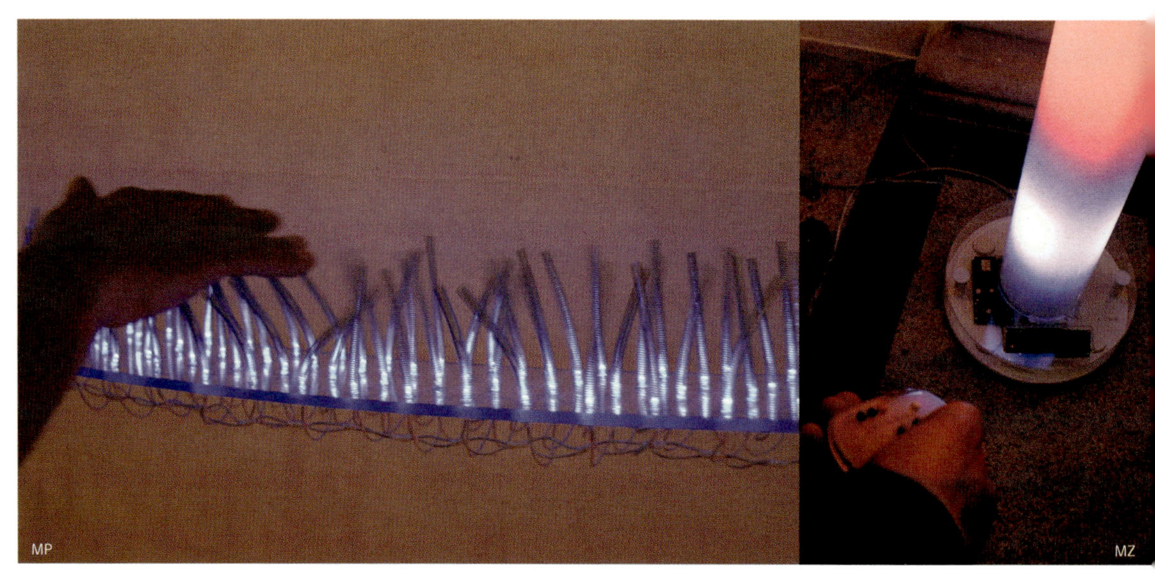

Puff Buff design @ Satellite

Artemide

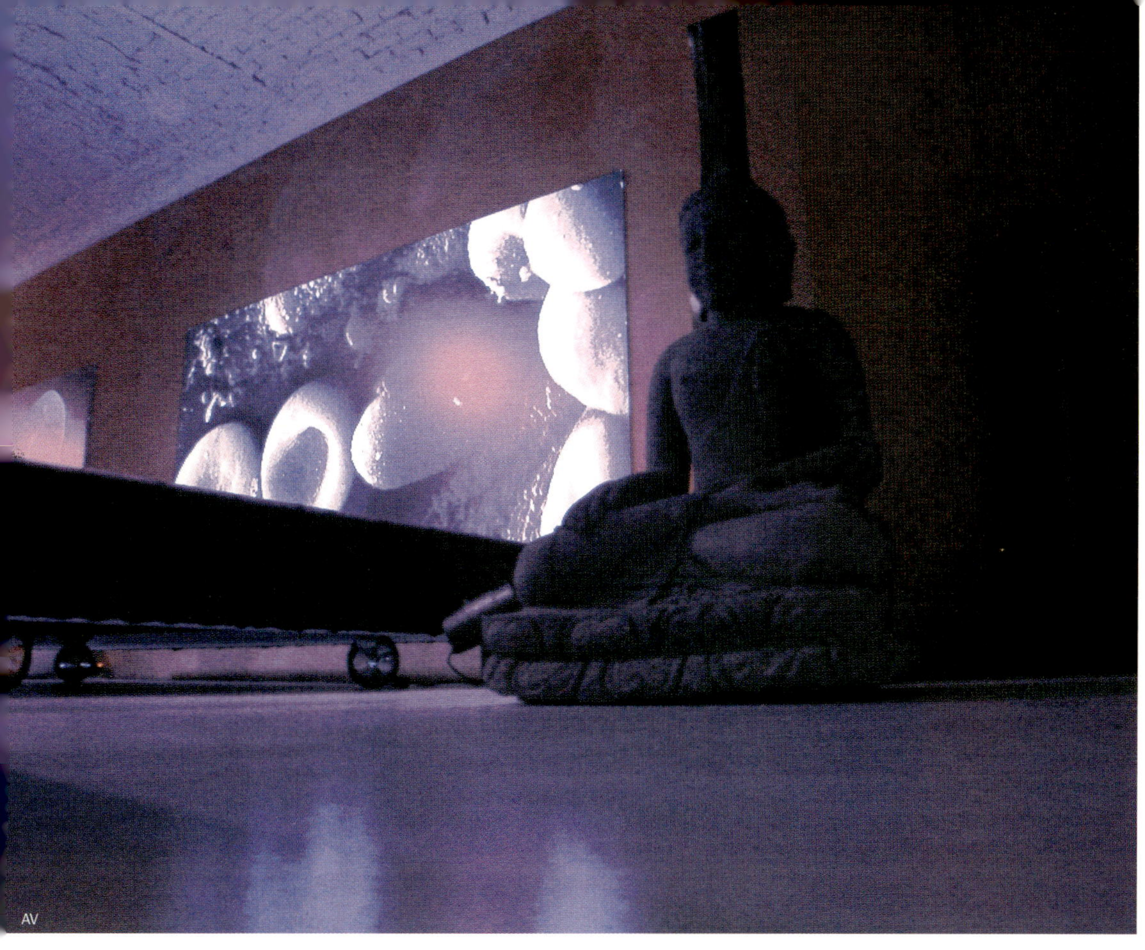

Dreams

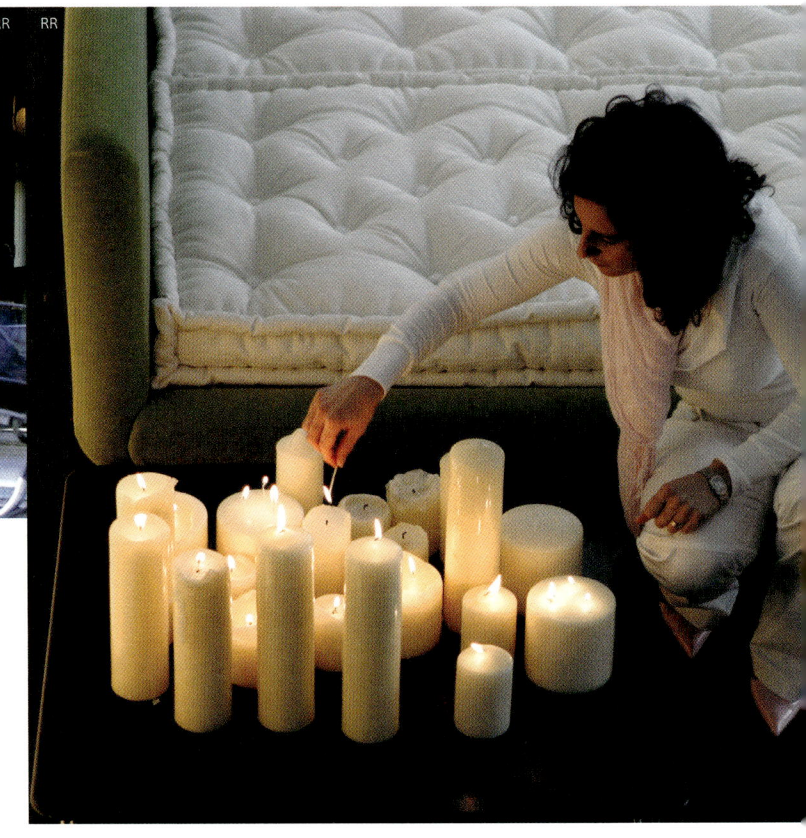

????

Living Divani

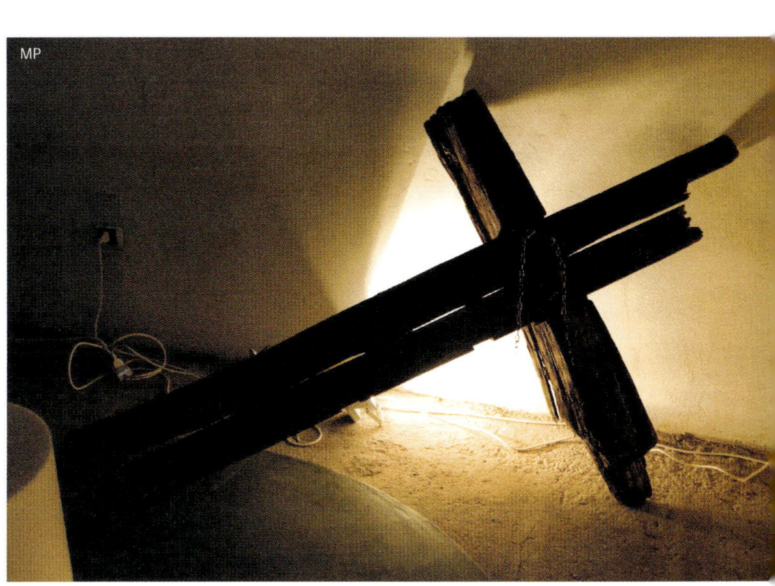

Ora italiana - Michela Formia

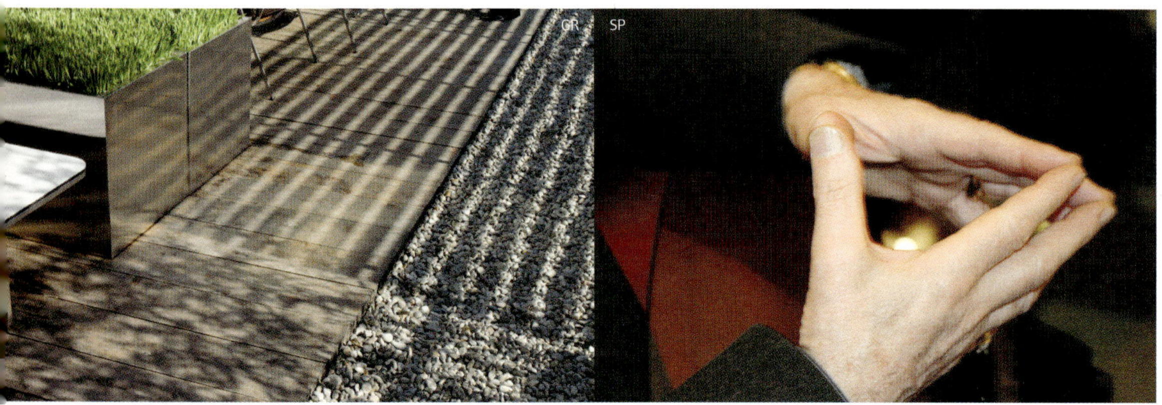
GR   SP

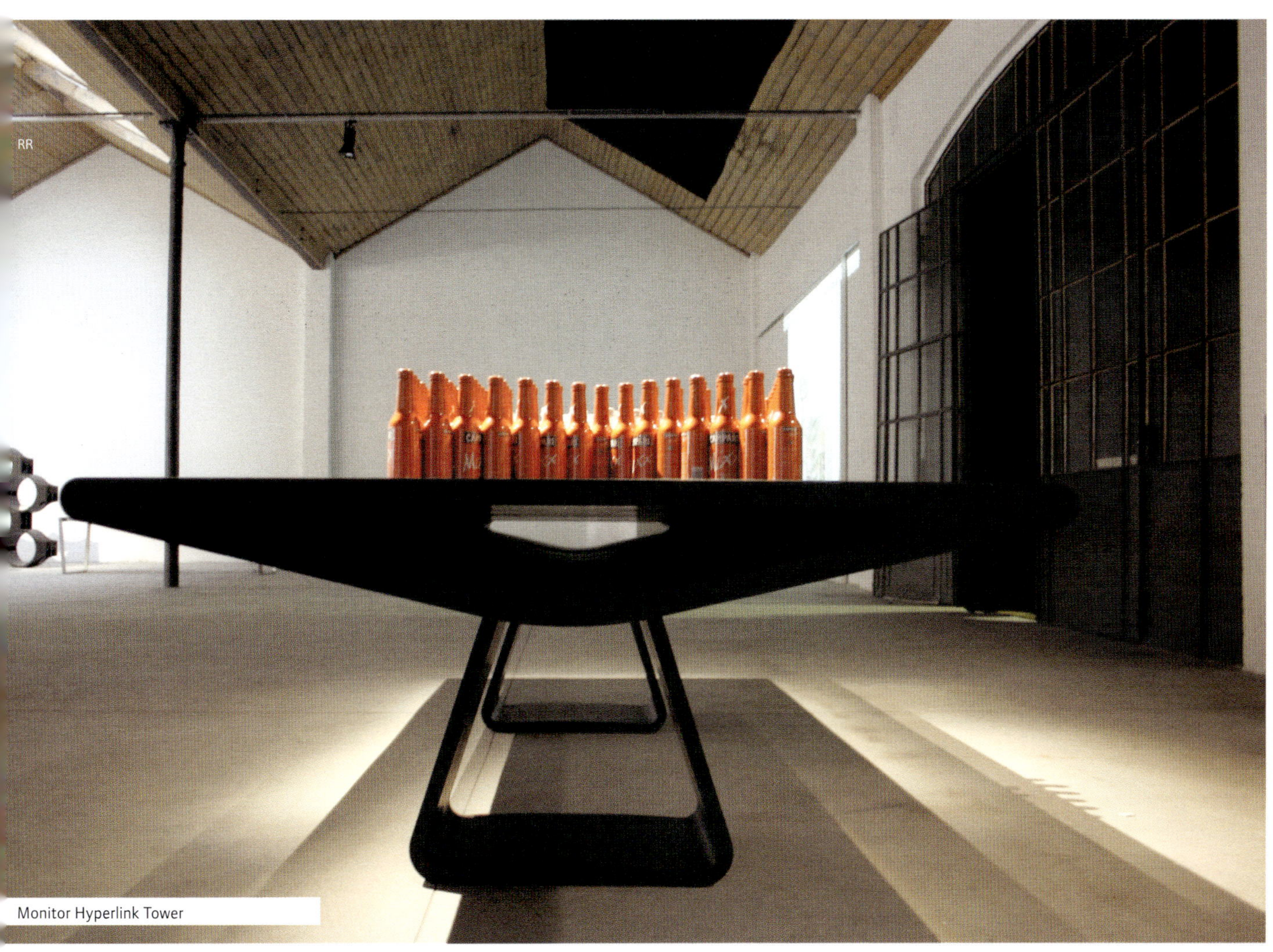

Monitor Hyperlink Tower

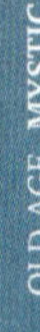

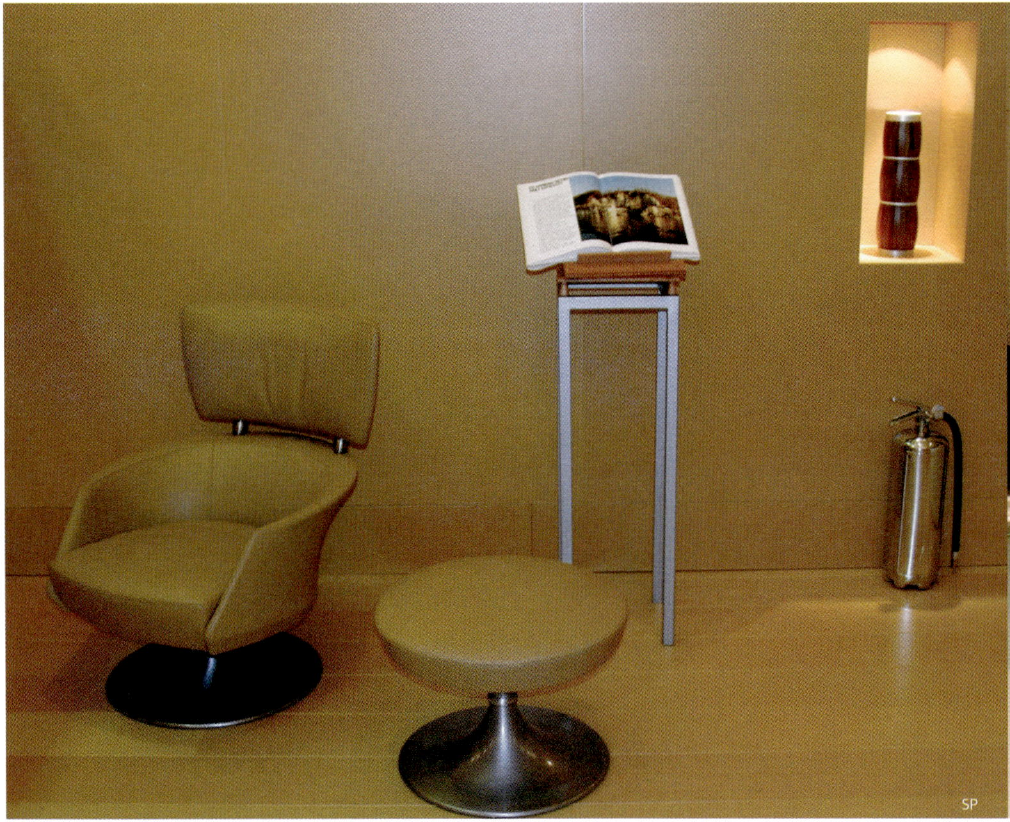

Giorgetti

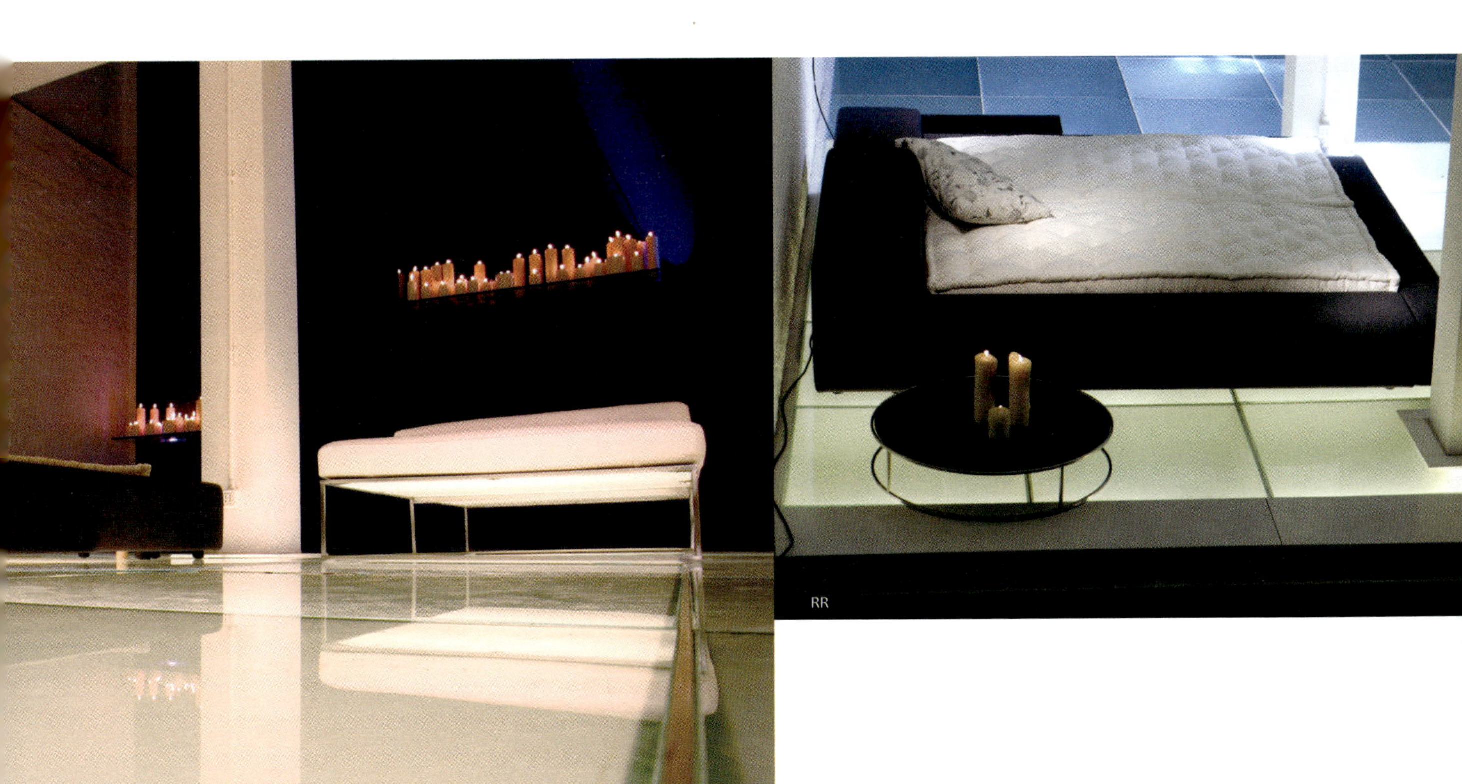

Living Divani   Living Divani

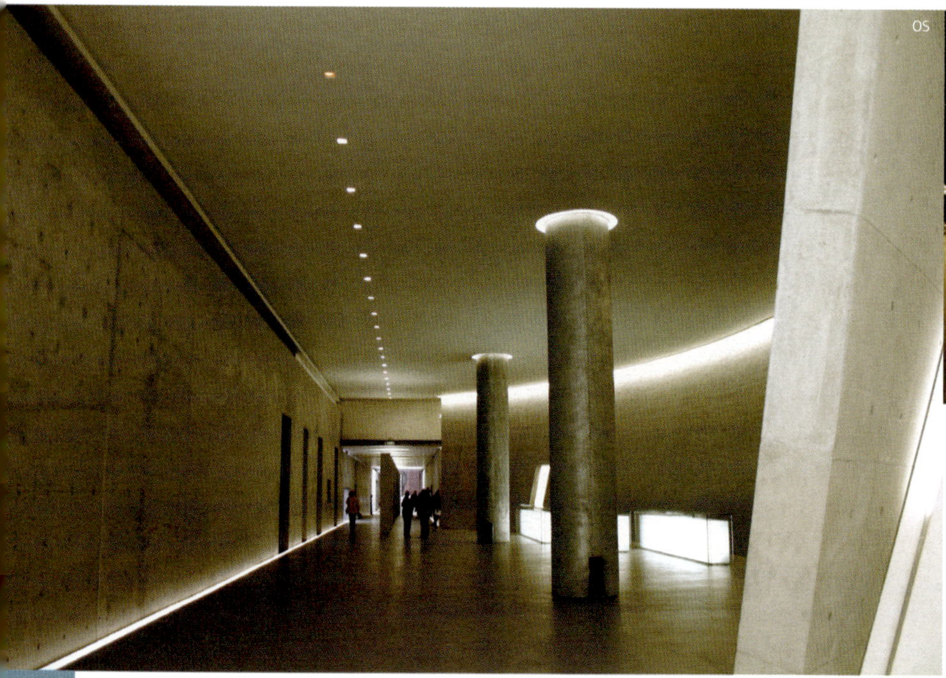

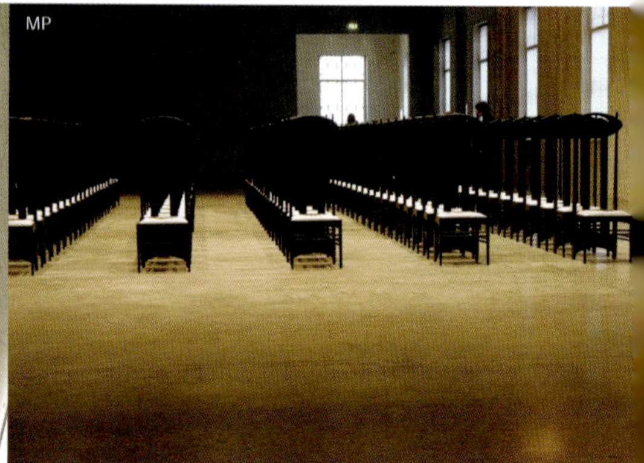

Armani

Prada

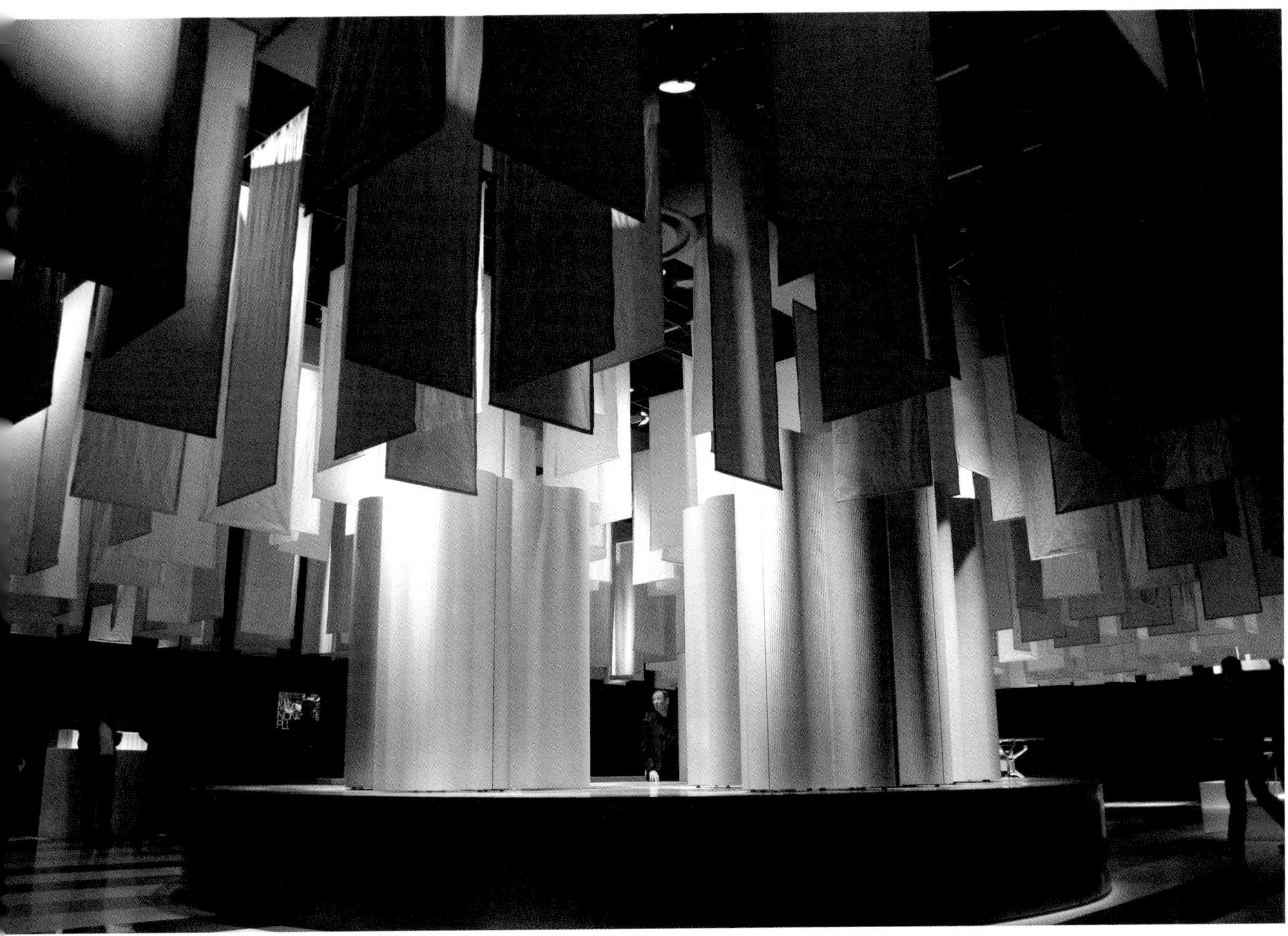

Alias

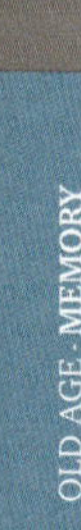

SV

@ Salone del Mobile

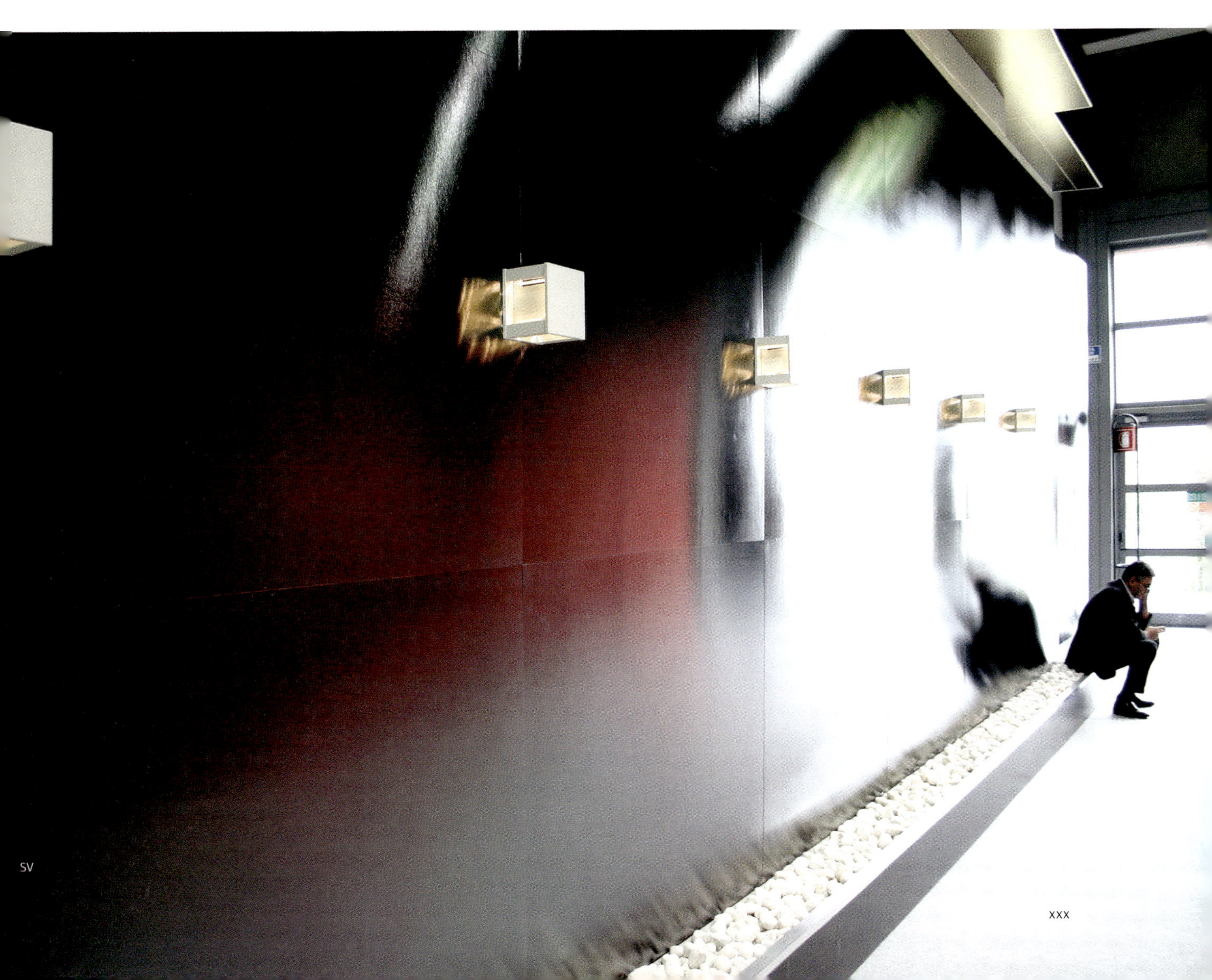
SV
XXX

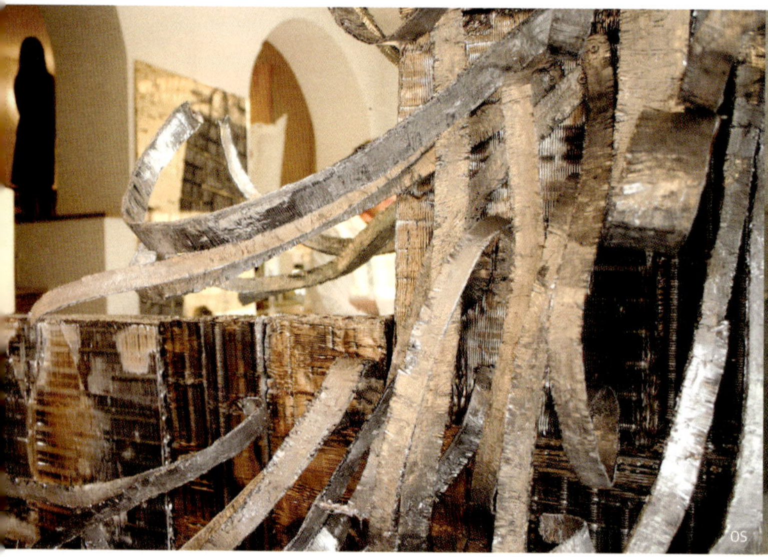

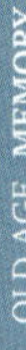

Visionnaire

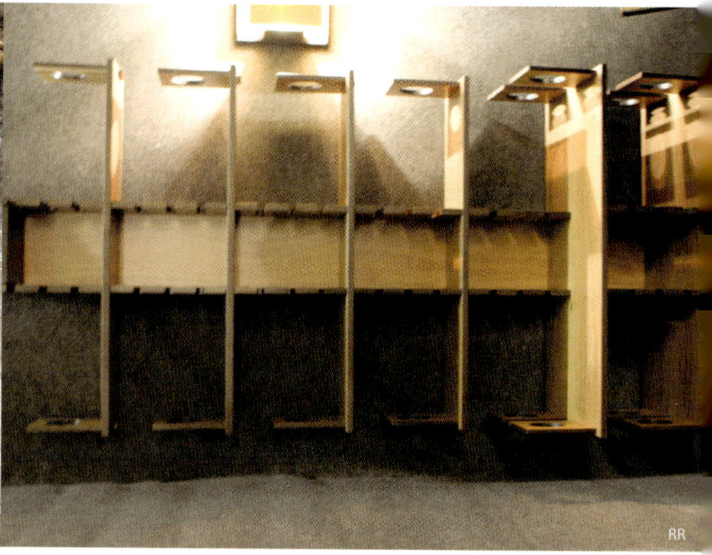

Jacopo Gardella

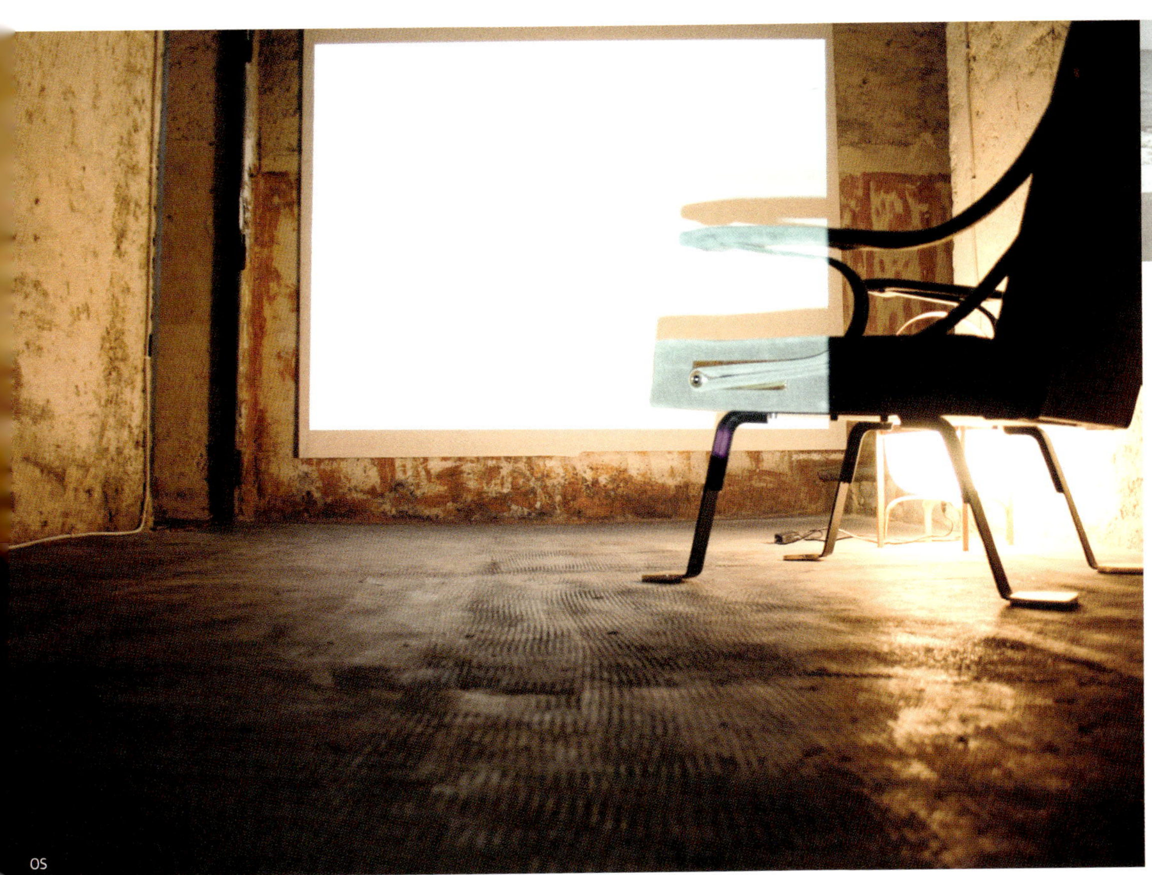

05

Santa & Cole

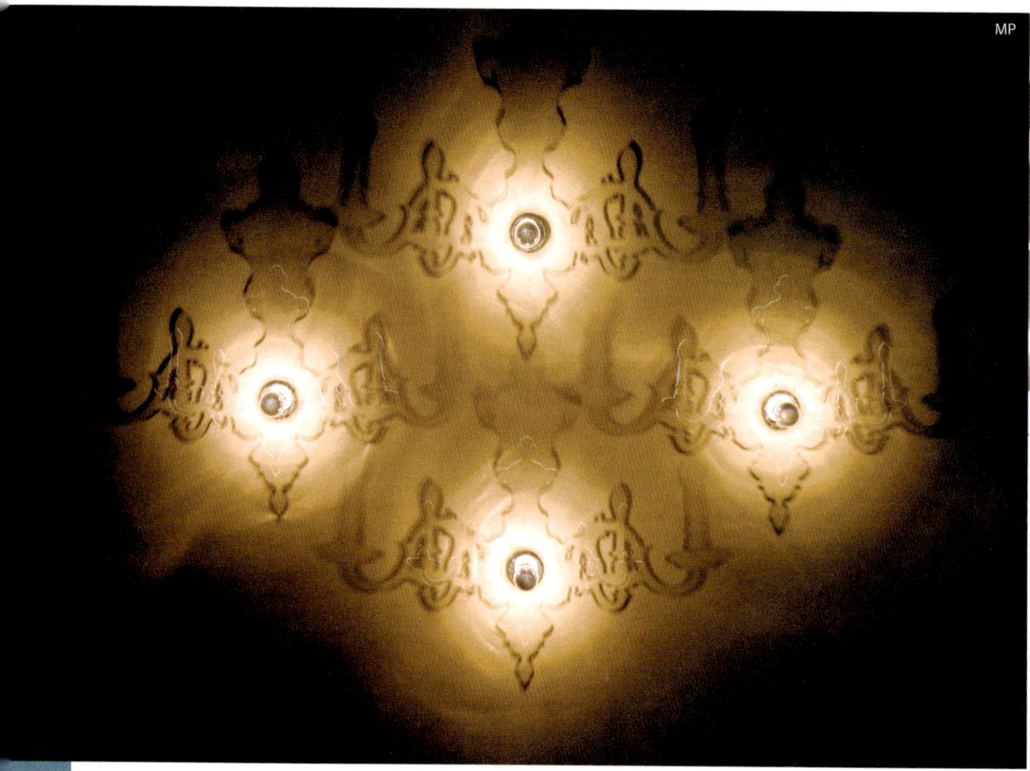

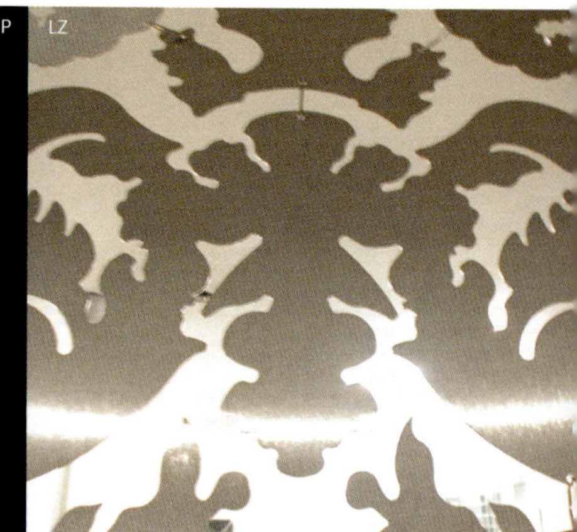

VIA

@ Dilmos

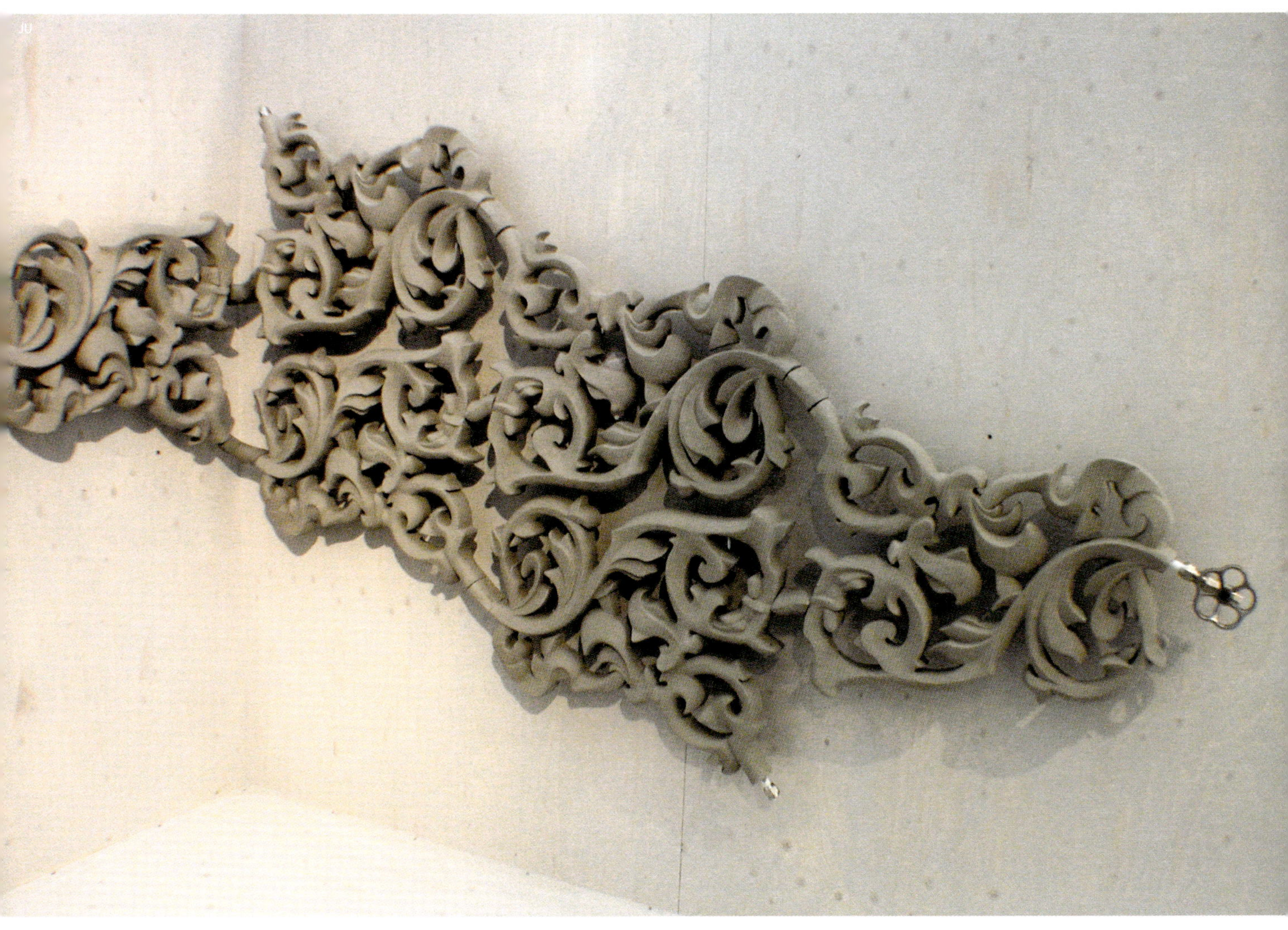

Joris Laarman @ Design Academy Eindhoven

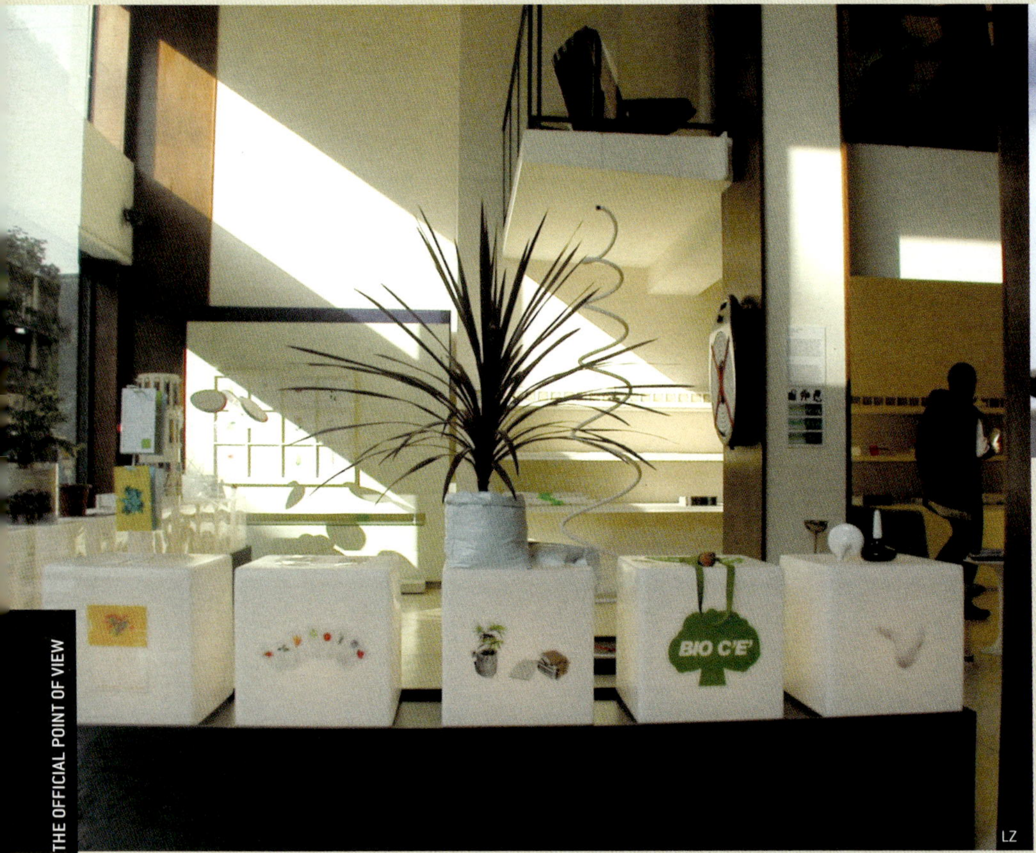

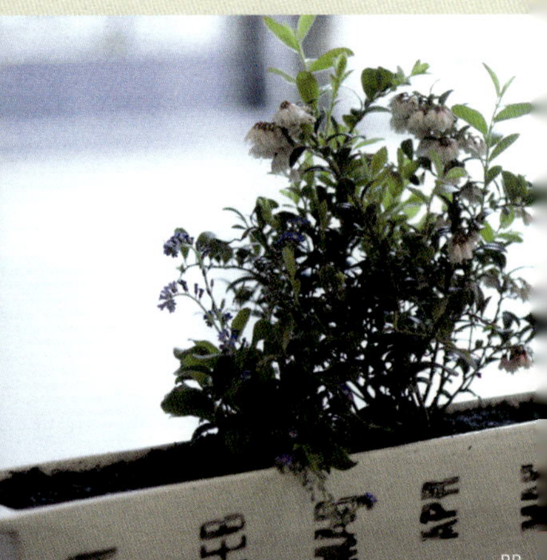

Asapstore shopwindow

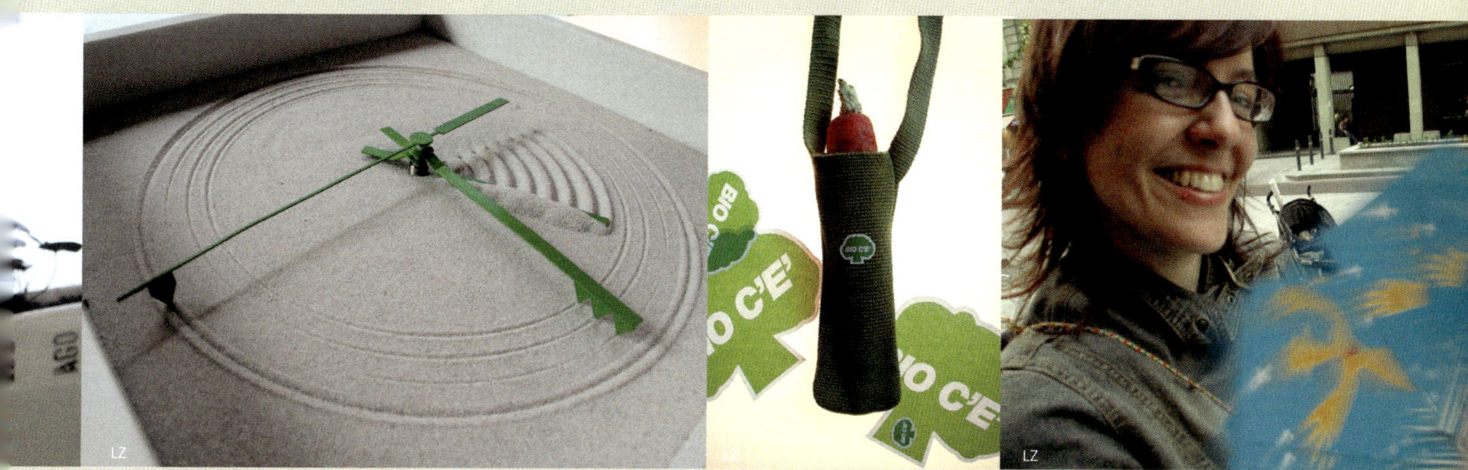

New agriculture in the sense of imagining and **rethinking the relationship that exists between people and the natural terrain**

- with its activities, its rhythms, its matter and its aesthetic.

More and more often places, professions, cultures and lifestyles that were a part

of the agricultural world are being undermined by a strong thrust of change.

The theme of the exhibition is one that proposes an analysis of **how this change is occurring** and to define a

projectual proposal that images new scenes and new products.

OPOS believes that this theme is absolutely essential to imagine a future model of human and natural development.

This way we are refocusing attention on themes of strong social and cultural impact.

Clock by Aroundesign   jtyjyj   Monica Moschini -

bassam Fellows

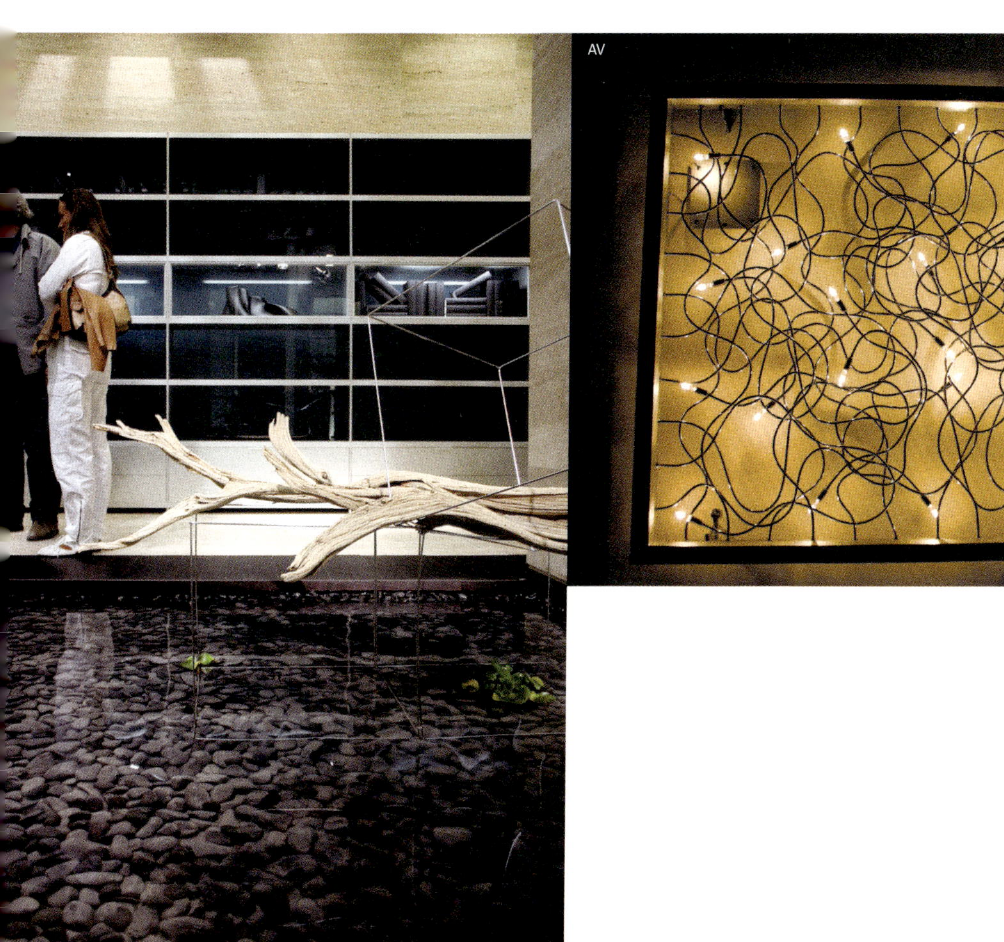

Rimadesio

Lumen Center

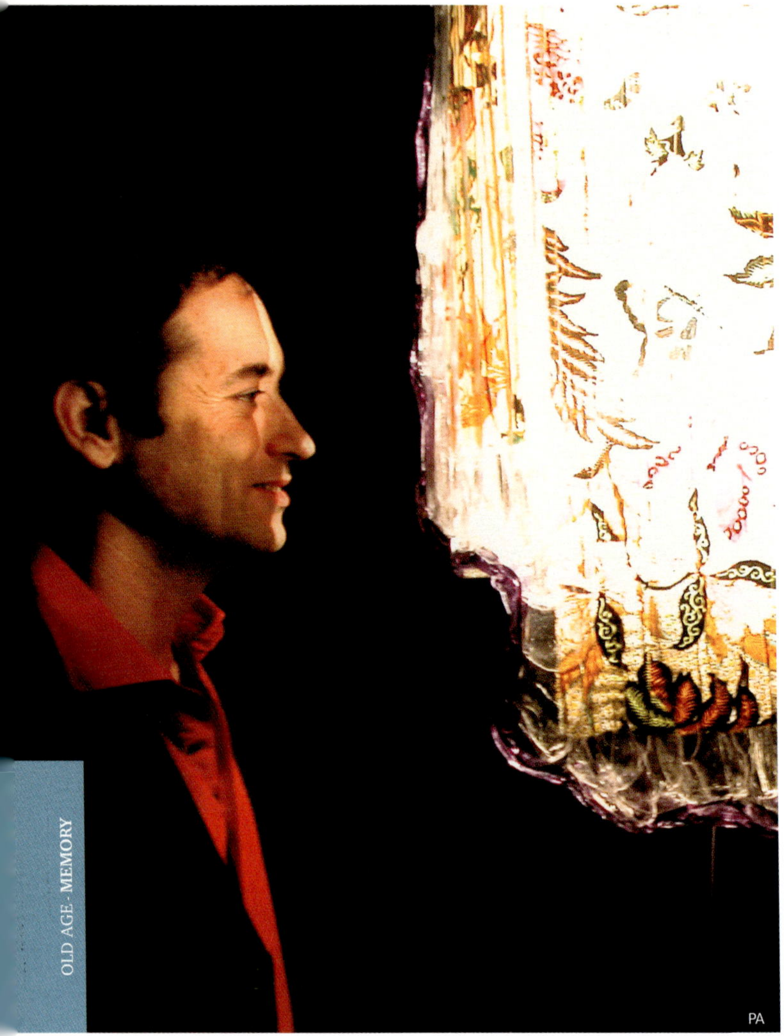

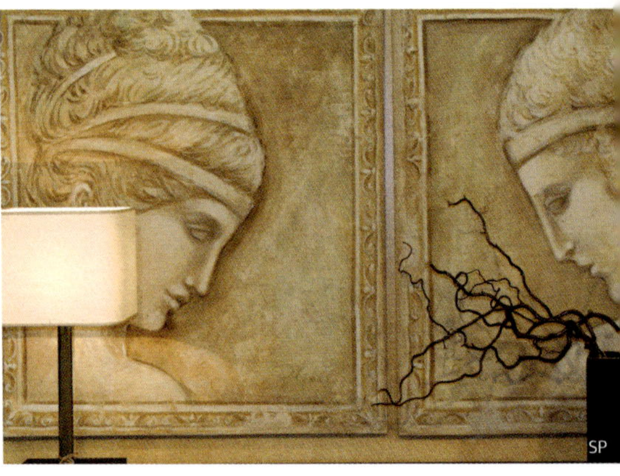

Jacopo Foggini

Consorcio

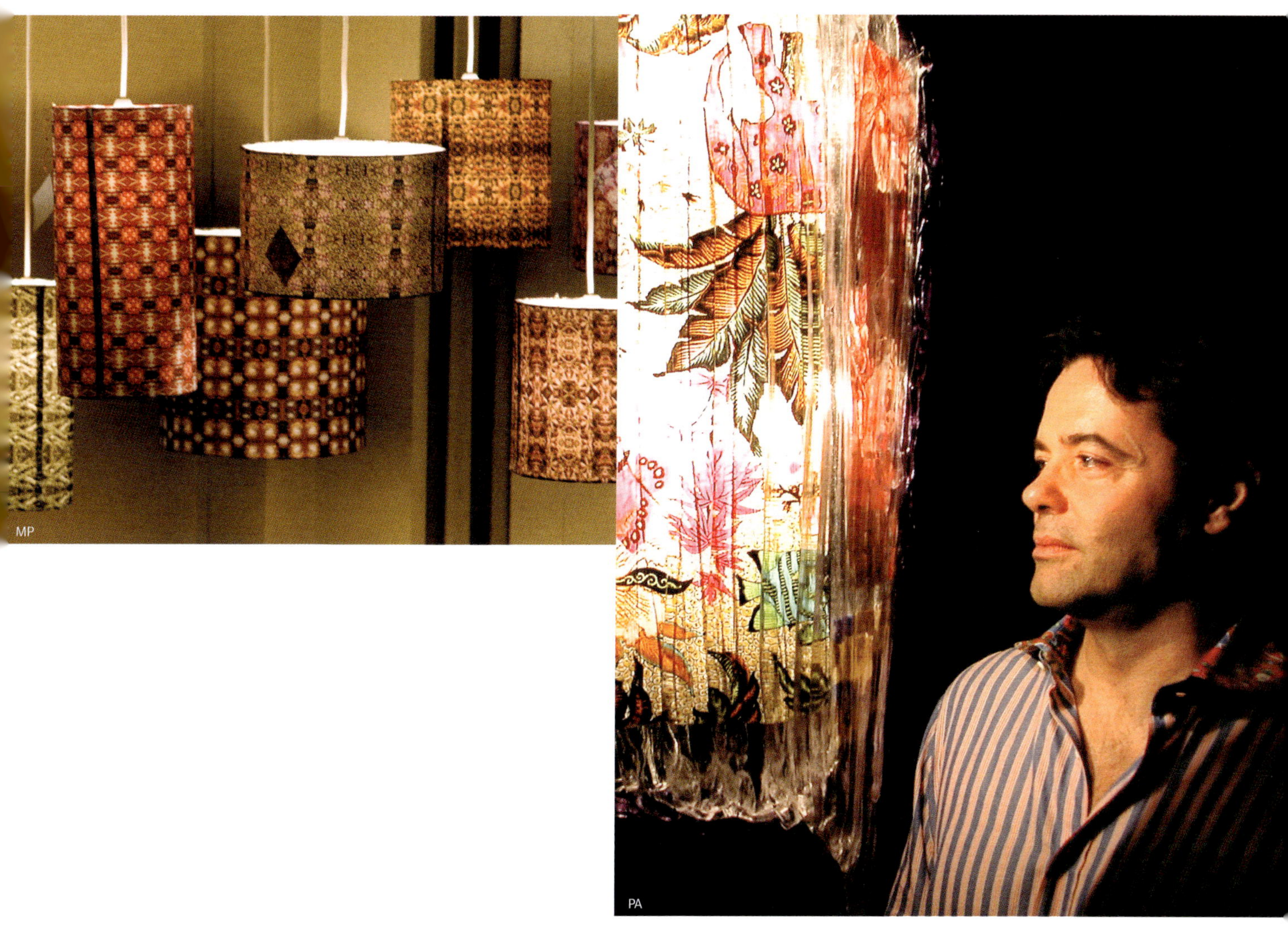

Design London

Jacopo Etro

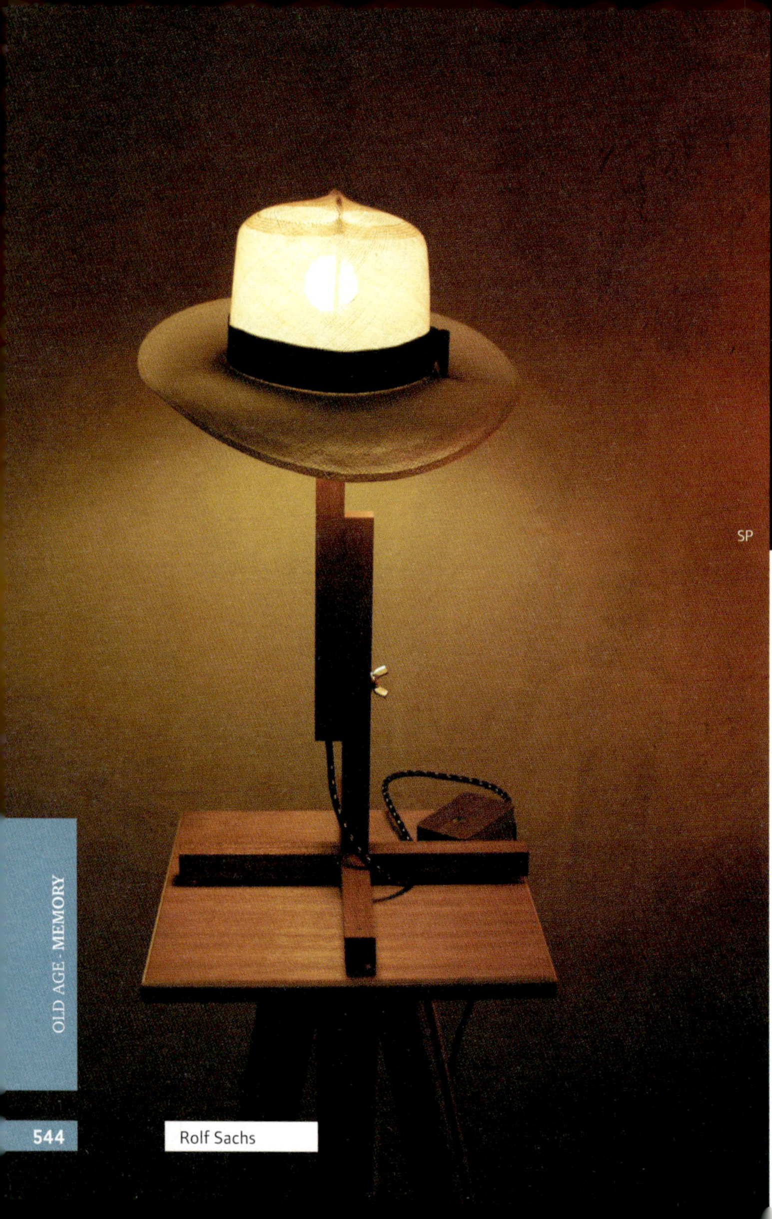

SP

Rolf Sachs

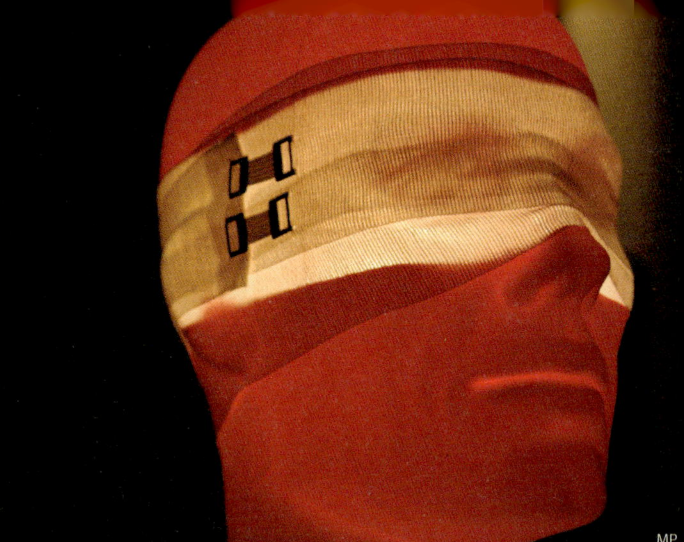

MP

@ Zona Tortona

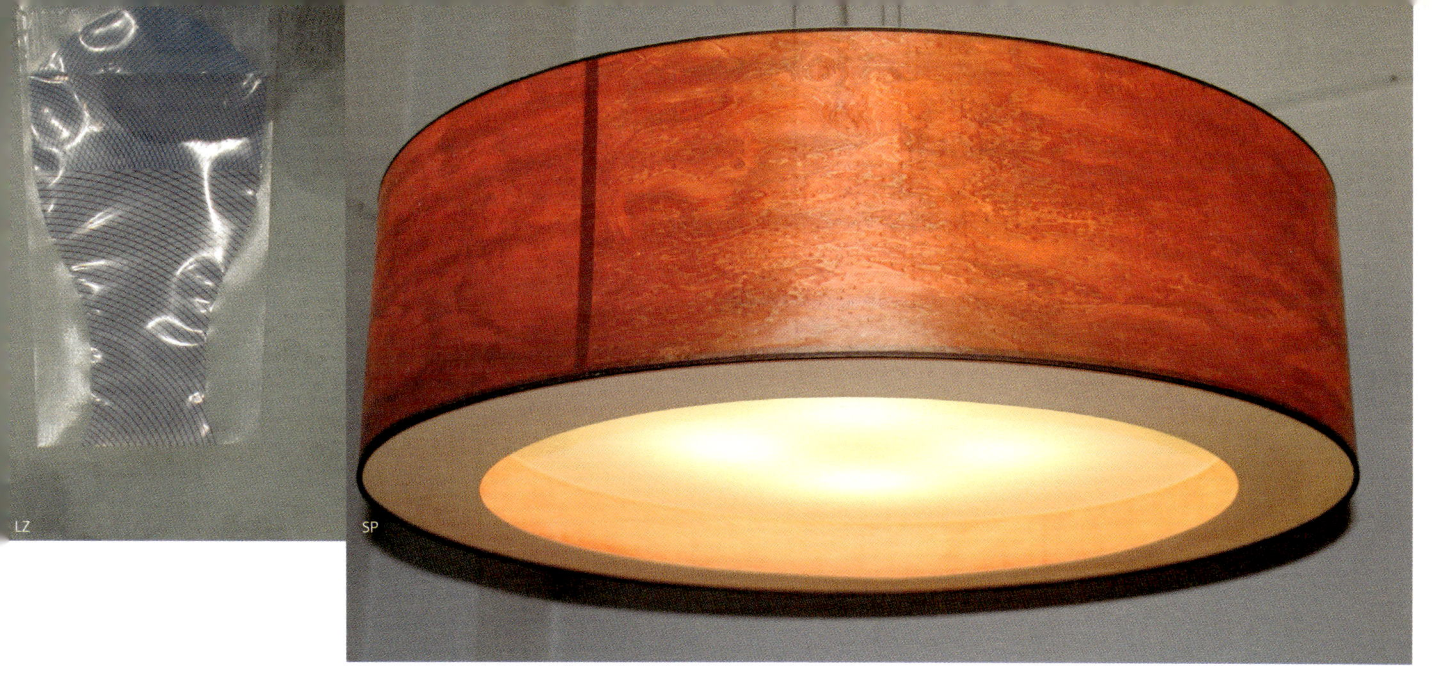

Flexible vase

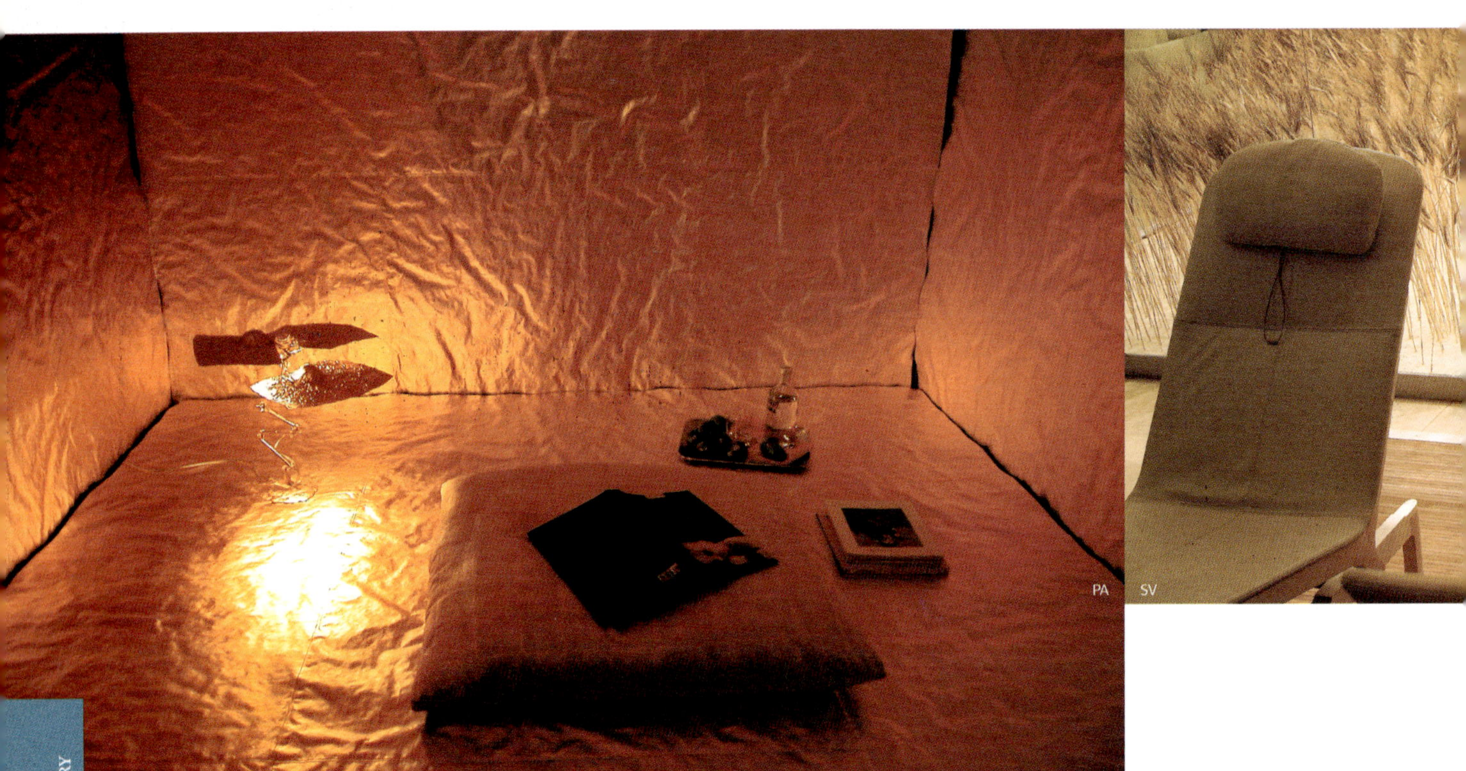

Ingo Maurer

Giorgetti

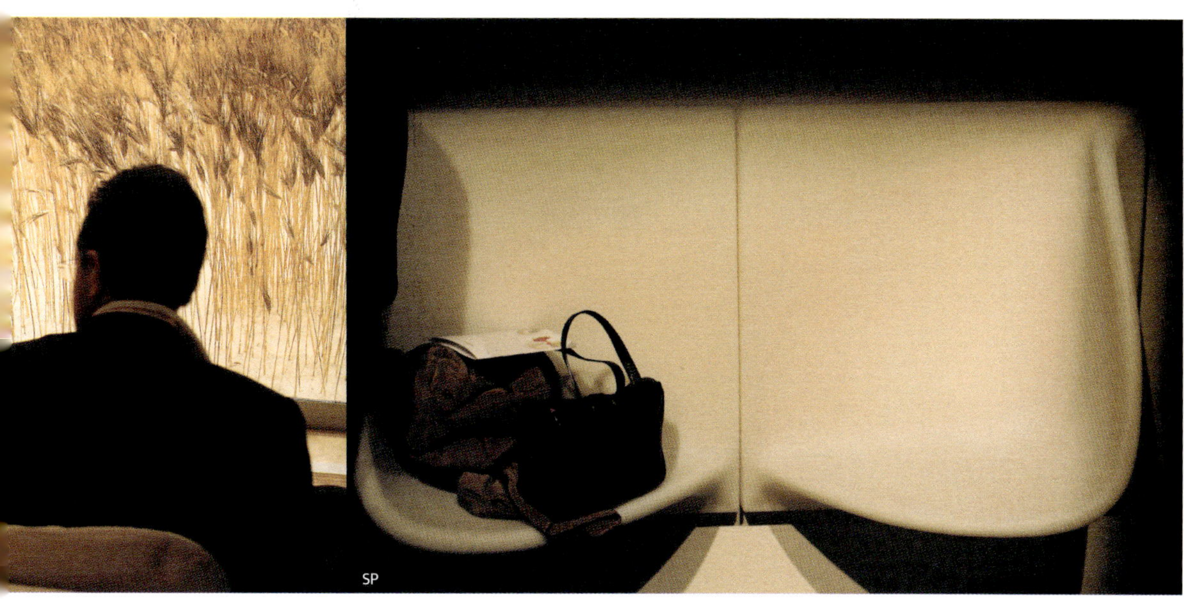

Rossi di Albizzate

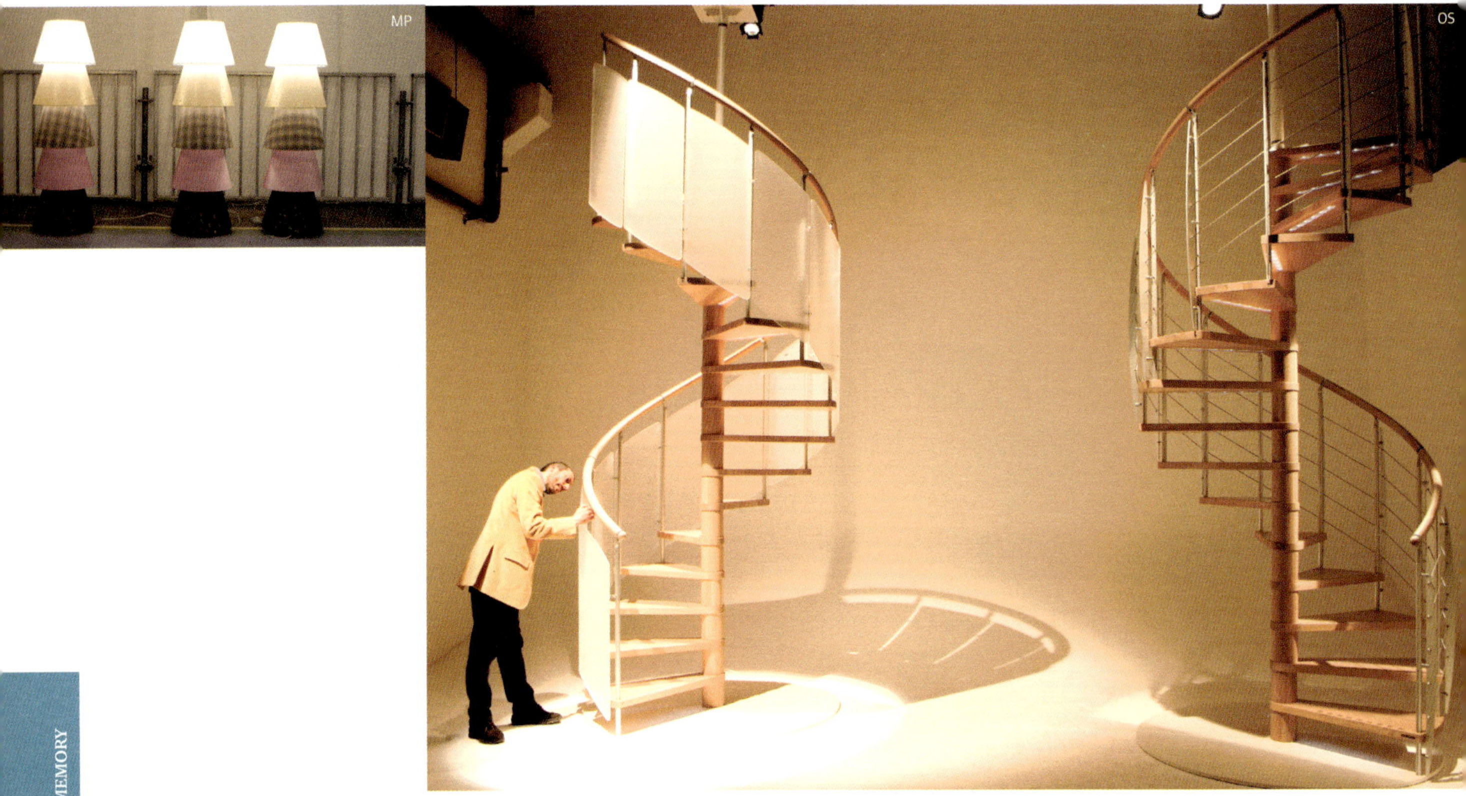

Moooi

Albini e Fontanot @ Zona Tortona

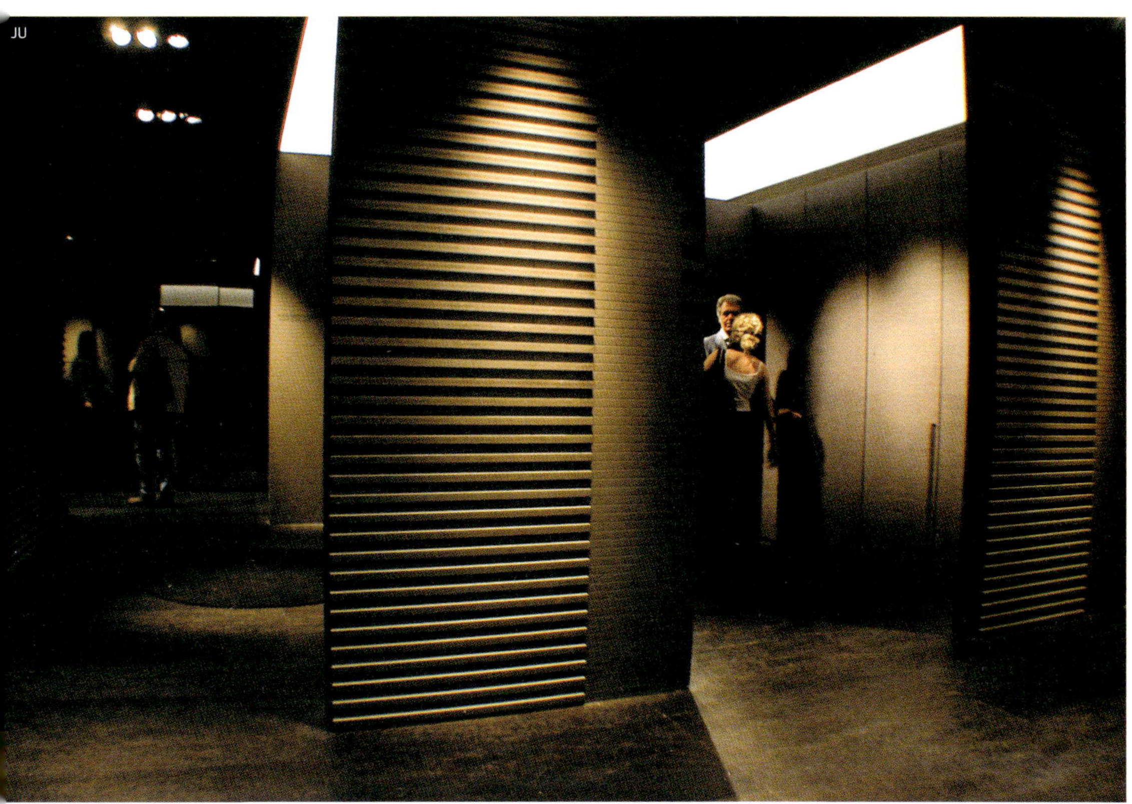

Poliform

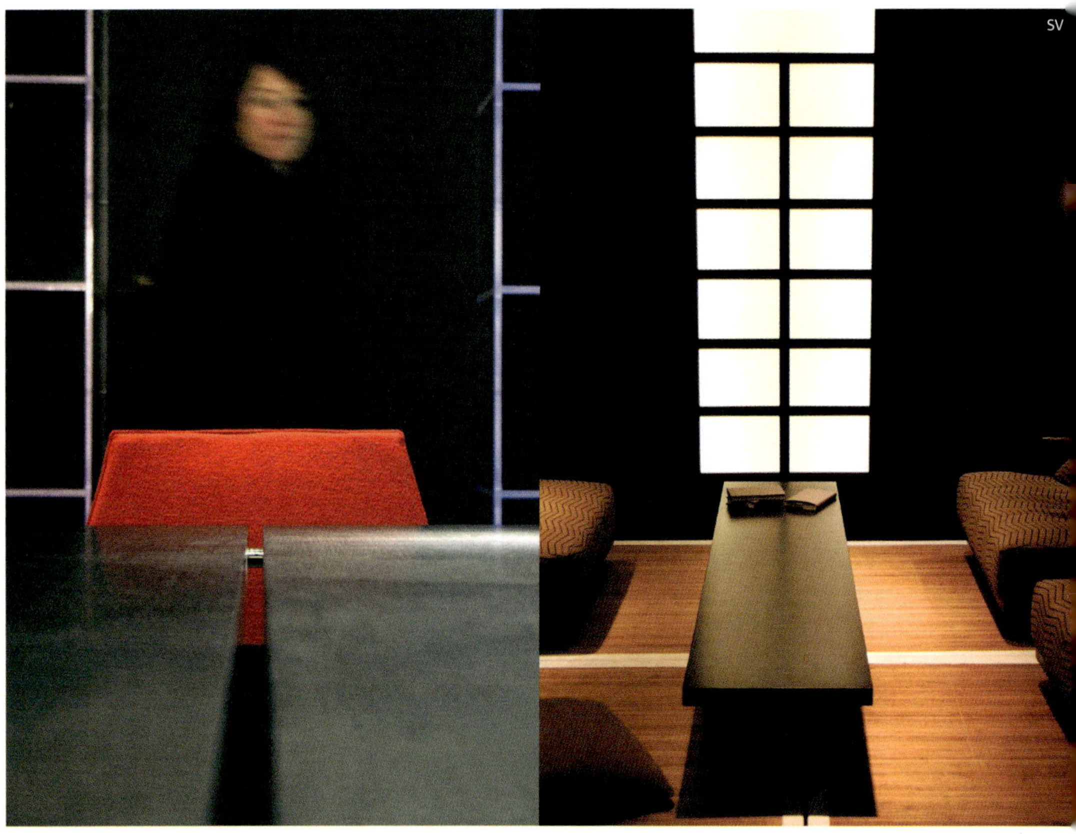

Acerbis

Giorgetti

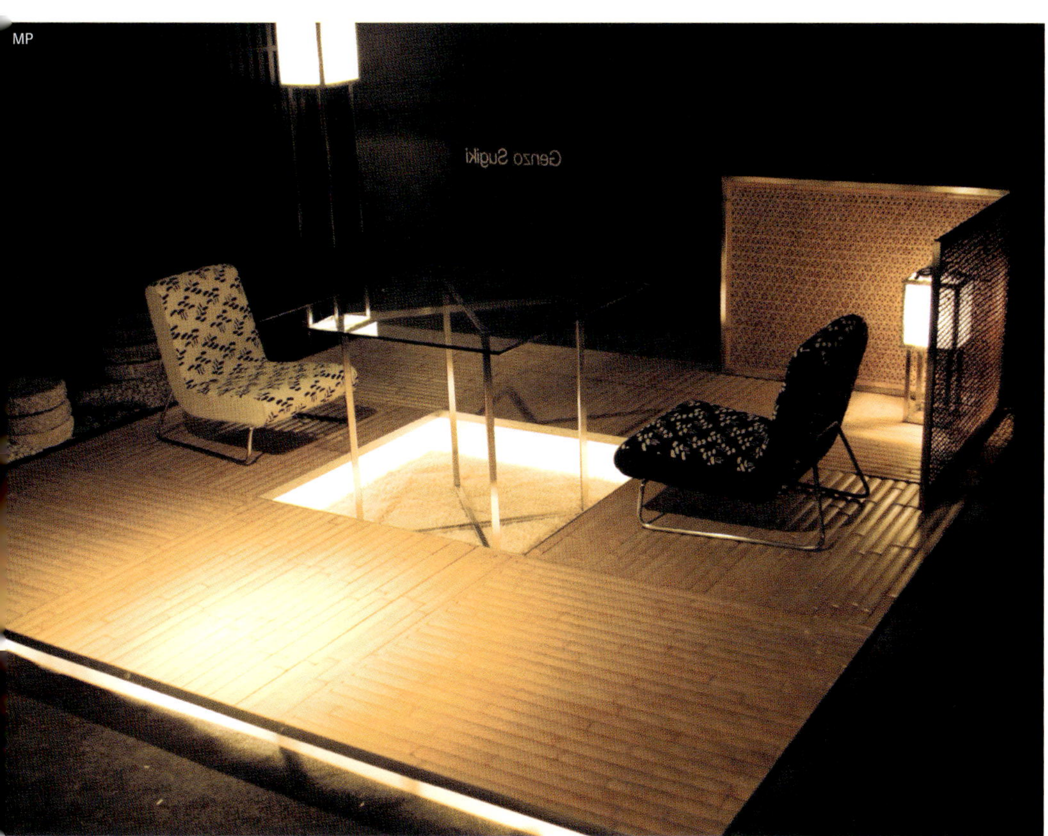

Wa-Qu Exhibition

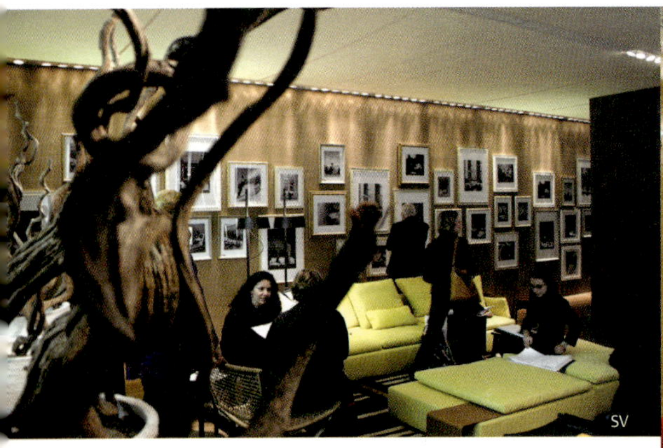

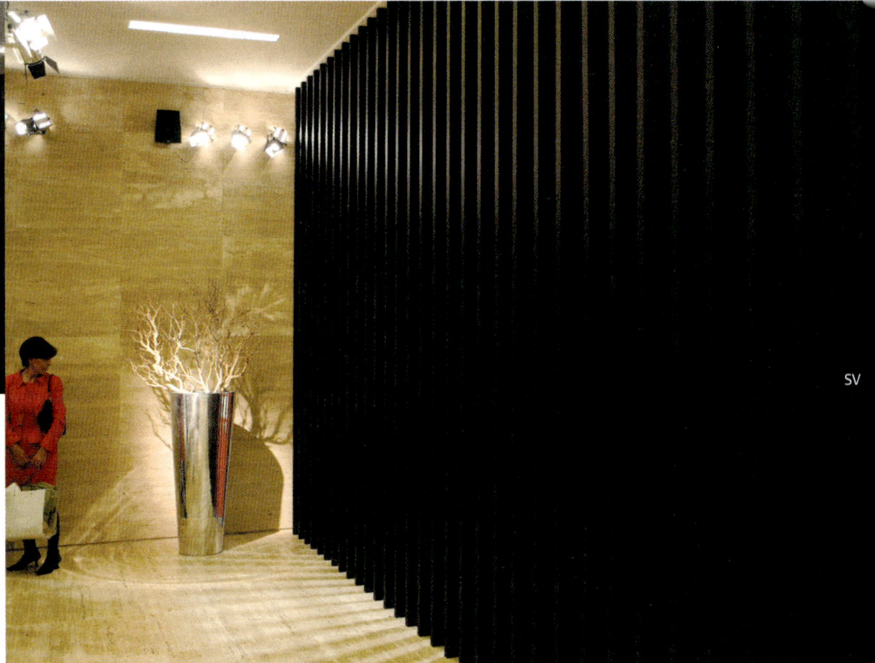

Flexform

Rimadesio

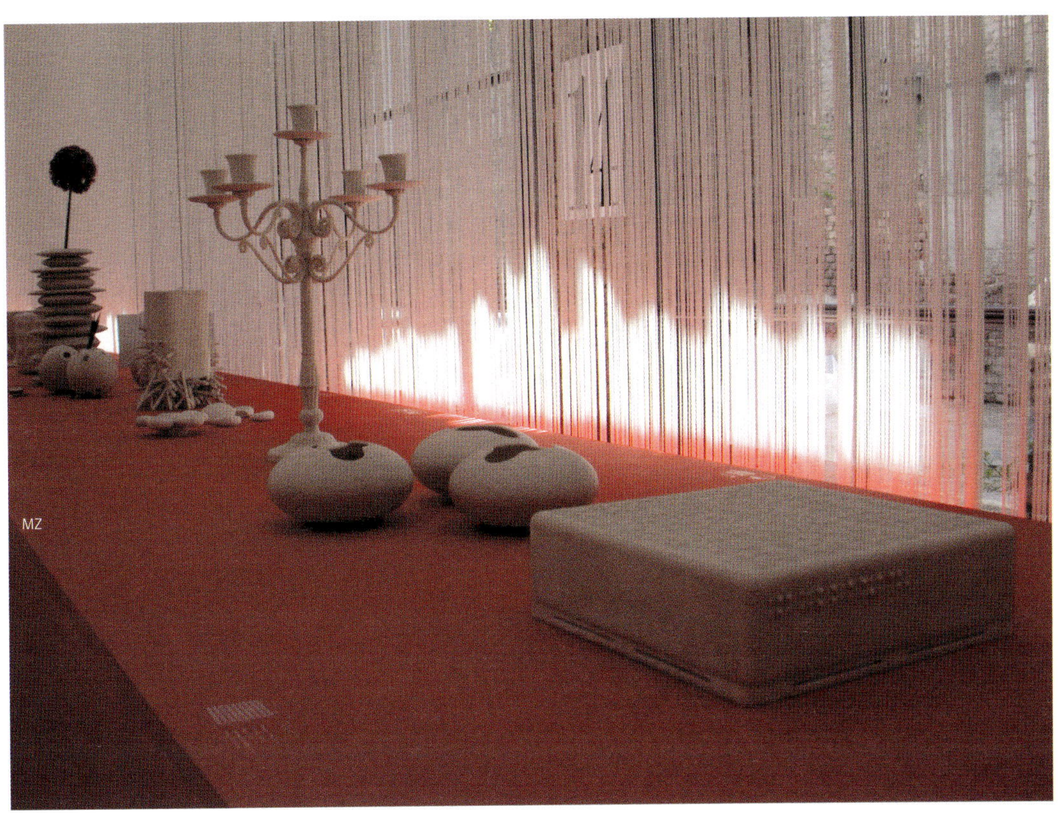

In dust we trust" by OneOff

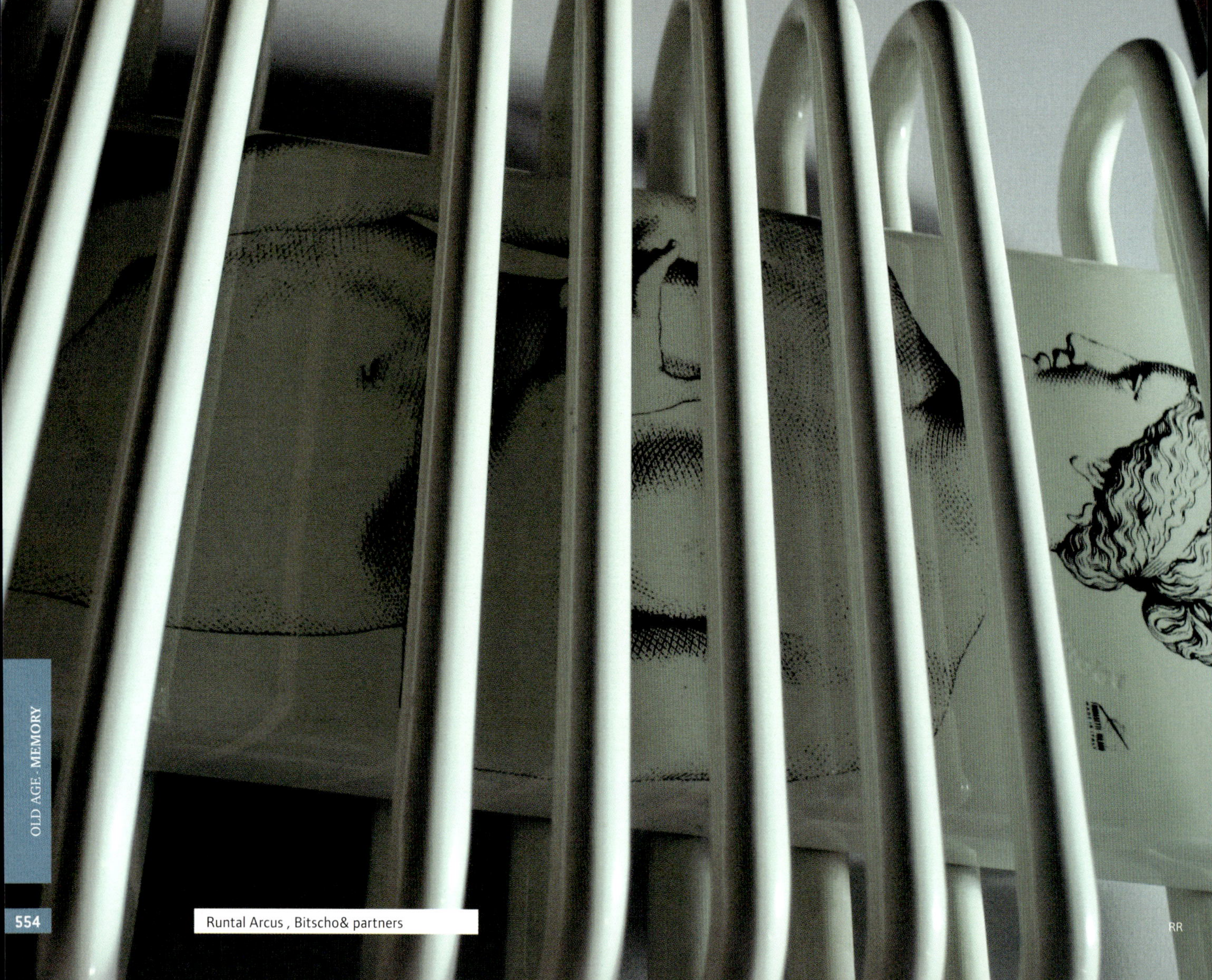

Runtal Arcus , Bitscho& partners

RR

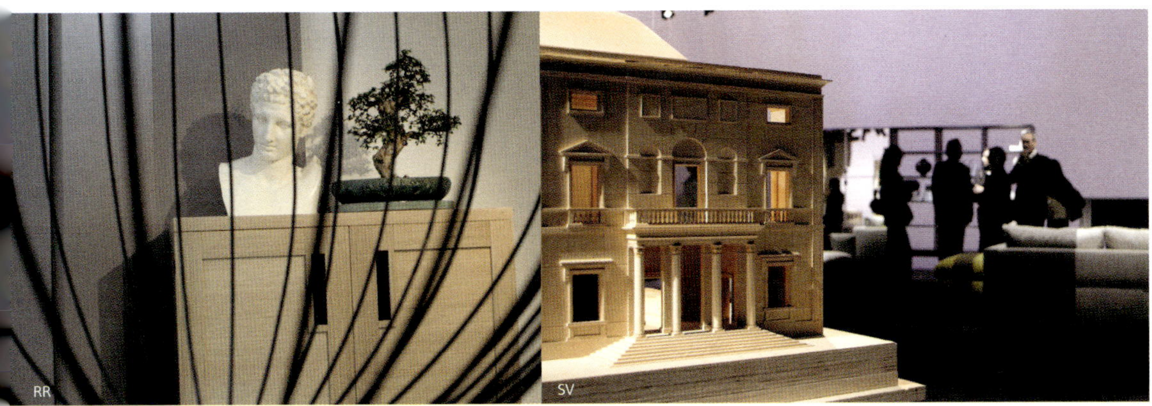

Malofancon   Molteni

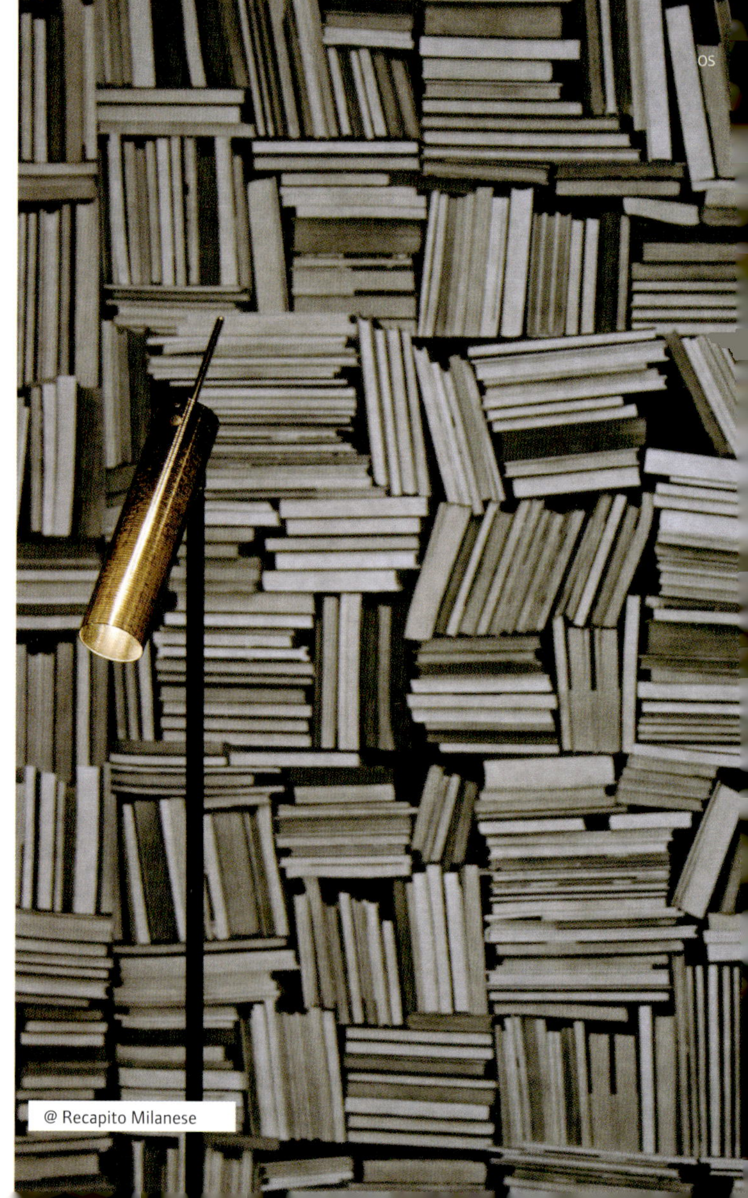

@ Recapito Milanese

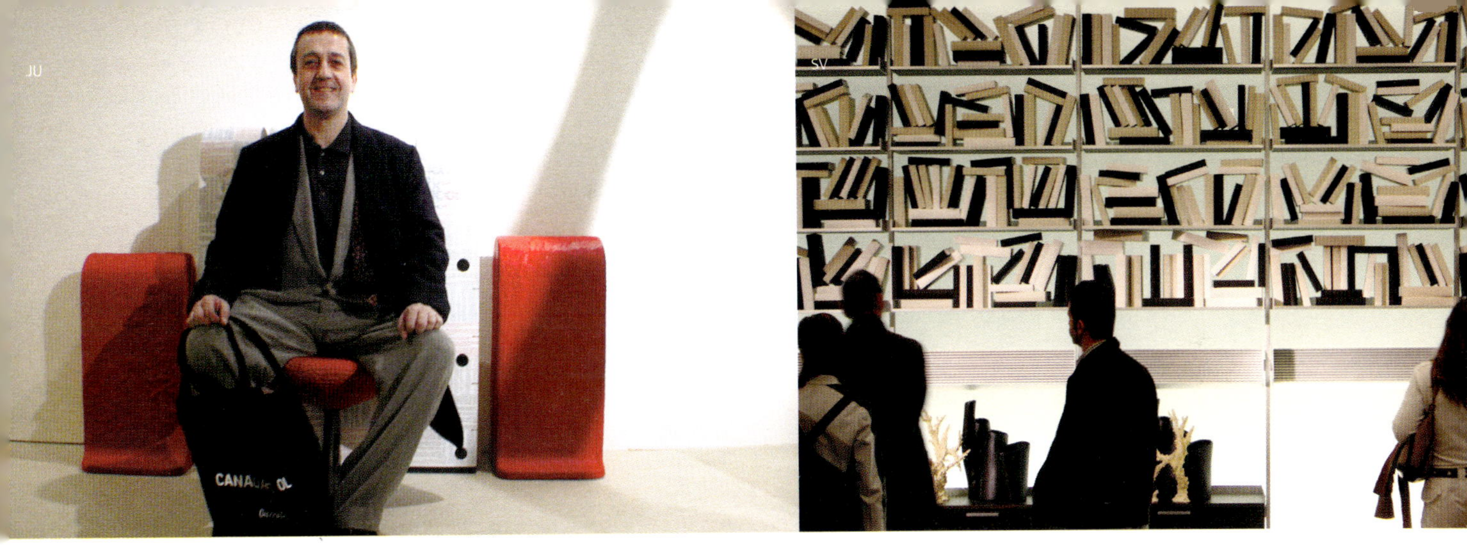

Alessandro Andrei

Rimadesio

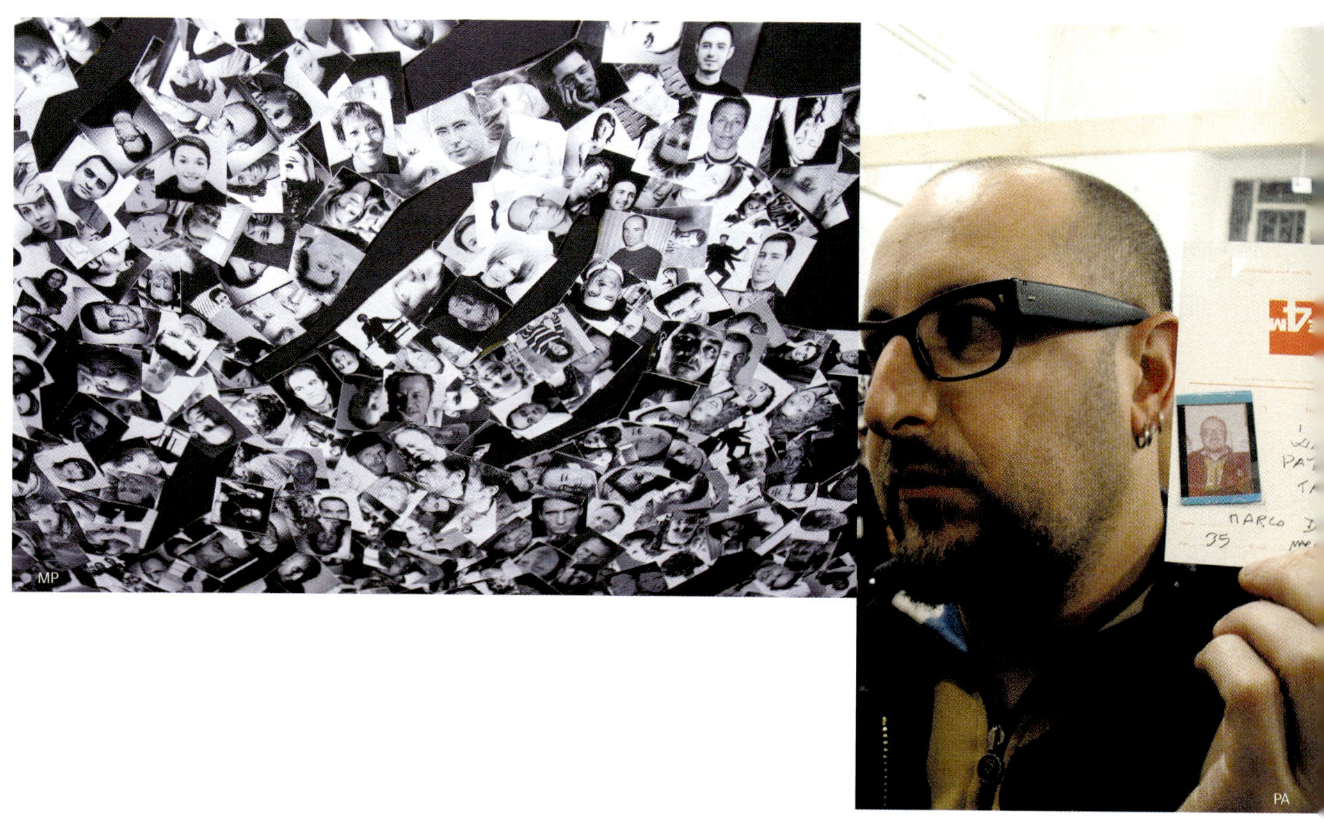

Via

Marco Donati

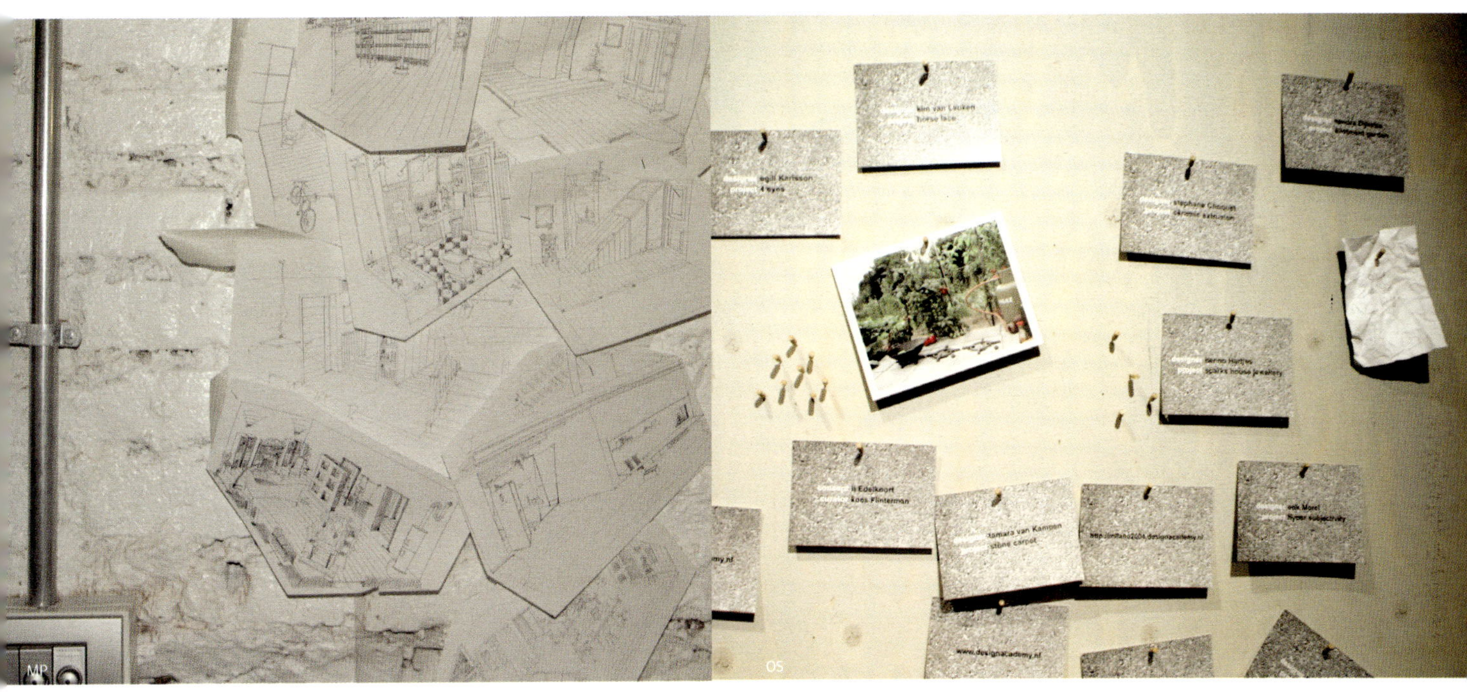

@ Design Academy Eindhoven

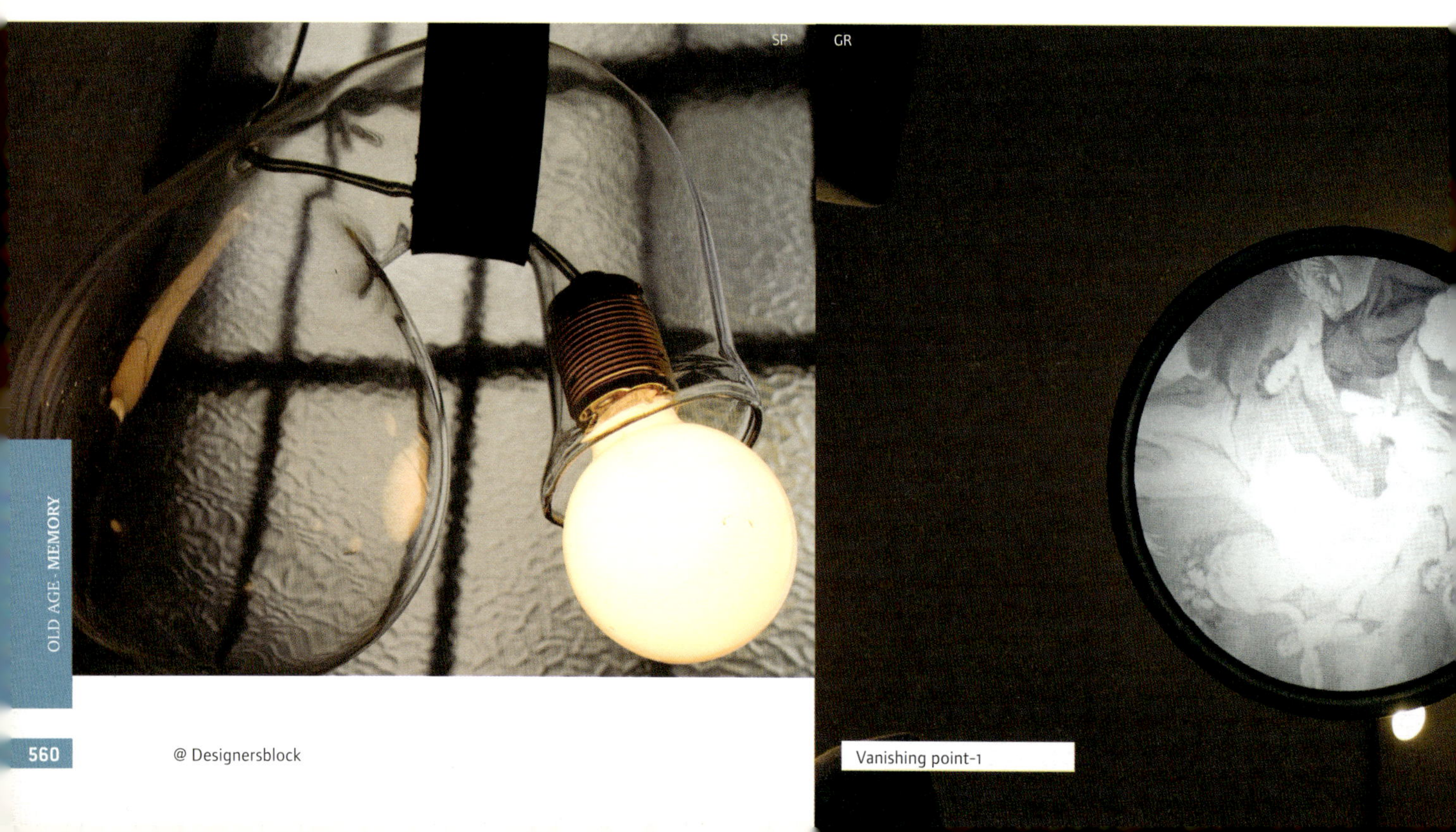

@ Designersblock

Vanishing point-1

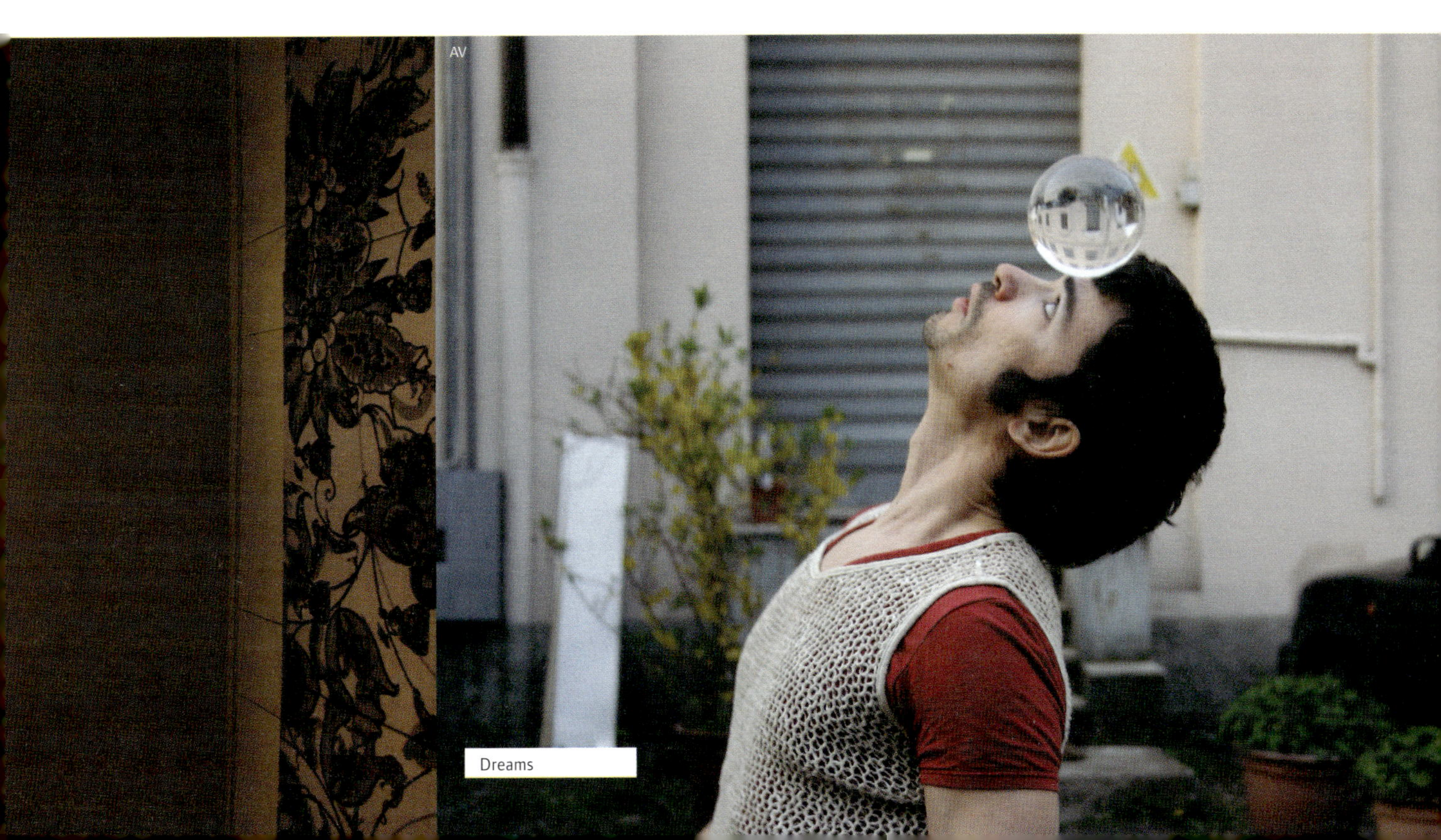
AV
Dreams

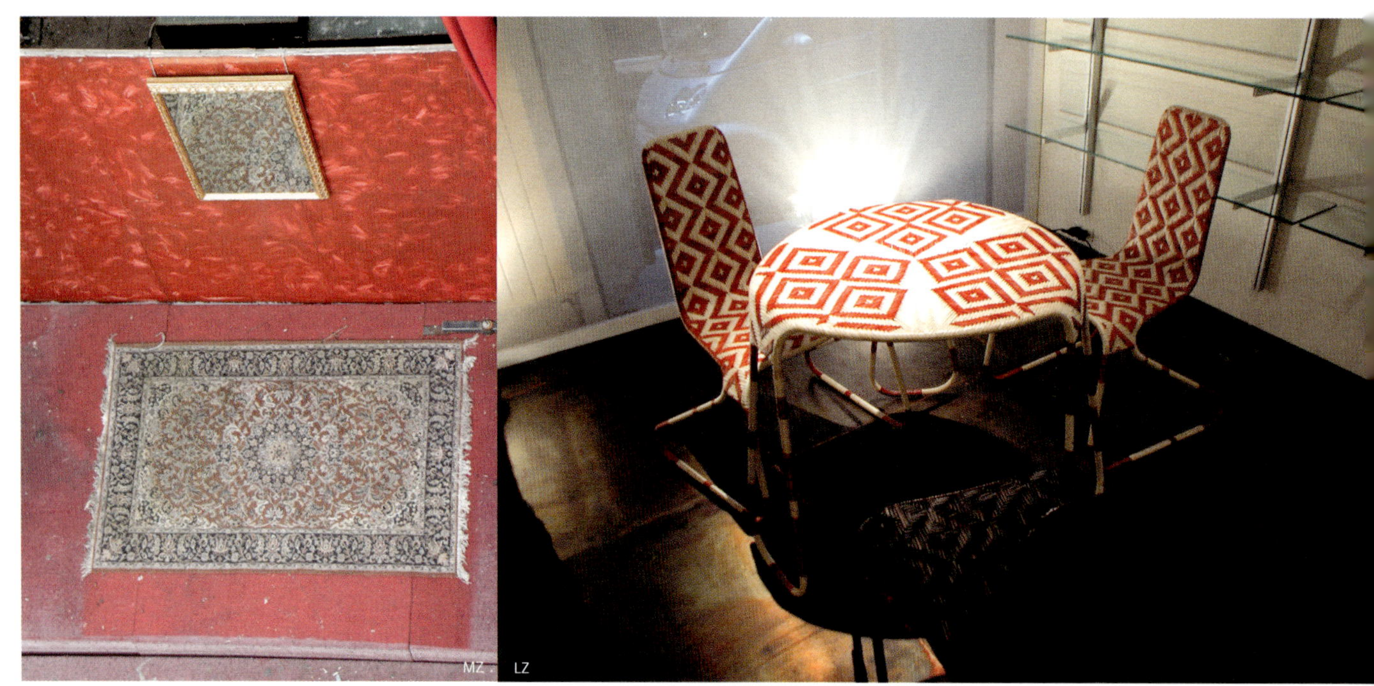

Driade

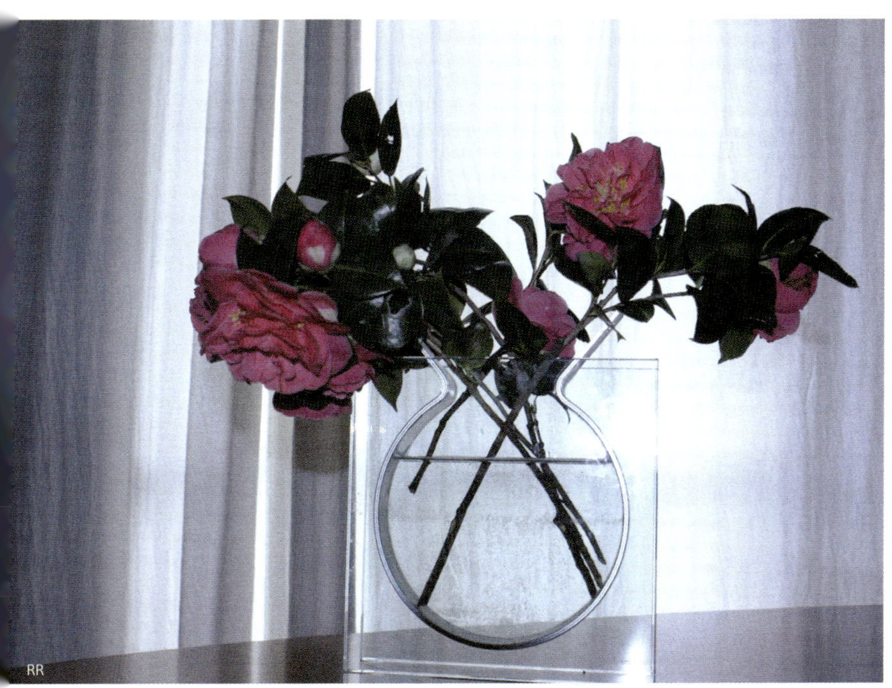

Rubber vase

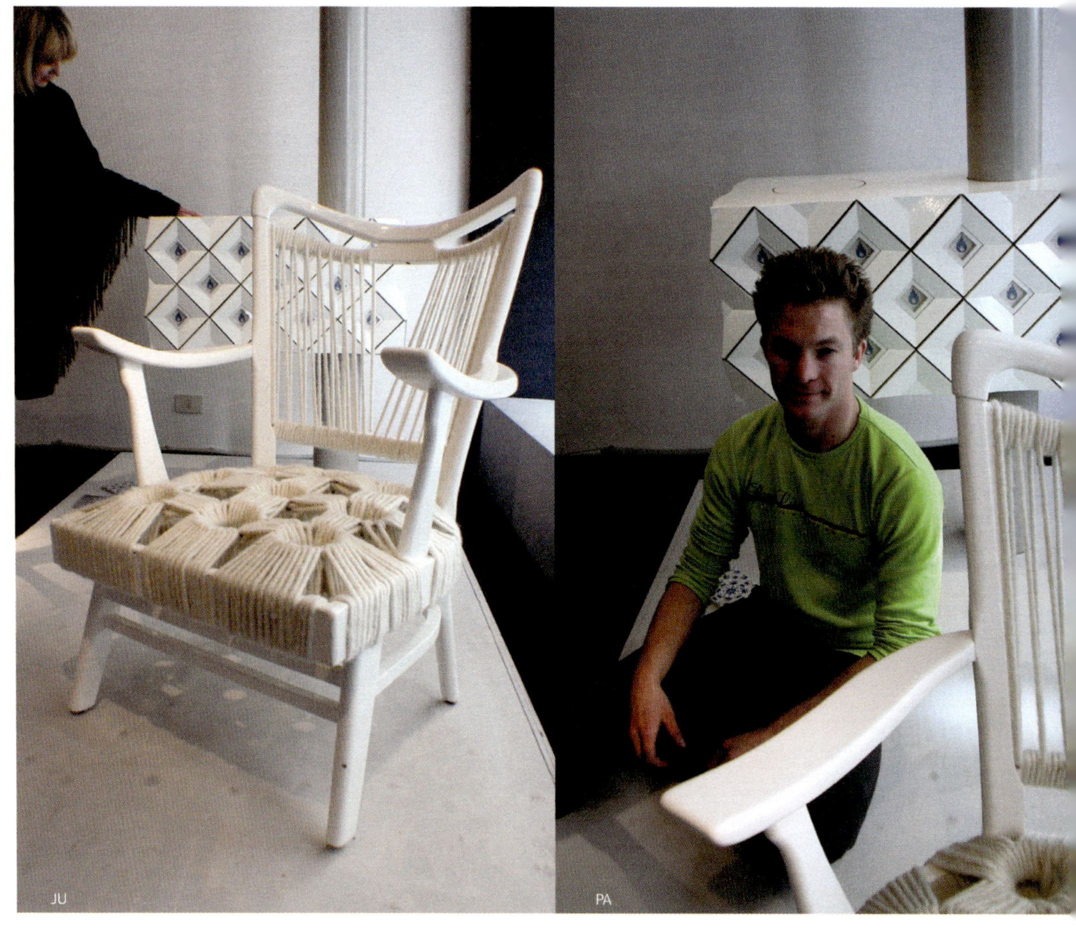

Gudrun Lilja Gunnlaugsdottir @ Design Academy Eindhoven   Niels Huneker @ Design Academy Eindhoven

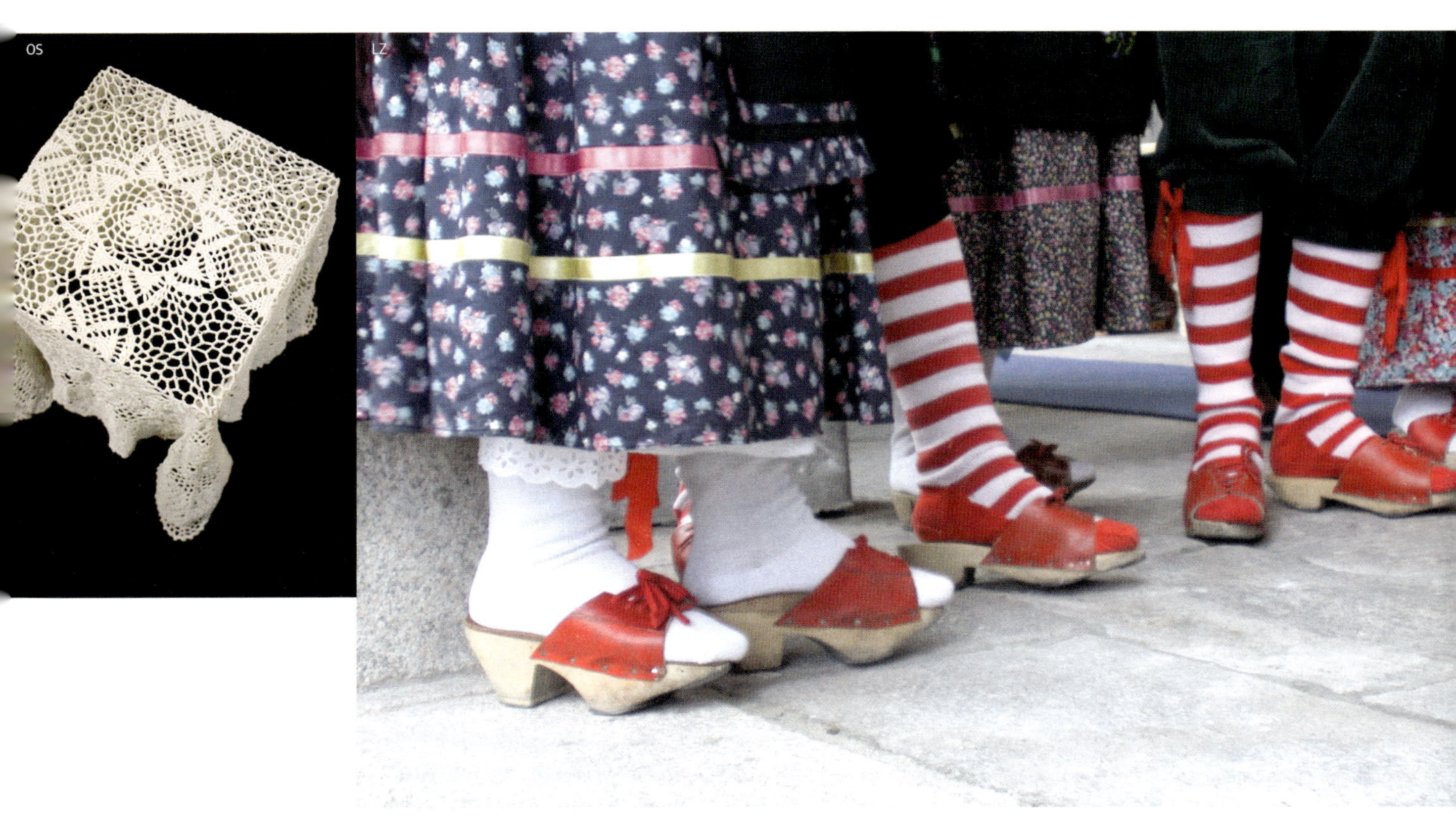

Demacker Design

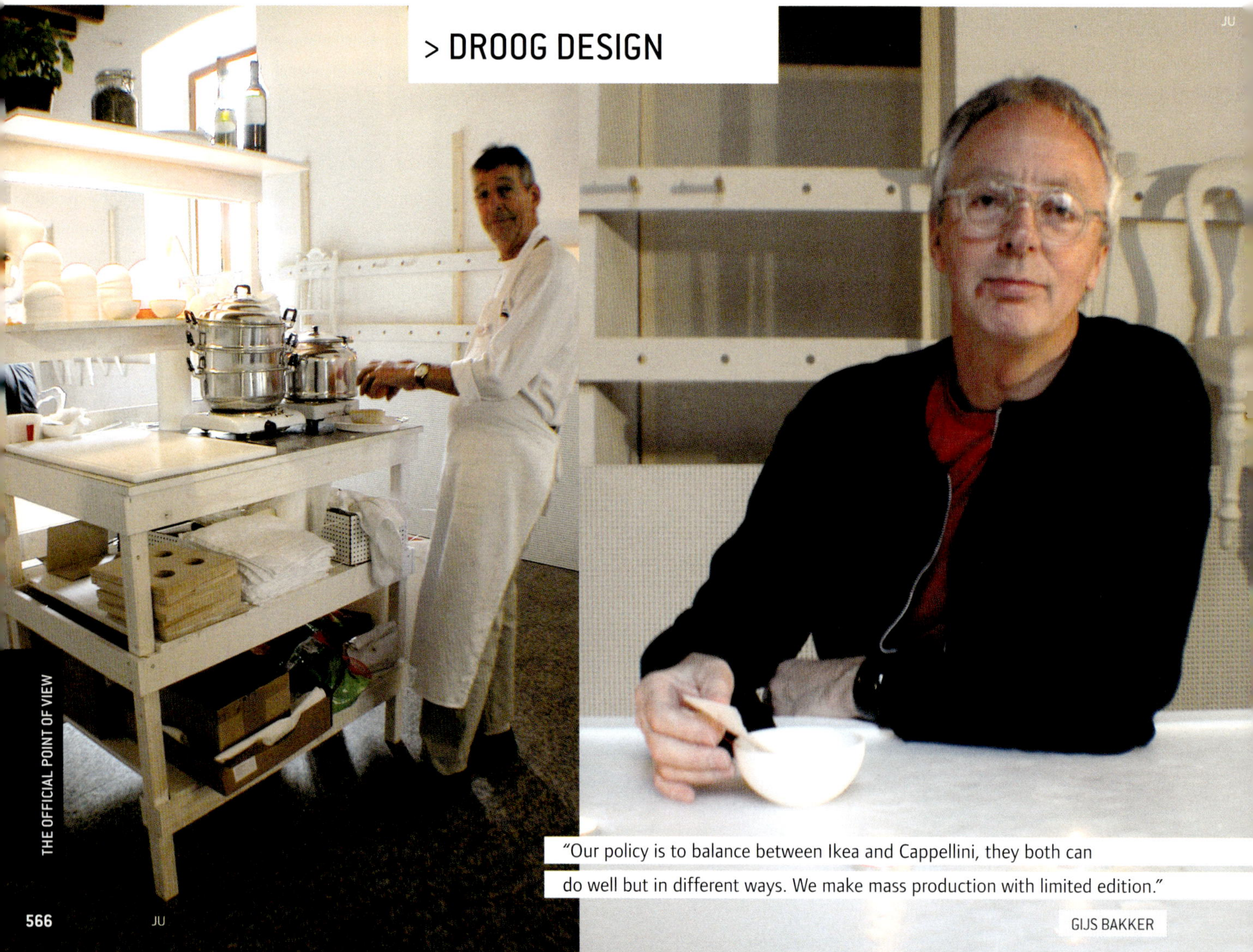

"Our policy is to balance between Ikea and Cappellini, they both can do well but in different ways. We make mass production with limited edition."

GIJS BAKKER

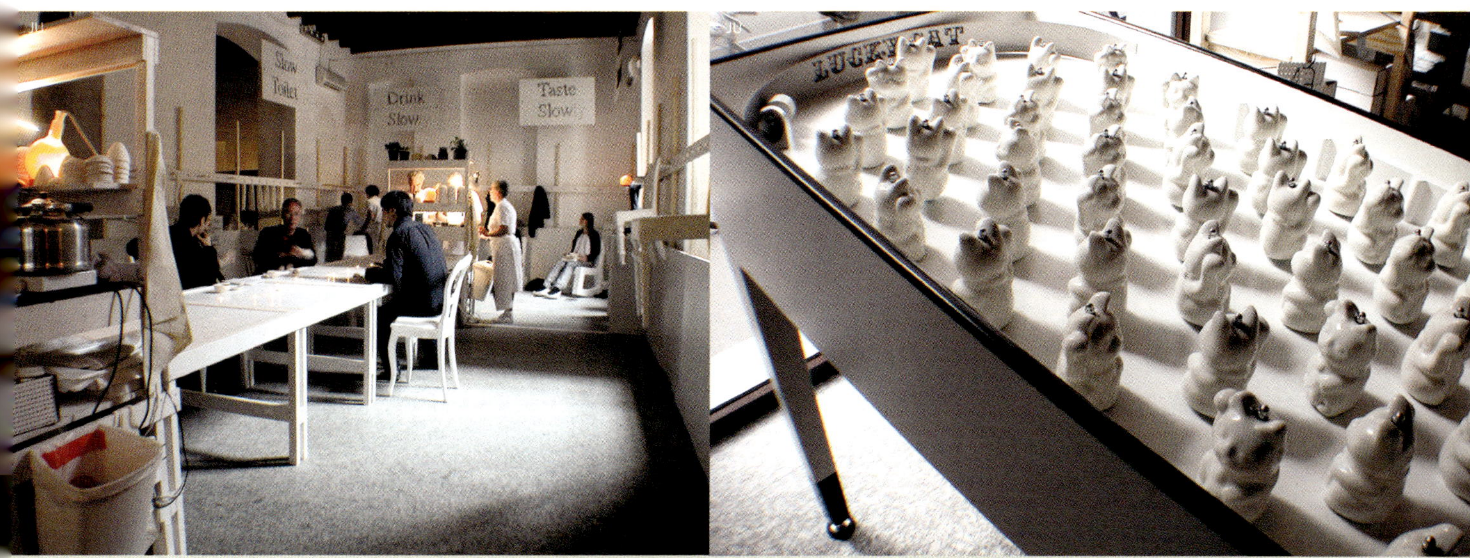

GO SLOW

Droog's **12th presentation** in Milan was based on the concept of going slow.

In a white environment you could enjoy a moment of rest in the hustle and bustle of Milan during the furniture fair.

Senior people flew in to offer you a bite and a drink.Their service is slow but attentive.

"Slowness is a quality that is hard to come by in our modern urbanized world which is dominated by speed and fast

consumption.We are extremely busy.We no longer follow processes.Our patience does not extend to "slow" and "difficult".

Things must be easy and complete. Slowness is luxury. You are invited to a slow experience.Take your time.

Experience processes.Enjoy attention and care. Enjoy relaxation.

Enjoy slowness."

DROOG DESIGN

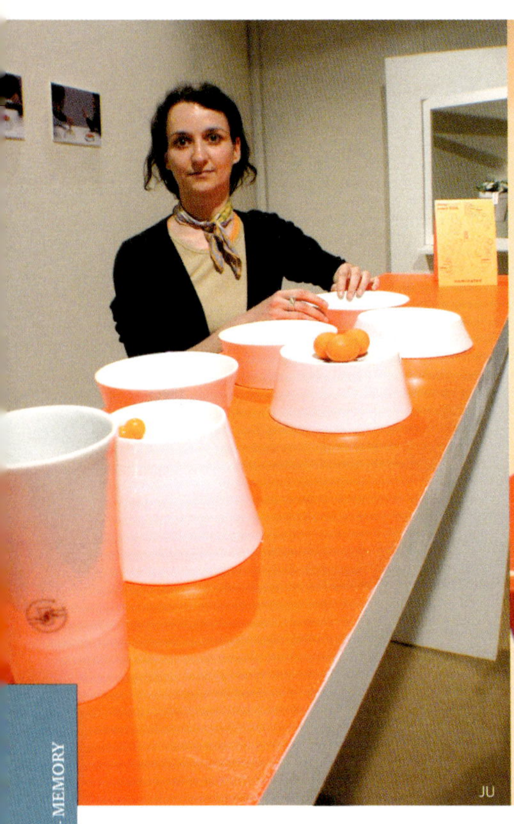

Brigit Jobst 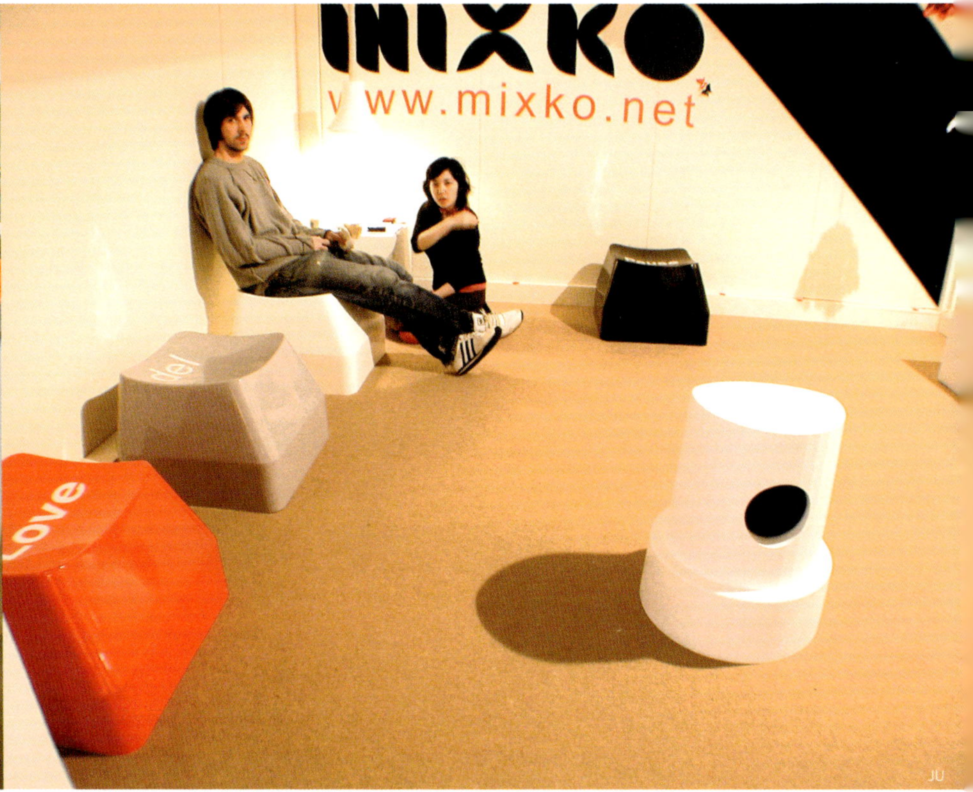　　　　Mixko

Press a button to find out.

It does not really work this way.

Actually I have no idea what it is happening while I am

sending you these few words.

The world now is made of buttons and cause-effect

reactions have no appearance anymore.

Certainly no one has a vague idea - please contradict me -

- of what makes the videorecorder videorecord,the lighter light,

the toaster toast, the player play, the fax fax.

Flavio Del Monte

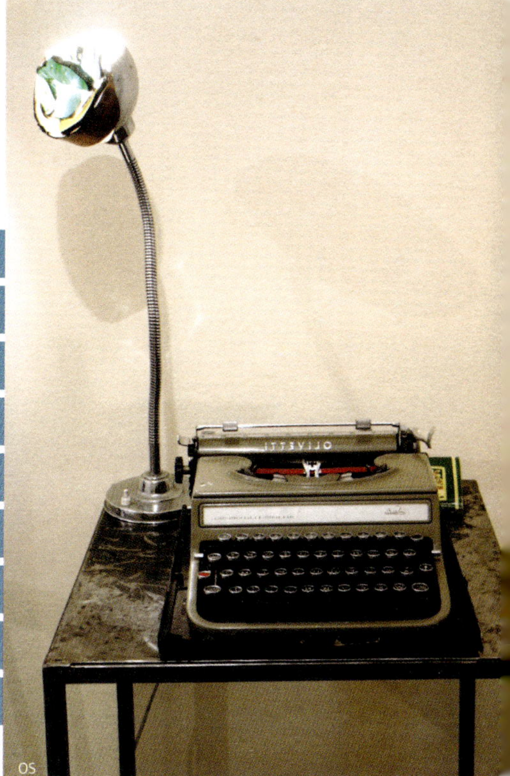

Cadrega

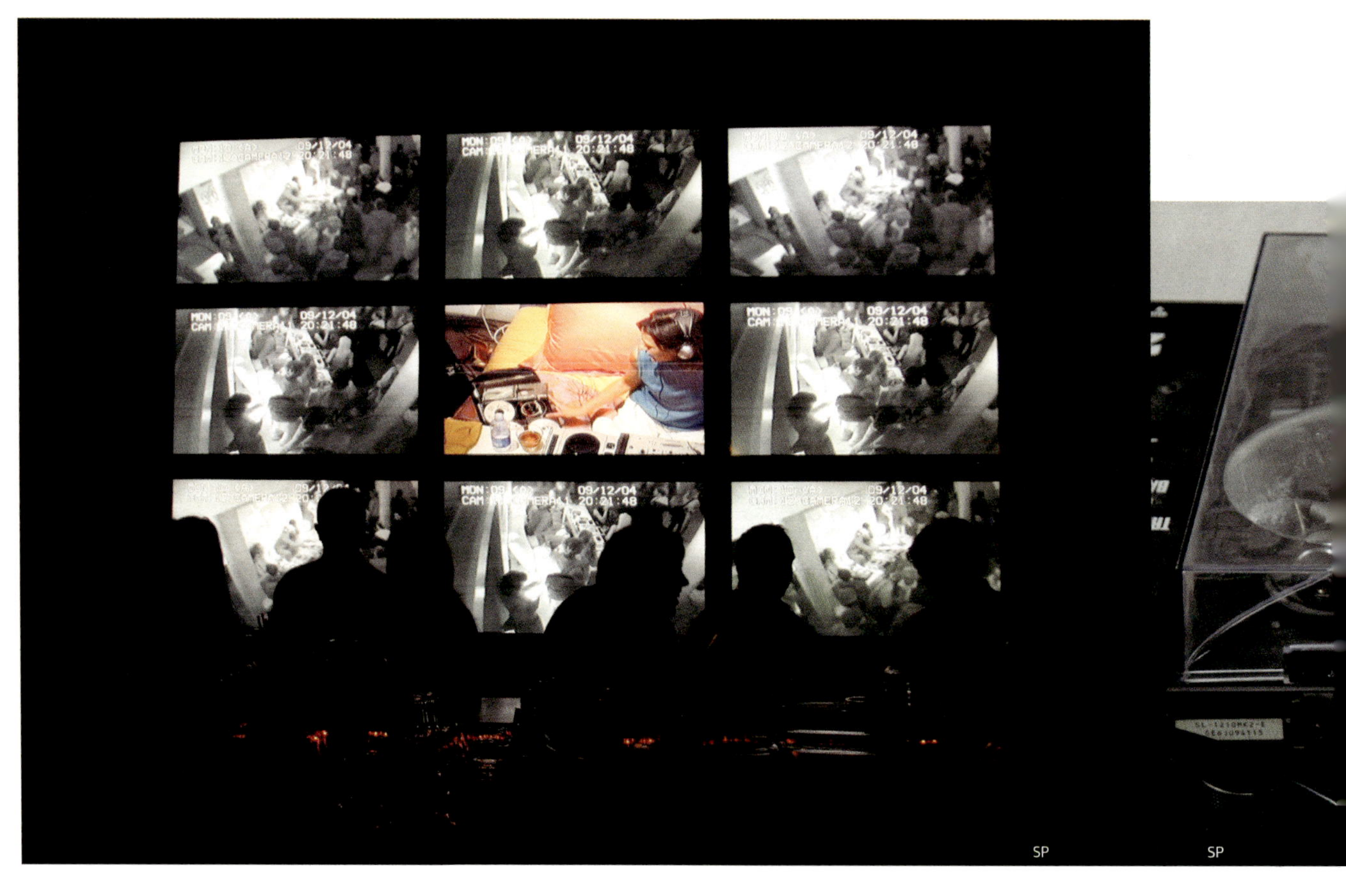

F1 @ Trussardi Palazzo Marino alla Scala

@ Designersblock

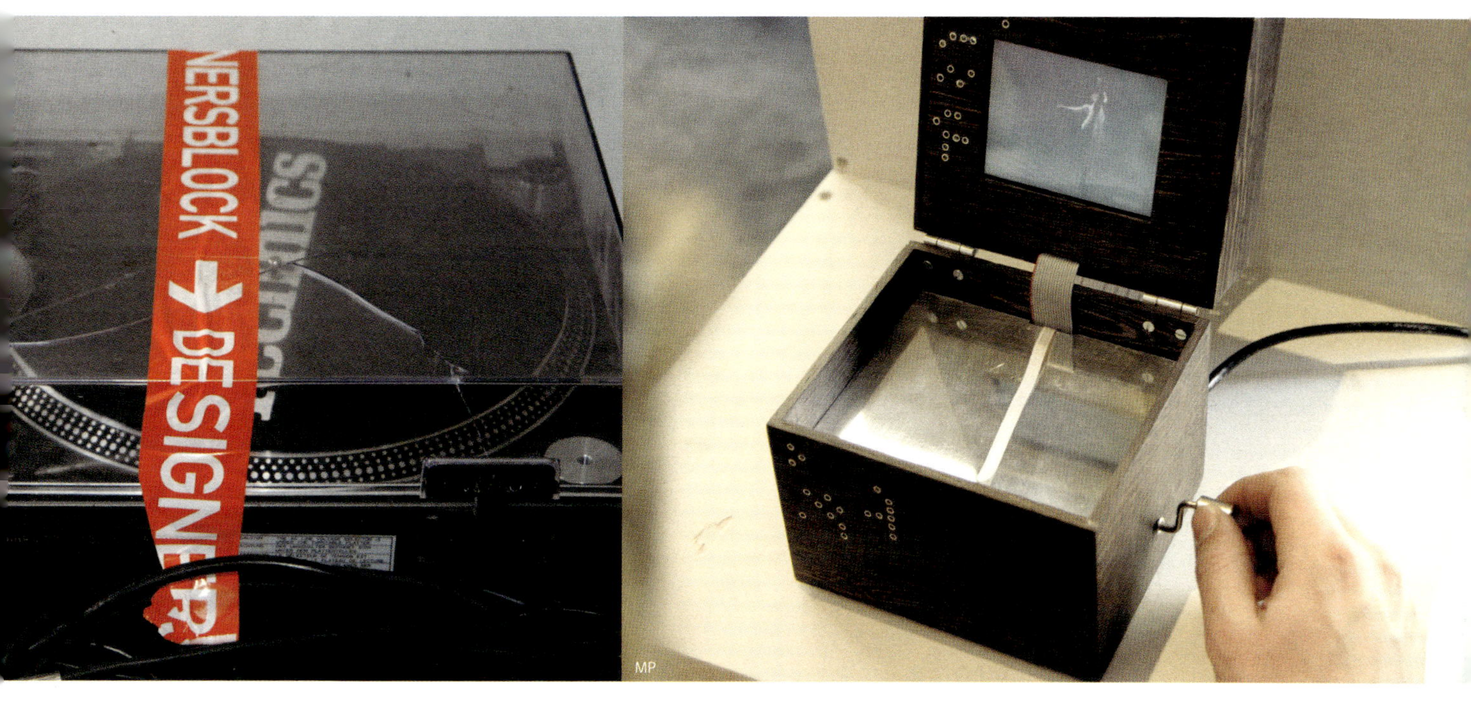

Erik Klarenbeek @ Design Academy Eindhoven

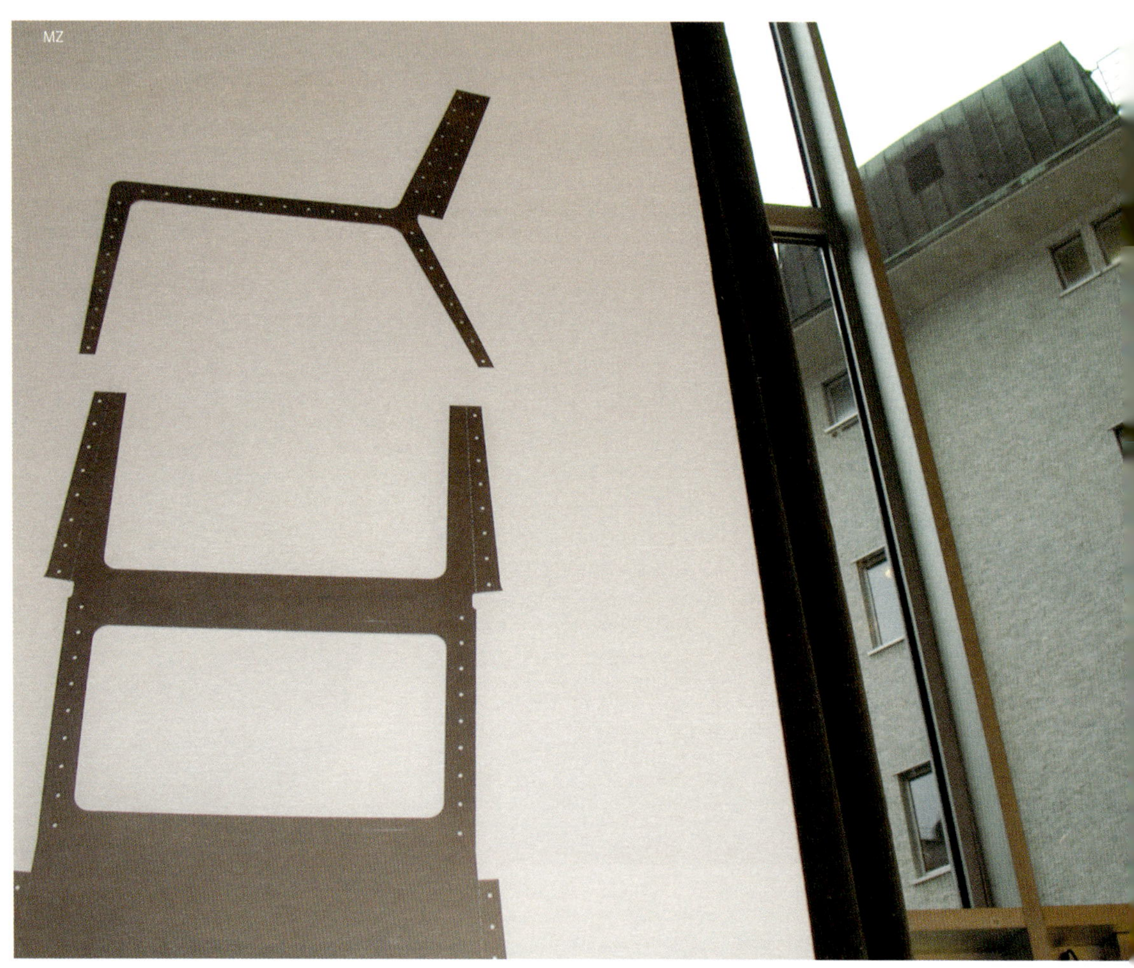

Swiss Design

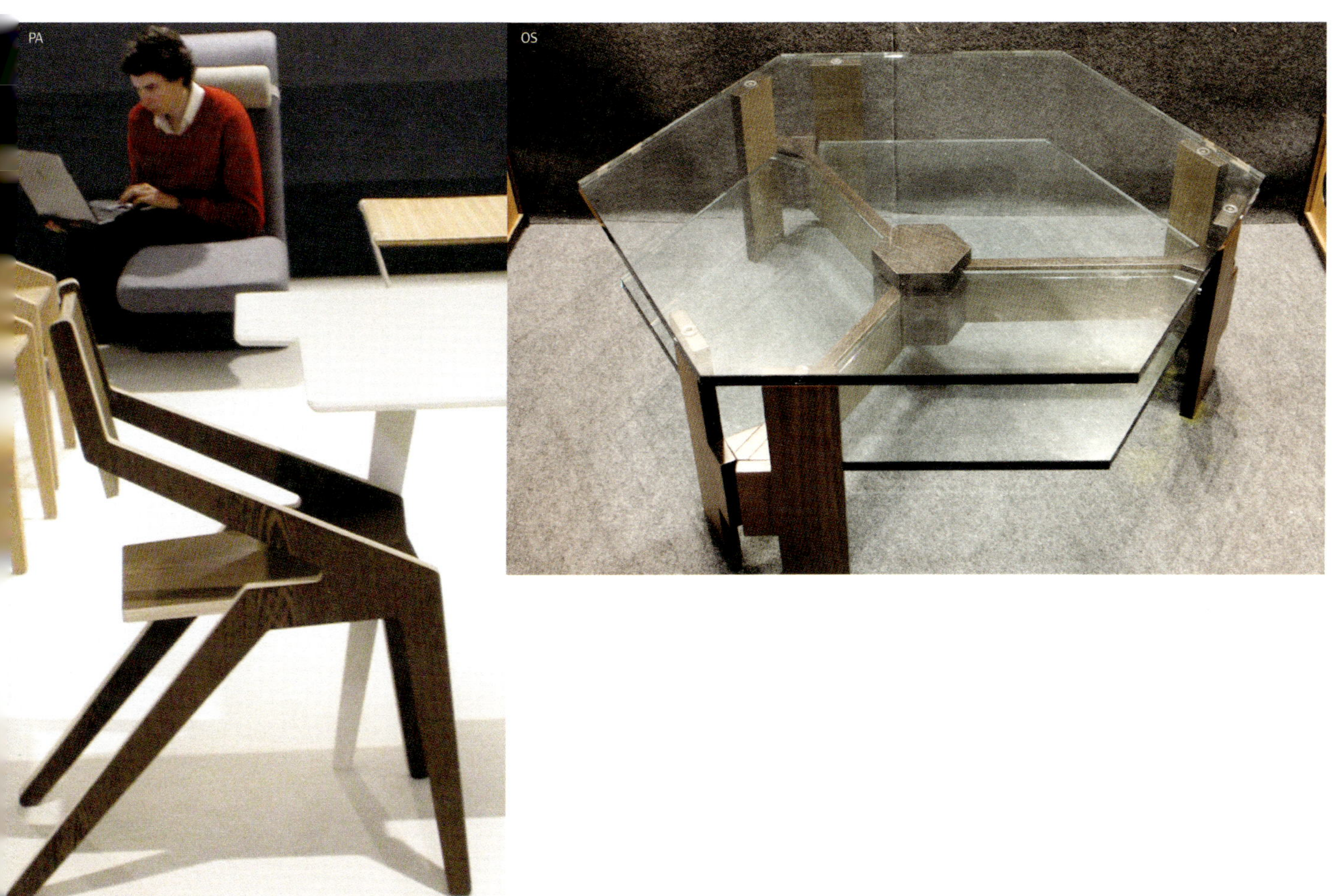

Bare Mobler

Jacopo Gardella

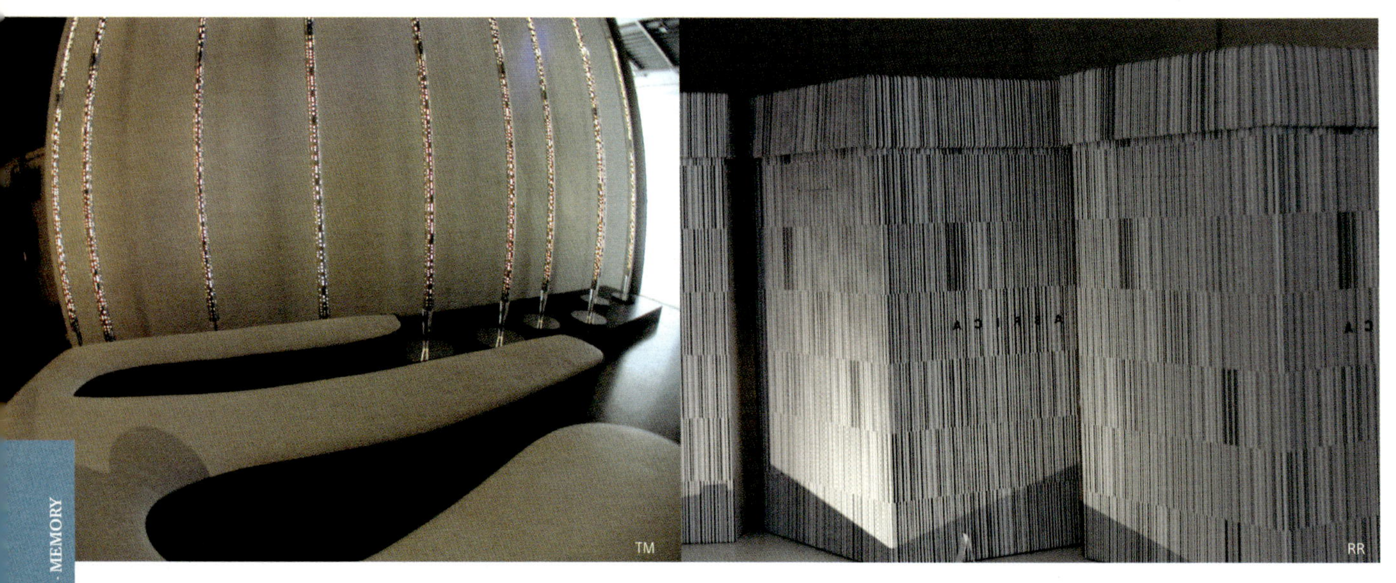

574   ??????

Cibic & partners

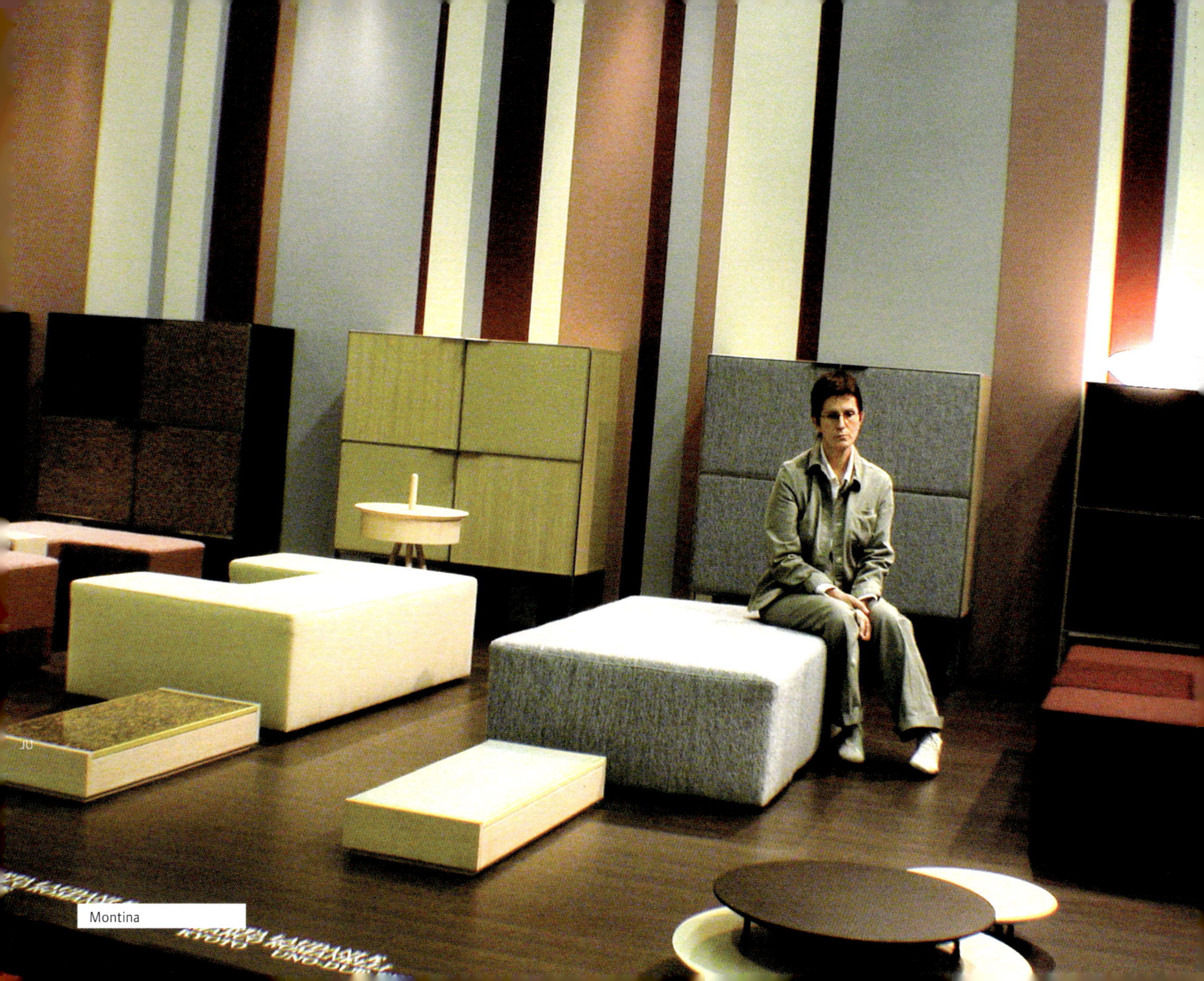

Montina

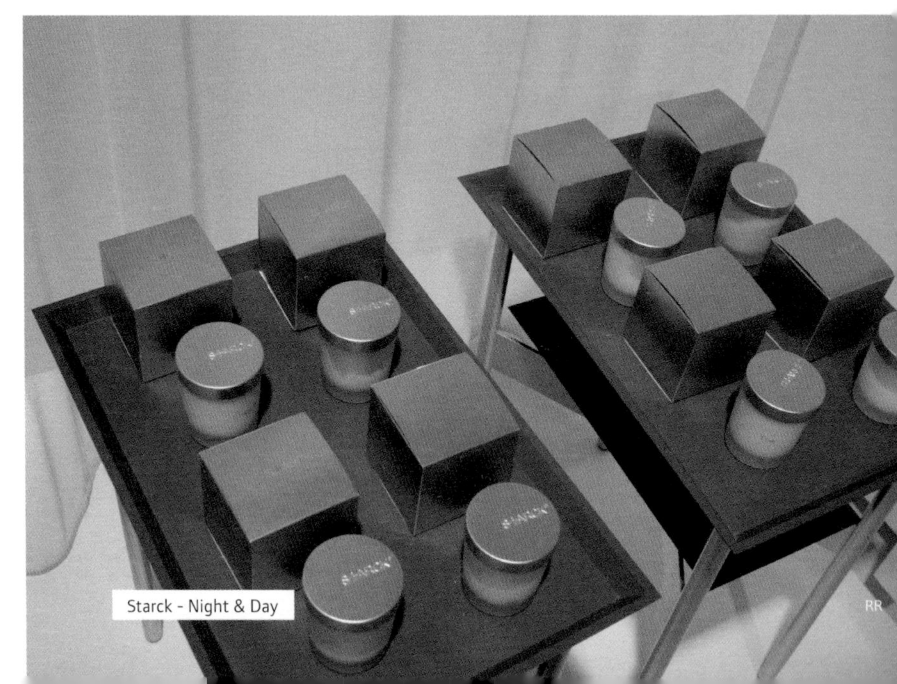

Starck - Night & Day

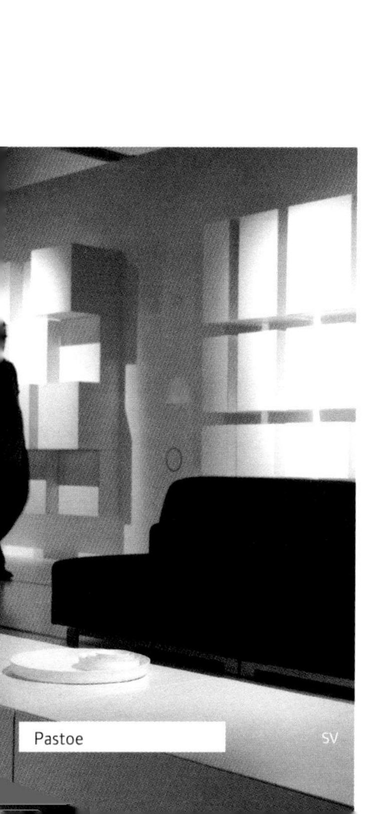

Pastoe
SV

Triennale
GR

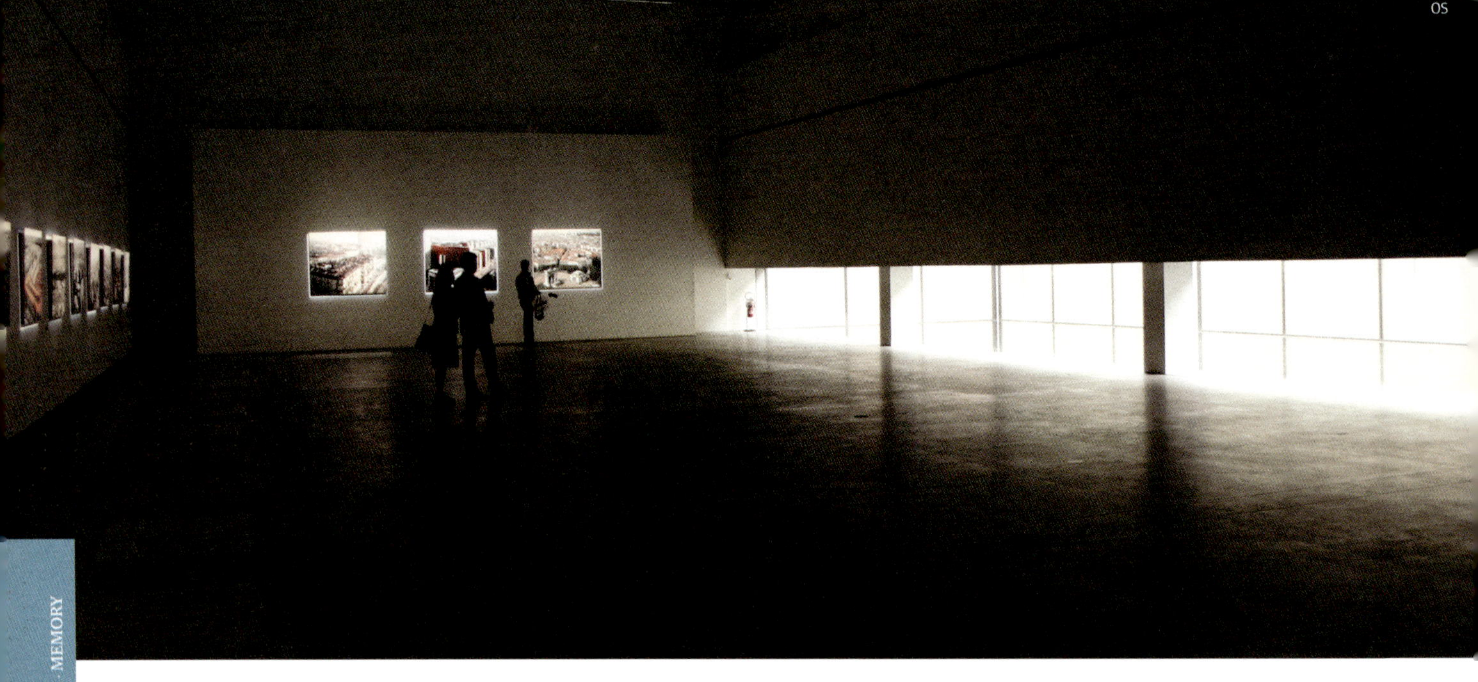

Castella

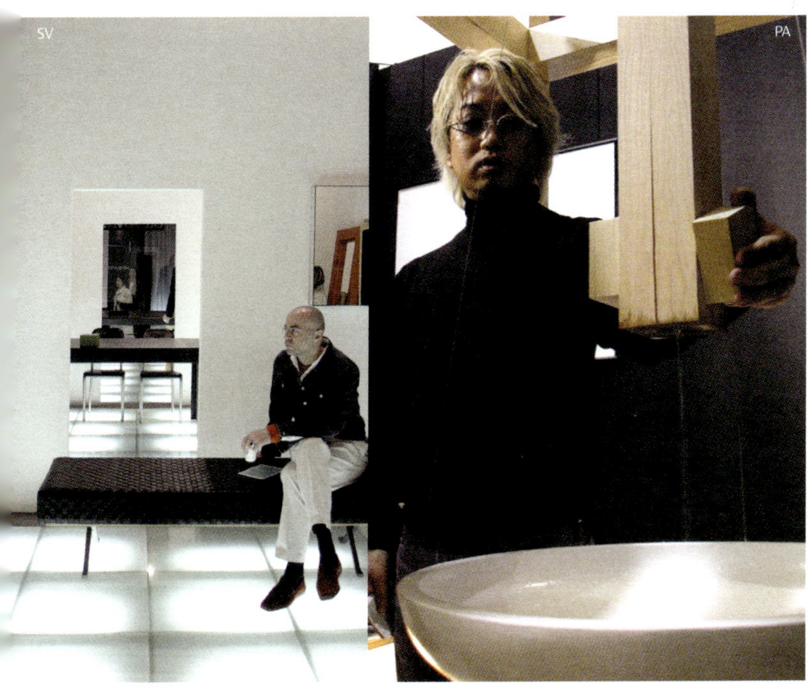

Triangolo   Yasutoshi Mifune @ Satellite

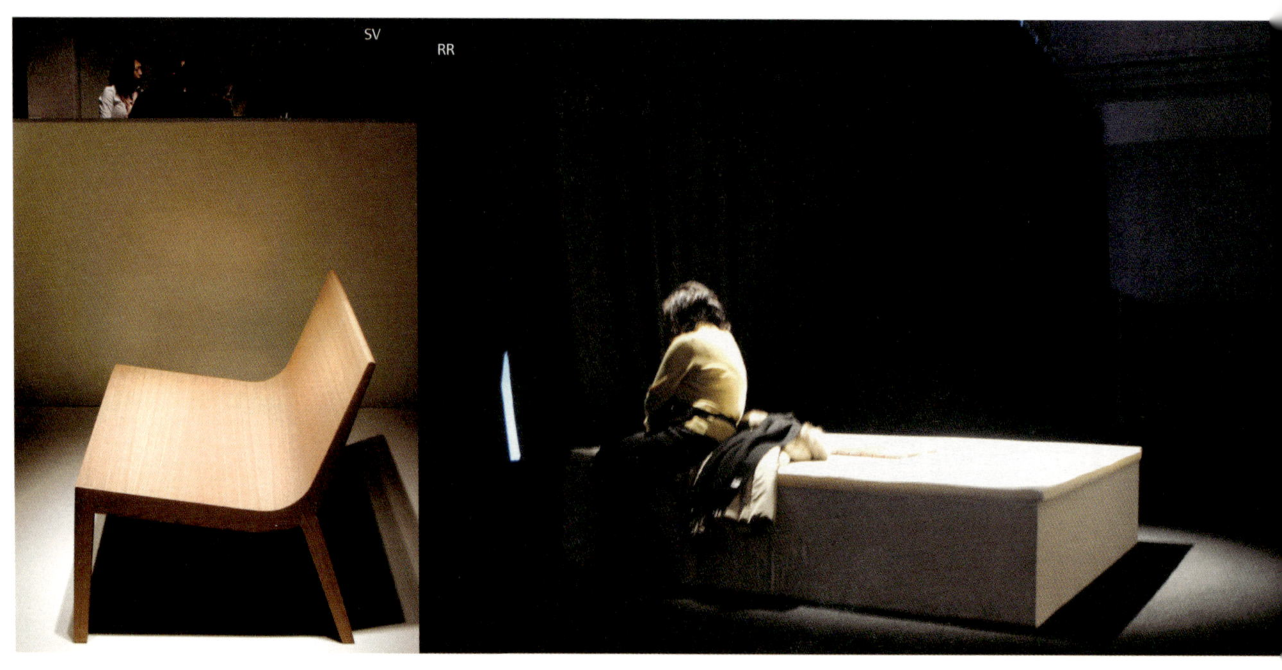

Andreu World

Morphosis by Jacuzzi @ Pelota

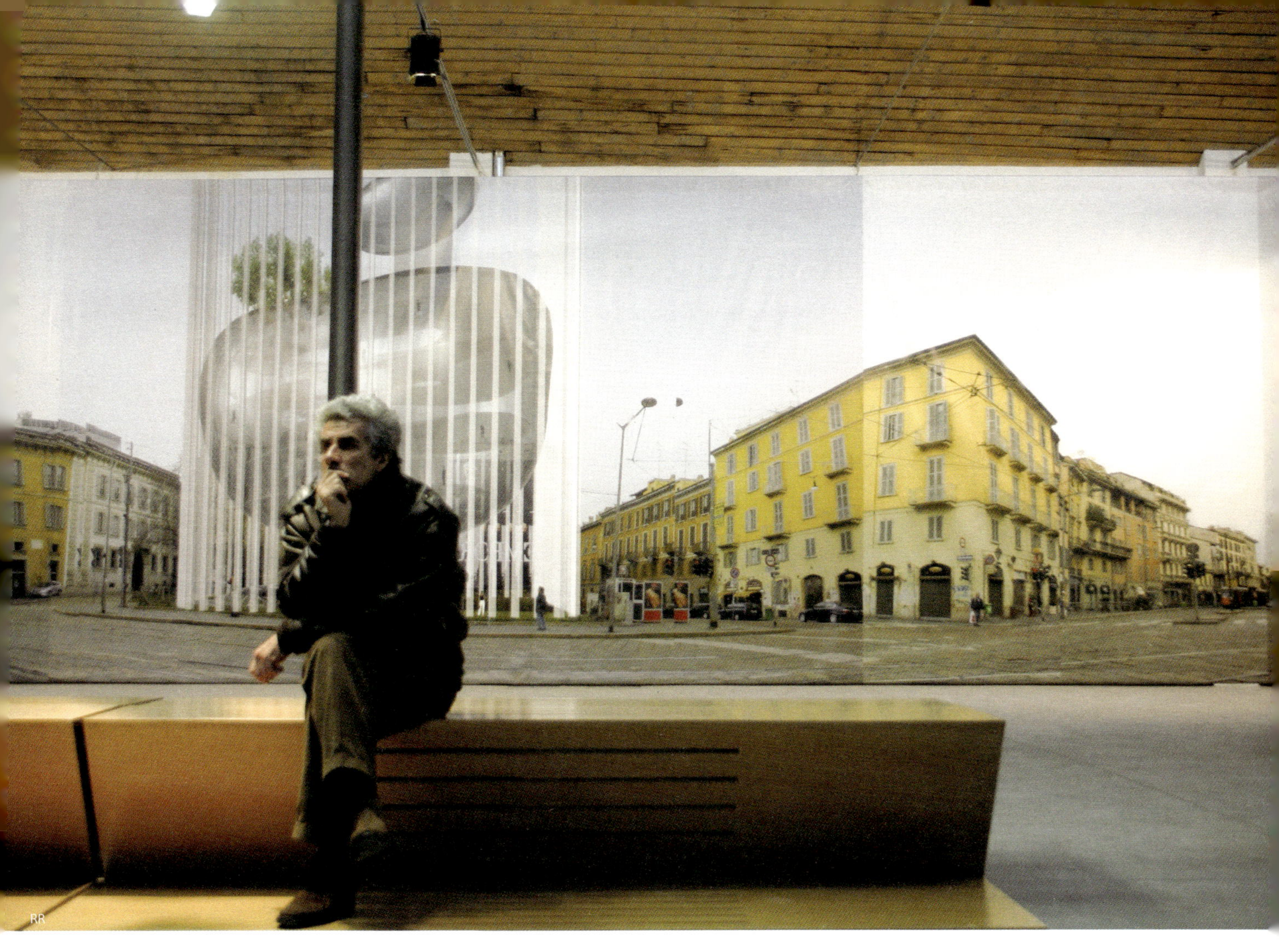

Monitor Hyperlink Tower

WHAT IS CURRENTLY REGARDED AS

THE BEST DESIGN CONCEPT OR OBJECT?

Its best consumer.

DAVID PALTERER

Constantly endeavouring to improve what is already there.

GALA FERNANDEZ

The Apple iPod is the world's first 3rd Millenium product.

JOZEPH FORAKIS

Spectacles, as one is always hoping to see better things through them.

MIGLIORE + SERVETTO

At Cologne 2004 I saw a polystyrene bookshelf/partition wall
designed by the Bouroullec brothers. I think it is a positive example of design object.

ROBERTO PAOLI

Anything, which involves a lot of hand labour, so there will be more jobs.

INGO MAURER

The product forcing its user to read the instructions.

DAVID PALTERER

The entire Bush Administration and it's campaign in Iraq has to be the worst design concept since the Third Reich.

JOZEPH FORAKIS

Minimal projects are the worst example of design concept.

ROBERTO PAOLI

The design of companies that copy.

ROSS LOVEGROVE

Design can never be pessimistic but I remember I had a student that brought me an unusual piece one day; he made a ceramic plate with a deep relieve on the border, as a funeral ghirlander, and in the middle of the plate ther was some cocaine; this is a negative object of design but with an optimistic concept since drugs heal you.

DROOG DESIGN

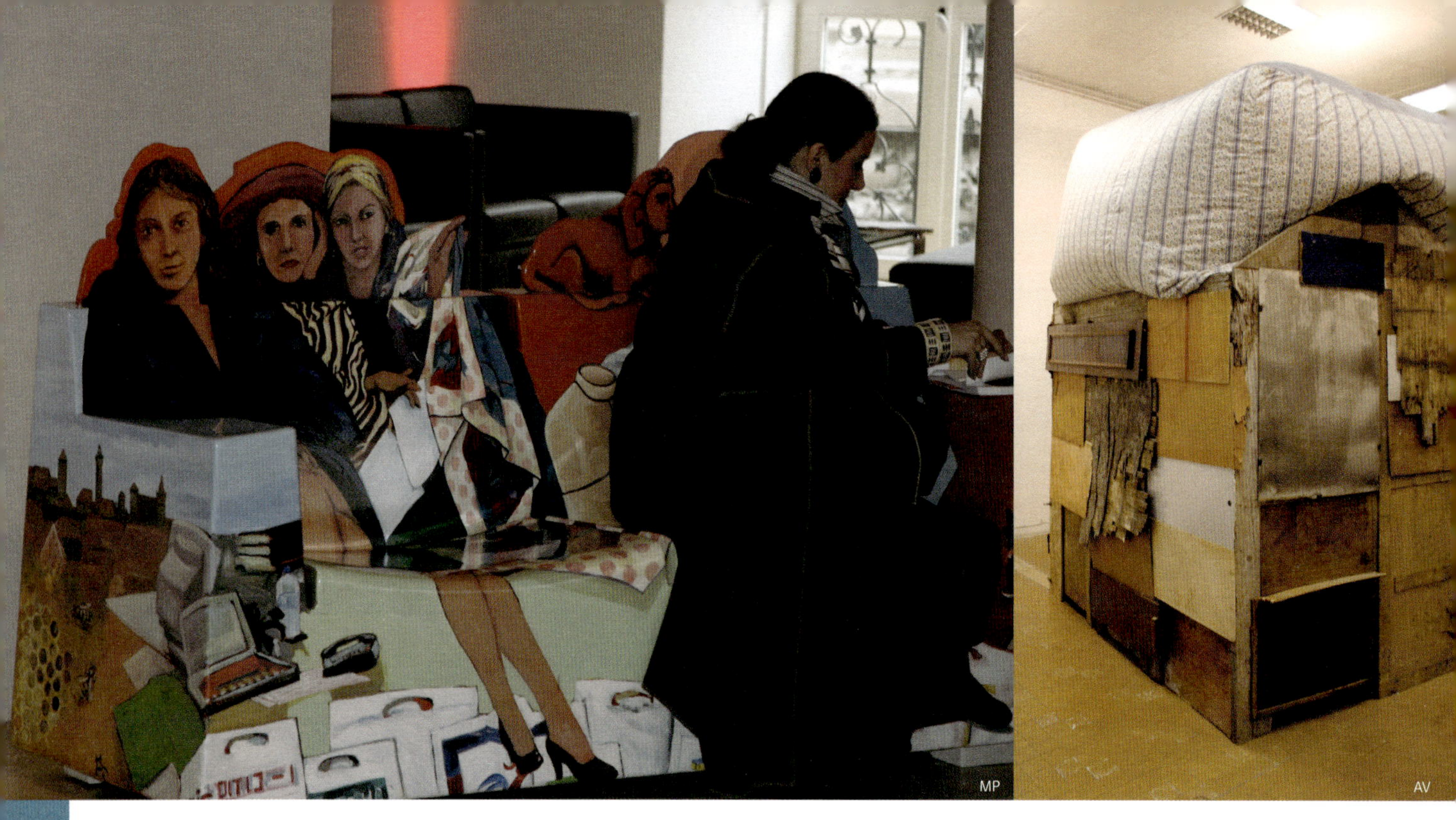

Edith Oellers

Fabbrica del Vapore

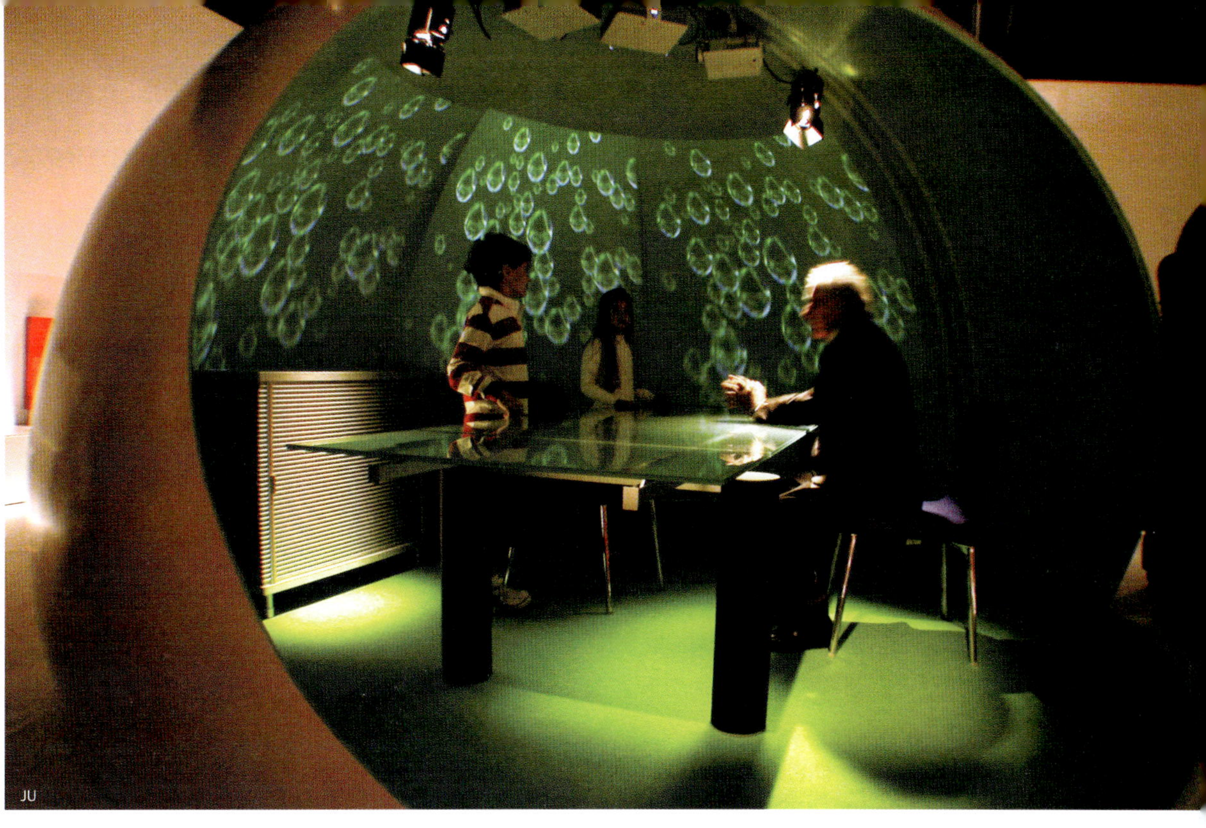

Ycami

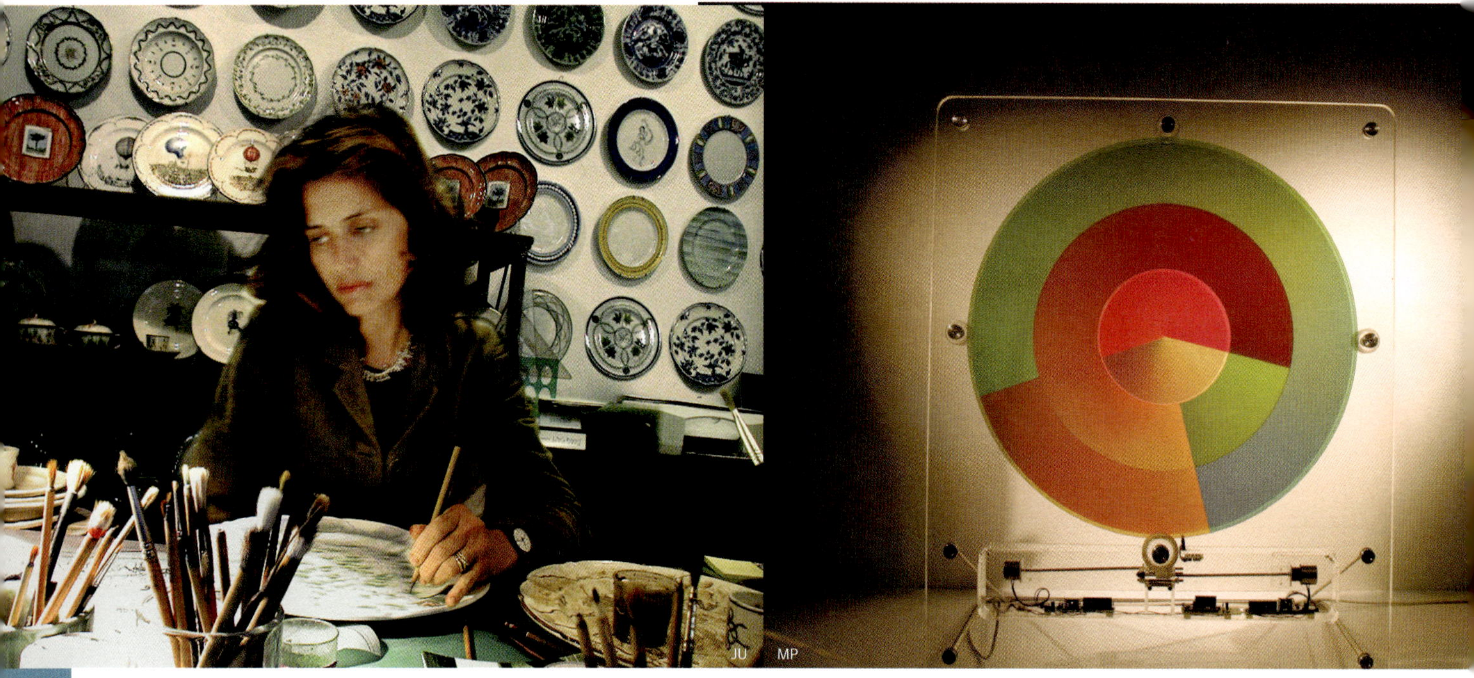

Costanza Paravicini for Paravicini Tableware

Bettina Dadon @ VIA

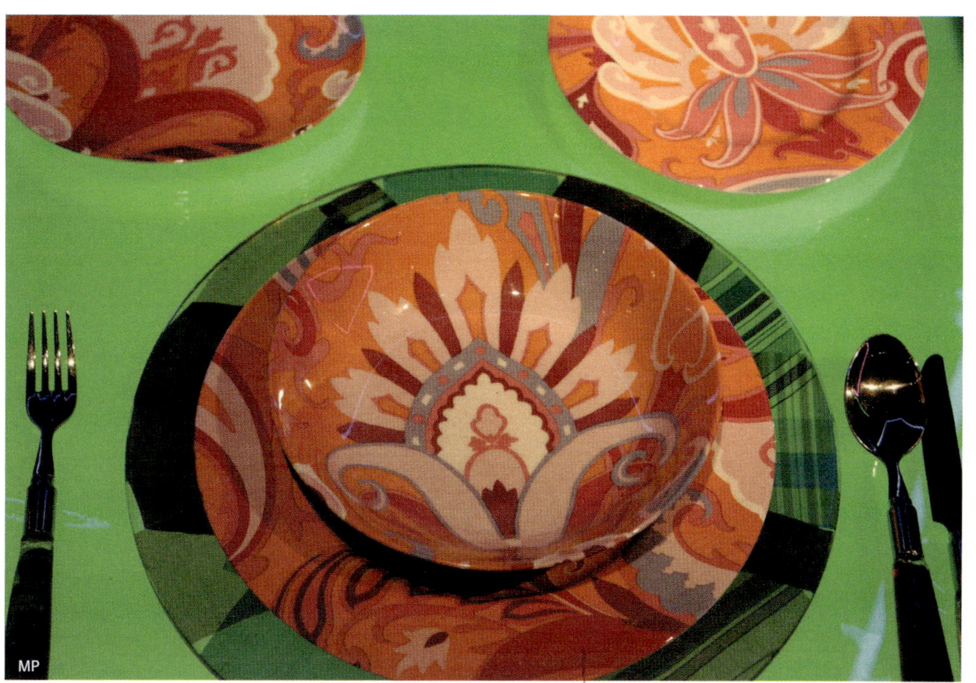

Paisley" by Etro Home Collection

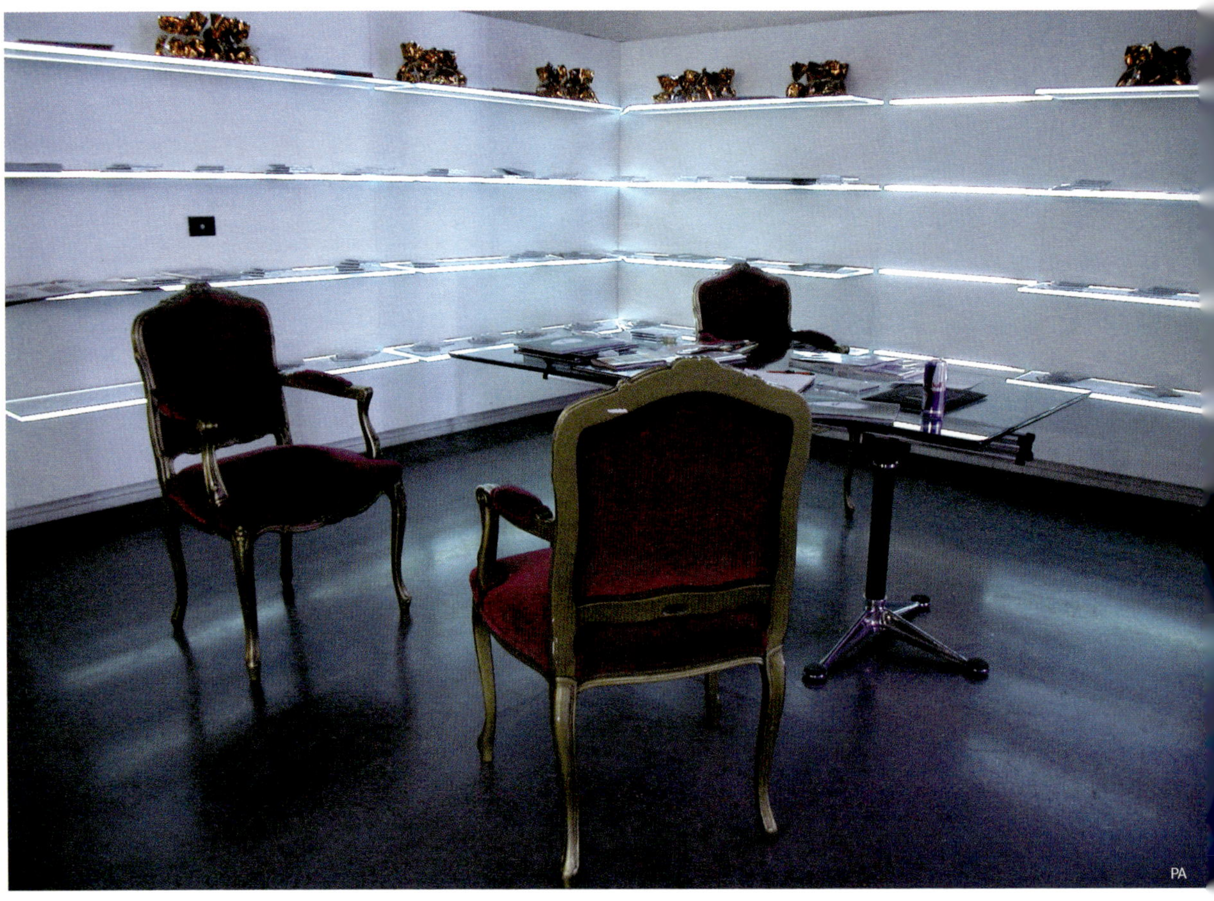

@ Nu Light

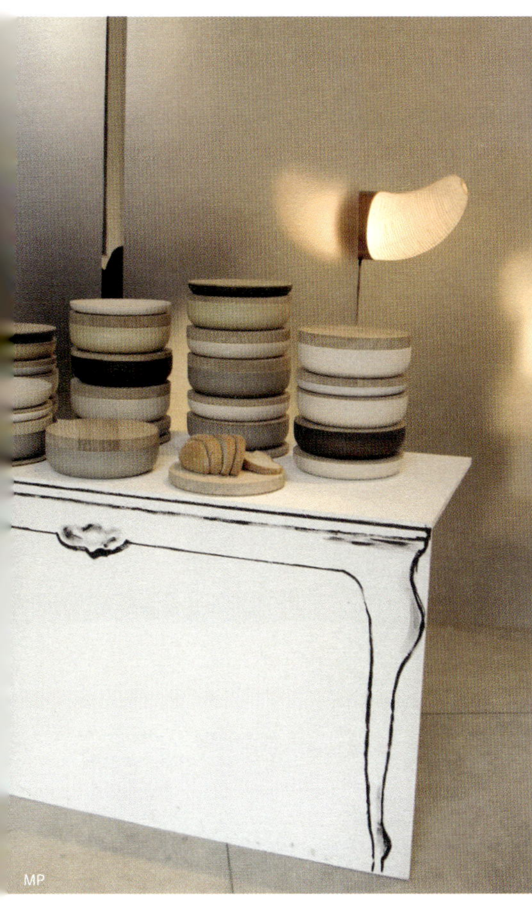

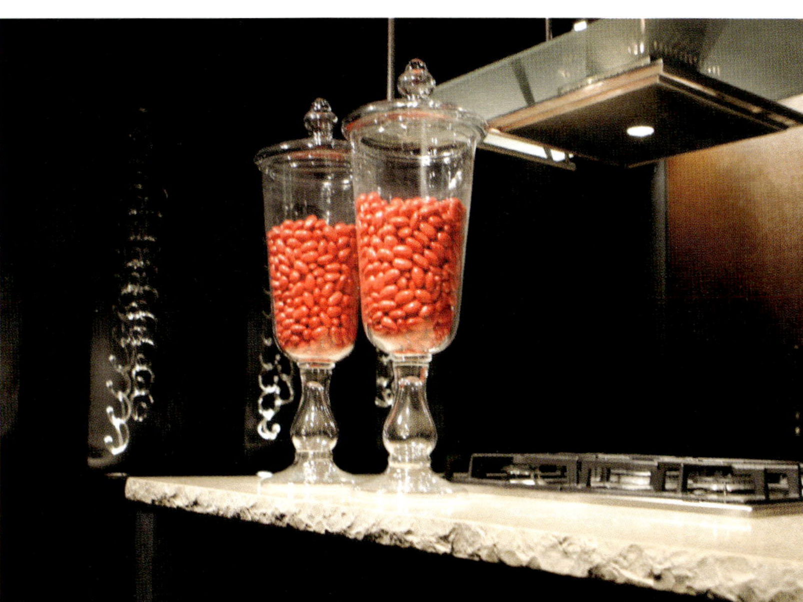

Vincent Van Duysen

Alta - Arros Group

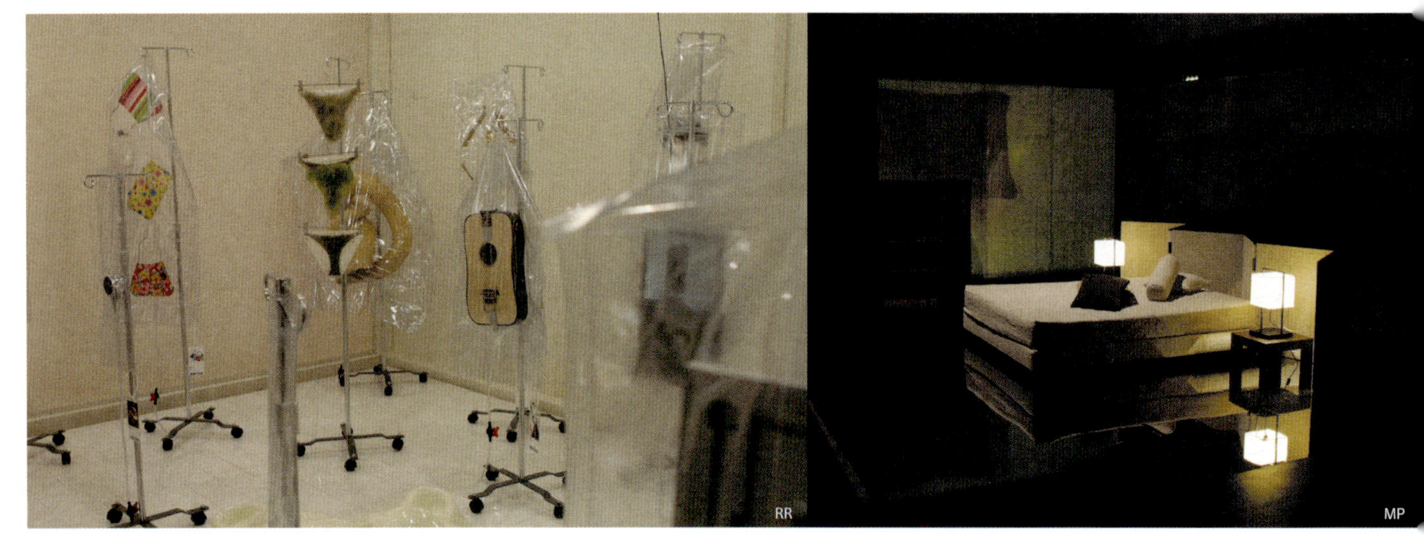

Holon Academic Institute of technology @ Satellite

Armani home collection

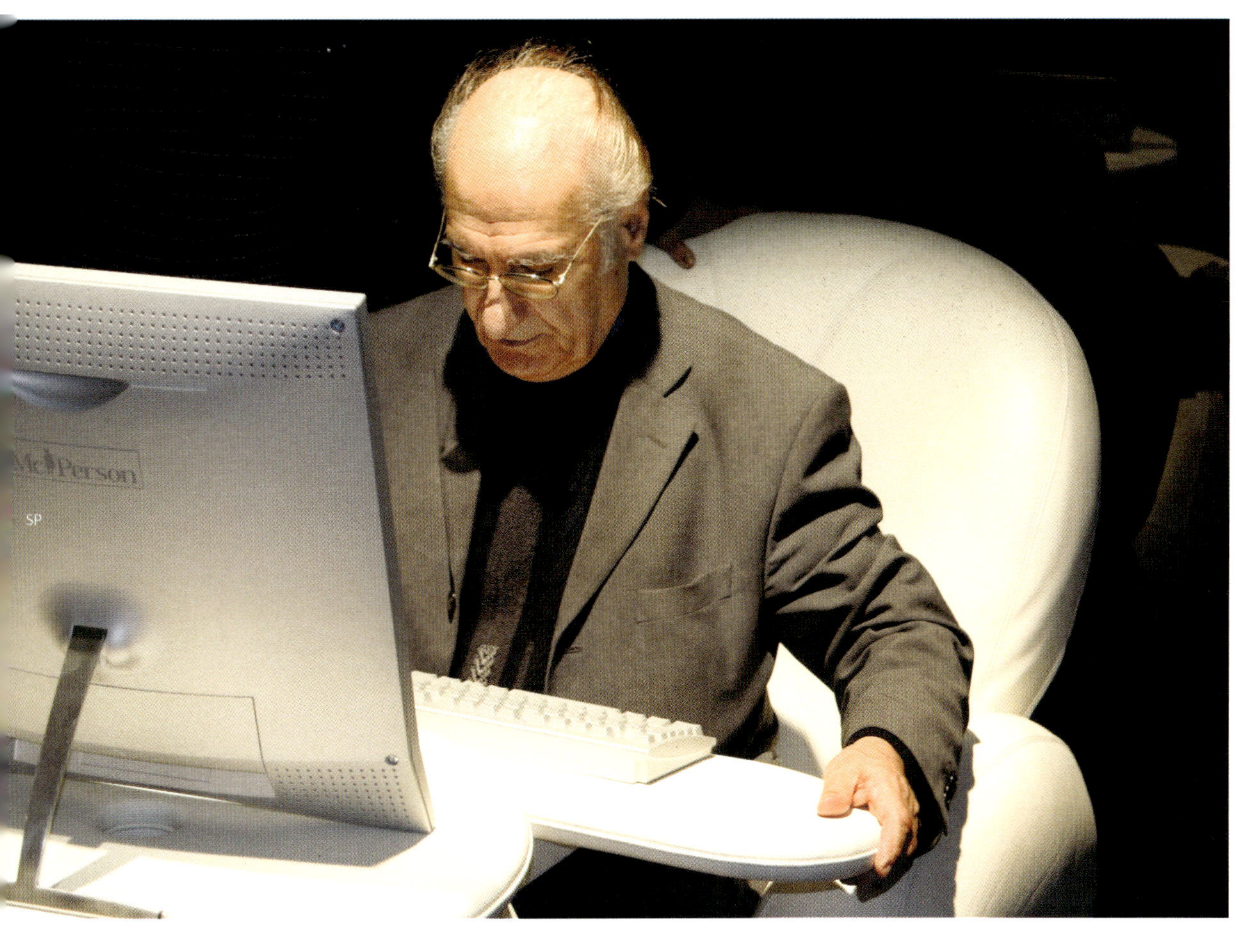

@ Rossi di Albizzate

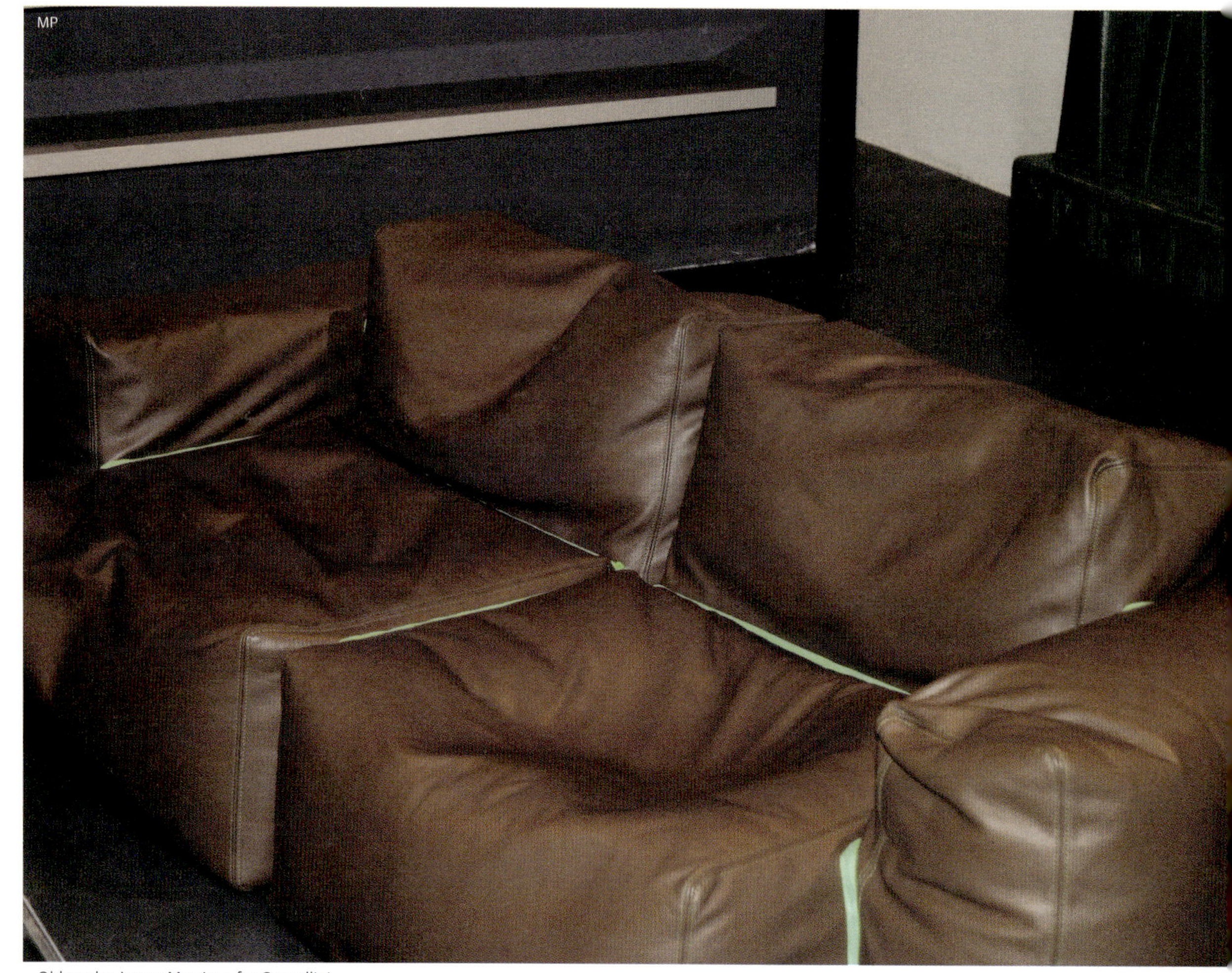

Oblong by Jasper Morrison for Cappellini

Many people commented on the low-energy at Salone this year.

I disagree. I saw many companies eschewing the orgiastic, self-inflated,

cult-of-personality bacchanalia of recent years, who were instead returning

to the business of focusing on strategies and products.

This can only be a positive thing. In fact there were a few notable examples of this,

namely James Irvine's chair for Thonet – quintessentially Irvine and Thonet

at the same time – as well as Jasper Morrison's stuffed armchairs and sofas

for the 'new' Cappellini – their iconic and unusual simplicity is just the kind

of low-investment product that company needs right now.

Jozeph Forakis

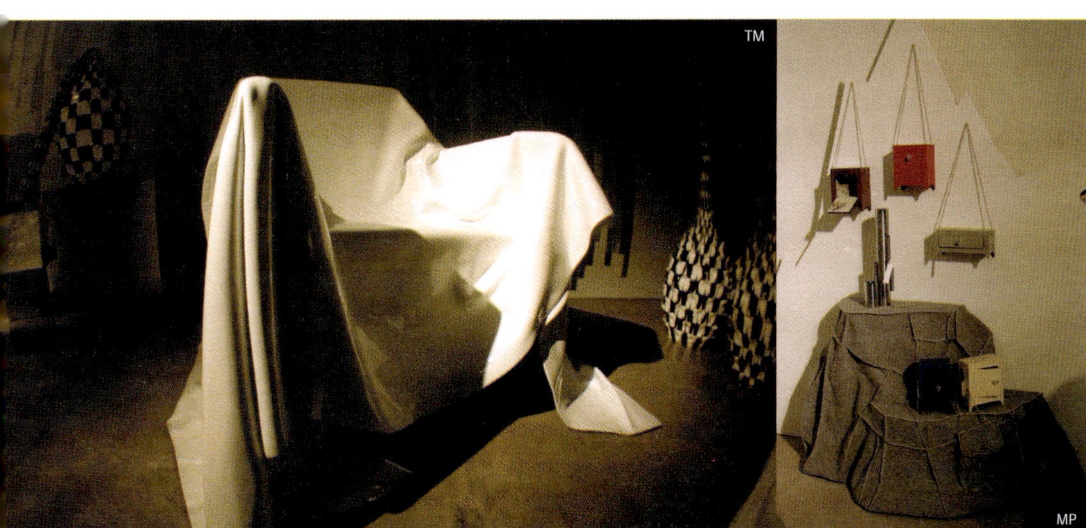

@ Dilmos   KiK

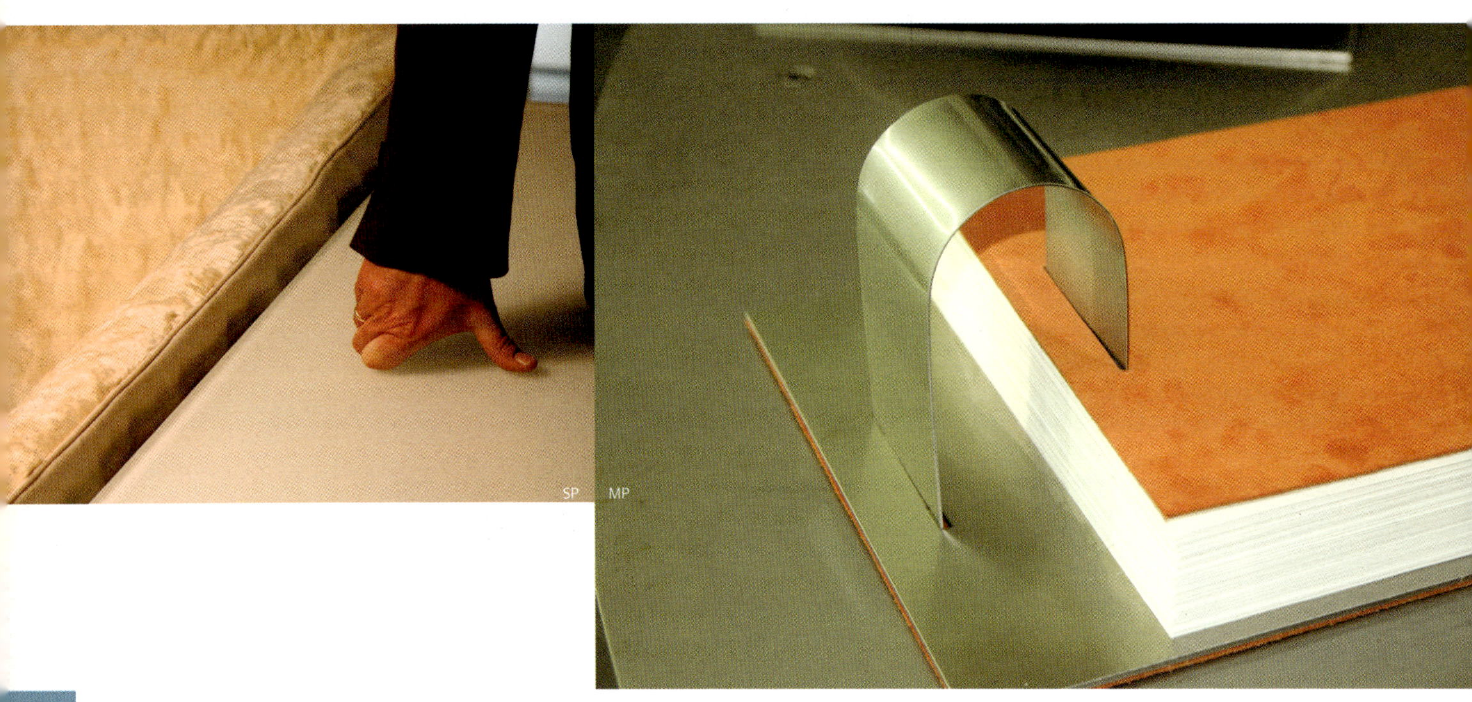

5 punto 6

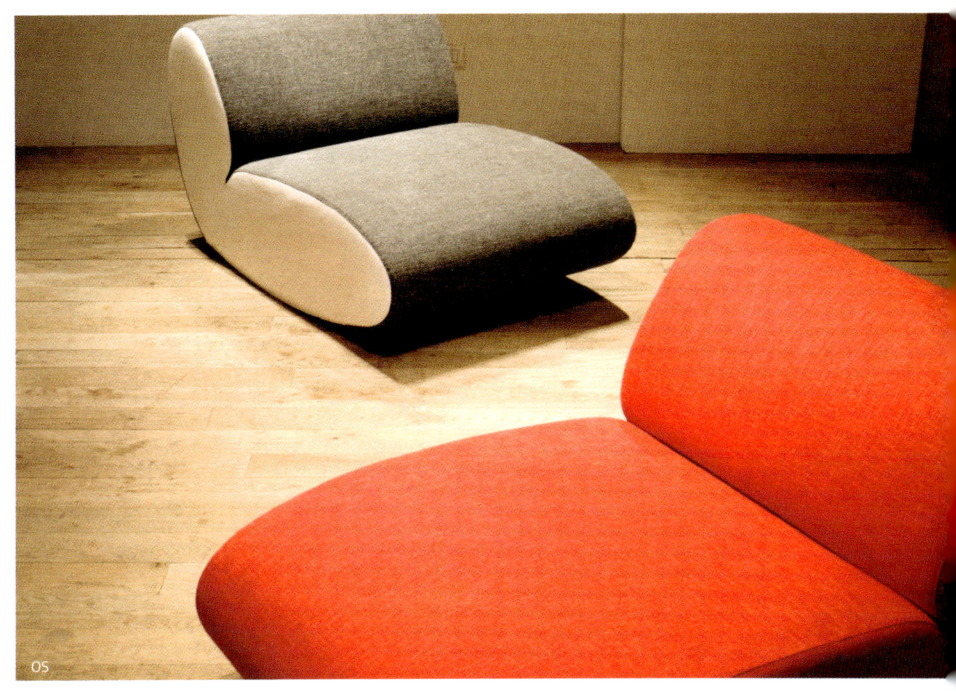

Maarten Kusters

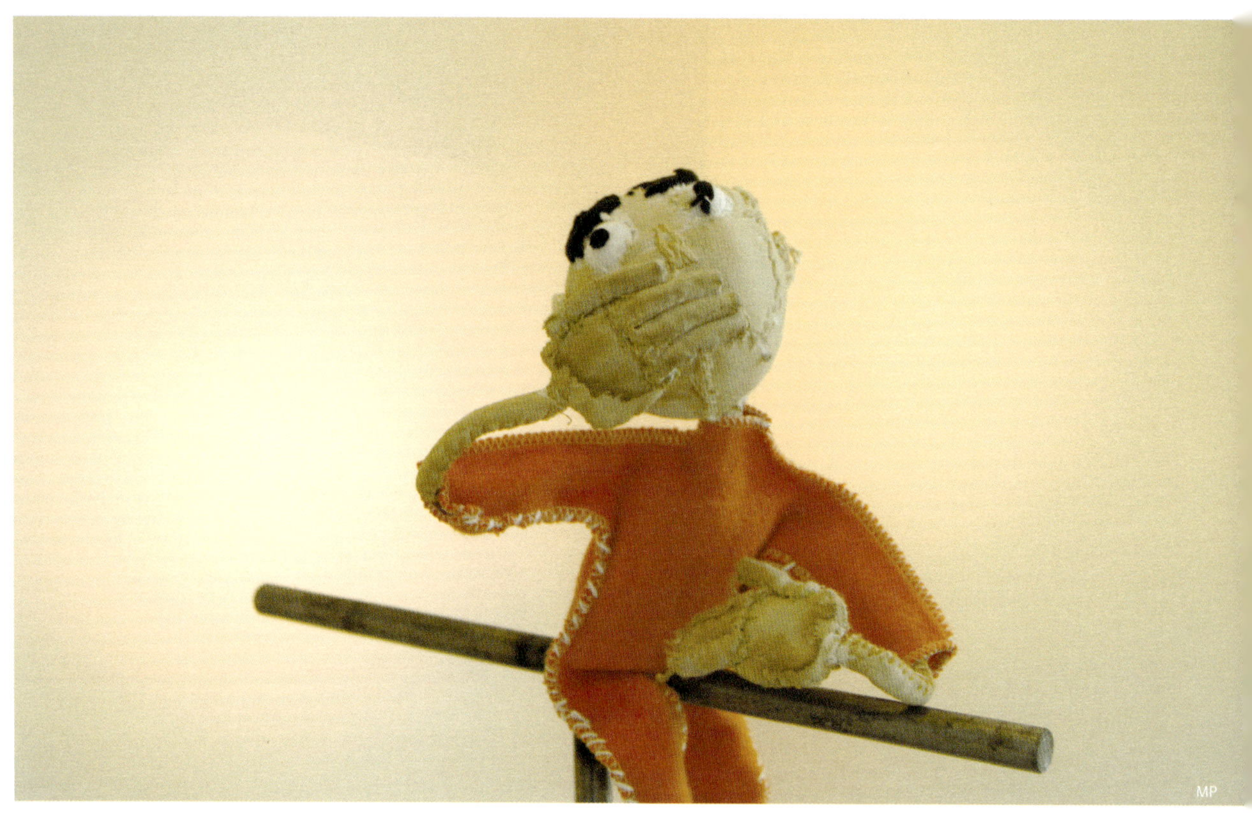

Cassia Maceira @ Dovetusai

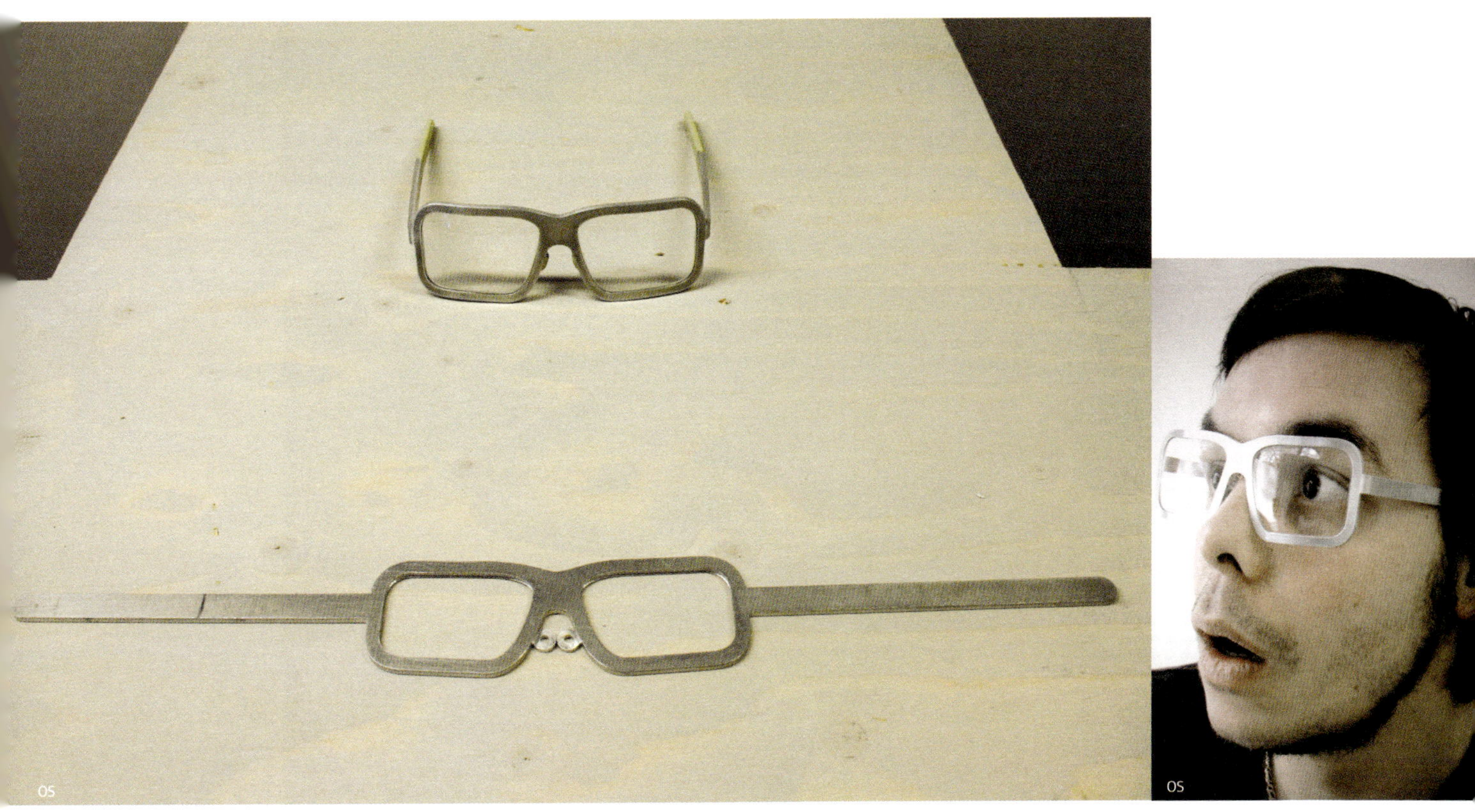

Egill Kalevi Karlsson @ Design Academy Eindhoven

I will never design a car, the tipical macho symbol.
If I'd be obliged I will project a car completely different
of the ones we see in the streets.

droog design

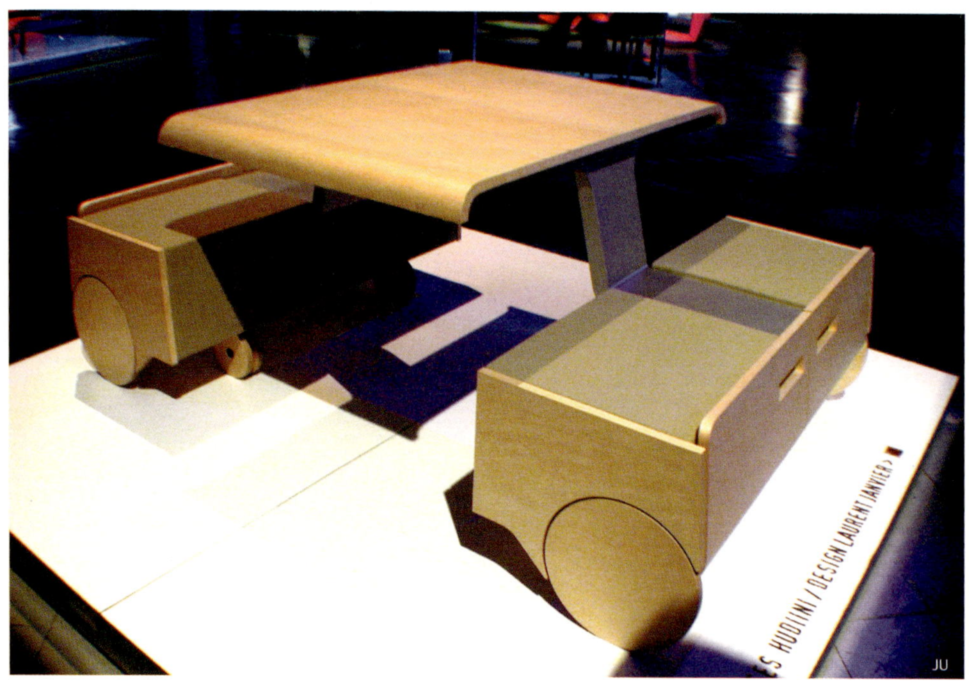

F1 Laurent Janvier @ VIA

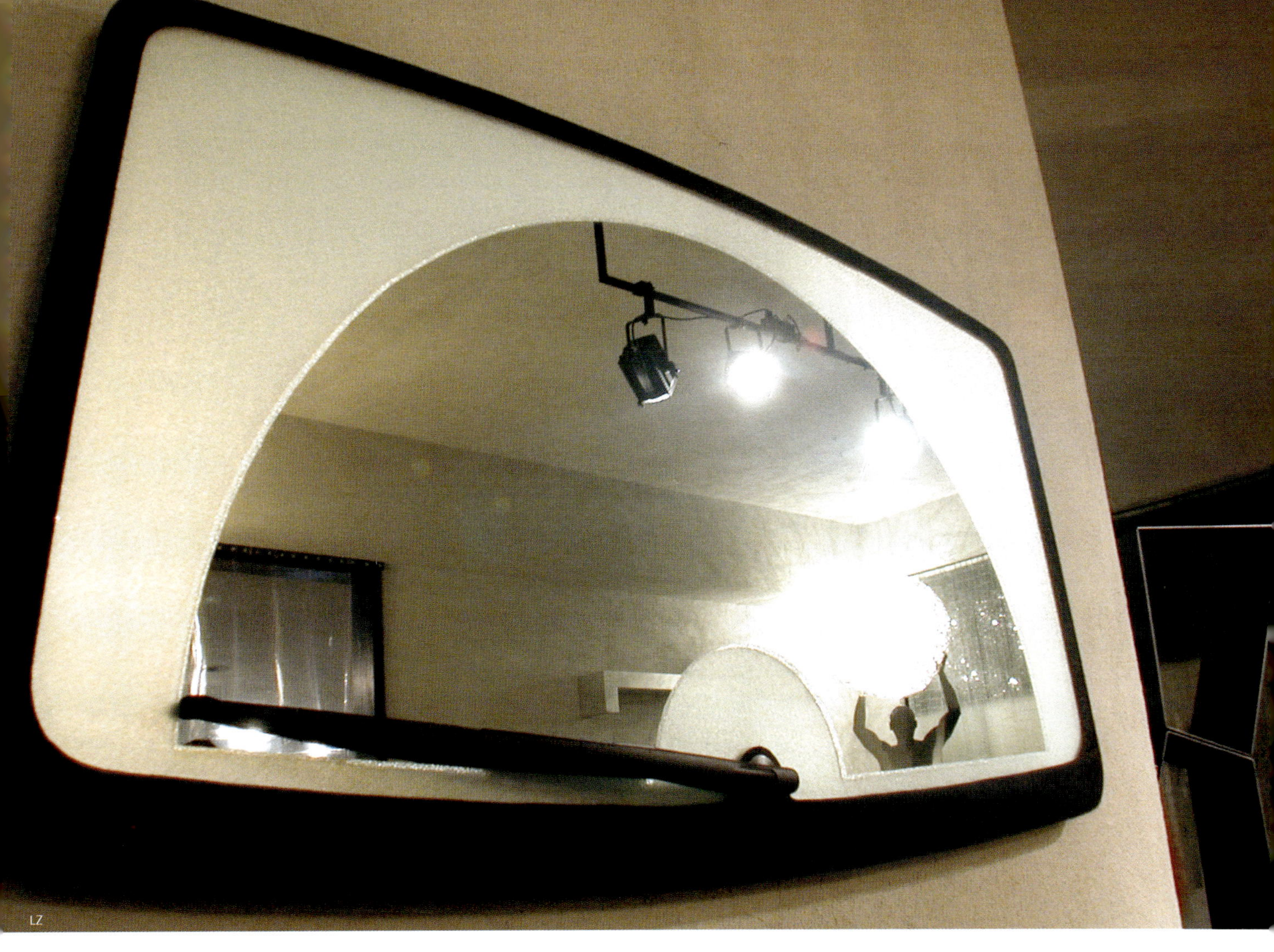

@ Dilmos

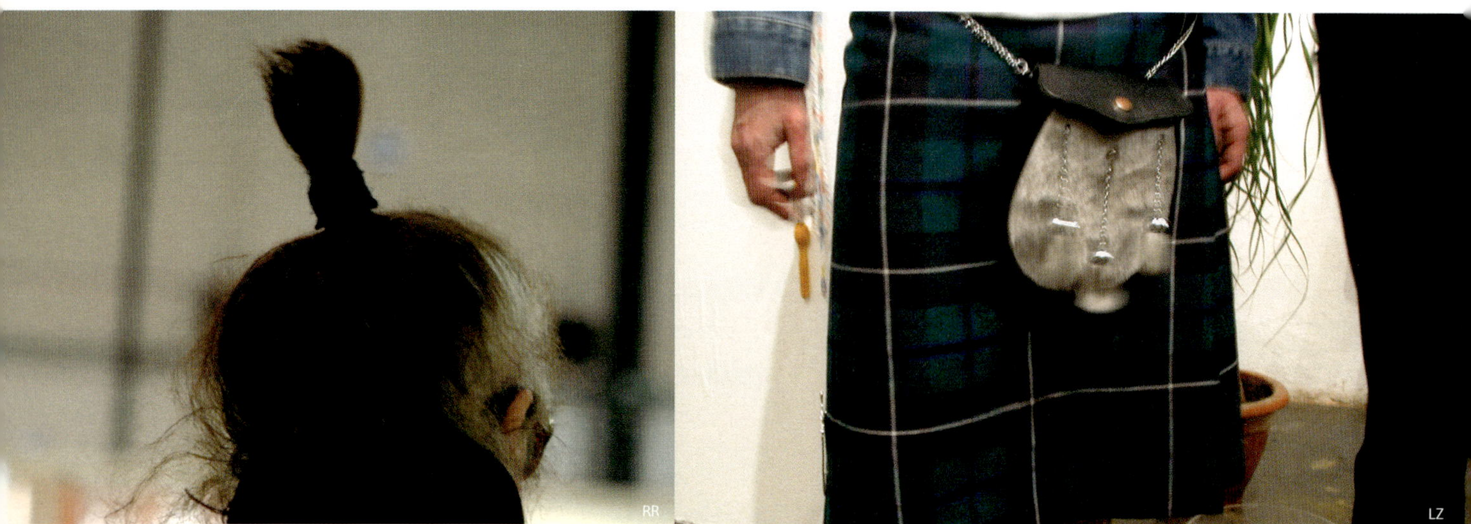

@ Designer Block

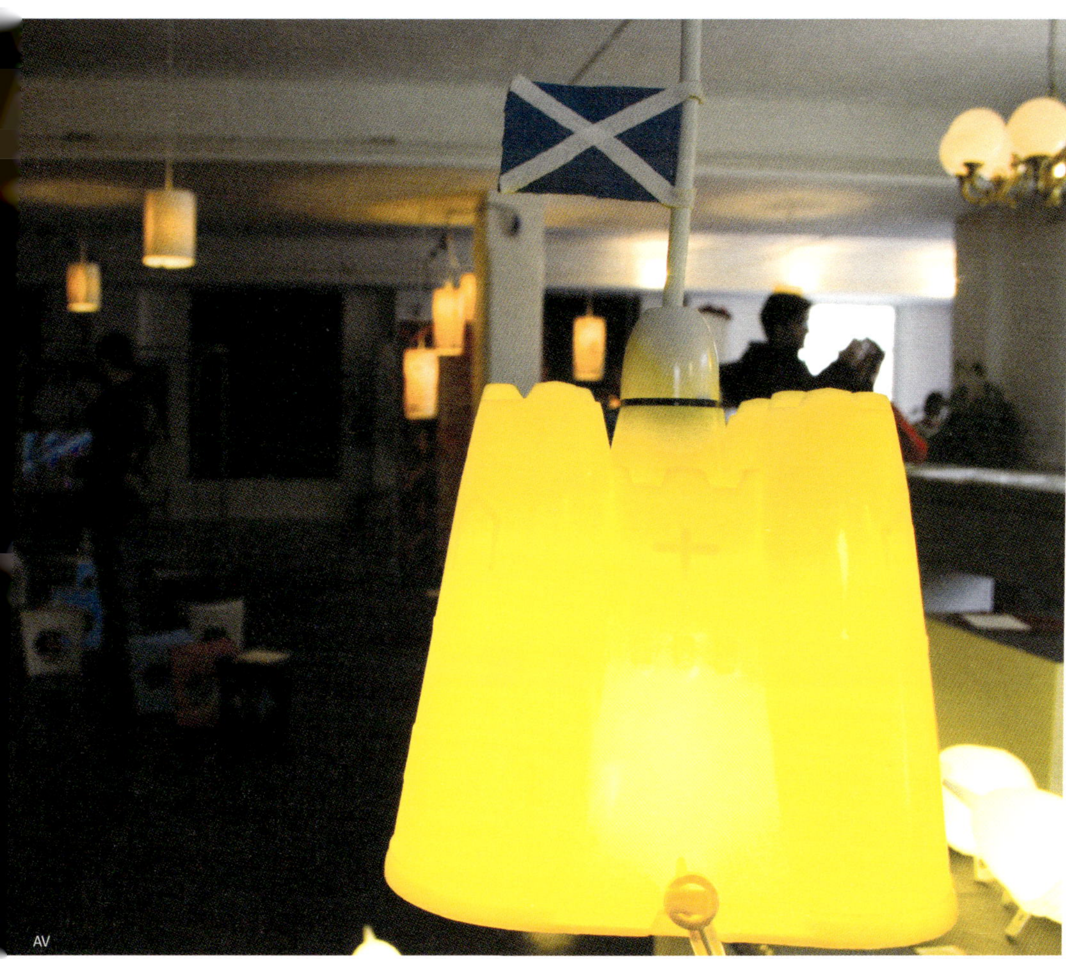

@ Designer Block

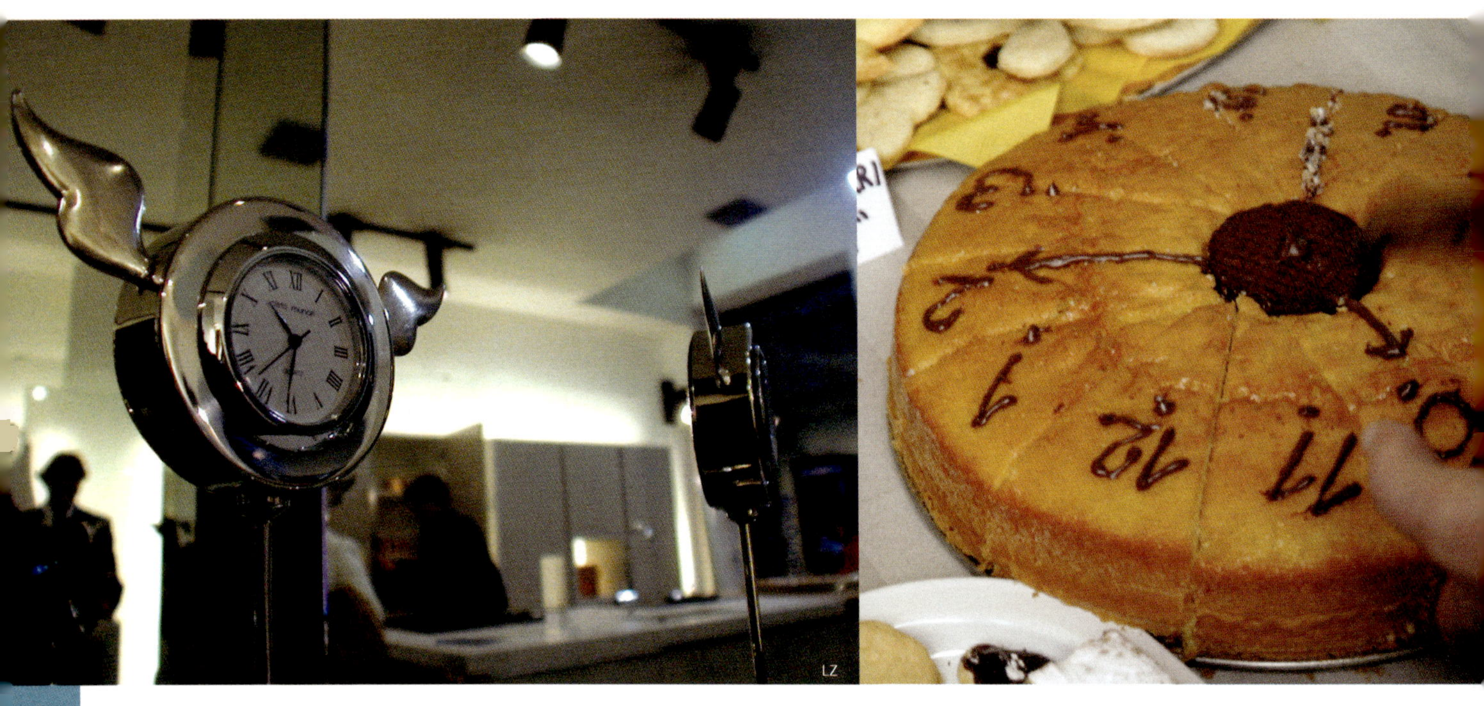

@ Domus Nova

Accademia delle Belle Arti

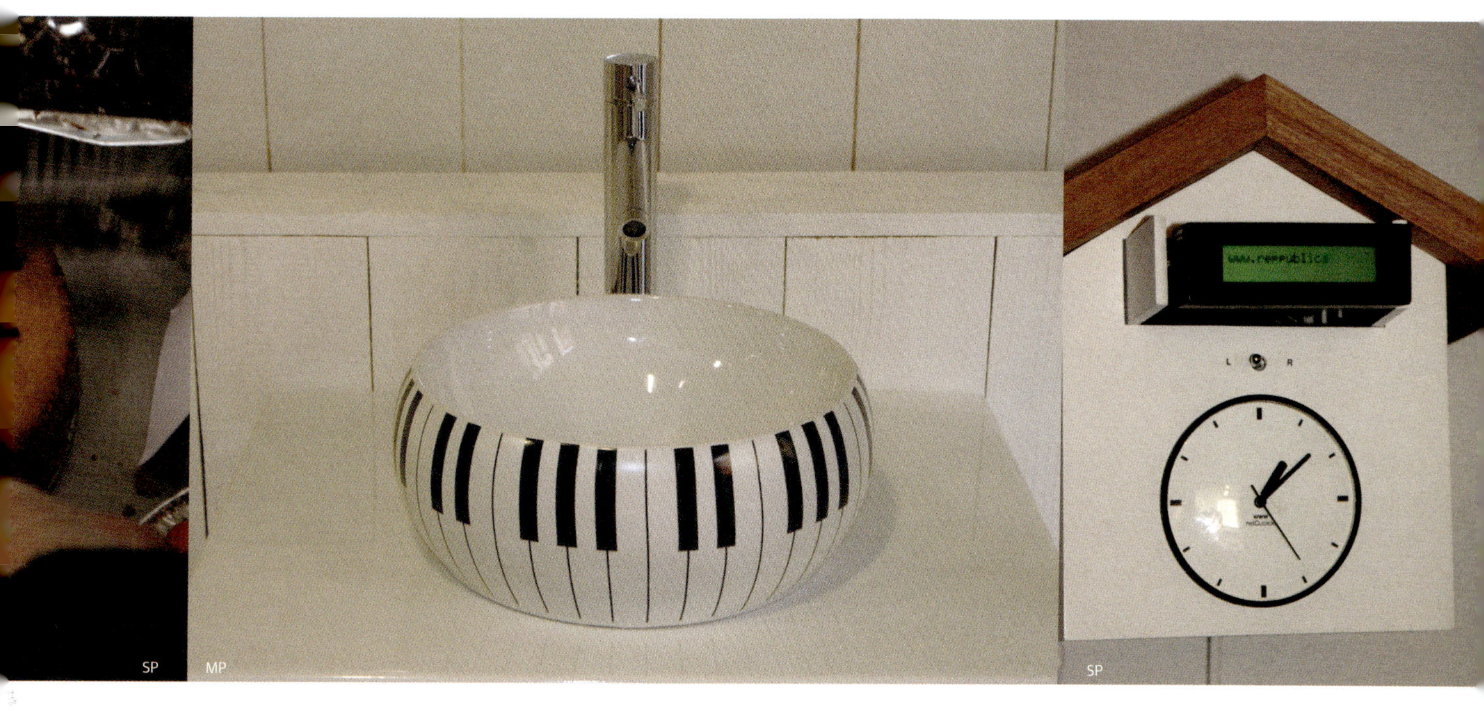

Joker Dinamo   netCuskoo@ Designersblock

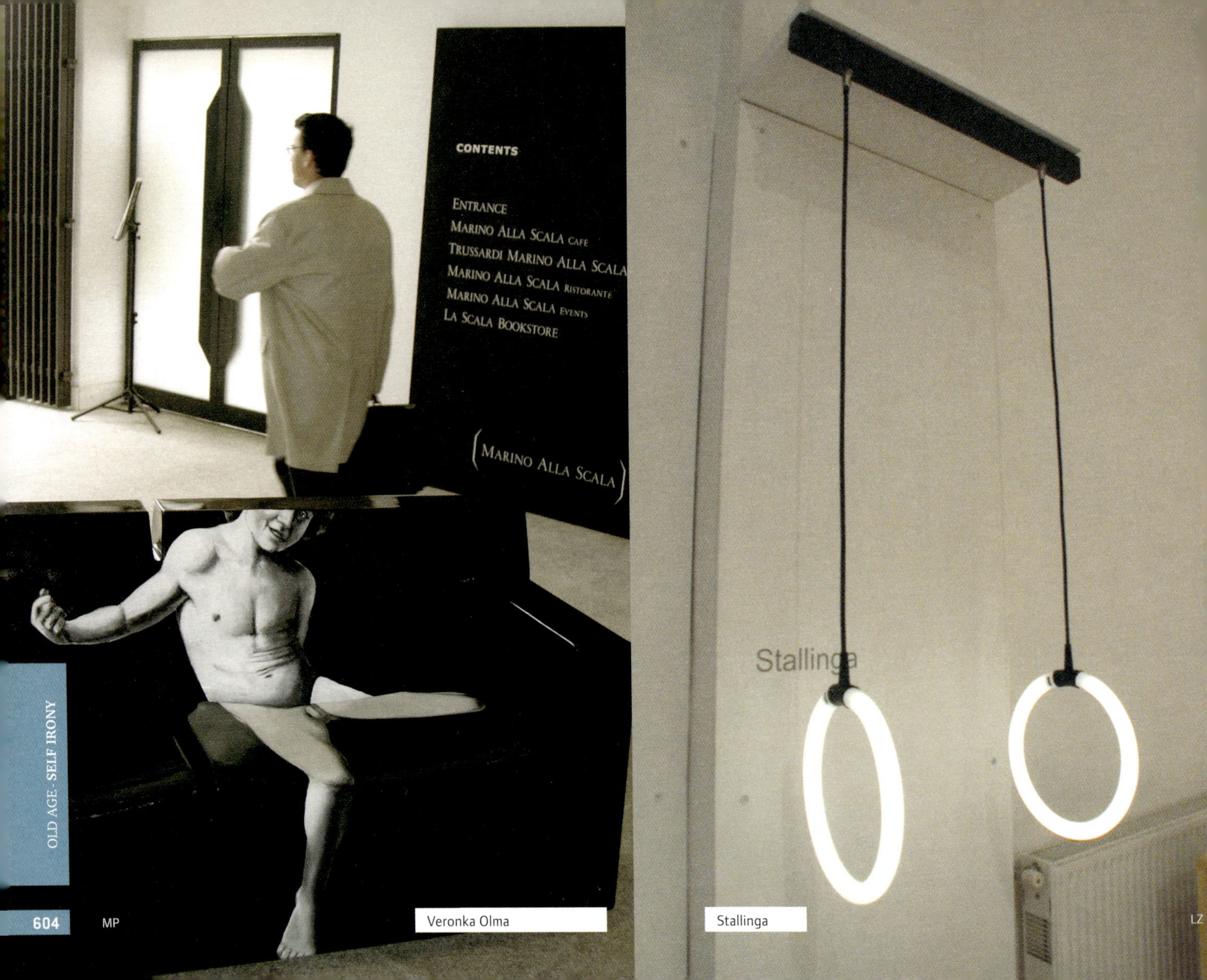

Veronka Olma

Stallinga

LZ

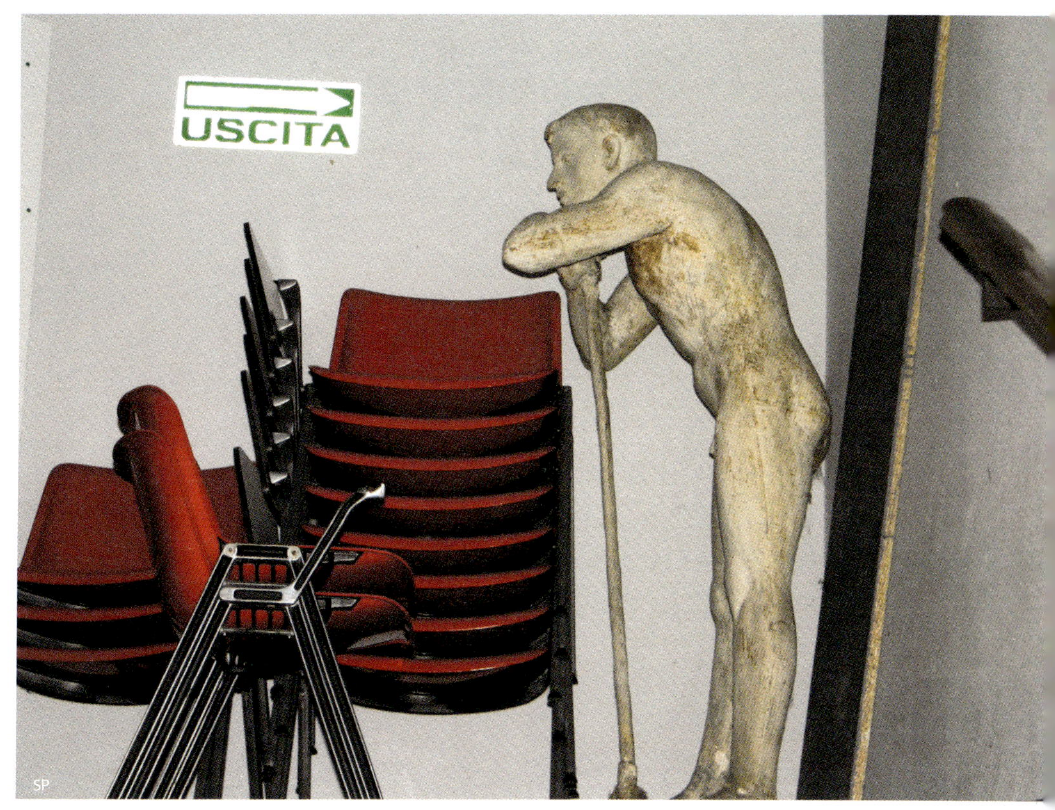

DesignPlaza

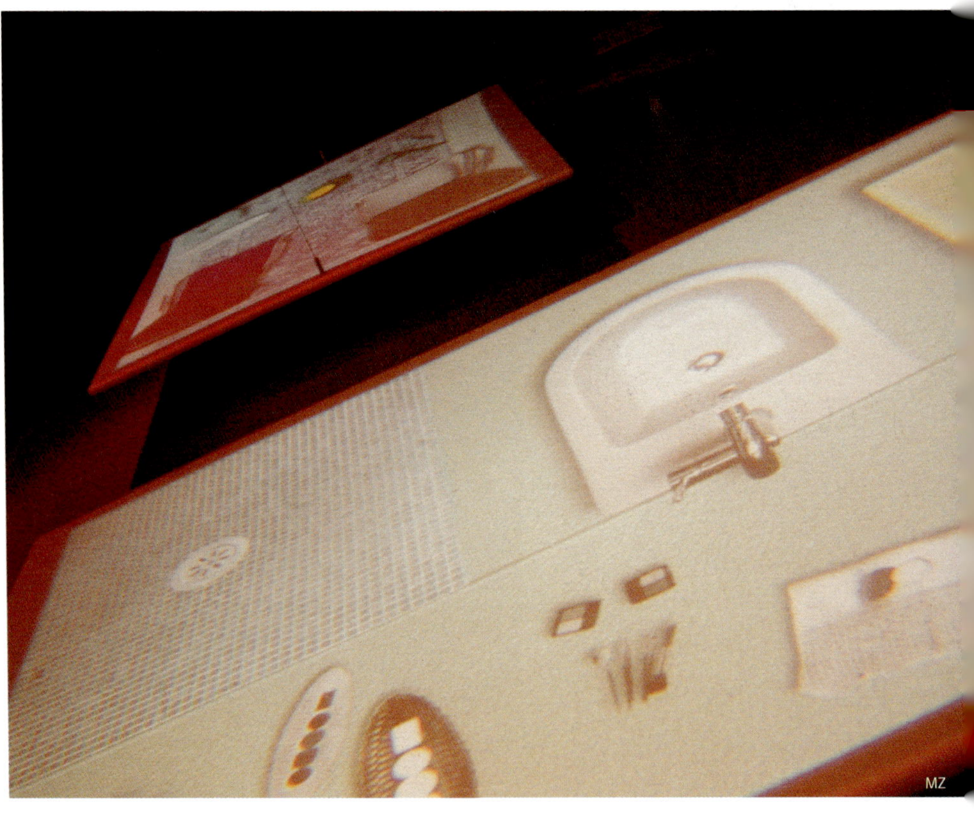

Axor

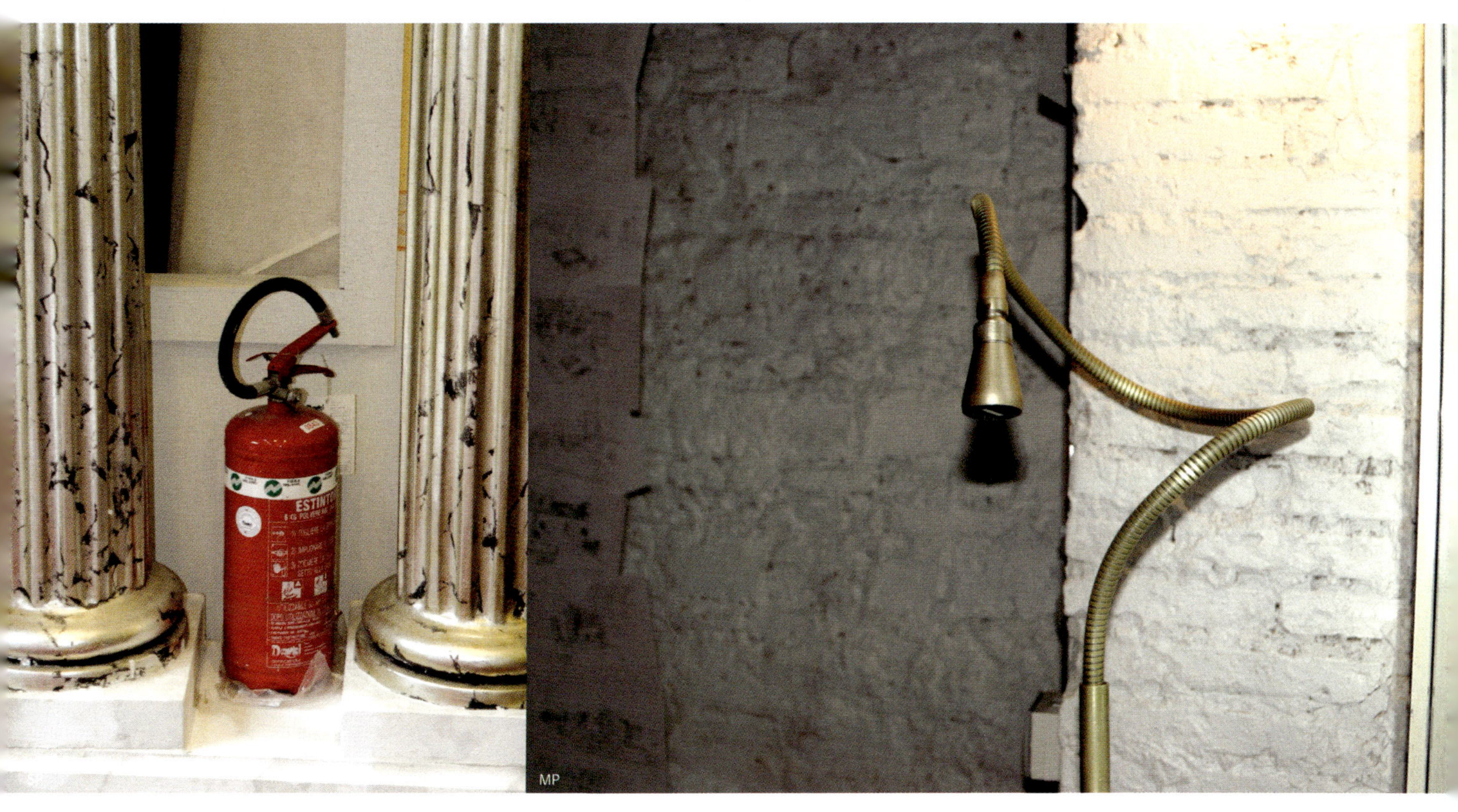

"Yogi" by Ari Tarvainen for Officine Creative

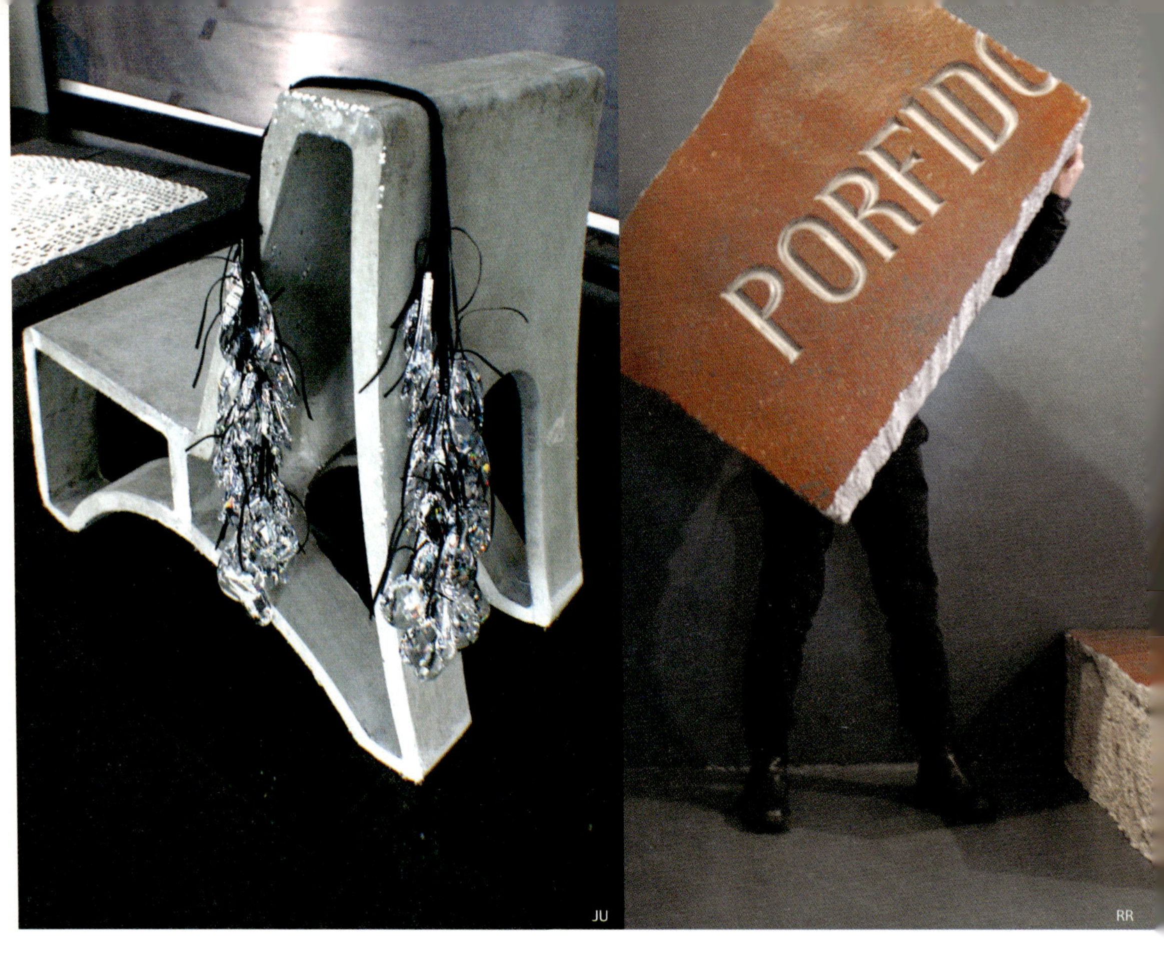

Thijs Bakker Ontwerpen @ Design Academy Eindhoven

Massolo - Piero Gilardi Gufram/Cappellini

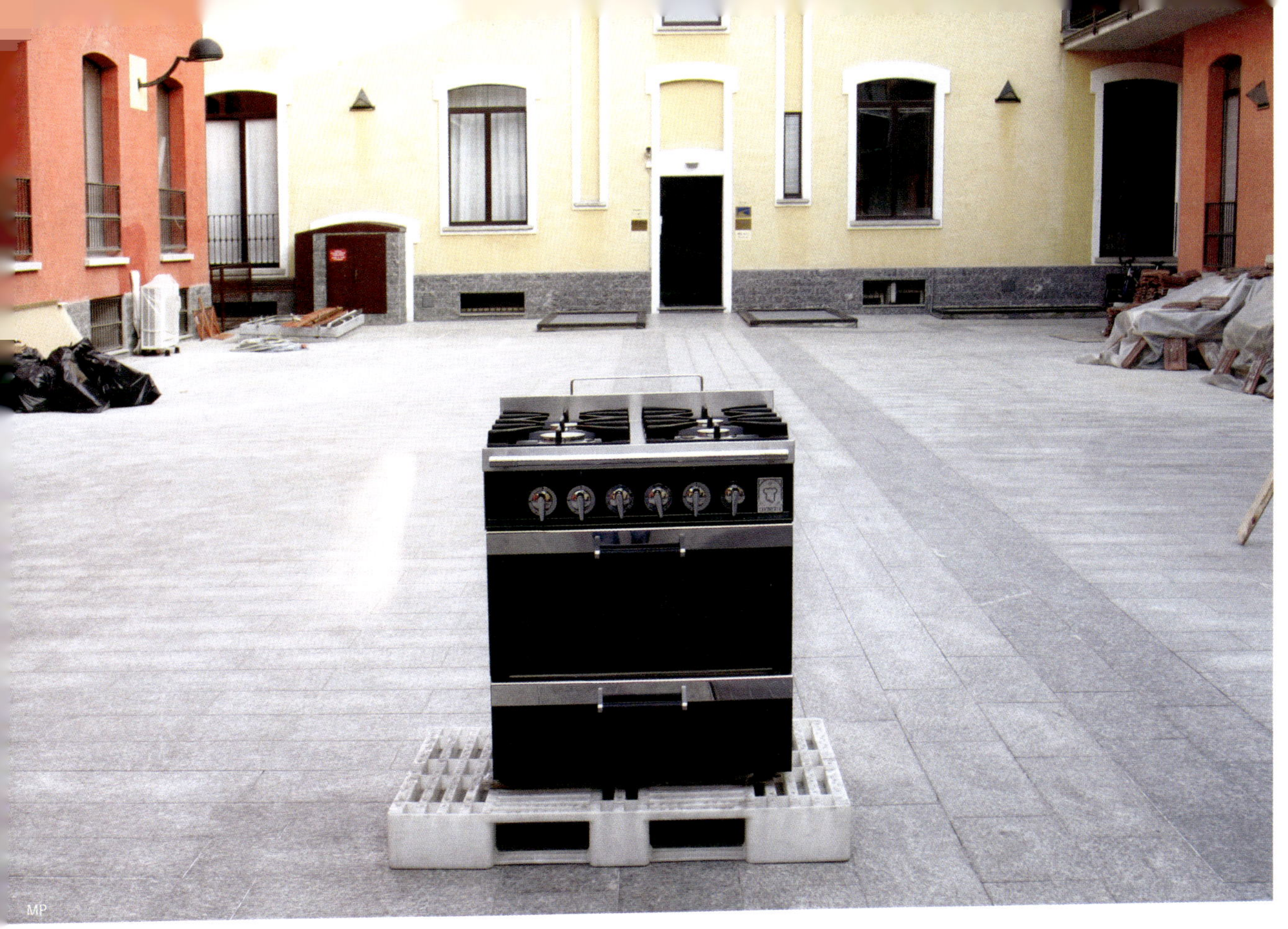

Cucineria Gourmet

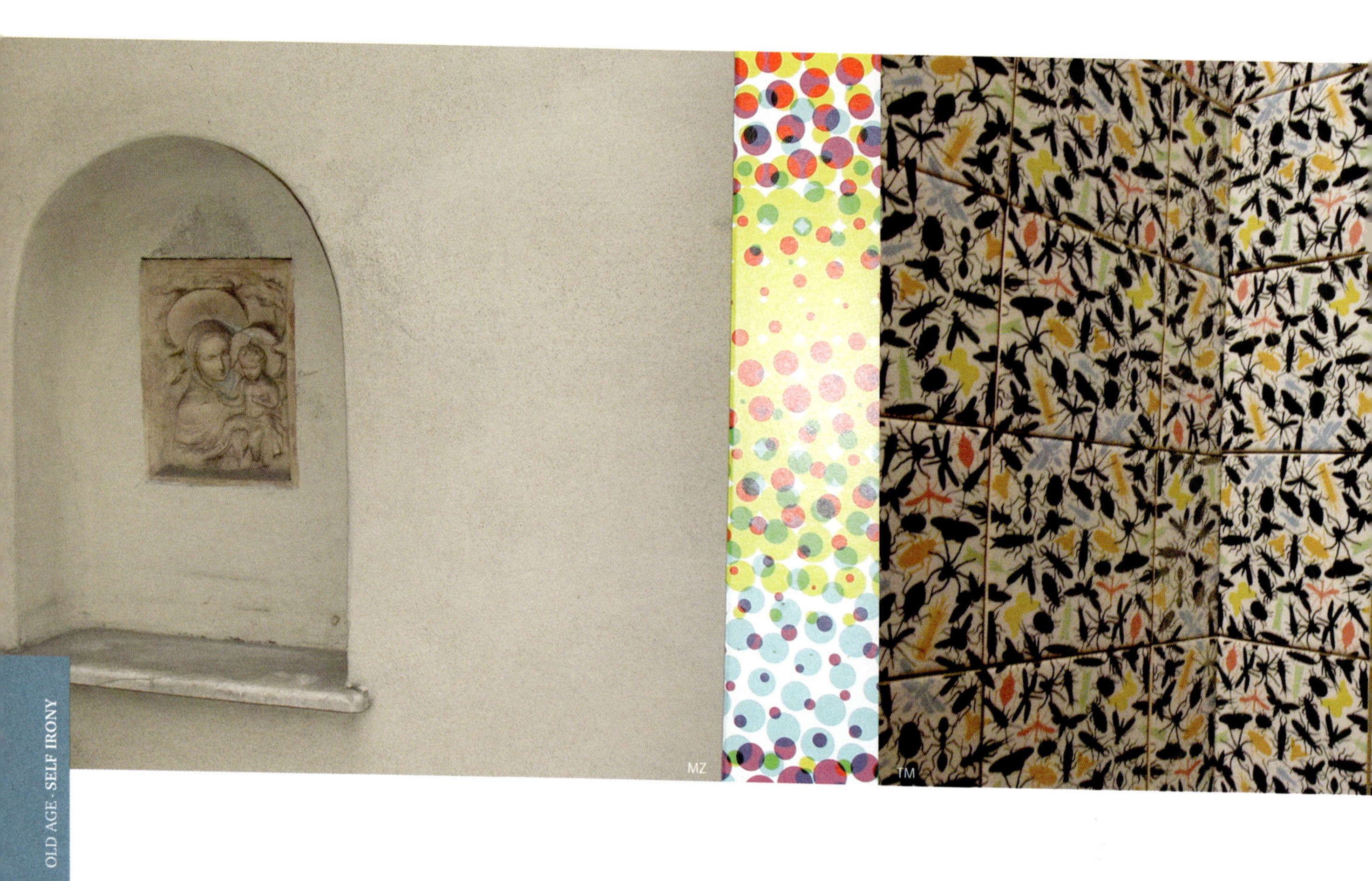

Internos

Studio Job

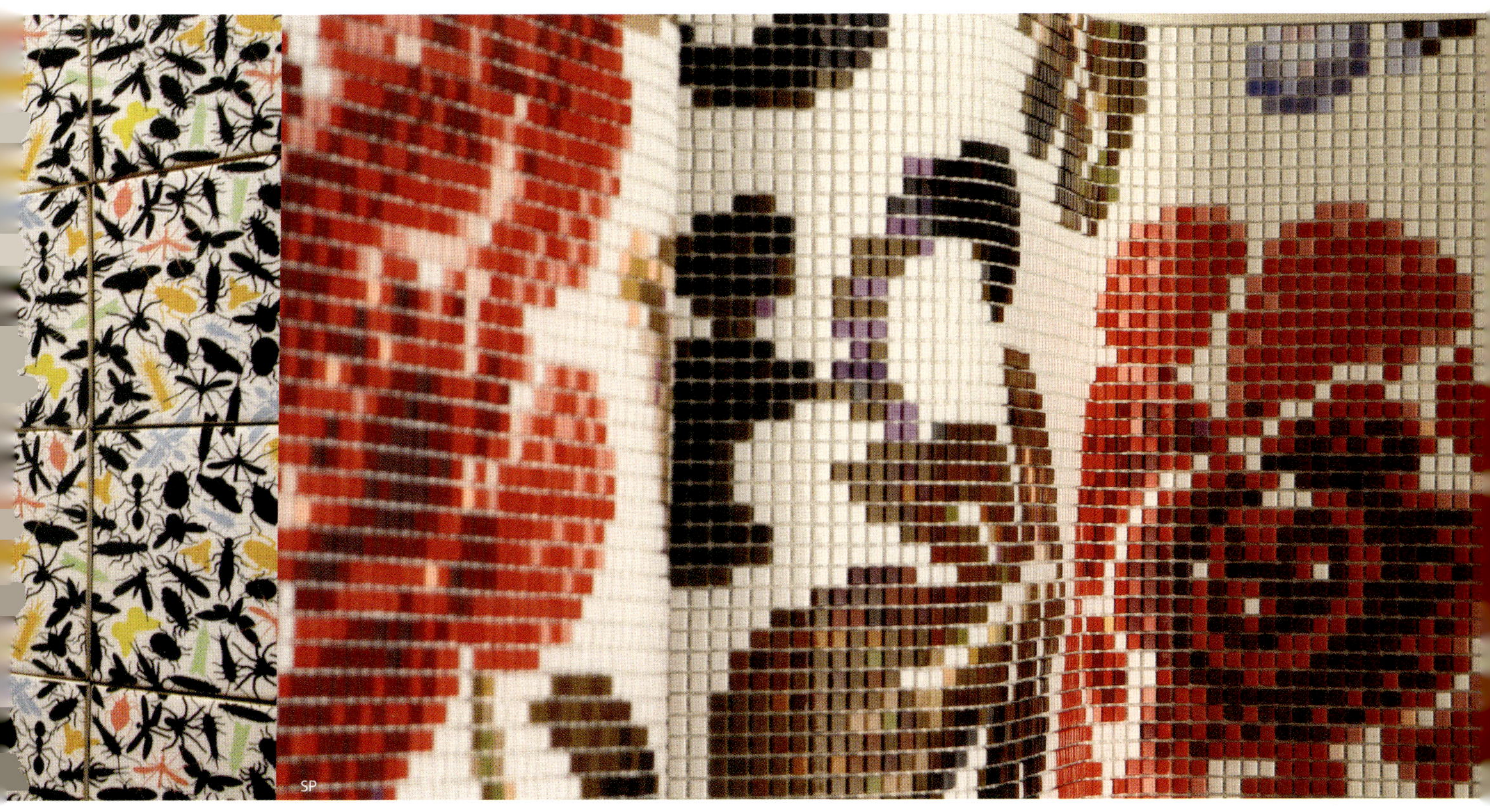

Bisazza 25 fiori

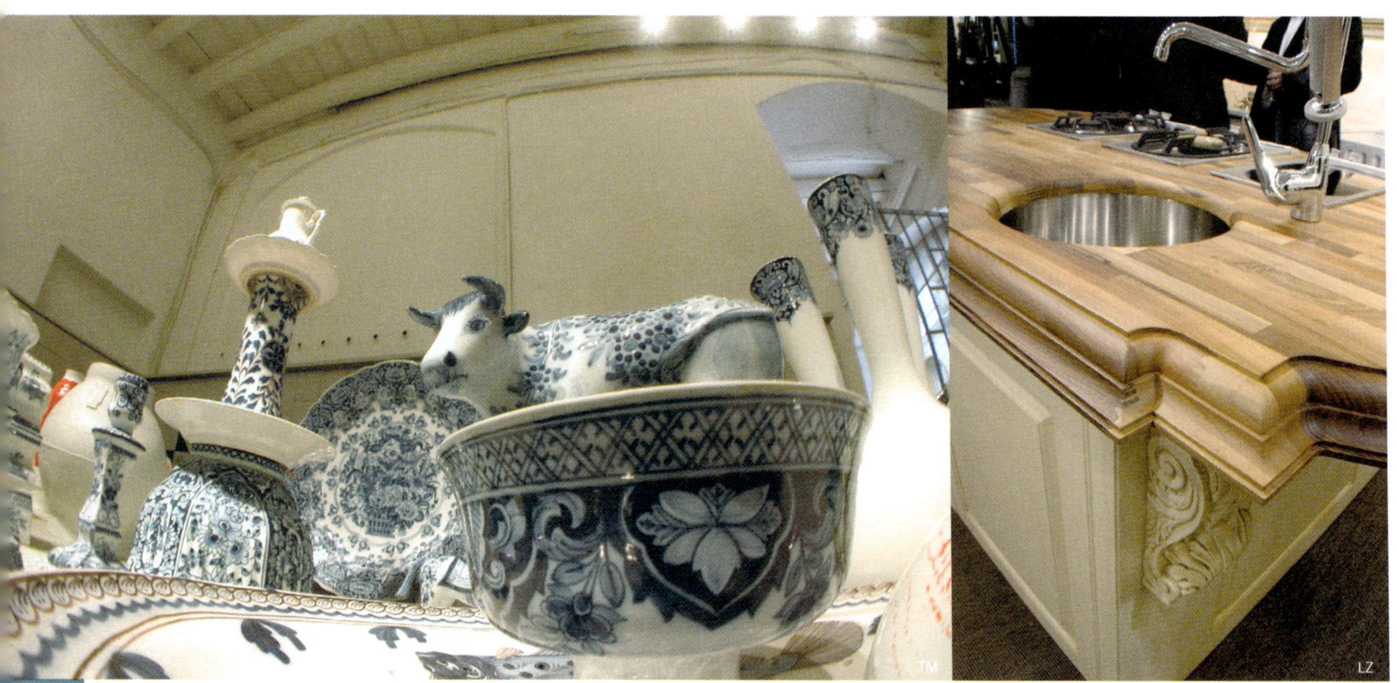

DomusNova

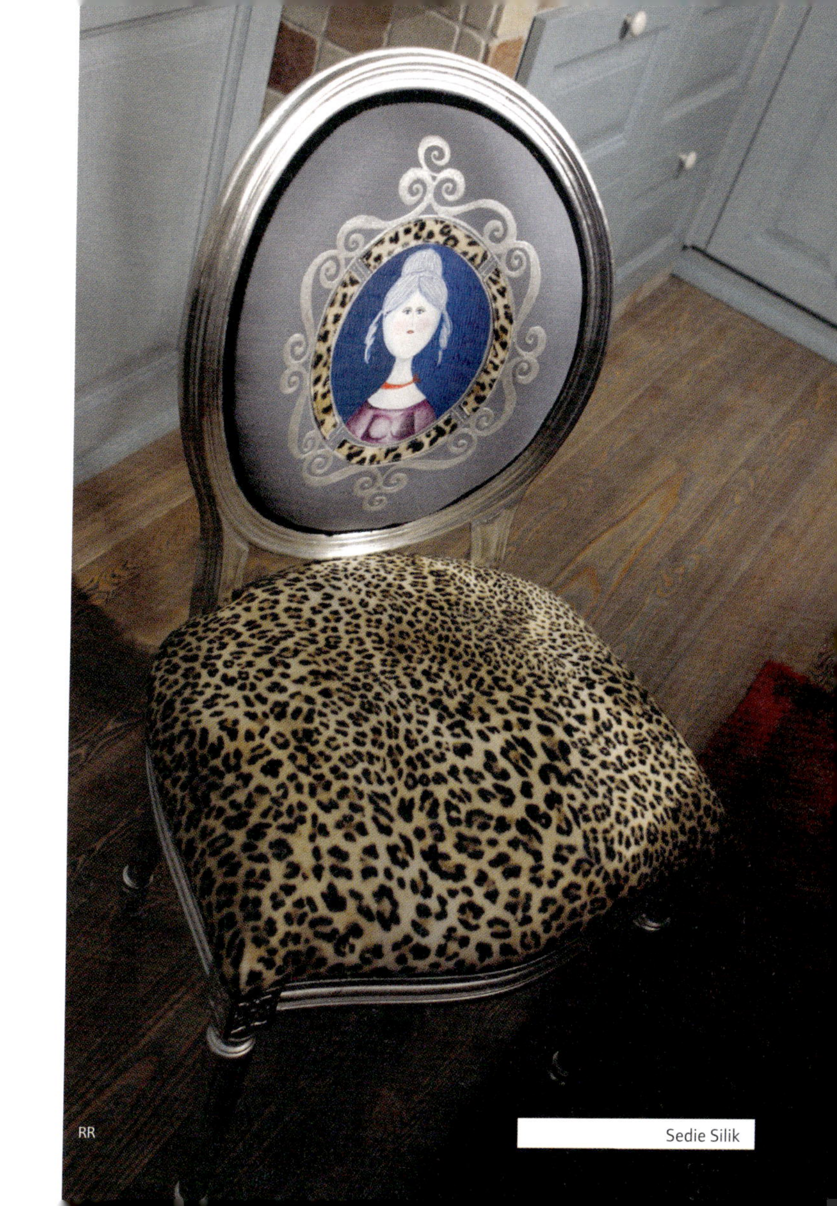

Sedie Silik

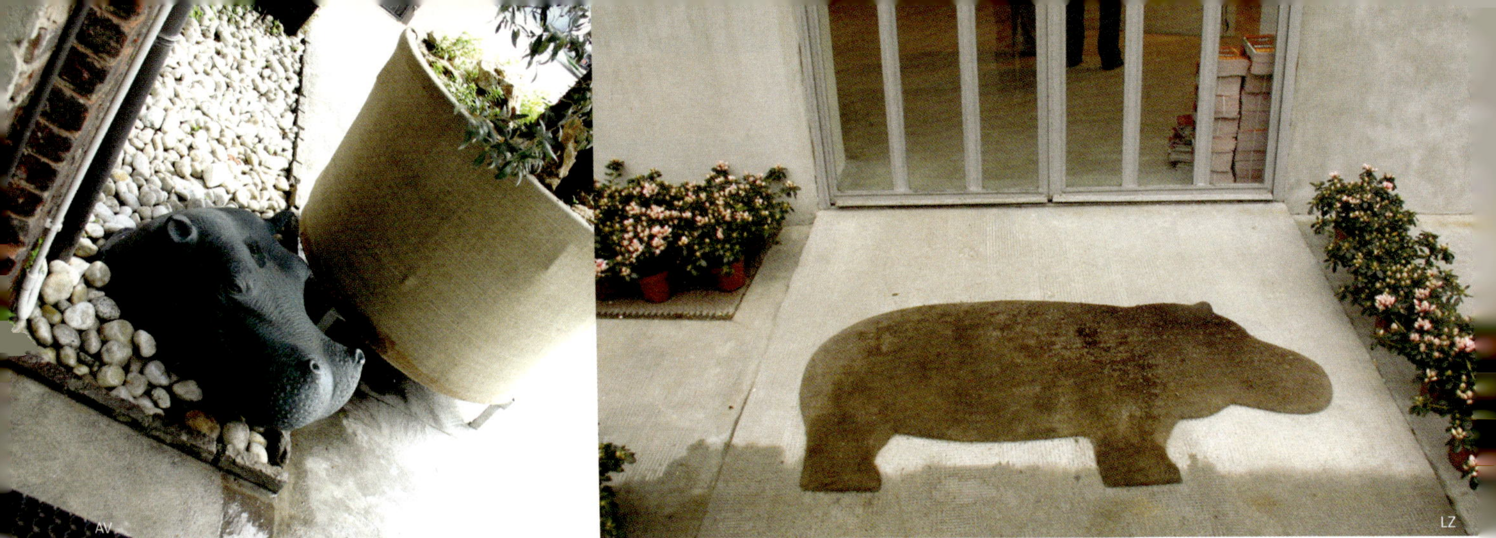

ADI

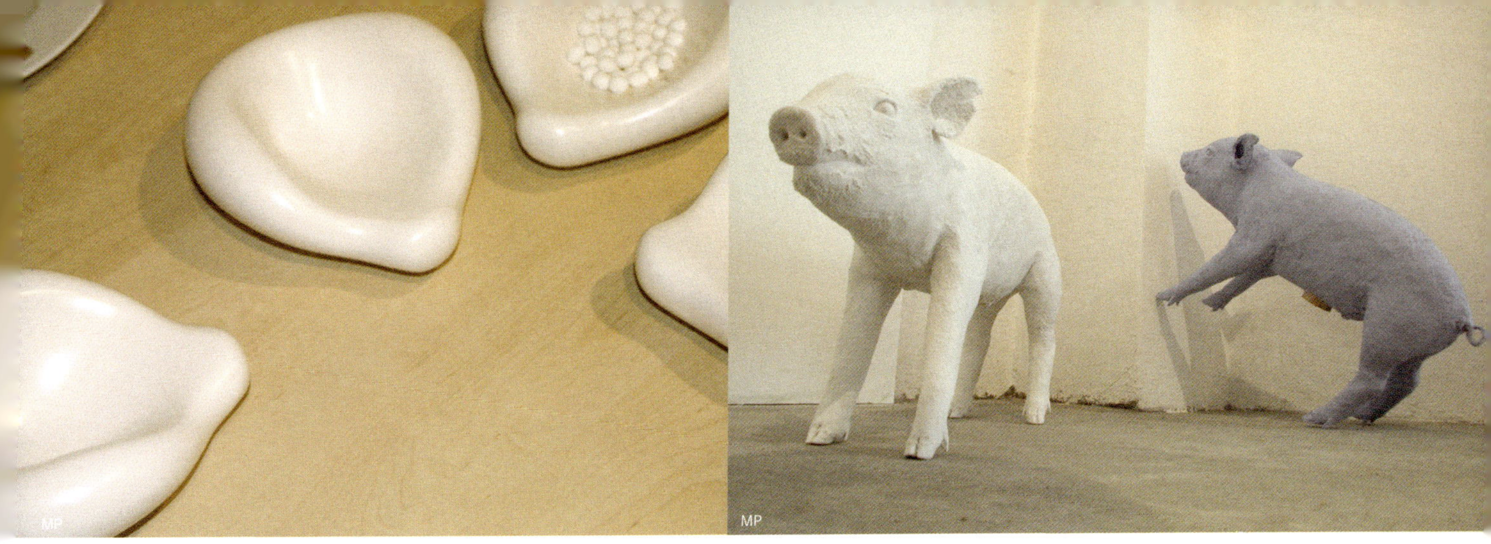

satellite

Harry Allen

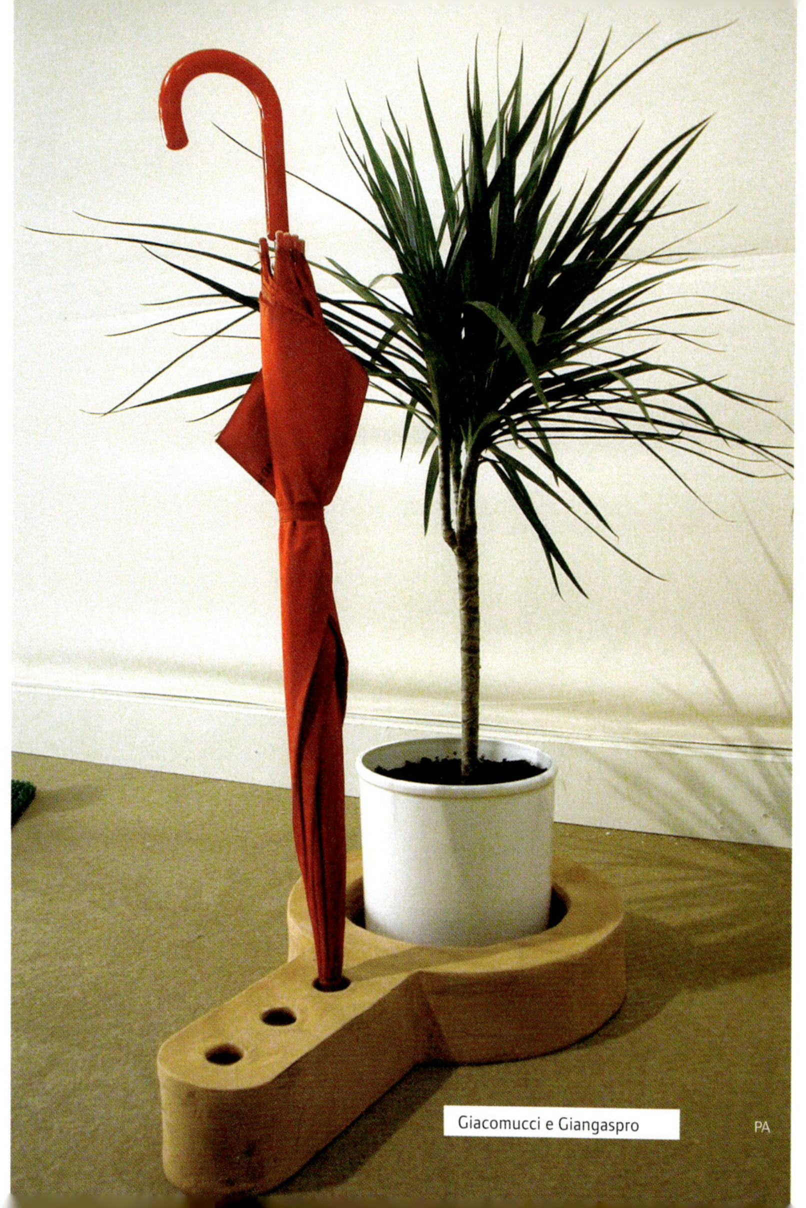

Giacomucci e Giangaspro

PA

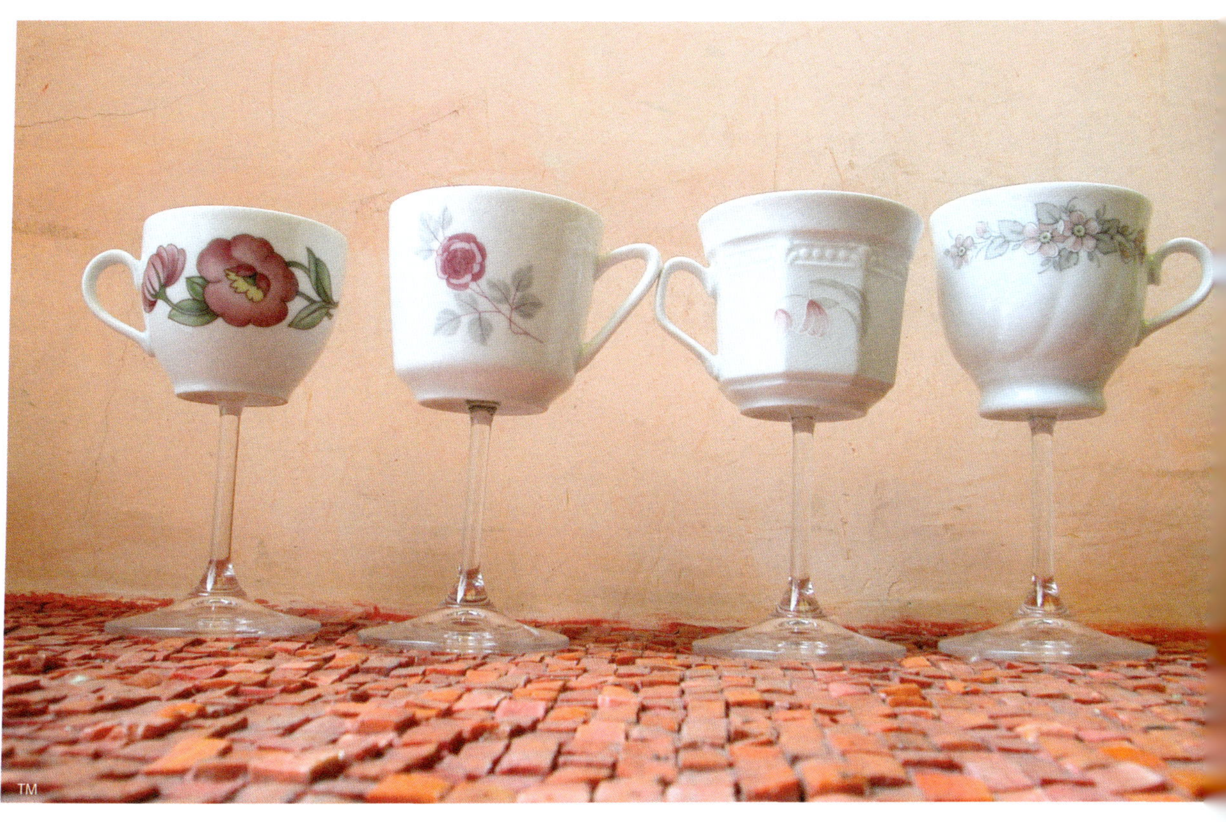

TM

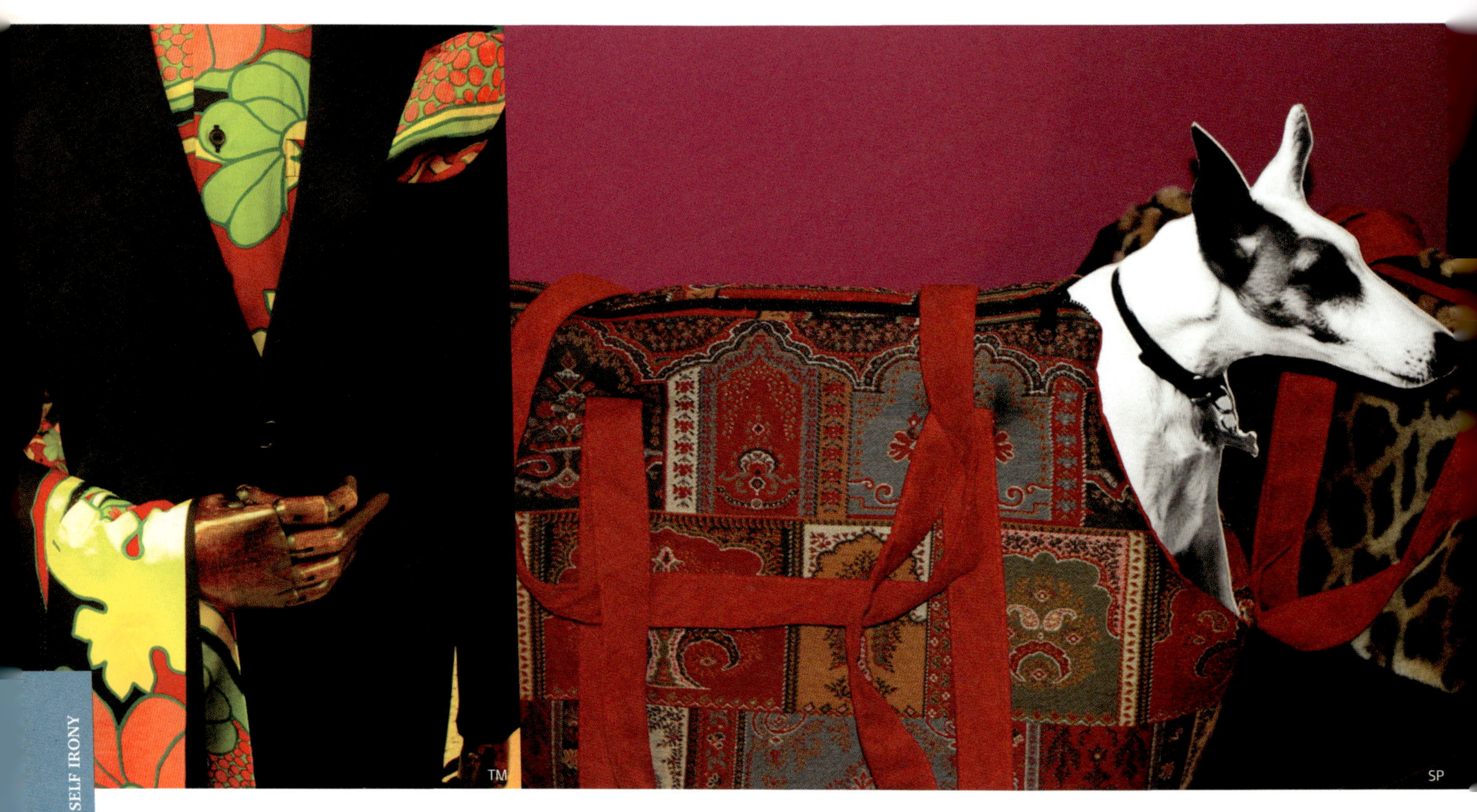

Etro

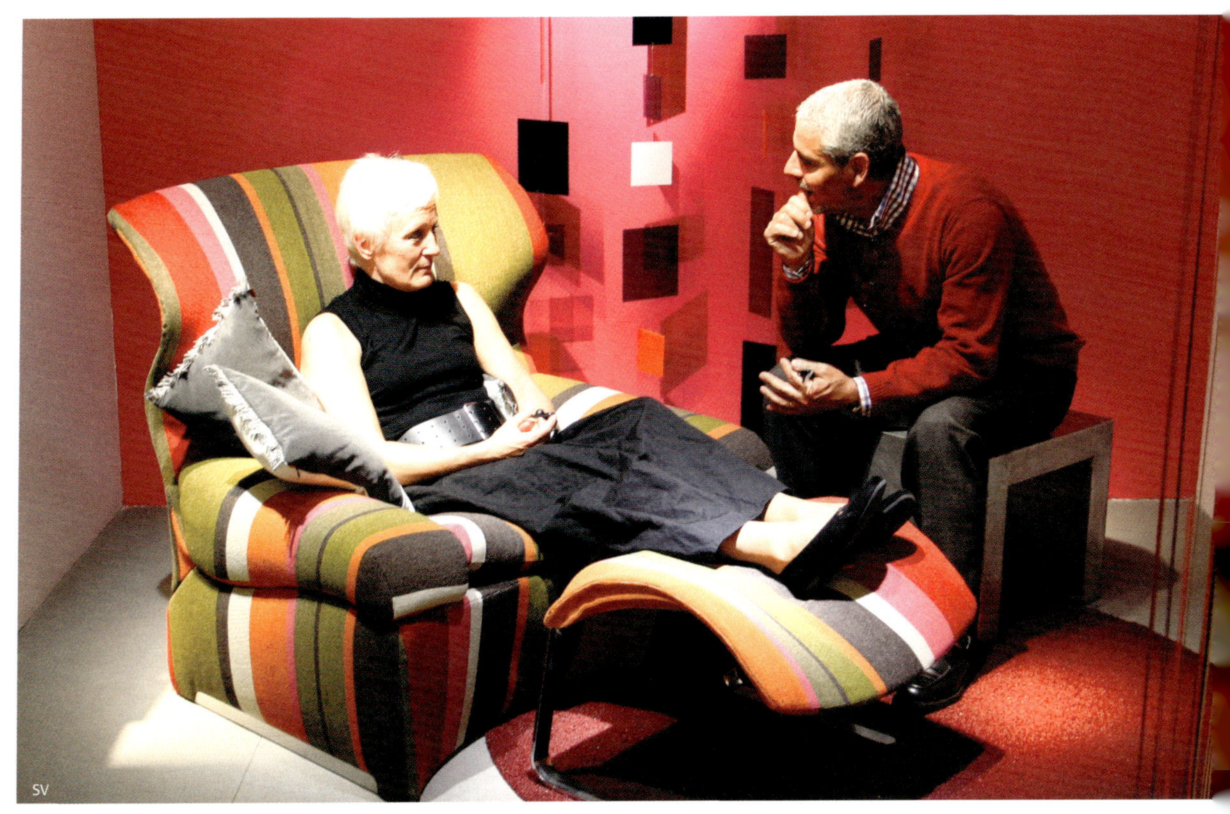

@ Designersblock

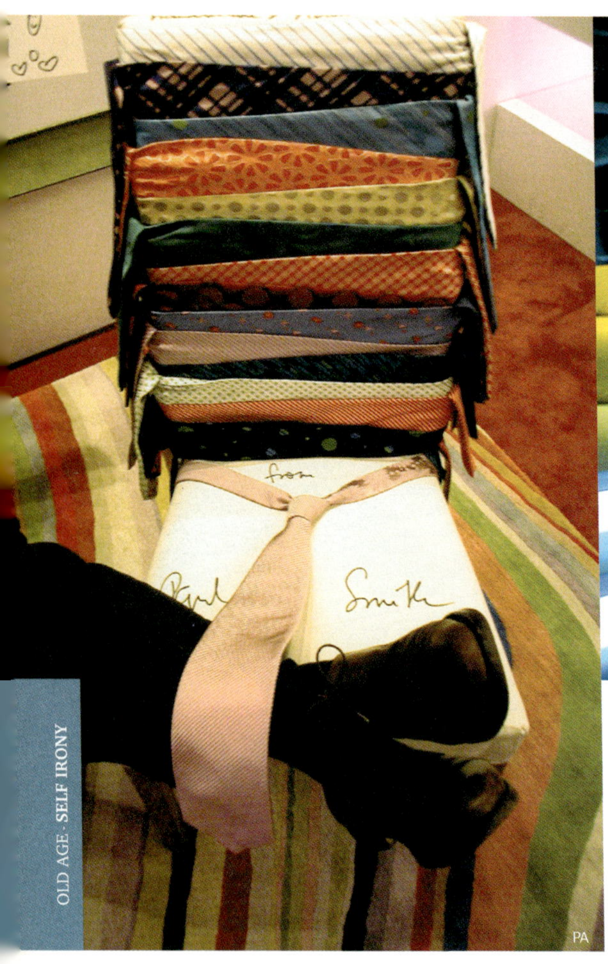

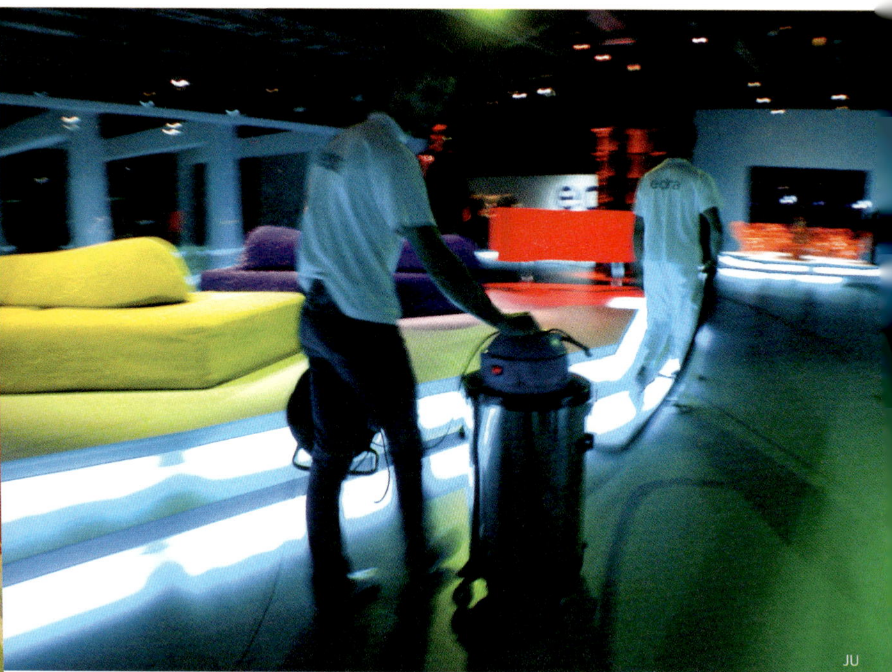

PA

JU

Paul Smith's chair

Edra

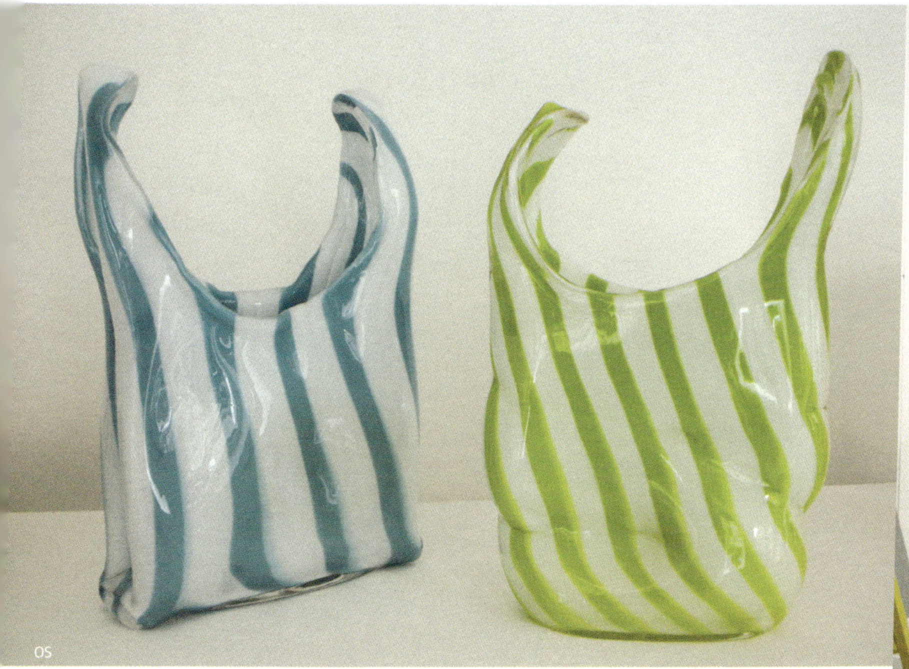

Marco Mencacci @ Galleria Blanchaert

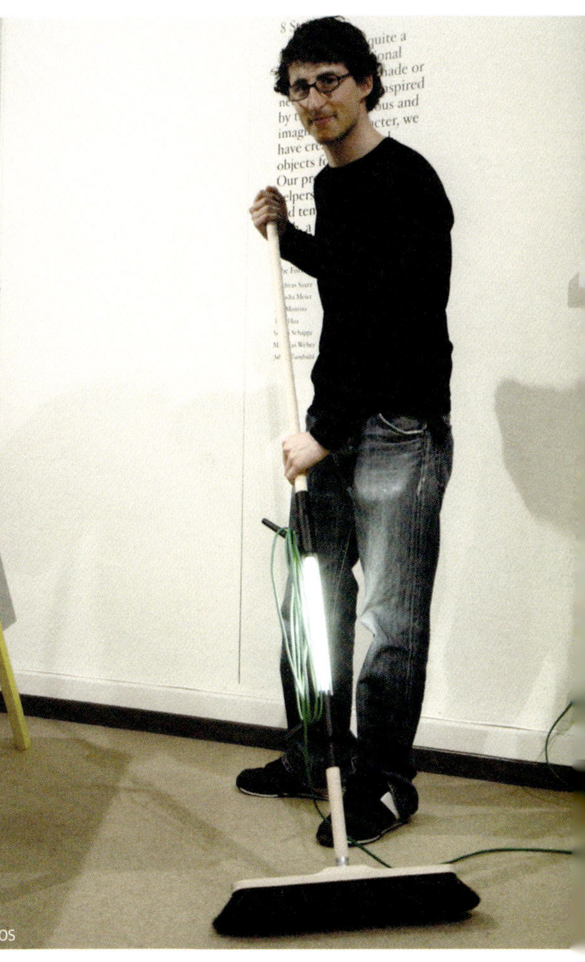

Jakob Zumbuhl of 8 Stazione @ Satellite

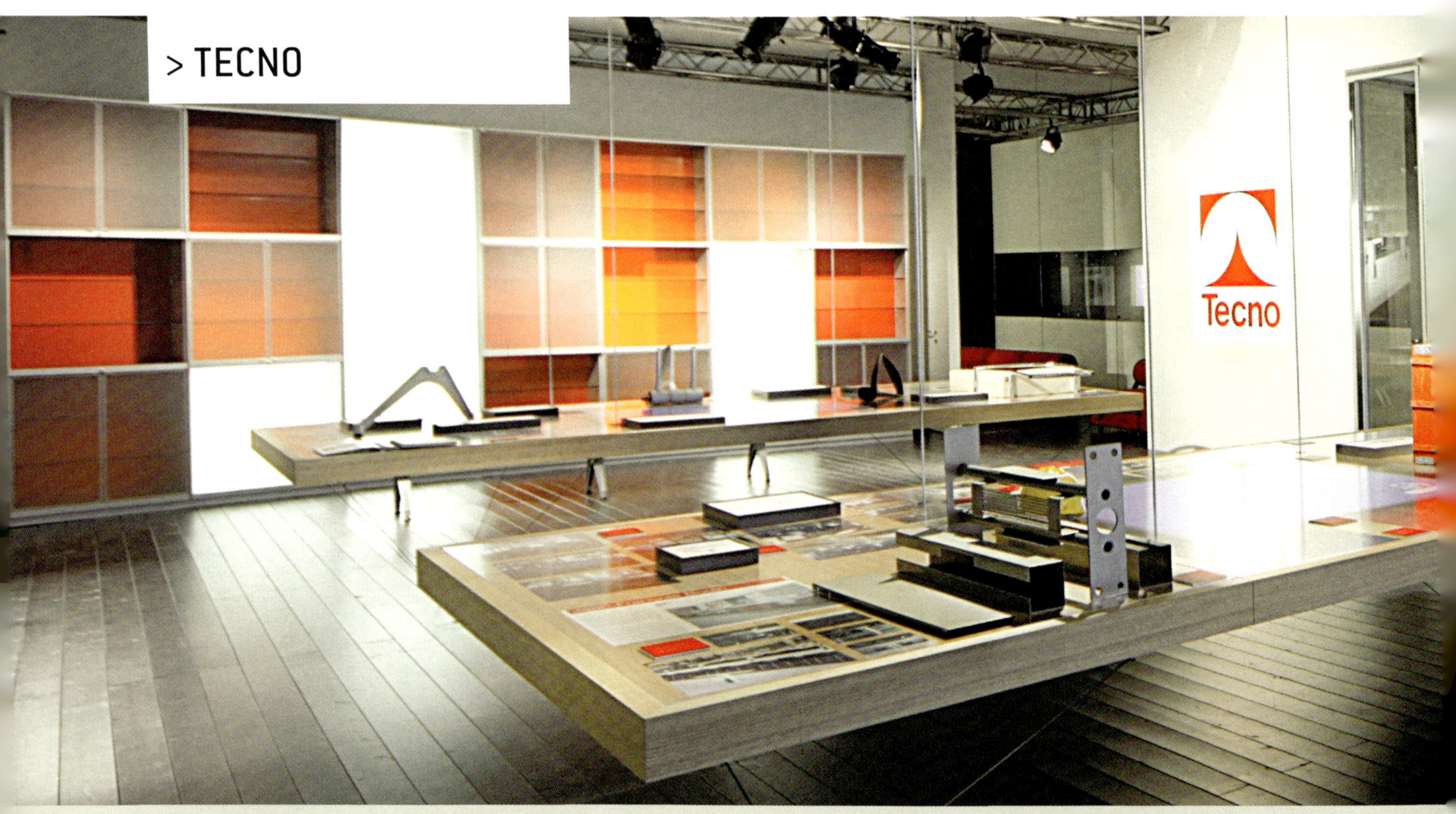

Tecno continues to have the leading edge in design culture, as much in its more established aspects as in its experimentations.

Over the past fifty years, Tecno's strength has always been its being tuned into architects, understanding their design objectives, foreseeing productive, marketing and cost developments and bringing their own expertise into the equation in terms of technology and knowledge of materials.

Tecno's entrepreneurial ethics have always been clear: to be of service to experts in the various countries as well as to the most important

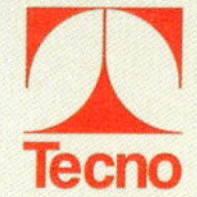

international studios, with the primary objective of highlighting the importance of the architects' work.

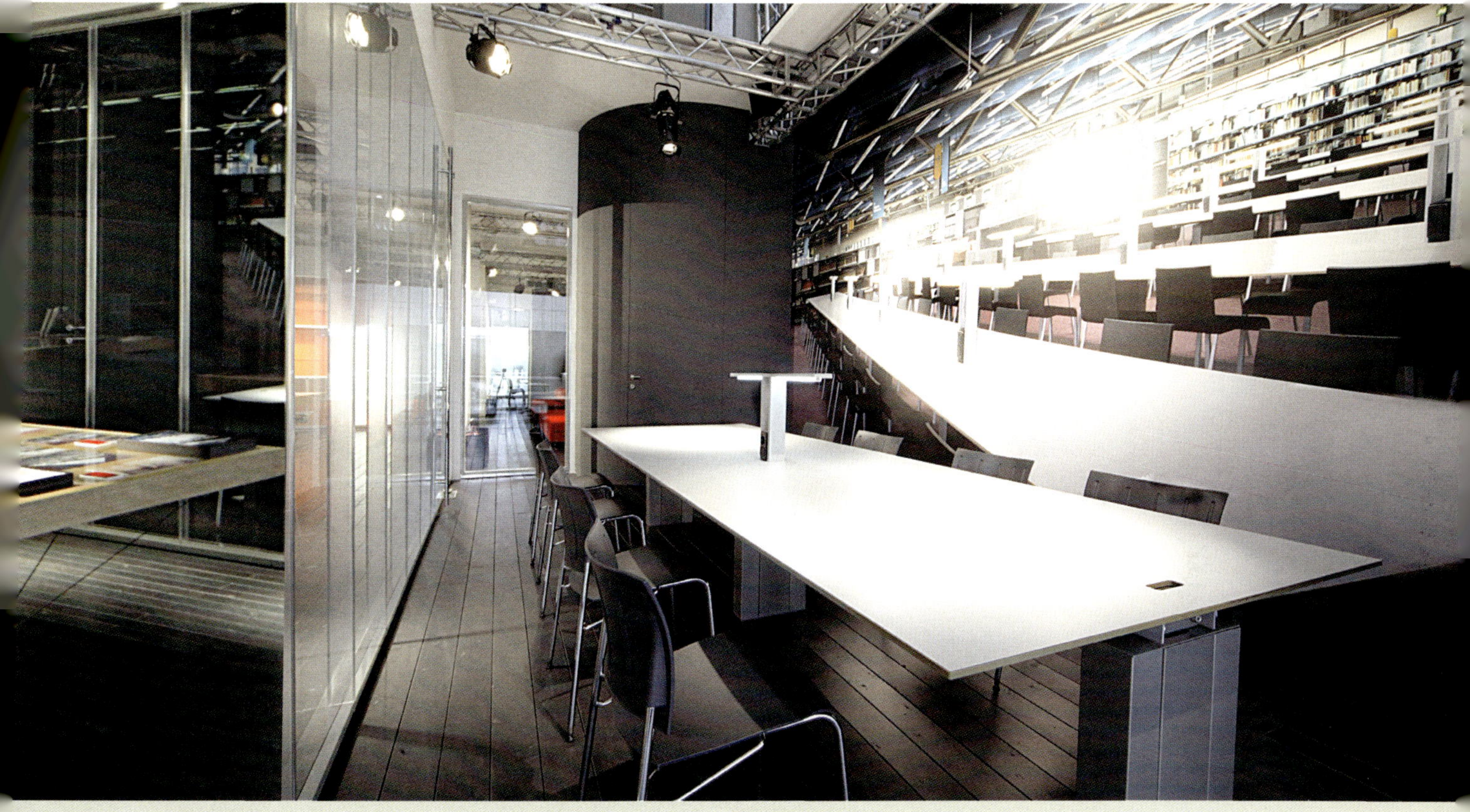

Tecno is currently experimenting at first hand an innovative 'business project', targeted at strengthening the presence of its

culture, products and brand over the coming decades, on the design scene in a globalised and highly competitive world.

Tecno answers the challenge of the Milan Design Week with a stand at Eimu and, outside the fair,

a presentation/performance at its own showroom in Fatebenefratelli 5.

photos Tilde De Tullio - Claudio Avancini

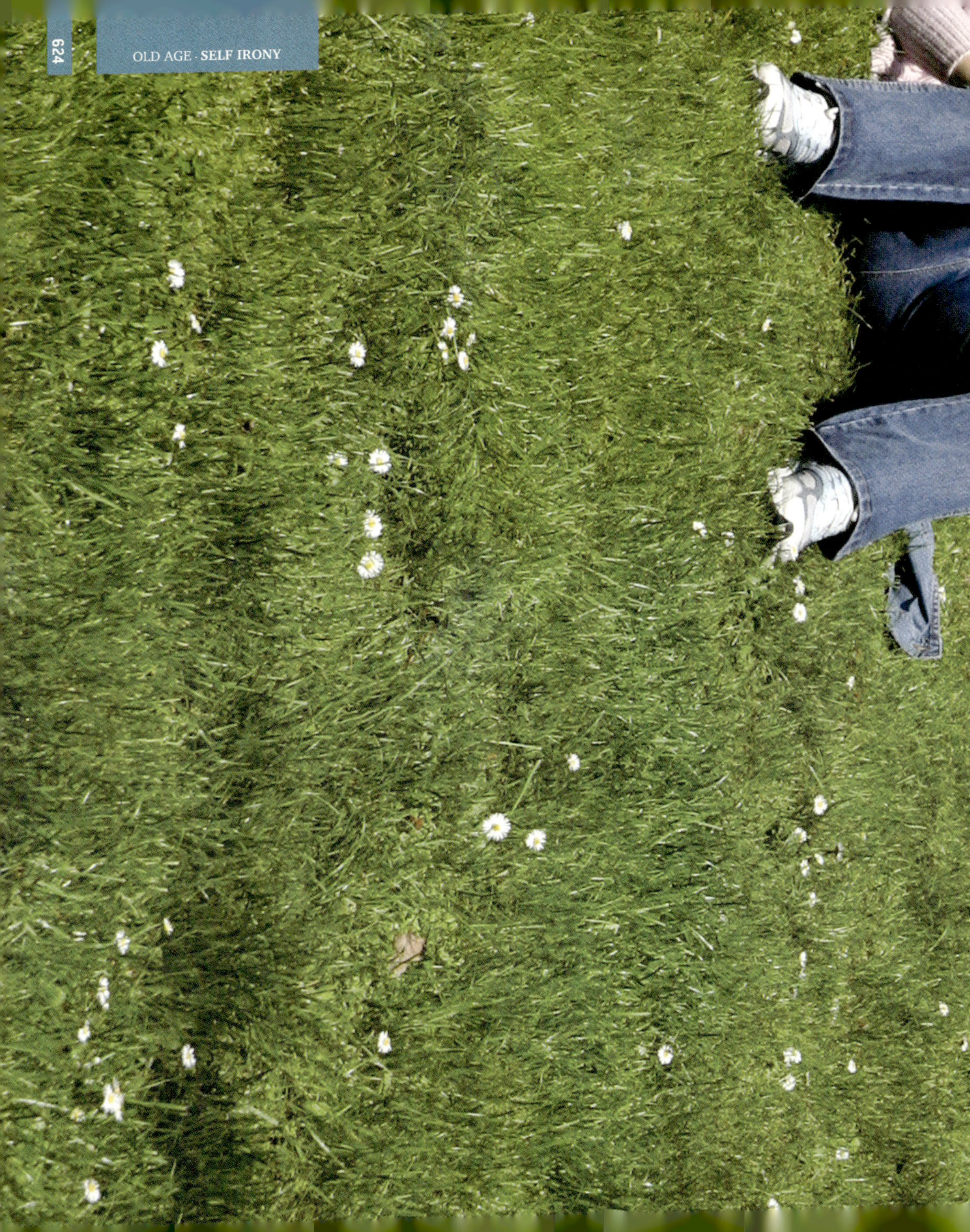

624   OLD AGE · SELF IRONY

SALONE SATELLITE

DESIGNERS

"4" DUPUIS, HARPER, NUEK, TURNER

Heidargerdi 25
IS190 Vogar
tel +354 692 77 66
maria@mariadupuis.com
www.mariadupuis.com

8 STAZIONE

Zeughalisstrasse 47
CH – 8004 Zürich
tel +41 78 626 15 39
claudiamei@gmx.ch

806 D

Via Fornace 25
33170 Pordenone
tel/fax +39 0434 542264
fucsia_d@libero.it

A TO Y

Frederiksborggade 46
DK – 1360 Copenhagen
tel +45 222 54779
yuriko19@hotmail.com

ALBERA, ARRIGONI, INDUNI, MONTI

Via Meravigli 14 - 20123 Milano
tel +39 02 86996670/574
n.monti@alberaemonti-assoc.com
www.alberaemonti-assoc.com

ALSO/ KITKABOODLE - JAMES ARMSTRONG

50 Stuart Road
UK SE15 3BE London
tel +44 020 7639 9491
js.armstrong@virgin.net

COLIN ANDERSON

Via Pacinotti 3
20059 Oreno di Vimercate (MI)
tel +39 3383084295
colin.anderson@idmilano.com
www.idmilano.com

DARIO ANTONIONI

1513 Berkeley – suite 5
USA – Santa Monica, CA 90404
tel +1 213 972 9922
fax +1 310 998 8419
dantonioni@orange22.com
www.orange22.com

CAROLA ARRIVAS BAJARDI

Viale dei Lillà 36
90100 Palermo
tel 091 4542253
arrivas@fastwebnet.it

ALESSANDRA BALDERESCHI

Viale Rimembranze 54/40
20099 Sesto San Giovanni (MI)
tel +39 02 2489 976
fax +39 02 2622 5515
alessandra.baldereschi@tin.it

LUCA BARBIERO

Corso Laghi 34
10051 Avigliana
tel/ fax +39 0119327625
info@lucabarbierodesign.com
www.lucabarbierodesign.com

ROSSANA BECCARI

Località Contovello 86
34017 Trieste
tel/ fax +39 040 225095
rossb@libero.it

MATTIA BEDEI

Via XX Settembre 34
48018 Faenza (RA)
tel 039 0546 660013
telabecks@hotmail.com

JOHN ANGELO BENSON

16 Sarre Road
UK – NW2 3SL London
tel +44 79 56 53 44 55
mail@johnangelobenson.com
www.johnangelobenson.com

ERIC BERTHES

84 bd de Sebastopol
F – 75003 Paris
tel +33 142789317
fax +33 142789310
eric@ericberthes.com
www.ericberthes.com

BIOTTI + KAUFMANN

Gewerbehaus Schachen
CH – 6033 Buchrain
tel +41 041 4484110
fax +41 041 4484111
mail@biotti-kaufmann.ch

LUCA BONATO

Via Rivarotta 11
36061 Bassano del Grappa (VI)
tel +39 0424 590163
fax +39 0424 829930

BOOMON DESIGN

Overtoom 239/1
NL – 1054 HV Amsterdam
tel/fax +31-20-683 6278
info@boomon.com
www.boomon.com

BRAM BOO

Basiliekstraat 14
B – 3800 St. Truiden
Mobile +32 496 407 773
fax +32 115 938 59
bram.bo@sttglobal.net

SHAWN-IAN BRUCE

390 N. Madison Ave. Apt.11
USA – Pasadena, CA 91101
tel +1 626 354 5570
fax +1 626 609 2342
ian@shawnbruce.com
www.shawnbruce.com

**ROBBY CANTARUTTI
& FRANCESCA PETRICICH**

Via Pavia 99
33042 Buttrio (UD)
tel +39 0432 673 339
fax +39 0432 683 256
robby@archazione.com
www.archazione.com

CATERINA CARBONI

Via Sicuri 42/A
43100 Parma, Italy
tel +39 521 970453
fax +39 521 907871
caterina.carboni@libero.it

SERGIO CATALANO

Via P. Melchiade 27
84018 Scafati, Salerno
tel +39 081 8508666
fax +39 081 8508666
s.catalano@awn.it
www.sergiocatalano.it

RICCARDO CENGIA

Via Renata Bianchi 77B/3-79
16152 Genova, Italy
tel +39 010 6506104
fax +39 010 6506437
acengia@tin.it
www.cengia.it

CENTO

Via Fara Sabina 1
00199 Roma, Italy
tel +39 335 7044347
pcento@libero.it

**MARIAVERA CHIARI
E SILVINA BOISSONNAS**

Alzaia Naviglio Grande 156
20144 Milano, Italy
Mobile 349 0679815
fax 02 7601144
mvchiari@libero.it
www.mv-ceramicsdesign.com

DARCY CLARKE/ STUDIOSOFT

1/4 Ti-tree Place
AUS – 2481 Byron Bay
tel/ fax +61 2 66807376
info@studiosoft.com.au
www.studiosoft.com.au

COMPOSITE DESIGN

24 McManus Street
AUS – 6107 Wilson, Perth
tel +61 8 9258 3137
fax +61 8 94375748
compositedesign@hotmail.com

CUBE, ARCHITETTURA + DESIGN

Tucholsky Strasse 41
D – 10017 Berlin
tel/ fax +49 30 29771919
cube.arch@t-online.de
www.cube-berlin.de

DEEPDESIGN

Via A. Vespucci 5
20124 Milano, Italy
tel/fax +39 02 29 00 12 21
info@deepdesign.it
www.deepdesign.it

DEFACTO.DESIGN

Reitmorstrasse 8
D – 80538 München
tel +49 89 49001309
fax +49 89 49001310
info@defactodesign.de
www.defactodesign.de

MATTHIAS DEMACKER

Richelstrasse 4
D – 80634 München tel +49 89
13958793
ax +49 89 13958793
md@demacker-design.de
www.demacker-design.de

**DESIGN FOR PEOPLE
MARC DE GROOT**

Van Bossestraat 97,1e
NL – JW 1051 Amsterdam
tel +31 20 475 2020
fax +31 20 475 2021
info@designforpeople.nl
www.designforpeople.nl

**DJONNE & SVEEN
BARE MOBLER**

Monrad Mjeldesvei 12
N – 5161 Laksevag
tel +47 92 21 68 62
orjan@baremobler.no
www.baremobler.no

DLITE PROJECT

Via Piave 44
28069 Trecate, Italy
tel/fax +39 0321 71570
info@dliteproject.com
www.dliteproject.com

SARAH DORKENWALD/RUTH SPITZER / WALLFURNITURE

95 Gore Vale Avenue
Toronto M6J 2R5-ON- Canada
tel +1 416 7032 479
wallfurniture@gmx.net

JEREMY EDWARDS / EVA SCHILDT

19, rue Chanzy
F – 75011 Paris
info@evaschildt.se
www.evaschildt.se

EN-MA / TANAKA TOSHIKAZU

601 Dai-2 Fukutomi Bldg.
2-2-6 Shinjuku Shinjuku-ku
J – 160 0022 Tokyo
tel +81 3 3357 0580
fax +81 3 3357 0816
kitano@en-ma.com

ANDREA EPIFANI

Via Umberto I°, 32
73100 Lecce, Italy
tel/fax +39 0832 24 34 43
cikli00@libero.it

FLATLIFE – ALMOST WALLPAPER

Contrada Ponticello 60
03017 Morolo (FR), Italy
tel/fax 39 0775 228040
info@flatlife.co.uk
www.flatlife.co.uk

CHARLOTTE FRIIS

Dybendalsvej 66, st. tv
DK – 2720 Vanlose, KBH
tel +45 26293987
charlottefriis@hotmail.com

FRONT

Runiusgatan 14
S – 11255 Stockholm
tel +46 873 674 90 07
everyone@designfront.org
www.designfront.org

FUHRMANN/ RUMOHR SCHOELL

Bahnhofstrasse 24
D – 35066 Frankenberg/ Eder
tel+49 6451 716152
fax +49 6451717623
Iris_schoell@yahoo.de
nicolaifuhrmann@yahoo.de

GABRIEL/ THIELE LAARMANN/ GROTTELL

C/O Rat für Formgebung /
German Design Council
Ludwig-Erhard-Anlage 1
D - 60327 Frankfurt an Main
tel +49 69 74 79 19
fax +49 69 741 09 11
info@german-design-council.de
www.german-design-council.de

JACOPO GARDELLA

Via Verdi 6
20121 Milano, Italy
tel +39 02 86995581
fax +39 02 86995589
studio.gardella@tiscalinet.it

GARISELLI ASSOCIATI

Via Mulino 3
42014 Castellerano (RE)
tel/fax +39 0536 859158
gino.gariselli@tin.it

JOERG GÄTJENS

Eifelwall 28
D – 50674 Köln
tel +49 221 800672
fax +49 221 9320912
joerg_gaetjens@yahoo.de

GHAADÉ, STÉPHANO NUVOLONI

62 rue d'Entraigues
F – 37000 Tours
tel +33 2 47 75 10 46
fax +33 2 47 75 17 46
ghaade@ghaade.com

PIERFRANCESCO GIANGASPRO ROBERTO GIACOMUCCI

Via Podesti 54
60122 Ancona (AN), Italy
tel +39 071 2071 514
fax +39 071 2077 183
psgianga@tiscali.it
gdesign@libero.it

FRANCESCO GIANNATTASIO

Via Luigi Guercio 84
84135 Salerno (SA), Italy
tel/ fax +39 089 405871
francescogi.arch@tin.it
www.francescogiannattasio.it

ANDREA GIANNI

Viale delle Rimembranze
di Lambrate 6 20134 Milano, Italy
tel/ fax +39 02 36507661

A.GIANNI @LABORATORILAMBRATE.IT

www.laboratorilambrate.it

GJOLDAHLE - PORT 29 - AAS

C/O Dtank
Pilestredet 75C
N – 0354 Oslo
tel +47 22 601944
fax +47 22 592652
post@dtank.no
www.gjoldahle-port29-aas.no

FRANCISCO GOMEZ PAZ E GIMENA

Via Mosè Bianchi 20
20149 Milano, Italy
tel +39 02 48000655
francisco@gomezpaz.com
www.gomezpaz.com

GO PING PONG APS

Nr. Farimagsgade 76, 5th
DK – 1364 K Copenhagen
tel +45 21436276
mail@gopingpong.dk
www.gopingpong.dk

GRANESE DESIGN STUDIO

Lungomare C. Colombo 211
84129 Salerno (SA), Italy
tel/ fax +39 089 331979
gastudio.granese@tin.it
www.granese-design.com

GROUP INC. GARTH ROBERTS

156 Allen street 15
USA – 10002 New York
tel +11 212 591 0362
groupie003@groupinc.com
www.groupinc.com

GRUPPO MIX

Via Carlo Bazzi 51
20141 Milano, Italy
tel +39 02 89503021
fax +39 02 89501462
ixisrl@tin.it www.ixisrl.com

GUGGENBICHLERDESIGNE

Schellhammergasse 3
A – 1170 Wien
tel +43 699 1924 15 30
fax +43 1 804 39 44
design@guggenbichler.at
www.guggenbichler.at

ANGELICA GUSTAFSSON STUDIO

Hantverkargatan 50
S- 112 31 Stockholm
tel/fax +46 8 654 03 00
info@angelicagustafsson.com
www.angelicagustafsson.com

HANS HAGEMEISTER

Märkisches Ufer 36
D – 10179 Berlin
tel +49 30 27593293
fax +49 30 27593295
hans.hagemeister@web.de

HAPPY FINISH DESIGN NICK RENNIE

21 Hillcrest Avenue
AUS – 3101 Kew
tel +61 3 9817 9780
fax +61 3 9817 5862
nick@happyfinishdesign.com
www.happyfinishdesign.com

SACHIO HIHARA

1-5-6 Shintori
J – 420 0065 Shizuoka
tel +81 54 652 0057
fax +81 54 652 0058
hihara@sachio.jp
www.sachio.jp

HOET

Niklaas Desparsstraat 19
B – 8000 Brugge
tel +32 50 334302
fax +32 50 338383
bieke@hoet.be
www.hoet.be

HELEN HÖGBERG/ JESSICA SIGNELL/ JOHANNA LINDGREN

Surbrunnsgatan 36
S – 11348 Stockholm
tel +46 70 516 55 84
helen.hogberg@bredband.net
info@jessicasignell.com
info@johannalindgren.se

CONSTANTINOS HOURSOGLOU

55 Sarantapihou Steet
GR – 11471 Athens
tel/ fax +30 210 6447 402
costantinos@chd.gr
www.chd.gr

GIL INBAL, ROY ROTH

23 Fierberg Street
IL – Tel Aviv
tel + 972 3 620 9238
info@sonicgarden.com
www.sonicgarden.com

IN-D

The Vicarage Spring Lane
Cookham Dean
GB - Maidenhead Berks 5L6 9PN
tel/ fax +44 1628 484084
andy.hale@mo-billy.com
www.mo-billy.com

INTERFERENZE

Fraz. Calacababbio 2
27050 Redavalle (PV)
tel/fax +39 0385 74208
vizzotto@tin.it

FLORENCE JAFFRAIN

3 rue Béranger F – 93500 Paris
tel +33 1 4845 2678
fax +33 1 4845 2680
contact@moaproduction.com
www.moaproduction.com

JAM

Havregatan 7 nb.
S – 118 59 Stockholm
tel +46 870 29700
JAM_swe@hotmail.com

JOBST/ OLZE & WILKENS

Alte Schönhauser Strasse 29
D – 10119 Berlin
tel +49 30 28044617
mail@birgitjobst.de
info@olzewilkens.de
www.birgitjobst.de
www.olzewilkens.de

NAMJOO JOH

Largo dell' Olgiata 15,
Isola 60 A 4/2
00123 Roma, Italy
tel +39 06 30880804
namjoo11@hotmail.com

MIHAJLO JURIC

Prvomajska 1
SER - 24414 Hajdukovo, Subotica
tel +38 1 64 213 20 19
mihajlojuric@hotmail.com
www.mihajlo.com

A. KANTAWALA, E. NG/ SEED

931 Massachusetts Avenue, Suite 604
USA – MA 02139 Cambridge
tel/ fax +1 617 5769668
seed@verizon.net
www.seed-international.com

TOMOKO KOIKE

Upsalagade 26 st. tv
DK – 2100 Copenhagen
tel +45 2665 8884
tomokokoike@hotmail.com
www.tomokokoike.com

HELEN KONTOURIS DESIGN

P.O.Box 316 Port Melbourne
AUS – 3207 Melbourne
tel +61 408664498
fax +61 398467780
helen@helenkontouris.com
www.helenkontouris.com

ALESSANDRO LABRICCIOSA TOSCA LEBORONI

Via Ugo Foscolo 7
62100 Macerata (MC), Italy
Mobile +39 347 6100680-
+39 340 4741237
tosca.progettazione@tiscali.it
alessandrodesign@virgilio.it

RUI LEAO – LEAO ATELIER DE ARQUITECTURA

Av. Da Praia Grande 291, Ed. Hon
Van 13° B Macau, China
tel +853 825199
fax +853 357023
carlotta@macau.ctm.net

LEE . HAE SEUNG

90-6 Youmgok Dong, Seocho Gu
137 170 Seoul, South Korea
tel +82 11 234 3573
fax +82 2 571 6249
haeseung27@empal.com

JOOHEE LEE

Third Floor, 76 Barons Court Road
GB – London W14 9DU
tel +44 77 9619 7679
joohee_lee@hotmail.com

LENS INC° EDEN

Dr. Willemsstraat 19
B – 3500 Hasselt
tel +32 11 247760
fax +32 11 262137
info@lensass.bt
www.lensass.bt

SABINE LEUTHOLD

Müllerstrasse 34
CH – 8004 Zürich
tel +41 1 241 4705
fax +41 1 241 4710
hello@sabineleuthold.com
www.sabineleuthold.com

LIUTHA

Am Erlenberg 29
D – 64285 Darmstadt
tel +49 179 3285797
contact@liutha.com www.liutha.com

M+K DESIGN

Via B. Cellini 4
20129 Milano, Italy
tel/fax +39 02 54120271
Mobile 340 0031172
mk_d@rmail.plala.or.jp

MADE IN NEWCASTLE

16 Westfield Avenue
GB – TD15 1PU
Berwick upon Tweed
tel +44 79 50913563
fax +44 191 2274655
designedinnewcastle@hotmail.com

MAOS CONTEMPORARY ART

Rua Ribeiro do Vale 1140
BR – 04568 003 Sao Paulo
tel +55 11 5561 3115
fax +55 11 5093 7776
luisfernando@laco.com.br

MARTON ELEK, MATÉ ELEK ILDIKO BUZOGANY

Geppetto design group
Radnoti Miklos v.26, N/1
H - 1137 Budapest
tel +36 1 2700107
fax +36 1 27 00 107
info@geppetto.hu
www.geppetto.hu

MAXJENNY SUPERSTUDIO

Tessinsway1b
SE–217 58 Malmoe
tel +46704829848; +4640265671
max@maxjenny.com
www.maxjenny.com

NADINE MEISEL

Putlitzstrasse 26
D – 76137 Karlsruhe
tel +49 721 815281
Mobile +49 175 6376744
mail@nadinemeisel.de
www.nadinemeisel.de

KEN MICHIDA

1-7-25 Shin-machi
J – 514 0042 Tsu, Mie
tel/fax +81 59 224 6660
michida@leef.jp http://
wing.zero.ad.jpmichida

YASUTOSHI MIFUNE

1-1-5-107 Takaminosato
J–580 0021 Matsubara City Osaka
tel +81 72 335 1029
fax +81 72 335 1069
fwnd9694@mb.infoweb.ne.jp

MIR-STUDIO.COM

Hoffeldstrasse 46
D – 40235 Düsseldorf
tel +49 211 239 61 26
fax +49 211 239 62 87
info@david-caspar-schaefer.de
www.mir-studio.com

MIXKO

11 Church Hill, Pinhoe
GB – EX4 9EX Exeter, Devon
tel +44 1392 660738
alex@mixko.net
www.mixko.net

MODAN, DESIGN
FOR NOMAD LIVING

Via Disciplini 9 20123 Milano, Italy
tel/fax +39 02 5843 3112
hannah@hidesignworld.com
michelangelo@giombinikind.com

ANDREA MODICA

Via Roma 41
20010 Marcallo con Casone (MI)
tel/fax +39 02 9761 851
andrea.modica@tiscali.it

ROBERTO MONTE

Via T. Cauciello 44
84016 Pagani, Italy
tel +39 081 954761
fax +39 081 916558
roberto_monte@libero.it
www.m2design.it

MOOPAK

83A Keong Saik Road
089137 Singapore
tel +65 62242156
june@moopak.com
www.moopak.com

MORE – GUALTIERO SACCHI

Via Emilia S. Pietro 22
42100 Reggio Emilia, Italy
tel/fax +39 0522 431591

ARTUR MOUSTAFA/ AÄÖ DESIGN

Drottninggatan 82
S – 25221 Helsingborg
tel +46 42 270820
fax +46 42 270821
artur@aaodesign.com
www.aaodesign.com

MTDESIGN®

Via Spada 52
31050 Vedelago (TR), Italy
tel/fax +39 0423 476666
intdesign_68@hotmail.co

MYONG, PAWLOWSKY, ZINK

c/o CHT
Bismarckstrasse 102
D – 72072 Tübingen
tel +46 7071 154 263
fax +46 7071 154 434

NENDO

4-1-20-2A Mejiro Toshimaku
J – 171 0031 Tokyo
tel/ fax +81 3 3954 5554
info@nendo.jp
www.nendo.jp

INA NIKOLIC

Via Gavirate 21
20148 Milano, Italy
tel +39 329 78 46 927
inanicol@hotmail.com

NONPRODUCTION

Linnesgade 14°. 5
DK – 1361 Copenhagen
tel +45 33328082
mail@nonproduction.dk
www.nonproduction.dk

JOACHIM NORDWALL

Jungfrugatan 7b
S – 11444 Stockholm
tel +46 86620812
fax +46 708181484
joachim@jnordwall.com
www.joachim@nordwall.com

ODA/ ERIC BREWER JUAN MACHADO

Calle Pomagas, Qta 28
Urb. Alta Florida, Dis. Capital
1050 Caracas, Venezuela
tel +58 212 7305545
fax +58 212 7306067
brewer@odaonline.com
www.odaonline.com

OVERBOARD

27 Isaac street
AUS – 4000 Spring Hill, Brisbane
tel +61 7 3839 0400
fax +61 7 38390399
contact@steendyk.com
www.steendyk.com

KEIKO OYABU

Tamagawagakuen 7-30-14,
Machidashi
J – 194 0041 Tokyo
tel +81 42 725 9655
fax +81 42 725 5769
info@keikooyabu.com
www.keikooyabu.com

DANIELE PARIO PERRA

Contraconcept
Via Montenero 9
40131 Bologna
tel +39 051 557442
info@contraconcept.org
www.contraconcept.org

PARK + (PARK PLUS)

Flat II, 160 Lavender Hill
GB – SW11 5TF London
tel +44 7919 160694
parkplus@hotmail.com

PERMAFROST DESIGNSTUDIO

Waldemar Thranes gt.75
N – 0175 Oslo
tel +47 22 36 45 45
fax +47 22 36 45 46
mail@permafrost.no www.permafrost.no

PLUS TIC MINUS TIC

Court Annex Oyama-cho 1 E 18-23
J – 157 0065 Shibuya-ku Tokyo
tel +81 354 52 31 71
fax +81 354 52 31 37
tt_atelier@hotmail.com

FERNANDO POGGIO

Av. Larrazabal 3159
AR – 1439 Buenos Aires
alox@sion.com
www.fernandopoggio.com

POLKA/ MARIE RAHM MONICA SINGER

Mariahilferstrasse 9/7
A – 1060 Wien
tel +43 69911699096
tel +43 69911156936
office@polkaproducts.com
www.polkaproducts.com

POLY-SITE

5-9-20-208 Kamisoshigaya
Setagaya-ku
J – 157 0065 Tokyo
tel/fax +81 3 5384 2745
info@fdl-italform.net
www.poly-site.com

PUFF-BUFF DESIGN

Ul. Andersa 10/41
PL – 00 201 Warsaw
tel +48 22 635 38 74
puff-buffdesign@op.pl
www.puff-buffdesign.art.pl

PUN/ ANTOINETTE PRATTIS

145 East 23rd Street, 20-1
USA – 10010 New York
tel +1 646 431 7766
fax +1 212 406 1962
antoinette@punfun.com
www.pun-design.org

PUTTI FACTORY

Toftes Gate 69 D
N – 0552 Oslo
tel +47 97016081
fax +47 22690006
are.h@puttifactory.com
www.puttyfactory.com

RANCH BOX DESIGN STUDIO

3-22-17 Nakaizumi, Komae-city
J – 201 0012 Tokyo
tel +81 3 3430 9278
fax +81 3 3430 9278
info@ranch-box.com
www.ranch-box.com

LEON RANSMEIER

General Bothastraat 7e
NL – 5642 NJ Eindhoven
tel/fax +31 40 2857993
leon@leonransmeier.com
www.leonransmeier.com

SALONE DA PRANZO

Via Marconi 30
21010 Besnate (VA), Italy
tel +39 0331 274019
contact@stefanosculati.it

FAUSTO SALVI / SILVIA ZOTTA

Via Venini 83
20127 Milano, Italy
tel/fax +39 02 2613565
salvizotta@infinito.it
misterfa@libero.it

SANNIA DESIGN

Via Savona 73
20144 Milano, Italy
tel +39 02 4234156
info@sanniadesign.com
www.sanniadesign.com

SATELIGHT DESIGN
SAMANTHA PARSONS

P.O.Box 306
AUS – 3206 Albert Park. Victoria
tel/fax +61 3 9399 5805
info@satelight.com.au
www.satelight.com.au

J. SCHAUB/ GREENFORM
+ S. STRAUBE/ FOORM.COM

Fürther Strasse 22
D – 90429 Nürnberg
tel +49 172 8229152
fax +49 911 5301612

MARIE-LOUISE SCIÒ

Via Pietro Paolo Rubens 44
00197 Roma, Italy
tel +39 335 8443104
fax +39 06 3211228
mscio@hotmail.com

SIGLA YOUNG

Via Asiago 24
20128 Milano, Italy
tel +39 02 2552 593
fax +39 02 25707336
info@designsigla.com

HUGO SILVA & ISABEL LUCIO

Av. Duque Avila 40, 1° Dt°
P – 1050 083 Lisboa
tel +351 933264410
fax +351 21 3582116
mail@hi-designteam.com
www.hi-designteam.com

SCOTT SMITH &
URSULA MARTINEZ

Flay 12, 24 York Grove
Queens Road Peckham
GB – London SE15 2 NZ
tel +44 207 207 1168
scottsclone@yahoo.co.uk
www.martinezsmith.com

SO-DESIGN

406 5-10-32 Minamiazabu Minato
J – 106 0047 Tokyo
tel +81 03 5420 6406
fax +81 03 5420 6407
mail@so-design.jp
www.so-design.jp

STORE

4 Alseich Street
IL – 63307 Tel Aviv
tel/fax +972 3 5106867
store_it@netvision.net.il

STUDIOBALL

177 Waller Road
GB – London SE 14 5LX
tel/ fax +44 207 207 1360
info@studioball.co.uk
www.studioball.co.uk

CAROLINA SUELS

Via G. Govone 37
20155 Milano, Italy
tel/fax +39 02 33601894
info@suelslab.com
www.suelslab.com

TOSHIHIKO SUZUKI

200 Kamisakurada
J – 990 9530 Yamagata
tel +81 23 627 2000
fax +81 23 627 2251
tsuzuki@product.tuad.ac.jp
www.product.tuad.ac.jp/suzuki_lab/

TAKEMI & ILARIA + TSM

Via Rosmini 7
20100 Milano, Italy
Mobile +39 349 4746401
ilariacostan@hotmail.com
ciaotakemi@hotmail.com

FLYNN TALBOT

2 Trident Terrace, Willethon
AUS – 6155 Perth
tel/fax +618 9310 6416
flynntalbot@iinet.net.au
www.flynntalbot.com

TF-PRODUCTDESIGN
FRANCK THORSTEN

Lautensackstrasse 21
D – 80687 München
tel +49 89 5786 9194
fax +49 89 5786 9195
thorsten_franck@t-online.de

THELERMONTHUPTON

114 Rutland Gardens
GB – London N4 1JR
tel +44 20 83740422
david@thelermonthupton.com
www.thelermonthupton.com

FRANK TJEPKEMA

Weesperzijde 80b
NL – 1091 EJ Amsterdam
tel +31 20 362 4296
fax +31 20 362 4299
frank@tjepkema.com
www.tjepkema.com

TONERICO: INC.

601 Grand Mansion Harajuku
6-18-2 Jingumae Shibuya-ku
J – 150 0001 Tokyo
tel +81 3 5468 0608
fax +81 3 5468 0609
tonerico.inc@nifty.com
www.tonerico-inc.com

TRICOIREDESIGN

61 rue de Reuilly
F – 75012 Paris
tel +33 1 48590408
alexis@tricoiredesign.com
www.tricoiredesign.com

TUTTAFUFFA DESIGN

Via G. Pellizza da Volpedo 2
10154 Torino
tel +39 339 2713822 / +39 347
8646 783
francescasignori@yahoo.it

ULTIMI

Ripa di Porta Ticinese 51
20143 Milano, Italy
tel +39 02 89422508
mobile +39 380 2594912
ultimi5@hotmail.com
www.ultimi.com

DANNY VENLET

C/o MNM Lifestyle Solutions
Valerius de Saedeleerstraat 97
B – 9300 Aalst
tel +32 53 700 719
info@mode-management.com

ARCH. IVANO VERDE

Via Ugo Foscolo 66
81031 Aversa (CE), Italy
tel/fax +39 081 8901842
iverdi@tin.it

ALFONSO VITALE

Via Fucilari 125
84014 Nocera Inferiore (SA)
tel/fax +39 081 5178473
info@alfonsovitale.it
www.alfonsovitale.it

VOON WONG & BENSON SAW

Unit 27, Istannary Street
GB – SE11 4AD London
tel +44 2075870116
fax +44 2078400178
info@voon-benson.com
www.voon-benson.com

W+B DESIGN ASBL

Rue de Suisse 10
B – 1060 Bruxelles
tel +32 2 5387991
fax +32 2 5377784

WOLF UDO WAGNER

Hanauer Landstrasse 161-173
D – 60314 Frankfurt/Main
tel: +49 69 9287 0574
fax: +49 69 9287 0575
wagner@wagner-design.de
www.wolf-udo-eagner.com

WANNFORS/ NEUSCHÜTZ FRYKLUND

Sofiagatan 3
SE – 11640 Stockholm
tel +46 8 4420980
fax +46 70 7474728
jonas@wannforsdesign.com
www.wannforsdesign.com

WEMAKE

11 Woodlands, Clapham Common
Northside
GB –Sw4 0RJ London
tel/fax +44 207 72 01 367
www.wemake.co.uk
wemake@wemake.homechoice.co.uk

WIENEKE VAN GEMEREN

Via Gazzo 18
36060 Pianezze S.L. (VI)
tel/fax +39 0424 702418
wieneke@realwieneke.com
www.realwieneke.com

KAICHIRO YAMADA

3-10-13 Taira, Miyamae-ku,
Kawasaki-shi
J – 216 0022 Kanagawa
tel +81 44 9770813
fax +81 44 9770856
kaichiro@bb.excite.co.jp

GIOVANNI ZANNINI

Vico Pallonetto Santa Chiara 32
80133 Napoli, Italy
tel +39 081 49 77 100
fax +39 081 55 11 417
deltagroove@iol.it

ZUII/ MARCEL SIGEL & ALANA DI GIACOMO

GPO Box 5156
AUS – 3001 Melbourne
tel +61 407 771649
fax +61 3 96991813
info@zuii.com
www.zuii.com

ALTERSTUDIO
Via Pinamonte da Vimercate 4
20121 Milano, Italy
tel +39 02 29011250
alterstudio@libero.it

RON ARAD ASSOCIATES
62 Chalk Farm Road
London NW1 8AN - UK
T. (44) 207 284 4963
F. (44) 207 379 0499
email: info@ronarad.com

ARCHILAB
Via J. Dal Verme 15
20159 Milano, Italy
tel +39 02 69005672
www.archilab.it
archilab@archilab.it

DODO ARSLAN
Piazza della Repubblica 5
20121 Milano, Italy
studio +39 02 36533352
fax +39 02 6575819
dodo@arslan.it

GAE AULENTI
P.zza San Marco 4
20121 Milano, Italy
tel +39 02 8692762

ANTONIA ASTORI DRIADE
Via G. Rossini 3
20122 Milano, Italy
tel +39 02 795005

MIKI ASTORI
Via C. Correnti 7
20123 Milano, Italy
tel +39 02 89404251
miki.astori@tiscalinet.it

AATTAK
www.aattak.com

ATTIVO CREATIVE RESOURCE
Via privata Rutilia 10/8
20141 Milano, Italy
tel +39 02 54116645
milano@attivocreative.com

KARIM AZZABI DESIGN NETWORK
Via Ausonio 6
20123 Milano, Italy
tel +39 02 89421599

EMMANUEL BABLED
Via G. Segantini 71
20143 Milano, Italy
t+ 39 02 58111119

ENRICO BALERI BALERI ITALIA S.P.A.
Via F. Cavallotti 8
20122 Milano, Italy
tel +39 02 76014672

BASE
Via A. Fumagalli 2
20143 Milano, Italy
tel +39 02 8394799
info@8a5e.com
www.8a5e.com

MARIO BELLINI
P.zza Arcole 4
20143 Milano, Italy
tel +39 02 89410387
atelier@bellini.it

BENZA INC.
www.benzadesign.com

GUGLIELMO BERCHICCI
Via Valparaiso 9
20144 Milano, Italy
tel +39 02 48019284

BRANCO STUDIO
d'architettura e design
Via Cardinale A. Sforza 81/A
20141 Milano, Italy
tel +39 02 89516831

BRASS CLARE DESIGN STUDIO
architettura d'interni e design
Via G.B. Bertini 19
20154 Milano, Italy
tel +39 02 34934013

RAOUL BRETZEL
via Mantova, 16 00198 Roma
tel/fax +39/06/8541127
rbretzel@libero.it

ANTONIO BRIZZI E BABETTE
Riefenstahl
Via C. d'Adda 9
20143 Milano, Italy
tel +39 02 89429253

ANDREA BRANZI
Via Solferino 25
20121 Milano, Italy
tel +39 02 6592227
Anbranzi@tin.it

SERGIO BRIOSCHI
Via G.B. Bertini 19
20154 Milano, Italy
tel +39 02 33101454

CAMBIOFACCIA
www.cambiofaccia.it

MARIO CANANZI

Alzaia Naviglio Grande 156
20144 Milano, Italy
tel +39 02 4239671

CHIARA CANTONO

Via M. Malpighi 3
20129 Milano, Italy
tel +39 02 29518792

CARUZZO RANCATI

Via G.B. Pergolesi 2
20124 Milano, Italy
tel +39 02 66713092

ANNA CASTELLI FERRIERI

C.so di Porta Romana 87/B
20122 Milano, Italy
tel +39 02 5510451

ACHILLE CASTIGLIONI

P.zza Castello 27
20121 Milano, Italy
tel +39 02 8053606
Achillecastiglioni@libero.it

PIERLUIGI CERRI

Via A. Saffi 25
20123 Milano, Italy
tel +39 02 48519800
cerri.associati@flashnet.it

ALDO CIBIC
CIBIC & PARTNERS

Via Varese 18
20121 Milano, Italy
tel +39 02 6571122
aldocibic@cibicdesign.com

ANNA CITELLI

via Fumagalli,1
20143 Milano, Italy
tel/fax +39 02 83241521
anncitel@tin.it
www.annacitelli,com

ANTONIO CITTERIO & PARTNERS

Via Cerva 4
20122 Milano, Italy
tel +39 02 7638801
citterio@mdsnet.it

CLS ARCHITETTI

via S.Maurilio, 24
20123 Milano, Italy
tel +39 02 866247
fax +39 02 866204
studio@clsarchitetti.com
www.clsarchitetti.com

CODICE 31

Via Cadore 40
20135 Milano, Italy
tel +39 02 5456727
codice31@freemail.it

MARCO COLOMBO STUDIO ABC

Via A. Stradella 13
20129 Milano, Italy
tel +39 02 29523200
mcolombo@planet.it

CONNEXINE

via Cadore 33
20135 Milano, Italy
tel +39-02-55184662
connexine@connexine.com
www.connexine.com

DAVID DESIGN

www.daviddesign.net

MICHELE DE LUCCHI
STUDIO DE LUCCHI

Via G. Pallavicino 31
20145 Milano, Italy
tel +39 02 43008230
sdl@studiodelucchi.it

GABRIELE DE VECCHI

Via E. Lombardini 20
20143 Milano, Italy
tel +39 02 8323365
gabrieledevecchi@libero.it

PAOLO DEGANELLO

Via G.B. Tiepolo 30/B
20129 Milano, Italy
tel +39 02 70009324

DERIM

www.derindesign.com

TOM DIXON

A: 28 All Saints Road,
 W11 1HG London,
tel +44 20 7792 5335
fax +44 7792 2156
www.tomdixon.net
info@tomdixon.net

FRANCESCA DONATI STUDIO

C.so G. Garibaldi 44
20121 Milano, Italy
tel +39 02 6590978

DDL - STUDIO
D'URBINO LOMAZZI

C.so XXII Marzo 39
20129 Milano, Italy
tel +39 02 76110543
durbilon@tin.it

RODOLFO DORDONI

via Solferino, 11
20121 Milano, Italy
tel +39 02 878581
dordoni@tin.it

GILLO DORFLES

P.le Lavater 3
20129 Milano, Italy
tel +39 02 29400351

DROOG DESIGN

www.droogdesign.nl

TERRY DWAN

C.so G. Garibaldi 60
20121 Milano, Italy
tel +39 02 6597452

CECILIA FABIANI

Via Gaudenzio Ferrari 7
20123 Milano, Italy
tel +39 02 8393696

MARIO FALCI

Via Generale G. Govone 100
20155 Milano, Italy
tel +39 02 33603600

GUIDO FERRANTE

Via G.B. Vico 2
20123 Milano, Italy
tel +39 02 4815329

PAOLO FERRANTE

Via San Marco 50
20121 Milano, Italy
tel +39 02 6575925

MADDALENA FERRARESI

V.le Pasubio 16
20154 Milano, Italy
tel +39 02 6597999

LUIGI FERRARIO

Via Castelfidardo 10
20121 Milano, Italy
tel +39 02 6572806
luigiferrario@luigiferrario.it
www.luigiferrario.it

MASSIMILIANO FISICHELLA

Via G. Pacini 36
20131 Milano, Italy
tel +39 02 70638409

JACOPO FOGGINI

Via Sannio 24
20100 Milano

JOZEPH FORAKIS STUDIO

via Canonica 67
20154 milan italy
tel +39.02.83240543
tel +39.02.89422389
www.forakis.com

GIANNI FORCOLINI

C.so G. Garibaldi 89
20121 Milano, Italy
tel +39 02 6571980

DUILIO TOMMASO FORTE

Via A. Corelli 34
20134 Milano, Italy
tel +39 02 70208099
www.duilioforte.com

FRANCESCADONATISTUDIO

www.francescadonatistudio.com

AGFRONZONI STUDIO

Via Solferino 44
20121 Milano, Italy
tel +39 02 6597962

GffILAB

www.glab.it

JACOPO GARDELLA

Via G. Verdi 6
20121 Milano, Italy
tel +39 02 86995581

GIUGIARO DESIGN

Via A.Grandi 21
10024 Moncalieri (TO), Italy
tel +39 011 6893311
www.giugiarodesign.it

GRASSI ALFONSO.

Via Lodovico il Moro 13
20143 Milano, Italy
tel +39 02 89127624

EZIO GRASSI

V.le L. Scarampo 19
20148 Milano, Italy
tel +39 02 4697976

GREGORIETTI ASSOCIATI

Via Montebello 27
20121 Milano, Italy
tel +39 02 29004813

GREGOTTI ASSOCIATI INTERNATIONAL

Via M. Bandello 20
20123 Milano, Italy
tel +39 02 4814141

HARRY & CAMILA CREATORS OF SIGNS

Via G. Meda 43
20141 Milano, Italy
tel +39 02 8464141

HIDDEN

www.hiddenart.com

HIVE

www.hive@hivespace.com

IACCHETTI+RAGNI AROUNDESIGN

Via Gardone 3
20139 Milano, Italy
tel +39 0256819180
www.aroundesign.it
info@aroundesign.it

MASSIMO IOSA GHINI

Via Gentilino 6
20136 Milano, Italy
tel +39 02 58106183
info@iosaghini.it
www.iosaghini.it

JAMES IRVINE STUDIO

James Irvine
Via G. Sirtori 4
20129 Milano, Italy
tel +39 02 29534532
james@james-irvine.com

LISSONI PEIA ASSOCIATI

Via Goito 7/9 - 20121 Milano
tel +39 02-6598647
fax +39 02-45478501
www.peja.it>

INGO MAURER GMBH

Kaiserstrasse 47
80801 Munchen Germany
tel +49 (0)89 381 606-0
fax. +49 (0)89 381 606-20
postmaster@ingo-maurer.com
www.ingo-maurer.com

MAKOTO KAWAMOTO

Via dell'Aprica 8
20158 Milano, Italy
tel +39 02 6080246
026080246@iol.it

MONKEY BOYS

www.monkeyboys.nl

KIM HIROMI

Via G. Romano 17
20135 Milano, Italy
tel +39 02 58302113
info@hiromikim.com
www.hiromikim.com

PERRY ALAN KING E SANTIAGO MIRANDA

Via privata V. Forcella 3
20144 Milano, Italy
tel +39 02 8394963
kingmiranda@iol.it
www.kingmiranda.com

KITA TOSHIYUKI

C.so G. Garibaldi 12
20121 Milano, Italy
tel +39 02 72023466

KOMODA KAZUYO

Via F. Filzi 7
20124 Milano, Italy
tel +39 02 66713655
kkomoda@micronet.it

LAR CENTER

www.larcenter.com.br

MAARTEN KUSTERS MK

Designstudio
Via F. De Sanctis 24
20141 Milano, Italy
tel +39 02 89500917
mk_designstudio@yahoo.com

CLAUDIO LA VIOLA

P.zza 5 Giornate 10
20129 Milano, Italy
tel +39 02 59902621

FERRUCCIO LAVIANI

Via E. De Amicis 53
20123 Milano, Italy
tel +39 02 89421426
laviani@internetforce.com

UGO LA PIETRA

Via Guercino 7
20154 Milano, Italy
tel +39 02 3360 8400

VICO MAGISTRETTI

Via Conservatorio 20
20122 Milano, Italy
tel +39 02 76002964

ANGELO MANGIAROTTI

Via Cesare da Sesto 15
20123 Milano, Italy
tel +39 02 89400449

ENZO MARI

P.le F. Baracca 10
20123 Milano, Italy
tel +39 02 4817315

SAMUELE MAZZA

www.visionnairehomephilosophy.com

ALESSANDRO E FRANCESCO MENDINI

Via Sannio 24
20137 Milano, Italy
tel +39 02 55185185
www.ateliermendini.it

DAVIDE MERCATALI

Ripa di Porta Ticinese 13
20143 Milano, Italy
tel +39 02 8360220
www.davide.mercatali.com

MIGLIORE+SERVETTO

Viale Col di lana 8,
20136 Milano Italy
T +39 0289420174
f +39 0245490251
www.miglioreservetto.com

MASSIMO MOROZZI MOROZZI & PARTNERS

Via Morimondo 21
20143 Milano, Italy
tel +39 02 89128572
morozzi@planet.it

NAVONE ASSOCIATI

Via Varese 18
20121 Milano, Italy
tel +39 02 29060748
navone@tin.it

PAOLA NAVONE

C.so San Gottardo 22
20136 Milano, Italy
tel +39 02 58104926
paolanavone@tin.it

**JOHANNES NORLANDER
ARKITEKTUR & FORM**

www.nordlander.se

FABIO NOVEMBRE

Via Mecenate 76/3
20138 Milano, Italy
tel +39 02 504104
www.novembre.it

OFFECCT

www.offecct.se

GIAMPIERO PEJA

Via Goito 9 20121
Milano, Italy
peja@peja.it

PERMAFROST

www.permafrost.no

MICHELE PIVA

Via Corno di Cavento 6
20148 Milano, Italy
tel +39 02 4981971

**PAOLO PIVA
E FRANCESCO OBERON**

Via G. Compagnoni 30
20129 Milano, Italy
tel +39 02 70125117

PIERO PINTO

Via G. Donizetti 33
20122 Milano, Italy
tel +39 02 782703

GIACOMO POLIN

Via D. Manin 3
20121 Milano, Italy
tel +39 02 29000162
arcpolin@tin.it

TIM POWER

Via Canonica 67
20154 Milano Italy
t: +39. 02.336.19063
tim.power@iol.it
www.tim-power.com

DANIELA PUPPA

Via Savona 97
20144 Milano, Italy
tel +39 02 4234244

NICOLA QUADRI / PIA SPREAFICO

Via Maffei ang. Via Clusone,
Milano, Italy
tel +39 02 5515486

ARNE QUINZE

www.quinzeandmilan.tv

MASSIMO RANDONE

Via Cadore 33 20135
Milano, Italy
tel +39 02 5518 4662
www.connexine.com

FRANCO RAGGI

Via Savona 97
20144 Milano,
tel +39 02 4234244

STEFANO REBOLI

www.stefanoreboli.com

UMBERTO RIVA

Via Vigevano 10
20144 Milano, Italy
tel +39 02 89406844

PAOLO RIZZATTO

Via Bramante da Urbino 7
20154 Milano, Italy
tel +39 02 3452580

FRITZ ROSSI

via Spontini, 4
ITA-20131 Milano, Italia
tel +39 3338455480

ITALO ROTA

Via M. Melloni 35
20129 Milano, Italy
tel +39 02 76115332

RUDE BRAVO DESIGN

www.rudebravo.com

MARC SADLER

Via Savona 97
20144 Milano, Italy
tel +39 02 4224199
m.sadler@tin.it

**SANO TAKAHIDE
STUDIO SANO**

Via F. Ingegnoli 13
20131 Milano, Italy
tel +39 02 26145827
sano@sano.com
www.studiosano.com

DENIS SANTACHIARA

Alzaia Naviglio Grande 156
20144 Milano, Italy
tel +39 02 4221727

RICHARD SAPPER

Via A. Beretta 3
20121 Milano, Italy
tel +39 02 72023101

WILLIAM SAWAYA PAOLO MORONI

Via Andegari 18
20121 Milano, Italy
tel +39 02 86395231
www.sawayamoroni.com

LUCA SCACCHETTI

Via Marcona 12
20129 Milano, Italy
tel +39 02 54108585
scacchetti@scacchetti.com
www.scacchetti.com

PATRIZIA SCARZELLA SIGLA

C.so Sempione 70
20154 Milano, Italy
tel +39 02 31810030

LUIGI SERAFINI

Via A. Ponchielli 3
20129 Milano, Italy
tel +39 02 29406204

JERSZY SEYMOUR

Via Vigevano 39
20144 Milano, Italy
tel +39 02 89422105
jerszyseymour@tin.it

BENJAMIN SHAFFER

www.pantoneb.com

SARAH SONG

www.sarahsongdesign.com

PETER SOLOMON DESIGN

viale Lombardia 66
Milano, 20131 Italia
tel: 02 28510047
fax: 02 700423502
www.petersolomondesign.it

ETTORE SOTTSASS SOTTSASS ASSOCIATI

Via Melone 2
20121 Milano, Italy
tel +39 02 72599201

FLAVIA ALVES DE SOUZA

falvesdesouza@yahoo.com

GEORGE SOWDEN

C.so di Porta Nuova 46/B
20121 Milano, Italy
tel +39 02 653089

STEW

www.stewDesignWorkshop.com

SUMAMPA

www.sumampa.com

SWEDESE

www.swedese.se

MATTEO THUN

Via A. Appiani 9
20121 Milano, Italy
tel +39 02 29000270
www.matteothun.com

TOUCK DESIGN STUDIO.INC.

www.touckdesignstudio.com

UNIFORM

www.uniform.nl

PATRICIA URQUIOLA

Via G. Uberti 33
20129 Milano, Italy
tel +39 02 29511012

WIDIANTO UTOMO

49 Imam Bonjol
Banyuwangi 68416
Indonesia

PETER VALOIS

www.touchdesignstudio.com

NIELS VAN EIJK

www.ons-adres.nl

VIRTUALLY DESIGN

www.virtuallydesign.com

STUDIO VUDAFIERI

Via N.A. Porpora 64
20131 Milano, Italy
tel +39 02 70635767

WUNDERKAMMER STUDIO

Via E. Lombardini 24
20143 Milano, Italy
tel +39 02 8372781

PAOLO ZANI

Via Montevideo 4
20144 Milano, Italy
tel +39 02 58112775
www.paolo.zani.it

MARCO ZANIN SOTTSASS ASSOCIATI

Via Melone 2
20121 Milano, Italy
tel +39 02 72599201

ANTONIO E PAOLA ZANUSO

Via dell'Orso 16
20121 Milano, Italy
tel +39 02 29002115

MARCO JR. ZANUSO

Via Soncino 1
20123 Milano, Italy
tel +39 02 8900847

ZIG ZAG

www.zigzagdesign.org

ACCORNERO

Via Umberto I 1/2,
15035 Frassinello Monf. (AL), Italy
tel +39 014 2933581
fax +39 014 2928369
info@accornero.it
www.accornero.it

ALESSI SPA

Via privata Alessi 6,
28882 Crusi. Omegna (VB), Italy
tel +39 0323 868611
fax +39 0323 641605
info@alessi.com
www.alessi.com

ALIAS SPA

Via L. da Vinci 29/33,
24064 Grum. del Monte (BG), Italy
tel +39 035 4422511
fax +39 035 4422590
info@aliasdesign.it
www.aliasdesign.it

ARC LINEA SPA

Via Pasubio 50,
36030 Caldogno (VI), Italy
tel +39 0444 394111
fax +39 0444 394263
arclinea@arclinea.it
www.arclinea.it

ARMANI / VIA MANZONI 31

Via A. Manzoni 31,
20121 Milano, Italy
tel +39 02 72318600
www.armani-viamanzoni31.com

B ITALIA CONTRACT SPA

Via don Minzoni 4,
20020 Misinto (MI), Italy
tel +39 02 967691
fax +39 02 96328071
contract@bebitalia.it
www.bebitalia.it

B ITALIA SPA

Strada Provinciale 32,
22060 Novedrate (CO), Italy
tel +39 031 765111
fax +39 031 795224
beb@bebitalia.it www.bebitalia.it

BISAZZA SPA

Via Milano 56,
36041 Alte (VI), Italy
tel +39 0444 707511
fax +39 0444 492088
nfo@bisazza.it www.bisazza.it

BOFFI SPA

Via Oberdan 70,
20030 Lent. sul Seveso (MI), Italy
tel +39 036 25341
fax +39 036 2565077
www.boffi.it

BONACINA PIERANTONIO & C.

Via Sant'Andrea 20/A,
22040 Lurago d'Erba (CO), Italy
tel +39 031 699225
fax +39 031 696151
www.bonacinapierantonio.it

BONTEMPI CASA SPA

Via Direttissima del Conero 71,
60021 Camerano (AN), Italy
tel +39 071 7300032
fax +39 071 7300036
info@bontempi.i t
www.bontempi.it

ROCCO BORMIOLI SPA

Via Genova 4/A,
43100 Parma (PR), Italy
tel +39 0521 7901
fax +39 0521 527821
www.bormiolirocco.com

CAPPELLINI SPA

Via Marconi 35,
22060 Arosio (CO), Italy
tel +39 031 759111
fax +39 031 763333
cappellini@cappellini.it;
www.cappellini.it

CASSINA SPA

Via Busnelli 1,
20036 Meda (MI), Italy
tel +39 036 23721
fax +39 0362342246
info@cassina.it
www.cassina.it

CINOVA SRL

Via Missori 2,
20035 Lissone (MI), Italy
tel +39 039 461031
fax +39 039 480889
info@cinova.it
www.cinova.it

CULTI AGRATI SRL

Via G. Leopardi 8,
20030 Seveso (MI), Italy
tel +39 036 2551985
fax +39 036 2551420

CYRUS COMPANY

Via Mottarone 60,
21010 Voghera di Samarate (VA),
Italy
tel +39 0331 224911
fax +39 0331 721136
info@cyruscompany.it;
www.cyruscompany.it

DALMAR SPA

Via Marconi 1/3
20090 Segrate (MI), Italy
tel +39 02 2133151

DANESE

Via A. Canova 34,
20145 Milano, Italy
tel +39 02 34939534
fax +39 02 34538211 i
info@danesemilano.com

DASSI MOBILI MODERNI

Via G. Matteotti 134, 20035
Lissone (MI), Italy
tel +39 039 481173
fax +39 039 464611
dmmdassi@tin.it

DOVETUSAI

Via Sigieri 24,
20135 Milano, Italy
tel +39 02 59902432
fax +39 02 59902442
info@dovetusai.it
www.dovetusai.it

EDRA

Via Livornese Est 108,
56030 Perignano (PI), Italy
tel +39 0587616660
fax +39 0587617500
www.edra.com

FEG

Strada Valassina, ang. Via Pascoli
20034 Giussano (MI), Italy
tel +39 036 28691
fax +39 036 2869280
info@gruppofeg.com
www.gruppofeg.com

FLEXFORM SPA

Via L. Einaudi 23/25,
20036 Meda (MI), Italy
tel +39 036 23991
fax +39 036 2730555
flexform@flexform.it www.flexform.it

FLOU SPA

Via Cadorna 12
20036 Meda (MI), Italy
tel +39 036 23731
fax +39 036 272952
info@flou.it
www.flou.it

FONTANAARTE SPA

Alzaia Trieste 49,
20094 Corsico (MI), Italy
tel +39 02 45121
fax +39 02 4512660
info@fontanaarte.it
www.fontanaarte.it

FOPPA PEDRETTI SPA

Via A. Volta 9,
24064 Grumello del Monte (BG), Italy
tel +39 035 830497
fax +39 035 831283
www.foppapedretti.it

FRATELLI GUZZINI SPA

Contrada Mattonata 60,
62019 Recanati (MC), Italy
tel +39 071 9891
fax +39 071 989260 f
ratelliguzzini@fratelliguzzini.com
www.fratelliguzzini.it

IKEA ITALIA (RETAIL)

Strada Provinciale 208 3,
20061 Carugate (MI), Italy
tel +39 02 929271
www.ikea.com

INSA

Località Canova 1,
27017 Pieve Porto Morone (PV), Italy
tel +39 0382 727411
fax +39 0382 788111
info@insa.it - www.insa.it

ITALHOME LE SEDIE

L.go C. Treves 2,
20121 Milano, Italy
tel +39 02 6551787
italhome@pianetasedia.it
www.pianetasedia.it

KARTELL SPA

Via delle Industrie 1,
20082 Noviglio (MI), Italy
tel +39 02 900121
fax +39 02 9053316
kartell@kartell.it
www.kartell.it

KNOLL INTERNATIONAL

P.zza G. Missori 3,
20123 Milano, Italy
tel +39 02 7222291
fax +39 02 72222930
talia@knoll.com - www.knoll.it

LA MURRINA

V.le Isonzo 11,
22078 Turate (CO), Italy
tel +39 02 969751
fax +39 02 96975211 l
lamurrina@lamurrina.com
www.lamurrina.com

LAGOSTINA SPA

Via 4 Novembre 45,
28887 Omegna (VB), Italy
tel +39 0323 6521
fax +39 0323 61046
info@lagostina.it www.lagostina.it

LEMA SPA.

S.S. Briantea 342,
22040 Alzate Brianza (CO), Italy
tel +39 031 630990
fax +39 031 632492
lema@lemamobili.com
www.lemamobili.com

MANDARINA DUCK

Via don Minzoni 36,
40057 Cad. Granarolo (BO), Italy
tel +39 051 764411
fax +39 051 766056

MATTEOGRASSI SPA

Via Padre Rovagnati 2,
22066 Mariano Com. (CO), Italy
tel +39 031 757711
fax +39 031 748388
info@matteograssi.it
www.matteograssi.it

MERITALIA S.P.A.

via Como 76
Mariano Comense (CO), Italy

MC SELVINI

Via C. Poerio 3,
20129 Milano, Italy
tel +39 02 76006118
fax +39 02 781325
www.mcselvini.it

MH WAY

Via Puecher 1; Via Rosselli 37,
20090 Fizzonasco (MI), Italy
tel +39 02 90781960
fax +39 02 90724782
mhway@mhway.it www.mhway.it

MISURA EMME

via IV Novembre 72,
35011 Mariano Com (CO), Italy
tel +39 031 754111
www.misuraemme.it

MOLTENI & C. SPA

Via Rossini 50,
20034 Giussano (MI), Italy
tel +39 036 23591
fax +39 036 2355170
www.molteni.it

MOROSO SPA

Via Nazionale 60,
33010 Cavalicco di Tav. (UD), Italy
tel +39 0432 577111
fax +39 0432 570761
info@moroso.it
www.moroso.it

NARDI INTERNI SPA

Via Refrontolo 5,
31053 Pieve di Soligo (TV), Italy
tel +39 0438 83546
fax +39 0438 83021
info@nardinterni.it

OLTREFRONTIERA

Via C. Cattaneo 30,
22066 Vigh. di Cantù (CO), Italy
tel +39 031 737311
fax +39 031 737329
info@oltrefrontiera.it
www.oltrefrontiera.it

PANDORA DESIGN

Via Canonica 40,
20154 Milano, Italy
tel +39 02 316157
fax +39 02 34939492
www.pandoradesign.it

PLANK

Via Nazionale 35,
39040 Ora (BZ), Italy
tel +39 0471 803500
fax +39 0471 803599
info@plank.i - www.plank.it

POLIFORM SPA

Via Montesanto 28,
22044 Inverigo (CO), Italy
tel +39 031 6951
fax +39 031 699444
info.poliform@poliform.it
www.poliform.it

POLTRONA FRAU SPA

S.S. 77, Km 74,500, 62029
Tolentino (MC), Italy
tel +39 0733 9091
fax +39 0733 909246
info@poltronafrau.it
www.poltronafrau.it

PRESOTTO INDUSTRIE MOBILI

via Puia 7
33070 Brugnera (PN), Italy
tel +39 04346181111
fax +39 0434613558
www.presotto.com
info@presotto.com

RIMADESIO SPA

Via Furlanelli 96,
20034 Giussano (MI), Italy
tel +39 036 23171
fax +39 036 2317317
rimadesio@rimadesio.it
www.rimadesio.it

STURM UND PLASTIC SPA

Via Coti Zelati 90,
20030 Palazz. Milanese (MI), Italy
tel +39 02 99044222
fax +39 02 99045611
www.sturmundplastic.it

TACCHINI

Via Domodossola 7,
20030 Barucc. di Seveso (MI),Italy
tel +39 036 2504182
fax +39 036 2552402
tacchini@tacchini.it www.tacchini.it

TECNO SPA

via Milano 12
20039 Varedo (MI), Italy
tel +39 0362 5351 -
fax +39 0362 535220
www.tecnospa.com
tecnospa@tin.it

THONET VIENNA GMBH CO.

Berggasse 31, A-1090 Wien
tel +43 1 310 200230
fax +43 1 310 200213
www.thonet-vienna.at

TRUSSARDI HOME DESIGN

P.zza E. Duse 4,
20122 Milano, Italy
tel +39 02 76004691
fax +39 02 7614249

VISMARA DESIGN

Via Carducci 3,
20030 Seveso (MI), Italy
tel +39 036 2503726
fax +39 036 2551452
vismara@vismara.it www.vismara.it

YCAMI

Via provinciale 31/33,
22060 Novedrate (CO), Italy
tel +39 0317897311
fax +39 0317897350
www.ycami.com
info@ycami.com

ZANI SPA

Via del Porto 51/53,
25088 Tosc Maderno (BS), Italy
tel +39 036 5641006
fax +39 036 5644281

ZANOTTA SPA

Via Vittorio Veneto 57, 20054
Nova Milanese (MI), Italy
tel +39 036 24961
fax +39 036 2451038
www.zanotta.it

9 NET AVENUE ITALIA SPA

Via Torri Bianche 9,
20059 Vimercate (MI), Italy
tel +39 039699901
fax +39 03969990229
www.9netweb.it

INSA

LocalitÓ Canova 1,
27017 P. Porto Morone (PV), Italy
tel +39 0382 727411
fax +39 0382 788111
info@insa.it; www.insa.it

KREON ITALIA

Via Forcella 5,
20144 Milano, Italy
tel +39 02 89420846
fax +39 02 89428785
Mailbox@kreon.it

KRIPTONITE ITALIA

Vi a Milano 6/13,
20068 Pesc. Borromeo (MI), Italy
tel +39 02 55309880
fax +39 02 5471501
www.kriptonite.com
info@kriptonite.com

KUNDALINI

Via De Sanctis 34
ITALY - 20141 Milano
Tel +39 02 848 000 88
fax +39 02 848 000 96
gregorio@kundalini.it
www.kundalini.it

LA MURRINA

V.le Isonzo 11,
22078 Turate (CO), Italy
tel +39 02 969751 f
fax +39 02 96975211
lamurrina@lamurrina.com
www.lamurrina.com

LASER ENTERTAINMENT

Via Licurgo 6,
20126 Milano, Italy
tel +39 0227007064
fax +39 0227002128
www.laserent.com
info@laserent.com

LUCEPLAN

Via E.T.Moneta 44/46,
20161 Milano, Italy
tel +39 02662421
fax +39 0266203400
www.luceplan.it
luceplan@luceplan.it

LUXO ITALIANA

Via delle More 1,
24030 Presezzo (BG), Italy
tel +39 035603511
fax +39 035464817
www.luxo.it - office@luxo.it

MARTINELLI LUCE

Via Bandettini 145,
55100 San Concordio Lucca, Italy
tel +39 0583418315
fax +39 0583419003
www.martinelliluce.it
info@martinelliluce.it

9NET WEB SOLUTIONS

Via Caldera, 21,
20153 Milano, Italy
tel +39 023890321
fax +39 02 38903229
www.9netweb.it

NOVALUX

Via Marzabotto 2,
40050 Funo di Argelato (BO), Italy
tel +39 051860558
fax +39 051863347
www.novalux.it
novalux@novalux.it

OLUCE

Via Cavour 52,
20098 S.Giul. Milanese (MI), Italy
tel +39 0298491435
fax +39 0298490779
www.oluce.com
info@oluce.com

PLANK

Via Nazionale 35,
39040 Ora (BZ), Italy
tel +39 0471 803500
fax +39 0471 803599
info@plank.it - www.plank.it

REGGIANI ILLUMINAZIONE

Viale Monza 16,
20050 Sovico (MI), Italy
tel +39 03920711
fax +39 0392071999
www.reggiani.net
point@reggiani.net

SOLZI LUCE

Via del Sale 46,
26100 Cremona, Italy
tel +39 037225712
fax +39 037237880
www.solziluce.com
solziluce@solziluce.com

TACCHINI

Via Domodossola 7,
20030 Bar. di Seveso (MI), Italy
tel +39 036 2504182
fax +39 036 2552402
tacchini@tacchini.it www.tacchini.it

TARGETTI

Via Pratese 164,
50145 Firenze, Italy
tel +3905537911
fax +39 0553791266
www.targetti.it
targetti@targetti.it

TERZANI

Via Castelpulci int.9,
50010 Scandicci (FI), Italy
tel +39 055722021
fax +39 0557311161
www.terzani.com
terzani@terzani.com

VIABIZZUNO

Via Fosse Ardeatine 8,
40061 Minerbio (BO), Italy
tel +39 0516607911
fax +39 0516606197
www.viabizzuno.com
viabizzuno@viabizzuno.com

VISTOSI VETRERIA

Via Galilei 9,
30121 Mogliano Veneto (TV), Italy
tel +39 0415900170
fax +39 0415900992
www.vistosi.it
vistosi@vistosi.it

ZOLTAN

Strada Padana Sup.,
20090 Vimodrone (MI), Italy
tel +39 027400160
fax +39 027400184
www.zoltan.it
safe@zoltan.it

ZONCA

Via Lomellina 145,
27058 Voghera (PV), Italy
tel +39 038348441
fax +39 0383647336
www.zonca.com
zonca@zonca.com

DESIGN GALLERIES

SHOWROOMS

DE PADOVA

C.so venezia 14,
20121 Milano, Italy
tel +39 02 777201
www.depadova.it

DESIGN GALLERY

Via Manzoni 46,
20121 Milano, Italy
tel +39 02 798955
www.designgallerymilano.com

DILMOS

P.za S.Marco 1,
20121 Milano, Italy
tel +39 02 29002437
www.dilmos.com

DRIADE

Via Manzoni 30,
20121 Milano, Italy
Tel +39 0276023098
www.dadriade.it
www.driade.com

MDF

Via della Chiusa
ang. Via Crocefisso,
20123 Milano, Italy
tel +39 02 58317168
www.mdfitalia.it

POST DESIGN

Via Moscova 27,
Milano, Italy
tel +39 02 6554731
Postdesign@tiscalinet.it

GALLERIA CARLA SOZZANI

Corso Como 10, Milano, Italy
tel +39 02 653531
www.galleriacarlasozzani.com

UNDERSTATE

Viale Crispi, Milano, Italy
tel +39 02 62690435
www.understate.it

PIT 21

Via Santa Marta 21,
20121 Milano, Italy
tel +39 02 89013169

YAKY

(Galleria S. Marco)
Via Solferino 2,
20121 Milano, Italy
tel - fax 02 654103

ACCADEMIA DI BELLE ARTI DI BRERA

Brera 2 (Istituto Zappa)
Corso Sperimentale di Design
Viale Marche 71,
20159 Milano, Italy
tel - fax +39 02 6684898

ACCADEMIA DI BELLE ARTI FROSINONE

Viale Marconi
03100 Frosinone (FR)
tel +39 0775 211167
fax +39 0775 211168
accademia.bellearti.fr@micanet.it
www.accademiabellearti.fr.it

ACCADEMIA DI COMUNICAZIONE

Via Savona 112/a
20144 Milano, Italy
tel +39 02 4815232
fax +39 0223006200
www.hdemia.it

ART ACADEMY OF LATVIA RIGA DESIGN SCHOOL OF ART

Kalpaka Boulv. 13
1867 Riga - Lettonia
tel +371 9153500
fax +371 7322196
abele@latnet.lv www.lma.lv

ART CENTER COLLEGE OF DESIGN

1700 Lida Street, P.O. Box 7197
USA - Pasadena, CA 91109-7197
tel +1 626 3962343
fax +1 626 7950819

BEZALEL ACADEMY FOR ART AND DESIGN

Industrial Design Department
Mount Scopus
P.O. Box 24046
91240 Jerusalem, Israel
tel +972 2 5893333
fax +972 2 5823094
www.bezalel.ac.il

BRISBANE CITY GALLERY

Ground Floor, City Hall
King George Square
Brisbane Qld 4000, Australia
tel +61 7 34035330
fax +61 7 34035325

CRANBROOK ACADEMY OF ART

P.O. Box 801
Bloomfield Hills,
MI 48303.0801, USA
tel +1 248 6453335
fax +1 248 6460046
sklinker@cranbrook.edu

DESIGN ACADEMY EINDHOVEN

Emmasingel 14, 5600 CC
Eindhoven, The Netherlands
tel +31 0 40 2393939
www.designacademy.nl

DOMUS ACADEMY

GRUPPO WEBEGG
Via Savona 97,
20144 Milano, Italy
tel +39 02 42414001
fax +39 02 4222525
www.domusacademy.it

ECOLE DES BEAUX-ARTS

7 rue des Beaux-Arts,
33000 Bordeaux, France
tel +33 5 56334911
fax +33 5 56314623
ecole.bxarts@mairie-bordeaux.fr

EINA – ESCUELA DE DISEÑO Y ARTE

Paseo Santa Eulalia 25
08017 Barcelona
Spagna
tel +34 93 2030923
fax +34 93 2800554
info@eina.edu
www.eina.edu

ENSAD, ECÔLE NATIONALE SUPERIEURE DES ARTS DÉCO RATIFS

31 rue d'Ulm
75240 Paris Cedex 05, France
tel +33 1 42349700
fax +33 1 42349785
info@ensad.fr – www.ensad.fr

ESTGAD,

Escola Superior de Tecnologia,
Gestr,o, Arte de Design
Rua Dr. Isidoro Inacio
Alves de Carvalho
2500 Caldas da Rainha, Portugal
tel +351 262 830900
fax +351 262 830904

FACHHOCHSCHULE AACHEN

Boxgraben 100
52064 Aachen, Germany
tel +49 241 60091510
fax +49 241 60091532
dekovic@fh-aachen.de

FACHHOCHSCHULE COBURG -

Dpt Interior Space Design
Am Hofbrauhaus 1
D - 96450 Coburg
tel +49 9561 317434
fax +49 9561 317441

GENESIO

ISTITUTO NUOVE TECNOLOGIE
Via Pietrasanta 14,
20141 Milano, Italy
tel +39 02 55230369
fax +39 02 55230410
www.genesio.org

GEORGE BROWN COLLEGE

200 King Street east, Room 313 A
CDN - M5T 2T9 Toronto, Ontario
tel +1 416 4152000-2165
fax +1 416 4152094
lferrara@gbrown.on.ca

GERRIT RIETVELD ACADEMIE

Fred Roeskestraat 96
NL - 1076 ED Amsterdam
tel +31 20 3624296
fax +31 20 3624299
joost.van.haaften@12move.n

THE GLASGOW SCHOOL OF ART

167 Renfrew Street
UK - G3 6RQ Glasgow
tel +44 141 3534589
fax +44 141 3534655
design@gsa.ac.uk
www.gsa.ac.uk

**HOCHSCHULE FÜR KUNST
UND GESTALTUNG**

Vogelangstrasse 15
CH - 4021 Basel
tel +41 61 6956347
fax +41 61 6956347

HOLON ACADEMIC

Institute of technology
52 Golomb Street
IL - 58102 Holon
tel +972 3 50265878
fax +972 3 5026690
givati@matav.net.il

HONG-IK UNIVERSITY

258-110 Itaewon 2 dong.
Yongsan-gu
Seoul – Corea del Sud
tel +82 11 2060530
fax +82 31 7887099

ICELAND ACADEMY OF THE ARTS

Skipholt 1
105 Reykjavik, Iceland
tel +354 552 4000
fax +354 562 3629
loaauduns@hotmail.com

**INTERACTION DESIGN
INSTITUTE IVREA**

Via Montenavale 1,
10015 Ivrea(TO), Italy
Tel.+39 012542211
www.interaction-ivrea.it

I.P.S.I.A. "G. MERONI"

Via Alfieri 14
20035 Lissone (MI)
tel +39 039 793948
fax +39 039 795683
ipsiameroni@ipsiameroni.it
www.ipsiameroni.it

**ISIA _ ISTITUTO
SUPERIORE PER LE
INDUSTRIE ARTISTICHE**

Via degli Alfani 58,
50121 Firenze, Italy
tel +39 055 218836
fax +39 055 218740
www.isia.it

ISTANBUL TECHNICAL UNIVERSITY

Ta.ki.la
34437 Istanbul, Turkey
tel + 90 212 2931310
fax +90 212 2514895
alpayer@itu.edu.tr

ISD

Istituto Superiore di Design
Via Duomo 61
80138 Napoli, Italy
tel +39 081 440495
fax +39 081 446449
isd@dial.it - www.dial.it/isd

ISTITUTO EUROPEO DI DESIGN

Via A. Sciesa 4,
20135 Milano, Italy
www.ied.it

ISTITUTO EUROPEO DI DESIGN

Via G.Pomba 17,
10123 Torino, Italy
tel +39 011 8125668
fax +39 011 835720
www.ied.it

**ISTITUTO ITALIANO
DI FOTOGRAFIA**

Via Bugatti 3,
Milano, Italy

KAUNAS ART INSTITUTE OF VILNIUS ACADEMY OF ARTS

MuitinÅs g. 4
3000 Kaunas, Lithuania
tel - fax +370 37 749296
sanojv@takas.it

L'ÄCOLE BLEUE

29, bd Saint Jacques
75014 Paris, France
tel +33 1 45893132
fax +33 1 53801609
info@ecole-bleue.com

LUND UNIVERSITY

P.O. Box 118
221 00 Lund, Sweden
tel +46 46 2228519
fax +46 46 2228060
claus.eckhardt@design.lth.se
www.ide.lth.se

MARANGONI SCHOOL

Via M.Gonzaga 6,
20123 Milano, Italy
tel +39 02 861090
fax +39 02 89010611
Info@istitutomarangoni.com
www.istitutomarangoni.com

METU – MIDDLE EAST TECH. UNIVERSITY

Faculty of Architecture
Department of Industrial Design
06531 Ankara Turkey
tel +90 312 2106534
fax +90 312 2101251
velasco@metu.edu.tr

OSAKA UNIVERSITY OF ARTS

469 Higashiyama Kanan-Cho
Minamikawachi-Gun
Osaka 585-8555, Japan
tel +81 721 933266
fax +81 721 935380
isao-y@osaka-geidai.ac.jp

PARSONS SCHOOL OF DESIGN

66 Fifth Avenue
New York NY 10011, USA
tel +1 212 2295885
fax +1 212 2295374
www.parsons.edu

POLITECNICO DI MILANO

Facoltà del Design
Via Durando 38/a
20158 Milano, Italy
tel +39 02 23995961
fax +39 02 23995977
www.design.polimi.it

RHODE ISLAND SCHOOL OF DESIGN

Two College Street
Providence, Rhode Island
02903-2784, USA
tel +1 401 454 6102
fax +1 401 454 6566
mgrear@risd.edu

RMIT UNIVERSITY

Bdg 8, Lev. 12 360
Swanston Street
AUS - Melbourne 3000
tel +61 3 99253555
fax +61 3 99253507

SEINÄJOKI POLYTECHNIC SCHOOL OF CULTURE AND DESIGN

Kotikouluntie 1, box 4
66301 Jurva Finlandi
tel +358 201 245944
fax +358 201 245901
leena.vainionpaa@seamk.fi

THE LEEDS SCHOOL OF ART ARCHITECTURE AND DESIGN

City Campus
Leeds LS1 3HE, UK
tel +44 113 2835990
fax +44 113 2833139
l.raine@lmu.ac.uk

TAMA ART UNIVERSITY

Dept. of Environmental Design
2-1723 Yarimizu, Hachioji
J - 192-0394 Tokyo
tel +81 426 768611
fax +81 426 762935

TONGIJ UNIVERSITY

Art and design department
1239 Siping Road
200092Shanghai
Cina Repubblica Popolare
tel +86 21 65982931
fax +86 21 65986707
nuqqun@yahoo.com.cn

UNIVERSIDAD DE LOS ANDES

Escuela de Diseño Industrial
Nucleo La Hechicera
«Dr. Pedro Rincon Gutierrez»
YV - 5101Merida
tel +58 274 2401902
fax +58 274 2401932

UNIVERSIDADE TUIUTI DO PARANÁ

Rua Amazonas Marcondes 9
BR - 80035-230 Curitiba - PR
tel +55 41 3317700
fax +55 41 2536498
Ivens.Fontoura@utp.br

UNIVERSITÀ DI GENOVA

Stradone S.Agostino 37, 16123
Genova, Italy
tel +39 010 2095731
fax +39 010 2095905
www.arch.unige.it

UNIVERSITÄT
DER KÜNSTE BERLIN

Stasse des 17. Juni 118
10623 Berlin, Germany
tel +49 30 31852914
fax +49 30 31852782
kruhland@udk-berlin.de

UNIVERSITÄT FÜR
ANGEWANDTE KUNST WIEN

Oskar Kokoschka-Platz 2
1010 Wien, Austria
tel +43 1 711330
fax +43 1 711332009
www.angewandte.at

UNIVERSITÉ DE MONTREAL

Faculté de l'amànagement
Ecole de Design Industriel
2940, ch. Côte Ste-Catherine
Montréal (Québec) H3T 1B9,
Canada
tel +1 514 3437905
fax +1 514 3435694
diane_bisson@mlink.net

UNIVERSITY OF WEST-HUNGAR

Sopron, Deakter 32
H - 9400 Sopron
tel +36 99 345180
fax +36 99 345180
ami@fmk.nyme.hu

VITRA DESIGN MUSEUM

Charles-Eames-Strasse 1
79576 Weil am Rhein, Germany
tel +49 7621 7023351
fax +49 7621 7024351
info@design-museum.de
www.design-museum.de

ƎƐ ш we take care
communication behind the scenes
the iperactive ipermedia company www.bew.it

ZETA_LAB
IS A DESIGN ORIENTED STUDIO DEVOTED TO BRANDING AND VISUAL DESIGN PROJECTS.
ZETA_LAB PROMOTES AN ANALYTICAL APPROACH RATHER THAN A STYLE
www.zetalab.com

THAT'S
ALL
FOLKS

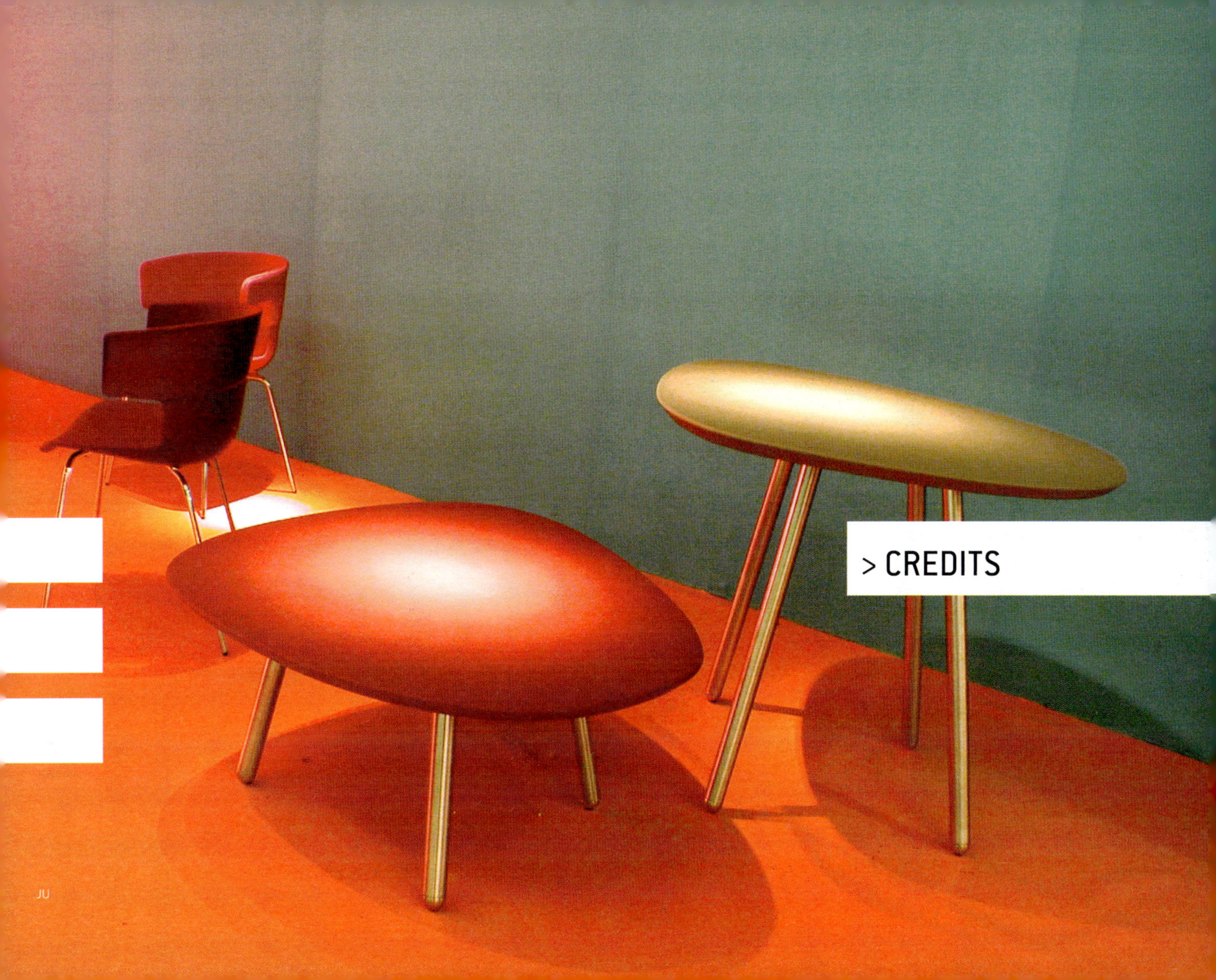

> CREDITS

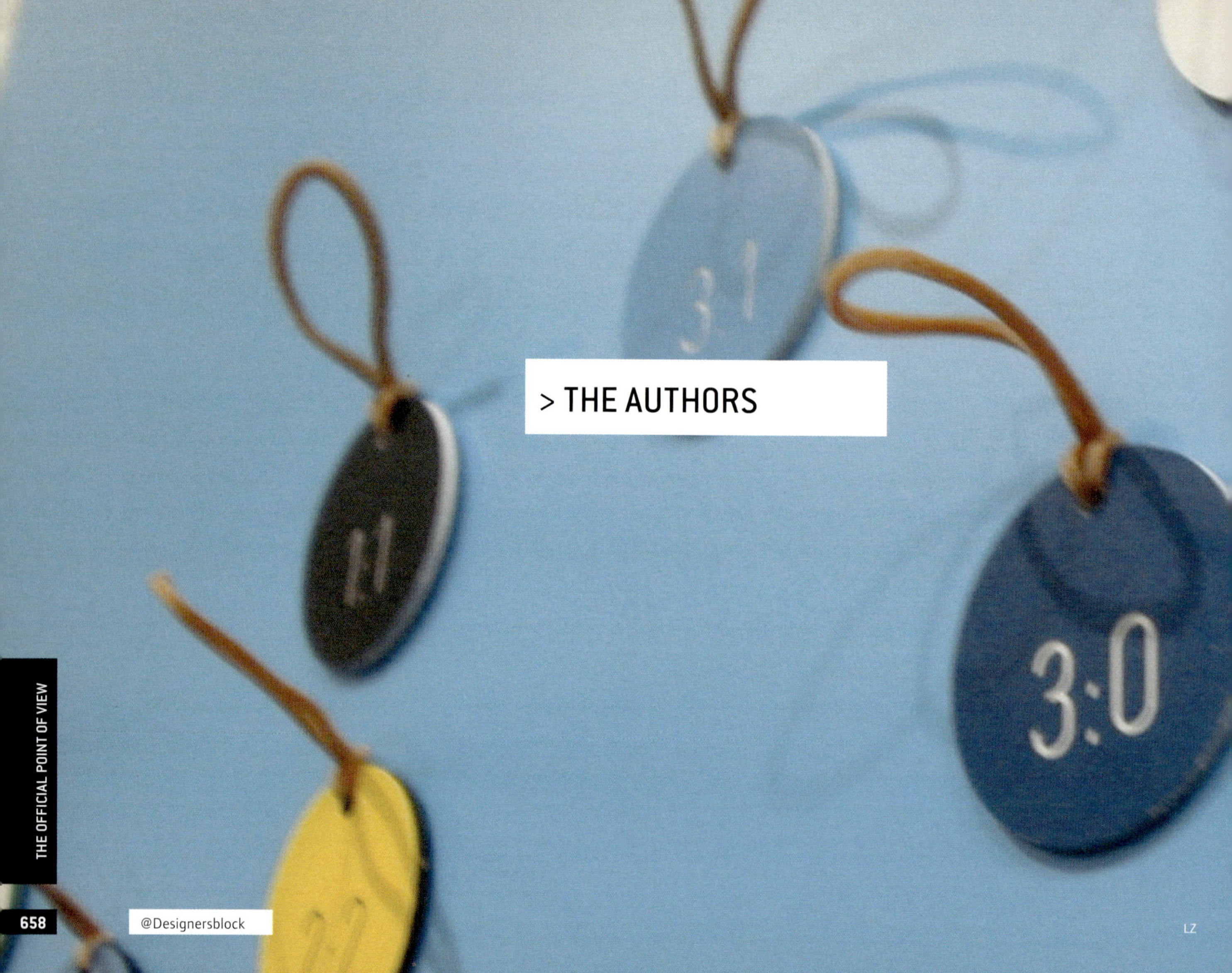

@Designersblock

LZ

GIULIA BER TACCHINI - JU

Is a designer and creative director working in fashion design - mainly accessories - (Dior, Ferré, Sazaby-Tokyo, Prada, Costume National, etc)

and industrial design (Fontana Arte, Arflex, Habitat, Barovier&Toso, Sturm und Plastic, etc.),

researching particular innovative materials and their applications. She has designed silver jewelry and tabletop for William Spratling.

She is doing artistic research work in the fields of photography and videofilm.

julia@theofficialpointofview.it

PAOLO CALCAGNI - PA

is co-founder of Central Production and since 1990 director of music and advertising films for over 100 national and international clients.

From 1992 he collaborated with many international production firms to produce ads for multinational brands.

He has directed actresses of international fame: Letizia Casta, Isabel Pasco', Catherine Zeta Jones, Penelope Cruz, Liv Tyler.

He has earned recognition in advertising film festivals in Milan and Cannes. In 1995 he created the company Enorme Film Arts.

Since 2002 he is the publisher of The Official Point of View".

paolo@theofficialpointofview.it

LUCIO LUZO LAZZARA - LZ

is the founder and art director af Zeta_Lab, Milano. He develops visual communication for many insitutions and firms, designing

complete visual identities, in a wide span going from company brands to editorial design via video and tv trailers.

Since 2001 is a teacher at Politecnico di Milano and Istituto Europeo di Design.

LuZo@theofficialpointofview.it

RICCARDO RINETTI - RR

Is principally an advertising and corporate film director while at the same time comes out his own personal research as a photographer

on black and white images of portraits and "poetic reportage". He began his career as a journalist and music critic, and also worked

as a record producer for various Italian singers. He worked for many years for the advertising agency McCann Ericksson, first as a copywriter

and then as creative co-director.

riccardo@theofficialpointofview.it

> THE PHOTOGRAPHERS

MAURIZIO COSTA -CO-

Expert in panoramic and internal photography, still life and digital elaborations.
Since 1999 he has been a teacher of photographic techniques at the Istituto Europeo di Design of Milan and is in charge of the laboratories there.

mauriziotcs@hotmail.com

SAVERIO LOMBARDI VALLAURI -SV-

Architectural photographer, photography teacher and author of manuals of photographic techniques.
Since 1998 he has been the official COSMIT photographer.

saveriolombardi@tiscalinet.it

TOMMASO MANGIOLA -TM-

Born in Calabria, he now lives in Milan.
He has worked with clients such CondéNast, GFT, Amica, Cappellini, Armani, Prada, and with various other entrepreneurs, not as wellknown but equally interesting, such as tattooers, bakers, gardeners, tailors, entertainers, jewellers and editors

tommasomangiola@libero.it

EMMANUEL MATHEZ -MZ-

Born in 1969, he works as a freelance photographer.
His photos appeared on the covers of many Italian records and in italian and international magazines.
Shortlisted for Kodak European Young Photographers Award 1993, Biennale Giovani Artisti del Mediterraneo '94
Shortlisted for SanCarlo BorromeoAward '95
Kodak Immaginando Award 1996

mathez@tiscalinet.it

The Temple by Hill Jephson Robb

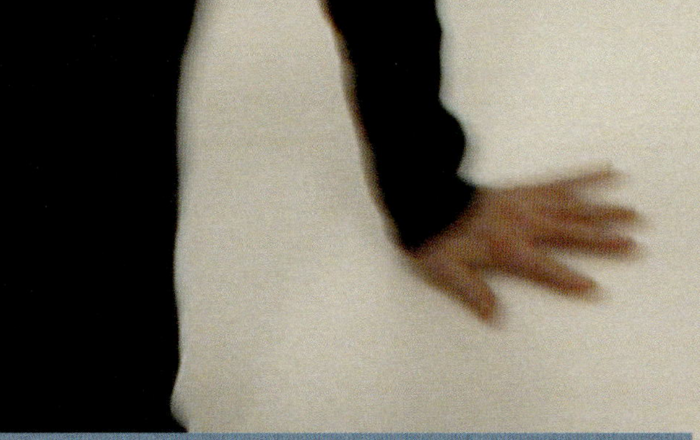

MARCO PIETRACUPA -MP-

He works in the fields of portraits and fashion photography .

After graduating from the Italian Institute of Photography

he has used the themes of his artistic-photographic research

for private exhibitions.

His appear in fashion and design magazines.

Personal exhibition: "Mondi2" Galleria Modigliani Due/art.

marco.pietracupa@tiscalinet.it

AGOSTINO OSIO -OS-

Born in 1978, he lives and he works in Milan, where he

studied photography at the European Institute of Design.

He mainly works in artistic photography films.

Osiago@hotmail.com

GIULIANO RADICI -GR-

"Photograpys that's job and curiosity for everything

beautiful and ugly". His search for the beautiful without avoiding

the ugly often takes histo wander in the Orient on personal

person-focused researches.

His photographs can be found in in art collections worldwide,

including the Brazilian collector Joaquin Piva, the Museum of San

Marino, and the Fotokunst Museum in Denmark.

SEBASTIANO PAVIA -SP-

Born in Catania in 1972, he has worked with Fabrica di

Oliviero Toscani, Grazia Neri agency, Upside Down,

for different companies and many international and Italian

newspapers and magazines from Photografia, Zoom, Private,

to Polaroid, Photo Espana, and Nu Attitudini Morbose.

He has directed videos such as 'Razzismo' for MTV and

"Giornalismo" for Arte' France.

sebbapavia@katamail.com

ALESSANDRO VIGANÒ -AV-

Born in 1972, he lives in Milan.

He studied at the NCAD in Dublin and then graduated in

architecture from the Politecnico of Milano..

He is interested in different fields of creative disciplines.

ale@zetalab.com

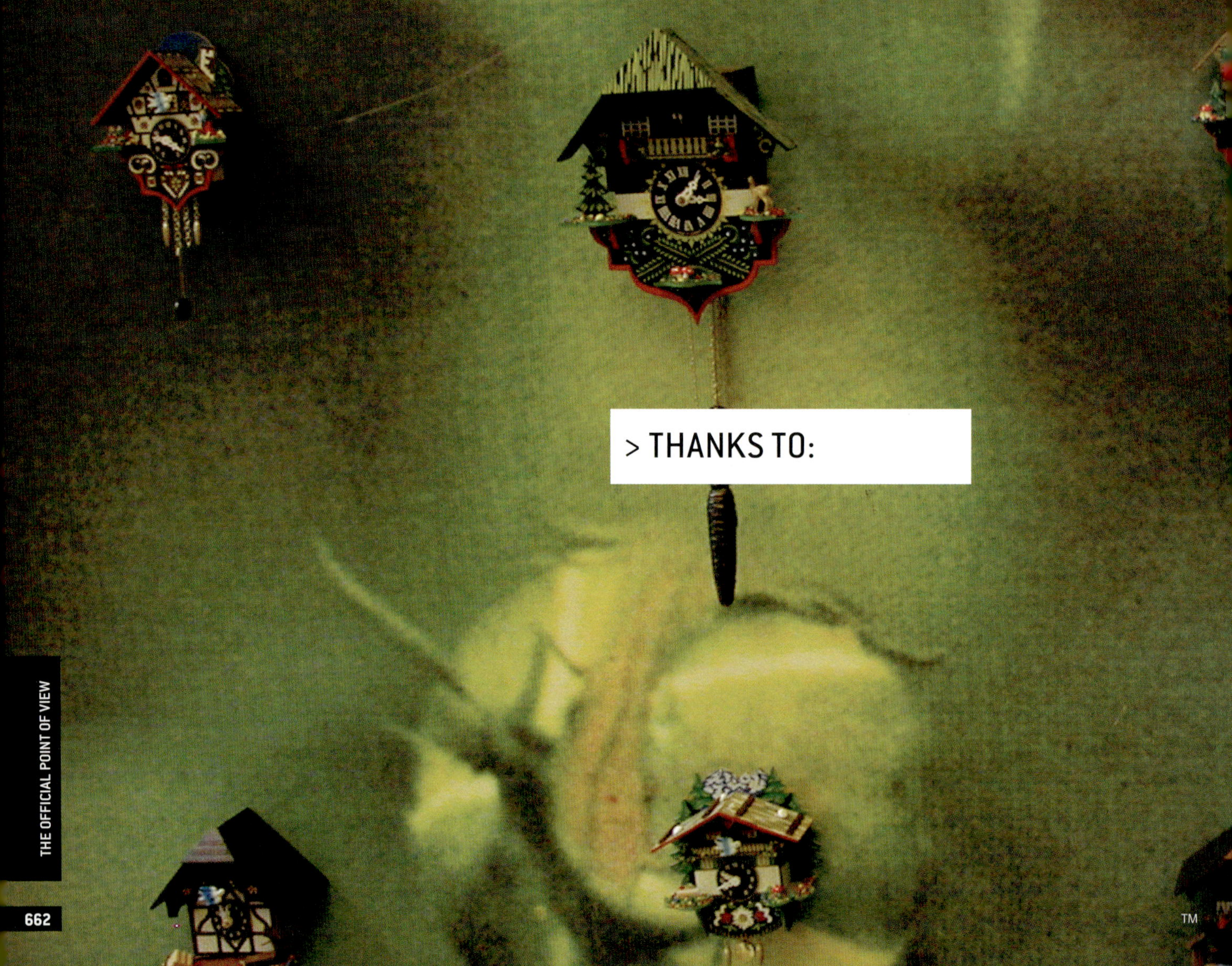

> THANKS TO:

INTERVIEWS

Maria Cristina Didero is a freelance photography curator.
For several years now, she has been in charge
of Vitra Design Museum exhibitions for Italy, besides
working on editorial projects and contributing to a
number of newspapers both in Italy and abroad.
Interviews on the Official Point of View texts.

GRAPHIC DESIGNERS

Marco Boldrini

Heraclio Atencio

Emanuele Radaelli

THANKS TO

Darren Almond

Marco Arno`

Silvia Ber

Michela Brogi

Gero Caccia

Gianandrea Castellazzi

COSMIT

Danila Crotti

Max Crotti

Marika Gherardi

Marinella Gori

Leo Kosaref

Flavio Del Monte

Droog Design

Ettore Favini

Gala Fermandez

Jozeph Forakis

Ernst Gampler

Vittorio Linfante

Ross Lovegrove

Filippo Masci

Ingo Maurer

Samuele Mazza

Ico Migliore+Mara Servetto

Dr.Monteleone

Silvia Morandi

Fabio Novembre

David Palterer

Roberto Paoli

Gaetano Pesce

Daniele Pignatelli

Alberto Pedrini

Roberta Robbie Ricciuti

Fabio Rotella

Claudio Sadler

Tania Solci

Studio MVM

Luisa Taliento

Veronica Valenza

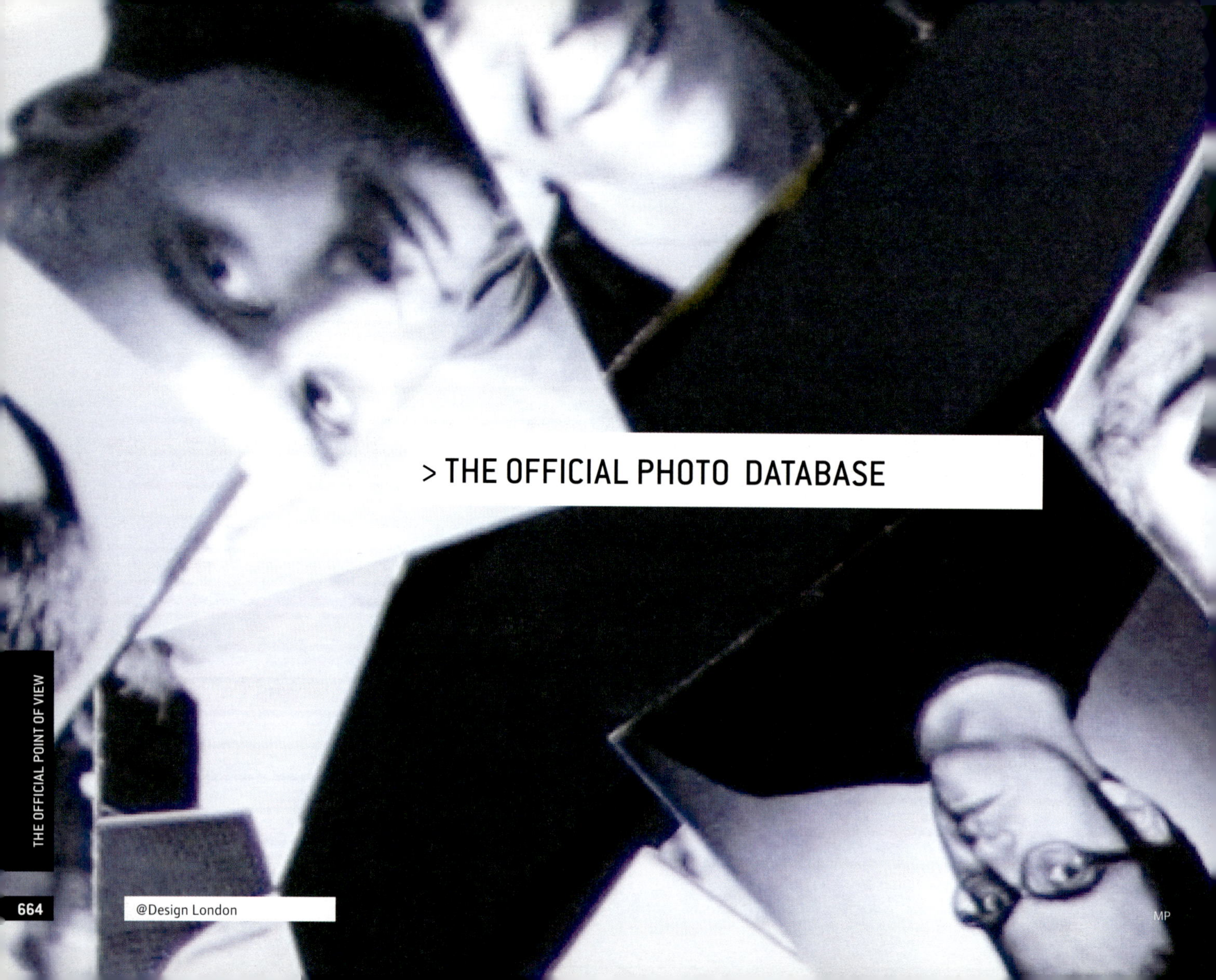

> THE OFFICIAL PHOTO DATABASE

@Design London

MP

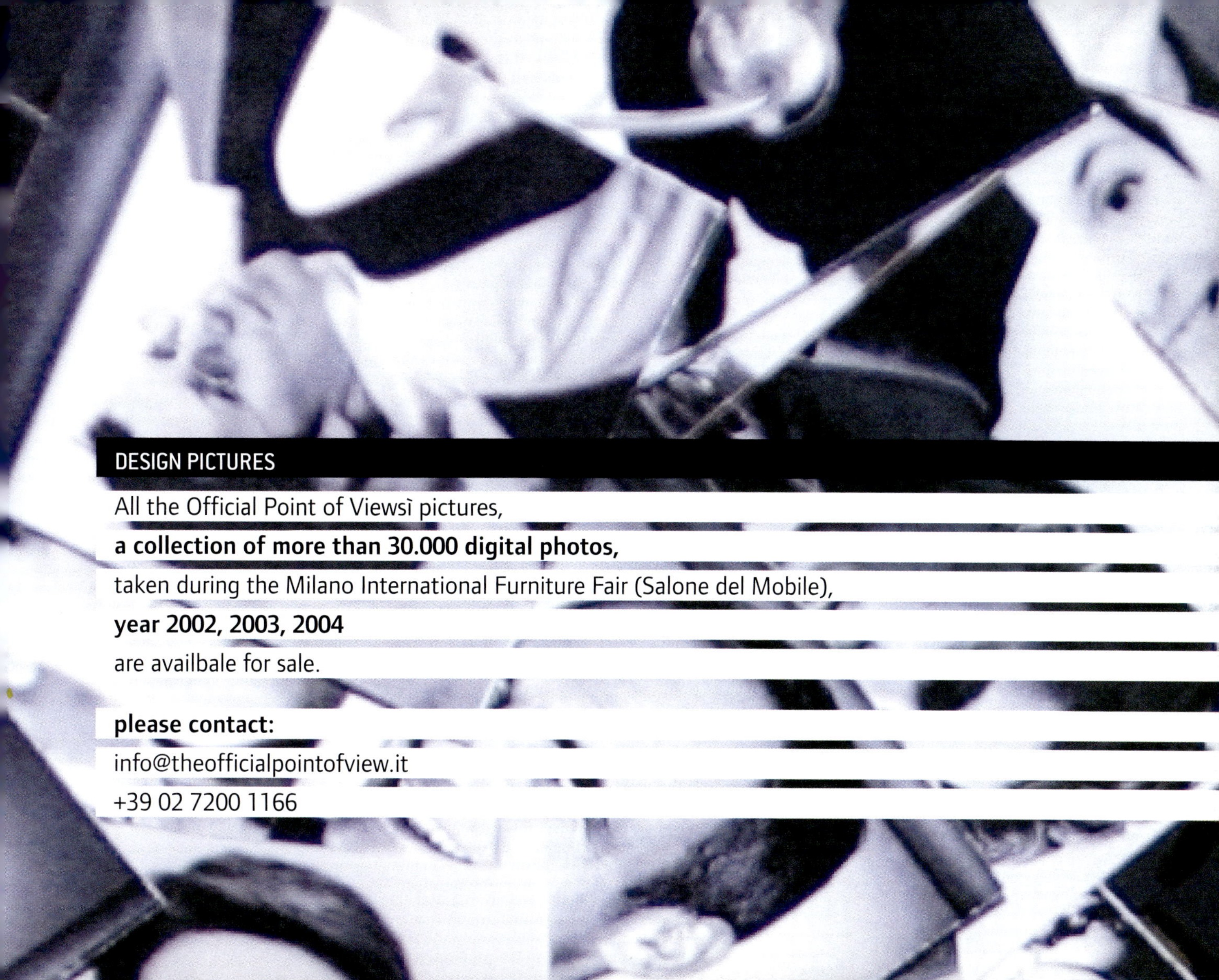
DESIGN PICTURES

All the Official Point of Viewsì pictures,

a collection of more than 30.000 digital photos,

taken during the Milano International Furniture Fair (Salone del Mobile),

year 2002, 2003, 2004

are availbale for sale.

please contact:

info@theofficialpointofview.it

+39 02 7200 1166

> WITH THE CONTRIBUTION OF
THE OFFICIAL POINT OF VIEW
@Design London

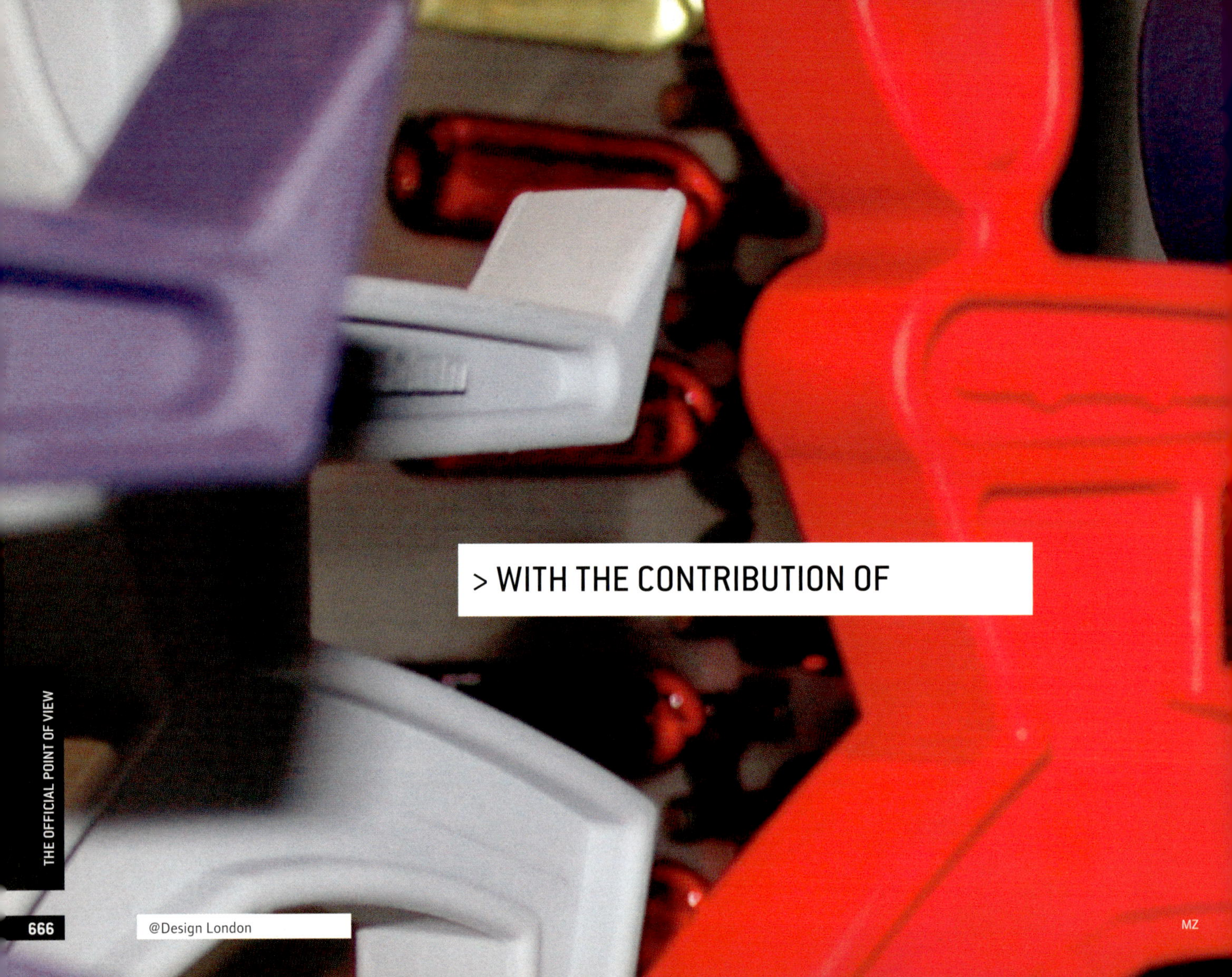

MZ

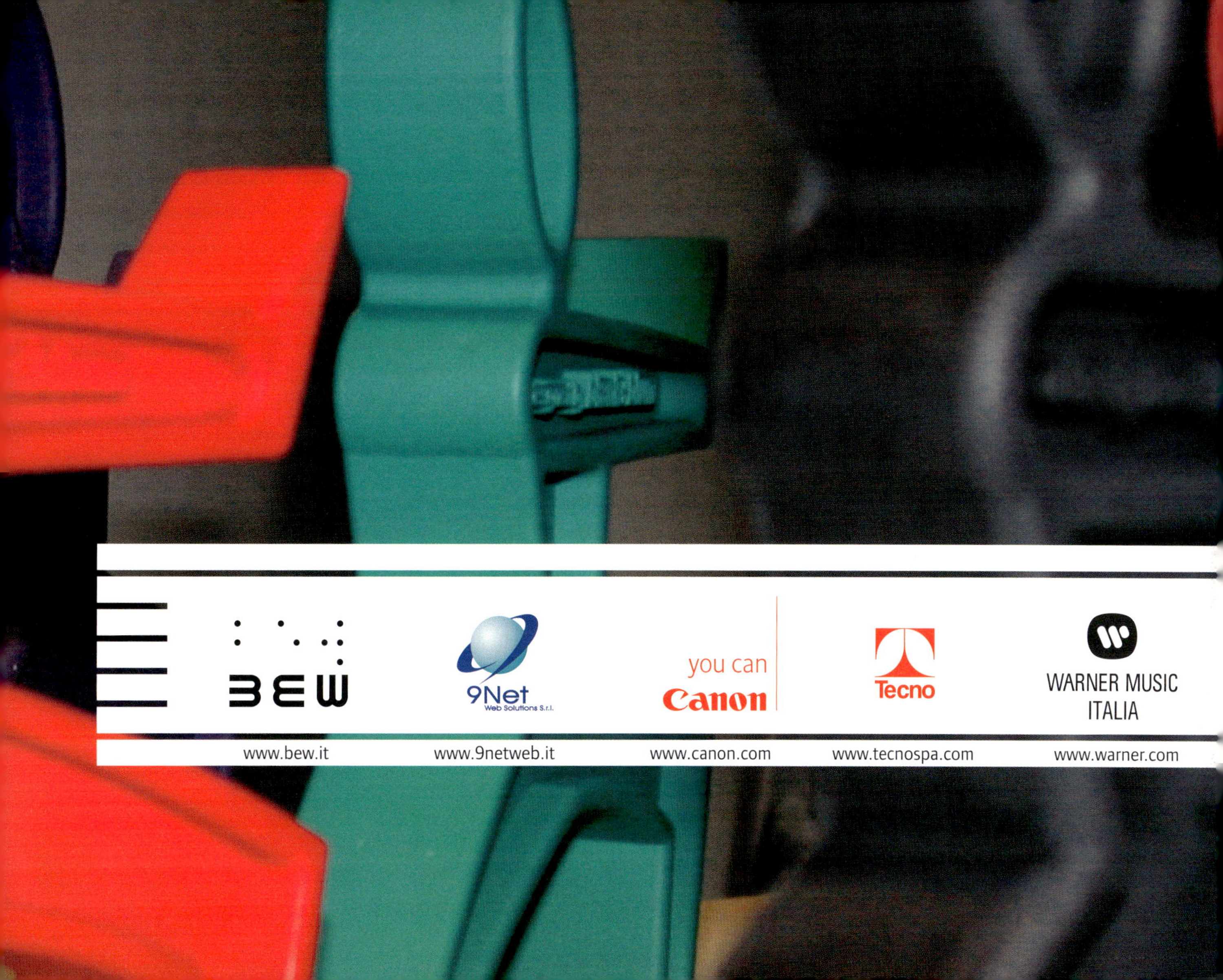
BEW
9Net
Web Solutions S.r.l.
you can
Canon
Tecno
WARNER MUSIC
ITALIA
www.bew.it
www.9netweb.it
www.canon.com
www.tecnospa.com
www.warner.com

THE OFFICIAL POINT OF VIEW

© Giulia Ber Tacchini

© Paolo Calcagni

© Lucio LuZo Lazzara

© Riccardo Rinetti

© 2004 Enorme Film Arts Snc

Milano - Italy

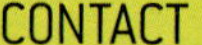

Enorme Film Arts©

CONTACT

The Official Point of View

via Nerino, 8

20123 Milano - Italy

tel +39 02 7200 1166

info@theofficialpointofview.it

www.theofficialpointofview.it

GRAPHIC DESIGN

Zeta_Lab

via Spallanzani 36/A

ITA-20129 Milano - Italy

tel +39 02 2048 0012

www.zetalab.com

PRINTED AND DISTRIBUTED WORLDWIDE BY

Actar

Roca i Batlle, 2-4

08023 Barcelona, Spain

Tel +34 93 418 7759

Fax +34 93 418 6707

info@actar-mail.com

printed in July 2004

ISBN-88-900822-9-1

MZ

> CD ROM CONTENTS

Inside the CD-ROM you will find THE OFFICIAL 360° VIEWS,

a selection of **116 interactive panoramic views** of the most important

and rappresentative exhibitions of the Milano Furniture Fair 2004:

Acerbis, Albini & Fontanot, Alessi, Artek, Arflex, Artenciel, Arte's, Bisazza, Bonacina, Cappellini,

Cecchini, Cinova, Coro, CP Company, Dada, Derin, Designosaurus by Ross lovegrove, Dining Design,

Dining design-IED, Edra, Emporio 31, Estel, Flexform, Fendi, F.lli Boffi, F.lli Graziano, Frette,

Gervasoni, Grohe, Hartwort, Herman Miller, IED/ Tubor, Kartell, Koinoor, Lema, Liv'it,

London design, Malofancon, Meritalia, Missoni Restaurant, Misura Emme, MK Mia, Molteni, Moroso,

Move, Monica Armani, Philippe Plein, Poliform, Poltrona Frau, Porro, Salvarani, Salone Satellite,

Scavolini, Scic, Segis, Signoria, Sphaus, Street dining design _KonoPizza, , Street dining design _Enoteca d'Italia,

Stua Svad-Dondi, T iSettanta, Tecno, Teuco, Thonet, Titan, Trussardi, Unifor, Ycami, Zanotta

photos by **Maurizio Costa**

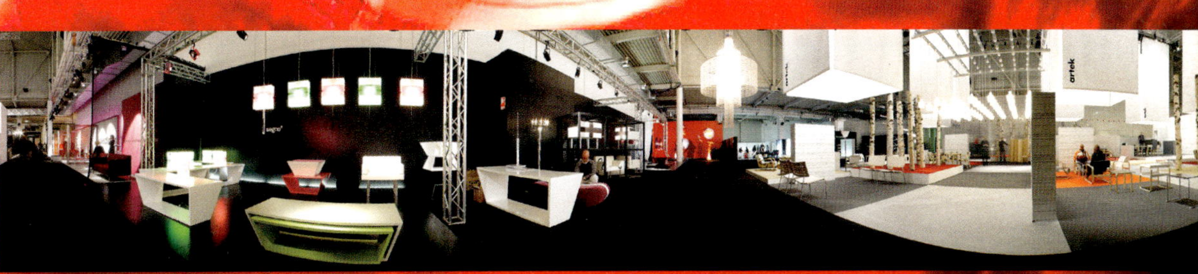

Artek

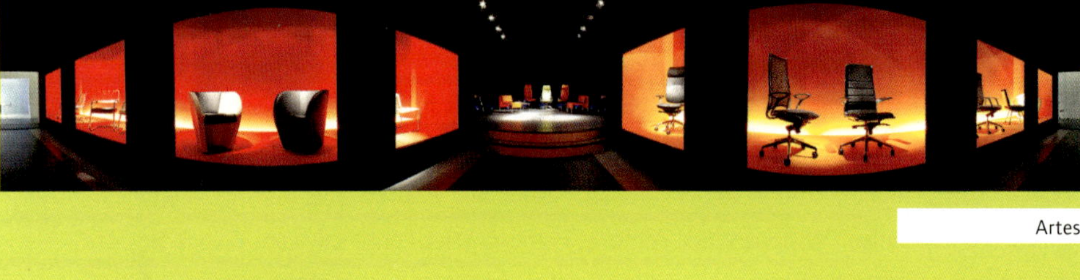

Artes

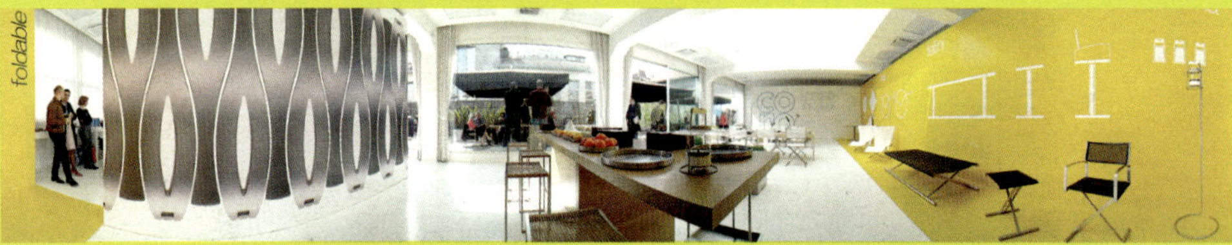

Coro

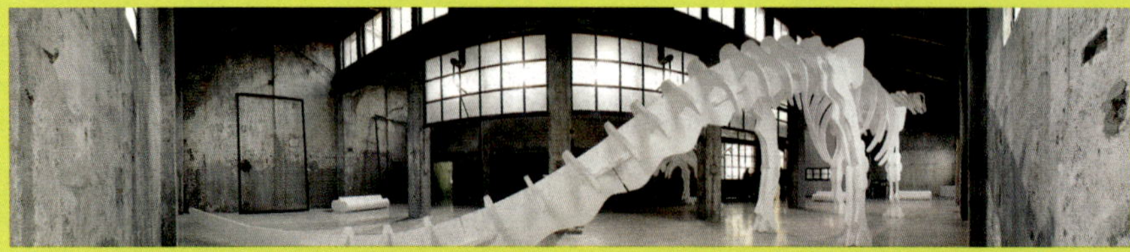

Designosaurus @ Segheria

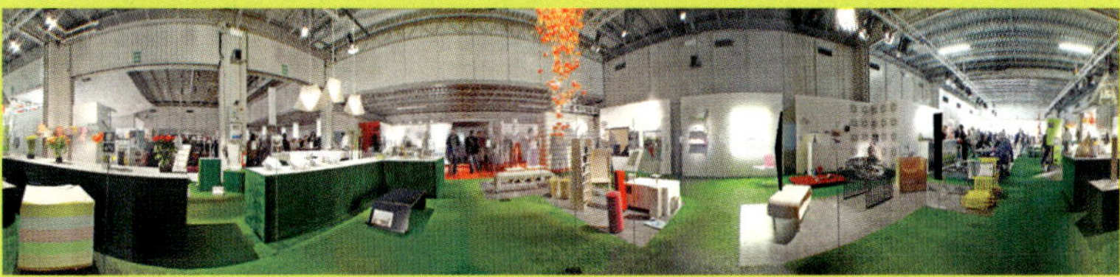

London Design

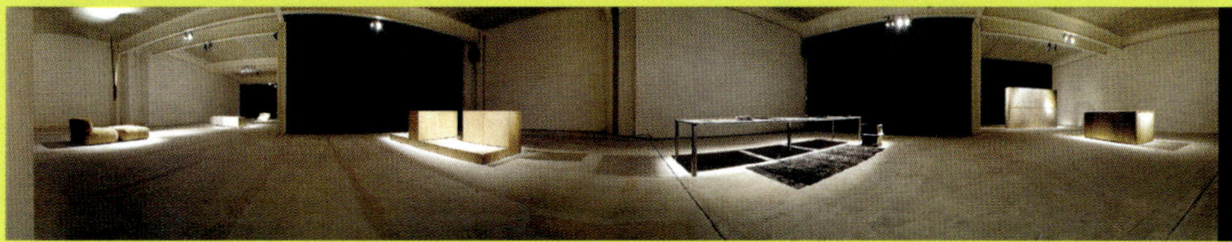

Progetto Domestico

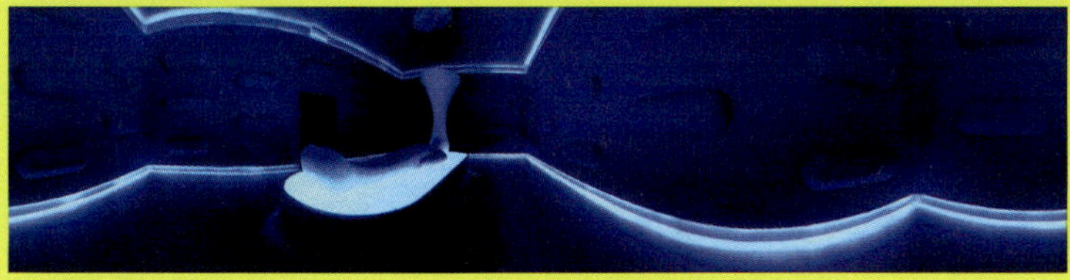

@ Triennale

...and 100 more>>

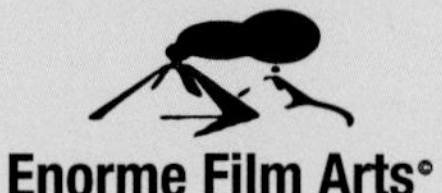

Enorme Film Arts©